BG JAN 2 1 1999

For Reference

Not to be taken from this room

R 909.0496 Jen

Jenkins, Everett, 1953-

Pan-African chronology
II :

D1064885

PALM BEACH COUNTY
LIBRARY SYSTEM
3650 SUMMIT BLVD.
WEST PALM BEACH, FLORIDA 33406

Pan-African Chronology II

PAN-AFRICAN CHRONOLOGY II

*A Comprehensive Reference to
the Black Quest for Freedom
in Africa, the Americas,
Europe and Asia, 1865–1915*

by
EVERETT JENKINS, JR.

McFarland & Company, Inc., Publishers
Jefferson, North Carolina, and London

British Library Cataloguing-in-Publication data are available

Library of Congress Cataloguing-in-Publication Data

Jenkins, Everett, 1953–
    Pan–African chronology II : a comprehensive reference to the
Black quest for freedom in Africa, the Americas, Europe and Asia,
1865–1915 / by Everett Jenkins, Jr.
      p.   cm.
    Includes bibliographical references and index.
    ISBN 0-7864-0385-3 (library binding : 50# alkaline paper) ∞
    1. Afro–Americans — History —1863–1877 — Chronology.
2. Afro–Americans — History —1877–1964 — Chronology.
3. Blacks — History —19th century — Chronology.   4. Blacks —
History — 20th century — Chronology.
    E185.2.J46   1998
    909'.049608'0202 — dc21   97-34101
                                                CIP
Note: The companion volume by the same author,
    Pan-African Chronology ... 1400–1865, published in 1996
    (ISBN 0-7864-0139-7), bears these classification numbers:
    DT17.J46 1996 and 909'.0496'00202 — dc20 (LC 95-8294).

©1998 Everett Jenkins, Jr. All rights reserved

*No part of this book, specifically including the index, may be reproduced
or transmitted in any form or by any means, electronic or mechanical,
including photocopying or recording, or by any information storage and
retrieval system, without permission in writing from the publisher.*

Manufactured in the United States of America

McFarland & Company, Inc., Publishers
  Box 611, Jefferson, North Carolina 28640

To God,
for the blessing
that is this life

TABLE OF CONTENTS

PREFACE

In 1905, George Santayana, the famed historian, wrote, "Those who cannot remember the past are condemned to repeat it." By this, he meant that the study of history is necessary if we are to avoid the mistakes of the past.

I suppose that Santayana is right. I suppose that one of the reasons we should read and study history is to learn from the mistakes that are seemingly rife in the story of man. But, for me, such a motivation for reading history tends to be depressing and often counterproductive. If all we can learn from history is a litany of mistakes, ultimately the mind and the spirit will rebel and refuse to ingest any more.

I prefer a more optimistic perspective of history—a perspective that reflects a faith in the inherent goodness and strength of men and women throughout the march of time. For me, the study of history should be an attempt to understand what is good and right in the story of man and to provide some guidance as to how such goodness and righteousness may be repeated. Indeed, contrary to the wisdom of Santayana, I assert that we should strive to remember the past so that certain lessons of life may not only be duplicated but also spread throughout the world for the benefit of mankind.

This is the approach that I have undertaken in preparing this book. While not overlooking the evils that have been perpetrated, I have attempted to tell the story of an African diaspora that is filled with examples of courage, endurance, intelligence, and hope. It is my belief that the story of the African diaspora contained herein is an inspirational story of a people who, despite tremendous obstacles and egregiously unjust burdens, pressed onward in their irresistible march to freedom.

It is my hope, and my prayer, that the lessons of courage and perseverance that this story tells will encourage others of like mind, body and spirit to initiate quests for freedom of their own.

EVERETT JENKINS, JR.
Richmond, California
September 1997

INTRODUCTION

This book is the second volume of a work that my editors and I have entitled *Pan-African Chronology*. In this volume of *Pan-African Chronology*, the story of the African diaspora continues with a number of surprising twists.

This volume covers the period from 1865 to 1915. During this period, in the United States, the Civil War came to an end, Reconstruction began and ended, the doctrine of "separate but equal" took root, and the NAACP was formed. Many historians have called this period the "nadir"—the lowest point in the African American experience. But such historians often forget that 1865 to 1915 was the period of some of the greatest artists (Henry Tanner, Edmonia Lewis), writers (Paul Laurence Dunbar, James Weldon Johnson) and leaders (Frederick Douglass, Booker T. Washington, W. E. B. DuBois) Afro-America has ever known. It was also the period that gave birth to that thing called jazz.

This period also saw the emergence of some trail-blazing black athletes. Isaac Murphy, the first jockey, black or white, to win the Kentucky Derby three times; Major Taylor, the champion cyclist; and Jack Johnson, the first black heavyweight champion of the world, all reigned during this period of time.

During this period, black enterprise blossomed and black towns were formed. Black churches grew stronger, and black colleges were built. This was the time of the great migration — a time when hundreds of thousands of African Americans left the farms of the South and migrated to the cities of the North. No, this was not the nadir of the African American experience. Instead, in many ways, it was the genesis. After all, this period saw the establishment of social structures that have come to define the African American experience in the United States.

Throughout the Americas, this period was notable as the era when slavery was finally eradicated as a legal institution. In the period covered by this volume, Puerto Rico, Cuba, and Brazil abolished the practice of slavery. Such pillars of Pan-African history as Antonio Maceo, Machado de Assis, and Marcus Garvey would arise, and the concepts of black nationalism and black pride would first be espoused in such West Indian locales as Jamaica and Haiti.

This volume of *Pan-African Chronology* also tells the story of the struggle to end the enslavement of Africans in Asia. It examines the role of the British in curtailing the slave trade in the Indian Ocean and especially focuses on the British attempts to end the mass trafficking of African slaves in India, Arabia, and the ever-shrinking Ottoman Empire.

As for Africa, 1865 to 1915 was the time in which the European powers carved up the continent, creating artificial boundaries that cause conflicts to this day. This imperialistic "scramble for Africa" ironically coincided with humanitarian European efforts to eradicate slavery and the slave trade on the African continent.

Along with the subjects that are customarily covered in texts pertaining to African and African American history, this volume of *Pan-African Chronology* reports on such arcane topics as Americana, Brazil, the Lost Colony of the Confederacy; Matthew Henson and Robert Peary, the Arctic explorers whose Eskimo descendants have united the explorers in life as well as legend; and the 1909 liberation of the black eunuchs of the Seraglio, the grand harem of the Ottoman Sultans.

This volume provides details on the lives of Peter Jackson, the Afro-Australian who dazzled the boxing world; Ch'en Yu-jen (Eugene Chen), an Afro-Chinese diplomat in Sun Yat-sen's China; and Juan Caballo, the Black Seminole whose odyssey took him from the swamps of Florida to the green hills of Oklahoma and, finally to his death bed in a Mexico City hospital — the final end to his own peripatetic search for freedom.

*   *   *

Before reading *Pan-African Chronology,* it is advisable to understand the structure of this book and the references made in the text.

This book is divided into years. Events in each year are grouped by region — the United States, the Americas, Europe, Australia, Asia, and Africa — or as "Related Historical Events." For the United States, there are additional divisions pertaining to such categories as the Socialist Movement, the Labor Movement, the Civil Rights Movement, the Ku Klux Klan, Notable Births, Notable Deaths, Notable Cases, Miscellaneous State Laws, Publications, Scholastic Achievements, the Black Church, the Arts, the Performing Arts, Music, Scientific Achievements, Technological Innovations, Black Enterprise and Sports.

For the Americas, the continents are divided by current national designations such as Canada, Cuba, Brazil, etc. For Africa, the continent is divided into separate regions, North Africa, Egypt and Sudan; West Africa; Central Africa; East Africa; and Southern Africa.

Because there are fewer entries for Europe, Asia, and Australia, no divisions are provided for those continents.

*   *   *

With regard to the use of language, when reading history from an African American perspective, one is frequently confronted with a vocabulary that reflects the racial biases and misunderstandings of the times. Columbus, believing he had landed in the East Indies, called the people he encountered "Indians." His error became a part of the language. Africans were called "Negroes" because "negro" is the Spanish word for "black," which was perceived to be the color of the skin of most Africans. Today the term "Negro" is in disrepute, but its English equivalent "black" is still commonly used even though the skin color of most African Americans is obviously not black.

In this book, I have preferred to use the terms "African" or "person of African descent" when referring to a person with some measure of African blood.

As for the term "African American," in the spirit of frank disclosure, I must admit that I have used the term in this volume because, in 1997, it is the phrase preferred by most. However, for me the phrase "African American" is also inaccurate. In researching history, one finds that most persons of African descent in the United States also have European and Indigenous American blood. By labelling these individuals "African" Americans, society may be denying other essential elements of their being. Nevertheless, as part of the language of the day, the term "African American" is used in this book.

In this book, I have also liberally used the phrase "Indigenous American." The use of the phrase "Indigenous American" reflects this author's discomfort with both "Indian" and "Native American." For me the phrase "Indigenous American" most aptly describes the people the Europeans found inhabiting this land.

In addition to, or in lieu of, the general term "Indigenous American," wherever possible I have used the specific name of the Indigenous American nation when describing the people the Europeans encountered.

As for the terms "whites" or "white people," I have resisted using those terms because they too are inaccurate and have certain racial and psychological connotations. Instead, I have preferred to use the term "European" or "Euro-American."

One term that I encountered frequently in my research was the word "illegitimate" in describing the heritage of individuals. Typically, this term would be applied to the children of European men and women of African descent. The more I saw this term applied to the notable people who inhabit the pages of this book, the more I found it objectionable. The term

"illegitimate" has historically been used to stigmatize the child, whereas the stigma, if any, should have fallen on the father who abandoned his responsibilities. Accordingly, in the interest of justice, I have not used the word "illegitimate" to describe any child born out of wedlock.

For similar reasons the word "mulatto" has been replaced by the phrase "child of two worlds" or "COTW" for short. This phrase is used in an overt attempt to eliminate any stigma associated with the word "mulatto" as it has historically been applied to people of dual heritage — to those who are part–African and part–European.

* * *

Occasionally the reader will notice an italicized phrase instructing the reader to see another year. These references are provided to assist the reader in finding further information on a particular subject.

Most of the information in this book has been compiled using secondary sources such as other chronologies. Without meaning any disrespect to the sources I have relied upon, I must admit that I have encountered a number of errors and some outdated information. To the best of my ability, I have attempted to make corrections and updates. However, it is inevitable that errors and outdated information continue to exist within this text. For any such flaws, I, as the author, take full responsibility. However, I do make a special request of you, the reader. If you find errors, I would greatly appreciate your informing me of them by writing to me in care of the publisher of this book. As I envision the life of this book, it will be subject to revisions for future editions. Therefore, your assistance in correcting any deficiencies would be most appreciated.

In the course of reading this book you will find certain interpretations and elaborations of historical events. Such interpretations and elaborations immediately follow bulleted items. From the outset, it must be noted that these comments are based upon my own particular African American perspective, which may not necessarily comport with the traditional perspective on the same event. Given the complexity of history, it is quite understandable that differing viewpoints may arise concerning the same historical event. The comments I have made simply set forth my particular opinion with regard to the significance of the event. You, as an independent reader, are encouraged to read and develop opinions of your own.

As a student of history, the most important lesson I have learned is that history is not written in stone. After all, even basic facts are often contested, numbers are frequently estimates, and the historical records almost invariably reflect the interests and biases of the historian.

Given all this, the study of history must be an evolving process which is best approached from different perspectives as well as from different times. The study of history must be a never-ending examination of the ramifications of events, not only for the conquerors, but also for the conquered.

In this book, I have continued my endeavor to present a chronological study of African and African American history as I believe it should be presented. However, I remain humbled by the knowledge that this book is not finished, that much work remains to be done. While I am confident that my books provide more information about Pan-African history than has been set forth in one place before, I am equally aware that my own limitations of time, resources, and strength have resulted in these books being less than they could possibly have been. Ultimately, I remain mindful of the fact that with these books — with this book — I am on a life journey, and that, during this journey, my own personal quest for freedom has become synonymous with this never-ending, ever-evolving quest for truth.

1865–1899

THE UNITED STATES

On January 31, 1865, the House of Representatives passed the Thirteenth Amendment to the United States Constitution. The Senate had already approved the amendment. The Thirteenth Amendment abolished slavery. It reads:

Amendment XIII

Section 1. Neither slavery nor involuntary servitude, except as a punishment for crime whereof the party shall have been duly convicted, shall exist within the United States, or any place subject to their jurisdiction.

Section 2. Congress shall have power to enforce this article by appropriate legislation.

Upon passage by the Thirty-eighth Congress, the Amendment was submitted to the states for ratification. In a proclamation of the Secretary of State dated December 18, 1865, the Thirteenth Amendment was declared to have been ratified by the legislatures of twenty-seven of the thirty-six States and was, therefore, the law of land. The States which ratified the Thirteenth Amendment, and the dates of ratification, are as follows:

Illinois	February 1, 1865
Rhode Island	February 2, 1865
Michigan	February 2, 1865
Maryland	February 3, 1865
New York	February 3, 1865
Pennsylvania	February 3, 1865
West Virginia	February 3, 1865
Missouri	February 6, 1865
Maine	February 7, 1865
Kansas	February 7, 1865
Massachusetts	February 7, 1865
Virginia	February 9, 1865
Ohio	February 10, 1865
Indiana	February 13, 1865
Nevada	February 16, 1865
Louisiana	February 17, 1865
Minnesota	February 23, 1865
Wisconsin	February 24, 1865
Vermont	March 9, 1865
Tennessee	April 7, 1865
Arkansas	April 14, 1865
Connecticut	May 4, 1865
New Hampshire	July 1, 1865
South Carolina	November 13, 1865
Alabama	December 2, 1865
North Carolina	December 4, 1865
Georgia	December 6, 1865

The Legislatures for the following States ratified the Thirteenth Amendment after December 6, 1865:

Oregon	December 8, 1865
California	December 19, 1865
Florida	December 28, 1865
Iowa	January 15, 1866
New Jersey	January 23, 1866
Texas	February 18, 1870
Delaware	February 12, 1901
Kentucky	March 18, 1976

The Arkansas State Legislature adopted the Thirteenth Amendment by unanimous vote, and, in Alabama, the Legislature passed the Amendment by a vote of 75 to 15 with the following proviso:

Be it further resolved, that this amendment to the Constitution of the U.S. is adopted by the Legislature of Alabama, with the understanding that it does not confer upon Congress the power to legislate upon the political status of freedmen in this state.

As for the State of Mississippi, for almost two decades Mississippi remained the only State among the thirty-seven States in existence in 1865 that had never ratified the Thirteenth Amendment. However, in March of 1995, this was rectified when the Mississippi State Legislature finally ratified the Amendment. At long last it could be said that *all* of the United States agreed that the concept of slavery was a concept the time for which had come to an end.

• General Lee said that it was "not only expedient but necessary" that the Confederate Army use African American slaves as soldiers (January 11).

A bill was introduced in the Confederacy which would permit the voluntary enlistment of slaves in the Confederate Army with freedom guaranteed at the end of hostilities. This bill was buried in a committee.

However, General Robert E. Lee desperately needed additional soldiers and made a plea for African American troops. In response to General Lee's plea, the State of Virginia passed a resolution which allowed the Army to enlist slaves if agreeable settlement was made with the slave's owner. After Virginia passed this resolution, the House and Senate of the Confederacy allowed the Army to enlist African Americans. The Confederate resolution stipulated that no change was to be made in the slave-slaveowner relationships and that the slaves were to receive the same pay and rations as the European American troops.

On March 13, Confederate President Jefferson Davis signed a bill allowing the Confederate States to fill their military quota by using slaves, but the number of slaves recruited was not to exceed twenty-five percent (25%) of the able-bodied male slave population between the ages of 18 and 45. This measure came too late to help the Confederacy. However, on the eastern seaboard a number of slaves were recruited and were mustered into Confederate service (March 24).

• John Sweat Rock became the first African American to practice before the United States Supreme Court (February 1).

• Martin Robinson Delany received a commission as a major in the Union Army and was ordered to Charleston, South Carolina where he served as an Army physician. Delany was the first African American to achieve the rank of major in the regular United States Army.

• On February 12, Henry Highland Garnet preached a sermon in the House of Representatives commemorating the passage of the 13th Amendment and the end of slavery. Garnet was the first African American to preach in the Capitol.

• The first three drafts of the Reconstruction Bill, introduced in the House of Representatives on January 16, February 21, and February 22, all limited the right to vote to European American males, although one draft did give African American soldiers the right to vote.

• Four companies of the 54th United States Colored Troops became the first African Americans to participate in an inaugural parade (March 4).

• After much debate, Congress passed a bill giving freedom to wives and children of African American soldiers in Union service (March 13).

• Aaron Anderson, a landsman on the U.S.S. *Wyandanch*, was awarded the Navy Medal of Honor for bravery at Mattox Creek (March 17).

• With the Civil War at a virtual end, Confederate General Robert E. Lee surrendered his army to Union General Ulysses S. Grant at Appomattox Court House in Virginia (April 9).

During the Civil War, 178,895 African Americans served with the Union Army. This number represented approximately ten percent (10%) of the total Union forces.

It is estimated that 3,000 African Americans were killed in battle. However, more than 26,000 died from disease associated with the War.

There were 14,887 African Americans who were deserters. This number represents about seven percent (7%) of the total desertions.

Between November, 1864, and April, 1865, more than 49,000 African Americans enlisted into Union service; 4,244 of these African American enlistees were from Confederate states.

On July 15, 1865, the 123,156 African Americans serving in the Union Army were assigned as follows:

120 infantry regiments	98,938
12 heavy artillery regiments	15,662
10 batteries of light artillery	1,311
7 cavalry regiments	7,245

• President Lincoln was shot and mortally wounded by John Wilkes Booth while attending the comedy "Our American Cousin" at Ford's Theater in Washington, D.C. (April 14). The President died the following morning.

At 7:22 A.M., Abraham Lincoln died from wounds received when shot at Ford's Theater in Washington D.C. by the actor John Wilkes Booth (April 15).

In Lincoln's funeral procession, the Irish Immigrant Organization refused to march with African Americans. The New York City Council refused to allow African Americans to march. It was only due to the intervention of the police commissioner, that a place in the procession was assigned to African Americans. Police protection was necessary to insure the safety of the African American marchers.

• On May 4, Joseph Smith III, the son of the Mormon prophet Joseph Smith, had a revelation that African Americans were truly equal and not banned from the priesthood. This was accepted into the doctrine of the Reorganized Church of the Latter Day Saints, which soon had many African American members. However, it was not the position of the regular Mormon Church located in Salt Lake City, Utah, which continued to deny the priesthood to African Americans.

• Two European American regiments and an African American regiment, the 62nd USCT, fought the last action of the Civil War at White's Ranch, Texas. Sergeant Crocket, an Afro-American, is believed to have been the last man to shed blood in the War (May 13).

1865 shall always be remembered as the year in which the institution of slavery came to an end in the United States. In celebration of that fact and in celebration of their obtaining their freedom, African Americans began a tradition which serves as a reminder of their heritage and their hope.

For African Americans, Juneteenth came to symbolize their "Independence Day." In communities throughout the land where there exists a significant African American population, Juneteenth is a day of civic celebrations. There are parades and family gatherings. There are speeches and there are picnics in the park. And there are performances — both contemporary and from an era that existed a long time ago.

Juneteenth is a holiday of great significance for African Americans but its history is little known to most African Americans and is virtually unknown to anyone else.

*   *   *

Abraham Lincoln issued the Emancipation Proclamation on January 1, 1863, and Confed-erate General Robert E. Lee surrendered to Union General Ulysses S. Grant on April 9, 1865. However, neither of these dates is celebrated as the day on which African Americans secured their freedom. Instead a day in June is honored as the day to celebrate African American freedom. The significance of the day in June is as follows:

History tells us that the last battle of the Civil War took place in Texas and did not conclude until May 15, 1865. After the last battle had been fought, Union Major General Gordon Granger with 1,800 soldiers marched into Galveston, Texas to take command of the District of Texas. The date of Granger's arrival in Galveston was June 18, 1865. The next day, June 19, from his headquarters in the Osterman Building at the corner of Strand and 22nd Street, the lives of countless Texans, starting with a quarter of a million African Americans changed.

The African Americans were, for the first time, informed that, in accordance with Lincoln's Emancipation Proclamation, they were free. They were informed that there were no more masters, that there would be no more whips and that there were no more chains. They were free.

For the African Americans of Texas it was a time of celebration. With joy, these last American slaves celebrated the demise of the institution which had chained them in body, mind and spirit for so long. They were free and for the first time a world of grand possibilities was truly within their grasp.

The next year, African Americans in Texas remembered June 19 as their own emancipation day and celebrations were organized. From Galveston to the Red River, former slaves marched and celebrated. Newspaper accounts in Houston reported that thousands of American flags waved as the African Americans paraded down Main Street to the uplifting music of a brass band.

The first official Texas Emancipation Day — the first official Juneteenth — was celebrated on June 19, 1869, and Lottie Brown was named the first "Juneteenth Queen."

After Reconstruction, when the dark days of racial oppression once again settled upon the South, Juneteenth lost its official state sanction. However, for the better part of the late 1800s and early 1900s, African Americans in Texas continued to celebrate the unofficial holiday by gathering together at parks for picnics, barbecues, baseball games and reunions.

Although the popularity of Juneteenth briefly

waned during the 1960s, local groups kept the Juneteenth tradition alive. After the showing of the television program *Roots* in 1977, interest in African American history and culture revived, and the interest in the Juneteenth holiday received new life.

In 1979, the Texas legislature recovered from a century long neglect of African American history and made June 19 "Black Heritage Day"— an official Texas holiday. Since that time, Juneteenth has become a symbolic holiday for African Americans throughout the nation.

The importance of Juneteenth is that it serves as a reminder of how precious freedom is and how much African Americans have sacrificed to achieve it. In the history of the United States, there is no other people for whom freedom has been so long denied. And, in the history of the world, there is no other people for whom the concept of freedom has been so dear.

If there are problems in our contemporary world, a major factor in those problems is that so many have come to take for granted the freedom that was so difficult to obtain. It must never be forgotten that freedom cannot be assumed and it should not be abused. Freedom must be cherished and it must be vigilantly maintained.

This is one of the great lessons of history and Juneteenth is the day on which this lesson may be reiterated for the benefit and betterment of us all.

• President Andrew Johnson announced his Reconstruction plan (May 29).

President Johnson followed the ideas on Reconstruction outlined in the Wade-Davis Bill, but he followed Lincoln in insisting that Reconstruction was the function of the President.

In 1865, Arkansas, Louisiana, Tennessee, and Virginia already had governments loyal to the United States. President Johnson recognized them as legal and legitimate.

In May and June of 1865, President Johnson also appointed governors in North Carolina, Mississippi, Georgia, Texas, Alabama, South Carolina, and Florida. By the end of 1865, these governors had convened State Conventions which nullified secession, abolished slavery, and repudiated debts.

In May of 1865, President Johnson issued his Amnesty Proclamation which granted amnesty to all Confederates who took the oath of allegiance to the United States. The exceptions to the Amnesty Proclamation were those individuals who were (1) civil and diplomatic officers of the Confederacy; (2) Confederates who left

United States judicial posts; (3) officers above the rank of colonel in the Army, or lieutenant in the Navy; (4) Confederates who left Congress; (5) Confederates who left the armed services of the United States; (6) Confederates who mistreated war prisoners; (7) Confederates who fled the United States; (8) Confederates who attended West Point or the Naval Academy; (9) Confederates who were governors of Confederate states; (10) Northerners who fought for the South; (11) persons whose taxable property value was over $20,000.

By mid–1866, because of President Johnson's liberal view on amnesty, very few Confederates remained unpardoned. Indeed, the former Confederate states were to send to the Thirty-ninth Congress such men as Alexander Stephens, the former Vice-President of the Confederacy, and four former Confederate generals, five Confederate colonels, 6 Confederate Cabinet officers and 58 former Confederate Congressmen.

• 1,800 African Americans were settled on confiscated plantations in Davis Bend, Mississippi. By the end of the year, they had a cash balance of $159,200. Despite the wishes of Stevens and Sumner, land confiscation and redistribution to African Americans was never authorized by Congress. Thus, no real land reform was carried out. When President Johnson pardoned the owners of plantations such as those at Davis Bend, the land was returned to them.

• General Sherman issued Special Field Order No. 15, by which the South Carolina and Georgia Sea Islands, south of Charleston, and the abandoned lands along the rivers for a distance of 30 miles inland were to be used for the settlement of African Americans on plots of not more than 40 acres. General Rufus Saxton was appointed Inspector of the settlements. In January 1866, President Johnson removed Saxton and most of the land was returned to its original owners.

• The Freedmen's Bureau was formed.

The Freedmen's Bureau was established as part of the War Department. The Commissioner of the Bureau was to be appointed by the President, with the consent of the Senate. The Commissioner had the authority to "control all subjects relating to refugees and freedmen." The Commissioner could set aside abandoned tracts of land up to 40 acres to be leased to freedmen at a low rent, giving them the right to buy the land at the end of three years.

As part the Freedmen's Bureau's authorizing

legislation, Union army officers would be used as assistant commissioners, and the Secretary of War could issue provisions, clothing and fuel to the freedmen and refugees.

The Freedmen's Bureau established schools, hired teachers, made provisions for transportation, issued food and clothing and with an expenditure of over $2,000,000 treated 450,000 medical cases.

Due to the efforts of the Freedmen's Bureau, the death rate of freed slaves was reduced from a high of thirty-eight percent (38%) in 1865 to a little more than two percent (2.03%) in 1869.

- Edward G. Walker and Charles L. Mitchell were elected to the Massachusetts House of Representatives thus becoming the first African Americans elected to an American legislative assembly.
- From 1865 to 1877, Robert Small, an African American Civil War hero, served in the South Carolina State Militia, rising to the rank of Major General.
- Michael Augustine Healy was appointed to the United States Revenue Service, the forerunner to the Coast Guard.
- James Lewis received an appointment as inspector of customs for the Port of New Orleans.

When the Union troops occupied New Orleans in 1862, James Lewis (1832–1914) abandoned the Confederate ship on which he was serving as a steward, raised two companies of African American soldiers, and led the First Regiment of the Louisiana National Guard during the battle of Port Hudson.

After the Civil War, Lewis became active in Louisiana politics and received a number of federal appointments.

- Alexander Thomas Augusta, an African American, became the director of the Freedmen's Hospital which was located on the grounds of Howard University.
- In December 1865, Thaddeus Stevens submitted a plan to the Republican caucus which (1) claimed Reconstruction as the business of Congress; (2) regarded the President's steps as provisional; (3) postponed consideration of admission of members from Southern states; (4) suggested a joint committee of fifteen be appointed to study conditions in the Confederate States. A resolution creating the joint committee passed the House of Representatives by a vote of 129 to 35, with 18 abstaining. It was subsequently passed by the Senate in February of 1866.

The Stevens Plan was not a great deviation in Congressional policy. Congress had, in fact, followed a policy independent of the Reconstruction Plans of Presidents Lincoln and Johnson by forbidding Virginia, North Carolina, South Carolina, Georgia, Florida, Alabama, Mississippi, Louisiana, Texas, Arkansas, and Tennessee representation in the Electoral College.

- *The Civil Rights Movement:* An African American convention held in Raleigh, North Carolina, adopted resolutions for the repeal of discriminatory laws, for proper wages, protection and education.
- An African American convention in Charleston, South Carolina, protested the results of the state constitutional convention.
- *The Ku Klux Klan:* The Ku Klux Klan was organized in Pulaski, Tennessee. It was formed to control African Americans through terror and intimidation and to minimize Union influence in the South.

The threat posed by Reconstruction which sought to raise southern African Americans to political power while destroying the European American power structure of the ante-bellum South, compelled a group of six Confederate veterans to organize the Ku Klux Klan on Christmas Eve in 1865.

The Ku Klux Klan was originally formed as a social club to shield European Americans against perceived humiliation at the hands of African Americans. As African Americans gained political power, the Ku Klux Klan was transformed into a political group which had the purpose of undermining African American power and reasserting European American supremacy.

In May of 1867, an organizational plan was adopted and General Nathan Bedford Forrest was elected Grand Wizard of the Order.

Klansmen were known for wearing white robes, masks, and high cardboard hats. Typically, they operated at night to frighten superstitious African Americans and to conceal their identity from federal troops.

Although the Klan proved effective in frightening and intimidating African Americans and loosening their alliance with the Republican Party, its use of terrorism and violence alienated many Southerners.

In 1869, General Forrest formally dissolved the Order. However, local groups remained active throughout the country and by 1915, the Order was restored — stronger than ever.

• *Notable Births:* Adam Clayton Powell, Sr., the famed pastor of the Abyssinian Baptist Church, was born.

Adam Clayton Powell, Sr., (1865–1953) was born in Franklin County, Virginia. As a youth, Powell worked his way through Rendville Academy in West Virginia by working in the neighboring coal mines. He graduated in 1885. Three years after his graduation from the Rendville Academy, Powell entered the Wayland Seminary in Washington, D.C. In 1892, he became pastor of his first church, the Ebenezer Baptist Church in Philadelphia. A year later, Powell accepted the post of minister at the Immanuel Baptist Church in New Haven, Connecticut. He would hold this position until 1908.

While in New Haven, Powell gained a reputation as a lecturer and writer. In 1895, he published *Souvenir of the Immanuel Baptist Church.* Powell lectured all over the East Coast and in California.

Powell also tried to organize the New Haven African Americans to become a political force, but factionalism and jealousy of Powell destroyed the effort.

In November 1908, Powell became pastor of the Abyssinian Baptist Church in New York City. One of his first political acts in New York was to lead a campaign to force the city to rid the area (40th Street on the West Side) in which the church was then located of prostitutes.

In 1910, Powell joined the newly formed National Association for the Advancement of Colored People and was appointed to its Finance Committee. Powell remained active in community work, trying to convince European American merchants in African American neighborhoods to hire African American help and trying to have a Harlem Community Center built.

By 1920, Powell had become a figure of national prominence. His sermons were often published in pamphlet form, and he made over $1,200 from the sale of *Watch Your Step* and *The Valley of Dry Bones.*

In 1932, Powell was nominated as a Presidential elector-at-large by the Republican Party of New York.

In 1937, Powell retired from the pulpit and was succeeded by his son, Adam Clayton Powell, Jr.

• *Notable Deaths:* James McCune Smith (1813–1865), an abolitionist writer considered by some to be the most scholarly African Americans of his time, died.

James McCune Smith was born in New York City. Smith was the son of a slave who owed his freedom to the Emancipation Act of the New York state and a self-emancipated bondswoman. Smith was educated in the African Free School, and entered the University of Glasgow in Scotland in 1832. In 1835, Smith received a Bachelor of Arts degree; in 1836, a Master of Arts; and, in 1837, a Doctorate of Medicine.

Smith soon returned to New York to practice medicine. He opened a pharmacy in New York and served for twenty-three years on the medical staff of the Free Negro Orphan Asylum. An opponent of the American Colonization Society, Smith became active in the New York Underground Railroad and a contributor to *The Emancipator.* In 1839, Smith was made the editor of the *Colored American*, to which he contributed "Abolition of Slavery and the Slave Trade in the French and British Colonies."

Smith was a prolific writer. Two of his more influential writings included a pamphlet entitled *A Lecture on the Haytien Revolutions: with a Sketch of the Character of Toussaint l'Ouverture* (1841); an article entitled "Freedom and Slavery for Africans," published in 1844 in the *New York Tribune*, and reprinted in the *Liberator* in 1844. Some of Smith's other works were "Civilization: Its Dependence on Physical Circumstances," "The German Invasion," "Citizenship, a Discussion of the Dred Scott Decision," "On the 14th Query of Thomas Jefferson's Notes on Virginia," and "The Influence of Climate upon Longevity."

Henry Highland Garnet, an abolitionist contemporary of Smith's, considered Smith to be the most scholarly African American of the era. Smith accepted an appointment as professor of anthropology at Wilberforce University in 1863.

Miscellaneous State Laws:

The Black Codes

With the demise of slavery, the states of the former Confederacy sought new legislative ways to control African Americans without resorting to abject enslavement. These states developed what has become known as the Black Codes.

The Black Codes were regulations written into the State Constitutions that regulated the lives of African Americans. Generally, the Black Codes relegated the freed slaves to virtual slavery if not legal slavery.

Under the Black Codes, any African American convicted of vagrancy was made subject to a period of indefinite servitude. Any African

American child that was separated from its parents could be subjected to a period of indefinite servitude. African Americans could come into court as witnesses only in cases in which African Americans were involved.

Under the Black Codes, access to land was limited, and the right to bear arms was forbidden. African American employment, which was previously, relatively unlimited, was limited to contract labor under the Black Codes.

Some of these Codes were so onerous that the Southern states were compelled to repeal them under pressure from the North.

- The South Carolina Constitution provided that no African American could enter the state unless, within twenty days after arrival, the African American put up a bond of $1,000 to ensure his good behavior. An African American had to have a special license for any job except as a farmer or a servant. The license included an annual tax of from $10 to $100. African Americans were prohibited from manufacturing or selling liquor. Work licenses were granted by a judge, revocable on complaint, and in case of revocation, the penalty was a fine double the amount paid for the license, half of which went to the informer.

- South Carolina created special courts for African Americans. The local magistrate was commissioned and "especially charged with the supervision of persons of color in his neighborhood, their protection, and the prevention of their misconduct."

- The Mississippi Constitution required every African American to submit evidence annually from the mayor or member of the police board proving that he had a lawful home and means of employment.

- The property provision of the Mississippi Black Codes provided that African Americans were prohibited to rent or lease land, except in incorporated towns or cities, in which places the corporate authorities controlled the land.

- In a Louisiana Black Code, all agricultural workers were required to make contracts with employers during the first ten days of each January; workers could not leave their employers until the contract expired; refusal to work would be punished by forced labor on public works. African Americans were required to work ten hours a day in summer and nine hours a day in the winter.

- In South Carolina, the rules for contract-

ing African American servants to European American employers were as follows: Employers were allowed to work servants under 18 "moderately." A servant over the age of 18 could be whipped on judicial authority. The wages and time period for the servants had to be specified in writing. Sunday and night work were forbidden. Unauthorized attacks on servants and the provision of inadequate food to servants were prohibited. The wages to be paid a servant were to be approved by a judge. Failure to make contracts was made a misdemeanor, punishable by fine. Farm labor was required from sunrise to sunset, with intervals for meals. Visitors were not allowed without the employer's consent. Enticing away another's servants was punishable by fine. To sell farm products without the written consent of the employer was forbidden. The contract between the European American employer and the African American servant had to be in writing, witnessed by European Americans and certified by a judge (invariably another European American). Any European American could arrest any African American that the European American saw commit a misdemeanor.

- Mississippi and Florida enacted laws segregating public transportation.

- Texas passed a law requiring every train to have special cars for freed slaves, but it did not specifically prohibit African Americans from riding in other cars.

- Wisconsin rejected a proposal to allow African Americans to vote. Minnesota and Connecticut also voted against African American suffrage.

- *Miscellaneous Publications:* George Moses Horton published *Naked Genius*, a volume of poetry. In this book, Horton lampooned Jefferson Davis, the former President of the Confederacy for attempting to escape the Union forces by dressing up as a woman. One poem in the book, "The Slave," expresses Horton's bitterness on being a slave.

- Thomas Morris Chester, an African American journalist writing for the *Philadelphia Press,* described the Union army's triumphant occupation of the Confederate capital at Richmond.

- In New Orleans, Louisiana, the first convention of African American journalists was chaired by P. B. S. Pinchback. Pinchback would later found the New Orleans *Louisianan.*

• *The Performing Arts:* African American singer and entertainer Charles Hicks organized the Georgia Minstrels, a travelling troupe that would go on to tour Europe as Haverly's European Minstrels.

Organized in Indianapolis, Indiana, the celebrated Georgia Minstrels' tours included performances in Germany and Great Britain. However, Charles Hicks experienced great difficulties in dealing with European American theater managers, and was eventually compelled to sell his rights to Charles Callender in 1872. Afterwards, The Georgia Minstrels were known as "Callender's Georgia Minstrels."

• *Scholastic Achievements:* Fisk University opened (April 20).
• Patrick Henry Healy became the first African American to earn the Doctor of Philosophy (Ph.D.) degree when he passed his final examination in Louvain, Belgium (July 26).
• The American Missionary Association founded Atlanta University at Atlanta, Georgia.
• Francis Louis Cardoza was named principal of the Avery Normal Institute in Charleston, South Carolina.

Francis Louis Cardoza (1837–1903) was born in Charleston, South Carolina, of a Jewish father and a COTW mother. Cardoza was educated abroad and, after the Civil War, became very active in Reconstruction politics. Cardoza would come to hold several government positions including Secretary of State for South Carolina.

• The American Baptist Home Mission helped establish Virginia Union University and Shaw University in Raleigh, North Carolina.
• Howard University was founded as Howard Seminary in Washington, D. C. (November 20).

In 1865, one in every twenty African Americans could read and write. By 1900, one in every two African Americans could read and write.

• *The Black Church:* In 1865, there were 250,000 members of the African Methodist Episcopal Church in the South.
• Daniel Alexander Payne published *The Semi-Centenary of the African Methodist Episcopal Church in the U.S.A.*

Black Enterprise: In 1865, various assessments were made concerning the economic health of African Americans.

In Cincinnati, African Americans owned taxable property valued at a half million dollars.

In New York, African Americans had invested $755,000 in African American owned businesses. In Brooklyn (a separate municipal entity at that time), African Americans had invested $76,000 in African American businesses. In New York, African Americans owned $733,000 in unencumbered property. In Brooklyn, they owned $276,000 in unencumbered property and, in Williamsburg, $151,000.

According to the June 1865 census, there were 16,509 freedmen in Memphis, Tennessee, of which only 220 were indigent. For the previous three years, 1863 to 1865, the African American poor and indigent had been essentially supported by African American benevolent societies who contributed $5,000 for the support of the African American poor.

• The Chesapeake Marine Railroad and Dry Dock Company was founded in Baltimore. It was an African American owned company and it employed over 300 African American mechanics — men who were normally discriminated against in the Baltimore shipyards. The Chesapeake Marine Railroad and Dry Dock Company would record a profit for 12 years.
• The Freedmen's Savings and Trust was chartered by Congress.

In 1865, the federal government established the Freedmen's Savings and Trust Company. Freedmen's was chartered to do business exclusively with African Americans. The Freedmen's Savings and Trust Company was headquartered in Washington, D. C. and over the following years it would grow to where, at one time, it had forty branch offices and total deposits of over three million dollars.

Unfortunately, in 1874, during the nationwide economic depression, the bank failed.

• An estimated 100,000 of the 120,000 artisans in the South were African Americans. However, by 1890, the skilled African American worker had been eliminated as competition for Southern European Americans.

THE AMERICAS

• *Canada:* By 1865, there were an estimated 40,000 persons of African descent living in Canada. The census of 1861 had counted approximately 11,000 persons of African descent living in Canada. The more than three-fold increase in the Afro-Canadian population was essentially due to escaped slaves leaving the United States during the Civil War.

- *Cuba:* Jose Ricardo O'Farrill and Miguel Aldama organized the Reformist Party, whose mouthpiece was the periodical *El Siglo.*

O'Farrill and Aldama proposed tariff reform, the cessation of the slave trade, representation in the Spanish Cortes, and the gradual abolition of slavery with compensation. The Cuban sugar mills had grown without restraint, and the introduction of new technologies reduced the need for slaves. Change and competition demanded new forms of organization.

- *Dominican Republic:* The Dominican Republic re-asserted its independence from Spain.

The struggle for Dominican liberation was led by Juan Pablo Duarte. Duarte is regarded as "the father of the Dominican Republic" and is indisputably the country's greatest national hero.

Duarte was ably assisted in his efforts by Ramon Matias Mella and Francisco del Rosario Sanchez. Led by this trio of heroes, the people of the Dominican Republic were able to proclaim their independence from Haiti on February 27, 1844.

Duarte's dream of establishing a liberal, democratic republic soon vanished with his permanent exile to Venezuela and his replacement by two caudillos (Pedro Santana and Buenaventura Baez). For decades, Santana and Baez would battle each other for control of the country.

The instability produced by the struggle between Santana and Baez was aggravated by the threat of frequent armed incursions by Haiti. Since neither Baez nor Santana believed in the viability of the Dominican Republic, they searched for foreign protectors. Whereas Baez hoped for annexation by France or the United States, Santana looked to Spain for salvation.

In 1861, Spain reannexed its former colony of Santo Domingo. Most Dominicans objected to the reestablishment of Spanish control over the country. Hostilities ensued and on August 16, 1863, the War of Restoration — the war to restore Dominican independence — began.

The War of Restoration would last for two years. In the end, Spain would be forced to withdraw from Santo Domingo.

- *Guatemala:* Jose Rafael Carrera (1814–1865), the ruler of Guatemala, died.

Jose Rafael Carrera was considered by many to be a zambo— a person of African and Indigenous Guatemalan heritage. However, he was more likely a person of triple heritage, part African, part Indigenous Guatemalan and part European.

Carrera was born to poor parents in Guatemala City on October 24, 1814. He joined the Central American federal army as a drummer at the age of twelve and rose rapidly through the ranks during the civil war of 1826.

The army, dominated by the Guatemalan conservative elite, not only provided military training but also indoctrinated Carrera in conservative ideology. After Francisco Morazan defeated the army in 1829, Carrera drifted for several years, eventually settling in Mataquescuintla. In Mataquescuintla, Carrera became a swineherd. Father Francisco Aqueche influenced him there and was instrumental in Carrera's marriage to Petrona Garcia, the daughter of a local landowner.

Carrera soon emerged as a leader of the peasants and landowners of eastern Guatemala against the liberal reforms of the Gautemalan governor, Dr. Mariano Galvez. The rural population, spurred on by the clergy, opposed Galvez's anticlericalism, taxes, judicial reforms, and land, labor, and immigration policies that appeared to favor foreigners over natives. The grievances of the populace were exacerbated by the Galvez government's efforts to check the cholera epidemic that broke out in 1837. The government's efforts at quarantines led to uprisings, especially in eastern Guatemala.

Carrera did not instigate the 1837 revolt. Indeed, at the time that the uprisings began, Carrera was in the employ of the Galvez government as commander of a government quarantine patrol. However, the local residents soon persuaded the young Carrera to join the revolt.

At Santa Rosa, on June 9, 1837, Carrera led a ragged band of insurgents to a stunning victory, sending the government troops fleeing back to the capital.

Aided by serious divisions between Galvez and Jose Francisco Barrundia, Carrera's peasant army took Guatemala City on February 1, 1838, thereby bringing down the Galvez government.

The demise of the Galvez government temporarily resulted in a more liberal government ruling Guatemala. Lieutenant Governor Pedro Valenzuela succeeded in persuading Carrera to leave the capital in return for promised reform and military command of the district of Mita. Resurgent strength of the conservative elite of the capital, however, and failure of the Valenzuela government to move fast enough with the reforms caused Carrera to resume the rebellion in March of 1838.

President Morazan brought federal troops from El Salvador into the struggle. However, on April 13, 1839, Carrera once more took the capital, this time installing a conservative government under Mariano Rivera Paz. In March, 1840, Carrera decisively defeated Morazan at Guatemala City, effectively ending the Central American national government.

From 1840 until his death in 1865, Carrera was essentially the military master of Guatemala. He consolidated the power of his army during the early 1840s, especially by the Convenio de Guadelupe of March 11, 1844.

In December 1844, Carrera assumed the presidency of Guatemala. Although his policies were conservative, during this period he sometimes supported moderate liberal political leaders as a check against the pretensions of the conservative ecclesiastical and economic elite of the capital. On March 21, 1847, Carrera completed the process of Guatemalan secession from the defunct Central American union by establishing the Republic of Guatemala.

Liberal opposition, combined with continued rebel activity in eastern Guatemala, led to Carrera's resignation and exile in Mexico in August 1848. The new Liberal government, however, failed to achieve unity or solve the country's problems, and Carrera re-entered the country in March 1849 at the head of an "army of restoration" composed heavily of Indigenous Guatemalans.

When Carrera captured Quetzaltenango, several generals defected to Carrera and an agreement was reached in June of 1849 that made Carrera a lieutenant general in the Guatemalan army. This arrangement was followed in August by Carrera's appointment as commanding general of the army.

Thereafter, Carrera strengthened the army as he carried out campaigns against continuing rebellions within Guatemala and against the liberals' attempts to revive the Central American union in El Salvador, Honduras, and Nicaragua. Carrera dealt those forces a major blow with a stunning victory against the "national army" at San Jose la Arada on February 2, 1851. This victory assured the dominance of the conservatives in Guatemala for many years to come.

After 1850, Carrera allied himself closely with the conservative and ecclesiastical elite of Guatemala City. Carrera's government restored close relations with Spain and signed a concordat with the Vatican guaranteeing the clergy a major role in the regime. Although Carrera was often described as reactionary by his opponents, Guatemala enjoyed considerable economic growth during the next twenty years as coffee began to replace cochineal as its leading export.

Carrera once again became president of Guatemala on November 6, 1851. He consolidated his strength and greatly increased his power when he became president for life, a virtual monarch, on October 21, 1854.

As the most powerful caudillo in mid–nineteenth century Central America, Carrera affected the development of neighboring states as well. Carrera's forces frequently intervened to assure conservative rule in El Salvador and Honduras.

When the North American adventurer William Walker came to the aid of Nicaraguan liberals and subsequently became president of Nicaragua, Carrera provided substantial aid to the combined Central American force that routed Walker in 1857. Although he declined an invitation to command the Central American army, leaving that to Costa Rica's Juan Rafael Mora, Carrera sent more troops than any other state in the "National Campaign."

In 1863, Carrera challenged the rise in El Salvador of General Barrios. Barrios had begun to pursue liberal, anti-clerical reforms. Although initially repulsed at Coatepeque in February, Carrera returned to conquer San Salvador later in the year, removing Barrios from office.

When he died from dysentery in 1865, Carrera had achieved considerable stability and economic growth for Guatemala. However, he had also established a stifling political dictatorship that had reserved many of the benefits of the regime for a small elite in Guatemala City. Nevertheless, Carrera deserves credit for protecting the rural Indigenous Guatemalan masses of the country from increased exploitation of their land and labor and for bringing Indigenous Guatemalans and meztisos into positions of political and military leadership. However, Carrera's most enduring legacy was the establishment of the military as the dominant political institution in the country.

• *Haiti:* Beaubrun Ardouin published *Etudes sur l'Histoire d'Haiti*, an eleven volume work on the history of Haiti.

• *Jamaica:* Riots erupted in Jamaica. These riots became known as the Morant Bay Rebellion.

• Paul Bogle (1822–1865), the leader of the Morant Bay Rebellion, died.

Paul Bogle was probably born a free man. He became a lay preacher in the Native Baptist Church and a peasant proprietor.

Bogle was listed as one of only 104 voters in the parish of St. Thomas. In the 1850s, Bogle became associated with George William Gordon, a wealthy COTW planter who was a member of the Legislative Assembly.

During the 1860s, economic conditions in Jamaica were deteriorating. As the peasant population's grievances grew, Bogle was selected to present their problems to the governor. However, the governor refused to see Bogle.

In anger over the rejection, Bogle and his followers began to organize small armed groups which met secretly in the hills. On October 7, 1865, the insurgents marched into Morant Bay and disrupted a court case against an Afro-Jamaican peasant. Policemen attempting to make arrests were beaten back, and Bogle and his followers fled.

Three days after the revolt began, police attempting to arrest those involved were overpowered by peasants in the village of Stony Gut where Bogle lived.

On October 11, Bogle and 400 followers, armed with sticks and a few guns, marched on the Morant Bay courthouse which was protected by members of the colony's militia. After a verbal confrontation between the Custos — the chief parish official — and the demonstrators (along with some throwing of stones), the militia was ordered to open fire.

The demonstrators moved in, killing some militiamen and forcing the rest into the courthouse which was set ablaze. Over 28 persons were killed, including the Custos, and 30 were wounded. Martial law was declared resulting in the execution of nearly 500 persons, the flogging of over 500, and the destruction of more than 1,000 homes. Bogle was finally captured on October 22 and was summarily executed two days later.

In 1965, Bogle was named a national hero of Jamaica.

• George William Gordon (1820–1865), a national hero of Jamaica, died.

George Gordon was born into slavery in Jamaica. He was born out of wedlock, the son of a wealthy European planter and an African slave woman.

Gordon taught himself to read and write and mastered the rudiments of accounting. In 1836, two years before the formal end of slavery, Gordon set himself up as a produce dealer in King-

ston. He later became a planter in the parish of St. Thomas. By 1842, Gordon had accumulated enough wealth to provide European educations for his twin sisters and an older sister, and to save his European father from bankruptcy. Gordon became a magistrate in St. Thomas Parish and, after 1850, a member of the Jamaican House of Assembly.

Instead of affiliating with the European rural ("Country") political party, Gordon joined the so-called "Town" party of fellow Afro-Jamaicans. The Town party was mostly composed of merchants, government officials, and lawyers. The Town party's early role was one of close support for critics of the harsh, conservative economic policies of Governor Eyre. Gordon, who together with a peasant leader, Paul Bogle, led the struggle for the rights of impoverished Afro-Jamaicans, predicted rebellion if more enlightened policies were not adopted.

Gordon's words proved to be prophetic. In October 1865, the Morant Bay uprising, led by Paul Bogle, occurred. Dozens of lives were lost.

Martial law was declared. Although Gordon was in Kingston at the time of the uprising and was not directly linked to the disturbance, he was arrested, taken to Morant Bay, and court-martialed for conspiracy.

George Gordon was hanged.

In 1969, the government of independent Jamaica recognized George William Gordon by naming him a Jamaican National Hero.

AFRICA

• *North Africa, Egypt and Sudan:* The Sudanese cotton industry was greatly expanded.

One of the consequences of the American Civil War was the temporary disruption of American cotton production. This disruption enabled the new African (Sudanese) cotton industry to expand in order to fulfill the European demand for cotton.

• American College was founded at Asyut.
• Suakin was leased to Egypt by Turkey.
• There was a mutiny at Kassala.
• Ahmad Mumtaz, became the governor of Suakin. Under his leadership the Sudanese cotton industry would experience rapid growth.
• Jafar Pasha Mazhar was made the Governor-General of the Sudan.

"Pasha" is a title that is conferred by the Ottoman Turkish government on officials. Holders of the title were divided into four grades, of which administrators in Sudan, for instance, Charles Gordon *(see 1885),* usually held the lowest grade.

• *Western Africa:* Pinet-Laprade became governor of Senegal. Saloun was again subdued. The Prophet Maba was defeated.

Maba Diakhou Ba (the Prophet Maba) (1809–1867) was a religious and military leader responsible for the spread of Islam in much of Senegambia.

The Prophet Maba was a Qur'anic scholar of the Tukolor clerical class. He was raised in the Mandingo states of the Senegambia. Maba's family came from Futa Toro in present day Senegal, a center for the dispersion of Islam in West Africa.

Around 1850, Maba met the famous Islamic revolutionary, al-Hajj Umar. It is believed that al-Hajj Umar made Maba the representative of the rapidly developing Tijani Islamic brotherhood for the Senegambia. Also around this time, the people of the Gambia states were divided into two factions — the Soninke who were non–Muslims or apathetic Muslims and the Marabout who were orthodox Muslims. The Prophet Maba was a member of the Marabout sect.

Maba soon founded his own town, Kirmaba, and began to gather his own followers.

In 1861, Maba was attacked by a Soninke group. After he defeated the Soninke, other Muslim religious leaders and their followers joined him. Thus, with one small victory a great Muslim revolution began.

The Prophet Maba's charisma and his belief in his divine mission appealed to Muslims in persecuted communities, whether they be Mandingo, Fula, or Wolof. After conquering a number of smaller Mandingo and Wolof states, Maba turned on the larger Serer states, which had no Muslim minorities.

By 1865, Maba had extended his control to the important state of Saloum (Saloun). During that time, Maba offered asylum to another famous military figure, Lat Dyor. At the time, Lat Dyor was fighting the French.

Maba, too, would soon encounter the forces of imperialistic France. An early alliance, with the French was broken and, in 1866, Maba's forces were forced to retreat to the south. Weakened by his losses to the French, Maba, nevertheless, resumed his attacks on the Serar state of Sine. It was during the 1867 attack on Sine that Maba was killed.

The victory for Sine was also a victory for the French. With the demise of Maba, the French no longer had to deal with the threat of a unified Muslim force in the Senegambia. However, even though Maba was unsuccessful in maintaining and expanding his Islamic empire, his influence was lasting. His campaign permitted a new Muslim elite to seize power in their societies. This Muslim elite was largely responsible for the conversion of the people of Senegambia to Islam.

* * *

"Marabout" is a term designating a Muslim religious leader. The word may be a French corruption of the Arabic word "murabit" which refers to a type of monastic community.

In the nineteenth century religious wars in the Senegambia, the term Marabout came to refer to any member of the orthodox Muslim faction.

• The British dispatched a company of the West India Regiment to assist the Egba siege of Ikorodu, near Lagos, Nigeria.

The British presence in Nigeria was officially established in 1849 when a consul was appointed for the Bight of Biafra. Lagos was annexed in 1851 and made a crown colony in 1862.

A consul had been appointed for the Bight of Benin in 1852. In 1885, Benin and Biafra were combined into the Oil Rivers Protectorate (after 1893 being called the Niger Coast Protectorate). The protectorate was combined in 1900 with the southern territory of the Royal Niger Company to form the Protectorate of Southern Nigeria. Lagos was added in 1906.

The northern territories of the Royal Niger Company were made into the Protectorate of Northern Nigeria in 1900. The Fula emirates were added after their conquest by British troops. In 1914, Northern and Southern Nigeria were combined under one governorship.

• The Mandingo near Sancorla were massacred by the Fulas under the command of Mussa Molo.

• Geraldo de Lema, a Brazilian slaver, was driven out of Ada. Lema then raised an army to take Ada. On March 17, Lema's forces were bombarded by the British.

• The Ewe effected an alliance with the Asantehene.

The Asante kingdom was formed in the 1670s when Osei Tutu united a number of petty Akan states which had been tributary to neighboring Denkyira. Through conquest, the Asante came to control an area of some 390,000 square kilometers and some three to five million people.

In the 19th century, the Asante kingdom fought a number of wars with the British. These wars came to an end in 1896 when the British declared a protectorate over Asante, dismembered the kingdom, and deposed its ruler.

The term "asantehene" is the title of the ruler of the Akan kingdom of Asante. When the kingdom first emerged as a confederation of Akan states in the 1670s, the power of the asantehene was greatly limited both inside and outside the capital of Kumasi. A series of rulers, beginning with Osei Kwadwo (c. 1760) instituted reforms which increased the power of the Asantehene and limited that of the nobility, both within Kumasi and in the conquered provinces of the kingdom.

- The French temporarily abandoned Porto Novo.
- The British blockaded Cotonou.
- Rohlfs's expedition from Tripoli reached Bornu, Sokoto, Baguirmi, Benue, and Lagos.

Kanem-Bornu was ruled for over a thousand years by the Sefawa dynasty. The Sefawa dynasty would prove to be the longest reigning dynasty in African history.

The kingdom of Kanem-Bornu was founded in Kanem in the eighth century. However, the Sefawa rulers retreated to the holdings in Bornu in the late 1300s to escape the raids of neighboring Bulala nomads.

The Sefawas ruled from there until the early nineteenth century when their power was usurped by al-Kanemi, the first ruler of the Shehu dynasty, who defended Bornu from the attacks of the Fula fighting under 'Uthman dan Fodio.

The last Sefawa king was executed in 1846 by al-Kanemi's son, 'Umar. The rule of the Shehu dynasty was interrupted in 1893, when Rabeh Zubair conquered Bornu. The Shehus were restored artificially by the Europeans who killed Rabeh and claimed Bornu in 1900.

*   *   *

Sokoto was comprised of former Hausa states. The Fula Islamic revolution in the Hausa states was begun in 1804 by 'Uthman dan Fodio. 'Uthman dan Fodio's son and successor, Muhammad Bello, administered the caliphate at its zenith. Muhammad and his successors used the title Sultan of Sokoto.

The caliphate of Sokoto was conquered by British forces under Frederick Lugard in the first years of the 20th century. However, the office of Sultan of Sokoto remains a great source of power and prestige to this day.

*   *   *

"Sultan" is an Islamic term which is applied to sovereign rulers. The term is roughly equivalent to the term "king" and is occasionally seen in early European descriptions of African rulers who were only nominally Muslim.

- *Central Africa:* Around 1865, Tippu Tip (Tippu Tib) began trading with the Bemba and Lundaland.

Tippu Tip (c.1830–1905) was the most powerful of the late 19th century Arab and Swahili traders in the east central African interior. Tippu Tip, who was also known by the names Tippu Tib and Hamid bin Muhammed al-Murjebi, built a vast mercantile empire which dominated eastern Zaire until the European occupation of Africa in the 1890s.

Tippu Tip was born in Zanzibar (Tanzania) to an Afro-Arab man and a mainland African woman. His commercial career began when he was twelve. His initial involvement was to accompany his father on short trading trips. Later though, he was a member of major expeditions into western Tanzania.

Around 1850, Tippu Tip separated from his father to undertake his own enterprises. Over the next fifteen years, Tippu Tip steadily accumulated wealth and experience until he was able to finance and organize large and well-armed caravans.

By the late 1860s, the operations of Tippu Tip extended to northeast Zambia. It was in Zambia that Tippu Tip engaged and defeated the Bemba. By defeating the Bemba, Tippu Tip captured a store of ivory—a store which greatly added to his wealth.

From Zambia, Tippu Tip moved into the Congo basin in the land which is today known as Zaire. In the Manyema region of eastern Zaire, Tippu Tip persuaded an African chief to abdicate for the purpose of allowing Tippu Tip to rule. Having thus established a political base, Tippu Tip began to expand his commercial empire.

Around 1874, Tippu Tip moved farther north into Manyema and secured recognition as unofficial governor over the region from other coastal traders. With Kasongo, on the Lualaba River, as his headquarters, Tippu Tip traded widely for ivory, raided for slaves, and established wide ranging alliances with the local chieftains and other traders. By the early 1880s, Tippu Tip was the de facto ruler of eastern Zaire.

In 1882, Tippu Tip ended his twelve year hiatus and returned to the eastern coast. The purpose of his return was to negotiate with the Zanzibari Sultan, Sultan Barghash. For his journey to the coast, Tippu Tip assembled the largest caravan to ever traverse Tanzania. Along the way, Tippu Tip made an alliance with the Nyanwezi chief Mirambo.

Once in Zanzibar, Tippu Tip accepted Barghash's proposal to serve as the sultan's agent in Zaire.

Around this same time, European imperialist pressure began to mount on the interior from all sides. Europeans assumed that Tippu Tip had even greater control over Arab slave traders than was the case. While Tippu Tip visited Zanzibar in 1886, his subordinates clashed with the forces of the Belgian King Leopold. At Zanzibar, Leopold's agent, Henry Stanley, persuaded Tippu Tip to accept the official governorship of eastern Zaire and to curb slaving in return for a salary. Returning to Zaire in 1887, Tippu Tip found that Leopold's government was unwilling to give him the material (financial) support he needed to satisfy his allies and supporters. Tippu Tip found himself increasingly challenged by revolts amongst his African subjects and by aggressive Arab slavers.

In 1890, Tippu Tip left Zaire for the last time. After his departure, Leopold's government overwhelmed the Arabs and dismantled Tippu Tip's empire. Tippu Tip lost most of his wealth and retired to Zanzibar.

Tippu Tip's commercial role in eastern Zaire may not have been a lasting one. However, he is remembered even today for the permanent contribution he made to the development of the Swahili language in Zaire. He did this by writing his autobiography — a book which became a classic in Swahili literature.

- Ziber Pasha was established at Rabah as the master of the Azande trade of some 25,000 slaves per year.
- *Eastern Africa:* Emperor Theodore II of Ethiopia made an unsuccessful attempt to oust Menelik, the Muslim, from Shoa. *See 1913.*
- The British Consul Cameron was arrested.
- Massawa was purchased from Turkey.

Massawa (Mits'iwa) is the main Red Sea port of Eritrea, a province of Ethiopia.

- *Southern Africa:* The British Kaffraria was incorporated into the Cape Colony (March 27).
- The Orange Free State — Basuto war was waged (June).

Masupha, the Basuto sub-chief and military commander of Moshoeshoe's forces, was defeated during the 1865 war with the neighbor-ing Orange Free State Republic, but re-established his reputation two years later in an action which saved the Sotho from conquest by the Free State.

During the Free State wars with Moshoeshoe in 1855 and 1865, Moroka, the Rolong chief, sided with the Afrikaners. In 1865, the Orange Free State President Johannes Brand rewarded Moroka with formal recognition of Rolong independence within the republic's borders. However, Rolong independence was lost four years after Moroka's death in 1880, when the Orange Free State annexed Thaba Nchu.

The Orange Free State was first settled by Afrikaners during their emigration from the Cape Colony around 1836. No attempt was made to establish a central government until 1848 when the British Governor Henry Smith annexed the country, together with Basutoland, as the Orange River Sovereignty.

When the British abandoned the territory, the Orange Free State Republic was formed and its first president elected. The Free State lost its independence during the South African War (the Boer War) and has since existed as a province of South Africa.

- The British treaty with Rasoherina was negotiated.
- There was an economic depression throughout South Africa.
- Dalindyebo (1865–1920), a future Thembu paramount chief, was born.

Dalindyebo was educated in a local Methodist mission school. Dalindyebo professed Christianity, but was never baptized.

Dalindyebo succeeded his father, Ngangelizwe, in 1884. Eight months later Thembu country was formally annexed to the Cape Colony.

Dalindyebo's peaceful reign contrasted sharply with that of his father. His policies were generally progressive. Immediately after his succession, Dalindyebo accepted the temporal leadership of Nehemiah Tile's Thembu National Church. However soon thereafter, Dalindyebo broke from the church and gave his support of the older Methodist churches.

RELATED HISTORICAL EVENTS

- *The United States:* Abraham Lincoln (1809–1865), the "Great Emancipator," died.

Abraham Lincoln (1809–1865) was born in a log cabin on a farm located about 5 miles south of Elizabethtown, Kentucky. Raised on the Indiana frontier, as a young man Lincoln settled in

Illinois. Self-educated, Lincoln began his practice of law in 1837, in Springfield, Illinois.

In 1846, Lincoln was elected to the House of Representatives as a member of the Whig Party. However, Lincoln joined the new Republican Party in 1856 when the Whig Party split over the issue of slavery.

Although Lincoln's public anti-slavery views were limited to a stated desire to keep the institution of slavery from spreading to the new territories, he was seen by Southerners as a dangerous enemy. Lincoln's refusal to concede to Confederate demands for the evacuation of the federal garrison at Fort Sumter, South Carolina, led to the eruption of hostilities which became the Civil War.

At the inception of the Civil War, Lincoln's chief concern was the preservation of the Union as opposed to the abolition of slavery. However, as the war dragged on, the abolition of slavery became more and more a political necessity. Thus, Lincoln's issuance of the Emancipation Proclamation was more a political document than a grand statement of moral principle.

Despite common misconceptions, the Emancipation Proclamation did not end slavery. The Emancipation Proclamation merely set free those slaves who were located in states still engaged in rebellion against the federal government. The slaves who were located in the border states that remained loyal to the Union remained enslaved. However, with the Emancipation Proclamation, the Union cause became a moral cause and the Proclamation served to end European sympathies for the Confederacy.

Lincoln was re-elected with a large majority in 1864 on a National Union platform. With a Union victory in sight, in his second inaugural address, Lincoln advocated a policy of reconciliation with the South stressing a need to a reconcile "with malice toward none, with charity for all."

The Confederate forces of Robert E. Lee surrendered to Ulysses S. Grant on April 9, 1865. Five days later, Abraham Lincoln was shot in a Washington, D. C. theater by an actor and Confederate sympathizer, John Wilkes Booth.

In the intervening years since Lincoln's death, much has been written concerning Lincoln's pre-occupation with the preservation of the Union over the eradication of slavery — concerning Lincoln's desire to maximize the opportunities of European Americans as a reason for his opposition to the expansion of slavery — concerning Lincoln's reticence at issuing the Emancipation Proclamation. However, despite the criticisms, in reading Lincoln's words and reviewing his career, one cannot help but be persuaded by his overriding humanity.

In African American history, one finds Lincoln to be a compelling person. Lincoln was a man who was a product of his time but whose life legacy transcends time.

Lincoln, better than any other person, enunciated the arguments against slavery in a manner which made them comprehensible to the common person — to the average American. His words often communicated not just to the mind but to the soul of European America.

In the long run, history will record that the greatness of Lincoln rests with his emancipation of his people. To the extent that Lincoln's words (and deeds) led to the spiritual emancipation — the uplifting — of the European American, — and to the extent that the spiritual emancipation of the European American, in turn, led to the physical emancipation of African Americans — it is to this extent that the greatness of Abraham Lincoln cannot be denied.

Four score and seven years ago our fathers brought forth, upon this continent, a new nation, conceived in Liberty, and dedicated to the proposition that all men are created equal.

Now we are engaged in a great civil war, testing whether that nation, or any nation, so conceived, and so dedicated, can long endure. We are met here on a great battle-field of that war. We have come to dedicate a portion of it as a final resting place for those who here gave their lives that that nation might live. It is altogether fitting and proper that we should do this.

But in a larger sense we can not dedicate — we can not consecrate — we can not hallow this ground. The brave men, living and dead, who struggled here, have consecrated it far above our poor power to add or detract. The world will little note, nor long remember, what we say here, but can never forget what they did here. It is for us, the living, rather to be dedicated here to the unfinished work which they have, thus far, so nobly carried on. It is rather for us to be here dedicated to the great task remaining before us — that from these honored dead we take increased devotion to that cause for which they here gave the last full measure of devotion — that we here highly resolve that these dead shall not have died in vain; that this nation shall have a new birth of freedom; and this government of the people, by the people, for the people, shall not perish from the earth.

— Lincoln's Gettysburg Address

• *The Americas:* The Paraguayan War (War of the Triple Alliance) began.

The War of the Triple Alliance played a significant role in the liberation of slaves in Brazil. In 1852, having invaded Uruguay and having put a puppet in charge, the government of the Second Empire of Brazil, then in league with Argentine rebels, won a major victory over the Uruguayan dictator, Juan Manuel de Rosas.

In 1864, Brazil again invaded Uruguay. This invasion provoked the Paraguayan dictator Francisco Solano Lopez, who feared for the survival of his own country, into invading both Argentine and Brazilian territory. The ensuing War of the Triple Alliance (Argentina, Brazil and Uruguay versus Paraguay) lasted for five years. When it ended most of the male population of Paraguay had been killed.

The slices of territory gained from Uruguay and Paraguay cost the Brazilian empire much of its stability. The war had been fought largely by troops of mixed race, some of them slaves recruited with the promise of freedom, who, in Argentina and Paraguay, encountered societies free of the taint of slavery. Additionally, the war had been an extremely expensive endeavor. As a result, a large increase in the foreign debt had become necessary. Finally, the officer class had grown and become a formidable and potentially challenging political force. These factors would all contribute to dramatic changes in Brazil.

• *Europe:* Spain created the Junta de Informacion.

• *Africa:* Heinrich Barth (1821–1865), a German explorer of Africa, died.

Heinrich Barth set out from Tripoli in 1850 as part of a British expedition to explore central Sudan. When the British leader died in northern Nigeria, Barth assumed command.

Barth explored the southern Lake Chad region and the upper Benue River (in today's Cameroon). He then headed for Timbuktu.

Barth arrived in Timbuktu in 1853. He stayed there for six months with Ahmad al-Bakka'i before recrossing the Sahara.

Barth returned to London in 1855 and set about writing his account of his travels. Barth published the five volume *Travels and Discoveries in North and Central Africa* over a two year period in 1857 and 1858. *Travels and Discoveries in North and Central Africa* is considered to be the most accurate and comprehensive explorer's accounting of West Africa during the mid–nineteenth century.

• Alfred Bryant (1865–1953), an English missionary and historian of the Zulu, was born.

Alfred T. Bryant arrived in South Africa in 1883 as a Roman Catholic missionary. Bryant worked first among the southern Nguni of the eastern Cape Province. Bryant then moved to Zululand (in 1896) where he remained for the rest of his life.

Bryant's works documenting Zulu language, ethnography, and history became classics. His most influential work was *Olden Times in Zululand and Natal* which was published in 1929. *Olden Times in Zululand and Natal* detailed the northern Nguni history through the time of the legendary Zulu chief, Shaka.

1866

THE UNITED STATES

• Several prominent African Americans, including Frederick Douglass, met with President Johnson to ask him to grant and guarantee suffrage for African Americans.

• President Johnson dispatched Carl Schurz on a tour of the South. Schurz's report on the observations made during this tour indicated that Johnson's Reconstruction Plan had failed especially with regards to integration of the African American into the mainstream of Southern society. This report was influential in forming the basis for the Radical position that the African American needed Federal assistance to achieve equality of opportunity.

The original Freedmen's Bureau Bill was amended in February of 1866. The bill amendment extended the Bureau's life. The provisions of the bill amendment set salaries of Bureau officials at $500 to $1200 per year and validated titles granted pursuant to General Sherman's orders of January 1865.

The amended Freedmen's Bureau Bill also provided that land be procured and schools and asylums to be erected. The bill mandated that the President provide military protection where the civil rights of African Americans were denied. According to the bill, any person depriving another's civil rights was to be punished by a $1,000 fine and/or one year in prison. The Bureau's power to oversee labor contracts was increased and it was authorized to establish special courts if justice was unobtainable in regular courts.

The amended Freedmen's Bureau Bill was a strong piece of civil rights legislation and President Andrew Johnson disagreed with it. Johnson vetoed the bill claiming that Congress did not have the authority to legislate for the states — the Southern states — which were not, at that time, represented in Congress.

Despite its Reconstructionist pronouncements, Congress was unable to override Johnson's veto in large part because six Republican Senators deserted their party. The vote in the Senate was 30 to 18. In other words, the vote to override the veto failed by three votes.

• In May, the House of Representatives passed a revised bill on the Freedmen's Bureau to replace the one vetoed by President Johnson. The new Freedmen's Bureau Bill provided that (1) the Bureau's life was limited to two years; (2) land held under General Sherman's field orders was to be restored to the original owners; (3) some property was to be appropriated for educational purposes; and (4) military protection of civil rights was to be guaranteed. The vote in the House was 96 to 32. President Johnson vetoed this revised version of the bill as well. However, unlike its predecessor, this bill was passed over his veto and became law.

What is not commonly understood about the Freedmen's Bureau was that it benefitted European Americans as well as the newly emancipated African American populace. In 1866, the federal government through the Freedmen's Bureau issued some 4,000,000 rations to an average of 21,000 people per month. Of this 21,000, 14,000 were European American while only 7,000 were African American.

It is sad and tragic that almost from the very beginning the government programs which were theoretically designed to benefit only African Americans strangely, invariably wound up benefitting European Americans the most. This historical precedent would repeat itself over and over again and continues to exist in the government programs which are being implemented to this day.

• During the 39th Congressional session, some 140 different proposals to change the Constitution were made. Among these 140 proposals, 45 dealt with apportionment and 31 were concerned with civil and political rights.

During the course of the debate over the Constitutional Amendments, the conservative Republicans advocated two amendments under which (1) African Americans were to be guaranteed equal civil rights but not necessarily equal political rights and (2) states which did not provide for African American suffrage — which denied African Americans the right to vote — were to suffer reduced representation in Congress and in the Electoral College.

The proposals advanced by the radical Republicans who were led by Thaddeus Stevens and Charles Sumner included amendments under which (1) Southern European Americans were to be disenfranchised — denied the right to vote — and (2) a new South would be created which was to be based upon universal suffrage for African Americans.

Ultimately, out of the dialogue and debate came the Civil Rights Act of 1866. Passed by both Houses of Congress on March 14, 1866, the Act conferred citizenship on African Americans (on "all persons born in the United States and not subject to any foreign powers, excluding Indians not taxed"). The Act also gave citizens "of every race and color" equal rights to make contracts, sue, testify in court, purchase, hold and dispose of property, and to enjoy "full and equal benefit of all laws."

The Civil Rights Act of 1866 also provided that all citizens were to be subject to "like punishment, pains and penalties" and it made any violations of its provisions punishable by fine and/or imprisonment. The Act gave jurisdiction for its enforcement to the United States District Courts and gave power of arrest to United States marshals and attorneys.

President Johnson vetoed the Civil Rights Act of 1866. However, Congress overrode his veto on April 6 and April 9.

With the passage of the Civil Rights Act of 1866, the insidious Black Codes were essentially nullified.

Upon his taking office following the assassination of Abraham Lincoln, Andrew Johnson enjoyed widespread support and popularity. However, this support and goodwill quickly evaporated as Johnson's Southern upbringing came to the fore on the issue of civil rights for African Americans.

One of the first acts which caused widespread criticism of Johnson, was his decision to grant amnesty to all but a few wealthy and leading former Confederates. In doing so, Johnson seemingly invited the remaining Confederates to re-assume their control over the governance of the South. Johnson exacerbated the criticism on this issue by requiring very little of the ex–Confederates while at the same time permitting them to exclude African Americans from voting. Additionally, Johnson took the egregious step of ordering the land which had been awarded to former slaves returned to the European Americans who were the previous owners.

With the ex–Confederates back in control, many Southern states enacted Black Codes — laws which authorized discrimination on a racial basis. The Republican Congress, shocked by the enactment of the Black Codes and the election of prominent ex–Confederates, refused to seat any Southern representatives. A clash between the President and the Congress was rapidly approaching.

Johnson helped to precipitate the clash by vetoing the rather moderate Freedmen's Bureau and Civil Rights bills. In overriding Johnson's veto on the Civil Rights bill, Congress essentially established its own Reconstruction Plan — the framework of which would later become the Fourteenth Amendment to the Constitution.

Johnson continued his efforts to block the Republican Reconstruction Plan. To that end, in the Fall of 1866, Johnson attempted to form a new political party — but without success.

In retaliation to Johnson's obstinacy, Congress then passed a Tenure of Office Act and other measures designed to curtail the power of the Presidency. Congress also instituted an even more radical Reconstruction policy which was based upon universal suffrage for African Americans.

The Civil Rights Act of 1866

The following are excerpts taken from the Civil Rights Act of 1866 which was approved by Congress (by a veto override) on April 9. The Civil Rights Act conferred citizenship upon African Americans and was designed to supersede the Dred Scott decision of 1857. The Civil Rights Act of 1866 also served to strike down several of the Black Codes which had been enacted in Southern states following the Civil War.

The Civil Rights Act of 1866 was the first federal statute to define citizenship and to guarantee civil rights within states. Due to its perceived infringement on the authority of the individual states, there was some doubt that its provisions could withstand a constitutional challenge. Given this concern, Congress later on in 1866 passed the Fourteenth Amendment to the United States Constitution — an amendment which contained a number of the more prominent provisions of the Civil Rights Act of 1866.

An Act to Protect all Persons in the United States in their Civil Rights, and Furnish the Means of their Vindication.

Be it enacted by the Senate and House of Representatives of the United States of America in Congress assembled, that all persons born in the United States and not subject to any foreign power, excluding Indians not taxed, are hereby declared to be citizens of the United States; and such citizens, of every race and color, without regard to any previous condition of slavery or involuntary servitude, except as a punishment for crime whereof the party shall have been duly convicted, shall have the same right, in every state and territory in the United States, to make and enforce contracts; to sue; be parties, and give evidence; to inherit, purchase, lease, sell, hold, and convey real and personal property; and to full and equal benefit of all laws and proceedings for the security of person and property as is enjoyed by white citizens, and shall be subject to like punishment, pains, and penalties, and to none other, any law, statute, ordinance, regulation, or custom to the contrary notwithstanding.

Section 2. *And be it further enacted,* that any person who, under color of any law, statute, ordinance, regulation, or custom, shall subject, or cause to be subjected, any inhabitant of any state or territory to the deprivation of any right secured or protected by this act, or to different punishment, pains, or penalties on account of such person having at any time been held in a condition of slavery or involuntary servitude, except as a punishment for crime whereof the party shall have been duly convicted, or by reason of his color or race, than is prescribed for the punishment of white persons, shall be deemed guilty of a misdemeanor, and, on conviction, shall be punished by fine not exceeding $1,000 or imprisonment not exceeding one year, or both, in the discretion of the court.

Section 3. *And be it further enacted,* that the district courts of the United States, within their respective districts, shall have, exclusively of the courts of the several states, cognizance of all crimes and offenses committed against the provisions of this act, and also, concurrently with the circuit courts of the United States, of all causes, civil and criminal, affecting persons who are denied or cannot enforce in the courts or judicial tribunals of the state or locality where they may be any of the rights secured to them by the 1st Section of this act; and if any suit or prosecution, civil or criminal, has been or shall be commenced in any state court, against any such person, for any cause whatsoever, or against any officer, civil or military, or other person, for any arrest or imprisonment, trespasses, or wrongs done or committed by virtue or under color of authority derived from this act or the act establishing a bureau for the relief of freedmen and refugees, and all acts amendatory thereof, or for refusing to do any act upon the ground that it would be inconsistent with this act, such defendant shall have the right to remove such cause for trial to the proper district or circuit court in the manner prescribed by the "Act relating to habeas corpus and regulating judicial proceedings in certain cases," approved March 3, 1863, and all acts amendatory thereof. ...

Section 4. *And be it further enacted,* that the district attorneys, marshals, and deputy marshals of the United States, the commissioners appointed by the circuit and territorial courts of the United States, with powers of arresting, imprisoning, or bailing offenders against the laws of the United States, the officers and agents of the Freedmen's Bureau, and every other officer who may be specially empowered by the President of the United States, shall be, and they are hereby, specially authorized and required, at the expense of the United States, to institute proceedings against all and every person who shall violate the provisions of this act, and cause him or them to be arrested and imprisoned, or bailed, as the case may be, for trial before such court of the United States or territorial court as by this act has cognizance of the offense.

And with a view to affording reasonable protection to all persons in their constitutional rights of equality before the law, without distinction of race or color, or previous condition of slavery or involuntary servitude, except as a punishment for crime, whereof the party shall have been duly convicted, and to the prompt discharge of the duties of this act, it shall be the duty of the circuit courts of the United States and the superior courts of the territories of the United States, from time to time, to increase the number of commissioners so as to afford a speedy and convenient means for the arrest and examination of persons charged with a violation of this act; and such commissioners are hereby authorized and required to exercise and discharge all the powers and duties conferred on them by this act, and the same duties with regards to offenses created by this act, as they are authorized by law to exercise with regard to other offenses against the laws of the United States. ...

Section 8. *And be it further enacted,* that whenever the President of the United States shall have reason to believe that offenses have been or are likely to be committed against the provisions of this act within any judicial district, it shall be unlawful for him, in his discretion, to direct the judge, marshal, and district attorney of such district to attend at such place within the district, and for such time as he may designate, for the purpose of the more speedy arrest and trial of persons charged with a violation of this act; and it shall be the duty of every judge or other officer, when any such requisition shall be received by him, to attend at the place and for the time therein designated.

Section 9. *And be it further enacted,* that it shall be lawful for the President of the United States, or such persons as he may empower for that purpose, to employ such part of the land or naval forces of the United States, or of the militia, as shall be necessary to prevent the violation and enforce the due execution of this act.

Section 10. *And be it further enacted,* that, upon all questions of law arising in any cause under the provisions of this act, a final appeal may be taken to the Supreme Court of the United States.

• Congress declared that no Representatives or Senators from any Southern state were to be seated until both Houses of Congress declared that the state was entitled to such representation. However, later in the year, the representatives from Tennessee (President Johnson's home state) were re-admitted to Congress.

• A bill was introduced in Congress which provided that African American males were entitled to vote in the District of Columbia. This bill was passed in December by both Houses of Congress. A referendum was held in December of 1866 in which only the European American voters of Washington, D. C. were allowed to participate. The vote was 6,591 against the enfranchisement of African Americans while only 35 were in favor of African American suffrage.

• The Joint Committee of 15 (composed of Radical and Conservative Republicans) issued an 800 page report in which the Committee concluded that (1) Constitutional amendments were needed to protect African Americans from discrimination and (2) the ultimate control of Reconstruction was within the jurisdiction of Congress as opposed to the President.

The Fourteenth Amendment to the Constitution was introduced to the Thirty-ninth Congress in the Spring of 1866. The Fourteenth Amendment incorporated the substance of the Civil Rights Act of 1866 into its first section and then went on to (1) prohibit the states from enacting laws which abridged the privileges or immunities of United States citizens, from depriving persons of life, liberty or property without due process, from denying any person the equal jurisdiction of its laws; (2) enable Congress to reduce a state's Congressional representation if the state denied an adult male the right to vote for any reason other than crime or rebellion; and (3) declared anyone who held Federal or state office and had joined the Confederacy, ineligible for public office until pardoned by two-thirds of Congress. The Fourteenth Amendment reads:

Amendment XIV

Section 1. All persons born or naturalized in the United States, and subject to the jurisdiction thereof, are citizens of the United States and of the State wherein they reside. No State shall make or enforce any law which shall abridge the privileges or immunities of citizens of the United States; nor shall any State deprive any person of life, liberty, or property, without due process of law; nor deny to any person within its jurisdiction the equal protection of the laws.

Section 2. Representatives shall be apportioned among the several States according to their respective numbers, counting the whole number of persons in each State, excluding Indians not taxed. But when the right to vote at any election for the choice of electors for President and Vice President of the United States, Representatives in Congress, the Exec-utive and Judicial officers of a State, or the members of the Legislature thereof, is denied to any of the male inhabitants of such State, being twenty-one years of age, and citizens of the United States, or in any way abridged, except for participation in rebellion, or other crime, the basis of representation therein shall be reduced in the proportion which the number of such male citizens shall bear to the whole number of male citizens twenty-one years of age in such State.

Section 3. No person shall be a Senator or Representative in Congress, or elector of President and Vice President, or hold any office, civil or military, under the United States, or under any State, who, having previously taken an oath, as a member of Congress, or as an officer of the United States, or as a member of any State, to support the Constitution of the United States, shall have engaged in insurrection or rebellion against the same, or given aid or comfort to the enemies thereof. But Congress may by a vote of two-thirds of each House, remove such disability.

Section 4. The validity of the public debt of the United States, authorized by law, including debts incurred for payment of pensions and bounties for services in suppressing insurrection or rebellion, shall not be questioned. But neither the United States nor any State shall assume or pay any debt or obligation incurred in aid of insurrection or rebellion against the United States, or any claim for the loss or emancipation of any slave; but all such debts, obligations and claims shall be held illegal and void.

Section 5. The Congress shall have power to enforce, by appropriate legislation, the provisions of this article.

The Fourteenth Amendment was passed by the House of Representatives on May 10, 1866 by a vote of 128 to 37 with 19 not voting. The Amendment was passed by the Senate on June 8, 1866 by a vote of 33 to 11 with 5 not voting. The amendment was then proposed to the legislatures of the then existing states on June 13, 1866. The ratification process lasted two years. On July 21, 1868, the Fourteenth Amendment was ratified and became the law of the land.

President Andrew Johnson denounced the Fourteenth Amendment and urged the Southern states not to ratify it. Most of the Southern states heeded Johnson's call. However, ironically, the one Southern state which did not heed Johnson's call was Johnson's home state of Tennessee.

Tennessee was one of the first to ratify the Fourteenth Amendment, doing so on July 19, 1866.

• On July 4, President Andrew Johnson issued another proclamation granting general amnesty to the Confederate participants in the Civil War.

• As evidence of the growing rift between the President and the Congress, in August, President Andrew Johnson attempted to form a new party. The National Union Convention was held in August in Philadelphia with representatives from both North and South, but mostly Democrats. In its Declaration of Principles, the National Union Convention declared that Congress had no right to deny Congressional representation to any state; that each state had the right to decide voting qualifications; and that the Constitution could not be amended unless all the states were represented in Congress. The convention attendees also endorsed Andrew Johnson, denied a desire to restore slavery, and ratified the invalidity of the Confederate debt.

• President Johnson officially declared the Civil War to be ended (August 20).

• In Congress, Thaddeus Stevens forwarded a proposal to distribute public and confiscated lands in the South to freedmen in 40 acre lots. The proposal was defeated in the House of Representatives 126 to 37.

• In September, in Philadelphia, a convention of Southern Loyalists and Northern Republicans met.

The delegates to this convention included Horace Greeley, John Jacob Astor, Carl Schurz, Frederick Douglass, and Thomas Benton. Douglass was elected from Rochester, New York—an act which was deemed to be a great "honor" which was being bestowed upon him. However, the conveners asked Douglass not to actually attend the convention because of their concern over the controversy and uproar which might become attached to the convention due to Douglass' attendance. To this request, Douglass replied:

> *"Gentlemen, with all respect, you might as well ask me to put a loaded pistol to my head and blow my brains out, as to ask me to keep out of this convention, to which I have been duly elected."*

The convention would ultimately adopt a declaration which called for universal male suffrage—the right to vote for all men.

• Massachusetts became the first Northern state to elect African Americans to its Legislature. These first African American legislators were Edward Garrison Walker (1830–1910) and Charles Lewis Mitchell (1829–1912).

Edward Walker is said to have been the first African American elected on the grounds that the polls in his ward closed a few hours earlier than those in Mitchell's. Walker was the son of David Walker, the author of the inflammatory tract known as *David Walker's Appeal.* Edward Walker became a prominent Boston attorney and was a Democrat in an era when most prominent African Americans were Republicans.

As for Charles Mitchell, Mitchell, who lost his foot during service in the Civil War, would later serve as the first African American inspector of customs in Boston.

• In a riot in Memphis, Tennessee, 46 African Americans and two European American sympathizers were killed. Another 75 African Americans were injured while 90 homes, 12 schools and four churches in the African American sector of the city were burned.

• In New Orleans, 35 African Americans were killed and more than 100 were wounded as a result of a race riot.

• Two African American cavalry units, the 9th and 10th Cavalry, were organized. These units were comprised primarily of African American Civil War veterans.

• In 1866, cotton sold for thirty cents per pound. In this year, the cotton crop was only 1.9 million bales in comparison to the 5 million bales which had been produced in 1861.

• *Labor Movement:* The National Labor Union which had been organized in Baltimore, Maryland, proclaimed that African Americans had to be unionized in order to prevent them from being used as scabs—as strike breakers.

• *Notable Births:* Henry Thacker Burleigh (1866–1949), a famed African American concert baritone and composer, was born (December 2).

Henry Thacker Burleigh was born in Erie, Pennsylvania. As a youth, Burleigh began singing in local choirs. The richness of his voice soon attracted attention and Burleigh was able to secure a scholarship to study with Dvorak at the National Conservatory of Music in New York.

Henry Burleigh would later come to teach at the conservatory and was the soloist from 1894 to 1946 at Saint George's Church in New York City. Burleigh also served as soloist for the Temple Emanuel for over twenty years.

In his long concert career, Burleigh sang his own compositions and became famous for his arrangements of such African American (Negro) spirituals as *Deep River* and *Were You There?*

• Matthew Alexander Henson (1866–1955), a legendary African American explorer, was born (August 8).

Matthew Alexander Henson was born in Culver City, Charles County, Maryland. He was orphaned at an early age which led to his shipping out as a cabin boy. The captain of the vessel came to recognize Matthew's abilities and encouraged him to read and study.

While working at a naval supply shop in New York City, Henson met Robert Peary, a naval engineer. Henson and Peary developed a close friendship. This friendship led Henson to become Peary's "right-hand man" on Peary's geographical expeditions to Central America and Greenland for the United States Navy.

In 1888, Peary and Henson went to Baffin Bay. Henson, because of his knowledge of the Eskimo language and his experience as a navigator, was an invaluable aid to Peary.

Over the next twenty-five years, Peary and Henson would make some seven Arctic explorations. On their famous 1908–1909 expedition, Henson was the one who was the first to set foot on the North Pole and it was Henson who planted the United States flag at the site which is deemed to be "the top of the world."

During their period of collaboration, Peary lectured widely while Henson became a consultant on Arctic geography to the American Museum of Natural History in New York.

Because of his exploits, Matthew Henson became an acknowledged expert on the Arctic and its people. On April 6, 1954, his noted career was honored by President Dwight Eisenhower who bestowed upon Henson a medal commemorating his landmark achievement of 1909.

In most books, the biography of Matthew Henson, reads like any other recitation of historical facts and accomplishments. The recitation marks the noteworthiness of the individual but fails to capture the essence of the man. In doing so, much — so very much — can be lost.

The historical biography of Matthew Henson is one of those tales which similarly impresses us but fails to fully inform us. For the full story, we need to go beyond what is reported in most history texts.

In the September, 1988 edition of National Geographic Magazine, a triad of articles appeared concerning the eightieth anniversary of Peary's expedition to the North Pole. The articles noted that the relationship between Peary and Henson was more than just collaborators. These two men had spent much of their adult lives together in harsh, unpredictable circumstances. The experiences of these two men had come to solidify the bond between them, and while they were in Greenland and on their Arctic expeditions, their differing skin colors did not matter. During those trying and sometimes exhilarating times, these two men were brothers — brothers in a sense that transcends blood or skin.

As the National Geographic articles relate, the legacy of Robert Peary and Matthew Henson is not a static recitation of history but rather a living, breathing testament to the brotherhood of man. For, as articles report, in Greenland, there lives today the descendants of Robert Peary and Matthew Henson. These men who had left part of their souls in the frozen North had also left children from their liaisons with the Eskimo women. These children bear the undeniable physical traits of their forefathers. They also bear their forefathers last names. Thus, in Greenland, one can today find scores of Hensons and Pearys who are directly descended from the two great explorers.

And indeed, perhaps most fittingly — most poignantly — of all, one can find a Kitdlaq Henson who is married to Kista Peary and see that they now have children of their own.

Thus, the essential part of the story — the lasting legacy — of Robert Peary and Matthew Henson is not just that they were brothers in spirit but that today, through their descendants, they have become brothers in blood and will be so — forevermore.

• *Notable Deaths:* Samuel Ringgold Ward (1817–1866), the "Black Daniel Webster," died. He was one of the most noted abolitionists (October 17).

In 1839, Samuel Ringgold Ward, an escaped slave, became a professional anti-slavery agent for the American Anti-slavery Society. Ward had been educated in New York and became a Presbyterian minister there. Ward pastored a European American church in South Butler, New York. Ward was also one of the first African Americans to join the Liberty Party. Ward later lived abroad, first, in England and, lastly, in Jamaica. He would die in poverty in Jamaica.

• *Miscellaneous State Laws:* New Mexico repealed a statute which prohibited interracial marriage.

• Nebraska's Constitution of 1866 granted the right to vote to European Americans only.

• The Tennessee Legislature confined suffrage to European Americans.

• *Scholastic Achievements:* James Milton Turner was appointed to the Kansas City School Board and was, subsequently, authorized to conduct a school for African American children — the first such school reported to exist in Missouri (April). *See 1915.*

• The Methodist Episcopal Church founded the Centenary Biblical Institute in Baltimore, Maryland. This Institute later became Morgan State College. The Methodist Episcopal Church would also later establish Rust College in Holly Springs, Mississippi. Rust College was initially named Shaw University but, in 1890, the name was changed, presumably to avoid confusion with the school of the same name located in Raleigh, North Carolina. The renamed college was named for Richard Rust, a European American anti-slavery advocate who supported the Freedmen's Aid Society of the Methodist Episcopal Church.

• The American Missionary Association established Trinity College in Athens, Alabama; Gregory in Wilmington, North Carolina; and Fisk University in Nashville, Tennessee. Fisk was founded on January 9.

• Edward Waters College of Jacksonville, Florida, became the first institution of higher learning in Florida for African Americans. It was founded in Live Oak, Florida, by the African Methodist Episcopal Church. It was renamed Brown University and moved to Jacksonville. In 1892, the University was again renamed and was incorporated as Edward Waters College.

• Jonathan Jasper Wright (1840–1885) was admitted to the state bar of Pennsylvania.

• *The Arts and Sciences:* The *London Art Journal* named Robert Duncanson, an African American, as one of the outstanding landscape artists of the times.

• *Black Enterprise:* By 1866, African Americans in Florida had secured homesteads covering 160,000 acres of land.

• Military banks that could safeguard the deposits made by African Americans were established in New Orleans (Louisiana), Norfolk (Virginia) and Beaufort (South Carolina). The Beaufort bank received deposits in excess of $200,000.

• The Chesapeake Marine Railway and Drydock Company of Baltimore, Maryland, became the first major African American shipfitting company. It was organized by Isaac Myers and it stayed in business until 1884. The company was formed by and for African American workers driven from the longshoremen and caulkers trades by European American laborers.

• Biddy Mason (1818–1891) became the first African American woman to own property in Los Angeles, California.

Born into slavery in Georgia or Mississippi, Biddy Mason and her owner moved to the Utah Territory and then to California. In California, Mason legally gained her freedom on January 21, 1856.

Mason worked as a nurse and midwife. It was her thriftiness which enabled her to purchase property in Los Angeles and which led to her son Robert being called the richest African American in Los Angeles in 1900.

A very religious and charitable woman, Mason opened her home for the establishment of the first African Methodist Episcopal church in Los Angeles in 1872.

THE AMERICAS

• *Antigua:* George Alexander McGuire, the first bishop of the African Orthodox Church, was born in Antigua (March 26).

• *Canada:* After the Civil War in the United States had essentially come to an end, the African Americans who had gone north to Canada on the Underground Railroad began to drift back to the United States. It is estimated that two-thirds of the 30,000 African Americans who had gone to Canada eventually made their way back to the United States.

• Mifflin Wister Gibbs was elected to the city council of Victoria, British Columbia.

• *Cuba:* In 1866, the Board of Information on Reforms in Cuba and Puerto Rico, convened by Spain, met with Cuban reformers who sought gradual abolition with compensation, cessation of the slave trade, an immigration plan, free commercial exchange, and assimilation giving Cuba the character of a Spanish province. Spain responded with the application of a direct tax of ten percent on revenue without eliminating tariffs, and it acceded to none of the other suggestions of the Board. This failure and the new tax led to a separatist rebellion — the "Grito de Yara" — which began on October 10, 1868. Led by Carlos Manuel de Cespedes, the uprising started the Ten Years War.

• *Haiti:* Georges Sylvain (1866–1925), a poet, was born in Puerto-Plata in the Dominican Republic.

Georges Sylvain was educated in Puerto-Plata and then in Paris. After obtaining a degree in law in France, Sylvain returned to Haiti in 1888. Upon his return, Sylvain founded the law school of Haiti, the periodical *La Patrie,* and, in 1922, the periodical *l'Union Patriotique.*

Sylvain belonged to the famous literary circle, *La Ronde.* His most noted literary accomplishment was the publication of a compilation of twenty-nine poems entitled *Confidences et Melancolies* (1901).

AFRICA

In 1866, financed mostly by friends and admirers, David Livingstone began an expedition to discover the sources of the Nile. Traveling along the Rovuma River, the explorer made his way toward Lake Tanganyika, reaching its shores in 1869.

During this Nile expedition, little was heard from Livingstone and his welfare became a matter of international concern. In 1870, Livingstone journeyed to Ujiji, on Lake Tanganyika, into the region lying west of the lake, thereby becoming the first European to visit the Lualaba River (in present day Zaire).

After enduring great privations, Livingstone made his return to Ujiji. Upon his arrival, he was met by a "rescue party" led by Henry Morton Stanley, a European American journalist. The story goes that at this meeting Stanley reportedly greeted Livingstone with the famous question, "Dr. Livingstone, I presume?"

• *North Africa, Egypt and Sudan:* The Assembly of Delegates, a quasi-parliament, was established for Egypt (November). It was composed of seventy-five members, principally village headmen. Under the Organic Law, the powers of the Assembly were limited.

• An Egyptian military mission was dispatched to Europe. The Egyptian army was re-equipped with Krupp armaments and United States made Remington rifles.

• The first Egyptian stamps were issued.

• Baqqara raided Kordofan.

• *Western Africa:* France acquired the River Caramance, Rio Cassinie, Rio Nunez, Rio Pongo and River Mellacorte on the Guinea coast.

• The governor of Sierra Leone became the Governor in Chief of West African settlements. A separate Legislative Council was established for Sierra Leone.

Sierra Leone was founded in 1787 as a settler colony for persons of African descent living in England and the British colonies (principally Nova Scotia and the West Indies). In 1808, Sierra Leone became a crown colony. At various times between 1821 and 1888, the governors of Sierra Leone had jurisdiction over Lagos, the Gold Coast (Ghana), and the Gambia. The colony's interior was annexed in the form of a protectorate in 1896.

Sierra Leone achieved independence in 1961.

• George Pepple became the ruler of the Ijo trading state of Bonny (Nigeria).

George Pepple succeeded his father, William Dappa Pepple, who died in 1866. William Pepple had sent George to England, where he was educated and became a Christian. However, these changes alienated George from many of his subjects upon his return to Bonny.

George Pepple is generally regarded as a weak personality and a weak ruler. He allowed his kingdom to be controlled by Oko Jumbo, head of one of the two rival trading houses of the city state. The result was warfare between the two houses, and the situation led Jaja, the head of the second house, to leave Bonny and found Opobo. In later years, Opobo would eclipse Bonny as a trading center and the fortunes of Bonny soon declined.

*   *   *

Oko Jumbo was the de facto ruler of the Niger trading state of Bonny during the civil war of the mid–1800s. Oko Jumbo was one of the new class of men who had risen from slavery to become the leading member of the Manilla Pepple House, one of the two main palm oil trading houses in Bonny.

Despite his slave origins, Oko Jumbo strongly supported the traditional monarchy against Jaja *(see 1891),* another ex-slave who headed a rival house.

In 1866, Oko took control of Bonny affairs when Bonny's weak ruler, George Pepple, placed the Manilla Pepple House in a favorable position relative to Jaja's house. The hostility between Jaja and the monarchy led to civil war in 1869. This civil war gave Jaja the excuse to transfer his house to a new locale, which was strategically chosen to block Bonny's access to the palm oil producers of the interior. Bonny declined in importance thereafter.

• Joseph Ephraim Casely Hayford (1866–1930), the founder of the National Congress of British West Africa, was born.

Joseph Casely Hayford was born in the Gold Coast (now Ghana). He was descended, on his mother's side, from the Brew family *(see 1881),* a family long prominent in local trade and politics. His father was a minister.

Casely Hayford was educated at Cape Coast schools and at Fourah Bay College in Sierra Leone. Returning to the Gold Coast, Casely Hayford served as a high school principal. He lost his job after engaging in political activity. After working as a journalist, he went to England to study law, returning home in 1896.

The late 1890s and early 1900s were a period when the British were abandoning a policy of partnership with the educated elite in favor of alliances with traditional tribal chiefs. Casely Hayford entered local politics trying to unite the two elites.

In 1910, Casely Hayford achieved some success when he got the government to withdraw a forestry bill which would have removed African jurisdiction over certain categories of lands.

An increasingly vocal advocate of African control of governmental structure, Casely Hayford and colleagues from other British West African colonies planned, in 1913, a National Congress of British West Africa. The National Congress of British West Africa was organized to press for African political representation and equality in employment.

World War I delayed the formation of the National Congress of British West Africa. It would not begin functional operations until 1920.

By the time the National Congress of British West Africa began functioning, Casely Hayford and his colleagues had become convinced that it was the educated elite in whose hands the future of Africa lay. Casely Hayford was not opposed to the government granting increased recognition to the traditional elite as long as the rights and opportunities of the educated elite were not infringed upon. As a demonstration of this position, in the early 1920s, Casely Hayford agitated for the return from exile of Prempe I, the former Ashanti ruler who had been deposed in 1896.

The British governors of the colonies derided the claims of the National Congress that the Congress spoke for the African masses. However, in the 1920s, some concessions were made to the educated elite and the West African colonies were granted new constitutions which provided for legislative councils. Since governmental representatives on these legislative councils outnumbered elected ones, many members of the Congress boycotted the elections. However, Casely Hayford himself ran for office in the Gold Coast and was elected.

The National Congress of British West Africa never truly exerted effective political pressure. Eventually, it turned into a sort of social club with the encouragement of British administrators. Casely Hayford died in 1930 and soon thereafter the National Congress dissolved.

• William Dappa Pepple (1817–1866), the ruler of the Niger delta trading state of Bonny, died.

William Pepple's ascendancy to power ended an interregnum which had followed the death of his father, Opobo, in 1830. William Pepple found he needed British support to rid himself of the regent who had been ruling since Opobo's death. He reciprocated by negotiating three anti-slave trade treaties with the British from 1839 to 1844. Only the last was ratified in England.

Economic and social organization in Bonny was centered in its trading houses, which acted as brokers between the Europeans on the coast and the African palm oil producers of the interior. Two rival houses, the Manila Pepple house and the Anna Pepple house, came to dominate in Bonny.

In 1852, William Dappa had a stroke. As a result, William appointed two men from the Manila Pepple house as regents. The rival Anna Pepple house and the European traders were antagonized by this action, which upset the delicate balance. William Dappa also made a number of enemies when he took measures to enrich himself after his recovery from the stroke.

The British traders eventually sent for Consul John Beecroft. Beecroft presided over a court hearing in which William Dappa was deposed and exiled to England.

The ouster of William Dappa was one of the first steps in British intervention in Niger delta politics. The two powerful Pepple trading houses remained at odds and later the Manila house petitioned for the return of King William Dappa.

In 1861, William Dappa was permitted to return. However, by then the real power in Bonny rested elsewhere in the Manila and Anna Pepple houses. These two houses would fight with each other for supremacy for the remainder of William Dappa's life.

• *Central Africa:* War erupted between the Akwa and Bell tribes.

• The Portuguese abandoned Mpinda, San Salvador, Bembe, and Encoje.

• *Eastern Africa:* Hormuzd Rassam, the Assistant Political Officer in Aden, was sent to Ethiopia with Dr. Blanc to obtain Cameron's release. However, both Rassam and Blanc were arrested and imprisoned. Emperor Theodore upbraided the British captives and demanded that the British workmen make munitions for him (April 17). Subsequently, Gondar rebelled. The British prisoners were taken to Magdala. Theodore had Gondar razed by fire (December 2). He then fortified Magdala. *See 1868.*

• The building of Dar es Salaam was begun by Sayyid Majid.

Sayyid Majid Ibn Said (c.1835–1870) was the second Busaidi ruler of Zanzibar (Tanzania). During Majid's tenure as Sultan of Zanzibar, the first serious attempts were made by Zanzibar to dominate the Tanzanian mainland. Majid began to develop Dar es Salaam as a future capital, but died before the project was completed.

Today, Dar es Salaam, the pride of Sayyid Majid Ibn Said is the largest town and main port of Tanzania. It is Majid's greatest legacy.

The Busaidi dynasty of which Majid was a part originated in Oman. The Busaidi dynasty usurped the older Yarubi dynasty in 1741.

During the eighteenth century, the Busaidi intensified long-standing Omani commercial operations along the East African coast. The early Omani Sultans held the dynastic title of "Imam." "Imam" is a general Arabic term for Muslim prayer-leaders. However, the term "imam" is sometimes used as a dynastic title by secular rulers of Islamic states.

The use of the title "imam" as a designation was later changed to "Sayyid" (of "Seyyid") by Sayyid Said. Said moved his capital to Zanzibar in 1840, but he continued to exercise control over Oman.

On Said's death in 1856, the Busaidi divided into two lines. Sayyid's son Thuwain ruled in Oman, while another son, Majid, ruled in Zanzibar. This separation was formalized by British arbitration in 1861. Thereafter the Zanzibari line was independent of Oman.

During the late nineteenth century, the Busaidi maintained territorial "governors" on the African mainland, but their effective control was limited to a few coastal towns, such as Dar es Salaam and Mombasa.

In 1890, the Busaidi accepted a British protectorate. Independence was restored in 1964, but an immediate African revolution threw the Busaidi out and led to the merger of Zanzibar and Tanganyika as the United Republic of Tanzania.

*   *   *

"Seyyid" or "Sayyid" is the Islamic honorific title taken by learned men. The title was adopted as a dynastic title by the Busaidi dynasty of Zanzibar.

• A Zanzibari expedition against Witu proved to be unsuccessful.

• Swedish Lutheran missionaries were established at Massawa.

• Suakin and Massawa were granted by Turkey to Khedive Ismail as hereditary possessions.

• Mwanga II (c.1866–1903), the last independent ruler of the Ganda kingdom, is believed to have been born in this year. *See 1903.*

• The love affair of Salima gained international prominence.

Seyyida Salima (Emily Ruete) was the daughter of Sultan Seyyid Said. Salima was a pawn in European-Zanzibari relations. During the reign of her brother, Sultan Majid, Salima entered into a romantic affair with a German trader, Heinrich Reute. After becoming pregnant, in 1866, Salima, followed by Reute, made a dramatic escape from her brother on a British warship.

In exile in Aden, Salima was baptized a Christian and married Reute. She took the name Emily Reute (later changed to Ruete).

Prevented from returning to Zanzibar (now Tanzania) because of her serious breaches of Islamic law and her affronts to family honor, Salima accompanied her husband to Germany and became a German subject.

When Heinrich died in 1870, leaving Salima with three children and little money, Salima began a prolonged appeal for a share of her father's inheritance to the new Zanzibari sultan Barghash — another of Salima's brothers. Salima's persistence in this matter helped to strain Barghash's relations with British and German officials.

In 1885, the German chancellor Bismarck sent Salima and her children to Zanzibar on a German warship in a ploy to get Barghash *(see 1888)* to assent to German territorial demands on the mainland. Salima's son — a German subject —

was, after all, a potential candidate for the Zanzibari throne.

Before Salima arrived, Barghash submitted to the German demands. Nevertheless, Barghash agreed to pay Salima only token compensation.

Salima returned to Germany and, in 1886, she published her autobiography. This autobiography was translated in 1888 as *Memoirs of an Arabian Princess.*

> • *Southern Africa:* Amaxolo was annexed by Natal (January).
> • The Treaty of Thaba Bosiu was executed (April). Under the terms of the treaty, Moshoeshoe accepted the Orange Free State annexations.

In 1866, Molapo, Moshoeshoe's son, renewed the war between the Orange Free State and the Sotho by attacking the Afrikaners on his own initiative. Molapo brought down a retaliation he could not handle and was defeated.

Molapo then made his own peace with the Orange Free State President Johannes Brand *(see 1888)*. As a result of this peace, Molapo essentially became a vassal of the Orange Free State.

Moshoeshoe (see 1870) had no choice but to recognize the cession of Molapo's district to the Orange Free State.

> • Ciskei was annexed to Cape Colony.

As high commissioner for South Africa, Philip Wodehouse promoted the consolidation of border territories under the Cape administration. In 1866, Wodehouse succeeded in transferring the Xhosa territory of the Ciskei (British Kaffraria) from the imperial government to the Cape Colony. However, he failed to obtain sanction to annex Xhosa territories north of the Kei River.

> • Bishop Colenso was reinstated.

John William Colenso (1814–1893) was consecrated to the new diocese of Natal in 1853. Colenso came to settle there in 1855.

Bishop Colenso promoted an active missionary campaign among the Zulu, translated many religious works into Zulu, and published a number of non-orthodox treatises which aroused considerable controversy.

Colenso's tolerance of polygamy among converts and his frank and non-canonical replies to the converts questions about the Bible led to Colenso's being tried for heresy, deposed and eventually ex-communicated in 1863.

In 1866, London courts reinstated Colenso. This holding set a major precedent in the English courts because it broke the hold of the Church of England on the overseas dioceses. The publicity associated with the case brought Natal and Zululand permanently to the attention of the English people.

Bishop Colenso was an outspoken and influential advocate of African rights. In 1873, Colenso vigorously protested Natal's banishment of Chief Langalibalele and was later instrumental in securing Langalibalele's release.

Colenso opposed the Zulu War of 1879 and was of great assistance in securing the reinstatement of Cetewayo to the Zulu kingship in 1883.

Many members of Colenso's family were also active advocates of African causes. Most notably, was Colenso's daughter, Harriette Colenso. Harriette Colenso (1847–1932) was a prolific pamphleteer. Harriette took an active role in organizing the defense of the Zulu chief Dinuzulu after the rebellion of 1906.

> • Coolie supply to Natal was stopped by the Indian government.
> • The United States executed a treaty with Rasonerina.
> • Sekgoma was deposed as the Ngwato chief. Macheng *(see 1873)* became chief for a second time.

The Tswana-speaking Ngwato people were named after their founder. The Ngwato broke away from the Kwena people in the 1600s to settle in what is today eastern Botswana.

During the nineteenth century, the Ngwato chiefdom became one of the most powerful states in Botswana and its chiefs were influential over a large area. The greatest of these chiefs, Kgama III, helped to establish a British protectorate over what was then called Bechuanaland in 1885.

Kgama's grandson, Seretse Khama, became the first president of the independent Republic of Botswana in 1966.

> • In Mwembe, Mataka, the ruler of the Yao, was visited in 1866 by David Livingstone — the first European to visit the region since the early 1600s.

RELATED HISTORICAL EVENTS

> • *The Americas:* A large number of ex–Confederates arrived in Brazil to start their own colony in Americana.

In 1866, Villa Americana was founded in Brazil. Villa Americana was the home of Confederate emigres from the United States. Villa Americana was the Lost Colony of the Confederacy.

Between 1866 and 1867, some 3,500 Confederate refugees engineered the most notable organized exodus of Americans in the history of the United States. Drawn by the promise of cheap land, a booming cotton industry, and the existence of slavery, these Confederate emigres left their pillared mansions and plantations and immigrated to the country of Brazil.

Not all of the immigrants were able to make the transition. Tropical diseases, drought and the remoteness of their settlements compelled up to eighty percent of the refugees to return to the United States. However, some did stay and today their descendants provide a glimpse at both America's past and America's future.

In the fertile soil north of the city of Sao Paulo, a Confederate colony took hold; 94 Confederate families remained and struggled to carve out a place for themselves in their new land. In so struggling, these staunch Confederates were transformed. Their fortunes having been depleted, few could afford the number of slaves that they had enjoyed in the South. For the first time in their lives, these Confederates were compelled to do much of their own farm labor often working side by side with their slave laborers. In time, the colonists succeeded, — the colony began to grow.

Today, the Confederate colony of Brazil goes by the name of Americana and it is now a city of some 160,000. The growth of the city is due to the obstinacy of the Confederates as well as to waves of Portuguese, Italian and Japanese immigrants. It is also due to the existence of the Afro-Brazilians who predominate throughout the land.

As for the Confederate descendants, intermarriage has resulted in a number of darker skinned grandsons and granddaughters of the Confederacy. In the intervening years, many of the former Confederates came to recognize that it is not the color of the skin that matters but rather the content of one's character. Thus, amongst many of the descendants of the Confederates, persons of African descent could, depending upon their deeds and their character, be accepted as "white" and welcomed, by marriage, into the family.

- *Africa:* James Hertzog (1866–1942), a future prime minister of South Africa, was born.

James Hertzog was a native of the Orange Free State. He was trained in law in Amsterdam. After a brief stint in the Transvaal, he became a judge in the Free State.

After the outbreak of the South African (Boer) War in 1899, Hertzog served as legal adviser to the military commander. Within a year, however, Hertzog was himself appointed a general by President Steyn and became second in command to De Wet. Hertzog initiated Afrikaner raids into the Cape Colony and carried out guerrilla activities until the end of the war. Hertzog opposed negotiating with the British at Vereeniging, but nevertheless obtained important concessions and then signed on behalf of the Orange Free State.

After the Boer War, Hertzog concentrated on politics in the Free State. At this time, Hertzog stressed two issues: (1) restoration of self-government to the Afrikaners and (2) equal recognition for the Dutch language.

When government was restored in 1907, Hertzog became attorney-general and minister of education. In his capacity as minister of education, Hertzog caused an uproar by enforcing his Dutch language policy.

When the Union of South Africa was formed in 1910, with Botha as prime minister, Hertzog opposed Botha's policy of conciliation with the British. Despite his opposition to Botha's policy, Hertzog was brought into Botha's first cabinet.

Hertzog was forced out of the cabinet two years later. With this expulsion, Hertzog broke from Botha's party to found the National Party in 1914.

The National Party gained steadily in the elections. In 1924, the National Party reached a pinnacle when Hertzog was called upon to form a coalition government as South Africa's new prime minister.

In Hertzog's South Africa, Afrikaans was raised to an official language; a national flag was adopted; and new racially discriminatory legislation was passed.

Hertzog's government was opposed by Jan Smuts and Smuts' South African Party. The South African Party insisted that South Africa remain a loyal dominion within the British Empire.

The world economic crisis eventually forced Hertzog to take South Africa off the gold standard in 1932. The crisis also forced Hertzog to bring Smuts into his government as deputy prime minister in 1933. This was done in order to obtain broader support for the government and its policies.

In 1934, the Status Act affirmed South Africa's national sovereignty.

During the last years of his administration,

Hertzog developed a policy of segregating Africans — one of his lifetime goals.

Hertzog broke with Smuts over war policy. Hertzog favored neutrality towards Nazi Germany, while Smuts advocated a declaration of war against Germany.

In 1939, Hertzog's government ended when Smuts was allowed to form his own government.

─────── **1 8 6 7** ───────

THE UNITED STATES

• Andrew Johnson issued another amnesty proclamation which essentially left only a few hundred Confederates unpardoned.

In March, just before the session was to come to an end, the 39th Congress passed the Tenure of Office Act. Pursuant to the Tenure of Office Act, the President was required to obtain the consent of the Senate in order to remove officials from office. Violation of the Act was made a misdemeanor and, accordingly, grounds for impeachment. The Congress also passed the Army Appropriations Act. This statute prohibited the President from issuing orders to the Army except through the General of the Army. Violation of this Act was also deemed to be a misdemeanor and grounds for impeachment.

To insure an uninterrupted session of the Legislature, the 39th Congress passed an act convening the 40th Congress immediately. By doing so, the Radical Republicans ensured that the Congress was ready to impeach President Johnson should he choose to violate either the Tenure of Office Act or the Army Appropriations Act.

Upon convening, the 40th Congress passed the First Reconstruction Act. The First Reconstruction Act, in effect, abolished Southern state governments which had been operating for one and half years and returned the South to governance by martial law. The Act also provided that (1) new state conventions were to be held; (2) all males were eligible to vote (except certain Confederates); (3) all Constitutions were to guarantee African Americans the right to vote; (4) state Constitutions were to be submitted to the electorate for approval, and only then could the governor and legislature be elected; (5) Congress had to approve the final state structure, and only after Congressional approval would military governors be removed, Southern Congressmen seated, and Southern states accepted back into the Union; and (6) new State Legislatures had to ratify the Fourteenth Amendment. The First Reconstruction Act was passed by Congress, vetoed by President Johnson, and repassed by Congress on a veto override. The Act became law on March 2, 1867.

The 40th Congress also passed two supplementary Reconstruction Acts. The Act of March 23 divided the South into five military districts and gave the district commanders powers to "protect all persons in their rights of person and property, to suppress insurrection, disorder and violence, and to punish … all disturbers of the public peace." The military commanders were also empowered to remove civil office holders, make arrests, try civilians in military courts, and use Federal troops to preserve order. The supplementary act gave the military commanders the responsibility of enrolling qualified voters and excluding from the voting lists those barred by the Fourteenth Amendment. It authorized commanders to hold elections for delegates to state constitutional conventions. President Johnson, in appointing commanders for the military districts, removed General Sheridan and appointed General Thomas, a Virginia Democrat, in his place. General Hancock, a loyal Johnson ally, was appointed for the District of Louisiana and Texas. He also removed General Sickles in the Carolinas and replaced him with General Canby.

In the second supplementary Act of Reconstruction, Congress provided that the district commanders were subject to the General of the Army, and not the President. This bill was vetoed by President Johnson but was repassed by the 40th Congress over the President's veto.

Three times Charles Sumner tried to no avail to amend the Reconstruction Acts to include provisions that the Freedmen's Bureau provide homes and schools for African Americans.

The First Reconstruction Act

An act to provide for the more efficient government of the Rebel states.

Whereas no legal state governments or adequate protection for life or property now exists in the Rebel states of Virginia, North Carolina, South Carolina, Georgia, Mississippi, Alabama, Louisiana, Florida, Texas, and Arkansas; and *whereas* it is necessary that peace and good order should be enforced in said states until loyal and republican state governments can be legally established; therefore,

Be it enacted by the Senate and House of Representatives of the United States of America in Congress assembled, that said Rebel states shall be divided into military districts and made subject to the military authority of the United States as hereinafter prescribed, and for that purpose Virginia shall constitute the first district; North Carolina and South Carolina the second district; Georgia, Alabama, and Florida the third district; Mississippi and Arkansas the fourth district; and Louisiana and Texas the fifth district.

Section 2. *And be it further enacted,* that it shall be the duty of the President to assign to the command of each of said districts an officer of the Army, not below the rank of brigadier general, and to detail a sufficient military force to enable such officer to perform his duties and enforce his authority within the district to which he is assigned.

Section 3. *And be it further enacted,* that it shall be the duty of each officer assigned as aforesaid to protect all persons in their rights of person and property, to suppress insurrection, disorder, and violence, and to punish or cause to be punished all disturbers of the public peace and criminals; and to this end he may allow local civil tribunals to take jurisdiction of and to try offenders, or, when in his judgment it may be necessary for the trial of offenders, he shall have power to organize military commissions or tribunals for that purpose, and all interference under color of state authority with the exercise of military authority under this act shall be null and void.

Section 4. *And be it further enacted,* that all persons put under military arrest by virtue of this act shall be tried without unnecessary delay, and no cruel or unusual punishment shall be inflicted, and no sentence of any military commission or tribunal hereby authorized affecting the life or liberty of any person shall be executed until it is approved by the officer in command of the district, and the laws and regulations for the government of the Army shall not be affected by this act, except insofar as they conflict with its provisions: *Provided,* that no sentence of death under the provisions of this act shall be carried into effect without the approval of the President.

Section 5. *And be it further enacted,* that when the people of any one of said Rebel states shall have formed a constitution of government in conformity with the Constitution of the United States in all respects, framed by a convention of delegates elected by the male citizens of said state, twenty-one years old and upward, of whatever race, color, or previous condition, who have been resident in said state for one year previous to the day of such election, except such as may be disfranchised for participation in the rebellion or for felony at common law, and when such constitution shall provide that the elective franchise shall be enjoyed by all persons as have the qualifications herein stated for electors of delegates, and when such constitution shall be ratified by a majority of the persons voting on the question of ratification who are qualified as electors for delegates, and when such constitution shall have been submitted to Congress for examination and approval, and Congress shall have approved the same; and when said state, by a vote of its legislature elected under said constitution, shall have adopted the amendment to the Constitution of the United States, proposed by the Thirty-ninth Congress and known as Article Fourteen, and when said article shall have become a part of the Constitution of the United States, said state shall be declared entitled to representation in Congress, and senators and representatives shall be admitted therefrom on their taking the oath prescribed by law, and then and thereafter the preceding sections of this act shall be inoperative in said state: *Provided,* that no person excluded from the privilege of holding office by said proposed amendment to the Constitution of the United States shall be eligible to election as a member of the convention to frame a constitution for any of said Rebel states, nor shall any such person vote for members of such convention.

Section 6. *And be it further enacted,* that, until the people of said Rebel states shall be by law admitted to representation in the Congress of the United States, any civil governments which may exist therein shall be deemed provisional only, and in all respects subject to the paramount authority of the United States at any time to abolish, modify, control, or supersede the same; and in all elections to any office under such provisional governments all persons shall be entitled to vote, and none others, who are entitled to vote under the provisions of the 5th Section of this act; and no person shall be eligible to any office under any such provisional governments who would be disqualified from holding office under the provisions of the 3rd Article of said constitutional amendment.

• Of the 65,000 troops in federal service, only 25,000 were stationed in the South.

• The Freedmen's Bureau issued some 3.5 million rations. This number was down from 1866. By 1867, 46 hospitals with 5,292 beds had been set up by the Bureau.

• After voter registration was carried out under the provisions of the Reconstruction Act and its supplements, African Americans constituted a majority of electors, although a minority in population in South Carolina, Georgia, Florida, Alabama, Mississippi and Louisiana. In Virginia, Arkansas, Texas and North Carolina, European Americans still constituted a larger part of the registered voters, but in these four states sizable numbers of European Americans in the mountain regions voted Republican. As a result of this legislation, there was a preponderance of Republicans in all State Constitutional Conventions except Virginia.

In South Carolina, the voter registration was as follows: 78,982 African Americans and 46,346 European Americans. Ten counties had a majority of European American voters, 21 counties had a majority of African American voters.

Mississippi voter registration was as follows: 60,167 African Americans and 46,636 European Americans. African American voters were in a majority in 33 out of the 61 counties. Significant African American majorities existed in the following counties: Adams, Bolivar, Claiborne, Hinds, Issaquena, Lowndes, Noxubee, Warren, Washington, Yazoo and Tunica. Two prominent African American Congressmen, Senator Hiram Revels and Representative John R. Lynch were from Adams County while another, Senator Blanche K. Bruce, was from Bolivar.

• The Union League began to organize clubs in the South.

• At the first Republican Party convention ever held in Mississippi, one third of the members were former slaves.

• In July, the Republican Party of South Carolina was organized at Columbia. A state committee was formed which included J. H. Rainey, an African American.

• Monroe Baker became the mayor of St. Martin, Louisiana. Baker was probably the first known African American to be elected mayor of an American town.

• Edward V. C. Eato (d.1914) became the first African American delegate to an international convention of the Young Men's Christian Association. Eato was a prominent leader of New York African American social life. In addition to the YMCA, Eato was a member of the Ugly Club, Masons, and Society of the Sons of New York. For twenty-five years, Eato was the president of the African Society.

Congress approved the first all African American units in the regular army. The African American soldiers comprised the Ninth and Tenth Cavalry Regiments as well as the Twenty-fourth and Twenty-fifth Infantry Regiments of the United States Colored Troops. These soldiers would come to be known as "Buffalo Soldiers." Their nickname came from the Indigenous Americans who believed their short curly hair was similar to that on the buffalo's neck and that their brave and fierce fighting matched the buffalo. Eleven of these African American soldiers earned the Congressional Medal of Honor in combat against Utes, Apaches, and Comanches. African American soldiers would serve in all African American regiments until the integration of the United States Armed Forces in 1952. A monument honoring the Buffalo Soldiers was unveiled at Fort Leavenworth in 1992.

• In 1867, the Pullman Palace Car Company introduced African American porters to its cars in the United States.

• *Civil Rights Movement:* William Still led a successful campaign against segregated streetcars in Philadelphia.

• In Charleston, Richmond, New Orleans, Mobile, and other cities, African-American demonstrators staged ride-ins on streetcars.

• *Crime and Punishment:* General Canby, the military district commander for North and South Carolina, reported that for the first 18 months ending June 30, there were 197 murders and 548 cases of aggravated assault.

• *The Ku Klux Klan:* In April, the Ku Klux Klan held its first national convention in Nashville. Its first Grand Wizard was ex–Confederate General Nathan Bedford Forrest.

• *Labor Movement:* The National Labor Union held its second annual conference in Chicago, Illinois. At this conference, the Union formed a special committee to work on issues related to African American labor.

• *Notable Births:* Robert Moton (1867–1940), an educator, was born (August 26).

• Maggie Lena Walker (1867–1934), the first woman bank president in the United States, was born in Richmond, Virginia (September 26). Walker was the founder of the Saint Luke Penny Savings Bank in Virginia.

• Sarah Breedlove Walker (1867–1919), a

pioneer African American business woman, was born (December 23).

Sarah Breedlove Walker, known throughout her later life as Madame C. J. Walker, was born in Delta, Louisiana, in abject poverty. She was orphaned at 6 and married at the age of 14. When she was 20, she became a widow with a small daughter.

With her child, Walker moved to Saint Louis, Missouri, and worked for a while as a laundress. While working as a laundress she attended school at night.

In 1905, Madame C. J. Walker developed a formula for a preparation which improved "the appearance of the hair" of African Americans. Convinced in the effectiveness of her product, Walker spent the next two years travelling around the country promoting it. Soon her mail order business began to grow. By 1910, she had become successful enough to establish laboratories for the manufacture of various cosmetics and hair products for African Americans.

• *Notable Deaths:* Frederick Ira Aldridge (1807?–1867), the great Shakespearean actor, died in Poland (August 7).

Frederick Ira Aldridge, a great African American thespian (actor), was born in New York City. He was educated as a freeman in the African School in New York. While in his teens, Aldridge made his acting debut with an all African American cast in New York in Sheridan's *Pizzaro.*

The young Aldridge went to Scotland to study, and in 1826 he made his London debut at the Royalty Theater, playing Othello. Aldridge played at Covent Garden and toured the English and Irish provinces.

Aldridge's reputation as an actor grew. He traveled throughout the European continent. A star of the first magnitude, Aldridge was decorated by the King of Prussia and the Czar of Russia, and he was knighted by the King of Sweden.

In Sweden, Aldridge married a Swedish baronness by whom he had three children. By 1857, Aldridge was commonly regarded as one of the two or three greatest actors in the world.

• James P. Beckwourth (1798– 1867), a famous African American scout and explorer, died.

In 1867, Jim Beckwourth died. James (Jim) Beckwourth was one of the great explorers of the American West. His life story is one of the truly remarkable stories in the history of the United States.

Jim Beckwourth was born in Virginia to a slave woman of African descent and a European American slave holder. Beckwourth's father was an officer in the Revolutionary Army. In the early years of the 19th century, the Beckwourths (who had 13 children) relocated to a settlement near what is the present-day city of St. Louis, Missouri.

In 1816, Jim Beckwourth, who had been apprenticed to a blacksmith, ran away to New Orleans. Once in New Orleans, Beckwourth soon found that there was no work so, in desperation, Beckwourth signed up as a scout for General Henry Ashley's Rocky Mountain expedition.

Beckwourth discovered that he liked the nomadic life of a expeditionary scout. As a scout, Beckwourth was independent — he was his own man. Like a number of his fellow African Americans, one of the prime motives for Beckwourth's nomadic existence was an unwillingness to accept the role assigned to African American males in Euro-centric American society.

During the 1820s and 1830s, the heyday of the mountain men and the fur trade, Beckwourth became a legendary figure. Like his friends Jim Bridger and Kit Carson, Beckwourth was one of the great scouts, hunters and "Indian fighters" of his time. During the Second Seminole War of 1835, Beckwourth served as a scout for the United States Army in its struggle against the Seminoles. Later when Beckwourth moved to the West, he endeared himself with the Indigenous Americans of the region. The Indigenous Americans respected him so highly that he was accepted into their tribes, first by the Blackfeet and later the Crow. Among the Crow, Beckwourth was an honorary chief.

In 1848, Beckwourth became the chief scout for John C. Fremont's exploring expedition in the Rockies.

In 1851, Beckwourth discovered a pass between the Feather and Truckee Rivers in California which provided a gateway through the Sierra Nevadas. Beckwourth discovered the pass while on a prospecting expedition as he and his party crossed the mountains from the American River valley to the Pit River valley. The pass, which is today known as Beckwourth Pass, is at an elevation of 5,212 feet and is the lowest pass over the summit of the Sierras.

The Beckwourth Pass is about two miles east of Chilcoot, California. Fifteen miles to the west of the pass is the town of Beckwourth, a town which was also named in honor of James Beckwourth.

After discovering the pass, Beckwourth proposed to the residents of Bidwell Bar and Marysville that a wagon road be made through this pass, across the Sierra Valley to the Middle Fork of the Feather River, and down the ridge east of the river past Bidwell Bar to Marysville. The citizens of Bidwell Bar and Marysville eventually adopted Beckwourth's plan and a trail was constructed.

Soon after completion of the trail, Beckwourth, while at Truckee in the Sierra Nevada, persuaded a passing emigrant train to try the new pass. The party liked the pass and spread the word of the relatively easy crossing. Others soon followed in their footsteps. Beckwourth Pass soon became a well-beaten trail.

The popularity of Beckwourth Pass, led Beckwourth to build a cabin (the first house in the Sierra Valley) on the pass route. This cabin served as a trading post and a hotel for the passersby. The cabin stood on a hillside two and a half miles west of what is today the town of Beckwourth. Beckwourth soon built a second cabin near to the first. Both of these cabins were eventually burned down by the local Indigenous Americans. However, undaunted, Beckwourth built a third cabin — a cabin which is today maintained as a historical landmark by the State of California.

A year after the discovery of Beckwourth Pass, an emigrant train of ox-drawn schooners from St. Louis, Missouri, came through the pass carrying an eleven-year-old child named Ina Coolbrith. Coolbrith was destined to become California's first poet laureate and her passage through Beckwourth Pass was an event which she was never to forget.

At a luncheon given in her honor in San Francisco, California, on April 24, 1927 — some seventy-five years after going through the pass — Coolbrith recalled:

Ours was the first of the covered wagon trains to break the trail through Beckwourth Pass into California. We were guided by the famous scout, Jim Beckwourth, who was an historical figure, and to my mind one of the most beautiful creatures that ever lived. He was rather dark and wore his hair in two long braids, twisted with colored cord that gave him a picturesque appearance. He wore a leather coat and moccasins and rode a horse without a saddle.

When we made that long journey toward the West over the deserts and mountains, our wagon train was driven over ground without a single mark of a wagon wheel until it was broken by ours. And when Jim Beckwourth said he would like to

have my mother's little girls ride into California on his horse in front of him, I was the happiest little girl in the world.

After two or three days of heavy riding we came at last in sight of California and there on the boundary line he stopped, and pointing forward, said: 'Here is California, little girls, here is your kingdom.'

- Armand Lanusse (1812–1867), the originator of *Les Cenelles*, an anthology of poetry by African American poets in New Orleans, died.

Miscellaneous Laws: In 1867, a number of state Constitutional Conventions convened. In general, the state Constitutional Conventions provided for universal suffrage; granted equal rights to African Americans; set up a system of public education; organized the judiciary on a popular basis; and instituted democratic reforms in government machinery.

The racial composition of the state Constitutional Conventions varied from state to state as follows:

State	European Americans	African Americans
Alabama	83	17
Arkansas	68	7
Florida	29	17
Georgia	133	33
Louisiana	52	40
Mississippi	68	17
North Carolina	107	13
South Carolina	34	63
Texas	81	9
Virginia	80	25

- Iowa and the Dakota Territory granted the right to vote to African Americans.
- Ohio voted against suffrage for African Americans.

African American males were enfranchised in Washington, D.C. African American males were first granted the right to vote by the act of January 8, 1867, which was "to regulate the elective franchise in the District of Columbia." The right was given to every male person twenty-one years of age, except those who were paupers, under guardianship, convicted of infamous crimes, or who had voluntarily comforted rebels.

President Andrew Johnson vetoed the bill on January 5, 1867, but both the Senate and the House of Representatives voted to override the veto, and the bill became law.

- *Miscellaneous Cases:* Threatened with Congressional re-organization, the United States Supreme Court played a passive role in

Reconstruction. In two significant cases, *Mississippi v. Johnson* (April 15, 1867) 71 U.S. 318, 18 L.Ed. 816 and *Georgia v. Stanton* (February 17, 1868) 73 U.S. 18 L.Ed. 721 the Court was asked to enjoin the President and the Secretary of War from enforcing the Reconstruction Acts on the grounds that they were unconstitutional. The Court evaded the issue, however, deciding in both cases that it had no power to enjoin an executive officer "in the performance of his official duties."

• *Miscellaneous Publications:* William Wells Brown published *The Negro in the American Rebellion, His Heroism and His Fidelity.*

• William Still published *A Brief Narrative of the Struggle for the Rights of the Colored People of Philadelphia in the City Railway Cars.*

• Benjamin Tucker Tanner published *An Apology for African Methodism. An Apology of African Methodism* was one of the first intellectual and theological accounts of the schisms between African American and European American branches of the Methodist Church.

• *Clotel, or the President's Daughter, A Narrative of Slave Life in the United States* by William Wells Brown, the first novel by an African American, was published for the first time in the United States.

Clotel, or the President's Daughter was basically an abolitionist book which told the story of the "mythic" unacknowledged daughter of Thomas Jefferson. In the story, Clotel tries to escape slavery but is killed, ironically within the sight of her father's (Jefferson's) house. Much of the text of the book was given over to a detailed description of the "peculiar institution" of slavery of which Brown had first hand experience.

Because of its content, the *Clotel* was first published in London, England. When *Clotel* was published in the United States in 1867, the story was altered. In the place of Jefferson, an anonymous Senator became Clotel's father.

• *Scholastic Achievements:* Howard University was chartered by the Federal Government and was established in Washington, D. C. (January 8). Howard University was named in honor of General Oliver O. Howard, the head of the Freedmen's Bureau. Howard University became the first African American school to establish undergraduate, graduate, and professional schools.

• The American Missionary Association established a number of schools (colleges) for the education of African Americans. The schools so established were Emerson at Mobile, Alabama; Storrs at Atlanta, Georgia; Beach at Savannah, Georgia; and Talladega in Alabama.

• Morehouse College was founded first as the Augusta Institute in Augusta, Georgia. The College was supported by the American Baptist Home Mission Society.

• Talladega and Morehouse Colleges opened (February).

• The Peabody Educational Fund was established for the South (February 7). The Peabody Fund was created to finance educational endeavors for freed slaves.

• Johnson C. Smith College was founded in Charlotte, North Carolina.

• Fisk University was incorporated under the laws of the State of Tennessee (August 22). Fisk University was named in honor of General Clinton B. Fisk of the Freedmen's Bureau.

• Presbyterians added Biddle University to Lincoln University which had been established in 1854.

• Rebecca J. Cole (1846–1922) graduated from the Female Medical College of Pennsylvania. Cole was the first African American woman to establish a medical practice in Pennsylvania.

• *The Black Church:* State Baptist organizations were created in Virginia and Alabama.

• The Consolidated American Baptist Convention was created in August of 1867 in Nashville, Tennessee. The Consolidated American Baptist Convention lasted until 1880, when it was replaced by the National Baptist Convention.

• *Sports:* The Excelsiors of Philadelphia beat the Brooklyn Uniques 37 to 24 in an all African American baseball club championship.

In October 1867, the Brooklyn Uniques were hosts to the Excelsiors of Philadelphia in a contest called "the championship of colored clubs." These two teams were among the first known African American baseball clubs, and the game between the Excelsiors and the Uniques was the first known intercity contest.

THE AMERICAS

• *Haiti:* The Haitian Constitution of 1867 was approved.

- Fabre Geffrard, the ruler of Haiti, was overthrown by Silvain Salnave (May 6).

The last former slave to rule Haiti was Faustin Soulouque. Soulouque ruled from 1847 to 1859. Soulouque was preoccupied with national territorial integrity. Twice Soulouque invaded the Dominican Republic which had broken away after the fall of Boyer. These incursions may have been primarily for the purpose of Soulouque's self-aggrandizement, but also arose from the old concern that the neighbor state would become a base for foreign intrusion.

Soulouque's defeats in the Dominican Republic led to his overthrow by General Fabre Geffrard, a dark COTW — a griffe — who spent much of his presidency gaining international respectability and favor. Geffrard detested voodoo as barbarism and signed a concordat with the Holy See in 1860. Two years later, President Abraham Lincoln finally gave United States diplomatic recognition to Haiti, and Geffrard encouraged the immigration of African Americans with little success. Geffrard was overthrown by another COTW general, Silvain Salnave, on May 6, 1867. Geffrard fled to Jamaica.

Salnave, who also declared himself president for life, was unusual in that he was a COTW who had support from some black factions. Salnave seems to have enjoyed some popularity among the poor of Port-au-Prince. Such was not the case, however, with the cacos, the successors to the southern piquets of the 1840s. These bands of middling peasants, or habitants, opposed Salnave, and played a large if intermittent role in politics until after the United States occupation of Haiti which lasted from 1915 to 1934.

The goals of the cacos were often obscure. They gave their support, first to one general then to another, on the basis of promises of short-term advantages. Perhaps what the cacos cherished most of all was benign neglect — the assurance that peasant land tenure and political arrangements would not be disturbed. Once their man was installed in the presidency these rural groups usually disbanded. Being primarily subsistence farmers, the cacos were unable to sustain a presence in the capital which would allow them to maintain their influence upon their leader. Only periodically would the opportunity arise for the cacos to band and once again exert influence throughout the land.

- Massillon Coicou, an Afro-Haitian poet, was born (October 9).

Massillon Coicou (1867–1908) was born in Port-au-Prince, Haiti, and was educated at Freres de l'Instruction Chretienne and Lycee Petion.

Like many of the prominent Caribbean and Latin American literary figures, Coicou was also a politician. He was in the Cabinet of President Thiresias S. Sam and served as the Haitian Minister to Paris.

Coicou founded the literary intellectual magazine *L'Oeuvre* and wrote two collections of poetry, *Les Poesies Nationales* (1891) and *Impression et Passion* (1902). *Les Poesies Nationales* was a work full of enthusiasm for Haiti and Coicou's revolutionary idealism, while *Impression et Passion* was more thoughtful, more meditative poetry.

In 1904, *Dessalines Liberte*, the best of Coicou's dramatic works was published. The theme of *Dessalines Liberte* was Haitian independence. *Dessalines Liberte* premiered in Paris and became a classic of the Haitian theatre.

Coicou spent his last years as a popular, outspoken professor of philosophy at the most prominent lycee in Port-au-Prince. He had a strong passion for politics and publicly announced his intentions to overthrow the government of Nord Alexis. Coicou's popularity and outspokenness led to his being executed, along with his two brothers, by a firing squad in 1908.

EUROPE

- Alexandre Dumas, fils, published *The Ideas of Madame Aubray*.

AFRICA

- *North Africa, Egypt and Sudan:* While officially neutral, Egypt assisted the British in the Anglo-Ethiopian war. *See 1866.*
- Sir Samuel Baker's expedition departed from Cairo for Gondokoro (April).

Samuel White Baker (1821–1893) was a British explorer of the upper Nile and an administrator in Sudan under the Egyptian government.

After a multi-faceted career, Baker utilized his own financial resources to support the search for the sources of the Nile. From 1862 to 1867, Baker and his wife explored southern Sudan and northern Uganda, naming Lake Albert and advancing the theory that Lake Albert was the ultimate source of the Nile River.

Upon his return to Cairo, the Khedive Ismail named Baker the governor of the Equatoria province of southern Sudan and gave him the title of *Pasha*. Baker thus became the first of a series of Englishmen to hold high office under the Egyptian government.

Baker worked to bring the Sudan under administrative control and tried unsuccessfully to end the slave trade there.

In 1872, Baker proclaimed an Egyptian protectorate over the Nyoro kingdom (of Uganda) but was driven out by Kabarega, the King of the Nyoro.

Baker was succeeded as governor of Equatoria by Charles Gordon. Baker returned to England and became an ardent advocate for continued British involvement in Sudan.

Baker wrote several books which remain valuable as sources of material for the history of the regions he visited.

- The first Sudanese became a pasha along with the first two Sudanese provincial governors.
- An elementary school was started in Khartoum.
- A post office was opened in Suakin.
- A Sudanese regiment, which had been reduced to the size of a company because of the casualties suffered during a tour in the Mexican war, returned to Sudan via Paris.
- *West Africa:* An exchange of Gold Coast forts between the British and the Dutch occurred (March 5). The British took Mari, Kormantin, Apam, and Accra while the Dutch took Beyin, Dixcove, Sekondi and Kommenda.

The British crown assumed jurisdiction over a number of Gold Coast settlements in 1821. These settlements were placed under the administration of Sierra Leone until 1850 when the adjacent ex–Danish settlements were added.

From 1866 to 1874, the British Gold Coast settlements were again administered from Sierra Leone as part of the federation of West African Settlements. After 1874, the Gold Coast again became a separate entity, and later expanded northward to include Ashanti and the Northern Territories.

The colony of Lagos (Nigeria) was subordinate to the Gold Coast from 1874 to 1896. The Gold Coast achieved independence in 1957 when its name was changed to Ghana.

- The Fante confederacy movement began.

The Fante confederacy movement lasted from 1867 to 1872. The purpose of the Fante confederacy movement was to reconstitute Fante government along national lines. The Fante confederacy movement was largely responsible for drawing up the confederacy's constitution. However, the confederacy movement was soon undermined by the annexation of the Gold Coast to the British Empire.

- The Egbas expelled all European traders and missionaries from Abeokuta.
- The reign of Kofi Karikari, the ruler of the Akan kingdom of Asante (Ashanti) during the British invasion, began.

Kofi Karikari ascended to the throne when his predecessor, Kwaku Dua I died during a campaign to reconquer Ashanti's southern territories, lost some forty years before. Kofi Karikari continued the wars, which soon brought him into conflict with the British on the coast.

In 1871, the British secured a document which they claimed was signed by Kofi Karikari, renouncing the Ashanti's title as landlord of the British Elmina fort. The document was a forgery and resulted in an Ashanti attack on the British in 1873. General Garnet Wolseley led the combined British and Fante forces which repulsed the Ashanti, and then advanced into Kumasi, the Ashanti capital.

The British demanded a monetary indemnity and declared the entire area south of Ashanti a British colony. Much of the old Ashanti empire broke away. Kofi Karikari was shortly thereafter accused of robbing the royal tombs, and deposed.

Kofi Karikari was succeeded by his younger brother, Mensa Bonsu. Mensa Bonsu began immediately to rebuild the shattered empire by reconquering its breakaway parts. Mensa Bonsu was especially concerned with the Akan states which made up the nucleus of the old empire.

After 1875, Mensa Bonsu abandoned warfare for diplomacy due partly to British pressure. Mensa Bonsu's lack of success, combined with his reputation for greediness, resulted in his being deposed in 1883.

Mensa Bonsu's successor, Kwaku Dua II, died after a year in office, and a four-year war broke out in Ashanti, lasting until the ascension of Prempe I.

- Maba Diakhou Ba (1809–1867), a religious and military leader responsible for the spread of Islam in much of the Senegambia, died.

It was during the 1867 attack on Sine that the Prophet Maba was killed. The victory for Sine was also a victory for the French. With the demise of Maba, the French no longer had to deal with the threat of a unified Muslim force in the Senegambia. However, even though Maba was unsuccessful in maintaining and expanding his Islamic empire, his influence was lasting. His campaign permitted a new Muslim elite to seize power in their societies. This Muslim elite was largely responsible for the conversion of the people of Senegambia to Islam. *See 1865.*

- *Central Africa:* The French negotiated a treaty with the King of the M'Goumbi and N'Doumbal Rakenga on the River Ogooue (May 10).
- David Livingstone discovered Lake Mweru (November 8). *See 1873.*
- Bunza (Munza), the King of the Mangbetu, constructed a new capital at Nangazizi.
- Tippu Tip began trading with Tabwa. *See 1865.*
- The James Holt Limited was founded at Douala.
- Livingstone visited Kazembe Mulonga. *See 1865.*
- *Eastern Africa:* Between 1862 and 1867, 97,203 slaves were exported from Kilwa.
- In January, David Livingstone travelled up the River Ruvuma. By April 1, he had reached Lake Tanganyika. *See 1873.*
- In Ethiopia, Menelik proclaimed himself independent as King of Shoa. *See 1865.*
- Yohannes declared the Tigre province of northern Ethiopia independent from Emperor Theodore.
- The British landed an expeditionary force of 32,000 under the command of Robert Napier *(see 1890)* at Zulla (December). *See 1866.*
- *Southern Africa:* In April, diamonds were found at Hopetown.
- Carl Mauch reported finding gold at Tati and in Mashonaland (December).

Carl (Karl) Mauch (1837–1875) was a German geologist and explorer of southern Africa. In 1866 and 1867, Mauch explored the land which is today called Zimbabwe. In Zimbabwe, Mauch confirmed the existence of gold deposits. Mauch published his findings and it was this publication which initiated a gold rush into Ndebele and Shona (Mashonaland). The gold rush eventually led to the occupation of Zimbabwe by agents of Cecil Rhodes.

In 1871–1872, Mauch re-visited Shona and became the first European to describe the impressive ruins of Great Zimbabwe to the outside world.

Mauch's records of his explorations were also among the first written descriptions of eastern Zimbabwe since those of the Portuguese explorers of the 17th century.

- The Native Foreigners Act was passed. Pursuant to provisions of the Act, passes had to be carried upon one's person in the Cape Colony.
- The Maseko Ngoni migrated from near Songea to south of Lake Malawi.

The term "Ngoni" could be applied to some eight different kingdoms in southeastern Africa. The term is a corruption of the term "Nguni."

In its narrowest sense, the name "Ngoni" is applied only to the followers of the three early Nguni-speaking kings: Zwangendaba, Nqaba and Maseko Ngwana. These three men's careers crossed many times, but their respective followers were essentially distinct.

Nqaba's Ngoni ceased to exist as a group during the 1840s. Around 1860, Maseko's followers settled in southern Malawi. They are today known as the Maseko, or Gomani Ngoni. Zwangendaba's Ngoni eventually separated into six kingdoms, which settled in Tanzania, Malawi and Zambia.

- Dr. Jose Lacerda published *Examen das viagens do Doutor Livingstone.*
- In Mozambique, between 1867 and 1869, Bonga, the leader of the da Cruz family empire, repelled four major invasions by the Portuguese government and the rival empire builder, Manuel Antonio de Sousa. *See 1879.*

Portuguese occupation of present day Mozambique began in 1505 when they built a fort at Sofala to trade with the interior. Other posts followed along the coast and on the Zambezi River.

Until 1752, Mozambique was administered through Portuguese India at Goa. After 1752, Mozambique was administered locally.

Through the mid–19th century, Portuguese rule was largely restricted to the coastal and Zambezi River towns. Many settlers of Portuguese descent lived around the Zambezi valley, out of effective government reach.

During the late 19th century, the Portuguese began expanding inland and the colony of Mozambique assumed the shape that the country of Mozambique has today.

- Faku (c.1780–1867), the paramount chief of the Mpondo, died.

Faku became the king of the Mpondo upon the death of his father Ncqungqushe in the early 1820s. Faku's ascension coincided with the rise of Shaka in nearby Zululand. As a consequence, Faku's Mpondo immediately faced Zulu attacks and a huge influx of northern Nguni refugees.

Although he was dangerously situated between the Zulu in the north and the Xhosa and Tembu in the south, Faku was able to hold his own against several invasions. Indeed, it was Faku who repelled Shaka's last southern campaign in 1828.

After Dingane became the Zulu king in 1828, the Qwabe chief Nqeto revolted and moved south with a large army into Mpondo country. Faku drove Nqeto off towards the neighboring Bhaca chief Ncaphayi. Ncaphayi killed Nqeto in 1829 and, consequently, the last Zulu threat to the Mpondo came to an end.

In 1830, Faku permitted Wesleyan Methodists to establish a mission among the Mpondo. Faku used the missionaries as his diplomatic agents and advisers. During the 1830s, Faku acted as a suzerain — as a feudal lord — over the Bhaca and other neighboring groups. Faku soon became known as the most powerful ruler between Natal and the Xhosa.

The Afrikaner Voortrekkers who began to settle in Natal after 1838 initiated a new threat to Faku's sovereignty and Mpondo security. In late 1840, the Voortrekker leader, A. W. J. Pretorius, launched a surprise attack on the Bhaca. This attack caused Faku to fear for the security of the Mpondo.

Faku appealed to the British governor of the Cape, G: T. Napier, for protection. The British occupied Natal and formed an alliance with Faku in 1844.

Faku's alliance with the British was a mutual aid alliance and relied on certain assurances that each party would aid the other. For the British, this meant that Faku was to aid them in their struggles against the Xhosa. However, during two British-Xhosa wars, Faku failed to provide material support to the British.

The alliance between the British and the Mpondo began to deteriorate. After the Xhosa were rendered less dangerous in 1857, the treaty between the Mpondo and the British essentially became valueless. Thereafter the British recognized Faku's sovereignty only over actual Mpondo settlements along the coast.

In 1861, Faku handed over the vast tract of land to his west, known as "Nomansland," to the British government. The Griqua of Adam Kok III were then settled there and the land became known as Griqualand East.

During his last years, Faku gradually lost personal control over the Mpondo and allowed a son, Ndamasa, to found a separate settlement west of the Mzimvubu River. Faku's eldest son, Mqikela, began to rule in Faku's place.

When Faku died in 1867, the Mpondo chiefdom was divided into two independent states under Faku's sons, Ndamasa and Mqikela.

RELATED HISTORICAL EVENTS

- *The Americas:* Canada became a dominion in the British empire (July 1).
- *Europe:* Garibaldi marched on Rome (October 22).
- Karl Marx published *Das Kapital.*
- The British House of Commons voted two million pounds to relieve (to ransom) British prisoners who were being held by Theodore II, the Emperor of Ethiopia.
- Spain disbanded the Junta de Informacion.
- *Africa:* Charles John Andersson (1827–1867), an Anglo-Swedish trader and adventurer, died.

Charles Andersson recorded one of the earliest accounts of Lake Ngami. It was there that he met the Tawana chief Letsholathebe in 1853. During the remainder of his life, Andersson worked as a trader in Walvis Bay. He occasionally explored the Okavango River and other parts of Namibia.

Several of Andersson's books became important sources for the history of Namibia. *Lake Ngami* (1856) and *Okavango River* (1861) were the most notable.

In 1863, Andersson was made "paramount chief" of the Herero people when he assisted chief Maherero against the Oorlam led by Jan Jonker Afrikaner. *See 1889.*

1868

THE UNITED STATES

- On February 24, the House voted to institute impeachment proceedings against President Johnson. Throughout 1867, a House Committee had gathered evidence about Johnson's political and private life. On March 13, 7 Republican Senators voted with the Democrats against impeachment. The final vote was 35 to 19, 1 short of the necessary two-thirds majority.
- Alabama was re-admitted to the Union in March. The Alabama state government had been organized by the Union League Republican Organization with John C. Keffer as its leader.
- Congress passed a law denying the United States Supreme Court jurisdiction in cases

involving the writ of habeas corpus. This law was intended to prevent the Supreme Court from ruling on certain cases concerning the constitutionality of the Reconstruction Act (March 27).

• Oscar J. Dunn (c.1821–1871), an ex–slave, became Lieutenant Governor of Louisiana, the highest elective office then held by an Afro-American (June 13).

Oscar Dunn was a music teacher before the Civil War. During his term as Lieutenant Governor, Dunn won a reputation for integrity. His sudden death, in 1871, after a violent two day illness came at a moment when it seemed that he might become the Republican nominee for Governor.

• The South Carolina General Assembly convened with a majority of African American legislators: 88 African Americans to 67 European Americans (July 6). This was the only time in American history where an African American majority existed in a state legislature.

• The Fourteenth Amendment, an amendment guaranteeing due process of law, became part of the United States Constitution (July 28). *See 1866.*

• The Republican Party platform for 1868 did not include a demand for universal African American suffrage in the Northern states because a number of Northern states had rejected the idea. Instead the platform said: "The guarantee by Congress of equal suffrage to all loyal men in the South was demanded by every consideration of public safety, of gratitude and of justice, and must be maintained; while the question of suffrage in all the loyal states properly belongs to the people of those states." P. B. S. Pinchback and James J. Harris became the first African American delegates to the Republican National Convention which was held in Chicago.

• The Democratic Party platform for 1868 labeled the Thirteenth and Fourteenth Amendments "unconstitutional, revolutionary and void."

• John Willis Menard (1839–1893) of Louisiana became the first African American elected to Congress. However, he was not seated. The committee on elections ruled that it was too early to admit an African American to Congress. When he was allowed to plead his own case on February 27, 1869, Menard became the first African American to speak on the floor of the House of Representatives.

John Menard was born of French creole parents living in Illinois. After the Civil War, Menard moved to Louisiana to work for the Republican Party. During his political career in Louisiana, Menard would serve as the inspector of customs of the port of New Orleans.

• Arkansas' Representatives and Senators were re-admitted to Congress.

• European Americans re-gained control of the Georgia state legislature and ejected all the African American members on the basis that the right to hold office had not been specifically bestowed upon the newly enfranchised African Americans. Congress subsequently declared that Georgia did not have a republican form of government, denied their Congressional Representatives their seats in Congress, and placed the state under martial law again. Georgia was only re-admitted to the Union upon its ratification of the Fifteenth Amendment.

• Francis L. Cardoza was appointed secretary of state in South Carolina, the first African American cabinet officer in a state government.

• Louisiana's Congressional Representatives and Senators were re-admitted to Congress.

• At the Mississippi Constitutional Convention, 17 of the 97 delegates were African Americans.

• North Carolina was re-admitted to the Union.

• The Freedmen's Bureau issued some 2.5 million rations in 1868.

• *Crime and Punishment:* In a June report, the Congressional Committee on Lawlessness and Violence reported that 373 freedmen between 1866 and 1868 had been killed by European Americans while only ten European Americans had been killed by freedmen.

• While attending the Mississippi state constitutional convention, Charles Caldwell, an African American, killed the son of a European American judge in self-defense. Tried before an all European American jury, Caldwell was found "not guilty"—a rather surprising verdict given the circumstances and the times.

In 1870, Charles Caldwell was elected to the Mississippi State Senate. Caldwell's career and life were cut short when, on Christmas Day, 1875, he was assassinated in Clinton, Mississippi.

• *The Ku Klux Klan:* Despite the prevalence of violence against freedmen, Florida was re-admitted to the Union. Due to Florida's Ku Klux Klan violence, Governor Reed was compelled to ask for Federal troops. But his request was denied. Between 1868 and 1871, some 235 racially motivated murders were committed in the State of Florida.

• Prior to the November 1868 election in Louisiana, 2,000 persons were killed or wounded. In the parish of Saint Landry, the Ku Klux Klan killed or wounded over 200 Republicans, hunting and chasing them over a two day period through fields and bayous. A pile of 25 dead Republicans was found half-buried in the woods. A "Negro hunt" took place in Bossier Parish. 120 African American corpses were found in the woods or taken out of the Red River. Some 297 persons were slain in the parishes adjacent to New Orleans during the month before the election.

• The "Organization and Principles" of the Ku Klux Klan were enunciated.

Organization and Principles of the Ku Klux Klan

Appellation

This organization shall be styled and denominated, the Order of the —

Creed

We, the Order of the —, reverentially acknowledge the majesty and supremacy of the Divine Being and recognize the goodness and providence of the same. And we recognize our relation to the United States government, the supremacy of the Constitution, the constitutional laws thereof, and the Union of states thereunder.

Character and Objects of the Order

This is an institution of chivalry, humanity, mercy, and patriotism; embodying in its genius and its principles all that is chivalric in conduct, noble in sentiment, generous in manhood, and patriotic in purpose; its peculiar objects being:

First, to protect the weak, the innocent, and the defenseless from the indignities, wrongs, and outrages of the lawless, the violent, and the brutal; to relieve the injured and oppressed; to succor the suffering and unfortunate, and especially the widows and orphans of Confederate soldiers.

Second, to protect and defend the Constitution of the United States, and all laws passed in conformity thereto, and to protect the states and the people thereof from all invasion from any source whatever.

Third, to aid and assist in the execution of all constitutional laws, and to protect the people from unlawful seizure and from trial, except by their peers in conformity to the laws of the land.

Titles

Section 1. The officers of this Order shall consist of a Grand Wizard of the Empire and his ten Genii; a Grand Dragon of the Realm and his eight Hydras; a Grand Titan of the Dominion and his six Furies; a Grand Giant of the Province and his four Goblins; a Grand Cyclops of the Den and his two Night Hawks; a Grand Magi, a Grand Monk, a Grand Scribe, a Grand Exchequer, a Grand Turk, and a Grand Sentinel.

Section 2. The body politic of this Order shall be known and designated as "Ghouls."

Territory and Its Divisions

Section 1. The territory embraced within the jurisdiction of this Order shall be coterminous with the states of Maryland, Virginia, North Carolina, South Carolina, Georgia, Florida, Alabama, Mississippi, Louisiana, Texas, Arkansas, Missouri, Kentucky, and Tennessee; all combined constituting the Empire.

Section 2. The Empire shall be divided into four departments, the first to be styled the Realm and coterminous with the boundaries of the several states; the second to be styled the Dominion and to be coterminous with such counties as the Grand Dragons of the several Realms may assign to the charge of the Grand Titan. The third to be styled the Province and to be coterminous with the several counties; *provided*, the Grand Titan may, when he deems it necessary, assign two Grand Giants to one Province, prescribing, at the same time, the jurisdiction of each. The fourth department to be styled the Den, and shall embrace such part of a Province as the Grand Giant shall assign to the charge of a Grand Cyclops.

Questions To Be Asked Candidates

1. Have your ever been rejected, upon application for membership in the —, or have you ever been expelled from the same?

2. Are you now, or have you ever been, a member of the Radical Republican Party, or either of the organizations known as the "Loyal League" and the "Grand Army of the Republic"?

3. Are you opposed to the principles and policy of the Radical Party, and to the Loyal League, and the Grand Army of the Republic, so far as you are informed of the character and purposes of those organizations?

4. Did you belong to the Federal Army during the late war, and fight against the South during the existence of the same?

5. Are you opposed to Negro equality, both social and political?

6. Are you in favor of a white man's government in this country?

7. Are you in favor of constitutional liberty, and a government of equitable laws instead of a government of violence and oppression?

8. Are you in favor of maintaining the constitutional rights of the South?

9. Are you in favor of the reenfranchisement and emancipation of the white men of the South, and the restitution of the Southern people to all their rights, alike proprietary, civil, and political?

10. Do you believe in the inalienable right of self-preservation of the people against the exercise of arbitrary and unlicensed power?

• *The Labor Movement:* At the Third Annual Conference of the National Labor Union in New York City, the topic of African American labor was not brought up, even though at the 1867 Conference a special committee on African American labor had resolved to consider the problem at this meeting.

• *Notable Births:* Charles "Buddy" Bolden (1868–1931), one of the founding fathers of jazz, was born in New Orleans (September 6).

Charles "Buddy" Bolden was born in New Orleans. Bolden grew up amid the brass band craze, playing cornet.

At the time, horns were the favorite instruments of New Orleans African Americans because they were easily carried in parades and because they were inexpensive. In 1897, Bolden organized the first jazz band and for seven years he was considered the "King of Jazz" in New Orleans.

Bolden's first band consisted of cornet, trombone, clarinet, guitar, string bass and drums. Bolden's musical accomplishments were notable

because neither Bolden nor his band members could read music.

One of Bolden's noted protégés was Bunk Johnson.

• William Edward Burghardt (W.E.B.) Du Bois (1868–1963), a noted African American scholar, was born (February 23).

On February 23, 1868, William Edward Burghardt ("W. E. B.") Du Bois was born. W. E. B. Du Bois is, without question, one of the greatest African Americans and Americo-Africans to have ever lived.

Du Bois was born in Great Barrington, Massachusetts. He received a bachelor of arts degree from Fisk University in 1888 and, in 1895, he became the first African American to be awarded a doctorate from Harvard University. Du Bois' dissertation was entitled *The Suppression of the African Slave Trade to the U.S.A., 1638–1870.* This doctoral dissertation was published as the first volume of the Harvard Historical Studies in 1896.

In the last decade of the 19th century, and the first decade of the 20th century, Du Bois gained a reputation as a prominent African American scholar and civil rights activist. Du Bois was an eloquent defender of and proponent for the full civil rights of African Americans through the Niagara Movement, which he founded in 1905, and which enlisted prominent African Americans, and through *The Horizon*, a magazine which Du Bois edited from 1907 until it ceased publication in 1910.

In addition to his demands for full equality, Du Bois was known for his opposition to Booker T. Washington and for his exposition of the theory of "the talented tenth." In Du Bois' mind, it was the responsibility of the African Americans who had gained success — it was the responsibility of "the talented tenth" — to lead the struggle to liberate African Americans.

In 1910, Du Bois joined the newly formed National Association for the Advancement of Colored People (NAACP) and became the editor of its official publication, the *Crisis*. It was a position he held until 1934. Du Bois' stint with the NAACP was a stormy one due to his militancy.

In partial response to his dissatisfaction with the NAACP, in 1919, Du Bois formed the Pan-African Conference. The Pan-African Conference lasted until 1929. The Pan-African Conference never became an important force, and the NAACP only half-heartedly supported it.

In 1926, Du Bois visited Russia for two months

and began to speak of socialism as a prerequisite for African American liberation.

In 1934, Du Bois shifted his focus from African American liberation to African American autonomy. His nationalistic sentiments along with his apologetics for Japanese imperialism (Du Bois admired Japan for being a powerful, assertive non–European nation) created a rift between Du Bois and the NAACP. Du Bois was forced to resign.

From 1934 to 1944, Du Bois taught at Atlanta University. During this period, he wrote his major work, *Black Reconstruction in America*, and an autobiography, *Dusk of Dawn* (1940).

In 1944, Du Bois was fired from Atlanta University. It was at this time that Walter White brought Du Bois back into the NAACP fold by appointing him as head of the NAACP's Department of Social Research. But Du Bois was still too militant — too radical — for the NAACP and, in 1948, he was dismissed.

By 1948, however, Du Bois had become involved in the world peace movement attending various international peace conferences and forming, in 1950, the Peace Information Service, a group which worked to ban nuclear weapons.

In 1950, Du Bois, then 82 years old, ran for the United States Senate from New York on the American Labor Party ticket.

In 1951, Du Bois was indicted by a Federal grand jury for failing to register the Peace Information Center as the American agent of a foreign principal. Du Bois was ultimately acquitted of the charges set forth in the indictment.

By 1952, Du Bois rejected all forms of the African American civil rights in favor of a world socialist movement. In 1957, he joined the Communist Party. However, even in the Communist Party, Du Bois remained contentious. He came to condemn the Communist proposal for an autonomous African American state.

In 1960, Du Bois moved to Ghana. He lived there until the day he died — August 28, 1963 — a day which was arguably the most momentous day in the history of the African American Civil Rights Movement.

Today, most people learn of Du Bois through his seminal work *The Souls of Black Folk,* a book of essays which made Du Bois the black intellectual of his day. However, the writing which served to inspire African Americans for most of two generations was his "Credo." Du Bois "Credo" would come to be framed and mounted in the homes of countless African Americans. The "Credo" has served as a declaration of principle which continues to withstand the test of time.

Credo (1904)

I believe in God who made of one blood all races that dwell on earth. I believe that all men, black and brown and white, are brothers, varying through Time and Opportunity, in form and gift and feature, but differing in no essential particular, and alike in soul and in the possibility of infinite development.

Especially do I believe in the Negro Race; in the beauty of its genius, the sweetness of its soul and its strength in that meekness which shall yet inherit this turbulent earth.

I believe in pride of race and lineage and self; in pride of self so deep as to scorn injustice to other selves; in pride of lineage so great as to despise no man's father; in pride of race so chivalrous as neither to offer bastardy to the weak nor beg wedlock of the strong, knowing that men may be brothers in Christ, even they be not brothers-in-law.

I believe in Service — humble reverent service, from the blackening of boots to the whitening of souls; for Work is Heaven, Idleness Hell, and Wage is the "Well done!" of the Master who summoned all them that labor and are heavy laden, making no distinction between the black sweating cotton-hands of Georgia and the First Families of Virginia, since all distinction not based on deed is devilish and not divine.

I believe in the Devil and his angels, who wantonly work to narrow the opportunity of struggling human beings, especially if they be black; who spit in the faces of the fallen, strike them that cannot strike again, believe the worst and work to prove it, hating the image which their Maker stamped on a brother's soul.

I believe in the Prince of Peace. I believe that War is Murder. I believe that armies and navies are at bottom the tinsel and braggadocio of oppression and wrong; and I believe that the wicked conquest of weaker and darker nations by nations whiter and stronger but foreshadows the death of that strength.

I believe in Liberty for all men; the space to stretch their arms and their souls; the right to breathe and the right to vote, the freedom to choose their friends, enjoy the sunshine and ride on the railroads, uncursed by color; thinking, dreaming, working as they will in a kingdom of God and love.

I believe in the training of children, black even as white; the leading out of little souls into the green pastures and beside the still waters, not for self or peace, but for Life lit by some large vision of beauty and goodness and truth; lest we forget, and the sons of the fathers, like Esau, for more meat barter their birthright in a mighty nation.

Finally, I believe in Patience — patience with the weakness of the Weak and the strength of the Strong, the prejudice of the ignorant and the ignorance of the Blind; patience with the tardy triumph of Joy and the mad chastening of Sorrow — patience with God.

• John Hope (1868–1936), an educator, was born in Augusta, Georgia (June 2). During his career, Hope would serve as president of Morehouse College and, later, the Atlanta University.

• Sissieretta Jones (1868–1933), a famous African American opera singer, was born.

Sissieretta Jones was born Matilda S. Joyner in Portsmouth, Virginia. She received her musical training at the Academy of Music in Providence, Rhode Island, and the New England Conservatory.

Sissieretta Jones was the first African American singer to appear at Wallach's Theater in Boston. During her career, she made concert tours in the United States, South America, the West Indies and Europe. In Europe, she became known as "Black Patti," a comparative tribute to the then great Italian soprano, Adelina Patti.

In 1892, Sissieretta Jones sang at the White House. Afterwards, she organized Black Patti's Troubadours. This travelling group toured the United States for 19 years.

• Scott Joplin, (1868–1917) the great ragtime composer and pianist, was born in Texarkana, Texas (November 12).

• *Miscellaneous State Laws:* An Alabama statute made it unlawful to unite, in one school, European American with African American children.

• Minnesota, Maine, New Hampshire, Vermont, Massachusetts, Rhode Island and Nevada permitted African Americans to vote while the concept of African American suffrage was denied in Missouri and Michigan.

• *Miscellaneous Cases:* In the case of *Ex Parte McCardle* (February 17, 1868) 73 U.S. 318, 18 L.Ed. 816, the United States Supreme Court refused to hear a case contesting the constitutionality of the Reconstruction Act. In this case, McCardle, a Mississippi newspaper editor who had been tried before a military tribunal for criticizing Reconstruction, challenged the jurisdiction of the tribunal and asked for a writ of habeas corpus. Relying upon the laws passed, the Court deemed that it did not have jurisdiction to hear the case.

• Threatened with Congressional re-organization, the United States Supreme Court played a passive role in Reconstruction. In two significant cases, *Mississippi v. Johnson* (1867) 71 U.S. 318, 18 L.Ed. 816 and *Georgia v. Stanton* (February 10, 1868) 73 U.S. 18 L.Ed. 721 the Court was asked to enjoin the President and the Secretary of War from enforcing the Reconstruction Acts on the grounds that they were unconstitutional. The Court evaded the issue, however, deciding in both cases that it had no power to enjoin an executive officer "in the performance of his official duties."

• *Miscellaneous Publications:* The famous slave narrative, *Behind the Scenes by Elizabeth Keckley, Formerly A Slave, but More Recently A Modiste and Friend to Mrs. Abraham Lincoln; or Thirty Years A Slave and Forty Years in the White House*, was published.

• *Scholastic Achievements:* The University of South Carolina was opened to all races (March 3).

• The American Missionary Association founded Hampton Normal and Agricultural Institute in Hampton, Virginia. At this institution, Booker T. Washington was educated. Hampton Institute opened in April.

• The American Missionary Association founded Knox College at Athens, Georgia, and Burwell at Selma, Alabama.

• Howard University Medical School opened.

• John Mercer Langston (1829–1897) founded and organized the Law Department at Howard University (October).

• *The Arts:* Edmonia Lewis completed her sculpture *Forever Free*, celebrating the Emancipation Proclamation.

THE AMERICAS

• *Cuba:* The government of the first Spanish republic decreed its commitment to the gradual emancipation of slaves (September). This decree effected both Cuba and Puerto Rico, the two remaining Spanish possessions in the Americas.

• In Cuba, Carlos Manuel de Cespedes, granted his slaves freedom. Cespedes also advocated and agitated for a revolution against Spain.

• The Grito de Yara began the Ten Years War.

The Ten Years' War was the first major Cuban struggle for independence. The Ten Years' War lasted from 1868 to 1878. It was a manifestation of serious social, economic, and political grievances on the island. While it failed to win independence, the Ten Years War did begin the process of slave emancipation in Cuba.

By the 1850s, Cuba had become the world's leading sugar exporter, tied increasingly to the United States market. But many agrarian workers had been displaced in the shift from a more diversified agricultural economy to one dominated by slave-produced sugar at the same time that Cuba's population was growing rapidly. Eastern Cuba was suffering especially in comparison to the newer sugar-producing regions of the west.

Additionally, abolitionists demanded an end to slavery while many Creoles wanted political and economic reform. Indeed, some of the Creoles even favored independence or annexation to the United States, which had showed repeated interest in acquiring Cuba.

The liberal Spanish government of General Enrique O'Donnell raised Cuban expectation of reform, but the subsequent conservative government pursued a repressive policy that alienated Cubans of many classes, especially in eastern Cuba.

Political turmoil in Spain contributed to the breakdown of order in Cuba. On September 18, 1868, naval officers at Cadiz revolted and ten days later revolutionaries took Madrid, proclaiming a liberal republic. The new government's refusal to grant reforms, however, led an eastern Cuban creole planter, Carlos Manuel de Cespedes, to proclaim Cuban independence on October 10, 1868. Cespedes proclamation of independence came to be known as the "Grito de Yara."

Calling for independence as well as gradual emancipation of slaves and universal male suffrage — universal male voting rights — Cespedes rallied the Cubans against Spain and a guerrilla war began at Bayamo.

On April 20, 1869, a constitutional convention organized a republican government at Guamarro. This government advocated the annexation of Cuba to the United States. Bitter guerrilla warfare followed. Meanwhile, in Spain, the government vacillated between monarchy

and republic until the Bourbons were finally restored with the coronation of Alfonso XII in January 1875.

In Cuba, the slavery issue created a deep division within the revolutionary movement. Because of their vested interest in the slave system, many of the planters would not support the revolution as long as the abolition of slavery was a principle goal. On the other hand, many of those fighting for independence were COTWs for whom the complete and immediate abolition of slavery was a primary objective of the revolution. The chief military leaders Maximo Gomez and Antonio Maceo *(see 1896)* represented the position of the Afro-Cubans. However, the rebel government leaders, who were dominated by the planters, repeatedly refused to allow Gomez and Maceo to carry the war into the west were most of the slaves were.

The United States, Britain and France were all interested in Cuba but none were interested enough to intervene in the Ten Years War. The Virginius Affair of October 31, 1875, in which Spanish naval forces seized a ship flying the United States flag off the coast of Jamaica came the closest to enticing one of the major powers to intervene. The American public was aghast at the execution by Spanish authorities of more than fifty of the officers, crew and passengers of the *Virginius*. Relations between the United States and Spain became strained. Only the diplomatic influence of England and France averted United States intervention in Spain's war with the Cubans.

By 1878, the war had severely damaged the sugar industry and had cost 250,000 lives. On February 11, 1878, at El Zanjon, the Spanish agreed to some political reform, to freedom for all those slaves who had fought with the rebels and gradual emancipation for the rest with compensation to the owners. This agreement with the creole leadership, however, fell far short of giving Cubans autonomy. It also failed to provide the social reforms for which so many had fought. Thus, the Pact of Zanjon itself became an issue for continued dissent in Cuba.

Immediately after the Pact of Zanjon was signed, General Antonio Maceo issued the "Protest of Baragua" and continued to fight on for nearly three more months before finally succumbing to Spanish forces in May of 1878.

The Ten Years War ultimately led to a major reorganization of the sugar industry in the 1880s, with major capital investment from the United States. But the Spanish failure to implement the reforms and the continued social and economic problems would contribute to a resumption of the Cuban War for Independence in 1895.

- *Haiti:* Pierre Faubert (1806–1868), a noted poet, playwright, died at Vanves, near Paris (July 31).

Pierre Faubert was the son of a general of the Haitian War of Independence. He was born in Cayes and studied in France.

Faubert became the Secretary of President Boyer and was chosen by President Geffrard as a negotiator for the Concordat between Haiti and the Vatican.

Faubert's most noted works are *Poesies Fugitives*, a book of poems, and *Oge ou le Prejuge de Couleur,* a drama.

EUROPE

- In Spain, the government of the first Spanish republic decreed its commitment to the gradual emancipation of slaves (September).

Almost from the beginning, the abolition of slavery in what remained of the once great Spanish Empire was tied to the liberal movement, and, it is an historical fact, that the most influential and vocal abolitionists in Spain were invariably Cuban and Puerto Rican creoles.

In 1811, it was Spain's colonial delegates who demanded gradualist emancipation in all the Americas. This movement failed.

In 1815 and 1817, treaties against the slave trade were executed between Spain and Great Britain, the leading anti-slavery crusading nation. One of the provisions of these treaties, called for the creation of a joint commission in Havana, Cuba, to oversee the seizure and disposal of slave ships. As a result of these treaties and the creation of the commission, British consuls in Havana thereafter became sentinels for the abolition movement in Cuba.

Despite the efforts of the British and the liberal elements in Spanish government, slavery in the Spanish West Indies continued. It was only the intervention of the Union navy during the United States Civil War which brought a final end to the slave trade in Cuba.

As for slavery itself, the United States Civil War is also responsible for stimulating the creation of the first Spanish abolitionist society. Established by a Puerto Rican in Madrid in 1864, the society would be instrumental laying the groundwork for the gradual emancipation decree of 1868.

- Robert Browning, the great Afro-English poet, published "Deaf and Dumb."

AFRICA

- *North Africa, Egypt and Sudan:* The *Jamiyyat al-Maarif* publishing house was founded in Cairo. The *Jamiyyat al-Maarif* was established principally for the publication of Arabic manuscripts.
- A state system of education was established in Egypt.
- The White Fathers (the Society of Missionaries of Our Lady of Africa) was founded by Cardinal Lavigerie at Algiers.
- The Sudan Company was liquidated.
- Elementary schools were opened at Berber and Dongola.
- *Western Africa:* Gle-Gle (Glele), the King of Dahomey, ceded Cotonou to the French to prevent the British from establishing themselves there.
- Minas sold Agoue to France.
- France established outposts at Boke and Bente, Guinea.
- France enacted protectorate treaties for the Ivory Coast area.
- The first educational grants-in-aid were awarded in Sierra Leone.
- The Ashanti renewed armed hostilities against the British.
- Around 1868, Creoles emerged as a distinctive people in Sierra Leone.
- In 1868, Benjamin Anderson set out from Monrovia, Liberia, on a thirteen-month journey which took him beyond the forest belt to the upland grasslands. During this exploration, Anderson visited the Mandinka kingdom of Musardu.

The status of the colony of Liberia in international law was never fully resolved. Because it received little support from the United States government, the settlers at Monrovia combined with neighboring settlements to form the Republic of Liberia in 1847.

Liberia's first president was inaugurated in 1848.

In the early 20th century, the government instituted a system of indirect rule over the Liberian hinterland. However, effective administration did not reach the interior until the presidency of William Tubman which began in 1944.

- James Horton *(see 1882)* published *West African Countries and Peoples.*

The most important of James Horton's publications was *West African Countries and Peoples*. *West African Countries and Peoples* proved to be a valuable description of the West African coast. In this book, Horton also argued that Africans were capable of governing under a Western form of government.

• William Edward Burghardt Du Bois, the great African American civil rights leader who became a citizen of Ghana, was born.

As an outspoken advocate of black equality, W. E. B. Du Bois opposed the gradualist approach of Booker T. Washington, who advocated technical training for African Americans. During his career, Du Bois also criticized the black separatist movement of Marcus Garvey.

In 1900, Du Bois participated in the first Pan-African Conference in London. In 1919, Du Bois and Blaise Diagne *(see 1872)*, the Senegalese politician, organized another conference in Paris. Others were held in 1921, 1923, 1927, and finally 1945 when Du Bois served as co-chairman with the future Ghanaian leader Kwame Nkrumah. Du Bois' pan-African movement was probably most important for linking up expatriate African nationalists.

After World War II, Du Bois became increasingly alienated from American society. In 1960, at the age of ninety-two, Du Bois having joined the Communist Party, moved to Ghana and became a Ghanaian citizen. Du Bois died in Ghana in 1963.

During his lifetime, Du Bois published or edited more than twenty books dealing with Africa or Afro-America.

• *Central Africa:* On January 14, a new treaty was executed between France and the Kings of Camma and Rembi. Under this treaty, the River Ogooue was opened to European commerce.

• On July 18, David Livingstone reached Lake Bangweulu.

• A trade treaty between Bunza and Abdal-Samad, a Sudanese ivory merchant, was executed.

• Beginning in 1868, a war erupted which pitted the Arabs and Swahili people against the Kazembe. The war would last until 1870.

• *Eastern Africa:* In Ethiopia, the collapse of Theodore's regime in 1868 was followed by a civil war which allowed Menelik to build Shoa into one of the strongest powers in Ethiopia.

• As a result of the collapse of Theodore's reign, 500 manuscripts and other Ethiopian treasures were seized by Britain.

• Napier supplied Yohannes IV (Ras Kassa) with weapons before departing for Britain.

"Ras" is the Ethiopian title conferred upon heads of important families, government ministers, territorial governors, etc. The title is roughly equivalent to the European title of "duke."

• Gondar was sacked by Menelik.

• A mission and orphanage for slave children was opened at Bagamoyo.

• Maglia, the first UMCA mainland mission was founded.

• John Kirk became the Acting British Consul in Zanzibar.

• Yohannes IV (Ras Kassa) became the Emperor of Ethiopia.

• France entered into a commercial treaty with Madagascar (August 8).

• Kimweri ye Nyumbai, the ruler of the Kilindi empire, died (1868).

Kimweri came to power very early in the nineteenth century. Kimweri was the fifth member of the Kilindi clan to rule Usambara in northeastern Tanzania. The Kilindi clan was founded by Mbega in the 1700s.

During his reign of almost 60 years, Kimweri extended Kilindi rule from his capital at Vuga over the Swahili and Arab towns on the coast.

Little is known about Kimweri before 1848. However, in 1848, Kimweri was visited by a literate European and his history began to be known.

During the early 1850s, Kimweri clashed with the Zanzibari ruler Sayyid Said over control of the coastal towns but in 1853 an accommodation was worked out by which a sort of condominium (joint) administration was established along the coast.

Kimweri oversaw an extensive trade in ivory, and some slaves, to the coast. During this period, Kimweri took the title Sultan. Thereafter his successors were also known as Sultan.

After his death in 1868, Usambara fell into a civil war, which ended only when the Germans occupied the country in 1890.

• The Ethiopian Emperor Theodore (c.1818 –1868) committed suicide while resisting the British expeditionary force at Magdala.

Theodore II (Tewodros) (c.1818–1868) was the Emperor of Ethiopia from 1855 to 1868. During his reign, Ethiopia was re-unified ending a century of political chaos.

Theodore's rise to power ended a period known as the "age of princes"—an age when Ethiopia was ruled by feudal chiefs while the old imperial dynasty maintained a tenuous hold on the capital at Gondar.

Theodore (who was born with the name Kassa) was born into an important northern family, but had no claim to membership in the Solomonic dynasty which traditionally ruled Ethiopia. However, Theodore was able to exploit the general political chaos that existed in Ethiopia and emerged as the Emperor—the single most powerful figure in the country.

By the early 1840s, Theodore was operating essentially as a bandit in the northwest. He alternately allied with, and rebelled from, the recognized local rulers. Theodore's military exploits were almost uniformly successful and his armed following grew rapidly.

In 1852, Theodore made his final break from the major northern ruler. Theodore began a series of decisive military victories which allowed him to consolidate power in his own right. By 1855, Theodore had defeated every major rival in central Ethiopia. Having vanquished all his competitors, Theodore was then crowned by the head of the Ethiopian Church as the *negus nagast*—the Emperor of Ethiopia. Upon his ascension, the man with the birth name of Kassa became the Emperor Theodore.

After his coronation, Theodore reduced the kingdom of Shoa to subjugation—taking the future emperor Menelik II prisoner in the process. However, this move did not resolve the persistent rebellions which erupted in other areas. Theodore's reign was all too frequently marked by an all too constant state of rebellion. Theodore found himself fighting campaigns almost every year that he reigned.

Faced with recurrent rebellions, Theodore sought military answers to the unification of his country. His reprisals against rebel territories became increasingly harsh. In an attempt to finance his campaigns, Theodore attempted to curb the power of the church and to tap the church's wealth. However, Theodore encountered strong clerical opposition and consequently lost considerable support from the population at large.

Theodore's ambition to unify Ethiopia was coupled with his broader goal of building a larger Christian empire and eventually recapturing Jerusalem from the Islamic Turks. Turkish control of Egypt, Sudan and the Red Sea posed a strong threat to Ethiopia and caused Theodore to turn to Europe for assistance.

Because of their strategic position, the Ottoman Turks had long been able to block Theodore's access to outside sources of modern arms. In an attempt to get around the Turkish barrier, Theodore sought craftsmen to manufacture weapons locally for him.

Upon his ascension to the throne, Theodore received Protestant missionaries from Europe. Theodore allowed them to do mission work for a few years, but as his desire for modern weapons grew, his attitude toward the missionaries changed. Theodore began to demand that the missionaries make him mortars and bombshells.

The missionaries manufactured a number of serviceable weapons for Theodore but they could not satisfy all his needs. In 1862, during a lull in his struggle with rebel factions, Theodore sent emissaries to Europe appealing for additional craftsmen and more direct assistance against the Turks.

Theodore was greatly disillusioned when his requests for arms were ignored. Exasperated, Theodore detained the resident British Consul (Consul Cameron) along with some missionaries as a protest gesture. This action precipitated an international incident and led to British reprisals. The reign of Theodore began to crumble.

By 1865, Theodore found himself battling not only his enemies within his country but also the antagonist Europeans. Theodore was soon completely encircled by rebellious territories and found himself steadily losing his grip on his army.

Theodore's continuing conflict with the clergy led to his imprisoning the head of the national church (Abuna Salama) in 1864 and later to plundering the churches of Gondar in 1866.

When Theodore transferred his British detainees into prisons, the British government mounted a massive expeditionary force against him.

By 1867, Theodore's grasp on his empire was gone. Theodore gathered together the remnants of his army to the naturally fortified plateau of Magdala. Meanwhile, a large British-Indian expeditionary force, under Robert Cornelius Napier, landed on the coast and prepared to march against Theodore. The end of Theodore's reign came in April of 1868. Theodore released his British prisoners and then led a futile token resistance against the British forces.

Theodore committed suicide as the British forces stormed Magdala.

*   *   *

"Negus" is the Ethiopian term for "King."
"Negus Nagast" ("king of kings") is the title of
the emperor. The usage of the term "negus"
appears to predate the time of Ezana in the
fourth century.

- *Southern Africa:* Mahehero, the Herero
chief, defeated Jan Jonker, the chief of the
Khoikhoi of Namibia. This Herero victory
resulted in the Herero obtaining their independence.
- Beginning in 1868 and lasting until 1870,
a war between the British and the Herero
raged.
- In 1868, the British finally annexed the
Sotho lands. Thereafter the region was officially known by the name the British gave it
"Basutoland" (March 12).

The country which is today known as Lesotho
originated during the 1820s. The first king of
Lesotho was Moshoeshoe. Moshoeshoe was
chief of a minor Sotho branch known as the
Mokotedi.

As Moshoeshoe built his kingdom out of
diverse elements, the generic name "Sotho"
came to be applied to his people. The British
annexed Lesotho in 1868, naming it the Basutoland Protectorate. Lesotho was administered
briefly by the Cape Colony, but it reverted to the
British crown until 1966, when it again became
an independent kingdom.

- Mswati (c.1820–1868), considered by many
to be the greatest king of the Swazi, died.

Mswati was the son of Sobhuza I, the founder
of the Swazi kingdom. Mswati's mother was a
daughter of the Ndwandwe king Zwide.

Mswati succeeded Sobhuza in 1840 after a
brief interregnum. During the interregnum, the
Swazi repelled an attempt by the Zulu king Dingane to occupy Swaziland. The subsequent
death of the Zulu ruler enabled Mswati to profit
from the temporary decline of Zulu military
power. He built his foreign policy around the
goal of protecting Swazi independence against
the Zulu.

Mswati successfully appealed to the new British
agent in Natal, Theophilus Shepstone, to restrain
the Zulu from attacking him, and created a heritage of Swazi trust in the British .

Mswati reorganized the Swazi army along
Zulu lines by converting the formerly clan based
military units into more efficiently mobilized
age regiments. Mswati absorbed many new

Sotho and Nguni followers into his kingdom
under a popular policy of tolerating non–Swazi
chiefs and non–Swazi customs. Mswati avoided
military engagements to his south and extended
his conquests into the eastern Transvaal as far
north as the Limpopo River.

Mswati's only major setback was at the hands
of the Pedi chief Sekwati in the 1850s. Around
1859, Mswati assisted the Gaza usurper Mawewe
to seize the Gaza kingship on the death of Soshangane, with whom the Swazi had been informally allied.

Later, however, when the Gaza heir Mzila
brought in Portuguese troops to drive Mawewe
out, Mswati stayed out of the conflict. Instead
Mswati, gave Mawewe and his followers asylum
in Swaziland and used their presence there as a
hedge against further trouble with Mzila. By the
time of his death in 1868, the Swazi were one of
the most powerful kingdoms in southern Africa,
with borders larger than those of present day
Swaziland.

Swazi contacts with Europeans began during
the 1840s, when the Afrikaner Voortrekkers were
occupying the Transvaal. Mswati hoped to use
the Afrikaners as allies and sold them a strip of
land to his south to create a buffer zone against
the Zulu. Other concessions followed.

Mswati also assisted the new Transvaal Republic in some of its wars against Sotho chiefs.

During the six years between Mswati's death
and the succession of his son Mbandzeni, the
Swazi were divided by a bitter succession dispute and European pressure on Swaziland began
in earnest.

- Umzilikazi (Mzilikazi) (c.1795–1868), the
founder king of the Ndebele (Matabele) state
of Zimbabwe, died. Uncombata (Mncumbathe) was proclaimed regent.

Mzilikazi was the founder-king of the Ndebele
(Matabele) state. He was perhaps the most successful of the 19th century Nguni migrant
empire-builders. Mzilikazi conquered much of
the Transvaal and came to dominate half of the
land which is today the country of Zimbabwe.

Mzilikazi was the son of Mashobane, the ruler
of a section of the Khumalo in South Africa's
Zululand. Mzilikazi grew up at the court of his
maternal grandfather, Zwide. At the time, Zwide
was building a powerful confederation among
the northern Nguni. However, Zwide distrusted
Mzilikazi's father. Around 1817, Zwide had
Mashobane killed and in Mashobane's place
installed his son, Mzilikazi, as the Khumalo chief.

During the late 1810s and early 1820s, Zwide fought a series of wars with the great Zulu king Shaka. During these wars, Mzilikazi defected and joined forces with Shaka. Mzilikazi served Shaka only briefly, however, and, around 1821, fled to the Transvaal with several hundred followers.

Employing the advanced discipline and military tactics developed by the northern Nguni, Mzilikazi fought his way north accumulating new followers and livestock. Mzilikazi occupied Pedi country for about a year. While occupying the Pedi country, Mzilikazi clashed with another migrant leader, Nqaba.

In 1823, Mzilikazi and his followers turned southwest, reaching the middle Vaal River. At the Vaal River, Mzilikazi built his first settlements and his people came to be known as "Matabele" to the Sotho.

After being harassed incessantly by mounted Griqua raiders armed with guns, Mzilikazi moved his expanding entourage north to the site of present day Pretoria. There he came to rest in 1827.

In 1829, Mzilikazi received his first European visitors. Among the visitors was the missionary Robert Moffat. Mzilikazi and Moffat struck upon a lasting friendship. Moffat essentially became Mzilikazi's informal ambassador. Throughout the 1830s, Mzilikazi (with Moffat's assistance) solicited missionaries to settle among the Ndebele and encouraged European visitors.

In 1831, while most Ndebele troops were campaigning north of the Limpopo River, Mzilikazi's reserve troops shattered a major Griqua army led by Barend Barends. Mzilikazi's victory effectively removed the Griqua threat and the Griqua's inept use of firearms essentially led Mzilikazi to disdain the use of firearms for his own forces.

In 1832, the Zulu chieftain, Dingane, attacked Mzilikazi. The war was inconclusive but the Zulu threat compelled Mzilikazi to move his people further west to the Marico River. By 1832, Mzilikazi had become the ruler of 20,000 people and directly or indirectly controlled most of the western Transvaal.

By 1835, disaffected Afrikaner (Boer) farmers in the British-ruled Cape Colony had begun to migrate inland, posing a threat to Mzilikazi's security. In 1836, Mzilikazi dispatched his senior adviser Mncumbathe to Cape Town to sign a treaty of friendship with Governor D'Urban. However, by mid 1836, advance Afrikaner parties crossed the Vaal and were annihilated by Mzilikazi's patrols. The following year the Afri-kaners, under the command of Andries Potgeiter retaliated against Ndebele towns, driving Mzilikazi down the Marico River. In the same year, new Zulu and Griqua assaults greatly weakened Mzilikazi's tenuous position.

At the end of 1837, Mzilikazi divided his people into two major migrant parties as the Ndebele fled into Ngwato territory. Most of the Ndebele went directly to what is present day Matabeleland in southwestern Zimbabwe. However, Mzilikazi himself led the remainder to Botswana.

When Mzilikazi rejoined the Ndebele in Zimbabwe, he found that his son Nkulumane had been installed as king in his absence. Mzilikazi quickly executed the usurpers and encountered no further serious challenges to his authority over the Ndebele during his lifetime.

Because the Ngoni had previously passed through Zimbabwe as a result of the Mfecane, the indigenous Shona people were too disorganized to effectively resist the advance of Mzilikazi. Mzilikazi established his capital near present Bulawayo and proceeded to raid the Shona for captives and cattle to rebuild his kingdom.

Several times during the 1840s, Mzilikazi initiated military campaigns against Sebitwane's Kololo in western Zambia, but each of these initiatives ended in disaster.

In 1847, Andries Potgeiter, the Voortrekker leader, attacked the Ndebele. However, the Voortrekkers were easily repelled and the Afrikaners ceased to be an active military threat to Mzilikazi.

During the 1850s, Mzilikazi negotiated peace treaties with the Transvaal Republic.

In 1854, Mzilikazi was visited by his old friend Robert Moffat. With this visit, Mzilikazi began a reconciliation with South Africa. Afterwards, increasing numbers of European and African traders entered Matabeleland.

In 1859, Robert Moffat's London Missionary Society established an outpost among the Ndebele. However, no Ndebele were converted to Christianity until the 1880s.

During the 1860s, Mzilikazi stepped up his campaign against the Shona, some of whom had begun raiding Ndebele cattle. Mzilikazi himself took a less active role in Ndebele affairs as his health deteriorated. During his last years, Mzilikazi was virtually confined in the wagon which he used to travel throughout his kingdom.

Mzilikazi died in 1868 without having publicly designated his successor. At the time of his death, Mzilikazi was the acknowledged ruler of some 100,000 people.

Uncertainty over his son Nkulumane's fate threw the Ndebele into political turmoil. Mnucumbathe, Mzilikazi's trusted adviser, served as regent until 1870 when Mzilikazi's son Lobengula was installed as king.

* * *

The Ndebele kingdom rose and fell in the nineteenth century. Under the founder-king Mzilikazi, a few hundred Nguni refugees fled from Zululand to the Transvaal, where they conquered and incorporated many thousands of non–Nguni peoples.

In 1838–1840, the Ndebele (Matabele) settled in Zimbabwe. The kingdom was conquered by the British in 1893–1896 but Nguni language and culture remained firmly implanted in Zimbabwe.

RELATED HISTORICAL EVENTS

• *The United States:* President Andrew Johnson was impeached. By one vote, the Senate found Johnson not guilty of the offenses for impeachment.

• Ulysses S. Grant was elected president.

• *The Americas:* In Brazil, a political crisis was triggered by the fall of the Zacarias de Goes e Vasconcelos cabinet.

In 1868, the Emperor — Dom Pedro II — expelled the Liberals from power. Although this action was constitutional, some Liberals interpreted it as a coup.

The Liberals reacted by forming, in 1870, the Republican Party. In its principles, the Republican Party was decidedly ideological. It was a clear alternative to liberalism, and most of its leading members were inspired by Comtian positivism, secularism, and social Darwinism. Unlike that of other Liberals, the position of the Republican Party on slavery was muted.

The Republican Party members were greatly concerned with the question of decentralization or federalism. Their insistence on devolution of powers and revenues to the provinces (to be called states when the republic was at last formed) was an expression of the annoyance of the southeastern and southern provinces at the overrepresentation of the economically decadent northeast.

Republicanism also appealed to opportunism, as the more prosperous and politically ambitious foresaw a decline of a dynasty that lacked a male heir. Even so, the Republican Party won few local or provincial elections during the 1870s and 1880s. Its only notable successes occurred in

Sao Paulo, Minas Gerais, and Rio Grande do Sul. Nevertheless, the existence of Republican Party served to lay the foundation for the Republic of Brazil that was to follow. *See 1889.*

1869

THE UNITED STATES

• Congress passed the Fifteenth Amendment which guaranteed to citizens the right to vote regardless of "race, color, or previous condition of servitude." The Amendment would become law on March 30, 1870. The Amendment did not specify that it applied only to "male inhabitants" as did the Fourteenth, however, it would be administered as if it did (February 26).

After going through some eleven different amendments, the Fifteenth Amendment to the United States Constitution was approved by Congress and proposed to the States. The Amendment was intended to safeguard African Americans from some of the oppression which would be omnipresent with a European American majority by guaranteeing that the right to vote could not be "denied or abridged by the United States or any State." The Fifteenth Amendment reads:

Amendment XV

Section 1. The right of citizens of the United States to vote shall not be denied or abridged by the United States or by any State on account of race, color, or previous condition of servitude.

Section 2. The Congress shall have power to enforce this article by appropriate legislation.

• Jefferson F. Long from Georgia was seated as the first African American to serve in the House of Representatives.

The 41st Congress included two African American Representatives: Jefferson F. Long of Georgia and Joseph H. Rainey of South Carolina. There was one African American in the United States Senate: Hiram R. Revels of Mississippi.

During the Reconstruction Era some twenty-two African Americans would come to serve in Congress. They were Bruce, Cain, Cheatham, DeLarge, Elliot, Haralson, Hyman, Langston, Long, Lynch, Miller, Murray, Nash, O'Hara, Rainey, Ransier, Rapier, Revels, Smalls, Turner, Walls, and White.

Of these twenty-two, Bruce, Cheatham, De-Large, Haralson, Hyman, Long, Lynch, Murray,

Nash, Rainey, Smalls, Turner, and White were born slaves while Cain, Elliot, Langston, Miller, O'Hara, Ransier, Rapier, Revels, and Walls were born free.

- James Garfield introduced a resolution in the House of Representatives which called for the reduction in the representation of the Southern states as a penalty for denying African Americans the right to vote in accordance with Section 2 of the Fourteenth Amendment *(see 1866)*. No action was taken on Garfield's proposed resolution.
- The American Anti–Slavery Society was dissolved.
- By 1869, the Freedmen's Bureau according to a report by the commissioner, General Oliver Howard, had spent $13.5 million on freedmen.
- Ebenezer Don Carlos Bennett (1833–1908) was the first African American to receive an appointment in the diplomatic service when he became Minister to Haiti (April 16).

After completion of his Haitian diplomatic mission in 1877, Bennett served for ten years as the general consul from Haiti to the United States.

- In 1869, Joseph Jenkins Roberts, the first President of Liberia, addressed the annual meeting of the African Colonization Society in Washington, D.C.
- In Mississippi, John R. Lynch, an African American, was nominated for secretary of state on the Republican Party ticket. Lynch was a well-educated Methodist preacher who had come to Mississippi from Indiana. Hiram R. Revels was nominated as Republican candidate for the State Senate. He was an African Methodist Episcopal pastor in Natchez. Revels was elected.
- In Mississippi, 716 officers and men comprised the total contingent of Federal troops stationed in Mississippi. By contrast, in Texas, there were 4,612 Federal troops but they were there primarily to protect the settlers from the Indigenous Americans.
- The South Carolina State Legislature consisted of 10 African Americans and 21 European Americans in the Senate and 78 African Americans and 46 European Americans serving as representatives.
- In Tennessee, the Democratic Party regained control of the state from the Republican Party.

- In 1869, two African American infantry regiments were formed. When combined with the African American cavalry units that were already in existence, the total number of African Americans in the army totalled 12,500 men.
- The first official Texas Emancipation Day (Juneteenth) was celebrated on June 19, 1869. Lottie Brown was named the first "Juneteenth Queen." *See 1865.*
- Robert Brown Elliott (1842–1884) was appointed assistant adjutant-general of the South Carolina National Guard. In this capacity, Elliott was charged with the formation and maintenance of the state militia — the "Black Militia" — whose commission was to protect European American and African Americans from the terrorist organization known as the Ku Klux Klan.

Robert Brown Elliott was a brilliant lawyer who was born in Liverpool, England, of West Indian parents. Elliott was educated in England.

Elliott was elected to the South Carolina legislature in 1868 and served as a United States Congressman from 1871 to 1875.

- Henry McNeal Turner was appointed to serve as a United States postmaster for Macon, Georgia. However, Turner resigned after serving for only a few months because European American racism prevented him from performing his duties.
- *Labor Movement:* At the Fourth Annual Conference of the National Labor Union in Philadelphia, Pennsylvania, there were 142 representatives of whom 9 were African American. At this conference, it was decided that African Americans should form their own unions and these unions would send their own delegates to future conferences. In general, in 1869, organized labor ignored the interests and concerns of African Americans and only accepted them when they were in segregated unions. An example of the segregation within the labor movement was Lewis H. Douglass, the son of Frederick Douglass. Lewis Douglass, despite working in the Government Printing Office, was not allowed to join the printer's union.
- The Colored National Labor Union was organized in Washington, D. C. Isaac Myers was elected president. The Colored National Labor Union recommended cooperatives, loan associations and the purchase of land by African Americans.

• *Miscellaneous State Laws:* Indiana authorized the establishment of separate schools for African Americans.

• *Miscellaneous Cases:* In the case of *Texas v. White* (April 12, 1869) 74 U.S. 700, 19 L.Ed. 227, the United States Supreme Court ruled that the Southern ordinances of secession had been null and void, and that the Southern states had never ceased to be in the Union. Although this rejected the basis of the Reconstruction Acts (that the states had left the Union, and thus the Union had the right to set standards for readmission), the Court declined to consider the constitutionality of the Reconstruction Acts, fearing Congressional reorganization.

• *Miscellaneous Publications:* Sarah Hopkins Bradford published *Scenes in the Life of Harriet Tubman.*

• Francis Ellen Harper published an epic poem entitled *Moses, a Story of the Nile.* Harper's *Poems on Miscellaneous Subjects* was published in 1854 and had sold 10,000 copies over a five year period.

• *Scholastic Achievements:* Straight (Dillard) University in New Orleans received a charter from the State of Louisiana. The law school was granted the right to qualify any of its graduates for immediate admission to the Louisiana bar.

• The American Missionary Association founded Le Moyne College in Memphis, Tennessee, and Tougaloo University in Mississippi.

• George Lewis Ruffin (1834–1886) graduated from Harvard University Law School. Ruffin was perhaps the first African American to graduate from a university law school and obtain a law degree.

George Ruffin went on to establish a law practice in Boston. He later became a judge of the District Court of Charlestown, Massachusetts (November 19, 1883), and he was a member of the Common Council of Boston in 1875 and 1876. Ruffin married Josephine St. Pierre Ruffin (1842–1924), who herself was a leader of the African American women's club movement.

• Alexander Thomas Augusta, the first African American surgeon in the United States Army and the former administrator of the Freedmen's Hospital, received an honorary degree from Howard University.

• Fanny Jackson (Coppin) (1837–1913) was promoted to principal of the Institute for Colored Youth of Philadelphia. The Society of Friends founded the school in 1837, and when Coppin graduated from Oberlin College in 1865, she became principal of the Institute's women's department. The Institute for Colored Youth was a prestigious school. Its faculty comprised some of the most highly educated African Americans of the time. Fanny Jackson (Coppin), who is said to have been the first African American woman to head a major educational institution for African Americans, remained in her position until she retired in 1902.

• *The Black Church:* The Colored Cumberland Presbyterian Church was founded. The Colored Cumberland Presbyterian Church broke from the European American denomination. It was one of the first to split away in the South when separate black churches became legally possible after the Civil War. Some contact with the parent denomination was maintained, and the separation of the churches was not absolute until 1874.

• *Sports:* The Philadelphia Pythons, an all African American baseball team, defeated the Philadelphia City Items, an all European American baseball team, 27–17. This was the first recorded encounter between African American and European American baseball teams.

THE AMERICAS

• *Cuba:* There were 363,000 slaves in Cuba.
• The Guaimare Constitution was drafted.

Dominican Republic: During Ulysses S. Grant's presidency, in 1869, the president of the Dominican Republic (Buenaventura Baez) offered to sell his country to the United States. Grant's secretary, General Orville Babcock, signed a treaty of annexation with the black republic. Charles Sumner, who was then chairman of the Senate Foreign Relations Committee, attacked the treaty and denounced Grant. Sumner, always the staunch supporter of political rights for persons of African descent, was angered at the thought of an African dominated republic losing its independence. Based on Sumner's opposition, the Senate rejected the treaty and the Dominican Republic remained seemingly independent.

• *Jamaica:* Edward Jordan (1800–1869), a Jamaican political leader, died.

Edward Jordan was one of a very small number of Afro-Jamaicans who held elective office during and immediately following the abolition of slavery. The son of a COTW freedman from Barbados, Jordan was jailed for a short while in 1831 on charges of fomenting slave rebellion. However, he was elected to the Jamaican House of Assembly in 1835, three years before the formal end of slavery.

Jordan also served on the Kingston Common Council and, ultimately, became mayor of Kingston, serving for twelve years beginning in 1854.

Jordan and fellow COTW, Robert Osborn, attempted to provide leadership for previously unrepresented Afro-Jamaicans. Together, the two men published a newspaper, *The Watchman.* However, despite his efforts, some critics accused Jordan of compromising too much with the European colonial establishment.

EUROPE

• Robert Browning completed a four volume poetry collection entitled *The Ring and the Book.*

AFRICA

• *North Africa, Egypt and Sudan:* On November 17, the Suez Canal was opened by Empress Eugenie.

• One hundred Sudanese boys were admitted to primary school in Cairo, Egypt.

• Tunis went bankrupt. Britain, France and Italy took control.

• Beginning in 1869, Gustave Nachtigal (1834–1885) led an expedition which took him from Tripoli to Bornu and back by way of Lake Chad, Darfur and the Nile.

Gustave Nachtigal was a German explorer and political agent. A doctor by profession, Nachtigal departed from Tripoli to cross the Sahara Desert in 1869. He arrived in Bornu in 1870 after exploring the Lake Chad region. From Bornu, Nachtigal crossed Wadai to Egypt and returned to Europe in 1875.

In 1884, Nachtigal was dispatched by his government to Douala, Cameroon, to help secure the new German West African territories. Nachtigal died aboard ship on the voyage back to Germany.

Nachtigal's three volume record of his trans-Saharan expedition, *Sahara und Sudan,* became an important reference work for the central Sudan and particularly for Bornu.

• *Western Africa:* W. H. Simpson, the Acting Administrator of the Gold Coast, was detained for five days by Akwamu (March-April). In June, the Ashanti attacked Anum and Ho.

• Bolama was made the capital of Portuguese Guinea (December 1). The government of Guinea was subsequently re-organized.

• Jaja founded Opobo.

In 1869 war broke out amongst the traders of Bonny. Jaja, one of the leading traders, lost most of his weapons in a fire and was forced to ask for peace. However, Jaja used the peace negotiations to leave Bonny and establish a new trading state which was located in a strategic position where Jaja was able to cut off Bonny from the sources of palm oil situated in the interior. Jaja founded Opobo.

• Lat Dior, instigated by Ahmadu Shehu of Toro, attacked the French. Lat Dior (c.1842–1886) was defeated and forced to flee abroad.

Lat Dior (Lat Dyor Diop) was the ruler of the Wolof kingdom of Kayor and was a resistance leader who was responsible for the Islamization of western Senegal.

Because his mother was of Kayor royal blood, Lat Dior was eligible to become King of the Wolof and was so chosen in 1862. Two years later, after coming into conflict with the French imperial forces, Lat Dior was forced to flee to Saloum, where he took refuge with the Muslim leader Maba Diakhou Ba. At the time, Maba Diakhou Ba was engaged in armed conflicts with both the French and local non–Muslims.

Under the influence of Maba Diakhou Ba, Lat Dior converted to Islam. When Maba was killed in 1867, Lat Dior came to terms with the French. However, the agreement was always tenuous and Lat Dior frequently found himself in opposition to French imperial designs.

In 1871, Lat Dior reached another accord with the French and was reinstated as the Wolof king. Four years later, Lat Dior allied himself with the French against Ahmadu Ibn 'Umar Tall, who was struggling to maintain the Tukolor empire against the French.

In 1877, Lat Dior won control over the neighboring state of Baol. Lat Dior's power and position enabled him to affect the Islamization of a large segment of western Senegal.

In 1882, Lat Dior again found himself in conflict with French colonial policy when he objected to the French plans to build a railroad through Kayor to connect Saint Louis with Dakar. Realizing the threat to his sovereignty posed by the railroad, Lat Dior refused to allow passage through his lands. The French refused to accept this and with their superior military forces were able to depose Lat Dior.

Lat Dior fled and became essentially a guerrilla warrior. He fought the French sporadically until he was killed in 1886.

- Gustave Nachtigal visited Sheikh Omar of Bornu.

"Sheik" is an Arabic Islamic title connoting religious or political leadership. In the form "Shehu" the term was the title taken by al-Kanemi of Bornu in the beginning of the nineteenth century and was retained by his descendants.

- In 1869, Joseph Jenkins Roberts, the first President of Liberia, addressed the annual meeting of the African Colonization Society in Washington, D.C.
- John Aggrey, the former ruler of the Fante community of Cape Coast (Ghana), died.

When John Aggrey became the ruler of the Fante around 1865, he immediately endeavored to clarify the relationship between his people and the British. At the time, the relationship between the British at Cape Coast Castle and the surrounding Fante community was nebulous. John Aggrey attempted to clarify the situation by claiming all the land surrounding the castle and by sending representatives to London to appear before the 1865 Commons Select Committee. These representatives were sent to London to assert John Aggrey's sovereignty over the Cape Coast region.

The 1865 Commons Select Committee eventually recommended a withdrawal from political responsibilities in West Africa. However, by that time, John Aggrey had become enmeshed in a number of disputes with the British agents at Cape Coast.

Aggrey had the agents arrested and tried. Considering themselves subject only to the laws of Britain, the agents refused to accept the decisions of the Fante courts. This on-going disobedience led to the deterioration of relations between Aggrey and the British administrator of the Cape Coast, Edward Conran. Ultimately, Aggrey was compelled to petition the British government against Conran in particular and the British presence in general.

Aggrey followed the petition with an even stronger letter alluding to the then recent rebellion in Jamaica. Conran deemed the letter seditious and when Aggrey refused to appear before him, Conran deposed him and had him deported to Sierra Leone.

Aggrey did not return to the Cape Coast until 1869, the year that he died. Today he is remembered as a hero of Ghanaian nationalists — the first Fante chief to rely upon Western educated advisers to assist him in fighting the British encroachment on Fante lands.

- *Central Africa:* Msiri proclaimed himself Mwami (King) of Garaganza (or Garenganze) with his capital at Bunkeya.

In the early 1870s, Msiri entered into a trade relationship with the powerful Swahili trader Tippu Tip and obtained the support of other coastal Swahili and Arab traders. Msiri exported slaves, ivory and copper to both the east and west coasts and imported large quantities of cloth and firearms.

- Bunza received Schweinfurth.
- An Arab trading post was established at Nyangwe by Mwine Dugumbi. From this post, raids were launched against the Manyema, Lega and Songola.
- Tippu Tip led a trade caravan which traded with the Bemba, Lungu, and Kazembe. The caravan was comprised of some 4,000 individuals.
- Schweinfurth explored the Azande country.
- *Eastern Africa:* The Italians purchased Assab.
- Djibouti replaced Obock as a French coaling station.
- David Livingstone reached Ujiji in March.

In 1866, financed mostly by friends and admirers, the explorer David Livingstone led an expedition to discover the sources of the Nile. Traveling along the Rovuma River, the explorer made his way toward Lake Tanganyika, reaching its shores in 1869.

- Sir Samuel Baker was appointed the Governor of the Equatorial Nile Basin. He would hold this position until 1873.
- Apolo Kagwa (c.1869–1927), a future prime minister of the Ganda kingdom (Buganda), was born.

In 1877, Apolo Kagwa became a page at the court of the Kabaka (king) Mutesa I about the same time as Christian missionaries began work in Buganda. Kagwa's rise to power is an example of the opportunities open to commoners in the very bureaucratic Ganda kingdom during the nineteenth century.

In 1884, Kagwa was baptized a Protestant

about the time Mwanga II acceded to the kingship. Two years later, Mwanga purged the Christians at his court, but Kagwa — who seemed always to have been only nominally religious — escaped with only a beating.

In 1887, Kagwa was made a commander in Mwanga's royal guards. Mwanga's reign was dominated by a complex power struggle between Protestant, Catholic, and Muslim chiefs. In 1888, Mwanga was overthrown by a temporary Christian-Muslim alliance and a general civil war commenced. Kagwa fled into neighboring Ankole with other Christian refugees.

In 1889, Kagwa re-entered the kingdom at the head of the Christian faction and helped to replace Mwanga on the throne. For this service, Kagwa was rewarded with the office of Katikiro — prime minister — of the Ganda kingdom.

As the struggle continued, Kagwa increasingly identified his Protestant faction with the English. When the British officer, Frederick Lugard arrived in 1890 to obtain a treaty of protection, Kagwa signed for the Protestants and then allied with Lugard to defeat the other faction.

A new treaty laid the basis for the future government of the Ganda kingdom and a British protectorate was formally declared in 1894. Three years later, when Mwanga revolted against this arrangement, Kagwa opted to ally with the British to defeat and depose him.

After the deposition of Mwanga, Kagwa added to his offices the position of senior regent over Mwanga's heir. Thus, when Henry Johnston negotiated the "Uganda Agreement" in 1900, Kagwa was the supreme Ganda chief and the leading signatory of the agreement.

The Uganda Agreement, which enunciated the rights of the Ganda chiefs under the colonial administration, allotted to Kagwa an immense tract of land and brought him to the height of his power. Kagwa continued to add to his landholdings and was an enthusiastic advocate of modernization. Kagwa's prestige among the British was unrivalled. Indeed, after a visit to London in 1902, Kagwa was knighted.

In 1914, Daudi Chwa II formally became king of the Ganda, ending Kagwa's regency. The new king began to demand curbs on Kagwa's power. Lesser Ganda chiefs — resentful of the terms of the 1900 agreement — also opposed Kagwa's dominance.

As the new British administration became more settled, it too became disenchanted with him. In 1926, Kagwa was forced to resign his office after a dispute with the king over a minor matter. The following year, Kagwa set off for

England to argue his case, but fell and died while passing through Kenya.

At the turn of the century, Kagwa had begun to write books on the history and customs of the Ganda and their neighbors in the Ganda language. These books are considered the first modern histories written by an east African. He wrote partly to justify the unique autonomy accorded Buganda under colonial rule, but his works are deemed to be seminal contributions to the history of the whole region.

- Kamurasi, the king of the Bunyoro, died.

Kamurasi came to power after defeating his brother in a civil war in 1852. His position was never completely secure, and he had to contend with rebellious outlying provinces throughout his reign.

Kamurasi also had to deal with the aggression of the increasingly powerful Ganda kingdom to his east. At one point, the Ganda actually chased Kamurasi out of his kingdom. However, he recovered and drove the invaders back. Cut off by the Ganda from easy access to traders from the east coast, Kamurasi traded for firearms with Arabs based in Khartoum.

In 1862, Kamurasi received at his court John Speke and J. A. Grant — the first Europeans to visit the Nyoro kingdom and to describe Bunyoro. A year later, Kamurasi was visited by Samuel Baker and his wife.

Baker regarded Kamurasi with contempt. Baker's unfavorable opinions helped to foster negative European attitudes about Bunyoro which later had disastrous consequences for his son and successor, Kabarega, who was conquered by the British.

Around 1869, Kabarega succeeded his father Kamurasi as the mukama — the king — of Bunyoro. The ascension followed a bitter civil war between Kabarega and his brother. The civil war, while securing the throne for Kabarega, also left his kingdom economically ruined.

Once secure upon the throne, Kabarega embarked on a campaign to restore the former greatness of Bunyoro by reorganizing his administration and army in an effort to recapture provinces his predecessors had lost to rebel chiefs over the previous century.

Kabarega curbed the power of the traditional aristocracy by appointing commoners as chiefs, and created a standing army such as was previously unknown in Uganda. While rebuilding his kingdom, Kabarega had to resist both the continued aggression of the powerful Ganda Kingdom (Buganda) to his east under King

Mutesa I and encroachments by the Egyptians from the north.

* * *

The first Nyoro (Bunyoro) kings — the first "mukama" — appear to have been both the earliest and the most powerful rulers in the land that is today known as Uganda. The Nyoro dynasties may have originated as early as the thirteenth century. Traditions record three dynastic periods. The first, that of the Tembuzi (Batembuzi) kings appears to be purely mythical. The second period was that of the Chwezi (Bachwezi) kings. This period borders on being a mythical time and has been loosely dated between the thirteenth and fifteenth centuries. The two great Chwezi kings — Ndahura and his son Wamara — are credited with having built an empire larger even than present day Uganda.

The last period of the Nyoro kings was that of the Bito kings. The Chwezi were said to have mysteriously disappeared before the arrival of the Bito, who may have been Nilotic-speaking immigrants from the north.

According to tradition, the Nyoro fell into decline in the eighteenth century as provinces broke away and the Ganda kingdom arose to challenge it. The Nyoro experienced a brief resurgence under its last independent king, Kabarega, but it was conquered by the British in 1899 and absorbed into the Uganda Protectorate.

Five years after Uganda became independent, the Nyoro and the other Uganda kingdoms were formally abolished.

- *Southern Africa:* The London and Limpopo Mining Company sponsored an expedition to Tati.
- Dr. William Macrorie was consecrated as the Bishop of Maritzburg. Macrorie would soon become a rival to Bishop Colenso.
- The diamond known as "The Star of South Africa" was discovered. With this key find, the gold and diamond rush in South Africa began.
- The Transvaal treaty with Portugal defined the borders of the Transvaal and of Gazaland. Also, under the treaty civil liberty was granted to Roman Catholics.

Gazaland was also the home of the Gaza kingdom — a heterogeneous empire built in the early 1820s by the Nguni leader Soshangane in southern Mozambique. The center of the Gaza kingdom shifted several times between the Limpopo and Sabi Rivers. The Gaza kingdom ceased to exist in 1895 when the Portuguese conquered it. After a disastrous revolt two years later, the Gaza kingdom broke into its component ethnic parts.

- Idols were burned in Madagascar.
- Kgamanyane, the chief of the Kgatla, was publicly flogged.

In 1848, Kgamanyane succeeded his father Pilane as chief of the Kgatla branch of the Tswana. His ascension came at a time when the Afrikaners were building the Transvaal Republic around his territory. At first, Kgamanyane accommodated the Afrikaners. He even assisted them in their campaigns against other chiefs. However, Kgamanyane resisted involuntary recruitment of his men as laborers. As a consequence, Kgamanyane was publicly flogged by the Transvaal government in 1869.

- From 1869 to 1872, Thomas Baines (1820–1875) explored the Shire River.

Thomas Baines was a British explorer and an artist. From 1842 to 1850, Baines lived in the Cape Colony. From 1850–1853, Baines served as the official artist during the Frontier War against the Xhosa.

From 1858 to 1859, Baines briefly served in David Livingstone's Zambezi expedition and from 1861 to 1863 Baines explored Namibia and Botswana.

Later on (around 1869), Baines obtained the first mining concession from the Ndebele king Lobengula.

Baines eventually retired to the Transvaal Republic. Due to his artwork, Baines left a unique pictorial record of all the peoples whom he encountered.

RELATED HISTORICAL EVENTS

- *The United States:* On March 4, Ulysses S. Grant assumed the office of President of the United States of America.
- *The Americas:* On March 9, the Hudson Bay Company territory was ceded to Canada.
- *Europe:* Portugal declared that all slaves were *libertos*. As *libertos*, the former slaves were entitled to wages before liberation.
- *Asia:* Mohandas Karamchand Gandhi (1869–1948), the Mahatma, was born.

In 1869, Mohandas Karamchand Gandhi, the Mahatma, was born. Today Gandhi is known mostly for his seemingly divine career as the leader of the nationalist movement in India. However, Gandhi's career as a civil rights activist actually began in South Africa.

Gandhi arrived in South Africa in 1893 after completing his legal studies in England. At first, Gandhi only planned on staying in South Africa for the short time that was required to resolve a lawsuit between two Natal Indian firms. However, his experience with racial discrimination in South Africa influenced him to remain.

During his twenty-one years in South Africa, Gandhi wage a legal and propaganda campaign against the disfranchisement of Indian voters. It was during this time that he developed the philosophy and tactics which he would later employ in his native India.

Gandhi lectured often, wrote pamphlets, and edited a newspaper. Over time, he became Natal's leading Indian spokesman. During his struggle in South Africa against legal repression, Gandhi remained loyal to the British government. He organized and led an Indian ambulance corps for British troops in both the South African (the Boer) War of 1899 and the Zulu rebellion of 1906.

In 1907, Gandhi responded to a new pass law in the Transvaal by organizing his first passive resistance *(satyagraha)* campaign. Passive resistance became Gandhi's main strategy in all his later civil rights and nationalistic campaigns.

Gandhi's South African campaign reached a climax in 1913 when he was imprisoned. While in prison, he met with South Africa's deputy prime minister, J. C. Smuts and succeeded in obtaining some legal concessions.

Shortly afterwards, Gandhi departed for India where he would begin his series of nationalistic campaigns. Gandhi's Indian campaigns were successful. In 1947, India became an independent nation.

In 1948, the Mahatma was assassinated by a dissident Hindu nationalist.

It is important to understand that history is filled with links — that the history of one people is invariably connected with the history of another. Thus, it should not be surprising that the movement which gave rise to the independence of India was born in South Africa and that, in turn, the movement which would lead to African Americans achieving their civil rights should be modeled upon the Indian movement developed by Gandhi.

• *Africa:* Frederick Gordon Guggisberg (1869–1930), the future governor of the Gold Coast, was born.

Frederick Guggisberg first arrived in Africa as an army engineer in 1902 on assignment to survey the Gold Coast and Asante.

Until the outbreak of World War I, Guggis-berg spent most of his time in Ghana and Nigeria directing pioneering surveying operations. After serving on active duty in the war, Guggisberg was appointed governor of the Gold Coast in 1919.

Guggisberg's administration of the Gold Coast is remembered for a number of major achievements. During his tenure, cocoa farmers access to markets was improved and the Gold Coast's first deep water port was constructed. Guggisberg also founded Achimota College, the predecessor to the University of Ghana, and, in 1925, he formulated the "Guggisberg Constitution" — the first such document to give Africans elected representation in the legislative council.

Ill health forced Guggisberg's resignation in 1927. He accepted the governorship of British Guiana (Guyana) in 1928, but again had to give up his position because of poor health.

Guggisberg died in 1930.

• Howard Unwin Moffat (1869–1951), a future prime minister of Southern Rhodesia, was born.

Howard Moffat was born in South Africa at Kuruman, the mission station founded by his father John Smith Moffat. In 1893, Howard Moffat moved to Rhodesia (Zimbabwe).

During the last years of the British South Africa Company's administration in Rhodesia, Moffat was elected to the legislative council (in 1920) and then to the legislative assembly (in 1924) after responsible self-government was granted by the British.

Howard Moffat joined Charles Coghlan's cabinet as minister of mines and public works and succeeded to the premiership on the death of the latter in 1927.

The greatest problem Moffat faced as premier was the distribution of land between Africans and the tiny European minority. Moffat opposed territorial segregation in principle, regarding it as the only practical means of preserving Africans' rights.

Following the initiative of a British commission, Moffat's administration passed the Land Apportionment Act of 1931. The Land Apportionment Act laid the basis for the future segregation policies of the country.

Moffat's policies during the world economic crisis of the early 1930s cost him the support of many members of his party.

Moffat resigned from office in 1933 due to ill health. A caretaker administration under George Mitchell was replaced by Godfrey Huggins the following year.

1 8 7 0

THE UNITED STATES

The Mississippi State Senate was convened in January with State Senator Hiram R. Revels opening the session with a prayer. About one-fourth of the State legislators were African Americans. These African American legislators demanded that one of the three possible United States Senate vacancies be filled by an African American. The three Senate vacancies were made possible by a vacancy created from the unexpired term of Jefferson Davis. Thus, at the time, the legislature was considering a short unexpired term, a normal term, and the normal term which was to follow the short unexpired term.

John Lynch, the African American then serving as the Secretary of State, was considered for the short term but the legislature decided not to fill the vacancy at the Senate by creating another vacancy at the state level which would require a new election to fill the vacated position. John Lynch's position as Secretary of State would have required a new statewide election.

In lieu of John Lynch, the legislature chose Hiram R. Revels, the State Senator from Adams County and, on January 20, 1870, Revels was elected to the United States Senate to fill the unexpired term of the former President of the Confederacy, Jefferson Davis.

Revels presented his credentials for his seat in the United States Senate on February 23, 1870. This presentation sparked a three day debate. The debate centered on essentially two issues: (1) whether the certification of the Revels election by General Ames, the military governor of Mississippi was valid and (2) whether Revels was eligible to serve in the Senate since, as an African American, Revels was deemed not to have been a citizen of the United States for the requisite nine years.

On February 25, Revels was accepted by a vote of 48 to 8. Revels was assigned to the Committee on Education and Labor. He made several reports to the Senate for the Committee and introduced three minor bills. None were passed.

On March 16, Hiram R. Revels made the first official speech by an African American before the United States Senate when he argued against Georgia's readmission to the Union without assurances to protect African American citizens.

Revels served in the Senate from February 21, 1870 to March 3, 1871. Among Revels' important votes in the Senate were (1) the readmis-

sion of Texas under Reconstruction government; (2) the enforcement of the Fifteenth Amendment; (3) a change in the naturalization laws by striking out the word "white"; (4) the abolition of the franking privilege; (5) a Federal election law with penalties; (6) Federal aid for steamship service to Mexico; and (7) the eligibility of General Ames to become governor of Mississippi. Revels voted against making public the proceedings of the Committee on Southern Outrages. *See 1901.*

• Alonzo J. Ransier, an African American and a South Carolina Republican, was elected Lieutenant Governor for the State of South Carolina.

• Benjamin S. Turner, an African American and an Alabama Republican, was elected to the House of Representatives. He would serve in Congress until 1872.

• In South Carolina, Robert B. Elliot was nominated to run for the House of Representatives in Columbia's Third District. Elliot was elected by a margin of 7,000 votes. Robert C. DeLarge and Joseph H. Rainey, both were elected to Congress.

• Joseph Hayne Rainey, an African American and a South Carolina Republican, was elected to the House of Representatives. Elected to fill an unexpired term, Rainey was sworn in on December 12, 1870. He would serve in Congress until 1879. *See 1887.*

• Josiah T. Walls from Florida was also elected to serve in the 42nd Congress, while Jefferson F. Long from Georgia was elected to fill an unexpired term in the 41st Congress.

• The Fifteenth Amendment was adopted, giving African Americans the right to vote (March 30). Ten days later, the American Anti-Slavery Society disbanded (April 9). By this time, the members believed that their work was done.

Thomas Mundy Peterson was the first African American to vote in the United States the day after the Fifteenth Amendment was ratified. Peterson was a school custodian in Perth Amboy, New Jersey. He became the first African American person to vote as a result of the adoption of the Fifteenth Amendment when he voted in the special election held to ratify a city charter. Peterson was appointed to the committee to revise the charter, which was adopted in the election. He later became a delegate to the Republican convention.

• In the Enforcement Acts of May 31, 1870, and February 28, 1871, the use of force or intimidation to prevent citizens from voting was made punishable by a fine or imprisonment. The President was authorized to use the military to enforce the Fifteenth Amendment. Congressional elections were placed under Federal supervision.

• Senator Charles Sumner introduced a bill providing equal rights in transportation, hotels, theaters, schools, churches, cemeteries and juries. This bill was not passed until 1875, and in its final version the school desegregation provision had been deleted.

• Georgia's, Mississippi's and Texas' Representatives and Senators were readmitted to Congress.

• Virginia was readmitted to the Union.

• Because of the war against the Indigenous Americans, the recruitment of African American soldiers increased in 1870. Between 1870 and 1890, eleven African American members of the Ninth Cavalry, one African member of the Tenth Cavalry, and two African American members of the 24th Infantry Regiment were awarded Congressional Medals of Honor for their bravery in the Indian Wars.

• The Freedman's Bureau expired by law.

The Freedmen's Bureau was established as part of the War Department. The Commissioner of the Bureau was to be appointed by the President, with the consent of the Senate. The Commissioner had the authority to "control all subjects relating to refugees and freedmen." The Commissioner could set aside abandoned tracts of land up to 40 acres to be leased to freedmen at a low rent, giving them the right to buy the land at the end of three years.

As part of the Freedmen's Bureau's authorizing legislation, Union army officers would be used as assistant commissioners, and the Secretary of War could issue provisions, clothing and fuel to the freedmen and refugees.

The Freedmen's Bureau established schools, hired teachers, made provisions for transportation, issued food and clothing and with an expenditure of over $2,000,000 treated 450,000 medical cases.

Due to the efforts of the Freedmen's Bureau, the death rate of freed slaves was reduced from a high of thirty-eight percent (38%) in 1865 to a little more than two percent (2.03%) in 1869.

• The Liberal Republican Party was organized in Missouri. This party was composed of a coalition of Democrats and dissatisfied Republicans who won control of the state and restored full political and civil rights to the ex–Confederates.

In 1870, the racial composition of the various state legislatures in the South was a follows:

State	European Americans	African Americans
Alabama	73	27
Arkansas	71	9
Georgia	149	26
Mississippi	77	30
North Carolina	101	1
South Carolina	49	75
Texas	82	8
Virginia	116	21

• Several African Americans were denied admission to the Supreme Lodge of the Knights of Pythias in New York. Undaunted by this rejection, some African Americans who had light complexions and could "pass for white" joined the Knights of Pythias and learned the organization's rituals. In 1880, these African Americans helped to organize the Colored Knights of Pythias. By 1905, there were 1,628 lodges with some 70,000 members.

• Robert H. Wood was elected mayor of Natchez, Mississippi (December).

• James W. Mason, an African American, was nominated to serve as Minister to Liberia by President Ulysses S. Grant (March). However, Mason never took his post.

• Jonathan Jasper Wright (1840-1865) won election to a seat on the South Carolina Supreme Court to fill an unexpired term (February 1). Wright resigned on December 1, 1877, after the overthrow of the Reconstruction South Carolina government.

• Emanuel Stance (c.1848-1887), a sergeant of Company F, Ninth United Cavalry stationed at Fort Kavett, Texas, was awarded the Congressional Medal of Honor. As a "Buffalo Soldier," Stance and a small group of soldiers dispersed a band of marauding Indigenous Americans.

The Census

In 1870, there were 4,880,009 African Americans in the United States who represented 12.7% of the total United States population. Twelve percent of the African Americans (584,049) were classified COTWs. The number of COTWs was lowest in the South. 125 COTWs per 1,000 in the South as compared to 255 per 1,000 in the North.

The percentage of African Americans born in the South but living in the North and West was 3.3%. The percentage of African Americans born in the North and West but living in the South was 4.9%.

Chicago had 3,696 African Americans. Between 1870 and 1900, the African American population of Chicago would double every ten years.

The percentage of the total population that attended school in the Southern states was 13.5% European American — 3.07% African American.

The Ku Klux Klan

The Democratic Party in North Carolina regained control of the state from the Republicans. 12,000 fewer Republicans voted than in the previous elections, largely because of Klan intimidation. Between April and May, in Caswell County in northern North Carolina, a strongly Republican area, the Klan whipped or beat 21 men (European and African American) and killed two (including one European American). In Alamance County, North Carolina in February, the African American Republican leader, Wyatt Outlaw, was lynched. The Klan violence was widespread in these two Republican counties. Thirteen known murders committed by the Klan caused Governor Holden to declare that these counties were in a state of insurrection and to send in the militia. Upon gaining control of the State Legislature, the Democrats impeached Governor Holden.

• In October, Governor Reed of Florida asked for Federal troops to cope with Klan violence. This request was not granted.

• *Notable Births:* Robert S. Abbott (1870–1940), founder of the *Chicago Defender*, was born on St. Simon's Island off the coast of Georgia (November 24).

Robert Sengstacke Abbott spent his childhood in Savannah, Georgia and went to school first at the Beach Institute (then known as Claflin Institute) in Orangeburg, South Carolina, and finally Hampton Institute in Virginia. It was at Hampton Institute that Abbott learned the trade of printing.

Abbott served as an apprentice at the *Savannah News* between 1890 and 1896. In 1896, Abbott went to Chicago where he believed that race would not be as great a barrier to jobs in the newspaper field. However, once in Chicago, Abbott was denied full membership in the International Typographical Union and was unable to find full-time employment in his profession.

Between 1898 and 1903, Abbott attended Kent College. He graduated from Kent College with a law degree and practiced for a short period in both Chicago, Illinois, and Gary, Indiana.

In 1905, Abbott decided to resume his life in print by starting up his own newspaper. The paper was entitled *Chicago Defender* and its first issue appeared on May 5, 1905. The newspaper was the first large-city African American newspaper and its timing was propitious.

It was at this time that Chicago began to receive an influx of African Americans fleeing the repressive climate of the South. The *Chicago Defender* came into existence just as the flood of African American immigrants from the South came to reside within Chicago. The newspaper served a great need and it prospered accordingly.

Abbott's *Chicago Defender* was not just a newspaper. It was an instrument for change. Abbott used the paper to crusade for the civil rights of African Americans not only in Chicago but throughout the United States.

During his lifetime, Abbott received many honors. He was appointed a member of the Illinois Race Relations Commission by Governor Lowden in 1919 and received honorary degrees from several colleges. In 1941, the Robert S. Abbott Memorial Award was set up by the *Chicago Defender*. The award is given annually to a person who has made a distinguished contribution to improve race relations. Additionally, a Robert S. Abbott scholarship was established at Lincoln University in Missouri and is awarded annually to a journalism student.

• Will Marion Cook (1870 [1869?]-1947), a famous composer, was born in Detroit, Michigan (January 27).

Will Marion Cook was born of educated parents who were graduates of Oberlin. Cook studied violin and after three years at Oberlin College went to the Berlin Conservatory of Music to study under the great German violinist Joachim.

Ill health forced Will to return to the United States in 1898. Upon his return, Cook briefly studied orchestration with Dvorak and began to compose musical scores. Over the next two decades, Will Cook would come to write several of the best musicals of the era. Cook's operetta *Clorindy, or the Origin of the Cakewalk* is credited with introducing syncopated ragtime to New York audiences in the 1890s.

Cook adopted, refined and wrote music from

the traditional African American (Negro) folk songs for large orchestras with a great deal of success. His style and his method of musical composition was a forerunner for such noted composers as William Dawson and George Gershwin. Four of Cook's most successful works were the art songs, *Rain Song, Swing Along, Wid De Moon,* and the adaptation to orchestra of an African American sermon, *Exhortation.*

• Bill Pickett (1870–1932), an internationally known rodeo performer and the originator of "bulldogging," was born.

Bill Pickett was born on December 5, 1870, in Williamson County, Texas, the second child of thirteen born to Thomas Jefferson Pickett and his wife Mary. Thomas Jefferson Pickett was a former slave said to have been of African, European and Indigenous American (Cherokee) heritage. Mary (Janie) Virginia Elizabeth Gilbert was a small, very dark, woman of African, Mexican, European and Indigenous American blood.

After going through the fifth grade, Bill Pickett became a ranch hand, developed his roping and riding skills, and invented a type of steer wrestling known as "bulldogging."

Wrestling steers or bulls down by hand, sometimes popularly called bulldogging, goes back to the Roman arena, but "bulldogging" as performed by Bill Pickett involved the contestant's riding up alongside a running bull, throwing himself onto its back, gripping its horns, and twisting its neck until he could sink his teeth into its upper lip or nose, and then throwing his hands wide and toppling off its back, his weight and the painful grip of his teeth bringing the animal over on its side.

The various accounts of how and when Pickett originated this technique agree only that he got the idea from seeing a cattle dog holding a "cow critter" by the nose or upper lip. According to one account, Pickett developed this feat out of the exigencies of working cattle in the Texas brush country, where roping was often impossible and the cowboy sometimes had to throw an animal by wrapping its tail around his saddle horn or wrestling it to the ground by its horns. Pickett was grappling ineffectually with an unusually stiff necked longhorn cow when he remembered a big mastiff which could bring rebellious steers to the ground by gripping their noses in their teeth, in the manner of the bulldogs which thus "baited" English bulls. Pickett accordingly sank his teeth into the animal's nostrils or lip and immediately brought the steer down.

Pickett eventually began regularly to use his bulldogging skills both in catching wild cattle in the brush and in putting on exhibitions at various stockyards. Sometime in the late 1880s, Pickett became at least a semi-professional, appearing at county fairs and other similar occasions.

On December 2, 1890, Pickett married Maggie Turner. Bill and Maggie would have nine children. The burden of raising an ever growing family apparently compelled Pickett to seek out greater opportunities to showcase his cowboy skills.

Under a series of managers, Pickett began bulldogging at various Texas cowtowns and — sometimes in association with some of his brothers — in other western states, Canada and Mexico.

Pickett stood five feet seven inches tall and weighed less than one hundred and fifty pounds. However, while relatively small in stature, he was "hard and tough as whalebone, with ... powerful shoulders and arms." Pickett wore a small mustache and for exhibition purposes "dressed as a Spanish bullfighter."

In 1907, Pickett was signed to a contract with the Miller brothers' famous 101 Ranch Wild West Show, with headquarters in Oklahoma's Cherokee Strip. Pickett became one of its principal attractions and, arguably, its star performer. Under the auspices of the 101 Ranch Wild West Show, Bill Pickett would attain national and international fame, appearing for a decade all over the United States, Canada, Mexico, Argentina, and England.

During this period, the technique which Pickett had invented became accepted as a regular and leading rodeo event albeit somewhat modified. Few (if any) of Pickett's contemporaries were willing, at least for long, to follow the original technique of "taking a mouthful" of a steer's upper lip or nostrils and depending on the grip of the teeth and the weight of the body to throw the animal. Instead, the "new" bulldoggers simply twisted the steers down by hand.

Objections by humane societies may also have contributed to abandonment of the true bulldog style. Advancing years and increasing dental deficiencies eventually forced even Pickett to depend on the leverage of his powerful hands rather than the grip of strong jaws and teeth, although for some time he continued at least to simulate his old bulldog stunt. Indeed, for publicity purposes, Pickett would simulate the technique simply to evoke a fine for "cruelty to animals."

Bill Pickett became a legendary figure and was

credited with such fabulous feats as throwing a buffalo bull and a fully antlered bull elk. Although at various times nearly every bone in his body was broken, Pickett so thoroughly dominated the animals that no steer or bull ever tried to gore him after a bulldogging.

Pickett's most grueling experience was undoubtedly in the Mexico City bullring on December 23, 1908. Joe Miller, for publicity purposes, had callously bet that Pickett could "stay with" a Mexican fighting bull for fifteen minutes, during five minutes of which Pickett was to be actually wrestling with the bull. The Mexican audience, enraged at this arrogant insult to their national sport, showered Pickett and his horse with missiles ranging from fruit and cushions to bottles, brickbats, and knives. As a result, Pickett's horse was badly gored.

As for Pickett, he was severely gashed and had three ribs broken. Although he won the bet by staying on the bull's back for seven and a half minutes, he never succeeded in throwing the animal. Given the animosity of the crowd, Pickett and his horse were lucky to escape with their lives.

Bill Pickett retired from the rodeo circuit shortly after 1916. He went back to the 101 Ranch where he worked until near the end of the 1920s. Pickett then settled on a little ranch he had bought near Chandler, Oklahoma.

In 1931, when the 101 Ranch was in serious financial difficulties, Pickett returned to help out.

On April 2, 1932, while roping a stallion on foot, the animal turned on Pickett and smashed in his head. He was buried at White Eagle Monument, Marland, Oklahoma. The Cherokee Strip Cowboy Association erected a marker at his gravesite and Colonel Zack Miller, who had declared Pickett to be "the greatest sweat-and-dirt cowhand that ever lived" wrote a poem in his honor which long adorned bunkhouse walls.

Bill Pickett's principal legacy is the rodeo event without which no rodeo is deemed complete. Homer Croy's verdict was that Bill Pickett contributed more to rodeos than any other one person. Wherever rodeos are held, the spirit of Bill Pickett lives on.

• *Notable Deaths:* Abraham (1790–1870), chief counsellor of the Seminoles, died.

Abraham, or Abram, (also known as Sohanac or Souanakke) was born of slave parents in Pen-sacola, Florida. As a young man, while serving as a slave to a Dr. Sierra, Abraham escaped from slavery to live among the Seminoles.

Among the Seminoles, Abraham was still enslaved. However, among the Seminoles, slaves were considered the dependents, or even the protégés, of their owners.

Among the Seminoles, Abraham served as an interpreter. As an interpreter, he played a key role for the Seminole delegation that traveled to Washington, D.C. in 1826.

On his return from Washington, Abraham was freed as a reward for his meritorious service. Abraham married a Seminole woman who was the widow of the former chief of the Seminole nation. Abraham was also appointed to a position amongst the Seminoles which combined the duties of private secretary, chief counsellor, and spokesman.

• James W. C. Pennington, a leader in the Free Negro Convention Movement which outlined an ideology and tactics for African American protest in the 19th century, died.

James W. C. Pennington (1809–1870), was a teacher, preacher, and author who was born into slavery on the Eastern Shore of Maryland. At the age of 21, Pennington escaped from his enslavement, but he was soon recaptured. However, with the help of a Pennsylvania Quaker, Pennington persisted and eventually won his freedom.

Upon gaining his freedom, Pennington left Maryland. After leaving Maryland, he spent a brief time in Pennsylvania, and then moved to western Long Island in New York, where he worked during the day and attended night school. At the age of 26, Pennington was certified to teach in the schools which had been established to teach African American children. Pennington first taught in Newton on Long Island, New York. He later taught in New Haven, Connecticut.

While in New Haven, Pennington studied theology. His eloquence attracted favorable attention, and Pennington served twice as president of the Hartford Central Association of Congregational Ministers, of which he was the only African American member. Pennington was five times elected a member of the General Convention for the Improvement of Free People of Color, and in 1843 represented Connecticut in the world Anti–slavery Convention at London. Pennington's published works were *The Fugitive*

Blacksmith (London 1849) and *Textbook of the Origin and History of the Colored People* (1841).

• James Whitfield, an African American poet, died.

Although born in New Hampshire, James Whitfield (1830 [1822?]–1870) came to live in Buffalo, a city which, at the time, was a center of the abolitionist movement.

With his friend and co-worker, Martin Delany, Whitfield engaged in a dialogue with Frederick Douglass concerning African American nationalism. Whitfield and Delany were strong nationalists while Douglass was not.

In his book, *America and Other Poems*, Whitfield's most successful poems were those which were blatantly nationalistic and propagandist. In the title poem, Whitfield wrote of American hypocrisy. It is said that in some respects Whitfield's poetry bore great resemblance to the verse of Lord Byron.

• Harriet E. Adams Wilson (c. 1827–1870), an African American author, died. In 1859, Wilson published a novel, *Our Nig; or, Sketches from the Life of a Free Black, In a Two Story White House North, Showing That Slavery's Shadows Fall Even There.* This novel depicted the social, racial, and economic oppression experienced by a COTW woman living in the North.

• *Miscellaneous State Laws:* Tennessee enacted a poll tax. The poll tax was suspended in 1871 and was repealed in 1873 due to pressure from poor European Americans.

• *Scholastic Achievements:* In 1870, the literacy rate among African Americans stood at 18.6%.

• In the schools sponsored by the Freedmen's Bureau, there were 3,300 teachers and 149,581 pupils.

• The Methodist Episcopal Church founded Clark College, in Atlanta, Georgia.

• The American Baptist Home Mission established Benedict College in South Carolina.

• LeMoyne-Owen College was established in Memphis, Tennessee.

• In 1870, Richard Theodore Greener (1844–1922) became the first known African American to receive an undergraduate degree from Harvard College.

After graduating from Harvard, Richard Theodore Greener became professor of metaphysics at the University of South Carolina. In addition to his teaching duties, Greener assisted in the departments of Latin, Greek, mathematics, and constitutional history.

Greener also served as acting librarian, arranging the university's rare book collection of 27,000 volumes, and began preparation of a catalog. During this same time, Greener studied law.

In 1876, Greener graduated from the university's law school. He was admitted to the Supreme Court of South Carolina in 1877. The next year, he practiced at the District of Columbia bar.

Greener remained in South Carolina until March 1877, when the Wade Hampton legislature abruptly closed the door of the university to African American students. Greener went on to head the Howard University Law School and developed a considerable reputation as a speaker and writer.

Later in his career, Greener became involved in the diplomatic service. In this capacity, Greener came to be stationed in Bombay (India) and Vladivostok (Russia).

Greener retired in 1905.

• James Webster Smith was admitted to West Point. Smith, the first African American to be so admitted, left the academy after being subjected to unbearable hazing and ostracism.

• The Freedmen's Bureau hired William Henry Crogman (1841–1931) to teach at Claflin College in South Carolina.

William Henry Crogman was a scholar and writer. He would later become the president of Clark College in Atlanta, Georgia, from 1903 to 1910. He is known for his early histories on African Americans: *Progress of a Race* and *Citizenship, Intelligence, Affluence, Honor and Trust.* Crogman's last work was revised and published as *The Colored American.*

• Julia Britton Hooks (1852–1942) became an instructor of instrumental music at Berea College, Berea, Kentucky. Berea College was, at the time, a multi-racial (integrated) college.

• Susan Maria Smith McKinney Steward (1848–1918) graduated from New York Medical College for Women.

After graduating from New York Medical College for Women, Steward practiced in Brooklyn for more than twenty years. In 1873, Steward became the first African American woman doctor to be formally certified.

Steward undertook postgraduate work at the Long Island Medical School Hospital (1888), the only woman in the entire medical school.

Steward was the founder of the Women's Loyal Union of New York and Brooklyn and, in 1881, she co-founded the Women's Hospital and Dispensary in Brooklyn. Steward married a prominent African Methodist Episcopal minister, Theophilus Gould Steward, in 1896, and became the resident physician at Wilberforce University (Ohio).

- Snowden School became the first state school for African Americans in Virginia.
- *The Black Church:* By 1870 there were a half million members of the African American (Negro) Baptist Church. In 1850, there had only been 150,000.
- The Colored Methodist Episcopal Church permitted the Southern churches to form their own conference — the Methodist Episcopal Church, South. The first general conference of the Methodist Episcopal Church, South was held in Jackson, Tennessee. Henry Miles and Richard Vanderhorst were elected bishops.
- The African Methodist Episcopal Zion Church had 200,000 members. In 1860, it had only had 26,746 members.
- *The Arts:* Edmonia Lewis, the noted Afro-Chippewa sculptress, went to study abroad. *See 1890.*

THE AMERICAS

- *Brazil:* Carlos Gomes, the great Afro-Brazilian composer, achieved his greatest success when his opera *Il Guarany* was performed at La Scala, in Milan, on March 19, 1870.
- Joaquim Machado de Assis *(see 1908)* published *Falenas (Moth)* and *Contos fluminenses (Tales of Rio de Janeiro).*
- *Canada:* The Red River census of 1870 listed five Afro-Canadians.
- *Cuba:* The Spanish government passed the Moret law which "theoretically" abolished slavery in Spanish America.

The Moret law was named after Segismundo Moret. Segismundo Moret became Spain's Minister of the Colonies during the Ten Years' War. The Moret law was Spain's attempt to counteract the article in the Guaimaro Constitution of 1869 in which the Cuban freedom fighters declared all men free and equal.

Moret's law provided for the freeing of all slaves born after its enactment and for the apprenticeship of these former slaves as *patrocinados* up to the age of 22. Patrocinados were consigned to work under the "tutelage" of the slave owners, the *patronatos*. The patrocinados were to be paid half-wages from the time they were 18 until they reached the full emancipation age. The Moret law also freed all slaves who attained the age of 65 or who served Spain during the Ten Years War.

In 1879, Arsenio Martinez Campos, the prime minister in Spain, announced that the patronato would end in 1888. However, it officially ended two years earlier, in 1886. By 1886, there were only 26,000 slaves that remained.

- *Haiti:* Silvain Salnave, the former ruler of Haiti, was executed.

Between Salnave's execution in January 1870 and the chaotic politics that began in August 1911 and ended in the United States invasion of 1915, the Liberal Party, often the representative of the COTW elite, faced opposition from the National Party, the organ of the black elites. With a few exceptions, these political struggles became violent.

- Selected by the National Assembly in 1870 after a provisional government, Nissage Saget became the president of Haiti. Saget would complete his term of office and step down voluntarily in 1874.

EUROPE

- In April 1870, Thomas Morris Chester became the first known person of African descent to be admitted to practice before the English courts.

Thomas Morris Chester (1834–1892) was born in Harrisburg, Pennsylvania, to abolitionist parents. He attended Alexander High School in Monrovia, Liberia, then at the Thetford Academy in Vermont.

During the Civil War, Chester was the first and only African American correspondent for a major daily, the *Philadelphia Press.* His dispatches covered the period from August 1864 through June 1865. For eight months, Chester reported on African American troop activity around Petersburg and the Confederate capital, both before and after Richmond, Virginia, was taken.

After the Civil War, Chester read law under a Liberian lawyer and then spent three years at Middle Temple in London, England. In April 1870, Chester became their first African American barrister admitted to practice before English courts.

- *Notable deaths:* Alexandre Dumas (1802–1870), the famous Afro-French author of the *The Three Musketeers* and *The Count of Monte Cristo,* died.

Alexandre Dumas was a famous French author and playwright. To distinguish him from his namesake son, the Alexandre Dumas of *The Three Musketeers* fame is known as Alexandre Dumas, pere. Alexandre Dumas, pere, the most widely read of all French writers, was best remembered for his historical novels.

Dumas was born at Villers-Cotterets in France on July 24, 1802. Dumas' father was General Alexandre Dumas, a COTW who was born in Haiti, the son of a French marquis and an African woman.

Dumas grew up in poverty. He was educated by a local priest who befriended him. Dumas read voraciously and was especially attracted to the 16th and 17th century adventure stories.

In 1827, Dumas went to Paris. While working as a clerk, he attended performances of an English Shakespearean company and became inspired to write drama. At first, Dumas began by writing vaudeville sketches and plays. But soon the Duke of Orleans became a patron of Dumas and Dumas' career began to blossom. His *Henri III et sa cour (Henry III and His Court)* (1829) and the romantic drama *Christine* (1830) were both resounding successes.

Dumas became a prolific playwright. *Antony*, *Richard Darlington*, and *Mademoiselle de Belle Isle* were among his most well received plays.

Dumas soon turned his attention to the writing of historical novels. His novels were revisionist in nature, but were extremely popular. In 1844, he wrote the immortal *The Three Musketeers* and *The Count of Monte Cristo*. It was these two works by which Dumas is best known and best remembered.

Dumas was an astoundingly prolific writer. At one time some 1200 volumes were published under his name. Although many were the result of collaboration or the production of a "fiction factory" in which hired writers produced fiction under Dumas' name, almost all of the works that were produced bear the unmistakable imprint of Dumas' genius.

As a prolific and commercially successful writer, Dumas made enormous sums of money. However, he also spent enormous sums of money. Dumas lavished a fortune in maintaining his estate outside Paris (Monte Cristo), supporting numerous mistresses (one of whom was the mother of his son Alexandre), purchasing artworks, and making up the losses incurred by ill advised business ventures.

When Dumas died on December 5, 1870, he was virtually bankrupt.

AFRICA

In 1870, David Livingstone journeyed from Ujiji, on Lake Tanganyika, into the region lying west of the lake, thereby becoming the first European to visit the Lualaba River (in present day Zaire).

After enduring great privations, Livingstone made his return to Ujiji. Upon his arrival, he was met by a "rescue party" led by Henry Morton Stanley, a European American journalist. The story goes that at this meeting Stanley reportedly greeted Livingstone with the famous question, "Dr. Livingstone, I presume?"

• *North Africa, Egypt and Sudan:* The Khedivial Mail Line was founded.

• American Staff Officers under Brigadier Charles P. Stone were recruited to reorganize the Egyptian army.

• Khedivial Library (now known as the Egyptian National Library) was founded.

• A telegraph line was erected connecting Khartoum to Cairo.

• Sir Samuel Baker was made Governor of the Equatorial Province.

• The Decret Cremieux naturalized all Algerian Jews as French citizens (October 14).

• Upon the fall of Napoleon III, settlers attempted to govern Algeria through Commune d'Alger.

• The French captured El Golea.

• *Western Africa:* Around 1870, the National African Company acquired practical though unofficial control of the River Niger.

• The Portuguese recovered Bolama from the British.

• The French temporarily evacuated the Ivory Coast.

• There was a disastrous fire in Lagos, Nigeria.

• In 1870, Ahmadu ibn 'Umar Tall, the ruler of the Tukolor Empire, began a campaign against his half-brothers which brought Kaarta back within the Tukolor Empire by 1874.

• Benjamin Anderson wrote *Narrative of a Journey to Musardu.* Anderson's account of his 1868 expedition provides one of the few descriptions of the Liberian hinterland in the 1800s.

• In 1870, Jaja, the former leading trader of Bonny, officially proclaimed his new kingdom. By naming it Opobo (the name of a famous king of Bonny), Jaja maintained his links with the traditions of the Bonny monarchy.

• Suluku Konte became the chief of the Biriwa of Sierra Leone.

Suluku's success as a warrior enabled him to claim the chieftaincy around 1870. At that time, the Biriwa chiefdom of Sierra Leone already controlled an important stretch of the trade route between Freetown and the northern interior.

Suluku expanded Biriwa through warfare, but also through diplomacy, for he apparently did less fighting after he became chief. Suluku maintained an elaborate alliance system with surrounding Limba, Yalunka, and Kuranko chiefdoms, marrying into a number of them.

Suluku also took care to maintain good relations with the British at Freetown. Suluku viewed the British as a powerful — but not overwhelming — neighbor.

• *Central Africa:* Around 1870, Bunza killed Dakpara and reunited the Mangbetu kingdom.

• In 1870, it was estimated that there were some 2,700 slave traders between Ubangi and Bahr al-Ghazal.

"al-" is a definite article preceding many Arabic names such as "al-Ghazal." This article is usually ignored for purposes of alphabetization.

• *Eastern Africa:* It is estimated that some 4,000 slaves per year were exported from Jimma (in Ethiopia) during the 1870s. The typical destination for these slaves were the Arab nations.

• In 1870, Sayyid Barghash became the Sultan of Zanzibar. He would remain in that position until 1888. *See 1888.*

Barghash succeeded Majid ibn Said in 1870. Once upon the throne, his reign was plagued by two problems: (1) the continuing threat to his position from the Omani portion of his father's partitioned domain and (2) his efforts to expand Zanzibari commercial activity on the African mainland.

• Ajuran and Boran Galla drove Warday out of Wajir.

• Egyptians occupied Zaila and North Somalia as far as Cape Guardafui.

• Italians occupied Assab.

• There was an outbreak of cholera at Kilwa Kivinje.

• Around 1870, Kimweri became the Sultan of Vuga.

• During the early 1870s, the various independent pastoral Masai groups were threatened by a major invasion of their agricultural kinsmen, the Kwavi. Mbatian united these groups and directed a successful military campaign to drive the invaders away. The pastoral Masai did not remain united, but Mbatian continued to be recognized as their greatest laibon until his death in 1889.

• Majid Ibn Said (c.1835–1870), the Sultan of Zanzibar, died.

Sayyid Majid Ibn Said was the second Busaidi ruler of Zanzibar (Tanzania). Majid was the first son of Sayyid Said to reign as the Sultan of Zanzibar and to hold his father's title *Sayyid* — an Islamic honorific title taken by learned men which was adopted as a dynastic title by the Busaidi dynasty of Zanzibar.

Upon his succession in 1856, Sayyid Said's commercial empire was divided between Majid in the materially wealthy lands of east Africa and his half-brother Thuwain in the previous Busaidi capital of Muscat in southern Arabia. Majid relied greatly on the support of the British consular officials to maintain his position vis-à-vis his jealous brother. Majid became beholden to the British navy for its assistance in foiling an attempted invasion by Thuwain in 1859. In 1861, the dispute between Majid and Thuwain was resolved by British arbitrators. The arbitration affirmed Zanzibar's independence from Muscat but required Majid to pay an annual tribute to Thuwain to compensate Thuwain for their economically unequal inheritance. The payment of these tributary amounts ended in 1866 when Thuwain was assassinated by his own son. It was this termination of the payment of the tributary amounts which enabled Majid to embark upon a period of construction on the Tanzanian mainland.

During Majid's tenure as Sultan of Zanzibar, the first serious attempts were made by Zanzibar to dominate the Tanzanian mainland. Majid began to develop Dar es Salaam as a future capital, but died before the project was completed.

Upon his death in 1870, Majid was peacefully succeeded by another brother, Barghash.

Today, Dar es Salaam, the pride of Sayyid Majid Ibn Said is the largest town and main port of Tanzania. It is Majid's greatest legacy.

• *Southern Africa:* The Anglican Synod in Cape Town rejected the Privy Council decision regarding Bishop Colenso.

• The Diggers' Republic was proclaimed in Klipdrift with Stafford Parker as the President (June).

• The Orange Free State proclaimed sovereignty over Campbell Lands (August).

- Diamonds were discovered in the Orange Free State (December).
- Lobengula was installed as the successor to Mzilikazi. Lobengula became the king of the Ndebele.

After Mzilikazi died in 1868, Lobengula was unexpectedly nominated by the national council to succeed him. The acknowledged heir to the Ndebele throne had been Lobengula's half-brother Nkulumane, but Nkulumane had disappeared in the 1840s, presumably at Mzilikazi's behest.

Mzilikazi never revealed the fate of Nkulumane. Mzilikazi also failed to designate another heir before he himself died. The fact that Lobengula's mother was a Swazi made his own nomination for the kingship unpopular to many Ndebele. In recognition of this fact, Lobengula wisely refused to be formally installed as king until the fate of the missing Nkulumane was settled.

Lobengula sponsored a delegation to Natal to search for the missing heir in 1869, but the latter was not found. After a year of such searching, the populace became satisfied that Nkulumane was nowhere to be found. Thus, early in 1870, Lobengula was made king.

- Letsie became chief of the Sotho.

When Letsie succeeded his father Moshoeshoe in 1870, Basutoland was a newly proclaimed British protectorate and just recovering from an exhausting war with the neighboring Orange Free State Republic. Moshoeshoe had built the kingdom largely on the strength of his own personality, but family factions had started to tear the kingdom apart before Moshoeshoe died.

The year after Letsie assumed office, the British crown turned over administration of Lesotho to the Cape Colony. The inability of the Cape to enforce its policies aggravated Letsie's problems by enabling his brothers to oppose him from their positions as district chiefs. One brother, Masupha, controlled Thaba Bosiu — Moshoeshoe's fortified mountain stronghold — and resisted all efforts to impose magistrates, setting an example which other sub-chiefs followed.

- The London and Limpopo Mining Company obtained the rights at Tati.
- The South African Gold Fields Exploration Company obtained the rights between the River Gwelo and River Hunyani.

After succeeding P. E. Wodehouse as governor of the Cape Colony in 1870, Henry Barkly quickly annexed the diamond fields in Griqualand to prevent them from falling into the hands of the Afrikaners.

- Standard Bank of South Africa became the national bank.
- Grandidier began exploring the Imerina country.
- When a truce between the Herero and the Oorlam (Khoikhoi) was reached in 1870, Jan Afrikaner, the chief of the Oorlam, found that the Oorlam had lost much of their power in central Namibia. Mahehero, the chief of the Herero leased Windhoek to Jan Afrikaner. After this truce, Mahehero stood as the single most powerful figure between the Orange and Kunene Rivers.
- Around 1870, Mpezeni, the king of the Chipata Ngoni, abandoned his campaigns against the Bemba and moved into the present Chipata district farther south. From this area, Mpezeni conquered the local Chewa chief Mkanda. Afterwards, Mpezeni was able to build his kingdom into the greatest power in southeast Zambia.
- Mzila, the king of the Gaza empire of Mozambique, demonstrated his independence from the Portuguese by sending a delegation to Theophilus Shepstone in Natal, inviting British trade and diplomatic contacts.
- There was an unsuccessful coup attempt against Sipopa of the Lozi.

Old sectional rivalries in the Lozi kingdom resurfaced, resulting in an unsuccessful coup attempt in 1870.

Sipopa reacted to the failed coup attempt by busying the Lozi with aggressive wars and by building up his arms supply through external trade.

Reluctant to participate in the slave trade with Angolans from the west coast, Sipopa turned to Europeans from the south.

- Hosea Kutako (1870–1970), a chief of the Herero people, was born.

Kutako was born into a Christian aristocratic Herero family before the German occupation of South West Africa. In 1904, Kutako joined the Herero revolt against German rule. He was wounded and captured, but was released after the Germans had either killed or driven off three-quarters of the Herero population.

Kutako turned to school teaching after the Herero war. During World War I, the Germans were driven out of South West Africa by South African forces. South Africa then assumed administration of the country under a League of Nations mandate.

Kutako was appointed government chief over the Herero in 1917, and was confirmed in this position by the exiled paramount chief, Samuel Mahehero, who was then in what is today Botswana.

Kutako gradually emerged as the outstanding African leader in the country. He urged moderation in dealings with the government, but resolutely rejected proposals for resettling the Herero or having South West Africa absorbed into the Union of South Africa.

After World War II, the South African government refused to recognize United Nations authority over the mandate system of the defunct League of Nations. Kutako petitioned the United Nations to take over South West Africa — which Africans call Namibia — in order to bring it to independence. Kutako's persistence in this matter brought South West Africa into international politics and helped to create a growing confrontation between South Africa and the rest of the world.

• Isiah Shembe (1870–1935), a South African separatist church leader, was born.

Isiah Shembe had no formal education. During his youth, Shembe became famous as a visionary prophet and healer. He was baptized into the African National Baptist Church in 1906 but later broke away to found the Nazirite Baptist Church.

Five years later, Shembe announced some revelations. He established a holy village near Durban and developed into one of the most prominent Zulu figures of his time.

Upon his death in 1935, Shembe was revered as a black messiah. His son Johannes Galilee Shembe inherited leadership of his church. Johannes — a Fort Hare College graduate — lacked his father's charisma and had trouble maintaining his leadership. Nevertheless, Johannes still had 80,000 followers by 1970.

• Moshoeshoe (1786–1870), the great Lesotho chief, died.

Moshoeshoe (also Mshweshwe or Moshesh) was born near the upper Caledon River in what is today Lesotho. His original name was "Lepoqo." Lepoqo was the son of a lesser chieftain (Mokgachane) who won a reputation for leadership by conducting cattle raids upon the neighboring tribes. According to tradition, in 1806, Lepoqo visited the chief and a wise man named Mohlomi and asked them how he could

become a great chief. Mohlomi advised Lepoqo to be gentle and benevolent and, most importantly, to extend his influence by marrying many wives. It was this advice that would guide Lepoqo (Moshoeshoe) throughout his life.

In 1809, Lepoqo took the name Moshoeshoe, an imitation of the sounds made by a knife when shaving and under this new name the legend would grow. A series of cattle raids and conquests brought Moshoeshoe great prestige.

In the early 1820s, the traditional patterns of the Sotho were shattered when the Nguni wars of the eastern coast reached Sotho lands. Militaristic Nguni bands under Matiwane and Mpangazitha swept through the Caledon valley and set off a chain reaction of Sotho-Tswana wars. These Sotho-Tswana wars came to be known as the Difaqane and they lasted for the better part of two decades.

Around 1824, Moshoeshoe along with his father, Mokgachane moved to Thaba Bosiu, a naturally fortified mountain. Using the virtually impregnable Thaba Bosiu as a base of operations, Moshoeshoe continued to raid his neighbors' cattle while he attracted new followers from the thousands of homeless refugees.

Moshoeshoe eventually united the various small groups to form the Sotho nation — the nation known as Basutoland. Ruling from his mountain citadel, Thaba Bosiu ("Mountain of the Night"), Moshoeshoe ruled his kingdom with a policy which pursued peace and prosperity.

In 1827, Moshoeshoe scored a major triumph by repelling an assault by Matiwane. Matiwane was compelled to return to the coast. Only the Tlokwa chief Sekonyela was left to challenge Moshoeshoe. Sekonyela would do so for thirty years. But in the end, Moshoeshoe prevailed because of his wiser tactics and his ability to attract followers.

By the mid–1830s, Moshoeshoe ruled over 25,000 people. Before he died, this number would increase more than six fold.

Moshoeshoe never drank or smoked but did follow Mohlomi's advice and had between 30 and 40 wives.

As evidence of his sagacity, when Moshoeshoe's kingdom was threatened by a powerful neighboring chieftain named Ngwane, Moshoeshoe concentrated on developing good relations with the all powerful Zulu king Shaka by sending Shaka gifts. When the gifts stopped arriving, Shaka sent a messenger to inquire as to why. Moshoeshoe then told Shaka that Ngwane was preventing him from sending the gifts. Naturally, this angered Shaka. Shaka attacked Ngwane and eliminated him as a threat to Moshoeshoe. Moshoeshoe had defeated his enemy without shedding the blood of his people.

Aware of the growing presence of the English and Boers in South Africa, in 1833, Moshoeshoe welcomed French missionaries affiliated with the Paris Evangelical Mission into his land. Although he encouraged the French in their evangelizing activities, Moshoeshoe continued to support the old customs and religion. His principal interest in the French was in the advice they could provide with regards to how to deal with the encroaching British and the Boers.

With characteristic diplomacy, Moshoeshoe maintained his power by playing the British and the Boers against each other until 1843 when he aligned himself with the British to prevent increased encroachment by the trekking Boers. This alliance was necessitated by the increased land pressure being exert by the Boers.

By 1843, many thousands of the Boers had crossed the Orange River. At first Moshoeshoe had tolerated them but this tolerance soon became annoyance when Moshoeshoe saw that the Boers were there to stay. As friction between the Boers and the Sotho mounted, Moshoeshoe sought the assistance of the British.

The tenuous alliance between Moshoeshoe and the British ended five years later when a dispute led to hostilities between Moshoeshoe and British. In 1848, the then Cape Colony governor Harry Smith declared a British sovereignty over the territory between the Orange and Vaal Rivers theoretically to provide a legal framework within which to resolve disputes. Moshoeshoe eventually took exception to this usurpation of his authority and hostilities ensued.

To the surprise of the over confident British, Moshoeshoe had taken the precaution of arming his warriors with some modern weapons. Moshoeshoe defeated the British.

Moshoeshoe continued to fight against the encroaching British and Boers. However, the creation of the Orange Free State in 1854 led to a series of debilitating wars which began to weaken Moshoeshoe. An early Free State president, Jacobus Boshof (*see 1881*), initiated a new border conflict with Moshoeshoe in 1855. But by 1858, Boshof had still failed to defeat Moshoeshoe. The new Cape governor, George Grey, mediated a settlement, and then personally staked out a new boundary line between the Sotho and the Afrikaners.

Sotho-Afrikaner conflicts over land erupted again in the 1860s when Johannes Brand (*see 1888*) became the Free State president. In 1865, Brand attacked Moshoeshoe. By then Moshoeshoe was too old to maintain firm control over his Sotho followers. While his prestige among his people remained great, they were being torn by the dissenting viewpoints of Moshoeshoe's sons and brothers. Many of the Sotho even abandoned Moshoeshoe and joined the Afrikaners.

When the conflict obviously began to go against him, Moshoeshoe appealed to the British to annex his lands.

In 1868, the British did finally annex the Sotho lands. Thereafter the region was officially known by the name the British gave it Basutoland.

After the annexation of Basutoland, the Afrikaners of the Orange Free State continued to attempt to dominate the Sotho by exploiting their internal factions. However, Moshoeshoe resisted these attempts. Two months before he died, Moshoeshoe abdicated in favor of his senior son Letsie (*see 1891*) and publicly defined the legal basis for future succession.

Although Moshoeshoe's power did diminish with age, he continued to be revered by his people. When he died in 1870, Moshoeshoe was 84 years old and had managed to keep his people and his nation together for over forty years. However, just as important Moshoeshoe had left a legacy which assured the permanent preservation of Sotho autonomy within a region otherwise dominated by Europeans.

Almost a hundred years after Moshoeshoe's death, Lesotho again became an independent nation and Moshoeshoe's descendant, Moshoeshoe II was chosen to serve as the new nation's constitutional monarch.

- Mbigo Masuku, a leading figure in the Ndebele civil war, died.

Little is known about Mbigo's early career. However, he appears to have been with Mzilikazi when the Ndebele founder left Zululand around 1820.

In 1847, Mbigo was the commander of the Zwangendaba regiment, which attained immense prestige by repelling Andries Potgieter's raid into Zimbabwe. By the 1860s, Mbigo was linked to King Mzilikazi by marriage and was the commander of an elite division of army regiments.

After Mzilikazi died in 1868, Mbigo steadfastly supported the installation of Nkulumane as king. However, the man claiming to be "Nkulumane" was not accepted by most leading Ndebele councillors as authentic, and Lobengula was made king early in 1870.

Mbigo refused to acknowledge Lobengula's authority and led his army division in open defiance to Lobengula. Mbigo was killed when loyalist troops crushed his forces in a single great battle in June of 1870.

RELATED HISTORICAL EVENTS

• *The United States:* Henry Morton Stanley was dispatched by the *New York Herald* to search for the missionary David Livingstone.

• Robert E. Lee, the commander of the Confederate forces during the Civil War, died.

• *The Americas:* The Paraguayan War came to an end.

• In Brazil, construction of telegraph lines linking North and South began.

Europe

On June 25, 1870, Spain's Queen Isabella II abdicated. Her son Alphonse, age twelve, succeeded Isabella but in name only. The duke of Aosta, the son of Italy's Victor Emmanuel II was induced to accept the crown and began a brief reign as Amadeo I.

The Hohenzollern prince Leopold who had made a claim to the Spanish throne was persuaded by Prussia's Wilhelm I to withdraw his acceptance of the Spanish crown after the French protested.

On July 13, the French sent an ultimatum to Prussia. France's Napoleon III wired Wilhelm demanding that Wilhelm prohibit Leopold from accepting any future offer of the Spanish crown. This ultimatum was made public by Prussia's Count von Bismarck. The clear attempt by Napoleon to humiliate Kaiser Wilhelm infuriated the Prussian populace. Wilhelm adamantly refused Napoleon's demands.

On July 19, France declared war on Prussia. Three Prussian armies invaded France while the French invaded the Saar basin and earned a victory at Saarbrucken. However, the taste of French victory was very brief. On September 1, at the Battle of Sedan, the French First Army Corps under the command of Marshal MacMahon was utterly defeated.

On September 2, Napoleon himself surrendered along with his 80,000 man force. On September 4, a revolution erupted in Paris and the Third Republic was proclaimed. Napoleon III's Second Empire had come to an end.

The Franco-Prussian War of 1870 is of particular significance in Pan-African history because France's defeat in Europe compelled France to attempt to regain its stature by conquering foreign lands — the foreign lands of Africa. The subsequent French interest in Africa was soon accompanied by the interest of other European powers and the "scramble for Africa" was on. By the end of the century, the continent would be carved up into colonies governed by the European imperialist powers. The die would thus be cast for European-African relations for the next seventy years.

• *Africa:* Maurice Delafosse (1870–1926), a French administrator who became a pioneer in African studies, was born.

Maurice Delafosse spent much of his career as a soldier, explorer and administrator in West Africa. His experiences enabled Delafosse to write a number of valuable historical, ethnographic and linguistic studies of the Western Sudan and the Guinea Coast.

Delafosse's best known work was the three volume *Haut Senegal-Niger* which was completed in 1912. *Haut Senegal-Niger* is sometimes listed under the name of Delafosse's supervisor, Francois Clozel. *Haut Senegal-Niger* is considered to be one of the best scholarly sources for parts of the Western Sudan.

• Lord Delamere (1870–1931), a leading English settler of Kenya, was born.

Lord Delamere was born Hugh Cholmondeley. After a successful hunting trip in the Kenya highlands in 1898, Lord Delamere returned as a settler in 1903.

Drawing upon his personal fortune, Lord Delamere pioneered new agricultural crops and experimented in stock raising. His efforts are credited with making a permanent contribution to the economy of Kenya.

From the time of his arrival in Kenya, Lord Delamere was a leading voice of European settler opinion. He was able to exert great influence on the colonial administration.

For a time, Lord Delamere served as an elected member of the legislative council. He was a strong advocate of the supremacy of European interests in Kenya and of the union of the three British ruled East African territories.

• Jan Christiaan Smuts (1870–1950), one of the most prominent political and military leaders in South African history, was born.

Jan Smuts was born to an Afrikaner farming family in the western Cape Colony. He studied law at Cambridge and was called to the Cape bar in 1895.

Smuts was shocked by British bad faith during the Jameson Raid of 1895. Because of his disenchantment with the British, Smuts moved to the Transvaal.

In the Transvaal, Smuts soon came to the attention of President Kruger. In 1898, Kruger appointed Smuts to be the Transvaal state attorney.

Shortly after being appointed to this position, the Boer War began. During the second phase of the war, Smuts gained celebrity by commanding a successful raid deep into the Cape Colony.

Smuts fought to the end. However, towards the end, he joined with Louis Botha in advocating negotiations in which he then played a leading part.

After the war had come to an end, Smuts and Botha founded a political party which came to power in the Transvaal when self-government was restored in 1907.

During the National Union Convention, both Smuts and Botha were leading advocates of cooperation with the British, and their plan for union was adopted as the basis for discussion.

Botha became prime minister when the Union of South Africa was formed in 1910. Smuts assumed several important ministerial portfolios.

It was Smuts who met with the Indian leader Mohandas Gandhi in 1913. Gandhi was the spokesman for the Indians of South Africa. At the time, the Indians were dissatisfied with their treatment by the South African government. Smuts eventually acceded to Gandhi's demands for relief of Indian grievances.

In contrast to his image as a political moderate, Smuts was draconian in suppressing rebellions of Rand miners and Afrikaner extremists in 1914.

In 1915, Smuts assisted Botha in occupying German South West Africa. The British then gave Smuts command over their forces in east Africa.

Smuts drove the German commander Von Lettow-Vorbeck out of Tanzania after a long and costly campaign. Smuts then joined the British War Cabinet where he came to exercise considerable influence.

At the conclusion of World War I, Smuts participated in the Versailles Conference and was a chief sponsor of the newly created League of Nations.

Smuts was largely responsible for the creation of the mandate system, by which South Africa assumed administration of South West Africa. Later, however, Smuts refused to recognize

United Nations trusteeship over South West Africa.

When Botha died in 1919, Smuts became prime minister. Smuts confirmed his reputation for ruthlessness by putting down another miners' revolt in 1922. He also suppressed a tax protest by the Bondelswarts people in South West Africa with machine guns and bombers.

During this time, the anti–British Nationalist Party of James Hertzog gained in electoral strength and was able to force Smuts out of office in 1924.

Later problems posed by the world economic crisis forced Hertzog to take Smuts into his government in order to broaden his own base of support. From 1933 to 1939, Smuts served as Hertzog's deputy premier.

Throughout his career, Smuts regarded the majority non–European population of South Africa as a disagreeable menace which needed to be denied political power. In 1936, Smuts joined with Hertzog to help remove the last African voters from the common roll in the Cape Province.

At the outbreak of World War II, Smuts favored declaring war on Germany. Hertzog, on the other hand, preferred neutrality. Hertzog's ministry fell on this issue and Smuts became prime minister once again.

In 1941, Smuts was made a field marshal in the British army. He served in North Africa and was a close adviser to Churchill throughout the rest of the war.

After World War II, Smuts played a leading role in founding the United Nations. Smuts wrote the preamble to the United Nations' Charter. Ironically, the preamble that Smuts wrote proclaimed fundamental human rights which Smuts' own government then denied to the majority of the people in South Africa. Meanwhile, the reactionary faction of the Afrikaner electorate had again grown stronger at home.

In 1948, Smuts' party lost to the reconstituted National Party of Daniel Malan. Smuts spent the last two years of his life leading the parliamentary opposition.

• Paul Emil von Lettow-Vorbeck (1870–1964), the commander of the German forces in East Africa during World War I, was born.

After service in Cameroon and South West Africa, Lettow-Vorbeck was given command of colonial forces in German East Africa (present day Tanzania) on the eve of World War I in 1914.

A British naval blockade quickly isolated the

Germans there. Governor Schnee advocated declaring German East Africa neutral. However, Lettow-Vorbeck, who was determined to tie up allied troops as long as possible, took the initiative by raiding Kenya.

The British maintained their blockade and prepared a massive counter-offensive. The counter-offensive was finally launched under the command of Jan Smuts early in 1916. Smuts quickly cleared most of Tanzania of German troops, but Lettow-Vorbeck continued a guerrilla campaign in the south.

Although his predominantly African forces were outnumbered ten to one, Lettow-Vorbeck maintained his resistance for the duration of the war. Lettow-Vorbeck retreated into Mozambique late in 1917, but later re-entered Tanzania and invaded northeastern Zambia, where he surrendered two days after the European armistice in November 1918.

After the war, Lettow-Vorbeck participated in the Kapp Putsch of 1920 and served briefly in the German Reichstag before retiring.

---

1 8 7 1

THE UNITED STATES

The following African Americans were elected to the 42nd Congress:

Robert C. De Large was elected to Congress as a representative of the State of South Carolina. During his term in office, De Large returned to South Carolina to investigate voting irregularities which occurred during his own election. The House Commission on Elections declared his seat vacant in 1873.

In 1871, Robert B. Elliott was elected to the United States House of Representatives representing South Carolina. He served two terms in the House. Afterwards, Elliott retired to New Orleans where he practiced law.

Jefferson F. Long of Georgia became the first African American to make an official speech in the House of Representatives (February 1).

Josiah T. Walls, of Florida, was elected to Congress and served in that body from 1871 to 1877. During his time in office, Walls advocated support for the Cuban Revolution.

R. S. Turner of Alabama and J. H. Rainey also served in the 42nd Congress.

• James Garfield again proposed a resolution in the House to reduce the representation of Southern states as a penalty for denying African Americans the right to vote in accordance with Section 2 of the Fourteenth Amendment. The resolution was not adopted.

• The Georgia Democratic Party regained control of the state from the Republican Party.

• In 1871, P. B. S. Pinchback was elected president pro tem of the Louisiana State Senate and subsequently became the Lieutenant Governor when the incumbent died.

• In the Mississippi Legislature, 38 out 115 members were African American.

• Virginia re-apportioned its election districts to minimize the African American vote.

• In 1871, the Knights of Liberty, a secret militant organization formed by African Americans to free the slaves, emerged into public light as the Temple and Tabernacle of the Knights and Daughters of Tabor. The Reverend Moses Dickson, of Independence, Missouri, founded the organization with the purpose of spreading Christian religion and education, and acquiring real estate and avoiding intemperance. 200,000 members were claimed by 1900.

• In Mississippi, a race riot broke out in Meridian, Mississippi.

• John Jones was elected to a one year term on the Cook County Board.

• James Milton Turner was named minister resident and consul-general for Liberia (March 1).

• *Organizations:* Alpha Lodge of New Jersey, Number 116, Free and Accepted Masons, an African American Masonic lodge, was recognized by European American Masons. The first meeting of the Alpha Lodge was held on January 31, 1871, under Nathan Mingus.

The Ku Klux Klan

The Report of the Congressional Investigating Committee on the Ku Klux Klan was published in 1871. This committee studied nine counties in South Carolina for a six-month period. The findings of the committee were as follows:

The Klan lynched and murdered 35 men and whipped 262 men and women; shot, mutilated, or burned the property of 101 people; and committed two sexual offenses. For the same period, African Americans were said to have killed four men, beat one man, and committed 16 other offenses but none of a sexual nature.

The committee also found that the Klan had

murdered 74 men in Georgia and 109 in Alabama between 1868 and 1871.

• The Third Enforcement Act (also known as the Ku Klux Klan Act) was enacted. The Act authorized the President to suspend habeas corpus for certain offenses and imposed heavy penalties on persons "who shall conspire together, or go in disguise … for the purpose … of depriving any person or any class of persons of the equal protection of the laws, or of equal privileges or immunities under the laws." This Ku Klux Klan Act expired in 1872. (But *see 1871:* The United States: Miscellaneous Cases.)

• Governor Reed of Florida again asked for Federal troops to cope with Klan violence. This was Governor Reed's third request for assistance since 1868. Like his previous requests, the third request was also denied. Jonathan Gibbs, the Florida Secretary of State who was an African American, reported before a Congressional Committee that 153 African Americans had been murdered in Jackson County, Florida, alone.

• In Mississippi, some 640 people were indicted under the Enforcement Acts but none were convicted. In Kemper County, Mississippi, between 1869 and 1871, 35 African Americans were known to have been killed by the Klan and the beating or whipping of African Americans was reported to be a nightly occurrence.

• According to the records of A. W. Cummings, President of Spartanburg Female College in Spartanburg County, South Carolina, from October 1870 to July 1871, there were 227 known victims of Klan aggressions.

• *Labor Movement:* The second meeting of the Colored National Labor Movement convened on January 9. Congress was petitioned for a national system of educational and technical training for African Americans.

• *Notable Births:* Oscar De Priest (1871–1951), the first African American Congressman elected from a northern state (Illinois), was born (March 9).

Oscar De Priest was born in Florence, Alabama. De Priest moved to Kansas in 1877 with his parents, Alexander R. and Mary De Priest. As a youth, he ran away from home and went to Chicago, Illinois.

In Chicago, De Priest became a painter and a master decorator. He invested in the stock market and in real estate and amassed a small fortune. Financially secure, he entered into politics and was twice elected Cook County Commissioner.

In 1915, De Priest became Chicago's first African American alderman. He was elected to the United States Congress and served in that body from 1929 to 1934. De Priest's affiliation with the Republican Party ultimately led to his defeat in the Depression years.

• Joseph H. Douglass, the grandson of Frederick Douglass and a renowned violinist, was born in Washington, D. C. (July 3).
• Isaac Hathaway, a noted sculptor, was born.

Isaac Hathaway was born in Lexington, Kentucky. He studied art at the New England Conservatory and ceramics at Pittsburgh Normal College.

Hathaway eventually became the head of the ceramics department of Alabama State Teachers College. He is famous for his portrait busts of Frederick Douglass, Paul Laurence Dunbar and Booker T. Washington. It was Hathaway who designed the Federal memorial coins of Booker T. Washington and George Washington Carver.

• James Weldon Johnson (1871–1938), poet, educator, civil rights fighter, and the first African American consul to Nicaragua, was born (June 17).

James Weldon Johnson was born in Jacksonville, Florida. He was educated at Atlanta and Columbia Universities.

For the first forty-five years of his life Johnson was known primarily for the lyrics for songs. However, in 1917, Johnson's first book of poetry was published. The book was entitled *Fifty Years and Other Poems. Fifty Years and Other Poems* became one of the most important books of African American literature. Known for its expression of racial pride, *Fifty Years and Other Poems* contained many beautiful lyrics which had no reference to race.

Johnson constantly protested against "southern justice" and the inferior status granted to the African American. Johnson was the first African American poet who took pride in his blackness without apology. Indeed, one of his poems, *Lift Every Voice and Sing,* (1900), became the epitome of black pride and is known today as the African American — the Negro — National Anthem.

Between 1916 and 1930, James Weldon Johnson was an active and influential member of the NAACP as a field secretary, and then the executive secretary. During this period, Johnson conducted an extensive study of African American culture. The 1920s was the era of the Harlem Renaissance, and Johnson found himself devoting much of his time to non-creative editorial work. Among the works that Johnson edited during this time were *The Book of American Negro Poetry* (1922), the first anthology of African American verse ever published; *The Book of American Negro Spirituals* (1925), the first anthology collected by an African American which focused on the African and African American oral literary tradition; and *Second Book of American Negro Spirituals* (1926). It was through these three books that Johnson was able to demonstrate to the literate public the scope and diversity of African American literature.

In addition to his editing, in 1920, Johnson published *Self-Determining Haiti*, a work based on Johnson's personal observations and a good background in Latin-American affairs. In 1927, Johnson's *God's Trombones: "Seven Negro Sermons in Verse"* was published. Offered as a reconstruction of sermons which were recorded in Johnson's memory, the sermons appear more to be creative works from Johnson's imagination. The rhythm of these poems are cadenced with long beat measures, giving them a striking chant-like quality. These were Johnson's last published collection of poetry.

In addition to his literary accomplishments, Johnson served as a school principal and a lawyer. Johnson also served as United States consul at Venezuela and Nicaragua.

The words to *Lift Every Voice and Sing* were set to music by the brother of James Weldon Johnson, J. Rosamund Johnson *(see 1873).* This anthem has been sung for decades to unify and inspire African Americans. Its role has been an important one and its words are similarly important to understand. The words to *Lift Every Voice and Sing* are

> *Lift every voice and sing, till earth and heaven ring.*
> *Ring with the harmonies of liberty;*
> *Let our rejoicing rise, high as the list'ning skies,*
> *Let it resound loud as the rolling sea.*
> *Sing a song full of the faith that the dark past has taught us;*
> *Sing a song full of the hope that the present has brought us;*
> *Facing the rising sun of our new day begun,*

> *Let us march on till victory is won.*
> *Stony the road we trod, bitter the chast'ning rod,*
> *Felt in the days when hope unborn had died;*
> *Yet with a steady beat, have not our weary feet*
> *Come to the place for which our fathers sighed?*
> *We have come over a way that with tears has been watered;*
> *We have come, treading our path thro' the blood of the slaughtered,*
> *Out from the gloomy past, till now we stand at last,*
> *Where the white gleam of our bright star is cast.*

> *God of our weary years, God of our silent tears,*
> *Thou who hast brought us thus far on the way;*
> *Thou who hast by Thy might, led us into the light,*
> *Keep us forever in the path, we pray.*
> *Lest our feet stray from the places, our God, where we met Thee,*
> *Lest our hearts, drunk with the wine of the world, we forget Thee;*
> *Shadowed beneath Thy hand, may we forever stand,*
> *True to our God, true to our native land.*

• Miles Vandahurst Lynk was born in Texas (June 3). Lynk was the founder of the first African American medical journal, the *Medical and Surgical Observer.* Lynk also helped to organize the National Medical Association — the African American counterpart to the American Medical Association.

• *Notable Deaths:* Rebecca Cox Jackson (1795–1871), the founder of an African American Shaker family in Philadelphia, died.

• James Whitfield (1822–1871), an African American poet and abolitionist, died.

• *Miscellaneous Cases:* In the *United States v. Souders* (April 1871) 2 Abb. U.S. 456, 27 Fed. Cas. 1267, a federal court held that the Enforcement Acts applied only to Congressional elections. *See also 1871:* The United States: The Ku Klux Klan.

• In *United States v. Hall* (May 1871) 3 Chi. Leg. News 260, 13 Int. Rev. Rec. 181, 26 Fed. Cas. 79, a federal court ruled that all the rights guaranteed by the first eight amendments were the "privileges and immunities" mentioned in the 14th Amendment. This decision was overruled by the 1899 case of *Maxwell v. Dow* (February 26, 1900) 176 U.S. 581, 44 L.Ed. 571.

• *Publications:* The Hampton Institute Press was founded.

• It is believed that Albery Allson Whitman published his first book *Essays on the Ten Plagues and Miscellaneous Subjects* in 1871.

• *Scholastic Achievements:* Howard University established a law school.

• Alcorn Agricultural and Mechanical College, the first land grant institution, began classes in Lorman, Mississippi.

Ironically, Alcorn A & M was named in honor of James I. Alcorn, a Reconstruction governor of the state who led the European American branch of the Republican Party and who opposed African American legislators during his term in office. Hiram Rhodes Revels served as Alcorn A & M's first president.

• Patrick Francis Healy was inaugurated as president of Georgetown University in Washington, D. C., the oldest Catholic University of America (July 31).

• Daniel Alexander Payne Murray (1852–1925) was hired by the Library of Congress in a professional capacity.

Under the mentorship of the librarian of Congress, Ainsworth R. Spofford, Murray became proficient in several languages and acquired invaluable research skills. In 1881, Murray was promoted to assistant librarian, a position he held until his retirement in 1923. Murray was asked to prepare an exhibit on African American achievements for the 1900 Paris Exposition, and an accompanying bibliography was a cornerstone for future African American bibliographies by Murray and others.

• *The Arts:* Edmonia "Wildfire" Lewis, the Afro-Chippewa sculptress, exhibited her works in Rome, Italy.

• *The Performing Arts:* The Fisk Jubilee Singers made their first appearances under the direction of George L. White. The Fisk Jubilee Singers would go on to tour throughout Europe and America, bringing Negro spiritual music to new and larger audiences.

• *Black Enterprise:* In 1871, the Freedmen's Savings and Trust Company, an African American owned bank, had 34 branches and reported deposits of $20 million. However, by 1874, the bank had failed.

THE AMERICAS

• *Barbados:* Samuel Jackman Prescod (1806–1871), the first non–European to be elected to the House of Assembly of Barbados, died.

Samuel Jackman Prescod was born out of wedlock. His father was a European planter.

Prescod was largely self-educated. He began his campaign in support of the rights of the Barbadian colored population in 1838. He soon became the acknowledged leader of the free colored population, and it was largely through his efforts that in 1831, the franchise was extended to them and all civil restriction on their activities was removed.

With the abolition of slavery in 1834, Prescod fought for the rights of the ex-slaves and against the system of apprenticeship required of the slaves prior to full emancipation. Prescod saw the struggle against apprenticeship as one of the "poor and middle classes of all complexions against the unjust assumptions of the wealthy few." His goal was to unite the coloreds, the ex-slaves, and the Europeans into a "grand radical alliance" against the privileged.

Prescod became the editor of the first colored newspaper on the island and for 25 years was editor of a radical journal, *The Liberal.* Prescod saw *The Liberal* as a vehicle for bridging the racial divide among Afro-Barbadians, coloreds, and Euro-Barbadians. As a result, The *Liberal* became one of the most influential journals in Barbados and the West Indies.

Prescod's prosecution on libel charges intensified his popularity. He won a seat in the Barbados Assembly from Bridgetown, the capital city, in 1843. By so winning, Prescod became the first non–European to sit in the Assembly.

As a legislator, Prescod quickly developed ties with persons of enlightened opinion in the British Parliament and came to be the leader of the Liberal Party in the Barbados House. Prescod fought unsuccessfully for universal adult suffrage and for an Executive Committee system of government.

The Executive Committee system of government was not finally adopted in Barbados until 1881.

Prescod retired from the Assembly in 1860, to become judge of the assistant court of appeals.

• *Brazil:* Joaquim Machado de Assis published his first novel — *Ressurreicao (Resurrection).*

• Maria do Carmo Geronimo, a woman who would become known as the world's oldest human being, was born (March 5).

On March 5, 1996, the diminutive (four foot tall) Maria do Carmo Geronimo celebrated her 125th birthday near the grassy hills of Carmo de Minas, Brazil, where she was born into slavery.

"Let freedom ring," Geronimo said as she was welcomed by a crowd of 100 in the town where she celebrated her birthday — a town located 250 miles southwest of Rio de Janeiro.

"It feels good to be alive — and free," Maria said as she completed the 60-mile ride from Itajuba, the small town where she had lived for eighty years. "I don't wish slavery on anyone."

The Reverend Francisco Alves da Cruz of the Roman Catholic Church gave Maria a special blessing for "showing the Lord's work in her 125 years of humility and simplicity."

After the blessing, Geronimo blew out the candles on a huge cake with white icing. She gathered enough strength to blow out the three candles shaped in the numbers of her age.

"God is showing us His values through this woman," da Cruz said. "The oldest person in the world is female, black and during the first 17 years of her life suffered the greatest ill man has known — slavery."

Maria's back was a testament of her suffering — her 125-year-old back still bore the scars of lashes inflicted by her owner. Just hearing the name of her owner — "Jose Garcia" — was enough to send chills down Maria's curved spine.

Maria was born on March 5, 1871, some seventeen (17) years before slavery was abolished in Brazil. At the time, birth certificates were not issued in the part of Brazil where Maria was born. However, officials of the Catholic Church were able to find Maria's baptismal records — records which were signed and dated March 15, 1871. These documents verified Maria's claim of an extraordinarily long life.

In addition to the church documents, interviews with people who knew Maria when they were young also verified her claim to longevity. As the 96-year-old Francisca De Andrade Pereira remarked, "When I arrived in town at the start of the century Maria do Carmo was a grown woman. She was adored by all of the children because she would play with us."

The verification of Maria's claim was necessary because, at the time, the recognized oldest human being was the then 121-year-old Jeanne Calmet of Arles, France.

Maria's longevity may be partly attributable to her lifestyle. She worked for decades as a nanny and a maid. She spent her retirement years in the one-room house built by the family that took Maria in around 1916 when she was a vagrant. Her principal hobby was tending her garden of medicinal herbs in her bare feet.

In the case of Maria do Carmo Geronimo, simplicity and serenity led to a long, blessed life.

• In Brazil, the Rio Branco Law was issued (September). This law stipulated that children of slaves were to be set free.

While the Rio Branco Law ostensibly emancipated the slaves, the emancipated slaves — the *ingenuos* — were still required to serve an apprenticeship until 21 years of age before effective freedom was to be granted. A state-supported emancipation fund was also established to purchase freedom for those born before 1872.

The Rio Branco Law was also known as the Law of the Free Womb (Ventre Livre). Its passage may have been partially attributable to the role that Afro-Brazilians had played in the war against Paraguay along with the historical contribution of Afro-Brazilians to Brazilian culture.

What is known for certain is that pressed by foreign opinion, the threat of slave rebellion, and the realization that wage labor had to be gradually introduced, the legislature passed the Free Birth Law in 1871. The Free Birth Law was a very gradual measure since the children were obliged to work for their keep until age twenty-one, but it was a major step, nevertheless.

Because of the significance of this legislation, it is presented here in its entirety.

*   *   *

The Princess Imperial, Regent, in the name of His Majesty the Emperor Senhor D. Pedro II, makes known to all the subjects of the Empire, that the General Assembly has decreed, and that she has sanctioned, the following Law:

Art. I. The children of women slaves that may be born in the Empire from the date of this Law shall be considered to be free.

§1. The said minors shall remain with and be under the dominion of the owners of the mother, who shall be obliged to rear and take care of them until such children shall have completed the age of eight years.

On the child of the slave attaining this age, the owner of its mother shall have the option either of receiving from the State the indemnification of 600 dollars, or of making use of the services of the minor until he shall have completed the age of twenty-one years.

In the former event the Government will receive the minor, and will dispose of him in conformity with the provisions of the present Law.

The pecuniary indemnification above fixed shall be paid in Government bonds, bearing interest at six per cent, per annum, which will be considered extinct at the end of thirty years.

The declaration of the owner must be made within thirty days, counting from the day on which the minor shall complete the age of eight years; and should he not do so within that time it will be understood that he embraces the option of making use of the service of the minor.

§2. Any one of those minors may ransom himself from the onus of servitude, by means of a previous pecuniary indemnification, offered by himself, or by any other person, to the owner of his mother, calculating the value of his services for the time which shall still remain unexpired to complete the period, should there be no agreement on the quantum of the said indemnification.

§3. It is also incumbent on owners to rear and bring up the children which the daughters of their female slaves may have while they are serving the same owners.

Such obligation, however, will cease as soon as the service of the mother ceases. Should the latter die within the term of servitude the children may be placed at the disposal of the Government.

§4. Should the female slave obtain her freedom, her children under eight years of age who may be under the dominion of her owners shall, by virtue of §1, be delivered up, unless she shall prefer leaving them with him, and he consents to their remaining.

§5. In case of the female slave being made over to another owner her free children under twelve years of age shall accompany her, the new owner of the said slave being invested with the rights and obligations of his predecessor.

§6. The services of the children of female slaves shall cease to be rendered before the term marked in §1, if by decision of the Criminal Judge it be known that the owner of the mothers ill-treat the children, inflicting on them severe punishments.

§7. The right conferred on owners by §1 shall be transferred in cases of direct succession; the child of a slave must render his services to the person to whose share in the division of property the said slave shall belong.

II. The Government may deliver over to associations which they shall have authorized, the children of the slaves that may be born from the date of this Law forward, and given up or abandoned by the owners of said slaves, or taken away from them by virtue of Article I, §6.

§1. The said associations shall have a right to gratuitous services of the minors, until they shall have completed the age of twenty-one years, and may hire out their services, but shall be bound —

1st. To rear and take care of said minors.

2ndly. To save a sum for each of them, out of the amount of wages, which for this purpose is reserved in the respective statutes.

3rdly. To seek to place them in a proper situation when their term of service shall be ended.

§2. The associations referred to in the previous paragraph shall be subject to the inspection of Judges of the Orphans' Court, in as far as affects minors.

§3. The disposition of this Article is applicable to foundling asylums, and to the persons whom the Judges of the Orphans' Court charge with the education of the said minors, in default of associations or houses established for that purpose.

§4. The Government has the free right of ordering the said minors to be taken into the public establishments, the obligations imposed by §1 on the authorized associations being in this case transferred to the State.

III. As many slaves as correspond in value to the annual disposable sum from the emancipation fund shall be freed in each province of the Empire.

§1. The emancipation fund arises from —

1st. The tax on slaves.

2ndly. General tax on transfer of the slaves as property.

3rdly. The proceeds of six lotteries per annum, free of tax, and the tenth part of those which may be granted from this time forth, to be drawn in the capital of the Empire.

4thly. The fines imposed by virtue of this Law.

5thly. The sums which may be marked in the general budget, and in those of the provinces and municipalities.

6thly. Subscriptions, endowments, and legacies for that purpose.

§2. The sums marked in the provincial and municipal budgets, as also the subscriptions, endowments, and legacies for the local purpose, shall be applied for the manumission of slaves in the provinces, districts, municipalities, and parishes designated.

IV. The slave is permitted to form a saving fund from what may come to him through gifts, legacies, and inheritances, and from what, by consent of his owner, he may obtain by his labor and economy. The Government will see to the regulations as to the placing and security of said savings.

§1. By the death of the slave half of his savings shall belong to his surviving widow, if there be such, and the other half shall be transmitted to his heirs in conformity with civil law.

In default of heirs the savings shall be adjudged to the emancipation fund of which Article III treats.

§2. The slave who, through his savings, may obtain means to pay his value has a right to freedom.

§3. It is further permitted the slave, in furtherance of his liberty, to contract with a third party the hire of his future services, for a term not exceeding seven years, by obtaining the consent of his master, and approval of the Judge of the Orphans' Court.

§4. The slave that belongs to joint proprietors, and is freed by one of them, shall have a right to his freedom by indemnifying the other owners with the share of the amount which belongs to them. This indemnification may be paid by services rendered for a term not exceeding seven years, in conformity with the preceding paragraph.

§5. The manumission, with the clause of services during a certain time, shall not become annulled by want of fulfilling the said clause, but the freed man shall be compelled to fulfill, by means of labor in the public establishments, or by contracting for his services with private persons.

§6. Manumissions, whether gratuitous or by means of onus, shall be exempted from all duties, emoluments, or expenses.

§7. In any case of alienation or transfer of slaves, the separation of husband and wife, and children under twelve years of age from father or mother, is prohibited under penalty of annulment.

§8. If the division of property among heirs or partners does not permit the union of a family, and none of them prefers remaining with the family by replacing the amount of the share belonging to the other interested parties, the said family shall be sold and the proceeds shall be divided among the heirs.

§9. The ordination, Book 4th, title 63, in the part which revokes freedom, on account of ingratitude, is set aside.

V. The Emancipation Societies which are formed, and those which may for the future be formed, shall be subject to the inspection of the Judges of the Orphans' Court.

Sole paragraph. The said societies shall have the privilege of commanding the services of the slaves whom they may have liberated, to indemnify themselves for the sum spent in their purchase.

VI. The following shall be declared free:

§1. The slaves belonging to the State, the Government giving them such employment as they may deem fit.

§2. The slave given in *usufruct* to the Crown.

§3. The slaves of unclaimed inheritances.

§4. The slaves who have been abandoned by their owners. Should these have abandoned the slaves from the latter being invalids they shall be obliged to maintain them, except in case of their own penury, the maintenance being charged by the Judge of the Orphans' Court.

§5. In general the slaves liberated by virtue of this Law shall be under the inspection of Government during five years. They will be obliged to hire themselves under pain of compulsion; if they lead an idle life they shall be made to work in the public establishments.

The compulsory labor, however, shall cease so soon as the freed man shall exhibit an engagement of hire.

VII. In trials in favor of freedom —

§1. The process shall be summary.

§2. There shall be appeal *ex officio* when the decisions shall be against the freedom.

VIII. The Government will order the special registration of all slaves existing in the Empire to be proceeded with, containing a declaration of name, sex, age, state, aptitude for work, and foliation of each, if such should be known.

§1. The date on which the registry ought to commence closing shall be announced beforehand, the longest time possible being given for preparation by means of edicts repeated, in which shall be inserted the dispositions of the following paragraph.

§2. The slaves who, through the fault or omission of the parties interested, shall not have been registered up to one year after the closing of the register, shall, *de facto*, be considered as free.

§3. For registering each slave the owner

shall pay, once only, the emolument of 500 reis, if done within the term marked, and one dollar should that be exceeded. The produce of those emoluments shall go towards the expenses of registering, and the surplus to the emancipation fund.

§4. The children of a slave mother, who by this Law became free, shall also be registered in a separate book.

Those persons who have become remiss shall incur a fine of 100 dollars to 200 dollars, repeated as many times as there may be individuals omitted: and for fraud, in the penalties of Article CLXXIX of the Criminal Code.

§5. The parish priests shall be obliged to have special books for the registry of births and deaths of the children of slaves born from and after the date of this Law. Each omission will subject the parish priest to a fine of 100 dollars.

IX. The Government, in its regulations, can impose fines of as much as 100 dollars, and the penalty of imprisonment up to one month.

X. All contrary dispositions are revoked.

Therefore, order all authorities to whom, &c. Given at the Palace of Rio de Janeiro, on the 28th September, 1871. 50th of the Independence and of the Empire.

— Princess Imperial, Regent.
Theodoro Machado Freire Pereira da Silva.

• As part of the Rio Branco Law, Brazilian abolitionists pushed through legislation which made owners free any slave who was capable of paying his market value.

Slavery was ingrained in Brazilian society. As a consequence, the attack on slavery in Brazil occurred much later than in the rest of Latin America.

Until 1850, an elite group of liberal urban intellectuals fought for the abolition of the Atlantic slave trade. The signing of a treaty, in 1831, with the British outlawing the slave trade had little effect. As a result, pressure began to build within Brazil itself until final abolition of the slave trade was forced on Brazil in 1850.

The abolition of the slave trade in Brazil was followed by a decade of relative calm with regards to the issue of slavery itself. However, the U.S. Civil War disrupted this calm and brought the issue to the forefront in Brazilian politics.

In September of 1871, Brazil adopted the Rio Branco Law which freed all those born to slaves after the effective date of the law. With the passage of the Rio Branco Law, Brazilian govern-ment leaders believed that they had resolved the issue, and, in fact, serious abolition agitation did disappear temporarily, so that until 1880 the planter class enjoyed relative peace and control over their slave force.

• *Canada:* By 1871, Wilson Abbott, a wealthy Afro-Canadian real estate broker, owned forty-two houses, five vacant lots, and a warehouse, largely in Toronto, but also in Hamilton and Owen Sound.

EUROPE

• Robert Browning published *Balaustion's Adventure* and *Prince Hohenstiel-Schwangau, Saviour of Society.*

AFRICA

• *North Africa, Egypt and Sudan:* Beginning in March 1871 and lasting until September of 1879, Jamal-al-Din al-Afghani, the pan-Islamic propagandist in Cairo, stirred up unrest and civil disturbances, especially at al-Azhar University.

• The *Muqabala* law granted ownership of land to Egyptian peasants who paid the *Muqabala* tax and redemption of half tax in perpetuity.

• In April, Baker Pasha (Sir Samuel Baker) annexed Gondokoro for Egypt.

• Khartoum, Sennar and the White Nile provinces were merged into the "Southern Sudan" and Ahmad Mumtaz was made the governor.

• On October 25, Tunis received a firman — an order issued by the Turkish Sultan — from Istanbul renouncing Tunis' obligation to pay tribute. However, the Bey of Tunis was still to be invested by the Turkish Porte and was forbidden to cede territory or make war or peace.

• There was a general uprising against the French in Algeria.

• The Sultan of Morocco requested that the United States establish a protectorate for his country. The State Department declined.

• *West Africa:* In January, the governor of Portuguese Guinea was assassinated by a grummet. In February, the uprising was suppressed.

• Senegal dispatched a Deputy to Paris.

The colony of Senegal was established in the 1600s. The colony changed hands between France and England several times until 1817 when the French seized it for a final time.

French authority was limited to the coast until the governorship of Louis Faidherbe when it rapidly expanded inland. Senegal was administered by the governors of French West Africa beginning in 1895.

Senegal became an independent nation in 1960.

• The French reached agreement with Lat Dior (Lat Dyor).

After Maba's death in 1867, Lat Dyor came to terms with the French. Returning to Kayor, Lat Dyor was reinstated as the ruler of the Wolof kingdom in 1871.

• Lagos (Nigeria) was again partly destroyed by fire.

• There was an attack on the steamer *Nelson* on the River Niger.

• Edward James Roye was elected President of Liberia (January).

As President of Liberia, Roye undertook the complete financial reconstruction of Liberia. He also introduced measures for improving the schools and the system of roads in Liberia. However, despite this initial promise, Roye's Presidency was destined to be brought down by scandal and tragedy.

The cause of Roye's demise lay in his dealings before assuming the Presidency. In 1870, Roye had gone to England to negotiate a loan. He was successful in securing a $500,000 loan. However, the very severe terms for the repayment of the loan caused great resentment in Liberia. Roye was accused of embezzlement. Roye became defensive and autocratic. He issued an edict which extended his term in office, but the people of Liberia would not obey it. An insurrection ensued and Roye was deposed from office.

Summoned to a trial for his crimes, Roye fled. He attempted to find a safe haven with an English ship that was in the nearby harbor. However, as Roye paddled out to the ship in a native canoe, the canoe was overturned by the waves. Roye was drowned.

While not generally known, another reason for Roye's demise was racism. During the 1870s, Liberia became bitterly factionalized along color (skin tone) lines. Roye happened to be the first dark skinned president of Liberia. Roye's COTW (fair skinned) opponents charged Roye with the crime of embezzlement described above. They also charged a Roye protégé, Edward Blyden with committing adultery with Roye's wife. Blyden was dragged through the streets of Monrovia by a mob and nearly lynched. *See 1912.*

• In 1871, Joseph Jenkins Roberts was once again elected President of Liberia and he served in that capacity until his death in 1876.

• In 1871, James Milton Turner, an African American educator, was appointed minister resident and consul general to Liberia. He would serve in this position until 1878.

• In 1871, the British secured a document which they claimed was signed by Kofi Karikari, renouncing the Ashanti's title as landlord of the British Elmina fort. The document was a forgery and resulted in an Ashanti attack on the British in 1873. General Garnet Wolseley led the combined British and Fante forces which repulsed the Ashanti, and then advanced into Kumasi, the Ashanti capital.

• Prempe I (c.1871–1931), the future ruler of the Akan state of Asante, is believed to have been born in this year.

At the age of seventeen, Prempe inherited a disintegrating empire. His predecessor had been his older brother, Kwaku Dua II, who died of smallpox in 1884 after reigning for only a year.

For the next four years, warfare was waged throughout the empire. The war was caused by a successional dispute, attempts of the original Akan founder states to secede from the Asante union and efforts of conquered neighbors to break away.

Because of his youth, Prempe, at first, relied heavily on advisers. Initially Prempe re-established the union by defeating the breakaway Kokofu, Mampong, and Nsuta states, which had not supported his candidacy. The rebel states, however, were offered protection by the British on the coast.

The British offered protection to the Asante rebel states as part of its effort to weaken Asante. In 1890, when Prempe sent a delegation to Accra to protest, the British offered to include Prempe's lands within its protected sphere.

Prempe refused the British offer. Instead, in 1892, he attacked and defeated the Brong states to the north, which had broken away earlier. These were especially important because of their location among the northern trade routes. In 1894, with the empire to a large measure restored, Prempe was officially installed on the Golden Stool — the great throne of the Asante Empire.

After becoming the asantehene, Prempe began to become less dependent on his advisers. In 1894, the British attempted to place a resident in Kumasi, offering Prempe a stipend. Prempe refused the offer, fearing a threat to Asante's sovereignty. Meanwhile Prempe sent his own envoys, led by John Owusu-Ansa *(see 1895),* to England.

Prempe's delegation to London unsuccessfully attempted to see Queen Victoria. They sought an audience with the Queen to refute British reports of Asante misrule and human sacrifice.

Prempe also tried to ally with Samori Toure, the great Mandinka ruler, who was building his second empire in the Ivory Coast interior. Prempe's overture to Samori failed. Its failure was largely due to the fact that Prempe hoped to befriend the French to counteract the British, while Samori wanted to do the exact opposite.

In 1896, a British expedition arrived in Kumasi to demand that the Asante accept British protection and to extort a large sum of gold to pay British expenses. Prempe decided that armed resistance was futile. Prempe accepted the protectorate, but claimed he had not the gold to pay the indemnity. Prempe was thereupon arrested and deported to Sierra Leone.

When, in 1900, the British demanded that the Asante surrender the Golden Stool, the symbol of Asante unity, the people unsuccessfully rebelled. Britain then dismantled the former empire and ruled it directly.

After 1921, the British re-visited the policy of direct rule of Asante. Relying upon the advice of government anthropologist George Rattray, the British reconstructed the nucleus of the Asante state.

At this same time, Asante leaders and the new Gold Coast elite, including the Fante lawyer Joseph Casely Hayford *(see 1866)*, lobbied for the release of Prempe.

In 1924, Prempe was permitted to return to Kumasi. Although the British officially regarded him as a private citizen, the thousands of people who turned out to greet Prempe clearly thought otherwise. By 1926, Prempe was installed as the ruler of the Kumasi division of Asante.

Given a great deal of power under the system of indirect rule, Prempe was regarded by his subjects as the ruler of all of Asante. At his death in 1931, he was succeeded by his nephew, Prempe II.

• Laminu Njitiya, the de facto ruler of the Kanuri state of Bornu, died.

Laminu Njitiya was of Shuwu Arab and Kanembu descent. He began his career as a bandit. However, he later became a part of a noble household. It was while he was a part of this noble household that Laminu became the first assistant to Shehu 'Umar's chief adviser.

Shehu 'Umar was a weak and indecisive man. He was deposed in 1853 but regained the throne in 1854. Because Laminu had remained loyal to

'Umar, 'Umar rewarded Laminu with a large fief and an untitled position as his most trusted confidant. In this position, and because of 'Umar's weak personality, Laminu became the de facto ruler of Bornu.

Laminu was a highly popular figure. He increased Bornu's holding by conquering some of the Marghai country to the south. After Laminu's death, Bukar, 'Umar's son and successor, became the de facto ruler of the Kanuri state of Bornu.

• Edward James Roye (1815–1871 or 1872), a champion of Liberia's dark skinned citizens and president of Liberia, died.

Edward Roye was born of a wealthy family in Newark, Ohio, and educated at Oberlin College in Ohio. After a successful career as a businessman, Roye emigrated to Liberia in 1846. There he established himself in business and studied law. He entered politics and became speaker of the House of Representatives in 1849.

At the age of fifty, Roye was elected to the supreme court, and became chief justice two years later. In 1870, Roye ran for president as the candidate of the True Whig Party. The True Whigs represented black-skinned citizens against the lighter skinned aristocracy which controlled the Republican Party.

As President, Roye undertook the financial reconstruction of Liberia. However, despite this initial promise, Roye's Presidency was destined to be brought down by scandal and tragedy.

The cause of Roye's demise lay in his dealings before assuming the Presidency. In 1870, Roye had gone to England to negotiate a loan. He was successful in securing a $500,000 loan. However, the very severe terms for the repayment of the loan caused great resentment in Liberia. Roye was accused of embezzlement. Roye became defensive and autocratic. He issued an edict which extended his term in office, but the people of Liberia would not obey it. An insurrection ensued and Roye was deposed from office.

Although official accounts claim that Roye drowned while trying to escape with some of the loan money, it is also reported that he died in prison after being beaten by a mob, or was murdered there. Roye was succeeded briefly by his vice-president and then by Joseph J. Roberts, a Republican who had been Liberia's first president.

• *Central Africa:* In March, David Livingstone reached the Lualaba River.

• Sudanese merchants erected a zariba at Tangasi, near Nangazizi.

• Abd al-Samad was replaced by the Coptic Ghattas Co.

• In 1871, Nyangwe was the largest slave market in central Africa.

• The American Presbyterian Mission started work in the Cameroon.

• *Eastern Africa:* From 1871 through 1874, Nyungu ya Mawe was a prominent leader of a *ruga-ruga* warrior band in Unyamwezi.

• On October 23, David Livingstone arrived back at Ujiji. On November 10, Henry Stanley met Livingstone at Ujiji in the famous encounter highlighted by Stanley's immortal question: "Dr. Livingstone, I presume?"

• Mirambo destroyed Tabora.

By 1871, coastal Arabs had allied with southern Nyamwezi chiefs to make Tabora in central Tanzania a major trade center. Mirambo, who at the time was the most powerful Nyamwezi chief, opposed this Arab-Nyamwezi presence. Mirambo's subsequent career was dominated by his rivalry with this Arab-Nyamwezi coalition over control of the new trade routes.

Mirambo harassed the Arab and Nyamwezi traders and initiated open warfare in 1871. The explorer Henry Stanley participated in the war as an ally of the Arabs who were fighting Mirambo.

Mirambo scored several early successes in this war, but eventually failed to follow them up. As a result of this lack of diligence, the war ultimately became a stalemate.

• Munzinger, a Swiss adventurer, became governor of Massawa. During his tenure, a bridge was built across Keren hills.

• Menelik, initiated a five year military campaign against the Wallo Galla.

• *Southern Africa:* In 1871–1872, Carl Mauch, the German geologist and explorer, re-visited Shona and became the first European to describe the impressive ruins of Great Zimbabwe to the outside world (September 5, 1871). *See 1867.*

• In October, Cecil Rhodes trekked from Natal to Kimberley.

• Basutoland was annexed to the Cape Colony and governed separately by proclamations.

The year after Letsie (*see 1891*) became chief of the Sotho, the British crown turned over administration of Lesotho (Basutoland) to the Cape Colony. The Colonial government divided Lesotho into four districts, and Letsie's brothers, became chiefs of the districts.

The inability of the Cape to enforce its policies aggravated Letsie's governance problems by enabling his brothers to oppose him from their positions as district chiefs. One brother, Masupha (*see 1899*), controlled Thaba Bosiu — Moshoeshoe's fortified mountain stronghold — and resisted all efforts to impose magistrates, setting an example which other sub-chiefs followed.

• Great Britain annexed the diamond fields of Kimberley and Griqualand West.

In 1871, Marthinus Pretorius, the president of the Transvaal Republic, resigned after mishandling the Transvaal's case in a dispute over possession of the recently discovered diamond fields.

• The Kgatla migrated to Botswana.

The humiliation of having been publicly flogged in 1869 made the position of Kgamanyane, the chief of the Kgatla, simply untenable as long as he remained in the Transvaal. Kgamanyane was compelled to move into the lands which comprise the present day Botswana. It was there that the Kwena chief Sechele allowed Kgamanyane's followers to settle at Mochudi in 1871.

• Sipopa, the ruler of the Lozi, granted George Westbeech a virtual monopoly over the Lozi ivory trade. Afterwards, Sipopa relied on Westbeech as a friend and adviser.

• John Langalibalele Dube (1871–1946), the first president of the African National Congress, was born.

In 1889, John Dube went to the United States to study theology. He returned to Zululand as a Methodist minister and immediately set about to improve secondary education. Dube founded and edited the first Zulu newspaper in Natal in 1904 and established for himself a reputation as a radical in his editorials criticizing the British policy in the Zulu rebellion of 1906.

In 1912, Dube responded to Pixley Seme's call to form an African union. He was elected the first president of the South African Native National Congress, an organization which became known as the African National Congress in 1923.

In 1914, Dube led an unsuccessful deputation to London to protest against new discriminatory legislation. Under fire from Seme, Dube resigned from the ANC presidency in 1917. However, he remained active in the ANC for most of the rest of his life.

By the 1930s, Dube was regarded by the rank and file of the Congress as a reactionary and his influence was minimal.

• Tiyo Soga (c.1829–1871), the first ordained Bantu-speaking South African, died.

The father of Tiyo Soga was a high counsellor in the Ngqika branch of the Xhosa people. Tiyo's mother was the first member of the family to be converted to Christianity.

Tiyo was trained at the United Presbyterian Church of Scotland mission schools in the Cape Colony. He later attended a seminary in Glasgow where he was baptized in 1848.

Afterwards, Tiyo did evangelical work among the Xhosa. He returned to Scotland for further study in 1851. He was ordained in 1856.

In 1857, Soga married a Scottish woman. He returned to Africa and founded a successful mission station among the Xhosa.

Although his health declined badly during the 1860s, Soga managed to open a new station among the Gcaleka Xhosa of chief Sarili three years before he died in 1871.

Tiyo Soga's translations of the Four Gospels and the first part of *Pilgrim's Progress* were among the earliest in the Xhosa language.

RELATED HISTORICAL EVENTS

• *Europe:* On January 18, Wilhelm I was proclaimed the German Emperor at Versailles.

• On January 28, Paris surrendered to the Prussians and, on May 10, the Franco-German Peace treaty was executed.

• Charles Darwin published *The Descent of Man.*

• *Africa:* Edouard Bouet-Willaumez (1808–1871), a French imperialist, died.

As a naval officer, Bouet-Willaumez, explored the upper reaches of the Senegal River in 1836. From 1838 to 1842, Bouet-Willaumez negotiated treaties with African chiefs between Cape Palmas in Liberia and the Gabon River. These treaties established a French foothold along the west coast of Africa.

Bouet-Willaumez was also the governor of Senegal from 1842 to 1844.

───────── **1 8 7 2** ─────────

THE UNITED STATES

• On June 5, the Republican National Convention convened in Philadelphia. This convention became the setting for major participation by African-American delegates. Robert B. Elliott (who chaired the delegation from South Carolina), Joseph Rainey (also from South Carolina), and John R. Lynch (from Mississippi) all spoke at the convention.

• The Democratic Party endorsed Horace Greeley, the Presidential candidate of the Liberal Republicans. The Democratic Party also accepted the platform of the Liberal Republicans. The platform of the Liberal Republicans included adherence to the Thirteenth, Fourteenth and Fifteenth Amendments.

• Congress passed a sweeping Amnesty Act, which pardoned almost all of those made ineligible for office under the Fourteenth Amendment. Thus, the officials of the Confederacy could re-enter politics.

• The Freedmen's Bureau ceased to exist. African Americans could no longer rely on the Freedmen's Bureau for sustenance in an emergency. With the extinction of the Freedmen's Bureau, African Americans, often tenants of European American landowners, were often compelled to cease any political activity under threat of expulsion from the land.

• In 1872, George Washington established the town of Centralia, Washington, when the Northern Pacific Railroad crossed his land. Today in Centralia, Washington, a city park bears his name.

• P. B. S. Pinchback became Acting Governor of Louisiana on the impeachment of the Governor (December 9). Between December 9, 1872 and January 13, 1873, Pinchback served as Governor of Louisiana while Governor Henry Clay Warmoth was being subjected to impeachment proceedings.

• James T. Rapier of Alabama was elected to the United States House of Representatives.

• The first African American police officer was appointed in Chicago.

• Macon B. Allen was chosen, by the State General Assembly, as a judge of the Inferior Court of Charleston, South Carolina (November 26).

• In Chicago, Illinois, Mayor Joseph Medill appointed the first African American fire company of nine men.

• In 1872, Frederick Douglass was nominated as a vice-presidential candidate by the Woman Suffrage Association.

• *The Ku Klux Klan:* In March, pursuant to the Enforcement Acts, habeas corpus was suspended and Federal troops were mobilized in South Carolina to combat the activities of the Ku Klux Klan. Some 500 Klansmen were arrested, but only 55 were eventually convicted.

• The North Carolina Legislature enacted a law which granted pardons and amnesty for any crimes committed on behalf of European American secret organizations such as the Ku Klux Klan.

• Congress allowed the Ku Klux Klan Act to expire.

• *Notable Births:* Paul Laurence Dunbar (1872–1906), the nationally known poet and short story writer, was born (June 27).

He sang of life, serenely sweet,
With, now and then, a deeper note.
From some high peak, nigh yet remote,
He voiced the world's absorbing beat.
He sang of love when earth was young,
And Love, itself, was in his lays.
But ah, the world, it turned to praise
A jingle in a broken tongue.
                              "The Poet"

Paul Laurence Dunbar was born in Dayton, Ohio. Dunbar's father had been a slave on a Kentucky plantation before escaping to Canada before the Civil War.

After the outbreak of the Civil War hostilities, Dunbar's father joined the 55th Massachusetts Infantry. After the War, the elder Dunbar worked in Dayton as a plasterer.

Dunbar was educated in the schools of Dayton, and served as president of the Literary Society. In 1893, Dunbar published *Oak and Ivory.*

In 1894, Dunbar was employed by Frederick Douglass in the Haiti Building at the World's Columbian Exposition in Chicago. Dunbar's second book of poems, *Majors and Minors,* was published in 1895.

In 1896, *Lyrics of a Lowly Life,* was published, followed by *The Uncalled,* in 1898.

Dunbar was the first American poet to investigate the African American subculture and to handle its folk-life with any degree of fullness or comprehension. Ironically, the poetry reflected what is known as the "plantation school" influence. The "plantation school" was a group of southern Ku Klux Klan writers who, through novels like *Red Rock* and *The Clansman* perpetuated the myth of the ante-bellum South concerning the contentment of the slaves. Similarly, in Dunbar's poetry, the African Americans are also happily resigned to their condition in life. Expressing an attitude which would one day be perceived as being characteristic of Uncle Toms — of betrayers of the race —, Dunbar's poetic characters were often depicted complaining

about the ante-bellum days when they did not have the burden of freedom.

Unlike the "plantation school" writers, Dunbar's treatment of his characters and themes was far more sympathetic. Although Dunbar was not from the South, he was able to access the memory and experiences of his mother, a former slave, in eliciting a certain feel that runs through his work. With great artistry, Dunbar managed to idealize such rural experiences as spelling bees, church services, and cotton picking.

Dunbar's *Complete Poems* was published in 1913. His novels were *The Uncalled* (1896); *The Love of Landry* (1900); *The Fanatics* (1901); and *The Sport of Gods* (1902). He also wrote a one-act musical sketch, *Uncle Eph's Christmas* (1900).

One of the haunting facts of African American existence is that African Americans are often defined by what European Americans want them to be rather than by what they are. History is replete with examples of African Americans who have had to project a certain image in order to succeed. There are plentiful examples of such compromised African Americans even today.

History also records that as the times change, the more "modern" social critics have a tendency to treat such compromised individuals harshly. The compromised African Americans are often called "Uncle Toms" and their art and accomplishments become tainted. And yet, any such re-assessment is rarely accurate. There is often much more to the compromised African American than one can at first see.

The poetry of Paul Laurence Dunbar is an example of the artistry of a compromised African American. There is no question but that his dialect poetry — his "plantation school" poetry — is a type of poetry which would be greatly criticized today. And indeed, Dunbar himself grew to find that the acclaim afforded his dialect poetry was to some extent a badge of shame. As he wrote,

Because I had loved so deeply,
Because I had loved so long,
God in His great compassion
Gave me the gift of song.
Because I have loved so vainly,
And sung with such faltering breath,
The Master in infinite mercy
Offers the boon of Death.
                              "Compensation"

But in reading the non-dialect poetry of Paul Laurence Dunbar, one is often overwhelmed by the power and the Afro-centric pride that is exhibited in his verse. This man was no Uncle

Tom. This man was a man of insight and sensitivity — a blessed soul — whose expressed talent is truly a gift from God.

• William Monroe Trotter (1872–1934), a civil rights activist and editor, was born in Chillicothe, Ohio (April 7).

• *Notable Deaths:* 12 African Americans were reported to have been lynched in the South.

• Robert Duncanson (1820 [1817]–1872), a noted African American landscape artist, died.

Robert Duncanson was born in Cincinnati. His father was a Scotsman and his mother was a COTW. Duncanson studied in Canada, Great Britain and Scotland and first became prominent in Canada with his painting *Lotus Eaters.* In 1857, Duncanson returned to Cincinnati and painted commission portraits. During the Civil War, Duncanson stayed in England. While in England, he became very successful and included Tennyson and the Duchesses of Sutherland and Essex among his patrons. The *London Art Journal* of 1866 selected Duncanson as one of the outstanding landscapists of his day.

Duncanson also painted murals and historical subjects. Among his surviving historical paintings are *Shylock and Jessica, Ruins of Carthage, Lotus Eaters, Trial of Shakespeare,* and *Battleground of the Raison River.*

• *Miscellaneous State Laws:* Alabama's law against miscegenation was declared void by a state court. However, in 1877, the court reversed itself.

• Georgia instituted school segregation.

• *Miscellaneous Publications:* Frederick Douglass published *U. S. Grant and the Colored People.*

• William Still published the records of fugitive slaves in the classic book, *Underground Railroad.*

Between 1851 and 1861, William Still served as chairperson and corresponding secretary of the Philadelphia branch of the Underground Railroad. His account of the activities of the Underground Railroad was published in 1872 under the highly appropriate title of *Underground Railroad.*

• *Scholastic Achievements:* John Henry Conyers became the first African American admitted to the United States Naval Academy (October 21). Conyers did not graduate.

• Charlotte E. Ray (1850–1911), the first African American woman lawyer, graduated from Howard University Law School. She was the first African American woman to graduate from a law school. As a graduate of Howard Law School, Ray was automatically admitted to practice in the lower courts of the district and on April 23, Ray became the first African American woman admitted to practice before the district Supreme Court.

Charlotte Ray was born in New York City. Hampered by her gender and race in trying to establish a legal practice, she eventually became a teacher in the Brooklyn schools. Her father, Charles Bennett Ray, was a noted abolitionist, minister and editor. Ray's sister, Florence T. Ray (1849–1916) was an accomplished poet.

• Henry Fitzbutler (1842–1901) graduated from the Medical School of the University of Michigan. Born in Canada, Fitzbutler moved to Louisville, Kentucky, and began his practice of medicine. Fitzbutler was devoted to the cause of medical education for African Americans. In 1888, the Kentucky legislature granted Fitzbutler and his associates permission to establish a school of medicine, the Louisville National Medical College.

• *The Black Church:* Richard Henry Boyd organized the first Negro (African American) Baptist Association in Texas.

• In Los Angeles, California, Biddy Mason opened her house for the establishment of the first African Methodist Episcopal church.

• *Technological Innovations:* Elijah McCoy (1843–1929) earned a patent for a steam engine lubricator (July 2).

During his lifetime, Elijah McCoy was granted over 72 patents. Most of his inventions were related to lubricating appliances for engines. McCoy was a pioneer in the art of steadily supplying oil to machinery from a cup so as to render it unnecessary to stop a machine to oil it.

Many of McCoy's inventions were long in use on locomotives of the Canadian and Northwestern Railroads and on the steamships of the Great Lakes.

During his lifetime, McCoy's name became synonymous with quality machine work. The association of his name to quality led to the creation of an American phrase indicating that an article was genuine and good — that the article was "the real McCoy."

• T. J. Byrd received four patents for improvements or new devices related to coupling horses to carriages.

• *Black Enterprise:* George Washington founded the town of Centralia, Washington.

The town was founded when the Northern Pacific Railroad crossed his land.

• The African American owned Freedmen's Savings and Trust Company had 70,000 depositors.

• Rebecca J. Cole (1846–1922) established a medical practice in Pennsylvania. Cole was the first African American to graduate from the Female Medical College of Pennsylvania (1867). Cole practice medicine for fifty years in Philadelphia, Pennsylvania; Columbia, South Carolina; and Washington, D. C.

• *Sports:* Bud Fowler played for a Newcastle, Pennsylvania, professional baseball team.

THE AMERICAS

• *Brazil:* In 1872, the first general census of Brazil's population was performed. According to the census, the racial composition of the population of Brazil was 38.2% Euro-Brazilian, 19.7% Afro-Brazilian, and 42.2% mestizos or bi-racial.

• *Haiti:* Justin Lherisson (1872–1907), a novelist, was born in Port-au-Prince on February 10.

Justin Lherisson earned a degree in law and devoted his career to practicing law, journalism and teaching. As a history teacher, Lherisson published a textbook on the Spanish period. As a journalist, he was the founder of the periodical, *Le Soir.*

As a poet, Lherisson wrote two compilations of poems, *Les Chants de l'Aurore* (1893) and *Passe-temps* (1893). Lherisson was acclaimed for his two notable novels, *La Famille des Pititecaille* (1905) and *Zoune Chez sa Ninnaine* (1906). Justin Lherisson was praised for writing the text of the Haitian National Anthem, *La Dessalinienne.*

• Etzer Vilaire (1872–1951), a poet, was born in Jeremie (April 7).

Etzer Vilaire attended law school and wrote poetry in his free time. Vilaire joined the literary circle *La Ronde* and published several of his poems. Vilaire is acclaimed in Haitian literature for his ability to colorfully express the "soul" of his time. His poetry celebrates nature, love for the motherland, melancholy, Christianity, humanity, love and death. Among his acclaimed works are *Annees Tendres* (1907); *Nouveaux Poemes* (1910); *Dix Hommes Noirs* (1901); and *Page d'Amour* (1897).

• *Jamaica:* Richard Hill (1795–1872), an Afro-Jamaican scientist, judge, and champion of human rights, died.

EUROPE

• Robert Browning published *Fifine at the Fair.*

AFRICA

• *North Africa, Egypt and Sudan:* Ahmad Mumtaz Pasha was dismissed as governor of the Southern Sudan (October). He was replaced by Adham Pasha al-Arifi.

• Jafar Pasha Mazhar sent an expedition to Bahr al-Ghazal which was defeated by the trader Zubair Rahma Mansur.

• Ismail Pasha Aiyub became the governor general of the Sudan. During his tenure, Ismail Pasha Aiyub pursued a policy of economic retrenchment.

• Daniele Comboni was appointed Vicar Apostolic of Central Africa.

• The Verona Fathers took charge of missionary work in the Sudan.

• The Sanitary Council, a body composed of resident foreign diplomats, were charged with public health in Tangier.

• In 1872, Samuel Baker proclaimed an Egyptian protectorate over the Nyoro kingdom but was driven out by King Kabarega. *See 1893.*

• In 1872, the British general Charles Gordon *(see 1885)* accepted the Egyptian Khedive Ismail's appointment to replace Samuel Baker *(see 1893)* as governor of the Equatoria province of southern Sudan, arriving there two years later.

• *Western Africa:* The British took over the Dutch forts on the Gold Coast (April 6).

• There was a riot at Elmina (April 26).

• The Asantehene threatened the British with war (September 2).

• The Ashanti army departed from Kumasi (December 9).

• King Jaja set himself up as chief of Opobo.

• Blaise Diagne (1872–1934), the first "black" African to serve in the French Chamber of Deputies, was born.

Blaise Diagne was born on the island of Goree, off Dakar, to a Serer father and a Lebou mother.

In his early years, Diagne came under the

patronage of a wealthy metis. Diagne's patron sent him to a Catholic grammar school in France.

Once in France, Diagne became homesick. He returned to Senegal where he completed his education in Saint Louis in 1890.

In 1892, Diagne was hired by the French customs service and posted to various stations in West Africa. French assimilation theories had taught Diagne that as an educated African he would be accepted as an equal. However, in fact, Diagne was passed over for promotion because of his color. Disillusioned, Diagne frequently quarrelled with his supervisors. After serving for short periods in Reunion and Madagascar, Diagne was finally posted to French Guiana in South America where his supervisors felt he could cause no embarrassment.

Diagne married a French woman. In 1913, he went to France on leave. In France, he decided to return to Senegal to run for deputy to the French Chamber.

Senegal had been sending deputies to the French Chamber since 1848. The deputies that were sent had always been French colonists or metis. The indigenous Senegalese electorate had a reputation for selling its vote to the highest bidder.

In Senegal, Diagne allied with a group of nationalistic African civil servants. He procured the support of local political and religious leaders including the head of the Mouride sect, Ahmadu Bamba. The campaign centered largely on the race issue. Diagne's alliance triumphed and he became the first "black" African to achieve a high post in the government of a European imperial nation.

Diagne used his new position to institute a number of reforms in Senegal. One of Diagne's reforms was to buttress the right of French citizenship shared by inhabitants of the four communes of Senegal, namely Dakar, Saint Louis, Goree, and Rufisque. For some time, the French had been trying to undermine the citizenship rights of the Senegalese citizens.

In return for the increased enfranchisement, the Senegalese were subjected to military service. In 1918, France's manpower needs for World War I became desperate. Diagne agreed to become commissioner for recruitment of African troops. He was commissioned as the governor-general and secured an additional commitment from France that the social services in Senegal would be improved.

Diagne's recruitment efforts proved to be highly successful even though his involvement was criticized by other African leaders.

In 1919, with the war over and new elections pending, Diagne enlisted African veterans to form the nucleus of the Republican-Socialist Party, the first African party in a French sub–Saharan colony. Diagne was re-elected and his colleagues won the contests for municipal offices. Senegalese politics were for the first time dominated by "black" Senegalese.

French politicians and businessmen responded by uniting effectively to block Diagne's further attempts at social reform. In 1923, he was forced to compromise. Diagne signed the famous "Bordeaux Pact" by which he agreed to end his attacks on the Bordeaux merchants who controlled the Senegalese economy in return for their support. From the signing of the Pact, Diagne was thereafter, labelled as a conservative and was bitterly attacked by his African rivals, notably Lamine Gueye.

In 1928, Diagne recaptured his seat in the French Chamber of Deputies. However, this time his victory was attributed to the fact that the French rigged his election.

In 1930, at Geneva, Diagne defended France's hated forced labor policy. Diagne's loyalty had its rewards. The next year, Diagne was made under-secretary of state for the colonies.

During the depression, Diagne greatly aided Senegalese farmers by negotiating the first subsidies for their peanut crops.

By 1934, the year of his death, Diagne rarely visited Senegal. He had become a virtual Frenchman rather than an African.

• John Ezzidio, the first African to take part in representative government in Sierra Leone, died.

John Ezzidio was a Nupe (Nigerian) slave recaptured by the British while being transported to the Americas. Ezzidio was freed and sent to Freetown in Sierra Leone in 1827.

In Sierra Leone, Ezzidio became a prosperous trader and Methodist church leader, attracting the attention of Europeans. Some European sponsors sent Ezzidio to England in 1842. In England, Ezzidio obtained credit directly from exporters which enabled him to expand his commercial enterprises.

In 1845, Ezzidio was chosen mayor of Freetown, a position which, at the time, was a largely ceremonial position.

In 1863, the government created a legislative council, to which the mercantile community was permitted to elect a member. Voting was along racial lines, and Ezzidio was elected.

Ezzidio served on the legislative council until his death.

During the 1850s and 1860s, Ezzidio was a strong supporter of the Methodist Church. Ezzidio helped create an atmosphere of interfaith co-operation which long survived him.

John Ezzidio is deemed by historians to be a representative of the class of West African "self-made men" who flourished in the 1800s before the large European trading houses drove them out of business.

• Lawal (1797–1872), the ruler of the Fula emirate of Adamawa, died.

Lawal's father, Adama, had been sanctioned by Fula revolutionary 'Uthman dan Fodio to create the Adamawa emirate, at the southeastern limit of 'Uthman's empire. When Lawal succeeded Adama in 1848, the problems Lawal faced were essentially the same as those of his father — expansion of the emirate and suppression of rebellions.

Although Lawal was nominally under the control of 'Uthman's successors at Sokoto, the explorer Barth claimed that he ruled almost independently of them.

Lawal was a strict fundamentalist in matters of Islamic law; moral conduct and dress were closely regulated, and Lawal himself eschewed ostentation. Islamic schools were opened throughout the emirate.

Lawal died in 1872 and was succeeded by his brother, Sanda.

• Cleveland Luca, the founder of the Luca Family Quartet and the composer of the Liberian national anthem, died in Liberia (March 27).
• Edward James Roye, the fifth President of Liberia, died. {See 1871.}
• *Central Africa:* The Kibali basin was explored by Giovanni Miani.
• *Eastern Africa:* Werner Munzinger, the governor of Massawa (Ethiopia), calculated that about 1,000 slaves per year were being exported. The French Consul De Sarzec reported the arrival in Massawa of 500 slaves. De Sarzec also noted that a eunuch of the Egyptian Queen Mother had come to purchase 200 eunuchs *(see 1909)* and slaves.
• A hurricane devastated Zanzibar, Pemba and Mafia. Two-thirds of the clove and coconut plantations were destroyed.

In 1872, the troubles confronting the Zanzibari Sultan Barghash ibn Said were aggravated when a hurricane destroyed many of his island's valuable clove and coconut trees and sank most of his fleet. With both his military and economic position severely weakened, Barghash had to rely more closely on the British for support.

The British took advantage of Barghash's problems by coercing Barghash into negotiating an anti-slavery treaty. In 1872, Henry Frere, a former governor of Bombay, India, was sent to Zanzibar to negotiate an anti-slavery treaty with Sultan Barghash. In 1873, the negotiations were concluded with the execution of a treaty outlawing seaborn traffic in slaves.

• A regular monthly mail service to Zanzibar was begun by the British India Steam Navigation Company.
• Mbarak of Gazi rebelled and then swore allegiance to Zanzibar.
• Menelik corresponded with Victor Emmanuel II of Italy.
• Ras Kassa was crowned the new Emperor of Ethiopia and became Yohannes IV.

In 1868, Ras Kassa assisted the British expeditionary force under Robert Napier in the British campaign against Theodore (Tewodros). Napier was successful, and on his return march he rewarded Kassa with a large supply of firearms and ammunition. Ras Kassa's new weapons gave his army a considerable advantage in the ensuing struggle for the vacant imperial throne.

The first claimant to Tewodros' throne was the ruler of Lasta — an heir to the old Zagwe dynasty of Lalibela — who had himself crowned as Takla Giorgis III. When Takla moved against the Tigre province in 1872, Kassa crushed his army and seized the throne. Kassa had himself crowned emperor (negus nagast) at Axum and took the imperial name Yohannes (John) IV.

As emperor, Yohannes worked to restore the unity briefly achieved by Tewodros. Unlike Tewodros, however, Yohannes made fewer demands on his subject rulers, who resembled feudal lords. A devout Christian, Yohannes flirted with the idea of forcing the country's many Muslims to convert to Christianity. However, Yohannes abandoned this policy so as not to jeopardize national unification.

After Yohannes IV became the Ethiopian emperor, Menelik, the King of Shoa, maintained an uneasy autonomy in the south. Menelik expanded his control over the Galla-speaking regions and dealt with Europeans as an independent ruler, inviting foreign technical assistance and importing large numbers of modern firearms.

- Munzinger seized the Keren-Bilen region for Egypt.
- The Egyptian forces occupied Massawa.
- In 1872, Sir Samuel Baker proclaimed an Egyptian protectorate over the Nyoro kingdom (of Uganda) but was driven out by Kabarega, the King of the Nyoro.

In 1872, Samuel Baker arrived with Sudanese troops on behalf of the Egyptian government in order to gain control of the headwaters of the Nile. Kabarega made a bad impression on Baker. This initial bad impression permanently damaged Kabarega's reputation among Europeans and led Baker to ally himself with a rebel chief, Ruyonga, against Kabarega. Kabarega eventually drove Baker off, but the problem of Egyptian expansionism remained.

- *Southern Africa:* After Mpande's death in 1872, Cetewayo was proclaimed the King of the Zulus according to tribal custom. A coronation ceremony performed by Sir Theophilus Shepstone, British secretary of native affairs in Natal, was the key event marking Cetewayo's ascension to the throne.

Cetewayo was the eldest son of King Mpande. King Mpande had reigned from 1840 to 1872. Mpande's reign was mainly a period of peace and internal consolidation. Mpande never designated an heir to his throne and took little interest in his kingdom's political factions.

Cetewayo began to compete for political support twenty years before his father died. Cetewayo's main rival was Mbulazi, a half-brother by his father's favorite wife. Ignoring Mpande, Cetewayo and his brother freely organized their supporters into formal parties. Cetewayo had the advantage of living in the most populous part of the kingdom. Accordingly, his Usuthu party became three times larger than Mbulazi's Izigqoza party.

The rivalry erupted into civil war in 1856. Cetewayo virtually annihilated Mbulazi's faction at the Tugela River. Mbulazi was killed. From that moment, Cetewayo was the de facto ruler of Zululand. Cetewayo proceeded to purge other potential rivals. As for his father, Mpande continued to reign but only as a figurehead king.

Cetewayo became king in his own right in 1872, when Mpande died. In 1872, the Zulu were perhaps more closely united than at any time in their long history. Cetewayo's main concern was to forestall Afrikaner encroachments from the Transvaal Republic to the northwest.

Making an alliance with the British adminis-

tration in Natal the key to his foreign policy, Cetewayo invited Theophilus Shepstone, Natal's secretary for native affairs, to his official coronation in 1873. He also enlisted John Dunn to serve as an adviser on European affairs.

Anticipating war with the Transvaal Afrikaners, Cetewayo renovated the military system created by his uncle Shaka. He called up new regiments and reimposed rigid training and discipline.

In 1877, when Cetewayo perceived that the Transvaal people were unable to defeat the Pedi chief Sekhukhune in their own country, he proposed to Shepstone a joint Zulu-Natal invasion of the Transvaal. Shepstone declined. However, a few months later Shepstone personally annexed the Transvaal to the British crown in a bloodless coup. This move merged the governments of the Transvaal and Natal and destroyed the basis of Cetewayo's foreign policy, as Shepstone now endorsed Afrikaner claims on Zulu territory.

The renovation of Cetewayo's army alarmed Shepstone. Shepstone appealed to the new British high commissioner for South Africa, Bartle Frere, to launch a pre-emptive attack on the Zulu. Frere endorsed the idea as a positive step towards reconciling British and Afrikaner interests in South Africa. A Natal commission revealed that Afrikaner claims on Zulu territory were worthless, but Frere suppressed its report and cited minor incidents on the Zulu-Natal border to justify a belligerent policy.

In 1878, Frere issued Cetewayo an ultimatum to disband the Zulu army within thirty days. Cetewayo rejected the ultimatum and prepared for war. In early 1879, the British invaded. The British forces were commanded by Lord Chelmsford.

At the Battle of Isandhlwana, the Zulu wiped out a British column. However, this victory was short lived. The British soon received reinforcements and gradually wore down the Zulu forces. Chelmsford broke the last serious resistance at Cetewayo's capital in July of 1879, forcing Cetewayo to go into hiding.

Cetewayo was captured by Chelmsford's successor, General Wolseley. General Wolseley formally deposed Cetewayo and sent him to prison in Cape Town.

Despite their victory, the British did not annex Zululand. Instead, Wolseley divided the country among thirteen independent chiefs who were designated by Wolseley. Wolseley then appointed a resident for Zululand and left the Zulu to renew old factional rivalries.

In 1882, Cetewayo was released to go to London. In London, Cetewayo was lionized by the public and entertained by Queen Victoria. Cetewayo made a grand impression. In response, the British government decided to reinstate Cetewayo as King in Zululand where the political situation had deteriorated badly.

Upon his return to Zululand, Cetewayo found his position untenable. The British had separated northern Zululand from the rest of Zululand and had given it to Zibhebhu, Cetewayo's cousin and the leader of the rival Mandlakazi faction. The British had also separated part of south Zululand and placed it under John Dunn. But Cetewayo had no army to assert a claim to these separated lands nor did he have an army to enforce control over the lands which were ostensibly his. Factional infighting erupted.

Cetewayo was chased out of his capital and, by 1884, Cetewayo was dead.

Despite his ignoble end, Cetewayo remains one of the prominent African leaders of modern times. As a proud leader of the Zulu, his name reverberates in the annals of South Africa and in the annals of Pan-Africa.

• "Nkulumane" attempted to seize the Ndebele throne.

Nkulumane was the son of the Ndebele king, Mzilikazi *(see 1868)* by the daughter of another king, Zwide. Nkulumane was Mzilikazi's undisputed heir. Perhaps the greatest mystery in Ndebele history is what happened to Nkulumane around 1840 when the Ndebele settled in Zimbabwe. The Ndebele had migrated to Zimbabwe from the Transvaal in several parties. Mzilikazi's party was temporarily lost and many people thought him dead.

Nkulumane — although a minor — was installed as king in his father's place. When Mzilikazi rejoined his people he executed many of the officials responsible for the premature coronation. Whether he also had Nkulumane executed is debated. Mzilikazi's senior counselor Mncumbathe later claimed to have executed Nkulumane by his own hand. However, others claimed that Nkulumane had been sent into exile to await his succession to the kingship.

Mzilikazi died in 1868 without publicly resolving the mystery.

In the interregnum between 1868 and 1870 Nkulumane's fate became a political issue. A delegation went to Natal to search for him. These envoys found in the employ of the government official Theophilus Shepstone a man named Kanda. Kanda claimed to be a son of Mzilikazi but, at the time, denied that he was Nkulumane.

When the envoys returned to Matabeleland, another royal son, Lobengula, accepted the Ndebele crown and was installed. However, not all Ndebele were satisfied that Nkulumane was dead. Lobengula soon had to suppress a revolt led by a powerful military officer, Mbigo.

Back in Natal, Kanda changed his story and asserted that he was indeed Nkulumane. Kanda obtained the support of Shepstone and other Europeans interested in mining gold in Zimbabwe. Assuming he had merely to appear in Zimbabwe to be recognized as the Ndebele king, Kanda prepared for a triumphal entry. He collected some dissident Ndebele as supporters and went to the Ngwato capital at Shoshong. The Ngwato chief Macheng *(see 1873)* — whose own history provided Kanda with a legal precedent for his claims — lent Kanda troops.

In 1872, Kanda led a small force into Ndebele country. Quickly routed by Lobengula, Kanda beat an ignominious retreat to Shoshong. Soon thereafter, Kanda's Ngwato patron, Macheng, was himself overthrown. Kanda then fled to the Transvaal, where the republican Afrikaner government granted him asylum.

During the remainder of his life, Kanda was the focus for a few dissident Ndebele. The Transvaal government occasionally used his political claims as a lever in its dealings with Lobengula.

Kanda died in the Transvaal in 1883. A happier ending was invented by Henry Haggard whose novel *King Solomon's Mines* was partly inspired by Kanda's attempt to overthrow Lobengula.

* * *

When the Ndebele king Mzilikazi died in 1868, Macheng, the Ngwato chief, sought to increase his influence among the Ndebele in order to strengthen Ngwato claims on the disputed territory. Macheng gave material support to the Ndebele royal pretender "Nkulumane." In Kanda/Nkulumane, Macheng saw a man whose background was similar to his own.

Kanda/Nkulumane attempted to seize the Ndebele kingship in 1872. The result was a disaster. Macheng's former allies, the Kwena, turned against Macheng and assisted Kgama III to drive Macheng out of the Ngwato capital.

• On July 1, Thomas Francois Burgers was elected President of Transvaal.

In 1872, Burgers was invited to become president of the Transvaal when M. W. Pretorius resigned. Burgers' term of office was dominated by a costly and unsuccessful war against the Pedi chief Sekhukhune which demonstrated to the British the weakness of the republic.

*   *   *

The "Pedi" are a branch of the Sotho speaking peoples in northeastern Transvaal Province. The Pedi established a centralized state around the 17th century, but little is known of the rulers before the 19th century. The Pedi were conquered by the British during the latter's occupation of the Transvaal Republic beginning in 1877.

• In October, John Charles Molteno became the first premier — the first prime minister — of the Cape Colony.

Henry Barkly, the governor of the Cape Colony, oversaw the establishment of responsible parliamentary government in the Cape Colony in 1872. The head of this inaugural government was John Molteno who became prime minister.

During his tenure as prime minister, Molteno resisted regional factionalism. He promoted the expansion of the railway, organized the Colony's finances, and opposed imperial interference.

• Griqualand West was annexed to the Cape Colony.
• Sekgoma regained the throne of the Ngwato kingdom.
• Elliott Kamwana (c.1872–1956), the Christian separatist leader who introduced the Watch Tower movement to central Africa, is believed to have been born in this year.

Elliott Kamwana's first Christian affiliation was with the Free Church of Scotland Mission in northern Nyasaland (Malawi). It was with the Free Church of Scotland Mission in Nyasaland that Kamwana led a Presbyterian revival between 1899 and 1903. Kamwana was then baptized an Adventist by Joseph Booth.

Kamwana visited South Africa with Booth and there joined the Jehovah's Witnesses. On his return to Nyasaland in 1909, Kamwana introduced the Witnesses' Watch Tower Movement and preached that the millennium would come in 1914 when all Europeans were to leave Africa. Within a few months, Kamwana baptized more than 10,000 people. British authorities grew alarmed and sent him back to South Africa.

Kamwana next went to the lower Zambezi River in Mozambique and preached until 1914, when the Portuguese returned him to Malawi.

After the outbreak of World War I, the British blamed Kamwana for their difficulties in recruiting Africans into the army and imprisoned him in the Seychelles and Mauritius. The failure of the millennium to arrive in 1914 had only a slight impact on Kamwana's adherents.

Kamwana returned to Malawi in 1937 to find his movement still alive. Kamwana himself led a much reduced Watch Tower movement until his death in 1956.

• Mncumbathe, a leading Ndebele councillor and ambassador, is believed to have died in this year (1872).

Mncumbathe's origins are clouded in uncertainty. However, his position as hereditary regent in the Ndebele kingdom suggests that he was with Mzilikazi when Mzilikazi left Zululand around 1820.

Mncumbathe served as Mzilikazi's leading adviser for over forty years. In 1829, Mncumbathe was sent by Mzilikazi to Kuruman to establish diplomatic contact with the missionary Robert Moffat.

In 1835, Mncumbathe went to Cape Town to sign a treaty of friendship on Mzilikazi's behalf with the governor D'Urban. Although the Ndebele kingdom was highly militaristic, Mncumbathe's duties appear to have been strictly non-military.

After Mzilikazi's death in 1868, Mncumbathe became regent while a successor was chosen. Mncumbathe claimed to have personally executed the missing royal heir Nkulumane on Mzilikazi's orders around 1840. Mncumbathe's testimony concerning Nkulumane's execution enabled Lobengula *(see 1894)* to become king in 1870.

• Mpande (c.1800–1872), the longest ruling Zulu king, died.

Mpande was the third son of Senzangakhona to rule the Zulu kingdom. Mpande served his half-brother Shaka as a soldier during the early years of Zulu consolidation, but afterwards took little active part in Zulu affairs.

Mpande seemed to have been regarded as a fool. When another half-brother, Dingane, seized the kingship in 1828, Mpande was ignored as inconsequential during the ensuing purge of the royal family, and remained inconspicuous throughout Dingane's reign.

Mpande began to emerge as a leader in 1838 during Dingane's war with Afrikaner migrants — the trekkers. British traders based at Port Natal (Durban) attempted to capitalize on the disorder, but Mpande rebuffed them and razed their settlement.

Later in 1838, the Zulu under Dingane were defeated by the Afrikaners in a major battle. After this battle, Dingane attempted to shift the Zulu base into Swaziland. Mpande refused to support Dingane and remained behind with half of the Zulu army. Mpande allied with the fledgling Afrikaner republic at Natal, which recognized him as Zulu king. Early in 1840, Mpande's army met and defeated Dingane's forces and he became undisputed king of the Zulu.

Mpande began his reign as an Afrikaner vassal, but this relationship ended when the British occupied Natal and abolished the Afrikaner republic in 1843. The British made Natal a colony and recognized Mpande's independence in return for his cession of St. Lucia Bay — the only potential port in Zululand. About this same time, Mpande eliminated his last remaining brother, Gqugqu. Several thousand Zulu then panicked and fled into Natal under the leadership of his aunt, Mawa.

Mpande's long reign was a period of rebuilding after the exhausting wars of his predecessors. Two abortive attacks on the Swazi in 1853 and 1854 were the only notable campaigns initiated during his reign. Nevertheless, Mpande preserved the essentials of the military system.

Mpande eventually lost interest in internal Zulu politics and allowed divisive factions to arise by failing to provide for his own succession. He never officially took a "great wife" to beget his royal heir. As a result, Mpande's two oldest sons, Mbulazi and Cetewayo, were compelled to vie against each other for popular support.

In 1856, Cetewayo crushed Mbulazi's factions in an exceptionally bloody civil war. Afterwards, Cetewayo was generally acknowledged as the de facto ruler of the Zulu.

RELATED HISTORICAL EVENTS

• *Africa:* Donald Charles Cameron (1872–1948), a future governor of Tanganyika and Nigeria, was born.

After serving in the administrations of British Guiana and Mauritius, Donald Cameron joined the Nigerian civil service and became imbued with Frederick Lugard's ideas about indirect rule. From his service in Nigeria, Cameron was appointed governor of Tanganyika in 1925. In Tanganyika, Cameron organized the African civil service, introduced a legislative council, and blocked a proposed union of Tanganyika, Kenya and Uganda.

In 1931, Cameron returned to Nigeria to this time serve as governor. Once back, he immediately insisted on reforming administrative policy. Cameron felt that the then existing administrative policy ignored the positive, westernizing aspects of indirect rule as envisioned by his mentor Lugard.

Cameron was particularly concerned with the lack of development in the north. He believed that the government had permitted the creation of anachronistic fiefdoms.

Cameron's most significant reform was his abolition of the system whereby British administrators sat as judges. He substituted a separate judiciary branch.

Cameron articulated his concepts on indirect rule in his book *Principles of Native Administration and their Application. Principles of Native Administration and their Application* was published in 1934 and became a highly influential text among colonial administrators.

• Albert-Pierre Sarraut (1872–1962), a French statesman, colonial administrator, and colonial theorist, was born.

Albert-Pierre Sarraut served as governor of Indochina from 1911 to 1914 and from 1916 to 1917. He also served as French minister for the colonies from 1920 to 1924 and from 1932 to 1933. During his tenure as minister for the colonies, Sarraut was noted for his liberal views on colonial administration.

In 1923, Sarraut published *La Mise en valeur des colonies francaises*. In *La Mise en valeur des colonies francaises,* Sarraut argued that France should develop her colonies so that they could make a financial contribution to France as well as providing her with raw materials and manpower to combat Germany. The book has been compared to Frederick Lugard's *Dual Mandate in British Tropical Africa*.

Sarraut was premier of France in 1933 and 1936.

1873

THE UNITED STATES

1873 was notable as being the year of the Colfax Massacre. The Colfax Massacre took place in Colfax, Grant Parish, Louisiana, a town about 350 miles northwest of New Orleans. In 1873, the parish population was approximately 500 and it was evenly divided — half European American and half African American.

In the Louisiana elections of 1872, fraud was

claimed by both Democrats and Republicans. Both parties claimed that they had won the Governorship, and both gubernatorial candidates, McEnery, the Fusion Democrat claimant, and Kellogg, the Republican claimant, commissioned a judge and a sheriff for Grant Parish.

On March 23, 1873, Kellogg's — the Republican's — appointees arrived in Colfax and took possession of the courthouse. The Republican appointees were guarded by a contingent of armed African Americans. The presence of the armed African Americans helped to heighten the tensions in the area and several shooting incidents were reported toward the end of March and the beginning of April.

Christopher Nash, as the Democratic sheriff of Grant Parish, formed a posse of European American residents of the parish at Summerfield Springs, a town four miles north of Colfax. Nash also sent out a call for assistance to the neighboring parishes. Some 100 men answered his call.

On April 13, the armed European Americans entered Colfax and engaged the armed African American contingent. A battle ensued and after all-day fighting, the European Americans emerged victorious.

That evening the European Americans decided to reap additional vengeance against the African Americans who had dared to oppose them. The European Americans slaughtered the African Americans that they had captured. Over 60 African Americans lost their lives.

The next day, Federal troops were sent in. However, in a typical conspiracy of silence, the troops never caught any of the European American leaders who were responsible for the bloodshed.

• Seven African Americans were elected to the 43rd Congress: Robert B. Elliott, Richard H. Cain, Alonzo J. Ransier, J. H. Rainey, James T. Rapier, Josiah T. Walls and John R. Lynch.
• Alonzo J. Ransier, an African American and a South Carolina Republican, was elected to the House of Representatives. Ransier would work for civil rights protection, a national tariff, a six year presidential term, and funding to improve Charleston Harbor.
• From 1873 to 1875 Richard Harvey Cain, an African American, served in the House of Representatives as a representative of the State of South Carolina.
• John Roy Lynch, of Mississippi, was elected to the House of Representatives from 1873 to 1877 and again from 1881 to 1883.

In January 1873, P. B. S. Pinchback, of Louisiana, was elected to the United States Senate. Upon his arrival in Washington, D.C. to assume his post, Pinchback was refused his seat. One of the reasons why Pinchback was denied his seat in the Senate was the resentment caused by his marriage to a European American woman. Pinchback fought for three years to be seated — but he never was.

• Mifflin Wistar Gibbs (1823– 1915) was elected a municipal court judge in Little Rock, Arkansas.
• Sampson W. Keeble became the first African American member of the Tennessee state house of representatives (January 6).
• *Notable Births:* William C. Handy (1873–1957), the "Father of the Blues," was born (November 16).

William C. Handy was born in Florence, Alabama. He was the son of a minister. At school Handy came under the influence of a musician and refused to follow in his father's footsteps. Handy became a musician instead of a minister.

Handy purchased a cornet and began to study music. In his late teens, Handy left for Birmingham, Alabama, where he taught school and worked in the ironworks.

The Depression of 1893 put Handy out of work and, out of desperation, Handy organized a band of musicians which Handy took to the Columbian Exposition in Chicago.

Handy returned South after the exposition and became a bandleader with a successful minstrel group, Mohara's Colored Minstrels. He moved to Memphis and wrote the campaign songs for Mayor Edward Crump in 1909. These songs came to be known as *The Mayor Crump Blues* and they became the initial basis for Handy's national success when Handy transformed them into *The Memphis Blues.*

Over the next twenty years, Handy's music became a popular fixture on the American music scene. His *Evolution of the Blues* was performed in 1924 by Vincent Lopez at the Metropolitan Opera House in New York City — a notable achievement of the time.

By 1926, Handy had his own music publishing house and, in 1928, Handy's concert illustrating the development of African American music was deemed to be the pinnacle of his illustrious career.

Handy's most famous song is undoubtedly *The St. Louis Blues,* a song which Handy wrote in 1914 with the original title of *The Saint Louis Woman.*

   • William A. Harper (1873–1910), a protégé of Henry Ossawa Tanner, was born in Chicago, Illinois. Harper was educated at the Chicago Art Institute. He met Tanner in Paris and developed into a gifted landscape artist. His *Avenue of Poplars, Last Gleam, The Hillside,* and *The Grey Dawn* reflected a unique and promising talent. Unfortunately, his death in 1910 cut short what could have been a brilliant career.

   • J. Rosamund Johnson (1873–1954), an African American composer, was born (August 11).

J. Rosamund Johnson was born in Jacksonville, Florida, the son of a Baptist minister. He was the brother of James Weldon Johnson, another famous African American composer *(see 1871).* Both Johnson brothers received a good education and ultimately both attended the New England Conservatory of Music.

In 1900, Johnson began collaborating with Robert Cole. In 1902, the Cole-Johnson collaboration produced *The Red Moon,* a song which met with some success.

Among the early popular songs of Cole and Johnson were *Under the Bamboo Tree, Congo Love Song, Nobody's Looking but the Owl and the Moon,* and *My Castle on the Nile.*

After Cole's death, Johnson collaborated with his brother on *God's Trombones.* J. Rosamund also taught at the New York Conservatory of Music, and in the 1930s acted in *Porgy and Bess, Mamba's Daughters* and *Cabin in the Sky.*

   • "Bert" Williams (1873–1922), described by *Billboard* magazine as "the greatest comedian on the American stage" in the early 1900s, was born.

Bert Williams was born Egbert Austin Williams in Antigua, British West Indies. He moved to California with his family and studied civil engineering. He abandoned this engineering career, however, and, in 1895, formed a vaudeville team with George Walker.

Between 1895 and 1909, Williams and Walker starred in and produced vaudeville shows throughout the United States and England. They were famous for their characterizations with Walker posing as the dandy and Williams in black-face, using a "Negro dialect."

After Walker's death in 1909, Williams sang and toured for ten years with the Ziegfeld Follies.

Williams appeared in *In Dahomey* in 1902. *In Dahomey* opened in a Times Square theater and had a command performance during a tour abroad in 1903.

In 1914, Williams became the first African American to star in a movie, *Darktown Jubilee. Darktown Jubilee* is said to have caused a race riot when it was shown in Brooklyn. It was Williams' only movie.

Williams' trademark was the song *Nobody* which he wrote and sang.

During his career, Williams was something of an anomaly. The only African American in an almost entirely European American field, Williams' talent allowed him to transcend the anti–African American sentiment of the times. Bert Williams is widely regarded as being the greatest African American vaudeville performer in American history.

   • John W. Work, musician and African American folk singer, was born (August 6).

   • *Notable Deaths:* Charles Lenox Remond (1810–1873), a noted African American anti-slavery leader, died.

Charles Lenox Remond was born as a free African American in Salem, Massachusetts. In 1838, Remond was appointed an agent of the Massachusetts Anti-slavery Society. As an agent of the Society, Remond canvassed Massachusetts, Rhode Island, and Maine.

Remond became a delegate to the American Anti-slavery Society and attended the World Anti-slavery Convention in London in 1840. Afterwards, Remond lectured in England and Ireland on the subject of slavery. In 1841, he returned to the United States and continued his work. During the Civil War, Remond recruited African American men to serve as soldiers in the 54th Massachusetts Infantry, the first African American regiment to be sent into action during the war (and later the subject of a popular theatrical release entitled *Glory*).

   • *Miscellaneous Cases:* The United States Supreme Court in the *Slaughter-House Cases* (April 14, 1873) 83 U.S. 36, 21 L.Ed. 395, ruled that the Fourteenth Amendment privileges and immunities clause referred only to the inherent characteristics of United States citizenship. The minority opinion stated that the amendment applied to privileges and immunities which citizens enjoyed as citizens of states, agreeing with Congress that African Americans needed protection from hostile state laws.

• *Miscellaneous Publications:* Frances Ellen Watkins Harper published *Sketches of a Southern Life,* a series of verse portraits of African Americans in the South.

• Alberry Whitman published his first volume of poetry. It was entitled *Leelah Misled* and was an apolitical volume of verse.

• *Scholastic Achievements:* The Branch Normal School was founded at Pine Bluff, Arkansas. The school later became the Arkansas Agricultural, Mechanical and Normal College.

• Richard T. Greener, the first African American graduate of Harvard University, was named professor of metaphysics at the University of South Carolina.

• Patrick Henry Healy, the first African American to earn a Ph.D. degree *(see 1865),* was inaugurated as President of Georgetown University, the oldest Catholic university in the United States (July 31). {But see 1874.}

• Susan Maria Smith McKinney (Steward) was formally certified to practice medicine by the State of New York.

• *The Performing Arts:* The Colored American Opera Company of Washington, D. C. was organized. The opera troupe received critical acclaim for its production of Julius Eichberg's *The Doctor of Alcantara.*

• *Black Enterprise:* The Freedman's Bank of Charleston, South Carolina, reported having $350,000 in deposits and 5,500 depositors.

THE AMERICAS

• *Brazil:* Joaquim Machado de Assis *(see 1908)* published *Historias da meia-noite (Midnight Tales).*

• *Canada:* Anderson Abbott, the first Canadian-born person of African descent to receive a license to practice medicine in Canada, became president of the Wilberforce Educational Institute in Chatham, Ontario.

• *Cuba:* The rebel boat *Virginius* was captured and fifty-two crewmen, mostly Americans and Englishmen, were shot by Spanish authorities.

• *Haiti:* Fernand Hibbert (1873–1928), a novelist, was born (October 3).

Fernand Hibbert was born in Miragoane. He completed his education in Paris where he studied law and political science. On his return to Haiti in 1894, Hibbert performed several teaching, political and diplomatic functions. He earned national fame by publishing a rich collection of satiric, hilarious novels. Hibbert was one of the most widely read Haitian authors. His principal works are *Sena* (1905); *Les Thazar* (1907); *Romulus* (1908); *Masques et Visages* (1910); *Manuscrit de mon Ami* (1923); and *Simulacres* (1923).

• Faustin Soulouque (1788–1873), the ruler of Haiti, died.

Faustin Soulouque ruled Haiti for twelve years after a period of turmoil following a revolution that deposed President Jean-Pierre Boyer in 1843, ending a period of COTW domination that had begun with Alexandre Petion in 1806. The choice of Faustin Soulouque as president was made by the COTW-dominated Senate almost on a whim. They chose Soulouque in the belief that he would be completely subservient to the COTW political elite.

Soulouque was illiterate, superstitious, and widely recognized to be almost totally incompetent. He was born to slave parents who had newly arrived from Africa just before his birth. Soulouque managed to move up in the predominantly black army to become general of the Palace Guard of his predecessor, General Riche.

Soon, Soulouque made it clear that he was nobody's puppet. He named his own council of advisers and staffed the army with his own loyal black generals. Soulouque organized a secret police and a system of personal tyranny to ensure loyalty among his advisers and to suppress organized opposition. The COTWs, realizing their mistake, soon made an effort to get rid of Soulouque by military means.

The COTW revolution was brutally quashed. Most prominent COTWs were either executed or forced to go into exile.

With potential and actual opposition neutralized. Soulouque turned his attention to reestablishing Haitian domination of the Dominican Republic. The Dominican Republic had declared its independence from Haiti in 1844.

On March 9, 1849, Soulouque invaded the Dominican Republic. Soulouque's forces were defeated and had to retreat, leaving a path of pillage and destruction in their wake.

Despite the defeat, Soulouque declared the invasion a success and began a campaign to make himself emperor. Soulouque declared that his becoming emperor was the will of God.

On September 20, 1849, a new Haitian constitution was approved and Soulouque declared himself to be Emperor Faustin I. Black generals, eager for prestige, were provided with peerages, mostly in exchange for a fee; 4 princes, 59 dukes,

2 marquises, 90 counts, 215 barons and 30 chevaliers were awarded in the court of Faustin.

Under Faustin, voodoo, which had merely been tolerated by his predecessors, was openly practiced and encouraged by Soulouque and his wife, Adelina. Voodoo priests were installed in his household, and voodoo beliefs and practices became one of the pillars of the emperor's power.

Soulouque, always intent on re-capturing Santo Domingo, engaged in frequent unsuccessful but costly invasions. There was also enormous expenditure on court rituals and royal pomp. Corruption and graft were rampant. Soulouque's printing of money greatly devalued Haitian currency. Revenue was also raised through state monopolization of exports and imports, steep increases in import duties, and heavy taxes on capital.

With a world depression during 1857 hitting prices of coffee and cotton particularly hard, with corruption running rampant, a bankrupt treasury, and escalating international debt, Soulouque found himself isolated from his former supporters. In December 1858, Soulouque was deserted by one of his most trusted ministers, Fabre Nicholas Geffrard. Geffrard pronounced an end to the empire. Geffrard made Soulouque a virtual prisoner while becoming president by acclamation.

Soulouque and his family, after signing an Act of Abdication, left Haiti for Jamaica. Soulouque returned to Haiti in 1867 and lived there until his death in 1873.

- *Puerto Rico:* Slavery was abolished in Puerto Rico (March 23).

EUROPE

- Robert Browning published *Red Cotton Night-Cap Country, or Turf and Towers.*
- Alexandre Dumas, fils, published *The Wife of Claude.*

AFRICA

- *North Africa, Egypt and Sudan:* The Mixed Courts (*Tribunal Mixte*) were established in Egypt.
- The first girls' schools were opened in Cairo.
- A peace was reached with Bahr al-Ghazal. Zubair Pasha Rahma Mansur was made governor.
- Baker Pasha reached Gondokoro and then returned to England.
- Zubair Pasha invaded Darfur.

- Post offices were opened at Korosko, Wadi Halfa, Dongola, Berber and Khartoum.
- A hospital with 270 beds was constructed in Khartoum. Other hospitals were soon erected in other Sudanese provincial capitals.
- General George Gordon was appointed Governor of the Equatorial Nile Basin.
- The Egyptian General Staff, with the assistance of Americans, mapped the Sudan.
- Joubert's expedition commenced.
- *West Africa:* War erupted between the Ashanti and the British.

In 1871, the British secured a document which they claimed was signed by Kofi Karikari, renouncing the Ashanti's title as landlord of the British Elmina fort. The document was a forgery and resulted in an Ashanti attack on the British in 1873. General Garnet Wolseley led the combined British and Fante forces which repulsed the Ashanti, and then advanced into Kumasi, the Ashanti capital.

On February 9, the Ashanti army defeated the British at Assin Nyankumasi. However, by June 9, the first British reinforcements arrived and, on June 13, minor actions between the two nations occurred at Elmina.

On October 20, an ultimatum was sent to Asantehene. This was followed by a British attack at Abakrampa (November 5) and, on November 26, the British began an advance on Kumasi.

The Ashanti army, having lost some 40,000 troops primarily from disease, was forced to retreat before the advancing British forces. The retreat of the Ashanti emboldened its neighbors to begin assisting the British. Notably, Gbanya, the chief of the Kpa-Mende, sent a contingent of warriors of his own to aid the British in their war against the Ashanti.

After defeating the Ashanti, the British demanded a monetary indemnity and declared the entire area south of Ashanti a British colony. Much of the old Ashanti empire broke away. Kofi Karikari was shortly thereafter accused of robbing the royal tombs, and deposed.

- Major General Sir Garnet Wolseley was sworn in as Civil Administrator (October 2).
- *Central Africa:* Bunza was killed by his own nephew.
- Nangazizi was burned. Mangbetu was again divided.
- Lieutenant Grandy explored the River Congo.
- 456 boys and 33 girls, both African and European, were recorded as being enrolled in schools in Angola.

• Marche and de Compiegne explored the River Ogooue.

• *Eastern Africa:* Over a period of thirty days, British Vice-Consul Frederic Elton saw 4,096 slaves marching north from Tanganyika.

• J. Kirk became the British Consul at Zanzibar.

• V. L. Cameron departed from Bagamoyo to explore central Africa (March 15).

• A diplomatic mission under the leadership of Sir Bartle Frere to Zanzibar negotiated a treaty which prohibited the exportation of slaves and which closed the slave market.

• Mbarak of Gazi again rebelled.

• The last holder of the title Mwenyi Mkuu died (1873).

Mwenyi Mkuu is the dynastic title of the rulers of the Hadimu people of the island of Zanzibar. The Mwenyi Mkuu was the dominant political authority on Zanzibar prior to the invasion of the Omani Sultanate of Sayyid Said in 1840. The Mwenyi Mkuu continued to reign as a vassal of Sayyid Said and his successors until 1873 when the last holder of the title died.

• *Southern Africa:* Around 1873, it was reported that 400 pupils, of African and European stock, were enrolled in schools in Mozambique.

• John Henry de Villiers, the first local born Chief Justice of the Cape Colony, was appointed to the post.

• Molapo, the brother of the Sotho chief Letsie, greatly embarrassed Letsie in 1873 by betraying a non-Sotho chief, Langalibalele, to the European government. This incident gave the Sotho a reputation for untrustworthiness and seriously impaired Letsie's relations with other African rulers.

• Barnett Barnato, the future diamond baron, arrived in South Africa.

Several years after diamonds were discovered in Griqualand West, Barnett Barnato (a.k.a. Barney Isaacs) arrived at Kimberley and began to operate as a dealer in 1873. By the 1880s, Barnato controlled nearly half the industry.

• An Anglican synod was established at Cape Town.

• Macheng (c.1828–c.1873), a noted Ngwato chief, is believed to have died in this year.

Macheng's actual father was the brother of the deceased Ngwato chief Kgari Kgama. However, since Macheng's mother was the senior wife of Kgari, Macheng was recognized as the Kgari's legal son and heir.

During his youth, one of Macheng's half-brothers, Sekgoma Kgari, drove Macheng and his mother out of Ngwato country and usurped the chieftainship for himself. Macheng lived among the Kwena people until 1842, when he was captured by the Ndebele of Mzilikazi. Macheng was taken to present day Zimbabwe and raised as an Ndebele soldier.

However, his claim to the Ngwato chiefdom was not forgotten.

During the 1850s, the Kwena chief Sechele, anxious to influence Ngwato politics, appealed to the missionary Robert Moffat to obtain Macheng's release from the Ndebele. In 1857, Moffat secured Macheng's release and Macheng went back to Botswana.

Although he had been away from his people for over twenty years, Macheng was readily acknowledged by the Ngwato as their rightful ruler and the usurper Sekgoma was forced to abdicate in his favor.

As chief of the Ngwato, Macheng quickly made himself unpopular. He ignored his councillors and aroused fears that he wanted to impose a Ndebele style autocracy. By 1859, Macheng was deposed and Sekgoma was made chief again.

Macheng returned to the Kwena.

Sekgoma also came to be an unpopular chief with the Ngwato people. Sekgoma was deposed in 1866 and Macheng became chief a second time.

A few years later, the discovery of gold on the Ngwato-Ndebele border produced a serious border conflict. When the Ndebele king Mzilikazi died in 1868, Macheng sought to increase his influence among the Ndebele in order to strengthen Ngwato claims on the disputed territory. Macheng gave material support to the Ndebele royal pretender Nkulumane. In Nkulumane, Macheng saw a man whose background was similar to his own.

With Ngwato aid, Nkulumane attempted to seize the Ndebele kingship in 1872. The result was a disaster. Macheng's former allies, the Kwena, turned against Macheng and assisted Kgama III to drive Macheng out of the Ngwato capital.

Macheng died in obscurity around 1873.

• Macoma (1798–1873), a prominent Xhosa leader during the 1834–1835 Frontier War with the British, died.

Macoma was the eldest son of the Rarabe Xhosa paramount chief Ngqika. However, he was the son of a junior wife and was, therefore, not eligible for succession.

Macoma distinguished himself in a war with the breakaway chief Ndlambe. Afterwards, Macoma opposed the settlement his father made with the Cape Colony to create a "neutral territory" in the frontier zone.

During the 1820s, Macoma violated the neutral territory by settling in it with his own followers. From the neutral territory, Macoma launched raids against the European settlers and the neighboring Thembu for cattle.

In 1829, a colonial force drove Macoma's people east. Later that year, Macoma's father died. Macoma's half-brother Sandile was Ngqika's successor, but as Sandile was a minor, Macoma, two of his brothers, and his mother were named to form a regency.

Macoma quickly became the most powerful leader among the Rarabe. Friction with the European settlers and the Cape government continued and a drought in 1834 accentuated the pressure on Rarabe land.

In late 1834, Macoma led the biggest Xhosa invasion ever against the eastern Cape Colony in a futile attempt to push back European settlement. The result was a Xhosa defeat and a brief Cape annexation of the Rarabe territory in the present Ciskei known as the "Queen Adelaide Province."

In 1840, Macoma's brother, Sandile, formally acceded to the chieftainship and Macoma's influence began to decline. Macoma applied to the British for permission to retire to the Cape Colony, but he was refused.

During the 1846 Frontier War, Macoma was the first Rarabe chief to sue for peace with the British. The Ciskei was again annexed this time by the British imperial government. Macoma resumed his defiance of the British and strongly supported the prophet Mlanjeni during the Frontier War of 1850.

In 1853, Macoma played a leading role in the Rarabe negotiations with British governor George Cathcart as the 1850 Frontier War came to an end.

In 1856, Macoma supported the great cattle killing initiated by the Gcaleka Xhosa prophet Mhlakaza to effect a religious solution to Xhosa problems. Afterwards he was accused by the British of having led the Xhosa into a desperate situation in order to incite a war with the Cape Colony even though no hostilities actually resulted from his actions. Nevertheless, Macoma was imprisoned on Robben Island.

Macoma died on Robben Island in 1873.

RELATED HISTORICAL EVENTS

• *Africa:* Sydney Percival Bunting (1873–1936), a noted Communist leader in Africa, was born.

Sydney Bunting first arrived in South Africa as a British lieutenant in the South African War (1899–1902). After the war, Bunting remained in Johannesburg, where he became a lawyer. As a lawyer, Bunting became active in radical labor organizations and he became a champion for African rights.

After World War I, Bunting visited Communist Russia. It was during this trip that Bunting became a Communist.

Upon his return to South Africa, Bunting established and led the Communist Party of South Africa. During the 1920s, he worked to build up the Indigenous African membership in the Communist Party. It was due to these efforts that Bunting soon found himself in trouble with the Euro-African South African regime and with the International Communist movement because of his independent behavior.

Bunting was expelled from the Communist Party in 1931.

• Dr. David Livingstone, a Scottish explorer of Africa, traveller and writer, died near Lake Bangweulu (April 30).

David Livingstone (1813–1873) was a Scottish doctor and missionary who is considered to be one of the most important explorers of Africa.

Livingstone was born on March 19, 1813, in Blantyre, Scotland. In 1823, Livingstone began to work in a cotton-textile factory. Later, during his medical studies in Glasgow, Livingstone also began attending theology courses. In 1838, Livingstone offered his services to the London Missionary Society. Upon the completion of his medical course in 1840, Livingstone was ordained and was sent as a medical missionary to South Africa.

In 1841, Livingstone reached Kuruman, a settlement founded in Bechuanaland (Botswana) by the Scottish missionary Robert Moffat (1795–1883).

Livingstone began his missionary work among the Africans of Bechuanaland (the Kwena of Sechele) and began to make his way northward despite opposition from the Boer settlers of the region. In 1845, he married his mentor's daughter, Mary Moffat, and together they traveled into regions where no Europeans had ever been before.

In 1849, Livingstone crossed the Kalahari

Desert and became the first European to see Lake Ngami. In 1851, accompanied by his wife and children, Livingstone became the first European to encounter the Zambezi River. At the Zambezi, Livingstone met the Kololo king Sebitwane. Livingstone became enthused by the idea of opening a mission among the Kololo. He thereafter set as his life's work expanding Christian frontiers in Africa.

On another expedition (1853–1856), while looking for a route to the interior from the east or west coast, Livingstone traveled north from Cape Town to the Zambezi River, and then west to Luanda on the Atlantic coast. Livingstone then retraced his journey to the Zambezi. On this expedition, Livingstone again visited the Kololo. By this time, the Kololo were ruled by Sebitwane's son, Sekeletu. It was with the aid provided by the Kololo that Livingstone was able to walk to Luanda on the Atlantic coast and then to Quelimane on the east coast.

On the trip to the east, Livingstone followed the Zambezi River to the point where it emptied into the Indian Ocean. In the process, Livingstone was the first European to cast his eyes upon the glory of the great Victoria Falls.

Livingstone's explorations resulted in a revision of the European's understanding of the African continent and enable cartographers to give definition to what was then largely unknown territory. Upon his return to Great Britain in 1856, Livingstone was welcomed as a great explorer and his book *Missionary Travels and Researches in South Africa* (1857) made him famous.

Livingstone's lectures inspired the immediate founding of the Universities' Mission to Central Africa. His own London Missionary Society launched missions to the Kololo and to the Ndebele of Mzilikazi. Royalties from his popular book made Livingstone independently wealthy. Livingstone soon thereafter resigned from the London Missionary Society.

In 1858, the British government appointed Livingstone Consul to Quelimane (Mozambique) and made him the commander of an expedition to explore east and central Africa. Upon his return to Africa, Livingstone led an expedition up the Shire River, a tributary of the Zambezi. On this expedition, Livingstone became the first European to see Lake Nyasa. Then, in 1859, Livingstone explored the Rovuma River and "discovered" Lake Chilwa.

During these later explorations, Livingstone became concerned with the plight of the Indigenous Africans who were being exploited by Arab and Portuguese slave traders. In 1865, while on a visit to England, Livingstone wrote *Narrative of an Expedition to the Zambezi and Its Tributaries*. In this book, Livingstone issued a condemnation of the still thriving slave trade and offered an expository on the commercial possibilities of the east African coast.

In 1866, financed mostly by friends and admirers, Livingstone led an expedition to discover the sources of the Nile. Traveling along the Rovuma River, the explorer made his way toward Lake Tanganyika, reaching its shores in 1869.

During this Nile expedition, little was heard from Livingstone and his welfare became a matter of international concern. In 1870, Livingstone journeyed to Ujiji, on Lake Tanganyika, into the region lying west of the lake, thereby becoming the first European to visit the Lualaba River (in present day Zaire).

After enduring great privations, Livingstone made his return to Ujiji. Upon his arrival, he was met by a "rescue party" led by Henry Morton Stanley, a European American journalist. The story goes that at this meeting Stanley reportedly greeted Livingstone with the famous question, "Dr. Livingstone, I presume?"

Stanley and Livingstone went on to explore the country north of Lake Tanganyika together. Upon Stanley's return to England, he portrayed Livingstone as a saintly martyr in the cause of African redemption and Livingstone achieved legendary status.

Later Livingstone set out on his own again to continue his search for the source of the Nile.

Livingstone died in Chitambo's village (in Zambia) sometime around April 30, 1873. His body was found on May 1. Livingstone's African followers cut out his heart and buried it at the foot of the tree where his body was found. They then transported his body first to Zanzibar and accompanied the body all the way back to England. A fitting tribute to this great man.

In 1874, Livingstone's remains were finally laid to rest in Westminster Abbey.

Livingstone's name reverberates through history as a great explorer of the continent of Africa. But his name reverberates through African and African American history because of his poignant opposition to the east African slave trade.

• Leo Frobenius (1873–1938), the German discoverer of the famous bronze sculptures at Ife (the Yoruba fatherland), was born.

The anthropological field work of Leo Frobenius included twelve trips to Africa from 1904 to 1935. From these trips, Frobenius brought back to Germany many valuable pieces of Ife art.

Frobenius' many anthropological writings posited the diffusionist theory that the cultures of West Africa and Oceania stemmed from one source. Frobenius also theorized that southern Nigerian culture was influenced by Mediterranean culture in the first millennium B.C.E.

1 8 7 4

THE UNITED STATES

• Martin Robinson Delany was nominated for Lieutenant Governor of South Carolina on the Independent Republican ticket, but was defeated in the election.

• Blanche Kelso Bruce, of Mississippi, was elected to the United States Senate. Bruce was the only African American to serve a full term in the United States Senate during the Reconstruction Era. Bruce was chosen by the Republican Party caucus to run for the Senate after receiving some 52 of the 80 caucus votes cast. Bruce was elected on February 3.

• Joseph Hayne Rainey became the first African American to preside over the proceedings of the House of Representatives.

• Charles E. Nash, of Louisiana, was elected to the House of Representatives. He would serve only one term.

• Jeremiah Haralson, an African American from Alabama, was elected to the House of Representatives in 1874. Accused of fraud and of maintaining a close friendship with Jefferson Davis, the former President of the Confederacy, Haralson only served two terms.

• Governor Ames, a Republican, dismissed the ex–United States Senator Hiram Revels from his position as president of Alcorn College.

• The Democratic Party regained control of Alabama, Arkansas, and Texas.

• Virginia again reapportioned its election districts, thereby minimizing the African American vote. Virginia also abolished the New England township system, thus seizing control of local government especially those towns which were under the control of African Americans.

• *Notable Births:* Charles Clinton Spaulding (1874–1952), an insurance magnate, was born.

• *Notable Deaths:* Robert C. De Large (1842–1874), a Reconstruction Congressman from South Carolina, died.

Robert C. De Large was born a slave in Aiken, South Carolina. With some education, he became a successful planter in South Carolina during the Reconstruction era. Elected first to the South Carolina State Legislature, De Large subsequently was elected to the United States Congress in 1871.

During his term in office, De Large returned to South Carolina to investigate voting irregularities which occurred during his own election. The House Commission on Elections declared his seat vacant in 1873.

De Large became a Charleston city magistrate in 1873. He would serve in this capacity for only one year. He died in 1874.

• William C. Nell (1816–1874), publisher of *Services of Colored Americans in the Wars of 1776 and 1812,* the first full length study of the African American soldier, died.

William Cooper Nell (1816–1874) was born in Boston, Massachusetts, the son of William G. Nell and Louisa Nell. He attended a primary school for African American children and, ultimately, read law in the office of William I. Bowditch. Nell became affiliated with the antislavery movement, but concentrated his efforts on opening public schools for the education of African American children.

In 1851, Nell assisted Frederick Douglass in the publication of the *North Star.* His pamphlet *Services of Colored Americans in the Wars of 1776 and 1812* was published in May of 1851.

In 1855, *Colored Patriots of the American Revolution,* with an introduction by Harriet Beecher Stowe, was published.

Nell became the first African American to hold a civil service post under the Federal Government when he was made a postal clerk by John G. Palfrey, the postmaster of Boston.

• Victor Sejour (1817–1874), a Creole poet and dramatist, died.

Victor Sejour was born in New Orleans. In 1834, Victor was listed on the membership role of an organization of free African American mechanics. The organization was called "Les Artisans." But Victor's destiny lay in another "artistic" arena.

Victor's parents sent him to Paris to study in an attempt to avoid Victor being handicapped by the social disadvantage of his race. In Paris, Victor became enchanted with the theatre. He frequented drama circles and was often in the company of successful dramatists such as Dumas *(see 1870)* and Emile Augier. In 1844, Le Theatre-Francais produced Sejour's first play. The play was entitled *Diegareas* and it launched Sejour on to a successful career. Sejour became one of the most commercially successful dramatists in Paris during the 1800s and on this basis rests his claim to fame.

> • *Miscellaneous Publications:* William Wells Brown published *The Rising Son, or the Antecedents and the Advancements of the Colored Race.*
> • William Still published *An Address on Voting and Laboring.*
> • *Scholastic Achievements:* Archibald Henry Grimke received an LL.B. (bachelor of laws) degree from Harvard Law School.
> • Patrick F. Healy, an African American priest and a member of the renowned Healy family was inaugurated as president of Georgetown University in Washington, D. C.

1874 marked two notable achievements for one very notable African American family. In 1874, James Augustine Healy was appointed bishop of Maine while in this same year his brother, Patrick Francis Healy was inaugurated as president of Georgetown University in Washington, D. C.

The Healy family was one of the most distinguished families in African American history. In addition to James Healy, two other Healy brothers became ordained Catholic priests: Alexander Sherwood Healy was ordained for the diocese of Massachusetts while Patrick Healy was ordained in Belgium. One of their sisters, Eliza became a nun (Sister Mary Magdalen) and a notable school headmistress, and another brother, Michael Alexander Healy, became a captain in the United States Revenue Cutter Service, the forerunner to the United States Coast Guard.

The three Healy brothers, James, Patrick and Michael would leave the most indelible marks. James would ascend the Catholic faith hierarchy to become the Bishop of Portland, Maine. Patrick would earn a Ph.D. from Louvain University in Belgium and would eventually become the President of Georgetown University. Michael, while serving in the Revenue Cutter Service, would become the de facto chief law enforcement officer in the coastal waters of Alaska. As such, Michael would serve as the model for Jack London's *Sea Wolf* (see also James Michener's *Alaska*).

Two of the factors contributing to the Healys'

success were the support of their parents and the relative acceptability afforded to them due to the color of their skin. The Healys were born to an Irish planter (Michael Morris Healy) and a COTW slave (Mary Eliza Smith) on the Healy plantation near Macon, Georgia. Unlike other plantation owners, Michael Morris Healy genuinely cared for his COTW children and took pains to see that they received an education. This care and education enabled the Healys to attain a measure of success.

As for the color of their skin, it is an unavoidable fact of history that part of the reason for the Healys success was attributable to the fact that the color of their skin was more European in appearance than African. While the racial identity of the Healys was not concealed, neither was it widely broadcast. Their fair skinned appearance no doubt contributed in no small measure to the Healys' ability to attain a measure of success which was uncommon for their darker skinned contemporaries.

> • Edward Alexander Bouchet (1825–1918) received a doctorate from Yale University (November). Bouchet's graduate work in physics was supported by the Institute for Colored Youth of Philadelphia, the institution with which Bouchet was associated for twenty-six years as a teacher of chemistry and physics.
> • Alabama State University was founded at Salem, Alabama, as the State Normal School and University for Colored Students and Teachers. The school was established to train African American teachers. The institution would move to Montgomery, Alabama, in 1887.
> • *The Black Church:* In 1874, James Augustine Healy was appointed bishop of Maine and was consecrated in the Cathedral at Portland, Maine, on June 2, 1875.
> • *The Arts and Sciences:* In 1874, Justin Holland published *Comprehensive Method for the Guitar,* a book which became recognized as a fundamental text for guitar playing.
> • *Technological Innovations:* Elijah McCoy received a patent for an ironing table.
> • *Black Enterprise:* By 1874, Georgia African Americans owned more than 350,000 acres of land.
> • In 1874, Frederick Douglass was elected president of the Freedmen's Saving and Trust Company as a last ditch effort to save the bank failed. The Charleston branch of the bank owed over $250,000 to 5,296 depositors

while the Beaufort, South Carolina branch owed $77,000 to some 1,200 depositors.

THE AMERICAS

• *Brazil:* Joaquim Machado de Assis published *A mao e a luva* (The Hand and the Glove).

• *Canada:* Anderson Abbott, the first Canadian-born person of African descent to receive a license to practice medicine in Canada, became the coroner for Kent County in 1874.

• *Haiti:* Nissage Saget relinquished the Executive seat and retired to Saint-Marc. The Constituent Assembly elected General Michel Domingue who as President promulgated the Constitution of 1874, seven years after the former Constitution of 1867.

• James Theodore Holly (1829–1911) was elected Episcopal Bishop of Haiti. Holly held this position until his death in 1911.

As rector of Saint Luke's Episcopal Church in New Haven, Connecticut, Holly baptized W. E. B. Du Bois in 1868. Holly championed African American emigration and dreamed of establishing a colony in Haiti. Holly's consecration made him the first person of African descent to serve as bishop in the Episcopal church.

• Stenio Vincent(1874–1959), a future president of Haiti, was born.

Stenio Vincent was a member of the COTW elite of Haiti. Vincent had an extensive career as a lawyer and diplomat. He served in Paris, Berlin, and the Hague.

During the United States occupation, Vincent headed the anti-interventionist Nationalist Party and the Patriotic Union. The Patriotic Union was a major advocate for the withdrawal of United States troops from Haiti.

In November 1930, Vincent was elected president by the National Assembly, and, in 1934, Vincent visited the United States and convinced President Franklin D. Roosevelt to withdraw the United States Marines occupation force. In 1935, Vincent's tenure in office was extended for five years by a referendum.

As president, Vincent was widely regarded as anti-black. He was particularly suspicious of the army which the United States Marines had left behind because the army was predominantly officered by blacks. Vincent built up his own special presidential guard, and his policy was to deposit the army's weapons in the presidential palace.

When, in 1941, Vincent again sought to have

his period in office extended, the United States government suggested that another extension would be unwise.

Vincent finally retired, pleading "ill health," giving way to President Elie Lescot, another member of the COTW elite.

• *Puerto Rico:* Bibliophile, journalist and lecturer Arthur A. Schomburg (1874–1938) was born in Puerto Rico (January 24).

AFRICA

• *North Africa, Egypt and Sudan:* Zubair Pasha destroyed the Darfur army at Shaka (January).

• General George Gordon arrived in Egypt (February). In March, Gordon went to Khartoum and proceeded to establish a series of military outposts from Gondokoro to within sixty miles of Lake Victoria.

In 1872, Gordon accepted the Egyptian Khedive Ismail's appointment to replace Samuel Baker *(see 1893)* as governor of the Equatoria province of southern Sudan, arriving there two years later.

In Equatoria, Gordon continued Baker's work of suppressing the slave trade. He extended Egyptian administration in the area and attempted to impose an Egyptian protectorate over Uganda.

• The *Ruznameh* tax was imposed in Egypt.

• The Egyptian railway reached Asyut.

• The Sudan Railway was inaugurated.

• El Fasher was occupied (November 2).

• Paul Soleillet's expedition began.

• A Moroccan military campaign against the Rif was initiated.

• D. Mackenzie established a factory at Tarfaya, Morocco.

• Ceuta was made the seat of the Spanish Captania General de Africa.

• Mustafa Kamil (1874–1908), an Egyptian nationalist, was born.

• *Western Africa:* The war between the British and the Ashanti came to an end.

On January 31, the British defeated the Ashanti at Amoafo. Wolseley entered Kumasi and found the town evacuated (February 4). He released the Fante prisoners who were still in the town and the Fante burned the town down. Wolseley then returned to the coast (February 6).

On February 13, the Asantehene agreed to pay a fine to the British as well as agreeing to free trade; to end the practice of human sacrifice;

and to open the road to Kumasi. This treaty was executed at Cape Coast on March 14.

• Lagos (Nigeria) was put under the auspices of the Governor of the Gold Coast Colony while the colony of Sierra Leone became a separate colony in its own right.

• *Central Africa:* Nyangwe came under the control of Tippu Tib.

• Beginning in 1874, George Grenfell initiated his explorations of Cameroon.

• Henry Stanley began his exploration of the Congo.

Stanley's 1874–1877 exploration of Africa was one of the single most productive explorations ever undertaken in Africa. During this exploration, Stanley resolved many questions about the great African lakes system and traced the Congo (Zaire) River to its mouth. Along the way, Stanley visited the Ganda king Mutesa I.

During his visit with Mutesa, Stanley assisted Mutesa in a local war, and persuaded Mutesa to invite Christian missionaries to Uganda in 1875. In an incident which tarnished his reputation, Stanley was responsible for the massacre of a party of Africans.

From Uganda, Stanley entered present day Zaire and joined the Swahili trader Tippu Tip down the Congo River. Stanley's trans-continental journey revealed to Europe the commercial possibilities of Zaire.

• Savorgnan de Brazza commenced his exploration of the Osgooue and Alima rivers along with the Congo basin.

• The exploration of Angola and the Congo by Pogge and Linx began. Their explorations would take them as far as Katanga.

• V. L. Cameron explored Katanga.

• *Eastern Africa:* V. L. Cameron reached Lake Tanganyika (February 18).

• Henry Stanley's second expedition departed from Bagamoyo (November 17).

• Yohannes IV appealed for Russian help against the Muslims. He received no reply.

• Edward Steere, a theologian, linguist, printer and architect, was appointed Anglican Bishop of Zanzibar.

• *Southern Africa:* The campaign began for the confederation of South Africa.

• Mbandzeni succeeded his father Mswati as king of Swazi in 1874 after a long and bitter succession dispute. Mbandzeni first attempted to continue his father's policy of allying with the Transvaal Republic against the Zulu kingdom, but later found his posi-

tion largely dictated by the Anglo-Afrikaner struggle for mastery in South Africa.

The ruling dynasty of the modern Swazi kingdom is the Ngwane (Nkosi Dlamini) clan. The Ngwane clan traces its chiefs back as much as 400 years.

Under Ngwane III, who reigned in the late 1700s, the Dlamini settled in the southeast of present day Swaziland. Ngwane's successors built the small northern Nguni chiefdom into a powerful state.

The Swazi lost their independence during the 1890s, when the neighboring Transvaal Republic attempted to annex their country in its drive to secure a sea port. The British annexed Swaziland in 1902.

The British restored Swazi independence in 1968 with Sobhuza II reigning as a constitutional monarch.

• In Mozambique, Cypriano Caetano Pereira (Kankuni) became king of the Makanga kingdom. Cypriano allied with the Portuguese government, thus obtaining arms which he used against his neighbors, while maintaining his independence.

• Around 1874, Manuel Sousa, an Indo-Portuguese adventurer, was recognized as the titular sovereign of Manica. During this year, he also married a daughter of the ruler of Barue. Sousa would later use this connection to place his infant son on the Barue throne with himself acting as regent. This regency essentially made Sousa the de facto ruler of the entire region between the Pungwe and Zambezi Rivers.

• Kgamanyane (c. 1820s–1874), the ruler of the Kgatla, died.

In 1848, Kgamanyane succeeded his father Pilane as chief of the Kgatla branch of the Tswana. His ascension came at a time when the Afrikaners were building the Transvaal Republic around his territory. At first, Kgamanyane accommodated the Afrikaners. He even assisted them in their campaigns against other chiefs. However, Kgamanyane resisted involuntary recruitment of his men as laborers. As a consequence, Kgamanyane was publicly flogged by the Transvaal government in 1869.

The humiliation of being flogged made Kgamanyane's position in the Transvaal untenable. He was compelled to move into the lands which comprise the present day Botswana. It was there that the Kwena chief Sechele allowed Kgamanyane's followers to settle at Mochudi in 1871.

Kgamanyane was not popular among all his people, some of whom remained in the Transvaal. In Botswana, Kgamanyane soon clashed with the Kwena ruler over the issue of sovereignty. Kgamanyane died before the war broke out, and was succeeded by his son Lentswe.

• Letsholathebe (c.1820–1874), the chief of the Tawana, died.

The Tawana broke from the Ngwato in the late 18th century. The Tawana then moved into northern Botswana. While Letsholathebe was a child his people were conquered by the Kololo of Sebitwane during the latter's march north. Letsholathebe escaped with his mother and became a fugitive.

Meanwhile, Letsholathebe's father, Sedumendi, was killed by Sebitwane and many Tawana fled to Lake Ngami, where they settled.

Eventually, Letsholathebe was found and made chief. He rallied refugee Tawana at the lake. The lake's complex water system was used for defensive purposes.

Kololo harassment finally ended in 1864, when Sebitwane's successor Sekeletu was overthrown by the Lozi. Many Kololo then found refuge under Letsholathebe.

Letsholathebe further strengthened his chiefdom by developing a profitable trade with Europeans on the Atlantic coast. His son and successor, Moremi II, used breechloading rifles obtained through this trade to repel two major attacks by the Ndebele of Lobengula. The autonomy of the Tawana was guaranteed by the establishment of the Bechuanaland Protectorate in 1885.

RELATED HISTORICAL EVENTS

The United States

• Charles Sumner (1811–1874), the great European American advocate of African American rights, died.

Charles Sumner was a statesman and anti-slavery leader. Sumner was born in Boston, Massachusetts.

After a career as a lawyer who championed anti-slavery causes, in 1851, Charles Sumner was elected to the United States Senate. In 1856, Sumner made a Senate speech which included several sneering references to Senator Andrew P. Butler of South Carolina. Three days later, Representative Preston S. Brooks, Butler's nephew, attacked Sumner in the Senate, beating Sumner senseless.

Sumner was one of the founders of the Republican Party. Sumner favored freeing the slaves and giving them the right to vote.

As the Civil War neared its end, Sumner advocated treating the South harshly. He opposed President Lincoln's moderate plans for the reconstruction of the South. Later Sumner also opposed President Andrew Johnson's reconstruction plans.

During Ulysses S. Grant's presidency, in 1869, the president of the Dominican Republic offered to sell his country to the United States. Grant's secretary, General Orville Babcock, signed a treaty of annexation with the black republic. Charles Sumner, who was then chairman of the Senate Foreign Relations Committee, attacked the treaty and denounced Grant. Sumner, always the staunch supporter of political rights for persons of African descent, was angered at the thought of an African dominated republic losing its independence. Based on Sumner's opposition, the Senate rejected the treaty and the Dominican Republic remained independent.

The Americas

• *Europe:* David Livingstone was buried in Westminster Abbey (April 18). *See 1873.*

• Glasgow merchants subscribed 10,000 pounds to purchase a steamer for operation on Lake Nyasa.

• *Africa:* Daniel Francois Malan (1874–1959), the prime minister of South Africa, was born.

Daniel Francois Malan was raised in the western Cape Colony. During his youth, Malan was a childhood companion of his later political rival, Jan Christian Smuts.

Malan earned a divinity degree in Holland in 1905. He then worked as a Dutch Reformed minister at the Cape.

After formation of the Union of South Africa in 1910, Malan became an early follower of James Hertzog's National Party. In 1915, Malan began to edit *Die Burger*, the National Party's first newspaper. Also, in 1915, Malan became a member of the South African parliament.

When Hertzog came to power in 1924, Malan joined the cabinet as minister of interior.

Malan broke away from Hertzog in 1933 when the latter took Smuts into his government and fused Hertzog's National Party with Smuts' South African Party.

Malan and other Afrikaner extremists formed a secret organization, the Broderbond. Malan worked to "purify" what was left of the old

National Party. He began with the still independent Cape branch which he led.

During the 1940s, Malan's party gathered electoral strength throughout the country. In 1948, the reconstituted National Party won the first of an uninterrupted series of victories, and he replaced Smuts as prime minister.

Malan increased his majority in the 1953 election, but resigned the next year and was succeeded by J. G. Strydom. While he was in power, Malan named to the ministry of Bantu Affairs, Hendrik Verwoerd. Verwoerd began to elaborate and to refine the country's discriminatory racial laws. Perhaps the most notable law passed during Malan's administration was the Registration Act of 1950. Under the Registration Act, the government set about classifying every individual in the country according to race.

--- **1 8 7 5** ---

THE UNITED STATES

• The Civil Rights Act (which had been originally proposed by Charles Sumner in 1870) was enacted by Congress and contained provisions pertaining to equality of accommodations for the races (March 1). The Act was drafted to guarantee African Americans protection from social barriers which might be erected by states or municipalities. The Act guaranteed equal rights in conveyances, theaters, inns, and juries. The Act also went beyond the rights granted by Congress in the Reconstruction Amendments — the Thirteenth, Fourteenth and Fifteenth Amendments.

• James Garfield re-introduced a resolution in the House of Representatives which called for reducing representation of Southern states as a penalty for denying suffrage to African Americans, in accordance with Section 2 of the Fourteenth Amendment. Once again, no action was taken on this resolution.

• The following African Americans served in the 44th Congress: Senator Blanche K. Bruce of Mississippi and Representatives J. R. Lynch of Mississippi; J. T. Walls of Florida; Jeremiah Haralson of Alabama; John A. Hyman of North Carolina; Charles E. Nash of Louisiana; J. H. Rainey and Robert Smalls of South Carolina.

• From 1875 to 1887, Robert Smalls, an African American Civil War hero, served as a Member of Congress representing the state of South Carolina. Smalls was one of the vocal supporters of the Civil Rights Bill of 1875.

• Blanche K. Bruce became a member of the United States Senate from Mississippi, the first African American to serve a full term in the Senate (March 15).

• John A. Hyman, of North Carolina, was elected to the House of Representatives. He would serve one term.

John A. Hyman (1840–1891) was born a slave in North Carolina. He was sold and sent to Alabama where he remained until after the Civil War. Hyman, a self-educated man, was elected to the 44th Congress. During his term in Congress, Hyman served on the Committee of Manufacturers. Hyman held several federal appointments in North Carolina.

• Former United States Senator Hiram R. Revels left the Republican Party and joined the Democratic Party. In a letter to President Grant, Revels claimed that the Republicans had become corrupt and dishonest.

• In 1875, there were 16 African Americans and 17 European Americans in the South Carolina Senate while there were 61 African Americans and 63 European Americans in the South Carolina House.

• African Americans were massacred at Hamburg, South Carolina (July 9).

• Major Charles Redman Douglass, Frederick Douglass' youngest son, was appointed consul to Santo Domingo by President Grant.

• The Convention of Colored Newspapermen was held in Cincinnati to help make African American newspapers self-sustaining.

• Three Black Seminole scouts earned the Congressional Medal of Honor for their service in the war against the Comanche.

Those who saw the Black Seminole scouts called them the best trackers and Indian fighters ever engaged along the Mexican border. These scouts were often called upon to track the trail of raiding Comanches for hundreds of miles across the desert. In doing so, they suffered extremes of heat and cold. The Black Seminole scouts moved quickly, undetected by the enemy, and stayed in the field for months without support. Frequently outnumbered, the Black Seminole scouts often had to rely upon surprise and bravado to defeat war parties of Apache and Comanche. During an eight year period of active campaigns, the Black Seminole scouts fought in twenty-five (25) actions without a man killed or seriously wounded.

In 1875, Lt. John L. Bullis, the European

American commander of the Black Seminole scouts, took Sergeant Ward, a Black Seminole, and two other Black Seminole scouts out on a reconnaissance mission to find the Comanche who had reportedly stolen horses from outlying ranches. Bullis was highly regarded by his men and for the eight years that they served in the Apache and Comanche wars, Bullis served as their commander.

Bullis' party discovered fresh tracks and followed the trail to the Pecos River. There they found about thirty (30) Comanche with a large herd of stolen horses. The officer and his men dismounted and crawled close enough to open fire.

The surprise attack initially threw the Comanche into confusion. However, they soon caught on to the sparsity of the men firing upon them. Soon the Comanche began to encircle the scouts. The scouts reached their horses and rode clear of the attackers, but Bullis was cut off. Bullis' horse bolted and Bullis was left virtually helpless to the advancing Comanche.

The scouts, seeing their commander in danger, turned around and charged back. Under intense fire, Sergeant Ward pulled Bullis up behind him on his horse. One bullet shattered Ward's carbine rifle stock. Another bullet cut his rifle strap. Nevertheless, the outnumbered scouts fought their way out a second time without losing a man.

Sergeant Ward, Trumpeter Isaac Payne and Private Pompey Factor, the Black Seminole scouts who saved Lieutenant Bullis, were awarded the Medal of Honor for extraordinary bravery under fire.

Today the exploits of the Black Seminole scouts along with the legendary Buffalo Soldiers of the Ninth and Tenth Cavalry are cited with pride by African Americans as demonstrating the contribution made by African Americans in taming the American West. However, such prideful remembrances should give pause to the thoughtful person.

The taming of the American West to a large extent involved the elimination of the Indigenous American population as a threat to the expansion of United States territorial claims. The elimination of the Indigenous Americans as a threat all too often involved the use of military forces to unjustly oppress and kill Indigenous Americans. To the extent that the Black Seminole scouts and the Buffalo Soldiers were tools that were used in such oppression, their story is similarly tainted with blood. And to the extent that innocent blood was shed, the story

of these African Americans cannot be said to be glorious.

Nevertheless, the history of the Black Seminoles is one of the more intriguing stories of American history and it is a story which begs to be told.

*   *   *

Slavery, as practiced in the Americas, could not bind all slaves. Some were able to escape. Many of those who did, found refuge among the native peoples. Among these native peoples, the Africans lived and, after a time, became one with them. Such was the case with the Black Seminoles of Florida.

During the 1700s, Florida was a Spanish colony bordering the English colonies. The relationship between the two countries was never cordial and, as a result, Florida was perceived as a haven for those slaves who escaped from the plantations in Georgia and the Carolinas.

In Florida, the escaped slaves encountered a branch of the Creek (Native American) nation. These Creeks accepted the escaped slaves into their communities and, after time, the two peoples became one. The presence of Africans among the Creeks was so prevalent that the Spaniards began calling both groups "cimarrones"—"run aways"—the Spanish term for self-liberated slaves. This Spanish word was transformed by the English into the word "Seminole."

The First Seminole War

In 1816, Florida was a Spanish possession eyed by the United States as prime lands for expansion. Additionally, there was ever mounting hostility between the Seminoles and the European Americans along the Florida-Georgia border over the issue of the Seminoles harboring escaped slaves.

Negotiations for the purchase of Florida between the United States and Spain had been going on for a number of years with little immediate prospects of closure. However, even though Florida remained the sovereign territory of Spain, incidents involving the Seminoles provided the United States with a golden opportunity to establish a military presence near and in Florida. Under the orders of President James Monroe and Secretary of War John Calhoun, the President's favorite general, the Hero of New Orleans, Andrew Jackson, was sent to Florida to stabilize the situation.

In 1816, a detachment of United States troops crossed the Florida border in pursuit of escaped slaves and destroyed Negro Fort—the maroon fortifications along the Apalachicola River which would later become the site of Fort Gadsden. Of the 300 maroon inhabitants of Negro Fort, only 40 remained alive after the ten day siege of the United States Army.

In 1817, troops from Fort Scott attacked the Seminole village of Fowltown in northwest Florida when Chief Neamathla insisted that the soldiers stop trespassing on Seminole hunting grounds. Both black and red Seminoles, along with a number of European American soldiers, were killed in the battle. Thus began the First Seminole War.

In March of 1818, General Jackson, having had recent success in the Creek War of 1813, gathered an armed force at Fort Scott. It consisted of 800 regular Army personnel, 900 Georgia militiamen, as well as a force of Creeks under the command of William MacIntosh, an individual of mixed European and Indigenous American heritage. Jackson took his forces across the border and marched on St. Marks, a settlement on the Apalachee Bay south of Tallahassee which was reputedly held by the Seminoles.

However, the Seminoles were clever fighters and knew that a direct confrontation with such a large force was not advisable. The Seminoles learned of Jackson's plans and abandoned the fort at St. Marks. When Jackson's forces arrived at St. Marks, they were met by an old Scottish trader, Alexander Arbuthnot, and two Creek chiefs who had been active in the Creek War. Jackson executed the Creeks at once and held Arbuthnot for trial.

Jackson then directed his forces in a southeasterly direction to the village of a Chief Boleck on the Suwanee River. However, once again the Seminoles eluded Jackson by simply vanishing into the Florida jungle. This time Jackson captured only two Englishmen who had been living among the Seminoles, Lieutenant Robert Ambrister of the Royal Marines and Peter Cook. The troops burned the village and then returned to St. Marks. At St. Marks, a "trial" was convened under which Arbuthnot and Ambrister were sentenced to death. They were hanged for ostensibly aiding and abetting the Seminoles.

Frustrated by the Seminoles unwillingness to fight, Jackson turned his attention towards the hapless Spanish. He marched his forces westward to the Spanish fort at Pensacola. After a three day siege, the Spanish surrendered and Jackson boldly claimed all of West Florida for the United States.

Of course, Jackson's actions were illegal under international law. Both Spain and England protested his incursion. However, the new Secretary of State John Quincy Adams backed Jackson and sent an ultimatum to Spain to either control the Seminoles or to cede the territory. In 1819, a treaty between the United States and Spain was signed which provided for the sale of the remainder of Florida to the United States. Official occupation took place in 1821 and Florida was organized as a territory in 1822.

As soon as Florida became a possession of the United States, European Americans began flooding into the land. The European Americans laid claim to and took over the lands which had been the Seminoles'. In 1823, some of the Seminole chieftains were pressured into signing the Treaty of Tampa, in which they assented to move to a reservation inland from Tampa Bay. It was no coincidence that the pressure was being asserted by the then Governor of the Florida Territory—none other than the man known as "Sharp Knife," Andrew Jackson, the soon to be President of the United States.

The Second Seminole War

In 1830, the United States Congress passed the Indian Removal Act which called for the relocation of eastern Indigenous Americans to the "Indian Territory" west of the Mississippi River. In 1832, James Gadsden, a representative of Secretary of War, Lewis Cass, forced some of the Seminole leaders to agree to the Treaty of Payne's Landing. Under this treaty, the Seminoles were required to evacuate Florida within three years in exchange for lands out west, a sum of money, plus blankets for men and frocks for women. The Treaty of Payne's Landing also established that any Seminoles with African blood were to be treated as escaped slaves subject to a return to slavery. Because of the fairly common intermarriage of Seminoles and Africans, this provision of the Treaty meant that many Seminole families would have been disintegrated. Such a disintegration was abhorrent to most of the Seminoles and most of them resolved not to abide by the Treaty.

By the end of the three year period set forth in the Treaty of Payne's Landing, no Seminoles had moved west. In 1835, the Indian agent General Wiley Thompson convened the Seminole leaders at Fort King for the purpose of reaffirming the terms of the Treaty of Payne's

Landing. At this meeting, a Creek who had become affiliated with the Seminoles rose and voiced his opposition to the relocation of the Seminoles. The Creek who spoke was named Osceola and he said:

> My brothers! ... The white man says I shall go, and he will send people to make me go; but I have a rifle, and I have some powder and some lead. I say, we must not leave our homes and lands. If any of our people want to go west we won't let them; and I tell them they are our enemies, and we will treat them so, for the great spirit will protect us.

For this demonstration of defiance, General Thompson locked up Osceola and warned Osceola that he would not be released unless he agreed to relocation.

After a night of incarceration, Osceola agreed. However, his agreement was only given by him to effect his escape. Soon after he was released, Osceola killed Charley Emathla, one of the Seminole leaders who supported removal, and, as a symbolic gesture, scattered to the wind the money the European Americans had paid him. With this act of violence, the Second Seminole War began.

The Seminoles sequestered their women and children deep into the Florida swamps and forests. Meanwhile, the Seminole men formed small marauding parties which relied upon guerrilla tactics to achieve military success. Three of the earliest Seminole victories took place during the last week of 1835. Osceola and a small band of warriors got revenge for the humiliation suffered at the hands of General Thompson by ambushing and killing the General and four other European Americans at Fort King. On the same day, a contingent of 300 Seminoles under the command of Micanopy, Alligator Sam Jones, and Jumper attacked and massacred a column of 100 soldiers under the command of Major Francis Dade. Only three of Dade's soldiers were able to escape (by feigning death). Three days later, on New Year's Eve, several hundred Seminoles under Osceola and Alligator Sam Jones surprised a superior force comprised of 300 regular army troops and 500 militia men. The American forces under the command of General Clinch were routed by the smaller Seminole force.

This war between the United States and the Seminoles would last for the next seven years. A whole contingent of American generals would be frustrated by the guerrilla war of the Florida swamps. The old Indian fighter, President Andrew Jackson, would send Generals Edmund Gaines, Duncan Clinch, Winfield Scott, Robert Call, Thomas Jessup, Alexander McComb, Walker Armistead, and William North (along with Colonel Zachary Taylor) against the Seminoles but to little avail. The Seminole warriors, though small in number, fought skillfully. They would cut up any small groups of soldiers that ventured from the forts while avoiding any direct confrontation with the main body of the army. The inability of the army to subdue the few hundred naked, hungry Seminole warriors soon became a national joke.

One general, Thomas Jessup, attempted to bring a halt to the war by capturing what he perceived to be the Seminole's leader. In December of 1837, Jessup invited Osceola to a truce parley. Osceola, weary from two years of constant warfare and inadequate food, agreed to the parley. However, when Osceola appeared for the parley, Jessup had him seized. Osceola, weakened by the war, made no effort to resist.

Jessup sent Osceola to St. Augustine with a guard contingent of two columns of troops. Osceola, who was too ill to walk, rode on horseback.

While in captivity, Osceola grew weaker and weaker. Wracked by malaria and a throat disease, Osceola knew that the time for his death was near. On January 30, 1838, Osceola called for his battle dress, and rising from his bed, he pulled on his shirt, leggings, and moccasins, and strapped his war belt around his waist. According to Dr. Frederick Weedon, the post surgeon, Osceola then

> called for red paint, and his looking-glass, which was held before him, then he deliberately painted one-half of his face, his neck and throat — his wrists — the backs of his hands, and the handle of his knife, red with vermilion; a custom practiced when the irrevocable oath of war and destruction is taken.

After recovering his strength for a moment, the dying Osceola

> rose up as before, and with most benignant and pleasing smiles, extended his hand to me and to all the officers ... and shook hands with us all in dead silence .... He made a signal for them to lower him down upon his bed, which was done, and he then slowly drew from his war belt his scalping knife, which he firmly grasped in his right hand,

laying it across the other on his breast, and a moment later smiled away his last breath, without a struggle or groan.

Dr. Weedon's touching account of Osceola's death apparently did not quite touch the good doctor's heart. Almost as soon as Osceola breathed his last breath, Dr. Weedon cut off his head. Dr. Weedon would keep this grisly souvenir for years.

The capture and death of Osceola did not end the Second Seminole War. The deception perpetrated by General Jessup and the brave martyrdom of Osceola only served to enrage and inspire the Seminoles.

In May of 1838, the tired and beleaguered General Jessup turned over his command to Colonel Zachary Taylor — an Andrew Jackson protégé. In 1837, Taylor had achieved some success against the Seminoles at the Battle of Lake Okeechobee when Taylor's forces surprised the Seminoles and won the ground. However, even this victory was tainted by the fact that the American troops suffered more casualties than the Seminoles.

Taylor divided Florida into a grid of squares twenty miles on a side and assigned a garrison to patrol each square. Using this method, Taylor took scores of Seminole prisoners and sent them west. But despite this success, the war went on.

The American public became outraged by the length of the war and the cost. The public was also embarrassed by the way the war had been conducted. The capture of Osceola under a flag of truce was a shameful affair. Zachary Taylor's subsequent use of bloodhounds to track down Seminoles was also deemed deplorable.

But to a certain extent Taylor's tactics began to work. The tactics forced the Seminoles to go deeper and deeper into the swamps of southern Florida. Eventually, the war of attrition forced most of the Seminoles to surrender and be subjected to relocation. The last notable surrender occurred in 1841, when a Seminole chieftain named Coacoochee (also known as Wild Cat) and his chief lieutenant were captured. The capture of Wild Cat and John Horse ended the hostilities of the Second Seminole War.

The Second Seminole War was the costliest Indian war ever fought by the United States government. For every two Seminoles relocated to the Indian Territory of Oklahoma, one American soldier died. (From 1835 to 1842, some 3,000 Seminoles were transported to Oklahoma.) The cost of the war in monetary terms is estimated to have been $40 million dollars. And even though the hostilities came to an end, the war was never officially concluded. In 1842, the United States government decided that the task of flushing out the remaining Seminoles from the swamps of the Florida Everglades was too costly and so the United States simply gave up trying. Thus, the Second Seminole War ended, but the Seminoles were never formally conquered.

Today, Seminoles, red, black and mixed, still live in the Florida Everglades. They point with pride and distinction to the fact that they never surrendered, and many of these Seminoles claim with arrogance that they and their lands are a sovereign nation — independent and free from the United States.

The Capture of Wild Cat

The story of the Black Seminoles did not end with the cessation of hostilities between the Seminoles and the United States Army in 1841. Indeed, in many respects the story had only begun, and the story essentially became the story of Wild Cat and John Horse.

By 1837, the Second Seminole War had been waged for two years in the miserable swamps of Florida. Thomas S. Jessup, the general who commanded the American forces, had grown frustrated by his inability to defeat the greatly outnumbered Seminoles. Something had to be done to halt the guerrilla war which had cost so much money and had embarrassed both Jessup and his predecessors.

In 1837, Jessup found a way to end the war. Disregarding the rules of war, he had his men seized several Seminole leaders (including the debilitated Osceola) when they came in to parley under a flag of truce. A Seminole war leader Coacoochee, known to the soldiers as Wild Cat, was among those captured. In years to come, the fate of the Black Seminoles would be tied to his.

Wild Cat was the son of a prominent chief and had a mesmerizing effect on those he met. He was a handsome man and a charismatic leader. It is said that Wild Cat could charm the ladies with a graceful bow just as effectively as he could ambush a column of soldiers.

Wild Cat shared a taste for fine clothes and whiskey with fellow prisoner John Horse, a Black Seminole leader noted for his valor and intelligence. In war, John Horse was coolheaded and deadly accurate with a rifle, while Wild Cat had the unsettling habit of erupting into laughter in the heat of battle. Although darker skinned and taller than the Seminoles, John Horse was a Seminole in both dress and spirit.

Sitting in a prison cell at Fort Marion, with their great leader Osceola dying and betrayed and cut off from their own people, John Horse, Wild Cat and 18 other prisoners of war knew they would have to escape if they were to avoid being executed. After darkness fell, one of the warriors climbed to a high window using handholds chipped in the cell wall. The warrior worked loose a bar and squeezed through the narrow opening. The others followed, often leaving behind scraped skin on the rough stone of the cell window. The band descended using a makeshift rope to the moat below and escaped into the night.

This dramatic breakout, along with the martyred death of Osceola, inspired many Seminole to continue with the war. Wild Cat was a key leader in rounding up the Seminole and encouraging them to continue with the struggle. Less than a month after the escape from Fort Marion, Wild Cat led a force of Red and Black Seminoles in a major battle against the United States Army 200 miles to the south.

The forces of Wild Cat fought bravely and with desperation. However, despite their courage, the Seminoles were badly outnumbered and pitifully supplied. As casualties mounted, many Seminole surrendered rather than face starvation. However, Wild Cat fought on. For three additional years Wild Cat waged his own guerrilla war — a war which would not end until Wild Cat was captured.

Only with the capture of Wild Cat could the Second Seminole War be considered to have ended. The war had lasted seven years and had cost the United States $40 million and the lives of 1,500 soldiers.

It is said that when Wild Cat and two of his followers finally surrendered to the United States Army they were dressed in the theatrical costumes which they had stolen from a trunk. Dressed as Hamlet, Richard III, and Horatio, these three men represented the tragedy, and the rather pathetic farce, that comprised the Seminole "surrender" to the United States.

The Black Seminoles of Mexico

At the conclusion of the Second Seminole War, the United States sought to relocate the Seminoles to Oklahoma. Gathering up those Seminoles that had been captured, the Army transported the Seminoles (including the Black Seminoles) up the Mississippi and Arkansas rivers to the Oklahoma Indian Territory. How-

ever, this relocation would soon prove to be problematic because the Black Seminoles still considered themselves free.

As soon as the Black Seminoles arrived at Fort Gibson, agents hired by slave owners were waiting for them to enslave them. Additionally, the Creek, old enemies of the Seminoles, and "civilized" slave keepers in their own right, were ready to enslave the Black Seminoles. Many of the Black Seminoles were kidnapped and sold into slavery. When the Seminole leaders protested to the government, the government said that despite the military's promise, those Black Seminoles who had been slaves before the Second Seminole War remained slaves and could be recaptured.

However, some of the Black Seminoles were able to remain relatively free and intact. Under the leadership of John Horse, some 300 Black Seminoles stayed together and settled in the village of Wewoka. These 300 Black Seminoles were not only together, they were armed. As General Arbuckle, the commanding officer of Fort Gibson noted:

> The negroes well know what to expect after being deprived of their arms, and they are not disposed to yield peaceably to any.

Arbuckle's words proved to be prophetic. Not long after settling in at Wewoka, a party of about 200 Creek attacked the town. Promised a bounty of $100 a head by slave hunters, the Creek seized a number of men, women and children. This attack and the prospect of many more, convinced John Horse that his band of Black Seminoles must leave the Indian Territory or perish.

As it happened, a number of the Red Seminoles were also ready to leave the Indian Territory. The Seminoles had been promised their own land when they surrendered but, when they arrived in the Indian Territory, they discovered that their land allotment was located within the Creek Nation.

Realizing that their old enemies now, essentially, controlled them, Wild Cat, the leader of the Red Seminoles, decided to act. Wild Cat and John Horse got together and decided that the best hope for their people was to find a new homeland — in Mexico.

In the fall of 1849, Wild Cat and John Horse and their Seminole followers broke free. 200 strong, the Seminoles warned that they would kill anyone who tried to stop them. John Horse led the Black Seminole contingent under the overall command of Wild Cat.

The Seminoles who left with Wild Cat and John Horse, left without the permission from either the Army or the Indian agent in charge. Their future was uncertain, the Creek might pursue them, the Plains Indians might attack them or the Mexicans might turn them away. All was unknown and all was risked. All was to be given in the quest to be free.

For the next nine months, scattered reports of the whereabouts of the Seminole band were spread across Texas. At one time, the Seminoles were reported on the Texas prairie; another they were seen on the Nueces River; and for a while it was reported that they were encamped for the winter near the Brazos River. Naturally, given the uncertainty of their whereabouts, along with the reputation of the Seminoles, the citizenry of Texas became alarmed.

But the Seminoles were not found, at least not until one day when they just suddenly appeared at Eagle Pass on the Texas side of the Rio Grande. After consulting with the Mexican authorities, the Seminoles were invited to settle on land near the Rio Grande. This they did, first near Piedras Negras and later at Nacimiento.

The cimarrones — the Seminoles — were now in Mexico where slavery was forbidden.

* * *

The Seminoles resided in Mexico throughout the Civil War years. However, after the end of the Civil War and the abolition of slavery, many of the Black Seminoles began looking for an opportunity to return to the United States. One chance that arose was with the United States Army. At the time, the United States Army needed men who knew the desert country, understood the ways of the Apache and Comanche and spoke the border language. The recruiting officer guaranteed pay and rations for those who joined and served as scouts.

Many of the Black Seminoles accepted the offer. On July 4, 1870, — on Independence Day — a band of Black Seminoles crossed the Rio Grande into Texas. The Seminoles had returned to the United States.

Today, Black Seminoles can be found in Florida, Oklahoma, Texas, and in the deserts of northern Mexico. However, most importantly, the spirit of the Black Seminoles can be found wherever men and women choose to accept nothing less than being free.

• Mary McLeod Bethune (1875–1955), a noted educator, was born (July 10).

Mary McLeod Bethune was born in Mayesville, South Carolina. She attended Scotia Seminary in North Carolina and the Moody Bible Institute in Chicago, Illinois.

Upon her graduation from the Moody Bible Institute, Bethune applied to the Presbyterian Board of Missions to become a missionary. Her application was denied. Having been so rejected, Bethune devoted her efforts to the education of African Americans.

In 1904, Bethune established the Daytona Normal and Industrial Institute for Negro Girls. This institution would later merge with Cookman Institute to become Bethune-Cookman College in Daytona Beach, Florida.

From 1930 to 1944, Bethune served as a Presidential advisor. She was instrumental in assisting President Franklin Delano Roosevelt in organizing the National Youth Administration and served as the Director of the Division of Negro Affairs from 1936 to 1944.

Among her many awards, Mary McLeod Bethune was also the 1935 recipient of the Spingarn Medal. In awarding the Spingarn Medal to Mary McLeod Bethune, it was noted that:

In the face of almost insuperable difficulties she has, almost single-handedly, established and built up Bethune-Cookman College … In doing this, she has not simply created another educational institution. Both the institution's and Mrs. Bethune's influence have been nationwide. That influence has always been on a high plane, directed by a superb courage. Mrs. Bethune has always spoken out against injustice, in the South as well as the North, without compromise or fear.

• Alice Ruth Moore Dunbar-Nelson, a writer, was born in New Orleans, Louisiana (July 19).

• Carter G. Woodson (1875–1950), a noted historian, was born (December 19).

Carter Goodwin Woodson was born in New Canton, Virginia, the son of a tenant farmer who was an ex-slave. Woodson was too poor to afford an education and spent most of his youth working in Virginia's coal mines. What little formal education he was able to attain came from attending for four months out of the school year.

Woodson entered Douglass High School at age 20 and was graduated with honors when he was 22. He matriculated at Berea College and again was graduated with honors.

In 1901, Woodson was sent to the Philippines as a school supervisor. In 1907, Woodson received his bachelor of arts degree from the University of Chicago and, in 1908, he received his master's degree.

Woodson went on to do graduate work at the Sorbonne and received his doctorate from Harvard in 1912. Primarily interested in African American history, Woodson would become one of the first academics to champion the creation of an academic discipline in African American studies.

In 1915, Woodson was a moving force behind the creation of the Association for the Study of Negro Life and History. He became its director and editor of its primary publication, *The Journal of Negro History.*

In 1922, Woodson published *The Negro in our History,* the first textbook of its kind. In 1926, Woodson helped to establish the National Negro History Week and, for all his efforts, was awarded the NAACP Spingarn Medal.

• *Scholastic Achievements:* The United Presbyterians established Knoxville College in Knoxville, Tennessee.

• Thomas Ezekiel Miller was admitted to the South Carolina state bar.

• *The Black Church:* In 1874, James Augustine Healy was appointed bishop of Maine and was consecrated in the Cathedral at Portland, Maine, on June 2, 1875. Healy would hold this position until his death in 1900.

• *Technological Innovations:* The inventor A. P. Ashbourne received a patent for a process for preparing coconut oil for domestic use.

• *Black Enterprise:* The Fisk Jubilee Singers raised enough money to construct the first important building at Fisk University.

• *Sports:* Oliver Lewis, an African American jockey, rode Aristides to victory in the first Kentucky Derby horse race. Thirteen of the fourteen jockeys who rode in the first Kentucky Derby were African Americans.

THE AMERICAS

• *Brazil:* Joaquim Machado de Assis *(see 1908)* published *Americanas (American Poems).*

• *Haiti:* President Michel Domingue signed a treaty of peace and friendship with the Dominican Republic (January 20).

• Charles Moravia (1875–1938), a poet, was born in Jacmel (June 17).

Charles Moravia became a teacher in Jacmel and became seriously involved in writing poetry.

He founded the periodicals *La Plume* in 1914 and *Le Temps* in 1922. Moravia was appointed Minister Plenipotentiary to Washington in 1919 and fiercely defended his country. Moravia became a Senator of the Republic during the government of President Vincent. Moravaia published poetry and plays. His works include: *Roses et Camelias* (1903), a compilation of poems; *La Crete a Pierrot* (1903), a play; *Au Clair de Lune* (1910), a play; and *L'Amiral Killick* (1943), a play.

EUROPE

• Samuel Coleridge Taylor (1875– 1912), a gifted Afro-English composer, was born (August 15).

Samuel Coleridge-Taylor was born in London, England. His father, a native of Sierra Leone, was a doctor. His mother was an Englishwoman. Samuel's mother was left to raise Samuel on her own when her husband returned to Africa.

Samuel grew up in Croydon. He studied the violin with Joseph Beckwith and sang in the choir of St. George's Presbyterian Church beginning at the age of ten. After his voice broke, Samuel sang alto in the parish choir of St. Mary Magdalene, Addiscombe.

In 1890, Samuel entered the Royal College of Musicians (RCM) as a violin student. Coleridge-Taylor's first important composition, *Te Deum,* dates from this year. Novello published one of his anthems, *In thee, O Lord,* in 1891, and brought out four more in the following year. He began to study composition with Stanford in 1892 and was awarded an open scholarship for composition at the college in March 1893. Frequent public performances of Coleridge-Taylor's music followed. A chamber concert in Croydon on October 9, 1893, included his Piano Quintet, part of his Clarinet Sonata, and three of his songs, with Coleridge-Taylor himself at the piano.

Between 1894 and 1897, some of Coleridge Taylor's works were heard at the RCM, notably the Nonet, the Clarinet Quintet, *Five Fantasie-stucke* for string quartet, the first three movements of the Symphony in A minor, and the String Quartet in D minor. In 1895 and 1896, Samuel Coleridge-Taylor won the Lesley Alexander composition prize.

In 1897, Samuel left the RCM and, in the following year, received his first commission, from the Three Choirs Festival. Samuel had received much help and advice from A. J. Jaeger, through whom his music became known to Elgar. It was Elgar who recommended Coleridge-Taylor for the festival commission, and the result, the Bal-lade in A minor for orchestra, was well received at its first performance.

Two months later, Stanford conducted the first performance of *Hiawatha's Wedding Feast* at the RCM. This cantata, on which the fame of Coleridge-Taylor came to rest, soon became widely acclaimed in England and the USA, and many festival commissions followed, including the *Overture to the Song of Hiawatha, The Death of Minnehaha, Hiawatha's Departure,* and a number of cantatas, of which *A Tale of Old Japan* was deemed the best. None of these later works, however, was as enthusiastically received as *Hiawatha's Wedding Feast.*

In addition to composing, Coleridge-Taylor was an excellent conductor of catholic tastes and came to be described as the "black Mahler." Coleridge-Taylor was permanent conductor of the Handel Society from 1904 until his death, of the Westmoreland Festival from 1901 to 1904, and of many choral and orchestral societies. Coleridge-Taylor also undertook teaching. He was appointed professor of composition at Trin-ity College of Music in London, in 1903, and at the Guildhall School of Music in 1910.

Coleridge-Taylor made three successful visits to the United States in 1904, 1906, and 1910 at the invitation of the Coleridge-Taylor Choral Society which had been founded in 1901 for African American singers.

Coleridge-Taylor saw it as his mission in life to help establish the dignity of people of African descent. He was greatly influenced by the African American poet, Paul Laurence Dunbar, by the Fisk Jubilee Singers, by W. E. B. Du Bois, Frederick Douglass, and Booker T. Washington. Samuel studied their works assiduously. African American musical ideas permeate his composi-tions, and his introduction to *24 Negro Melodies* is evidence of the importance with which he regarded this music.

Many musicians in the United States looked upon Coleridge-Taylor as a beneficent influ-ence. Henry Burleigh frequently sang for Coleridge-Taylor.

Coleridge-Taylor suffered many rebuffs on account of his race.

At one time, recognizing the obstacles in the way of a composer of African descent in Eng-land, Coleridge-Taylor contemplated emigrat-ing to the United States.

On December 30, 1899, Coleridge-Taylor married Jessie Walmisley, a relative of T. A. Walmisley. Their son Hiawatha and daughter Avril both followed musical careers.

On September 1, 1912, Samuel Coleridge-Tay-lor died. His death, at age 37, from pneumonia was probably due to overwork. In addition to his musical accomplishments, Samuel Coleridge-Taylor was remembered as a man of great dig-nity and patience.

• Robert Browning published *Aristophanes' Apology* and *The Inn Album.*

AFRICA

• *North Africa, Egypt and Sudan:* Khedive Ismail accepted General Gordon's plan to extend Egypt to include eastern Africa.

• The Khedive Geographical Society was founded. The Khedive Geographical Society would later be known as the Royal Egyptian Geographical Society.

• Rohlf commenced his travels in the Libyan desert.

• Largeau began his North African expedi-tion.

• Great Britain purchased 176,602 Suez Canal shares from the Khedive for 4 million pounds (September 19).

• Ismail Sidky Pasha (1875–1950), an Egyptian stateman, was born.

• *Western Africa:* Jaja, the king of Opobo, was given a sword of honor by Queen Victo-ria for his aid in the Ashanti war. Jaja had sent an armed contingent to help Britain in the Ashanti War.

• The French conducted a military cam-paign against Ahmadu Shehu of Toro.

• The Ashanti attacked Juaben.

• There was a war in the Bagru country.

• The steamer *Sultan of Sockatoo* was attacked on the River Niger.

• In 1875, Lat Dyor allied with the French against Ahmadu ibn 'Umar Tall, who was struggling to maintain the Tukolor empire against the French.

• James Aggrey (1875–1927), an advocate for cooperation between Africans and Euro-peans, was born.

James E. Kwegyir Aggrey was a Christian edu-cator who became a noted interpreter of Africa to western audiences. James Aggrey was born at Ahamabu in the Gold Coast, the land which is today known as Ghana.

James Aggrey was educated in Wesleyan Methodist schools. He taught in mission schools until sailing for the United States in 1898.

Aggrey studied at Livingstone College, Salis-bury, North Carolina, an institution sponsored by the African Methodist Episcopal Zion Church. He graduated from Livingstone College in 1902.

James Aggrey married an American woman and remained in Salisbury on the faculty of Livingstone College. Later on, he enrolled at Columbia University in New York and commenced work on a doctorate.

Through his friendship with T. Jesse Jones, Aggrey was invited to become a member of the Phelps-Stokes Commission on education in Africa. Aggrey toured Africa in 1920 and in 1924.

As the only African on the Phelps-Stokes Commission, Aggrey attracted great interest when he addressed African audiences, and in Great Britain and the United States he became a renown interpreter of Africa.

In late 1924, Aggrey return to Ghana as a senior member of staff for the newly established Achimota College. However, his long absence from Ghana made for certain difficulties and Aggrey's American wife found it impossible to live in Ghana.

In May 1927, Aggrey went on leave intending to write his Ph.D. dissertation, but he died suddenly in New York in July.

The life of James Aggrey has been used as an example to African schoolchildren of what they can achieve through education, and of the necessity for cooperation between the races. One of the greatest inspirational speeches ever given was given by James Aggrey and a paraphrased text of the speech follows:

A farmer went into the forest seeking any bird of interest that he might find. He came upon an eagle's nest and noticed that a young eaglet still resided therein. The farmer caught the young eagle and took it back to his farm where he put it amongst his chickens and ducks. The farmer thereafter treated the eaglet like a chicken. He even gave the eaglet chickens' food to eat even though it was an eagle, the king of birds.

Five years later, a naturalist came to see the farmer. While walking around the farm, the naturalist noticed the eagle amongst the farm fowl and asked, "Good friend, what is that big bird doing over there?"

"That is my prize chicken," replied the farmer.

"But that bird is an eagle, not a chicken," said the naturalist.

"Ah, yes," said the farmer, "it looks like an eagle but I have trained it to be a chicken. It is no longer an eagle. It is a chicken, even though it measures fifteen feet from wingtip to wingtip."

The naturalist took a closer look at the bird and said, "No my friend, it is an eagle still; it still has the heart of an eagle, and it still can soar high up to the heavens."

The farmer scoffed, "No, you are wrong. It is a chicken, and it will never fly."

The farmer and the naturalist agreed to resolve their dispute by putting the bird to a test. The naturalist picked up the eagle, held it up, and said with great intensity: "Eagle, thou art an eagle; thou dost belong to the sky and not to this earth; stretch forth thy wings and fly."

The eagle turned this way and that, and then looking down, saw the chickens eating their food, and down he jumped.

The farmer, in triumph, said: "I told you it was a chicken."

The naturalist again stared at the bird and said: "No, it is an eagle. Give it another chance tomorrow."

On the next day, the naturalist and the farmer took the bird to the top of the farmer's house and exhorted the bird by saying: "Eagle, thou art an eagle; stretch forth thy wings and fly." But again, the bird seeing the chickens feeding below, simply jumped down to eat with them.

With some irritation, the farmer said: "I told you it was a chicken."

"No," asserted the naturalist, "it is an eagle, and it has the heart of an eagle; only give it one more chance, and I will make it fly tomorrow."

The next morning, the naturalist and the farmer rose early and took the big bird away from the farm to the foot of a high mountain. The sun was just rising, gilding the top of the mountain with gold, and every crag was glistening with the joy of the beautiful morning.

The naturalist picked up the bird and with great passion said: "Eagle, thou art an eagle; thou dost belong to the sky and not to this earth; stretch forth thy wings and fly!"

The big bird looked around and trembled as if new life were coming to it, but it did not fly. The naturalist then made the bird look directly at the rising sun. Suddenly the bird stretched out its wings and, with the screech of an eagle, it took off. The eagle flew, and, as it flew, it mounted ever higher and higher towards the heavens. It was once again an eagle and it would live the life of a chicken no more.

My people of Africa, we were created in the image of God, but men have made us think that we are chickens, and we still think we are; but we are eagles. Don't be content with the food of chickens! Be an eagle! Stretch forth your wings and fly!

• Galandou Diouf (1875–1941), the first black African to be elected to a Senegalese colonial government position, was born.

Galandou Diouf was born in Saint Louis. He entered politics in 1909 when he was elected to the general council of the four communes of Senegal (Dakar, St. Louis, Rufisque, and Goree). Diouf was a frequent critic of French policy, especially of administrative attempts to disfranchise African voters.

Around 1910, Diouf founded the Young Senegalese, an elitist pressure group which lobbied for equal pay for equal work, more political participation, and African access to scholarships for study in France.

In 1913, Diouf enlisted the support of the Young Senegalese to engineer the election of Blaise Diagne *(see 1872)* as the first black African to be sent to the French Chamber of Deputies. Subsequently, Diouf became the mayor of Rufisque.

Like many Senegalese, Diouf broke with Diagne in the 1920s as the latter moved to the right — as Diagne identified more with France than with Senegal. In 1928, the two men were opponents for the position of Chamber Deputy. Diagne defeated Diouf amid charges that the election was rigged by French business and political interests.

Diouf lost to Diagne again in 1932. However, Diagne died in 1934 and Diouf was elected to replace him.

Once a Deputy, Diouf also began to change. He too began to identify more with the interests of France rather than the interests of Senegal. As a result, Diouf also came to lose his popular support.

Diouf served in the French Chamber of Deputies until the fall of France in 1940 when the Nazis abolished colonial representation.

• *Central Africa:* Cameron reached Katombela, having crossed Africa (November 6).

Verney Cameron *(see 1894),* a British explorer, crossed Zaire and reached the Atlantic Ocean in 1875. Cameron's expedition added to the European understanding and knowledge of the African interior. His expedition also sparked the interest of Leopold, the King of Belgium, in the commercial possibilities associated with Zaire.

• Tippu Tib established himself at Kasongo, becoming the virtual ruler of the area.

• Slavery and forced labor were abolished in Angola.

• The Chokwe began their expansion westward beyond the Kasai River.

• Beginning in 1875, Pierre de Brazza, a French explorer, explored the region of the Ogooue River.

• *Eastern Africa:* George Gordon, the governor-general of the Sudan estimated that between 80,000 to 100,000 slaves were exported from Bahr el Ghazal (a region southwest of Ethiopia) during a four year period extending from 1875 to 1879.

• Henry Stanley visited Kabaka Mutesa of Buganda (April 5).

In 1862, the explorers John Speke and J. A. Grant visited Mutesa's court and brought Uganda to the attention of the outside world. By the time Europeans next visited him, thirteen years later, Mutesa was seriously concerned with Egyptian-Sudanese encroachments in northern Uganda and was anxious to form new alliances.

Henry Stanley visited Mutesa in 1875 and made a favorable impression by actively aiding Mutesa in a military campaign. Mutesa assented to Stanley's proposal to introduce Christian missionaries, hoping that they would assist him militarily.

• Barawa was annexed by Egypt, followed by Kisimayu and Lamu (November).

• The first Protestant missionaries arrived in the Ganda kingdom.

• Zanzibari troops were disarmed.

• Sayyid Barghash, the Sultan of Zanzibar, paid a state visit to Queen Victoria at Windsor.

• Three Egyptian expeditions were sent against Ethiopia. Munzinger's expedition was annihilated by the forces of the Sultan of Aussa. The expedition from Massawa was wiped out by Yohannes IV. Only the expedition under Rauf Pasha against Harar was successful.

• A UMCA mission was set up on the Ruvuma River.

• Nyungu ya Mawe occupied Kirurumo.

• Henry Stanley wrote letters to *The Daily Telegraph* appealing for missionaries for Uganda (November 15).

• LMS missions were established on Lake Tanganyika.

• Mirambo, the ruler of the Nyamwezi, reached an accord with the coastal Arabs which brought to an end their armed hostilities.

In 1875, Mirambo reached an accommodation with the Tabora Arabs and then worked to improve his trading position through ambitious negotiations. Mirambo's efforts to construct an alliance with the Ganda king Mutesa I came to nothing, but he received the support of the British consul John Kirk at Zanzibar.

After 1875, Mirambo received a succession of European visitors — traders, missionaries and imperialist agents — most of whom he favorably impressed. Meanwhile, Mirambo kept his armies busy raiding northern neighbors for cattle and arranging alliances and tributary relationships with rulers to the west and southwest.

• Musajjakawa Malaki (c.1875–1929), the founder of the Malakite church of Uganda, is believed to have been born in this year.

Musajjakawa Malaki was educated by Anglican missionaries, however, he twice failed the Anglican baptismal test.

After working as a school teacher and government official, Malaki helped to found a separatist revival movement in 1914 which emphasized rejection of European medical techniques. The movement developed into a formal church, "The Society of the One Almighty God," or the Malakite Church.

Malaki's followers were called "Bamalaki" or "Malakites." By the early 1920s, Malaki claimed over 90,000 followers.

Eventually, the church was suppressed by the colonial government when it opposed a vaccination program. Malaki himself died while engaged in a hunger strike.

• *Southern Africa:* The United Free Church of Scotland Missions were established at Blantyre and Livingstonia on Lake Nyasa.
• The Anglican Synod in Cape Town adopted a new constitution.
• Lord Carnarvon held talks concerning the South African Federation (August).
• Ngangelizwe *(see 1884),* the Thembu paramount chief, was deposed.

In 1866, Ngangelizwe took as his chief wife Novili, the daughter of the Gcaleka chief, Sarili, but treated her so badly that she fled back to her father in 1870. This episode strained relations between the Thembu and the Gcaleka and exacerbated the disputes between the two people over land and cattle.

Ngangelizwe fought several unsuccessful engagements against the Gcaleka during the early 1870s and then appealed to the Cape Colony government for "protection." In 1875,

the Cape government granted Ngangelizwe's request on the condition that Ngangelizwe abdicate.

• Lentswe became the chief of the Kgatla.

Lentswe succeeded his father Kgamanyane as chief in 1875 and immediately inherited a major dispute with the Kwena of Sechele I. Several years earlier, the Kgatla had moved from the western Transvaal Republic to Mochudi in present Botswana to escape Afrikaner harassment.

The Kwena allowed the Kgatla to settle at Mochudi. However, the Kwena did demand that the Kgatla pay tribute to the Kwena. The Kgatla's refusal and insistence that the Kgatla were an independent people led to hostilities between the Kgatla and the Kwena.

Lentswe defeated the Kwena in the first engagement, but sporadic fighting continued for years.

• Khama became the ruler of the Ngwato.

Khama spent three years in exile, but returned in 1875 to drive his father, Sekgoma I, out of office for the last time. Except for an attempted coup by his brother Kgamane in 1882, Khama reigned without further opposition for the rest of his life.

Khama's long reign was progressive from a European point of view. Khama imposed stern reforms upon his people, abolishing circumcision, rainmaking and bridewealth, and prohibiting alcohol. Khama closely supervised the activities of the many outsiders who used his capital at Shoshong as a center for journeys into northern Botswana, Rhodesia and western Zambia.

• Sipopa, the ruler of the Lozi kingdom, was deposed.

Sipopa's final rift with the Lozi aristocracy came in 1875. In that year, Sipopa moved his capital down the Zambezi River. He refused to consider returning to the central kingdom.

Late in 1875, Sipopa's faction was defeated in a revolt emanating from the center of the kingdom. Sipopa was wounded and died early the next year.

• Charles Domingo, a separatist church leader, was born.

Charles Domingo was born in Mozambique and was brought to present day Malawi by his father in 1881. As a youth, Domingo became attached to the Free Church of Scotland mission at Livingstonia where he was baptized.

By the time he was twenty, Domingo was considered one of the mission's leading protégés.

However, around 1907, Domingo began to break from the mission to preach on his own.

Domingo was influenced by the teaching of Joseph Booth and seems to have affiliated with both the Seventh Day Adventists and the Watch Tower Movement.

From 1910 to 1916, Domingo organized a chain of Seventh Day Adventist missions in northern Malawi. Around this time, Domingo also took an increasingly vocal stance against the European administration of the country.

Domingo was never connected with the violent uprising of John Chilembwe *(see 1915)* in southern Malawi, but the government which at the time was greatly alarmed by dissident Africans, deported Domingo in 1916.

• Thomas Mokopu Mofolo (1875–1948), a novelist who is regarded as the first modern African writer, was born.

Thomas Mofolo was born in Lesotho (Basutoland) to Christian parents. Mofolo studied theology at Morija and obtained a teaching diploma in 1899. Afterwards, Mofolo taught in a school at Morija and worked in the mission press. A natural story teller, Mofolo was encouraged to take up writing.

Mofolo published three full length novels in Sotho. The first *Moeti oa Bochabela,* appeared in a newspaper in 1906 and was later published in a translation as *Traveller of the East* in 1934.

Moeti dealt with a man searching for an alternative to traditional religion. The book revealed a strong Christian moralizing tone which characterized Mofolo's subsequent work.

An as yet untranslated book, *Pitseng,* followed in 1910. After *Pitseng* came Mofolo's major work, *Chaka. Chaka* was published in 1925 and in translated form became *Chaka: an historical romance* which was published in 1931.

In *Chaka,* Mofolo examined the conflict between good and evil within the person of the infamous Zulu king Shaka.

Mofolo wrote what he felt to be his best novel about the Sotho king Moshoeshoe *(see 1870).* However, this manuscript was lost in a fire.

• Jumbe I (Salim bin Abdallah) (c. 1800–c.1875) died.

"Jumbe"—Swahili for "chief" or "official"—was the title taken by four successive rulers of the town of Nkhota Kota (Kota Kota) on the southwest coast of Lake Nyasa. By virtue primarily of their superiority in firearms, the Jumbes dominated the ivory and slave trades of central Malawi and established a sort of protec-

torate in the name of the sultan of Zanzibar (Tanzania) to whom they paid nominal allegiance. The Jumbes are credited with introducing Islamic culture to modern Malawi.

Salim bin Abdallah (Jumbe I) occupied Nkhota Kota during the 1840s. Salim came from Zanzibar by way of western Tanzania where Salim had traded at Tabora and Ujiji during the 1830s.

Initially, Salim traded across the lake at the sufferance of the Chewa chief Malenga, but gradually Salim became recognized as a protector against the aggressive Ngoni kingdoms and was paid tribute by local chiefs.

At first, Salim styled himself "the Sultan of Marimba." However, later he took the name "Jumbe" to represent himself as an agent of the Zanzibar government.

During the 1860s, Jumbe I was visited twice by David Livingstone. Livingstone was the first European to describe the country that is today known as Malawi.

• Adam Kok III (c.1810–1875), the Griquaruler, died.

Adam Kok III was the nominal ruler of the territory between the Orange and Modder Rivers, but the Griqua were too few to effectively settle the entire area. As the Voortrekkers poured over the Orange River, the Griqua carelessly leased out much of their land. The Afrikaners soon challenged Kok's authority, but he was supported by the Cape government.

In 1843, Kok and his Sotho neighbor Moshoeshoe signed treaties with the governor, George Napier, delimiting their boundaries. Three years later, however, Kok signed a new treaty with the next governor, Peregrine Maitland, in which his country was effectively partitioned between his people and the Afrikaners.

In 1848, Governor Harry Smith annexed the whole region between the Orange and Vaal Rivers as the "Orange River Sovereignty." When the British abandoned the Sovereignty in 1854, they left the new Afrikaner Orange Free State Republic in control of much of Kok's territory.

Kok recognized that he was losing his control over his remaining land. In anticipation of the Afrikaner advance, Kok scouted the lands to the east of Lesotho for a new home. In 1861, Kok sold all title to Griqua territory to the Free State. He then led 3000 followers across the Drakensberg Mountains to the region known as "Nomansland." By then, Kok, through the auspices of Governor George Grey, had obtained permission of the Mpondo chief Faku which allowed the Griqua to settle.

In this new territory, later known as "Griqualand East," Kok founded the town of Kokstad and attempted to rebuild his community. The hardships of the migration and the barrenness of the new land left the Griqua greatly impoverished.

In Griqualand East, Kok was nominally a British subject. However, he received no assistance from the Cape government. Once again the Griqua allowed their lands to slip into Euro-African ownership.

Griqualand East was formally annexed by the Cape shortly after Kok's death in 1875.

• Kido Witbooi (c.1780–1875), a leader of the Witbooi family of Namibia, died.

Kido Witbooi became the hereditary chief of an Oorlam group sometime before 1800. Little is known about his early career beyond the fact that he lived near the Orange River in the northwest Cape Colony and that he established a friendship with another Oorlam chief, Jager Afrikaner.

About 1840, Witbooi led his people into southern Botswana. After a decade of nomadic life he settled in southern Namibia. In Namibia, the Oorlam constructed a permanent town at Gideon.

From Gideon, Witbooi would venture out to conquer the neighboring Nama Khoikhoi communities.

A few years before he died, Kido Witbooi converted to Christianity.

The Witbooi family which Kido Witbooi founded went on to become a powerful ruling family in the Oorlam branch of the Khoikhoi through the 1800s and early twentieth century. The Witboois, along with other Oorlam groups, having migrated from the Cape Colony into Namibia, introduced Dutch language and culture into their new homeland.

RELATED HISTORICAL EVENTS

The United States

• Andrew Johnson (1808–1875), the 17th President of the United States, died.
• *Africa:* Thomas Baines (1820–1875), an English explorer and artist, died.

Thomas Baines lived in the Cape Colony from 1842 to 1850. He served as official artist during the 1850–1853 Frontier War against the Xhosa. Baines served briefly in Livingstone's Zambezi expedition (1858–1859) and then explored in Namibia and Botswana (1861–1863). Later on, Baines obtained the first mining concession from the Ndebele king Lobengula.

Baines retired to the Transvaal Republic. Baines' most lasting memorial was his extensive pictorial record of the peoples that he encountered during his explorations.

• Albert Schweitzer (1875–1965), a theologian, missionary and musician, was born.

After receiving a doctorate in philosophy in 1899, Albert Schweitzer achieved world recognition for his organ interpretations of Johann Sebastian Bach and for his studies of the life of Bach and of Jesus.

In 1905, Schweitzer entered medical school with the aim of becoming a missionary doctor. He graduated in 1913.

With his wife, Schweitzer established a hospital at Lambarene on the Ogooue River in French-ruled Gabon. Because of his German nationality, Schweitzer was forced evacuate the hospital during World War I.

Schweitzer returned to Germany and published a number of philosophical works.

In 1924, he went back to Gabon to resume his medical work. Although considered eccentric and paternalistic by some, Schweitzer won international acclaim for his work and was awarded the Nobel Peace Prize in 1954.

1 8 7 6

THE UNITED STATES

During the Congressional session of this year, Blanche K. Bruce, the African American who served as a United States Senator from Mississippi, introduced a bill on racial affairs which was reported out of committee with a negative recommendation. Bruce also presented two petitions but neither received any legislative support.

In an executive session of the United States Senate, Bruce denounced the Grant administration and the Republican Party for not caring more for the African Americans who continued to reside in the South. In protest, Bruce refused to go to the White House when summoned by the President.

On March 3, Bruce made his first speech before the assembled Senate. He argued for upholding the validity of P. B. S. Pinchback's election. Pinchback was an African American who had been elected to serve as the Senator from Louisiana. However, due to opposition generally attributed to opposition to Pinchback's interracial marriage, Pinchback was never admitted to the United States Senate.

In his second major speech, Bruce spoke in favor of a resolution to investigate the Mississippi elections of 1875 in which the Republican Party had dropped from a majority. Bruce charged that the decline of the Republican Party was due to voter fraud and intimidation. His resolution was passed.

As evidence of the intimidation, a letter from E. M. Albretta, an African American member of the Mississippi Republican Party, was sent to George W. Boutwell, a United States Senator. The letter was dated June 29, 1876 and it read:

The Democrats told the colored voters, if they went to the polls on election day they would be killed. They intended to carry this election with powder and shot, and that they would kill every Republican speaker in the country if it did not go Democratic .... The chairman of our county committee ... was shot in the last canvass.

- In Mississippi, the Democratic Party regained control of the state legislature.
- Between 1876 and 1894, some 52 African Americans served in the lower house of the North Carolina Legislature.
- A letter from D. Alleber, of the Tax Collector's Office of the parish of West Feliciana, in Saint Francisville, Louisiana, expressed the tenor of the times in much of the South. In the letter dated May 18, 1876, Alleber wrote to Senator O. P. Morton: "Sir: The telegraph has no doubt informed you of the wholesale slaughter of Negroes on the line of Louisiana and Mississippi. We have ascertained that 38 Negroes were shot and hung. The lives of the few European American Republicans now left are in imminent danger."
- President Grant dispatched federal troops to restore order in Hamburg, South Carolina, after a heavily armed European American mob killed several African Americans.
- In order to further diminish the impact of the African American vote, Virginia reapportioned election districts for the third time.
- Former United States Senator Hiram R. Revels was re-appointed president of Alcorn College by the Democratic governor of Mississippi (August).
- The Reverend Washington Brown established the Grand Foundation of True Reformers by consolidating local, existing groups of True Reformers. The Grand Foundation of True Reformers was an African American secret society. Reverend Brown's attempt to create a mutual benefit organization on a national scale would prove not to be successful.
- Isaiah Dorman, an African American cavalry soldier serving as an Indian scout for General George Armstrong Custer, warned Custer of the presence of hostile Sioux near the Little Bighorn River in Montana. Dorman's warning went unheeded and the so-called massacre at the Little Big Horn became history.
- In Philadelphia's Freemont (Fairmont) Park, a monument was dedicated to Richard Allen, one of the founders of the Free African Society and the first bishop of the African Methodist Episcopal Church (June 12). This was the first known monument erected by African Americans to honor an African American leader.

Richard Allen (1760–1831) was born a slave near Philadelphia (February 14). As a youth, Allen was sold to a farmer in Dover, Delaware. Allen became a religious worker and was converted by Methodists. The Methodists permitted Allen to conduct services at his home, where he converted the farmer who purchased him. Allen eventually bought his freedom by hauling salt, wood, and other products and by laboring in a brickyard.

Allen studied privately and preached to European Americans and African Americans alike. He traveled throughout Delaware, New Jersey, Pennsylvania and Maryland. In 1784, at the first general conference of the Methodist Church in Baltimore, Allen was accepted by the hierarchy as a minister of promise.

He returned to Philadelphia in 1786 and was occasionally asked to preach. Allen began conducting prayer meetings among African Americans and sought to establish a separate place of worship for his African American congregation. Both African Americans and European Americans opposed the establishment of an African American church. However, Allen attracted large numbers of African Americans to his church services and, when he tried to integrate a church service where he was preaching to a predominantly European American congregation, the European Americans objected to the presence of the African Americans by pulling the African Americans from their knees while they prayed and ordering them up to the gallery. Rather than submit to this insult, the African Americans withdrew and, in 1787, established an independent organization, the Free African Society.

Some of Allen's congregation later broke away and formed the Independent Bethel Church.

Allen was ordained a deacon of the African Methodist Episcopal Church in 1799 and an elder in 1816. By 1816, there were some 16 congregations of the church and, later in that same year of 1816, Allen became its first bishop.

• *Organizations:* The Young Men's Christian Association (YMCA) was organized at Howard University in Washington, D. C. By 1911, there would be over one hundred African American branches of the YMCA.

• *Notable Deaths:* Joseph Jenkins Roberts (1809–1876), the first President of Liberia, died.

The parents of Joseph Jenkins Roberts were free African Americans who resided in Petersburg, Virginia. In 1829, Roberts migrated to Liberia with his widowed mother and younger brothers, and became a merchant. In 1842, he became the first President of the colony of Liberia — a colony created by the American Colonization Society to accept freed African slaves from the United States.

The colony of Liberia experienced some difficulty with the native inhabitants of the area, and in an attempt to raise money, they decided to lay import duties on goods brought into Liberia. This caused international problems, because Liberia was not a sovereign nation nor was it actually an official colony of the United States.

In 1844, Roberts returned to the United States on a diplomatic mission. He hoped to resolve the dispute concerning Liberia's import tax but the American government avoided taking a stand in defense of Liberia ostensibly because the annexation of Texas had compelled the issue of slavery to the forefront of political debate. Eventually, the American Colonization Society gave up all claims on the Liberian colony and left the African American colonists on their own.

Roberts returned to Liberia and resumed purchasing land for the colony. In 1847, he convened a conference at which the new Republic of Liberia was proclaimed and he was elected its first President. Roberts was re-elected in 1849, 1851, and 1853.

In 1849, under Roberts leadership, the Republic of Liberia agreed to a commercial treaty with Great Britain. Subsequent visits by Roberts to France and Belgium were instrumental in achieving recognition for Liberia as a sovereign country. In 1856, Roberts was elected the first president of the new College of Liberia. On another subsequent visit to the United States, in 1869, Roberts addressed the annual meeting of the African Colonization Society at Washington. In 1871, Roberts was once again elected President of Liberia and he served in that capacity until his death in 1876.

• *Miscellaneous State Laws:* An Alabama law stated that African American and European American prisoners were not to be confined in the same "apartments."

• *Miscellaneous Cases:* The United States Supreme Court in the case of *United States v. Cruikshank* (March 27, 1876) 92 U.S. 542, 23 L.Ed. 588, held that "the right to suffrage is not a necessary attribute of national citizenship; but that exemption from discrimination in the exercise of that right on account of race, etc., is. The right to vote in the States comes from the States; but the right of exemption from prohibitive discrimination comes from U. S. ... The 14th Amendment prohibits a state from denying to any person within its jurisdiction the equal protection of the laws, but this provision does not, any more than the one that preceded it, ... add anything to the rights which one citizen has under the Constitution against another. ... The power of the national government is limited to the enforcement of the rights guaranteed."

• In the *United States v. Reese* (March 27, 1876) 92 U.S. 214, 23 L.Ed. 563, the United States Supreme Court decided that "the 15th Amendment to the Constitution does not confer the right of suffrage. The power of Congress to legislate at all upon the subject of voting at state elections rests upon this Amendment and can be exercised by providing a punishment only when the wrongful refusal to receive the vote of a qualified elector at such election is because of his race, color or previous condition of servitude." The Court thereby held that Sections 3 and 4 of the Enforcement Act of 1870 were unconstitutional. The Court reasoned that these Enforcement Act provisions authorized Congressional action against discrimination in voting in general, without specifically mentioning the type of election or the conditions of the 15th Amendment: race, color or previous condition of servitude.

• *Scholastic Achievements:* Edward A. Bouchet received a Doctor of Philosophy degree in physics from Yale University, the first African American to earn a doctorate from an American university.

- Meharry Medical College was founded at Central Tennessee College in Nashville. The school opened with only twelve students and was administered by George W. Hubbard. Hubbard would serve as the administrator for the next forty-five years.
- Richard Theodore Greener was admitted to the South Carolina bar.
- *The Black Church:* By 1876, the property owned by the African Methodist Episcopal Church had increased seven-fold in value since 1856. The membership of the church had also increased from 75,000 in 1866 to 200,000 in 1876.
- *The Arts:* Edward Mitchell Bannister, an Afro-Canadian landscape painter residing in the United States, exhibited and received a first prize medal for his *Under the Oaks* at the Philadelphia Centennial Exposition (July 4).

Like Edward M. (Robert) Bannister, Edmonia Lewis, an Afro-Chippewa sculptress, had a successful showing at the Philadelphia Centennial Exposition in 1876. Her *Death of Cleopatra* drew critical praise as "the grandest statue in the exposition." The statue weighed over two tons and stood over twelve feet tall.

- *Technological Innovations:* D. C. Fisher received a patent for a furniture caster.
- *Sports:* It was reported that, in 1876, Nat Love (a.k.a. "Deadwood Dick") became a rodeo champion.

Nat Love (Deadwood Dick) was born in a log cabin in Davidson County, Tennessee, in 1854. Love was the youngest of three children. He worked as a cowboy for twenty years, excelling in roping, shooting, and other skills of his trade, earning the title of champion in 1876 in contests in Deadwood, South Dakota.

Despite the laws of the pre–Civil War South, Love obtained a modest ability to read and write at his father's knee. These lessons and whatever educational experiences he may have had were sufficient to enable Love to write a presentable autobiography in 1907. The book was entitled *The Life and Adventures of Nat Love: Better Known in the Cattle Country as "Deadwood Dick."*

Love's father Sampson worked as a foreman in the fields. His mother was a cook. When his father returned from service as a laborer in support of the Confederate forces, the destitution of a sharecropper followed the distress of slavery and the deprivation of war.

At the age of fourteen, upon his father's death,

Nat became head of the family and supported his mother and his widowed sister and her two children. His family's precarious living depended upon sharecropping and an off season job at $1.50 per month. Love earned additional income by breaking horses to ride, and acquired a skill that would later be of great importance to him.

A lucky raffle ticket brought Love enough money so that, after dividing it with his mother, he was able to clothe himself and to seek greater opportunities.

Love started on foot for the West in February 1869. Upon his arrival in Dodge City, Kansas, Love found work as a cowboy. At once, he earned admiration for his unsuspected ability to ride a bucking bronco which his new companions had furnished him for his initiation. By this extraordinary feat, the "tenderfoot" Love was accepted by the Duval outfit at the "astronomical" wage of $30 month.

Not long after Love's initiation, an Indian attack occurred. As Love wrote: "At the first blood curdling yell, I lost all courage and thought my time had come to die." While under attack, Love's companions taught him how to use a handgun.

In 1872, Love was employed by the Pete Gallinger Company on the Gila River in southern Arizona. Love found the cowboy's life agreeable. The long days in the saddle, the narrow escapes, risky rescues, mustang hunts, roundups, long cattle and horse drives with the "wild sons of the plains whose home was in the saddle and their couch, mother earth, with the sky for a covering" all suited Love. His superior physique, his keen eye, quick wit, and alert mind, carried him successfully through an early cowboy's life on the open range, with its attendant adventures.

Love eagerly accepted the hardships of extremes of weather and geography, wild animals, stampedes, outlaws and Indigenous Americans. Recognizing the need for proficiency with the tools of his trade, Love set a high standard for himself. As a result, he had the trust, confidence and acclaim of his peers and employers. Love became the Gallinger "chief brand reader," a position important in roundups on the open range in the identification and care of his employer's property.

At a Fourth of July celebration in 1876, after a cattle drive to Deadwood, South Dakota, Love found himself in competition with the best cowboys in the West. Love won the contest to rope, throw, tie, bridle, saddle, and mount an untamed bronco, a feat Love accomplished in nine minutes — a record.

Love also won the shooting contests with a rifle at 100 and 250 yards and with the Colt .45 at 150 yards. He entered and finished three matches with the confidence of a man who declared that "if a man can hit a running buffalo at 200 yards, he can hit pretty much of anything he shoots at." For his extraordinary abilities with a gun, Love was named "Deadwood Dick" by his admiring fans.

During his famous career, Love was captured by Indigenous Americans and unwillingly adopted into the tribe. He escaped after a breakneck ride of a hundred miles during the dead of night. He rode while carrying with him two new bullet holes, part of his career collection of "fourteen bullet wounds on different parts" of his body.

As the high tide of the cowboy's world began to pass with the coming of trains, Love quit the fading wave of the horse of the flesh and joined the crest of the new horse of iron. Love became a railroad porter and rode the trains with the same enthusiasm that he rode the range.

THE AMERICAS

• *Brazil:* Joaquim Machado de Assis published *Helena.*

• *Canada:* Wilson Abbott (1801–1876), a wealthy Toronto real estate broker, died.

Wilson Abbott was a pillar of Canadian society and he was another of the unsung heroes in Pan-African history whose life is little known but who manages to send ripples through the waters of time.

Wilson Abbott was born of a Scotch-Irish father and a free African American mother in Richmond, Virginia, in 1801. Although apprenticed as a carpenter, Abbott left home at fifteen to work as a steward on a Mississippi River steamer. Seriously injured aboard the vessel, Wilson Abbott was nursed back to health by Ellen Toyer, the maid of a Boston lady who was travelling on the steamer at the time.

Wilson Abbott and Ellen Toyer fell in love and got married. They began their life together by opening up a grocery store in Mobile, Alabama. The grocery store was profitable. However, as was the case in the South, the successful business served to provoke the envy and anger of the town's European Americans. Wilson and Ellen were forced to leave town.

After a short time in New York, the Abbotts moved to Toronto, Canada, in 1835. Their first endeavor was to open a tobacco shop, but the shop soon failed. It was after this failure, that

Wilson Abbott embarked upon the career which would make him a wealthy man. Wilson Abbott became a real estate broker.

By 1871, Wilson Abbott owned forty-two houses, five vacant lots and a warehouse. His principal area of business was in Toronto but he also had property in Hamilton and Owen Sound. With his wealth, Abbott was able to purchase the freedom of a number of escaped slaves, to keep his wife's sister as a well-paid housekeeper, and to engage extensively in community affairs.

Wilson Abbott became a true Canadian. He devoted himself entirely to Canadian affairs. During the uprising of 1837, Abbott served in defense of the Crown. In 1838, he helped to establish the Colored Wesleyan Methodist Church of Toronto.

Ellen Abbott was also active in community affairs. She organized the Queen Victoria Benevolent Society in 1840 to aid indigent Afro-Canadian women and was known for her contributions to the British Methodist Episcopal Church.

In addition to purchasing the freedom of escaped slaves, Wilson Abbott supported the Anti-Slavery Society of Canada. He taught his four sons and five daughters to think of themselves as Canadians. One of his proudest accomplishments was his election to the Toronto City Council from Saint Patrick's Ward. He also served as a member of the Reform Central Committee.

One of Wilson and Ellen's children was Anderson Ruffin Abbott *(see 1913)* the first Canadian-born person of African descent to receive a license to practice medicine.

It was through men such as Wilson Abbott that so many African Americans were able to obtain their freedom in Canada, and while the exploits of such men rarely fill the pages of "standard" history, their deeds are recorded here and, hopefully, in eternity.

• *Haiti:* Edmond Laforest (1876–1915), a poet, was born in Jeremie on June 20, 1876. He was educated in Haiti and later taught French and mathematics. Among his writings are *Poemes Melancoliques* (1901), *Sonnets-Medaillons* (1909), and *Cendres et Flammes.*

EUROPE

• Robert Browning published *Pacchiarotto and How He Worked in Distemper.*

AFRICA

• *North Africa, Egypt and Sudan:* Caise de

la Dette Publique was established in Cairo with Austrian, British, French and Italian members (May).

• In October, British and French controllers were appointed to supervise Egyptian revenue and expenditures. The system that was devised came to be known as Dual Control.

• G. J. Goschen and Joubert arrived in Egypt to establish dual control.

• General Gordon resigned because of ill health.

• *Al-Ahram*, a principal Egyptian newspaper, was founded.

The Secret Society was founded by Egyptian military officers.

• A Moroccan military expedition was initiated against the Rif.

• Cave reported on Egyptian finances (March).

• *Western Africa:* Briere de l'Isle became governor of Senegal.

• Cotonou was ceded to France.

• Fourah Bay College, an affiliate of Durham University, was founded.

• The steamer *Sultan of Sockatoo* was again attacked. Commercial trade on the River Niger essentially came to a standstill until the completion of a punitive expedition by the Royal Niger.

• The *West African Reporter,* a newspaper, was founded. It would last until 1884.

• Joseph Jenkins Roberts (1809–1876), the first President of Liberia, died.

Joseph Jenkins Roberts was born in Virginia. At the age of twenty, Roberts emigrated to Monrovia, where he became a successful trader and an active officer in the militia. In 1839, Roberts was elected lieutenant-governor of the colony. When Thomas Buchanan, the colony's last European governor, died in 1841, Roberts succeeded him.

Six years later independence was thrust upon Liberia because its undefined international status had permitted stronger nations to take advantage of it and because the United States, embroiled in the question of domestic slavery, was wary of sponsoring a black colony.

A constitution for Liberia was drafted by a Harvard law professor. Roberts was elected president of the new nation. Liberia incorporated three previously autonomous black settler colonies, although a fourth, Maryland refused to join.

Roberts' first task was to achieve international recognition. A state visit to England yielded British support. By 1849, most of Europe recognized Liberia. The United States, however, did not do so until 1862.

In 1854, Maryland joined the republic. Roberts worked to improve relations with the interior, but his government was unable to exercise any control over Africans living there. Roberts was re-elected for consecutive two-year terms until 1856 when he stepped down in favor of his vice-president, Stephen Allen Benson.

In 1857, Roberts became the first president of the new Liberia College. Around this time Liberian politics became more factionalized along color lines. Roberts exacerbated the situation by favoring lighter-skinned citizens like himself both while he was president of the nation and president of the college.

In 1871, President Edward Roye, acting on the results of a national referendum, proclaimed the extension of his term of office to four years. Roye also negotiated an unpopular loan from Britain. Roye was a dark-skinned Americo-Liberian and the color conscious legislature deposed him *(see 1871).*

After deposing Roye, the government invited Roberts to re-assume the presidency, which he did.

Roberts became seriously ill not long after taking office in 1872. He continued to direct his efforts, not always successfully, to improving relations with interior Africans. Too ill to stand for election in 1876, Roberts was succeeded by James S. Payne. He died later that year.

• *Central Africa:* Papagiotis Potogos explored the sources of the Bili River.

• *Eastern Africa:* Sayyid Barghash issued proclamations prohibiting the conveyance of slaves by land and slave caravans from the interior coming to the coast. These edicts caused riots in Mombasa.

• During the late 1870s, Abushiri led a division of the Zanzibari Sultan Barghash's troops against the Nyamwezi chief Mirambo.

• General Gordon arrived in Bunyoro.

By 1876, Kabarega, the king of Bunyoro, had reconquered the Toro kingdom, which had broken away from his great-grandfather in 1830 under Kaboyo.

Charles Gordon, the next governor of southern Sudan, renewed Egyptian pressure on Bunyoro. However, in 1876, Kabarega met Gordon's successor, Eduard Schnitzer (Emin Pasha) and was able to establish a friendly rapport.

• In January, Egyptians withdrew from Barawa, Kisimayu and Lamu.

• Ethiopian forces defeated the Egyptians near Gura (March 5–7).

• Egypt formally annexed territory near Lake Victoria and Lake Albert without sending any troops.

• In September, an Italian exploratory mission under Count Orazio Antinori arrived in Ethiopia.

• A fresh Egyptian expedition against Ethiopia was defeated at Gura. This defeat ended any Egyptian attempts to annex east Africa.

• Yohannes IV, the Emperor of Ethiopia, again requested assistance from Russia in his fight against the Muslims. But again, his request received no reply.

• The Church Missionary Society (CMS) started work at Mpwapwa.

• The first CMS missionaries reached Uganda.

• Zauditu (1876–1930), the Empress of Ethiopia, was born.

Zauditu (Judith) was the daughter of the Emperor Menelik II who left no surviving sons to inherit his throne. Zauditu's step-mother, Taitu, championed Zauditu's claims to the royal succession, but her father was reluctant to name a woman as his successor.

On Menelik's death in 1913, his grandson Iyasu V became emperor. Iyasu was toppled three years later. Zauditu was then crowned empress on the condition that she renounce her husband Gugsa Wolie, whom she had married in 1902. Additionally, the real power behind the throne was given to Ras Tafari Makonnen, the man who would later be known as Haile Selassie. Ras Tafari Makonnen was designated as the "regent and heir apparent."

Zauditu gradually became alarmed at Tafari's accretion of power. In 1928, Tafari staged a palace coup — possibly in response to Zauditu's hostile initiative. Tafari successfully demanded that she crown him negus (king) and hand over to him her last vestiges of power.

Two years later, Zauditu's estranged husband attempted to raise an anti–Tafari revolt in the northern provinces where he was governor-general. He was defeated and killed.

Zauditu died the day after she heard the news. Some say she died of a broken heart.

Tafari then became emperor in his own right. It was then that he became known as Haile Selassie — the Lion of Judah.

Twenty-five years later, Haile Selassie promulgated a constitution prohibiting females from becoming monarchs in Ethiopia.

• *Southern Africa:* Blantyre was founded.

• War erupted with the Secocoeni.

• In 1876, Du Toit founded the first Afrikans language newspaper, *Die Afrikaanse Patriot.* The next year, Du Toit published an Afrikans history of South Africa which was the forerunner of modern Afrikans nationalist historiography. *See 1911.*

• In 1876, Transvaal President Burgers *(see 1881)* attacked the Pedi, led by Sekhukhune, in order to complete Afrikaner domination of the Transvaal. Sekhukhune's dynastic rival Mampuru allied with Burgers. For over a year, the Pedi resisted conquest.

The Transvaal Republic, along with the Orange Free State, originated during the Afrikaner emigration from the Cape Colony during the 1830s. The emigrant settlers (Voortrekkers) established a number of petty republics throughout the Transvaal after 1838. No attempt to establish a central government was made until 1852, when Great Britain formally recognized the independence of the "South African Republic" north of the Vaal River.

After a constitution had been developed in 1857, a state president was elected. The administration at Pretoria was gradually recognized by all the Afrikaners in the Transvaal.

The Transvaal lost its independence to Great Britain twice. The first time was from 1877 to 1881 and the second time was from 1902 to 1910.

Since the Union of South Africa was formed in 1910, the Transvaal Republic has been administered as a province.

• Solomon Tshekisho Plaatje (1876–1932), a prominent member of the early African National Congress, was born.

Solomon Plaatje belonged to the Rolong branch of the Tswana people, but took the Dutch name "Plaatje" from a nickname his father used. After attending school in the 1880s, Plaatje served the Cape Colony government first as a postal clerk in Kimberley, then as a court interpreter for the British high command.

In 1904, Plaatje launched the first independent Tswana language newspaper, *Koranta ea Bechuana.* Plaatje used the paper as a platform to oppose European encroachments on African rights.

When, in 1912, John Dube *(see 1871)* formed the South African Native National Congress (later renamed the African National Congress — the ANC), Plaatje became correspondence secretary. Considered a lucid orator, Plaatje became a part of a delegation to London to oppose a new South African land bill in 1913.

The British government, distracted by the approaching world war, ignored the delegation, but Plaatje remained in England throughout the war. He supported himself by publishing several books, one of which was *Native Life in South Africa*. *Native Life in South Africa* was published in 1916 and it outlined African opposition to the South African land bill.

In 1919, Plaatje made a second trip to Europe in a futile attempt to bring South African issues into the Versailles treaty conference. Afterwards, Plaatje travelled through Europe, Canada and the United States.

Plaatje also wrote poetry and translated five of Shakespeare's plays into Tswana. Among his many books, *Mhudi: An Epic of Native Life 100 Years Ago* is noted as being one of the first English novels written by an African. *Mhudi* was published in 1930 and dealt with the Rolong at the time Mzilikazi's Ndebele were occupying the western Transvaal. Plaatje's characters were later used by Peter Abrahams in the latter's novel, *Wild Conquest*.

- Sipopa Lutangu (c.1830–1876), the ruler of the Lozi kingdom, died.

The father of Sipopa Lutangu, Mulambwa, was one of the greatest of the early Lozi kings. During Sipopa's youth (around 1840), the Lozi kingdom (Bulozi) was conquered and occupied by the migrant Kololo. Sipopa established a good rapport with the Kololo founder-king Sebitwane, but he fled Bulozi when Sebitwane's successor Sekeletu initiated a purge of Lozi princes in 1859.

During Sipopa's exile, the Lozi rebelled under the leadership of Sipopa's kinsman, Njekwa. Under Njekwa, the Lozi drove the Kololo out of Bulozi in 1864.

Njekwa declined the throne of the restored kingship. In lieu of Njekwa, the Lozi chiefs offered the kingship to Sipopa.

Sipopa's rule was popular for the first five years, but he gradually alienated his people by acting capriciously and greedily. Old sectional rivalries in the kingdom re-surfaced, resulting in an unsuccessful coup attempt in 1870.

Sipopa reacted to the failed coup attempt by busying the Lozi with aggressive wars and by building up his arms supply through external trade.

Reluctant to participate in the slave trade with Angolans from the west coast, Sipopa turned to Europeans from the south. In 1871, Sipopa granted George Westbeech a virtual monopoly in the country's ivory trade and afterwards relied on Westbeech as a friend and adviser.

Sipopa's final rift with the Lozi aristocracy came in 1875. In that year, Sipopa moved his capital down the Zambezi River. He refused to consider returning to the central kingdom.

Late in 1875, Sipopa's faction was defeated in a revolt emanating from the center of the kingdom. Sipopa was wounded and died early the next year.

Sipopa's successor, Mwanawina, ruled less than two years before he too was overthrown and replaced by Lewanika.

RELATED HISTORICAL EVENTS

- *The United States:* In the United States, the National Baseball League was founded.
- *Europe:* The International Geographical Conference convened at Brussels and created the International African Association.
- *Asia:* Abd al-Hamid II (1876–1909), an Ottoman Sultan, was born.

---

1 8 7 7

THE UNITED STATES

Historians tell us that Reconstruction came to an end in 1877. The end of Reconstruction was essentially a political act which was the result of a compromise. The demise of Reconstruction was an act which would hamper reconciliation between African Americans and European Americans for the succeeding one hundred years and, indeed, for the hundred years of which we are a part of now.

In 1877, Rutherford B. Hayes' election to the United States presidency was contested in the electoral college by Samuel J. Tilden, the Democratic candidate. Resolution of the dispute was complicated by the fact that there were two sets of electors presented from Louisiana, South Carolina, and Florida. To end the dispute, the Democrats traded the presidency for Republican assurance that Democrats would be able to control southern state governments without federal interference. Hayes was chosen as president, but the trade off effectively brought an end to Reconstruction.

In conferences at the Wormley Hotel in Washington, D. C. on February 26 and 27, Rutherford B. Hayes promised Southern delegates that he would remove Federal troops from the South and would leave the states alone in return for support from Democratic Southern Congressmen when the House voted for President. Upon Hayes' election, Hayes removed Federal troops from South Carolina and Louisiana. During his first five months in office, one-third of the appointees to the Hayes administration were Southern Democrats.

Reconstruction is deemed to have officially come to an end with the withdrawal of all Union troops from the South. The withdrawal of the troops led to European Americans regaining control of state governments in the South and to the reinstatement of oppressive (segregationist) laws regulating the rights and activities of African Americans.

• Richard Harvey Cain, J. H. Rainey, and Robert Smalls of South Carolina were elected to the House of Representatives.

• Senator Blanche K. Bruce, the African American legislator from Mississippi, was appointed chairperson of a select committee on Mississippi River levees. When the chairman of the Manufacturers Committee resigned, Bruce, being the senior member, served as acting chair until a successor was appointed. Bruce presented a petition asking for Federal aid for emigrants to Liberia. Bruce voted against reducing the Army.

• Frederick Douglass was appointed Marshall of the District of Columbia by President Rutherford B. Hayes.

• From 1877 to 1879, Richard Harvey Cain, an African American, served a second term in the House of Representatives as a representative of South Carolina.

• From 1877 to 1885, John Mercer Langston served in the diplomatic corps as Minister Resident to Haiti and charge d'affaires to Santo Domingo.

• In 1877, an African American was elected Grand Sire of the Independent Order of Good Samaritans and Daughters of Samaria. The Independent Order of Good Samaritans and Daughters of Samaria was organized by African Americans and European Americans to promote temperance. In separate district grand lodges, at first, African Americans could vote only on matters which concerned African Americans. However, as the African American membership increased, the European Americans dropped out, and the African

Americans eventually gained control of the Order.

• *Crime and Punishment:* While in office, in 1877, Congressman Robert Smalls was convicted of accepting a bribe. However, he was pardoned by Governor W. D. Simpson and was, therefore, able to continue his service in Congress until 1887.

• *Notable Births:* Meta Vaux Fuller (1877–1968), a noted sculptress, was born (June 9).

Meta Vaux Warrick Fuller was born in Philadelphia, Pennsylvania. She graduated with honors from the Pennsylvania School of Industrial Art.

In 1899, Fuller went to Paris to study for three years at Colarossi's Academy. While at Colarossi's Academy, Fuller's sculptures began to attract some critical acclaim. Her sculptures *The Medusa* and *Christ in Agony* were particularly impressive.

In 1903, Fuller's *The Wretched,* a sculpture exhibited at the Paris Salon, made Fuller famous in Parisian art circles. One of the admirers of her art was none other than the great Auguste Rodin.

Fuller soon fell under the influence of Rodin and Rodin's influence soon became evident in her work. Such sculptures as *Secret Sorrow, Oedipus, Death on the Wing, The Man Who Laughed, John the Baptist, Three Gray Women* and a group sculpture of the Fates are noteworthy examples of her work during this period.

In 1907, Fuller received a commission to do a series of commemorative figures illustrating the history of the African American for the Jamestown Tercentennial Exposition.

Over time, Fuller's style became less symbolic and more realistic. Her work during the 1920s and 1930s dealt mostly with African American subjects and was commissioned by African American and other liberal (pro–African American) organizations.

• May Howard Jackson (1877–1930), a sculptress, was born.

May Howard Jackson was born in Philadelphia, Pennsylvania. She graduated from the Pennsylvania Academy of Fine Arts in 1899.

May soon married Sherman Jackson and moved to Washington, D. C., where she maintained a studio for the duration of her life. Partly because she never studied in Paris, her sculpting style never came to reflect the European style which was so prevalent during the day. Instead, her work was very much an American artform in line with much of the art being produced by her European American contemporaries.

African American themes dominated Jackson's work throughout her career. She is best known for her busts of Paul Laurence Dunbar and W. E. B. DuBois along with the thematic sculptures of *The Mulatto Mother and Her Child* and *Head of a Child*.

• Garrett A. Morgan, the inventor of the traffic light and gas mask, was born in Kentucky.

• *Publications:* In 1877, Alberry Whitman published *Not a Man and Yet a Man* a 20 volume epic. In *Not a Man and Yet a Man*, Whitman relates the story of a COTW slave who rescues his owner's daughter during an Indian (Indigenous American) uprising. The COTW slave falls in love with the young woman and the long narrative follows the lovers travails as the slave suffers tribulations which eventually lead him to Canada — and freedom.

• *Scholastic Achievements:* Henry O. Flipper, born a slave in Georgia, became the first African American graduate of West Point (June 15). Flipper endured four years of ostracism by his European American classmates.

Henry Ossian Flipper (1856–1940) was a student at Atlanta University at the time of his appointment to West Point. Flipper graduated fiftieth out of a class of seventy-six after suffering four years of hostility and ostracism by European American cadets.

After graduation, Flipper joined the Tenth Cavalry in 1878. He served in Oklahoma and Texas. The only African American officer in the army, Flipper became a target for unfair treatment. In 1882, he was accused of embezzlement. He was cleared of the charges but was convicted of conduct unbecoming an officer and gentlemen and discharged.

After his discharge, Flipper remained in the West. For the next fifty years, he engaged himself in engineering, mining and survey work.

For a while, Flipper also resided in Atlanta with his well-established brother, Josephus Flipper, a bishop in the African Methodist Episcopal Church.

In 1976, Henry Flipper was posthumously exonerated by the army. On May 3, 1977, — the centennial of his graduation — a bust was unveiled in Flipper's honor at West Point. The bust was a tribute to Flipper's unblemished honor.

Flipper wrote a book about his experiences at West Point. *Colored Cadet at West Point* was published in 1878 and gives a poignant insight into Flipper's then young life.

• George Washington Henderson was elected to Phi Beta Kappa. Henderson was elected by the University of Vermont. Edward Alexander Bouchet was elected on the basis of his work as a member of Yale University's Class of 1874, however, his election did not occur until 1884 when Yale reactivated its chapter of Phi Beta Kappa.

• Fayetteville State was established in North Carolina.

• *Black Enterprise:* Six African American entrepreneurs in northwestern Kansas founded the American Nicodemus Town Company.

During the late 1800s and early 1900s, African American town promoters established at least eighty-eight, and perhaps as many as two hundred, black towns throughout the United States and Canada. Black towns, all African American incorporated communities with autonomous African American city governments and shopkeeper economies, were created out of a combination of economic and political motives. The founders of towns such as Boley, Oklahoma, and Mound Bayou, Mississippi, like the entrepreneurs who created Chicago, Denver, and thousands of other municipalities across the nation, hoped their enterprises would be profitable, and appealed to early settlers with the promise of rising real estate values. However, these promoters added some special attractions for African Americans. The promoters offered an opportunity to escape racial oppression, control their economic destinies, and prove that African Americans possessed capacity for self-government.

The first attempts at establishing all-black communities were in Upper Canada (Ontario). These communities were generally associated with the abolitionist movement. In 1829, the settlement of Wilberforce was created to resettle African American refugees from Cincinnati, Ohio. Wilberforce, as well as most of the later Canadian settlements such as Dawn and Elgin, were operated largely by Euro-Canadian charities. These communities were designed to give African Americans land and to teach them usable skills. However, they were poorly funded and managed, and none survived.

The first black town in the United States was created in 1835, when Free Frank McWhorter, an ex–Kentucky slave, established the short-lived town of New Philadelphia, Illinois.

More black towns were settled in the first years after the Civil War. Texas led the way in the late 1860s, with the founding of Shankleville in 1867 and Kendleton in 1870. These arose from the desire of emancipated slaves to own land without interference.

However, the vast majority of black towns emerged following the end of Reconstruction. Like European Americans, African Americans were lured by the promise of the West, and many towns were planned in western areas. African Americans, largely unable to secure land and economic opportunity in settled areas, looked to the West, with its reserves of land obtainable cheaply (or free) through the Homestead Act. Furthermore, the society of the frontier had a reputation for egalitarianism and individual autonomy. To African Americans in the ex-Confederate states who had briefly tasted political power before being overwhelmed by European Americans, the possibility of African American run areas was attractive.

Nicodemus, Kansas, was the first all-black community that gained national attention. Nicodemus was founded by W. R. Hill, a European American minister and land speculator. During the mid-1870s, Hill joined three African American Kansas residents — W. H. Smith, Simon P. Rountree, and Z. T. Fletcher — in planning an African American agricultural community in western Kansas, near the frontier. This foursome founded a land company to create Nicodemus and recruited settlers from the South.

Nicodemus was named after a legendary African slave prince who purchased his freedom. The first group of settlers in Nicodemus consisted of thirty colonists who arrived from Kentucky in July of 1877. Undaunted by the treeless, windswept countryside, another 150 Kentucky settlers reached the site in March 1878. Later in 1878, more pioneers arrived from Tennessee, Missouri, and Mississippi as part of the "Exoduster" migration.

In the 1880 census it was reported that some 258 African Americans and 58 European Americans resided in Nicodemus and its surrounding township. Both the townspeople and the neighboring wheat and corn farmers helped Nicodemus emerge as a small, briefly thriving community. The first retail stores opened in 1879. Town founder and postmaster Z. T. Fletcher opened the Saint Francis Hotel in 1885. Two European American residents established the town's newspapers, the *Nicodemus Western Cyclone,* in 1886 and the *Nicodemus Enterprise* one year later. By 1886, Nicodemus had three churches and a new schoolhouse.

Nicodemus' success attracted other African Americans, including Edwin P. McCabe, a man who would achieve a modicum of notoriety of his own as the most famous African American politician outside of the South.

A native of Troy, New York, Edwin McCabe arrived in Nicodemus in 1878 and began working as a land agent, locating settlers on their claims. In 1880, when Kansas governor John P. St. John established Graham County (which included Nicodemus), McCabe was appointed acting county clerk, beginning a long career of elective and appointive officeholding.

In November of 1881, McCabe was elected clerk for Graham County, and the following year, at age thirty-two, he became the highest-ranking African American elected official outside the South when Kansas voters chose him as state auditor.

Nicodemus' fortunes began to decline in the late 1880s. An 1885 blizzard destroyed 40 percent of the wheat crop, prompting the first exodus from the area. By 1888, three railroads had bypassed the town, despite its commitment of $16,000 in bonds to attract a rail line. Moreover, toward the end of the decade Oklahoma began to appeal to prospective African American homesteaders and Nicodemus began an irreversible decline.

• *Sports:* Isaac Murphy, an African American jockey, won the Saint Leger Stakes at Churchill Downs.

THE AMERICAS

• *Brazil:* In 1877, Jose Do Patrocinio, an Afro-Brazilian, published *Motta Coquiero. Motta Coquiero* was a story concerning the murder of a plantation owner as retaliation for a murder the story's central character did not commit. Its importance lies in the careful examination of racial tensions and conflicts on a plantation in Brazil among Euro-Brazilians, Afro-Brazilians, and COTWs.

• *Cuba:* In 1877, Afro-Cubans represented 32.2% of Cuba's population.

• *Haiti:* Luis Dantes Bellegarde (1877–1966), a Haitian educator, politician, diplomat, and author, was born.

Luis Dantes Bellegarde was born on May 18, 1877, in Port-au-Prince. Bellegarde taught at the secondary and university levels before entering politics. He joined the Ministry of Foreign Affairs around 1905 and was minister of public instruction and agriculture in 1918–1921.

In 1950, Bellegarde became president of the

Constituent Assembly. Bellegarde's diplomatic activity included service as ambassador to France and the Vatican as well as ambassador to the United States and to the United Nations.

Bellegarde was co-author of almost 20 books on Haitian history, politics, and sociology. Among these are *La nation haitienne* which was published in 1938 and written with Stenio Vincent, and *Haiti et son peuple* which was published in 1953 and written with Mercer Cook.

Bellegarde was controversial for his pro-French, Christian, and Western views. Nevertheless, his contributions to Haitian social thought; foreign, financial, and economic policy; and education are clear and indisputable.

Luis Bellegarde died on June 14, 1966, in Port-au-Prince.

EUROPE

• Robert Browning published *The Agamemnon of Aeschylus.*

ASIA

• In 1877, Hafiz Beheram, a Sudanese African, became the Grand Eunuch of the Ottoman Empire. In this capacity, Hafiz Beheram was the second most powerful man in the empire — second only to the Ottoman Sultan. *See 1909.*

AFRICA

• *North Africa, Egypt and Sudan:* General Charles George Gordon became the Governor-General of the Sudan.

In 1877, Gordon *(see 1885)* became governor-general of Sudan, while Eduard Schnitzer (Emin Pasha) succeeded him in Equatoria. Gordon's main concern was to negotiate an end to the Egyptian-Ethiopian war, but an interview with the Ethiopian Emperor, Yohannes IV, proved fruitless. Frustrated by the lack of Egyptian support for his work, Gordon resigned in 1880 and returned to British service.

• Lyons missionaries (SMA) work in Egypt.
• *Western Africa:* In 1877, Lat Dior won control over the neighboring state of Baol. Lat Dior's power and position enabled him to affect the Islamization of a large segment of western Senegal.
• War erupted between Ibadan and Egbas and Ijebus. The Fulani from Ilorin attacked Ibadan.
• The first visit of George Goldie Taubman to the upper Niger occurred in 1877.

George Goldie (1846–1925) arrived in Nigeria in the 1870s, at a time when British traders were competing fiercely for economic control of the hinterland.

By 1879, Goldie had united all the important British companies into a single corporation, the United Africa Company. However, competition from the French remained strong.

In the early 1880s, Goldie tried to convince the British government to charter the company to rule the Nigerian interior as a protectorate — a method the British had used in their earliest days of colonization. The government refused, so Goldie, after failing to come to terms with the French, commenced a price war financed by his personal fortune.

By 1884, the French had abandoned their stations on the Niger. In the same year, Goldie began a campaign to sign treaties of "protection" with local rulers. By aiding the chiefs in local conflicts, Goldie obtained their economic cooperation.

The treaties obtained by Goldie proved to be immensely beneficial to the British government. During the Berlin Conference of 1884–1885 — the conference which formally initiated the "Scramble for Africa," England used the treaties obtained by Goldie as proof of Britain's prior occupation of much of Nigeria.

In 1885, Great Britain formally declared a protectorate over the Oil Rivers Districts. The next year Goldie's company — now called the Royal Niger Company — took over administration of the protectorate inland from the Niger Delta. Despite official prohibitions, the company soon established a trade monopoly which excluded African as well as other European traders, and aroused a great deal of bitter resentment.

In 1894, Goldie again confronted French competition, this time in Borgu. The result was the famous English-French race to Nikki to obtain a treaty with the supposed overlord of Borgu. Goldie engaged Frederick Lugard to lead the expedition. The expedition succeeded in nosing out the French. Afterwards, Goldie's company continued to expand its holdings by treaty and conquest. Two particularly important conquests were Nupe and Ilorin in 1897.

In 1895, African traders of the city-state of Nembe (Brass) — being strangled by Goldies' monopolistic policies — organized under Frederick Koko to attack the company's headquarters. The attack was brutally repressed.

An official inquiry into the repression of Koko's attack exposed Goldies' unfair trade practices. Goldie's company charter was revoked in 1899 and the British government immediately declared a protectorate over northern Nigeria. In compensation for the loss of his monopoly, Goldie received a huge financial settlement.

• Abdul Bubakar was forced to recognize a French protectorate over his provinces in Senegal.

Abdul Bubakar was the ruler of Futa Toro. During his reign, he attempted to revive the Tukolor confederation to oppose the French.

Although Futa Toro had been united in a *jihad* by the end of the 1700s, the Islamic confederation of states which resulted was always tenuous. Each clan leader was territorial in nature and determined to guard his own interests.

The most powerful of the clan leaders in the 1870s was Abdul Bubakar. Fearing the French advance up the Senegal River, Bubakar attempted to unite the Tukolor into a more cohesive resisting force. His efforts met with little overall success for in 1877, Abdul Bubakar was compelled to recognize France and its protectorate over his provinces.

Nevertheless, Abdul Bubakar continued to fight the French. Allying himself with the Fula and the Wolof, Bubakar "resisted" until the 1890s.

• Charles D. B. King (1877–1961), a future President of Liberia, was born.

Shortly after he assumed the presidency of Liberia in 1920, King welcomed emissaries from Marcus Garvey. At the time Garvey wanted to use Liberia as a base for his "Back to Africa" movement.

In the early 1920s, Liberia was in deep financial trouble. Garvey's plans to pump funds into the economy seemed a solution to Liberia's financial problems. However, four years later, King's administration banned Garvey's movement because Liberia's economy managed to recover independently and because the Americo-Liberians feared the loss of their privileged position over indigenous Africans.

The basis for the new prosperity in Liberia was an agreement with the Firestone Rubber Company for the exploitation of Liberian rubber. Negotiations began in 1923 and were concluded three years later on terms that were very advantageous to Firestone.

In 1929, international criticism of alleged domestic slavery and forced labor caused King to request a League of Nations investigation. Although King was not personally implicated,

King's vice-president, Allen Yancy, was implicated. At the end of 1930, both King and Yancy resigned.

King was succeeded by Edwin Barclay. Barclay's first years were spent warding off European and American schemes for an international take-over of Liberia. Pressure eventually diminished with Liberia's improving economic situation and the friendly administration of the United States president, Franklin D. Roosevelt.

• *Central Africa:* Henry Stanley arrived at the place which would become known as Stanley Falls (January 1). On March 12, Stanley reached Stanley Pool and, on October 17, he arrived at Boma. All in all, it had taken Stanley 999 days to cross Africa.

• *Eastern Africa:* In 1877, slaves were still being smuggled from Kilwa.

• The Holy Ghost Fathers mission was opened at Mhonda.

• Police, water supply and street lighting were organized and provided in Zanzibar.

• The Eastern Telegraph Company linked Zanzibar to Aden.

• Menelik was confirmed in his title by Yohannes IV.

• The Crepel-Cambier expedition to Lake Tanganyika began.

• General Matthews began training the regular army of Zanzibar.

• *Southern Africa:* Sir Henry Bartle Frere arrived in South Africa with instructions to work for federation (March 31).

In 1877, the Secretary of State for the Colonies, Lord Carnarvon, dispatched Sir Henry Bartle Frere *(see 1884)* to South Africa to succeed Henry Barkly as governor and high commissioner. Frere was given the special task of uniting the various British possessions and the Afrikaner republic into a federation.

Two weeks before Frere arrived at Cape Town, his position was undermined when the Natal agent, Theophilus Shepstone, annexed the Transvaal Republic to the British Crown. Shepstone's action made the Afrikaners distrustful of the British and uncooperative in federation discussions. Indeed, the annexation of the Transvaal prompted Marthinus Pretorius, the former president of the Transvaal, to come out of retirement to lead Afrikaner resistance to British annexation of the Transvaal.

With Stephanus (Paul) Kruger and P. J. Joubert, Pretorius formed a triumvirate government which led the Transvaal back to independence.

• The South African Republic (the Transvaal) was annexed by Great Britain (April 12).

When Cetewayo, the great Zulu chief, perceived that the Transvaal people were unable to defeat the Pedi chief Sekhukhune in their own country, he proposed to Theophilus Shepstone, the British agent, a joint Zulu-Natal invasion of the Transvaal. Shepstone declined. However, a few months later Shepstone personally annexed the Transvaal to the British crown in a bloodless coup and became the Transvaal governor. This move merged the governments of the Transvaal and Natal and destroyed the basis of Cetewayo's foreign policy, as Shepstone now endorsed Afrikaner claims on Zulu territory.

Seeing Shepstone's reversal as a betrayal, Cetewayo began assembling a large armed force — an army which came to number some 40,000 strong. The resurgence of Cetewayo's army alarmed Shepstone. Shepstone appealed to the new British high commissioner for South Africa, Bartle Frere, to launch a pre-emptive attack on the Zulu. Frere endorsed the idea as a positive step towards reconciling British and Afrikaner interests in South Africa. A Natal commission revealed that Afrikaner claims on Zulu territory were worthless, but Frere suppressed its report and cited minor incidents on the Zulu-Natal border to justify a belligerent policy.

• The first Kaffir War began (August).
• Great Britain negotiated a treaty of commerce with Madagascar (October).
• Francois Coillard explored Mashonaland.
• Zanzibar Arabs established a slave-raiding base at Karonga on Lake Malawi.
• Augusto Cardoso initiated his expedition to Lake Nyasa.
• War commenced with Gcalekas.

In 1877, Sarili's dispute with the Mfengu people over land drew in a new British intervention, which produced the last Xhosa Frontier War. Again the British forces chased Sarili into exile and the governor and high commissioner Bartle Frere declared Sarili deposed as the paramount chief of the Gcalekas.

RELATED HISTORICAL EVENTS

• *The Americas:* In Brazil, a railroad between Sao Paulo and Rio de Janeiro began operation.
• *Europe:* The Livingstone Inland Mission (LIM) was founded in London.

1 8 7 8

THE UNITED STATES

• The Democratic Party became the majority party in the 46th Congress. In that capacity, the Democrats attached riders to appropriation bills which left the Army without funds and took away the President's power to use Federal troops to insure fair elections. Although President Hayes approved of these initial changes, he would subsequently come to veto certain follow-up bills which sought to attack other provisions of the Enforcement Acts.
• In the 1878 Congressional elections, only 62 of the 294 Southern counties with an African American majority were claimed by the Republican Party as compared with 125 in 1876.
• A bill introduced by Horace Page of California that would have empowered Congress to reduce the representation of any state that abridged suffrage was tabled in the House Judiciary Committee.
• Federal troops were removed from Louisiana and South Carolina. After the removal of the troops, the Republican governors of the states were removed from office and the African American citizens of the state were disenfranchised.
• Two pension bills that were introduced by Blanche K. Bruce were passed by the United States Senate. Bruce reported a bill for the improvement of the Mississippi River and the development of the channel and levee system. The Senate passed the bill, but the session ended before the House had considered it. Bruce also presented petitions on prohibition and the refund of the cotton tax. Bruce argued for the integration of the Army, but met with little success. Bruce did make some history in 1878 when he became the first African American to preside over the United States Senate.
• In 1878, there was an influx of African Americans from North Carolina to Indiana. A United States Senate committee investigating aspects of African American immigration to the North, heard conflicting testimony as to the reasons for the mass exodus from North Carolina. Some Republicans actually acknowledged that the migration had, in part, been instigated by Indiana Republicans seeking to develop a Republican majority in the state.

• From 1878 to 1885, John Henry Smyth served in the diplomatic corps as Minister Resident and Consul General in Liberia.

• Between 1876 and 1878, South Carolina had four African American and 14 European American state Senators and 58 African American and 64 European American representatives in its state legislature.

• In Abbeville County, South Carolina, where there were twice as many African Americans as there were European Americans, only three (3) ballots were cast for the Republican Party. In 1874, 1,500 votes for the Republican Party had been cast. In Fairfield County, South Carolina, where there was a three to one ratio of African Americans to European Americans, not a single vote was cast for the Republican Party. In 1874, two-thirds of the vote had gone to the Republican Party.

• Virginia again re-apportioned its election districts to minimize the African American vote.

On December 2, 1878, a report issued by the United States Attorney General revealed that Southern Democrats had stuffed ballot boxes and committed political murders in South Carolina, Louisiana, Texas, and Virginia. On this same day, President Rutherford B. Hayes, in his annual message to Congress, specifically and generally accused the South of abrogating the rights of African Americans.

A Senate committee was appointed to investigate the Southern elections. The committee found that fraud, murder, and intimidation had been used in South Carolina, Louisiana, and Mississippi to prevent African Americans from voting. The committee also found that, in Louisiana alone, some forty political murders had been committed. The committee called for a renewal of Federal protection for African American citizens of those Southern states.

• *Notable Births:* William Stanley Beaumont Braithwaite (1878–1962), a noted poet, was born.

William Stanley Beaumont Braithwaite was born in Boston, Massachusetts. Braithwaite was greatly influenced by the English poets such as Swinburne and Ernest Dowson.

In 1904, Braithwaite published *Lyrics of Life and Love,* his first collection of poetry. This collection of poetry is notable because it stood in stark contrast to the dialect poetry that was so prevalent among African American poets of the day *(see 1872:* Notable births: Paul Laurence Dunbar).

In 1908, Braithwaite's *House of Falling Leaves* was published. In this body of work, Braithwaite elaborated on his theme of mystical aestheticism.

Braithwaite was one of the first critics to acclaim the poetry of James Weldon Johnson as a new voice in African American poetry.

While Braithwaite is considered to be one of the great African American poets, it is interesting to note that Braithwaite never wrote a poem or an essay which would lead the reader to believe that he was an African American. To the extent that his poetry achieved some acclaim, William Braithwaite stands as a testament to the transcendancy of talent over the obstacles of race.

Braithwaite also wrote prose. Some of his more prominent works are *Our Essayists and Critics of Today* (1920), a critique of prominent American and British essayists and literary critics; *Story of the Great War* (1919), a popular history of World War I; and *Bewitched Personage* (1959), a biographical study of the Bronte family.

While Braithwaite was a notable poet and essayist in his own right, his most important contribution may be his work as an anthologist. From 1913 to 1929, Braithwaite edited *Anthology of Magazine Verse.* In this anthology, Braithwaite culled poems from popular and little magazines of the day. Poems by such poets as Edgar Lee Masters, Vachel Lindsay, and Carl Sandburg came to grace the pages of *Anthology of Magazine Verse* long before these author's works appeared in a book form.

Some of Braithwaite's other anthologies include *Elizabethan Verse* (1906); *Georgian Verse* (1908); *Restoration Verse* (1909); *Massachusetts Poets* (1931); and *Anthology of Magazine Verse of 1958.*

• Charles Sidney Gilpin (1878–1930), a noted African American actor, was born (November 19).

Charles Sidney Gilpin was born in Richmond, Virginia. His father was African American and his mother was European American. After attending Saint Francis School for Catholic Children, Gilpin went to work for the *Richmond Planet.*

In 1903, Gilpin became associated with the Canadian Jubilee Singers of Hamilton, Ontario, Canada. Later on he worked with Williams and Walker's Abyssinia Company and, between 1905 and 1906, he was a member of Gus Hill's Smart Set.

After becoming a member of the Pekin Stock

Company in Chicago in 1907, Gilpin came to tour with the Pan-American Octette and joined a group known as the Old Man's Boy Company.

In 1916, Gilpin settled in New York City and became manager of the Lafayette Theater Company in Harlem. The Lafayette Theater Company was an African American drama company in New York.

Gilpin first appeared on Broadway as William Custis, the African American clergyman in the American production of John Drinkwater's *Abraham Lincoln* (December 15, 1919). Playing Brutus Jones in Eugene O'Neill's *Emperor Jones*, Gilpin opened at the Provincetown Playhouse on MacDougall Street (November 1, 1920). The play would subsequently move "uptown" to the Princess Theater on January 29, 1921.

In 1921, Charles Gilpin was one of ten people chosen to receive the Drama League Award. Later that same year, Gilpin was awarded the Spingarn Medal from the NAACP.

- Jack Johnson (1878–1946), the first African American boxer to reign as heavyweight champion of the world, was born.

Jack Johnson was born in Galveston, Texas. Johnson learned how to fight by working out with professional boxers while he lived as a vagabond travelling all over the United States. From 1899 to 1908, Johnson fought 100 bouts and lost only 3.

On December 26, 1908, Johnson won the heavyweight boxing championship from Tommy Burns. He held the title for almost seven years. Johnson lost his championship to Jesse Willard in 1915.

- Bill "Bojangles" Robinson (1878–1949), a famous dancer, vaudevillian, and movie star, was born (May 25).

Bill "Bojangles" Robinson was born in Richmond, Virginia, and was raised by his grandmother, a former slave. Robinson first appeared in vaudeville in 1896 on the Keith circuit. He was a fabulous dancer and came to be known as the "King of Tap Dancers."

In 1927, Robinson starred in Broadway's *Blackbirds*. However, his greatest claim to fame would come from the movies. His best known movies were *Harlem is Heaven* (1932) and a trio of movies with Shirley Temple, *The Little Colonel, The Littlest Rebel,* and *Rebecca of Sunnybrook Farm.*

- Marshall "Major" Taylor, an international cycling champion, was born in Indianapolis, Indiana (November 8).

- *Notable Deaths:* George Vashon (1824–1878), an African American lawyer and poet, died in Mississippi (October 5).

On January 11, 1848, George Vashon became the first African American licensed to practice law in the state of New York. However, his most lasting tribute was his poetry.

George Vashon emphasized Haitian history as the subject matter of his poetry. Vashon visited Haiti during the early 1850s and immersed himself in Haitian culture. At the time, Haiti was an ideal for African Americans because it was a country which proved that people of African descent could govern themselves.

Based upon his Haitian experiences, Vashon wrote his most famous poem *Vincent Oge. Vincent Oge* was a romantic narrative about a real life COTW hero of the Haitian Revolution. The significance of *Vincent Oge* is essentially twofold: First, it was the first narrative, non-lyrical poem ever written by a prominent African American writer and, secondly, the poem was the first poetic tribute written by an African American concerning a revolutionary of African descent.

Vincent Oge was published in 1856 as part of Vashon's *Autographs of Freedom*. The poem remains one of the best examples of anti-slavery poetry.

- *Miscellaneous Cases:* In *Hall v. DeCuir* (January 14, 1978) 95 U.S. 485, 24 L.Ed. 547, the United States Supreme Court sanctioned segregation by ruling that states cannot outlaw segregation on streetcars, railroads, and similar forms of public transportation.

- *Miscellaneous Publications:* James Monroe Trotter published *Music and Some Highly Musical People*, a collection of biographical sketches of African American composers and musicians who specialized in European and European American classical music.

- The *Conservator*, a newspaper, began publication in Chicago. Richard De Baptiste assumed editorial control later in 1878.

- William Lewis Eagleson (1835–1899) began publishing a newspaper in Kansas (January).

- *The Black Church:* John Jasper (1812–1901) preached his famous sermon *De Sun Do Move.* Jasper would deliver this sermon 253 times before his death in 1901.

Born a slave in Virginia, Jasper converted in 1837 and became a powerful and popular preacher.

Jasper spoke in the language of the uneducated, rural African American. However, his sincerity and the power of his oratory made a lasting impression on even those educated listeners who initially came to scoff at his sermons.

- *The Performing Arts:* Sam Lucas (1840–1916) became the first African American to play Uncle Tom in *Uncle Tom's Cabin* on the American stage.

Sam Lucas (a.k.a. Samuel Milady) was born in Washington, Ohio. Lucas performed with major minstrel troupes, wrote one of the most popular minstrel songs of the 1870s (*Carve dat 'Possum*), appeared in vaudeville, and starred in musical comedies, including *A Trip to Coontown*. Lucas also was known as one of the first African American composers of popular ballads.

- *Music:* James Bland published his classic song *Carry Me Back to Old Virginny*. *Carry Me Back to Old Virginny* was adopted by Virginia as the state song in April 1940. When it was adopted, few people realized that it was composed by an African American.
- *Technological Innovations:* J. R. Winters devised a fire escape ladder.
- W. A. Lavalette received a patent for a variation on the printing press.

Sports

In April 1878, the African American John W. "Bud" Fowler, playing for a local team from Chelsea, Massachusetts, defeated the Boston club of the National League in an exhibition game. Fowler also played second base and his semi-professional career lasted until 1891. Fowler, whose real name was John W. Jackson, was the first of more than seventy African American players on interracial teams in organized baseball during the nineteenth century. Bert Jones of Atchison in the Kansas State League was the last being forced out in 1899.

THE AMERICAS

- *Brazil:* In 1878, Joaquim Machado de Assis published *Yaya Garcia*. In this novel, a faithful slave, Raymundo, is the only fully drawn Afro-Brazilian character that appears in any of Machado's works.
- *Cuba:* The Peace of Zanjon ended the Ten Years War. However, General Antonio Maceo rejected the Peace and called for the abolition of slavery.

On February 11, 1878, the Peace of Zanjon was signed and the war — The Ten Years War — between the Cuban revolutionaries and the Spaniards came to an end. Most of the generals of the Cuban army accepted the pact. But not the Afro-Cuban general, Antonio Maceo.

Maceo refused to capitulate. He continued to fight. He fought not just for the freedom of his country but also for the freedom of his people who still remained enslaved.

Maceo held an historic meeting, known as the "Protest of Baragua," in which he met with the leader of the Spanish forces, Marshal Arsenio Martinez Campos. In this meeting, Maceo boldly demanded the independence of Cuba and the complete abolition of slavery. When these two conditions were rejected, Maceo resumed fighting with his rag tag guerrilla army.

Maceo's efforts, while heroic, were futile. Ultimately realizing the futility and confronted with overwhelming Spanish forces, Maceo was soon compelled to surrender.

Maceo left Cuba and went into exile. Nevertheless, his gesture remained a source of inspiration for future Cuban freedom fighters and earned Maceo the respect and acclaim of Cubans and foreigners alike. *See also 1896.*

- By 1878, there were 228,000 slaves remaining in Cuba. In 1869 there had been 363,000. About half of the reduction was attributable to the application of the Moret law *(see 1870)* reforms.

At the end of the Ten years War, the situation in Cuba became critical. Many criollos lost their capital to the skyrocketing war taxes. Additionally, crop areas that had seen combat were devastated.

One of the consequences of the Pact of Zanjon, which put an end to the Ten Years War, was a change in metropolitan policies that made possible the formation of political parties. Freedom of the press, assembly, association, and worship were also granted. Two parties developed: the Autonomist Party, which sought self-governance, and the Constitutional Union Party, which proposed some reforms but opposed independence.

The Autonomist Party and the Constitutional Union Party represented the opposing interests of Cubans and Spaniards. The Autonomists, with Rafael Montoro, Eliseo Giberga, and Enrique Jose Varona among them, demanded civil and economic rights for Cubans equal to those that existed for Spaniards. Their few representatives to the Cortes repeatedly protested Cuba's wrongs and defended her interests. Among their ranks were a number of outstanding intellectuals and brilliant orators.

On the economic scene, the differential right of flags — a scale of tariffs, based on the national flag under which a ship sailed, that charged less for ships flying the Spanish flag — was suspended and the fiscal system was streamlined. Also, negotiations began toward the forging of treaties with the United States.

Until 1890, relations between the United States and Cuba would be defined by policies that favored exports to the United States.

All of these factors would set the stage for the conflict that was to follow.

• *Haiti:* Fabre Nicholas Geffrard (1806–1878), a president of Haiti, died.

Fabre Geffrard was born in the south of Haiti. He was the son of a COTW father and a black mother. Coming from an elite family, Geffrard acquired an education before joining the army.

Geffrard served as a general in the campaigns of President Faustin Soulouque to re-establish Haitian dominion over the Dominican Republic. When the Haitian empire was established by Soulouque, Geffrard was given the title Duke of Tabara. Geffrard became the emperor's most trusted adviser. As bankruptcy, corruption, graft and military, political, and administrative incompetence intensified, the idea of Geffrard as a possible successor to Soulouque began to grow. The emperor ordered Geffrard's arrest, but Geffrard led a successful insurrection and was made president by acclamation of January 20, 1859.

Geffrard's administration, while more partial to the COTW elite, incorporated many powerful blacks from the Soulouque government. The army, the bastion of black elitism, survived.

Geffrard inherited a pattern of state decision making that subverted the rule of law and the constitution. He re-introduced, with minor changes, the relatively progressive constitution of Jean Baptiste Riche, who had preceded Soulouque. Although the government had less dictatorial power, Geffrard was President for Life.

Geffrard halved the army from 30,000 to 15,000 men. He was moderately successful in improving roads and the coastal steamboat service. However, he failed in his attempts to introduce electric telegraphy and to improve irrigation and the city's water supply.

Geffrard did improve the educational system, starting a number of primary and high schools, re-establishing a medical school, and founding a law school, a school of navigation, and a school of art. However, education still retained its elite character.

Geffrard acted to curb the influence of voodoo which had gained under Soulouque. He signed a concordat with the Vatican in 1860 which restored the power of the Catholic Church.

President Geffrard paid considerable attention to international affairs. He reached an accord with the Dominican Republic. However, when the Dominican Republic returned to being a Spanish colony, Geffrard provided crucial assistance to insurgents there. Spain sent a squadron to Haiti's capital city and obtained a commitment from Geffrard not to support the rebels, to grant Spain an apology, and to pay a $200,000 indemnity. Five months later, however, Geffrard managed to get diplomatic recognition of Haiti by the United States for the first time.

Problems that plagued previous regimes persisted; use of state funds for personal enrichment, and the fiscal deficit which quadrupled between 1859 and 1865. In 1865 and 1866, devastating crop failures particularly affected the country's export of cotton.

Geffrard was faced with 15 attempted coups during his years in power. Because of constant rebellion, he dissolved the elected legislature in 1863, replacing it with one guaranteed to rubber stamp his edicts. In 1865, an insurrection led by Sylvain Salnave, was put down with British help. In 1867, with Salnave again rebelling and with a mutiny of his palace guard, Geffrard left for Jamaica. Geffrard died on Jamaica in 1878.

EUROPE

• Robert Browning published *La Saisiaz* and *The Two Poets of Croisic*.

ASIA

• Ch'en Yu-jen (Eugene Chen) (1878–1944), an Afro-Chinese statesman, was born.

Ch'en Yu-jen was born of African, Chinese and Spanish parentage in San Fernando, Trinidad in the British West Indies. His father, Ch'en Kan-ch'uan, was a native of Shunte hsien, Kwangtung province and is believed to have served in the army of the Taiping rebels.

Ch'en Kan-ch'uan was forced to flee China when the Taiping rebellion failed. He fled to the West Indies. Making his living as a barber, Ch'en Kan-ch'uan going by the name Achan, went first to Jamaica and then to Martinique. In Martinique, Achan married a woman of African and Spanish heritage who belonged to a family of

Cantonese immigrants. Achan and his wife moved to Trinidad where they raised a family of six children, five boys and a girl. Ch'en Yu-jen was the eldest child — the number one son.

Known first as Eugene Bernard Achan, Ch'en Yu-jen attended the San Fernando borough school, then went to the Roman Catholic College of Saint Mary's in Port-of-Spain. After leaving college, Ch'en worked in a solicitor's office in Trinidad. Around this time, Ch'en also began contributing articles to the local press.

In time, Ch'en qualified as a solicitor, conveyancer, and notary public in the supreme court of Trinidad and Tobago. Later Ch'en also qualified as a barrister and practiced law until 1911, when he left Trinidad.

Ch'en's departure from Trinidad was probably due to the jealousy his success engendered amongst his fellow barristers and the racial discrimination that accompanied that jealousy.

In 1911, Ch'en went to London, England, where he practiced as a barrister. Toward the end of 1911, Ch'en met Sun Yat-sen. Sun Yat-sen had just received news of the Wuchang revolt and was returning to China from the United States by way of England and France to become the acknowledged leader of the revolution.

Sun Yat-sen was impressed by Ch'en's grasp of legal matters and succeeded in persuading him to go to China and employ his talents for the benefit of his father's land.

In 1912, Ch'en went to Beijing where he was employed as a legal adviser to the Ministry of Communications. Ch'en held this position until 1913 when the Kuomintang's second revolution against Yuan Shih-k'ai was defeated and Sun Yat-sen, along with many of his followers was forced to flee the country.

Ch'en Yu-jen, however, remained in Beijing. In Beijing, he became the editor of the English language journal, *The Peking Gazette.* Using *The Peking Gazette* as a vehicle Ch'en launched a vigorous and bold attack. He selected as his chief target the *North China Daily News,* the chief spokesman of British imperialist interests in the Far East.

During this time, Chinese commerce was centered in Shanghai which was then an international settlement. However, the Chinese commerce of the day was chiefly for the benefit of Great Britain rather than China. Financial power rested with the British Hong Kong and Shanghai Bank.

Ch'en's articles rankled the government. The breaking point occurred on May 18, 1917, when Ch'en published an article entitled "Selling China." "Selling China" reported on the secret negotiations that Tuan Ch'i-jui had engaged in with Japan. Tuan Ch'i-jui was the premier of China and the negotiations centered on China's relinquishing its control over China's armed forces. The reporting of these negotiations embarrassed the Chinese government.

The next day Ch'en was arrested and thrown into a narrow cell with lice-covered assassins. Due to the fact that Ch'en was still a British citizen and because extraterritoriality still existed in China, Ch'en asserted that he was being illegally held. His protest reached a sympathetic ear and, shortly thereafter, by the order of Li Yuanhung, the president of China, he was released.

Under orders from the northern warlords, Li Yuan-hung dissolved the Chinese Parliament. In response, Sun Yat-sen launched the "constitution protection movement." With the support of the navy, Sun Yat-sen brought a number of the members of the Parliament to Canton. This move led to the formation of a new military government in the south with Sun Yat-sen as its head.

Ch'en Yu-jen joined Sun Yat-sen at Canton. In the summer of 1918, together with Quo T'ai-ch'i and C. T. Wang, Ch'en went to the United States to secure American support for the southern government at Canton, but with no success.

In 1919, Ch'en was in France, serving as a technical expert on the southern group, headed by C. C. Wu, of the Chinese delegation to the Paris Peace Conference. Ch'en prepared several documents for the delegation. The most noteworthy of his contributions was China's demand for abrogation of all treaties derived from Japan's Twenty-one Demands of 1915.

During his European sojourn, Ch'en visited London and other European cities. He did not return to China until the summer of 1920.

Upon his return to China, Ch'en went to Shanghai where he established the *Shanghai Gazette.* The *Shanghai Gazette* essentially continued the editorial policies of the *Peking Gazette.*

In 1922, Ch'en Yu-jen rejoined Sun Yat-sen as his foreign affairs adviser and attended the meetings in Shanghai between Sun and Adolph Joffe, an envoy from the Soviet Union. The Sun-Joffe declaration of January 1923 coincided with a pronounced political shift to the left by Ch'en. It also marked the appearance of the anti-imperialist nationalism that was to characterize Ch'en's political attitude for remainder of his life.

In February 1923, Sun Yat-sen returned to

Canton after his loyal troops had ousted Ch'en Chiung-ming from the city and adjacent areas. Sun revived the old military government and re-assumed the title of generalissimo. Ch'en Yu-jen returned to serve as Sun's foreign affairs adviser.

In August 1924, the Canton Merchants Corps attempted to stage a revolt, but the government halted the supply of arms to them. The British authorities sought to intervene and threatened to use British naval forces against Sun.

On September 1, 1924, Sun Yat-sen issued a declaration to the world and also sent a note to British Prime Minister Ramsay MacDonald lodging a strong protest against the "bloody imperialism" of the British. These documents were drafted by Ch'en Yu-jen.

In October of 1924, the Merchant Corps again attempted to revolt. Sun then organized a special committee, which he headed, to deal with the situation. In addition to Ch'en Yu-jen, membership included Hsu Ch'ung-chih, Liao Chung-k'ai, Wang Ching-wei, Chiang Kai-shek, and T'an P'ing-shan. The Merchant Corps staged an armed uprising on October 15, but it was suppressed quickly.

Later in October of 1924, Sun Yat-sen accepted the invitation of Feng Yu-hsiang and Tuan Ch'i-jui to visit Beijing for discussions. Ch'en Yu-jen was a member of Sun's entourage. Ch'en served as Sun's English secretary while Wang Ching-wei served as the senior Chinese secretary.

While in Beijing, Sun became ill. His condition grew steadily worse. In the latter part of February 1925, two wills, one political and one personal, were prepared by Wang Ching-wei and approved by Sun. On March 11, 1925, the day before he died, Sun Yat-sen signed these documents in the presence of a group of his intimate associates. Ch'en Yu-jen wrote Sun's farewell message to the Soviet Union, which re-affirmed the Kuomintang's policy of cooperation with the Soviet Union in its struggle to liberate China from Western imperialism. Sun Yat-sen signed this document after T. V. Soong had read it. This message was later the subject of great controversy among Kuomintang members, some claiming that Sun Yat-sen, since he was on his deathbed, had not been able to study its contents adequately.

After Sun's death, Ch'en remained in Beijing to edit the bilingual Kuomintang newspaper, *Min Pao — The People's Journal.* In August of 1925, Ch'en published an erroneous report which claimed that Chang Tso-lin was dead. Ch'en had previously called Chang Tso-lin a "butcher."

Because of this false report, Ch'en was arrested and imprisoned in Tientsin.

Ch'en secured his release from prison in December 1925 when the forces of Feng Yu-shiang occupied Tientsin and released Ch'en. Upon his release, Ch'en returned to Canton.

At the Second National Congress of the Kuomintang, which was held in January 1926, Ch'en Yu-jen was elected to the Central Executive Committee. In May of 1926, Hu Han-min, the foreign minister of the Canton government, left Canton for Shanghai, and Ch'en Yu-jen was appointed foreign minister.

In June of 1926, Ch'en Yu-jen was named to membership on a three-man delegation, with T. V. Soong and Ch'en Kung-po to discuss with the Hong Kong authorities a settlement of the anti–British strike which had begun in 1925. The strike ended in September 1926. In his capacity as foreign minister, Ch'en also protested to the American consul at Canton against a projected tariff conference in Beijing.

In July 1926, the Northern Expedition under the over-all command of Chiang Kai-shek was launched. By October, Hankow had come under the control of the Nationalists. In mid–November, the Canton government dispatched a five-man committee to Wuhan to investigate the matter of moving the government there. Its members were Ch'en Yu-jen, T. V. Soong, Sun Fo, Hsu Ch'ien, and Borodin.

On December 13, 1926, the leaders who had arrived at Wuhan organized a joint council of the Kuomintang and the National Government to act as the interim authority pending re-establishment of central control. Hsu Ch'ien was made chairman, and the members included Madame Sun Yat-sen, as well as Ch'en and the other members of the advance group from Canton. This council was the nucleus of the National Government that began to function officially at Wuhan on January 1, 1927.

During this time, Ch'en Yu-jen gave fuller scope to his policy of anti-imperialism. In December of 1926, while acting in the name of the National Government, Ch'en lodged a protest with the British government because 14 Kuomintang members in the British concession in Tientsin had been arrested and handed over to Fengtien army authorities. In no uncertain words, Ch'en said that the British would be held responsible for the consequences.

Sir Miles Lampson, the new British minister to China, was visiting Wuhan on an inspection tour about this time, and Ch'en met with him on December 11, 1926. In the course of the interview, Ch'en presented to the British minister a demand that the National Government have access to a share of the customs surplus. On December 31, Ch'en sent a message to United States Secretary of State Frank B. Kellogg voicing his government's opposition to the British implementation of the decision made at the Washington Conference on the imposition of surcharges to the customs duty and the handing over of these sums to the authorities at the port of collection.

At the beginning of January 1927, a demonstration by workers at Hankow led to a clash with marines guarding the British concession. The Nationalists took over the concession, and a committee composed of Ch'en, Sun Fo, and T. V. Soong assumed responsibility for its administration. A few days later, a similar mass action brought the British concession at Kiukiang into Chinese hands. The Japanese and French consuls at Hankow asked Ch'en for information as to any intended changes in the Japanese and French concessions; they were told that the concessions must be handed over unconditionally. By mid–January, foreign warships had begun to concentrate at Shanghai.

By mid–January of 1927, Owen St. Clair O'Malley, the acting counselor of the British legation at Beijing, had taken over the negotiations from the British consul at Hankow. The Ch'en-O'Malley notes of February 19 and March 2 confirmed the retrocession to China of the two concessions in question. For the moment, Ch'en's diplomatic triumph seemed complete, and it appeared that he had begun a new era of revolutionary diplomacy for China.

The March 1927 incident at Nanking, in which a number of foreign nationals were killed or injured and foreign property was destroyed, reflected the prevailing spirit of anti-imperialism in China. Foreign enterprises, particularly in the industrial center of Hankow, were forced to close their doors, and foreign citizens began to leave the Yangtze valley.

Countervailing forces were also at work, however. The foreign powers had concentrated effective military forces at Shanghai. Additionally, several of them had intervened to protect their nationals at Nanking by naval bombardment. When Chinese demonstrators attacked the Japanese concession at Hankow on April 3, 1927, they were cut down by the Japanese machine gun fire. Ch'en's revolutionary foreign policy had begun to arouse powerful opposition.

In light of the difficulties being experienced by the Nationalist regime in its relations with the foreign powers, Ch'en was prepared to soften his policies. However, by then, a change of policy was no longer feasible. Chang Tso-lin's raid on the Soviet embassy at Beijing in April 1927 led Ch'en to extend "profound regrets" to the Soviet commissar for foreign affairs. Ch'en also had to denounce the Beijing diplomatic corps for its involvement in the disastrous affair.

The incident at Beijing was just the first of a series of domestic setbacks for the Wuhan regime. A few days later Chiang Kai-shek established a rival National Government at Nanking. With the establishment of Chiang Kai-shek's government, Ch'en found himself competing with the moderate Nanking foreign minister, C. C. Wu.

In April 1927, Wang Ching-wei returned from Europe to head the Wuhan regime. During the next few weeks Wang, himself a moderate, grew disturbed about the increasingly radical policies urged by the Communists and the left-wing Kuomintang members of his government, and in July he began a purge of these elements. Ch'en Yu-jen, Madame Sun Yat-sen, Borodin, and others departed for the Soviet Union.

From Moscow, Ch'en went to Western Europe, where he remained for the next three years. When the Wuhan-Nanking reconciliation along conservative lines was made official in February of 1928, Ch'en was elected to both the central Executive Committee and the Central Political Council of the Kuomintang. However, these appointments were essentially pro forma and did not confer any real power to the absent Ch'en.

Ch'en did not return to China until February 1931 when he arrived in the British crown colony of Hong Kong. In March 1931, Chiang Kai-shek's arrest of Hu Han-min at Nanking precipitated a new anti–Chiang coalition at Canton. The coalition commenced with the participation of Wang Ching-wei, Sun Fo, C. C. Wu, T'ang Shao-yi, and the support of the military leaders of Kwangtung and Kwangsi, Ch'en Chi-t'ang and Li Tsung-jen. An opposition government was set up at Canton in May 1931 and Ch'en Yu-jen was made foreign minister.

In July of 1931, Ch'en went to Japan to get arms and military advisers for Canton. This move was rationalized by the opposition government as being in accord with Sun Yat-sen's Pan-Asian principle. However, Ch'en's mission was a departure from Ch'en's previous anti-imperialism. Additionally, Ch'en's diplomacy was initiated at a time when China and Japan were engaged in bloody clashes in both Korea and Manchuria. With some justification, Ch'en received widespread condemnation in China for this act.

Threatened civil war between Canton and Nanking was averted by the Japanese attack at Mukden in September 1931. The dissident Canton regime was dissolved.

On December 29, 1931, Sun Fo was appointed president of the Executive Yuan at Nanking, and Ch'en Yu-jen was made foreign minister in that cabinet. However, on January 24, 1932, Ch'en resigned because the policies he advocated found little support among the government leaders. Sun Fo followed Ch'en by resigning on the next day.

Ch'en lived for a time in Shanghai after leaving Nanking. In May 1932, Ch'en demanded the re-organization of the Kuomintang and he predicted that there would eventually be war between the United States and Japan.

In March 1933, Ch'en urged American intervention in the Sino-Japanese conflict as a means of avoiding the larger war which he foresaw coming. Meanwhile, some of the southern leaders had established the Southwest Political Council, which maintained virtual autonomy in the local administration of the provinces of Kwangtung and Kwangsi. Although actually controlled by the military leaders of the two provinces, the council had the support of some veteran political leaders, including Hu Han-min and T'ang Shao-yi. Ch'en Yu-jen was appointed a member of the council in May 1933.

In November 1933, with military support provided by the famous Nineteenth Route Army commanded by Chiang Kuang-nai and Ts'ai T'ing-k'ai along with the cooperation of Li Chishen, Ch'en Ming-shu launched the Fukien revolt. The movement began with the formation of a people's revolutionary government at Foochow. Ch'en Yu-jen and his Wuhan colleague Hsu Ch'ien were among the prominent participants, and Ch'en became the foreign minister of the insurgent regime. The Fukien rebellion was short-lived. It was easily suppressed by Chiang Kai-shek at the beginning of 1934. For his participation in the Fukien rebellion, Ch'en was expelled by the Kuomintang. Ch'en was forced to return to Europe.

At the outbreak of the full blown Sino-Japanese war in July of 1937, Ch'en was in Paris. He was invited by T. V. Soong and Wang Ch'unghui to return to China, and he arrived in Hong Kong in October 1938.

Although reinstated in the Kuomintang, Ch'en declined to participate in China's wartime government. Instead, Ch'en issued a statement from Hong Kong demanding that Chiang Kaishek turn over the leadership of the government to a five-member commission.

When war broke out in Europe in 1939, Ch'en advocated that China issue a declaration favoring England and France. Ch'en condemned the Hitler-Stalin pact of August 1939 as well as the Soviet invasion of Finland in November.

After the outbreak of war in the Pacific in December 1941, and the Japanese occupation of Hong Kong, Ch'en was detained by the Japanese and taken to Shanghai. In Shanghai, Ch'en resisted all efforts by the Japanese to persuade him to join the Japanese-sponsored regime of Wang Ching-wei in Nanking.

Even while in enemy-occupied territory, Ch'en remained characteristically outspoken. He denounced the peace policy of the Wang Ching-wei regime as a "puppet peace." On one occasion, in 1943, he was said to have referred to members of the Japanese War Office as "a pack of liars" for circulating a report that he had joined the Nanking regime.

Ch'en Yu-jen remained detained in Shanghai until his death on May 20, 1944.

Aside from his political legacy, Ch'en Yu-jen also left behind his children. Ch'en Yu-jen's wife was of African descent and his children reflected their African blood.

One of Ch'en's children would come to leave his own mark on China. Percy Chen was born in Trinidad in 1901. He was Ch'en Yu-jen's eldest son. Percy studied law in England and was made a member of the Middle Temple. Percy was called to the English bar at the age of 21. He later practiced law for several years in Trinidad.

Percy Chen went to China in the fall of 1926. He was appointed a member of the staff of the Foreign Office of the Nationalist Government and followed the Nationalist armies to Hankow during their Northern Punitive Expedition.

In 1927, Percy was commissioned by the Nationalist Government to conduct Borodin and other Russian advisors to their own country. Percy subsequently served as an advisor to the General Motors Corporation in their negotiations with the Soviet Commissariat of Heavy Industry.

AFRICA

• *North Africa, Egypt and Sudan:* In March, the British and French governments demanded an international commission of inquiry into Egyptian finances.

• On August 18, Nubar Pasha became the premier of Egypt with Sir Rivers Wilson as Minister of Finance.

• On December 11, Dual Control in Egypt was suspended because of the introduction of ministerial government.

• Cleopatra's Needle, given to England in 1819, was dispatched from Alexandria to London.

• Dem Ziber was occupied by Gessi Pasha and, subsequently, became the capital of Bahr al-Ghazal.

• Rohlfs visited Kufra oasis.

• A plan was forwarded for a railway from Algeria to Senegal.

• *Western Africa:* A quarrel between the people of Bolor and Jufunco led to the massacre of Portuguese troops (December 30).

• The British were besieged by Awuna at Fort Prinsensten, Keta.

• The Ibadan army beat the Fulani at Ikirun.

• Yoko became the ruler of the Kpa Mende confederacy of Sierra Leone.

Yoko made alliances with her neighbors and built a large confederacy. Perhaps the most important of these alliances was with the British who were playing a continually larger role in the politics of the Sierra Leone hinterland. Yoko aided the British in their diplomatic and peace-keeping missions, and received their support in return, including a contingent of Frontier Police stationed in her capital.

• *Central Africa:* The Livingstone Inland Mission started work in the Congo.

• Serpa Pinto began his journey from Luanda (Angola) to Durban (South Africa) via Bie.

• The *Comite d'Etudes du Haut- Congo* was formed in the Congo (November 25).

• Henry Stanley agreed to serve Leopold of Belgium for five years.

• *Eastern Africa:* Lieutenant Cambier's expedition departed Bagamoyo (June 28).

• Nyungu ya Mawe attacked the White Fathers caravan.

• The first White Fathers' mission was established at Tabora.

• An Italian trade expedition arrived in Ethiopia.

In 1878, Menelik was persuaded to acknowledge Yohannes as the Emperor of Ethiopia. But this acknowledgment was not an overwhelming vote of approval. Indeed, Menelik's own strong position was too solid for Menelik to completely subordinate himself to Yohannes.

In return for Shoa's support, Yohannes granted Menelik considerable autonomy and promised Menelik the Ethiopian crown on his death. Revolts continued to arise in other provinces, but generally Yohannes' position was stronger than that enjoyed by any previous nineteenth century Ethiopian emperor.

Nevertheless, around this same time, European imperialists began to encroach upon Ethiopia from all sides. The Italians saw Menelik as an ally against Yohannes, while the French saw him as a potential ally against the British who were, at the time, advancing into southern Sudan. During the 1880s, continued arms imports would give Menelik the best-equipped African army in northeast Africa.

• The Council of Ethiopian Churches convened at Borumieda. The conveners ordered that heretics were to be compelled to submit. Muslims, Jews and pagans were to be baptized.

• The Hehe warded off the Ngoni, but their war would last until 1881.

• In 1878, William Mackinnon, the founder of the British East Africa Protectorate, leased mainland territory from the Sultan of Zanzibar, Barghash. This venture came to nothing, but his agents continued to collect treaty rights in Kenya and Uganda.

• *Southern Africa:* Walwis Bay was annexed (March 18).

• Kruger and Joubert petitioned Westminster against annexation of Transvaal (May).

• On December 11, Great Britain sent an ultimatum to the Zulus.

The British military became fearful of the Zulu build-up begun by Cetewayo in 1877. The British high commissioner, Sir Bartle Frere decided to eliminate what was perceived to be a threat to the British colonists of South Africa. On the pretext that Cetewayo had violated earlier agreements with Transvaal Governor Shepstone, an ultimatum was sent in December 1878 demanding what amounted to the disbanding of the Zulu military forces that had been gathered by Cetewayo. When the demand was not met, the British invaded Zululand.

• The Livingstonia Central African Trading Company (LCATC) was founded at Mandala near Blantyre.

• J. Stevenson founded a company for trade on Lake Nyasa.

• In 1878, John Molteno, the prime minister of the Cape Colony, broke with Governor Henry Frere *(see 1884)* over the employment of imperial troops in the Xhosa frontier war. Molteno's administration was dismissed by Frere and Molteno was replaced as the Cape Colony prime minister by John Sprigg.

The Xhosa are the most populous southern Nguni branch of Bantu-speaking peoples. The senior royal dynasty of the Xhosa goes back to the 1400s when the Xhosa were living in the land which is today known as Natal.

Until the late eighteenth century, most Xhosa recognized a single paramount chief, but their political system was never highly centralized. A few small groups moved south to form new chiefdoms, which usually took the names of their founders, such as Ndlambe.

In the late 1700s, a major division among the Xhosa led to the creation of two dominant chiefdoms — the Gcaleka, north of the Kei River, and the Rarabe (Ngqika), south of the Kei River. Over time, some additional divisions occurred, but the Gcaleka and Rarabe chiefs remained dominant.

From the 1770s to the 1870s, the Xhosa fought a succession of frontier wars with the Europeans of the neighboring Cape Colony. Each war cost the Xhosa some of their land and autonomy. By 1886, all Xhosa territories were annexed to the Cape Colony and the surviving lineages were on the payroll of the Cape Colony administration.

• Civil war erupted in Barotseland (the land of the Lozi).

The Lozi (also known as the Aluyi, Balozi, Barotse, Luyana, Luyi or Rotse) is the collective name for the peoples living under a western Zambian kingdom ruled by an intrusive aristocracy known as Luyi, or Luyana. Their country was known as Barotseland.

The origins of Barotseland are rather obscure. According to tradition, the Luyi were founded by Mbuyu, who came from the Lunda of southern Zaire. One of her sons, Mboo, was the first ruler — the first "litunga" — of the Lozi kingdom. Despite the apparent Lunda origins of the kingdom, many of its institutions evolved spontaneously during a long period of relative isolation, amidst the special conditions of the Zambezi floodplains.

After the death of the great litunga Mulambwa around 1835, Barotseland fell into a long and bitter civil war. The war was interrupted when the Kololo king Sebitwane occupied Barotseland from 1840 to 1864.

After the restoration of Lozi rule, civil war continued until 1885. In 1885, Lewanika Lumbosi came to power.

In 1890, Lewanika signed the first of a series of treaties with the British South Africa Company. These treaties brought Barotseland under a protectorate and eventually into the colony of Northern Rhodesia (present day Zambia).

• Mataka I Nyambi (c.1805– c.1878), the founder of the strongest Yao chiefdom, is believed to have died in this year.

Prior to the nineteenth century, the Yao of northern Mozambique had a tradition of long-distance trade, but their chiefdoms were typically small and weak. During the mid–19th century, many Yao leaders of various backgrounds capitalized on the growth of the coastal slave trade to build new chiefdoms of unprecedented strength. Some of these leaders carried Yao commerce and settlements into southern Malawi and southern Tanzania. Mataka, whose successors bore his name as their dynastic title, built his own chiefdom in northern Mozambique.

Around the 1850s, Mataka left the village of his grandmother to form a separate community. He moved about frequently and gathered followers. His people traded woven baskets for iron hoes, which in turn they traded for slaves. Eventually, however, Mataka acquired his trade slaves directly by armed raiding. By the 1860s, Mataka controlled much of the territory east of Lake Nyasa by relying upon terror and the threat of brutal discipline.

Formal administrative structure was limited to his immediate capital, Mwembe.

In Mwembe, Mataka was visited in 1866 by David Livingstone — the first European to visit the region since the early 1600s.

Mataka retained Swahili and Arab scribes. He was a man who was deeply influenced by coastal Islamic (Swahili) culture. However, while he appreciated the aesthetics of Islam, he never personally converted to the faith.

Shortly before his death, Mataka made an appeal for Christian teachers — teachers who came but who Mataka never saw. On his death, a nephew was made chief with the title Mataka II Che Nyenje. Nyenje ended Mataka's war and was himself converted to Islam despite the arrival of Christian missionaries in 1880.

• Sandile (c.1820–1878), the last Rarabe Xhosa paramount chief, died.

Sandile was only about nine years old when his father Ngqika died in 1829. Because of his young age, a regency was formed which included Sandile's half-brother Maqoma *(see 1873)*.

Maqoma dominated Rarabe politics over the next decade and led a major but unsuccessful war against the Cape Colony. During this war, Sandile remained neutral. For this neutrality, Sandile was rewarded with Cape support after the war was concluded.

Sandile formally acceded to the chieftainship in 1840 and then gradually outstripped Maqoma in influence among his people.

Sandile supported cattle raiding from white settlers and became the central Xhosa figure in another frontier war in 1846. After Xhosa resistance had been worn down, Sandile surrendered to the British.

The British betrayed Sandile by imprisoning him. When the new Cape Governor and High Commissioner Harry Smith arrived, Sandile was forced to kiss his feet and to acknowledge British sovereignty over "British Kaffraria." These humiliations intensified Xhosa resentment against the British and led to another war in 1850.

In the war of 1850, the Xhosa were once again defeated. Sandile was forced to withdraw his people into a smaller area.

In 1856, the great cattle killing began among the Gcaleka Xhosa north of the Kei River. Sandile was urged by the Gcaleka chief Sarili to comply with the prophecies of Mhlakaza, who promised the Xhosa the millennium in return for total destruction of their wealth. Sandile reluctantly assented, but only part of his own people killed their cattle.

In 1860, Sandile visited Cape Town, and six years later his territory was annexed to the Cape Colony. In 1878, Sandile was reluctantly drawn into a last frontier war, although it primarily involved the Gcaleka. Sandile died fighting. For his valor, Sandile's corpse was decapitated.

RELATED HISTORICAL EVENTS

• *Europe:* A labor code was instituted for all Portuguese colonies. Forced labor was abolished.

----------- **1 8 7 9** -----------

THE UNITED STATES

In 1879, the exodus of African Americans from the South became a matter of national concern. Encouraged by such activists as Henry Adams of Louisiana and Benjamin "Pap" Singleton of Tennessee, thousands of African Americans began a mass exodus from what was becoming an increasingly oppressive South. These migrating African Americans fled for the North and West, especially the state of Kansas.

Somewhat in response to this mass exodus, in May, General James Chalmers of Mississippi and a group of Southern European Americans "closed" the Mississippi River by threatening to sink all vessels carrying African Americans. Chalmers and his group terrorized ship owners into stranding 1,500 African Americans along the banks of the Mississippi. General Thomas Conway, of New Jersey, described the situation in a letter to President Hayes: "Every river landing is blockaded by white enemies of the colored exodus; some of whom are mounted and armed, as if we were at war …" Only under threats of Federal intervention did the shipping companies resume service.

A resolution was introduced by Senator Windom of Minnesota to study the practicability of encouraging Southern African American emigration to other parts of the United States.

It is estimated that during this time over 40,000 African Americans fled to the Midwest to escape the political and economic conditions of the South.

• In February, Vice President Wheeler was absent, and for a time, Blanche K. Bruce presided over the United States Senate (February 15). During this session of the Senate, Bruce voted against a bill to restrict Chinese immigration. Bruce was also appointed chair of a Select Committee on the Freedmen's Bank — a bank which had failed in 1874.

• House Democrats attached a rider to the Army Appropriation Bill which forbade the use of Federal troops at elections. President Hayes vetoed the bill on April 29.

• The African Americans who served in the 45th Congress included Representatives R. H. Cain, J. H. Rainey and Robert Smalls of South Carolina; as well as Senator B. K. Bruce of Mississippi.

• Around 1879, the Readjusters, a dissenting Southern Democratic group, gained some prominence in Virginia. They captured 56 of the 100 seats in the Virginia House of Delegates, and 24 of the 40 seats in the Virginia Senate. Led by William Mahone, they advocated repudiation of the state debt and openly appealed to African Americans.

• *The Labor Movement:* The Colored Farmer's Alliance was established as the African American counterpart to the European American Farmer's Alliance, a forerunner of the Populist political movement. Almost 1.25 million African Americans would eventually join the Colored Farmer's Alliance.

• *Notable Births:* Nannie Burroughs, a noted civil rights activist and religious leader, was born in Orange, Virginia (May 2).

• William Geary "Bunk" Johnson (1879–1949), an African American jazz musician, was born (December 27).

William Geary "Bunk" Johnson was born in New Orleans. Johnson studied with Wallace Cutchey. In 1896, Johnson became the second cornetist in the Buddy Bolden Band.

From 1911 through 1914, Johnson played with the Eagle Band in New Orleans. After touring with the Eagle Band, Johnson became associated with minstrel shows and played in county fairs until he retired from music in 1931.

Johnson was "rediscovered" in 1938, and as late as 1945, Johnson was playing in New York City and Boston with Sidney Bechet.

• *Notable Deaths:* John Jones (1816–1879), "the most prominent citizen of Chicago" during his lifetime, died. Jones was born free in North Carolina. His parents were a free African American woman and a European American man. Jones apprenticed with a tailor in Tennessee and arrived in Chicago in 1845. Jones was a civil rights advocate and the first African American elected Cook County commissioner. He was elected to a one year term on the Cook County Board in 1871 and to a three year term in 1872.

• *Miscellaneous State Laws:* South Carolina re-enacted a statute which prohibited interracial marriage.

• *Miscellaneous Publications:* Martin Robinson Delany published *Principia of Ethnology: The Origin of Races and Color, etc.* This publication espoused Delany's views on race.

• *Scholastic Achievements:* The African Methodist Episcopal Church established Livingston College in North Carolina.

• Richard Theodore Greener became dean of the Howard University Law School.

• Josephine Silone Yates (1859–1912) was certified to teach in the public schools of Rhode Island.

• Mary Elizabeth Mahoney (1845–1926) graduated from the New England Hospital for Women and Children. Of the forty original aspirants, only three remained to receive their nursing diplomas, two European American women and Mary Mahoney.

Today, the Mary Mahoney Medal, a medal named in honor of Mary Mahoney by the American Nurses' Association, is given biennially to the person making the most progress toward opening full opportunities in nursing for all, regardless of race, creed, color, or national origin.

• *Sports:* Isaac Murphy won the Travers Stakes at Saratoga. During 1879, Murphy would win 35 of the 75 races he entered.

• Frank Hart set an American record for marathon walking. Nicknamed "O'Leary's Smoked Irishman," in tribute to his coach, the former marathon walking champion O'Leary, Hart won a contest in New York City which had contestants walk as far as they could in three or six days for a prize of several thousand dollars.

THE AMERICAS

• *Cuba:* La Guerra Chiquita began.

• In 1879, Arsenio Martinez Campos, the prime minister in Spain, announced that the patronato (the last vestiges of slavery) would end in 1888. However, the patronato officially ended two years earlier, in 1886. By 1886, there were only 26,000 slaves that remained in Cuba.

• *Dominican Republic:* Ulises Heureaux terminated the presidency of Cesareo Guillermo in 1879. Heureaux then became the minister of the interior and the police during the presidency of Archbishop Fernando Arturo de Merino (1880–1882).

• *Haiti:* President Boisrond Canal resigned in disgust in July 1879 because he could not make his constitutional relationship work with a hostile legislature.

Between Salnave's execution in January 1870 and the chaotic politics that began in August 1911 and ended in the United States invasion of 1915, the Liberal Party, often the representative of the COTW elite, faced opposition from the National Party, the organ of the black elites. With a few exceptions, these political struggles became violent.

Selected by the National Assembly in 1870 after a provisional government, President Nissage Saget completed his term of office and stepped down voluntarily in 1874.

President Boisrond Canal resigned in disgust in July 1879 because he could not make his constitutional relationship work with a hostile legislature. Apart from these exceptions, presidencies began and ended by force or the threat of it.

Once in office, a president of Haiti was typically faced with the need to implement policies, to collect money to run the government and to pay off political creditors and hungry, potentially hostile officeholders. Peasants were hard to tax, unless the president could find a way to tax or seize their export produce which for most Haiti's history was coffee. However, interfering with exports or imports alienated the small but important bourgeoisie, mainly in Port-au-Prince.

Foreign interference was another problem. The British and the French still held colonies in the Caribbean and insisted on the payment of loans. The tendency of deposed presidents to flee to Jamaica, or invading armies to come from the Dominican Republic, presented additional opportunities for foreign interference.

Of growing importance was the United States. As an exporter of capital by the 1890s, and as a power that increasingly saw the Caribbean as its own sphere of influence, the United States government and business community found the sporadic unrest in Haiti to be a threat to United States citizens and their commercial enterprises. In the 1890s and early 1900s, the United States especially found Haiti's black nationalism to be an affront and the United States considered many of the Haitian government policies, such as the prohibition against the ownership of land by foreigners of European descent, to be an obstacle to investment. Additionally, Haiti's strategic geographical position commanding the entrances to the northern Caribbean also provoked interference from the United States and other powers.

The need for money, the relationship with the national bourgeoisie, and fear of foreign power, faced each president, whatever his ethnic politics and proclamations. The welfare of the majority was often forgotten, and several presidents found themselves appeasing foreign governments, negotiating new loans with them, or even negotiating leases of national territory. Such was the rivalry for the presidency and the precariousness of tenure once in office that some Haitian leaders treacherously called in foreign military support against their compatriot opponents.

• Louis Etienne Lysius Felicite Salomon

became the president of Haiti. Salomon served as president of Haiti from 1879 to 1888.

When President Boisrond Canal stepped down after a turbulent period in office, Salomon returned an overwhelming number of Nationalists to the National Assembly, which in October of 1879, by a vote of 74–13, elected Salomon president.

Salomon had served in Soulouque's cabinet and was a noted black nationalist. Salomon survived an invasion from Jamaica backed by the British. Salomon also suppressed dissidence and claimed to fight for national integrity.

Nevertheless, Salomon found it expedient to support the concordat with the Holy See in spite of the anticlerical, pro-voodoo opinions of many of his followers. Salomon negotiated with the United States for the lease of national territory, founded the Banque Nationale backed by French capital, and, in return for the liquidation of the French indemnity, accepted a French military mission. Salomon even permitted foreign companies to own Haitian land.

Ultimately, Salomon's regime was characterized by a certain degree of subservience to French interests and ideas. It was, after all, Salomon who brought together a group of French bankers to capitalize and administer a national bank. And it was Salomon who resumed payment on outstanding debts to France which were entirely liquidated. And it was Salomon who recruited French teachers and established an expanded French-style system of education which still prevails.

EUROPE

• Robert Browning published *Dramatic Idyls.*

AFRICA

• *North Africa, Egypt and Sudan:* Nubar Pasha and Sir R. Wilson were mobbed in Cairo (February 17) and the next day the ministry of Nubar Pasha collapsed.

• In April, Sharif Pasha formed a ministry.

• Khedive Ismail was deposed (June 29). Muhammed Tewfiq became the new Khedive and the International Committee of Liquidation was appointed.

• In July, the Assembly of Delegates was dismissed and, in August, so also was Sharif Pasha. Riyad Pasha became the premier.

• On September 4, Dual Control was reimposed. Sir Evelyn Baring was named the British representative.

• A secret society of Egyptian army officers emerged as the Patriotic Party (*al-Hizb al-Watani*). The Patriotic Party was hostile to the Khedive and foreigners.

• The Egyptian General Staff was disbanded.

• Azande recognized Egyptian suzerainty. The trade in ivory was made a state monopoly.

• There was an uprising against the French in Algeria. It was ultimately quelled.

• *Western Africa:* Senegal was granted financial autonomy.

• The United Africa Company (UAC) was founded by Sir George Goldie.

By 1879, George Goldie (*see 1877*) had united all the important British companies of West Africa into a single corporation, the United Africa Company. However, competition from the French remained strong.

• The UAC station at Onitsha was evacuated because of local hostility.

• Cocoa was introduced into the Gold Coast from Fernando Po and Sao Tome.

• French establishments in the Gulf of Benin were attached to Gabon.

• The British occupied Ketonou.

• The French went to war against the Moreah.

• Cinque (Joseph Cinquez or Sengbe), the leader of the famous *Amistad* slave ship rebellion, died.

Cinque was a Mende from the land that today is the country of Sierra Leone. Cinque was enslaved and transported to Havana, Cuba.

In 1839, Cinque and fifty-one other slaves were put on the *Amistad*, a small transport, to sail for another Cuban port. Seizing machetes, Cinque and his comrades killed the captain and cook, and ordered the two remaining crew members to steer the ship to Africa.

The helmsman, however, landed the ship on Long Island, New York, deceiving Cinque. Cinque and the other slaves were seized by the United States Navy.

President Martin Van Buren wanted to accede to Spanish demands to return the slaves. However, former President John Quincy Adams won the release of Cinque and his followers by arguing their case before the United States Supreme Court.

Cinque and the others were sent back to Africa accompanied by some clergymen who wanted to use them in a missionary movement. Fortunately for Cinque, the destination was Sierra Leone.

Upon their arrival in 1841, the missionaries set up a station on the borders of Mendeland. However, Cinque left them to return home.

It is believed that for a while Cinque became a slave trader. However, eventually, he returned to the mission and worked with the missionaries as an interpreter.

• *Central Africa:* King Akwa requested the protection of Queen Victoria.

• Rubber was first exported from Angola.

• Henry Stanley, with Zanzibari porters, began the exploration of the Congo River (August 4).

• Fernando Po was made into a penal settlement.

• Junker explored the Ouelle and Chari Rivers.

• By 1879, Lewanika, the king of the Lozi, had smashed an attempted counter-coup by Mwanawina. Mwanawina died shortly thereafter. After disposing of this threat, Lewanika took additional precautionary steps by purging many of his potential rivals.

• *Eastern Africa:* The first White Fathers reached Entebbe (February 17).

Henry Stanley visited Mutesa, the king of the Ganda kingdom, in 1875 and made a favorable impression by actively aiding Mutesa in a military campaign. Afterwards, Mutesa assented to Stanley's proposal to introduce Christian missionaries, hoping that they would assist him militarily.

The first Protestant missionaries arrived in 1877. Catholic missionaries soon followed in 1879 and the seeds for a cultural and political revolution were planted.

• Cambier departed from Tabora (May 27). He arrived in Ujiji on August 12. Cambier was joined by another expeditionary party led by Captain Poperlin in November.

• Fort Leopold was constructed at Karema as a post of the International African Association.

• Mkwawa succeeded Munyigamba (Munyigumba) as the chief of the Hehe.

Munyigumba died in 1879. Upon his death, Mkwawa briefly fled north while a subordinate chief usurped power. Mkwawa soon returned, however, and drove the usurper out. Mkwawa then proceeded to consolidate his position by military means.

• General Gordon visited Yohannes IV to

make peace with Ethiopia for Egypt. Yohannes refused and demanded recognition of Ethiopia's ancient frontiers.

• Henry Stanley left Zanzibar for the Congo.

• Joseph Thomson explored southern Tanzania and eastern Zaire.

Joseph Thomson's first expedition in 1879 took him through southern Tanzania and eastern Zaire and clarified a number of geographical questions about the interior's lake systems.

• *Southern Africa:* In 1879, the Zulu War erupted. On January 22, British troops were massacred at Isandhlwana.

On the basis of his colonial experience in India, the British High Commissioner for South Africa, Sir Henry Bartle Frere *(see 1884)* advocated disarming native societies. Because he saw the humbling of the powerful Zulu kingdom as the key to obtaining the cooperation of the Afrikaner republics, in 1878, Frere issued an ultimatum to Cetewayo, the king of the Zulu. In the ultimatum, Cetewayo was ordered to disband and disarm the Zulu army. Frere's action precipitated the Zulu War of 1879.

Armed with little more than spears, the Zulus under the leadership of the Zulu King Cetewayo, in a surprise attack at Isandhlwana (Isandlana), wiped out an entire British regiment (January 22, 1879). Stunned by this defeat, the British regrouped and subsequently soundly defeated the Zulus at Ulundi (July 4, 1879). Cetewayo was captured in August (August 28) of 1879 and confined, in exile, near Cape Town. Cetewayo's kingdom, Zululand, was then divided among 13 chiefs.

• Prince Imperial was killed (July).
• The principles of the Afrikaner Bond were published (July 4).
• The Zulu War officially came to an end (September 1).
• The Transvaal Republic was proclaimed (December 16).
• Fingoland and Griqualand East were annexed.

The Cape government annexed Griqualand East in 1879 and the British high commissioner, Bartle Frere, demanded that Mqikela, the chief of the Mpondo, cede Port St. John to him. Mqikela refused, so Frere shifted British recognition to his rival Nqiliso (the son of Ndamase), who sold the port to the British in return for recognition of his own independence.

After this episode, the British pressed Mqikela

for the right to open a road between their port and newly acquired territory inland.

Mqikela — allegedly a drunkard — gradually lost control of his chiefdom to his nephew Mdlangaso. Mqikela was succeeded upon his death by his son Sigcawu.

• A Jesuit mission was established at Bulawayo.
• The British resumed hostilities against the Pedi.

Fresh from his occupation of the Zulu kingdom, Garnet Wolseley attacked the Pedi with two British regiments and 6000 Swazi troops. A thousand Pedi, including Sekhukhune's heir, were killed. Sekhukhune himself was captured and taken to Pretoria, while his rival, Mampuru, was made Pedi chief.

• Antonio Vicente da Cruz (c.1825–1879) died.

The da Cruz family was comprised of Portuguese settlers who, over time, came to identify primarily with African culture and politics. The da Cruz family established themselves among the Tonga chiefdoms between the Indian Ocean and the town of Tete. Essentially, the da Cruz family prospered because they held a key location astride the major interior trade routes.

Antonio Vicente da Cruz, went by the African name of Bonga, — a name which was later applied to the whole family. Bonga was the son of Nhaude. Bonga at first maintained good relations with the Portuguese while extending the family's influence through diplomatic marriages with African rulers.

Bonga's firm control of the Zambezi trade routes angered the coastal Portuguese. This led to a number of invasions. Between 1867 and 1869, Bonga repelled four major invasions by the Portuguese government and the rival empire builder, Manuel Antonio de Sousa.

After the 1860s, Bonga's power subsided. He ultimately was forced into a treaty with the Portuguese.

Upon his death in 1879, Bonga was succeeded briefly by Luis Vicente da Cruz (Muchenga) and then by Vitorino da Cruz (Nhamisinga) in 1880. During these years, peace was maintained. However, the peace was only temporary since da Sousa's power in the south was growing stronger.

• Sayyid Ali al-Mirghani was born.
• Moorosi (c.1790s–1879), the last ruler of the Phuthi of Basutoland, died.

After the Sotho wars of the 1820s, Basutoland

came to be dominated by Moshoeshoe *(see 1870)*. Moorosi, however, maintained Phuthi autonomy in southern Basutoland, where he defended himself on a naturally fortified mountain.

At first, Moorosi resisted Moshoeshoe's expansion. However, gradually he became the latter's ally.

In 1869, Moorosi's territory — along with that of Moshoeshoe — was incorporated into the British Basutoland Protectorate. Later the Protectorate was transferred to the administration of the Cape Colony.

In 1878, the Cape Colony unilaterally decreed severe limits on Africans' rights to possess firearms within the Protectorate. Moorosi adamantly refused to comply. The next year, British forces stormed his mountain and routed his people. Moorosi was killed and decapitated.

After Moorosi's death, the Phuthi chiefdom ceased to exist and the Phuthi were gradually absorbed into the dominant Sotho kingdom.

RELATED HISTORICAL EVENTS

• *The United States:* William Lloyd Garrison (1805–1879), abolitionist and publisher of the *Liberator*, died (May 24).

William Lloyd Garrison was an American journalist and reformer who became famous in the 1830s for his denunciations of slavery. Before his time, abolitionists had made moderate appeals to slaveholders and legislators on behalf of slaves. This method was employed in the hope of achieving the gradual abolition of slavery.

Garrison changed this attitude. Garrison said that slavery was evil and that it should be ended "immediately." Garrison also took umbrage with all who did not entirely agree with him.

Garrison was raised in Newburyport, Massachusetts. As an impoverished youth, Garrison was apprenticed to a printer at the age of 13. By 1827, Garrison had become a veteran journalist. He soon became the editor of the *National Philanthropist*, America's first temperance newspaper.

In 1828, Garrison met Benjamin Lundy, a Quaker and a pioneer anti-slavery propagandist and organizer. Not long afterwards, Garrison became an ardent abolitionist.

Writing for Lundy's newspaper, Garrison wrote scathing attacks on the institution of slavery. His attacks on slave dealers caused Garrison to be jailed for seven months.

In 1831, Garrison began publishing *The Liberator* in Boston. *The Liberator* had a small cir-

culation, but it was influential and at times aroused violent public reaction.

In 1832, Garrison was instrumental in organizing the first society for the immediate abolition of slavery. Garrison was able to attract associates such as Wendell Phillips and influenced such individuals as Theodore Parker and Henry David Thoreau.

Garrison was also an advocate of women's rights. His fight to give women equal rights within the American Anti-Slavery Society split the abolitionist movement.

Garrison was a non-Unionist. He believed that the Northern states ought to separate from the South. Garrison refused to vote, and opposed the United States government because it permitted slavery. Eventually, however, Garrison did come to support Abraham Lincoln and Lincoln's efforts during the Civil War.

• *Europe:* Fabri published a pamphlet entitled *Germany's Need for Colonies.*

• *Africa:* In the Cape Colony, George Theal became the keeper of the Cape archives.

When George Theal was made keeper of the Cape archives in 1879, he undertook more ambitious ethnographic and historical projects. He organized the vast holdings of the Cape archives and collected material on southern Africa in European centers.

During his lifetime, Theal wrote and edited more than eighty volumes. Among his works are the three volumes of *Basutoland Records* (1883); the thirty-six volumes of *Records of the Cape Colony* (1897–1905); the nine volumes of *Records of South East Africa* (1898–1903); and his monumental eleven volume *History of South Africa* (1892–1919).

Theal's writings were massively detailed, but he generally treated his sources uncritically and he rarely identified them. Additionally, his work was characterized by a strong Euro-African settler bias.

Nevertheless, Theal's unequaled mastery of documentary records gave his histories a seminal influence over the whole development of modern South African historiography.

——— **1 8 8 0** ———

THE UNITED STATES

1880 marked both the zenith and the end of the political career of Senator Blanche Bruce of Mississippi. In this year, Bruce introduced 21 bills in the United States Senate, although none became law. Bruce also spoke on behalf of admitting duty-free clothing sent from England and destined for destitute African Americans in Kansas.

Bruce supported a more enlightened government policy towards Indigenous Americans and urged the division of land among the various Indigenous American nations.

On May 4, 1880, Bruce presided over the Senate. In the second session of the Senate, Bruce introduced a bill to have the Freedmen's Bank property bought by the government. The bill was passed in the Senate but was never considered by the House.

At the Republican National Convention of 1880, Bruce settled his differences with Grant and came out in support of him. However, in one of those odd moments which crop up occasionally in history, Bruce was asked to briefly chair the convention proceedings. While serving as chair, Bruce recognized a certain James Garfield. During the ensuing moments, James Garfield made a lasting impression upon the convention delegates. The impression buoyed Garfield's prospects tremendously. He became the Republican Party nominee.

As for Blanche Bruce, he received 8 votes in an unsuccessful bid to become the Republican nominee for Vice-President.

In the Presidential election of 1880, James Garfield won the Presidential election by a plurality of less than 10,000 votes out of a total of 9 million votes that were cast. Garfield had campaigned on a "bloody shirt" platform and had promised to protect Southern African Americans. Thus, in more ways than one, Garfield owed his election, in large part, to his command of the African American vote.

Despite these successes, by the end of the year, the Congressional career of Blanche Bruce had come to an end. In 1880, the Democrats regained control of three fourths of the seats in the Mississippi Legislature. The Mississippi Legislature then decided against re-electing Bruce to the United States Senate.

• In the 1880 Georgia gubernatorial election, the Democratic incumbent, Governor Colquitt, was re-elected even though he received a minority of the European American vote. However, through force, intimidation and bribery, Colquitt garnered the great majority of the African American vote.

• In Florida, protests by poor European Americans were successful in getting officials to ignore the literacy tests for voting written into the 1868 state constitution to prevent African Americans from voting. The tests were slated to go into effect in 1880.

• In 1880, William Still helped to establish the first African American YMCA.

• In 1880, African Americans organized the Colored Knights of Pythias. By 1905, there were 1,628 lodges with some 70,000 members.

• In Virginia, of those employed as oystermen (a profitable profession of the day), about half were African Americans.

• The Pea Island, North Carolina, Lifesaving Station was established. The Pea Island Lifesaving Station was an all African American Coast Guard facility. Richard Etheridge, a former slave, established it.

• Samuel R. Lowery (1832–c.1900) became the first African American to argue a case before the Supreme Court (February 2). John Rock *(see 1865)* was admitted to practice before the Supreme Court in 1865 but did not actually argue a case before the court at that time.

• During the 1880s, a Tennessee African American named Benjamin "Pap" Singleton began advocating that Kansas African Americans colonize Canada, Cyprus or Liberia.

The Census

In 1880, the Census issued its decennial report. There were 6,580,793 African Americans in the United States representing 13.1% of the population.

The African American literacy rate was thirty percent up from the 18.6% in 1870. The percentages of total population attending school in the Southern states was European American 18.3% (up from 13.5% in 1870); African American 13.07% (up from 3.07% in 1870).

Of all the African Americans in the United States, three out of four lived in the former Confederate States. In those states African Americans formed the following proportion of the population:

Alabama	47.5%
Arkansas	26.3%
Florida	47.0%
Georgia	47.0%
Louisiana	51.5%
Mississippi	57.5%
North Carolina	37.9%
South Carolina	60.7%
Tennessee	26.2%
Texas	24.7%
Virginia	41.8%

Of particular note was the presence of substantial African American majorities in several regions of the South. The central portion of Georgia, northern Florida, western Mississippi, south central Alabama, east central Louisiana, eastern North Carolina and southeastern Virginia all contained overwhelming African American majorities. Indeed, some commentators have dubbed these areas as constituting a "black belt." The following chart indicates some of the counties which comprised the "black belt" and the numerical predominance of African Americans in those counties:

Alabama		47.5%
Dallas	82.6%	
Greene	82.8%	
Lowndes	81.9%	
Florida		47.0%
Alachua	60.8%	
Georgia		47.0%
Burke	77.5%	
Lee	83.5%	
Louisiana		51.5%
Tensas	91.1%	
East Carroll	91.4%	
Madison	90.9%	
Mississippi		57.5%
Bolivar	85.6%	
Washington	86.2%	
Adams	78.8%	
Tunica	91.7%	
Sharkey	77.6%	
Coahoma	82.2%	
North Carolina		37.9%
Edgecombe	69.6%	
Craven	66.2%	
Halifax	69.8%	
South Carolina		60.7%
Aiken	54.0%	
Charleston	69.9%	
Beaufort	91.9%	
Sumter	73.1%	
Virginia		41.8%
Amelia	70.7%	
Prince Edward	67.6%	

The percentage of African Americans born in the South but living in the North and West was 3.2%. The percentage of African Americans born in the North and West but living in the South was 5%.

Of particular interest in the 1880 Census was the reporting on the migration of African American males between the ages of 15 and 34. From 1870 to 1880, the number of African Americans males decreased by 20.9% in Alabama and by 4.6% in Georgia. At the same time, the number of African American males increased by 4.0% in Mississippi; 37.1% in Illinois; 12.5% in Michigan; and 23.9% in New York. Because the immigration of Africans into the United States was virtually non-existent at the time, the implications of the 1880 Census was that a great northward migration of African American males had occurred during the 1870s.

One reflection of the northward migration was the City of Chicago in Illinois. In 1870, Chicago had an African American population of 3,696. By 1880, there were 7,400 African Americans in Chicago.

• *Notable Births:* The poet Angelina Weld Grimke was born in Boston, Massachusetts (February 27).

• Aida Overton Walker, a dancer and ragtime singer, was born in New York (February 14).

• *Miscellaneous State Laws:* Mississippi re-enacted a law which had been "omitted" in 1871. Mississippi re-enacted its prohibition against interracial marriage.

• *Miscellaneous Cases:* In *Strauder v. West Virginia* (March 1, 1880) 100 U.S. 303, 25 L.Ed. 664, the United States Supreme Court held that laws which excluded African Americans from juries violated the equal protection clause of the Fourteenth Amendment. This Court decision would be the last court decision deemed favorable to the interests of African Americans until after the turn of the century.

• *Miscellaneous Publications:* William Wells Brown published *My Southern Home.*

• *The Black Church:* Along with the founding of the National Baptist Convention at Montgomery, Alabama, two smaller groups were established, the Baptist Foreign Mission Convention of the United States of America and the American National Baptist Convention.

The Baptist Foreign Mission Convention of the United States of America was formed at a meeting in Montgomery, Alabama, on November 24, 1880. W. W. Colley became the first corresponding secretary. The convention was noted for supporting African missions abroad and for supporting anti-liquor and anti-tobacco measures at home.

• By 1880, the African Methodist Episcopal Church reported 40,000 members.

• *Sports:* Riding Fonso, Barrett Lewis won the Kentucky Derby.

THE AMERICAS

• *Brazil:* A Brazilian anti-slavery society was established.

• *Canada:* During the 1880s, Benjamin

"Pap" Singleton, a Tennessee African American, who had resided in Windsor, Ontario, began advocating that Kansas African Americans colonize Canada, Cyprus or Liberia.

• Daniel Williams, a giant ex-slave, was hanged for murder at Fort Saskatchewan. Daniel Williams became known as a western Canadian bogeyman. Many Euro-Canadian mothers would frighten their children by telling them that "Nigger Dan" would get them if they did not behave.

• In 1867, the Pullman Palace Car Company introduced African American porters to its cars in the United States. When new rail connections were completed in the 1880s and Pullman service from New England and New York to Montreal began, the black porters came with the trains.

During the 1880s, the railroads began unifying not only the United States but also Canada. In so unifying these nations, the railroads also served the purpose of liberating many of the African Americans who were fortunate enough to work for them.

Indicative of the liberation wrought by the advent of the railroads was the Afro-Canadian experience. In Canada, the Canadian Pacific Railroad system made Montreal its general employment center, while the Canadian National used the city to hire for its Central and Atlantic divisions. Accordingly, persons of African descent who sought work with the railroads also came to be concentrated in Montreal.

By 1900, Saint Antoine Street had essentially been made into an Afro-Canadian quarter. This area was known as a "sporting district" in Montreal. It was here that prostitution, gambling, and other illicit activities abounded. During the summer, the Saint Antoine district grew, with temporary porters, redcaps, and the "flitting element" who came for the horse races. In 1897, the first Afro-Canadian cabaret opened its doors. However, for all its vitality and attractiveness, very few of the porters who inhabited the area were inclined to become citizens or to enter into the mainstream of Afro-Canadian life.

A number of persons of African descent moved to Montreal to be near the rail center. Others settled in Winnipeg, Calgary and Vancouver for the same reason. One of the attractions of the railroad life — the porter's life — was the mobility. Due to his mobility, the porter was cut loose from many of the forms of social control which normal communal life creates. Additionally, a porter generally received a higher salary than others. These attributes gave porters a higher status than fellow Afro-Canadians.

The development of this "liberated" class of Afro-Canadians and Afro-Americans would have great significance in the civil rights movement that was to come. It was, after all, the Brotherhood of Sleeping Car Porters which was organized by A. Philip Randolph in 1925 which would become the strongest of the African American labor unions. As such, the porters were often in the forefront with regards to improving the working conditions and the lives of African Americans.

Additionally, it was A. Philip Randolph, the leader of the porters union, who would play a key role in the civil rights struggle from the 1920s through the 1960s. Randolph's role in such actions as the March on Washington in 1963 was instrumental in the Civil Rights Movement achieving the success that was achieved.

• *Cuba:* In Cuba, the Moret law *(see 1870)* was fully applied. Slavery was abolished by royal decree and the patronato system was instituted by which slaves could remain under the "protection" of their owners for a period of years. In the period of 1880 to 1884, 60,550 slaves were emancipated in Cuba.

The 1880 law calling for the establishment of a patronato — a trusteeship — began a process of economic change that led to the social division of labor in the sugar industry, marking the transition from slave manufacture to capitalist industry. Patronatos, which offered monthly stipends and conditions for gaining freedom, replaced traditional slavery. The Ten Years War had already contributed to the elimination of inefficient mills in the east and hastened the development of business districts. These economic changes made the atmosphere ripe for the effective abolition of slavery in 1886. With the abrogation that year of the patronato came a massive immigration of laborers from Spain for the processing of the sugar crops.

• *Haiti:* The Haitian Central Bank (the National Bank of Haiti) was organized by President Salomon (Lysius Felicite Salomon Jeune).

EUROPE

• Robert Browning published *Dramatic Idyls: Second Series.*

AFRICA

By 1880, the European colonization of Africa was in full progress. One consequence of the European influx into Africa, was the "divestment" of African art from missionaries for inclusion in ethnological museums in London and Paris. The creation of these ethnological museums was attributable to the new discipline of anthropology.

African art was sent to ethnological museums rather than to art museums because, at the time, African art was considered aesthetically "immature."

- North Africa, Egypt and Sudan: The Law of Liquidation in Egypt allotted 50% of revenues to administration and 50% to Caisse de la Dette.
- Rivalry between France and Italy began in Tunis.
- Muhammed Rauf became the Governor-General of the Sudan.
- *Western Africa:* Around 1880, Freetown harbor was fortified to serve as a naval coaling depot.
- Around 1880, trade wars in the hinterland of Sierra Leone began.
- There was freer competition between British and French companies on Oil Rivers.
- France obtained the railway concession in Guinea.
- Lyons mission (SMA) began work on the Gold Coast.
- Dio was attacked by Bambara (May 11). However, the attack was halted by order of Ahmadu, the Tekrur Sultan. The post of Bamako was founded by Gallieni.

In 1880, Joseph Gallieni (1849–1916), a French military commander, set out on a mission to establish alliances with the African allies of Ahmadu ibn 'Umar, the ruler of the Tukolor empire.

When the plan failed Gallieni continued to Segu, Ahmadu's capital, where he tried to get a one-sided treaty which would have effectively undermined Ahmadu's Tukolor empire. Both France and the Tukolor empire rejected Gallieni's treaty.

Gallieni was, however, instrumental in persuading the French government to adopt his militant stance towards the West African Islamic empires.

- Benjamin Anderson, a noted Liberian explorer, died.

Benjamin Anderson was born and educated in Liberia. He served two years as secretary of the treasury before visiting the United States, where he and the Liberian intellectual Edward Blyden persuaded two philanthropists to support an expedition into the uncharted Liberian interior.

Anderson set out from Monrovia in 1868 on a thirteen-month journey which took him beyond the forest belt to the upland grasslands. During this exploration, Anderson visited the Mandinka kingdom of Musardu.

Anderson's account of the expedition, *Narrative of a Journey to Musardu* (1870) provides one of the few descriptions of the Liberian hinterland in the 1800s.

Anderson made another journey into the interior in 1874. He also helped to conduct a survey of the Saint Paul River at the end of the decade. Upon his return, Anderson became a tutor in mathematics at Liberia College.

- *Central Africa:* Around 1880, Msiri's kingdom reached its greatest extent and caravans were dispatched to Angola and Zanzibar.

Around 1880, Msiri's father died and Msiri was confirmed as mwami (king) of the region. Msiri reduced the Luba states to his north to tributary status and even raided deeply into the Mwata Kazembe's central territory.

- The Tyo warred against the Bobangi.
- A post was established at Mswata (April 19).
- Leopold II was proclaimed sovereign at Vivi (April 30). Sir Francis de Winton was appointed the Administrator-General.
- Brazza set up a post at Franceville (June) and, in September, negotiated treaties with the Congolese Kings.

In 1880, Pierre de Brazza raced Henry Stanley to the upper Congo River where he signed treaties with local chiefs, most notably with the Bateke ruler, Makoko. The execution of this treaty gave France claims to the north bank of the Congo and led to the founding of the French Congo.

- On October 1, Brazzaville was founded.
- Stanley and Brazza met (November 9).
- The first missions of the Holy Ghost Fathers in the Congo were established.
- Thirstland Trekkers, under the leadership of Jacobus Botha, settled on the Huila plateau in Angola. Portuguese immigration to the plateau subsequently increased.
- Serpa Pinto's second journey began.
- H. von Wissmann explored the Congo.

Hermann von Wissmann was known for crossing central Africa from Angola to Zanzibar from 1880 to 1882.

Eastern Africa

It is estimated that Bonga, a major slave market in southwestern Ethiopia, handled 8,000 slaves annually.

• The International African Association set up posts at Kondoa (French); Tabora and Kakoma (German).

• In 1880, Mirambo, the ruler of the Nyamwezi, was implicated in the killing of two Englishmen. This incident cost Mirambo the support of John Kirk and forced Mirambo to take a more aggressive stance towards his neighbors.

• Freetown mission in Mombasa, was attacked during Ramadan by Arabs and Swahili for harboring escaped slaves.

• Menelik defeated the Galla and prepared to take Harar. Menelik also sent an expedition against Kaffa.

• Around 1880, 50,000 Muslims, 20,000 pagans and a half million Galla were said to have been baptized in forced conversions performed by the Ethiopian Church.

• Rohlfs visited Ethiopia.

• By 1880, Egypt abandoned its attempts to control Bunyoro and began to withdraw its posts in northern Uganda. This allowed Kabarega to concentrate on improving his position with regards to Buganda.

• Siti binti Saad (1880–1950), a Swahili poetess, was born.

• *Southern Africa:* The Transvaal Republic declared its independence (October 13). On October 16, Britain and Transvaal went to war.

• By December 16, the prospects of the Transvaal Republic appeared optimistic and, accordingly, the Republic was again proclaimed. This was followed on December 30 by the proclamation of Paul Kruger as the Republic's President.

• De Beers mining corporation was formed by Cecil Rhodes.

In 1880, Rhodes joined with Alfred Beit to form the DeBeers Mining Company. Eight years later, Rhodes amalgamated — merged — with his chief rival, Barnett Barnato, to found the monopoly De Beers Consolidated Mines.

• In 1880, in the land which is now known as Namibia, hostilities between the Herero and the Oorlam (Khoikhoi) broke out again.

Jan Afrikaner, the chief of the Oorlam allied himself with another Khoikhoi chief, Moses Witbooi, against the Herero. However, by this time, the Herero were more united and much stronger. Some costly battles ensued. The position of Jan Afrikaner and his Oorlam became tenuous.

In 1880, difficulties with the Khoikhoi were renewed over disputed grazing land. This time, Moses Witbooi was Mahehero's major adversary.

After an initial Khoikhoi raid, Mahehero, the Hehero chief, massacred many of Witbooi's people. This united the Khoikhoi against Mahehero, but they did not become a serious threat until Hendrik Witbooi rose to power after 1884.

• The British High Commissioner for South Africa, Sir Henry Bartle Frere used his influence to have the Cape prime minister, John Sprigg, issue a disarmament ultimatum to the Sotho kingdom. This ultimatum resulted in the disastrous "Gun War" of 1880.

In 1878, the Cape prime minister, John Gordon Sprigg, passed a law which severely restricted African ownership of firearms. After Sprigg had overwhelmed the Sotho neighbor, Moorosi, Sprigg ordered the Sotho to turn in their guns and to pay a hut tax. Letsie, the chief of the Sotho, was inclined to compromise, but strong factions in the country adamantly opposed the Euro-African government and thus precipitated the "Gun War" of 1880.

The Sotho emerged victorious from the Gun War and protectorate administration was restored to the British Crown in 1884.

During the "Gun War," Masupha, Letsie's brother, was the focus of resistance to the Cape Colony's attempts to disarm the Sotho. The Sotho emerged victorious, but their divided response to this war made their factional disputes even more bitter. Seemingly above the internal strife while perched upon Thaba Bosiu — the legendary mountain stronghold, Masupha ignored the political rivalries which ravaged the kingdom below.

• Pixley ka Izaka Seme (c.1880– 1951), a co-founder of the African National Congress, is believed to have been born in this year.

After a mission education in Zululand, Pixley ka Izaka Seme went to the United States, where he graduated from Columbia University. Seme then studied law at Oxford and became one of the first black South Africans called to the bar.

Originally, Seme's political sentiments were directed towards Zulu nationalism. However, he returned to South Africa as the Union government was forming and he was jolted into a wider political consciousness by new restrictions on African political rights. In response to the exclusively Euro-African Union government, Seme called for a convention of Africans to form the South African Native National Congress. (The South African Native National Congress would be renamed the African National Congress in 1923.)

Over one hundred delegates to the Congress met in 1912. At Seme's suggestion, the delegates patterned the new organization after the United States Congress. John Dube *(see 1871)* became the first Congress president and Seme was elected treasurer.

Later in 1910, Seme founded the first African newspaper with a national circulation, *Abantu-Batho*. *Abantu-Batho* was printed in four languages. Over the ensuing years, Seme edited the newspaper, practiced law, and participated in ANC activities.

In 1928, Columbia University awarded Seme an honorary doctoral degree. The prestige associated with this degree helped him to be elected ANC president-general in 1930. During this period, the ANC competed with more radical African organizations, such as the ICU (Industrial and Commercial Union) of Clements Kadalie.

Seme's conservative views and authoritative management of the ANC disappointed his followers. The Congress declined seriously, and Seme, considered reactionary by many, was voted out of office in 1936.

• Matthew Chigaga Zwimba (c.1880–1930), the founder of the first independent Christian church among the Shona, is believed to have been born in this year.

Matthew Zwimba was the son of the government appointed paramount chief of the Zwimba reserve in eastern Zimbabwe, where he became a catechist under the Wesleyan Methodist Missionary Society. Zwimba established the first mission school in his district, working with enthusiasm among his own relatives and friends. However, when he was transferred to a strange district, Zwimba clashed with his supervisors. Eventually, Zwimba was dismissed as a teacher in 1907.

Zwimba was in constant trouble with the European authorities until 1915 when he founded his own church and physically occupied the Methodist station in his own district. His Original Church of the White Bird Mission (Shiri Chena Church) incorporated both Christian and traditional Shona symbolism and was the first of a large number of independent churches among the Shona.

Zwimba was persistently harassed by the Euro-Rhodesian government. As a consequence, Zwimba became a leading spokesman for the people in his reserve.

• Molapo (c.1815–1880), a Sotho prince, died.

Molapo was the son of the great Sotho king Moshoeshoe *(see 1870)*. When Moshoeshoe admitted the first missionaries to Basutoland in 1833, Molapo was one of the princes sent to oversee the missionaries' activities. Molapo was also instructed to obtain a Western education.

Afterwards Molapo was appointed chief over the Leribe district in northern Lesotho. Molapo was an able military leader. However, he was considered too ambitious and unreliable to be fully trusted.

In 1848, Molapo caused his father considerable trouble by attacking the Tlokwa chief Sekonyela without authorization. In the early 1850s, however, Molapo distinguished himself in several actions against British forces and in 1858 fought against the Orange Free State Republic.

The Orange Free State and the Sotho fought again in 1865. Neither side prevailed, and Moshoeshoe was glad for a respite.

In 1866, Molapo renewed the war between the Orange Free State and the Sotho by attacking the Afrikaners on his own initiative. Molapo brought down a retaliation he could not handle and was defeated.

Molapo then made his own peace with the Orange Free State President Johannes Brand *(see 1888)*. As a result of this peace, Molapo essentially became a vassal of the Orange Free State.

Moshoeshoe had no choice but to recognize the cession of Molapo's district to the Orange Free State. Fortunately, in 1869, the British intervened and salvaged the Sotho position by establishing a protectorate over Basutoland and restoring Molapo's district.

In 1870, Moshoeshoe died and was succeeded by Molapo's elder brother Letsie. Molapo greatly embarrassed Letsie in 1873 by betraying a non–Sotho chief, Langalibalele, to the European government. This incident gave the Sotho a reputation for untrustworthiness and seriously impaired Letsie's relations with other African rulers.

Molapo supported the Cape government when it tried to force the Sotho to disarm in 1879, but died shortly before the war which ensued. His sons, Jonathan and Joel took opposite sides on this issue, and their continuing feud aggravated the problem of Sotho disunity after Molapo's death.

- Moroka II (c.1795–1880), the Seleka Rolong chief who collaborated with Europeans to become one of the few African rulers to remain independent in the midst of the developing Afrikaner republics, died.

Moroka II succeeded his father Sefunelo after several decades of war, during which the Rolong lived as nomads around the middle Vaal River. Sefunelo had obtained help from Wesleyan missionaries who acted as diplomatic agents for the Rolong. After his father's death in 1829, Moroka followed the missionaries to a permanent home at Thaba Nchu (in present Orange Free State) where the southern Sotho king, Moshoeshoe granted the missionaries land in 1833.

Thaba Nchu became the center for many Sotho and Griqua refugees and Moroka emerged as one of the strongest rulers in the region. During his entire reign, Moroka depended closely on the missionaries for support, but never converted to Christianity.

When Afrikaner migrants crossed the Orange River, Moroka immediately befriended them. In 1836, Moroka rescued an Afrikaner party after it had been attacked by the Ndebele of Mzilikazi.

The next year, Moroka participated in A. H. Potgeiter's successful counter-attacks against the Ndebele. These services earned for Moroka the lasting gratitude of the Afrikaners, who then settled the region.

During the 1840s, Moshoeshoe contested Moroka's title to Thaba Nchu. However, this dispute was resolved when the British governor, Harry Smith, annexed the entire region.

When the British abandoned the region, the Afrikaners proclaimed the Orange Free State Republic, allowing the Rolong to maintain their autonomy. During the Free State wars with Moshoeshoe in 1855 and 1865, Moroka sided with the Afrikaners.

In 1865, the Orange Free State President Johannes Brand rewarded Moroka with formal recognition of Rolong independence within the republic's borders. Rolong independence was lost four years after his death, when the Orange Free State annexed Thaba Nchu.

RELATED HISTORICAL EVENTS

- *Europe:* The *Compagnie francaise de l'Afrique equatoriale* was founded.
- *Asia:* Ibn Saud (1880–1953), the King of Saudi Arabia, was born.

——————— **1 8 8 1** ———————

THE UNITED STATES

- In his inaugural address, President James Garfield claimed that only education could solve the African American problem in the South. Regrettably, Garfield was assassinated before he could expand on his idea.
- In his first message to Congress, President Chester Arthur, James Garfield's successor, implied that, until African Americans became more literate, African Americans might justifiably be disenfranchised — denied the right to vote.
- The only African Americans to serve in the 47th Congress were Representatives Robert Smalls of South Carolina and John R. Lynch of Mississippi.
- Ex–Senator Blanche K. Bruce of Mississippi was offered the post of either minister to Brazil or third assistant to the Postmaster General. Bruce refused both positions. However, he did subsequently accept an appointment as Register of the Treasury. He took office in May.
- Frederick Douglass was appointed Recorder of Deeds for the District of Columbia (May 17).
- Henry Highland Garnet was appointed Minister to Liberia.
- Charles Burleigh Purvis was appointed as surgeon-in-chief of the Freedmen's Hospital in Washington, D. C. Purvis was also called upon, in 1881, to tend to the fatally wounded President James A. Garfield when Garfield was wounded by an assassin's bullet in 1881.

Charles Burleigh Purvis (1842–1929) was the son of the prosperous abolitionist Robert Purvis. He attended Oberlin College in Ohio and, desiring to pursue medical training, transferred to Western Reserve Medical School in Cleveland, Ohio, graduating in 1865. Purvis served in the army until 1869, when he became the assistant surgeon at Freedmen's and a faculty member at Howard University in Washington, D. C. In addition to his many other achievements, in 1897, Purvis was appointed to serve on the District of Columbia's Board of Medical Examiners.

• James Sidney Hinton was elected to the Indiana House of Representatives.

• Good Samaritan Hospital, a privately run hospital established exclusively for African Americans, was opened in Charlotte, North Carolina.

• *Notable Births:* Julian Francis Abele, a noted architect whose designs would contribute to the construction of Philadelphia's Museum of Art, the Free Library and campus buildings at Duke University, was born in Philadelphia.

• Bandleader James Reese Europe was born in Alabama (February 22).

• William Pickins (1881–1954), orator, author and equal rights advocate, was born (January 15).

• *Miscellaneous State Laws:* Rhode Island repealed a law which prohibited interracial marriage.

• Tennessee enacted the first Jim Crow law. The Tennessee statute segregated railroad coaches. The law directed railroad companies to provide for equivalent first class accommodations to African Americans and European Americans instead of relegating African Americans to the second class cars as had been the custom.

• *Publications:* William Sanders Scarborough (1852–1926) published a Greek language textbook entitled *First Lessons in Greek. First Lessons in Greek*, won recognition for Scarborough.

An African Methodist Episcopal minister, Scarborough was active in African American intellectual circles and served as president of Wilberforce University (Ohio) from 1908 to 1920.

Scholastic Achievements

Booker T. Washington began his work at Tuskegee Institute (July 4). On September 19, Tuskegee opened its doors to some 30 students and one teacher, Booker T. Washington. With an annual budget of only $2,000 which was provided by the Alabama legislature, Washington was nevertheless able to rapidly develop Tuskegee Institute. Washington's emphasis on industrial training and economic self-reliance helped the Institute to succeed. Within its first twenty years, some forty buildings were erected on the campus — most of these buildings were erected by the students of Tuskegee themselves.

Washington built his school and his influence by tapping the generosity of northern philanthropists. He pursued and received donations from wealthy New Englanders and from some of the leading industrialists and businessmen of his time. Men such as Andrew Carnegie, William H. Baldwin, Jr., Julius Rosenwald, and Robert C. Ogden were all major contributors to Tuskegee and to the career of Booker T. Washington.

• The African Negro Methodist Episcopal Church established Allen University in Columbia, South Carolina.

• Spelman College opened in Atlanta, Georgia. Spelman College was the first institution of higher education established exclusively for the education of African American women. Sponsored by philanthropist John D. Rockefeller, Spelman opened on April 11, 1881 as the Atlanta Baptist Female Seminary. In 1884, the name Spelman was adopted in honor of Mrs. John D. Rockefeller's parents.

• *The Performing Arts:* Jack Haverly's Callender Minstrels, an African American minstrel company, made its first European tour with critical and commercial success. The Callender Minstrels were the most famous and successful of all minstrel companies.

• *Technological Innovations:* In 1881, Norbert Rillieux devised a system for the production of beet sugar. This invention was highly successful and became a common sight on sugar beet plantations.

• Lewis Latimer patented the first incandescent electric lamp with carbon filament. Latimer also made drawings for the first telephone for Alexander Graham Bell, and was the chief draftsman for General Electric and Westinghouse. Latimer also wrote the first textbook on the lighting system used by the Edison company.

• *Sports:* Moses Fleetwood Walker (1857–1924) became a member of the Oberlin College varsity baseball team.

THE AMERICAS

Brazil

In the 1880s, Brazil finally began to experience a popular movement of abolitionism. Once this movement began, it shook the very foundations of slavery as it had existed in Brazil.

Although the leadership of the Brazilian abolitionist movement typically came from elite families, Brazilian abolitionism was unusual in having a significant minority of COTW and black leaders. Such men as the engineer, Andre Reboucas, the pharmacist Jose de Patrocino, and the politician Luiz Gama were instrumental figures in the drive towards freedom for the Afro-Brazilians that were still enslaved.

Another key Afro-Brazilian abolitionist leader was the fugitive-slave leader Quintano Lacerda and his 10,000 strong fugitive-slave community in the port city of Santos.

The abolitionist cause also included, by the last half of the decade, large numbers of free black workers on the docks and in the railroads. These workers were inclined to refuse to transport slaves and to assist those slaves who were attempting to escape.

All of these players were instrumental in leading Brazil to its abolition of slavery.

- In 1881, aided by his wealthy father-in-law, Jose do Patrocinio acquired *Gazeta de Tarde*. Under Patrocinio, *Gazeta de Tarde* would become the principal anti-slavery journal in Brazil until it was replaced by his equally effective *A Cidade do Rio* in 1887.
- In 1881, Joaquim Machado de Assis published *Memorias postumas de Braz Cubas*. In this work, one of the ancillary themes is the pernicious effects of slavery on both the slave and the slave owner.

Memorias postumas de Bras Cubas was completed in 1881. In this novel, Machado gives the reader a fictional autobiography which is written by the dead hero. Starting with the hero's death and subsequent funeral, *Memorias posthumas de Bras Cubas* represents a complete break with the literary conventions of the time. This novel revolutionized Brazilian literature by allowing for an exploration of themes which had heretofore not been utilized. With psychological acuity, Machado was able to observe people in trivial, cynical, and egocentric conditions. His novel, in essence, became a time capsule of Brazilian society at the end of the second Brazilian empire with an accompanying psychological insight into the people of the era.

When reviewing Machado's rise to literary genius as evidenced by *Memorias postumas de Bras Cubas,* most critics interpret Machado's change in fortunes to being a consequence of his long desire for perfection and as the result of Machado's internal struggle between romantic ideals and his creative intuition. From this perspective, Machado's newly found brilliance as reflected in *Memorias Postumas de Bras Cubas* was merely a reflection of his progression and maturation as a writer.

- Teixeira E. Sousa, a noted Afro-Brazilian novelist, died.

Teixeira E. Sousa (1812–1881) published the first Brazilian novel, *Filha do Pescador*, in 1843. Sousa's masterpiece, the epic *A Independencia do Brasil*, dealt with the nation on the eve of its break with Portugal. Sousa emphasized the multi-racial nature of the populace and showed his desire that the races mix so that the true Brazilian, a COTW, would ultimately emerge.

In 1852, Sousa published *Maria ou a Menina Rouhada* in Paul Brito's magazine, *Marmota Fluminense. Maria* was the first novel in Brazilian literature in which Afro-Brazilians were the leading characters. The novel dealt with Afro-Brazilian customs, religion and sorcery.

- *Jamaica:* Mary Seacole (d. 1881), an Afro-Jamaican heroine of the Crimean War, died.

AFRICA

- *North Africa, Egypt and Sudan:* In February, Colonels Ahmad Pasha Urabi, Ali Fahmi and Abd al-Al Hilmi, the leaders of the Patriotic Party, were court-martialled. However, a mutiny of the Egyptian army secured the Colonels release.
- Muhammed Ahmad bin Abdallah, a *faqih* from Dongola, proclaimed himself the Mahdi in Sudan (June 19). This pronouncement began the period in Sudanese history known as the Mahdia.

Around 1880, Muhammed toured the central provinces of Sudan and became incensed at the evils of the Egyptian administration and the general social chaos he found. Early in 1881, Muhammed proclaimed himself to be the Mahdi — the awaited redeemer of Islam.

The Mahdi launched a jihad against the alien rulers of the Sudan with the aim of restoring the theocratic state to Islam. The Mahdi's followers easily repelled several feeble attempts by the Egyptian administration to suppress him and his prestige grew rapidly among the religiously devout and political dissenters alike.

*   *   *

The word "bin" is the Swahili form of the Arabic word "ibn." Both "bin" and "ibn" are particles indicating "son of," often abbreviated as "b.." Ibn sometimes constitutes the first part of proper names, as in Ibn Battuta. "Ibn" and "bin" are interchanged in many east African names.

"Mahdi" is an Islamic title meaning "the

divinely guided one." The term "Mahdi" was applied to the awaited deliverer and restorer of pure Islam. The concept of the Mahdi does not appear in the Qur'an nor in any of the orthodox traditions, but belief in the coming of such a redeemer has been widespread among Muslims. Since the tenth century several self-proclaimed Mahdis have appeared in northern Africa. The best known self-proclaimed Mahdi was the late nineteenth century Sudanese leader Muhammed 'Ahmad.

- In August, an expedition was sent to seize the Mahdi. The expedition failed.
- On September 9, there was a nationalist uprising in Egypt under Ahmad Pasha Urabi. The uprising led to the creation of a new ministry under Sharif Pasha.
- On April 30, the French navy seized Bizerta. The French army invaded Tunis from Algeria.
- The Treaty of Bardo was executed. Under the Treaty of Bardo, the Bey of Tunis agreed to the establishment of a French protectorate (May 12).
- In July, there was an uprising against the French in Algeria.
- The *Code de l'indigenat* was established in Algeria.
- Beginning in 1881, the administrative services in Algiers came under the direct authority of ministries located in Paris.
- In 1881, when Muhammed 'Ahmad proclaimed himself the Mahdi in Sudan, Hayatu became his protégé in the central Sudan. Hayatu attracted many adherents to the town of Balda and maintained a large following throughout Adamawa.
- *Western Africa:* UAC gave aid to the Amir of Nupe in a struggle against rebels.
- Captain Lonsdale visited the Asantehene on a mission of peace and to open northern trade routes.
- A French expedition to Kita began. Bosseyabes was subdued in Guinea.
- In 1881, annual slave raids continued to occur from Dahomey into Yorubaland.
- Kwa Ibo territory was raided by King Jaja.
- French expeditions against Alimamy (Almamy) Samory began.

"Alimamy" (or "Almamy") is a title assumed by political leaders in many parts of West Africa. The title Alimamy is derived from the Arabic *al-Imam* (leader of prayer at a mosque), or possibly from *amir al-mu'minim* (commander of the faithful). The most famous West African to assume the title was the 19th century revolutionary Samory (Samori Toure).

- Samuel Collins Brew (c.1810– 1881) died.

The Brew family comprised a Gold Coast (Ghana) elite which was long prominent in trade, politics and the professions. The Brew family were the Fante descendants of Richard Brew (c.1725–1776) an Irish merchant who lived on the Gold Coast. Because of their dual heritage, the Brew family had the early advantage of Western education. This advantage enabled them to play important roles in Gold Coast (Ghana) activities for over two hundred years.

Samuel Collins Brew was one of the prominent members of the Brew family. During the 1860s and 1870s, Brew joined the British Gold Coast administration. In his official capacity, Brew served largely in a judicial function as a Western educated link between the British and the Africans of the Gold Coast interior.

- Umar ibn Muhammed al-Amin al-Kanemi, the ruler of the Kanuri state of Bornu, died (1881).

Umar succeeded his father al-Kanemi. Al-Kanemi had usurped power from the thousand year old Sefawa dynasty of Bornu. Umar, like his father, permitted the Sefawa kings to remain as titular rulers. But when one of these Sefawa kings (Ibrahim) tried to regain power by allying with the state of Wadai. Umar killed both Ibrahim and Ibrahim's son. This act ended the ancient dynasty of the Sefawa kings.

Umar was a weak and indecisive ruler who came to rely heavily on his unpopular wazir— his unpopular chief advisor. The nobles of the court became so dissatisfied that, in 1853, they supported a coup led by Umar's brother, Abdurrahman.

Abdurrahman proved to be a tyrannical ruler. Support soon swung back in favor of Umar, who had seemed all the more preferable because his wazir had died. The next year Abdurrahman was deposed and Umar was reinstated. Abdurrahman was killed shortly afterwards.

For the next thirteen years, the most powerful man in Bornu was Laminu Njitiya. Laminu Njitiya was a former bandit who rose to become Umar's new advisor. A capable and popular man, Laminu died in 1871.

In the last years of Umar's reign the power of the nobility increased at the king's expense. Umar was succeeded at his death by his own son, Bukar. Bukar had made his reputation as a military commander while his father was still alive.

Bukar was probably the de facto ruler of Bornu during Umar's last years.

- *Central Africa:* Around 1881, Simon Kimbangu, a revivalist, was born at Nkamba.
- Many posts were established by the International African Association in the Congo.
- Henry Stanley reached Brazzaville. Stanley proceeded to found Leopoldville on the opposite bank of the River Congo.
- In December, Henry Stanley reached Stanley Falls in three boats.
- BMS started work in the Congo.
- *Eastern Africa:* Menelik commenced his expedition against Arusi.
- Yohannes IV, the Emperor of Ethiopia, paid the Coptic Patriarch 12,000 Maria Theresa thalers for consecration of four abunas (bishops).

"Abuna" is the title conferred upon bishops and archbishops in the Ethiopian church. The word "abuna" literally means "our father." Until the 1950s, all the heads of the Ethiopian Coptic Church were Egyptians nominated by the patriarch in Alexandria.

- France required Egypt to remove the Egyptian flag from Ras Bir, near Obock.
- France occupied Obock.
- In 1881, Joseph Thomson, a British explorer, surveyed for coal around the Ruvuma River on behalf of the Zanzibari Sultan Barghash.
- *Southern Africa:* In 1881, armed conflicts continued between the British and the Boers.

On January 28, Boers repulsed the British at Laing's Neck and again, on February 27, at Majuba Hill. As a result, on February 27, an armistice was negotiated between the British and the Boers.

On March 21, the Transvaal became self-governing under a Triumvirate. In April, the Treaty of Pretoria was executed. Under the terms of the treaty, Britain formally recognized the Boer Republic. In August, the Pretoria Convention defined the boundaries between the two people and their lands.

- Around 1881, caravans of up to 5,000 slaves passed through Mwembe to Kilwa.
- Work in Nyasaland was resumed by UMCA.

Nyasaland was the name given to the land that today comprises the nation of Malawi. British administration of Nyasaland began in 1889 when Henry Johnston declared a protectorate.

From 1893 to 1907 the territory was known as British Central Africa. Thereafter, it was called Nyasaland until its independence in 1964 when it became known as Malawi.

- In 1881, fighting was reported on the western Transvaal border.

Mbandzeni, the king of the Swazi, assisted the Transvaal — which was administered by the British from 1877 to 1881— to fight with Pedi chief Sekhukhune and was rewarded with two Anglo-Afrikaner treaties which "guaranteed" Swazi independence. Nevertheless, despite these treaties, European infiltration into Swaziland intensified, especially after the discovery of gold in 1882.

- During the British annexation of the Transvaal, Paul Kruger regained his popularity by leading the resistance movement. He joined a triumvirate government in opposition to the British and was credited with negotiating the settlement which restored Afrikaner independence in 1881.

RELATED HISTORICAL EVENTS

- *The United States:* The President of the United States, James Garfield was assassinated.

At his funeral, thirteen bands from the African American fraternal organizations of New Orleans played.

- *Africa:* A. A. da Rocha de Serpa Pinto, a Portuguese explorer, published *How I Crossed Africa*.
- Jacobus Boshof (1808–1881), a former president of the Orange Free State, died.

During the great Afrikaner trek into the interior of South Africa, Boshof remained in the British civil service in the Cape Colony and Natal.

In 1855, Boshof accepted the invitation to become president of the newly formed Orange Free State Republic.

During Boshof's administration, Boshof resisted pressures to merge with the Transvaal, then governed by M. W. Pretorius, and fought the Sotho of Moshoeshoe to a stand-off mediated by the British Cape Governor George Grey in 1858. The following year, Boshof resigned and returned to Natal.

- Thomas Francois Burgers (1834–1881), the former president of the Transvaal Republic, died.

Thomas Burgers was originally a Dutch Reformed Church minister in the Cape Colony. In this capacity, he established a reputation for his liberal views.

In 1872, Burgers was invited to become president of the Transvaal when M. W. Pretorius resigned. Burgers' term of office was dominated by a costly and unsuccessful war against the Pedi chief Sekhukhune which demonstrated to the British the weakness of the republic.

When Theophilus Shepstone annexed the Transvaal in 1877, Burgers offered no resistance and retired from public life.

• George Rattray (1881–1938), a British anthropologist who was largely responsible for the restoration of the Asante state, was born.

George Rattray was a member of the government department of anthropology, who in 1921 proposed that it would serve the best interests of the British and Asante to reunite the kingdom. Asante had been dismembered and ruled directly by the British since 1896 when Prempe I, its ruler was exiled.

Rattray suggested that the government give up its demand for recovery of the Golden Stool — the Asante throne — the traditional symbol of Asante nationhood which had been hidden from the colonists. He also proposed the reestablishment of the Kumasi Division of Asante to provide for an African administrator under indirect rule.

In 1924, Prempe was allowed to return to Kumasi, the Asante capital. Two years later, Prempe was made head of the Kumasi division of Asante, and the de facto leader of all of Asante.

The position of asantehene — the Asante king — was officially restored to Prempe's successor, Prempe II, in 1935.

Rattray, in addition to his influential reports, wrote a number of important scholarly anthropological studies on Asante, which were published in the 1920s.

1882

THE UNITED STATES

In 1882, United States Attorney General Brewster attempted to safeguard free elections. In Charleston, South Carolina, Brewster prosecuted a group of influential men arrested who had attempted to obstruct the election process,

but he was unable to secure any convictions. Brewster then ordered the United States Marshal in Charleston to immediately arrest anyone who interfered with free elections. But again Brewster met with little success with regards to securing convictions.

Discouraged by his inability to safeguard the elections, Brewster soon abandoned the cause. During the summer of 1882, the pleas of disenfranchised African Americans went unheeded. In one particularly glaring case, Brewster promised to investigate the complaints made by Daniel Payne, the senior bishop of the African Methodist Episcopal Church. Payne was forced off a Florida train because he refused to ride in a second-class car after having purchased a ticket for a first-class passenger seat. Brewster promised to investigate Payne's complaint, but never did.

• From 1882 to 1886, James E. O'Hara served in the House of Representatives for the state of North Carolina.

• In Georgia, the Populists, led by Tom Watson, actively campaigned for the African American vote, advocating free education for African Americans and the abolition of the convict lease system. In 1882, the African American vote would be instrumental in electing Watson to the lower house of the Georgia Legislature.

• Edward (Edwin?) P. McCabe (1850–1920) was elected to the position of Kansas State Auditor.

McCabe moved to Oklahoma in 1889 and became one of the founders of Langston City, Oklahoma.

• *Military Achievements:* Thomas Boyne, a cavalry sergeant, received the Congressional Medal of Honor for bravery in the Indian Wars of New Mexico.

• *Notable Births:* Benjamin Brawley (1882–1939), a noted social historian, was born (April 22).

Benjamin Brawley was born in Columbia, South Carolina. Brawley was a clergyman and a very scholarly man noted for his pioneering studies of African American history. Most notable of his publications were *A Short History of the American Negro* (1913); *The Negro in Literature and Art in the United States* (1918); and *A Social History of the American Negro* (1921).

Brawley also wrote the first biography of Paul Laurence Dunbar which was published in 1936. Brawley also was an accomplished poet who wrote in a style of the late Victorians. His most acclaimed poem was *Seven Sleepers of Epheuses.*

• Charlotte Hawkins Brown, founder of the Palmer Institute at Sedalia, North Carolina was born.

• Father Divine (1882–1965), a famous religious leader, was born.

In 1882, one of the more mercurial figures in Pan-African history was born. His name was George Baker but the world would come to known him as Father Divine.

Father Divine was born under the birthname of George Baker near Savannah, Georgia. George Baker was an itinerant garden worker and sometime preacher until, in 1907, he moved to Baltimore where he became a "God in Sonship" with Father Jehovah.

By 1919, when he moved to Sayville, Long Island, New York, George Baker had proclaimed himself to be God and he had become "Father Divine." It was also at this time that Father Divine began his Peace Mission movement.

Father Divine's Peace Mission was non-denominational and interracial, and the theme of the movement was universal peace. In 1931, Father Divine and some 80 of his followers were arrested on a disorderly conduct charge stemming from a raucous singing session. Divine was sentenced to a prison term, but four days later the sentencing judge dropped dead from a heart attack. Upon hearing of the demise of the judge, Divine was reported to have said, "I hated to do it."

The publicity that Divine received from this incident swelled the ranks of his movement. Father Divine moved into Harlem. Using the funds donated by his followers, Divine supported missions which provided cheap meals and rooms for African Americans who were hard hit by the Depression.

Father Divine's life had always been somewhat out of the ordinary — somewhat unusual. In 1949, Divine again made news when he appeared at the Federal Trust Company in Newark with $500,000 in cash.

A judge once called Father Divine a "methodical home-breaker." And indeed, Divine was known for his notorious trysts with female followers.

In 1941, Divine moved into a Philadelphia mansion that was the gift of one of Divine's European American followers, a certain John De Voute. The house was known as Woodmont, it had 32 rooms and was situated on a 73 acre estate. Divine would remain at Woodmont for the next twenty-four years.

At his death in 1965, Divine's religious empire was an impressive one. One out of every four of his followers was a European American. The holdings of his Peace Mission were valued at $10 million. The Peace Mission also ran a great many businesses in such diverse locales as Austria, Australia, Sweden, Germany, Switzerland, England as well as the United States.

• The novelist Jessie Fauset was born in Camden, New Jersey (April 27).

• Mrs. Violette A. Johnson, the first African American woman admitted to practice before the United States Supreme Court was born (July 16).

• *Notable Deaths:* Forty-eight African Americans were lynched in 1882.

• Henry Highland Garnet (1815–1882), clergyman, anti-slavery advocate, and Minister to Liberia, died.

Henry Highland Garnet was an educator and a clergyman. He was born a slave at New Market in Kent County, Maryland. Garnet's grandfather was said to have been a ruler of a tribe in the Mandingo Empire of West Africa.

In 1824, Garnet, with his father, escaped and went to New York. In New York, Garnet sought and obtained an education. After finishing his studies, he divided his time between preaching the Gospel in church and advocating the abolition of slavery with the American Anti-slavery Society.

Garnet continued with his dual avocations until 1843 when he made an address at the National Convention of the Free People of Color at Buffalo, New York, in which he called upon slaves to rise up and slay their masters. The National Convention refused to endorse these sentiments, and he was especially criticized by Frederick Douglass. Garnet's popularity fell and his influence waned.

Garnet returned to the pulpit and concentrated more upon preaching the Gospel. He served as pastor of the Liberty Street Presbyterian Church in Troy, New York from 1843 to 1848. In 1848, Garnet published *The Past and Present Condition, and the Destiny of the Colored Race.* Garnet also published *The National Watchman* with William G. Allen.

In 1852, Garnet was sent as a missionary to Jamaica. On February 12, 1865, Garnet preached a sermon in the House of Representatives commemorating the passage of the 13th Amendment. In 1881, Garnet was appointed Minister of Liberia.

• Robert Morris, the first African American to practice in the courts of the United States, died (December 11).

• Alonzo J. Ransier (1834–1882), a former South Carolina Congressman, died.

Alonzo J. Ransier was born to free parents in Charleston, South Carolina. Before the Civil War, he worked as a shipping clerk. In 1865, Ransier served as a Registrar of Elections. In 1866, he attended the first Republican Convention in South Carolina. After the convention, Ransier went to Washington, D.C., to lobby for federal protection of African Americans.

In 1868, Ransier became a presidential elector and the chairman of the State Executive Committee. In 1870, he was elected Lieutenant Governor of the State of South Carolina.

Ransier was elected to the House of Representatives in 1873. While in Congress, he worked for civil rights protection, a national tariff, a six-year presidential term, and funds for the improvement of Charleston Harbor.

• James T. Rapier (1837–1882), a former Alabama Congressman and a labor organizer, died.

James T. Rapier (1837–1882) was born of free parents in Florence, Alabama. Rapier's father was a wealthy planter and provided Rapier with a tutor for his primary education. Later on, Rapier was sent to Montreal College in Canada, the University of Glasgow in Scotland, and Franklin College in Tennessee.

As a successful cotton planter, Rapier became involved in reform of the Alabama State Constitution and the founding of the state Republican Party, serving as its Vice President.

Interested in organizing urban and rural workers, Rapier helped to establish, and chaired, the first state African American labor convention. Rapier edited and published the *Montgomery Sentinel* to present his views on African American solidarity and was elected to the House of Representatives in 1872.

Although the power of the Ku Klux Klan and the Democratic Party ended his political career after only one term in Congress, Rapier continued to dabble in politics. He would later serve as a United States revenue officer in Alabama.

• *Miscellaneous State Laws:* A special election law passed in South Carolina created a separate ballot and ballot box for each office. The law authorized election managers to speak to voters only when requested to read titles, and said that ballots in the wrong boxes would not be counted.

• *Publications:* George Washington Williams published a two-volume history of the African American people entitled *History of the Negro Race in America.*

George Washington Williams (1849–1891) was born in Bedford Springs, Pennsylvania. During the Civil War, Williams was one of a number of underaged soldiers who served in the United States Army.

In 1875, Williams became an ordained Baptist minister. He subsequently turned to law and politics, serving a term in the Ohio legislature. His active life facilitated the collection of materials for his histories. His other writings include the valuable *History of the Negro Troops in the War of the Rebellion* which was published in 1877.

One of Williams last efforts was an attack on the inhumane government of the Congo Free State following an 1890 visit there.

• *Scholastic Achievements:* The John F. Slater Fund of one million dollars was created for the education and uplifting of the African Americans residing in the South.

• The Colored Methodist Episcopal Church founded Lane College in Jackson, Tennessee.

• Nathan Francis Mossell graduated from the University of Pennsylvania with a medical degree.

Nathan Francis Mossell (1856–1946) was born in Canada. After receiving his medical degree, Mossell waged an acrimonious fight to be admitted to the Philadelphia Medical Society. The fight was a successful one, he was admitted in 1885.

Mossell studied at prestigious hospitals in London, England, before he attacked the problem of founding a hospital. In 1895, Mossell established Philadelphia's first hospital devoted primarily to the care of African American patients. The Frederick Douglass Memorial Hospital and Training School for Nurses became his most lasting legacy.

In 1905, Mossell travelled to Niagara Falls with W. E. B. Du Bois as one of the organizers of the Niagara Movement.

As a side bar to history, it is notable that Nathan Francis Mossell was the uncle of Paul Robeson, the famous singer, actor and activist.

• *The Performing Arts:* In 1865, Charles Hicks, an African American, organized the Georgia Minstrels. In 1882, the Georgia

Minstrels became part of Callender's Consolidated Spectacular Colored Minstrels.

• *Technological Innovations:* William B. Purvis patented a device for fastening paper bags (April 25). Ultimately, Purvis would receive some eleven patents for the manufacturing of paper bags. Most of the patents were sold to the Union Paper Bag Company of New York.

• Lewis H. Latimer patented the first cost-efficient method of producing carbon filaments for electric lights (June 17).

Lewis H. Latimer (1848–1928) was the son of George Latimer, an escaped slave whose capture precipitated the first of the highly publicized fugitive slave trials in 1842. It was the trial of George Latimer which provoked Frederick Douglass' first appearance in print.

During the Civil War, Lewis Latimer enlisted in the Navy as soon as he was old enough. He then became an office boy in a patent office and, later on, was a patent draftsman.

Latimer made patent drawings for many of Alexander Graham Bell's telephone patents. He also worked for the United States Electric Lighting Company, where he made many significant innovations in the development of electric lighting. While working for the United States Electric Lighting Company, Latimer supervised the installation of electric light plants in New York and Philadelphia.

In 1884, Latimer began to work for the Edison Electric Light Company, and entered its legal department in 1890. From 1896 to 1811, he was the head draftsman for the Board of Patent Control.

• *Sports:* The jockey Babe Hurd won the Kentucky Derby riding Apollo.

THE AMERICAS

• *Brazil:* Joaquim Machado de Assis published *Papeis avulsos.*
• Luis Gonzaga de Pinto Gama (1830–1882), the Afro-Brazilian poet whose poems advanced the concept of negritude (black pride), died.

Luis Gonzaga de Pinto Gama (1830–1882) was born free in Bahia, Brazil. Luis was the son of a Portuguese aristocrat and a free Afro–Brazilian woman, Luiza Mahin, who participated in the Hausa uprising in Bahia.

In 1840, Gama was sold into slavery by his father and sent to Sao Paulo. While in Sao Paulo, Gama was taught how to read by his owner's friend and, by the age of 17, had secured his freedom.

Gama became a lawyer and became prominent for defending escaped slaves. During his career, he is credited with retrieving some 500 slaves from forced servitude. He was also noted for advocating slave revolts.

In his poetry, Gama was the first poet to glorify African women and to refer to the beauty of African women as being superior to that of European women. His poems *Junto a Estatua* and *Laura* were prime examples of his pride in the beauty of "black" women.

Gama also wrote satires about Afro-Brazilians who tried to pass for "white." *Pacotilha* and *Bodarrada* are two of the more noted satires.

Luis Gama was the first known writer of African descent to advocate black pride — to advance the notion of negritude.

• *Canada:* John Ware, the "Negro Cowboy," arrived in Canada. Ware became a legend in his lifetime. He was one of the finest riders in Alberta's range history. Ware died in 1905 when his horse fell on him. Ware was honored by having a mountain, a creek and a coulee named after him under the name "Nigger John." His log cabin was moved to adorn a provincial park.

• *Dominican Republic:* Ulises Heureaux became the president of the Dominican Republic. Heureaux's first term as president of the Dominican Republic lasted from 1882 to 1884.

The frequent turmoil that had plagued the nation ever since it attained independence was suspended temporarily during the last two decades of the nineteenth century, when General Ulises Heureaux came to power.

Ulises Heureaux exercised an iron-fisted rule over the Dominican Republic. His rule was a dictatorship which was marked by assassinations, bribery, and secret police surveillance. Nevertheless, the stability of the political situation under Heureaux led to a flurry of foreign investments that resulted in the building of telegraph lines, railways, roads, and the first large sugar mills in the southern Dominican Republic.

• *Haiti:* Port-au-Prince and Haiti were dedicated to Our Lady of Perpetual Help during a mass celebrated by the Archbishop of Port-au-Prince, Jean-Marie Guilloux, in the chapel of St. Francis of Assisi of Bel Air (February 5).

• *Mexico:* Juan Caballo (John Horse) (c. 1812–1882), a leader of the Black Seminoles, died. *See also 1875.*

Juan Caballo (John Horse) was born in Florida. He was reported to be a "slave" under chief Charles Cavallo. However, some historians believe that Charles Cavallo was actually Juan Caballo's father. In any event, Juan Caballo's father was most certainly a Seminole and his mother was a person of African descent.

Juan Caballo presumably experienced the dislocations caused by the American invasions of Florida in 1812 and in 1818. In 1826, while living in Thlonotosassa, Caballo won the nickname of "Gopher John" by selling a brace of "gopher" terrapins over and over again to an officer at Fort Brooke in Tampa Bay.

Juan Caballo grew up to be a tall, slim, "ginger-colored" man, with long wavy hair and a proud way of carrying himself. Caballo was noted for his tact and diplomacy as well as for his deadly accuracy with a rifle.

The Second Seminole War gave Caballo an opportunity to make a name for himself and that is precisely what he proceeded to do. By 1837, he was one of the leaders of the Black Seminoles and, on March 6, 1837, Caballo was one of the signers of the Treaty of Fort Dade.

When the Treaty of Fort Dade was violated by the re-enslavement of Black Seminoles who had surrendered, Caballo joined Osceola *(see 1875)*, Wild Cat and others in carrying away the Seminole hostages and renewing the war.

On October 21, while on a mission from the Seminole head chief Micanopy to the St. Johns River Indians, Caballo was captured under a flag of truce with Wild Cat and others and imprisoned in Fort Marion in St. Augustine. However, on the night of November 29, Caballo escaped with Wild Cat and others *(see 1875)*.

On December 25, Caballo was a commander with Wild Cat, Alligator, and Sam Jones, at the hard-fought Battle of Okeechobee. But the following April (April 1838), Caballo, along with Alligator, surrendered on a promise of freedom to the Black Seminoles who would surrender.

After his surrender, Juan Caballo was quickly shipped off to the Indian Territory of Oklahoma.

In the fall of 1838, Juan Caballo volunteered to return to Florida to help persuade the Seminole holdouts to surrender and from 1839 to 1842, Caballo served with great success as a United States guide and interpreter, even participating on April 19, 1842 in a daring mounted attack on Halleck Tustenuggee's Mikasuki.

After being sent west for a second time, Caballo soon found himself being once again allied with Wild Cat, Alligator, and other militants in striving for Seminole independence and greater protection for the Black Seminoles.

Caballo went to Washington again a year later and remained for nearly a year, pleading the cause of himself and his relatives in particular and that of the Black Seminoles in general. After the attorney general of the United States announced the illegality of the war time promise of freedom to the Black Seminoles, Caballo founded the Oklahoma city of Wewoka. Founded in 1849, Wewoka later became the Seminole capital and county seat of Seminole County, as a "city of refuge" where persons of African descent could come together and defend themselves against seizure.

Juan Caballo soon realized that there could be no "city of refuge" in the United States. So, in the fall of 1849, Juan Caballo, in association with Wild Cat, led an exodus of Black Seminoles to Mexico.

The Mexican government settled the Seminoles on the border of Coahuila as military colonists recognizing Wild Cat as the principal leader with Juan Caballo as commander of Seminole forces.

As commander of the Seminole forces, Juan Caballo often led his band against other Indigenous Americans as well as against the Texans. However, Caballo was careful not to become involved in the Mexican civil wars.

The proximity of the Black Seminoles and their ability to protect themselves alarmed the citizens of Texas. On September 19, 1851, on a visit to Eagle Pass, Juan Caballo was seized as a slave. Wild Cat was forced to pay a large ransom for his release.

This episode was a factor in the Mexican government's decision to move the Seminoles to the less exposed location of Nacimiento at the headwaters of the Sabina. However, even this precaution did not guarantee their safety. In November of 1852, at a fandango in Piedras Negras, Juan Caballo was shot and wounded by a visiting Texan.

After Wild Cat's death from smallpox early in 1857, many of the Seminoles gradually drifted back to the area around Coahuila. In 1859, Governor Santiago Vidaurri relocated the Black Seminoles to the Laguna de Parras, where under Juan Caballo's command they operated effectively against the Apache.

The Imperialist invasion scattered the Black Seminoles and some of them returned to the

United States. Beginning in 1870, a number of Black Seminoles served with distinction as "Indian" scouts for the United States Army (*see 1875*).

As for Juan Caballo, he was too old for active scouting. After being badly wounded at Fort Clark on May 19, 1876, in an assassination attempt, Caballo returned with other disillusioned Black Seminoles to Mexico.

Although in his later years, Juan Caballo was remembered as a "doctor," "philanthropist" and "father of his people," rather than as a warrior, Caballo was sufficiently active and alert to take a leading part in the destruction of a band of dangerous marauders near San Carlos, Chihuahua.

When, in 1882, claimants to the Seminole land at Nacimiento backed by the local caudillo Jose Maria Garza Galan ordered the removal of the Black Seminoles, Juan Caballo went to Mexico City where he obtained from the federal government confirmation of the Seminole claims. Although many conflicting accounts of his death were long current, it is virtually certain that he was the "Juan Caballo" who died of pneumonia in a Mexico City hospital on August 9, 1882.

AFRICA

• *North Africa, Egypt and Sudan:* In 1882, relations between Egypt and the Dual Control countries of France and Great Britain deteriorated.

The deterioration of relations between Egypt and the Dual Control parties accelerated in January when Ahmad Pasha Urabi, one of the leaders of the Patriotic Party, became Egypt's Secretary of War. This ascension led to the following sequence of events.

In response, on January 8, the Anglo-French Note was sent to the Khedive.

On February 21, a Ministry of the Sudan was created in Egypt.

On May 19, an Anglo-French fleet arrived at Alexandria and, on July 11, bombarded Alexandria.

On July 22, Ahmad Pasha Urabi was proclaimed a rebel.

On September 13, the British defeated an Egyptian army under the command of Ahmad Pasha Urabi at Tel el-Kebir. With the defeat of the Egyptian army, the British occupation of Egypt and Sudan began.

On September 15, the British seized Cairo.

Ahmad Pasha Urabi was banished to Ceylon (Sri Lanka).

On November 9, Lord Dufferin arrived to re-establish Dual Control.

• Jules Ferry proposed a school in every hamlet in Algeria.

• *Western Africa:* In January, the Portuguese initiated a military campaign against Jubada.

• An Anglo-French agreement was reached regarding the boundaries of Sierra Leone and Guinea.

• Friction developed between the Ashanti and Gyaman.

• Hostilities erupted between Abomey and Porto Novo.

• The First Gold Coast Education Ordinance was enacted.

• The UAC store at Asabu was destroyed. The town was bombarded by the HMS *Flirt*.

• The UAC was reorganized as the National African Company, Limited.

• Lat Dior was deposed.

In 1882, Lat Dior again found himself in conflict with French colonial policy when he objected to the French plans to build a railroad through Kayor to connect Saint Louis with Dakar in Senegal. Realizing the threat to his sovereignty posed by the railroad, Lat Dior refused to allow passage through his lands. The French refused to accept this and with their superior military forces were able to depose Lat Dior.

• James Africanus Beale Horton (1835–1882), a pioneer West African political philosopher, died.

James Horton's father had been an Ibo slave who was rescued at sea by a British anti-slave patrol and freed to Sierra Leone. In was in Sierra Leone that James Horton was born.

Horton received a classical education in missionary schools. He went on to study for the Christian ministry at Fourah Bay Institute (later Fourah Bay College) in Freetown.

In 1853, Horton was one of three Africans selected to study medicine in England. Horton spent five years in London and one at Edinburgh University from where he received his degree in 1859. He returned to West Africa as an army physician and worked at various stations along the coast for the next twenty years, retiring as a lieutenant-general.

During his lifetime, Horton published a variety of books and articles. The most important of his publications was *West African Countries and Peoples* which was published in 1868. *West African Countries and Peoples* proved to be a valuable description of the West African coast. In this book, Horton also argued that Africans were capable of governing under a Western form of government.

Horton advocated the establishment of six new nations similar to Liberia along the west coast of Africa. Unlike his friend and fellow intellectual, Edward Blyden *(see 1912)*, Horton believed that there was no such thing as a separate African identity. He considered that African nations should develop along European lines with European technology and education. In this respect, Horton subscribed to the argument of African cultural inferiority.

Horton's ideas were probably most influential in designing the short-lived Fante Confederation in the Gold Coast in 1871. Horton's death in 1882, prevented the development of his views in light of then imminent advent of European imperialism.

• *Central Africa:* Great Britain refused the request of the Cameroon kings and chiefs for the creation of a British protectorate over the Cameroon (March 1).

• A French post was established on the Alina River in the Congo (Zaire).

• International African Association posts were established at Mpala (by Storme) and Stanley Falls (by Henry Stanley).

• Kirundu was founded.

• The Tyo kingdom accepted a French protectorate.

• Azanga, the King of Mangbetu, submitted to Sudanese mercenaries in Egyptian pay.

• Harry Johnston explored Angola and the Congo.

• In 1882, Lewanika, the king of the Lozi, personally led a large army eastward against the Ila people gaining an immense booty and enhanced prestige.

• *Eastern Africa:* Italy established a colony at Eritrea (December).

• Menelik's expedition against Gojjam began. The Galla kingdom of Gudru was seized and the Sultan of Jimma became a vassal of Menelik.

• Mkwawa, the chief of the Hehe, began a military campaign against the Nyamwezi and Ngoni.

• In 1882, Bwana Heri focused Zigua animosity towards Zanzibari domination and organized a successful revolt against Sultan Barghash.

• Tippu Tip returned to the east coast of Tanzania.

In 1882, Tippu Tip, the de facto ruler of eastern Zaire, ended his twelve year hiatus and returned to the eastern coast. The purpose of his return was to negotiate with the Zanzibari Sultan, Sultan Barghash. For his journey to the coast, Tippu Tip assembled the largest caravan to ever traverse Tanzania. Along the way, Tippu Tip made an alliance with the Nyamwezi chief Mirambo. Once in Zanzibar, Tippu Tip accepted Barghash's proposal to serve as the sultan's agent in Zaire.

• In 1882, Abushiri the leader of the coastal people — the Swahili — repelled a force sent by Barghash to punish him for defaulting on some commercial loans. The defeat suffered by Barghash at the hands of Abushiri dissuaded Barghash from attempting, in the future, to administer the mainland region.

• Joseph Thomson explored Lake Victoria.

Joseph Thomson's most important expedition began in 1882. During this expedition, Thomson went from Mombasa to Lake Victoria and demonstrated the possibility of opening commercial routes through the Masai country of western Kenya.

• *Southern Africa:* Marianhill Abbey was founded by the Trappists.

• Friction mounted between the French and the government of Madagascar.

• General Charles Gordon became commander of the British forces in the Cape Colony.

At the time that Gordon *(see 1885)* became the British commander, the British forces were engaged in a costly war with the Sotho. Gordon attempted to negotiate a settlement with Masupha, a Sotho chief. However, Gordon soon resigned when he discovered that his negotiations were being undercut by another British official with another Sotho chief.

• Cetewayo went to London.

In 1882, Cetewayo, the King of the Zulu, was released from his imprisonment to go to London. In London, Cetewayo was lionized by the public and entertained by Queen Victoria. Cetewayo made a grand impression. In response, the British government decided to reinstate Cetewayo as King in Zululand where the political situation had deteriorated badly.

• Sekhukhune (c.1814–1882), the former paramount chief of the Pedi, died.

Sekhukhune seized power on the death of his father, Sekwati, in 1861. The succession was disputed by his half-brother Mampuru but the latter's claim to the throne was questionable at best.

Sekhukhune drove Mampuru away, but not forever.

Alarmed by the influence of Europeans on the Pedi, Sekhukhune ousted the German missionaries admitted by his father. Meanwhile, new friction developed with the neighboring Afrikaner republican government. In 1876, President Burgers *(see 1881)* attacked the Pedi in order to complete Afrikaner domination of the Transvaal. Sekhukhune's dynastic rival Mampuru allied with Burgers. For over a year, the Pedi resisted conquest.

Outside the Transvaal, the British noted the weakness of the Afrikaners with interest. In 1877, Theophilus Shepstone, an official in Natal, annexed the Transvaal Republic in a peaceful coup. Two years later, The British renewed the war against Sekhukhune.

Fresh from his occupation of the Zulu kingdom, Garnet Wolseley attacked the Pedi with two British regiments and 6000 Swazi troops. A thousand Pedi, including Sekhukhune's heir, were killed. Sekhukhune himself was captured and taken to Pretoria, while his rival, Mampuru, was made Pedi chief.

In 1881, the British restored independence to the Afrikaners in the Transvaal and simultaneously returned Sekhukhune to his people. Sekhukhune was then assassinated by Mampuru. Mampuru was tried and hanged by the Afrikaner government and the unity of the Pedi was effectively ended.

RELATED HISTORICAL EVENTS

• *Europe:* Charles Darwin (1809–1882), explorer, naturalist, scientist and one of the originators of the Theory of Natural Selection, died.

Charles Darwin was born on February 12, 1809, in Shrewsbury, England. He was the son of Robert Waring Darwin, a renowned London physician. Darwin was also the grandson of Erasmus Darwin, the author of *Zoonomia, or the Laws of Organic Life.* Because of his father and grandfather, Darwin enjoyed a relatively easy entree into the professional upper middle class that provided him with considerable social and professional advantages.

Darwin's mother died when he was eight years old. However, aside from this tragedy, Darwin seems to have enjoyed a charmed childhood. He was coddled and encouraged by adoring sisters, an older brother and the large Darwin clan.

Darwin was keenly interested in specimen collecting and chemical investigations, but at the Shrewsbury school, where he was an uninspired student, the headmaster, Dr. Samuel Butler, stressed the classics and publicly rebuked Darwin for wasting his time with chemical experiments.

Darwin's father was somewhat puzzled by the singular interests of Charles as well as by Charles' undistinguished career in the classical curriculum of the Shrewsbury school. Robert Darwin sent Charles to Edinburgh to study medicine.

At Edinburgh, Darwin collected animals in tidal pools, trawled for oysters with Newhaven fishermen to obtain specimens, and made two small discoveries which he incorporated in papers read before the Plinian Society. Darwin put forth very little effort to learn medicine.

With frustration, Dr. Darwin proposed the vocation of clergyman as an alternative. The life of a clergyman appealed to Charles. After quieting his doubts concerning his belief in "all the dogmas of the Church," Darwin began his new career at Cambridge.

Despite his divinity studies, Darwin proved unable to repress his scientific interests and developed into an ardent entomologist. He was particularly devoted to collecting beetles. Darwin's first brush with academic success came when one of his rare beetle specimens was published in Stephen's *Illustrations of British Insects.*

As at Edinburgh, Darwin enjoyed many stimulating associations with men of science. It was a professor of botany at Cambridge, John Stevens Henslow, who arranged for Darwin's appointment as naturalist aboard the government ship, H. M. S. *Beagle.*

From 1831 to 1836, the *Beagle* voyaged in Southern waters. Charles Lyell's researches into the changes wrought by natural processes, set forth in *Principles of Geology,* gave direction to Darwin's own observations of the geological structure of the Cape Verde Islands. Darwin also made extensive examinations of coral reefs and noted the relations of animals on the mainland to those of the adjacent islands, as well as the relation of living animals to the fossil remains of the same species.

Darwin described the voyage of the *Beagle* as "by far the most important event in any life." Besides making him one of the best qualified naturalists of his day, the voyage also developed in him the "habit of energetic industry and of concentrated attention." This new purposefulness on the part of Charles was noted by Dr. Darwin who remarked upon first seeing him after the voyage: "Why, the shape of his head is quite altered."

After his return, Charles settled in London and began the task of organizing and recording his observations. He became a close friend of Charles Lyell, the leading English geologist, and later of Hooker, an outstanding botanist.

In 1839, Charles Darwin married his cousin, Emma Wedgwood, and toward the end of 1842, because of Darwin's chronic ill-health, the family moved to Down, where Charles lived in seclusion for the rest of his life.

However, during the six years that Darwin was in London, he prepared his *Journal* from the notes of the voyage and published his carefully documented study of *Coral Reefs*.

The next eight years were spent in the laborious classification of barnacles for his four volume work on that subject. "I have been struck," Darwin wrote to Hooker, "with the variability of every part in some slight degree of every species." After this period of detailed work with a single species, Darwin felt prepared to attack the problem of the modification of species which he had been pondering for many years.

A number of facts had come to light during the voyage of the *Beagle* that Darwin felt "could only be explained on the supposition that species gradually become modified." Later, after his return to England, Darwin had collected all the material he could find which "bore in anyway on the variation of plants and animals under domestication." Darwin soon perceived "that selection was the keystone of man's success. But how selection could be applied to organisms living in a state of nature remained for some time a mystery."

One day while reading Thomas Malthus' *An Essay on the Principle of Population,* it suddenly occurred to Darwin how, in the struggle for existence, which he had everywhere observed, "favorable variations would tend to be preserved and unfavorable ones to be destroyed. The result would be the formation of a new species. Here then I had at last a theory by which to work."

Darwin confided this theory to Hooker and Lyell, who urged him to write out his views for publication. But Darwin worked deliberately. He was only half through his projected book when, in the summer of 1858, he received an essay from Alfred Russel Wallace at Ternate in the Moluccas, containing exactly the same theory as Darwin's own. Darwin submitted his dilemma to Hooker and Lyell, to whom he wrote: "Your words have come true with a vengeance — that I should be forestalled." It was their decision to publish an abstract of his theory with Wallace's essay, the joint work being entitled: *On the Tendency of Species to form Varieties and on the Perpetuation of Varieties and Species by Natural Means of Selection.*

A year later, on November 24, 1859, *The Origin of Species (On the Origin of Species by Means of Natural Selection, or The Preservation of Favoured Races in the Struggle of Life)* appeared. The entire first edition of 1,250 copies was sold on the day of publication. A storm of controversy arose over the book, reaching its height at a meeting of the British Association at Oxford, where the celebrated duel between T. H. Huxley and Bishop Wilberforce took place. Darwin, who could not sleep when he answered an antagonist harshly, took Lyell's advice and saved both "time and temper" by avoiding the debates.

Darwin continued the theme of *The Origin of Species* in his next three books. He expanded the material of the first chapter of the *Origin* into a book. The book was entitled *The Variation of Animals and Plants Under Domestication. The Variation of Animals and Plants Under Domestication* was published in 1868.

Darwin met the issue of human evolution head-on in *The Descent of Man, and Selection in Relation to Sex.* Published in 1871, *The Descent of Man* expanded the scope of evolution to include moral and spiritual as well as physical traits and underscored man's psychological as well as physiological similarities to the great apes, predicting, "the time will before long come when it will be thought wonderful that naturalists, who were well acquainted with the comparative structure and development of man and other animals, should have believed that each was the work of a separate act of creation."

The last of Darwin's sequels to the *Origin of Species* was *The Expression of the Emotions in Man and Animals. The Expression of the Emotions in Man and Animals* was published in 1872. It was an attempt to erase the last barrier presumed to exist between human and non-human animals — the idea that the expression of such feelings as suffering, anxiety, grief, despair, joy, love, devotion, hatred, and anger is unique to human beings. Darwin connected studies of facial muscles and the emission of sounds with the corresponding emotional states in man and then argued that the same facial movements and sounds in non-human animals express similar emotional states. This book laid the groundwork for the study of ethology, neurobiology, and communication theory in psychology.

Darwin's existence at his home at Down was peculiarly adapted to preserve his energy and give direct order to his activity. Because of his continual ill-health, his wife took pains "to shield him from every avoidable annoyance."

Darwin observed the same routine for nearly forty years. His days being carefully parcelled into intervals of exercise and light reading in such proportions that he could utilize to his fullest capacity the four hours he devoted to work.

Darwin's scientific reading and experimentation, as well, were organized with the most rigorous economy. Even the phases of his intellectual life non-essential to his work became, as he put it, "atrophied," a fact which he regretted as "a loss of happiness." Such non-scientific reading as Darwin did was purely for relaxation, and he thought that "a law ought to be passed" against unhappy endings to novels.

With his wife and seven children, Darwin's manner was so unusually "affectionate and delightful" that his son, Francis, marvelled that he could preserve it "with such an undemonstrative race as we are."

When Darwin died on April 18, 1882, his family wanted him to be buried at Down. However, the public demanded a more honored — a more public — burial site. Darwin was interred in Westminster Abbey. He was laid to rest beside Sir Isaac Newton.

Today there is little debate about the fact that Charles Darwin was the most influential scientist of the 1800s. His legacy — "Darwinism" — has continuing importance over one hundred years after his death. Its importance is such that it should not be ignored in any book covering the 1800s.

The term "Darwinism" has both a narrow and a broad meaning. In the narrow sense, it refers to a theory of organic evolution presented by Charles Darwin and by other scientists who developed various aspects of Darwin's views. The term "Darwinism," in its broadest sense, refers to a complex of scientific, social, theological and philosophical thought that was historically stimulated and supported by Darwin's theory of evolution.

Biological Darwinism — Darwinism in its narrowest sense — was the outstanding scientific achievement of the nineteenth century and is now the foundation of large regions of biological theory.

Darwinism in its broadest sense is a major philosophical problem which continues to confront mankind to this day.

The biology and cosmology of Darwinism is capable of being many things to many people. Like the sayings of the Bible, Darwinism has the ability to inspire and to lend a measure of support for a number of sometimes conflicting propositions.

In the annals of Pan-African history, Social Darwinism has played an all too significant role, particularly during the latter half of the nineteenth century and the early half of the twentieth century. Darwin's process of natural selection came to be reduced to the simplistic phrase "survival of the fittest." This skewed version of the theory led people to see society as the outcome of a social struggle in which each man, in pursuing his own good, can succeed only at the expense of others. The fittest in this social struggle are the ruthless, the imaginative, the industrious, and the frugal. People with these character traits will invariably climb to the top of the social order and, more importantly, their rise would be deemed good and part of the natural order.

As for those who do not have such character traits, the idle, the infirm, and the extravagant are deemed to be losers — individuals who have not adapted to the realities of their world. In a society where the law of nature reigns, the "losers" were considered to be legitimate subjects for elimination by "social selection."

Sadly, in Pan-African history, the definition of "losers" has been based upon criteria which were established by Europeans. Accordingly, the European conceived concept of Darwinism has all too often been used by Europeans as "scientific" justification for social policies by which people of African descent have been the subjects of persecution, discrimination, neglect, and elimination.

Today historians claim that Social Darwinism is now no more than a historical footnote. But the reality is that the forces of a Social Darwinism are still at play throughout the world and that people of African descent continue to be disparately affected by them.

Perhaps one day, the world will focus on the work that Darwin did later in his life. Later in his life, Darwin discovered that plants exhibit complicated characteristics that are adaptive and that increase the survival of a species. One such characteristic was cross-pollination. Darwin observed that flowers that are pollinated by the wind have little color, while those that need to attract insects have brightly colored petals and sweet smelling nectaries.

Darwin went on to experiment in his own garden. He raised two large beds of *Linaria vulgaris*, one from cross-pollinated and the other from self-pollinated seeds, both of which he obtained from the same parent plant.

Darwin then observed: "To my surprise, the crossed plants when fully grown were plainly taller and more vigorous than the self-fertilized ones." Ultimately, Darwin came to the conclusion that there are hereditary advantages in having two sexes in both the plant and animal kingdom. Darwin theorized that the presence of two opposites was necessary to ensure cross-fertilization, which produced healthier, more vigorous offspring.

Perhaps, one day the world will realize the merit of cultural and racial diversity throughout the spectrum of human experience. Perhaps one day the world will begin to understand the need for cross-fertilization amongst the people of the world as a means of ensuring a healthier, more vigorous world. Perhaps one day will come. Perhaps, one day is now.

- A House of Commons resolution recommended the transfer of all administrative responsibility in West Africa to the "natives" except "probably" in Sierra Leone.
- Adolf Luderitz secured Chancellor Bismarck's support to buy land for trading stations on the South West African coast.

Adolf Luderitz established the basis for German occupation of South West Africa by collecting treaties in 1883. Luderitz sold out to a private company in 1885. Chancellor Bismarck sent an administrator to protect German interests, and soon declared an official protectorate over the land.

The Germans were driven out of South West Africa during World War I. The country was later administered as an integral part of South Africa.

Today South West Africa is the country of Namibia.

- Leopold II established the International Association for the Congo.
- Henry Haggard published *Cetewayo and His White Neighbours.*

Henry Haggard (1856–1925) became famous for his highly imaginative adventure novels, but many of his story ideas can be traced to authentic African settings and episodes about which Haggard learned during his brief stay in South Africa.

Haggard first arrived in Natal in 1875. He spent two years in the civil service at Durban.

In 1877, Haggard was with Theophilus Shepstone when the latter annexed the Transvaal Republic to the British Crown. Haggard served in the Transvaal administration until 1879, then returned to England permanently.

Haggard's first book, *Cetewayo and His White Neighbours* was published in 1882. *Cetewayo and His White Neighbours* dealt with the Zulu war.

Haggard then experimented with light romantic fiction, producing the enormously successful *King Solomon's Mines* in 1885. *King Solomon's Mines* told a story which was inspired by early reports of the Shona mines and ruins in Zimbabwe and which dealt with the actual life story of the Ndebele royal pretender Nkulumane. The Nkulumane pretender had been Shepstone's employee in Natal.

Haggard modelled the fabulous queen of *She* (1887) on the Mujaji (queen) of the Lobedu people of the northern Transvaal.

The hero of one of Haggard's most popular books, *Allan Quartermain* was apparently modelled on the hunter, F. C. Selous.

Haggard wrote dozens of other books, many set in South Africa. He is one of the most widely read authors in the English language and made a significant impact in shaping popular Western images of Africa.

1883

THE UNITED STATES

- Angered at President Chester Arthur's refusal to aid African Americans, the National Convention of Colored People, meeting in Louisville, refused to endorse Arthur's Administration (September). Some of the participants called for African Americans to form their own political party.
- The Virginia Readjusters were defeated by the regular ("Bourbon") Democrats in the 1883 Virginia state elections. A race riot that erupted in Danville, Virginia, on the Saturday prior to the elections was credited with leading to the Republican defeat.
- Once again, the Virginia legislature reapportioned the legislative districts in an effort to minimize the African American vote. Additionally, a number of city charters

were amended to reduce African American representation on city councils.

• The only African Americans elected to serve in the 48th Congress were James E. O'Hara of North Carolina and Robert Smalls of South Carolina.

• *Notable Births:* Pianist and composer Eubie Blake was born in Baltimore, Maryland (February 7).

• The activist and educator, Hubert Henry Harrison (1883– 1927), was born in St. Croix, Virgin Islands (April 27).

• Edwin Bancroft Henderson, a noted coach and athletic event organizer, was born in Washington, D. C. (November 24). Henderson is considered to be the "Father of Black Sports." He was instrumental in organizing the Negro Athletic Conference, the Interscholastic Athletic Association, and the Colored Inter-Collegiate Athletic Association.

• William A. Hinton (1883–1959), a noted doctor, scientist, and professor, was born.

William A. Hinton was born in Chicago and was educated at the Harvard Medical School. For a while, Hinton served as a voluntary assistant in pathology at Massachusetts General Hospital before practicing for eight years at the Boston Dispensary and the Massachusetts Department of Health Laboratories.

From 1916 to 1952, Hinton served as the director of the Boston Dispensary Laboratory. During this time, Hinton became a world-renowned authority on venereal disease. In that regard, Hinton developed the Hinton Test (and later on, the Davies-Hinton Test) for the detection of syphilis.

In 1949, after serving as an assistant lecturer in preventive medicine and hygiene, Hinton became the first African American professor at Harvard University Medical School.

• Ernest Everett Just (1883–1941), a biologist known for research in cellular biology, was born (August 14).

Ernest Everett Just was born in Charleston, South Carolina and was educated in the public schools that were open for African Americans — the segregated schools — of Orangeburg, South Carolina.

By 1900, Just had worked his way from South Carolina to New York. In New York, Just applied to, and was accepted at, the Kimball Academy. Just would graduate from the Kimball Academy in 1903.

After graduating from the Kimball Academy, Just went to Dartmouth College in New Hampshire. In 1907, Just graduated *magna cum laude* from Dartmouth.

In 1908, Ernest Just became a member of the faculty at Howard University. For the next thirty-three years, Just would remain at Howard.

Just wrote many major treatises on the chromosome makeup of animals and cellular theory. His work in this area garnered Just an international academic reputation.

Just published a number of papers on experiments with protoplasm. In these experiments, Just demonstrated how living cells absorb and retain water. This work led to the determination of the structural relations of water to the colloids of the cell and to electrolytes.

In 1915, Ernest Everett Just was awarded the first Spingarn Medal.

• Arthur W. Mitchell, the first African American to be elected to Congress as a Democrat, was born (December 22).

Arthur W. Mitchell was born in Alabama and educated at Tuskegee Institute and the universities of Columbia and Harvard.

In 1934, Mitchell was elected to Congress as a Democrat serving a Congressional district in Illinois. Mitchell was the first African American to serve in Congress as a member of the Democratic Party. He would serve in Congress until 1942.

Mitchell was also a prosperous landowner and lawyer in Washington, D.C. In Congress and in the court, Mitchell was a champion for civil rights. In a notable case in which Mitchell was the name plaintiff, and in which Mitchell personally argued his own case before the United States Supreme Court, Mitchell successfully obtained a decision against Jim Crow railroad regulations. In *Mitchell v. United States* (April 28, 1941) 313 U.S. 80; 61 S.Ct. 873, the United States Supreme Court held that the Interstate Commerce Act prohibits discrimination against African American passengers because of their race and that the Act requires carriers to provide equality of treatment with respect to transportation facilities, furnishing African Americans who purchased first-class tickets with accommodations equal in comforts and conveniences to those afforded to first-class European American passengers.

Mitchell retired to his estate in Virginia in 1942.

• Blues singer Mamie Smith, the first African American woman to record a blues song, was born in Cincinnati, Ohio (May 26).

• The poet Anne Spencer was born in Henry County, Virginia (February 6).
• *Notable Deaths:* In 1883, some 52 African Americans were lynched.
• Josiah Henson (1789–1883), the model for Harriet Beecher Stowe's "Uncle Tom" of *Uncle Tom's Cabin*, died.

Josiah Henson was born on June 15, 1789 in Charles County, Maryland, on the farm of Francis Newman. As a youth, Henson saw his parents brutally assaulted by Newman.

In 1828, Henson became a preacher. When Henson tried to purchase his emancipation, the Newmans sent him to New Orleans to be sold. He then decided to escape. On October 28, 1830, Henson crossed over into Canada.

Henson helped other slaves to escape and tried to start a community. He traveled to England, where he was honored by Lord John Russell, the Prime Minister, and invited by Lord Grey to go to India to supervise cotton raising.

During his travels, while passing through Andover, Massachusetts, Henson happened to tell his story to Harriet Beecher Stowe. She referred to him in *A Key to Uncle Tom's Cabin*, published in 1853.

In 1849, Henson published *The Life of Josiah Henson, Formerly a Slave, Now an Inhabitant of Canada as Narrated by himself*, and in 1858 an enlarged edition appeared with an introduction by Harriet Beecher Stowe, under the title *Truth Stranger than Fiction, an Autobiography of the Rev. Josiah Henson.*

• George Moses Horton (1797–1883), a noted African American poet, died.

George Moses Horton was born a slave and lived at Chapel Hill, North Carolina. He worked as a janitor at the University of North Carolina where the college president was his owner. Horton made money writing love poems for the male students; the prices for his poems ranging from 25 cents to 50 cents a lyric, depending upon the warmth desired. His first book of poems, published in 1829, was to raise funds for his manumission. Unfortunately, it was a financial failure.

Horton was well into his 60s when Union soldiers finally freed him. During his literary career prior to liberation, there were only a few general statements against slavery in Horton's poetry, but these were too vague and mild to cause any controversy. However, in his second volume of poems, *Naked Genius*, published after the Civil War, Horton was more outspoken. He lampooned Jefferson Davis' attempt at escape (dressed as a woman), and in one poem, "The Slave," he expressed his true feelings on being a slave.

• Sojourner Truth (1797–1883), the abolitionist and advocate for women's rights, died in Battle Creek, Michigan. She was 86 years old (November 26).

Sojourner Truth was born a slave in Hurley, New York. Sojourner Truth was born Isabella Baumfree (Bomefree). She lived in New York City after having been freed in 1827 by the New York State Emancipation Act. After receiving a divine revelation in 1843, Isabella Baumfree changed her name to Sojourner Truth and began traveling and speaking for emancipation and women's rights.

During the Civil War, Sojourner Truth helped emancipated slaves who had emigrated to the North and made visits to army camps. After the Civil War, Sojourner Truth lectured and toured, advocating better educational opportunities for African Americans.

• *Miscellaneous State Laws:* Maine and Michigan repealed laws which prohibited interracial marriages.
• *Miscellaneous Cases:* In *Pace v. Alabama* (January 29, 1883) 106 U.S. 583, 27 L.Ed. 207, the United States Supreme Court held that an Alabama statute providing harsher punishment for interracial fornication than fornication with the same race did not violate the equal protection clause of the Fourteenth Amendment.
• In *United States v. Harris* (January 22, 1883) 106 U.S. 629, 27 L.Ed. 290, the United States Supreme Court held unconstitutional the provisions of the Enforcement Act of April 20, 1871 which penalized individuals who conspired to impede the exercise of those civil rights guaranteed under the Fourteenth and Fifteenth Amendment. The Court reasoned that the Fourteenth and Fifteenth Amendments were directed at curtailing state sponsored discrimination as opposed to individual discrimination and, as such, they could not be applied to individual private citizens.
• In *The Civil Rights Cases* (October 15, 1883) 109 U.S. 3, 3 S.Ct. 18, the Republican dominated United States Supreme Court declared the Civil Rights Act of 1875 to be unconstitutional. The Court held that the Act's guarantees of equal rights went beyond the powers granted to Congress in the Reconstruction Amendments. Justice Bradley,

speaking for a majority of the Court, declared that Congress could not properly "cover the whole domain of rights appertaining to life, liberty, and property, defining them and providing for their vindication."

• *Miscellaneous Publications:* George Washington Williams wrote a *History of the Negro Race in America,* the first serious history undertaken by an African American.

• John Mercer Langston, the Minister to Haiti, published *Freedom and Citizenship,* a collection of his speeches. *See 1829.*

• *Scholastic Achievements:* William Adger graduated from the University of Pennsylvania.

William Adger (1857–1885) was a native of Philadelphia. He graduated from the Institute for Colored Youth. Adger died during his senior year at the Episcopal Seminary.

• *The Black Church:* The Conference of Churchworkers Among Colored People became the first African American caucus in the Protestant Episcopal Church. The leader in the formation of the Conference of Churchworkers Among Colored People was Alexander Crummell (1819–1898).

Technological Innovations

In the 1880s, some of the most important inventions were developed by African Americans. Men such as Norbert Rillieux, Jan Matzeliger, John J. Parker, Granville T. Woods and Lewis Latimer made significant technological innovations which helped propel the industrialization of the United States—and the world.

It is ironic that the contributions made by these innovative pioneers were developed during a time in United States history when, for the most part, the fellow African Americans of these great innovators were being barred from employment in skilled industrial jobs.

The systematic segregation of African Americans from skilled industrial jobs would have long term consequences. Not only did it make the labor skills of the African American populace more marginal, it also potentially deprived the world of other technological innovations which may have been developed by nonmarginalized African Americans.

• The shoe lasting machine was patented by Jan Matzeliger, an African American inventor (March 20). The shoe lasting machine would revolutionize the shoe manufacturing industry.

• Humpfrey H. Reynolds patented an improvement for railroad car window ventilators (April 3).

Reynolds' innovation was soon adopted on all Pullman cars. However, Reynolds received no compensation from the Pullman company for the use of his patent. Accordingly, Reynolds quit his job as a railroad porter and sued. Reynolds won $10,000.

• *Black Enterprise:* Eatonville, Florida, was incorporated. Eatonville was, at the time, an all African American town.

THE AMERICAS

• *Brazil:* Slavery was abolished in Amazonas and Ceara.

• Andre Reboucas *(see 1898),* an Afro–Brazilian abolitionist and engineer, authored *Agriculture nacional. Agricultura nacional* was an anti-slavery book which called for the democratization of Brazil's agriculture for the benefit of ex-slaves, immigrants, and the rural poor.

• Goncalves Crespo (1846–1883), an Afro-Brazilian poet considered to be a major poet in the Portuguese language, died.

Goncalves Crespo was educated at the University of Coimbra. Crespo is considered by many to be the finest poet of the Parnassian school and one of the major poets of the Portuguese language. Of his poems, *A Sesta, Na Roca,* and *Cancun,* deal nostalgically with plantation Afro-Brazilians, their earthiness, durability and beautiful women.

• *Cuba:* In 1883, because of the Moret law reforms *(see 1870),* only 100,000 slaves remained in Cuba. In 1869, there had been 363,000, and, in 1878, there had been 228,000.

• *Haiti:* An agrarian law was enacted which facilitated foreign ownership of land, previously proscribed. Despite the best intentions, this policy along with a pro–French stance taken by the Salomon government were blamed for undermining Haitian independence and are seen by many as the beginning of a pattern of foreign intervention which culminated in United States occupation of Haiti in 1915.

• Oswald Durand, a noted Haitian poet, composed *Choucoune,* a famous poem which came to be set to music.

• In 1883, a major rebellion in Haiti resulted in the pillaging and burning of

COTW properties and murdering of COTWs by black soldiers and mobs. The rebellion ended only when the United States and European powers threatened intervention. The rebellion forced the expenditure of enormous amounts on the military, did irreparable damage to commerce and industry, further intensified racial animosities, and precipitated a spiral of inflation and state bankruptcy from which the regime of Louis-Felicite Salomon never recovered.

- Elie Lescot (1883–1974), a future president of Haiti, was born.

Elie Lescot was a member of the Haitian COTW elite. He went to primary and secondary school in Cape Haitien and then joined his uncle's import-export business. He became an interpreter for the customs service in 1905 and six years later was a member of the Chamber of Deputies. Subsequently, Lescot was director of the major secondary school in Port-au-Prince, justice of the peace, consul in Cuba, and a judge of a civil tribunal. Lescot also held various cabinet posts and was Haiti's ambassador to the United States.

Lescot developed strong ties with Rafael Leonidas Trujillo, the dictator of the Dominican Republic. Trujillo provided Lescot with funds which Lescot used to bribe members of the Haitian Assembly to elect him president in 1941.

After the failure of an unconstitutional attempt by President Stenio Vincent to remain in office, Vincent, under pressure from the United States government, resigned. On May 15, 1941, Vincent was succeeded by Lescot.

Lescot's regime was tyrannical and corrupt. He established military tribunals with jurisdiction over all offenses and persons, thus circumventing the judiciary. There were numerous arbitrary arrests of political opponents, critical journalists, and the clergy. Corruption and nepotism were rampant. Ostensible social security and economic development schemes became mechanisms for enriching Lescot, his family, and a small clique of elites.

Lescot took exclusive personal control over the Haitian budget. In 1944, using the excuse of the war, he appropriated all foreign assets in the country. Lescot also created six regional delegates with absolute power in their local jurisdictions, who answered directly to him through his minister of interior.

Lescot established strong ties with the United States. The United States and Haitian entry into World War II proved highly opportune. Declaring "extraordinary powers," Lescot virtually suspended the constitution and negotiated with the United States for increased economic aid and military assistance. The United States agreed to buy all of Haiti's cotton and sisal. Haiti was provided artillery, military aircraft, and a detachment of the United States Coast Guard.

During the war, Lescot also suspended national elections to the assembly in 1944, giving himself the power to appoint its members, and extended his presidential term from five years to seven. As soon as the war ended, however, Lescot came under attack from the local newspaper, *La Ruche*. His move in January of 1946 to ban the paper and detain its editors sparked massive demonstrations by students and civil servants. On January 11, three high ranking officers, including the commander of the Presidential Guard, Mayor Paul Eugene Magliore, deposed the president.

Lescot left Haiti for Miami. He later took up residence in Montreal before returning to Haiti.

- *Virgin Islands:* The activist and educator, Hubert Henry Harrison (1883–1927), was born in St. Croix, Virgin Islands (April 27).

EUROPE

- Robert Browning published *Jocoseria*.

AFRICA

- *North Africa, Egypt and Sudan:* The Mahdi *(see 1881)* captured Bara (January).
- Pursuant to "Organic Law," a Legislative Council and General Assembly were established in Egypt under the authority of the British Agent (May 1).
- After the Convention of Marsa (June 5), France gained effective control of Tunisia.
- Sir Evelyn Baring (Lord Cromer) arrived in Egypt as the British Agent (September 11).
- The Mahdi defeated an Anglo-Egyptian force at El Obeid (November 5). Britain subsequently evacuated Sudan.

By early 1883, the movement of Muhammed 'Ahmad ibn 'Abdallah was the focus of a Sudanese revolt against the Egyptian government and his developing army controlled central Sudan. Later that year, the Mahdi's troops annihilated an Anglo-Egyptian army and then moved against the capital, Khartoum.

- Rudolf von Slatin Pasha, the Governor of Darfur, having converted to Islam, submitted to the Mahdi.

• Nubar Pasha began his tenure as Premier of Egypt.

• General Charles Gordon was recalled to the Sudan.

During 1883, Gordon *(see 1885)* considered working for Leopold, the King of Belgium and the ruler of the Belgian Congo. However, before accepting commission, Gordon was recalled to Sudan by the British government which had assumed the administration of Egypt.

• Abd al-Qadir (1807–1883), an Algerian resistance leader, died.

• *West Africa:* The Asantehene Mensah Bonsu was deposed by chiefs who wanted to demonstrate their friendliness towards the British (February).

• The deposing of Mensah Bonsu was followed by a year of anarchy among the Ashanti.

• In March, there was a Fula uprising against the Portuguese at South Belchier.

• France began the conquest of the upper Niger (December).

• Gallieni occupied Bamako.

In 1883, Joseph Gallieni, a French military commander, occupied Bamako, the future capital of Mali. Later, when he became military commander (*Commandant-Superieur du Haut-Fleuve*), Gallieni modified his views to include peaceful economic development as a means of extending French imperial aims.

As part of his economic scheme, Gallieni concentrated on constructing a railroad which he hoped would reach Bamako. However, he continued to believe that eventually the Islamic empires would have to be taken by force.

• France reoccupied Grand Bassam, Assinie and Dabou, Ivory Coast.

• Consul Hewett recommended deportation of King Jaja of Opobo for cruelty to Africans.

• The French declared a protectorate over Porto Novo.

In 1883, Toffa, the ruler of the Aja kingdom of Porto Novo, asked the French to proclaim a new protectorate, and they obliged. Porto Novo thrived as a port under French protection. Toffa, meanwhile, sent insulting messages to Behanzin, the ruler of Dahomey (Benin). These taunts were ostensibly an attempt to goad Behanzin into an attack on Porto Novo, which Toffa knew the French would answer.

• *Central Africa:* A commercial agreement was reached between King Akwa and the German merchant E. Schmidt (January 30).

• A treaty was negotiated between the Germans and Pass-All, the Cameroon chief (August 23).

• Brazza was named Commissioner-General in West Africa.

In 1883, Pierre de Brazza returned to the French Congo to mount more expeditions. These expeditions would greatly extend and bolster French claims in the region.

• Joseph Thomson explored the region between Lakes Nyasa and Tanganyika.

• H. von Wissmann explored northern Cameroon.

• Brazza, along with others, explored and occupied the French Congo.

• *Eastern Africa:* The French vessel *l'Inferne* was sent to reconnoiter Obock with a view to setting up a post.

• There was a Mahdist raid on Gondar.

• Bukumbi, the first White Fathers' mission on Lake Victoria, was founded.

• Vicariate Apostolic of Uganda was established.

• In Ethiopia, Taitu married Menelik (who was then King of Shoa).

• In 1883, Mirambo's *(see 1884)* troops suffered setbacks at the hands of the northern Ngoni and the resurgent southern Nyamwezi.

• *Southern Africa:* Paul Kruger became the President of the South African Republic (April 16).

• Germany began to establish settlements in Southwest Africa at Angra Pequena (April 24). Britain warned that the settlements were an infringement on its territorial rights.

In 1883, the agent of Adolf Luderitz collected treaties around Angra Pequena Bay (what is today Luderitz Bay) and built up a claim to a large amount of territory in what is today Namibia. Luderitz then sold these rights to a private company—the German Colonial Society for South West Africa—which attempted to establish an administration there in 1885.

• France went to war against the government of Madagascar (June 1).

• The Boer republic of Stellaland was founded in Bechuanaland (September).

• Portugal granted a railway concession from Delagoa Bay to Transvaal to a United States promoter (December 14).

• British consul was appointed to Malawi region.

• In 1883, John Jabavu founded his own paper, *Imvo Zabantsundu* — "the views of the Bantu People." *Imvo Zabantsundu* quickly became a popular mouthpiece for Xhosa opinion.

• The Oblates of St. Francis de Sales began work on the Orange River.

• A civil war erupted in Zululand.

The British restored Cetewayo, the great Zulu chief, as ruler of central Zululand in January 1883. However, after a three year absence, the displaced Zulu chiefs refused to accept his leadership. A struggle ensued and Cetewayo was beaten in battle by a rival. Fleeing his enemies, Cetewayo sought asylum with the British at Eshowe.

• Sarili, the former paramount chief of the Gcaleka Xhosa, was pardoned.

• Kanda, the man who pretended to be Nkulumane, the heir to the Ndebele throne, died. *See 1872.*

• Pasipamire, the Chaminuka medium, was killed by the Ndebele.

• Sekgoma Kgari I (c.1815–1883), the ruler of the Ngwato, died.

Sekgoma Kgari was a junior son of the Ngwato chief Kgari Kgama, who died fighting the Shona around 1828. Soon afterwards, the Ngwato were scattered by the invading Kololo of King Sebitwane. Sekgoma himself was captured by the Kololo, but escaped and returned home.

While recovering from the effects of the Kololo invasion, the Ngwato were torn by a succession dispute. Sekgoma's half-brother Macheng was the rightful heir to the Ngwato throne, but he was only an infant. Taking advantage of the situation, Sekgoma seized power around 1834 and ruled without challenge for over twenty years, while Macheng was later carried off by the Ndebele around 1842.

Although an usurper, Sekgoma was at first a popular ruler. He reunified the Ngwato and strengthened them militarily. His capital at Shoshong grew to about 30,000 inhabitants. When the powerful Ndebele of Mzilikazi attempted to collect tribute from him in 1842, he killed the envoys and suffered no reprisals. However, eventually, Sekgoma came to be regarded as too harsh a ruler.

When Macheng was released from the Ndebele in 1857, the Ngwato enthusiastically made him chief. Sekgoma and his sons went into voluntary exile among the Kwena. After a year, however, the Ngwato ousted Macheng, and Sekgoma was recalled to power.

When Sekgoma returned to Shoshong, he brought with him a German missionary who baptized his sons, Khama and Kgamane. John MacKenzie and another agent of the London Missionary Society opened a permanent mission among the Ngwato in 1862. The mission proved a success, but Sekgoma held to his traditional religious beliefs.

Sekgoma's sons proved to be enthusiastic supporters of the mission and religious differences created a family rift. In 1866, Khama helped his uncle Macheng oust Sekgoma for a second time. Sekgoma went back into exile.

Six years later, Macheng was again out of favor. Khama helped Sekgoma to regain his throne.

Finally, in 1875, Sekgoma was ousted for the third and last time. This time his son, Khama, became chief. Sekgoma spent the remaining years of his life living in obscurity on the fringe of Ngwato territory.

RELATED HISTORICAL EVENTS

• *Europe:* Lord Granville announced Britain's intention to withdraw from Egypt as soon as the state of the country would allow (January 3).

• Karl Marx (1818–1883), the father of Communism, died.

• Godfrey Martin Huggins (1883–1971), a future prime minister of Southern Rhodesia, was born.

Godfrey Huggins was born in England where he began a career as a surgeon. In 1911, Huggins went to Rhodesia (Zimbabwe). Huggins entered the legislature in 1924.

Huggins was a supporter of the ruling party of Charles Coghlan. Dissatisfied with the economic policies of Coghlan's successor, Howard Moffat, Huggins defected to the Reform Party and became its leader in 1931. Two years later, he came to power at the head of a coalition. Anxious to maintain strong personal control, Huggins called another election in 1934 and, ironically, emerged the leader of essentially the same party he had previously opposed.

Throughout his exceptionally long tenure of office, Huggins articulated his own vision of race relations in what he called the "two pyramid" theory. The "two pyramid" theory called for the separate but interdependent Euro-African and African political development.

Huggins was fearful of Southern Rhodesia being sucked into the Union of South Africa and regarded some form of amalgamation with Northern Rhodesia (Zambia) as a means of preserving Rhodesia's autonomy.

By the late 1940s, Huggins joined with Roy Welensky of Northern Rhodesia to advocate federation, for which he relentlessly lobbied in England. In 1953, Huggins' goal was achieved with the formation of the Federation of Rhodesia and Nyasaland.

Huggins resigned from his Southern Rhodesian premiership to become the Federation's first prime minister. Despite his talk about partnership, Huggins worked to keep political control out of the hands of Africans.

Huggins was made a viscount in 1955. As Lord Malvern, he retired from public life.

- *Africa:* Olive Schreiner, South Africa's first great novelist, published *The Story of an African Farm.*

In 1881, Olive Schreiner went to England to find a publisher for her novel, *The Story of an African Farm.* Two years later, the book was published under the pen-name "Ralph Iron." *The Story of an African Farm* is sometimes regarded as a classic in English literature. This novel depicts the lonely and hard life of Afrikaner farmers, and draws heavily on Schreiner's own experiences. It was an immediate international success, popular largely because of its exotic setting and its non–Victorian views on marriage.

- George Theal *(see 1879)* published *Basutoland Records,* a three volume historical record of Basutoland.
- Robert Moffat (1795–1883), the pioneering British missionary, died.

Robert Moffat began his career with the London Missionary Society (LMS) among the Khoikhoi of Namaqualand in South West Africa in 1817. Moffat soon moved to the northern Cape Colony to live among the Tlhaping.

In 1824, Moffat founded a station at Kuruman. This station would long serve as the northernmost European outpost in South Africa. Moffat became an unofficial diplomatic agent between Europeans and northern peoples and used his local prestige to help launch new missions in all directions.

In 1829 and 1835, Moffat visited the Ndebele king Mzilikazi — who was then located in the Transvaal — and established a life-long friendship with him.

In 1854, Moffat was the first European to visit Mzilikazi in Matabeleland, where the Ndebele had settled around 1840.

Later on (around 1859), Moffat helped to establish a permanent LMS mission among the Ndebele.

Robert Moffat travelled widely within South Africa, but always retained his headquarters at Kuruman. He retired in 1870.

One of Moffat's more notable achievements was his prodigious linguistic work which made Tswana one of the first Bantu languages to be reduced to writing.

1 8 8 4

THE UNITED STATES

- Between 1876 and 1884, African American voting dropped by one-third in Louisiana, by one-fourth in Mississippi, and by one-half in South Carolina.
- The Medico-Chirugical Society of the District of Columbia, the oldest African American medical society, was organized (April 24).
- John Roy Lynch, former Congressman, was elected temporary chairman of the Republican convention, the first African American to preside over deliberations of a national political party (June 3).
- Senator Blair introduced a bill for Federal Aid to Education. The bill passed in the Senate but was defeated in the House of Representatives.
- Ex–Senator Blanche K. Bruce was put in charge of the African American exhibit at the World's Cotton Exposition, held in New Orleans, from November 1884 through May of 1885. Bruce received critical acclaim for his display of the achievements of African Americans.
- *Notable Births:* Rose McClendon, an actress, was born in North Carolina (August 27).
- Oscar Micheaux, the trailblazing filmmaker, was born in Illinois (January 22).
- William Edouard Scott (1884–1964), an African American artist, was born in Indianapolis, Indiana.

William Scott studied art in Indianapolis, Chicago and Paris. During his career, Scott exhibited his works at the Paris Salon (1912–1913).

William Scott was greatly influenced by the work of Henry Ossawa Tanner. Tanner's influence on Scott is quite evident in Scott's landscape *Rainy Night at Etaples.*

Upon his return to the United States from Europe, Scott received a series of commissions for murals for the City Hospital in Indianapolis, the Illinois State House, Fort Wayne Court House, and later several African American colleges and YMCAs.

During the 1930s, after spending some time in the West Indies while on a Rosenwald Grant, Scott began a series of memorable sketches of West Indian inhabitants and the colorful tropical landscapes of the islands.

- *Notable Deaths:* In 1884, 50 African Americans were lynched.
- Elijah Abel (?–1884), an African American who became an elder (priest) in the Mormon Church while the Mormons were located in Nauvoo, Illinois, died.

Elijah Abel was an undertaker who was converted to Mormonism in 1832. After becoming an elder, Abel moved with the Mormons to Salt Lake City, Utah. In Salt Lake City, he became a hotel manager. Abel would be active in the Mormon church throughout his life.

- William Wells Brown (1816?–1884), the author of *Clotel*, the first novel by an African American, and the publisher of *The Escape*, the first play written by an African American, died in Cambridge, Massachusetts.

William Wells Brown was a noted African American author and historian. He was born in Lexington, Kentucky. His mother was an attractive COTW slave and his father was said to be a European American slaveholder by the name of George Higgins.

William Wells Brown was taken to St. Louis and, once he became old enough to hire out for work, he was hired out on a steamboat. For a time he also worked for Elijah P. Lovejoy, the editor of the *St. Louis Times*. However, his stay there was brief and he was once again hired out on a steamboat.

In 1834, Brown escaped to Ohio. His original purpose was to go to Canada. He was sheltered by a Quaker who inspired him to assist other slaves to escape.

Between 1843 and 1849, Brown worked as a lecturer for the Western New York Anti-slavery Society and the Massachusetts Anti-slavery Society.

William Wells Brown was also interested in temperance, women's suffrage, and prison reform. In 1849, he visited England and represented the American Peace Society at the Peace Congress in Paris. Brown stayed abroad until 1854.

Although Brown also studied medicine, his fame rests largely on his reputation as an historian. His works include *Narrative of William Wells Brown, a Fugitive Slave* (1847); *Three Years in Europe* (1852) (also known as *The American Fugitive in Europe: Sketches of Places and People Abroad*); and *Clotel, or the President's Daughter, A Narrative of Slave Life in the United States*, a novel published in 1853.

Brown wrote a number of plays. His plays include *The Dough Face* and *The Escape, or a Leap for Freedom*. His historical works include: *The Black Man, His Antecedents, His Genius and His Achievements* (1863); *The Negro in the American Rebellion, His Heroism and His Fidelity* (1867); and *The Rising Son, or the Antecedents and the Advancements of the Colored Race* (1874).

- Robert Brown Elliott (1842–1884), a Reconstruction Congressman from South Carolina, died (August 9).

Robert Brown Elliott was the son of West Indian parents living in Boston, Massachusetts. Elliott was educated abroad in Jamaica, at the High Holburn Academy in London, and at Eton.

Upon returning to the United States, Elliott became the editor of the *Charleston Leader*. He was made a delegate to the South Carolina Constitutional Convention in 1868, and became a member of the State Legislature.

In 1871, Elliott was elected to the United States House of Representatives representing South Carolina. He served two terms in the House. Afterwards, Elliott retired to New Orleans where he practiced law.

- *Miscellaneous State Laws:* In Alabama, the chaining together of African American and European American convicts was made illegal. Additionally, African American and European American convicts were henceforth housed in segregated jail cells.
- *Miscellaneous Publications:* Timothy Thomas Fortune began publication of the *New York Freeman*, a newspaper which would eventually be better known as the *New York Age*.
- Timothy Thomas Fortune published *Land, Labor and Politics in the South*.
- James Walker Hood published *The Negro in the Christian Pulpit*.
- In 1884, Alberry Whitman published a long narrative poem, *The Rape of Florida*. *The Rape of Florida* was done in Spenserian stanzas and was focused on the European American oppression of the Seminoles. The significance of the poem was that Whitman

saw the Seminoles in a position analogous to that of his own people. He saw the position of the Seminoles was similar to the position of African Americans. *See 1875.*

• In 1884, Benjamin Tanner launched the *A.M.E. Church Review,* the only national magazine published for African Americans at that time.

• Moses Grandy, a former slave, published an account of his experiences.

• *The Arts:* James Conway Farley, a photographer, won first prize at the Colored Industrial Fair in Richmond.

James Conway Farley (1854–1910) of Richmond, Virginia, also won a premium at the New Orleans World Exposition of 1885, where he exhibited with European American photographers. Of the many photographs Farley made, only one remains that is attributable to him.

• *Music:* Gussie Davis wrote *When Nellie Was Raking the Hay,* a popular musical piece of the time.

• *Scholastic Achievements:* The Southern Methodist Episcopal Church established Paine College in Augusta, Georgia.

• *The Black Church:* Henry Vinson Plummer was appointed to serve as a chaplain in the regular United States army (July 8).

Henry Vinson Plummer (1844–1905) was born a slave in Maryland. During the Civil War, Plummer escaped. He taught himself to read while serving in the navy. A strong advocate for temperance, Plummer, a captain in the army, was court-martialed and discharged from the army on a charge of drunkenness — a charge supported by one witness, who had a ten year grudge against him.

• *Technological Innovations:* John J. Parker invented a screw for tobacco presses and set up his own foundry to manufacture it.

• Granville Woods received his first two patents. One was for a steam boiler, the other was for a telephone transmitter (December 2).

In the 1880s, Granville T. Woods began producing inventions in electronics, telegraphy, steam boilers and air brake systems. Many of Woods inventions were sold to such companies as American Bell Telephone Company, General Electric Company, and Westinghouse Air Brake Company.

• *Black Enterprise:* Granville T. Woods founded the Woods Electric Company in Cincinnati, Ohio.

• *Sports:* In 1884, the Toledo professional baseball team — the champions of the Northwestern League of the American Association, had an African American player. Moses Fleetwood Walker was the catcher for the team. At the time, Walker caught the ball without using a mitt.

• Trainer William Bird, an African American, and Jockey Isaac Murphy, another African American, won the Kentucky Derby with their mount, Buchanan.

THE AMERICAS

• *Brazil:* In 1884, Brazil's slave population was estimated to be about 3,000,000.

In 1884, Brazilian abolitionists succeeded in proclaiming the northeastern state of Ceara as a free state. Immediately following, an active underground railroad developed with free persons helping individual slaves to escape their owners and reach Ceara.

• Joaquim Machado de Assis published *Historias sem data.*

• *Haiti:* Louis-Joseph Janvier published the striking *L'Egalite des Races* (Equality of the Races), a thesis in which he vehemently defended those of African descent.

• Thomas Madiou (1814–1884), a noted historian, died.

Thomas Madiou was born in Port-au-Prince on April 30, 1814. At the age of ten, Madiou was sent to France to study at the College Royal d'Angers.

In 1833, at Rennes, France, Madiou was awarded a Bachelor of Arts Degree in Letters, and for two years took classes at the Law School of Paris.

Madiou returned to Haiti to write the history of his country. He carried out several public functions as the Director of Le Moniteur — the official paper of the government — in 1849.

Madiou's manuscript, *Histoire d'Haiti,* is deemed to be one of the most valued works in Haitian literature.

• *Jamaica:* William Alexander Bustamante (1884–1977), the first prime minister of independent Jamaica, was born.

William Alexander Bustamante was the son of an Irish planter and a COTW mother. Bustamante's birthname was William Alexander Clarke.

After attending elementary school and doing some private studies, Bustamante worked as a store clerk and in a sugar factory. He left Jamaica in 1905 and lived in several countries during the next 30 years. When Bustamante returned to Jamaica in 1934 he had a sizable fortune and set up a real estate and money lending business.

By 1936, Bustamante was taking part in protest marches against the colonial government and intervening in strikes. In 1937, "Busta" became treasurer of the Jamaica Workers' and Tradesmen's Union (JWTU) which he had helped organize. During 1937 and 1938, there was an escalation of labor and political unrest not only in Jamaica but throughout the West Indies. Bustamante became deeply involved in this turmoil. On May 23, 1938, Bustamante was arrested, charged with sedition, and held without bail. Intense labor and political pressure brought his release a week later. Regarded as a martyr as a result of this experience, Bustamante gained even more status as a charismatic hero.

Soon afterward, Bustamante formed the Bustamante Industrial Trade Union (BITU), and he served as its president until his death. With his cousin, Norman Washington Manley, Bustamante joined in forming the Peoples National Party (PNP) in September 1938. For a time, the BITU was the union arm of the PNP. In February 1939, Bustamante attempted to organize a general strike which failed. In 1940, after threatening to call a general strike, Bustamante was arrested and detained for 17 months for "impeding the war effort." Upon release in February 1942, Bustamante attacked the leaders of the PNP, accusing them of a betrayal of trust. In 1943, Bustamante founded the Jamaica Labour Party (JLP) to contest the impending elections, the first under universal adult suffrage.

Bustamante's charismatic oratory and wit, together with the decision of portions of the Jamaican middle class to support the JLP out of fear of the socialist ideology of Manley's Peoples National Party, brought victory to Bustamante and his party who captured 22 of the 32 seats in the House of Representatives. The PNP won in only four constituencies. Bustamante became minister of communication and works and leader of the elected members of the Executive Council under a new constitution. Bustamante's party was victorious again in 1949, winning 18 of 32 seats in the House, although the PNP won a majority of the popular votes. Bustamante was then appointed chief minister and presided over a largely elected Executive Council.

In office, Bustamante considerably modified his positions. A confrontation with strikers of the PNP controlled Trade Union Congress in 1946 that resulted in the death of one of the strikers generated a scandal. Moreover, Bustamante was avowedly anti-socialist and a firm believer in the British Crown. He resisted the PNP campaign for increased self-government and accepted a new constitution only at the urging of the governor.

Only after a narrow victory in 1949 did Bustamante begin to implement modest social welfare programs for workers. Finally, in 1955, the JLP lost to the PNP, getting only 14 seats to the PNP's 18. Bustamante became Leader of the Opposition and was knighted by the queen.

Despite reservations, Bustamante had been one of the West Indian leaders who in 1947 had agreed to form a regional federation as the basis for eventual independence. After his 1955 electoral defeat, Bustamante served as the leader of a federal coalition of parties. When federal elections were held in 1958, Bustamante's JLP won 12 of the 17 Jamaican seats in the federal Parliament, but parties allied with his JLP lost to parties in the rival Federal Labor Party elsewhere.

Bustamante became highly critical of the federation. After losing another election to the PNP in 1959, Bustamante forced the Manley government to call a referendum on the issue on September 19, 1961. Bustamante won a resounding victory as voters supported secession. This was the death knell of the federation, which came to a formal end on May 31, 1962.

Bustamante then joined with Manley to petition for Jamaica's full independence. Bustamante served on the committee to draw up the independence constitution, joined the delegation that went to Britain to negotiate, and was one of the signatories to the agreement for independence. The leaders of the JLP and PNP agreed on an election prior to independence. Bustamante's JLP was swept to power, winning 26 seats to 19 for PNP. The country became independent on August 6, 1962, and Bustamante became its first prime minister. In 1964, the 80 year old Bustamante became ill and never returned to full-time involvement in government. He finally retired as prime minister in 1967.

EUROPE

• Robert Browning published *Ferishtah's Fancies.*

AFRICA

• *North Africa, Egypt and Sudan:* General Gordon reached Khartoum (Sudan) with orders to evacuate Egyptians (February 18). The Mahdi refused to negotiate.

During Gordon's three year hiatus from the Sudan, a large scale Islamic revolution had erupted under the leadership of Muhammed 'Ahmad, the Mahdi. British forces were cut off at Khartoum and Gordon was assigned to relieve them.

Gordon reached Khartoum early in 1884. However, instead of relieving the beleaguered British troops, Gordon soon found himself trapped. After a siege which lasted almost a year, the Mahdists took the city of Khartoum and Gordon was killed.

- The Mahdi captured Qedaref and, on October 13, Omdurman.
- *Western Africa:* Germany occupied Togo (April).
- In April, the Portuguese mounted an expedition against Jebelor, Jeboucer and Beri.
- The merchants of the Benin River protested that they had had no consular visit since 1879.
- A treaty was negotiated between Britain and Opobo (July 1).

By 1884, the French had abandoned their stations on the Niger. In the same year, George Goldie *(see 1877)* began a campaign to sign treaties of "protection" with local rulers. By aiding the chiefs in local conflicts, Goldie obtained their economic cooperation.

The treaties obtained by Goldie proved to be immensely beneficial to the British government. During the Berlin Conference of 1884–1885 — the conference which formally initiated the "Scramble for Africa" — England used the treaties obtained by Goldie as proof of Britain's prior occupation of much of Nigeria.

One of the treaties negotiated was with Jaja, the king of Opobo. Jaja signed a treaty placing himself under British protection. However, he explicitly refused to guarantee free trade. The same year, the European merchants on the coast combined to boycott the purchase of oil at Opobo. Jaja broke the boycott by finding a European buyer.

- Germany entered into a treaty with Chief Nlapa in Togo (July 5).
- A treaty was executed between Britain and Asabu (November 1).
- An additional treaty between Britain and Opobo was negotiated which stipulated a freedom of trade (December 19).
- Treaties between the National African

Company and Sokoto and Gwandu were effected.
- The Rio de Oro was occupied by Emilio Bonelli. A Spanish protectorate was established over the area between Cape Bojador and Cape Blanco.
- Samory converted his empire into a theocratic Islamic state.

Up until this time, the unifying principle which Samory had employed was loyalty to his person. With the expansion of his empire, Samory felt that personal loyalty would not suffice and, in 1884, he attempted to turn the empire into an Islamic theocracy.

- Samory conquered the Sierra Leone hinterland.

Samory conquered the Sierra Leone hinterland in order to ensure the supply of arms from Freetown, the most important terminus of his caravans. In exchange for arms, Samory offered gold and ivory. The slaves that Samory captured were his most important source of capital, although these had to be exchanged for products acceptable in Freetown.

When Samory's forces (the Sofa) invaded the Sierra Leone interior in 1884, Suluku Konte, the chief of the Biriwa, realized early on that the Biriwa were not powerful enough to stop them. A Sofa contingent occupied a town in Biriwa and Suluku was at first forced to pay nominal allegiance to Islam. However, Samory's forces were never able to dominate Biriwa because Suluku called on the British for intervention whenever the Sofa threatened.

By playing off the British against Samory, Suluku was able to maintain himself in power during the nine-year Sofa occupation even though many neighboring chiefs fell or became Sofa puppets. Ultimately, in 1894, the French drove out the Sofa.

- In 1884, Frederick Lugard accepted his first West African assignment when he was hired by the Royal Niger Company to race up the Niger River in Nigeria to obtain treaties of "protection" from local rulers before the French could do so. Lugard succeeded in bringing Borgu under British chartered company rule.
- Nana Olumu became the "Governor of the River."

The office of "Governor of the River" was created among the Itsekiri of Nigeria at the suggestion of the British to regulate the palm oil trade. When Nana Olumu became governor in

1884 the office was the highest in the land, for the formerly strong monarchy had suffered an interregnum since 1848.

The governor was chosen from among the leading traders, thus, commercial skill came to replace heredity as the prerequisite for power.

Itsekiri society was factionalized, however, and Nana could not command the obedience of all his people. He also had to contend with European pressures during a period of militant imperialism.

In his first year as Governor of the River, Nana Olumu was compelled to sign a treaty bringing Itsekiriland under British "protection." In 1886, Nana ordered a trade stoppage against the British to protest against falling palm oil prices. Although his action was not unprecedented, the British consul took unusually strong exception to it, and pressured Nana to end it six months later.

In 1889, the British denied Nana his claim to authority over the neighboring Ijo people, despite the British having earlier used that claim as their basis for extending their "protection" to the Ijo. When Nana continued to resist British encroachment, they viewed it as a selfish attempt to protect his personal trade monopoly. Eventually, the British came to see Nana as standing in the way of their goal of increased economic and political control of the western Niger delta.

In 1894, Nana was deposed. He resisted but was forcibly suppressed. The British were aided by Dogho, leader of a rival Itsekiri trading house. Nana surrendered, and after his trial, was stripped of his wealth and deported. Nana was permitted to return home in 1906, where he spent the last ten years of his life.

- *Central Africa:* Henry Stanley departed the Congo for Europe (June 8). During his Africa career, Stanley established 40 outposts and negotiated 400 treaties.
- Douala chiefs signed a protectorate treaty with the firm of E. Woermann (July 12), and, on July 14, a German protectorate over Cameroon was inaugurated by Dr. Gustave Nachtigal.

Due to European politics and the desire to protect economic interests from imperial politics, Germany came to occupy the land that today includes the country of Cameroon. After its establishment, the colony was augmented by military conquest and by cession of French territory. During World War I, Cameroon was conquered by Britain and France who subsequently partitioned it. The two British parts were ruled as part of Nigeria while the French part became the new territory of Cameroon and was governed independently. All three were League of Nations (later United Nations) mandates. After independence, one of the British parts joined Nigeria, while the other became a part of the Cameroon Republic.

- On July 19, the British initiated an unsuccessful attempt to proclaim a protectorate of their own over the Cameroon.
- Grenfell explored Oubangui in order to set up missions.
- Mangbetu again became independent as a result of the Mahdia.
- H. von Wissman explored Lake Tanganyika and Lake Nyasa, ultimately reaching the coast at Quelimane.
- Tippu Tip arrived at Stanley Falls. Tippu Tip was commissioned by the Sultan of Zanzibar to seize the eastern half of the Congo in the name of the Sultan.
- The expedition of Dias de Carvalho reached Katanga.
- Felix Eboue (Adolphe-Felix-Sylvestre Eboue) (1884–1944), a future Governor-General of French Equatorial Africa, was born.

The grandparents of Felix Eboue were brought as slaves from Africa to French Guiana, where he was born a French citizen. Showing unusual abilities as a youth, Eboue was awarded a scholarship to Bordeaux where he received a bachelor's degree in 1905.

In 1906, Eboue entered the special government training school for colonial administrators, graduating in 1908. During his early career, Eboue became a close friend of Blaise Diagne, the Senegalese politician and senior French government official. Diagne was instrumental in helping Eboue secure promotions.

Eboue's first ministerial assignment was to a remote section of Oubangui-Chari (the Central African Republic). In 1932, he was appointed acting governor of Martinique, and then afterwards, he was assigned to the French Sudan (modern day Mali).

In addition to his administrative duties, Eboue pursued anthropological and ethnographic studies, many of which were published. In 1936, he was promoted to the rank of governor and assigned to Guadeloupe. However, in 1938, he was recalled because of a political dispute and was reassigned to Chad.

When World War II began, France quickly surrendered to Germany. In the aftermath, the Vichy government was formed. Pierre Boisson, the Vichy high commissioner for Africa, tried to force Eboue to declare for Vichy, but Eboue instead sided with General de Gaulle's Free French forces. Eboue rallied support for General de Gaulle. In the process of doing so, Eboue helped to stem the wave of defeatism which had spread through French Africa.

De Gualle rewarded Eboue by making him Governor-General of French Equatorial Africa. During his administration, de Gualle formulated ambitious new programs to advance African welfare. Eboue never had a chance to implement the new programs. He died of pneumonia while attending a conference in Cairo in 1944.

In 1949, Felix Eboue was buried in the Pantheon in Paris.

• *Eastern Africa:* The Sultan of Gobad recognized French authority at Obock (April 9).
• Yohannes signed a treaty with Britain for an alliance against the Mahdi and suppression of the slave trade (June 3).
• Lagarde opened a French post at Obock. On September 21, the Sultan of Tadjoura recognized France.
• Gobad and Tadjoura were ceded to France.
• Dr. Karl Peters landed in Zanzibar and negotiated treaties with eleven mainland cities (November).

In 1884, the Germans began entering into treaties with mainland chiefs in Zanzibari territory. These actions were the precursor to the German declaration of a protectorate over the land known today as Tanzania.

Karl Peters went to East Africa privately with two associates to collect treaties from chiefs in the northeast of present day Tanzania. These treaties were recognized by Chancellor Bismarck the next year.

Peters' company was given an imperial charter to found a protectorate. The protectorate became German East Africa (later Tanganyika and then Tanzania).

• Britain established the British Somaliland Protectorate based in Zaila (December).
• Abdallah ibn Muhammed ibn Ali Abd al-Shakur was made ruler of Harar.
• The Keren-Bilen territory was restored by Egypt to Ethiopia.
• Mwanga became the king of the Ganda kingdom.

When Mwanga succeeded his father Mutesa I as king — as Kabaka — of Buganda in 1884, Mwanga inherited an administrative structure undergoing a fundamental transformation. Before the time of Mutesa, the Ganda kings had ruled through a powerful class of hereditary territorial chiefs.

The arrival of Christian missionaries in the late 1870s gave rise to a new class of younger religiously oriented officials. Educated Catholics, Protestants, and Muslims formed distinct administrative cadres within the kingdom. Though hostile to each others' creeds, they shared the common goal of reforming Ganda society. Mwanga's often capricious dealings with these groups incurred their hostility. A four way power struggle of shifting alliances developed between him and each of the religious factions.

Mwanga's father had patronized the newly educated officials and had allowed them to undermine the traditional deference which subjects accorded the kings, giving these men unprecedented influence in the kingdom. At first Mwanga allowed this new elite to carry on as under his father, but soon he became apprehensive of the increasing influence of Christianity.

• Mirambo (c.1840–1884), the most powerful of the nineteenth century Nyamwezi chiefs, died.

The chronicle of Mirambo's early life is subject to dispute. Although it is clear that his military career was influenced by Ngoni techniques, there is no evidence to support the frequent claim that Mirambo was raised among one of the off-shoot Ngoni groups which entered Tanzania during the 1840s.

Whatever the case may be, around 1850, Mirambo succeeded his father as chief of a minor Nyamwezi chiefdom. Employing innovative techniques in military organization and fighting, Mirambo expanded his control over neighboring chiefdoms and became by the late 1860s the strongest Nyamwezi ruler.

During this same period of time, coastal Arabs had allied with southern Nyamwezi chiefs to make Tabora in central Tanzania a major trade center. Mirambo's subsequent career was dominated by his rivalry with this Arab-Nyamwezi coalition over control of the new trade routes.

Mirambo harassed the traders and initiated open warfare in 1871. One of the notable footnotes to this war was that the explorer Henry Stanley participated in the war as an ally of the Arabs who were fighting Mirambo.

Mirambo scored several early successes in this war, but eventually failed to follow them up. As a result of this lack of diligence, the war ultimately became a stalemate.

The Arabs were hampered by their inability to unite or to gain the unqualified support of the Zanzibari sultan Barghash *(see 1888)*. In 1875, Mirambo reached an accommodation with the Tabora Arabs and then worked to improve his trading position through ambitious negotiations. Mirambo's efforts to construct an alliance with the Ganda king Mutesa I came to nothing, but he received the support of the British consul John Kirk at Zanzibar.

After 1875, Mirambo received a succession of European visitors — traders, missionaries and imperialist agents — most of whom he favorably impressed. Meanwhile, Mirambo kept his armies busy raiding northern neighbors for cattle and arranging alliances and tributary relationships with rulers to the west and southwest.

In 1880, Mirambo's position began to deteriorate when he was implicated in the killing of two Englishmen. This incident cost Mirambo the support of John Kirk and forced Mirambo to take a more aggressive stance.

In 1882 and 1883, Mirambo allied with the powerful Swahili trader Tippu Tip. However, Tippu Tip's preoccupation with his own affairs in eastern Zaire prevented him from using his influence in Zanzibar on Mirambo's behalf. Meanwhile Mirambo's health hampered his ability to rule. In 1883–1884, Mirambo's troops suffered setbacks at the hands of the northern Ngoni and the resurgent southern Nyamwezi. In late 1884, Mirambo died of a throat ailment. Afterwards, Mirambo's empire crumbled because of the weak leadership of his successors and the advance of German occupation forces.

- Mutesa I (c.1838–1884), the ruler of the Ganda kingdom, died.

Mutesa was considered by many Ganda to be too young and too weak to become king when his father Suna II died in 1856. Nevertheless, Mutesa's election and installation by government ministers was achieved with relatively little disorder, demonstrating the power of appointed officials.

If Mutesa's supporters had counted on his being a compliant puppet, they were disappointed. Mutesa soon developed into one of the most powerful kings (Kabaka) in Ganda history.

Mutesa continued his father's military reforms. He imported increasing numbers of firearms — over which he maintained a monopoly — from Arab sources to the north and to the east. Mutesa also raided his neighbors and maintained pressure on the Nyoro kingdom of Bunyoro to the west.

During the 1870s, Mutesa — like his neighbors — was exposed to the threat of conquest from the north when Egypt began an attempt to control the headwaters of the Nile. During the last fifteen or so years of his life, Mutesa's foreign policy was dominated by his desire to improve his position over that of his neighbors. Mutesa was particularly concerned about besting the Bunyoro.

Mutesa had an eclectic attitude towards new ideas. The secularization of his state left him largely free of traditional ritual obligations. Muslim traders had been resident in Buganda since the time of Suna and Mutesa was attracted to Islam. However, his aversion to the rite of circumcision prevented his formal "conversion."

By the late 1860s, Mutesa was reading the Qur'an in Arabic and was faithfully observing Islamic practices. In 1862, the explorers John Speke and J. A. Grant visited Mutesa's court and brought Uganda to the attention of the outside world. By the time Europeans next visited him, thirteen years later, Mutesa was seriously concerned with Egyptian-Sudanese encroachments in northern Uganda and was anxious to form new alliances.

Henry Stanley visited Mutesa in 1875 and made a favorable impression by actively aiding Mutesa in a military campaign. Mutesa assented to Stanley's proposal to introduce Christian missionaries, hoping that they would assist him militarily.

The first Protestant missionaries arrived in 1877.

Catholic missionaries soon followed in 1879 and the seeds for a cultural and political revolution were planted.

Among the comparatively tolerant Ganda, the missions flourished. However, doctrinal infighting between the Protestants, Catholics and Muslims gave rise to sectarian political factions.

The Protestants assisted Mutesa to send emissaries to London in 1879, but Mutesa was disappointed by the failure of the missionaries to assist him militarily.

By the end of the decade, the Egyptian threat to the Ganda kingdom had subsided. However, internal factionalism had replaced the Egyptian threat as the dominant issue confronting Mutesa. Mutesa grew interested in Christianity, but was denied baptism by both Protestant and Catholic missions because of his political need to retain his many wives and because of his seemingly doubtful sincerity.

Mutesa ended his days sympathetic to Islam while many of his chiefs were converted to Christianity.

During Mutesa's last five years, deteriorating health weakened his ability to rule the Ganda kingdom. His infirmity allowed power to shift into the hands of his ministers. Meanwhile, cholera and plague epidemics ravaged his subjects. He kept his army increasingly busy, but his commanders suffered several major setbacks. These developments helped to prepare the way for changes after his death in 1884.

- Nyungu-ya-mawe (c.1840–1884), the unifier of the Kimbu people of Tanzania, died.

Although Nyungu was partly of Kimbu ancestry, he was born into a chiefly family of the Nyanyembe branch of the Nyamwezi people. Nyungu was associated with a Nyanyembe faction which contested Arab control of the ivory and slave trade routes passing through Tabora. After Nyungu's overlord Mnwa Sele was killed by the Arabs in 1865, Nyungu carried on the struggle with his own personal following.

Nyungu commanded an army of unattached soldiers. These soldiers were known as "ruga-ruga." Nyungu ruled his followers with an iron hand and maintained their loyalty through his redistribution of the spoils from their many successful raiding expeditions.

During the 1870s, Nyungu began a systematic conquest of the Kimbu people, who lived under more than thirty autonomous chiefdoms. By the end of his career, Nyungu brought more than 50,000 square kilometers of territory under his rule by replacing conquered chiefs with a much smaller number of governors who were personally chosen by him.

During the late 1870s, Nyungu turned his attention to the north. He began harassing caravans and attempted to seize control of the trade routes.

When Nyungu died in late 1884, Nyungu bequeathed to his daughter Mugalula an empire inherently more stable than that left by the Nyamwezi chief Mirambo.

- *Southern Africa:* Cetewayo was driven out of Zululand (February).
- A British protectorate was proclaimed in Basutoland (March).
- Dinuzulu, the son of Cetewayo, was crowned King of the Zulu in return for land ceded to settlers (May).

Dinuzulu became king when he was fifteen years old in 1884. By the time Dinuzulu became king, Zululand had recently been partitioned into sections of varying degrees of independence, and Dinuzulu's father, Cetewayo, had just been crushed by Zibhebhu, the leader of a rival faction of the Zulu royal family.

Dinuzulu was quickly installed as king by loyalists in his father's Usuthu faction. Dinuzulu then obtained military assistance from Afrikaners in the Transvaal Republic to drive Zibhebhu's party out of the country.

Unfortunately for Dinuzulu, the Afrikaners, as allies, proved to be far worse enemies than Zibhebhu. The Afrikaners proceeded to carve the "New Republic" out of northwestern Zululand as compensation for their services. The British government intervened, but the negotiated settlement between the British and the Afrikaners, ignored Zulu concerns.

- A German protectorate was proclaimed over Southwest Africa (August).
- Goshen was annexed by the Transvaal (September).
- A rebellion erupted against Lewanika in Barotseland (September).

The endemic Lozi factionalism surfaced again in 1884. Rebel chiefs occupied Lewanika's capital at Lealui forcing him into exile. The rebels enthroned a puppet, Tatila Akufunu, but loyalist forces staged a successful counter-coup the next year, allowing Lewanika to return.

- Britain annexed St. Lucia Bay to Natal to prevent Boer access to the east coast (November).
- The Maseko raided across the Kirk Mountains. This raid temporarily interrupted the Yao slave raiding operations.
- Galekaland and Tembuland were annexed by the Cape.

The Tembu (Thembu) are a major branch of the southern Nguni. Since the 1600s, the Thembu have lived in the Transkei region between the Mpondo and the Xhosa peoples. The Thembu are closely related to the Mpondo and the Xhosa.

During the 1800s, the Thembu developed increasingly closer ties with the British administration of the Cape, to which they were formally annexed in 1885.

In 1884, Dalindyebo succeeded his father, Ngangelizwe, as paramount chief of the Thembu (Tembu). Eight months later Thembu country was formally annexed to the Cape Colony. Dalindyebo's peaceful reign contrasted sharply with that of his father. His policies were generally considered to be progressive.

- *Imvo zaba Ntsundu,* the first Xhosa newspaper, was published.
- The Tembu National Church was formed in Transkei.

In 1884, Nehemiah Tile founded the Thembu National Church with Ngangelizwe's support. Tile's church was the forerunner of many independent churches among the coastal Nguni, but was unique in that it was closely identified with the traditional political authority rather than with westernized nationalists.

Tile attracted many followers and worked towards establishing his church as the official denomination of the Thembu chiefdom, but this effort failed shortly after his death.

The church continued to grow as a strong religious body, but became less closely identified with Thembu nationalism and politics.

Immediately after his succession as paramount chief of the Thembu (Tembu), Dalindyebo accepted the temporal leadership of Nehemiah Tile's Thembu National Church. However soon thereafter, Dalindyebo broke from the church and gave his support to the older Methodist churches.

- A. Schultz and A. Hammar explored Chobe River.
- H. Capello and R. Ivens crossed Africa from Angola to Quelimane via Barotseland.
- In 1884, Manuel Sousa, the Indo-Portuguese empire builder, crushed a revolt of the Massingire state between the Shire and Zambezi Rivers. Two years later, Sousa moved deeper into northeastern Zimbabwe.
- Gungunyane became king of Gaza.

When Gungunyane's father, Mzila, passed away in 1884, the question of succession to the throne of Gaza was unresolved. Gungunyane seized power in a coup. However, some potential rivals escaped his purge and their presence in enemy territories hampered his diplomatic efforts throughout his reign. *See 1906.*

- Cetewayo (1826–1884), a great king of the Zulus, died (February 8).

Cetewayo was born near Eshowe in the Zululand region of South Africa. As a young man of twelve, Cetewayo became inspired by the legendary exploits of his infamous uncle Shaka and took part in a number of fierce raids on European settlers. Later on (1853–1854), Cetewayo came to distinguish himself in wars against the Swazis.

Cetewayo's ascent to the throne of the Zulus was a stormy one. Due to the practice of polygamy, Cetewayo's father, Mpande, produced many heirs. Not until six of Cetewayo's half-brothers were killed and two others forced to flee, was Cetewayo's right to succeed Mpande secured.

After Mpande's death in 1872, Cetewayo was proclaimed the King of the Zulus according to tribal custom. A coronation ceremony performed by Sir Theophilus Shepstone, British secretary of native affairs in Natal, was the key event marking Cetewayo's ascension to the throne.

For the next five years, the relations between the British and the Zulus were fairly amicable. However, in 1877, Great Britain annexed the Transvaal and Sir Theophilus Shepstone became the Transvaal governor. Upon becoming governor, Shepstone reversed previous positions and began supporting Boer land claims against Zulu interests in disputed territories. Seeing this reversal as a betrayal, Cetewayo began assembling a large armed force — an army which came to number some 40,000 strong.

The British military became fearful of the Zulu build-up. The British high commissioner, Sir Bartle Frere decided to eliminate what was perceived to be a threat to the British colonists of South Africa. On the pretext that Cetewayo had violated earlier agreements with Shepstone, an ultimatum was sent in December 1878 demanding what amounted to the disbanding of the Zulu military forces that had been gathered by Cetewayo. When the demand was not met, the British invaded Zululand.

Armed with little more than spears, the Zulus, in a surprise attack at Isandhlwana (Isandlana), wiped out an entire British regiment (January 22, 1879). Stunned by this defeat, the British regrouped and subsequently soundly defeated the Zulus at Ulundi (July 4, 1879).

Cetewayo was captured in August of 1879 and confined, in exile, near Cape Town. Cetewayo's kingdom, Zululand, was divided among 13 chiefs. Refusing to submit to exile, Cetewayo beseeched the British to allow him to travel to Great Britain and present his case. Cetewayo traveled to London and made a great presentation. A proud and dignified warrior king, Cetewayo made an indelible impression on those he met.

Based upon Cetewayo's presence and his plea, and the general infeasibility of the division of Zululand, the British restored Cetewayo as ruler of central Zululand in January 1883. However, after a three year absence, the displaced Zulu chiefs refused to accept his leadership. A struggle ensued and Cetewayo was beaten in battle by a rival. Fleeing his enemies, Cetewayo sought asylum with the British at Eshowe.

On February 8, 1884, Cetewayo died of a heart attack. Today he is remembered as having been a strong military leader whose political abilities restored power and prestige to the Zulu nation. Cetewayo's grave, located deep in the Nkandla forest, is considered sacred ground by the Zulu people who maintain the grave under constant guard.

• Mzila (c.1810–1884), the king of the Gaza (Shangana) empire of Mozambique, died.

Mzila was the rightful heir to his father Soshangane who had founded the Gaza state. However, Mzila's half-brother Mawewe used Swazi troops to usurp the kingship when Soshangane died around 1859.

Mzila went into exile. He was able to obtain assistance from Portuguese gunman and, with Portuguese aid, succeeded in driving Mawewe out in 1862. This act earned him the enmity of the neighboring Swazi and also led the Portuguese to regard him as their vassal.

Mzila moved to the upper Sabi River in the north, away from both of his antagonists at the Limpopo. At the Sabi, Mzila received tribute payments from minor Portuguese posts on the Zambezi River and at Sofala. He extended his conquests to the Shona people of eastern Zimbabwe. Mzila established a détente with the Ndebele, who raided the Shona from Matabeleland, and later exchanged wives with king Lobengula.

In 1870, Mzila demonstrated his independence from the Portuguese by sending a delegation to Theophilus Shepstone in Natal, inviting British trade and diplomatic contacts. The next year, however, a British delegate to his court reported unfavorably on him to British officials, making it difficult for him and for his successor Gungunyane to deal with any Europeans other than the Portuguese.

Later Gaza delegations to the British were generally ignored. In the late 1870s, the Portuguese began to assert their old claims to sovereignty over Mozambique.

A Goan-Portuguese landowner — a prazeiro — Manuel Antonio de Sousa ("Gouveia"), built his own private empire in the Zambezi valley, from which he expelled Gaza tribute-collectors.

Mzila died in 1884 at a time when Portuguese pressures were just beginning to become intense.

• Ngangelizwe (c.1840–1884), the last independent Thembu paramount chief, died.

Ngangelizwe's father died in 1849 and a regent ruled the Thembu until Ngangelizwe was old enough to become chief in 1863.

During his reign, Ngangelizwe fought a desultory war with the neighboring Gcaleka Xhosa and increasingly turned to the British for support.

In 1866, Ngangelizwe took as his chief wife Novili, the daughter of the Gcaleka chief, Sarili, but treated her so badly that she fled back to her father in 1870. This episode strained relations between the Thembu and the Gcaleka and exacerbated the disputes between the two people over land and cattle.

Ngangelizwe fought several unsuccessful engagements against the Gcaleka during the early 1870s and then appealed to the Cape Colony government for "protection." In 1875, the Cape government granted Ngangelizwe's request on the condition that Ngangelizwe abdicate.

Ngangelizwe's deposition ultimately proved to be impractical. Ngangelizwe was reinstated in 1876.

Thereafter, Ngangelizwe supported the colonial government forces in several actions against his neighbors. Shortly before he died, Ngangelizwe accepted the temporal leadership of Nehemiah Tile's independent church.

RELATED HISTORICAL EVENTS

• *The United States: The Adventures of Huckleberry Finn* by Mark Twain was published.

On December 10, 1884, Mark Twain (Samuel Clemens) published what many considered to be the great American novel, — Mark Twain published *The Adventures of Huckleberry Finn.*

The Adventures of Huckleberry Finn was a sequel to *Tom Sawyer. The Adventures of Huckleberry Finn* was begun by Twain in 1876. Although it carries on the picaresque story of the characters first seen in *Tom Sawyer, The Adventures of Huckleberry Finn* is generally considered to be a more accomplished and a more serious work of art as well as a more realistic depiction of regional character and frontier experience on the Mississippi River.

The story is narrated by the title character, Huckleberry "Huck" Finn. It begins with Huck living with the Widow Douglas and her sister, Miss Watson.

When Huck's abusive, ne'er-do-well father

appears to demand Huck's share of the treasure found in the cave at the end of *The Adventures of Tom Sawyer,* Huck tricks his father by transferring his money to Judge Thatcher. In retaliation, his father kidnaps Huck and imprisons Huck in a lonely cabin.

During one of the old man's drunken spells, Huck stage manages his own apparent murder and escapes to Jackson's Island, where he meets another escapee, Miss Watson's slave, Jim. Fearing that a posse is after Jim, Huck and Jim make off on a raft in the hope of making it to the Ohio River and the freedom that awaited Jim on the Illinois shores.

Together Huck and Jim start up the Mississippi. However, after several adventures, including missing the turn at Cairo, Illinois, the raft is hit by a steamboat and the two travelling companions are separated.

Huck swam ashore where he finds shelter with the Grangerford family. The Grangerford family happens to be having a feud with the Shepherdson family and this feud results in blood being shed.

Huck stumbles upon Jim in the slave quarters and, after the raft is retrieved, the two resume their journey on the Mississippi. Along the way, Huck and Jim are hijacked by a couple of crooks. One was the "Duke of Bridgewater," an itinerant printer and fraud in his thirties, and the other was "Dauphin" ("Louis XVII of France"), a septuagenarian actor, evangelist and temperance faker.

At stops on their journey, the "King" lectures as a reformed pirate and the two impersonators present, as "Kean" and "Garrick," dramatic Shakespearean performances. These performances culminated in the fraudulent exhibition of the "Royal Nonesuch."

A little later on, Huck witnesses the murder of a harmless drunkard by an Arkansas aristocrat, whose contempt discourages a would be lynch mob. The rogues, the Duke and the Dauphin, learn of the death of Peter Wilks and decide to claim legacies as Wilks' brothers. Huck intervenes on behalf of the three Wilks daughters, and the scheme of the rogues is foiled by the arrival of the real brothers.

After this diversion, Huck learns that the "King" sold Jim to Silas Phelps. As Huck soon discovers Silas Phelps happens to be the husband of Tom Sawyer's Aunt Sally. In an attempt to rescue Jim, Huck goes to the Phelps farm where he impersonates Tom. When Tom happens to show up, Tom begins masquerading as Tom's brother, Sid.

At this point in the story, Tom takes control. Tom conceives a plan to free Jim. In the botched rescue that follows, Tom is accidentally shot while Jim is recaptured.

While he is recuperating, Tom reveals that Miss Watson died, setting Jim free in her will and that Huck's father had died. Tom failed to tell Huck this because he "wanted the adventure" associated with Jim's rescue. The story concludes with Huck saying, "But I reckon I got to light out for the Territory ahead of the rest, because Aunt Sally she's going to adopt me and civilize me and I can't stant it. I been there before."

*   *   *

As the twentieth century ends, the status of Mark Twain's *The Adventures of Huckleberry Finn* as an American classic has come under attack. Long a standard text used in classrooms throughout the nation, many African Americans object to its use in schools because of the frequency of the word "nigger" within the text.

The defenders of the book note that the message of the book is a good one; that the book shows the development of a healthy relationship between a European American child and an African American man; and that the language used in the book was a reflection of the times.

Frequently, the supporters of *Huckleberry Finn* and similar "American classics" will contend that the use of the derogatory language in the text should be used as an opportunity to discuss the historical and social context in which the book was written rather than exiling the book from the classroom. These contenders will often assert that to exile such works from the classroom is not only censorship but is also a denial of the historical heritage for both the European American and African American children.

African Americans, on the other hand, find abhorrent the notion that schools sanction the use of a book which contains epithets which are universally deemed to be derogatory and inflammatory when uttered by European Americans. For all too many African Americans, the memory lingers of the cruelties and embarrassments endured in the school setting whenever such works were read. The notion that works such as *Huckleberry Finn* might be used in a sensitive and constructive manner belies the personal experience held by African Americans that indicates exactly otherwise. The experience of African Americans tells them that, in the United States, there has rarely been a truly sensitive and constructive dialogue on race amongst adults and that it is extremely unlikely that such a constructive dialogue will take place in the schools. Additionally, if a constructive dialogue were to occur, it is unlikely that works such as *Huckleberry Finn* would enhance the dialogue that needs to occur. Accordingly, from the African American perspective, the continued presence of *Huckleberry Finn* in the classroom can only serve to perpetuate the pain and impose an unpleasant experience upon African American children — an experience which it would be best to avoid.

In time, the furor over *The Adventures of Huckleberry Finn* may subside. However, it seems clear that its status as a great American novel has been tarnished to the point where it can no longer be universally accepted as an American classic but instead is a book which European Americans perceive to be a classic.

For all too many African Americans, *The Adventures of Huckleberry Finn* has simply become a bitter reminder of a day and a use of language which should forever remain in the past. The book is also viewed as being dangerous to the extent that the use of the language in *Huckleberry Finn* is perceived to sanction a relationship between the races which no longer exists and which may cause psychological harm to African American children who are coerced into confronting the words and their connotations in perhaps hostile or formidable environments.

While it may be an accurate portrayal of the time for which it was written, *Huckleberry Finn* cannot escape its anachronistic language and the detracting flaws that are now associated with that language.

- *Europe:* An Anglo-Portuguese Treaty was finalized (February 26). Under the terms of the treaty, Britain recognized Portugal's right to the mouth of the Congo River. Leopold II and Germany protested the terms of this treaty.
- At the Convention of London, the status of the Transvaal was regulated.
- The Society for German Colonization was founded.
- Britain denounced the Anglo-Portuguese Congo Treaty (April 26).
- The International Conference on Egyptian finances convened in London (June 18).
- At the Berlin Conference, free trade was recognized on the Congo River. Slavery and the slave trade were abolished (November 15, 1884 to February 24, 1885).
- *Africa:* Henry Frere (1815–1884), the for-

mer high commissioner for South Africa, died.

Henry Bartle Edward Frere was sent to South Africa to consolidate all the European governments then in existence in South Africa. However, a succession of African wars and rebellions would mar Frere's efforts at federation.

Frere's early colonial experience was in India. In India, Frere rose to be the governor of Bombay from 1862 to 1867.

In 1872, Frere made a visit to Zanzibar to negotiate an anti-slavery treaty with Sultan Barghash. In 1877, the Secretary of State for the Colonies, Lord Carnarvon, dispatched Frere to South Africa to succeed Henry Barkly as governor and high commissioner. Frere was given the special task of uniting the various British possessions and the Afrikaner republic into a federation.

Two weeks before Frere arrived at Cape Town, his position was undermined when the Natal agent, Theophilus Shepstone, annexed the Transvaal Republic to the British Crown. Shepstone's action made the Afrikaners distrustful of the British and apprehensive of federation discussions.

Frere also faced a succession of African revolts. The Xhosa in the eastern Cape revolted in 1877; the Pedi under the leadership of Sekhukhune revolted in the Transvaal in 1879; the Griqua in both the west and the east Cape revolted in 1878; and the Phuthi of Moorosi revolted in southern Lesotho in 1879.

The revolts siphoned away Frere's federation energies and made it increasingly difficult to deal with the European politicians of the various South African states. One notable dispute arose between Frere and the prime minister of the Cape, John Molteno. The two clashed over the use of imperial troops in the Xhosa war. Frere eventually dismissed Molteno in favor of John Sprigg.

On the basis of his Indian experience Frere advocated disarming native societies. Because he saw the humbling of the powerful Zulu kingdom as the key to obtaining the cooperation of the Afrikaner republics, in 1878, Frere issued an ultimatum to Cetewayo, the king of the Zulu, in which Cetewayo was ordered to disband and disarm the Zulu army. Frere's ultimatum led to the Zulu War of 1879 in which the Zulu, despite some initial victories, were eventually defeated.

However, due to the unpopularity of the Zulu War, along with a spotted record on the issue of South African federation, Frere was relieved of his authority over Natal and the Transvaal. General Wolseley became the high commissioner in an effort to conclude the Zulu War.

Frere's last actions arose in the Cape where Frere used his influence to have the Cape prime minister, John Sprigg, issue a disarmament ultimatum to the Sotho kingdom after Moorosi's rebellion. This ultimatum resulted in the disastrous "Gun War" of 1880. By 1880, Frere's federation plans had collapsed. Soon thereafter, Frere was recalled to England.

1 8 8 5

THE UNITED STATES

• Robert Smalls of South Carolina and James E. O'Hara of North Carolina were elected to serve in the 49th Congress.

• Ex–Senator Blanche K. Bruce retired from his position as Register of the Treasury. Bruce had held this position since 1881. He went on to become a popular lecturer.

• Nathan Francis Mossell was admitted to the Philadelphia Medical Society. *See 1882.*

• Benjamin William Arnett was elected to represent Green County, Ohio, in the Ohio State Legislature.

Benjamin William Arnett was a bishop of the African Methodist Episcopal Church. In 1864, Arnett was the first and, for a period, the only African American teacher in Fayette County, Pennsylvania. As a legislator, Arnett helped to abolish discriminatory laws in Ohio. In addition to his purely religious work, Arnett remained influential in many fraternal organizations and in politics, especially through his friendship with William McKinley, Jr.

Notable Births

It could be argued that 1885 was the year in which American music was born. In this momentous year, three giants of the American music scene — Leadbelly, Jelly Roll Morton and King Oliver — were born and each would go on to leave an indelible mark on American music.

Huddie "Leadbelly" Ledbetter (1885–1949), a famous folk singer, was born in Louisiana and raised in Texas. He was the son of a former slave and, essentially, was self-educated. As an itinerant musician and singer, Leadbelly wandered throughout the South. During his wanderings, Leadbelly met Blind Lemon Jefferson, a Texas street singer, who took Leadbelly under his wings. Blind Lemon taught a number of his songs to Leadbelly and it was these songs which would form the basis for Leadbelly's pioneering career.

In 1918, Leadbelly was convicted of murder and sentenced to prison. He served seven years in prison for this crime.

In 1930, Leadbelly was convicted of attempted murder and again sentenced to prison. This time he served four years.

Leadbelly was paroled into the custody of a certain John Lomax. It was John Lomax who took Leadbelly North and launched Leadbelly on his singing career. Among Leadbelly's best known songs are *Good Night, Irene; Rock Island Line* and *On Top of Old Smoky.*

In 1949, Leadbelly went on a successful tour of France. It was this tour which helped to establish European interest in American folk music.

*   *   *

Ferdinand "Jelly Roll" Morton (1885–1941), a noted jazz musician who is credited with being the first great jazz composer, was born in Gulfport, Louisiana. His grandfather was a delegate to the Louisiana Constitutional Convention of 1868. His father was a small businessman. However, Jelly Roll was mainly a manual laborer in a barrel factory before embarking on his musical career in 1902.

Jelly Roll began his career in Storyville — a red light district in New Orleans. His profession and the locale of his performances were an embarrassment to his Creole family of New Orleans. Nevertheless, Jelly Roll persevered to become one of the luminaries of jazz music.

It is widely regarded that Jelly Roll's stint with the Victor label between 1926–1930 with his Red Hot Peppers group was the most significant period of his career. It was during this time that Jelly Roll established himself as the first great jazz composer.

Among the more notable of Jelly Roll's songs are *King Porter Stomp, Wolverine Blues, Millenburg Joys, Georgia Swing, Kansas City Stomps and Wild Man Blues.*

*   *   *

Joe "King" Oliver (1885–1938), a jazz musician and one of the pioneers of jazz, was born on May 11, 1885, on a Louisiana plantation. King Oliver grew up in New Orleans.

In 1923, King Oliver's Creole Jazz Band (which included the soon to be great Louis Armstrong as second clarinetist) made the first series of recordings by an African American jazz band.

The influence of King Oliver on American music, particularly on jazz musicians, is incalculable. However, by 1928, when he moved to New York his popularity had begun to wane.

The final years of King Oliver's life were spent working in a poolroom in Savannah, Georgia.

- *Notable Deaths:* In 1885, some 74 African Americans were reported to have been lynched.
- Martin Robinson Delany (1812–1885), newspaper editor, author and the first African American major in the United States Army, died (January 24).

Martin Robinson Delany was the first African American major in the United States Army, a medical doctor, an African American nationalist and a writer. He was born in Charlestown, Virginia. His parents were Samuel Delany, a slave, and Pati (Peace) Delany, a free African American. Martin's paternal grandfather was a prince of a Mandingo tribe who had been captured in the Niger Valley, sold into slavery, and subsequently brought to America.

Delany was educated in the African Free School of New York City, the Canaan Academy in New Hampshire, and the Oneida Institute in New York. Delany also studied under Reverend Louis Woodson, who was employed by a society of African Americans interested in education. Dr. Andrew McDowell taught him medicine. In 1843, Delany began publishing *The Mystery* in Pittsburgh. Between 1847 and 1849, Delany was associated with Frederick Douglass and assisted in the publication of *The North Star*.

In 1849, Delany studied medicine at Harvard University. Upon completion of his medical studies, in 1852, Delany was noted for doing outstanding work in battling a cholera epidemic in Pittsburgh.

Delany was an ardent black nationalist. His compatriot, Frederick Douglass, once remarked: "I thank God for making me a man simply; but Delany always thanks Him for making him a black man."

In 1854, Delany issued a call for a National Emigration Convention, which met in Cleveland in August. The second convention was also held in Cleveland in 1856.

Delany moved to Chatham, Ontario, Canada and practiced medicine. The third National Emigration Convention was held in Chatham in 1858. At this convention, Delany was chosen as the chief commissioner and was designated to explore the Valley of the Niger as a possible relocation site. According to his commission, Delany was to make inquiries "for the purpose of science and for general information and without reference to, and with the Board being entirely opposed to any emigration there as such."

Delany sailed to the Niger in 1859. He departed from New York aboard the *Mendi*, a vessel owned by three African merchants. While in Nigeria, Delany negotiated treaties with a number of African chiefs who granted lands for prospective African American immigrants. In 1861, Delany published the official report of the Niger Valley exploration.

During the Civil War, Delany helped recruit soldiers for the Union Army. On February 8, 1865, Delany received a commission as a major in the Union Army and was ordered to Charleston, South Carolina were he would serve as an Army physician.

After the Civil War, Delany served with the Freedmen's Bureau for three years for which he worked as trial judge in Charleston, South Carolina. Delany was a leader of the Honest Government League and a severe critic of the corruption of the Reconstruction period in South Carolina. Delany was nominated for Lieutenant Governor of South Carolina on the Independent Republican ticket in 1874, but was defeated.

In 1879, Delany published *Principia of Ethnology: The Origin of Races and Color, etc.* This publication espoused Delany's views on race.

- Jonathan Jasper Wright (1840–1885), the first African American to serve as a state (South Carolina) supreme court justice, died.
- *Miscellaneous Publications:* The *Philadelphia Tribune* began publication. The *Philadelphia Tribune* is the oldest continually published, non-church African American newspaper.
- Timothy Thomas Fortune published *The Negro in Politics*.
- Daniel Alexander Payne published *A Treatise on Domestic Education*.
- Henry McNeal Turner published *The Genius and Method of Methodist Policy*.
- George Washington Williams published *The Negro in the American Rebellion*.
- *The Arts:* The photographer James Conway Farley won an award at the New Orleans World Exposition.
- *The Performing Arts:* In 1885, African Americans were still performing in Congo Square. Beginning in 1817, slaves had been

allowed to do voodoo dances, using African drums, gourds, and other instruments. However, by 1885, the triangle, jew's harp, and other European musical instruments had been incorporated into the performances.

The blending of West African and European musical traditions would ultimately lead to a uniquely American musical invention. The blending of West African and European musical traditions led to jazz.

The dances that were held in Congo Square helped to preserve the African musical heritage of New Orleans. The Calinda and the Bamboula, both based on African dances, were frequently performed. Originally, the beat was provided by bones stuck on the head of a cask, the chanting of women and metal pieces on the ankles of men.

• *Scholastic Achievements:* Between 1885 and 1889, two African Americans in the United States received doctorates.

• The African Methodist Episcopal Church founded Morris Brown University in Atlanta, Georgia.

• *The Black Church:* Henry McNeal Turner published *The Genius and Method of Methodist Policy.*

• Samuel David Ferguson became the first African-American missionary bishop in the Protestant Episcopal Church when he was assigned to Liberia.

• *Technological Innovations:* Sarah Goode received a patent for a folding cabinet bed (July 14).

• *Black Enterprise:* D. Watson Onley constructed the first steam saw and planing mill owned and operated entirely by African Americans in Jacksonville, Florida. After the mill was destroyed by fire set by an incendiary, Onley worked for Florida State Normal and Industrial College, attended Howard University School of Dentistry, and established a practice in Washington, D. C.

• *Sports:* Jockey Erskine Henderson won the Kentucky Derby riding the horse Joe Cotton.

• The Cuban Giants, considered to be the first African American professional baseball team, was formed.

THE AMERICAS

• *Brazil:* The Saraiva-Cotegipe Law of Brazil declared that all slaves which reached the age of 60 were to be free.

However, in response to the establishment of an underground railroad to the northeastern free state of Ceara *(see 1884),* the Brazilian government also adopted a harsh fugitive slave law. This fugitive slave law punished anyone assisting an escaped slave.

The adoption of the fugitive slave law did not greatly curtail the assisting of escaping slaves, but it did provoke the abolitionist movement into becoming more strident in its quest for freedom for the Brazilian slaves.

• In 1885, there were 1.1 million Afro-Brazilian slaves.

• *Canada:* In Saint John, New Brunswick, Robert Whetsel died. Upon his passing, the *Daily Sun* noted, in a substantial obituary, that Whetsel was one of the city's "representative colored citizens" whose word was his bond.

• *Haiti:* Antenor Firmin published his monumental 650 page essay on the merit of the peoples of African descent. Entitled *L'Egalite des Races Humaines* (Equality of the Human Races), the essay was a response to the work of the French writer, Gobineau, *Essai sur l'Inegalite des Races Humaines,* "Essay on the Inequality of the Human Races."

EUROPE

• *France:* Alexandre Dumas, fils, published *Denise.*

AFRICA

• *North Africa, Egypt and Sudan:* The Mahdi captured Khartoum (January 26).

In 1881, Muhammed 'Ahmad proclaimed himself to be the Mahdi — the Muslim redeemer. Muhammed 'Ahmad set about to construct a theocratic state modelled on that of the Prophet Muhammed. 'Abdallahi was named one of Muhammed 'Ahmad's four caliphs and was given command of a major part of the growing Mahdist army.

Over the next four years, 'Abdallahi led a wave of Mahdist victories over Anglo-Egyptian forces, culminating in the taking of Khartoum in 1885.

After the unexpected death of the Mahdi in mid–1885, 'Abdallahi assumed the leadership of the incipient theocratic state and moved to consolidate his position against various internal factions, while declaring himself the Khalifa al-Mahdi — the Mahdi's successor.

• General Gordon was killed resisting the siege of Khartoum.

• British relief forces arrived in the Sudan to effect an evacuation (January 28).

• The Mahdi died (June 22). He was succeeded by Khalifa Abdallahi ibn Muhammad.

• On July 30, dervishes captured Kassala. This victory enabled the dervishes to effectively control all Sudan except ports.

• The plight of Emin Pasha received international attention.

Muhammed al-Amin, a German administrator of Equatoria, led several scientific expeditions and negotiated with the Nyoro king Kabarega and other rulers in present day Uganda. When the capital of Sudan, Khartoum fell to the Mahdists in 1885, Muhammed al-Amin was left isolated on the upper Nile. A mutiny among his Sudanese troops added to his difficulties.

During this time, Muhammed al-Amin received the Turkish title "Pasha." Now known as Emin Pasha, the plight of Muhammed al-Amin attracted worldwide attention.

A massive relief force under the command of the explorer Henry Stanley was sent to rescue Emin Pasha. Emin Pasha wanted to remain at the Nile to solve problems himself, but he reluctantly consented to accompany Stanley to Bagamoyo on the east African coast.

• Sayyid Abd al-Rahman al-Mahdi (1885–1959), the posthumous son of the Mahdi, was born.

• Muhammed 'Ahmad ibn 'Abdallah al-Mahdi (c.1844–1885), a revolutionary Muslim religious leader who conquered most of the Nilotic Sudan in order to establish a purified Islamic theocracy, died (June 22).

Muhammed 'Ahmad ibn 'Abdallah al-Mahdi — the "Mahdi"— was born in northern Sudan, where he spent his early life engaged in intense religious study.

Muhammed joined a Sufi brotherhood, but grew disgusted with the worldliness of its leaders and, around 1870, Muhammed retreated into isolation with a handful of devout followers.

Around 1880, Muhammed toured the central provinces of Sudan and became incensed at the evils of the Egyptian administration and the general social chaos he found. Early in 1881, Muhammed proclaimed himself to be the Mahdi — the awaited redeemer of Islam.

The Mahdi launched a jihad against the alien rulers of the Sudan with the aim of restoring the theocratic state to Islam. The Mahdi's followers easily repelled several feeble attempts by the Egyptian administration to suppress him and his prestige grew rapidly among the religiously devout and political dissenters alike.

The Mahdi's reputation as a religious redeemer reached as far as present day Nigeria. By early 1883, his movement was the focus of a national revolt against the Egyptian government and his developing army controlled central Sudan. Later that year, the Mahdi's troops annihilated an Anglo-Egyptian army and then moved against the capital, Khartoum.

General Charles Gordon arrived to evacuate Egyptian forces, but stayed to defend Khartoum personally. By early 1885, Khartoum fell and Gordon was killed. Muhammed 'Ahmad ibn 'Abdallah al-Mahdi — the Mahdi — was the master of Sudan.

Soon after achieving his victory over Gordon, the Mahdi became ill. He died at Omdurman.

The temporal leadership of the Sudan passed to one of the Mahdi's lieutenants, 'Abdallahi ibn Muhammed (see 1899). 'Abdallahi ibn Muhammed abandoned the theocratic ideal while building a powerful bureaucratic state.

• *Western Africa:* A treaty was finalized between Britain and Sokoto (June 1).

In 1885, Joseph Thomson, a British imperial agent, obtained treaties from the Sultan of Sokoto and the Emir of Gwandu in northern Nigeria for the Royal Niger Company.

• The British established a protectorate over the "Niger Districts" (June 5).

In 1885, Great Britain formally declared a protectorate over the Oil Rivers Districts — the "Niger Districts." The next year, the company of George Goldie (see 1877)— now called the Royal Niger Company — took over administration of the protectorate inland from the Niger Delta. Despite official prohibitions, the company soon established a trade monopoly which excluded African as well as other European traders, and aroused a great deal of bitter resentment.

• The German flag was raised at Agbanekin (July) while the Portuguese flag was raised at Whydah, Godomey and Cotonou (September). However, the Portuguese claims were later withdrawn in favor of France.

• The boundary between Sierra Leone and Liberia was defined (November 11).

• The French garrison was established at Cotonou.

• A Franco-German convention was convened. Pursuant to the convention, Germans received Porto Seguro and Little Popo; French Guinea possessions were recognized by Germany; and the boundaries of Togo were agreed.

The German government colonized Togo in 1885. This colonization was undertaken ostensibly to protect German economic interests and to further Germany's international position.

After World War I, Great Britain and France divided the tiny colony. Britain administered its portion through the neighboring Gold Coast (Ghana) while France created a new colony. Both Togo territories became League of Nations mandate territories.

- The British abandoned Ketonou.
- Trade treaties between Sokoto and Gwandu were negotiated on behalf of the Royal Niger Company.
- Further complaints were made by Benin concerning the lack of consular visits.
- The Court of Equity on Brass River was compelled by local chiefs to reverse decisions.
- King Jaja of Opobo objected to the freedom of trade agreed to at the Berlin Conference.
- Mamadu Lamine declared a jihad in Mali.

Mamadu returned to Kayes (Mali) in 1885 after having spent five years as a virtual prisoner of the Tukolor Empire. During his absence, the French had begun to compete militarily with the Tukolor for control of the Senegambia. A charismatic leader in his own right, Mamadu used anti–Tukolor and anti–French sentiment to build a large following. Within a few months, Mamadu declared a jihad — a holy war — against his Senegambian neighbors and the Tukolor Empire.

- *Central Africa:* Beginning in 1885, the German penetration of Cameroon commenced.
- Spain proclaimed a protectorate over Spanish Guinea (January 9).
- A Franco-German convention on boundaries of the Cameroon and Gabon commenced (December 24).
- The Chokwe invaded the land of the Lunda.
- *Eastern Africa:* Five CMS converts were murdered in Buganda (January 5).

When Mwanga succeeded his father Mutesa I as king — Kabaka — of Buganda in 1884, Mwanga inherited an administrative structure undergoing a fundamental transformation. Before the time of Mutesa *(see 1884),* the kings had ruled through a powerful class of hereditary territorial chiefs.

The arrival of Christian missionaries in the late 1870s gave rise to a new class of younger religiously oriented officials. Educated Catholics, Protestants, and Muslims formed distinct administrative cadres within the kingdom. Though hostile to each others' creeds, they shared the common goal of reforming Ganda society. Mwanga's often capricious dealings with these groups incurred their hostility. A four way power struggle of shifting alliances developed between him and each of the religious factions.

Mwanga's father had patronized the newly educated officials and had allowed them to undermine the traditional deference which subjects accorded the kings, giving these men unprecedented influence in the kingdom. At first Mwanga allowed this new elite to carry on as under his father, but soon he became apprehensive of the increasing influence of Christianity. His alarm mounted in 1885 when he learned of the German annexation of present day Tanzania.

Encouraged by his prime minister — his katikiro —, Mwanga rashly sanctioned the killing of the Anglican Bishop Hannington who was, at that time, on his way to Buganda.

- Italy occupied Massawa (February 6).
- Germany annexed German East Africa (February 25).

German interest in mainland Tanzania began in 1884. In 1885, Barghash virtually ceded the coast to the Germans — a move not recognized by Abushiri and other coastal peoples — other Swahili.

- Lagarde signed a treaty with Somali chiefs of Gubber-Kharab and Ambado (March 26).
- Tadjoura and Djibouti were occupied.
- A German naval demonstration was performed off the Zanzibar coast. The German claims on the mainland were recognized.

In 1885, Bismarck approved a German protectorate over present day Tanzania — the African mainland area ruled by the Zanzibari Sultan Barghash. With the declaration of the protectorate, German agents began to pressure Barghash to cede his territorial claims — his sovereignty — to Germany. Barghash ultimately conceded to the demands of the German agents.

- Bishop Harrington was murdered on the Buganda border (October 29).

- Germany acquired customs privileges at Dar es Salaam and Pangani.
- Yohannes IV gave permission for a Russian colony and monastery in Ethiopia.
- Italians occupied Massawa.
- The British occupied Berbera and Zaila.
- H. H. Johnston arrived in the Kilimanjaro region.
- Benedictine nuns started work in Dar es Salaam.
- Mwinyi Kheri (c.1820–1885), the ruler of Ujiji, died.

Mwinyi Kheri was born on the Tanzanian coast. He was among the first Arab traders to open trading stations at Lake Tanganyika during the 1840s. On Lake Tanganyika, the Arabs established the town of Ujiji among the Ha people and supervised a large trading network.

Mwinyi Kheri amassed a personal fortune and rose to leadership of the community by the 1870s. He pioneered trade routes north of the lake and exercised a nominal suzerainty over neighboring chiefs, who relied on Ujiji for imports.

When European missionaries arrived in 1878, he cooperated with them tacitly, allowing their enterprises to expire of their own accord.

In 1881, Mwinyi Kheri accepted the formal title of governor of Ujiji under the Zanzibari Sultan Barghash. However, despite the change in title, Mwinyi Kheri continued to run his affairs much as before.

- *Southern Africa:* A treaty of friendship was parlayed between the South African Republic and Germany (January 22).
- A British protectorate over North Bechuanaland brought to an end the Stellaland Republic (March 31).
- Bechuanaland was proclaimed a British Crown Colony (September).

In 1883, Paul Kruger was elected to the first of four terms as president of the Transvaal Republic. Kruger's first concerns were to remove the remaining British restrictions on Transvaal sovereignty and to secure access to a sea port. His efforts to subordinate Tswana chiefs to his west led directly to Bathoen's retaliatory cattle raid against Afrikaner farmers in 1884 and triggered a British expedition under Charles Warren which, in turn, led to the establishment of the British Bechuanaland Protectorate in 1885. *See 1910.*

When Charles Warren toured Botswana in 1885 to set up the Bechuanaland Protectorate,

Khama, the ruler of the Ngwato, welcomed him warmly.

As for the Kwena, when the Kgatla refused to acknowledge Sechele's sovereignty, a desultory Kwena-Kgatla war erupted. At the same time, the Transvaal Afrikaners began to encroach on Kwena territory. In order to forestall an Afrikaner conquest, Sechele reluctantly assented to the establishment of the British protectorate during Charles Warren's visit in 1885. Under the new British Bechuanaland Protectorate, Sechele's dispute with the Kgatla was soon resolved. The Kwena then enjoyed relative peace and an autonomy not shared by their kinsmen in the neighboring Transvaal.

- Pursuant to a French treaty with Madagascar, a Resident was installed (December 17).
- Gold was discovered in the Transvaal.
- The Cape railway reached Kimberley.
- The Transvaal formally denied all Indians civil and political rights.
- Cape Parliament Houses were completed.
- Lewanika regained control of Barotseland.

After regaining control of Barotseland, Lewanika adopted the praise-name "Lewanika." "Lewanika" means the "uniter." Lewanika also began to purge, without mercy, every possible rival. This was the last major challenge to his rule, but he lived ever afterwards in fear of a coup.

- The Independent Congregational Church of Bechuanaland began.
- In 1885, Jan Afrikaner, the chief of Namibian Khoikhoi, ceded territory to the Germans who were, at that time, expanding into southwest Africa. The following year, the lands of the Oorlam were made part of a German protectorate.
- Mahehero, the chief of the Herero of Namibia, signed a treaty of protection with the Germans.
- Antonio Vicente da Cruz (Chatara) became the ruler of the da Cruz family empire in Mozambique. *See 1879.*
- The Ndebele launched a disastrous raid against the Tswana.

After the Ndebele civil war of 1870, Lobengula, the king of the Ndebele, satisfied the inherently aggressive impulse of the Ndebele military system built by his father Mzilikazi by launching regular cattle raids. Lobengula directed these raids mainly against the Shona to his north and east, but he also raided western Zambia and Botswana.

Many of the military advantages Mzilikazi had enjoyed were lost as the Ndebele failed to keep pace with their neighbors development in tactics, weaponry and use of horses. Accordingly, over time, the Ndebele raids became progressively less successful as potential victims retreated to natural strongholds and obtained firearms to defend them. Lobengula had to send his army on increasingly distant and risky campaigns.

In 1885, Lobengula dispatched Lotshe on a campaign against the Tawana at Lake Ngami, six hundred and forty kilometers to the west. The campaign was a disaster. As a result, the morale of the Ndebele army became extremely low.

• Moletsane (c.1788–1885), the ruler of the Taung, died.

During the 1810s, Moletsane became the hereditary ruler of the Taung — one of many small Sotho-Tswana chiefdoms. Moletsane soon built his reputation as an exceptional military leader in the present Orange Free State region.

When the Difiqane wars of the 1820s erupted among the Sotho, Moletsane crossed the Vaal River and operated through the early 1820s as a wandering predator.

During this period, Moletsane seems to have allied briefly with Sebitwane, another Sotho chief who later built the Kololo kingdom. Moletsane also allied with the Griqua bandit Jan Bloem to raid cattle from the powerful Ndebele kingdom of Mzilikazi. At that time, Mzilikazi dominated the western Transvaal.

Around 1826, Mzilikazi's Ndebele chased the Taung back across the Vaal. However, Moletsane and Bloem re-attacked in 1828. This time the Ndebele chased the Taung deep into the Orange Free State and nearly annihilated them in 1829. Immediately after this setback, Moletsane's kingdom was pillaged by the Griqua chief Adam Kok III.

Moletsane lived as a vassal under Kok for several years with a vastly reduced following. In 1836, missionaries persuaded Moletsane to move to Lesotho (Basutoland). In Basutoland, the Sotho chief, Moshoeshoe granted Moletsane and his Taung some land.

In Basutoland, Moletsane rebuilt his chiefdom with new adherents while serving faithfully as Moshoeshoe's ally through wars with Europeans and other Sotho. Moletsane was semi-autonomous within Lesotho when it was declared the British Basutoland Protectorate in 1868.

RELATED HISTORICAL EVENTS

• *Europe:* Karl Peters' German East Africa Company was chartered (February 12).

• The International Congo Association was formally recognized (February 23).

• Leopold II was proclaimed the sovereign of the Congo Free State (April 30).

• The constitution of the Congo Free State was proclaimed (August 1).

• *Africa:* Isak Dinesen (1885–1962), a Danish writer who wrote about Africa, was born.

Isak Dinesen was born Karen Dinesen. Karen Dinesen became a Baroness when she married Bror van Blixen. The Blixens established a coffee plantation in the Kenya highlands in 1914.

The Blixens divorced in 1921. However, Karen continued to operate the farm in Kenya on her own.

When the world coffee market collapsed, Dinesen sold the farm and, in 1931, returned to Denmark. It was then that she turned to writing short stories in English and earned an international reputation as a stylist.

Dinesen's best known work, *Out of Africa*, was published in 1937. *Out of Africa* is considered to be a classic statement of Euro-African settler attitudes in colonial Kenya. This classic became the subject of a motion picture of the same title. The motion picture *Out of Africa* won the Academy Award for best picture of 1985.

Another noted Dinesen publication was a volume on East Africa entitled *Shadows in the Grass*. *Shadows in the Grass* was published in 1960.

• In Sudan, General Gordon was killed resisting the siege of Khartoum.

In 1860, Charles George Gordon (1833–1885) fought in the Anglo-Chinese war. He remained in the service of the Chinese government and received the nickname "Chinese Gordon" after putting down the Taiping Rebellion in 1864.

In 1872, Gordon accepted the Egyptian Khedive Ismail's appointment to replace Samuel Baker *(see 1893)* as governor of the Equatoria province of southern Sudan, arriving there two years later.

In Equatoria, Gordon continued Baker's work of suppressing the slave trade. He extended Egyptian administration in the area and attempted to impose an Egyptian protectorate over Uganda.

In 1877, Gordon became governor-general of

Sudan, while Eduard Schnitzer (Emin Pasha) succeeded him in Equatoria. Gordon's main concern was to negotiate an end to the Egyptian-Ethiopian war, but an interview with the Ethiopian Emperor, Yohannes IV, proved fruitless. Frustrated by the lack of Egyptian support for his work, Gordon resigned in 1880 and returned to British service.

In 1882, Gordon was made commander of British forces in the Cape Colony. At the time, the British forces were engaged in a costly war with the Sotho. Gordon attempted to negotiate a settlement with Masupha, a Sotho chief. However, Gordon soon resigned when he discovered that his negotiations were being undercut by another British official with another Sotho chief.

During 1883, Gordon considered working for the Leopold, the King of Belgium and the ruler of the Belgian Congo. However, before accepting such a commission, Gordon was recalled to Sudan by the British government which had, at that time, assumed the administration of Egypt.

During his three year hiatus from the Sudan, a large scale Islamic revolution had erupted under the leadership of Muhammed 'Ahmad, the Mahdi. British forces were cut off at Khartoum and Gordon was assigned to relieve them.

Gordon reached Khartoum early in 1884. However, instead of relieving the beleaguered British troops, Gordon soon found himself trapped. After a siege which lasted almost a year, the Mahdists took the city of Khartoum and Gordon was killed.

> • Henry Haggard published the enormously successful *King Solomon's Mines* in 1885. *King Solomon's Mines* told a story which was inspired by early reports of the Shona mines and ruins in Zimbabwe and which dealt with the actual life story of the Ndebele royal pretender Nkulumane.
> • Gustave Nachtigal (1834–1885), a German explorer and political agent, died.

A Prussian military doctor, Gustave Nachtigal left North Africa to cross the Sahara in 1869. He arrived at the capital of Bornu in 1870 after exploring the Lake Chad region. From the Lake Chad region, Nachtigal crossed Wadai to Egypt, and returned to Europe in 1875.

In 1884, Nachtigal was sent by his government to Douala, Cameroon, to help secure the new German West Africa territories. Nachtigal died aboard ship on the voyage home.

Nactigal's three volume record of his trans-Saharan expedition, *Sahara und Sudan*, became an important sourcework for the central Sudan, particularly Bornu. *Sahara und Sudan* was published between 1879 through 1889.

--- **1 8 8 6** ---

THE UNITED STATES

• James Milton Turner, a noted educator and the former Minister to Liberia, presented the claim of the African American members of the Cherokee Nation to President Cleveland. Turner was successful in securing $75,000 for the claimants from the federal funds allocated to the Cherokee Nation.

• Senator Blair, for the second time, introduced a bill for Federal Aid to Education. The bill, once again, passed in the Senate but was defeated in the House.

• The first electric trolley on the American continent was run by an African American, L. Clark Brooks (May 24).

• In 1886, Michael Healy was assigned to command the famous cutter *Bear* and became the chief federal law enforcement officer in the northern waters off the coast of Alaska. It was Michael Healy who served as the model for Jack London's *Sea Wolf.* (See also James Michener's *Alaska.*)

• *The Labor Movement:* The National Colored Farmers' Alliance and Cooperative Union was established.

• In 1886, there were some 60,000 African American members of the Knights of Labor. The total membership of the Knights of Labor was 700,000.

• *Notable Births:* William L. Dawson, a Congressman from Illinois, was born.

William L. Dawson was born in Albany, Georgia. He was educated at Fisk University, at Kent College, and the Law School of Northwestern University.

Dawson began his practice of law in Illinois. A Republican, Dawson became active in politics and became a Chicago city alderman in 1935. However, with the ever increasing popularity of Franklin Roosevelt, Dawson soon switched parties. He became a Democrat.

Dawson rose quickly through the Democratic ranks. He became the first African American to serve as vice chairman of the National Democratic Committee.

Elected to the House of Representatives in 1943, Dawson eventually became the Chairperson of the Committee on Government Operations. Dawson thereby became the first African

American to chair a standing congressional committee after the Reconstruction era.

• Timothy Drew, the founder of Moorish Science (the precursor of the Nation of Islam), was born in rural North Carolina (January 8).

• Georgia Douglas Johnson (1886–1966), a poetess, was born (September 10).

Georgia Douglas Johnson was born in Atlanta, Georgia. She was educated at Atlanta University and Oberlin Conservatory. While teaching in Alabama and working for the Government in Washington, D. C., Georgia Johnson published *The Heart of Woman* (1918); *Bronze* (1922); and *Autumn Love* (1928).

• Alain LeRoy Locke (1886–1954), a noted educator, was born (September 13).

Alain LeRoy Locke was born in Philadelphia, Pennsylvania.

In 1908, Locke became the first African American Rhodes Scholar. The impact of his selection was particularly significant because of the efforts of many European American scholars of the day to prove that African Americans were intellectually inferior and that because of this "inferiority" African Americans needed to be segregated from European Americans. Locke's selection served to dispel some of these racist notions.

Locke received a bachelor of arts degree with honors at Harvard University where he was also elected to Phi Beta Kappa. Later, he received a bachelor's in literature at England's Oxford University, where he was a Rhodes Scholar. Locke concluded his formal education by receiving a doctor of philosophy degree at Harvard.

Locke joined the faculty of Howard University where he would teach for 41 years. While at Howard University, Locke led a successful movement to establish a Phi Beta Kappa chapter at the university.

Locke is best known as a critic and popularizer of the writers of the Harlem Renaissance. His anthology of Harlem Renaissance writings, *The New Negro,* was published in 1925 and *The Negro in American Culture* was completed by Margaret Butcher two years after Locke's death and was published in 1956.

• Gertrude "Ma" Rainey (1886– 1939), a noted blues singer, was born (April 26).

"Ma" Rainey was born in Columbus, Georgia. Her parents were African American show people. At 15, Rainey married Will Rainey and began performing in his troupe, the Rabbit Foot Minstrels.

During her career, Rainey would be accompanied by such luminaries as Louis Armstrong, Buster Bailey, Charles Green and Fletcher Henderson.

Ma Rainey retired in 1933 and died in 1939.

• The photographer James VanDerZee was born in Lenox, Massachusetts (June 29). VanDerZee was known for his photographs of Harlem.

• *Notable Deaths:* In 1886, 74 African Americans were reported to have been lynched.

• Charles Bennett Ray (1807–1886), journalist, clergyman, and noted abolitionist, died.

Charles Bennett Ray was born in Falmouth, Massachusetts. Ray attended school in Falmouth and worked for five years on his grandfather's farm in Westerly, Rhode Island. Ray studied at Wesleyan Seminary and Wesleyan University in Middletown, Connecticut. In 1832, Ray went to New York and opened a boot and shoe store. While in New York, Ray joined the anti-slavery society and helped runaway slaves. In 1837, Ray became an ordained minister in the Methodist church. In 1846, he became pastor of the Bethesda Congregational Church in New York City.

In 1837, Ray became an appointed agent of the African American publication, *Colored American* and, between 1839 and 1842, Ray served as the sole editor of said publication. By 1843, Ray had also become the corresponding secretary of the Committee of Vigilance — an organization created to protect and assist slaves fleeing from bondage. In 1850, Charles Ray was made a member of the executive committee of the New York State Vigilance Committee.

Charles Bennett Ray is also known as being the father of Charlotte E. Ray, the first African American woman to become a lawyer, and Florence T. Ray, a noted poet.

• George Monroe (1843–1886), a famous pioneer of the American West, died.

After a stint with the Pony Express, George Monroe went on to become a famous stagecoach driver and gold miner. His name is today memorialized by a meadow (Monroe Meadows) which was named for him in Yosemite National Park.

• William Whipper, underground railroad leader; founder of the African American abolitionist group, the American Moral Reform Society; and publisher of "An Address on

Non-Resistance to Offensive Aggression," died.

• *Miscellaneous Publications:* George Washington Cable published a frank treatment of African American problems in *The Silent South.*

• William Sanders Scarborough published *Birds of Aristophanes.*

• A retitled revision of Sarah Hopkins Bradford's *Scenes in the Life of Harriet Tubman* was released as *Harriet, the Moses of her People.*

• *Scholastic Achievements:* Spelman Seminary (now Spelman College) in Atlanta, Georgia, began the first nursing school for African American women. African American women were forced to organize schools of their own for the training of nurses. As a result of the founding of all African American training schools, the number of African American graduate nurses steadily rose.

• *The Black Church:* The first meeting of the American National Baptist Convention was held in St. Louis, Missouri (August 25). The first president of the organization was William J. Simmons (1849–1890). The convention was the largest component of the three organizations that joined to form the National Baptist Convention, USA, in 1895.

• The United Holy Church was established in Method, North Carolina. The United Holy Church is known as the first African American holiness church. The church grew out of a revival conducted by Isaac Cheshier on the first Sunday in May of 1886.

• Augustus Tolton celebrated mass at Saint Mary's Hospital in Hoboken, New Jersey (July 7).

Augustus Tolton (1854–1897) was not the first African American priest but, at the time, he was the most widely recognized one. Tolton often held himself out as being the first African American priest even though the fair skinned Healy brothers were historically credited with being the first. Tolton became a priest on August 24, 1886 and served principally in Quincy and Chicago (Illinois).

• *Music:* George W. Chadwick's *Second Symphony* was published. *Second Symphony* was the first symphonic work which incorporated African American folksongs into symphonic arrangements.

• *Sports:* In 1886, Peter "The Black Prince" Jackson (1861–1901) won the Australian heavyweight title by beating Tom Leeds in thirty seconds of the first round (September 25).

THE AMERICAS

• *Brazil:* In 1886, strikes by free workers, many of them Afro-Brazilian, forced the city of Santos to declare itself a free city. By the end of the year, 10,000 escaped slaves were living within the borders of Santos.

• *Cuba:* In Cuba, the patronato system was terminated, and the patrocinados came under the protection of the state.

In October of 1886, the Spanish government in Madrid succumbed to the persistent abolitionist pressure and terminated the patronato—apprenticeship—program which had kept Afro-Cubans in technical bondage until the age of 22.

• *Haiti:* The Haitian constitution was redrafted.

Louis-Felicite Salomon, the president of Haiti, had the Haitian constitution rewritten in 1886 to allow his re-election after a seven-year term. From the beginning of his second term, there was internal turmoil and discontent, stemming partly from fears that Salomon might become president for life. By August 1888, the embittered Salomon, facing a rebellion from the predominantly black North, left for France. Salomon died in France a few months later.

• *Jamaica:* Walter Adolphe Roberts, a writer, was born.

Walter Adolphe Roberts was born in Kingston, Jamaica. From 1902 to 1918, Roberts was a reporter, first in his homeland of Jamaica and later in the United States. From 1914 through 1918, Roberts was foreign correspondent in France for the *Brooklyn Eagle.* Between 1918 and 1921, Roberts edited *Amslee's Magazine,* and later Hearst's *International Magazine.*

Roberts' most notable works include *Pierrot Wounded and Other Poems* which was published in 1919; *Pan and Peacocks* (1928), a second collection of poems; *Sir Henry Morgan, Buccaneer and Governor* (1933), a biography; *Semmes of the Alabama* (1938), a biography of a Confederate naval officer; *Six Great Jamaicans* (1952), a collection of biographical sketches; *Havana, Portrait of a City* (1953), a travelogue and social history; and *Jamaica, Portrait of an Island* (1955).

In 1956, Roberts became editor of the Pioneer Press in Kingston, Jamaica.

AUSTRALIA

- In 1886, Peter "The Black Prince" Jackson (1861–1901) won the Australian heavyweight title by beating Tom Leeds in thirty seconds of the first round (September 25).

Peter Jackson was born on July 3, 1861, in Christiansted, St. Croix in the Virgin Islands. At the age of six, Jackson was taken to Australia to live.

As a youth, Jackson developed into an excellent swimmer with a magnificent style. Jackson gave swimming exhibitions and during one of these exhibitions he caught the attention of Larry Foley, a boxing trainer.

Jackson began taking boxing lessons at age seventeen from Larry Foley. His first bouts were with mixed results. Indeed, in 1884, he was knocked out in three rounds by Bill Farnon. However, by 1886, he had developed enough to contest for the Australian heavyweight crown which he handily won from Tom Leeds.

Jackson was a magnificently sculpted boxer. He stood six feet one and half inches (187 centimeters) tall and weighed 190 pounds (86 kilograms). He was one of those rare fighters who combined both speed and strength. Jackson possessed a marvelous feint, a strong jab and a masterly left-right combination.

With no opponents worthy of him left in Australia, Jackson sailed for America in 1888 in search of fights against the leading heavyweights. However, the United States of the 1880s was an increasingly segregated society and the color line was used as both a sword and a shield.

The best European American boxers of the day avoided Jackson. The only boxer immediately available to give Jackson a good fight was George Godfrey, the best African American fighter of the time.

A match was arranged in San Francisco between Godfrey and Jackson. Jackson toyed with Godfrey. He beat him with such form and captivating ring grace that the audience was left in awe.

The call began to go out for a champion of European descent to take on Jackson. The first to answer the call was Jack McAuliffe, the leading heavyweight on the Pacific Coast. McAuliffe agreed to fight Jackson for $3000.

McAuliffe and Jackson met before the California Athletic Club and fought with bare knuckles as was then the custom. For twenty-four rounds, Jackson toyed with McAuliffe. But in the twenty-fourth round, Jackson utilized his famous one-two combination to dispose of

McAuliffe. First, Jackson hit McAuliffe with a right to the stomach. When McAuliffe doubled over from the force of the blow, Jackson straitened him up with an upper cut that hit McAuliffe between the eyes.

The bout was over.

Jackson's stunning victory over McAuliffe drove the Euro-American boxers behind the race shield. John L. Sullivan, the then reigning champion, simply avoided Jackson and announced that since he knew he could whip Jackson, there was no need to fight him.

Disappointed by Sullivan's refusal to fight, Jackson chased Sullivan to England. But the ever elusive Sullivan was not there.

Instead of fighting Sullivan, Jackson took on the best of England. He fought and defeated all comers, including Jem Smith, the English champion. Jackson destroyed Smith, knocking him out in two rounds. Having conquered England, Jackson once again set his sights on America.

By now, Jackson had developed a reputation and the sportsmen of the United States issued a call for a champion of European descent to come forth and put the upstart Jackson in his place.

The first to step forward was the Peoria Giant, Patsy Cardiff. Patsy had once fought the great John Sullivan to a draw. But the lumbering giant was no match for the cat quick Jackson. Jackson danced around with Cardiff for ten rounds. Then, in the tenth, Jackson sprang like a panther upon Cardiff. Using the lethal one-two combination, Jackson felled Cardiff.

More pressure was exerted upon Sullivan to come forward to face Jackson. But Sullivan continued to dodge. Instead, a future champion by the name of James J. Corbett, "Gentleman Jim Corbett," came to the fore.

On May 21, 1891, Corbett and Jackson met at the California Athletic Club for a fight to the finish with five-ounce gloves. The purse was $10,000 and the betting was against Corbett.

The smaller, quicker Corbett knew that he could not outslug the bigger, stronger Jackson. So using his brains, Corbett ran, dodged and ducked.

As Corbett himself would put it, "No matter in what direction I would dash, this big black thing was on top of me trying to one-two me to death."

In the sixteenth round, Jackson caught up to Corbett and landed a mighty blow. Corbett was stunned, but with the heart of a future champion, he was able to hold on.

Soon Corbett began to notice a pattern to Jackson's tactics. Exploiting a weakness in Jackson's tactics along with a fortunate turning of Jackson's ankle, Corbett began to wear Jackson down.

By the fortieth round, the fight had become an endurance contest. Jackson had a swollen ankle and was visibly slowed. Corbett had two broken ribs and was rightfully wary of the power that still resided in Jackson's blows.

In the sixty-first round, the bout was declared a draw.

The Corbett-Jackson bout was a turning point in boxing history. The bout introduced new tactics and methods of training. The gentlemanly and chivalrous nature of Corbett and Jackson created in the public a taste for something more than brawlers and maulers.

Corbett went on to defeat John Sullivan to become the world champion. Many commentators believe that Sullivan would have suffered the same fate if he had fought Jackson before fighting Corbett.

As for Jackson, his moment of glory in the United States was passed. He returned to England where a new challenge awaited him — Frank Slavin, an Australian.

Slavin was a magnificent athlete with a powerful punch. He was a brutal boxer and, being a product of his times, a virulent racist. Slavin despised black men and welcomed the opportunity to prove the superiority of whites.

On May 30, 1892, Slavin got his chance. At the National Sporting Club in London, Slavin met Jackson in a widely advertised fight which was attended by none other than the Prince of Wales, the future Edward VII. As Jackson stepped into the ring, Slavin shouted, "To be beaten by a nigger is a pill I will never swallow."

Such language was nothing new to Jackson. During his career, Jackson had always had to endure such language. Called all sorts of names, Jackson came to be known as "Peter the Great" or "The Black Prince" because of his courtly, gentlemanly manner in the ring. His great sportsmanship and modesty reflected his nature but it was also a role imposed upon him by the fact that he was a black fighter in a white world. Nevertheless, his deference, good looks, fine speaking manner, and skill made him universally popular. Indeed, Jackson was one of the few boxers, black or white, allowed to move freely in the National Sporting Club rooms in London.

However, by uttering the epithet "nigger," Slavin had set a stage on which Jackson's gentility would be sorely tested.

The betting on the bout was fast and furious.

The betting was two to one in favor of Slavin. After all, Slavin was stronger and he was white.

When the bell rang, the two approached each other cautiously. Slavin shot out a roundhouse right which if it had caught Jackson would surely have finished him. But it did not catch Jackson. With the moves of a panther, Jackson kept the more powerful Slavin at bay. Using a swift left jab, Jackson began to frustrate Slavin. Slavin was being outboxed.

Showing his lack of class, Slavin began taunting Jackson in the hope that Jackson might accept the bait and try to slug it out. But Jackson was too wily for that ruse. He continued to outbox Slavin and for the first five rounds, the fight was his.

In the sixth round, however, Slavin caught Jackson with a smashing blow that staggered Jackson. Quickly Slavin followed with another tremendous blow. All seemed lost for Jackson, but then the bell rang.

Sensing victory in his grasp, Slavin rushed out in the seventh round in an attempt to finish off Jackson. But by then Jackson had caught his breath and managed to regroup. He evaded Slavin's charge and resumed the tactic of keeping Slavin at bay with a straight left jab.

Round seven came and went. So also did the eighth and the ninth. With each round, Slavin's frustration and anger grew.

When the bell for the tenth round rang, Slavin made a mad charge for Jackson. But like a skilled matador, this time Jackson met Slavin head on. Flashing the famous one-two combination, Jackson stunned Slavin.

Slavin stood helplessly in the middle of the ring. His hands were at his side and he seemed unable to move. Slavin quite literally had been knocked out on his feet.

The crowd clamored for Jackson to finish him. The referee motioned for Jackson to continue the fight. But Jackson, seeing his opponent helpless — seeing the man who had viciously called him a "nigger" being unable to move — could not bring himself to hit Slavin again.

Jackson went up to Slavin and gently pushed him to the ground. He then picked Slavin up and carried him tenderly to his corner. The fight was over but the legend of Peter Jackson had begun.

Peter Jackson never duplicated the feats of the Corbett and Slavin fights. For the next five years, white fighters avoided Jackson like the plague, fearing being humbled by this great fighter.

After the Slavin fight, Jackson was unable to obtain any fights. Jackson began to engage in the dissipate life that so often accompanied inactive fighters. While living the fast life, Jackson did teach boxing, worked as a publican, and even toured as an actor in a stage production of *Uncle Tom's Cabin.*

After six years of relative inactivity and with his skills diminished by drink and indulgence, Jackson knew that his best fighting days were gone. Others, perhaps sensing his vulnerability and relishing the prospect of Jackson's defeat, arranged a bout with Jim Jeffries in 1898.

Jeffries was a mountain of a man. In his youth, Jackson would have danced around the lumbering Jeffries. But time had caught up with him. The 37-year-old, probably tubercular, Jackson could dance no more.

Jeffries knocked Jackson out in the third round.

After the bout, Jackson returned to his Australia. He had been a great fighter but because of the racism of the day, his life had been unfulfilled. Jackson gave himself up to drink and became a physical wreck. He was reduced to living in the back rooms made available by friends and had to rely on charity for a bite to eat.

Peter Jackson died of tuberculosis on July 13, 1901 and was buried in the Toowong Cemetery in Roma, Queensland, Australia. He was buried with Anglican rites and pomp. On the magnificent monument erected by his friends over his grave, there is an inscription which serves as a most fitting epitaph for this great boxer. The monument simply says, "This was a man."

AFRICA

• *North Africa, Egypt and Sudan:* The Prefecture Apostolic of the Nile Delta was established.
• Emin Pasha withdrew to southern Equatoria.

When the capital of Sudan, Khartoum fell to the Mahdists in 1885, Muhammed al-Amin, the governor of Equatoria, was left isolated on the upper Nile. A mutiny among his Sudanese troops added to his difficulties.

During this time, Muhammed al-Amin received the Turkish title "Pasha." Now known as Emin Pasha, the plight of Muhammed al-Amin attracted worldwide attention.

A massive relief force under the command of the explorer Henry Stanley was sent to rescue Emin Pasha. Emin Pasha wanted to remain at the Nile to solve problems himself, but he reluctantly consented to accompany Stanley to Bagamoyo on the east African coast.

• *Western Africa:* The Colony of Lagos separated from the Niger River Company (January 13). A governor independent of the Gold Coast was installed.
• A Franco-Portuguese convention was convened to discuss Dahomey and Guinea (May 12).
• British and Germans agreed to 2.5 miles of the Gold Coast-Togo boundary (July 14).
• An Anglo-German agreement on the boundary of Nigeria and Cameroon was reached.
• The Portuguese campaign against the Fulas led by Mussa Molo was initiated near Sancoria.
• King Agoue accepted the protection offered by the French.
• The Adansi massacred 150 Ashanti traders. The Ashanti army drove the Adansi people across the River Pra.
• A British arbitration ended the Yoruba War.
• A naval force attacked the Niger delta villages after attacks on the Royal Niger Company's vessels.
• The Royal Niger Company Constabulary was established.
• Between 1886 and 1887, the Togo-Dahomey border was delineated by France and Germany.
• From 1886 through 1888, Gallieni mounted military expeditions against Samory and Bambara.

By 1886, Mamadu Lamine, the Sarakole resistance leader, had become the ruler of a sizable portion of the Senegambia. He made his headquarters at Dianna on the upper Gambia.

In early 1886, Mamadu first encountered the French in battle. Mamadu Lamine's victories were sufficient to force Gallieni, the French commander, to come to terms with another imperialist, Samori Toure, so that the French could concentrate on the Senegambia.

More importantly, Gallieni temporarily allied with Mamadu Lamine's old enemy, Ahmadu.

• The *Sierra Leone Weekly News*, a newspaper, began publication.
• In the Niger River delta region, Nana Olumu, the Itsekiri "Governor of the River," ordered a trade stoppage against the British to protest against falling palm oil prices. Although his action was not unprecedented, the British consul took unusually strong exception to it, and pressured Nana to end it six months later.

• Lat Dyor Diop (c.1842-1886), the former ruler of the Wolof kingdom of Kayor, died.

Because Lat Dyor Diop's mother was of Kayor royal blood, Lat Dyor was eligible for the kingship and was chosen in 1862. Two years later, after coming into conflict with French imperial forces, Lat Dyor was forced to flee in Saloum, where he took refuge with the Muslim leader Maba Diakhou Ba. At the time, Maba Diakhou Ba was fighting both the French and local non-Muslims.

While with Maba Diakhou Ba, Lat Dyor converted to Islam.

Maba was killed in 1867. After Maba's death, Lat Dyor came to terms with the French.

Returning to Kayor, Lat Dyor was reinstated as the ruler of the Wolof kingdom in 1871.

In 1875, Lat Dyor allied with the French against Ahmadu ibn 'Umar Tall, who was struggling to maintain the Tukolor empire against the French.

In 1877, Lat Dyor won control over the neighboring state of Baol. His power and position enabled him to affect the Islamization of a large segment of western Senegal.

In 1882, Lat Dyor was again pitted against the French when they began to build a railway through Kayor to connect St. Louis with Dakar. Realizing the threat to his sovereignty, Lat Dyor refused the French passage, and was again forced to flee. Lat Dyor fought the French sporadically until he was killed in 1886.

After Lat Dior's death, Ahmadu Bamba returned to Baol. Soon after arriving in Baol, Ahmadu had a vision in which he was commanded to establish a new Islamic brotherhood. The brotherhood was to be called the Muridiyya. The Muridiyya preached that hard work and total submission to its leaders were the most important requisites to winning God's favor.

During this time, French colonialism had created unsettled conditions in Senegal as citizens were deprived of their chiefs and slaves were released from their households. In this chaos, Ahmadu attracted a following of thousands.

• *Central Africa:* A Franco-Portuguese convention was convened to discuss the boundary of the French Congo (May 12).
• The colonies of Gabon and French Congo came under single rule (June 29). Brazza was named Commissioner-General.

From 1886 to 1888, Pierre de Brazza was the commissioner-general of the French Congo. De Brazza's expeditions, which were quite popular in France, were greatly responsible for accelerating the European "scramble" for Africa.

• The post at Stanley Falls was attacked by Arab traders under the command of Rashid, the nephew of Tippu Tip (August 24).
• The Sanford Exploring Expedition was granted a concession in the upper Congo (December).
• Bremen mission started work in Douala (December 23).
• *Force Publique* was established in the Congo for military and police duties.
• A Plymouth Brethren mission was founded in Katanga.

In 1886, Msiri, the ruler of Katanga, admitted missionaries into his kingdom and began to receive European imperialist agents. Ultimately, Msiri attempted to hold off the imperialists. However, the disintegration of his kingdom weakened Msiri's bargaining position, and the known mineral wealth of Katanga made the Europeans more insistent on controlling it.

• The American Presbyterians were replaced by the *Societe des Missions Evangeliques* in Gabon.
• *Eastern Africa:* Catholic and Anglican converts were martyred in Buganda (June 3).

When Mwanga succeeded his father Mutesa I as king — Kabaka — of Buganda in 1884, Mwanga inherited an administrative structure undergoing a fundamental transformation. Before the time of Mutesa *(see 1884),* the kings had ruled through a powerful class of hereditary territorial chiefs.

The arrival of Christian missionaries in the late 1870s gave rise to a new class of younger religiously oriented officials. Educated Catholics, Protestants, and Muslims formed distinct administrative cadres within the kingdom. Though hostile to each others' creeds, they shared the common goal of reforming Ganda society. Mwanga's often capricious dealings with these groups incurred their hostility. A four way power struggle of shifting alliances developed between him and each of the religious factions.

Mwanga's father had patronized the newly educated officials and had allowed them to undermine the traditional deference which subjects accorded the kings, giving these men unprecedented influence in the kingdom. At first Mwanga allowed this new elite to carry on as under his father, but soon he became apprehensive of the increasing influence of Christianity. His alarm mounted in 1885 when he learned of the German annexation of present day Tanzania.

Encouraged by his prime minister — his katikiro—, Mwanga rashly sanctioned the killing of the Anglican Bishop Hannington — then on his way to Buganda. Then, in 1886, Mwanga sponsored a bloody purge of Christians in order to appease the older chiefs.

- Bethel Lutheran Mission started work in German East Africa.
- Yohannes IV declared war on the Mahdi.
- The Sultan of Harar defeated an Italian military expedition.
- In 1886, Kabarega, the king of Bunyoro, defeated a major invasion attempt by the Bugandan king, Mwanga II.
- In 1886, Salima (Emily Ruete), the outcast sister of Sultan Majid, published her autobiography. This autobiography was translated in 1888 as *Memoirs of an Arabian Princess.*
- *Southern Africa:* A French Protectorate was established over Grand Comoro (January 6). However, the French Resident was rejected by Anjouan (April 21) and French troops were forced to disembark.
- In Mozambique, Cypriano Caetano Pereira (Kankuni), the king of the Makanga kingdom, died. He was succeeded by Chanetta (Chicucuru). Chanetta ended the rapprochement with Portugal in 1888. Fearing the loss of his own independence Chanetta assisted the da Cruz family *(see 1879)* when the Portuguese invaded them.
- On April 26, a French Protectorate was established in Moheli.
- A German-Portuguese agreement was reached on the boundaries of Angola and German Southwest Africa.
- Part of Zululand was annexed.
- Gold was discovered in the Rand.

The discovery of gold in the Rand in 1886 solved the financial problems of the fledgling Transvaal Republic, but it also attracted an influx of foreigners (uitlanders) who threatened to outnumber the Afrikaners in the Transvaal. The Transvaal government's reluctance to grant these newcomers access to political rights angered the British and invited external meddling in Transvaal affairs.

- In 1886, Masupha accepted a British magistrate in his Sotho district.
- Recognizing the futility of trying to ignore the Cape, Mdlangaso, the leader of the Mpondo, went to Cape Town in 1886 to sign a treaty of friendship.

The Mpondo are a major branch of the southern Nguni who today occupy the northern Transkei. The genealogy of the Mpondo extends back almost thirty names, originating at least as early as the 17th century.

During the 1800s, the Mpondo preserved their independence longer than any other Nguni chiefdom in South Africa, until annexed by the Cape Colony in 1894.

On the death of their great chief Faku in 1867, the chiefdom split into two states. Both chiefdoms lost real power after the Cape administration divided the country into small magisterial districts.

RELATED HISTORICAL EVENTS

- *Europe:* The Royal Niger Company was chartered (July 10).
- An Anglo-German agreement was reached concerning spheres of interest in East Africa (November 1).
- H. de la Martiniere published *Essai de Bibliographie Marocaine* in which he suggested that France conquer Morocco.
- Spain abolished slavery.
- *Africa:* Adolf Luderitz (1834–1886), a German merchant who acquired the treaties which led to the creation of German South West Africa, died.

At a time when the German government was reluctant to colonize overseas territories, Adolf Luderitz, in 1882, secured Chancellor Bismarck's support to buy land for trading stations on the South West African coast.

In 1883, Luderitz's agent collected treaties around Angra Pequena Bay (what is today Luderitz Bay) and built up a claim to a large amount of territory in what is today Namibia. Luderitz then sold these rights to a private company — the German Colonial Society for South West Africa — which attempted to establish an administration there in 1885.

Luderitz himself apparently drowned in 1886 in the Orange River. When the German Colonial Society for South West Africa ran into difficulty, the German government stepped in, and eventually conquered Namibia.

- John Charles Molteno (1814– 1886), the first prime minister of the Cape Colony, died.

After migrating from Britain in 1831, John Molteno became a successful farmer in the western Cape. Molteno was elected to the first representative assembly in 1854. When responsible self-government was initiated in 1872, Molteno became the first prime minister of the Cape Colony.

Molteno resisted regional factionalism. He promoted the expansion of the railway, organized the Colony's finances, and stoutly opposed imperial interference in Cape affairs.

During Henry Barkly's governorship, Molteno refused to incorporate the diamond fields of Griqualand West into the Cape Colony. In 1878, Molteno broke with Governor Henry Frere *(see 1884)* over the employment of imperial troops in the Xhosa frontier war.

Molteno's administration was dismissed by Frere and Molteno was replaced as the Cape Colony prime minister by John Sprigg.

John Molteno retired from public life permanently in 1883.

1 8 8 7

THE UNITED STATES

• The first "Jim Crow" law to segregate Afro-American passengers from Euro-Americans on railway cars was passed by the Florida legislature.

• Tennessee had adopted the first Jim Crow law in 1875, and other Southern states had quickly followed. By the end of the 19th century, Afro-Americans would be barred from Euro-American hotels, barber shops, restaurants, and theaters.

• Isaiah Montgomery founded Mount Bayou on 30,000 acres of land in 1887 in the Mississippi Yazoo delta. Eventually, this primarily agricultural community grew to 3,000 persons and was self-sufficient. In time, Mount Bayou would have its own bank and farming cooperative.

• Sam Bass was elected mayor of Mount Bayou, Mississippi.

• *The Civil Rights Movement:* In 1887, Timothy Thomas Fortune formed the Afro-American League which worked for full civil rights for African Americans, including the right to vote, an anti-lynching bill and the equitable distribution of school funds. By 1890, the Afro-American League had representatives in 21 states.

• *The Labor Movement:* In 1887, the African American membership in the Knights of Labor increased by 30,000,

bringing the total African American membership to 90,000 out of a total mass membership of 500,000.

• *Notable Births:* The musician Cora "Lovie" Austin was born in Chattanooga, Tennessee (September 19).

• Marcus Garvey (1887–1940), an influential Afro-centric nationalist, was born (August 17).

In 1887, one of the most influential figures in Pan-African history was born. The figure was Marcus Garvey and his influence would teach persons of African descent throughout the world.

In 1887, Marcus Garvey was born in Jamaica in a large family. He attended school until he was fourteen.

In 1901, Garvey was apprenticed to a printer and later he became a print shop foreman in Kingston, Jamaica.

While working as a printer, Garvey became aware of the poor conditions under which his fellow Afro-Jamaicans lived. It was also at this time that Garvey participated in an unsuccessful strike by the printers' union. While working at the Government Printing Office, Garvey organized the National Club and began publishing *Our Own*.

Garvey soon left his job with the Government Printing Office and began a newspaper of his own which was entitled *The Watchman*. *The Watchman* proved to be a financial failure and Garvey was compelled to seek his fortune elsewhere.

After attempting to earn money in Central and South America, and after a stint of living in London, Garvey returned to Jamaica in 1911. It was while in Jamaica, in 1914, that Garvey founded the Universal Negro Improvement and Conservation Association and African Communities League — the Universal Negro Improvement Association (also known as "UNIA"). The purpose of the UNIA was to promote black unity through racial pride and to build a strong black nation in Africa.

While confined to Jamaica, the Universal Negro Improvement Association would prove to be an unsuccessful venture. However, once Garvey moved his operations to the United States, prospects began to change.

In 1916, Garvey moved to the United States to establish UNIA branches in Harlem and other black urban centers. He was a highly charismatic figure whose philosophy of black separatism and racial dignity appealed to many northern urban

African Americans. It was from this base that Garvey's organization was built.

In 1917, Garvey, now centered in New York City, founded the newspaper *The Negro World.* Through *The Negro World,* Garvey was able to advance his "Back to Africa" movement. This movement would lead to the establishment of 30 branch offices of the Universal Negro Improvement Association within the United States.

Eventually, the UNIA established branches abroad, making it the largest black movement ever. However, because of his black separatist beliefs (and perhaps because of his success) Garvey was disliked and criticized by many African American leaders, including W. E. B. Du Bois.

As part of his nationalistic stance, in 1919, Garvey founded a steamship company — the Black Star Line, the Negro Factories Corporation, and scores of small businesses.

By 1920, Garvey was at the height of his power and influence. In 1920, Garvey presided in glory over a UNIA national convention at Harlem.

In the same year, Garvey made contact with the poverty-stricken government of Liberia. In Liberia, Garvey obtained a commitment from the Liberian government which endorsed his proposals to funnel money into Liberia's economy in return for land for UNIA settlers. However, by 1924, the Liberian government became hostile to Garvey and expelled his emissaries.

The factors which contributed to the change in attitude were numerous. First, the Liberian economy had begun to recover independently of Garvey. Second, the Liberian government faced pressure from Britain and France to sever relations with the UNIA. Third, the Americo-Liberians (the descendants of emancipated slaves from the United States) saw an influx of new settlers as posing a threat to their control over Liberia.

As the relations between Garvey and Liberia soured so too did his financial empire begin to decline. The nadir occurred in 1925 when Garvey was imprisoned in the United States on a mail fraud charge in connection with stock sales for the Black Star Line. The Black Star Line had consisted of three ships which cruised a triangular route between New York, the West Indies and Africa. Although financed by $500,000 from various subscribers, the line ultimately failed.

Garvey was arrested and tried for fraud. Convicted, he served over 2 years in prison.

Garvey's sentence was commuted in 1927 and President Coolidge had him deported to Jamaica. A world tour in 1928 failed to raise enough money to pay the exorbitant debts that had been incurred by his New York UNIA staff and even the funds of the Jamaica branch of the UNIA were taken from Garvey in a series of adverse court decisions.

Garvey's other commercial endeavors, the African Communities League and the Negro Factories Corporation, also proved to be unsuccessful.

His plans for African colonization of Germany's former colonies were ignored by the League of Nations, and Liberia, fearing that Garvey desired to create his own personal African empire, withdrew its support of his proposal.

After these failures, Garvey essentially confined himself to improving the legal status and living conditions of his fellow Jamaicans. Garvey won a seat on a local council and proceeded to lead a more ordinary life.

Marcus Garvey died in near obscurity in Kensington, England in 1940.

• Thomas Montgomery Gregory, the founder of the Howard University Players, was born in Washington, D. C. (August 31).
• Roland Hayes (1887), a world famous singer, was born.
• Sargent Johnson (1887–1967), a sculptor, was born (October 7).

Sargent Johnson was born in Boston, Massachusetts. Johnson lived and worked in San Francisco and exhibited his works annually in various San Francisco Art Association exhibitions. From 1928 through 1935, Johnson also exhibited his works with the Harmon Foundation.

Johnson is noted for his busts. The busts created by Johnson display sensitive character portrayal. The subject matter of almost all of Johnson's sculptures are African Americans.

Johnson's other work includes drawings in which the dominant stylistic influence was African and Aztec art.

• *Notable Deaths:* In 1887, 70 African Americans were lynched.
• Richard Harvey Cain (1825–1887), an African American and a former Member of Congress from South Carolina, died.

Richard Harvey Cain was born the son of a Cherokee mother and a free African American father in Greenbriar County, Virginia. Cain was ordained a deacon of the African Methodist Episcopal Church in 1859 and transferred to

Brooklyn, New York in 1862. In Brooklyn, he became an elder of the church and also published a newspaper called *The Missionary Record*.

In 1865, Cain was sent to the South Carolina Conference and, in 1868, he was a member of the Constitutional Convention. In 1868, Cain became a State Senator representing the Charleston District of South Carolina. From 1873 to 1875 and from 1877 to 1879, Cain served in the House of Representatives as a representative of South Carolina.

Cain helped organize the Honest Government League. In 1880, he was appointed Bishop of the African Methodist Episcopal diocese of Louisiana and Texas.

• Joseph Hayne Rainey (1832–1887), an African American and a former Member of Congress from South Carolina, died.

Joseph Hayne Rainey was a barber at the outbreak of the Civil War. In 1862, Confederate authorities drafted him to work on the fortifications of Charleston. He escaped and went to the West Indies. In 1867, after returning to the United States, Rainey became a member of the executive committee of the newly formed Republican Party of South Carolina. The following year, Rainey was elected a delegate from Georgetown to the State Constitutional Convention. He was subsequently elected to the State Senate. In 1870, Rainey was elected to the United States House of Representatives where he took the place of B. F. Whittemore, a person whose credentials the House of Representatives refused to accept. Rainey continued to serve in the House until 1879 when he was replaced by a Democrat. In 1874, Rainey became the first African American to preside over the House of Representatives.

• *Miscellaneous State Laws:* Florida enacted a railroad car segregation law which was modeled after Tennessee's 1881 law. An additional provision of the law specified that no European American man was to be allowed to insult or annoy an African American while the African American was in the car designated for African Americans. Shortly after Florida's enactment of this law, the other Southern states passed similar legislation.

• Ohio repealed a statute which prohibited interracial marriage.

• *Miscellaneous Publications:* Charles Chestnutt's short story "The Goophered Grapevine" was published in the *Atlantic Monthly*. Chestnutt's story was the first work of fiction by an African American author which was disseminated to a largely European American audience.

• Gussie Davis wrote *The Lighthouse by the Sea.*

• George Washington Williams' *History of the Negro Troops in the War of Rebellion* was published.

• *Scholastic Achievements:* Rufus Lewis Perry was awarded a doctorate in philosophy (a Ph.D.) by the State University at Louisville, Kentucky.

• *Black Enterprise:* Mound Bayou (also known as Mount Bayou), Mississippi, was founded.

Mound Bayou, Mississippi, was the most successful all-black town. Founded by the Louisville, New Orleans & Texas Railroad in 1887, the town was situated along the rail line that extended through the Yazoo-Mississippi delta, an area of thick woods, bayous, and swamps that nonetheless contained some of the richest cotton-producing lands in the state.

When the fear of swampland diseases deterred European American settlement, the railroad hired two prominent African-American politicians, James Hill and Isaiah Montgomery, as land promoters. Hill had once been Mississippi's secretary of state, while Montgomery was the patriarch of a family of ex-slaves of Joseph Davis.

After the Civil War, the Montgomery family had acquired the Davis Bend plantations of their former master and of his more famous brother, Confederate president Jefferson Davis. The Davis heirs reclaimed the lands in the 1880s, prompting the Montgomery family to seek other business opportunities.

The railroad, which wanted settlers on the least populated lands along the route, chose a site fifteen miles east of the Mississippi River and ninety miles south of Memphis to establish a town. The four-square-mile area selected included two bayous and several Indigenous American burial mounds, inspiring Montgomery to name the town and colony Mound Bayou.

Montgomery, the more active of the two promoters, sold the first town to relatives and friends from the Davis Bend plantations. In the fall of 1887, Montgomery led the first twelve settlers to Mound Bayou. By 1888, Mound Bayou had forty residents, and about two hundred people had settled in the surrounding countryside. Twelve years later it had grown to 287 residents, with 1,500 African Americans in the vicinity.

With rail transportation assured and a sizable population of black farmers nearby, Montgomery and other promoters concentrated on efforts to increase business development. Those efforts were helped by Montgomery's close association with Booker T. Washington. Montgomery and Washington met in 1895 when the Mississippi planter served as a commissioner for the Atlanta Exposition. It was at the Atlanta Exposition that Washington gave the famous speech which launched his national career *(see 1895)*.

Washington who saw in Montgomery and Mound Bayou the embodiment of his philosophy of African American economic self-help, featured the Mississippian in exhibitions and conferences sponsored by Tuskegee Institute (now Tuskegee University). Montgomery, in turn, used Washington's fame and contacts to attract investors.

While Montgomery accepted a federal post in Jackson in 1902 and ceased his direct involvement in Mound Bayou promotional activities, Washington's interest in the town remained strong. Montgomery switched his support to merchant farmer Charles Banks, who settled there in 1904 and founded the Bank of Mound Bayou.

In 1908, following a visit to Mound Bayou, Washington prompted a number of flattering articles on the town in national magazines and profiled the community in books he published in 1909 and 1911.

Mound Bayou's population reached eleven hundred in 1911, with nearly eight thousand in the surrounding rural area. The sizable population ensured economic support for the town, which featured the largest number of African American owned businesses of any of the all-black towns in the United States.

Mound Bayou's businesses included its banks, a savings and loan association, two saw mills, three cotton gins, and the only black-owned cottonseed mill in the United States. By 1914, however, some businesses, including the Bank of Mound Bayou, closed, and the town experienced its first population losses. Booker T. Washington's death in 1915 initiated a period of estrangement between Isaiah Montgomery and Charles Banks, the promoters most closely identified with Mound Bayou's fortunes. By the early 1920s Mound Bayou lost its vitality and began to resemble other small delta communities.

• *Sports:* In Chicago, Frank Peters founded a semi-professional African American baseball team. The name of the team was the Union Giants.

• Isaac Lewis won the Kentucky Derby aboard the mount Montrose.

• Isaac Murphy won four big horse races including the St. Louis Derby.

• Pinto Jim and Bronco Jim Davis participated in a rodeo in Denver, Colorado (October). Pinto Jim could rope, bridle, saddle, and mount a horse in thirteen minutes. Bronco Jim Davis's contest was abandoned after thirty minutes of struggle in which the man and the horse appeared to be evenly matched.

THE AMERICAS

• *Brazil:* By 1887, the number of slaves in Brazil had declined to 723,000. This number was down from the 1.1 million reported for 1885.

• *Cuba:* By 1887, persons of African descent comprised some 32.4% of Cuba's population.

• *Dominican Republic:* Ulises Heureaux once again became the president of the Dominican Republic. Heureaux would rule the Dominican Republic as an iron-fisted dictator until his assassination on July 26, 1899 at Moca.

After decades of chaotic political strife, civil war, and fiscal irresponsibility, Heureaux's dictatorship provided the necessary climate for a great influx of foreign (especially the United States) capital into the Dominican Republic. Heureaux's reign also oversaw the rapid development of the sugar industry.

While progress was made under Heureaux, the die of dictatorship was cast by Heureaux and his rule would be the model for dictatorial aspirants to come. One such aspirant was one Rafael Leonidas Trujillo and Trujillo's dictatorial reign would point to Heureaux's as the model of the strong rule needed to run the "unruly" Dominican Republic.

• *Jamaica:* Marcus Garvey (1887–1940), an influential Afro-centric nationalist, was born (August 17). *See 1887:* The United States: Notable Births.

EUROPE

• Robert Browning published *Parleyings with Certain People of Importance in Their Day.*

• In France, Alexandre Dumas, fils, published *Francillon.*

AFRICA

- *North Africa, Egypt and Sudan:* Britain executed a convention with Egypt whereby Britain agreed to withdraw in three years (May 22).
- Fighting involving Ethiopia erupted on the Sudanese frontier.
- *Western Africa:* Civil war began among the Ashanti. The war would last until 1896.
- Binger travelled from Bamako to Grand Bassam, Ivory Coast, via Kong and the Mossi.

Louis Binger, a French explorer, first came to Senegal in 1880 as part of a military mapping expedition. He returned to Dakar in 1887 to lead a treaty-making expedition through present day Senegal, Guinea, Ivory Coast and Upper Volta.

In mid–1888, Binger arrived at the capital of the Mossi state of Ouagadougou. However, he failed to negotiate a treaty with the Mossi. The Mossi would be conquered by force in 1896.

Binger reached the coast of Grand-Bassam in 1889 after having traversed some 2500 miles. In 1892, he returned to the Ivory Coast as an administrator.

Binger's two volume account of his travels, *Du Niger au golfe de Guinee* was published in 1890–2. *Du Niger au golfe de Guinee* was an important historical sourcework on West Africa.

- Dakar separated from Goree and made a *commune de pleine exercice.*
- The Executive Council in Gambia was expanded to include two Africans.
- The Basel (Calvinist) Mission replaced the English Baptists in the Gold Coast.
- Samory besieged Sikasso, the capital of the Kenedugu kingdom of Mali.

In 1887, Samori, the leader of the Sofa, laid siege to Sikasso, one of the best protected towns in the region. Tieba, the ruler of the Kenedugu kingdom, and Samori waged a fifteen month war of attrition. During this conflict, Tieba signed a treaty with Gallieni placing himself under French protection. The treaty allowed Tieba to receive French arms.

- Glegle, the King of Dahomey, demanded French withdrawal from Cotonou.
- A dispute arose between Britain and King Jaja. In August, King Jaja was deported to the West Indies.

In an effort to remove obstacles to open trade on the Niger River, the British consul, Henry Hamilton Johnston induced the powerful merchant chief Jaja of Opobo to meet with him. During this meeting, Johnston seized Jaja, had Jaja arrested and deported him.

Jaja lived in the West Indies for the next four years on a pension of 800 pounds a year. In 1891, he was allowed to return home but he died in transit.

- In Sierra Leone, Kabalai became the leader of the Temne.

In 1887, the elders of the Temne chiefdom, unable to find a suitable successor to Bokhari, offered it to Kabalai. From that time onward, Kabalai became known as Bai Bureh — "Bai Bureh" being the designated title of the ruler of Kasseh.

As the ruler of Kasseh, Bai Bureh became a powerful war chief. He became one of the select few who were able to sell their services to neighboring rulers.

Bai Bureh's Kasseh had had a treaty of friendship with the British in Freetown. However, Bai Bureh soon came into conflict with the British because of his continued involvement in local wars. These local wars tended to create instability and disrupted the trade within the colony.

- The Governing Councils replaced the Courts of Inquiry on Oil Rivers.

In the early 1880s, the French resumed their eastward encroachment into the Tukolor Empire, establishing posts as far inland as Bamako. Ahmadu, beset with internal problems, was powerless to stop them, but the French themselves were not anxious to engage in hostilities because of their preoccupation with Samori Toure and Lat Dior elsewhere. A truce was effected between the two empires.

As evidence of the truce, in 1887, Ahmadu and the French joined forces to destroy Mamadu Lamine whose military ambitions in Senegambia threatened both French and Tukolor Empires.

The French forces led by Joseph Gallieni allied with Ahmadu to defeat Mamadu Lamine, the Islamic leader who had opposed both of them. In the same year, Gallieni made a treaty with Samori Toure who was then carving out an empire in Guinea.

- Edward Blyden published his best known work, a volume of essays entitled *Christianity, Islam and the Negro Race.*

Blyden's greatest legacy is an intellectual one rather than a political one. His ideas on race relations foreshadowed the philosophy of Aime Cesaire and Leopold Senghor. Blyden believed that blacks and whites had equal, but different, potentials, and that blacks could only attain their full potential in Africa.

Given his philosophy, Blyden became an advocate for the back-to-Africa movement. In this regard, he was a trailblazer for Marcus Garvey.

Blyden believed that the only way blacks could control their destinies was through Pan-African nationalism. He advocated the creation of a vast West African nation, or at least larger political groupings than those of colonial West Africa. Blyden hoped to accomplish this by linking Liberia with Sierra Leone, by encouraging European imperialism (which Blyden perceived as a tool for unifying the multitude of African peoples), by developing black racial pride, and by promoting Islam.

Although Blyden was a Christian minister, he felt that Christianity was unsuitable for Africa because of the discrimination practiced in the Christian churches.

Blyden's philosophical and political writings were voluminous. His best known work was a volume of essays, *Christianity, Islam and the Negro Race* which was published in 1887. Blyden was also a scholar in Arabic and classical languages.

• Ahmadu Tijani, the Tukolor ruler of Macina, died.

Ahmadu Tijani was a protégé of the great al-Hajj 'Umar ibn Said Tall, the founder of the Tukolor Empire. During the 1850s, Ahmadu Tijani assisted 'Umar in consolidating the Empire.

In 1864, 'Umar was killed while suppressing a revolt in the province of Macina. Ahmadu Tijani took command of the army and reconquered Macina within a few months.

Although 'Umar's son, Ahmadu ibn 'Umar Tall, inherited the Tukolor Empire, Ahmadu Tijani refused to relinquish his control of Macina to the new emperor. For the remainder of his life, Ahmadu Tijani independently ruled Macina from his capital at Bandiagara.

• Mamadu Lamine (c.1835–1887), a Sarakole resistance leader, died.

Mamadu Lamine (also known as Muhammed al-Amin) came from a village near Kayes in what is today Mali. Mamadu's father was a Muslim cleric. As a youth, Mamadu studied in Bondu and Bakel in the Senegal River region.

In the 1850s, Mamadu apparently met and served under al-Hajj 'Umar, the Tukolor Islamic imperialist.

After spending some time in Segu, Mamadu left in the 1860s on the pilgrimage to Mecca, passing through Wadai. Mamadu did not return to Segu until about 1880. Mamadu spent the next years in Segu as a virtual prisoner of Ahmadu *(see 1898)*. It is believed that Ahmadu may have resented Mamadu's Sarakole identity or his slightly different ideas about the nature of the Tijaniya Islamic brotherhood. This episode was pivotal in inculcating an anti–Tukolor sentiment in Mamadu Lamine.

Mamadu returned to his birthplace in 1885. During his absence, the French had begun to compete militarily with the Tukolor for control of the Senegambia. A charismatic leader in his own right, Mamadu used anti–Tukolor and anti–French sentiment to build a large following.

Within a few months, Mamadu declared a jihad — a holy war — against his Senegambian neighbors and the Tukolor Empire. By 1886, Mamadu was ruler of a sizable portion of the Senegambia. He made his headquarters at Dianna on the upper Gambia.

In early 1886, Mamadu first encountered the French in battle. Mamadu Lamine's victories were sufficient to force Gallieni, the French commander, to come to terms with another imperialist, Samori Toure, so that the French could concentrate on the Senegambia.

More importantly, Gallieni temporarily allied with Mamadu Lamine's old enemy, Ahmadu. After protracted fighting Mamadu Lamine was defeated by the French at Toubakouta in December 1887.

Although the accounts of his death conflict, Mamadu was probably caught and killed soon after the battle of Toubakouta. With his death, the Sarakole resistance movement died as well.

• *Central Africa:* Tippu Tip was made governor of the Stanley Falls District in the Congo Free State (February).

• A convention between France and the Congo Free State was convened to discuss the Congolese boundaries.

• Chokwe was expelled by brothers Mushiri and Kawele.

• The Baptist Mission in Ambas Bay was bought out by Germany. Subsequently, the British claim to Ambas Bay was withdrawn.

• *Eastern Africa:* Ras Alula defeated the Italians at Sagati (January). The Ethiopian army then withdrew because of an uprising of the Galla.

• In June, Gondar was attacked by the Mahdists. It was burned and pillaged. Harar was taken by Menelik and the Sultan was deposed.

By 1887, Menelik occupied the predominantly Muslim province of Harar. In Harar, Menelik appointed his cousin, Makonnen, as the governor of the province. Makonnen was the father of the future emperor, Haile Selassie. *See 1865.*

• Menelik subdued additional Galla and Sidama territory.

• Henry Stanley explored Lake Albert Edward Nyanza (December 13).

• France occupied Dougaretta. The British, in exchange for French evacuation, recognized French possession of Mouscha Island.

• Relief expeditions of Stanley and Karl Peters searched for Emin Pasha. *See 1886:* North Africa.

• The British declared a protectorate over North Somalia.

• The Benedictines of St. Ottilien arrived in Dar es Salaam.

• Yohannes' forces defeated the Italians at Dogali.

• *Southern Africa:* Anjouan accepted a French Protectorate and the French Resident (March 26).

• Britain annexed all Zululand (June 21).

• A treaty was negotiated between Lobengula and the Transvaal.

• Dinizulu was banished to St. Helena.

• Cecil Rhodes acquired control of De Beers.

• Gold Fields of South Africa, Ltd, later the Consolidated Gold Fields of South Africa, Ltd, was founded by Cecil Rhodes.

In 1880, Rhodes joined with Alfred Beit to form the DeBeers Mining Company. A few years later, Rhodes amalgamated — merged — with his chief rival, Barnett Barnato, to found the monopoly De Beers Consolidated Mines.

Rhodes then moved into the Transvaal gold fields, founding the powerful Gold Fields of Southern Africa Company in 1887. Rhodes retained leadership of both the diamond and gold mining companies and attracted considerable additional wealth from Britain to further his political enterprises.

• Fighting arose between the LCATC and Arabs under Mlozi at the north end of Lake Nyasa.

• In Mozambique, Antonio Vicente da Cruz (Chatara) quarrelled with internal factions. The factions abandoned Chatara when the Portuguese invaded with Gouveia

(Manuel Sousa) in 1887. Chatara was captured and exiled to the Cape Verde Islands while the rest of the da Cruz family fled north to asylum with the Pereiras. *See 1879.*

The Pereira family was a powerful Afro-Portuguese family who founded the Makanga kingdom in the lower Zambezi region. The Pereiras, like the da Cruz family, are examples of the cultural and political "Africanization" of European settlers.

Goncalo Caetano Pereira (Dombo Dombo) founded the family. Of partial Indian background, Goncalo came to Africa from Goa (India) around 1760 to prospect for gold. Unlike other powerful settlers, Goncalo never held title to an estate, but he became wealthy from gold mines north of Tete.

With his son, Manuel, Goncalo opened trade routes to the Bisa and Lunda of eastern Zambia. By the end of the 18th century, the Pereira family dominated trade north of the Zambezi River.

Another of Goncalo's sons, Pedro Caentano Pereira (Choutama), appears to have been the founder of the Makanga state. Pedro Caentano secured the title to the Chewa chiefdom in his own right and used it to extend Pereira political influence northwest of Tete. During the 1840s, Pedro Caentano's military conquests began the era of Zambezi wars, in which he used Makanga's strategic location along trade routes as a weapon against the Portuguese. Pedro Caentano Pereira died in 1849.

Pedro Caentano's son, Pedro (Chissaka), extended Makanga's wars against the Portuguese estate holders (prezeros) south of the Zambezi. In 1853, Pedro failed in an attempt to conquer the da Cruz family at Massangano but afterwards assisted the Portuguese government's efforts to do so.

Pedro died in 1858.

After Pedro's death, the power of the Pereira family declined for fifteen years. Leadership passed among various minor figures until Pedro's son, Cypriano Caetano Pereira (Kankuni) became king in 1874. Cypriano allied with the Portuguese government, thus obtaining arms which he used against his neighbors, while maintaining his independence.

Cypriano died in 1886. He was succeeded by Chanetta (Chicucuru). Chanetta ended the rapprochement with Portugal in 1888. Fearing the loss of his own independence Chanetta assisted the da Cruz family when the Portuguese invaded them.

Chanetta died in 1893. He was succeeded by

his nephew, Chegaga, for a brief time until Chegaga gave way to another of Pedro's sons, Chinsinga. Chinsinga became King of Makanga in 1893. At this point in time, the Portuguese government ceded administration of the region to a chartered company, which lacked the resources to control it. Chinsinga allied with the company in 1895 and assisted it in conquering the Ngoni chiefdom north of Makanga in 1898.

In 1901, Chinsinga was named the company's administrator in Makanga. The next year, Chinsinga was accused of embezzling company funds. The company, with Ngoni help, invaded Makanga. Chisinga's followers failed to support him. He was captured and executed in 1902.

The execution of Chisinga brought to an end the period of family-dominated states in the Zambezi valley.

• In 1887, a new man, Sigcawu, became chief of the Mpondo. Sigcawu insisted on ruling without Mdlangaso's assistance. Three years later, Mdlangaso attempted to seize power for himself.
• In 1887, the Cape Colony passed a franchise qualification bill which effectively denied the vote to all but a few Africans.
• In Namibia, Moses Witbooi, the ruler of the Oorlam, was forced to abdicate by his son-in-law, Paul Visser.
• Mqikela (1831–1887), a ruler of the Mpondo, died.

Mqikela succeeded his father Faku as paramount chief of the Mpondo in 1867. His half-brother Ndamase seceded to form a separate chiefdom. This split in the Mpondo state greatly hampered Mqikela's efforts to deal with mounting British pressure on his country.

Mqikela attempted to follow his father's (Faku's) policy of alliance with the British, but the decline of the neighboring Xhosa made it possible for the British to disregard the Mpondo as allies and to treat them roughly.

The Cape government annexed Griqualand East in 1879 and the British high commissioner, Bartle Frere, demanded that Mqikela cede Port St. John to him. Mqikela refused, so Frere shifted British recognition to his rival Nqiliso (the son of Ndamase), who sold the port to the British in return for recognition of his own independence.

After this episode, the British pressed Mqikela for the right to open a road between their port and newly acquired territory inland. Mqikela — allegedly a drunkard — gradually lost control of his chiefdom to his nephew Mdlangaso. Mqikela

was succeeded upon his death by his son Sigcawu.

RELATED HISTORICAL EVENTS

• *The United States:* Henry Ward Beecher (1813–1887), a European American clergyman and promoter of equal rights, died.

Henry Ward Beecher (1813–1887) was born in Litchfield, Connecticut. He was the son of Lyman Beecher, a prominent Presbyterian clergyman.

Beecher was educated at Amherst College and at the Lane Theological Seminary. In 1847, after serving as pastor to Presbyterian congregations in Lawrenceburg, Indiana, and Indianapolis, Indiana, Beecher became the pastor of the Plymouth Church of the Pilgrims in Brooklyn, New York. Beecher would hold this post for the rest of his life.

As his career progressed, Beecher became one of the most famous pulpit orators and lecturers in American history. Beecher's theological views were fairly orthodox, but nevertheless, he attracted and held huge audiences in the United States and England with his brilliant speeches and leadership at services and revival meetings and by his espousal of such controversial causes as the biological theory of evolution and scientific historical study of biblical texts.

One of the earliest and best-known supporters of the abolitionists, Beecher was also an effective proponent of women's rights, particularly woman suffrage.

From 1861 to 1863, Beecher was the editor in chief of the *Independent*, a religious and political periodical largely devoted to the abolition of slavery and the advancement of women's rights. From 1870 to 1881, Beecher edited *The Christian Observer*, another publication devoted to the advancement of civil rights.

In 1874, Beecher's former friend and successor as editor of the *Independent*, the American journalist and writer Theodore Tilton (1835–1907) sued Beecher and charged Beecher with having committed adultery with Tilton's wife. A trial held in that year ended in a hung jury, leaving Beecher's reputation besmirched. The cloud of adultery would hang over Beecher for the rest of his life.

• *Europe:* Agreement was reached on the French and Belgian Congo boundaries (April 29).
• The Imperial British East Africa Company was chartered.

- The *Compagnie du Congo pour le Commerce et l'Industrie* was founded in Brussels.
- Henry Haggard published *She*. Haggard modelled the fabulous queen of *She* on the Mujaji (queen) of the Lobedu people of the northern Transvaal.

"Mujaji" is the dynastic title of the female ruler of the Sotho-speaking Lobedu people of the northern Transvaal. The dynasty appears to have derived from the Shona ruling dynasties during the early seventeenth century, but its exact origins and early history are unclear.

During the nineteenth century, two women held the title of Mujaji. The second of these title-holders committed suicide in 1894.

The Lobedu were politically unimportant within the Transvaal. However, the Mujaji was widely recognized and honored as a rain-maker.

The Mujaji evidently inspired the character of "Ayesha" in Henry Haggard's novel *She*. The Mujaji reputedly possessed many of the mystical traits which Haggard assigned to his fictional heroine.

- Henry Haggard published one of his most popular books, *Allan Quartermain*. The hero of *Allan Quartermain* was apparently modelled on the hunter, F. C. Selous.
- *Africa:* John Mackenzie published *Austral Africa* in which he argued for total British control of Southern Africa.
- Johann Ludwig Krapf (1810– 1887), a German missionary and explorer, died.

Johann Krapf was a German Lutheran. He joined the Anglican Church Missionary Society (CMS) to participate in a new Protestant mission drive into Ethiopia.

Krapf reached Ethiopia in 1837 and, unable to work in the Tigre province, went instead to the Shoa kingdom, where he and other CMS agents were warmly received by the king, Sahle Selassie. All the Protestant missionaries were expelled from Shoa in 1842 for political reasons. Determined to work among the Galla of southwest Ethiopia, Krapf then went to Zanzibar (Tanzania) with the idea of reaching the Galla from the south.

After meeting the Zanzibari sultan, Sayyid Said, Krapf decided to remain in East Africa, opening a CMS station near Mombasa in 1844. There, two years later, Krapf was joined by Johannes Rebmann. The mission work of Krapf and Rebmann at Mombasa was only modestly successful, so Krapf and Rebmann began to look for new opportunities inland.

Between 1847 and 1849, Krapf and Rebmann became the first Europeans to penetrate the east African interior. In 1848, Krapf and Rebmann visited Kimweri ye Nyumba I in Usambara and then became the first Europeans to see Mount Kilimanjaro.

Krapf parted from Rebmann to enter present day Kenya. There Krapf was befriended by the Kamba trader Kivoi, who showed him Mount Kenya.

The reports of Krapf and Rebmann on the snow-capped peaks of Equatorial Africa aroused great skepticism in Europe. Nevertheless, their findings helped to stimulate further European interest in east Africa. Krapf returned to Europe in 1853 because of poor health, and later published a full account of his Ethiopian and east African experiences.

Krapf was an accomplished linguist. His writings on Ge'ez, Amharic, and Swahili were among the earliest scholarly works on those languages.

In 1867, Krapf returned to Ethiopia to serve as an interpreter in Robert Napier's expedition.

- Philip Edmond Wodehouse (1811– 1887), the British governor of the Cape Colony and high commissioner for South Africa, died.

After holding various colonial service posts in Asia and the West Indies, Philip Wodehouse succeeded George Grey as governor of the Cape Colony. In his capacity as governor, Wodehouse worked to solve fiscal problems in the face of a general economic slump. He strove to increase his executive powers at the expense of the new settler parliament.

As high commissioner, Wodehouse promoted the consolidation of border territories under the Cape administration. In 1866, Wodehouse succeeded in transferring the Xhosa territory of the Ciskei (British Kaffraria) from the imperial government to the Cape Colony. However, he failed to obtain sanction to annex Xhosa territories north of the Kei River.

Wodehouse mediated in the war between the Orange Free State and the Sotho of Moshoeshoe. He supported Moshoeshoe's request for annexation to the British Crown and helped to create the Basutoland Protectorate over Lesotho in 1868.

After he finished his second term in 1870, Wodehouse was succeeded by Henry Barkly.

Wodehouse later served as governor of Bombay.

1 8 8 8

THE UNITED STATES

• By dropping the issue of race and campaigning for a protective tariff, Benjamin Harrison, the Republican Presidential nominee, received more Southern votes than any other Republican candidate since the end of Reconstruction.

• Henry Cabot Lodge proposed a new Force Act, to protect African Americans living in the South. This proposal was rejected by Congress.

• Senator Blair of New Hampshire introduced his third bill for Federal aid to education. The bill was passed in the Senate but was again defeated in the House.

• In 1888, Boston erected a monument to honor those who died in the Boston Massacre of 1770. Among those honored was Crispus Attucks.

Crispus Attucks (1723–1770) was a person of African and Indigenous American (Natick) heritage. Contemporary accounts described Attucks as having been "owned" by a Deacon William Browne of Framingham, Massachusetts. Attucks was the leader of a group which precipitated the so-called Boston Massacre. On March 5, 1770, Attucks led a group of 50 to 60 men, mostly sailors, from Dock Square to State Street in Boston to harass British soldiers. In the fray which followed, an event now known as the "Boston Massacre," three people were killed, including Attucks. It is reported that Attucks was the first to be killed.

19th century historians transformed Attucks into a full-blooded Indigenous American from the Natick Nation but 20th century research, along with 18th century documentation, has brought the true African and Indigenous American heritage of Attucks to light.

• John Mercer Langston, former Minister to Haiti, was elected to Congress representing Virginia.

• Henry Plummer Cheatham was elected to Congress representing North Carolina.

• William Alphaeus Hunton became employed by the Young Men's Christian Association (YMCA) when he went to work for the Norfolk, Virginia, branch.

William Alphaeus Hunton (1863–1916) was born in Chatham, Ontario, Canada. He devoted his life to work with the YMCA, particularly in the Colored Men's Department. In 1893, Hunton became the first African American secretary of the International Young Men's Christian Association.

• Frederick Douglass was nominated to be the presidential candidate at the Republican convention. He received one vote during the balloting.

• *Notable Births:* Fenton Johnson (1888–1958), a poet, was born in Chicago (May 7). Johnson was educated at the University of Chicago. His poetical works include *A Little Dreaming* (1914); *Visions of the Dusk* (1916); *Songs of the Soil* and *WPA Poems.* Johnson's prose works include *Tales of Darkest America* (1920).

• Alcide "Slow Drag" Pavageau, a bassist, was born (March 7).

• Horace Pippin (1888–1946), a painter, was born (February 22).

Horace Pippin was born in Westchester, Pennsylvania. Partially paralyzed as a soldier, in World War I, Pippin began painting in 1920.

Pippin's war scenes, domestic still lifes and landscapes, all done in a primitive but vivid style received critical praise by art critics and were purchased by a number of major collectors such as the Whitney Museum and the Barnes Foundation.

Among Pippin's most notable works are *Cabin in the Cotton* (1944); *Buffalo Hunt* and *John Brown Goes to His Hanging.*

• *Notable Deaths:* In 1888, 69 African Americans were reported to have been lynched.

• *Miscellaneous State Laws:* Mississippi authorized the railroads to designate separate waiting rooms for African Americans and European Americans.

• *Miscellaneous Publications:* Daniel Alexander Payne, former president of Wilberforce University, published *Recollections of Seventy Years.*

• The *Freeman* began publication in Indianapolis, Indiana (July 14). The *Freeman* was founded by Edward Elder Cooper and was the first African American newspaper to make a feature of portraits and cartoons. The *Freeman* gained national prominence and made Cooper a wealthy man.

• *Scholastic Achievements:* Aaron Albert Mossell, Jr., graduated from the University of Pennsylvania Law School.

Aaron Albert Mossell, Jr., became a member of the Pennsylvania bar in 1895. He later served as attorney for the Frederick Douglass Memorial Hospital in Philadelphia, where his brother, Nathan Francis Mossell, was superintendent. Aaron Mossell was the father of Sadie Tanner Mossell, one of the first three African American women to earn a Ph.D. degree.

- *Black Enterprise:* In 1888, two African American banks were established. The Savings Bank of the Grand Fountain United Order of True Reformers in Richmond, Virginia, and the Capital Savings Bank of Washington, D. C. began operations. The True Reformers' Bank was chartered on March 2 and opened for business on April 3. The Capital Savings Bank was organized on October 17.
- *Sports:* Pike Barnes, an African American jockey, won the inaugural Futurity race at Sheepstead in Brooklyn.

THE AMERICAS

Brazil

By 1888, the Brazilian army and local police refused to enforce Brazil's fugitive slave law. Accordingly, a mass exodus from Brazilian plantations to the cities was underway. Almost all the major cities were declaring slavery abolished and pronouncing themselves to be free zones.

In addition to the disregard for the fugitive slave law, the level of violence began to escalate as arms were distributed to the growing number of escaped slaves. Conflicts between the police and armed escaped slaves became more frequent and nationwide chaos threatened.

When members of the imperial family came to side with the abolitionists, slavery, as a legalized institution in the Americas, was doomed.

On May 13, 1888, Princess-Regent Isabel rushed to the Brazilian Chamber of Deputies to sign the "Golden Law"—the law abolishing slavery. The majority of deputies wildly cheered the signing. Only the plantation owners stood back, disappointed and frustrated.

The imperial proclamation of 1888 decreed the immediate and totally uncompensated emancipation of all slaves. With this edict, the largest remaining slave regime in America was destroyed.

The Golden Law

The Princess Imperial Regent, in the name of His Majesty the Emperor Dom Pedro II, makes known to all subjects of the Empire that the General Assembly has decreed, and she has approved, the following Law: —

Art. 1. From the date of this Law slavery is declared abolished in Brazil.

2. All contrary provisions are revoked.

She orders, therefore, all the authorities to whom belong the knowledge and execution of the said Law to execute it, and cause it to be fully and exactly executed and observed.

The Secretary of State for the Departments of Agriculture, Commerce, and Public Works, and *ad interim* for Foreign Affairs, Bachelor Rodrigo Augusto da Silva, of the Council of His Majesty the Emperor, will cause it to be printed, published, and circulated.

Given in the Palace of Rio de Janeiro, May 13, 1888, the 67th year of Independence and of the Empire.

Princess Imperial Regent.
Rodrigo Augusto da Silva.

- Slavery was abolished in Brazil (May 13). Some 600,000 slaves were freed by Princess-Regent Isabel's declaration.

With the end of slavery in 1888, Jose do Patrocinio, an Afro-Brazilian abolitionist, organized the Guarda Negra (Black Guard). The Black Guard was an association of Afro-Brazilian militants dedicated to protecting Princess Isabel. At the time, Princess Isabel's succession to the throne was threatened by a growing republican movement.

- By 1888, the Emancipation Fund, which had been established in 1871 as a vehicle for gradual emancipation, had freed only 32,000 slaves.
- *Haiti:* Liautaud Etheart, a noted playwright, died.

Liautaud Etheart (1826–1888) was born in Port-au-Prince. He was the Haitian Secretary of State in 1879. Etheart is best known for his theatrical works. *Le Monde de Chez Nous* (1857), *Miscellanees* (1858), *La Fille de l'Empereur* (1860), and *Un Duel sous Blanchelande* (1860) were Etheart's most notable productions.

- Louis-Felicite Lysius Salomon (1815–1888), a president of Haiti, died.

Louis-Felicite Salomon was born to a wealthy black landowning family in southern Haiti. Well educated, Salomon early on committed to preventing political domination of Haiti by COTWs. When Faustin Soulouque re-established black dominance, Salomon served as his minister of finance for eleven years. Salomon was made duke of Saint Louis de Sud after Soulouque declared himself emperor in 1849.

After the overthrow of Soulouque in 1858,

Salomon lived in exile. In 1867, Salomon was named Haiti's diplomatic representative in Europe. Salomon used his European tour to broaden his knowledge, to travel, and to become acquainted with world affairs. Salomon also got married. He married Louise Magnus, a French-woman.

While abroad Salomon acquired the reputation as the leading defender of black interests in Haiti. This reputation, which elevated him in the twentieth century to the status of a patron saint of Haitian black nationalism, prolonged his exile.

During Salomon's period abroad, the Haitian elite coalesced into factions of COTWS — the "Liberals," and blacks, — into a coalition called the "Nationalists." When President Boisrond Canal stepped down after a turbulent period in office, Salomon returned an overwhelming number of Nationalists to the National Assembly, which in October, by a vote of 74–13, elected Salomon president.

Salomon's regime was characterized by a certain degree of subservience to French interests and ideas. Salomon brought together a group of French bankers to capitalize and administer a national bank. Salomon resumed payment on outstanding debts to France which were entirely liquidated. He recruited French teachers and established an expanded French-style system of education which still prevails. His military was re-organized with French assistance.

Salomon secured the admission of Haiti to the Universal Postal Union and granted a British company the concession to lay a cable between Haiti and Jamaica. An agrarian law of 1883 facilitated foreign ownership of land, previously proscribed. Despite the best intentions, these policies were blamed for undermining Haitian independence and are seen by many as the beginning of a pattern of foreign intervention which culminated in United States occupation of Haiti in 1915.

Salomon faced COTW rebellions early in his regime. In 1883, a major rebellion resulted in the pillaging and burning of COTW properties and murdering of COTWs by black soldiers and mobs. These disturbances ended only when the United States and European powers threatened intervention. The rebellion forced the expenditure of enormous amounts on the military, did irreparable damage to commerce and industry, further intensified racial animosities, and precipitated a spiral of inflation and state bankruptcy from which the regime never recovered.

Salomon had the constitution rewritten in 1886 to allow his re-election after a seven-year term. From the beginning of his second term, there was internal turmoil and discontent, stemming partly from fears that he might become president for life. By August 1888, the embittered Salomon, facing a rebellion from the predominantly black North, left for France. Salomon died in France a few months later.

AFRICA

• *North Africa, Egypt and Sudan:* Karl Peters explored southern Sudan.

In 1888, the German Karl Peters led an expedition from the Kenya coast to southern Sudan on the pretext of attempting to rescue his countryman, Eduard Schnitzer (Emin Pasha) who was isolated there by the Mahdists. When Peters learned of Henry Stanley's reaching Schnitzer first, he diverted his course to Uganda.

• *Western Africa:* Samory suppressed a rebellion in his empire.

Samory's attempt to take Sikasso, the capital of the Kenedugu kingdom of Mali, proved to be a major disaster. The defeat decimated his army and triggered off a massive revolt in his empire in 1888. As a consequence, Samory decided to abandon Islam as a unifying principle and return to one of personal loyalty.

• Archinard's expedition was launched against Samory.

Louis Archinard (1850–1932) was a French military commander who was one of the architects of the conquest of the Western Sudan. Driven largely by personal ambition, Archinard was a major force in converting France's policy of peaceful expansion to one of military conquest.

Archinard first arrived in the Western Sudan region in 1880 to supervise the construction of forts. In 1888, Archinard was appointed *Commandant-Superieur* for the Western Sudan.

After launching a military expedition against Samori Toure (Samory) in 1888, Archinard was forced to call a halt to his military endeavors against Samori in order to concentrate on the Tukolor Empire and the forces of Ahmadu ibn 'Umar Tall *(see 1898).*

By 1891, the war with the Tukolor Empire was under control and Archinard was once again able to concentrate on Samori, who at that time was in the process of creating his own West African empire. Archinard's forces penetrated to Kankan, deep into Samori's territory. However, despite the advance, Archinard was not immediately able to totally defeat Samori. The war with Samori would last for another seven years until Samori was captured.

- A French protectorate treaty was reached with the Almany of Futa, Guinea (December 11).
- A new Anglo-German agreement on the Gold Coast-Togo boundary was negotiated.
- The Treaty with the Alafin of Oyo placed all Yorubaland under British protection.

According to Yoruba tradition Oyo was founded by Oranyan, a prince who migrated to Ife, the Yoruba fatherland around 1200. During the 14th century, Oyo became an important power in northern Yorubaland.

Wars with neighbors forced the kings — the alafin — of Oyo to abandon the capital in the mid–16th century, but it was re-occupied around 1600. From 1600 onward, Oyo grew to be the most powerful state in the region, dominating both its Yoruba and non–Yoruba neighbors with the exception of Benin.

In the early 1700s, Oyo achieved suzerainty over the Aja kingdom of Dahomey. But Oyo collapsed in the early 19th century due to a mixture of internal and external factors, precipitated by the revolt of the province of Ilorin.

*   *   *

"Alafin" is the title of the ruler of the Yoruba kingdom of Oyo in Nigeria. The Alafin was a divine king. Succession to the throne was initially through primogeniture. However, after Igboho became the capital of Oyo in the 16th century, the Alafin was elected from among the royal princes by the Oyo Mesi, a 7-man council of state. The actions of the Alafin subsequently required the approval of the Oyo Mesi.

The head of the Oyo Mesi was the Basorun. As the head of the ruling council, there were times in the history of the Oyo that the Basorun was actually more powerful than the Alafin.

*   *   *

"Oba" is the title of the ruler of the Edo-speaking kingdom of Benin. Oba is also the term for "king" among the Yoruba peoples. The oba of each Yoruba kingdom was known by a specific title (e.g., the "Alafin" of the Oyo, the "Alaketu" of the Ketu, etc.). The principal Yoruba oba all claimed descent from the original oba of the Ife. Both the Benin and the Yoruba oba were considered to be "divine kings." These "divine" oba exercised a great deal of power, but their authority was checked by councils of chiefs.

- The Gambia became a separate colony.

English traders first built trading factories on the Gambia River in the early 17th century. From 1779 to 1816, the colony was controlled by the French. It became part of the Sierra Leone colony from 1821 until 1843, when it was separated. Beginning in 1866, it was administered as part of the West African Settlements, based at Sierra Leone.

In 1888, the Gambia once again became a separate colony. In 1894, a protectorate was declared over the colony's interior.

The Gambia became independent in 1965.

- Ovunramwen became the Oba of the Edo kingdom of Benin.

When Ovunramwen's father, Adolo, died in 1888, Ovonramwen secured his position as the new oba — king — by killing off leaders of rival factions, destroying whole villages in some cases.

Ovunramwen also strengthened himself by expanding the nobility in order to reward friends, and to placate some of his enemies. Nevertheless, the power of the many Benin palace chiefs remained sufficiently great that Ovunramwen could not entirely subdue opposing factions.

The kingdom which Ovunramwen inherited had recently been reduced in size because of Nupe and British encroachment. The British, who were quickly bringing the Niger delta states under their control, presented the major threat. When Ovonramwen asserted his authority by placing restrictions on trade to the coast, the British attempted to enforce a protectorate over Benin.

- *Central Africa:* Henry Stanley found Emin Pasha (April 29).
- Gabon and the French Congo were declared a single colony. Brazza was made the Commissioner General (December 11).
- All British mission were replaced by Germans in Cameroon.
- Tippu Tip claimed Rwanda as being his supplier of arms.

Rwanda was originally founded as the kingdom of the Banyarwanda people. The kingdom of the Banyarwanda was founded around the 1400s by an intrusive pastoralist minority known as the Tutsi (Watusi). The overwhelming majority of the country's population were agriculturalists known as Hutu. From the 15th through the 19th centuries, the Tutsi kings gradually expanded their domain at the expense of older Hutu states. During the reign of Kigeri IV the kingdom reached approximately the shape of the present nation of Rwanda.

Rwanda was long isolated from outside trade and contacts. The first European to reach the king's court arrived in 1894. With the eager collaboration of Yuhi IV Musinga, the Germans gradually imposed an administration between 1897 and 1906. The Germans were displaced by the Belgians during World War I. The Rwanda kingship was maintained throughout the colonial period, during which the country was administered as a part of Ruanda-Urundi.

The last king (Kigeri V Ndahindurwa) of Ruanda-Urundi took office in 1959. Within months, a mass Hutu uprising drove Kigeri V into exile and initiated a wholesale massacre of the Tutsi minority. A Hutu-sponsored referendum in 1961 favored creation of a republic and the Tutsi monarchy was officially abolished.

In 1962, Rwanda became an independent country.

• Njoya, the King of Foumbau, invented the Bamoun script with its seventy-three letters and ten figures.
• The Scheut Fathers replaced the Holy Ghost Fathers in the Congo.
• Yaounde was founded.
• *Eastern Africa:* The French moved the refueling post from Obock to Djibouti. This move was recognized by Great Britain (February 8).
• In 1888, Mwanga, the ruler of the Ganda kingdom, was overthrown by a temporary Christian-Muslim alliance and a general civil war commenced.

In 1888, Mwanga attempted to abolish all three (Catholic, Protestant and Muslim) religious factions in the Ganda kingdom. His plan miscarried disastrously. All three groups united to drive Mwanga out of the country.

A new king was installed in Mwanga's place. Within a month, the dominant Muslim faction staged another coup, installing yet another king. The Christians then fled from the country.

A four year civil war ensued. Mwanga was assisted by the Christians in his attempt to reclaim his throne. Mwanga rewarded the strongest Christian leader, Apolo Kagwa (*see 1869*), by making him his prime minister, even though his own position remained tenuous.

• In 1888, Bwana Heri again united the Zigua this time to defy German imperialism.
• Abushiri's rebellion in German East Africa began.

In mid–1888, the Germans occupied the coastal towns and attempted to collect customs duties. Faced with economic ruin, Abushiri and other Swahili townsmen spontaneously drove the Germans away.

The Germans then launched a counter-offensive under Hermann von Wissmann. Over the next year, Abushiri rallied the Swahili between Pangani and Dar es Salaam and waged a see-saw war with the Germans.

Eventually, Abushiri's support began to wane as his followers tired of German naval bombardment and costly battles.

• Ethiopians were sent to Russia to participate in the 900th anniversary celebration of the introduction of Christianity into Russia.
• IBEA established a base in Mombasa (Kenya). A "coastal strip" was subsequently leased from the Sultan of Zanzibar.

European administration of the lands which today comprise the country of Kenya began in 1888 under the charter granted to the Imperial British East Africa Company ("IBEA" or "BEAC") of William MacKinnon. Administration was turned over to the British government in 1895 and the office of commissioner was transformed into that of governor in 1906.

Until 1920, Kenya was known as the East African Protectorate. After 1920, the land became the Kenya Colony.

Kenya gained its independence in 1963 with Jomo Kenyatta as its first prime minister.

• Barghash Ibn Said (c.1837– 1888), the third Busaidi ruler of Zanzibar, died.

After the death of his father Sayyid Said in 1856, Barghash Ibn Said made two feeble attempts to usurp the Zanzibari throne from his brother, Majid ibn Said. From 1859 to 1861, Majid exiled Barghash to Bombay (India).

Barghash succeeded Majid in 1870. Once upon the throne, his reign was plagued by two problems: (1) the continuing threat to his position from the Omani portion of his father's partitioned domain and (2) his efforts to expand Zanzibari commercial activity on the African mainland.

In 1872, both of Barghash's problems were aggravated when a hurricane destroyed many of his island's valuable clove and coconut trees and sank most of his fleet. With both his military and economic position severely weakened, Barghash had to rely more closely on the British for support.

The British took advantage of Barghash. They

persuaded him to sign, in 1873, a treaty outlawing the seaborne trafficking of slaves. From the execution of this treaty, the British played an increasingly dominant role in his external relations and the British induced Barghash to implement this and later edicts which eventually ended the bulk of slave trading in East Africa.

The traditional dependence of the clove industry on mainland slaves made Barghash's economic plight more precarious and caused him to promote other forms of trade on the mainland. In an attempt to recoup, Barghash emphasized ivory and rubber as alternative commodities to cloves.

In his attempts to establish a Zanzibari presence on the mainland, Barghash encountered the fact that Zanzibari sovereignty on the mainland was always more nominal than real. Barghash was soon hard pressed to subdue his mainland rivals. The Nyamwezi chief, Mirambo, the Zigua chief, Bwana Heri, and the Arab (Swahili) leaders Mbaruk bin Rashid and Abushiri bin Salimu proved particularly troublesome for Barghash.

Nevertheless, despite the obstacles, Zanzibar's commerce flourished and its exports to Europe and the United States grew considerably.

During the 1880s, Barghash enlisted the support of powerful independent Arab and Swahili merchants, most notably Tippu Tip, to expand his commercial base. Barghash appointed territorial governors, such as Jumbe and Mwinyi Kheri, at various inland mainland stations.

In 1884, the Germans began entering into treaties with mainland chiefs in Zanzibari territory. In 1885, Bismarck approved a German protectorate over present day Tanzania — the African mainland area ruled by Barghash. With the declaration of the protectorate, German agents began to pressure Barghash to cede his territorial claims — his sovereignty — to Germany.

Barghash ultimately conceded to the demands of the German agents. Turning away from the mainland, Barghash concentrated his energies on consolidating his position on Zanzibar itself.

• *Southern Africa:* Lobengula of the Matabele accepted a British Protectorate (February 11).
• On October 30, Lobengula granted mining rights to Cecil Rhodes. Rhodes subsequently amalgamated the Kimberley diamond companies.

For a while, Barnett Barnato and Alfred Beit competed with Cecil J. Rhodes for control of the diamond business. However, the three titans eventually amalgamated (in 1888) to form the powerful De Beers Consolidated Mines.

Rhodes rewarded Barnato by obtaining for him the Kimberley seat in the Cape Colony parliament. Barnato held this seat from 1888 until 1897.

• Lobengula signed the "Rudd Concession" and essentially signed over all mines and metals in his kingdom to the Rhodes group.

Cecil Rhodes became obsessed with the goal of extending British rule north of the Limpopo River. In 1888, his partner Charles Rudd obtained a monopoly mining concession from the Ndebele King Lobengula. Rhodes used this concession as a lever to obtain a crown charter for his new British South African Company ("BSAC") in 1889.

The concession treaty signed by Lobengula ostensibly gave Cecil Rhodes exclusive rights to mine Zimbabwe. Rhodes broadly interpreted the concession granted by Lobengula as a grant of land itself. In 1890, Rhodes' private company occupied eastern Zimbabwe (Mashonaland).

Lobengula lacked enough Ndebele support to resist Rhodes' group decisively. Instead, he had to re-assert his claims to sovereignty over the Shona of eastern Zimbabwe by intensifying raids and punitive expeditions against them.

A sidebar to the Rudd Concession was the fate of Lotshe. Having experienced the debacle against the Tawana (*see 1885*), Lotshe, the Ndebele military commander, became a leading advocate of peaceful accommodation with Europeans who were then clamoring to enter Zimbabwe. Lotshe advised Lobengula to sign the concession treaty offered by Charles Rudd on behalf of Cecil Rhodes in 1888. When it was discovered that the Europeans had grossly misrepresented the terms of this document, Lotshe became the scapegoat.

In 1889, Lotshe was executed and his entire family was massacred.

• Rhodes gained control of the Kimberley mining industry.
• LCATC was absorbed by the British South Africa Company under the name African Lakes Corporation.
• The Portuguese refused passage to the African Lakes Company of the company's artillery which was intended for use against Mlozi.
• An expedition under Serpa Pinto was dispatched to occupy the Shire Highlands.
• The Bechuanaland Exploration Company was formed.

• Barotse (the Lozi) again campaigned against the Ila.

• Joao Sant'anna da Cruz (Motontora) re-organized the da Cruz family refugees and staged a brief re-occupation of Massangano. After the Portuguese chased Motontora out, Motontora returned to settle in the Pereira kingdom and the da Cruz family ceased to be an African power. *See 1879.*

• By 1888, the New Republic territory (formerly northwestern Zululand) was absorbed into the far larger Transvaal Republic, and the British had annexed the then existent Zululand. The British divided Zululand into magisterial districts with the reluctant assent of Dinuzulu, the Zulu king.

• Frederick Lugard led an expedition organized by British settlers in Nyasaland (Malawi) to drive out Arab slave traders.

• Because the Germans failed to provide security against the Witboois (the Khoikhoi), Mahehero renounced the treaty that had been reached in 1885.

• Moses Witbooi (c.1810–1888), a leader of the Witbooi family of Namibia, died.

The Witbooi family was a powerful ruling family in the Oorlam branch of the Khoikhoi through the 1800s and early twentieth century. The Witboois, along with other Oorlam groups, migrated from the Cape Colony into Namibia, where they introduced Dutch language and culture.

Moses Witbooi was the son of Kido Witbooi *(see 1875)*, the founder of the Namibia Witbooi clan. Moses Witbooi was the effective ruler the Witbooi community during his father's last years and formally became chief in 1875.

During the 1880s, Moses Witbooi allied with another Oorlam chief, Jan Jonker Afrikaner, against the Bantu-speaking Herero people. Witbooi was mistrusted by his own people. He gradually lost supporters to his son, Hendrik, and to his son-in-law, Paul Visser.

In 1887, Moses Witbooi was forced to abdicate by Visser. Visser had Moses Witbooi executed the next year.

Soon afterwards, Witbooi's son, Hendrik, killed Visser and re-united the Oorlam under his own rule.

RELATED HISTORICAL EVENTS

• *Europe:* The Suez Canal Convention, meeting at Istanbul, declared the canal open to all nations in war as well as in peace.

• The Missionary Sisters of the Precious Blood and African Society of German Catholics was founded.

• Cardinal Lavigerie was ordered by Pope Leo XIII to undertake a crusade against slavery.

• Manuel Sousa, the Indo-Portuguese empire builder, visited Lisbon (Portugal) where he was highly honored for his assistance in furthering Portuguese influence in Mozambique. Sousa was made a colonel in the Portuguese army in tribute to his service.

• Peter Claver was canonized and declared, by Pope Leo XIII, the patron saint of all missionary enterprises among persons of African descent, in whatever part of the world.

Saint Peter Claver (1581–1654) was born in Verdu, in Catalonia, Spain. As a youth, Peter demonstrated fine qualities of mind and spirit. His mental acuity led him to study at the University of Barcelona.

Peter graduated with distinction from the University and, after receiving minor orders, decided to join the Society of Jesus (the Jesuits). Peter was received into the novitiate of Tarragona at the age of twenty, and was sent to the college of Montesione at Palma, in Majorca.

In Majorca, Peter met Saint Alphonsus Rodriguez, who was then a porter in the college, though with a reputation far above his humble office. This meeting was to set the direction for Peter Claver's life.

Peter studied the science of the saints at the feet of the Alphonsus, and Alphonsus developed a corresponding regard for the capabilities of young Peter. In Peter, Alphonsus soon began to think that he had found the right person for a very difficult and arduous calling. Alphonsus commissioned Peter to go to the New World to minister amongst the many who were without spiritual guidance.

In later years, Peter would often recall that Alphonsus had actually foretold not only that Peter would go to the New World but also the precise location where he would work. Moved by the inspirational fervor of Alphonsus, Peter approached his superiors and offered himself for the West Indies. His superiors told him that his vocation would be chosen for him, in due course.

Peter returned to Barcelona to study theology. After two years, and after additional requests from Peter, his superiors chose Peter to represent the province of Aragon on the Jesuit mission to New Granada.

Peter left Spain forever in April of 1610. After a wearisome voyage, Peter landed with his companions at Cartagena, in what is now the Republic of Colombia.

The first five years of Peter's mission in Colombia was spent performing various tasks associated with the Jesuit mission located outside of Cartagena. However, in 1615, Peter returned to Cartagena, was ordained a priest, and began the calling for which he is today remembered.

By 1615, the slave trade had been established in the Americas for nearly a hundred years and the port of Cartagena was one of the principal centers of slave debarkation. By 1615, the enslavement of Indigenous Americans had subsided due to the inability of the Indigenous Americans to withstand the harsh environment of the silver and gold mines along with the debilitating European diseases. Thus, African slaves from Angola and the Congo were in great demand.

The conditions under which the African slaves were transported to the colonies were truly hellacious. It was estimated that in each cargo of slaves at least one third of the slaves would die during the six or seven week voyage. Nevertheless, each year some ten thousand slaves survived the trip and landed in Cartagena.

Slavery had been condemned by Pope Paul III as being a great crime and was termed a "supreme villainy" by Pope Pius IX. Nevertheless, slavery in Catholic America continued to flourish.

Despite the papal decrees and the ameliorating implorations of the Catholic clergy, most slave owners limited their religious instruction of their slaves to simply having them baptized. The slaves received no religious instruction and no religious ministration. Indeed, over time the very act of their religious conversion — their baptism — became synonymous to their oppression.

For the most part, the Catholic clergy were ineffective at changing the conditions of the slaves. The best that they could do was to express some compassion for the misery being suffered by the Africans.

At the time of Peter Claver's ordination, the leader in the field work among the African slaves was Father Alfonso de Sandoval, a great Jesuit missionary who spent forty years in the service of the slaves. After working with Father Alfonso, Peter declared himself "the slave of the Negroes for ever."

Although by nature shy and without self-confidence, Peter, nevertheless, threw himself into the work. He pursued it not with unbridled enthusiasm but with methodical organization.

Peter enlisted bands of assistants. As soon as a slave-ship entered the port of Cartagena, Peter would go to the docks. After the slaves had disembarked and were shut up in the yards, crowds of locals would gather to gape at them. These "idle gazers" were drawn by a morbid curiosity but were careful not to come to close. After all, when hundreds of men are transported like sardines in the hole of a slave ship for weeks on end, the "unpacking" of the slaves was not a particularly pretty sight.

The misery of the slaves did not end with their disembarkation. Despite the fact that they may have been malnourished, ill or dying, they were all herded together and confined in a crowded pen. The misery of the situation was increased by the damp heat and humidity. So horrible was the scene and revolting the conditions that a friend who came with Father Claver once could never face it again, and of Father Sandoval himself it was written in one of the "relations" of his province that, "when he heard a vessel of Negroes was come into port he was at once covered with a cold sweat and a death like pallor at the recollection of the indescribable fatigue and unspeakable work on the previous like occasions. The experience and practice of years never accustomed him to it."

Father Claver would venture into the yards to minister to the huddled masses of slaves. He would take medicines and food, bread, brandy, lemons and tobacco to distribute among the Negroes, some of whom were too frightened, others too ill, to accept them.

"We must speak to them with our hands, before we try to speak to them with our lips," Claver would say. When he came upon any slaves that were dying, he baptized them. During the time that the Africans were confined in the shed, penned so closely that they had to sleep almost upon one another and freely handed on their diseases, St. Peter Claver cared for the bodies of the sick and the souls of all.

Unlike many of his brethren, Claver did not consider that ignorance of the African languages absolved him from the obligation of instructing the Africans in the matters of the Catholic religion. Claver considered it his duty to bring to the abused Africans the consolation of the words of Christ.

Claver employed seven interpreters, one of whom spoke four African dialects. With the aid of his interpreters, Claver prepared the slaves for baptism, not only in groups but also individually. Often Claver would use pictures to get his message across. These pictures usually depicted

Jesus suffering on the cross for the slaves or showed popes, princes and other great Europeans rejoicing at the baptism of an African.

Claver's aim was always to instill in the slaves some degree of self-respect—to give them at least some idea that as redeemed human beings they had dignity and worth, even if as slaves they were outcast and despised. Claver showed the slaves that they were loved even more than they were abused and that the divine love of God must not be outraged by the slaves doing evil deeds.

It is estimated that in forty years St. Peter Claver instructed and baptized over 300,000 slaves. Claver never tired of preaching to the Africans to turn away from sin and he repeatedly urged the slave owners to care for the souls of the slaves.

When the slaves were sent off to the mines and plantations, St. Peter would appeal to them for the last time with renewed earnestness, to not sin. Claver had a steady confidence that God would care for the slaves.

Claver also believed that God would care for the slave owners. Claver did not regard the slave owners as despicable barbarians, beyond the mercy or might of God. Peter believed that slave owners also had souls that needed to be saved. Peter appealed to the slave owners and urged them to exercise physical and spiritual justice with the slaves—for their own sake if not for the sake of the slaves.

Of course, Peter's faith in his fellow human beings would often prove to be unfounded. Thousands of slaves would die in the mines and on the plantations of Colombia. In that respect, Peter was naive.

However, in some respects, Peter's work was ameliorative. It must be stated that while Spanish slavery was a most vile institution, it paled in comparison to the barbarity of the English practice of slavery. At least under the Spanish, the laws of the government and the auspices of the church provided for the marriage of slaves, prohibited the separation (disintegration) of slave families, and protected freed slaves from unjust seizure after liberation. In comparison, the moral indifference of the British (and later the Americans) was simply evil.

As the messenger of the church, Claver did all he could to provide for the observance of the laws. Every spring after Easter, he would make a tour of the plantations near Cartagena in order to see how the Africans were being treated.

Father Claver was not always well received by the slave owners. The slave owners complained that Father Claver wasted the slaves time with his preaching, praying and hymn singing, and when the slaves misbehaved, the owners blamed Father Claver for the slaves' bad behavior. But Father Claver was not deterred, not even when his superiors lent too willing an ear to the complaints of his critics.

Many are the stories of the heroism and of the miraculous powers of Saint Peter Claver concerning his nursing sick and diseased Africans, in circumstances often that no one else, black or white, could face. However, Saint Peter Claver also cared for others besides slaves.

There were two hospitals in Cartagena, one for general cases, served by the Brothers of Saint John-of-God—Saint Sebastian's—and another—Saint Lazarus's—for lepers and for those suffering from the complaint called "Saint Anthony's Fire." Father Peter visited both of these hospitals every week.

Claver also ministered to the traders and travellers who often visited Cartagena. He is credited with having converted an Anglican archdeacon but was less successful with the Muslim Turks and Moors who came to port.

Father Claver was also frequently requested to attend condemned criminals. It is reported that not one prisoner was executed in Cartagena during Claver's lifetime without his being present to console him. Under Claver's guidance, the most hardened and defiant criminals would spend their last hours in prayer and sorrow for their sins.

During his spring forays into the country side, Claver would often refuse the hospitality of the slave owners in order to reside with the slaves.

In 1650, Claver went to preach the jubilee among the slaves, but illness attacked his emaciated and weakened body. He was forced to return to Cartagena. In Cartagena, a virus epidemic was raging through the city. Claver in his weakened state soon contracted the virus. His death was near.

However, after receiving the last rites, Father Peter recovered, but he was never the same. For the rest of his life, pain hardly left him, and a trembling in his limbs made it impossible for him to celebrate Mass.

Father Claver became almost entirely inactive, but would sometimes hear confessions, especially of his dear friend Dona Isabella de Urbina, a generous patron. Occasionally, Father Claver would be carried to a hospital, a condemned prisoner, or some other sick person. Once when a slave ship arrived carrying slaves from an area of Africa which had not been contacted for thirty years, Father Peter became excited and shook off his infirmities. He was carted around until he found an interpreter and then went to the pens to minister to the newly arrived slaves. He baptized the children and gave brief moral instructions to the adults.

As his health declined and his activities became curtailed, the citizens of Cartagena and even his fellow brothers began to forget about him. At times, Father Peter would be left unattended for days on end. The treatment of Father Peter was simply deplorable.

In the summer of 1654, Father Diego Ramirez Farina arrived in Cartagena from Spain with a commission from the King of Spain to work among the slaves. Father Peter was overjoyed and dragged himself from his bed to greet his successor. Shortly afterwards, he heard the confession of his good friend Dona Isabella and told her it was for the last time. On September 6, after assisting at Mass and receiving communion, Father Peter confided to Nicholas Gonzalez, "I am going to die." That same evening, he became very ill and slipped into a coma.

The news of the impending death of the priest spread like wildfire through Cartagena. Suddenly, everyone remembered the saint again. Scores came to kiss his hands before it was too late. Some of the more greedy citizens stripped his meager cell of everything that could be carried off as a relic.

Saint Peter Claver never recovered. He died on September 8, 1654.

After his death, the civil authorities who had looked with disdain at his solicitations amongst the slaves and his fellow clergy who had criticized his zeal, now vied with one another to honor his memory. The city magistrates ordered that he should be buried at the public expense with great pomp, and the vicar general of the diocese officiated at the funeral. The slaves and the Indigenous Americans arranged for a Mass of their own. Father Peter's church was ablaze with lights, a special choir sang, and an oration was delivered which eloquently spoke of the virtues, holiness, heroism, and stupendous miracles of Father Claver.

Saint Peter Claver was never again forgotten and his fame spread throughout the world. He was canonized in 1888 and he was declared by Pope Leo XIII the patron of all missionary enterprises among persons of African descent, in whatever part of the world.

The work performed by Saint Peter Claver is simply unparalleled in the annals of African or African American history. In one way or another, he touched the lives of over 300,000 persons of African descent at a time when they were at their most vulnerable. His greatness cannot be denied and his memory should never be forgotten.

• Sir Richard Francis Burton completed his definitive translation of the collection of tales known as *The Arabian Nights* (1885-1888).

• *Africa:* Johannes Henricus Brand (1823–1888), the president of the Orange Free State, died.

In 1864, while still a British subject working as a barrister, Cape Town, Brand was elected president of the Orange Free State. Brand accepted the office and spent his first term in a prolonged war with the Sokoto king, Moshoeshoe. Peace finally came when the British annexed Lesotho in 1868.

During two subsequent terms of office, Brand contended with internal factions variously demanding annexation to the Cape Colony, merger with the Transvaal, and continued autonomy.

After diamonds were discovered at Kimberley in 1867, Brand waged a bitter and unsuccessful campaign to assert Free State sovereignty over the diamond fields. Eventually, the British put an end to Brand's efforts by annexing the region.

Despite the differences over the Kimberley diamond mines, Brand maintained good relations with the British. One of his diplomatic highlights came when he mediated in the British-Transvaal War of 1881.

1889

THE UNITED STATES

• The following African Americans served in the 51st Congress: Henry Cheatham of North Carolina; Thomas Miller of South Carolina; and John Langston of Virginia.

• In his annual message to Congress, President Benjamin Harrison became the first president since Grant to assert that the federal government had an obligation to protect the free exercise of the ballot — to protect the right to vote.

• Provident Hospital was incorporated in Chicago and began the first training school for African American nurses (January 23).

• President Harrison appointed ex–Senator Blanche K. Bruce Recorder of Deeds for the District of Columbia, a position which Bruce would hold until his retirement in 1893.

• Frederick Douglass was appointed United States Minister to Haiti.

• Senator M. C. Butler of South Carolina introduced a bill to facilitate the migration of African Americans from Southern states. Butler's bill failed to come to a vote.

• African Americans in North Carolina burned President Harrison and his Cabinet in effigy. Out of this protest, a committee was formed to go to Washington, D.C. and to petition the President and the Congress in an effort to address the abandonment of the African American by the Republican Party.

• The Southern Democrats sought to extinguish the Populist movement by utilizing the threat of African American labor against the European American farmer. As Henry Grady, a Georgia Democrat, put it, "There is no room for divided hearts in the South ... the only hope and assurance of the South [is] the clear and unmistakable domination of the white race."

• William Owen Bush was elected to the Washington state legislature.

William Owen Bush (1832–1907) was the son of the pioneer George Washington Bush. William Owen Bush was a master farmer. In 1876, he won a gold medal for his wheat at the 1876 Centennial Exposition in Philadelphia.

• Dr. Daniel Hale Williams was appointed to the Illinois State Board of Health.

• "Nigger Add" (Old Add, Old Negro Ad) became a range boss in the Southwest. Old Add was an exceptional rider and roper. He worked most of his professional life with cattleman George W. Littlefield or his outfits in the Texas Panhandle and eastern New Mexico.

• *Notable Births:* Asa Philip Randolph (1889–1979), a noted labor leader, was born (April 15).

Asa Philip Randolph was born in Crescent City, Florida. During his youth, Randolph worked as a section hand on a railroad. Upon completion of high school, Randolph moved to New York City and attended the City College of New York. It was during his student days that Randolph began his career in labor organizing. While at the City College of New York, Randolph organized a small union of elevator operators.

After college, Randolph edited *The Messenger* and wrote articles for *Opportunity* magazine.

Concerned over the treatment of African American employees on railroads, in 1925, Randolph organized the Brotherhood of Sleeping Car Porters. The Brotherhood of Sleeping Car Porters was the first union of predominantly African American workers to be granted a charter by the American Federation of Labor. After a decade long struggle, this union won recognition as the bargaining agent for the union members employed by the Pullman Company. With this victory, Randolph achieved prominence as the leader of the strongest of the African American labor unions.

In 1935, Randolph was made a member of the Mayor LaGuardia's New York City Commission on Race. A long time supporter of civil rights, Randolph was instrumental in persuading President Franklin Roosevelt to set up the Fair Employment Practices Committee. The creation of this committee led to an end of discrimination in defense industries during World War II. Upon the conclusion of the war, Randolph successfully lobbied for the creation of a permanent Fair Employment Practices Committee.

In 1947, A. Philip Randolph and Grand Reynolds organized the League of Non-Violent Civil Disobedience Against Military Segregation. As a leader of the growing civil rights movement, Randolph led a delegation of African American leaders in conferring with President Truman in March 1948 and told the President that African Americans would refuse to register for the draft if it meant serving in a Jim Crow army. Randolph also informed the Senate Armed Services Committee that he would personally aid draft resisters if the Jim Crow army remained. Randolph was true to his word.

In 1957, Randolph became a vice-president of the American Federation of Labor and Congress of Industrial Organizations (AFL-CIO) and later became a member of the union's executive council.

At the 1959 AFL-CIO convention, Randolph charged organized labor with discrimination. This charge provoked the anger of then labor President George Meany and brought forth a censure of Randolph by the AFL-CIO executive committee.

Also in 1959, Randolph met with more than seventy-five African American union leaders and chaired the National Steering Committee of the Negro American Labor Council (NALC). Randolph would lead this organization until 1963.

A. Philip Randolph was one of the principal organizers of the 1963 March on Washington. This civil rights gathering of over 200,000 was marked in history as the occasion for Martin Luther King's famous "I Have a Dream" speech.

In March of 1964, Randolph and Bayard Rustin led a march by 3,000 on Albany, New York to demand equal civil rights and social reforms from Governor Rockefeller and the New York Legislature.

- *Notable Deaths:* In 1889, 92 African Americans were lynched.
- Jan E. Matzeliger (1852–1889), an African American inventor, died at the young age of 37.

Jan E. Matzeliger was born in Dutch Guiana. Matzeliger came to the United States as a young man and served as a cobbler's apprentice, first in Philadelphia, and later in Lynn, Massachusetts.

Although Matzeliger died at the young age of 37, in his brief life his contributions made a "lasting" impact on the leather industry. Matzeliger's "sole machine" was a profound advancement in the shoemaking business. The sole machine was the first machine of its kind. It was capable of performing all the steps required to hold a shoe on its last, grip and pull the leather down around the heel, guide and drive the nails into place, and then discharge the complete shoe from the machine. This invention essentially automated the shoemaking process enabling shoes to be manufactured in mass.

Matzeliger's patent was bought by the United Shoe Machinery Company of Boston, which made millions on the basis of Matzeliger's invention. The company was soon able to expand. It rapidly grew to include 40 subsidiaries and employed tens of thousands of people in its plants.

- *Miscellaneous State Laws:* Texas enacted a railroad segregation law.
- *Miscellaneous Publications:* Henry McNeal Turner founded *The Southern Christian Recorder.*
- Henry O. Flipper published *The Colored Cadet at West Point.*
- *Scholastic Achievements:* Gaius C. Bolin graduated from Williams College (Massachusetts).
- Monroe Alpheus Majors passed the California state medical boards.

Monroe Alpheus Majors (1864–1960) was an 1886 Meharry College of Medicine graduate. Majors began his medical career in Texas but he was forced to leave Texas due to segregationist pressures which were exacerbated by Majors' efforts in founding the Lone Star State Medical Association. Majors was a Renaissance man. In addition to medicine, he was a newspaper editor (*Los Angeles Western News*), a compiler of an esteemed biographical dictionary (*Noted Negro Women: Their Triumphs and Activities, 1893*), a politician, a poet and a hospital administrator.

- Alfred O. Coffin was awarded a doctorate in biological sciences from Illinois Wesleyan University.
- Addie Hunton graduated from the Spencerian College of Commerce in Philadelphia.
- *The Black Church:* The first meeting of the Catholic Afro-American Lay Congress began on January 1, 1889, in Washington, D.C., under the presidency of William H. Smith. There were five congresses from 1889 to 1894. The most pressing problem for many of the delegates was the sparse number of African American priests. At the time, only one African American priest (Augustine Tolton in 1886) had been ordained since the ordination of the Healy brothers in the 1850s.
- *The Performing Arts:* The Theodore Drury Colored Opera Company began productions in Brooklyn, New York.
- *Black Enterprise:* Hampton Institute in Virginia created the People's Building and Loan Association. Over the next twenty years, the People's Building and Loan Association would loan some $375,000 to African Americans in the Hampton area thereby helping them to acquire 375 houses and lots.
- The Virginia Organization of True Reformers, a African American secret society, founded a bank.
- An African American bank, the Mutual Trust Company, was established in Chattanooga, Tennessee.
- *Sports:* Two African Americans played on the varsity football team at Amherst College. William Tecumseh Sherman Jackson and William Henry Lewis both played with distinction on the Amherst team. Lewis would also later play for the Harvard University team.
- Pike Barnes, an African American jockey, won the Champagne Stakes.
- The Cuban Giants became the first African American professional baseball team.

In 1885, Frank P. Thompson organized a group of waiters and bellmen at the Argyle Hotel on Long Island, New York, to form the Cuban Giants. Four years later, the team joined the Middle States League and became the first African American professional baseball team. The

Cuban Giants finished with a record of 55 wins and 17 losses.

THE AMERICAS

- *Brazil:* The Second Empire of Brazil came to an end.

By the late 1880s, Brazilian slavery had allowed for manumission and freedom through escape was becoming easier to achieve. In Sao Paulo, coffee planters contemplated final abolition as they observed that their slaves were willing to accept labor contracts and as the evident truth finally struck them that European immigration could be achieved only after slavery had been eliminated.

In 1885, sexagenarian slaves were freed, and finally, in 1888, Brazil became the last country in the Western world to abolish slavery entirely.

Had the franchise — the right to vote — been extended, and its free exercise guaranteed, the empire may have survived for a longer period of time than it did. After all, the proclamation abolishing slavery was signed by Princess Isabella, the daughter of the emperor, acting as regent while her father was ill. Isabella immediately became the idol of the emancipated slaves.

However, because the franchise had been restricted by certain "reforms" in 1881, the momentary goodwill and popularity generated by abolition was not enough to save the empire.

The instrument of the demise of the empire was the army. The inevitable cuts in its budget after the war had caused great anguish, which was exacerbated by Emperor Dom Pedro's inability to deal tactfully with an officer class that prided itself on its pridefulness.

Unfortunately, the Duke of Caxias, upon whom the emperor had depended for this chore had died in 1880.

The Republican Party used every opportunity to heighten tensions, and some of its leaders called openly for an army coup to bring about the downfall of the empire.

Many among the ruling elite did not expect the empire to deal effectively with the very rapid social and economic changes of the 1880s. Urban growth, the beginning of mass immigration, the enlargement of the free population of color, and the increase in factory production were all problems which the elite perceived that the empire was unable to adequately cope with. However, while these underlying forces may have been influential, the bottom line was that the an army general of limited political and economic awareness ended the empire on November 15, 1889, when the imperial family was dispatched into exile.

The year 1889 is traditionally considered a turning point in Brazilian history. The abolition of slavery in 1888 resulted in an increase in immigration and in-migration from the countryside to urban centers; the weakening of the old Rio de Janeiro coffee planter oligarchy, and the emergence of a military in alliance with the middle class essentially became preconditions for the proclamation of the republic in 1889.

On November 15, 1889, a military coup supported by small groups of civilian conspirators resulted in the establishment of the Republic.

- Tobias Barreto, an Afro-Brazilian jurist, lawyer, linguist, and poet, died.

Tobias Barreto (1839–1889) was a successful jurist, lawyer, linguist, and poet. A light skinned Afro-Brazilian, Barreto did his best to hide his African heritage in order to gain acceptance into upper-class Euro-Brazilian society. As a result, only one of his poems, *A Escraxidao*, deals with Africans and the subject of slavery.

EUROPE

- Robert Browning (1812–1889), a great Afro-English poet, died (December 12).

Robert Browning was born on May 7, 1812, in Camberwell, England. He was the son of Robert Browning. There were only two children in the Browning family, Robert and his sister, Sarianna. Their mother was part Scotch and part German.

From fourteen to sixteen, Robert expected to compose musical compositions for his life work. However, when, at seventeen, the question of his future was to be decided, Browning inquired as to whether the family income permitted his leading "a life of pure culture." When informed that it did, Browning decided to pursue the life of a poet.

In 1846, Browning was introduced to Elizabeth Barrett, the cloistered invalid whose poems he had so much admired and whom he already loved by description. Eventually, in defiance of her father, she would become his wife.

The story of Elizabeth Barrett Browning and

Robert Browning is one of the great love stories of the world — and of Pan-African history.

Both Elizabeth Barrett Browning and Robert Browning were products of the plantation system of Jamaica of the late 1700s and early 1800s. Edward Barrett, Elizabeth's great-grandfather, was an English planter and slaveowner who owned virtually the entire northwestern part of Jamaica.

Edward Barrett had three children, two sons and a daughter.

The daughter Elizabeth — the great poet's grandmother — married Charles Moulton, the scion of a wealthy shipping family and a free wheeling spirit who was probably of mixed ancestry. It was through Charles Moulton that Elizabeth Barrett Browning believed that she had African blood.

After abandoning his wife and children, Moulton, a rather shadowy figure, is believed to have become a slave trader in New York. He had a number of mistresses (and out of wedlock children), including the woman who became his last wife, Jane Clark, a Jamaican woman who bore him a son.

Robert Browning was a product of the same colonial system and it appears that his grandmother was a COTW.

Like the Barretts, the Brownings profited from slavery. Robert Browning's grandfather married into the Tittle family of St. Kitts, who were themselves great landowners and slaveholders.

The father of Robert Browning, Robert Browning, Sr., was of obvious African ancestry. He was so dark that when he visited his mother's plantation in St. Kitts, the church beadle made him sit with the "coloured people" rather than with the whites.

After he was caught teaching a slave to write, Robert Browning, Sr., was sent home to England and given a position as a bank clerk. Robert, Sr., later renounced his inheritance and was cut out of his family's will.

Like his father, the poet Robert was dark complexioned. The earliest known photograph, taken in 1856, captures his swarthy skin as well as his long, gnarled hair and curly beard. However, probably because his own father had renounced the plantation system and the wealth it brought — Robert Browning showed little concern or shame about having black blood.

In 1846, Browning began a secret courtship with Elizabeth Barrett, already an internationally known poet. Their courtship would produce 574 letters in 20 months as well as *Sonnets*

From the Portuguese, possibly the world's best loved volume of love poetry.

In 1846, Elizabeth Barrett and Robert Browning secretly married in London and then fled to Italy.

In 1849, after miscarriages, Elizabeth finally gave birth to their only child, to her father's first grandchild, Robert Wiedemann Barrett Browning, nicknamed "Penini" or "Penn."

So great was Elizabeth's concern about her lineage that throughout her life she made reference to her dark skin and full lips. In an 1845 letter to the English historical painter Benjamin Robert Haydon, Elizabeth described herself as "little and black."

Elizabeth believed that she had African blood through her grandfather Charles Moulton, and she linked her African heritage as to being "cursed from generation to generation." This sentiment was undoubtedly derived from her father who through his control of his children sought to extinguish the blood line.

The portraits of Elizabeth Barrett Browning which adorn most publications of her works do not evidence her African heritage. But the photographs of her and the descriptions of her provided by contemporaries leave little doubt that African blood flowed through her veins.

Elizabeth's self-described lack of nose, her overgenerous mouth, and her own writings in which she laments the darkness of her skin are evidence of her heritage.

The story of Elizabeth Barrett Browning and Robert Browning is a great love story, but to this day the story remains only half told. The other part of the story which remains to be told is the role that race played in the creative genius that was the mark of these two literary giants. Undoubtedly race impacted their personalities in ways which influenced their writing. Additionally, the similarity in racial heritage between the two presumably influenced the love that they shared for each other.

Finally, race has undoubtedly affected the history that has been written about the Brownings. It is understandable that European historians have wanted the face of genius to be represented by a European face. But the true Genius has given us something more beautiful and something far more eternal. In the story of the Brownings and in their poetry, one finds that through a bond of love, two people — two races — became one.

> I know there shall come a day
> — Is it here on homely earth?

Is it yonder, worlds away,
    Where the strange and new have birth,
That Power comes full in play?

Is it here, with grass about,
    Under befriending trees,
When shy buds venture out,
    And the air by mild degrees
Puts winter's death past doubt?

Is it up amid whirl and roar
    Of the elemental flame
Which star-flecks heaven's dark floor,
    That, new yet still the same,
Full in play comes Power once more?

Somewhere, below, above,
    Shall a day dawn — this, I know —
When Power, which vainly strove
    My weakness to o'erthrow,
Shall triumph, I breathe, I move,

I truly am, at last!
    For a veil is rent between
Me and the truth which passed
    Fitful, half-guessed, half-seen,
Grasped at — not gained, held fast.

I for my race and me
    Shall apprehend life's law:
In the legend of man shall see
    Writ large what small I saw
In my life's tale: both agree.

As the record from youth to age
    Of my own, the single soul —
So the world's wide book: one page
    Deciphered explains the whole
Of our common heritage.

> From *Asolando: Fancies and Facts*
> {Published on December 12, 1889,
> the day of the poet's death}

ASIA

• Sheik Hafiz Wahba (1889–1969) envoy for
Saudi Arabia in England, was born. Sheik
Hafiz Wahba was a journalist and a lawyer.
He became the minister of education for
Saudi Arabia and he served as a counsellor to
King Ibn Saud. In 1945, Sheik Hafiz Wahba
served in the Arabian delegation to the
United Nations Conference in San Fran-
cisco.

AFRICA

By the late 1880s, several European countries
had developed an interest in the economic and
political future of Africa.

The European "scramble for Africa" was well
underway and would soon lead to the large scale
partitioning of the continent along with the
widespread employment of colonialism and
imperialism.

However, one of the other consequences of
this European involvement in Africa was a European commitment to the abolition of the slave
trade.

This period of time also coincided with the
notion that Europeans were bound by the "white
man's burden" which required that European
Christianity be introduced into Africa as a way
of "civilizing" Africans. From these perspectives,
the demand arose that the dehumanizing slave
trade be brought to an end while the glory of
Christian brotherhood was propagated throughout the land.

With these sentiments and perspectives laying
the foundation, the Brussels Conference of 1889
came to be. While the Berlin Conference of
1884–1885 had dealt with the issue of slavery and
the slave trade in only a peripheral way, the
Brussels Conference aimed to put "an end to the
crimes and devastation engendered by the traffic
in African slaves." The result was the ratification, in 1890, of the General Act.

In the General Act, the participatory nations
at the Conference agreed to suppress the slave
trade by controlling the areas in which it originated, by intercepting and freeing slave caravans, and by prohibiting the importation of
slaves into areas controlled by the signatories.

The General Act also sought to suppress the
prevalent use of foreign flags on vessels engaged
in the trade by requiring that all users of foreign
colors prove that they had never been condemned
for slave trading. In order to prevent the transportation of slaves under the guise of African
crewmen, the General Act provided that "a list
of the crew shall be issued to the captain of the
vessel at the port of departure by the authorities
of the power whose color it carries."

The General Act was not immediately effective. It would take ten years before the slave
trade would diminish to the point where it was
no longer an international issue. However, the
General Act was a beginning of international cooperation and agreement on the issue of abolition and it established the worldwide principle
that slavery was not to be condoned anywhere
in the modern world.

• *North Africa, Egypt and Sudan:* al-
Muayyad, a political journal, was founded in
Cairo by Shaikh Ali Yusuf.

• Emin Pasha departed from Equatoria with Henry Stanley's relief mission.

• A budget surplus was restored in Egypt.

• 'Abdallahi's Sudanese army continued a border war with Ethiopia and killed the Ethiopian Emperor Yohannes IV in 1889.

• *Western Africa:* France declared a Protectorate over the Ivory Coast (January 10).

• An Anglo-French convention was convened to discuss the frontiers of Guinea, Sierra Leone, the Gold Coast, and Lagos (Nigeria) (August 10).

• Corraim, the ruler of Ganadu, revolted against the Portuguese.

• Glegle invaded Porto Novo just before he died. Glegle was succeeded by Behanzin.

By the time Behanzin came to power in 1889, the fate of Dahomey was essentially in the hands of Europeans.

Behanzin succeeded his father, Glegle, who ruled a powerful, centralized monarchy, but who could not resist the increasing French encroachment. Glegle died in 1889, possibly of suicide. It is theorized that Glegle did not want to negotiate with the French who had taken over the Dahomean port of Cotonou.

Behanzin adopted as his insignia the head of a shark. This symbol was adopted to indicate that he did not intend to let the Europeans penetrate his kingdom. Behanzin displayed his power by raiding the Egba for slaves in 1890. Some of these slaves were sacrificed at the funeral ceremonies for Behanzin's father, Glegle.

• Major MacDonald, the Special Commissioner, investigated allegations against the Royal Niger Company.

• Lieutenant Mizon entered the mouth of the River Niger with a French warship. Hostilities with local Africans ensued.

• Final pacification of the River Niger occurred at Opobo.

In 1889, the British denied Nana Olumu, the Itsekiri leader, of his claim to authority over the neighboring Ijo people, despite the British having earlier used that claim as their basis for extending their "protection" to the Ijo. When Nana continued to resist British encroachment, they viewed it as a selfish attempt to protect his personal trade monopoly. Eventually, the British came to see Nana as standing in the way of their goal of increased economic and political control of the western Niger delta.

• An Anglo-French agreement was reached concerning the boundary of Dahomey with Nigeria.

By 1889, the threat to the French posed by Lat Dior and Samori Toure had been dissipated. The French ended the truce that they had maintained with Ahmadu ibn 'Umar Tall of the Tukolor Empire. The French resumed hostilities.

The French captured Kaarta, Segu, and Jenne. Ahmadu was forced to flee to Macina and to negotiate an alliance with the Macina rulers. However, for all intents and purposes, the Tukolor Empire (of today's Guinea, Mali, Mauritania and Senegal) had come to an end.

• Glele (also Glegle or Gle-Gle), the great ruler of the Aja kingdom of Dahomey, died.

By the beginning of the 1800s, Dahomey had fallen on hard times. However, during the reign of Gezo, Glele's predecessor, Dahomey began to revive.

The revival would blossom into a full blown renaissance once Glele ascended to the throne. During Glele's lifetime, Dahomey would win a number of impressive military victories against its neighbors, most notably the state of Ketu in 1883 and 1886. Glele also tried to take Abeokuta, but — like his predecessor, Gezo — failed.

Glele continued Gezo's policy of supplementing slave exports with palm oil but revenue from palm products was never as profitable. Glele also continued his predecessor's administrative, economic, and agricultural reforms as well as those which he initiated on his own.

Glele's control over Dahomey's destiny dwindled as the state's wealth declined and Europeans encroached from the coast. It was probably for this reason that Glele isolated his seat of government far inland at Abomey where Europeans could not easily reach him.

Glele's barbarous displays of human sacrifice before European visitors also contributed to a hesitance by Europeans to venture into Glele's land. However, displays of barbarity were only temporary deterrents. Ultimately, the Europeans overcame their horror to intervene in the affairs of Dahomey.

Dahomey became a victim of British-French rivalry on the coast. The French first proclaimed a protectorate over Dahomey's port of Cotonou in 1878. At first, Glele ignored the protectorate, but years later the French sent a negotiator, Bayol, to discuss revenue payments which the French demanded that Glele pay.

By the time that Bayol arrived in Dahomey,

Glele was dead. It is said that he poisoned himself rather than admit that his once great kingdom had become subjugated to France.

• *Central Africa:* An eclipse was observed during the coronation of Mibambwe IV Rutarinda of Rwanda (December 22).

• Leopold II declared all "vacant" land in the Congo state property.

• The first hospital was built at Boma.

• Simon Kimbangu (1889–1951), the founder of one of the largest religious movements in modern Africa, was born.

Simon Kimbangu was educated at a mission of the Baptist Missionary Society. He was baptized in 1915 and he worked for the Mission as a teacher and evangelist.

Kimbangu later went as a migrant laborer to Leopoldville (Kinshasa). He returned to his home at N'Kamba in 1921.

In response to what he regarded as divine compulsion, Kimbangu embarked on a mission of healing and preaching. This mission would become a mass revival.

Anti–European feeling on the part of many Kongo found an outlet in the movement, and the Baptist missionaries were divided over the part Kimbangu was playing. Kimbangu's ministry lasted from April to September 1921.

Kimbangu continued to heal people and to teach against witchcraft and sorcery. As he attracted ever-increasing crowds, the Belgian administration became alarmed. In September of 1921, Kimbangu was arrested, tried for sedition and on October 3 sentenced to death. However, the death sentence was commuted and he was flogged and then imprisoned in the eastern Congo where he would remain for the rest of his life.

During his trial, Kimbangu consciously patterned his behavior after that of Christ during his passion. The martyr image Kimbangu created became idealized during the long imprisonment which cut him off from communication from his followers. Continued Belgian persecution of Kimbangu's adherents gave tangible support to the anti–European teachings of the Kimbanguists, and the movement flourished as an underground church.

Some erstwhile adherents, such as Simon-Pierre Mpadi, established their own churches, but all emphasized the symbolic leadership of Kimbangu.

Kimbangu also became a symbol of Kongo political separatism in western Zaire, northern Angola and the French Congo—an idea later taken up by Kasavubu *(see 1910).*

Before Kimbangu entered prison in 1921, he is said to have predicted that his youngest son Joseph Diangienda would become his successor. During the 1950s, Diangienda reunited various Kimbanguist groups under his own leadership and established the Church of Jesus Christ on Earth through the prophet Simon Kimbangu (EJCSK). When the Belgian government granted sudden independence to the Congo in 1960, the ban on Kimbanguism was lifted and the EJCSK emerged as a national church.

Under Diangienda's leadership the church's membership grew. As of 1986, the church claimed about three million adherents. In 1969, the EJCSK became the first independent African church to attain full membership in the World Council of Churches.

• *Eastern Africa:* A Russian military expedition settled in at Sagallo (January 18). But, on February 17, after a brief skirmish, the Russians surrendered to the French and, by March, the expedition had returned to Russia.

• Yohannes IV was killed in the battle of Metemna (March 10). Menelik proclaimed himself Emperor of Ethiopia. On May 2, Italy and Menelik signed the Treaty of Ucciali. Italy claimed this document created an Italian protectorate over Ethiopia.

In 1889, Yohannes, the Emperor of Ethiopia, died while fighting the Mahdists in the west. The death of Yohannes created a power vacuum which Menelik, the former King of Shoa, quickly sought to fill. Menelik had himself proclaimed the *negus nagast* — the emperor. Menelik then signed a friendship pact with the Italians known as the Treaty of Ucciali (Wichale).

The Treaty of Ucciali was a controversial document because it existed in two radically different versions. One version was in Amharic while the other was in Italian.

According to the Amharic version, Italy merely offered its services as Ethiopia's diplomatic intermediary with the outside world. However, pursuant to the Italian version, Menelik recognized an Italian protectorate over Ethiopia. The irreconcilable difference between the two documents led to an Italian invasion of Ethiopia in 1895.

Taitu, the wife of Menelik, was instrumental in Menelik's rise to the imperial throne. Taitu married Menelik (who was then King of Shoa) in 1883 after several previous marriages and liaisons. Taitu's associations with other powerful men gave her valuable political experience which she used to assist Menelik in his rise to the Ethiopian emperorship in 1889.

• Italians made a treaty of protection with the Sultan of Obbia, Somalia.

• Italians occupied Asmara (August 3).

• An Italian treaty of friendship and trade was signed with Shoa.

• Kabaka Mwanga of Buganda was deposed (September 6). He was succeeded by Kiwewa.

• Muslims expelled all Christian missionaries from Buganda (October 18). Kiwewa was deposed. He was succeeded by the Muslim Kabaka Kalema. The country was antagonized by compulsory circumcision.

• Kagwa re-entered the kingdom at the head of the Christian faction and helped to replace Mwanga on the throne. For this service, Kagwa was rewarded with the office of Katikiro — prime minister — of the Ganda kingdom.

• Religious freedom was restored to Muslims in Ethiopia.

• Abushiri was executed.

Abushiri bin Salimu bin Abushiri al-Harthi was a leader of the coastal resistance movement against German occupation.

Abushiri was the son of an African mother and Arab father. His father was a member of one of the oldest Arab families in East Africa.

As a young man, Abushiri organized and led trade caravans from the coast to Lake Tanganyika. The principal commodities that he traded for were ivory and slaves.

By the 1870s, Abushiri was operating a sugar plantation near Pangani. On this plantation, Abushiri commanded thousands of free men and slaves.

During the late 1870s, Abushiri led a division of the Zanzibari ruler Barghash's troops against the Nyamwezi chief Mirambo. However, while acting in this capacity, Abushiri never recognized Zanzibar's sovereignty over the mainland.

In 1882, Abushiri repelled a force sent by Barghash to punish him for defaulting on some commercial loans. The defeat suffered by Barghash at the hands of Abushiri dissuaded Barghash from attempting to administer the mainland region.

German interest in mainland Tanzania began in 1884. In 1885, Barghash virtually ceded the coast to the Germans — a move not recognized by Abushiri and other coastal peoples — other Swahili. In mid-1888, the Germans occupied the coastal towns and attempted to collect customs

duties. Faced with economic ruin, Abushiri and other Swahili townsmen spontaneously drove the Germans away.

The Germans then launched a counter-offensive under Hermann von Wissmann. Over the next year, Abushiri rallied the Swahili between Pangani and Dar es Salaam and waged a see-saw war with the Germans.

Eventually, Abushiri's support began to wane as his followers tired of German naval bombardment and costly battles. Additionally, his followers had become suspicious of Abushiri's own political motives.

By December of 1889, Abushiri was a lone fugitive. He attempted to flee north to join forces with the Zigua leader Bwana Heri, but was captured.

Abushiri was subsequently executed.

• In 1889, Frederick Lugard was hired by the Imperial British East Africa company to explore the Kenyan interior.

• Mbatian (c.1820–1889), a Masai religious and military leader, died.

Mbatian was the son of Supet. From Supet, Mbatian inherited the office of laibon — ritual leader — among a branch of the pastoral Masai. During the early 1870s, the various independent pastoral Masai groups were threatened by a major invasion by their agricultural kinsmen, the Kwavi. Mbatian united these groups and directed a successful military campaign to drive the invaders away. The pastoral Masai did not remain united, but Mbatian continued to be recognized as their greatest laibon until his death in 1889. Afterwards his sons quarrelled over succession to the office of laibon. These quarrels severely weakened Masai resistance to the impending European occupation of east Africa.

• Yohannes IV (c.1839–1889), the Emperor of Ethiopia, died.

As Ras Kassa, Yohannes first came into prominence when he declared the Tigre province of northern Ethiopia independent of Emperor Tewodros II (Theodore II) in 1867. The next year, Yohannes assisted the British expeditionary force under Robert Napier to march against Tewodros. Napier was successful, and on his return march he rewarded Kassa with a large supply of firearms and ammunition.

Tewodros committed suicide and Kassa's new weapons gave his army a considerable advantage in the ensuing struggle for the vacant imperial throne.

The first claimant to Tewodros' throne was the ruler of Lasta — an heir to the old Zagwe dynasty of Lalibela — who had himself crowned as Takle Giorgis III. When Takle moved against the Tigre province in 1872, Kassa crushed his army and seized the throne. Kassa had himself crowned emperor (negus nagast) at Axum and took the imperial name Yohannes (John) IV.

As emperor, Yohannes worked to restore the unity briefly achieved by Tewodros. Unlike Tewodros, however, Yohannes made fewer demands on his subject rulers, who resembled feudal lords. A devout Christian, Yohannes flirted with the idea of forcing the country's many Muslims to convert to Christianity. However, Yohannes abandoned this policy so as not to jeopardize national unification.

The deceptively easy success of Napier's expedition against Tewodros in 1868 invited further foreign invasions. Under the Khedive Ismail, the resurgent Egyptian state expanded into Sudan and down the Red Sea. The Egyptians tried to invade Ethiopia in 1875 and 1876, but Yohannes' army crushed each attempt, forcing the Egyptians to withdraw permanently.

In 1878, Yohannes obtained the submission of his main Ethiopian rival, Menelik II, then king of Shoa. In return for Shoa's support, Yohannes granted Menelik considerable autonomy and promised him his own crown on his death. Revolts continued to arise in other provinces, but generally Yohannes' position was stronger than that enjoyed by any previous nineteenth century Ethiopian emperor.

The 1880s introduced new dangers: the Mahdist revolution in Sudan and European imperialist expansion. The British had taken over the administration of Egypt in 1882. Alarmed by the Mahdist threat, the British signed a treaty of alliance with Yohannes in 1884 whereby his boundary with Sudan was adjusted.

A desultory Mahdist-Ethiopian border war ensued. Meanwhile, the Italians occupied Massawa in 1885 and prepared to expand inland. Yohannes' forces smashed the Italians at Dogali in 1887. However, increased Mahdist incursions forced him to turn his attention west again.

Yohannes mobilized almost his entire country against the Mahdists and personally led the counterattack early in 1889. He was on the verge of a major victory at Gallabat, but died from chance wounds. His demoralized army crumbled.

Afterwards, the war returned to border skirmishing and Menelik assumed the throne.

- *Southern Africa:* De Beers Consolidated Mines was formed (March).
- H. H. Johnston took up duties as Consul for Mozambique (May).
- The British South African Company under Cecil Rhodes was given a charter extending its territory at the expense of the Transvaal (October 29).
- A British Protectorate of Nyasaland was proclaimed (December).

In 1889, Henry Hamilton Johnston became the British consul in Mozambique. His charge was to subdue the slave trade around Lake Nyasa. At the same time, Johnston served as an agent for the British South Africa Company of Cecil Rhodes. As the BSA Company agent, Johnston negotiated treaties with chiefs between Lake Nyasa and Lake Tanganyika.

When the Portuguese agent Serpa Pinto showed an interest in Nyasaland (Malawi), Johnston declared it a British protectorate to forestall foreign occupation. Johnston was then made the first commissioner and consul-general over British Central Africa (Malawi). However, he was given rather meager resources to establish an administration.

Operating with a handful of Indian soldiers, Johnston fought and largely subdued Arab and Yao slavers in southern Malawi before turning his attention to the north. Johnston's efforts to bring the country under British control were largely successful, although he left the task of confronting the Ngoni kingdoms to his successor, Alfred Sharpe.

- H. H. Johnson made a treaty with Nyasaland chiefs.
- L. S. Jameson made treaties in Mashonaland.
- Salisbury (Zimbabwe) was founded.
- A truce was reached with the Arabs at Karonga.
- Britain declared the Makololo country and the Shire hills as part of its protectorate.
- Witwatersrand Chamber of Mines was formed.
- Between 1889 and 1918, some seventy-six Ethiopian (Coptic) churches were established in South Africa.
- In Bechuanaland, Bathoen succeeded his father Gaseitsiwe after having been the effective ruler of the Ngwaketse for almost a decade.

The Ngwaketse branch of the Tswana separated from the Kwena branch in the 1600s.

Settling in the southeast of the country which is today Botswana, the Ngwaketse, remained independent until 1885 when the British Bechuanaland Protectorate was declared over Botswana.

• The Gaza migrated to southern Mozambique.

In order to avoid de Sousa and the encroaching Portuguese, along with needing to re-establish Gaza control in the south, Gungunyane, the king of the Gaza, moved his people from the Manica highlands to near the mouth of the Limpopo River. This migration of about sixty thousand people had a tremendous impact on the entire region. The consequential economic dislocation left Gaza extremely weak.

• Bhunu became the ruler of Swaziland.

Due to his youth at the time of his ascension to the throne, Bhunu's reign began with the assistance of regents. By the time of his ascension, Bhunu's father, Mbandzeni, had sold almost all of Swaziland's economic resources to European concession hunters.

After Bhunu became king, the neighboring Transvaal Republic bought up most of the Swaziland concessions to establish a legal basis for annexing Swaziland in its drive to expand to a sea port. Bhunu and his regents worked futilely to regain control of their rights, but then quietly acquiesced while the Transvaal imposed its administration on Swaziland with British consent in 1895.

• Jan Jonker Afrikaner died.

The Afrikaner family was a prominent Oorlam Khoikhoi family of southwest Africa in what today is Namibia. The Afrikaners, the Witbooi, and other Khoikhoi families migrated from the Cape Colony into what is today Namibia early in the 1800s. Mostly Dutch speaking, the Afrikaner family introduced European culture into southwest Africa. The heads of these families were usually officially recognized by the Cape colonial government as chiefs.

Jan Jonker Afrikaner (c.1823–1889) became the Oorlam chief in 1863 when his brother Christiaan was killed in a war with the Herero. Jan had received some education from Rhemish missionaries during the 1840s. He became a close friend of the future Herero chief Mahehero.

Jan Afrikaner wanted to live at peace with the neighboring Herero. However, he found that the fundamental differences between the Oorlam and Herero over land rights prevented peace.

In 1863, Mahehero became the chief of his people. Soon thereafter, Mahehero launched a bitter seven year war to assert Herero independence from the Khoikhoi.

When a truce between the Herero and the Oorlam (Khoikhoi) was settled in 1870, Jan Afrikaner, found that the Oorlam had lost much of their power in central Namibia.

In 1880, hostilities between the Herero and the Oorlam (Khoikhoi) broke out again. Jan Afrikaner allied himself with another Khoikhoi chief, Moses Witbooi, against the Herero. However, by this time, the Herero were more united and much stronger. Some costly battles ensued. The position of Jan Afrikaner and his Oorlam became tenuous.

In 1885, Jan Afrikaner ceded territory to the Germans who were, at that time, expanding into southwest Africa. The following year, the lands of the Oorlam were made part of a German protectorate.

The German protectorate did not protect the Oorlam. The Germans failed to give Jan Afrikaner the military support he needed against the Herero, and, at the same time, the alliance with the Witbooi dissolved.

After a battle with the Witbooi in 1889, Jan Afrikaner was shot and killed by one of his own sons. Afterwards the people of Jan Afrikaner — the Oorlam — dissipated into other groups.

• Gaseitsiwe (c.1820–1889), the Ngwaketse chief and unifier, died.

During Gaseitsiwe's youth, his uncle, Sebego, usurped the throne and split the Ngwaketse into two groups. Gaseitsiwe eventually left Sebego to join another uncle, Segotshane, and the dissident Ngwaketse in the western Transvaal.

Around 1844, Gaseitsiwe returned to the Ngwaketse center at Kanye in southeastern Botswana and drove Sebego out, assuming the role of chief for himself.

Gaseitsiwe continued to fight a desultory war with Sebego's son, Senthufi. Gaseitsiwe finally defeated Senthufi in 1857.

Noted for his tact, Gaseitsiwe allowed the dissidents to return to Kanye two years later. By doing so, Gaseitsiwe permanently restored Ngwaketse unity.

The main problems of Gaseitsiwe's reign were boundary disputes with neighbors after the dislocations of the Mfecane wars of the 1820s and 1830s. Most of these disputes were finally resolved in 1885 when the British Bechuanaland Protectorate was proclaimed over Botswana.

• Langalibalele (c.1818–1889), a hero of African resistance to European rule in southern Africa, died.

Langalibalele was the hereditary ruler of a section of the Hlubi people. The Hlubi people had been scattered by the Mfecane wars during the 1820s while under Mpangazitha.

In 1845, Langalibalele returned his people to their original home in Zululand but was soon driven south into Natal by the Zulu king Mpande.

Theophilus Shepstone, the Secretary for Native Affairs in the fledgling British colony, got Langalibalele to settle at a location high in the Drakensberg Mountains. In the Drakensberg Mountains, Langalibalele's following grew to about 10,000 people. Langalibalele earned a reputation as a great rain-maker among his Sotho and Nguni neighbors.

After the discovery of diamonds in 1870, many Hlubi worked at the new Kimberley mines and used their earnings to buy guns. Shepstone feared Langalibalele was becoming a threat to the tiny European population of Natal. Shepstone ordered the Hlubi to register their guns. The Hlubi refused. To add to Shepstone's concerns, Langalibalele ignored Shepstone's repeated summonses to appear.

The Europeans panicked. Fearing the influence that Langalibalele's defiance would have upon other African groups, Shepstone mounted a strong invasion force. Langalibalele fled into Lesotho with many followers.

In Lesotho, a Sotho sub-chief, Molapo, offered Langalibalele protection. However, as the British forces pillaged Hlubi country, Molapo was persuaded to help arrest Langalibele in return for a share in the booty.

Langalibalele was then captured and taken to Pietermaritzburg, where he was given a sham trial for murder, rebellion and treason. Langalibalele was sent to prison on Robben Island, but due to the intervention of Bishop Colenso, the conditions of his exile were ameliorated. After thirteen years, Langalibalele returned to Zululand.

• Lotshe, the Ndebele military commander, died.

Lotshe rose to prominence during the last years of the reign of king Mzilikazi *(see 1868)*. In 1869, Lotshe led an Ndebele delegation to Natal to investigate the disappearance of the royal heir Nkulumane. Satisfied that the missing heir had long since died, Lotshe returned to Ndebele country (Matabeleland) to support Lobengula's elevation to the kingship.

When civil war erupted in 1870, Lotshe remained loyal to Lobengula *(see 1894)*. For this loyalty, Lotshe was rewarded with promotions within the officer corps of the powerful Ndebele army.

The civil war of 1870 was Lobengula's last personal participation in fighting. Thereafter, Lobengula satisfied the inherently aggressive impulse of the military system built by his father Mzilikazi by launching regular cattle raids. Lobengula directed these raids mainly against the Shona to his north and east, but he also raided western Zambia and Botswana.

Many of the military advantages Mzilikazi had enjoyed were lost as the Ndebele failed to keep pace with their neighbors development in tactics, weaponry and use of horses. Accordingly, over time, the Ndebele raids became progressively less successful as potential victims retreated to natural strongholds and obtained firearms to defend them. Lobengula had to send his army on increasingly distant and risky campaigns.

In 1885, Lobengula dispatched Lotshe on a campaign against the Tawana at Lake Ngami, six hundred and forty kilometers to the west. The campaign was a disaster. As a result, the morale of the Ndebele army became extremely low.

Having experienced the debacle against the Tawana, Lotshe became a leading advocate of peaceful accommodation with Europeans who were then clamoring to enter Zimbabwe. Lotshe advised Lobengula to sign the concession treaty offered by Charles Rudd on behalf of Cecil Rhodes in 1888. When it was discovered that the Europeans had grossly misrepresented the terms of this document, Lotshe became the scapegoat.

In 1889, Lotshe was executed and his entire family was massacred.

• Mbandzeni (c.1857–1889), the Swazi king, died.

Mbandzeni succeeded his father Mswati as king in 1874 after a long and bitter succession dispute. Mbandzeni first attempted to continue his father's policy of allying with the Transvaal Republic against the Zulu kingdom, but later found his position largely dictated by the Anglo-Afrikaner struggle for mastery in South Africa.

Mbandzeni assisted the Transvaal — which was administered by the British from 1877 to 1881 — to fight with Pedi chief Sekhukhune and was rewarded with two Anglo-Afrikaner treaties which "guaranteed" Swazi independence. Nevertheless, despite these treaties, European infiltration into Swaziland intensified, especially after the discovery of gold in 1882.

During the last five years of his life, Mbandzeni signed almost four hundred concessions granting Europeans practically every conceivable economic privilege.

Mbandzeni turned to the former British agent in Natal, Theophilus Shepstone, for help in dealing with Europeans. Shepstone sent Mbandzeni his own son, Theophilus ("Offy") Shepstone, Jr. to serve as an official Swazi adviser in 1887.

The younger Shepstone enriched himself at Swazi expense and advised Mbandzeni to sign one final, all encompassing concession in 1889. This final concession granted Europeans almost total financial control of the kingdom in return for 12,000 pounds per year. Mbandzeni died soon afterwards. At the time of his death, his country was controlled by concessionaires. Mbandzeni was succeeded by Bhunu.

RELATED HISTORICAL EVENTS

• *The United States:* Oklahoma was opened to settlement by non–Indigenous (non–Indian) Americans.

• *The Americas:* In Brazil, the Republic of Brazil was proclaimed (November 15).

• *Europe:* The International Colonial Congress met in Paris (July).

• The Colonial Conference convened in Brussels (November 18).

• The British South Africa Company was incorporated with powers in all southern Africa north of Bechuanaland.

• Louis L. Faidherbe (1818–1889), a former governor of Senegal, died.

After an undistinguished early military career, Louis Faidherbe went to Senegal in 1852. Two years after his arrival in Senegal, Faidherbe became governor.

Upon becoming governor, Faidherbe's immediate concerns were to secure France's position vis-à-vis the neighboring state of Walo, to subdue the Trarza Moors, and, most importantly, to forestall the threat of invasion posed by the Tukolor revolutionary al-Hajj 'Umar.

During his tenure as governor, Faidherbe succeeded in winning the respect of the Africans. This success was due, in no small measure, to Faidherbe's liberal attitude towards Islam. Faidherbe's success in Senegal enhanced France's reputation and influence northward through Mauritania and southward to Futa Jalon.

In 1860, Faidherbe came to terms with the Tukolor ruler 'Umar. The European imperialist and the African empire builder, demarcated their respective spheres of influence.

Within Senegal, Faidherbe presided over the cultural renaissance of Saint Louis. Faidherbe also encouraged the study of African culture and laid the foundation for the construction of the port of Dakar.

Faidherbe established an African (Senegalese) army, the renown *Tirailleurs Senegalais.* Faidherbe's plan for French control of the western Sudan by peaceful expansion was abandoned upon his retirement in 1865. Instead the French would pursue a far more aggressive — far more militaristic — posture towards the western Sudan in the years that followed.

---

1 8 9 0

THE UNITED STATES

In 1890, there were 7,488,676 African Americans reported to be living in the United States by the United States Census. This number represented 11.9% of the total population of the United States.

Of all the African Americans living in the United States, it was estimated that some 92.5% of them were born in the South. While overwhelmingly large, this percentage represented a decrease from the 93.3% of Southern born African Americans reported in 1880 and the 93.4% of Southern born African Americans reported in 1870.

Of the total number of African Americans, some 15.2% were reported to be COTWs — people of mixed (interracial) heritage. This number was up from the 12% COTW composition reported in 1870.

The death rate for African Americans was 32.4% as compared to 20.2% for European Americans.

The net intercensal migration for African American males between the ages of 15 and 34 for the decade between 1880 and 1890 was as follows:

Alabama	-8.8%
Georgia	+2.9%
Mississippi	-4.1%
Illinois	+28.7%
New York	+32.1%

In simpler terms, the census indicated that between 1880 and 1890, 9 out of every 100 African American males living in Alabama in 1880 left the state by 1890. Whereas, in New York, for every 100 African American males living in the state in 1880 another 32 African American males were added by 1890.

In 1890, the African American population for

the City of New York stood at about 23,000 while the African American population for the City of Chicago, Illinois stood at 14,800. The African American population of Chicago doubled between 1880 and 1890.

Of the Southern African American population, 18.7% attended school, compared with 13.07% in 1880 and 3.07% in 1870.

- In June, Representative Henry Cabot Lodge of Massachusetts introduced a bill for the Federal supervision of national elections. Lodge's bill authorized the appointment of Federal supervisors representing both parties if a specified number of voters petitioned for it. These supervisors were to have the power to judge the qualifications of voters and place in the ballot boxes ballots that had been wrongfully refused by local officials. The bill passed in the House of Representatives by a vote of 155 to 149. Senator Hoar of Massachusetts introduced a similar bill in the Senate but Hoar's bill was set aside and was not acted on.

In later sessions of Congress, an alliance between southern Democrats and Silver Republicans prevented Lodge's bill from being considered. By the election of 1892, the Democratic national platform officially denounced the election bill. African Americans in the South continued to suffer discrimination and intimidation at the ballot box until the late 1960s after the passage of the Voting Rights Act of 1965.

- In December, Senator Dolph of Oregon introduced a resolution to investigate elections and to ensure that the 14th and 15th Amendments were not being violated. This resolution was buried in committee.
- In Louisiana, there were 16 African American members of the Louisiana General Assembly.
- Ben Tillman was elected Governor of South Carolina through the support of impoverished European Americans. Surprisingly, Tillman, a renowned demagogic hater of African Americans, received the support of the National Colored Farmer's Alliance.
- By 1890 Timothy Thomas Fortune's Afro-American League had representatives in 21 states.

Timothy Thomas Fortune was an advocate of full equality for African Americans. In 1887, he formed the Afro-American League which worked for full civil rights for African Americans, including the right to vote, an anti-lynching bill and the equitable distribution of school funds.

In 1890, the National Afro-American League convened in Chicago and elected Joseph C. Price as its first president.

- Minnie Cox was appointed postmistress for the town of Indianola, Mississippi.
- *The Labor Movement:* In 1890, the African American membership in labor unions was as follows: 200 were in the barbers' union; 50 were brick and clayworkers; 1,500 were longshoremen; 33 were painters, decorators, and paperhangers; 1,500 were tobacco workers.
- In the Black Belt counties of southern Virginia, African American laborers were so numerous that wages averaged only $10 per month.
- The AFL (American Federation of Labor) passed a convention resolution which voiced disapproval of unions that denied membership on the basis of race.

In 1865, an estimated 100,000 of the 120,000 artisans in the South were African Americans. However, by 1890, the skilled African American worker had been eliminated as competition for Southern European Americans and European Immigrants.

- *Notable Births:* Palmer C. Hayden, an artist, was born in Tidewater, Virginia (January 15).
- Mordecai W. Johnson, Howard University's first African American president, was born in Paris, Tennessee (January 12).
- Claude McKay (1890–1948), a poet, novelist and major force in the Harlem Renaissance, was born (September 15).

Claude McKay was born in Jamaica. McKay came to the United States in 1913, having already published two books of poetry, *Songs of Jamaica* (1911) and *Constab Ballads.*

McKay studied at Tuskegee Institute and Kansas State before moving to New York City and devoting himself to poetry. McKay was an associate editor of the *Liberator* and a major figure in the Harlem Renaissance.

McKay's poetical works include *Harlem Shadows* (1922); *Selected Poems* (1953); and *Songs in New Hampshire* (1920).

McKay's prose works include the novels, *Home to Harlem* (1927); *Banjo* (1929); *Banana Bottom* (1933); and his autobiography, *A Long Way From Home* (1937).

- Nancy Elizabeth Prophet, a sculptor, was born in Rhode Island (March 19).
- The banjoist, Johnny St. Cyr, was born (April 17).

• *Notable Deaths:* There were 85 African Americans lynched in 1890.
• Alexander Thomas Augusta (1825–1890), the first African American surgeon in the United States Army, died.

Alexander T. Augusta was born a free person in Virginia. After serving a medical apprenticeship in Philadelphia, Augusta went to Trinity Medical College in Toronto, Canada, where he graduated in 1856.

In 1863, Augusta joined the Union forces and was commissioned with the initial rank of major but was soon promoted to lieutenant colonel.

In 1865, Augusta became the director of the newly created Freedman's Hospital which was located on the grounds of Howard University.

In 1868, Augusta became a demonstrator of anatomy at Howard University Medical School and, in 1869, Augusta received an honorary degree from Howard University.

• Edmonia Lewis (1845–1890), the noted Afro-Chippewa sculptress, died.

In 1890, Wildfire died. The world knew Wildfire as Edmonia Lewis, the African American sculptor, but the people who raised and nurtured her knew her as Wildfire.

Wildfire was the daughter of a Chippewa mother and an African American father. She was born near Albany, New York, in 1845.

Wildfire's mother died when she was only three years old. After her mother's death, Wildfire lived with her Chippewa aunts in upstate New York, making baskets and embroidering moccasins. During her time among the Chippewa, she was known by her Chippewa name — she was known as "Wildfire."

From 1860 to 1862, with money given to her by her brother, "Sunrise," Edmonia Lewis attended Oberlin College. It was at Oberlin that her interest in sculpting began.

While at Oberlin, Lewis was accused of attempting to poison two European American acquaintances. In a well-publicized trial, she won an acquittal.

Lewis left Oberlin for Boston where she soon frequented abolitionist circles. In 1865, she was introduced to William Lloyd Garrison, the noted abolitionist. While in Boston she received a number of commissions to do busts of prominent people.

In 1870, the Story family of Boston sent Lewis to Italy to study. She was to remain in Europe for most of the remainder of her life.

Like Robert Bannister, Edmonia Lewis had a successful showing at the Philadelphia Centennial Exposition in 1876. Her *Death of Cleopatra* drew critical praise as "the grandest statue in the exposition." The statue weighed over two tons and stood over twelve feet tall.

Among Lewis' other notable sculptures were *The Marriage of Hiawatha, The Madonna with Infant* and *Forever, Free.* Lewis' portrait busts done in Roman classical style include busts of Lincoln, Longfellow, John Brown, Charles Sumner and William Story.

A century after her death, the sculpture of Edmonia Lewis began to be re-noticed. As the world came to once again pay attention to her art, she was touted as a great example of African American artistry. But she was not simply an African American.

In so many ways, Edmonia Lewis was also a Chippewa, and in remembering her art we would do well to remember the red soul that resided within the black skin.

• *Miscellaneous State Laws:* In August, the Mississippi Constitutional Convention met to re-write the 1868 Reconstruction Constitution. Of the 133 delegates, only one was an African American, Isaiah Montgomery. At this time, African Americans represented 56.9% of the population of the State of Mississippi. On October 22, the convention decided that it was unnecessary to submit the Constitution to the electorate. On November 1, 1890, the Mississippi Constitution was approved. A suffrage amendment in the new Constitution imposed a poll tax of $2 on voters, barred voters convicted of bribery, burglary, theft, arson, perjury, murder, or bigamy. The Mississippi Constitution also barred from voting any person who could not read, understand or interpret a given section of the State Constitution. This "Mississippi Plan" would soon be adopted by other southern states.

Miscellaneous Cases

In the two decades stretching from 1890 to 1910, a total of 528 cases were brought before the United States Supreme Court which involved the 14th Amendment. Of these 528 cases, only 19 would actually involve an application of the Amendment to the securing of civil rights for African Americans.

• In *Louisville, New Orleans and Texas Railroad v. Mississippi* (March 3, 1890) 133 U.S. 587, 10 S.Ct. 348, the United States Supreme Court ruled that a Mississippi state statute which provided for segregation on the railroads within the state was constitutional. The Mississippi statute provided that "all railroads carrying passengers in this state, other than street railroads, shall provide equal, but separate, accommodation for the [European American and African American passengers], by providing two or more passenger-cars for each passenger train, or by dividing the passenger cars by a partition so as to secure separate accommodations."

• In *In re Green* (March 3, 1890) 134 U.S. 377, 10 S.Ct. 586, the United States Supreme Court held that electors for President and Vice-President are state officers who are appointed by the state in such manner as the state legislature may direct and that it is within the exclusive jurisdiction of the state to punish all fraudulent voting for such electors. The effect of this decision was to make possible the disenfranchisement of African Americans in Presidential elections because the Southern legislatures prevented African Americans from exercising their right to vote.

• *Miscellaneous Publications:* John Wesley Gaines published *African Methodism in the South.*

• Octavia Victoria Rogers Albert's *The House of Bondage,* a collection of slave narratives, was posthumously published.

Scholastic Achievements

The 1890 Census reported that out of those African Americans living in the South, 18.7% attended school, compared with 13.07% in 1880 and 3.07% in 1870. Additionally, the literacy rate among African Americans rose to 42.9% compared with the 30% reported in 1880. Regionally, illiteracy among African Americans was distributed as follows: North Atlantic states 21.2%; South Atlantic states 60.1%; North Central states 32.2%; South Central states 61.2%; West 23.2%.

• There were some 15,100 African American teachers and professors in 1890.

• Susie Elizabeth Frazier became the first African American woman appointed to teach in the New York City public schools.

• Although Senator Blair's bill for Federal aid to education was defeated (by a vote of 37 to 31) in the United States Senate, the Morrill Act was amended to assure equal land grant funds for the education of African Americans where a segregated system existed.

• Savannah State College was founded in Georgia.

• *Technological Innovations:* William B. Purvis was granted a patent for a fountain pen.

• *The Black Church:* The 1890 Census reported that there were 12,159 African American clergymen.

• By 1890, there were 90,000 African American practitioners of the Catholic faith although there were fewer than 30 African American priests.

• John Wesley Gaines published *African Methodism in the South.*

• *Black Enterprise:* According to the 1890 Census, 57% of the African American population was engaged in agriculture, fishing or mining as opposed to 47% of the native European American population and 26% of the European American immigrant population. 31% of the African American population was engaged in some form of domestic and personal service (compared with 12% of the native European American population and 27% of the European American immigrant population). 6% of the African American population was engaged in manufacturing (compared to 19% of the native European American population and 31% of the immigrant population). In trade and transportation, the percentage of African Americans was 5%, while 16% of the native European American population and 14% of the foreign born population were similarly employed. Only one percent of all African Americans were in the professions, in stark contrast to 6% of the native European Americans and 2% of the foreign born European Americans.

• The 1890 Census reported that African Americans owned 120,738 farms and that about 19% of the nation's African American households owned their own homes.

• In Virginia, African Americans were reported to own some 28,621 homes compared to 82,516 homes that were rented by African Americans.

• There were 909 African American doctors and 120 African American dentists in 1890.

• There were 134 African American journalists and 431 African American lawyers in 1890.

• The Alabama Penny Savings and Loan Company was established by African Americans in Birmingham, Alabama (October 15). This savings and loan was notable for surviving the 1893 financial depression which caused many of Birmingham's larger banks to fail.

• Thomy Lafon achieved notoriety as being the nation's first African American millionaire. Lafon was a New Orleans real estate speculator and moneylender. His estate was valued at nearly half a million dollars.

• Langston City, Oklahoma was founded.

Oklahoma was the most important center of black town activity. Thirty-two all-black towns, the largest number in the nation, emerged in the Twin Territories, (Oklahoma Territory and Indian Territory), that became the state of Oklahoma in 1907. The two most famous black towns in Oklahoma were Langston City in Oklahoma Territory and Boley in Indian Territory. Though the specific reasons for town founding varied, most grew out of the tradition of autonomy among the ex-slaves of the Indigenous Americans; anti-black violence in the South, which encouraged migration to the Twin Territories; and the political manipulations of Edwin McCabe *(see 1877)* and other African American politicians who settled in Oklahoma.

The government owned land in Oklahoma was a primary focus of African American leaders. These leaders lobbied for the creation of an all-black territory in the years before 1889. For African Americans like Edwin McCabe, the Oklahoma Territory, whose former Indigenous American reservations were opened to non–Indigenous American settlement in 1889, represented not only the last major chance for homesteading but also a singular opportunity to develop communities where African Americans could achieve their economic potential and exercise their political rights without interference. McCabe, who emerged as the leading advocate of black towns, would also become a town promoter, combining political and racial objectives with personal profit.

Edwin McCabe and his wife Sarah, moved to Oklahoma in April 1890 and six months later joined Charles Robbins, a European American land speculator, and William L. Eagleson, an African American newspaper publisher, in founding Langston City, an all-black community about ten miles northeast of Guthrie, the territorial capital.

Langston City was named after John Mercer Langston, the Virginia African American who as a Congressman supported migration to Oklahoma. The McCabe's, who owned most of the town lots, immediately began advertising for prospective purchasers through their newspaper, the *Langston City Herald,* which was sold in neighboring states. The *Herald* portrayed the town as an ideal community for African Americans. "Langston City is a Negro City, and we are proud of that fact," proclaimed McCabe in the *Herald.* "Her city officers are all colored. Her teachers are colored. Her public schools furnish thorough educational advantages to nearly two hundred colored children." The *Herald* also touted the agricultural potential of the region, claiming the central Oklahoma prairie could produce superior cotton, wheat, and tobacco.

By February of 1892, Langston City had six hundred residents from fifteen states including Georgia, Maryland, and California, with the largest numbers from neighboring Texas. The businesses established included a cotton gin, a soap factory, a bank, and two hotels. An opera house, a racetrack, a billiard parlor, three saloons, masonic lodges, and social clubs provided various forms of entertainment.

Similar to Nicodemus *(see 1877),* Langston City residents hoped a railroad would improve their town's fortunes. Between 1892 and 1900, McCabe waged a steady but ultimately unsuccessful campaign to persuade the St. Louis & San Francisco Railroad to extend its tracks through the town. When the rail line bypassed the town, Langston residents believed they lost their main opportunity to grow. Throughout the railroad campaign, however, town promoters urged other reasons for migration to their community. The *Herald* (no longer owned by the McCabes) continued to emphasize the superior racial climate of the area. McCabe, using his political connections as chief clerk of the territorial legislature in 1896, was able to obtain for Langston City the Colored Agricultural and Normal School (Langston University). The location of the school, the only publicly supported African American educational institution in the territory, in Langston City ensured the town's permanence.

• *Sports:* George "Little Chocolate" Dixon won the world bantamweight boxing championship. Dixon would hold the title from 1890 to 1892. In 1892, Dixon refused to fight in the New Orleans Olympia Club unless it agreed to set aside 700 seats for African American fans. The Club succumbed to Dixon's demands and, for the first time in the club's history, African American spectators were admitted to view an athletic contest.

George "Little Chocolate" Dixon (1870–1909) was born in Halifax, Nova Scotia. He became the world bantamweight champion when he defeated Nunc Wallace on June 27, 1890. On March 31, 1891, Dixon knocked out Cal McCarthy and became the first person of African descent to hold an American title in any sport. Dixon was also the first African American to win the featherweight and paperweight crowns.

• Pike Barnes won the Belmont Stakes aboard Burlington and later won the Alabama Stakes.

• Isaac Murphy won the Kentucky Derby aboard Riley.

Isaac Murphy (Isaac Burns) (c.1861–1896) was the first jockey to win the Kentucky Derby three times. Murphy was born on the David Tanner farm in Fayette County, Kentucky. He took the name Murphy to honor his grandfather, Green Murphy, a well-known auctioneer in Lexington.

Isaac learned to ride when he was fourteen. He won his first Kentucky Derby in 1884. In that year, Murphy became the only jockey to win the Kentucky Derby, the Kentucky Oaks and the Clark Stakes in the same Churchill Downs meeting.

Isaac Murphy is considered to be one of the greatest jockeys in history. During his career, he won forty-four percent of all the races in which he rode. His Kentucky Derby record of three victories stood until 1930.

In 1955, Murphy was the first jockey voted into the Jockey Hall of Fame at the National Museum of Racing in Saratoga Springs, New York.

• An unknown African American set a record in steer roping in Mobeetie, Texas. His time was one minute and forty-five seconds.

• William Henry Lewis and William Tecumseh Sherman Jackson played on the Amherst College football team.

William Henry Lewis (1868–1949) was made captain of the Amherst team in 1891. He was the first African American named to Walter Camp's All-American teams of 1892 and 1893. Lewis wrote *How to Play Football* in 1896. While studying law at Harvard, Lewis served as line coach for the Harvard football team. Lewis completed his law degree at Harvard and became an assistant district attorney in Boston. He later became an Assistant United States Attorney General.

THE AMERICAS

• *Canada:* An Afro-Canadian laborer was reported living near Killarney, Manitoba.

AFRICA

• *North Africa, Egypt and Sudan:* Riyad Pasha became the premier of Egypt.

• Uthman Digna became the governor of Dongola (April).

• King Idris I of Libya was born (March 12).

• Cardinal Lavigerie's *Algiers Toast* called upon all Frenchmen to rally to the Constitution in an attempt to improve relations between the Church and the State.

• *Western Africa:* Behanzin, son of Glegle, attacked Cotonou (March). The settlement made by the French included payment of rent for Cotonou and Porto Novo.

In 1890, Behanzin's forces attacked Cotonou in an unsuccessful attempt to regain it from the French. Later in the year, Behanzin signed a treaty enabling the French to remain in Cotonou in return for 20,000 francs annually. However, the French, concerned that another European power would claim Dahomey, created a pretext for invading Dahomey by crusading against Behanzin's continued slave raiding and exporting, and against Behanzin's attacks on territory already claimed by France.

• A Franco-British declaration was issued in London whereby France gave up its rights in Sokoto in exchange for recognition of a protectorate in Madagascar.

• The Asantehene refused the British protectorate (December).

At the age of about seventeen, Prempe, the asantehene of the Asante Empire, inherited a disintegrating empire. His predecessor had been his older brother, Kwaku Dua II, who died of smallpox in 1884 after reigning for only a year.

For the next four years, warfare was waged throughout the empire. The war was caused by a successional dispute, attempts of the original Akan founder states to secede from the Asante union and efforts of conquered neighbors to break away.

Because of his youth, Prempe, at first, relied heavily on advisers. Initially Prempe re-established the union by defeating the breakaway Kokofu, Mampong, and Nsuta states, which had not supported his candidacy. The rebel states, however, were offered protection by the British on the coast.

The British offered protection to the Asante rebel states as part of its concerted effort to weaken Asante. In 1890, when Prempe sent a delegation to Accra to protest, the British offered to include Prempe's lands within its protected sphere.

Prempe refused the British offer.

- There was an uprising in Carantamba, Chenhaba, Julabu, Denadu and Xime led by Moli Boia. In response, the Portuguese dispatched a punitive military expedition.
- The Sierra Leone Protectorate was proclaimed.
- Father Dorgere became the ambassador to the court of Abomey.
- Dr. Crozat explored Mossi.
- Archinard's second expedition against Ahmadu began. *See 1888.*

When the French military leader Archinard set out to conquer the Tukolor empire, Archinard used the rivalry between the two brothers, Ahmadu ibn 'Umar Tall and Muhammed Aguibu Tall, as a wedge. After the fall of Segu in 1890, Archinard contacted Muhammed and claimed that it was only Ahmadu and not the Tukolor nation whom the French were fighting. Muhammed answered amicably and formally submitted to the French the following year.

Muhammed's acquiescence to French rule, divided the Tukolor and facilitated the fall of Macina, Ahmadu's last base, in 1893.

- A treaty between the Royal Niger Company and the Sultan of Sokoto took place.
- An Anglo-German agreement on the boundaries of Nigeria and Cameroon was reached.
- Colonel Monteil began his exploration of Say, Kano, Bornu, and Chad. He would return to Tripoli in 1893 after making treaties with Kong and others.
- Between 1890 and 1894, exploratory expeditions were mounted in Guinea by Parvisse, Brasselard, Faidherbe and Madrolle.
- Around 1890, Syrian traders began arriving in Freetown.
- Wobogo became the ruler of the Mossi state of Ouagadougou in Burkina Faso.

Wobogo first competed with his brother Sanum for the crown at their father's death in 1850. Wobogo lost out, partially because of his youth. Forty years later, when Sanum died leaving no sons, Wobogo vied with his remaining brothers for the kingship.

Because Wobogo had led a civil war against Sanum years before and had been subsequently exiled from Ouagadougou, the council of electors was not well disposed towards him. However, they agreed to name him mogho naba

(king) after his soldiers surrounded their meeting place. At his elevation, Wobogo dropped his given name, Boukary Koutou, and chose the name Wobogo, meaning elephant.

- *Central Africa:* Tippu Tip returned to Zanzibar to answer a law suit filed by Henry Stanley (April).
- The Pallotine Fathers began work in Cameroon (October 25).
- The Ponel mission explored the Oubangui River.
- Cholet explored the Sangha River as far as N'Goko.
- Prince d'Arenbourg and H. Alis established the committee for French Africa; for French penetration to Lake Chad; and to join up Algeria, Sudan and the Congo.
- The *Nord-West Kamerun Gesellschaft* was founded.
- The Lemarinel mission was sent to Katanga. However, Msiri refused to recognize the Congo Free State.
- The Ovimbundu kingdoms in Angola were subjugated by Portugal.
- Around 1890, the budgets were balanced in the Congo Free State.
- *Eastern Africa:* Around 1890, a rinderpest plague destroyed many cattle in East Africa. This plague was followed by pneumonia and a serious outbreak of smallpox. The Masai, Kikuyu and Kamba were severely affected.
- Islam began to spread near Tanga and Dar es Salaam.
- Allidina Visram became a leading figure in the Zanzibar mercantile community.
- A revolt led by Bwana Heri was defeated (January 4).

"Bwana" is a Swahili form of address, roughly equivalent to "mister" in English. Occasionally, the word "bwana" is used as an honorific title connoting "master," or as part of a proper name.

Bwana Heri was the leader of the Zigua resistance against German occupation of Tanzania. Prior to the 1880s, Bwana Heri ruled one of many small chiefdoms into which the Zigua people of northeastern Tanzania were organized.

In 1882, Bwana Heri focused Zigua animosity towards Zanzibari domination and organized a successful revolt against Sultan Barghash.

In 1888, Bwana Heri again united the Zigua this time to defy German imperialism. Bwana Heri waged a successful guerrilla campaign against the Germans until his supplies became depleted in 1890.

In return for his negotiating a settlement with

von Wissman, Bwana Heri was retained by the Germans as a government chief. However, in 1894, Bwana Heri clashed with the new administration and attempted to raise a rebellion.

After being defeated by the Germans, Bwana Heri fled to Zanzibar. It was there that he died.

- Von Wissman occupied Kilwa Kivinje and Lindi (May).
- Italy reorganized its Red Sea territories as the Colony of Eritrea.
- The Sultan of Zanzibar signed the Anti-Slavery Decree (August 1).
- Emin Pasha, Langheld and Stuhlmann met at Tabora. The local Arabs agreed to accept German suzerainty (August 1).
- Langheld established outposts at Mwanza and Bukoba (September).
- Germany took over German East Africa from the German East Africa Company (October 28).
- A British protectorate was proclaimed over Zanzibar (November 4). The British Foreign office would be responsible for Zanzibar until 1913.
- Frederick Lugard occupied Uganda for the BEAC (December 18).

By 1890, Kabarega, the king of Bunyoro, was at the peak of his power. However, a new and greater danger appeared. European expansion into Africa brought the British into Uganda from the east coast.

Late in 1890, Frederick D. Lugard arrived to create a British protectorate. Lugard negotiated first with Buganda and adopted that kingdom's hostile stance towards Kabarega. Lugard intervened in a civil war among Ganda religious factions and persuaded Apolo Kagwa (*see 1869*) and other Ganda chiefs to accept a British protectorate and to deny accusations that he had used excessive violence there.

As for Kabarega, Kabarega's attempts to parley with Lugard were futile, and, in 1891, Lugard even assisted the Toro kingdom to regain its autonomy.

- In Uganda, Karl Peters obtained a treaty of protection from the Ganda king Mwanga. In the meantime, an Anglo-German agreement delimited Germany's interests in East Africa and nullified this agreement.
- Mbatian, Laibon of the Masai, died. Sendeu and Lenana quarreled to succeed Mbatian.
- *Southern Africa:* BSA Company signed treaty of protection with Barotseland (June 27).

In 1890, Frank Lochner, an agent of Cecil Rhodes' British South Africa Company (BSAC) arrived to negotiate a treaty. Though suspicious of Lochner's claims to represent Queen Victoria, Lewanika, the king of the Barotse (the Lozi) reluctantly signed a major mining concession treaty and obtained approval from his highly skeptical national council. The BSAC's tardiness in demonstrating that the Lozi were being "protected" ultimately produced a crisis for Lewanika.

- Cecil Rhodes became the premier of the Cape Colony (July 17).
- The first Swaziland convention convened (August).
- BSA Company Pioneer Column established posts at Fort Tuli, Fort Victoria, and Fort Charter and, on September 10, at Fort Salisbury. On September 12, the British flag was ceremoniously raised.

Cecil Rhodes's British South Africa Company obtained a concession from the Ndebele king Lobengula which was used to occupy Mashonaland in 1890. Manuel Sousa, the Indo-Portuguese empire builder, and a Portuguese agent, Paiva Andrada, rushed to Manica in eastern Shona territory to forestall a British takeover there. Both were captured by the British and sent to Cape Town.

In 1890, Khama, the ruler of the Ngwato, materially assisted Cecil Rhodes' "Pioneer Column" to occupy eastern Rhodesia.

- An Anglo-Portuguese agreement on the Zambezi and the Congo was reached. Bechuanaland was placed under the governance of a British Governor.
- A civil war erupted amongst the Mpondo.

In 1887, a new man, Sigcawu, became chief of the Mpondo. Sigcawu insisted on ruling without Mdlangaso's assistance. Three years later, Mdlangaso attempted to seize power for himself. A civil war ensued. The war would last for four years.

- The Gaza reached an agreement with the BSA Company.

In 1890, Gungunyane, the king of Gaza, was visited by agents of Cecil Rhodes British South Africa Company. These agents sought a concession similar to the one that had been obtained from the Ndebele king Lobengula two years before. Gungunyane was anxious to comply. But in doing so, he failed to understand that he was dealing with private interests and not the British government. *See 1906.*

• In 1890, Mpezeni, the ruler of the Chipata Ngoni, granted a generous concession to a lone German trader, Karl Wiese. However, aside from this concession, Mpezeni was generally able to ignore the increasing European imperialistic pressure at the same time that the same forces were reducing his neighbors to colonial dependents.

• Tomo Nyirenda (c.1890–1926), a messianic religious leader of southeastern Africa, is believed to have been born in this year.

Tomo Nyirenda was born and raised in Nyasaland (Malawi). In the early 1920s, he went to work on the Copperbelt in Northern Rhodesia (Zambia), where he became acquainted with the Watch Tower Movement which had been introduced into the country by Elliott Kamwana *(see 1872)*.

Nyirenda was baptized and began to preach the new faith in early 1925. British colonial authorities soon imprisoned him for failing to register as an "alien native."

Upon his release, Nyirenda declared himself to be the Mwana Lesa, — the Son of God. Nyirenda preached a apocalyptic creed which stressed opposition to the European regime and promised the coming of African American benefactors.

Nyirenda enhanced his rapidly growing reputation with the further claim — unusual among such messianic figures — that he could divine witches and sorcerers. He soon won a large following among the Lala of Central Province.

Nyirenda incurred the hostility of the government of Northern Rhodesia (Zambia) by drowning a number of "witches"— people who had failed to pass his test of baptism. Seeking to escape government scrutiny, Nyirenda shifted his movement to the Katanga province of the Belgian Congo (Zaire).

In Zaire, Nyirenda introduced the Watch Tower beliefs and again engaged in drowning people who failed his baptismal test. Over one hundred people failed his test and the Belgian authorities, like their Zambian counterparts, also chased Nyirenda out of the country.

Nyirenda was chased back to Zambia where he was arrested, tried and hanged in 1926.

• Mahehero (c.1820–1890), the Herero chief who freed the Herero from Khoikhoi domination and united most Herero chiefdoms under his leadership, died.

During his youth, the Bantu-speaking Herero (Damara) were divided into small chiefdoms subordinate to intrusive Dutch-speaking Khoikhoi chiefs. In the 1840s, Mahehero accompanied his father to Windhoek to join Jonker Afrikaner's Khoikhoi. There Mahehero learned about horses and guns from the Khoikhoi and became a friend of the future chief Jan Jonker Afrikaner.

When Mahehero's father died in 1861, Mahehero became ruler of one of many Herero chiefdoms. Mahehero resisted Khoikhoi domination. When his friend Jan Jonker became Khoikhoi chief in 1863, Mahehero launched the Herero seven year war of independence. Mahehero obtained Herero recognition for the prosperous Anglo-Swedish trader Charles Anderson *(see 1867)* and Anderson became the Herero's paramount chief.

Anderson provided the Herero with firearms and commanded them in several successful engagements until his death in 1867. Mahehero himself defeated Jan Jonker the following year. This defeat of the Khoikhoi broke the Khoikhoi hold over the Herero.

In 1870, a general truce was settled and Mahehero leased Windhoek to Jan Jonker. Mahehero then stood as the single most powerful figure between the Orange and Kunene Rivers.

For the next ten years, Mahehero's Herero were at peace. However, Mahehero had increasing problems with the new European settlers. Mahehero asked the British government at Cape Town for help but received only a resident magistrate. In 1880, difficulties with the Khoikhoi were renewed over disputed grazing land. This time Moses Witbooi was Mahehero's major adversary.

After an initial Khoikhoi raid, Mahehero massacred many of Witbooi's people. This united the Khoikhoi against him, but they did not become a serious threat until Hendrik Witbooi rose to power after 1884.

In 1885, Mahehero signed a treaty of protection with the Germans. The Germans were then occupying Namibia. However, the Germans failed to provide security against the Witboois, so he renounced the treaty in 1888.

Mahehero changed his mind when German troops began arriving the following year. Mahehero reaffirmed the treaty shortly before his death in 1890.

• Nyamazana (c.1835–1890), a Ngoni queen and migration leader, died.

Nyamazana was a relative — possibly a niece — of the great Ngoni migrant leader Zwangendaba.

Zwangendaba left Zululand around 1819. During Zwangendaba's migration through Rhodesia, Nyamazana became the leader of a section of the Ngoni. Zwangendaba crossed the Zambezi River in 1835, but Nyamazana remained behind with her followers. According to one tradition, Zwangendaba refused to allow Nyamazana to follow him any further.

Over the next few years, Nyamazana and her followers roamed and pillaged through Shona territory. When the Ndebele of Mzilikazi arrived in Zimbabwe, Nyamazana's Ngoni submitted to them and were incorporated into the Ndebele state. Nyamazana herself married the Ndebele king.

RELATED HISTORICAL EVENTS

• *The United States:* The Sioux (Indigenous American) chief, Sitting Bull, was arrested in a skirmish with United States troops and then shot dead as Sioux warriors tried to rescue him (December 15).

• At the "Battle" of Wounded Knee, some 300 Indigenous American men, women and children were massacred by the United States Seventh Cavalry (December 29).

• *Europe:* Kaiser Wilhelm of Germany forced Bismarck's resignation as Chancellor (March 18).

• The Mackinnon Treaty between Leopold of Belgium and BEAC recognized Leopold's rights west of the Upper Nile in return for territory near Lake Tanganyika (May 24).

• Pursuant to the Anglo-German convention, Britain ceded Heligoland in return for Zanzibar and Pemba (July 1).

• The Anti–Slavery Conference convened in Brussels in an effort to eradicate the slave trade and liquor traffic amongst underdeveloped peoples (July 2). *See 1889: Related Historical Events.*

• Part of the will of Leopold II was made public (July 9). In the will, Leopold bequeathed the Congo Free State to Belgium. This enabled Leopold to obtain a loan from the Belgian Parliament.

• An Anglo–French convention defined spheres of interest in Nigeria, Zanzibar and Pemba, and Madagascar (August 5).

• An Anglo-Portuguese agreement on Nyasaland and Mashonaland was reached (August 20).

• James Frazer published the first volume of *The Golden Bough.*

• *Notable Deaths:* Sir Richard Francis Burton (1821–1890), a British explorer of Africa, writer and anthropologist, died.

Richard Francis Burton was born in Torquay, Devonshire, England. He was educated at the University of Oxford.

In 1842, Burton joined the army maintained by the East India Company. Burton was stationed at Sind, India for seven years. During his stay in India, Burton mastered a number of Asian languages. This study of languages would prove to serve Burton well on his numerous journeys and explorations.

In 1853, Burton, disguised as an Afghan pilgrim, made the pilgrimage to Medina and Mecca. In doing so, Burton became one of the first Europeans to enter the most holy of Islamic cities.

Burton's next journey took him to Somaliland — a region of Africa which, at the time, few Europeans had ever explored. On Burton's 1854 exploration of Somaliland, he was accompanied by the English explorer John Hanning Speke, a person who would become a noted explorer in his own right. During this 1854 exploration, Burton became the first European to visit the city of Harar in Ethiopia.

After service in the Crimean War, Burton returned to Africa in 1858 with Speke. Together they became the first known Europeans to see Lake Victoria and to visit Lake Tanganyika.

By 1861, Burton had become a member of the British diplomatic service. During his diplomatic career, Burton would be assigned to such diverse places as Fernando Po, Africa; Brazil; Damascus, Syria; and Trieste, Italy.

In 1886, Richard Francis Burton was knighted in recognition of his explorations of Arabia and the African continent.

Burton is best known for his definitive translation of the collection of tales known as *The Arabian Nights* (1885–1888). Among his other works are *Personal Narrative of a Pilgrimage to El Medina and Mecca* (1855); *First Footsteps in East Africa* (1856); *The Lake Regions of Central Africa* (1860); *Wanderings in West Africa* (1863); and various studies of Brazil, Paraguay, Syria, Zanzibar, Etruscan Bologna, and the Gold Coast. *The Lake Regions of Central Africa* is a major source for Tanzanian history and is considered to be a classic. Indeed, of Burton's eighty volumes of original writings and translations, twenty center on Africa.

• Cornelius Napier (1810–1890), the commander of the British invasion of Ethiopia of 1867, died.

Robert Napier interrupted his career in the Indian army to secure the release of British subjects held captive by the Ethiopian emperor Theodore II (Tewodros) in the years 1867 and 1868. Arriving in Ethiopia at a moment when Theodore was neither able nor inclined to offer serious resistance, Napier led a force of 32,000 men against the emperor's headquarters at Magdala.

Theodore released the captives and led a token resistance before committing suicide. Napier razed Magdala, looted the monasteries of ancient manuscripts and returned to the coast.

For his actions in Ethiopia, Napier was given a peerage and the title "Lord Napier of Magdala."

——————— 1891 ———————

THE UNITED STATES

• Henry Cheatham of North Carolina was the only African American to serve in the 52nd Congress.

• At the Nationalist Populist Convention held in Cincinnati, Ohio, Southerners attempted to segregate the delegates from the National Colored Farmer's Alliance. At the time, the National Colored Farmer's Alliance had membership of 1.3 million. The Southern segregationist initiative was soundly defeated.

• An alliance of Southern Democrats and Silver Republicans was able to prevent Congressman Lodge's bill on the supervision of Federal elections from being brought up for consideration.

• In his third message to Congress, President Harrison proposed a non-partisan commission to examine the workings of elections, since Lodge's Federal elections bill had died (December 9). However, the commission was never appointed.

• Through the efforts of Daniel Hale Williams, Provident Hospital was established in Chicago (May 4). Provident Hospital was a hospital where African Americans could receive training as doctors and nurses and where African Americans could receive quality care without fear of racial bias.

• In protest of the exploitation of the Haitian people by American business interests, Frederick Douglass resigned his post as charge d'affaires.

• *The Labor Movement:* In 1891, there were 196 industrial employers in the South who employed some 7,395 African Americans.

These African Americans were largely used as menial workers.

• In Texas, cotton pickers unionized and struck for higher wages.

• *Notable Births:* Edwin (Edward) Richard Dudley, a diplomat who became the United States Ambassador to Liberia, was born.

Edwin Richard Dudley was born in South Boston, Virginia. Having received a law degree from St. John's Law School, Dudley worked on the legal staff of the NAACP and as Assistant Attorney General for New York State.

In 1948, President Harry S. Truman appointed Dudley Ambassador to Liberia.

During his career, Dudley also served as Borough President of Manhattan in New York City and on the State Supreme Court.

• Lillian Evanti, one of the founders of the National Negro Opera Company, was born in Washington, D. C. (August 12).

• Charles H. Garvin, the first African American physician to be commissioned during World War I was born in Jacksonville, Florida (October 27).

• Zora Neale Hurston, folklorist, novelist and short story writer, was born in Eatonville, Florida (January 7).

• James P. Johnson (1891–1955), a jazz pianist, was born.

James P. Johnson was born in New Brunswick, New Jersey. He studied music as a child and made his professional debut in 1904.

In the 1920s, Johnson recorded player piano rolls, toured with road shows and appeared in films.

In the 1930s, Johnson spent more time composing. His *Symphony Harlem* was written in 1932.

In 1949, Johnson wrote the music for the show *Sugar Hill.*

One of Johnson's most important disciples was the legendary Fats Waller. Johnson met Waller in 1919.

Johnson was also a major influence on Duke Ellington.

• Nella Larsen, a novelist, was born in Chicago, Illinois (April 13).

• Archibald Motley, a painter known for depicting the life of urban African Americans, was born (October 7).

Archibald Motley was born in New Orleans, Louisiana. Motley won the Chicago Art Institute's Francis Logan Medal for character study in 1925 for his *A Mulatress.*

In 1929, Motley's portraits, *My Grandmother* and *Old Snuff Dipper,* won the Harmon Gold Medal, and he was awarded a Guggenheim Fellowship for two years' study in Paris. Motley's best technical works, among them his portrait study *The Young Martiniquan,* were done at this time.

After he returned from Paris, Motley's work became more surrealistic, emphasizing the squalor and bizarre aspects of urban (ghetto) life. Motley's style, once restrained, became highly imaginative — a combination of Dutch realism and American humor.

In 1933, six of Motley's canvasses along with his WPA projects received wide acclaim. A series of murals on the life of Frederick Douglass at Howard University and murals for the State Street Library in Chicago were among the notable WPA projects completed by Motley.

- Alma W. Thomas, an artist, was born in Columbus, Georgia (September 22).
- Charles Wesley (1891–1987), an historian and educator, was born.

Charles Wesley was born in Louisville, Kentucky, and was educated at Fisk, Howard, Yale and other major universities. Wesley received numerous academic awards, including a Guggenheim Fellowship for 1930–1931.

A professor and dean at Howard University, Wesley became president of Central State (Wilberforce) College in 1942.

Among Wesley's notable works are *Negro Labor in the United States 1850–1925: A Study in American Economic History* (1927); *Richard Allen, Apostle of Freedom* (1935); *The Collapse of the Confederacy* (1938); and *The Negro in America* (1940).

- *Notable Deaths:* There were 112 African Americans lynched in 1891.
- John A. Hyman (1840–1891), a former Congressman from North Carolina, died in Washington, D. C. (September 14).

John A. Hyman was born a slave near Warrenton, North Carolina. Hyman was sold and taken to Alabama but still managed to educate himself.

In 1868, Hyman attended the North Carolina Constitutional Convention. He served in the North Carolina Legislature for six years. In 1875, Hyman was elected to the House of Representatives. He served one term.

At the end of his term in office, Hyman stayed in Washington, D.C., where he worked in a minor post in the revenue service.

- *Miscellaneous State Laws:* Alabama instituted railroad segregation.
- Georgia became the first state to segregate streetcars.
- In South Carolina, Governor Tillman failed to obtain legislative approval of a railroad segregation bill. However, Tillman did succeed in having a law enacted which placed a prohibitive tax on labor agents who were enticing African American farm laborers to migrate. Governor Tillman also convinced the state Democratic executive committee to require that an African American would be allowed to vote only if ten European American men would vouch for his loyalty.
- Virginia again re-apportioned its legislative districts in an effort to minimize the impact of the African American vote.
- *Miscellaneous Publications:* Archibald Henry Grimke published a biography of William Lloyd Garrison.
- Lucy A. Berry Delaney published *From Darkness Cometh the Light; or, Struggles for Freedom.*
- Daniel Alexander Payne published *The History of the AME Church from 1816 to 1856.*
- Lucius Henry Holsey compiled a *Hymn Book of the Colored Methodist Episcopal Church in America* and published in 1891.
- *Scholastic Achievements:* North Carolina Agricultural and Technical State University was founded in Greensboro.
- West Virginia State College was founded in Institute, West Virginia.
- The first three schools of nursing for African Americans attached to hospitals were established in 1891: Dixie Hospital in Hampton, Virginia; MacVicar Hospital, in connection with Spelman College in Atlanta, Georgia; and Provident Training School in Chicago.
- *The Black Church:* Daniel Alexander Payne published *The History of the AME Church from 1816 to 1856.*
- Lucius Henry Holsey compiled a *Hymn Book of the Colored Methodist Episcopal Church in America* and published in 1891.
- Charles Randolph Uncles was ordained as a Catholic priest in Baltimore, Maryland (December 19). Uncles was the first African American to be ordained as a priest in the United States. The previous four Catholic priests (the three Healy brothers and Augustus Tolon) had all been ordained in Europe.
- *The Performing Arts:* In Boston, *The*

Creole Show, a play by Sam T. Jack, opened. *The Creole Show* became the first African American production to feature African American women as lead performers and to feature African American women singing. Promoted by the European American, John Isham, the show was also known for its introduction of the theatrical cake walk. In the finale, Dora Dean and Charles Johnson performed the cake walk, a dance derived from the old plantation chalkline walk. *The Creole Show* was one of the first shows in which African American performers did not wear black face.

• In New Orleans, Charles "Buddy" Bolden formed what may have been the first real jazz band.

A plasterer by trade, Bolden developed a coronet style that influenced musicians such as King Oliver and Dizzy Gillespie. Many call Bolden the "Father of Jazz." His band incorporated blues and ragtime and the band's fierce, driving tone led to Bolden being called "King Bolden."

Diagnosed as paranoid in 1907, Bolden was committed to East Louisiana State Hospital. It was in this institution that Charles "Buddy" Bolden spent the remainder of his days.

• *Music:* The Onward Brass Band, an African American musical group from New Orleans, traveled to New York and won wide attention, and first place, in a band contest.

• *Black Enterprise:* In Virginia's 16 major cities and towns, African Americans owned land assessed at $3,207,069.

• *Sports:* Peter Jackson, a great Afro-Australian boxer, fought a sixty-one round draw with James J. Corbett (May 21). At the time, Jackson was the boxing champion of Australia. *See 1891: Australia.*

• Isaac Murphy capped an illustrious riding career by winning the Kentucky Derby for a record third time and by becoming the first person to win the race in two consecutive years. In this year, Murphy rode Kingman to victory.

• George "Little Chocolate" Dixon knocked out Cal McCarthy to win the American bantamweight title (March 31).

THE AMERICAS

• *Brazil:* Dom Pedro II (1825–1891), the former Brazilian emperor, died.

• Joaquim Machado de Assis published *Quincas Borba.*

In *Quincas Borba,* the hero of the story Rubiao, a teacher from Minas Gerais, inherits a huge amount of money from Quincas Borba. As he leaves for Rio, Rubiao meets a pair of con artists, Christiano Palha and his beautiful wife, Sofia. Rubiao falls in love with Sofia and, in an effort to be near Sofia, Rubiao allows Christiano and Sofia to become his closest friends.

Christiano and Sofia proceed to take Rubiao for everything that he has. In the process, a coterie of marginal and shifty people become peripherally involved. In the end, Rubiao winds up poor and insane. It is a story in which there is universal indifference in the face of human suffering and abandonment of man by the supernatural powers that be.

Canada

The often schizophrenic attitude of Canada towards persons of African descent was best illustrated in 1891 by the events in Chatham, Ontario.

In January, some members of the Chatham Literary Association, an Afro-Canadian club, organized the Kent County Civil Rights League to combat a rising tide of racial insults and discrimination. In May, an armed band of Euro-Canadians attempted to force an elderly Afro-Canadian couple from their land. However, the band was driven off by gunfire. The Kent County Civil Rights League approved of this action.

Around this time, the Kent County Civil Rights League also protested against the segregated schools of Chatham, but with little success. A few months later a police constable in nearby Raleigh attempted to arrest one George Freeman, who had kept a thirteen-year-old Euro-Canadian girl in his house and coerced her into fathering his child. Beaten off with an ax, the constable sought assistance from the Chatham police who, upon appearing in Raleigh, were attacked by Afro-Canadians wielding guns and meat cleavers. Two policemen escaped with wounds. One was killed.

As soon as the news reached Chatham, ten sleighloads of armed Euro-Canadian men set out in pursuit of any Raleigh Afro-Canadian who could be found. The chief of police, although cautioned by a lawyer standing at his side, declared that he would "get the murderers, dead or alive, if we have to burn their shack and every miserable wretch in it." The Euro-Canadians of Chatham lined the streets for the dead constable's funeral and thronged the inquest — at which seven Afro-Canadians ultimately were charged.

The Euro-Canadians battered upon the courthouse walls demanding to see the prisoners. Some five hundred Euro-Canadians encircled the jail threatening to lynch the Freeman family.

Most of the Afro-Canadians of Chatham offered their assistance to the authorities to help hold back the mob. During the furor, four large barns near Chatham were burned to the ground. On each of the barns was nailed the epithet "white trash" and a warning that the Afro-Canadians of the area were tired of mistreatment. However, a Euro-Canadian investigator forestalled any racial retribution for these fires by proving that one of the Euro-Canadian barn owners had burned down his own barn in an attempt to collect on the insurance. This same Euro-Canadian had burned down the other barns as a diversion.

Despite the anti–Afro-Canadian fever, and perhaps in embarrassment over the racial animus in the town and the criminal race baiting manipulations perpetuated by the Euro-Canadian barnowner, the Chatham school board agreed to admit Afro-Canadians to the common schools a few weeks after the conclusion of the Freeman trial.

- *Haiti:* Massillon Coicou, an Afro-Haitian poet, published *Les Poesies Nationales*, a work full of enthusiasm for Haiti and Coicou's revolutionary idealism. *See 1865.*
- *Puerto Rico:* Pedro Albizu Campos (1891–1965), the principal leader of the Puerto Rican Nationalist Party, was born.

Pedro Albizu Campos went to local schools in Puerto Rico before attending Harvard University in 1917.

After Puerto Ricans became recognized United States citizens in 1917, Albizu Campos entered the United States Army and became a lieutenant.

In the army, Albizu Campos was subjected to racial segregation. This experience was responsible for Albizu Campos' lifelong bitter enmity for the United States.

Returning to civilian life after his army stint, Albizu Campos became an advocate of Puerto Rican independence and spent several years preaching that idea. In 1930, Albizu Campos was elected president of the Puerto Rican Nationalist Party. The Puerto Rican Nationalist Party had been established two decades earlier.

The Puerto Rican Nationalist Party participated in the 1932 election and Albizu Campos was candidate for insular senator-at-large. However, the party received less than 10 percent of the total vote needed to make it a "legal" party.

Thereafter, under Albizu's leadership, the Nationalist Party turned to personal acts of violence. Their greatest "success" was the assassination of insular police chief, Colonel E. Francis Riggs, in February 1936.

As a result of these acts of nationalistic violence, Albizu Campos and seven of his supporters were sentenced to federal prison. Part of this sentence Albizu Campos spent in a hospital in New York City.

Albizu Campos was released in December 1947.

The Nationalists' attempts to murder President Harry Truman and Puerto Rican Governor Luiz Munoz Marin in 1950 resulted in Albizu Campos again being given a jail sentence. This time Albizu Campos served his time in Puerto Rico.

Albizu Campos was pardoned by Governor Munoz Marin in 1953. However, when the Nationalists made an armed attack on the United States Congress in March 1954, Albizu Campos was jailed once again.

Albizu Campos was pardoned for a final time by Governor Munoz Marin in November 1964.

AUSTRALIA

- Peter Jackson *(see 1886)* fought "Gentleman Jim" Corbett to a draw.

On May 21, 1891, James Corbett and Peter Jackson met at the California Athletic Club for a fight to the finish with five-ounce gloves. Corbett was an up and coming boxer known for his scientific boxing technique. Peter Jackson, the Australian champion who was known as the "Black Prince," was such a skilled fighter that the best Euro-American fighters had avoided fighting him for years.

The purse for the bout was $10,000 and the betting was against Corbett.

The smaller, quicker Corbett knew that he could not outslug the bigger, stronger Jackson. So using his brains, Corbett ran, dodged and ducked.

As Corbett himself would put it, "No matter in what direction I would dash, this big black thing was on top of me trying to one-two me to death."

In the sixteenth round, Jackson caught up to Corbett and landed a mighty blow. Corbett was stunned, but with the heart of a future champion, he was able to hold on.

Soon Corbett began to notice a pattern to Jackson's tactics. Exploiting a weakness in Jackson's tactics along with a fortunate turning of Jackson's ankle, Corbett began to wear Jackson down.

By the fortieth round, the fight had become an endurance contest. Jackson had a swollen ankle and was visibly slowed. Corbett had two broken ribs and was rightfully wary of the power that still resided in Jackson's blows.

In the sixty-first round, the bout was declared a draw.

The Corbett-Jackson bout was a turning point in boxing history. The bout introduced new tactics and methods of training. The gentlemanly and chivalrous nature of Corbett and Jackson created in the public a taste for something more than brawlers and maulers.

Corbett went on to defeat John Sullivan to become the world champion. Many commentators believe that Sullivan would have suffered the same fate if he had fought Jackson before fighting Corbett.

EUROPE

• Dom Pedro II (1825–1891), the former Brazilian emperor, died.

AFRICA

• *North Africa, Egypt and Sudan:* Mustafa Pasha Fahmi became the Premier of Egypt.
• A plot in Omdurman was developed to supersede the Khalifa.
• An Anglo-Egyptian expedition from Suakin routed Uthman Digna and captured his headquarters near Tokar (February).
• *Western Africa:* Dodd initiated his campaign in Senegal.
• The French finalized a treaty with Adrar (October 20).
• Beginning in 1891, there were numerous French explorations along the Ivory Coast.
• Dr. Ballay became the Governor of Guinea (December 12).
• Ballot became the Governor of Benin (Dahomey) (December 3).
• The Department of Native Affairs was established by the British in Sierra Leone.

In 1891, the British allied with Bai Bureh and used 1500 of Bai Bureh's troops to defeat one of Bai Bureh's chief Sierra Leone rivals. This alliance allowed Bai Bureh to study British fighting techniques. What he learned he soon began to employ.

• The Government of Oil Rivers was reorganized.
• The African Banking Corporation, the first bank in Nigeria, opened.
• Colonel Humbert under the orders of Louis Archinard launched an expedition against Samori. *See 1888.*

Archinard's second campaign against Samori was unauthorized and against the wishes of his superiors in France. This second campaign would result in a war that would last for another seven years.

After having conquered the Western Sudan, Archinard attempted to rule the land indirectly through "natural chiefs." However, his repression against local rulers and their frequent replacement limited the success of his policy.

In 1891, the French, hopeful of persuading Tieba, the ruler of the Kenedugu kingdom of Sikasso, to ally with them against Samori, aided Tieba in some local conflicts. However, the diplomatic errors committed by the French aroused Tieba's hostility. The net result was that the French were forced to fight Samori without Tieba's assistance.

• Lamine Gueye (1891–1968), the organizer of the first modern political party in Francophonic Africa, was born.

Lamine Gueye was born in French Sudan (Mali) of a Senegalese family. He studied law in France during World War I and became French Africa's first black lawyer.

Gueye returned to Senegal in 1922 as a supporter of Blaise Diagne. Diagne had won election to the French Chamber of Deputies as an advocate of African rights. When Diagne later turned conservative, Gueye broke with him and worked unsuccessfully to secure Diagne's defeat in the 1928 election.

Diagne and Gueye were later reconciled. As a result, Gueye was rewarded with a magistrateship in Reunion.

Gueye returned to Senegal after Diagne's death in 1934 to try to capture Diagne's Chamber seat. However, Gueye was defeated by a former political ally, Galandou Diouf.

In 1935, Gueye took over the nascent Parti Socialiste Senegalais (PSS) and organized it along modern lines to attract the young Senegalese elite. Gueye affiliated the PSS with the French Socialist Party, the SFIO. The new party failed its first test in 1936, when Diouf again defeated Gueye in a chamber election. After the election, the SFIO absorbed the PSS.

The fall of France in 1940 interrupted local politics. However, in 1945, Gueye, with the SFIO behind him, was elected deputy, and, in 1946, Gueye was elected mayor of Dakar.

In the French Chamber of Deputies, Gueye sponsored legislation to win African bureaucrats the same pay as their French counterparts in Africa. However, this legislation was atypical of Gueye's legislative career. Following the course of his mentor Diagne, Gueye continued to draw his principal support from the urban and traditional Senegalese elites while ignoring the plight of the Afro-Senegalese.

Due to Gueye's neglect of the black Senegalese, Leopold Senghor, Gueye's protégé and fellow deputy, broke with Gueye in 1948 to form his own party. Senghor's party defeated Gueye and the other SFIO candidates in the 1951 elections.

In 1958, Senghor and Gueye reunited to oppose those African leaders who favored total autonomy for each French African territory rather than a form of federation. Their opponents were led by Felix Houphouet-Boigny and it was their opponents' position which prevailed. Nevertheless, Senghor's party continued to dominate Senegalese politics.

In 1959, Senegal became a republic. Gueye was elected President of the national assembly. He remained active in Senegalese politics until his death in 1968.

• Samuel Ajayi Crowther (1809– 1891), the first Yoruban to become an Anglican bishop, died.

Samuel Crowther was born in Yorubaland. During the civil war of 1821 in Yorubaland, Crowther was captured and sold to Portuguese traders on the coast. The slave ship which was transporting Crowther to the Americas was seized by a British anti-slavery patrol. Crowther was released at Freetown in Sierra Leone.

In Sierra Leone, Crowther was educated by the Church Missionary Society (CMS). He was baptized in 1825.

Following a brief visit to England, Crowther matriculated in the Fourah Bay Institute. After graduation, Crowther became a school teacher.

Crowther impressed his supervisors as being intelligent and very devout. As a result, Crowther was invited to join the British Niger Expedition in 1841.

Crowther then went to England where he was ordained in 1845. He returned to West Africa as a missionary and served for a brief period of time at Badagry before being posted to Abeokuta in Yorubaland in 1846.

In 1854 and 1857, Crowther accompanied W. B. Baikie's exploration of the Niger River.

The mid–1800s was a period of grandiose European missionary plans for expansion in West Africa. When it was decided to create a West African diocese with an indigenous African pastorate, Crowther was selected as bishop and was consecrated in 1864.

Thoroughly Victorian in his perspective, Crowther was immensely successful in promoting Christianity, missionary education, and capitalism throughout the Niger valley.

In the 1880s, Crowther began to lose control of the diocese to younger missionaries who questioned the policy of establishing an indigenous African pastorate. Crowther also faced pressure from the European trading community led by Sir George Goldie. The trading community wanted to see British missionaries extending British influence throughout the region.

A number of Crowther's associates came under attack for moral turpitude. Crowther himself was accused of lax discipline. In response, Crowther noted that he himself had long complained that his associates were poorly trained and that he had no resources available to better train them. However, Crowther was essentially a soft spoken, retiring individual. He made little effort to fully counter the charges and, in 1890, he was forced to resign.

Although Crowther is best remembered for his missionary activities, he also made valuable scholarly contributions with his journals of the Niger expeditions and with his study of the Yoruba language.

• Jaja (c.1821–1891), a ruler of the Niger delta trading state of Opobo, died.

Jaja was born a slave. He was sold to a chief in the Bonny trading state at the age of twelve. Jaja was later transferred to the Anna Pepple trading house in Bonny. It was with the Anna Pepple trading house that Jaja began his rise as a trader.

In 1861, Alali, the head of the Anna Pepple trading house died. Two years later, Jaja, who had become one of the leading chiefs of Bonny, was elected to succeed Alali. As part of the succession, Jaja assumed the 10,000 pound debt which Alali had accumulated with the European palm oil merchants. Jaja paid off the debt immediately.

Jaja expanded his trading empire by absorbing other trading houses. His success aroused the antagonism of his major rival in Bonny, the Manilla Pepple trading house headed by Oko Jumbo.

King George Pepple, the titular ruler of Bonny, was unable to intercede. Instead, Pepple asked the British Consul, Charles Livingstone, to request British intervention. Livingstone refused, and in 1869 war broke out.

Jaja lost most of his weapons in a fire and was forced to ask for peace. However, Jaja used the peace negotiations to leave Bonny and establish a new trading state which was located in a position where Jaja was able to cut off Bonny from the sources of palm oil situated in the interior. Jaja founded Opobo.

The British traders had too much capital invested at Bonny to allow Jaja to monopolize the palm oil trade. The British boycotted Opobo.

Jaja broke the boycott by finding a trader who would continue to buy from him. Once again he went to war with Bonny. Meanwhile, Jaja continued to prevent palm oil shipments from reaching Bonny, bankrupting many European firms there.

In 1870, Jaja officially proclaimed his new kingdom. By naming it Opobo (the name of a famous king of Bonny), Jaja maintained his links with the traditions of the Bonny monarchy. In 1873, Jaja agreed to a settlement with Bonny. The settlement was in Jaja's favor — Opobo was unquestionably supreme.

Jaja developed good relations with the British once they recognized him as king of Opobo. In 1875, Jaja even sent a contingent to help Britain in the Asante War. However, Jaja's insistence upon maintaining strict control over the oil trade eventually caused relations to deteriorate.

In 1884, Jaja signed a treaty placing himself under British protection. However, he explicitly refused to guarantee free trade. The same year, the European merchants on the coast combined to boycott the purchase of oil at Opobo.

Once again, Jaja broke the boycott by finding a European buyer.

In 1885, Britain declared a protectorate over the Niger delta area. Two years later, the British consul, Henry Johnston, demanded that Europeans be allowed to buy their oil upriver, thereby avoiding the Opobo middlemen.

Jaja agreed to the demand. However, in fact, Jaja took measures to ensure his monopoly.

Johnston asked Jaja to meet with him. Johnston pledged not to detain Jaja. But, at the meeting, Johnston told Jaja that if he did not go to Accra for trial, Opobo would be bombarded.

Jaja was forced to accede.

In Accra, Jaja was found guilty of blocking trade. Jaja was deported to the West Indies.

Jaja lived in the West Indies for the next four years on a pension of 800 pounds a year. In 1891, he was allowed to return home but he died in transit.

- Umaru (c.1824–1891), the ruler of the Fula Sokoto empire, died.

Umaru was a great-grandson of Uthman dan Fodio. Uthman dan Fodio was the founder of the Fula empire in northern Nigeria. Uthman's successors had kept alive the traditions of the jihad (holy war) by assembling the armies of the Sokoto emirates for military campaigns each autumn. These campaigns had degenerated into raids on neighboring territories rather than attempts to extend Sokoto's boundaries. Umaru discontinued the raids.

To make up for lost revenues, Umaru extracted greater tribute within the empire. He also interfered more in the domestic affairs of the individual emirates. These policies were generally accepted, and the period was one of unprecedented security and flourishing trade. Expansion to the north and east continued on a peaceful basis.

Ironically, Umaru died while on a military expedition. He was succeeded by Abdurrahman.

- *Central Africa:* The first expedition of the Katanga Company was launched (May). Msiri refused to recognize the Katanga Company (October).
- Ivory and rubber were made state monopolies in the Congo (September 21).
- Basanga revolted against Msiri.
- Msiri refused to recognize Stairs mission (December).
- Msiri was killed by Captain Bodson (December 20). With Msiri's death, the kingdom of Garaganza (the Yeke kingdom of Katanga) essentially came to an end.
- The Crampel mission was established on the Oubangui and Chari rivers.
- French posts were founded at Ouesso and on the Kemo River.
- Albertville was established as an outpost by Captain Joubert.
- Between 1891 and 1894, the Arabs were at war with the Congo Free State.
- In 1891, the Bia-Francqui expedition to Katanga was initiated. During the expedition, copper deposits were described by J. Cornet.

• Msiri (c.1820s–1891), the founder and ruler of the Yeke kingdom in Katanga (Zaire), died.

Msiri was the son of Kalasa, a Sumbwa subchief and long-distance trader of western Tanzania. Kalasa was a pioneer in the development of Nyamwezi trade routes to Katanga, where Sumbwa and Nyamwezi were known as Yeke, or Garenganze. As a young man, Msiri accompanied his father to Katanga.

Around 1856, Msiri returned at the head of his own expedition, and obtained permission from the reigning Mwata Kazembe of the Zambian Lunda empire to trade in southern Katanga, which the latter ruled.

Msiri settled in Katanga, married into local ruling families, and collected other Nyamwezi traders around himself. The firearms he obtained from the east coast trade gave him a military advantage over his neighbors and he began to build his own domain.

By 1865, Msiri was an independent power. Over the next five years, Msiri separated the western part of the Mwata Kazembe's territory from the Lunda, while his followers extended his power throughout Katanga.

In the early 1870s, Msiri entered into a trade relationship with the powerful Swahili trader Tippu Tip and obtained the support of other coastal Swahili and Arab traders. Msiri exported slaves, ivory and copper to both the east and west coasts and imported large quantities of cloth and firearms.

Around 1880, Msiri's father died and Msiri was confirmed as mwami (king) of the region. Msiri reduced the Luba states to his north to tributary status and even raided deeply into the Mwata Kazembe's central territory.

Msiri's power reached its peak in the mid–1880s. By the end of that time, many of the peoples whom he had subjugated were in revolt.

In 1886, Msiri admitted missionaries into his kingdom and began to receive European imperialist agents. Ultimately, Msiri attempted to hold off the imperialists. However, the disintegration of his kingdom weakened Msiri's bargaining position, and the known mineral wealth of Katanga made the Europeans more insistent on controlling it.

In late 1891, Msiri was shot while negotiating with agents of King Leopold's Congo Free State. His son and successor Mukundabantu quickly came to terms with the Belgians and militarily assisted them in conquering the rest of Katanga.

Eastern Africa

• Julius von Soden became the first Governor of German East Africa.

• H. von Wissmann's began his expedition to Lake Nyasa via the Zambezi and Shire rivers. During this expedition, an outpost was set up at Langenburg.

• Menelik of Ethiopia denounced the Italian claims to a protectorate (February 9).

• IBEA Company set up an administration in Kisimayu (August).

• Emil von Zelewski was severely defeated by Hehe forces under the command of Mkwawa (August 16).

In 1891, Mkwawa annihilated a German column and emerged as the main obstacle to German occupation of southern Tanzania. Mkwawa relentlessly harassed trading caravans, German patrols, and Africans who accommodated the Germans. The Germans mounted ever larger forces against Mkwawa, and finally stormed his main fort in 1894.

After the loss of his main fort, Mkwawa resisted for four more years. But, in 1898, with his capture imminent, Mkwawa, the great Hehe leader, committed suicide rather than submit to capture. With Mkwawa's death, Hehe resistance to German aggression came to an end.

• The control of the Sultan of Zanzibar's finances was taken over by the British (October). Sir Lloyd Matthews was named the First Minister and the administration of Zanzibar was reorganized along British colonial lines.

• Sisal first introduced into German East Africa.

• The first British officer was posted in Busoga.

• Berlin Society Missionaries started work amongst the Makonde.

• Hugh Martin Thackeray Kayamba (1891–1939), a Tanzanian educator, was born.

Kayamba was the direct descendant of the great Shambaa ruler Kimweri. He was a member of an unusually well educated family and the leading representative of the country's early westernized elite.

Kayamba was born in Zanzibar. Both of his parents taught in English mission schools, at a time, when mainland Tanganyika (now Tanzania) was under German colonial rule.

Kayamba began his education at an early age. However, he left school when he was fifteen.

Kayamba then worked at various jobs throughout Kenya, returning to Zanzibar to teach briefly in 1912.

During World War I, Kayamba visited Tanga on mainland Tanganyika. Because he was a British subject, Kayamba was arrested by the Germans and detained from 1915 to 1916. Kayamba was liberated when German East Africa fell to the Belgians and British.

The substitution of British for German administration of the mainland gave Kayamba and other English educated Africans unique employment opportunities. Kayamba entered the civil service as an interpreter. By 1923, Kayamba was the head of an entirely African staff in the Tanga district office.

Kayamba formed the country's first African trade union and welfare organization. He came to prominence in 1929 when he was appointed to an advisory committee on colonial education in which he was an outspoken advocate of better educational facilities for Africans.

Two years later, Kayamba was one of three Tanganyikans to represent African interests in talks on East African union in London. In England, Kayamba adamantly opposed the merger of Tanganyika with Kenya and Uganda. He also argued for a more direct African voice in administration and opposed the forming of African reserves.

Kayamba's nationalistic and pro–African positions were often undermined by his deferential and humiliating statements to Europeans and Euro-Africans on the virtues of white rule.

When Kayamba returned to Tanga, he was made an assistant secretary to the government secretariat in Dar es Salaam. This office made Kayamba the highest ranking African in the civil service, but his real influence was minimal.

During the 1930s, Kayamba gradually became disillusioned with colonialism. In 1938, Kayamba retired to a farm near Tanga. He died eighteen months later.

• Jomo Kenyatta (c.1891–1978), the first president of Kenya, is believed to have been born in this year.

Jomo Kenyatta was born Kamau Ngengi in central Kenya. Kamau's parents were a Kikuyu speaking people.

Little is known about Kamau's very early life. However, Kamau was given some education and was baptized by the Church of Scotland Mission in 1914.

During the early 1920s, Kamau (Kenyatta) worked as an interpreter for the Nairobi municipal government. In 1922, Kenyatta joined a Kikuyu political group, becoming its general secretary by 1928. At that time, a dominant political issue was the alienation of Kikuyu land by Europeans and, in 1929, Kenyatta went to London to represent his people on the issue.

Kenyatta again went to England in 1931. He remained there for fifteen years. In London, Kenyatta studied anthropology under Malinowski and, in 1938, wrote *Facing Mt. Kenya*. *Facing Mt. Kenya* analyzed the negative impact of colonialism on Kikuyu life.

In 1945, Kenyatta joined with Kwame Nkrumah of the Gold Coast (Ghana) and other future African statesmen to form a pan–African organization.

Kenyatta returned to Kenya in 1946 and was immediately acknowledged as unchallenged leader of the nationalist movement. Rapidly Kenyatta transformed the predominantly Kikuyu Kenya African Union (KAU) into a truly national party.

After the outbreak of the so-called "Mau Mau" movement the European administration suspected the KAU of complicity. In 1952, the KAU was banned and Kenyatta and other leaders were arrested.

Kenyatta remained imprisoned and in detention until 1961. During his imprisonment and detention, Kenyatta's leadership in the nationalist movement was tacitly assumed by Tom Mboya.

When the Mau Mau emergency was declared over in 1959, most other detainees were released. Kenyatta's continued detention itself became a national political issue as the country moved towards independence.

In 1960, a new party, the Kenya African National Union (KANU) was formed and Kenyatta was named president *in absentia*. When Kenyatta was released in 1961, he was denied permission to head a government.

In the 1962 elections, KANU won. The KANU leaders refused to form a government without Kenyatta, so Kenyatta became leader of the parliamentary opposition.

After another KANU sweep in the 1963 elections, Kenyatta was allowed to form a government, becoming the first prime minister of Kenya upon the country's independence in that same year.

In 1964, Kenya became a republic and Kenyatta became Kenya's first president.

After independence, Kenyatta remained a powerful symbol of national unity and moderation. He increasingly delegated responsibility to his ministers, but his stature both in and out of Kenya remained high and Kenyatta remained an influential personage until his death in 1978.

• *Southern Africa:* Harry Johnston was appointed first Commissioner of the British Central Africa Protectorate (January).

• Sultan Abdallah of Anjouan died (February 2). A civil war erupted over his successor. Said Ali led an unsuccessful revolt in Grand Comoro and was, subsequently, deported.

• L. S. Jameson became administrator of BSA (British South Africa) Company's territories (June 10).

• An Anglo-Portuguese convention on the boundaries of North and South Rhodesia (Zimbabwe) was convened (June 11). Nyasaland was proclaimed a British Protectorate.

In 1891, the British and Portuguese governments also signed a treaty separating their zones of influence in southeastern Africa and giving the Portuguese a free hand in Gaza. Afterwards, the Portuguese mounted a major thrust to break the independent rulers of southern Mozambique. Gungunyane, the king of the Gaza, attempted to negotiate an accommodation with the Portuguese, but the Portuguese were not interested in accommodation — they were only interested in conquest.

• The first hospital in Salisbury was opened by Dominican nuns.

• The first Anglican Bishop of Mashonaland was appointed.

• The hut tax was introduced in Nyasaland.

• Joseph Booth began the Baptist Zambezi Industrial Mission at Blantyre.

Joseph Booth (1851–1932) was an English missionary. Throughout his career, Booth frequently shifted his affiliation among different Christian denominations, but consistently championed the rights of black Africans.

In 1891, Booth opened his first station for the Baptists in Malawi, where an early convert was John Chilembwe, the future leader of the 1915 rebellion against the British.

Booth traveled with Chilembwe to the United States in 1897. In the United States, a rift developed between Chilembwe and Booth. They separated — permanently.

Booth returned to southern Africa to launch a series of new missions under a succession of denominations. He frequently clashed with European authorities over political issues. Suspected of complicity in Chilembwe's 1915 uprising, Booth was expelled from South Africa.

Booth was forced to return to England impoverished.

• The BSA Company extended its operations into North Rhodesia.

• The Mozambique Company was established to exploit Manica and Sofala districts.

• The Niassa Company was established north of the Lurio River.

• A special mission on administrative reform was begun in Mozambique.

• Letsie I (c.1810–1891), the Lesotho king, died.

When Letsie succeeded his father Moshoeshoe in 1870, Basutoland (Lesotho) was a newly proclaimed British protectorate and just recovering from an exhausting war with the neighboring Orange Free State Republic. Moshoeshoe had built the kingdom largely on the strength of his own personality, but family factions had started to tear it apart before Moshoeshoe died. The year after Letsie assumed office, the British crown turned over administration of Lesotho to the Cape Colony.

The inability of the Cape to enforce its policies aggravated Letsie's problems by enabling his brothers to oppose him from their positions as district chiefs. One brother, Masupha, controlled Thaba Bosiu — Moshoeshoe's fortified mountain stronghold — and resisted all efforts to impose magistrates, setting an example which other sub-chiefs followed.

In 1873, another brother, Molapo, embarrassed Letsie's regime by betraying a foreign chief to the Euro-African government.

In 1878, the Cape prime minister Sprigg passed a law which severely restricted African ownership of firearms. After he had overwhelmed Letsie's neighbor, Moorosi, Sprigg ordered the Sotho to turn in their guns and to pay a hut tax. Letsie was inclined to compromise, but strong factions in the country adamantly opposed the Euro-African government and thus precipitated the "Gun War" of 1880.

The Sotho emerged victorious from the Gun War and protectorate administration was restored to the British Crown in 1884.

• Mbelwa Jere (c.1836–1891), the founder of an Ngoni kingdom in northern Malawi, died.

Mbelwa Jere was born in Zambia shortly after his father, Zwangendaba, crossed the Zambezi River during the great Ngoni migration from South Africa. Zwangendaba died in southern Tanzania around 1845 leaving the Ngoni to quarrel over his succession. One party favored Mbelwa, but a brother, Mpezeni Jere, was made king.

During the early 1850s, Mbelwa's faction, under the leadership of his regent Gwasa Jere, broke from the main Ngoni body and moved into northern Malawi. In northern Malawi, they settled among the local Tumbuka and Kamanga peoples. Soon thereafter, Mbelwa was formally installed as king.

During his reign, Mbelwa directed raids against most of his neighbors, whom he reduced to tributary status. In the late 1870s, however, Mbelwa was unable to quell a rebellion by the Thonga. This triggered a succession of revolts which forced him to wage bloody wars of reprisal.

During this same period, the first missionaries of the Free Church of Scotland commenced work among the Ngoni. In the 1880s, Mbelwa stabilized his relations with his neighbors and generally reduced the level of warfare.

Mbelwa died in 1891.

• Nehemiah Tile (c.1850–1891), the founder of the first independent African church in South Africa, died.

Nehemiah Tile is believed to have been a member of the Thembu branch of the southern Nguni, but his actual origins are uncertain. By the early 1870s, Tile was working as an evangelist for the Wesleyan Methodist mission in the Thembu region of the present eastern Cape Province.

Tile attended seminary and became a probationary minister in 1879. Tile became a full minister in 1883.

During the early 1880s, the Cape Colony government was informally attempting to impose an administration over the Thembu. Tile worked vigorously with the Thembu paramount chief Ngangelizwe to prevent this encroachment. He broke with his mission supervisors because of their disapproval of his political activity.

In 1884, Tile founded the Thembu National Church with Ngangelizwe's support. Tile's church was the forerunner of many independent churches among the coastal Nguni, but was unique in that it was closely identified with the traditional political authority rather than with westernized nationalists.

Tile attracted many followers and worked towards establishing his church as the official denomination of the Thembu chiefdom, but this effort failed shortly after his death.

The church continued to grow as a strong religious body, but became less closely identified with Thembu nationalism and politics.

RELATED HISTORICAL EVENTS

• *The Americas:* The Brazilian Constitution was finalized.

The Brazilian Constitution of 1891 reflected the ideal of restricted democracy. The constitution embodied the principle that political rights are granted by society to those deemed deserving of them. Accordingly, the right to vote was not permitted for the illiterate, common soldiers, clergy, and women. These limitations resulted in only two percent of the population voting for president in 1894. Deleted from an early version of the Constitution was the obligation of the state to provide education, which had figured in the empire's charter. The republic maintained the prohibition against the foundation of new monastic orders, the exclusion of the Jesuits, and the ban on religious teaching in public schools.

Additional features of the Brazilian charter were the establishment of three separate and independent powers: judicial, legislative (Chamber of Deputies and Senate) and executive.

During the operation of this constitution which was in effect from 1894 to 1930, the executive was supported by the wealthiest states — Sao Paulo and Minas Gerais — which formed a coalition with Rio Grande do Sul, Rio de Janeiro, and Pernambuco. It was this regionalism which hampered the formation of national parties. In Sao Paulo, politics were controlled by coffee plantation owners and export-import commercial concerns.

The Constituent Assembly elected the first president and vice president, Deodoro da Fonseca and Floriano Peixoto, respectively. Fonseca, who had been ruling since the fall of the empire, was supported by part of the army. Peixoto was backed by a substantial part of the army and by urban industrial and service sectors.

During Fonseca's rule from 1889 to 1891, Brazil was disturbed by economic and political crises. The old coffee plantations of the state of Rio de Janeiro declined due to the abolition of slavery, soil exhaustion, and plant disease.

To fight depression, Finance Minister Rui Barbosa launched a policy of economic recovery based upon an increase of currency emissions and credit. Barbosa attempted to redirect the economy toward activities other than agriculture for export.

The policies of Rui Barobosa that led to the

Encilhamento, a period of feverish, speculative economic activity, are a matter of some controversy. Public credit that had been restricted to coffee production and export was thenceforth extended to industry and other activities. The devaluation of currency and the imposition of tariffs to be paid in gold produced an increase in custom duties and deterred the importation of competitive manufactured goods. At the same time, special measures ensured the entry of capital goods and raw materials. Industrial expansion was further favored by declines in energy prices. Labor costs also fell due to a surplus of labor. The decrease in labor costs, however, sparked workers' strikes and conflict between labor and the federal government. Negative aspects of the Encilhamento included a high rate of inflation, increased speculation, formation of fictitious enterprises to gain favorable credits, corruption, and bankruptcies.

Bankruptcies were frequent but mostly related to fake or small, weak businesses, whereas the major industrial concerns acquired capital in spite of inflation and increased production. Nevertheless, popular discontent exploded as food prices and rent rose, salaries and wages remained low, and unemployment became extensive.

The executive, which lost the support of Congress, was closed by President Fonseca, who decreed a state of siege and announced new elections. Opponents sought support from the navy, which revolted under the command of Admiral Custodio de Melo.

To avoid civil war, Fonseca resigned in 1891 and Vice President Peixoto took over. Peixoto would govern Brazil from 1891 to 1894. During his tenure, Peixoto reversed the policy of enlarging the currency, suspended the state of siege, and deposed state governors who had supported the former president. In 1892, an unsuccessful uprising at two fortresses in Rio de Janeiro led to calls for immediate presidential elections.

All this turmoil began to erode the promise which existed after the abolition of slavery and the creation of the republic. In Brazil, in the 1890s, the seeds for recurring instability were sown.

- *Europe:* An agreement was reached between the British government and the BSA Company which extended the company's operations beyond the Zambezi River (February).
- An Anglo-Italian agreement was reached concerning Ethiopia (April 15). The agreement defined the colonial boundaries of the two European powers.

- The Katanga Company was founded.
- The powers to appoint magistrates and to raise revenue was granted to the British South Africa (BSA) Company (May 9).
- Portugal agreed to new boundaries for Angola and the Congo Free State (May 21).
- An Anglo-Portuguese convention met to set the Mozambique boundaries (June 1).
- A Franco-British agreement was reached on the boundaries for Guinea (June 26).
- The British sphere beyond the Zambezi was formally constituted (July 31).

1 8 9 2

THE UNITED STATES

Southern European Americans divided into Populist and Democratic parties with both attempting to gain the African American vote, first with friendship but later with bribery, intimidation and fraud.

In February, at the Populist Convention held in St. Louis, William E. Warwick of the Virginia National Colored Farmer's Alliance served as assistant to the secretary. Ignatius Donnely, a European American politician, declared: "I tell you, my friends, what we propose to do; we propose to wipe the Mason-Dixon line out of our geographies; we propose to wipe the color line off all our politics."

The initial initiative of the Populist Party was to effect an alliance of the poor African Americans and the poor European Americans living in the South. As Tom Watson, the Populist gubernatorial candidate in the state of Georgia explained: "Now the People's Party says to these two men, you are kept apart that you may be separately fleeced of your earnings. You are made to hate each other because upon that hatred is rested the keystone of the arch of financial despotism which enslaves you both. You are deceived and blinded that you may not see how this race antagonism perpetuates a monetary system which beggars you both."

When H. S. Doyle, an African American preacher who had been campaigning for Watson, was threatened with lynching, Watson issued a call for assistance and some 2,000 armed European American farmers guarded him for two nights.

Unfortunately, only in the state of Georgia was there a significant Populist appeal to the African American voter.

In Texas, two African Americans were appointed to the state executive committee at the first state convention. This practice of appointing one or two African Americans to the state executive committee became a standard procedure at other state Populist conventions.

In Arkansas, the Populist state platform included a resolution suggested by I. Glopsy, an African American, which included the provision: "That it is the object of the People's Party to elevate the downtrodden sons and daughters of industry in all matters before the people, irrespective of race and color."

While many European American Populists were supportive of African Americans, a great many were not. In Washington, Georgia, John Heard, a European American Populist, shot at some African Americans who attended a Democratic meeting. Similar incidents led African American political leaders in Douglas County, Greene County, and Athens, Georgia, to refuse to accept the endorsement of the Populists.

To counteract the Populist victories in the South, the Democratic Party made an appeal for the votes of African Americans. In an Alabama election, Democrats tried to attract African American voters by calling attention to the legislative measures that had benefitted African Americans, such as aid to African American education. Democrats also sponsored picnics and barbecues for African Americans.

In Georgia, the Democratic Party organized the Northern Club, a Democratic club for African Americans.

When the overtures to African Americans proved to be unsuccessful, the Democrats resorted to other tactics. A circular issued by a Wilkes County Democratic chairman recommended the use of economic power to intimidate voters: "This danger [of a Populist victory] ... can be overcome by the absolute control which you yet exercise over your property. It is absolutely necessary that you should bring to bear the power which your situation gives over tenants, laborers and croppers."

In Augusta, Georgia, Democrats stuffed the ballot boxes, creating a total number of votes which was twice the number of registered voters.

In Jackson, Mississippi, the *Clarion Ledger* attempted to frighten European American voters. The newspaper noted: "A division of the white vote means the balance of power in the hands of the Negro and this means the devil's own time wherever it exists."

• The Democratic platform of 1892

denounced Congressman Lodge's Federal elections bill. *See 1890 and 1891.*

• Congress granted a pension to Harriet Tubman for her work during the Civil War as a scout, nurse and spy.

• Matthew O. Ricketts, an ex-slave, was elected to the state legislature in Nebraska. A physician who graduated from the University of Nebraska College of Medicine in 1884, Ricketts served two terms as Omaha's representative.

• *The Labor Movement:* In St. Louis, African American longshoremen struck for higher wages.

• *Notable Births:* Mutt Carey, a jazz trumpeter, was born (August 28).

• Johnny Dodds, a jazz clarinetist, was born (April 12).

• Minnie Evans, a self-taught artist, was born in rural North Carolina (December 12).

• Luther P. Jackson, an African American historian, was born in Lexington, Kentucky (July 11).

• Augusta Savage, a noted sculptor, was born near Jacksonville, Florida (February 29).

Notable Deaths

In 1892, lynchings in the United States reached a peak. In this year, there were 160 lynchings of African Americans. Between 1882 and 1892, some 1,400 African Americans were lynched.

Outraged by an incident in which she knew the victim, Memphis journalist Ida Wells began her career of investigating lynchings in the South (March 9).

Ida B. Wells was born in Holly Springs, Mississippi. She was educated at Rust College. As an editor and part-owner of the Memphis Free Speech, Ida Wells exposed those behind the lynching of three African American Memphis businessmen. For her efforts, angry European American citizens of Memphis destroyed her offices and drove her out of the city.

Wells then went to Chicago and married Ferdinand Barnett, the founding editor of the Chicago Conservator. As Ida Wells Barnett, Barnett chaired the Anti-Lynching Bureau of the National Afro-American Council and proved statistically that the Southern European American fantasy that African American men raped European American women was not the cause of lynchings. As she came to say, "Nowhere in the civilized world, save the United States, do men go out in bands, to hunt down, shoot, hang to death a single individual."

Ida Wells Barnett was one of the founders of the NAACP (see 1909). She died in 1931.

On the national level, President Harrison presented a bill to Congress to prevent the lynching of foreign nationals.

The Republican Party platform stated: "We denounce the continued inhuman outrages perpetuated upon American citizens for political reasons in certain Southern States of the Union."

• In Georgia, European American Democrats murdered fifteen (15) African Americans during the Georgia gubernatorial campaign.

• Thomas Morris Chester (1834–1892), an African American who served as a correspondent for a major newspaper, the *Philadelphia Press*, during the Civil War, died. A previous editor of the *Star of Liberia*, Chester's dispatches covered a period of time from August 1864 through June 1865. His dispatches included reports on African American troop activity around Petersburg and Richmond, Virginia.

Thomas Morris Chester was born in Harrisburg, Pennsylvania. He studied at Alexander High School in Monrovia, Liberia, and then at the Thetford Academy in Vermont.

After the Civil War, Chester read law with a Liberian lawyer. Liking the law, he moved to England and spent the next three years at Middle Temple in London.

In April 1870, Chester became the first known person of African descent to be admitted to practice before the English courts.

• *Publications:* The Virginia Organization of True Reformers, an African American secret society, began publishing a newspaper, *The Reformer*. By 1900, *The Reformer* would have a weekly circulation of 8,000.

• Henry McNeal Turner founded the *Voice of the Missions*.

• Archibald Henry Grimke published *The Life of Charles Sumner, the Scholar in Politics*.

• *A Voice from the South,* by Anna Julia Cooper, was published.

• The newspaper, *Afro-American*, began publication in Baltimore, Maryland.

• Frances Ellen Watkins Harper published her only novel, *Iola Leroy: Or, Shadows Uplifted*.

• The *Medical and Surgical Observer* was published in Jackson, Tennessee (December). Miles Vandahurst Lynk was the first editor.

• *The Black Church:* Henry McNeal Turner founded the *Voice of the Missions*.

• *The Performing Arts:* The World's Fair Colored Opera Company gave the first performance by African Americans at New York's recently opened Carnegie Hall.

• In 1892, Sissieretta Jones, a famous African American opera singer known as "Black Patti," sang at the White House. Afterwards, she organized Black Patti's Troubadours. This travelling group toured the United States for 19 years.

• *Technological Innovations:* Andrew Beard was granted a patent for his rotary engine.

• *Sports:* In New York City, an African American athletic club, the Calumet Wheelmen, was organized.

• William Henry Lewis, an African American who had played football for Amherst College and Harvard University, was named to Walter Camp's All-American team.

• George "Little Chocolate" Dixon became the world featherweight boxing champion by defeating Jack Skelly, a person of European heritage, in New Orleans. The city's major newspaper criticized the event for bringing the two fighters together on equal terms. Dixon would hold this title until 1900.

• The first African American intercollegiate football game was played between Livingstone College and Biddle College (now known as Johnson C. Smith). The game was played on Thanksgiving Day.

THE AMERICAS

• *Cuba:* Jose Marti formed the Partido Revolucionario Cubano.

In the 1890s, among the Cuban emigres in the United States led by Jose Marti, the Cuban Revolutionary Party (the Partido Revolucionario Cubano) was already forming. The party was officially announced on April 10, 1892, and Marti was named its representative. From the start, the group dedicated itself to raising funds and unifying Cubans to prepare for war.

With the critical economic situation, the drop in the price of sugar, and the failure of the reform plan proposed by Overseas Minister Antonio Maura, armed struggle appeared to be the only option.

• *Haiti:* Leon Laleau (1892–1979), a poet and novelist, was born in Port-au-Prince (August 3).

Leon Laleau obtained a degree in letters and

sciences and a degree in law. Laleau was appointed to various political and diplomatic posts as Minister of Foreign Affairs, Minister of National Education, Agriculture, and Public Works, Chief of Diplomatic Missions in Rome, London, Paris, Santiago, and Lima.

Laleau was also the Special Mission Ambassador to Panama, Cuba, the United Nations and the UNESCO. He was one of the members who signed the Accord on July 24, 1934 for the end of the United States occupation of Haiti. Acclaimed as one of the most brilliant writers of his time, Laleau won many international awards, including the Edgar Allan Poe Prize in 1962.

Laleau was a member of the Ronsard Academy and the Mediterranean Academy (Academie Mediterranean).

Laleau's principal works include: *A Voix Basse* (1920), poetry; *Le Rayon des Jupes* (1928), poetry; *La Fleche au Coeur* (1926), poetry; *Abbreviations* (1928), poetry; *Musique Negre* (1931), poetry; *Ondes Courtes* (1933), poetry; *Jusqu'au Bord* (1916), a novel; *La Danse des Vagues* (1919), a novel; *Le Choc* (1932), a novel; *La Pluie et le Beau Temps,* a play; and *Le Tremplin,* a play.

AUSTRALIA

• Peter Jackson defeated Frank Slavin to become the British champion.

After fighting the American Jim Corbett to a draw, the Afro-Australian Peter Jackson *(see 1886)* went to England where a new challenge awaited him — Frank Slavin, an Australian, who had been trained by Jackson's former mentor, Jem Mace.

Slavin was a magnificent athlete with a powerful punch. He was a brutal boxer and, being a product of his times, a virulent racist. Slavin despised black men and welcomed the opportunity to prove the superiority of whites.

On May 30, 1892, Slavin got his chance. At the National Sporting Club in London, Slavin met Jackson in a widely advertised fight which was attended by none other than the Prince of Wales, the future Edward VII. As Slavin stepped into the ring, he shouted, "To be beaten by a nigger is a pill I will never swallow."

The betting on the bout was fast and furious. The betting was two to one in favor of Slavin. After all, Slavin was stronger and he was white.

When the bell rang, the two approached each other cautiously. Slavin shot out a roundhouse right which if it had caught Jackson would surely

have finished him. But it did not catch Jackson. With the moves of a panther, Jackson kept the more powerful Slavin at bay. Using a swift left jab, Jackson began to frustrate Slavin. Slavin was being outboxed.

Showing his lack of class, Slavin began taunting Jackson in the hope that Jackson might accept the bait and try to slug it out. But Jackson was too wily for that ruse. He continued to outbox Slavin and for the first five rounds, the fight was his.

In the sixth round, however, Slavin caught Jackson with a smashing blow that staggered Jackson. Quickly Slavin followed with another tremendous blow. All seemed lost for Jackson, but then the bell rang.

Sensing victory in his grasp, Slavin rushed out in the seventh round in an attempt to finish off Jackson. But by then Jackson had caught his breath and managed to regroup. He evaded Slavin's charge and resumed the tactic of keeping Slavin at bay with a straight left jab.

Round seven came and went. So also did the eighth and the ninth. With each round, Slavin's frustration and anger grew.

When the bell for the tenth round rang, Slavin made a mad charge for Jackson. But like a skilled matador, this time Jackson met Slavin head on. Flashing the famous one-two combination, Jackson stunned Slavin.

Slavin stood helplessly in the middle of the ring. His hands were at his side and he seemed unable to move. Slavin quite literally had been knocked out on his feet.

The crowd clamored for Jackson to finish him. The referee motioned for Jackson to continue the fight. But Jackson, seeing his opponent helpless — seeing the man who had viciously called him a "nigger" being unable to move — could not bring himself to hit Slavin again.

Jackson went up to Slavin and gently pushed him to the ground. He then picked Slavin up and carried him tenderly to his corner. The fight was over but the immortality that is the legend of Peter Jackson had begun.

AFRICA

• *North Africa, Egypt and Sudan:* The Health Commission comprised of representatives of foreign colonies met in Tangier.

• Abbas II became the Khedive of Egypt. His tenure was noted for the hostility shown to Britain.

• In 1892, Zubeiru, the governor of Adamawa (Sudan), felt he could no longer tolerate the presence of the Mahdists. Zubeiru challenged Hayatu, the leader of the Mahdists, on the battlefield. In the resulting battle, Hayatu was victorious.

When Zubeiru succeeded his brother, Sanda, he was considered unstable, and probably suffered from epilepsy. He began a program of Islamic fundamentalist reform. These reforms along with the perception of him held by his people, made Zubeiru unpopular and weakened his ability to withstand the challenge of Hayatu ibn Sa'id.

Hayatu was a great-grandson of the Fula Islamic revolutionary 'Uthman dan Fodio who had created the empire of which Adamawa was a part. Hayatu came to Adamawa and attracted a large following. Zubeiru felt compelled to fight him, but was disastrously defeated in 1892. Hayatu was unable to follow up his victory however and later was killed in Bornu.

- Muhammed Tewfik, the Khedive of Egypt, died (January 7). He was succeeded by his son Abbas II.
- *Western Africa:* The French negotiated a treaty with Tieba, the King of Sikasso.
- Prempe, the asantehene of the Asante, attacked and defeated the Brong states to the north, which had broken away from the Asante empire. Retaking the Brong states was especially important because of their location among the northern trade routes.
- Menard's expedition came to a tragic end as Menard was killed at Seguela (February 4).
- Binger's expedition helped to define the Ivory Coast frontier with the Gold Coast.
- Egbados was subdued by the British.
- Behanzin, the King of Dahomey, attacked the French (August 9). The French captured Cana and Abomey (November 17) forcing Behanzin to flee. On December 3, Dahomey was declared to be French protectorate.

Behanzin attacked the French at Cotonou in 1892. The French were aided by Toffa, the ruler of Porto Novo—a former Dahomean dependency.

After five battles, the French occupied Abomey, the inland capital. Behanzin surrendered in 1893. He was later deported to Martinique and then to Algeria.

When the French invaded Dahomey in 1892, Toffa supplied porters for the French. He was rewarded for his services by being allowed greater freedom than most of his neighbors who had come under French rule. Porto Novo's limited autonomy ended with Toffa's death in 1908.

- The administration of Portuguese Guinea was reorganized (May 21).
- A Franco-Liberian convention met to determine the Ivory Coast frontier (December 8).
- Civil war began in Kano following a disputed succession.
- An uprising was led by Moli Boia.
- The Divine Word Fathers (SVD) started work in Togo.
- The Oil Rivers Irregulars, later the Niger Coast Constabulary, was founded.
- The Combes expedition cut Samory's communications with Futa Jalon and Sierra Leone.
- Rabeh Zubayr, a powerful slave trader, attacked the Baghirmi state. Baghirmi allied with neighboring Wadai, but was nevertheless defeated.
- Prempe II (1892–1970), the ruler of the Akan Asante confederacy during the colonial and early independence period, was born.

Prempe II succeed his uncle, Prempe I *(see 1871)*, in 1931. Prempe II was an educated Christian. At the time of his succession, he was working as a storekeeper for a European firm.

In 1935, Prempe II was officially restored as asantehene — ruler of all of Asante — in a magnificent coronation ceremony. At the same time, the Asante Confederacy Council was created as a kind of parliament. There was at first some question as to the scope of Prempe's powers, but these proved to be extensive, largely because of Prempe's personal ability.

Prempe's interests usually coincided with those of the British. In 1932, in the midst of some controversy, Prempe supported them by favoring continued British administration of Asante as an autonomous unit.

In 1935, political rivals charged that Prempe was unfit to hold office because he was circumcised, a breach of Asante tradition. The circumcision allegation was untrue, and Prempe banished the dissidents with the approval of the British.

Despite his close ties to the British, Prempe was not a puppet. Prempe supported the cocoa hold-ups and boycott of European goods in 1934 and 1937 when cocoa prices were very low.

In 1937, Prempe was knighted. Soon afterwards, his powers began to wane in the face of nationalistic party politics. From 1948, Prempe and other traditional leaders came under attack from Kwame Nkrumah and the Convention People's Party (CPP).

In 1954, Prempe backed the National Liberation Movement (NLM) which formed in Kumasi to counter the CPP. The 1956 elections resulted in the NLM and an allied party winning majorities in Asante. However, the CPP was the overall victor.

Powerless against Nkrumah, in 1957, Prempe switched his allegiance to the CPP.

By the time Asante had become the independent nation of Ghana, Prempe's authority, like that of many other traditional African leaders, had diminished.

• *Central Africa:* Joubert was defeated by Rumaliza at Kalonda (April 5). Albertville was besieged and was not relieved until December when forces commanded by Lieutenant Long arrived.

• Ngongu Lutebo was defeated at Batugenge (May). Sefu ibn Tippu Tip, with a force of 10,000 Arabs, defeated the Belgian forces under Hodister.

• O. Baumann began exploring Burundi. Baumann came to be perceived by the Hutus as their liberator from Tutsi domination.

• Emin Pasha was murdered in Congo (October).

• Belgians suppressed the uprising of Arab slaveholders in the Congo (November 22).

• A general war began in Kasai.

• Delanghe's campaign began in northeast Congo.

• *Eastern Africa:* A German force was defeated by the Chagga people near Moshi (June). A new expedition was initiated to quell the Chagga.

• The Hehe raided Kilosa killing all of the German garrison.

• A quarrel arose between Catholics and Protestants in Uganda. After a complicated series of wars and treaties, Apolo Kagwa's Protestant faction emerged as the dominant force.

• Tafari Makonnen (later known as the Emperor Haile Selassie) (1892–1975) was born (July 23).

In 1892, the Lion of Judah was born.

Tafari Makonnen was born into the royal family of the former kingdom of Shoa. His father, Makonnen, was a cousin of emperor Menelik II. Makonnen served Menelik as an important general and councillor, and as governor of the Harar province.

The young Tafari made a favorable impression on Menelik whom he met through his father. Tafari's chances for political advance would have been weakened by his father's death in 1906 if not for the intervention of Menelik who called Tafari to his court.

Tafari continued his education at Addis Adaba and was appointed governor over a small province. Tafari later rose (in 1910) to the governorship of the important Harar province.

Menelik spent his last years on the verge of death while political factions grappled to name his successor. Tafari was a strong candidate, but he pledged his support to Iyasu, Menelik's choice as his successor.

When Iyasu ascended to the throne upon Menelik's death in 1913, he soon proved unacceptable to the dominantly Christian ruling class by appearing ready to transform Ethiopia into a Muslim state. In 1916, Tafari, feeling that Iyasu's heresy released him from his pledge to Menelik, led the Shoa faction in a successful revolt. Iyasu was deposed.

Instead of claiming the crown for himself, Tafari pledged his allegiance to Menelik's daughter, Zauditu. Zauditu was crowned Empress and, as his reward, Tafari was designated prince regent and heir apparent, with the title Ras.

Over the next fourteen years, Tafari served as the head of government and assumed an increasingly prominent role. By the standards of traditional Ethiopian society, Tafari was a progressive reformer. He worked to extend Ethiopia's contacts with the Western world. His first application for admission to the League of Nations in 1919 was rejected because of the existence of slavery in Ethiopia. However, Tafari finally obtained League membership in 1923 and then moved to abolish slavery.

In 1928, Empress Zauditu attempted to curb Tafari's powers. However, she was preempted when Tafari staged a successful palace coup. Subsequently, Tafari forced Zauditu to recognize his complete supremacy in Ethiopian affairs. By Zauditu's own hands, Tafari was crowned *negus* — King of Ethiopia.

In 1930, Tafari suppressed a revolt led by Zauditu's former husband, *Ras* Gugsa Wolie, the governor of the northern provinces. Not long afterwards, Zauditu died.

Tafari was then crowned *Negus Nagast* — "King of Kings" — and, as such, became the Emperor of Ethiopia. It was then that Tafari took his baptismal name, "Haile Selassie" — "Lion of Judah" — as his dynastic name.

In 1931, Haile Selassie introduced the first Ethiopian parliamentary body, with appointed members. However, his reform movement was interrupted in 1934, at the onset of a border dispute with Italian Somaliland.

Haile Selassie appealed to the League of Nations for assistance. But none came. Mussolini's army invaded Ethiopia the next year. The Lion of Judah led his army into the field against the invading Italians. However, his forces proved to be no match for the modern Italian army.

Haile Selassie left Ethiopia and went to Europe to plead his case to the League of Nations. While the Italians were overrunning Ethiopia, the League of Nations ignored Haile Selassie's pleas for intervention.

Only with the outbreak of the Second World War was Haile Selassie able to garner support. From his base in London, he lobbied the British government to supply forces to re-capture his country. With the aid of the British, Haile Selassie led the forces which successfully reconquered Ethiopia in 1941.

Once again upon the throne, Haile Selassie began to restructure his government. Throughout the 1940s, he promoted the development of a secular educational system and drew upon many Western nations for economic and technical assistance.

In 1955, Haile Selassie promulgated a new constitution which allowed for elected members of parliament beginning in 1957. However, despite this reform, the real power continued to reside with the Emperor until 1974.

Despite Haile Selassie's long record of progressive reform, many Ethiopians found the pace of change too slow. During his state visit to Brazil in 1960, officers of his palace guard attempted a coup and placed his son, Asfa Wossen, on the throne. However, the army remained loyal and Haile Selassie returned home to regain control.

Throughout the 1960s, Haile Selassie played an increasingly active role in inter-African affairs. The first conference of the Organization of African Unity (OAU) met in Addis Adaba. Addis Adaba subsequently became (in 1963) the headquarters for the OAU.

In 1968, Haile Selassie's negotiations with the independent government of Somalia helped to quell a major border dispute with that country. Haile Selassie also played a leading role as a mediator in the civil wars in Nigeria which lasted from 1968 to 1970 and the 1972 civil war in Sudan.

The predominantly Muslim province of Eritrea had been fully incorporated into Ethiopia in 1962. However, Eritrean nationalism continued to plague Haile Selassie.

The latent problem of internal radicalism resurfaced early in 1974 when an army mutiny forced Haile Selassie to make his first concessions of real power. By the end of the year, the military was in complete control, and Haile Selassie was placed under house arrest.

While under house arrest, Haile Selassie — the Lion of Judah — died (August 1975). The circumstances under which the Lion of Judah perished remain mysterious.

- *Southern Africa:* Ndebele began to raid Mashona in the Fort Victoria area (August 1).
- The French occupied Iles Glorieuses (August 23).
- The first trains reached Johannesburg (September) and Pretoria (December).
- The French occupied St. Paul Island on October 19 and, on October 27, Amsterdam Island was likewise occupied by France.
- The Primitive Methodist mission was set up in Barotseland.

Though he was always lukewarm towards Christianity, Lewanika, the king of the Barotse (the Lozi), perceived great advantages in the western education the missionaries offered, and he hoped a Christian influence would help "modernize" his country.

- The Berlin Missionary Society began its work in Southern Rhodesia.
- Lentswe, the chief of the Kgatla, converted to the Afrikaners' Dutch Reformed Church and declared it the Kgatla official church.
- Sarili (c.1815–1892), the paramount chief of the Gcaleka Xhosa and titular paramount chief of all the Xhosa through a long period of British wars, died.

Sarili became Gcaleka chief in 1835, when his father Hinta was killed by the British during a frontier war. Sarili quickly reaffirmed his father's treaty with the Cape governor D'Urban, agreeing to pay a large indemnity for the war. He never paid this indemnity, but northern Nguni refugees who had lived among the Xhosa migrated to the Cape Colony, taking about 30,000 Xhosa cattle with them. The Cape government's support of this theft left Sarili's Xhosa bitter.

In 1844, Sarili signed a treaty of friendship with the Governor, Maitland. Although he was merely the ritual head of the Xhosa people, the Cape government held him responsible for the actions of the Rarabe and other Xhosa groups whom he could not control.

During the 1850 Frontier War, Sarili was

accused of harboring Rarabe refugees. He was attacked and looted by the British. As European encroachment on Gcaleka territory mounted, Sarili turned to a seer, Mhlakaza, for advice. Sarili fully accepted Mhlakaza's prophecy that wholesale destruction of Xhosa wealth would bring the millennium to the Xhosa. Sarili strongly supported the ensuing cattle killing and persuaded the Rarabe chief Sandile to comply with the prophecy.

All but a few sections of the Gcaleka destroyed all their livestock and agricultural produce. Many thousands of Xhosa starved and others went to the Cape Colony for employment. The Xhosa were left economically broken and unable to resist effectively the continuing British pressure.

The Cape government suspected Sarili of having initiated the cattle-killing to induce the Xhosa to fight a desperate war with the Europeans. The Cape governor, George Grey, sent a force which chased Sarili into exile among his neighbors.

In 1864, Sarili was allowed to return home. Once home, Sarili began to recoup his political and military strength. During the 1870s, Sarili fought several successful actions against the Thembu chief Ngangelizwe, with whom Sarili competed for land and cattle.

In 1877, Sarili's dispute with the Mfengu people over land drew in a new British intervention, which produced the last Xhosa Frontier War. Again the British forces chased Sarili into exile and the governor and high commissioner Bartle Frere declared Sarili deposed.

Sarili remained in obscure exile among the Mpondo until 1883 when he was pardoned. Afterwards, Sarili avoided conflicts to escape imprisonment at Robben Island — a common fate amongst his fellow chiefs.

In 1885, Sarili's territory was annexed by the Cape Colony and Xhosa independence ended.

• Sechele I (c.1810–1892), the last independent ruler of the northern Kwena chiefdom, died.

During the first decades of the nineteenth century, the northern Kwena chiefdom was torn by internal strife. When Sechele's father Motswasele was assassinated around 1822, the chiefdom fragmented.

A succession of militaristic invaders then ravaged Kwena country in the western Transvaal in the era known as the Difaqane. Sechele himself was captured by the Kololo of king Sebitwane. Eventually, however, he was ransomed by the chief of the Ngwato, who assisted him to obtain the Kwena throne around 1831. Afterwards, Sechele maintained a strong interest in Ngwato politics.

Meanwhile the powerful Ndebele of Mzilikazi were occupying the western Transvaal. Sechele learned that the Ndebele had killed his uncle around 1834, so he fled north. The Ndebele pursued and scattered the Kwena, but Sechele eluded capture. His success in evading the Ndebele attracted to his banner other Tswana refugees, including the Kaa. By the late 1830s, the Ndebele had left the Transvaal. Sechele returned to his homeland and re-established Kwena unity.

In the early 1840s, the missionary David Livingstone opened a mission among the Kwena. Sechele learned to read and write and was baptized in 1848. Sechele was Livingstone's first convert.

Through the 1840s, Sechele traded for firearms with Europeans and aroused the anger of the Afrikaners in the developing Transvaal Republic to his east.

The Afrikaners attacked Sechele in 1852 and drove him into what is today known as Botswana. In 1864, Sechele established a permanent Kwena capital at Molepolole. Sechele eventually gathered more than 30,000 followers.

Sechele was instrumental in placing Macheng on the Ngwato throne in 1857. Later he sent Kwena troops to the Ngwato capital to assist Kgama III to overthrow Macheng. Meanwhile, Sechele allowed the Kgatla of Kgamanyane to settle in Kwena territory.

When the Kgatla refused to acknowledge Sechele's sovereignty, a desultory Kwena-Kgatla war erupted. At the same time, the Transvaal Afrikaners began to encroach on Kwena territory. In order to forestall an Afrikaner conquest, Sechele reluctantly assented to the establishment of a British protectorate during Charles Warren's visit in 1885. Under the new British Bechuanaland Protectorate, Sechele's dispute with the Kgatla was soon resolved.

The Kwena then enjoyed relative peace and an autonomy not shared by their kinsmen in the neighboring Transvaal.

On his death in 1892, Sechele was succeeded by his son Sebele. Sebele joined with the rulers of the Ngwato and Ngwaketse to prevent a takeover of Botswana by the British South Africa Company of Cecil Rhodes.

• Manuel Antonio de Sousa (1835–1892), a Portuguese-Indian builder of a powerful personal empire, died.

Manuel Sousa was born in India of Catholic Goanese parents. He went to Mozambique in the early 1850s to administer his uncle's estate (prazo) near Sena.

Sousa engaged in trade and developed a private army composed of hunters and slaves. Among Africans, Sousa became known as "Gouveia," an adaptation of "Goa."

In 1863, the Portuguese government, whose control of the Zambezi valley was tenuous, appointed Sousa as "captain major" over the Manica region. Despite his official title, Sousa remained an independent agent throughout his career.

During the 1860s, Sousa fought to curb Gaza raiding from the south. He constructed a chain of fortifications as a defensive line. From 1867 to 1869, Sousa participated in four Portuguese attacks on the da Cruz family whose Massangano kingdom was blocking trade on the Zambezi River.

During the 1870s, Sousa intervened in inter-Shona wars. Around 1874, Sousa was recognized as the titular sovereign of Manica. During this year, he also married a daughter of the ruler of Barue. Sousa would later use this connection to place his infant son on the Barue throne with himself acting as regent. This regency essentially made Sousa the de facto ruler of the entire region between the Pungwe and Zambezi Rivers.

During the 1880s, the Portuguese government turned to Sousa for support in asserting its control over the region as British and other interests began to show interest in central Africa.

In 1884, Sousa crushed a revolt of the Massingire state between the Shire and Zambezi Rivers. Two years later, Sousa moved deeper into northeastern Zimbabwe.

In 1887, Sousa failed to conquer the Shona Mtoko chiefdom, but with Portuguese help he drove the da Cruz family out of Massangano. The next year, he visited Lisbon (Portugal) where he was highly acclaimed. Indeed, he was made a colonel in the Portuguese army in tribute to his service.

Around this time, Cecil Rhodes' British South Africa Company obtained a concession from the Ndebele king Lobengula which was used to occupy Mashonaland in 1890. Sousa and a Portuguese agent, Paiva Andrada, rushed to Manica in eastern Shona territory to forestall a British takeover there. Both were captured by the British and sent to Cape Town.

During Sousa's involuntary absence from Zimbabwe subordinate chiefs defected and his private empire began to crumble. When the British released him in 1891, Sousa returned to the Zambezi to re-gain control of his empire.

After some initial military successes against the Barue chiefdom, Sousa was wounded in action. Manuel Sousa, the great empire builder, was slain by a child.

The demise of Manuel Sousa resulted in a collapse of Portuguese authority on the lower Zambezi.

RELATED HISTORICAL EVENTS

• *The United States:* John Greenleaf Whittier (1807–1892), a European American poet noted for his anti-slavery poetry, died.

John Greenleaf Whittier was born in Haverhill, Massachusetts. His parents were Quaker farmers. Whittier's poetry showed the influence of his Quaker religion and rural New England background. Whittier is often called the "Quaker poet."

The Scottish poet Robert Burns also influenced Whittier. Like Burns, Whittier wrote many ballads on rural themes. However, unlike Burns, Whittier's poems lacked a certain witticism.

From 1833 to 1863, Whittier was active in politics and the anti-slavery movement. Whittier called for the abolition of slavery in newspaper articles and while serving in the Massachusetts legislature in 1835. The abolitionist cause also dominated his poetry. In "Moral Warfare" (1838) and "Massachusetts to Virginia" (1843), Whittier attacked the injustices of slavery. Whittier also condemned what he considered to be the hypocrisy of the United States — a nation founded on the ideals of freedom but which perpetuated the evil institution of slavery.

Whittier's most noted poem was "Ichabod" (1850). In "Ichabod," Whittier criticized Senator Daniel Webster of Massachusetts for his pivotal role in the passage of the Compromise of 1850. Whittier objected to the compromise because it required that runaway slaves be returned to their owners. However, instead of being a hyperbolic polemic, Whittier's "Ichabod" uses a dignified, restrained tone that makes the poem seem more like an expression of sympathy for Senator Webster rather than an attack upon him.

• *Europe:* An Anglo-German Convention met to discuss the Cameroon (October).

• *Africa:* Eduard Schnitzer (1840–1892), the German administrator in Anglo-Egyptian

Sudan who was known as Emin Pasha, died.

After training as a doctor in Germany, Eduard Schnitzer went to Albania to serve under the Ottoman administration. In Albania, Schnitzer took the name Muhammed al-Amin (Mehemet Emin).

In 1875, Muhammed al-Amin arrived in Khartoum to practice medicine and was soon appointed a medical officer by Charles Gordon, the governor of Equatoria. Muhammed al-Amin himself became governor of the province in 1878 after Gordon rose to become governor-general of Sudan.

Muhammed al-Amin led several scientific expeditions and negotiated with the Nyoro king Kabarega and other rulers in present day Uganda. When the capital of Sudan, Khartoum fell to the Mahdists in 1885, Muhammed al-Amin was left isolated on the upper Nile. A mutiny among his Sudanese troops added to his difficulties.

During this time, Muhammed al-Amin received the Turkish title "Pasha." Now known as Emin Pasha, the plight of Muhammed al-Amin attracted worldwide attention.

A massive relief force under the command of the explorer Henry Stanley was sent to rescue Emin Pasha. Emin Pasha wanted to remain at the Nile to solve his problems himself, but he reluctantly consented to accompany Stanley to Bagamoyo on the east African coast.

Emin Pasha later joined the German administration in east Africa to help extend German control in the interior.

In 1892, Emin Pasha was killed by Arab slavers in eastern Zaire.

---

1 8 9 3

THE UNITED STATES

• Dr. Daniel Hale Williams performed the world's first successful heart operation at Chicago's Provident Hospital (July 9).

On July 9, 1893, Daniel Hale Williams opened the chest of James Cornish, a laborer who had been stabbed. Williams found the pericardial sac, emptied it of blood, and successfully sutured it.

"Doctor Dan" was a founder and first vice-president of the National Medical Association. He was also the first and only African American to be invited to become a charter member of the American College of Surgeons.

• Representative George W. Murray of South Carolina was the only African American elected to the 53rd Congress.

• C. H. J. Taylor was appointed by President Grover Cleveland to serve as minister to Bolivia. However, the Senate refused to confirm his nomination. Taylor would later accept the post of recorder of deeds for the District of Columbia.

Nancy Green (1831–1898), a former slave from Montgomery County, Kentucky, made her debut as the first Aunt Jemima. Green appeared as Aunt Jemima at the Columbian Exposition in Chicago, Illinois, where she served pancakes. The Aunt Jemima Mills Company distributed a souvenir lapel button which bore her photograph and the caption, "I'se in town honey." This slogan later became the slogan on the company's promotional campaign. Nancy Green, the world's first living trademark, was Aunt Jemima for three decades.

• William Alphaeus Hunton became the secretary of the International Young Men's Christian Association.

• *Organizations:* The first African American branch of the Young Women's Christian Association (YWCA) was opened in Dayton, Ohio.

• *The Labor Movement:* The American Federation of Labor (AFL), at its 13th national convention, unanimously adopted a resolution affirming unity of labor regardless of race.

• *Notable Births:* Perry Bradford, a songwriter, was born (February 14).

• William "Big Bill" Broonzy (1893–1957), a country blues singer, was born (June 26).

William "Big Bill" Broonzy was born in Scott, Mississippi. His mother was a former slave from whom he learned many African American songs.

Broonzy worked as a farmhand, janitor and preacher, during the course of his life. This life experience served as a backdrop to Broonzy's composing and singing of the blues. Over his lifetime, Broonzy wrote over 300 songs.

Broonzy went to Chicago in 1920, where he worked as a redcap. He made his first recordings for Paramount Records in 1926. He played guitar, accompanying Clarence La Font and Bumble Bee Slim. In the late 1930s, he was singing blues on Perfect and Vocalion Records, and in 1938 he sang in Carnegie Hall.

• Bessie Coleman, a pioneering aviator, was born in Texas (January 20). Coleman was the first African American woman to obtain a pilot's license.

• "Mississippi" John Hurt, a singer, was born (July 3).

• Charles S. Johnson, a noted sociologist, was born in Bristol, Virginia (July 24). Johnson founded the National Urban League's magazine, *Opportunity,* and served as president of Fisk University.

• Walter Francis White, long-time Executive Secretary of the NAACP, was born in Atlanta, Georgia (July 1).

• *Notable Deaths:* There were 117 African Americans lynched in 1893.

• John Mifflin Brown (1817–1893), a bishop in the African Methodist Episcopal Church, died.

John Mifflin Brown, a person of African American and European American parentage, was born in Cantwell's Bridge (now called Odessa), Delaware. In 1836, Brown joined the Bethel African Methodist Episcopal Church. He prepared for the ministry and attended Wesleyan Academy and Oberlin College.

Between 1844 and 1847, Brown served as principal of the Union Seminary, which is now known as Wilberforce University. Union Seminary was the first higher educational effort of the African Methodist Episcopal Church.

In 1864, Brown was chosen editor of the *Christian Recorder,* the oldest African American newspaper in the United States.

In 1868, Brown was ordained a bishop in the African Methodist Episcopal Church. During his twenty-five years of service as a bishop, Brown is credited with establishing the Payne Institute (now known as Allen University) at Columbia, South Carolina, and Paul Quinn College at Waco, Texas.

• Mary Ann Shadd Cary (1823–1893), a noted abolitionist lecturer and journalist, died. Cary was the publisher and editor of the *Provincial Freeman,* a Canadian newspaper published for those African Americans who had fled the United States for Canada after the passage of the Fugitive Slave Law of 1850.

• Thomy Lafon (1810–1893), an African American philanthropist who supported the American Anti–Slavery Society and the underground railroad, died.

• Daniel Alexander Payne (1811–1893), a bishop of the African Methodist Episcopal and a president of Wilberforce University, died.

Daniel Alexander Payne was a bishop of the

African Methodist Episcopal Church. Payne was born in Charleston, South Carolina to parents who were free African Americans. As a student, Payne attended the Minor's Moralist Society School—a school established by free African Americans. Under the tutelage of Thomas Bonneau, Payne excelled at mathematics, English, Latin, Greek and French. In 1826, Payne joined the Methodist Episcopal Church and, in 1829, he opened a school for African American children which became the most successful institution of its kind in Charleston. The school flourished until the South Carolina legislature passed a law in 1834 against teaching African Americans to read or write.

Payne soon left South Carolina. He went to Pennsylvania and attended the Lutheran Theological Seminary at Gettysburg. In 1839, Payne was ordained as a minister. In 1840, Payne opened a school in Philadelphia and, in 1842, he joined the African Methodist Episcopal Church. Chosen as historiographer of the African Methodist Episcopal Church in 1848, Payne traveled extensively throughout the United States. Payne was elected bishop in 1852.

In 1863, Payne purchased Wilberforce University and served as president of the university for thirteen years. Among his publications were *Pleasures and Other Miscellaneous Poems* (1850), *The Semi–Centenary of the African Methodist Episcopal Church in the U.S.A.* (1866), *A Treatise on Domestic Education* (1885), *Recollections of Seventy Years* (1888), and *The History of the AME Church from 1816 to 1856* (1891).

• Charles Lewis Reason (1818–1893), an African American writer, died.

• *Miscellaneous State Laws:* Arkansas made separate railroad waiting stations compulsory.

• *Miscellaneous Publications:* Rufus Lewis Perry published *The Cushite; or the Descendants of Ham as seen by Ancient Historians.*

• In 1893, Paul Laurence Dunbar published *Oak and Ivory. See 1872.*

• Peter Randolph published *From Slave Cabin to the Pulpit: The Autobiography of Reverend Peter Randolph: The Southern Question Illustrated and Sketches of Slave Life.*

• Gussie Davis published *The Fatal Wedding.*

• *Scholastic Achievements:* Ex–Mississippi Senator Blanche K. Bruce was made a trustee of the public schools of Washington, D. C. Bruce would serve in this capacity until 1898.

• Harriet (Hattie) Aletha Gibbs Marshall (1869–1941), a concert artist, pianist, and educator, graduated from the Oberlin Conservatory of Music.

Harriet Aletha Gibbs Marshall was born in Vancouver, British Columbia, the daughter of Mifflin Gibbs. She was a pioneer in her efforts to bring African American concert artists from all over the nation to Washington, D. C.

In 1903, Harriet Marshall established the Washington Conservatory of Music in Washington, D. C., which she directed until 1923. In 1923, Marshall moved to Haiti with her husband. In Haiti, Marshall founded an industrial school and collected folk music.

Marshall returned to the United States in 1936, and established a National Negro Music Center in association with the Washington, D.C. conservatory.

- William L. Bulkley was awarded a doctorate in Latin from Syracuse University, Syracuse, New York.
- *The Sciences:* In 1893, Daniel Hale Williams conducted the first open-heart surgery under rather primitive conditions. Williams ground breaking surgery involved the suturing of the pericardium of a stabbing victim.
- *The Black Church:* The American National Educational Baptist Convention was created.
- The Afro-Presbyterian Council was the first formal organization for African American Presbyterians in the North and West. The organization became the Council of the North and West in 1947, and was formally dissolved in 1957. The realization that the dissolution had been premature led to the formation of the Black Presbyterians United in 1968.
- *The Arts:* Henry Ossawa Tanner completed *The Banjo Lesson.*

In 1893, Tanner returned to the United States to recover from a bout with typhoid fever. While in the United States, Tanner was invited to speak at the Congress on Africa which was held at the World's Columbian Exposition in Chicago, Illinois in August of 1893. Tanner's experience at the Congress brought on a racial awareness which had heretofore been lacking in Tanner's work. This increased racial awareness led to Tanner's painting *The Banjo Lesson* (1893), one of Tanner's most recognized pieces, and *The Thankful Poor* (1894).

- *Black Enterprise:* Thomy Lafon (1810–1893), an African American tycoon from New Orleans, who was worth a million dollars at his death, had "contributed so much to the development of the city that the State Legislature ordered a bust of Lafon to be carved and set up in some public institution in New Orleans."
- E. P. McCabe, an African American entrepreneur, took part in the Oklahoma Land Rush. McCabe became the founder of two all-black Oklahoma towns, Liberty and Langston.
- The North Carolina Mutual Life Insurance Company was founded in Durham, North Carolina. The North Carolina Mutual Life Insurance Company was the first African American insurance company to attain one hundred million dollars in assets. The success of the company was largely due to the abilities of Charles Clinton Spaulding (1874–1952) who became general manager of the company in 1900 and was president from 1923 until his death in 1952.
- *Sports:* William Henry Lewis, an African American playing for Harvard, was named by Walter Camp to the All-American team for the second time.
- Willie Simms won the Belmont Stakes aboard Comanche.

THE AMERICAS

- *Brazil:* In 1893, Antonio Vicente Mendes Maciel, a messianic religious leader called the Counselor by his followers, settled the village of Canudos. An economically, self-sufficient peasant community, Canudos served as a refuge for the poor and unemployed.
- *Canada:* Mary Ann Shadd Cary (1823–1893), a noted abolitionist lecturer and journalist, died. Cary was the publisher and editor of the *Provincial Freeman,* a Canadian newspaper published for those African Americans who had fled the United States for Canada after the passage of the Fugitive Slave Law of 1850.
- *Cuba:* Mariana Grajales (1808–1893), one of the most outstanding women in Cuban history, died (November 28).

Mariana Grajales was born in Santiago de Cuba of Dominican parents on July 16, 1808. She was first married to Francisco Regueiferos. With Francisco Regueiferos, Mariana had four children before becoming a widow.

Mariana eventually remarried. She married Marcos Maceo and had nine children with him between 1845 and 1860. The oldest of Mariana's children with Marcos Maceo was Antonio Maceo, the great general of the Cuban independence army *(see 1878 and 1896).*

Mariana was an ardent participant in the Cuban struggle for independence. All of Mariana's children, along with her second husband Marcos, fought in Cuba's wars for independence. One of the touching moments of Cuban history was when Mariana's husband, Marcos Maceo, fell on the battlefield on May 14, 1869, during the Ten Years War. Marcos with his last dying breath whispered, "I have done all I can for Mariana."

Mariana would serve as an inspiration for many of the Cuban freedom fighters. Jose Marti, Cuba's greatest hero and most influential writer, wrote to Antonio Maceo of Mariana, "I will now see again one of the women who has moved my heart: your mother." On another occasion, Marti wrote: "I will remember her with love all my life."

Today, in Havana, there is a monument dedicated in honor of Mariana Grajales, an exemplary mother whose quest for freedom inspired the Cuban people to fight for their own.

- *Haiti:* Hannibal Price published *De la Rehabilitation de la Race Noire par la Republique d'Haiti* (On the Rehabilitation of the Black Race by the Republic of Haiti). *De la Rehabilitation de la Race Noire par la Republique d'Haiti* was a defense of the black race and a response to Spencer Saint-John, the English diplomat who in 1884 published the offensive book on Haiti entitled *Hayti or the Black Republic.*
- Hannibal Price (1841–1893), the author of *De la Rehabilitation de la Race Noire par la Republique d'Haiti,* died in Baltimore, Maryland (January 1).

Hannibal Price was a native of Jacmel. Price was educated in his native town. He landed a diplomatic career starting out as a Counselor to the Provisional Government of 1875 after the fall of President Domingue. Later, Price was appointed Minister Plenipotentiary of Haiti to Washington from 1890 to 1893.

It was during his mission in Washington that Price wrote his famous book *De la Rehabilitation de la Race Noire par la Republique d'Haiti.*

- *Jamaica:* Norman Washington Manley (1893–1969), the founder of Jamaica's first national party, was born.

Norman Manley was of Irish and African descent. He was born in rural Jamaica and grew up in modest circumstances. After graduation in 1913, from Jamaica College, Manley taught school

for nearly two years before leaving Jamaica on a Rhodes Scholarship at Oxford University.

Manley's university studies were interrupted by World War I. During the war, Manley served in an artillery regiment of the British Army.

Returning to Oxford after the war, Manley received a bachelor's degree in 1920 and was called to the bar at Gray's Inn in 1921.

Back in Jamaica by 1922, Manley rocketed to prominence as a lawyer and was appointed King's Counsel within only ten years.

The 1930s were a period of growing unrest in the West Indies, including Jamaica. An incident on May 2, 1938, in which rioting strikers were bloodily suppressed by the police, was the beginning of serious labor and political turmoil. Manley was retained by the West Indian Sugar Company to defend its actions against the rioters. Shortly afterward, however, Manley's cousin William Alexander Bustamante, the recognized labor leader at the time, was arrested, and Manley represented Bustamante, whose release he secured.

Manley led in forming the People's National Party (PNP) which, from its inception on September 19, 1938, had a socialist and nationalist ideology. The PNP became the model for nationalist parties throughout the West Indies in the postwar era. For a time, the Bustamante Industrial Trade Union (BITU), headed by Bustamante, served as labor wing of the party.

The two-party system was inaugurated in 1943, with formation of the Jamaica Labour Party (JLP) by Bustamante. By that time, Bustamante had split with Manley.

Around the same time, the PNP formed the Trade Union Congress. Largely as a result of the PNP's efforts, universal suffrage was granted for the 1944 elections under a new constitution.

The PNP lost the 1944 elections to the JLP, with Manley losing in his own constituency. The PNP also lost the election of 1949, despite winning a majority of the popular vote. Manley, however, was elected and was Opposition Leader between 1949 and 1955.

Manley campaigned for a West Indian Federation as the logical extension of Jamaican nationalism, and he became one of the most committed West Indian leaders to this cause.

In 1953, a ministerial system of government was inaugurated, and two years later Manley led his PNP to victory over Bustamante's JLP. He became chief minister and promptly began the task of reforming the economy, agriculture, and education.

Manley secured increased revenue from the

bauxite companies operating within Jamaica. There was substantial economic growth, particularly in manufacturing and tourism. Manley also pressed Britain for full internal self-government which was granted in 1959, at which time he became premier.

Manley contributed significantly to the inauguration of the West Indies Federation in 1958. This contribution was made even though the loosely linked federal party with which his PNP was associated (and over which Manley personally presided) lost badly to Bustamante's Jamaica Labour Party. Despite this defeat, Manley led the PNP to victory in the 1959 national elections.

Almost immediately after the creation of the West Indies Federation, however, Bustamante called for Jamaica's secession from it. In response, Manley agreed to call a referendum in 1961. In the referendum, the electorate overwhelmingly voted for secession.

The PNP and JLP jointly prepared the independence constitution, and Britain agreed to grant independence after elections were held in 1962. Manley and the PNP lost the elections, relegating him to Leader of the Opposition when the country received its independence in August 1962.

In opposition, Manley assumed the role of elder statesman and began to restructure his party to win back the support it had lost over the years. Manley decided to return to greater emphasis on democratic socialism, although supporting some private enterprises, as well as joint ventures between the private and state sectors. Manley resigned his position as party leader and member of the House of Representatives shortly before his death.

In 1969, Norman Manley was declared a National Hero of Jamaica.

EUROPE

• A chamber concert in Croydon, England on October 9, 1893, included Samuel Coleridge-Taylor's Piano Quintet, part of his Clarinet Sonata, and three of his songs, with the Coleridge-Taylor himself at the piano.

AFRICA

• *North Africa, Egypt and Sudan:* Riyad Pasha became the Premier of Egypt.
• Khedive Abbas dismissed the pro–British minister (January 17).

• Moroccans obstructed the extension to fortifications of Melilla. The war of Melilla between Spain and Morocco followed.
• *Western Africa:* The French colonies of Guinea and Ivory Coast were formally established (March 10).
• In 1893, Macina, the last stronghold of the Tukolor Empire, fell. The French, under the command of Louis Archinard *(see 1888),* installed Muhammed Aguibu Tall as the new ruler of the co-opted Tukolor Empire. Ahmadu ibn 'Umar Tall, the deposed ruler of the Tukolor Empire, was forced to flee.

When the French military leader Archinard set out to conquer the Tukolor empire, Archinard used the rivalry between the two brothers (Muhammed Aguibu Tall and Ahmadu ibn Umar Tall) as a wedge. After the fall of Segu in 1890, Archinard contacted Muhammed and claimed that it was only Ahmadu and not the Tukolor nation whom the French were fighting. Muhammed responded amicably and formally submitted to the French the following year.

Muhammed's acquiescence to French rule, divided the Tukolor and facilitated the fall of Macina, Ahmadu's last base, in 1893. Archinard rewarded Muhammed by making him the new ruler of Macina. This was a wise move on Archinard's part since, by making Muhammed the ruler of Macina, he averted further resistance from the population. The population of Macina appeared to be quite willing to accept the substitution of one son of al-Hajj 'Umar for another.

• An Anglo-German agreement on the boundaries of Nigeria and Cameroon was reached (November 15).
• A French governor was installed in Soudan (November 21).
• The French reached Timbuktu (December 12).
• The Oil Rivers Protectorate was renamed the Niger Coast Protectorate.
• Great Britain obtain treaties of trade and friendship with Abeokuta, Oyo and Ilorin.
• Rabeh, a former slave of Zubayr Pasha, led an army from the eastern Sudan into Bornu. The Shehu of Bornu was defeated and Rabeh was proclaimed the Sultan of Bornu.

In 1893, Hayatu *(see 1898),* the protégé of the Mahdi, decided to throw in his lot with Rabeh Zubair, a great Mahdist leader. Rabeh's forces although greatly outnumbered, were victorious against the Bornu forces through their tactical superiority, and Hashimi, the Bornu ruler, was forced to abdicate in 1893.

Hashimi was succeeded (and assassinated) by Kiyari. However, Kiyari was no more successful against Rabeh than Hashimi had been. He was captured and executed by Rabeh later in 1893.

The conquest of Bornu was complete.

- Hamallah (Hamahu'allah ibn Sharif Muhammed ibn Sidna Omar), the founder of the Hamallist Islamic protest movement, was born.

Hamallah (1893–1943) was the son of a Berber trader and a Fula slave woman. He received a modest Islamic education at Nioro du Sahil in present Mali before becoming a disciple of al-Akhdar, a former member of the Tijani Islamic brotherhood who had been ousted for adopting a different rosary. When al-Akhdar died in 1909, Hamallah became the leader of the movement based at Nioro.

The Tijani brotherhood under the famous revolutionary al-Hajj 'Umar had been in the forefront of resistance to the French, but after 'Umar's defeat the Tijaniyya came to support the colonialists. Any splinter groups distrusted by the Tijaniyya were also distrusted by the French. Hamallah's preaching differed from Tijaniyya orthodoxy in its emphasis on egalitarianism, mysticism and faith, in addition to the different rosary.

Hamallah himself never made anti–French statements nor did he preach in public. Hamallah's many followers, however, refused to acknowledge traditional Tijani Islamic leaders and it was those Tijani Islamic leaders who had the ear of the French.

Nevertheless, a 1916 report on the movement by the well-known ethnographer Paul Marty was favorable towards Hamallah. Meanwhile, Hamallah's following had spread throughout the western Sudan. Although Hamallists consciously ignored the colonialists, Hamallah avoided any illegal activity.

In 1925, amid fears of a worldwide Islamic conspiracy, the French authorities deported Hamallah to Mauritania. Hamallah's followers in the French Sudan (Mali), who at the time were not under the direct control of Hamallah, took a militant stance against the French and the Tijani brotherhood. Violence erupted. The most violent incident occurred in 1930 at Kaedi, Mauritania, where about thirty people were killed during an assault on the district office.

Hamallah denounced the violence. Nevertheless, the French relocated Hamallah to the Ivory Coast where it was hoped that his influence would become dissipated.

Instead of seeing his influence wane, Hamallah became something of a cause celebre. He won the support of some highly educated Islamic clerics and important Senegalese politicians such as Galandou Diouf and Lamine Gueye.

Diouf and Gueye intervened on Hamallah's behalf and Hamallah returned home in 1935.

In 1940, near Nioro, a Hamallist band apparently led by three of his sons, attacked a camp of Tenwajib pastoralists, a group which had been harassing the Hamillists for many years. Over four hundred Tenwajib, mainly women and children, were massacred.

In response, the French rounded up six hundred Hamallists, shot thirty-three leaders, including Hamallah's sons, and imprisoned the rest. Governor General Boisson deported Hamallah to Algeria, and two years later he was removed to France.

Hamallah's deportation did not stem the violence associated with his movement. In 1941, six Europeans were killed by Hamallists at Bobo Dioulasso (Upper Volta). Such incidences of violence would continue until 1951. However, after 1946, a new freedom of political expression in French West Africa permitted the creation of less violent channels of protest, and the Hamallist movement became integrated with the *Rassemblement Democratique Africain,* the largest anti-colonial party in French West Africa.

As for Hamallah, while in exile in France, Hamallah staged a fast protesting his deportation. It was complications resulting from this fast which led to Hamallah's death in 1943.

- Tieba, the ruler of the Kenedugu kingdom of Sikasso, died (1893).

Tieba's kingdom was a major goal in Samori's scheme for the conquest of the Guinea interior. In 1887, Samori laid siege to the capital, Sikasso, one of the best protected towns in the region. Tieba and Samori's armies waged a fifteen month war of attrition. During this conflict, Tieba signed a treaty with Gallieni placing himself under French protection. The treaty allowed Tieba to receive French arms.

In August of 1888, Samori was forced to withdraw from Tieba's kingdom with his army depleted and some of his best generals killed. Among the casualties were Samori's son and two of his brothers. This defeat sparked a major revolt in Samori's empire which monopolized Samori's attention for the next year.

In 1891, the French, hopeful of persuading Tieba to ally with them against Samori, aided Tieba in some local conflicts. However, the diplomatic errors committed by the French aroused Tieba's hostility. The net result was that the French were forced to fight Samori without Tieba's assistance.

At Tieba's death in 1893, he was succeeded by his brother, Ba Bemba. Ba Bemba had been sympathetic to Samori and adamantly refused to help the French against him.

In 1898, the French turned on Sikasso. After twelve days of fighting the walls of the capital fell and French forces entered the city. Inside the walls, the French found the body of Ba Bemba. Ba Bemba had taken his own life.

- *Central Africa:* There was some chaotic fighting between the Arabs and the *Force Publique* on the Lualaba River (February 26). On March 4, Nyangwe was occupied.
- The Arabs were expelled from Stanley Falls (May 18).
- An Arab camp was destroyed at Utia Mutongo (August 6).
- A revolt of Dahomey troops occurred in the Cameroon.
- The Jesuits began their work in the Congo.
- The Decazes mission commenced operation on the Oubangui River.
- The *Force Publique* began operations against Rumaliza.
- *Eastern Africa:* IBEA handed over Uganda to the British government (March 10).
- The Italians defeated a Mahdist attack on Eritrea near Agordat (December).
- The British built four forts in Bunyoro (December).

When the British withdrew their garrison from Toro in 1893, Kabarega, the king of Bunyoro, immediately re-occupied the province. The British then invaded Bunyoro with the assistance of the Ganda.

After an initial success, Kabarega withdrew from his capital and waged a long guerrilla campaign.

- Sayyid Ali of Zanzibar died. Sayyid Khalid ibn Barghash seized the palace. He was ejected by British and Zanzibari troops.
- Sayyid Hamid ibn Thuwaini was installed by the British and the sultan's power in Zanzibar was thereafter ceremonial in nature.
- Lieutenant Prince routed the Nyamwezi under the command of Siki.

- Meli, the Chagga chief, was defeated by the Germans.
- The first German government school was opened at Tanga.
- The Leipzig Mission began work in German East Africa.
- J. von Schele became Governor of German East Africa.
- Between 1893 and 1899, the Finance, Agricultural, Survey, Justice, Medical and Public Works Departments were organized in Dar es Salaam.
- Between 1893 and 1905, the Tanga-Mombo railway was constructed.
- Mugalula committed suicide.

When Nyungu, the unifier of the Kimbu people, died in late 1884, Nyungu bequeathed to his daughter Mugalula an empire (in Tanzania) which was inherently more stable than that left by the Nyamwezi chief Mirambo. Mugalula committed suicide in 1893 and was succeeded by another female ruler, Msavila. Msavila voluntarily submitted to the Germans in 1895 and renounced all claims to sovereignty over the Kimbu.

- *Southern Africa:* France occupied Kerguelen Island (January).
- Natal was granted self-government (May 10).
- There was a Matabele uprising against the BSA Company (July).
- Britain agreed to the annexation of Swaziland by Transvaal (November 13).
- Employing the use of machine guns, Leander Jameson crushed the Matabele revolt and occupied Bulawayo (November).
- An unproductive meeting of the Swaziland convention was held (November).
- Lobengula fled (November).

In 1893, Leander Jameson, an agent of Cecil Rhodes, used an Ndebele (Matabele) raid on the Shona as the pretext for invading the Ndebele.

Lobengula, the king of the Ndebele who attempted to negotiate until the end, offered only token resistance. Jameson's conquest was completed within six months. Jameson then became administrator of all of present day Zimbabwe.

An interesting footnote in history is that Khama, the ruler of the Ngwato, a Ndebele rival group, personally commanded Ngwato troops against the Ndebele during Rhodes' war with Lobengula.

As for Lobengula, he attempted to flee to the

land of the Ngoni king Mpezeni Jere in eastern Zambia. However, while in flight, Lobengula contracted smallpox.

Lobengula died of smallpox in 1894. He was the last Ndebele king.

- Zombe (Abercorn) and Ikawa (later Fife) were made into British posts.
- A treasury grant of 10,000 pounds was agreed to for the establishment of the Nyasaland Protectorate.
- In Mozambique, Chanetta, the ruler of the Makanga kingdom, died. He was succeeded by his nephew, Chegaga, for brief time until Chegaga gave way to another of Pedro Pereira's sons, Chinsinga.
- Alfred Bitini Xuma (c.1893–1962), a future president-general of the African National Congress, is believed to have been born in this year.

Born to an aristocratic but poor Xhosa family in the Transkei, Alfred Xuma saved money to travel to the United States, where he worked his way through high school and college. Xuma obtained a medical degree in Europe before returning to South Africa.

In 1940, Xuma was elected president-general of the ANC at a time when the congress movement was at a low ebb. He revised the constitution of the ANC and allied with the Indian National Congress, thus laying the basis for the mass protest movements of the 1950s.

In 1944, a Youth League formed within the ANC. Its leaders — Mandela, Sisulu, and Tambo — pushed for more militant action.

In 1949, the leaders of the Youth League gave their support to J. S. Moroka who was elected president of the ANC in Xuma's place.

RELATED HISTORICAL EVENTS

The Americas

In Brazil, with the support of Admiral Luis Filipe Saldanha da Gama, a monarchist who claimed that Floriano Peixoto's government was unconstitutional, the navy, under the leadership of Custodio de Melo revolted once again. In the same year, federalists in Rio Grande do Sul rebelled against the authoritarian local government and, after joining forces, dominated the south of the country. The decisive victory of federal forces in 1894 ended a period of troubled consolidation of the republic, although the hopeless resistance of Saldanha da Gama lasted until August 1895. The main urban centers were also disturbed by conflicts between the National Guard, police, and army and between Brazilians and Portuguese.

- *Europe:* An Anglo-German agreement was reached on the Shari District (November 15).
- The Vatican removed the ban on the translation of the Bible into African vernaculars.
- Antonio Enes published *Mocambique.* In *Mocambique,* Enes set out the bases for Portuguese colonial policy.
- *Africa:* Samuel White Baker (1821–1893), a British explorer of the upper Nile River and an administrator of Sudan under the Egyptian government, died.

Using his own financial resources, Samuel Baker decided to find the sources of the Nile River. From 1862 to 1865, Baker and his wife explored southern Sudan and northern Uganda. During their explorations, they named Lake Albert. It was Lake Albert which Baker advocated as being the ultimate source of the Nile River.

When Baker later returned to Cairo (Egypt), the Khedive Ismail named Baker governor of the Equatoria province of southern Sudan and gave him the title of Pasha. Baker would serve in this capacity from 1869 to 1873.

As an Egyptian Pasha, Baker was the first of what would become a long line of Englishmen to hold high office in the Egyptian government. In his official capacity, Baker worked to bring this large region under administrative control and tried unsuccessfully to end the slave trade there.

In 1872, Baker proclaimed an Egyptian protectorate over the Nyoro kingdom but was driven out by King Kabarega. Baker was succeeded as governor of Equatoria by C. G. Gordon and returned to England, where he was a persistent advocate of British involvement in Sudan.

Baker wrote several books which continue to be valued as source material for the history of the regions he explored.

- John William Colenso (1814–1893), the first Anglican Bishop of Natal, died. *See 1866.*
- William Mackinnon (1823–1893), the founder of the British East Africa Protectorate, died.

After running a prosperous trading firm in India for thirty years, William Mackinnon turned his attention to the commercial possibilities of east Africa. In 1878, Mackinnon leased mainland territory from the Sultan of Zanzibar,

Barghash. This venture came to nothing, but his agents continued to collect treaty rights in present day Kenya and Uganda.

Mackinnon formed the Imperial British East Africa Company, for which he received a royal charter in 1888. Mackinnon's company established the first European administration in Kenya but went bankrupt and turned over its protectorate to the British government.

• Theophilus Shepstone (1815–1893), an influential British civil servant in South Africa, died.

The family of Theophilus Shepstone settled in the eastern Cape region in 1820. It was there that he became intimate with the Nguni people.

Shepstone served as interpreter during the 1835 European-Xhosa War, and then served with a British force sent to Natal to help settle the Zulu-Afrikaner War of 1838.

After the creation of British Natal, Shepstone became Agent for Native Affairs. For over thirty years, Shepstone was the most influential European in Natal.

Shepstone confronted Natal's immense African refugee problem by establishing reserves, creating hereditary chiefs, and developing a system of indirect rule. Many of his innovations became models for future European-African relations throughout South Africa.

In the 1860s, Shepstone established an alliance with the neighboring Zulu. This alliance resulted, in 1873, in Shepstone being invited to "crown" Cetewayo *(see 1884)*. Thinking that the ceremony bestowed on him quasi-sovereignty over the Zulu, Shepstone pronounced a set of laws which had no relevance to the independent Zulu state.

Later in 1873, Shepstone feared that the refusal of a Hlubi chief, Langalibalele, to register his people's guns would incite a general African rebellion against the tiny European population. Shepstone proceeded to sack the Hlubi settlements and subjected Langalibalele to a sham trial and banishment.

Shepstone's treatment of Langalibalele badly damaged Shepstone's credibility with other African rulers and forced him to harden his policies.

In 1876, Shepstone instigated a war in the Transvaal Republic. The following year, he personally annexed the Transvaal to the British Crown.

In a new role as administrator of the Transvaal, Shepstone altered his relationship to the Zulu, whom he had previously supported in boundary disputes with the Transvaal. Shepstone convinced the new high commissioner for South Africa, Bartle Frere *(see 1884)*, to invade Zululand in order to advance the goal of British-Afrikaner federation. Shepstone and Frere then suppressed a government report which supported Zulu boundary claims vis-a-vis the Transvaal. Shepstone next cited Cetewayo's violations of the "laws" which he had promulgated in 1873 as a pretext for war.

In late 1878, Shepstone and Frere issued an ultimatum to Cetewayo to disarm. The next year the two men launched a successful invasion into Zululand.

Shepstone retired in 1880. He returned briefly in 1884 to administer a Zulu reserve which the British had separated from Cetewayo's kingdom.

• Johannes Gerhardus Strydom (1893–1958), a prime minister of South Africa, was born.

Johannes Strydom was born in the Cape province where he trained in law. Later he went to the Transvaal to work in the civil service. In 1929, Johannes Strydom was elected to the national parliament.

In the parliament, Strydom quickly gained a reputation as a hard-line Afrikaner nationalist. He opposed the alliance between Hertzog and Smuts in 1933 which fused the Nationalist Party together. When Malan came to power in 1948, Strydom became minister of lands and irrigation.

Strydom succeeded Malan as prime minister in 1954, when the latter retired. During his administration, Strydom worked towards making South Africa a republic, while his Bantu Affairs Minister, Hendrik Verwoerd, advanced the tide of discriminatory legislation.

In 1956, Strydom's government arrested more than 150 people for "treason." These arrests initiated a legal battle which lasted until 1961 and resulted in the dismissal or acquittal of all the defendants.

Strydom died in 1958. He was succeeded by Verwoerd.

1894

THE UNITED STATES

• Congress repealed one of the cornerstones of Reconstruction, the Enforcement Act of 1870, thereby making it easier for some states to disenfranchise Afro-American voters (February 8).

• The Populists gained control of the North Carolina Legislature with the support of the remnants of the old Republican organization and dismantled the Democratic election machinery.

• During the 1894 elections, African Americans were openly bribed. Indeed, in the Charlotte, Virginia *Dispatch,* an African American Democrat openly reported that African American votes could "be cornered at half-price."

• The *Louisiana Populist* commented on recent elections: "All the hill parishes where the [European Americans] are in the majority, the Populists polled big majorities, but in the river parishes, where the [African Americans] were in the majority, the Democrats succeeded in maintaining [European American] supremacy with the [African American] votes."

• In the election of 1894 in Texas, of 14 counties with African American populations of more than fifty percent, seven voted Democratic, four voted Republican and three voted Populist.

• Archibald Henry Grimke was named American consul to Santo Domingo.

• *The Labor Movement:* At its 14th convention, the American Federation of Labor unanimously adopted a resolution affirming the unity of labor regardless of race.

• In accord with other railroad unions, Eugene V. Debs' American Railway Union excluded African Americans from membership. The Brotherhood of Boilermakers and Iron Shipbuilders, the International Brotherhood of Electrical Workers and the International Association of Machinists followed the same policy.

• *Notable Births:* The musician Charles "Cow Cow" Davenport was born (April 23).

• E. Franklin Frazier (1894–1962), an African American historian and sociologist, was born (September 24).

E. Franklin Frazier was born in Baltimore, Maryland (or Washington, D. C.?). Educated at Howard University and the University of Chicago, Frazier taught in the sociology department of Howard and occasionally at Columbia University.

In 1940 and 1941, Frazier served as a Guggenheim Fellow.

In 1948, E. Franklin Frazier was elected to serve as president of the American Sociological Society.

Frazier is best known for his book, *Black Bourgeoisie.* His other works include: *The Negro Family in Chicago* (1932); *The Negro Family in the United States* (1948 rev. ed.); *The Negro in the United States* (1957 rev. ed.); *Race and Culture Contacts in the Modern World* (1957); and *The Negro Church in America* (1961).

• Lucille Hegamin, a singer, was born (November 29).

• James P. Johnson, a jazz pianist, was born in New Brunswick, New Jersey (February 1). Johnson's Harlem stride piano technique would influence Fats Waller and Duke Ellington.

• The comedienne, Jackie "Moms" Mabley, was born in Brevard, North Carolina (March 19).

• Nightclub hostess Ada Bricktop Smith was born in Alderson, West Virginia (August 14).

• Bessie Smith (1894?–1937), a trailblazing blues singer, was born (April 15).

Bessie Smith was born in Chattanooga, Tennessee. At the age of 13, Bessie was discovered by Ma Rainey. Bessie toured with the Rabbit Foot Minstrels and gradually achieved recognition on the African American vaudeville circuit.

Smith began her recording career in 1923 with *Down Hearted Blues.* Smith's accompanist on many of her recordings was James P. Johnson.

Smith's career declined during the Depression, partly because people were not buying records and partly because of personal problems.

In 1937, Bessie Smith died in Mississippi following an automobile accident. Her untimely death is largely attributable to the fact that she was denied entry into the hospital which was nearest to the accident scene because the hospital was for European Americans only.

Today Bessie Smith is generally recognized as one of the great jazz singers and many consider her to be the greatest blues singer to have ever sung.

• Jean Toomer, the author of the experimental novel *Cane,* was born in Washington, D. C. (December 26).

• Paul Revere Williams was born in Los Angeles, California (February 18). Williams was noted for designing the Hollywood YMCA and houses for Frank Sinatra, Lon Chaney and others.

• Jesse Ernest Wilkins (1894–1959), Assistant Secretary of Labor in the Eisenhower administration, was born.

Jesse Ernest Wilkins was born in Farmington, Missouri. He was educated at the University of Illinois and Chicago School of Law.

In 1953, President Eisenhower chose Wilkins as the first vice president of the Committee on Government Contracts.

In 1954, Eisenhower again turned to Wilkins and appointed Wilkins to the position of Assistant Secretary of Labor.

- *Notable Deaths:* In 1894, 135 African Americans were lynched.
- Macon B. Allen (1816–1894), the first African American admitted to the Massachusetts bar, died.
- Sarah Remond (1826–1894), an African American civil rights activist, died.
- Norbert Rillieux (1806–1894), an inventor and scientist, died in Paris.

Norbert Rillieux was the son of a wealthy European engineer and a COTW woman. Despite the fact that Norbert was born out of wedlock, his father, Vincent Rillieux, sent Norbert to Paris to study engineering.

1830 was a very significant year in the life of Norbert Rillieux. In 1830, Norbert became an instructor in Paris at the L'Ecole Centrale where he taught applied mechanics at L'Ecole Centrale. Also, in 1830, Norbert Rillieux published a series of articles on steam engine mechanics and steam economy. Finally, in 1830, Rillieux is credited with inventing the triple-effect evaporator used in sugar refining.

In 1846, Rillieux patented a vacuum cup which "revolutionized sugar refining methods in that day." By 1855, the Rillieux system of steam evaporation was installed in all the sugar refineries in the southern United States, Cuba, and Mexico.

In 1881, Rillieux devised a system for the production of beet sugar. This invention was highly successful and became a common sight on sugar beet plantations.

Despite his achievements, Rillieux remained unappreciated in his native Louisiana. Two of his suggestions for improvement of the state (a method of draining the bayous of Louisiana and a sewage system for the city of New Orleans) were rejected primarily because of Rillieux's race.

Rillieux died in his adopted country. Rillieux died in Paris in 1894.

- Benjamin S. Turner (1825–1894), a former Member of Congress, died.

Benjamin S. Turner was born a slave in Halifax, North Carolina, but was taken to Alabama, freed and given a basic education. Before becoming a prosperous small businessman in Selma, Alabama, Turner served as a tax collector and city councilman. In 1870, Turner was elected as a Republican to the House of Representatives. Defeated in 1872, Turner retired from politics.

- *Miscellaneous State Laws:* Virginia enacted new election codes in which: (1) registration certificates had to be secured far in advance of an election; (2) a change in residence, or changes in precinct boundaries required obtaining a new certificate; (3) candidates' names were to be arranged on ballots by office, not by party as had been previously done; and (4) the time allotted for voting in the polling booth was limited to two and a half minutes.
- *Publications*: Appointed, by Walter Stowers and William H. Anderson, was published in Detroit. *Appointed* was the first African American novel which dealt with the impact of Jim Crow racism and the "black peril phobia" of the 1890s. *Appointed* treated post-slavery serfdom, convict-labor, lynching, disenfranchisement and segregation as aspects of systematic repression.
- In 1894, Lucius Henry Holsey published a *Manual of the Discipline of the Colored Methodist Episcopal Church in America.*
- John Mercer Langston, a former Minister to Haiti and a Virginia Congressman, published *From the Virginia Plantation to the National Capitol,* his autobiography.
- *Scholastic Achievements:* George Washington Carver graduated from Iowa State College.
- *The Black Church:* In 1894, Lucius Henry Holsey published a *Manual of the Discipline of the Colored Methodist Episcopal Church in America.*
- *The Arts:* Henry Ossawa Tanner completed *The Thankful Poor.*
- *The Performing Arts:* Henry Burleigh, a noted African American singer became the soloist at Saint George's Church in New York City. He would remain in this position until 1946. Burleigh also served as soloist for the Temple Emanuel for over twenty years. *See 1866.*
- *Sports:* Willie Simms, an African American jockey, won the Belmont Stakes aboard Henry of Navarre. It was Simms' second consecutive victory at Belmont.

THE AMERICAS

• *Canada:* In 1894, Anderson Abbott, the first Canadian-born person of African descent to receive a license to practice medicine in Canada, became surgeon-in-charge at the Provident Hospital and Training School in Chicago, the first such institution for African Americans in the United States.

EUROPE

• Between 1894 and 1897, some of Samuel Coleridge-Taylor's works were heard at the Royal College of Musicians (RCM), notably the Nonet, the Clarinet Quintet, *Five Fantasiestucke* for string quartet, the first three movements of the Symphony in A minor, and the String Quartet in D minor.

• Annita Garibaldi (1821–1894), the Afro-Brazilian wife of the Italian liberator Garibaldi, died. An excellent rider, Annita Garibaldi was a captain in her husband's legion and rode to battle beside him.

AFRICA

• *North Africa, Egypt and Sudan:* Khedive Abbas Hilmi II inspected the Egyptian army after reform by Kitchener (January).

• Italians took Kassala from the Dervishes (July 17). Clashes also occurred between the Belgians and the Dervishes.

• Nubar Pasha became the Premier of Egypt.

• Abd al-Aziz ibn Hasan became the Sultan of Morocco. Bu Ahmad, a black African slaver, served as vizier for the fourteen-year-old sultan. In essence, Bu Ahmad was the regent of Morocco until 1900.

• The Agreement of Marrakesh between Spain and Morocco ended the war of Melilla.

• *Western Africa:* There was an uprising in Bissau (November).

• Colonel Bonnier was killed by the Tuareg (January 10).

• Behanzin was captured in Dahomey and, on June 22, Ballot became the governor of Dahomey. Subsequently, Dahomey was proclaimed a French colony.

• Captain Lugard signed a treaty with the French expedition under the command of Captain Decoeur (November 10).

In 1894, Britain's George Goldie again confronted French competition, this time in Borgu. The result was the famous English-French race to Nikki to obtain a treaty with the supposed overlord of Borgu. Goldie engaged Frederick Lugard to lead the expedition. The expedition succeeded in nosing out the French. Afterwards, Goldie's company continued to expand its holdings by treaty and conquest. Two particularly important conquests were Nupe and Ilorin in 1897.

• An expedition was sent against the Itsekiri in Nigeria (August).

Dogho, an Itsekiri trading rival of Nana Olumu, the ruler of the Benin River, aided the British when they moved to depose Nana by force in 1894. The British abolished Nana's office, but rewarded Dogho with appointments to other offices.

As for Nana Olumu, Nana surrendered, and after his trial, was stripped of his wealth and deported. Nana was permitted to return home in 1906, where he spent the last ten years of his life.

• The Fabert and Donnet missions were dispatched to Adrar.

• Prempe was officially installed on the Golden Stool — the great throne of the Asante Empire.

• The British attempted to place a resident in Kumasi.

In 1894, the British attempted to place a resident in Kumasi, offering Prempe a stipend. Prempe refused the offer, fearing a threat to Asante's sovereignty. Meanwhile Prempe sent his own envoys, led by John Owusu-Ansa (*see 1895*), to England.

Prempe's delegation to London unsuccessfully attempted to see Queen Victoria. They sought an audience with the Queen in order to refute British reports of Asante misrule and human sacrifice.

Prempe also tried to ally with Samori Toure, the great Mandinka ruler, who was building his second empire in the Ivory Coast interior. Prempe's overture to Samori failed. Its failure was largely due to the fact that Prempe hoped to befriend the French to counteract the British, while Samori wanted to do the exact opposite.

• Samory moved his empire.

In 1894, realizing he could not defeat the French, Samory decided upon a daring alternative. Samory moved his empire eastward to the Ivory Coast interior, pursuing a scorched earth policy in the lands he vacated. There he began the conquest of new lands, and briefly attempted to ally with Prempe I, the ruler of Asante in the Gold Coast.

• Wobogo, the ruler of the Mossi state of Ouagadougou (in Burkina Faso) signed a treaty of friendship with the British in 1894.

• *Central Africa:* A Franco-German agreement on the boundaries of French Congo and the Cameroon was finalized (March 15).

• Mahdist troops attacked the Congo Free State post at Mundu and were repelled with heavy losses (March 18).

• An Anglo-Congolese treaty on the boundary of the Congo with Uganda was negotiated (May 12). Germany and France protested the terms of the treaty.

• A Franco-Congolese convention gave French access to the Nile (August 14). France subsequently occupied the former Belgian posts on the Upper Oubangui.

• G. A. von Gotzen explored Rwanda. In June, Gotzen was received by Mwami Rwabugiri of Rwanda. On June 16, Gotzen "discovered" Lake Kivu.

• The *Force Publique* initiated a campaign against the Kibonge.

• The Arabs in Kasai were defeated.

• Between 1894 and 1900, France explored and occupied Chad.

• *Eastern Africa:* A treaty established the Toro Confederacy, bringing Toro into the British sphere of influence (March 3).

• Uganda was declared a British Protectorate (April 11).

In 1894, a new treaty laid the basis for the future government of the Ganda kingdom and a British protectorate was formally declared.

When Frederick Lugard secured treaty rights for the Imperial British East Africa Company of William MacKinnon, a protectorate was declared over the Ganda kingdom in 1894. Other territories were soon acquired as well.

• An Anglo-Italian agreement was reached on East Africa assigning Harar to Italy (May 5).

• A new German expedition was mounted against the Hehe (October). Mkwawa *(see 1898)* was defeated.

• An uprising under Hasan ibn Omari near Kilwa was suppressed.

• Sheikh Mbarak al-Mazrui was allowed to settle near Dar es Salaam with 1,000 followers.

• Captain Prince captured the Hehe fortress of Kalenga (October 30).

• Lugard partitioned Buganda among the Protestants, Catholics and Muslims, giving the Protestants the superior position.

Buganda was subsequently governed by two prime ministers — one Protestant, the other Catholic.

• There was an uprising on the coast of German East Africa under Bwana Heri.

In 1894, Bwana Heri clashed with the new German administration and attempted to initiate a rebellion. After being defeated by the Germans, Bwana Heri fled to Zanzibar.

• Menelik campaigned against Walamo in person.

• The boundary between Italian Somalia and Ethiopia was defined.

• The Mill Hill Fathers began their work in Uganda.

• Between 1894 and 1925, Sir Apolo Kagwa served as the Katakiro— the Prime Minister — of Buganda.

• *Southern Africa:* Cecil Rhodes won the election in the Cape and became the Minister for Native Affairs (January).

• Jameson completed the occupation of Matabeleland (January).

In 1888, the partner of Cecil Rhodes, Charles Rudd, obtained a monopoly mining concession from the Ndebele King Lobengula. Rhodes used this concession as a lever to obtain a crown charter for his new British South African Company in 1889.

Rhodes regarded this charter as giving him a free hand north of the Limpopo and sent agents north of the Zambezi to obtain further treaties. They succeeded in gaining concessions from the Lozi king Lewanika and the Lunda chief Mwata Kazembe in 1890. These concessions laid the basis for company administration in Zambia (Northern Rhodesia) until a protectorate was declared.

Around this same time, Rhodes interpreted Rudd's concession as conferring the right of his company to occupy eastern Zimbabwe (Mashonaland). After an administration was established in Mashonaland, Rhodes' agent Leander Jameson provoked a war with the Ndebele.

Rhodes' forces easily conquered the Ndebele in 1894. This victory gave Rhodes effective control of all of Zimbabwe. In tribute to this conqueror, Zimbabwe became "Rhodesia."

• After the fall of the Ndebele kingdom during the British occupation of 1893 and 1894, Mkwati established an oracular shrine at Thaba zi ka Mambo, the pre-Ndebele center of the Changamire empire.

The collapse of the Ndebele kingdom enabled

Mkwati to appeal to the broad mass of former Ndebele subjects, many of whom were originally Shona. Operating through Mwari cult priests, Mkwati organized a popular revolt against the British occupation and directed it through 1896.

• The Glen Grey Act inaugurated a new native policy (August). The Glen Grey Act was designed to westernize subject African communities by granting freehold land tenure to individuals and by establishing representative government among the Xhosa.

• Britain annexed Pondoland, connecting Natal and the Cape Colony.

In 1887, a new man, Sigcawu, became chief of the Mpondo. Sigcawu insisted on ruling without Mdlangaso's assistance. Three years later, Mdlangaso attempted to seize power for himself.

A civil war ensued. The war would last for four years. The war came to an end in 1894 when the Cape ministry of Cecil Rhodes annexed Mpondo land. Mdlangaso became the scapegoat for the war. He was banished from Mpondo country.

• France began its campaign of conquest in Madagascar (November 10).

• The BSA Company ceased to control the British Central African Protectorate (Nyasaland).

• Gold was discovered in the Transvaal.

• The French occupied Tamatave (December).

• Bulawayo began to be developed rapidly. 400 gold prospecting licenses were issued. 11,000 mining claims were registered. The Native Hut Tax was instituted in the BSA Company area.

• Coal was located in southern Rhodesia.

• Europeans began to occupy the "gold belt areas" and the richer lands in Matabeleland.

• Shangani and Gwaai Reserves were designated in southern Rhodesia.

• Lourenco Marques was attacked by Africans.

• In 1894, Mwene Heri became Jumbe IV. Mwene Heri was the son of Mwene Nguzo who was the short reigning Jumbe II. After becoming the Jumbe — the Swahili chief — in 1894, Mwene Heri revolted against the British administration only to be quickly captured and deposed. He was deported to Zanzibar and the rule of the Jumbes in Malawi came to an end.

"Mwene" is a common title for a chief, particularly in Zaire, Zambia, and Zimbabwe.

• Gungunhana, the chief of the Gaza, was deported to Lisbon (Portugal).

• German forces defeated the Khoikhoi in Namibia.

Shortly after his arrival in South West Africa in 1894, Theodore Leutwin defeated the powerful Khoikhoi chief Hendrik Witbooi. Afterwards, Leutwin forced Witbooi to accept a German protectorate. Thereafter, Leutwin's policy was to maintain close personal ties with African rulers, to use them against their fellow chiefs, and to make available as much land as possible for European settlement.

• Jumbe III (Tawakali Sudi)(c. 1845-1894), died.

"Jumbe" — Swahili for "chief" or "official" — was the title taken by four successive rulers of the town of Nkhota Kota (Kota Kota) on the southwest coast of Lake Nyasa. By virtue primarily of their superiority in firearms, the Jumbes dominated the ivory and slave trades of central Malawi and established a sort of protectorate in the name of the sultan of Zanzibar (Tanzania) to whom they paid nominal allegiance. The Jumbes are credited with introducing Islamic culture to modern Malawi.

Tawakali Sudi, the third Jumbe, ascended to the chieftainship in 1875. He asserted his link to the Sultan of Zanzibar more forcefully and built his trading city state to its greatest power and influence.

When British settlers arrived in Malawi about the time of his succession he co-operated with them and accepted a Christian missionary in his predominantly Muslim town. Henry Johnston declared a British protectorate over Malawi in 1889 and Jumbe III became one of the first rulers to collaborate with the new regime.

Jumbe III's economic ties with the local peoples were sufficiently diversified and strong for him to renounce slave trading in return for a government subsidy. Jumbe III also provided Johnston with some material support to help suppress other slave traders around the lake. Shortly before his death, however, Jumbe was unable to prevent his own people from resuming the trade.

• Lobengula (c. 1836-1894), the last ruler of the Ndebele kingdom, died.

Lobengula was the son of the founder of the Ndebele kingdom, Mzilikazi. He was born in the western Transvaal shortly before the Ndebele migrated to present day southwestern Zimbabwe.

After Mzilikazi died in 1868, Lobengula was unexpectedly nominated by the national council to succeed him. The acknowledged heir to the Ndebele throne had been Lobengula's half-brother Nkulumane, but Nkulumane had disappeared in the 1840s, presumably at Mzilikazi's behest.

Mzilikazi never revealed the fate of Nkulumane. Mzilikazi also failed to designate another heir before he himself died. The fact that Lobengula's mother was a Swazi made his own nomination for the kingship unpopular to many Ndebele. In recognition of this fact, Lobengula wisely refused to be formally installed as king until the fate of the missing Nkulumane was settled.

Lobengula sponsored a delegation to Natal to search for the missing heir in 1869, but the latter was not found. After a year of such searching, the populace became satisfied that Nkulumane was nowhere to be found. Thus, early in 1870, Lobengula was made king.

Shortly after Lobengula became king, a man claiming to be Nkulumane emerged in Natal and solicited European support to claim Lobengula's throne. Lobengula countered by granting mining concessions to a group represented by Thomas Baines *(see 1875)*, thus drawing off some of the pretender's support.

At home, a pro-Nkulumane faction led by a prestigious army commander, Mbigo Masuku, openly defied Lobengula. A brief civil war ensued in which Lobengula emerged victorious around June of 1870.

In 1872, the pretender "Nkulumane" attempted an invasion of Ndebele country (Matabeleland). However, Lobengula's forces easily repulsed the invasion. The pretender Nkulumane retreated to settle in the western Transvaal, where he attracted other Ndebele dissidents and planned new coups. However, these coups would never occur. The pretender Nkulumane never threatened Lobengula again.

Nevertheless, Lobengula's European enemies attempted to coerce him by threatening to support the Nkulumane. In 1878, Lobengula reluctantly assented to the killing of a semi-official British envoy, Captain R. R. Patterson, whose use of this threat was too blatant to be tolerated. Meanwhile, concessions which Lobengula had earlier granted to European miners gave rise to another problem, for the miners began to claim territorial rights on his southwestern border. Lobengula's difficulties with internal opposition were temporarily resolved by frequent purges. In a futile attempt to satisfy dissidents, Lobengula authorized the execution of his own sister, several brothers, and many other prominent persons.

Europeans vilified Lobengula as a blood thirsty despot. Missionaries who had become frustrated by their failure to make converts vehemently criticized Lobengula. A call went forth for military action to be initiated against Lobengula as part of a moral crusade.

During the late 1880s, Lobengula faced mounting pressure from British, Afrikaner, German and Portuguese imperialists, all of whom wanted land or concessions. In 1888, Lobengula signed a concession treaty offered by Charles Rudd which ostensibly gave Cecil Rhodes exclusive rights to mine Zimbabwe.

Rhodes broadly interpreted the concession granted by Lobengula as a grant of land itself. In 1890, Rhodes' private company occupied eastern Zimbabwe (Mashonaland).

Lobengula lacked enough Ndebele support to resist Rhodes' group decisively. Instead, he had to re-assert his claims to sovereignty over the Shona of eastern Zimbabwe by intensifying raids and punitive expeditions against them.

In 1893, the British administrator there, L. S. Jameson, used one of Lobengula's raids as a pretext for invading the Ndebele themselves. Lobengula offered only half-hearted resistance as the British overran the country. Lobengula attempted to flee to the land of the Ngoni king Mpezeni Jere in eastern Zambia. However, while in flight, Lobengula contracted smallpox.

Lobengula died of smallpox in 1894. He was the last Ndebele king.

RELATED HISTORICAL EVENTS

• *The United States:* Mark Twain published *Pudd'nhead Wilson.*

• *Europe:* An Anglo-Congolese agreement was reached on the boundaries of Uganda and the Congo (April 12).

• An Anglo-Italian agreement was reached on East Africa (May 5).

• A Belgo-French agreement was reached concerning the Congo boundaries (August 14).

• *Notable Births:* Margaret Ballinger (1894-1980), a South African politician, was born.

Margaret Ballinger was born Margaret Hodgson in Scotland. She emigrated to South Africa as child but returned to England for her higher education.

While teaching history in Johannesburg, Margaret married W. P. Ballinger, a British labor organizer who came to South Africa to assist Clements Kadalie's labor movement.

After the 1935 "Representation of Natives Act" took Africans off the common voting rolls in the Cape Province, Margaret Ballinger was asked by the leaders of the African National Congress to stand for one of the four parliamentary seats set aside for non-white voters. Ballinger did stand and won. She held this seat until it was abolished in 1960 at which time Ballinger retired from public life.

During her career, Ballinger was one of the few vocal advocates of Africans' rights in the South African parliament. In 1953, Ballinger, Alan Paton, and others founded the Liberal Party. Margaret Ballinger became the Liberal Party's first president and its only member of parliament.

• Pierre Francois Boisson (1894-1948), a governor of French West Africa, was born.

Pierre Boisson was a former governor of Cameroon who was made governor of French West Africa to replace Leon Cayla. Cayla had been reluctant to cooperate with the Vichy regime.

Having lost a leg in World War I, Boisson was no friend of the Germans. However, he believed that he was preventing German and Italian colonization by maintaining Vichy policy of strict neutrality in Africa.

In 1940, Boisson thwarted de Gaulle's Free French invasion of Dakar.

Boisson later switched his support to de Gaulle, but the switch was perceived as being too late. De Gaulle had Boisson imprisoned in 1943.

• *Notable Deaths:* Verney Lovett Cameron (1844-1894), a British explorer, died.

Verney Cameron interrupted his naval career to lead a Royal Geographical Society expedition in search of David Livingstone. However, upon his arrival in Africa, Cameron learned that Livingstone had been found by Henry Stanley.

Undeterred by the news, Cameron proceeded to Lake Tanganyika. It was at Lake Tanganyika, that Cameron learned of Livingstone's death in 1873.

Cameron went on to explore the southern shores and the effluents of Lake Tanganyika. He also crossed Zaire and reached the Atlantic Ocean in 1875.

Cameron's expedition added to the European understanding and knowledge of the African interior. His expedition also sparked Leopold's interest in the commercial possibilities associated with Zaire.

After retiring from the navy in 1882, Cameron devoted the remainder of his life to various commercial enterprises connected with Africa.

---

1 8 9 5

THE UNITED STATES

On September 18, 1895, Booker T. Washington delivered a speech entitled "The Road to Negro Progress" at the Cotton States and International Exposition in Atlanta, Georgia.

Washington was introduced to the audience by former Governor Rufus Bullock. Bullock introduced Washington as a "representative of Negro enterprise and Negro civilization." Washington's speech allayed any fear his European American audience might have had about the ambitions of the African Americans living in the South. Washington emphasized that the African American wanted responsibilities rather than rights and proposed a program of accommodation that was essentially music to the ears of the European American Southerners.

The end result of this speech was that Washington was thrust into the role of national spokesman for African Americans — a role which had been vacant since the death of Frederick Douglass in February.

This speech has come to be known as the "Atlanta Compromise" because many of Washington's critics felt it was a wholesale capitulation to European American oppression while his supporters believed that it was merely a practical statement of submission which was issued in light of the general climate that prevailed in the United States at the end of the 1800s.

Regardless of how it is viewed, it is undeniable that Booker T. Washington's speech is the second most famous speech by an African American. It is surpassed in its renown only by Martin Luther King's famous "I Have A Dream" speech of 1963. Here is "The Road to Negro Progress."

Mr. President and Gentlemen of the Board of Directors and Citizens:

One-third of the population of the South is of the Negro race. No enterprise seeking the material, civil, or moral welfare of this section can disregard this element of our population and reach the highest success. I but convey to you, Mr. President and Directors, the sentiment of the masses of my race when I say that in no way have the value and manhood of the American Negro been more fittingly and generously recognized than by the managers of this magnificent exposition at every stage of its progress. It is a recognition that will do more to cement the friendship of the two races than any occurrence since the dawn of our freedom.

Not only this, but the opportunity here afforded will awaken among us a new era of industrial progress. Ignorant and inexperienced, it is not strange that in the first years of our new life we began at the top instead of at the bottom; that a seat in Congress or the state legislature was more sought than real estate or industrial skill; that the political convention or stump speaking had more attractions than starting a dairy farm or truck garden.

A ship lost at sea for many days suddenly sighted a friendly vessel. From the mast of the unfortunate vessel was seen a signal: "Water, water; we die of thirst." The answer from the friendly vessel at once came back: "Cast down your bucket where you are." A second time the signal, "Water, water, send us water!" ran up from the distressed vessel, and was answered: "Cast down your bucket where you are." And a third and fourth signal for water was answered: "Cast down your bucket where you are." The captain of the distressed vessel, at last heeding the injunction, cast down his bucket, and it came up full of fresh, sparkling water from the mouth of the Amazon River.

To those of my race who depend on bettering their condition in a foreign land or who underestimate the importance of cultivating friendly relations with the Southern white man, who is their next-door neighbor, I would say: Cast down your bucket where you are; cast it down in making friends, in every manly way, of the people of all races by whom we are surrounded. Cast it down in agriculture, mechanics, in commerce, in domestic service, and in the professions. And in this connection it is well to bear in mind that whatever other sins the South may be called to bear, when it comes to business, pure and simple, it is in the South that the Negro is given a man's chance in the commercial world, and in nothing is this exposition more eloquent than in emphasizing this chance.

Our greatest danger is that, in the great leap from slavery to freedom, we may overlook the fact that the masses of us are to live by the productions of our hands and fail to keep in mind that we shall prosper in proportion as we learn to dignify and glorify common labor, and put brains and skill into the common occupations of life: shall prosper in proportion as we learn to draw the line between the superficial and the substantial, the ornamental gewgaws of life and the useful. No race can prosper till it learns that there is as much dignity in tilling a field as in writing a poem. It is at the bottom of life we must begin, and not at the top. Nor should we permit our grievances to overshadow our opportunities.

To those of the white race who look to the incoming of those of foreign birth and strange tongue and habits for the prosperity of the South, were I permitted I would repeat what I say to my own race, "Cast down your bucket where you are." Cast it down among the 8 million Negroes whose habits you know, whose fidelity and love you have tested in days when to have proved treacherous meant the ruin of your fireside. Cast down your bucket among these people who have, without strikes and labor wars, tilled your fields, cleared your forests, built your railroads and cities, and brought forth treasures from the bowels of the earth and helped make possible this magnificent representation of the progress of the South. Casting down your bucket among my people, helping and encouraging them as you are doing on these grounds, and, with education of head, hand, and heart, you will find that they will buy your surplus land, make blossom the waste places in your fields, and run your factories.

While doing this, you can be sure in the future, as in the past, that you and your families will be surrounded by the most patient, faithful, law-abiding, and unresentful people that the world has seen. As we have proved our loyalty to you in the past, in nursing your children, watching by the sickbed of your mothers and fathers, and often following them with tear-dimmed eyes to their graves, so in the future, in our humble way, we shall stand by you with a devotion that no foreigner can approach, ready to lay down our lives, if need be, in defense of yours; interlacing our industrial, commercial, civil, and religious life with yours in a way that shall make the interests of both races one. In all things that are purely social we can be as separate as the fingers, yet one as the hand in all things essential to mutual progress.

There is no defense or security for any of us except in the highest intelligence and development of all. If anywhere there are efforts tending to curtail the fullest growth of the Negro, let these efforts be turned into stimulating, encouraging, and making him the most useful and intelligent citizen. Effort or means so invested will pay a thousand percent interest. These efforts will be twice blessed — "blessing him that gives and him that takes."

There is no escape, through law of man or God, from the inevitable:

The laws of changeless justice bind
Oppressor with oppressed;
And close as sin and suffering joined
We march to fate abreast.

Nearly 16 million hands will aid you in pulling the load upward, or they will pull against you the load downward. We shall constitute one-third and more of the ignorance and crime of the South, or one-third its intelligence and progress; we shall contribute one-third to the business and industrial prosperity of the South, or we shall prove a veritable body of death, stagnating, depressing, retarding every effort to advance the body politic.

Gentlemen of the exposition, as we present to you our humble effort at an exhibition of our progress, you must not expect overmuch. Starting thirty years ago with ownership here and there in a few quilts and pumpkins and chickens (gathered from miscellaneous sources), remember: the path that has led from these to the invention and production of agricultural implements, buggies, steam engines, newspapers, books, statuary, carving, paintings, the management of drugstores and banks, has not been trodden without contact with thorns and thistles. While we take pride in what we exhibit as a result of our independent efforts, we do not for a moment forget that our part in this exhibition would fall far short of your expectations but for the constant help that has come to our educational life, not only from the Southern states but especially from Northern philanthropists who have made their gifts a constant stream of blessing and encouragement.

The wisest among my race understand that the agitation of questions of social equality is the extremist folly, and that progress in the enjoyment of all the privileges that will come to us must be the result of severe and constant struggle rather than of artificial forcing. No race that has anything to contribute to the markets of the world is long in any degree ostracized. It is important and right that all privileges of the law be ours, but it is vastly more important that we be prepared for the exercise of those privileges. The opportunity to earn a dollar in a factory just now is worth infinitely more than the opportunity to spend a dollar in an opera house.

In conclusion, may I repeat that nothing in thirty years has given us more hope and encouragement and drawn us so near to you of the white race as this opportunity offered by the exposition; and here bending, as it were, over the altar that represents the results of the struggles of your race and mine, both starting practically empty-handed three decades ago, I pledge that, in your effort to work out the great and intricate problem which God has laid at the doors of the South, you shall have at all times the patient, sympathetic help of my race; only let this be constantly in mind that, while from representations in these buildings of the product of field, of forest, of mine, of factory, letters, and art, much good will come — yet far above and beyond material benefits will be that higher good, that let us pray God will come, in a blotting out of sectional differences and racial animosities and suspicions, in a determination to administer absolute justice, in a willing obedience among all classes to the mandates of law. This, coupled with our material prosperity, will bring into our beloved South a new heaven and a new earth.

• In 1895, George Washington Murray, of South Carolina, was re-elected to Congress. While in Congress, Murray advocated better educational opportunities for African Americans. Murray left politics after an unsuccessful attempt to lead an African American faction away from the Republican Party.

• In 1895, the Populist controlled North Carolina Legislature passed an election law in which each party was represented on all registration boards and heavy penalties were prescribed for vote-buying and selling. As a result of this legislation, a number of African American officials and 300 African American magistrates were appointed. The State Legislature also passed a county government bill which took the power of appointing local officials from the Legislature and gave it to the residents of each county. Thus, the Democrats retained control of local government, but African American counties could now elect African American officials.

• In Georgia, despite strong Populist sympathy, the Democrats were able to control the African American vote. The Democrats often paid the taxes of African Americans so that the African Americans would vote Democratic. In Augusta's 4th Ward, heavily African American, the vote was 9 for the Populist candidate and 989 for his Democratic opponent.

• *Organizations:* The National Conference of Colored Women met in Boston, Massachusetts (August).

The moving force behind the Conference was Josephine St. Pierre Ruffin (1842-1924), the founder of the Women's New Era Club. The meeting led to the formation of the National Federation of Afro-American Women, which was merged into the National Association of Colored Women the following year.

• The National Medical Association was established (October). The National Medical Association was formed in Atlanta, Georgia, during the Cotton States and International Exposition. The first president of the National Medical Association was R. F. Boyd of Nashville, Tennessee. The National Medical Association was formed in reaction to the discriminatory practices of the predominantly European American medical associations.

• *The Labor Movement:* When the National Machinists' Union refused to remove a racial exclusion clause from its constitution, the American Federation of Labor (AFL) organized a new union, the International Machinists' Association. The National Machinists Union then dropped its exclusion clause, but retained a secret pledge whereby members nominated only European Americans for membership.

• *Notable Births:* Jodie Edwards, a vaudevillian known as "Butterbeans," was born (July 19).

• Charles Hamilton Houston (1895-1950), considered one of the great constitutional lawyers in American history and one of the architects of the legal challenges to segregation, was born in Washington, D. C. (September 3).

Charles Hamilton Houston was a Phi Beta Kappa graduate of Amherst College and was the first African American to serve as an editor of the prestigious *Harvard Law Review.* Houston received his law degree with honors from Harvard University Law School in 1922 and, in 1923, became the first African American to receive a Doctor of Judicial Science degree from Harvard.

In 1935, Houston became the NAACP's first paid full-time legal counsel. Houston's tenure with the NAACP was marked by the securing of Supreme Court victories in the following areas: (1) The admission of African American students to the University of Maryland and University of Missouri Law School; (2) the right of African American railroad firemen to organize; (3) against restrictive covenants in real estate documents; and (4) supporting African American representation on Southern juries.

The work of Charles Hamilton Houston paved the way for the 1954 Supreme Court decision in *Brown v. Board of Education* — the decision which overturned the doctrine of "separate but equal" public facilities and accommodations.

• Alberta Hunter, the noted singer, was born in Memphis, Tennessee (April 1).

• Rex Ingram, an actor who played "De Lawd" in the film version of *The Green Pastures* in 1936, was born near Cairo, Illinois (October 20).

• Eva Jessye, a choral director, was born in Coffeyville, Kansas (January 20).

• Lizzie Miles, a singer, was born (March 31).

• Florence Mills (1895-1927), a singer, dancer and comedienne, was born.

Florence Mills was born in Washington, D. C. Mills made her stage debut at the age of 6 with her sister in a singing act. Later, and until 1919, Mills led a cabaret act with Ada "Bricktop" Smith, Cora Greene and Matte Hight. This quartet played such places as Chicago's Old Panama Cafe. Mills subsequently joined a group known as the "Tennessee Ten," but achieved her first significant stage success in the musical comedy revue of 1922, *Shuffle Along.*

Florence Mills also had a long run with the Broadway production of *Plantation.* Mills later toured with her company in *Dixie to Broadway.*

By 1926, Florence Mills had become one of the most popular performers on the European continent. Mills had wide success with the revue *Blackbirds,* in London. This success came despite an attempt by the British Artists' Federation to bar Mills from the English stage.

Mills gave credit for her dancing expertise to Bill "Bojangles" Robinson *(see 1878).* It was

Robinson who taught Mills how to dance on the roof of a rooming house while she was performing at the Panama Cafe.

At her funeral in 1927, it was estimated that 3,000 attended while some 150,000 lined the streets in order to watch the procession.

Among the celebrities who attended her funeral were James Weldon Johnson, Johnny Dunn, Jack Benny, and Ethel Waters.

- Andy Razaf (originally Razafkeriefo), a songwriter of such popular hits as *Ain't Misbehavin'* and *Honeysuckle Rose*, was born in Washington, D.C. (December 16).
- William Grant Still, orchestral musician and composer of *Afro-American Symphony*, was born (May 11).

William Grant Still was born in Woodville, Mississippi. Educated at Wilberforce University, the Oberlin Conservatory of Music, and the New England Conservatory, Still began as an arranger for jazz orchestras. Still's original compositions were first played in 1926.

Since 1926, Still's songs, symphonies and opera have been performed by major orchestras in the United States and Europe.

In 1936, William Grant Still conducted a program of his own works at the Hollywood Bowl.

Still also wrote successful musicals, including *From Dixie to Broadway*—the musical which brought Florence Mills to stardom.

- *Notable Deaths:* There were 112 African Americans lynched in 1895.
- Frederick Douglass (1818-1895) died in Anacosta Heights, District of Columbia, where his home is now a national shrine (February 20).

Frederick Douglass was born Frederick Augustus Washington Bailey. However, Douglass assumed the name Frederick Douglass shortly after his escape to freedom. Douglass' father was an unknown European American, his mother, Harriet Bailey, an African American slave.

In his youth, Douglass was sent to Baltimore to serve as a house servant. It was while serving as a house servant that he learned how to read and write. Upon the death of the slaveholder who owned Douglass, Douglass was sent back to the country to work as a field hand.

Douglass despised the work he was consigned to do and decided to escape. Along with a dozen other slaves, he prepared an escape plan. But before the plan could be put into effect, Douglass and his fellow conspirators were betrayed. Douglass was jailed.

Upon his release from jail, Douglass was returned to Baltimore. However, despite the jail stay, Douglass was determined to be free. He disguised himself as a sailor and attempted his second escape on September 3, 1838. On this second attempt, Douglass was successful.

Douglass fled to New York City. He soon became involved in abolitionist causes. In 1841, he attended a convention of the Massachusetts Anti-slavery Society in Nantucket. He later was employed as an agent by the Society and took an active part in the Society's Rhode Island campaign against a new state constitution which would have disenfranchised African Americans. Douglass became a central figure in the famous 100 Conventions of New England Anti-slavery Society.

In 1845, Frederick Douglass published *Narrative of the Life of Frederick Douglass*. It added to Douglass' growing fame and stature. For the next two years after the publication of this book, Douglass spent two years lecturing in Britain and Ireland on slavery and women's rights issues. The money he received from his book and his lectures enabled Douglass to actually purchase his freedom from his former owner.

Douglass established a newspaper, the *North Star*, in Rochester, New York, which helped him to espouse his abolitionist views. Douglass also joined forces with Harriet Beecher Stowe to establish an industrial school for young African Americans.

Douglass was an ardent abolitionist and this passion brought him in contact with some of the more noted abolitionist personalities of the era. One such personality was John Brown. For a time, Douglass consulted with and counseled John Brown. This association was to create some problems for Douglass. After John Brown's failed insurrection and capture, Douglass was outlawed in the State of Virginia. Fearing for his general safety, Douglass fled to Canada.

Douglass returned to the United States upon the outbreak of initial hostilities of the Civil War. During the Civil War, Douglass helped to recruit the 54th and 55th Massachusetts Negro Regiments, the first African American units to serve in the Civil War.

After the War, Douglass held a number of posts. He was a member of the Territorial Legislature of Washington, D.C.; the secretary of the Santo Domingo Commission; police commissioner, marshal, and recorder of deeds of the District of Columbia; United States Minister to Haiti; and charge d'affaires for Santo Domingo.

While in Haiti, Douglass noted with disgust

the exploitation of the people and the land which was being perpetrated by American business interests. In protest to this exploitation, Douglass resigned his position as charge d'affaires in 1891.

Douglass published a number of works. Among his most noteworthy works are *Narrative of the Life of Frederick Douglass* (1845); *Lectures on American Slavery* (1851); *My Bondage and My Freedom* (1855); and *U.S. Grant and the Colored People* (1872).

By any measure, Frederick Douglass stands as not only a giant in the history of African American history but also a giant in American history as well.

• Rufus Lewis Perry (1834-1895), an African American clergyman, missionary, educator and journalist, died.

Rufus Lewis Perry was an African American missionary, educator, and journalist. His parents were Lewis and Mary Perry, slaves owned by Archibald Overton. Rufus' father, Lewis, was a Baptist preacher and an able mechanic and carpenter. Lewis Perry was allowed to work in Nashville where Rufus attended school until one day when Rufus' father fled to Canada, leaving his family behind.

The Perry family returned to the Overton plantation and, in 1852, Rufus was sold to a slave dealer who intended to take him to Mississippi. It was then Rufus who decided to flee.

Rufus went to Canada. In Canada, he became a teacher and was ordained a minister in 1861.

Perry served as editor of the *Sunbeam* and of the *People's Journal*. He was co-editor of the *American Baptist* from 1869 until 1871. From 1872 until 1895, Perry was joint editor of *The National Monitor*.

In 1887, Perry was awarded a doctorate in philosophy (a Ph.D.) from the State University at Louisville, Kentucky, and, in 1893, he published *The Cushite; or the Descendants of Ham as seen by Ancient Historians*.

• *Miscellaneous State Laws:* Florida enacted a law requiring segregated education in private schools as well as in public schools (a law segregating public education had been passed earlier). This law imposed penalties on teachers, administrators, and patrons of integrated schools.

• In 1895, South Carolina revised the Reconstruction Constitution of 1868. The new Constitution effectively disfranchised most African Americans. It required payment of all taxes, educational tests, property worth $300, a poll tax of $1 and two years residence.

In order to prevent African Americans from exercising their right to vote, many Southern states revised their state constitutions between 1895 and 1910 by adding "grandfather clauses." The 15th Amendment, ratified in 1870, had assured that no one could be denied the right to vote because of race or previous condition of servitude. However, the "grandfather clauses" restricted the right to vote to those who had voted on January 1, 1867, and to the descendants of those who had the right to vote on that date. In effect, this disqualified African Americans, who were unable to vote in the South until after the passage of the Fifteenth Amendment in 1870. Grandfather clauses were enacted in Alabama, Georgia, Louisiana, North and South Carolina, Oklahoma, Maryland and Virginia. In 1915, the United States Supreme Court declared "grandfather clauses" to be unconstitutional.

• *Publications:* Paul Laurence Dunbar's second book of poems, *Majors and Minors,* was published in 1895. It received a favorable, review in *Harper's Weekly* in its issue of June 27, 1897, by William Dean Howells.

• Ida B. Wells (Barnett) published the first statistics on lynching in her pamphlet, *The Red Record.*

• James Walker Hood published *One Hundred Years of the Methodist Episcopal Zion Church.*

• Adam Clayton Powell, Sr., published *Souvenir of the Immanuel Baptist Church.*

• *Scholastic Achievements:* In 1895, W. E. B. Du Bois became the first African American to be awarded a doctorate from Harvard University (June). Du Bois' dissertation was entitled *The Suppression of the African Slave Trade to the U.S.A., 1638-1870.* This doctoral dissertation was published as the first volume of the Harvard Historical Studies in 1896.

• The Frederick Douglass Memorial Hospital and Training School for Nurses was founded in Philadelphia, Pennsylvania, by Nathan Francis Mossell.

• By 1895, the school enrollment for African Americans had increased 59% from 1876. The increase for European Americans during this same period was 106%.

• Mary Church Terrell (1863-1954) began her tenure on the Washington, D. C., Board of Education.

• *The Black Church:* In Atlanta, Georgia, the National Baptist Convention, the Foreign Mission Baptist Convention of the U.S.A., the American National Baptist Convention, and the American National Educational Baptist Convention were combined in the formation of the National Baptist Convention of the U.S.A. The National Baptist Convention, USA, held its first meeting on September 28. E. C. Morris was the first president.

• James Walker Hood published *One Hundred Years of the Methodist Episcopal Zion Church*.

• *The Performing Arts:* Between 1895 and 1909, Bert Williams and George Walker starred in and produced vaudeville shows throughout the United States and England. They were famous for their characterizations with Walker posing as the dandy and Williams in black-face, using a "Negro dialect."

• John W. Ishaw produced the all-African American musical *The Octoroon*.

• *Technological Innovations:* The United States Patent Office advertised its first special exhibit of the inventions of African Americans.

THE AMERICAS

• *Cuba:* The Grito de Baire began the Cuban War of Independence (February 24).

The Cuban War of Independence was the culmination of the Cubans' struggle to gain their freedom from Spanish colonial rule. The armed separatists were committed to more than just independence. The Creole bourgeoisie was just as much the enemy of the Cuban freedom fighters — the Cuba Libre — as were the Spanish officeholders, and the revolutionaries recognized that inequity was not caused by Spanish political rule as much as by the Cuban social system. The revolutionaries thus believed that a transformation of Cuban society was the only remedy.

Originally, the War of Independence was primarily between the colony of Cuba and the metropolis of Spain, but after 1896 the conflict expanded to become a struggle between the creole bourgeoisie and a populist coalition over competing claims of hegemony within the colony. The rebellion offered oppressed groups — poor blacks and whites, peasants and workers, the destitute and dispossessed — the promise of social justice and economic freedom.

Jose Marti, the father of Cuban independence, Maximo Gomez y Baez, Antonio Maceo *(see 1896),* and other veterans of the Ten Years War *(see 1868)* coordinated the war efforts in Cuba.

On February 24, 1895, the war began with the Grito de Baire (Declaration of Baire). On March 24, Marti presented the Manifesto de Montecristi. The Manifesto de Montecristi set forth the revolutionaries war policies. Under the Manifesto de Montecristi, the war for independence was to be waged by Afro-Cubans and Euro-Cubans alike. Indeed, from the perspective of the revolution leaders, the participation of the blacks would be essential if the revolution was to succeed.

Pursuant to the Manifesto, Spaniards who did not object to the war effort were to be spared; private rural properties were not to be destroyed; and the revolution was to bring new economic life to Cuba. Marti stated: "Cubans ask no more of the world than the recognition of and respect for their sacrifices."

Marti's death in 1895 did not stop the independence movement. In September, representatives of the five branches of the Army of Liberation proclaimed the Republic in Arms. In July 1895, Gomez and Maceo sent orders to end all economic activity on the island that might be advantageous to the royalists. Defeat of the Spanish required destruction of the bourgeoisie's social and economic power, and so the insurrection became an economic war.

The insurgents burned fields to stop sugar production. The population continued to support the rebellion despite its economic consequences, and the war did in fact destroy the Spanish bourgeoisie as a social class as well as end colonial rule.

Spanish authorities were stunned by the insurrection. The Spaniards enlarged their army to 200,000 men and appointed General Valeriano Weyler y Nicolau to bolster the war effort.

Weyler y Nicolau instituted the re-concentration policy under which the rural population was ordered to evacuate the countryside and relocate in specially designated fortified towns. Subsistence agriculture was banned and villages, fields, homes, food reserves, and livestock were all destroyed.

Over 300,000 Cubans were relocated into these re-concentration camps. Mass deaths resulted because the municipal authorities were not prepared to assume the responsibility of caring for the internal refugees. The policy proved to be counterproductive. As a result of the camps, more Cubans came to support the insurrection. Additionally, in the United States and even in Spain, there was a strong public reaction against the Spanish policy in Cuba.

The Spanish controlled the cities and attacked the peasants, while the Cubans controlled the countryside and attacked the planters. By the end of 1897, Cuban victory was inevitable. Weyler was incapable of expelling the insurgents from the western area of the island, and the Cuban elites began appealing to the United States to intervene and restore order.

The explosion on February 15, 1898, of the U. S. S. *Maine* killed 260 enlisted men and officers. The *Maine* had been sent to the Havana harbor to protect United States citizens. The explosion on the *Maine* provided the United States with an excuse to enter the war.

On April 25, 1898, the United States Congress declared war against Spain, however, the Teller Amendment stated that the United States would make no attempt to establish permanent control over the island.

In June 1898, some 17,000 United States troops landed east of Santiago, Cuba. On July 3, 1898, the Spanish fleet was destroyed.

After a few more defeats, the Spanish surrendered on August 12, 1918.

Although the Cuban forces were instrumental in the outcome of the war, they were excluded from the peace negotiations that resulted in the Treaty of Paris. The terms of the treaty, which permitted the United States to dominate Cuba, reflected the view that the quick victory over Spain was attributable solely to the United States. This view did not acknowledge that the Cuban struggle for independence had been depleting the Spanish crown's resources for several decades, especially in the preceding three years.

On January 1, 1899, the Spanish administration retired from Cuba. General John R. Brooke installed a military government, establishing the United States occupation of the island, which ended in 1902.

• The Jimaguayu Constitution was drafted.

EUROPE

• In 1895 and 1896, in England, Samuel Coleridge-Taylor won the Lesley Alexander composition prize.

• Alexandre Dumas, fils (1824-1895), the son of the author of *The Three Musketeers* and the author, in his own right, of *The Lady of the Camellias* (also known as *Camille*), died.

Alexandre Dumas (1824-1895) was born in Paris, France, the unacknowledged son of the famous Afro-French writer Alexandre Dumas, the author of *The Three Musketeers*. Alexandre Dumas the younger is known as Alexandre

Dumas *fils*. "Fils" is the French word for "son." The senior Alexandre Dumas is known as Alexandre Dumas *pere*. "Pere" is the French word for father.

The stigma of his unacknowledged parental relationship clouded the childhood of the young Dumas. He suffered and his suffering made him empathetic to the suffering of fellow victims of society. Additionally, the lack of a stable family relationship became an ideal which is often reflected in his written works.

Dumas wrote both novels and plays. However, his principal claim to fame rests chiefly with his plays. His first play, *The Lady of the Camellias* (often called *Camille*), was an overnight success when performed in 1852. The tragic love story is set in the fashionable Parisian society of Dumas's era. The author based the play on his novel of the same name which had been published in 1848. This popular play would inspire the great composer Giuseppe Verdi and formed the basis for his opera *La Traviata*.

Dumas came to believe that plays should teach social and moral values. He defended the ideal of a stable family life in *The Wife of Claude* (1873), *Denise* (1885), and *Francillon* (1887). Although he often attacked the sinful acts of men, he also stressed forgiveness for those who repented. His *The Ideas of Madame Aubray* (1867) is a prime example of the repentance and forgiveness which Dumas advocated.

AFRICA

• *North Africa, Egypt and Sudan:* Mustafa Pasha Fahmi again became premier of Egypt. His tenure would last until 1908.

• D. Mackenzie's factory at Tarfaya was bought out by the Sultan of Morocco for 50,000 pounds.

• *West Africa:* Beginning in 1895, the construction of the Sierra Leone railway began. The construction would be completed in 1914.

• The British Niger Company proclaimed a protectorate over Busa and Nikki (January 1).

• Oyo was bombarded and temporarily garrisoned.

• The Brass towns attacked the Royal Niger Company's factory at Akassa (January 29). Forty-three African captives were killed and eaten. Sir John Kirk was sent to investigate as the Special Commissioner. On February 22, the British seized Nimbe and other Brass towns.

In 1895, African traders of the city-state of

Nembe (Brass)—who were being strangled by George Goldie's monopolistic policies—organized under Frederick Koko to attack the company headquarters of the Royal Niger Company.

Koko's army, consisting of about 1500 soldiers in thirty or forty canoes, attacked and destroyed the Royal Niger Company's trading depot at Akassa. The company counter attacked with the aid of the forces of the British Niger Coast Protectorate which claimed jurisdiction over Nembe.

Nembe was destroyed and Koko fled to the remote village of Etiema where he died in 1898.

The brief war with the Nembe drew attention to the Royal Niger Company's illegal monopoly in the delta. An official inquiry into the repression of Koko's attack exposed Goldies' unfair trade practices. Goldie's company charter was revoked in 1899 and the British government immediately declared a protectorate over northern Nigeria.

However, in compensation for the loss of his monopoly, Sir George Goldie *(see 1877)* received a huge financial settlement.

• The Ashanti sent a diplomatic mission led by John Owusu-Ansa to London (March).

John Owusu-Ansa, an adviser to the King Prempe I of the Akan kingdom of Ashanti, was born around 1850. Owusu-Ansa was the son of an Akan prince who had been educated in England in the 1830s. Owusu-Ansa himself received a western education, and served as a sergeant-major in the Gold Coast Rifle Corps.

In 1889, Owusu-Ansa went to the Asante capital, Kumasi, where he became an adviser to King Prempe. He served as Prempe's ambassador to the British on the coast on numerous occasions. Dressed in his bowler hat, English suits, patent-leather shoes, and carrying a walking stick, Owusu-Ansa never failed to leave an impression.

In 1895, Owusu-Ansa and his brother Albert headed Prempe's delegation to England to complain about British interference in Asante affairs. British officials had already given approval for an expedition to Kumasi, and they refused to meet the envoys.

The next year Prempe blamed Owusu-Ansa for having deceived the British. Prempe was, at the time, facing deportation by the British, and his accusation may merely have been an attempt to curry favor with the British colonialists.

Despite Prempe's accusations, Owusu-Ansa worked from London to secure Prempe's release from exile.

• There was an uprising in Bissau which was put down by troops from Angola (April). There was a revolt in Forrea led by Mamadu Pate Bulola. In August, a punitive expedition was launched.

• The *Afrique Occidentale Francaise (AOF)* (the French West African Federation) was founded (June 15). It was comprised of Senegal, Soudan, Guinea and Ivory Coast.

In accordance with the French practice of administrative centralization, French Sudan Guinea, Ivory Coast and Senegal were united under a governor-general in 1895. Dahomey (Benin), Mauritania, Niger and Upper Volta joined later when they became separate colonies.

• In 1895, after rumors spread concerning a planned *jihad* (holy war) the French exiled Ahmadu Bamba, the leader of the Muridiyya Islamic brotherhood of Senegal, to Gabon.

• An Anglo-French agreement was negotiated which defined the boundary of Sierra Leone.

• Joseph Danquah (1895-1965), the founder of the first modern Ghanaian political party, was born.

Joseph Kwame Kyeretwi Boakye Danquah was born to an important family in eastern Ghana which was then known as the Gold Coast. Danquah received his first education in Ghana. However, later, he went to the University of London.

Danquah received his law degree from the University of London in 1927. Three years later, he returned to Ghana where he established a newspaper and took up the banner of constitutional reform.

Danquah went to London in 1934 on a mission to protest Colonial Office policy. He remained in England to do African historical research for two years.

In 1937, nationalist sentiment was aroused in Ghana by the success of the famous cocoa hold-up. Immediately afterwards, Danquah created the Gold Coast Youth Congress, a broad based organization which brought together Ghana's elite.

Danquah successfully identified the Gold Coast Youth Congress with the entire Gold Coast region. However, at the same time, he rejected notions of pan-Africanism still shared by a number of other leaders.

In 1947, Danquah and some associates organized the United Gold Coast Convention (UGCC), comprised largely of intellectuals.

Also in 1947, Danquah persuaded Kwame Nkrumah, who was then studying in London, to return to take over the party leadership.

Upon his return to Ghana, Nkrumah called for a program of mass organization and public demonstrations for independence. The UGCC leaders, fearing Nkrumah's militancy, ousted him in 1949.

Nkrumah then formed his own party. Nkrumah's party essentially became the party for the nationalist movement.

Danquah's preference for a slower pace of constitutional reform was out of step with the mood of the Ghanaian people. Danquah's period of influence began to wane and the UGCC soon dissolved. The various political parties that Danquah joined after the dissolution of the UGCC proved to be ineffective with little popular support.

In 1960, Danquah ran against Nkrumah in the Ghanaian presidential elections. Nkrumah beat him badly.

With his popular mandate, Nkrumah became increasingly autocratic. Danquah, as the leader of the opposition, became a vocal critic of Nkrumah. In retaliation, Nkrumah imprisoned Danquah, without trial, under the Preventive Detention Act.

Danquah was imprisoned from October 1961 to June 1962. In 1964, Danquah was again imprisoned under the Preventive Detention Act. Danquah died in 1965 while still in prison.

• William Vacanarat Shadrach Tubman (1895-1971), the long reigning "president" of Liberia, was born.

William Tubman was born in Maryland County to a family of the Americo-Liberian elite who controlled the Liberian Government since its inception in 1847. Tubman was educated in a Methodist seminary. In 1913, Tubman left the seminary to teach while studying law.

Tubman became a lawyer in 1917 and five years later was elected to the Senate. In 1928, Tubman became a Methodist lay preachers.

Tubman was re-elected to the Senate in 1929 but resigned in 1930 in the wake of a political scandal involving forced labor during the administration of President Charles King.

Defeated when he attempted to regain his seat in 1934, Tubman, nevertheless, became deputy president of the Supreme Court in 1937.

In 1943, outgoing President Edwin Barclay chose Tubman to be the presidential candidate of the dominant True Whig Party. Tubman's designation as the True Whig candidate virtually assured him election. Barclay's choice of Tubman may have been an effort on Barclay's part to run Liberia from behind the scenes, but Tubman soon proved to be his own man.

During the next few years, Tubman moved to incorporate the citizens of the interior into Liberia's government, which had formerly extended little beyond the coast. Tubman introduced universal adult suffrage and secured interior representation in the national legislature. Communications and social services were instituted for the first time in many areas. Tubman also reduced Liberia's extreme dependence on the United States by encouraging other European nations to mine heavily in the country's iron ore deposits.

Tubman retained absolute control over politics in Liberia. In 1951, he engineered an amendment to the constitution abolishing the eight year limit for holders of the office of president. Afterwards, Tubman was continuously re-elected with only token opposition except in 1951 when he was opposed by Duhdwo Twe, a Kru.

Twe was indicted for sedition and forced to flee the country immediately after losing the election.

Tubman oversaw almost every detail of Liberian political life. He insisted on approving all items of public expenditure over $25. He intervened personally to settle individual citizens' complaints, as well as political and economic controversies.

Tubman supported the African independence movements of the 1950s and 1960s. He took a lead in establishing communications between heads of the newly independent states.

Although Tubman did not favor pan-African federation, he advocated close cooperation between African nations, including joint policy-making and customs unions.

Although there were a number of assassination attempts against him, Tubman remained a genuinely popular figure among both the Americo-Liberians and the interior peoples. At his death in 1971, he was succeeded by his vice-president, William R. Tolbert.

• *Central Africa:* A Franco-Belgian agreement was reached on Congolese possessions (February 5). A French post was erected at Tamboura.

• Batetela led the *Force Publique* revolt (July 4). On October 9, the mutineers were defeated at the Lomani River, and, on October 18, the mutiny came to an end.

- The Chokwe were defeated by Ngongo Letata, an ally of Tippu Tip.
- The slave trade was forbidden in Cameroon.
- Chaltin's campaigns commenced in northeast Congo.
- Kigeri IV Rwabugiri, the king of Rwanda, died (1895).

Kigeri IV Rwabugiri became *mwami*— king of Rwanda — after his predecessor (Mutara II Rwogera) had initiated a military resurgence. Kigeri's reign is remembered as one of uninterrupted military victory. Kigeri reorganized the army to provide conscripts for continuous warfare and to consolidate Tutsi control over previously independent Hutu states within present day Rwanda.

Like his predecessors, Kigeri kept outsiders out of Rwanda. However, he was able to obtain firearms indirectly through his eastern neighbors. By the end of Kigeri's reign, the Rwandan kingship was at its peak of power.

After receiving his only military check at the hands of the Burundi kingdom to his south, Kigeri turned his attention to his northern neighbors. By the 1880s, Kigeri was raiding deeply into southern Uganda and northwestern Tanzania.

In 1894, Kigeri received the first European explorers to reach Rwanda.

Kigeri's death in 1895 touched off a succession dispute in which one of his sons, Mibambwe IV Rutalindwa, was killed after reigning for only a year.

Another of Kigeri's sons, Yuhi IV Musinga ushered in the colonial era by collaborating with the Germans to strengthen his own kingship.

- *Eastern Africa:* The British installed Shaikh Rashid ibn Salim al-Mazrui as Shaikh of Takaungu (February 1).
- Italian troops entered Ethiopia (March 25).
- A quarrel with Shaikh Mbaruk ibn Salim al-Mazrui led to civil war (June).

In 1888, the chartered Imperial British East Africa Company (IBEAC) established an administration over the Kenya coast. Under its aegis, Mbaruk returned peacefully to settle at Gazi. Over the next seven years, Mbaruk cooperated with the IBEAC and occasionally lent it material support against his neighbors. This arrangement ended in 1895 when the company prepared to turn over its administration to the British crown.

Around this same time, the northern Mazrui community entered into a succession dispute. The IBEAC intervened, causing the northern Mazrui to revolt.

Some of the Mazrui sought refuge with Mbaruk. Through his refusal to betray his kinsmen, Mbaruk was reluctantly drawn into the rebellion.

- A British Protectorate was established over IBEA territory in Kenya (June 18). Proclaimed in Mombasa, the protectorate was named the East African Protectorate.
- A British vice-consul was appointed in Pemba.
- The British quarreled with Sayyid Hamid of Zanzibar. As a result, Sayyid Hamid formed a private bodyguard unit. On December 17, fighting erupted between the bodyguards and the British.
- The British East African Protectorate came to include present day Kenya, Uganda and Zanzibar. Sir Arthur Hardinge was named the first commissioner.

Unbeknownst to Mumia, the ruler of the Wanga kingdom of Kenya, Wanga was included in the British East Africa Protectorate in 1888. In 1894, a British official arrived at his capital to establish an administrative headquarters over the region.

Perhaps fearing the fate met by the Uganda kings Mwanga and Kabarega — who had resisted the British — Mumia acquiesced before the imposition of colonial rule, and instead became its most outstanding African champion. Mumia's capital served as a base for British military campaigns against his Bantu and Nilotic speaking neighbors and, by 1895, Mumia was lending thousands of his own troops to assist the British in their imperialistic campaigns.

As the chief ally of the British during the next decade, and as the ruler of the only centralized state in Kenya, Mumia stood in a unique position vis-à-vis the colonial administration.

- The Ethiopians defeated the Italians at Amba Alagi (December 7).
- The Uganda-Usoga Agreement was reached. Under the terms of the agreement, Busoga was incorporated into Uganda.
- Jubaland was declared a British Protectorate.
- The "Mad Mullah" settled at Berbera and began to propagate the "dervish" doctrines.
- The IBEA surrendered its charter.
- George Wilson became the Resident in

Buganda. The first *baraza* (National Council) was established as the *Lukiko*.

• Only 21 British officials were stationed in Uganda.

• The first bush schools were started by the CMS in Uganda.

• The British gradually came to occupy the Northern Frontier District of Kenya.

• Herman von Wissmann became the Governor of German East Africa.

• Msavila submitted to German sovereignty.

When Nyungu, the unifier of the Kimbu people of Tanzania, died in late 1884, Nyungu bequeathed to his daughter Mugalula an empire inherently more stable than that left by the Nyamwezi chief Mirambo. Mugalula committed suicide in 1893 and was succeeded by another female ruler, Msavila. Msavila voluntarily submitted to the Germans in 1895 and renounced all claims to sovereignty over the Kimbu.

• *Southern Africa:* The third Swaziland Convention made Swaziland a Protectorate of the Transvaal (February).

• The French occupied Majunga (February 15).

• The Battle of Ampasilova occurred (May 2).

• The BSA Company territory south of the Zambezi River was organized as Rhodesia in tribute to Cecil Rhodes (May 2).

• The Battle of Ambodimonty occurred (May 16).

• The Battle of Tsarasoatra took place (June 20).

• The BSA Company assumed control north of the Zambezi River.

• The Delagoa railway provided an outlet for the Transvaal (July 8).

• The Tananarive was bombarded and occupied (September 29).

• Mlugulu led a revolt against the British in Zimbabwe.

Mlugulu was a member of the Khumalo clan of the Ndebele royal family. By the late 1870s, Mlugulu commanded an important military town. According to one European source, Mlugulu personally led the force which killed a British envoy (R. R. Patterson) in 1878.

During the 1880s, Mlugulu succeeded Mtamjana as an official of the Ndebele national religion. In this capacity, Mlugulu presided over the annual national dances.

King Lobengula died in 1894. Lobengula's death occurred while the British South Africa Company was conquering the Ndebele kingdom. After Lobengula's death, the British prohibited the Ndebele from installing a new king.

Frustrated by the refusal of the British to respond to his petitions, Mlugulu and other senior Ndebele officials planned a revolt. Mlugulu carefully monitored British troop and police movements. When the British South Africa Company administrator, Leander Jameson, took most of the Rhodesian police into the Transvaal in late 1895, Mlugulu scheduled a national dance to install a new king for the Ndebele.

The coronation never occurred because other Ndebele precipitously initiated the revolt. Leadership of the revolt was divided between the established Ndebele hierarchy, which Mlugulu represented, and a Shona-derived religious cult led by Mkwati.

Mlugulu commanded Ndebele troops for several months and played a leading part in peace negotiations with Cecil Rhodes in late 1896. After the war, Mlugulu was made a salaried induna — a salaried chief — by the government. Through the remainder of his life, Mlugulu continued a peaceful, but unsuccessful, movement for restoration of the Ndebele kingdom.

• A treaty established the French Protectorate in Madagascar.

• The Arab half-caste Mlozi was defeated by Johnston at Karonga (November). Over 1,000 slaves were freed. Mlozi was hanged after a trial by Makonde chiefs.

• "British" Bechuanaland was annexed to the Cape Colony (November 11).

In 1895, Bathoen, the chief of the Ngwakatse, joined Kgama III (Khama) and Sebele in a visit to London. In London, the trio successfully blocked the proposal to turn the Bechuanaland Protectorate over to the privately controlled British South Africa Company.

• Jameson's raid went into the Transvaal from Bechuanaland (December 29).

Late in 1895, Jameson led a force of about five hundred Rhodesian police and volunteers into the Transvaal. Jameson and Cecil Rhodes had anticipated a general uprising of foreign Euro-Africans (uitlanders) to topple the Afrikaner regime of Paulus Kruger. Communications were poor, the local uprising failed to materialize, and the "raid" was a disaster. Jameson was forced to surrender to the Afrikaners.

The Afrikaner victory enabled Kruger to

emerge with much more unified support from his own people. Thereafter, Kruger used income from the Transvaal mines to equip his growing army with modern weapons, supplied by the new rail link he had established through Mozambique.

- The Transkeian General Council was formed.
- The telegraph reached Blantyre and Zomba.
- Swaziland became a protectorate of the South African Republic.
- The Northern Copper Company obtained 500 mile concession in the Kafue region.
- The "Kaffir Boom" in mining shares spread to London, Berlin and Paris.
- Civil circumscriptions were introduced in Mozambique.
- There were native uprisings in Mozambique.

In 1895, Gungunyane's army was overwhelmed by the machine guns and other modern weapons of the Portuguese. Gungunyane, the last king of Gaza, was captured and exiled to the Azore Islands. He would died there in 1906. *See 1906.*

- In 1895, Dinuzulu, the king of the Zulu, received a pardon. However, the efforts of the Natal colonial government to annex Zululand delayed Dinuzulu's return home from his imprisonment on St. Helena Island until 1898.
- John Dunn (c.1835-1895), a Euro-African chief of the Zulu nation, died.

John Dunn was born in Natal and first came to Zululand as a hunter in 1853. In Zululand, Dunn became active in Zulu politics, supporting Mbulazi's faction against Cetewayo in the Zulu civil war of 1856. Cetewayo won the war, but became reconciled with Dunn and made Dunn a territorial chief and his adviser on European affairs. Dunn married into dozens of Zulu families and eventually administered about 10,000 people.

When the British invaded Zululand in 1879, Dunn attempted to remain neutral, but soon went over to the British.

Cetewayo was defeated and the Zulu kingdom became splintered. The British general Garnet Wolseley divided Zululand into thirteen independent sections and made Dunn the chief of one section.

In 1881, Dunn unsuccessfully attempted to proclaim himself the paramount chief of all the Zulu. When Cetewayo was restored as paramount chief in 1884, Dunn remained an independent chief outside Cetewayo's territory.

At the time of his death, John Dunn was one of the most powerful people in Zululand.

RELATED HISTORICAL EVENTS

- *Europe:* The Anglo-Moroccan treaty was reached (March 13).
- On March 28, Sir E. Grey, the British Foreign Secretary, announced that Britain would regard any French occupation of the Upper Nile as an unfriendly act. On April 5, the French issued a protest to this announcement.
- Isaac Wallace-Johnson (1895-1965), a labor leader, was born.
- *Africa:* Joseph Thomson (1858-1895), a British explorer and imperial agent, died.

Joseph Thomson's first expedition in 1879 took him through southern Tanzania and eastern Zaire and clarified a number of geographical questions about the interior's lake systems.

In 1881, Thomson surveyed for coal around the Ruvuma River on behalf of the Zanzibari Sultan Barghash. His most important expedition began in 1882. During this expedition, Thomson went from Mombasa to Lake Victoria and demonstrated the possibility of opening commercial routes through the Masai country of western Kenya.

In 1885, Thomson obtained treaties from the Sultan of Sokoto and the Emir of Gwandu in northern Nigeria for the Royal Niger Company.

On his last important trip in 1890, Thomson obtained treaties in northeastern Zambia for the British South Africa Company of Cecil Rhodes.

Thomson published several books and numerous articles on his explorations. For many east African regions his are the earliest written records.

- Hermann von Wissmann (1853-1905), a German explorer and colonial administrator in East Africa, died.

Hermann von Wissmann was known for crossing central Africa from Angola to Zanzibar from 1880 to 1882. When the Germans began to administer mainland Tanzania, Von Wissmann ruthlessly suppressed massive resistance from the coastal peoples.

Late in 1889, Von Wissmann's forces captured and executed the Arab resister Abushiri bin Salimu. The next year, Von Wissman negotiated a truce with the Zigua resistance leader Bwana Heri.

During the early 1890s, Von Wissmann occupied himself with steamship ventures on the great African lakes. Von Wissmann served briefly as governor of German East Africa in 1895, continuing the suppression of African resistance.

1 8 9 6

THE UNITED STATES

On May 18, 1896, the United States Supreme Court decision of *Plessy v. Ferguson* (1896) 163 U.S. 537, 16 S.Ct. 1138, was rendered. The *Plessy* case upheld the doctrine of "separate but equal"—a doctrine which prevailed in the South for the next sixty years.

On June 7, 1892, Homer Plessy, a light skinned New Orleans African American (seven-eighths European, one-eighth African) who could easily have "passed for white," got on a railroad car, announced that he was an African American, and attempted to ride in the railroad car designated for European Americans. For this transgression, Plessy was arrested. Plessy was tried in the court of the Honorable John H. Ferguson, a judge of the criminal district court for the parish of Orleans, and was convicted of violating an 1890 Louisiana law which segregated railroad passenger cars.

Plessy appealed his conviction to the United States Supreme Court. Justice Henry Billings Brown, writing the majority opinion in the case which came to be known as *Plessy v. Ferguson*, called the creation of "separate but equal" accommodations a "reasonable" use of state police power. Additionally, Brown rejected the argument that the 14th Amendment had "been intended to abolish distinctions based on color, or to enforce social as distinguished from political equality, or a commingling of the two races upon terms unsatisfactory to either."

Brown noted that "If the two races are to meet upon terms of social equality, it must be the result of natural affinities, a mutual appreciation of each other's merits, and a voluntary consent of individuals. ... Legislation is powerless to eradicate racial instincts, or to abolish distinctions based upon physical differences, and the attempt to do so can only result in accentuating the difficulties of the present situation. If the civil and political rights of both races be equal, one cannot be inferior to the other civilly or politically. If one race be inferior to the other socially, the constitution of the United States cannot put them upon the same plane."

Justice John Marshall Harlan wrote the dissent in *Plessy*. In his dissent, Harlan prophetically wrote: "The judgment this day rendered will, in time, prove to be quite as pernicious as the decision made by this tribunal in the Dred Scott case."

Harlan later asserted that "The arbitrary separation of citizens, on the basis of race, while they are on a public highway, is a badge of servitude wholly inconsistent with the civil freedom and the equality before the law established by the constitution. It cannot be justified upon any legal grounds. ... If evils will result from the commingling of the two races upon public highways established for the benefit of all, they will be infinitely less than those that will surely come from state legislation regulating the enjoyment of civil rights upon the basis of race. We boast of the freedom enjoyed by our people above all other peoples. But it is difficult to reconcile that boast with a state of the law which, practically, puts the brand of servitude and degradation upon a large class of our fellow citizens, — our equals before the law. The thin disguise of "equal" accommodations for passengers in railroad coaches will not mislead any one, nor atone for the wrong this day done."

• South Carolina adopted the "white primary." In the "white primary" only European Americans could vote in the Democratic primary.

• The Republican Party platform stated: "We proclaim our unqualified condemnation of the uncivilized and preposterous practice well-known as lynching, and the killing of human beings suspected or charged with crimes without due process of law."

• In the 1896 Presidential election, William Jennings Bryan ran on both the Democratic and Populist tickets. Southern European Americans were divided, however, between Populists and Democrats. Both sought the vote of African Americans. For a while, the Populists upheld the cause of African Americans. Indeed, the Populist platform of Georgia contained a plank which denounced "lynch law." In Louisiana, African Americans held the balance of power between the Populist-Republican Fusion and the Democrats. This precarious position led to violence. On the day of the state election, the militia was sent into Saint Landry Parish after Republicans and Populists seized the town of Washington and forced the Democratic election official to register the African Americans. Two African

Americans were murdered and many beaten by European American Democrats.

• The Democrats were victorious in Louisiana, and between 1896 and 1904 adopted literacy, property, and poll tax requirements to disenfranchise African Americans. These restrictions and the "grandfather clause" of 1898 reduced the number of registered African American voters from 130,334 in 1896 to 1,342 in 1904.

• The North Carolina elections were also marked by violence. In Franklington, state troops were called out to prevent a race riot. A riot did occur in Pearson County. Nevertheless, the North Carolina Populists won a substantial victory in the election.

• George Washington Carver became the director of agricultural research at Tuskegee Institute.

• Austin Maurice Curtis (1868-1939) was appointed to the medical staff of Chicago's Cook County Hospital — a nonsegregated hospital.

Austin Maurice Curtis was an 1891 graduate of Northwestern University. Curtis was the first physician to intern with Daniel Hale Williams. He later succeeded Williams as head of Freedmen's Hospital in Washington, D. C., and taught at Howard University College of Medicine.

• African Americans were instrumental in the incorporation of Miami, Florida.

On July 28, 1896, Miami, Florida, officially made its transition from seaside village to city when 200 European American men gathered in a room above a pool hall. Bound by a law requiring at least 300 votes for incorporation, the European American fathers of Miami did something which was unheard of at the time in the segregated South. They asked more than 100 African American laborers to cast ballots.

The first African American vote recorded was that of the laborer Silas Austin. With the aid of the African American laborers Miami became a city.

• *Organizations:* The National Association of Colored Women was organized in Washington, D.C. by Dr. Mary Church Terrell (July 21). By 1901, the National Association of Colored Women had chapters organized in 26 states. A nurses' training school was set up in New Orleans, and hygiene teams were sent to four states to aid the African Americans there. Land was purchased in Memphis for an old folks' home, and in Tennessee and Louisiana

the Legislatures were petitioned for repeal of Jim Crow laws. Plans to establish Mothers' Congresses and to teach African American mothers how to care for their children were implemented.

• A Colored Young Men's Christian Association Building was constructed in Norfolk, Virginia.

• *The Labor Movement:* The Boilermakers and Shipbuilders Union was admitted to the American Federation of Labor. The members of the Boilermakers and Shipbuilders Union were pledged to propose — to nominate — only European American men for membership.

• Richard L. Davis, an Ohio African American, was elected to serve on the national executive board of the United Mine Workers. Davis, with other African American miners, had been a local union official since the United Mine Workers was organized in 1890.

• *Notable Births:* May Chinn, pioneering physician, was born (April 15).

• Ida Cox, a blues singer, was born in Georgia (February 25).

• "Blind" Gary Davis, a guitar player, was born in Laurens, South Carolina (April 30).

• Amy Jacques Garvey, a noted activist, was born in Kingston, Jamaica (December 31).

• Malvin Gray Johnson (1896-1934), an African American artist, was born.

Malvin Gray Johnson was born in Greensboro, North Carolina. He attended the National Academy in New York City and won the Otto Kahn special prize at the Harmon Show in 1928 for *Swing Low Sweet Chariot,* a depiction of plantation slaves' fantasies. During his life, Johnson experimented with many forms. His early work showed great impressionist influence. Later he evolved toward cubism; his last and most mature work utilized African pictorial elements.

The subject matter in Johnson's last works was plantation life in the contemporary South. The two most significant series of canvasses were *Virginia Landscapes,* of which "Red Road" and "Convict Labor" were most outstanding.

A second series was a gallery of African American portraits done in water color. Johnson was arguably the most talented African American painter of his generation.

• Evelyn Preer, a noted thespian, was born in Vicksburg, Mississippi (July 26).

• Eslanda Robeson, a writer, was born in Washington, D. C. (December 12).

• *Notable Deaths:* In 1896, 77 African Americans were lynched.

• *Miscellaneous Cases:* The United States Supreme Court decision of *Plessy v. Ferguson* (1896) 163 U.S. 537, 16 S.Ct. 1138, was rendered (May 18). The *Plessy* case upheld the doctrine of "separate but equal"—a doctrine which would prevail in the South for the next sixty years.

• In Washington County, Mississippi, 7,000 African Americans and 1,500 European Americans were declared competent for jury duty, but only European Americans were chosen. This exclusionary practice was contested before the United States Supreme Court in *Gibson v. Mississippi* (April 13, 1896) 162 U.S. 565, 16 S.Ct. 904. In *Gibson,* the Supreme Court effectively excluded African Americans from juries by ruling that there was no proof of exclusion on the grounds of race or color in this case.

• *Miscellaneous Publications:* In 1895, W. E. B. Du Bois became the first African American to be awarded a doctorate from Harvard University. Du Bois' dissertation was entitled *The Suppression of the African Slave Trade to the U.S.A., 1638-1870.* This doctoral dissertation was published as the first volume of the Harvard Historical Studies in 1896. These studies, which were published between 1896 and 1914, dealt with a different phase of African American life each year, and represented "the first real sociological research in the South."

• In 1896, *Lyrics of a Lowly Life,* was published by Paul Laurence Dunbar. This collection of poems received national attention.

• *Hearts of Gold* by J. McHenry Jones, was published in Wheeling, West Virginia. This work continued the trend started by Walter Stowers' and William H. Anderson's novel, *Appointed. Hearts of Gold* focused on the new reign of terror waged by poor European Americans who feared African Americans for economic reasons.

• Gussie Davis wrote *In the Baggage Coach Ahead.*

• William Henry Lewis wrote *How to Play Football.*

• The Atlanta University Press began publishing books.

• *Scholastic Achievements:* W. E. B. Du Bois established the Atlanta University Studies, a yearly series of scholarly conferences and publications on African American life.

• South Carolina State College was founded as the Colored Normal Industrial, Agricultural, and Mechanical College at Orangeburg.

• Booker T. Washington received the first honorary degree awarded to an African American by Harvard University.

• Lewis B. Moore received doctorates in Greek and Latin from the University of Pennsylvania in Philadelphia.

• Otelia Cromwell (1873-1972) graduated from Smith College (Northampton, Massachusetts). In 1950, Cromwell would receive an honorary LL.D. degree from Smith College.

• *The Black Church:* William S. Crowdy, a railroad cook, established the Church of God and Saints of Christ in Lawrence, Kansas.

The Church of God and Saints of Christ mixed Judaism, Christianity, and black nationalism and was sometimes called the first African American Jewish group.

A principal belief of the Church of God and Saints of Christ is that African Americans are the direct descendants of the lost tribes of Israel. A contemporaneous, and possibly earlier, church with similar views was the Church of God (Black Jews), founded by the Prophet F. S. Cherry.

• *The Arts:* Henry Ossawa Tanner's *Daniel in the Lion's Den* (*Daniel dans la Fosse aux Lions*) received honorable mention at the Paris Salon.

Music

Beginning in 1896, ragtime became popular throughout the United States. Ragtime was spread by itinerant pianists from the South and Midwest at midways and fairs. Ragtime represented a blending of West African rhythm and European musical form, with emphasis on the European.

Ragtime originated in the Midwest, not New Orleans. European Americans as well as African Americans were performers. Ragtime developed about the same time as jazz emerged in New Orleans. However, the styles of ragtime and jazz were disparate and would not merge for some 20 years.

Scott Joplin, an African American with classical training, was the greatest composer of ragtime. Attempts were made to incorporate ragtime into the European tradition. James P. Johnson composed choral works, concertos, and symphonies in ragtime. However, such works as Johnson's works proved to be too complex for most performers and the public did not embrace them.

A form of orchestral ragtime did manage to survive in a simplified form with complicated rhythms. Ragtime became what is today known as Dixieland jazz.

- The first known example of the spasm band began performing in New Orleans where Emile "Stale Bread" Lacoume, "Cajun," "Whiskey," "Warm Gravy," and "Slew Foot Pete" played improvised music on homemade instruments on street corners.
- *Black Enterprise:* An African American bank, the Nickel Savings Bank of Richmond, Virginia, was established.
- *Sports:* Willie Simms won the Kentucky Derby riding Ben Brush.

In 1896, the Kentucky Derby was shortened from one and one-half miles to one and one-quarter miles. The first winner of the race at this new distance was Ben Brush ridden by Willie Simms of Augusta, Georgia. During his career, Willie Simms won many of the best known horse races in the United States, such as the Kentucky Derby and Preakness in 1898, the Belmont Stakes in 1893 and 1894, and the Champagne Stakes at Belmont in 1895. Simms was also the first American jockey on an American horse to win on the English track. With his English victory, Willie Simms achieved international fame.

THE AMERICAS

- *Brazil:* Joaquim Machado de Assis published *Varias historias.*
- Antonio Carlos Gomes (1836-1896), the first Brazilian musician to achieve success in Italy as a composer of operas, died (September 16).

Antonio Gomes was the son of a bandmaster. Antonio learned the fundamentals of music and an elementary knowledge of several instruments from his father at an early age.

Gomes' *Hino academico,* an early composition, was well received. Gomes went to Rio de Janeiro in order to enroll in the Imperial Conservatory of Music. His conservatory studies in composition with Joaquim Giannini reinforced his interest in opera. Two of his operatic compositions, *A noite do castelo* (1861) and *Joana de Flandres* (1863) were well received and, as a result, Gomes was awarded a government subsidy for study in Italy.

The greatest success of Gomes' career was the performance of his opera *Il Guarany* at La Scala, in Milan, on March 19, 1870. *Il Guarany* was followed by *Fosca, Salvator Rosa, Maria Tudor, Lo schiavo,* and *Condor.* However, none of the later works achieved the success *Il Guarany.*

Gomes chose Brazilian subjects for some of his operas, but his style of writing and approach was Italian at a time of rising musical nationalism in Brazil. Expecting unqualified and enthusiastic acceptance in his native country during a time of rising republican sentiments, Gomes was instead considered an aristocrat out of touch with political realities. The fact that his family sought to forbid performances of his operas in the Portuguese language, insisting on Italian, only added to the disdain shown by Brazilians for the work of their native son.

- *Canada:* From 1896 until his death in 1915, Alfred Shadd, the great grandson of Abraham Shadd, practiced medicine in Kinistino and Melfort, Saskatchewan. Shadd experimented with breeding cattle, edited the *Melfort Journal,* and twice ran unsuccessfully for office as a Conservative.
- *Cuba:* General Antonio Maceo was killed on the battlefield near Havana.

Antonio Maceo (1845-1896) was an Afro-Cuban patriot who became a hero of the series of wars that ended Spanish domination of Cuba in 1898.

Antonio Maceo was born in Santiago de Cuba on June 14, 1845. He was the son of Marcos Maceo, a Afro-Venezuelan émigré, and a free Afro-Cuban Mariana Grajales *(see 1893),* one of the outstanding women in Cuban history. All of the children of Mariana Grajales played patriotic roles in the efforts to make Cuba an independent nation.

As a youth Maceo, lived on his father's small farm in Oriente. He received his education at home from private tutors. Maceo also worked at his father's farm making occasional trips to Santiago de Cuba to sell agricultural products.

During the 1860s, Cuba entered a period of revolutionary turmoil as Cuban patriots conspired to rid themselves of Spanish control. Unhappy with Spanish domination and horrified by the exploitation of the slaves, Maceo entered the Masonic Lodge of Santiago in 1864 and started to conspire with Cuban revolutionaries. When, on October 19, 1868, Carlos Manuel de Cespedes and other leaders began Cuba's Ten Years War, Maceo joined the rebellion.

Maceo soon showed superior ability in guerrilla fighting. Under the instructions of Maximo Gomez, a Dominican guerrilla expert who had joined the Cuban Forces, Maceo developed into one of the most daring fighters of the Cuban army. Showing extraordinary leadership and tactical abilities, Maceo defeated the Spanish in numerous battles. In recognition of his success, Maceo was soon promoted to the rank of captain.

Maceo won respect and admiration from his men as well as fear and scorn from the Spanish troops. He kept tight discipline in his encampment, constantly planning and organizing future battles. Maceo developed a knack for outsmarting and outmaneuvering the Spanish generals. On several occasions, Maceo's tactical brilliance enabled the Cubans to inflict heavy losses on the Spanish forces.

Maceo's forays into the sugar growing regions of Cuba not only disrupted the sugar harvest but also led to the freedom of the slaves in these regions. Many of these slaves could soon be found in the ranks of Maceo's army.

By 1872, Maceo had achieved the rank of general. His prominent position among revolutionary leaders soon gave rise to intrigue and suspicion. Conservative elements who supported the war efforts began to fear the possibility of the establishment of a black republic with Maceo at its head.

Maceo did closely identify with the plight of the men and women of African descent in Cuba. However, while many believed that his identification with the slaves was the precursor to the creation of a black state, Maceo's defense of the rights of Afro-Cubans was actually based on the theoretical notion of the rights of all men rather than any particular ethnic affinity. As Maceo said, "The revolution has no color."

Nevertheless, the suspicions remained. Thus, when General Gomez advocated a full invasion of western Cuba to cripple sugar production and to liberate all the slaves, this plan was met by opposition from the conservative supporters of the revolutionary army. Maceo, in particular, was ordered to remain in Oriente province and the invasion of western Cuba had to be postponed until 1875.

Even after the invasion of western Cuba got underway, the army only got as far as Las Villas province in central Cuba. The destruction of the sugar estates increased opposition from the landed and sugar interests who were supporting the rebels. Additionally, dissension within the revolutionary ranks and fear of the Afro-Cubans contributed to the slowing down of the revolutionary advance.

After a prolonged silence, on May 16, 1876, Maceo answered those who persisted in accusing him of attempting to establish a black republic. He wrote: "In planting these seeds of distrust and dissension, they [his accusers] do not seem to realize that it is the country that will suffer ... I must protest energetically that neither now nor at any other time am I to be regarded as an advocate of a [Black] Republic ... This concept is a deadly thing to this democratic Republic which is founded on the basis of liberty and fraternity."

The Ten Years War dragged on for ten long years. Neither the Cubans nor the Spaniards were able to win a decisive victory. Finally, on February 11, 1878, the Peace of Zanjon was signed and the war came to an end. Most of the generals of the Cuban army accepted the pact. But not Antonio Maceo.

Maceo refused to capitulate. He continued to fight.

Arrogantly, Maceo held an historic meeting, known as the "Protest of Baragua," in which he met with the leader of the Spanish forces, Marshal Arsenio Martinez Campos. In this meeting Maceo boldly demanded the independence of Cuba and the complete abolition of slavery. When these two conditions were rejected, Maceo resumed fighting with his rag tag army.

Maceo's efforts, while heroic, were futile. Realizing the futility, Maceo left Cuba and went into exile.

Maceo first went to Jamaica. From Jamaica, he traveled to New York to raise money and weapons to continue the struggle.

Maceo soon joined the efforts of Major General Calixto Garcia who was then organizing a new rebellion. The new rebellion, known as La Guerra Chiquita ("The Little War"), lasted from 1879 to 1880. La Guerra Chiquita ended in disaster. As a result, Maceo was once again exiled.

Disappointed and disillusioned. Maceo traveled to the Dominican Republic and finally settled in Honduras. In Honduras, Maceo joined General Gomez and was appointed to an army post in Tegucigalpa. Nevertheless, Maceo continued to see his exile as being only a temporary interruption in the struggle to liberate Cuba.

Maceo and Gomez soon began to organize a new Cuban rebellion. Maceo personally visited different Cuban exile centers in the United States seeking support for the cause of Cuban independence.

For most of the next decade, Maceo wandered throughout the Caribbean and Central America. Maceo lived in Panama, visited Santiago de Chile and Jamaica in 1890, and finally settled in Costa Rica where he engaged successfully in tobacco and sugar production.

While in Costa Rica, Maceo received a call from Jose Marti for a final effort to liberate Cuba. Marti had organized a revolutionary party in exile and now offered Maceo an important position in the movement. Maceo joined Marti and Gomez in organizing the Cubans in and out of the island until finally on February 24, 1895, the War of Independence began.

In March of 1895, Maceo and a group of expeditionaries landed in Oriente province to join the rebellion. Gomez and Maceo were able to implement their plan to invade the western provinces and carry the war to the other extreme of the island. The two generals and Marti met on Cuban soil to map the war effort.

For the purpose of managing the war, Maceo advocated a strong military junta rather than civilian control. Maceo argued that dissension and incompetence of the civilian government during the Ten Years War had led to the failure of the rebellion. Although the question of civilian versus military control was not resolved, Gomez was made Commander-in-Chief of the army, Maceo military commander of Oriente, and Marti head of the revolution abroad and in non-military matters.

Marti's death on May 19, 1895, dealt a blow to the morale of the Cuban forces. Nevertheless, Maceo and Gomez did not hesitate. In repeated attacks, the two generals undermined and defeated the Spanish forces.

For the next three months, Maceo and Gomez carried the war to the western provinces. The war in the western provinces is considered to have been Maceo's greatest military feat. It was a brilliant operation during which Maceo covered more than a thousand miles in 92 days while engaging the Spanish army in 27 battles or skirmishes and capturing more than 2,000 rifles and 80,000 rounds.

Beginning in January of 1896, Maceo waged a bitter but successful campaign against larger Spanish forces in the provinces of Pinar del Rio and Havana.

On December 7, 1896, while preparing for their next campaign, Maceo's troops were attacked near the small town of San Pedro del Cacahual. Maceo was killed in this skirmish.

Throughout his military career, it is estimated that Maceo fought in more than 900 military actions. Since he frequently led his troops in battle, Maceo sustained some twenty-six wounds.

Antonio Maceo was undoubtedly, one of the great men of Cuba.

- *Haiti:* President Florvil Hyppolite died of a heart attack during an expedition. General Tiresias Antoine Simon Sam was elected President to succeed Hyppolite.
- Alibee Fery (1818-1896), a playwright, narrator, poet, and storyteller, died.

Alibee Fery was born in Jeremie on May 28, 1818. He was self-taught. Fery authored several Haitian stories. He was the first to tell the story of Bouqui and Malice, the two famous characters of Haitian tales.

Fery's other works include: *Essais Litteraires*, a play; *Fils du Chasseur*, a story; *Les Bluettes*, a book of poems; *Les Echantillons*, a book of stories; and *Les Esquisses*, a group of historical stories.

- *Jamaica:* Amy Jacques Garvey, a noted activist, was born in Kingston, Jamaica (December 31).

AFRICA

During the late 1890s, Germany began to expand into Africa. As it did so, it amassed great African art collections. These collections would come to find homes in Berlin, Hamburg, Bremen, Leipzig, Frankfurt, Munich, and several smaller cities. The German African art collections would be the subjects of serious studies and treatises by German scholars and anthropologists.

- *North Africa, Egypt and Sudan:* Lord Cromer dispatched an Anglo-Egyptian force to the Sudan (March 16).
- Kitchener recaptured Dongola with an Anglo-Egyptian force (September 23).

In 1896, General Kitchener began the Anglo-Egyptian reconquest of the Sudan.

- Construction of the Aswan Dam began. The construction would be completed in 1903.
- *Western Africa:* A British expeditionary force was sent against the Ashanti. On January 20, the Asantehene was deposed and imprisoned with other notables. This led to disturbances in Borin in March and April.
- On August 16, the British created a British Protectorate over Ashanti. Similar protectorate treaties were effected with neighboring chieftains.

In 1896, a British expedition arrived in Kumasi to demand that the Ashanti (Asante) accept British protection and to extort a large sum of gold to pay British expenses. Prempe, the asantehene, decided that armed resistance was futile. Prempe accepted the protectorate, but claimed he had not the gold to pay the indemnity. Prempe was thereupon arrested and deported to Sierra Leone.

- In 1896, Great Britain proclaimed a protectorate over the Sierra Leone interior. Although Suluku Konte, the ruler of the Biriwa chiefdom, was now limited in his external dealings, he maintained much of his power and influence. The British recognized this by making no attempt to divide up his chiefdom as they did others (such as Bai Bureh's Kasseh [*see 1908*]) in the protectorate.
- An Anglo-French Convention on the boundary of Dahomey and Nigeria was convened.
- By 1896, Rabeh Zubayr *(see 1900)* had the whole state of Bornu under his control and Rabeh was well on his way to establishing a new Bornu dynasty.
- Bubakar Biro, the ruler of the Fula state of Futa Jalon, died.

Bubakar Biro shared power in alternating two year periods with Oumarou Bademba, the leader of the rival ruling house in Futa. During the last period of Bubakar's reign the French tried to enforce a protectorate over the state. Bubakar tried to negotiate, but was forced to fight. He was defeated and then killed by Oumarou Bademba who was supported by the French.

The death of Bubakar Biro brought to an end the unique political system in Futa Jalon, which had operated for over fifty years.

- French forces invaded Ouagadougou from the north.

When Wobogo, the ruler of the Mossi state of Ouagadougou, attempted to resist, the French commander, Voulet, burned the town in retaliation.

Wobogo continued to fight, but was forced to flee when some of his vassal kings surrendered. Voulet formally deposed Wobogo early in 1897, and placed his brother, Sighiri on the throne.

- Milton Augustus Striery Margai (1896-1964), a future prime minister of Sierra Leone, was born.

Milton Margai was the son of a Mende trader. He was educated in mission schools and at Fourah Bay College in Freetown before attending medical school in England. Returning to Sierra Leone, Margai soon joined government service, working in the southern interior for many years and gaining widespread popularity. Margai entered politics in 1946 when he joined

a protectorate political party working for limited reforms rather than independence.

In 1949, Margai was elected to the protectorate assembly, and retired from medicine the next year.

In 1951, Margai formed the Sierra Leone People's Party (SLPP). The SLPP would come to dominate Sierra Leone politics through the independence period. By forming a coalition of modern and traditional elites in the protectorate, Milton Margai overcame the political strength of the Freetown Creoles. The Freetown Creoles had previously dominated Sierra Leone politics for decades.

In 1954, after a SLPP election victory, Milton Margai became chief minister of the government.

Sierra Leone received a new constitution and held elections in 1957, and the SLPP won again. However, Milton's brother, Albert Margai *(see 1910)* challenged Milton for party leadership. Albert alleged that Milton was too conservative.

A vote of the SLPP membership favored Albert. However, Albert decided to yield to his older brother and Milton became prime minister in 1958.

Albert left the SLPP to form his own party. In 1960, Sierra Leone's parties formed a coalition to go to London for independence talks. When independence was declared in 1961, Milton continued as prime minister.

Milton remained one of Africa's more conservative heads of state. At his death in 1964, Albert, Milton's brother, succeeded him as prime minister of Sierra Leone.

- *Central Africa:* The Crown Lands Ordinance was adopted in Cameroon (June 15).
- The Marchand mission was sent to occupy Fashoda disembarked at Loango (July 24).
- Mibambwe IV Rutarindwa of Rwanda was murdered for "unpopularity and greed." He was succeeded by Yuhi V Musinga.
- A German post was established at Usumbura.
- The first White Fathers' Mission in Burundi was founded at Muyaga.
- The Trappists began their work in the Congo.
- The Pallotine Fathers started their work in the Cameroon.
- The Congo station was established at Uvira.
- *Eastern Africa:* An Indian regiment was brought in to end the Mazrui war (March).

In 1888, the chartered Imperial British East Africa Company (IBEAC) established an administration over the Kenya coast. Under its aegis, Mbaruk returned peacefully to settle at Gazi. Over the next seven years, Mbaruk cooperated with the IBEAC and occasionally lent it material support against his neighbors. This arrangement ended in 1895 when the company prepared to turn over its administration to the British crown.

Around this same time, the northern Mazrui community entered into a succession dispute. The IBEAC intervened, causing the northern Mazrui to revolt.

Some of the Mazrui sought refuge with Mbaruk. Through his refusal to betray his kinsmen, Mbaruk was reluctantly drawn into the rebellion.

Mbaruk conducted a successful guerrilla campaign until early 1896, when he fled across the border into German administered territory (present day Tanzania). In the German territory, Mbaruk surrendered to Governor von Wissmann and was granted asylum.

Mbaruk's retirement to Dar es Salaam on a German pension brought Mazrui political influence in colonial East Africa to an end.

- The Ethiopians defeated the Italians at Adowa (March 1). Italy was forced to ask for peace.

After serving as governor from 1892 to 1896 of Italian held Eritrea, Oreste Baratieri was named commander-in-chief over an invasion of Ethiopia.

At the Battle of Adowa, Baratieri was overwhelmingly defeated by the Ethiopian Emperor Menelik II. This defeat was the worst setback ever experienced by a European power in sub-Saharan Africa.

- The Kingdom of Koki and parts of Bunyoro were incorporated into the Kingdom of Buganda (April 9).
- A decree set up "Cote Francaise des Somalis et Dependences" and made it subject to the Minister of France to Ethiopia (May 20).
- Sayyid Hamid died (August 25). Sayyid Khalid again seized the palace. On August 26, the British bombarded Zanzibar and installed Sayyid Hamud ibn Muhammed as Sultan.
- An administrator was appointed for the French Somaliland (August 28).
- The Treaty of Addis Adaba was negotiated (October 26). Under the treaty, the Italian Protectorate over Ethiopia was withdrawn.

In 1895, Italy invaded Ethiopia. After some initial setbacks, Menelik, the Emperor of Ethiopia, launched a counter-offensive in 1896. This counter-offensive resulted in a major Ethiopian victory at Adowa. As a result of this crushing Ethiopian victory, the Italians were compelled to execute a new treaty — a treaty which acknowledged Ethiopia's complete independence. *See 1865.*

- Aussa was annexed by Menelik.
- A military post was established at Iringa.
- Construction of the Uganda railway was begun. The line from Mombasa to Kampala would be completed in 1901.
- Lij Iyasu (Iyasu V), the future Emperor of Ethiopia, was born.

"Lij" is the honorific title conferred upon the sons of important families in Ethiopia. The term "Lij" is sometimes confused for proper names as in "Lij" Iyasu.

Iyasu V (1896-1935) was the grandson by a daughter of the great Emperor Menelik II *(see 1913)*. After 1906, the health of Menelik deteriorated. Lacking sons of his own, Menelik, in 1908, nominated Iyasu as his successor.

Iyasu spent the next five years in the midst of a complicated palace power struggle as Menelik's wife, Taitu, fought against Iyasu's succession, and various factions put forward other candidates. Nevertheless, supported by the Galla army of his Muslim father, *Ras* Mikael, Iyasu ascended to the throne in 1914.

Iyasu's reign upon the throne was a turbulent one. Iyasu became increasingly sympathetic to Islam. He was said to have commissioned a fake genealogy to prove he was descended from the Prophet Muhammed rather than Solomon — the traditionally purported ancestor of the Christian Ethiopian kings.

Iyasu's apparent interest in transforming Ethiopia into an Islamic state alarmed the largely Christian nobility. When Iyasu moved to replace Tafari Makonnen (Haile Selassie), who was then the governor of the predominantly Muslim Harar province, with a Muslim, a coup was mounted against him.

Under the leadership of Tafari *(see 1892)*, Iyasu was deposed and replaced by Empress Zauditu. Iyasu's efforts to reclaim his throne failed. He was ex-communicated from the Ethiopian church and became a fugitive. However, he eluded capture for five years.

Iyasu died in prison in 1935. The official cause of death was typhoid fever, but many believe that he may have been murdered.

• David Zakayo Kivuli (c.1896-1974), an independent church leader, is believed to have been born in this year.

David Kivuli was educated in a mission school in western Kenya. Kivuli then worked as a migrant laborer. In 1925, Kivuli returned to school and was baptized by the Pentecostal Assemblies of Canada Mission, in which he served as a preacher and schools supervisor for over twelve years.

In 1932, Kivuli started "speaking in tongues" and became a popular faith-healer. His personal following grew until, Kivuli clashed with the mission leaders over his personal role in the church.

In 1942, Kivuli broke from the mission and founded the African Israel Church Nineveh. His church grew rapidly among the Luo and Luyia of western Kenya and spread into neighboring Tanzania and Uganda.

By 1970, Kivuli led perhaps 100,000 followers. His church had one hundred branches and was accepted as a probationary member of the National Christian Council of Kenya.

Kivuli died in 1974. In 1975, his church, the Africa Israel Church Nineveh, became an associate member church of the World Council of Churches.

• *Southern Africa:* Jameson surrendered at Doornkop (January 2).
• William II of Germany dispatched the "Kruger telegram" creating a strain in British-German relations (January 3).
• Rhodes resigned the premiership of the Cape Colony (January 6). A committee of the Cape Assembly reported that Rhodes engineered Jameson's raid. Pretoria and Johannesburg were fortified.
• Sir Gordon Sprigg became Prime Minister of the Cape (January 13).
• Rainilaiarivony, the Prime Minister of Madagascar, was deported to Algeria (February 21). A rebellion raged throughout the island.
• An offensive and defensive alliance was reached between the Transvaal and the Orange Free State (March 17).
• In March, the Matabele staged an uprising in Rhodesia. The uprising would not be suppressed until September of 1897.

One consequence of the disastrous Jameson raid of 1895 was that Jameson's expedition drained Rhodesia of its police force and allowed the Shona and Ndebele to revolt. The collapse of the Ndebele (Matabele) kingdom in 1894 had enabled Mkwati, a Ndebele religious leader, to appeal to the broad mass of former Ndebele subjects, many of whom were originally Shona. Operating through Mwari cult priests, Mkwati organized a popular revolt against the British occupation and directed it through 1896. At the same time, the remaining Ndebele hierarchy, under the leadership of Mlugulu, organized their own revolt.

The extent to which Mkwati and Mlugulu cooperated during this uprising is not certain. Indeed, by late 1896, Mlugulu's faction was ready to negotiate with Cecil Rhodes, but Mkwati refused to surrender. Instead, Mkwati angrily broke from the Ndebele and went to Shona country where another revolt had recently begun.

In central Mashonaland, Mkwati worked with Kagubi and other religious cult leaders to dissuade Shona chiefs from negotiating with the British. As the increasingly savage British suppression of the revolt induced many Shona chiefs to surrender, Mkwati went farther north, ever hoping to increase resistance to the British.

Mkwati died around September 1897. It is believed that he was killed by Shona who were disillusioned with the course the war with the British had taken.

• France annexed Madagascar (August 18).
• General Gallieni took control of Madagascar and became the Resident General (September 9).
• Slavery was abolished in Madagascar (September 27).
• In 1896, Khama, the ruler of the Ngwato, lent tacit support to Cecil Rhodes' group during their second war with the Ndebele.
• There was a serious rinderpest plague in the Ndebele territory.
• In 1896, when anti–British feeling was running high throughout the recently imposed colony of Rhodesia, Kagubi, a Shona spirit medium, initiated and led the Shona revolt near the town of Salisbury. Kagubi worked closely with the more established Nehanda medium, while other mhondoro mediums directed the Shona rising elsewhere.
• Expeditions were launched against the Yao and the Chewa.
• Resistance to the French began in Madagascar. The war of resistance would last until 1900.
• The Gaza kingdom ceased to exist in 1895 when the Portuguese conquered it. After a disastrous revolt two years later, the Gaza

kingdom broke into its component ethnic parts.

- Joachim Albuquerque became the governor-general of Mozambique.

Joachim Albuquerque (1855-1902) arrived in southern Mozambique to assist the special high commissioner, Antonio Enes, to conquer the Gaza kingdom. Albuquerque personally captured the Gaza king, Gungunyane.

During his tenure as governor-general, Albuquerque ruthlessly extended Portuguese conquests in southern Mozambique. A white supremacist, Albuquerque resigned his post in 1898 after clashing with higher authorities over the issue of provincial autonomy.

In 1899, Albuquerque wrote a book about his experiences entitled *Mozambique.* His book and a public parade of the captured Gungunyane in Lisbon in 1900 made Albuquerque a national hero.

- Clements Kadalie (c.1896-1951), the founder and national secretary of the Industrial and Commercial Workers' Union of Africa, was born.

Clements Kadalie was born in Malawi. He was educated in mission schools.

Kadalie had a brief career as a teacher. In 1915, Kadalie went south where he worked for three years in Southern Rhodesia before he reached Cape Town. The fact that some Africans could still vote at the Cape seems to have drawn Kadalie to the Cape. The franchisement led Kadalie to immediately become involved in electoral work for a Euro-African parliamentary candidate.

After this election, Kadalie organized two dozen African and colored dock workers into a union he called the Industrial and Commercial Union (ICU). In 1919, Kadalie began to solicit affiliate unions throughout South Africa.

In 1920, a national convention was held among labor leaders. The Industrial and Commercial Workers' Union of Africa — the "ICU" — was formed. Kadalie was excluded from office so he withdrew his delegation. The following year, however, the ICU was reorganized.

In 1921, Kadalie became the National Secretary of the ICU. Over the next few years, Kadalie consolidated his position in the Cape and sought to present his organization to Euro-Africans as a purely conventional trade union.

Kadalie avoided competing with the more political African National Congress. Nevertheless, Kadalie did use his position to influence Cape African voters.

Disenchanted with Jan Smut's administration for its handling of the 1922 Rand miners' strike, in 1924, Kadalie urged voters to support the Nationalist-Labour Party of James Hertzog. After Hertzog's election, Kadalie attempted to cooperate with the new government. These attempts soon dissolved as Kadalie came to realize that Hertzog's government was even more reactionary — more racist — than its predecessor. This disappointment caused Kadalie to turn against the entire Euro-African (white) power structure through more overtly political activities.

Under Kadalie's charismatic leadership, the ICU grew rapidly. Kadalie claimed 100,000 members by 1927, making his organization both the biggest African movement and the biggest trade union in South Africa. Also, in 1927, Kadalie moved the ICU's headquarters to Johannesburg to keep in closer touch with Euro-African (white) labor groups.

Although all Euro-African organizations except the Communist Party of Sidney P. Bunting refused to co-operate with the ICU, Kadalie insisted on purging the ICU of Communist members.

Also, in 1927, Kadalie attended an international labor meeting in Geneva. At the meeting, Kadalie sought in vain to obtain affiliation with an international body. He studied labor relations in Britain, where he got help to redraft the ICU's constitution.

During Kadalie's absence abroad there was trouble within the ICU's leadership. Kadalie returned to find that his control over the movement had waned. The Durban branch seceded and other defections followed.

In 1928, Kadalie was forced to take a harder line against pass laws than he desired to take. W. G. Ballinger, British labor organizer, arrived to help the ICU regenerate. His presence drove a wedge between Kadalie and other ICU leaders. Because of these differences, Kadalie resigned early in 1929.

The split in the ICU's national leadership broke the movement's momentum. Nevertheless, the short-lived success of the ICU provided a model for the mass movements of the 1950s.

As for Kadalie, he settled in east London where he led a local version of the ICU for the remainder of his life.

RELATED HISTORICAL EVENTS

- *The United States:* Harriet Beecher Stowe (1811-1896), the author best remembered for her anti-slavery novel *Uncle Tom's Cabin,* died.

Today Harriet Beecher Stowe is best remembered for her anti-slavery novel, *Uncle Tom's Cabin*. Stowe was born on June 14, 1811, in Litchfield, Connecticut. Her father, Lyman Beecher, was a Presbyterian minister and her siblings included the famous clergyman, Henry Ward Beecher, and the reformer and educator, Catherine Beecher.

Stowe was educated at the academy in Litchfield and at Hartford Female Seminary. From 1832 to 1850, Stowe lived in Cincinnati, Ohio, where her father served as president of Lane Theological Seminary.

In 1836, Harriet married Calvin Stowe, a member of the Lane Theological Seminary faculty. Harriet's years in Cincinnati would form the basis for many of the characters and incidents in *Uncle Tom's Cabin*, which was written while Harriet was staying in Brunswick, Maine.

After the publication of *Uncle Tom's Cabin*, Stowe became famous overnight. On a visit to England, she was welcomed by the English abolitionists and soon became a favorite of the abolitionists on both sides of the ocean.

Uncle Tom's Cabin is described as melodramatic and sentimental, but it is more than a melodrama. *Uncle Tom's Cabin* re-creates characters, scenes, and incidents with humor and realism. It analyzes the issue of slavery in the Midwest, New England, and the South during the days of the Fugitive Slave Law.

Uncle Tom's Cabin was published on the heels of the Compromise of 1850. The book served to intensify the disagreement between the North and the South which led to the Civil War. Stowe's name was anathema in the South, and many historians believe that the bitter feelings aroused by Stowe's book helped cause the Civil War.

It is important to understand that the images that most people have of the characters in *Uncle Tom's Cabin* are not the way the characters are actually portrayed in the book. After the Civil War, *Uncle Tom's Cabin* became known chiefly through abridgments of the novel and by plays (particularly George L. Aiken's play) based on the book. However, these versions distorted the original story and characters. By the late 1800s, most people believed that *Uncle Tom's Cabin* dealt primarily with the death of Tom and Little Eva, Topsy's antics, and Eliza's escape. The term "Uncle Tom" as derived from the plays and distortions came to stand for an African American man who, for selfish reasons or through fear, adopted a humble, often self-degrading, manner to gain favor of European Americans. However, in Stowe's novel, Uncle Tom is portrayed as a brave man who dies rather than betray two fellow slaves.

Stowe's other works dealt with New England in the late 1700s and early 1800s. These works include *The Minister's Wooing* (1859); *The Pearl of Orr's Island* (1862); *Oldtown Folks* (1869); and *Sam Lawson's Oldtown Fireside Stories* (1872). Another novel *Dred, A Tale of the Great Dismal Swamp* (1856) dealt with slavery in the South.

- *Europe:* The "Kruger telegram" provoked an Anglo-German crisis. In March, Britain decided to retake Sudan to prevent French encroachment.
- A Franco-Italian convention on Tunis was convened. Under the convention, Italy abandoned many of its African claims.
- The first modern Olympic Games were held in Athens, Greece.

---

1 8 9 7

THE UNITED STATES

- G. H. White of North Carolina, an African American, was elected to the 55th Congress.
- President McKinley re-appointed ex–Senator Blanche K. Bruce as Register of the Treasury. Bruce held the position until March 1898, when he died.
- H. A. Rucker served as Collector of Internal Revenue in Georgia.
- Charles Burleigh Purvis was appointed to serve on the District of Columbia's Board of Medical Examiners.
- *Crime and Punishment:* By the end of 1897, 7,372 cases had been tried under the Enforcement Acts. 5,172 of these cases originated in the South and 2,200 in the North. Of the 7,372 cases, only 1,432 resulted in convictions.
- *Notable Births:* Sidney Bechet (1897-1959), a noted jazz musician, was born (May 14).

Sidney Bechet was born in New Orleans, Louisiana. He began playing the clarinet at six. As a teenager, he played with Freddie Keppard's band and the Eagle Band, and in 1916 he joined King Oliver's Olympic Band in New Orleans.

In 1919, Bechet played with Will Marion Cook's Southern Syncopated Orchestra in New York. When he returned to New York in 1921 after a European tour, Bechet began playing soprano sax along with the clarinet.

In the mid-1920s, Bechet again toured Europe and Russia and, in 1928, he joined Noble Sissle's band in Paris. Bechet played with the Noble Sissle band until 1938, touring both in Europe and the United States.

During the 1940s, Bechet played with Eddie Condon, principally in New York, and then began to spend most of his time in Europe.

Sidney Bechet died in Paris in 1959.

- Willie Covan, a tap dancer, was born in Atlanta (March 4).
- Lizzie "Memphis Minnie" Douglas, one of the most important and influential country blues singers, was born (June 3).
- Rudolph Fisher, a novelist, was born in Washington, D. C. (May 9).
- Fletcher Henderson, a bandleader and jazz pianist, was born in Cuthbert, Georgia (December 18).
- "Blind Lemon" Jefferson was born in Texas (July 1). Blind Lemon would become one of the first to use the term "rock n' roll"—a sexual euphemism.
- Elijah Muhammed, a prominent leader of the Nation of Islam, was born (October 8).

Elijah Muhammed was born Elijah Poole in Sandersville, Georgia, the son of a Baptist preacher who had been a slave.

In 1923, Elijah Poole, with his wife and two children, moved to Detroit. Poole held several menial jobs, but with the arrival of the Depression he found himself out of work.

Around 1930, Elijah Poole met Fard Muhammed (Wali Fard). Fard Muhammed was the founder of a sect known as the Nation of Islam. Fard Muhammed converted Elijah Poole. Upon his conversion, Elijah Poole changed his name to Elijah Muhammed.

Elijah Muhammed became Fard's trusted lieutenant. In 1932, Elijah Muhammed was entrusted with establishing and running a temple in Chicago. Two years later Muhammed returned to Detroit to become Fard Muhammed's Minister of Islam and heir apparent.

In June 1934, Fard Muhammed disappeared. Several of the followers of Fard Muhammed who were jealous of Elijah's success and who were leary of his militancy, accused Elijah of being responsible for Fard Muhammed's disappearance. Elijah Muhammed was forced to leave Detroit and to leave the Nation of Islam.

Elijah Muhammed returned to Chicago and organized his movement, the Black Muslims. Elijah deified Fard as Allah and claimed quasi-divinity for himself for having known Allah.

In 1942, Elijah Muhammed was arrested for sedition. Elijah Muhammed had been openly sympathetic to Japan because Japan was a nation populated by people of color. Because of his Japanese sympathies, Elijah Muhammed had urged African Americans not to serve in the war against Japan. Elijah Muhammed was tried, convicted, and served three years in prison.

Elijah Muhammed was never well received by the mainstream civil rights community. Elijah Muhammed's black supremacist and anti-Jewish positions were often disavowed by the mainstream civil rights leaders. Nevertheless, Elijah Muhammed's Black Muslims have become recognized as a potentially powerful political force within the African American community.

In 1960, it was estimated that the Black Muslims numbered more than 100,000 nationwide with 50 temples, numerous storefront missions, and two universities of Islam in Detroit and Chicago.

- Willie "The Lion" Smith, a stride pianist, was born in Goshen, New York (November 25).
- *Notable Deaths:* 123 African Americans were lynched in 1897.
- John Mercer Langston (1829-1897) of Virginia, a soldier, educator, Haitian consul and Congressman, died (November 15).

John Mercer Langston was born a slave in Louisa County, Virginia. Langston's father was Captain Ralph Quarles, the European American plantation owner and Lucy Langston, a woman of African and Indigenous American heritage. Freed on the death of his father, Langston was sent to Ohio and educated in private schools. He graduated from Oberlin College and went on to study theology and law. In 1854, Langston was admitted to the Ohio bar.

In 1855, Langston was elected the town clerk of Brownhelm, Ohio, perhaps becoming the first African American to hold such a position.

During the Civil War, Langston left his practice of the law in Brownhelm, Ohio, to recruit African Americans into the Union cause. After the War, he served as an inspector general of the Freedmen's Bureau and, from 1869 to 1876, he was the dean of Howard University.

From 1877 to 1885, Langston served in the diplomatic corps as Minister Resident to Haiti and charge d'affaires to Santo Domingo. Upon returning to the United States, Langston was named president of the Virginia Normal and Collegiate Institute.

In 1888, Langston was elected to the House of

Representatives — the first African American to serve in that capacity for the Commonwealth of Virginia.

Langston's works include *Freedom and Citizenship* (1883), a collection of his speeches, and *From the Virginia Plantation to the National Capitol* (1894), an autobiography.

- Peter Randolph (1825-1897), a Baptist minister, a Justice of the Peace, and the author of *From Slave Cabin to the Pulpit: The Autobiography of Reverend Peter Randolph: The Southern Question Illustrated and Sketches of Slave Life* (1893), died.

Peter Randolph was born into slavery in Virginia. Freed in 1847, he moved to Boston where he would eventually become a Baptist minister with a ministry in Massachusetts, Connecticut, New York, Rhode Island, and Richmond, Virginia. Later in his life, Randolph took up the study of law and became a Justice of the Peace in Boston.

- *Miscellaneous Laws:* Arkansas adopted the "white primary."
- *Publications:* James Edwin Campbell wrote *Echoes from the Cabin and Elsewhere*. *Echoes from the Cabin and Elsewhere* was a collection of dialect poetry which employed Gullah speech of the South Carolina coast. Campbell's poetry was replete with superstitions and folklore of the Gullah people.
- Daniel Webster Davis published a collection of dialect poems entitled *Weh Down Souf*. *Weh Down Souf* was noted for depicting African Americans as simple-minded, happy-go-lucky characters.
- John Wesley Gaines published *The Negro and the White Man*.
- Richard Henry Boyd formed the National Baptist Publishing Board. The National Baptist Publishing Board issued the first series of African American Baptist literature ever published.
- *Scholastic Achievements:* The American Negro Academy was established by Alexander Crumwell (March 5). The purposes of the Academy were the promotion of literature, science, art, the fostering of higher education, and the defense of the African American. The officers were S. G. Atkins, principal of the Slater Normal School in Winston-Salem; L. B. Moore, the dean of Howard University; and W. H. Crogman, the president of Clark University, Atlanta, Georgia.

The American Negro Academy was founded in Washington, D. C. Among its presidents were such luminaries as Alexander Crummell, W. E. B. Du Bois, Archibald Grimke, John W. Cromwell, and Arthur Schomburg. Established when African Americans were being severely oppressed, the academy set out to counter the "scientific" racism of the day. The Academy sought to encourage a pride in African American culture, history and accomplishments.

The American Negro Academy often served as a forum for African American intellectuals. It achieved recognition for its exhibitions of African American books and it supported Kelly Miller's efforts to have Howard University establish a special collection of African and African American materials.

Over the years, the American Negro Academy published 5 monographs and 22 "occasional papers" from its own meetings.

The first African American intellectual society, it functioned until 1928.

- Anita Hemmings graduated from Vassar College in Poughkeepsie, New York.

Anita Hemmings was a very light-skinned African American who essentially "passed for white" during her stay at Vassar. Hemmings' declaration of her true racial identity upon graduation attracted the sensational press and caused "dismay" for the Vassar College administration.

- *The Black Church:* Richard Henry Boyd formed the National Baptist Publishing Board. The National Baptist Publishing Board issued the first series of African American Baptist literature ever published.
- *The Arts:* Henry Ossawa Tanner's *The Resurrection of Lazarus* (*La Resurrection de Lazare*) was awarded a medal at the Paris Salon and was purchased by the French government for the Luxembourg Gallery.
- *The Performing Arts: Oriental America* played on Broadway. The production followed the minstrel pattern, but the after-piece was a medley of operatic selections. *Oriental America* was credited with being the first African American production to play on Broadway instead of in burlesque theaters.
- *Music:* Charles "Buddy" Bolden organized the first jazz band. For the next seven years, Bolden would be known as the "King of Jazz" in New Orleans.
- Composer Thomas Million Turpin's *Harlem Rag* was published (December). Thomas Million Turpin (1873-1922) was a bar owner in St. Louis's tenderloin district and

eventually became the owner of the Booker T. Washington Theater in that city.

• Storyville, the official red-light district of New Orleans, was opened. In Storyville, the playing of jazz became a full-time profession instead of a mere avocation for solo pianists such as Jelly Roll Morton.

• *Technological Innovations:* Andrew J. Beard (1849-1941) received $50,000 for his invention of the "Jenny Coupler," an automatic device for coupling railroad cars.

• *Sports:* Willie Simms, a famous African American jockey, won the Brighton Handicap.

EUROPE

• Jose Thomaz de Sousa Martins (1843-1897), a noted Afro-Portuguese physician, died.

AFRICA

• *North Africa, Egypt and Sudan:* The Marchand mission reached Bangui (April). Dem Ziber was occupied. Kitchener's force advanced (May). Marchand's mission reached Semio (August 3). Marchand settled on the Such River at Wan (November).

In 1897, Marchand commanded an expedition which raced across the continent from Gabon to Fashoda on the White Nile in an attempt to counter the British occupation of Egypt by seizing control of the river. There Marchand came face to face with the British forces of Horatio Kitchener. Kitchener's forces greatly outnumbered his own and Marchand was forced to withdraw.

The encounter between Marchand and Kitchener marked the closest that Britain and France ever came to armed hostilities over possession of African territories.

• Italy ceded Kassala to Egypt (December 25).

• Jamal al-Din al-Afghani (1839-1897), an Egyptian religious teacher and one of the first Islamic modernist, died.

• *West Africa:* The British Consul-General Phillips, with a large party, was massacred attempting to reach Benin (January 4).

• Further trouble erupted in Ilorin (January). The British occupied Bida (January 27), and, on February 16, Ilorin.

• British forces captured Benin (February 18).

Ovonramwen, the ruler of Benin, came to power in 1888. The kingdom which Ovonramwen inherited had recently been reduced in size because of Nupe and British encroachment. The British, who were quickly bringing the Niger delta states under their control, presented the major threat. When Ovonramwen asserted his authority by placing restrictions on trade to the coast, the British attempted to enforce a protectorate over Benin.

A British mission to Benin city in 1892 secured the desired treaty, although it is unlikely that Ovonramwen was aware of its provisions for the surrender of Benin's sovereignty. Ovonramwen ignored the treaty's restrictions as well as British demands that he honor it.

The British came to see Benin as a challenge — the last important state in southern Nigeria to elude British control. Ovonramwen's extensive use of human sacrifice in Benin rituals gave them an added excuse for intervention.

In January 1897, J. R. Phillips, acting consul-general of the Niger Coast Protectorate, set out for Benin to warn Ovonramwen that he was assembling a military expedition to depose him if necessary. Phillip's party was massacred on the orders of a group of palace chiefs who opposed the oba.

In response, the British quickly assembled 1500 troops and launched an assault. The British overcame heavy resistance before reaching Benin City, which Ovonramwen abandoned.

Resistance continued until August when Ovonramwen surrendered. Although the British consul-general, Ralph Moor, at first offered to let Ovonramwen remain as chief of Benin City, the offer was withdrawn largely due to a misunderstanding between the two men. Subsequently, Ovonramwen was deported to Calabar.

• A fresh revolt led by Mamadu Pate Bulola occurred.

• The West African Frontier Force (WAFF) was enrolled to protect the British Protectorates.

• The Ashanti Goldfields Corporation started operations in the Gold Coast.

• Samuel Johnson *(see 1901)* completed *History of the Yorubas.*

In 1897, Samuel Johnson *(see 1901)* completed *History of the Yorubas. History of the Yorubas* is a chronicle of Yorubaland from its mythical beginnings to the 19th century civil wars. After Johnson finished his *History of the Yorubas*, he submitted it to his sponsor, the Church Missionary Society (CMS).

CMS refused to publish Johnson's treatise.

CMS claimed that the book was too long. Unwilling to take no for an answer, Johnson sent it to another publisher. Unfortunately, in this transmittal, it was lost.

After Samuel Johnson's death in 1901, Johnson's brother rewrote the *History* from notes and earlier drafts. The revised version of the *History* was published in 1921.

Today, Johnson's *History of the Yorubas* remains the most definitive source of pre–19th century Yoruba history.

• Mamadou Konate (1897-1956), a Malian writer and nationalist leader, was born.

Mamadou Konate was born in Bafoulabe. Konate graduated from the William Ponty School in Senegal in 1919. He worked as a teacher and gained a widespread reputation among the African intelligentsia as a poet and writer representing the non-Islamic Bambara tradition.

In the 1930s, Konate was the president of the *Fayer dur Soudan,* an association of Malian elites which was the forerunner of the territory's first political parties.

In 1945, Konate and Modibo Keita, the future president of Mali, formed a political party which they later affiliated with the inter-territorial RDA. Although the party was less popular than its rival led by Fily-Dabo Sissoko, Konate was elected to the French National Assembly in 1946, and later became one of Mali's vice-presidents.

After Konate's death in 1956, Keita took over the party leadership, and made it the dominant force in Malian politics.

• *Central Africa:* Rwanda was explored by Hauptmann Ramsay (January).
• There was a mutiny at Dirfi (February 14). Operations were begun against the mutineers.
• There was a mutiny of Congolese troops at Uvira.
• The Batelas rose in Upper Congo (September).
• *Eastern Africa:* The Ethiopian-French treaty was finalized (March 20). This treaty defined the Somali border.
• The legal status of slavery was abolished in Zanzibar (April 5). Slaves were freed upon their demand, while the owners were entitled to compensation.
• The Zanzibari courts were reorganized and a High Court was set up.
• An Ethiopian-British treaty was negotiated (May 14). Britain abandoned certain claims in Somaliland but Ethiopia declined to abandon claims on the Upper Nile.

• Kabaka Mwanga of Buganda rebelled against the British and fled to Buddu (July 6). His infant son, Daudi Chwa was made Kabaka.

When Mwanga revolted against British protectorate over Buganda, Apolo Kagwa, Mwanga's prime minister, opted to ally with the British to defeat and depose Mwanga. Mwanga drew widespread support from traditionalists, but not in sufficient numbers to carry his cause.

Mwanga withdrew into northwest Tanzania and later returned to carry on the struggle for two additional years. In the meantime, Mwanga was formally deposed and replaced by his one-year-old son Daudi Chwa II. The regency and real power in Buganda were then assumed by Apolo Kagwa and his faction.

After the deposition of Mwanga, Kagwa added to his offices the position of senior regent over Mwanga's heir.

• There was a mutiny amongst the British Sudanese mercenaries in Eldama Ravine, Kenya, and in Uganda (September).
• Mwanga was defeated by the British (December).
• Indian troops arrived in Mombasa and disarmed a number of the Sudanese.
• A German punitive expedition was launched against the Ngoni.

When the Germans arrived in Ngoni country in 1897, they neglected the titular Ngoni ruler and negotiated instead with Songea, the recognized leader of the Ngoni. Songea reluctantly assented to the German occupation and cooperated with the Europeans over the next seven years.

• The Native Courts Regulation in Kenya recognized "chiefs and headmen" in certain tribes.
• The translation of the Bible into Luganda was completed.
• Menelik's expedition under Walda Giorgis captured Kaffa.
• Ethiopia annexed much Somali territory in various expeditions.
• Operations were commenced against the Hehe under Mkwawa. Mkwawa committed suicide.
• There was a famine amongst the Kikuyu, Kamba and neighboring peoples.
• *Southern Africa:* The Queen of Hovas was deposed (February 28). Gallieni became Governor-General of Madagascar (July 30).
• Sir Alfred Milner arrived as the High Commissioner for South Africa (August).

During his career, Alfred Milner earned a reputation as a first rate administrator for his work in Egypt from 1880 to 1892 and as chairman of the Inland Board of Trade in England from 1892 to 1897. After Hercules Robinson retired as governor of the Cape and high commissioner for South Africa, Milner was selected for the delicate job of replacing him at a time when Anglo-Afrikaner relations were at a low ebb.

Milner started his work with a great deal of energy, learning to speak Dutch and Afrikaans, and making a good impression on Paul Kruger, the president of the Transvaal. However, Milner's British imperialistic bias hardened and he soon came to advocate British supremacy throughout South Africa.

- The Cape railway reached Bulawayo (November 4).
- Zululand was annexed to Natal (December 1).
- Natal made it a criminal offense for a European African to marry an Indian African.
- The first demand for a European African Legislative Council in South Rhodesia was made by the Bulawayo Literary and Debating Society.
- Early in 1897, Kagubi, a Shona spirit medium, was joined by Mkwati — an official of the Mwari cult — who had left Matabeleland as the Ndebele rebellion was ending there. Kagubi and Mkwati collaborated to sustain Shona fighting against the British.
- Maguiguana (c.1850s–1897), the commander in chief of the Gaza army and the leader of the anti–Portuguese rebellion, died.

Maguiguana appears to have been born an Ndau (Shona), one of the subject peoples ruled by the Ngoni speaking Gaza kingdom in southern Mozambique. Although the hierarchy of the Gaza kingdom was normally limited to men of Nguni origin, Maguiguana rose from a low position during the reign of king Mzila to become commander of the entire Gaza army under the last king, Gungunyane.

Maguiguana also served as Gungunyane's chancellor, strongly advocating belligerent policies towards European imperialists. In 1895, the Portuguese invaded the Gaza. The Gaza army was poorly equipped to meet Portuguese machine guns and other modern weapons. Maguiguana's forces were easily routed.

After the Portuguese victory, many of the Gazas' subject people deserted them. The Gaza kingdom was soon abolished and king Gungunyane was deported.

Maguiguana became the leading Gaza spokesman. He vigorously protested against the harsh economic conditions laid down by the Portuguese.

In 1897, Maguiguana roused the Gaza to a final, but futile, war against the Portuguese. The Gaza were again defeated and Maguiguana was killed.

- Mkwati, a religious figure who played a leading role in both the Ndebele and Shona revolts against the British, died (1897).

Described as an "ex-slave" of the Leya of Zambia, Mkwati was captured by Ndebele raiders and taken to the land which is today Zimbabwe. While living in an Ndebele military town, Mkwati became a functionary in the Mwari cult — the organization through which the Shona worshipped their high god.

After the fall of the Ndebele kingdom during the British occupation of 1893 and 1894, Mkwati established an oracular shrine at Thaba zi ka Mambo, the pre-Ndebele center of the Changamire empire.

Mkwati married the daughter of a prominent Shona chief and his prestige as a prophet grew rapidly.

The collapse of the Ndebele kingdom enabled Mkwati to appeal to the broad mass of former Ndebele subjects, many of whom were originally Shona. Operating through Mwari cult priests, Mkwati organized a popular revolt against the British occupation and directed it through 1896. At the same time, the remaining Ndebele hierarchy, under the leadership of Mlugulu, organized their own revolt.

The extent to which Mkwati and Mlugulu cooperated during this uprising is not certain. Indeed, by late 1896, Mlugulu's factions was ready to negotiate with Cecil Rhodes, but Mkwati refused to surrender. Instead, Mkwati angrily broke from the Ndebele and went to Shona country where another revolt had recently begun.

In central Mashonaland, Mkwati worked with Kagubi and other religious cult leaders to dissuade Shona chiefs from negotiating with the British. As the increasingly savage British suppression of the revolt induced many Shona chiefs to surrender, Mkwati went farther north, ever hoping to increase resistance to the British.

Mkwati died around September 1897. It is believed that he was killed by Shona who were disillusioned with the course the war with the British had taken.

RELATED HISTORICAL EVENTS

• *Europe:* A report of the Parliamentary Committee into the Jameson Raid censured Cecil Rhodes but cleared Chamberlain and the Colonial Office (July).

• An Anglo-French agreement was reached on Tunisia (September 18).

• *Africa:* Mary Kingsley published *Travels in West Africa. See 1900.*

• Olive Schreiner published the novel, *Trooper Peter Halket of Mashonaland.* In *Trooper Peter Halket of Mashonaland,* Schreiner condemned Rhodes' African policies in Zimbabwe.

• *Notable Deaths:* Barnett Barnato (1852-1897), a noted British financier, committed suicide by jumping off a ship.

Several years after diamonds were discovered in Griqualand West, Barnett Barnato (a.k.a. Barney Isaacs) arrived at Kimberley and began to operate as a dealer in 1873. By the 1880s, Barnato controlled nearly half the industry.

For a while, Barnato competed with Alfred Beit and Cecil J. Rhodes. However, the three titans eventually amalgamated (in 1888) to form the powerful De Beers Consolidated Mines.

Rhodes rewarded Barnato by obtaining for him the Kimberley seat in the Cape Colony parliament. Barnato held this seat from 1888 until 1897.

Barnato moved to Johannesburg. In Johannesburg, Barnato added newly discovered gold mines to his considerable assets.

• Hercules George Robert Robinson (Lord Rosmead) (1824-1897), the British governor of the Cape Colony, died.

Hercules Robinson had a long career in the British colonial service, holding posts in many parts of the world.

Early in 1881, Robinson succeeded Henry Frere as governor and high commissioner in South Africa. A month after his arrival British forces suffered a humiliating defeat at the hands of the Transvaal Afrikaners at Majuba. Robinson presided over peace negotiations which restored independence to Paul Kruger's regime in the Transvaal.

In 1884, Robinson went to London to participate in a convention to revise Anglo-Afrikaner relations in the Transvaal.

After Robinson's return to South Africa, he became concerned over Afrikaner encroachments on Tswana territory in eastern Botswana. Robinson authorized a British expedition under Charles Warren to negotiate treaties which led to the establishment of the Bechuanaland Protectorate in 1885.

During his term of office, Robinson supported the activities of Cecil Rhodes' group and endorsed Charles Rudd's treaty with the Ndebele king Lobengula in 1888. Rudd's treaty would later be used as a pretext for Rhodes' occupation of Zimbabwe.

In 1895, Robinson emerged from retirement to re-assume the governorship. Late that year, Leander Jameson — on behalf of Rhodes — led an abortive coup into the Transvaal against Kruger's government without Robinson's knowledge.

As a consequence of the Jameson fiasco, Robinson withdrew his support for Rhodes, even though Robinson did negotiate in Pretoria for the release of the Jameson party to the British authorities. He retired in 1897 and died shortly afterwards.

--------- **1 8 9 8** ---------

THE UNITED STATES

• In the Spanish-American War, in Teddy Roosevelt's charge up San Juan Hill, the 9th and 10th Negro Cavalry participated.

• At the Battle of El Caney, the 25th Negro Infantry took part and captured a Spanish fort.

• The following African Americans of the Tenth United States Cavalry received the Congressional Medal of Honor for bravery at Tayabacoa, Cuba: Private Dennis Bell, Private Fitz Lee, Private William H. Thompkins, and Private George Wanton. These soldiers received their medals for selflessly rescuing a stranded group of soldiers in the Cuban province of Puerto Principe — a maneuver that had been thwarted on three previous attempts. For rescuing a fellow soldier while under fire in Santiago, Cuba, Sergeant Major Edward L. Baker of the Tenth United States Cavalry was also awarded the Congressional Medal of Honor.

• Daniel Atkins, a ship's cook, and Robert Penn, a fireman First Class, were awarded the Navy Medal of Honor for bravery during the Spanish-American War.

On July 20, 1898, the USS *Iowa* was anchored off Santiago, Cuba, when an explosion occurred in the boiler room. Penn saved a coal handler, single-handedly averting an explosion that could have destroyed the *Iowa* and taken the lives of many crewmen. For his bravery, Penn was awarded the Naval Medal of Honor (December 14).

• A Congressional Amnesty Act removed the last disabilities on ex–Confederates.

• John Roy Lynch, a former Reconstruction Era Congressman, was appointed United States Paymaster.

• In North Carolina, as a result of the Populist-Republican victories in 1894 and 1896 and the County Government Bill, there were 300 African American magistrates and a total of 1,000 African American officeholders. However, in the elections held in 1898, "white supremacy" became the major issue. There were riots in Wilmington, North Carolina, and after the victory of the Democratic white supremacy advocates, 400 European Americans invaded the African American district and injured, burned, killed, and chased the African Americans out of town.

• Georgia adopted a "white primary."

Georgia's initiation of the "white primary" began a trend which was soon adopted throughout the South. With the "white primary," only European Americans were allowed to vote in Democratic primary elections, which, in the one-party South, in essence, determined the winning candidates.

• The Virginia Organization of True Reformers, a secret African American benevolent society, established a home for the aged outside Richmond, Virginia.

• *Crime and Punishment:* In Lake City, South Carolina, the appointment of an African American postmaster touched off a riot of European Americans. The African American postmaster and his family were murdered and his house was burned to the ground.

• *The Labor Movement:* Illinois coal companies, in Pana and Verden, used Southern African Americans as strikebreakers. The violence occasioned by the strikes and its ultimate failure caused hostility among European American and African American members of the United Mine Workers.

• In Galveston, Texas, African American longshoremen struck for higher wages and better working conditions.

• *Notable Births:* Sadie T. M. Alexander, a lawyer and activist, was born in Philadelphia, Pennsylvania (January 2).

• Lil Hardin Armstrong, a jazz pianist, was born in Memphis, Tennessee (February 3).

• Septima Clark, an activist, was born (May 3).

• Fletcher Henderson (1898-1952), a jazz musician, was born.

Fletcher Henderson was born in Cuthbert, Georgia. He attended Atlanta University where he majored in chemistry and mathematics.

In 1920, Henderson left Georgia for New York to do graduate work in chemistry. In 1922, he took a job as a song demonstrator for a New York music publisher, Black Swan, to pay his expenses. Henderson soon became a full-time pianist at the publisher's recording studio.

In 1924, Henderson took his nine piece band to Roseland in New York City, where he made famous his call-and-response arrangements with improvised soloists. His tenor saxophonist, Coleman Hawkins, made the saxophone a jazz instrument. Henderson's band frequently played at the Savoy Ballroom and the Apollo in Harlem after the Roseland's closing hour of one o'clock.

Fletcher Henderson's band was the first big band to become famous playing jazz. In the 1920s, he also made many recordings accompanying Bessie Smith. In the 1930s, Henderson arranged for the Benny Goodman band. Some of his most important arrangements for Goodman were *Sometimes I'm Happy, King Porter Stomp* and *Down South Camp Meeting.* While continuing to lead his own band, Henderson also played piano in the Goodman orchestra. Perhaps Henderson's greatest contribution to jazz music was as a pioneer in writing arrangements for large swing bands.

• Andy Kirk, a bandleader, was born in Waco, Texas (December 29).

• Hattie McDaniel, the first African American to win an "Oscar," was born in Wichita, Kansas (June 10). McDaniel won the Academy Award for Best Supporting Actress for her portrayal of "Mammy" in the classic *Gone with the Wind.*

• Audley "Queen Mother" Moore, an activist, was born in Louisiana (July 27).

• The entrepreneur, Otis J. Rene, was born in New Orleans (October 2). Rene and his brother Leon founded Exclusive and Excelsior Records in the 1930s. Their artists included Nat "King" Cole and Johnny Otis.

• Paul Robeson (1898-1976), a famous actor and concert singer, was born (April 9).

Paul Robeson was born in Princeton, New

Jersey. His father was a fugitive slave who worked his way through Lincoln University and became a Presbyterian minister.

Paul Robeson attended Rutgers University where he won many academic and athletic honors, including Phi Beta Kappa and selection to the All-American football team. Robeson paid for his education at Columbia Law School by playing professional football, but became interested in acting. Beginning in 1924, Robeson became acclaimed both in Europe and the United States as an actor and concert singer.

Robeson's major theatrical roles include Eugene O'Neill's *All God's Children Got Wings, The Emperor Jones, The Hairy Ape;* the musicals *Show Boat* and *Porgy and Bess,* and Shakespeare's *Othello.* He also appeared in the movie version of *The Emperor Jones, King Solomon's Mines* and the *Song of Freedom.*

• Arthur James "Zutty" Singleton, a noted drummer, was born (May 14).

• Beulah Thomas, a blues singer who was known as Sippie Wallace, was born in Houston, Texas (November 11)

• Melvin B. Tolson, a writer and educator, was born in Moberly, Missouri (February 6). As poet laureate of Liberia, Tolson would write that the epic poem *Libretto for the Republic of Liberia.*

• Chancellor Williams, an historian, was born in South Carolina (December 22).

• Clarence Williams, a jazz musician, was born (October 8).

• *Notable Deaths:* There were 101 lynchings of African Americans in 1898.

• Blanche K. Bruce (1841-1898), Senator from Mississippi during the Reconstruction era, died in Washington, D.C. (March 17). Bruce died as a result of diabetes. His funeral services at the Metropolitan African Methodist Episcopal Church attracted a large crowd composed of both African and European Americans. Congressmen acted as honorary pallbearers and a tribute by Senator Allison was read.

Blanche Kelso Bruce was born in Farmville, Prince Edward County, Virginia. A quadroon (a person with one-quarter African blood — one grandparent of African descent), Bruce was taken to Missouri several years before the Civil War. While in Brunswick, Missouri, Bruce learned the printer's trade.

In 1861, Bruce escaped and went to Hannibal, Missouri. In Hannibal, Bruce organized a school.

After the War, Bruce took a two-year course

at Oberlin College. After the course, he went to Mississippi.

In 1869, Bruce was made the sergeant-at-arms of the Mississippi State Senate. Bruce held many local positions in Mississippi. At different times, Bruce was a county assessor, a tax collector, a sheriff, a superintendent of schools, and a member of the Levee Board. Bruce also became a wealthy planter and a prominent member of the Republican Party.

In 1874, Bruce was elected to the United States Senate as the Senator from Mississippi. He was the only African American to serve a regular term in the United States Senate during the Reconstruction Era.

After his term as Senator, Bruce settled in Washington, D.C., where he became Register of the Treasury under President Garfield. In 1889, President Harrison appointed Bruce recorder of deeds for Washington, D.C., and, in 1895, he was recalled to be the Register of the Treasury.

• Alexander Crummell (1819-1898), an African American and an ordained Episcopal minister who later had a parish in New York, died in Red Bank, New Jersey (September 10). Crummell was born in New York, the son of Boston Crummell, an African from Sierra Leone, and a free African American woman.

• *Miscellaneous State Laws:* Throughout the South, segregation laws were strengthened and expanded, especially with regards to public transportation.

• Louisiana, in order to protect its poor European Americans from the stringent voting requirements of 1896, added a "grandfather clause" to its State Constitution. Under this clause, if a man's father or grandfather had voted on January 1, 1867, his name would be added to the permanent registration list, regardless of his ability to comply with the other voting requirements. By 1900, there were only 5,320 African Americans registered in Louisiana, compared to 130,344 African American voters registered in 1896.

• A South Carolina law established segregation for first-class railroad coaches. In 1900, a law extended segregation to all railroad coach classes.

• *Miscellaneous Cases:* In *Williams v. Mississippi* (April 25, 1898) 170 U.S. 213, 18 S.Ct. 583, the United States Supreme Court held that a provision of the Mississippi constitution and the laws passed pursuant thereto which prescribed the qualifications of voters (including the institution of a poll tax) and which invested the state officials with a "large discretion" in determining what citizens have the necessary qualifications did not violate the 14th Amendment merely because the plaintiffs made a showing that the provision operated as a discrimination against African Americans.

- *Publications:* The poet Paul Laurence Dunbar published a novel entitled *The Uncalled* and a collection of his magazine articles in a book entitled *Folks from Dixie. The Uncalled* is a spiritual autobiography of a boy who rejects the ministry for which he was groomed by his family. The hero and all the characters are European American. *The Uncalled* is considered to be Dunbar's best novel. It was widely read by European Americans.

- In 1898, there were three African American magazines, three daily newspapers, eleven school papers and 136 weekly papers. Two of the three magazines were quarterly Methodist reviews. Of the weeklies, 13 of the 70 were published by religious organizations, secret and fraternal societies.

- *The Black Church:* Henry McNeal Turner, the first African American chaplain in the United States Army, declared that God is black. According to Turner, "We had rather believe in no God, or ... believe that all nature is God than to believe in the personality of a God, and not to believe that He is a Negro."

- Mary J. Small, the wife of Bishop John B. Small, was the first Methodist woman to be ordained an elder.

- *The Performing Arts:* Bob Cole's *A Trip to Coontown,* the first musical comedy written by an African American for African American talent, debuted in New York (April). Cole also wrote in 1900 the highly successful *A Shoo Fly Regiment,* a musical about African Americans in the United States forces in the Spanish-American War. Several of its songs became hits including *Louisiana Lize, I Must Have Been a-Dreaming, No One Can Fill Her Place, Katydid, The Maiden with Dreamy Eyes, The Cricket and the Frog.*

- *Clorindy, the Origin of the Cakewalk,* with lyrics and book by Paul Laurence Dunbar and music by Will Marion Cook, was produced at the Casino Theater in New York City and created an immediate sensation.

Clorindy, the Origin of the Cakewalk, more than any other work bridged the gap between minstrel shows and musicals. Cook and Dunbar conceived of it as an operetta. The theme of the story was music, specifically the origin of the dance known as the cakewalk in New Orleans in the 1880s. The idea was primarily Cook's. *Clorindy, the Origin of the Cakewalk* was also the first show to introduce syncopated ragtime music to New York City theatergoers. It opened after *A Trip to Coontown* and ran the summer season at the Casino Theater.

- *Black Enterprise:* The North Carolina Mutual Life Insurance Company was organized by John Merrick and Dr. A. M. Moore in Durham, North Carolina. By the 1990s, the company would be one of the most prosperous insurance and investment companies in the United States.

- S. W. Rutherford started the National Benefit Insurance Company and C. C. Spaulding began the North Carolina Mutual Benefit Insurance Company.

- *Sports:* Willie Simms won the Kentucky Derby aboard Plaudit. Simms also won the Brighton Handicap in 1898.

- Marshall "Major" Taylor was declared the national cycling champion. However, the League of American Wheelmen refused to recognize Taylor as the champion and instead chose someone else.

Marshall W. "Major" Taylor of Indianapolis, Indiana, began his professional career as a trick rider for a local cycling shop and participated in a few amateur events. Taylor won his first professional start, a half-mile handicap held at Madison Square Garden. Taylor's 121 point score made him the first African American champion in cycling.

Toward the end of the year, Taylor had compiled twenty-one first place victories, thirteen second place berths, and eleven third-place showings. Taylor came to be known as the "fastest bicycle rider in the world" until his 1910 retirement.

THE AMERICAS

History tells us that 1898 was the year in which the Spanish-American War began. It is a war remembered as a great victory for the United States in which the heroics of Teddy Roosevelt and the glorious charge up San Juan Hill were featured. The Spanish-American War is also a war in which the United States began to re-assert itself imperialistically throughout the Western Hemisphere after the fratricidal Civil War.

However, what most histories fail to tell us is that this great American victory was achieved only after thousands of Cubans, black and white, had shed their blood during a thirty year struggle for their independence. What most histories fail to tell us is that the great American victory was primarily a victory against an already beaten and battered Spain.

By the end of 1897, Cuban victory was inevitable in the war between Spain and the Cuban insurgents. General Valeriano Weyler y Nicolau, the commander of the Spanish forces, was incapable of expelling the insurgents from the western area of the island, and the Cuban elites began appealing to the United States to intervene and restore order.

The explosion on February 15, 1898, of the *U.S.S. Maine* killed 260 enlisted men and officers. The *Maine* had been sent to the Havana harbor to protect United States citizens. The explosion on the *Maine* provided the United States with an excuse to enter the war.

On April 25, 1898, the United States Congress declared war against Spain, however, the Teller Amendment stated that the United States would make no attempt to establish permanent control over the island of Cuba.

In June 1898, some 17,000 United States troops landed east of Santiago, Cuba. On July 3, 1898, the Spanish fleet was destroyed.

After a few more defeats, the Spanish surrendered on August 12, 1898.

Although the Cuban forces were instrumental in the outcome of the war, they were excluded from the peace negotiations that resulted in the Treaty of Paris. The terms of the treaty, which permitted the United States to dominate Cuba, reflected the view that the quick victory over Spain was attributable solely to the United States. This view did not acknowledge that the Cuban struggle for independence had been depleting the Spanish crown's resources for several decades, especially in the preceding three years.

On January 1, 1899, the Spanish administration retired from Cuba. General John R. Brooke installed a military government, establishing the United States occupation of the island, which lasted until 1902.

• *Brazil:* Andre Reboucas (1838-1898), a noted Afro-Brazilian abolitionist, engineer, teacher, and land reform advocate, died (May 9).

In 1898, one of the leaders of the Brazilian abolition movement passed away.

Andre Reboucas was the son of Antonio Pereira Reboucas, an official in Bahia. Andre was educated at military school in Rio de Janeiro as a mathematician and engineer. Based upon these school ties, Reboucas became a close friend and adviser to many influential Brazilians, including Dom Pedro II, the Emperor.

After travel and study in Europe in the early 1860s, Reboucas returned to Brazil in time to play an important role in the War of the Triple Alliance as an adviser and strategist. Later, having supervised major engineering projects, including the construction of railroads and docks in Rio de Janeiro, Reboucas became a teacher at the Polytechnic School.

As an abolitionist, during the 1880s, Reboucas wrote articles, pamphlets, and manifestos against slavery. He also created immigrationist and antislavery organizations, advised fellow reformers, and donated his wealth to the abolition cause.

With the end of slavery in 1888, Reboucas and other major abolitionists worked for additional reforms, including popular education and a program of land reform called "rural democracy."

In 1889, Reboucas was forced to leave Brazil during the military revolt. He chose to accompany the imperial family into exile. Reboucas would spend the rest of his life in Europe, Africa, and on the island of Madeira.

Reboucas was the author of many articles, an informative diary, and *Agricultura nacional*, which was published in 1883. *Agricultura nacional* was an anti-slavery book which called for the democratization of Brazil's agriculture for the benefit of ex-slaves, immigrants, and the rural poor.

Reboucas died on Madeira on May 9, 1898. His death fittingly came on the ten year anniversary of the day on which the Brazilian Chamber of Deputies voted to abolish slavery.

• *Cuba:* The Cuban War of Independence came to an end.

"Independent" Cuba ceased being a Spanish colony only to become a protectorate of the United States. After the devastating War of Independence, the country was left in a lamentable condition. The war destroyed the economic base and casualties claimed a large part of the population, owing especially to epidemics and famine brought about by the decrees of General Valeriano to relocate the rural population.

One of the first measures of the new military government was to proceed with the country's reconstruction. A public administration was organized and an educational system was established. Measures were taken to strengthen the economic base of the island, and tariffs on United States goods were unilaterally reduced.

EUROPE

• In 1898, Stanford conducted the first performance of Samuel Coleridge-Taylor's *Hiawatha's Wedding Feast* at the Royal College of Musicians. This cantata, on which the fame of Coleridge-Taylor came to rest, soon became widely acclaimed in England and the United States, and many festival commissions followed, including the *Overture to the Song of Hiawatha*, *The Death of Minnehaha*, *Hiawatha's Departure*, and a number of cantatas, of which *A Tale of Old Japan* was deemed the best. None of these later works, however, was as enthusiastically received as *Hiawatha's Wedding Feast.*

AFRICA

• *North Africa, Egypt and Sudan:* Kitchener's reconquest of Sudan was completed when he took Omdurman, shattering the Mahdist government of the Khalif 'Abdallahi Muhammed.

On April 8, Horatio Kitchener defeated Amir Mahmud at Atbara River. The French under the command of Marchand occupied Fashoda on July 10 and, on July 12, the French flag was ceremonially hoisted. On August 7, an Anglo-Egyptian force captured Abu Hamed and, on September 2, Omdurman.

At the "Battle" of Omdurman, Kitchener employed the use of machine guns to devastating effect. Using Maxim machine guns, Kitchener's forces killed 11,000 of the Khalifa's dervishes while wounding 16,000 more. The British casualties amounted to only 48. The Khalifa's army was destroyed.

Marchand made a treaty with Shilluk (September 3). However, Kitchener reached Fashoda on September 19, and, on November 4, Marchand was ordered to evacuate Fashoda. On December 11, France evacuated Fashoda. The Khalifa—'Abdallah ibn Muhammed—fled south.

With these victories, the Mahdist administration of Sudan came to an end and the Anglo-Egyptian reconquest of Sudan was essentially complete.

• Ali Dinar, the last Sultan of Darfur, began his reign. Dinar's reign would last until 1916.

• *West Africa:* The Hut Tax was instituted in the Sierra Leone Protectorate (January 1). On April 27, there was a general uprising in Sierra Leone. The uprising was suppressed by a West African regiment.

The 1896 declaration of a British protectorate for Sierra Leone was followed, in 1898, by the imposition of a hut tax on most of the protectorate. The imposition of the hut tax precipitated the famous Hut Tax War.

The Hut Tax War was essentially a protest by the indigenous people of Sierra Leone (including the Temne) against not only the hut tax but also against their loss of freedom. Bai Bureh led the Temne campaign against the British. The Temne campaign spread from Kasseh in the north to Mende in the south and lasted for ten months.

Bai Bureh was successful at first because of his innovative use of guerrilla tactics. However, the tactics could not overcome the superior firepower and resources of the British. Bai Bureh was eventually captured. *See 1908.*

During the 1898 Hut Tax War, Suluku Konte, the ruler of the Biriwa chiefdom, abstained from fighting, and offered to mediate between the British and Bai Bureh, the Temne rebel leader. Suluku later rebuked the British for their inability to keep the peace.

• Sarkin Damagaram from Zinder launched an unsuccessful invasion of Kano.

• Railway construction began in the Gold Coast.

• Lagos (Nigeria) was lit by electricity.

• An Anglo-French agreement was reached on the Nigerian boundaries.

• Foureau and Lamy began their explorations of Bornu and Wadai.

• Samory, the ruler of the Mandinka, was captured.

The French military drive was relentless and, in 1898, when the British refused to sell him arms, Samory retreated into Liberia. The French captured him that year and exiled him to Gabon.

• In 1898, the French turned on Sikasso, the capital of the Kenedugu kingdom. After twelve days of fighting the walls of the capital fell and French forces entered the city. Inside the walls, the French found the body of Ba Bemba. Ba Bemba, the ruler of Sikasso, had taken his own life.

• Ahmadu ibn 'Umar Tall (c.1833-1898), the former ruler of the Tukolor Empire, died.

Ahmadu ibn 'Umar Tall was the son of and

successor to al-Hajj 'Umar ibn Said Tall, the founder of the Tukolor Empire of Guinea, Mali, Mauritania, and Senegal. Ahmadu's mother was a Hausa who had been a slave. Ahmadu's father married his mother in Sokoto (now Nigeria) while returning from a pilgrimage.

When 'Umar died in 1864 putting down a revolt at Macina, a succession dispute ensued. Ahmadu gained control over Segu, but his cousin Ahmadu Tijani recaptured and held Macina while some of 'Umar's ministers seized Kaarta. Because of the dispute, Ahmadu was forced to wait nearly two years before formally announcing the death of his father.

Ahmadu did not inherit his father's prestige. Ahmadu simply lacked 'Umar's charisma. However, Ahmadu did possess a high intelligence and he wisely surrounded himself with experienced and capable advisers.

Ahmadu spent the first years of his rule consolidating his kingdom and centralizing his government. In 1870, Ahmadu began a campaign against his half-brothers which brought Kaarta back within the Tukolor Empire by 1874. As for Macina, Ahmadu was never able to recapture it from Ahmadu Tijani.

Towards the end of the 1870s, Ahmadu faced a new challenge from the French, who had fought 'Umar in the 1850s, but who had afterwards come to terms with him while they concentrated on commercial development.

In the early 1880s, the French resumed their eastward encroachment into the Tukolor Empire, establishing posts as far inland as Bamako. Ahmadu, beset with internal problems, was powerless to stop them, but the French themselves were not anxious to engage in hostilities because of their preoccupation with Samori Toure and Lat Dior elsewhere. A truce was effected between the two empires.

As evidence of the truce, in 1887, Ahmadu and the French joined forces to destroy Mamadu Lamine whose military ambitions in Senegambia threatened both French and Tukolor Empires. However, by 1889, the threat to the French posed by Lat Dior and Samori Toure had been dissipated. The French ended the truce. They resumed hostilities with the Tukolor Empire.

The French captured Kaarta, Segu, and Jenne. Ahmadu was forced to flee to Macina and to negotiate an alliance with the Macina rulers. But this alliance was not long lasting. In 1893, Macina fell. The French installed Ahmadu's son, Muhammed Aguibu Tall as ruler of the Tukolor Empire. Once again Ahmadu was forced to flee.

Ahmadu moved about for a time. He finally came to settle in Sokoto in 1896 with the remainder of his followers.

• Hayatu ibn Sa'id (1840-1898), a Mahdist figure in the Central Sudanic region, died.

Hayatu ibn Sa'id was a great-grandson of the Fula Islamic revolutionary leader 'Uthman dan Fodio. He was born in the Sokoto Caliphate in northern Nigeria.

After his early ambitions for high political office in Sokoto were frustrated, Hayatu ibn Sa'id left for Adamawa in the southeastern part of the empire.

In 1881, when Muhammed 'Ahmad proclaimed himself the Mahdi in Sudan, Hayatu became his protégé in the central Sudan. Hayatu attracted many adherents to the town of Balda and maintained a large following throughout Adamawa.

The Sokoto empire, however, did not recognize Muhammed 'Ahmad. By 1892, Zubeiru, the governor of Adamawa, felt he could no longer tolerate the presence of the Mahdists.

Zubeiru challenged Hayatu on the battlefield. In the resulting battle, Hayatu was victorious. However, the victory only made the rulers of Sokoto's other emirates more fearful of him.

Hayatu decided to throw in his lot with Rabeh Zubair, another Mahdist leader. Their combined forces conquered Bornu in 1893.

Rabeh became the ruler of Bornu. Hayatu, frustrated with his subordinate role, attempted to break away.

In 1898, the forces of Hayatu and Rabeh met on the battlefield. Hayatu's forces were defeated and Hayatu was killed.

Hayatu left a legacy of consciousness and concern over the coming of the Mahdi in Sokoto at a time when the concept of the Mahdi had been on the verge of fading away. The Mahdist movement grew and became a rallying point for anti–British sentiment after Hayatu's death.

• Frederick William Koko (c.1853-1898), the ruler of the Niger delta trading state of Nembe, died.

When Frederick Koko became the ruler of Nembe, the Royal Niger Company under George Goldie was forcing Nembe traders out of their traditional palm-oil markets. Koko succeeded his uncle ruling as regent, but declined the kingship. Koko's selection was somewhat unusual, since he was not the head of any of the trading houses which formed the basic social and commercial units in Nembe. Indeed, many believe that Koko may have been chosen precisely because he was not affiliated with any particular trading house and was less likely to be identified with any one faction of Nembe traders.

Koko was raised as a Christian. He renounced the Christian faith after he became ruler. This renunciation was probably attributable to a desire to appease the more traditional factions within the Nembe state.

Koko postponed his campaign against the British until after 1894 when a powerful Nembe chief who opposed the plan died. Koko then persuaded or coerced the people of neighboring Okpoma to join him. Together they successfully sought allies in Bonny and Kalabari.

In 1895, Koko's army, consisting of about 1500 soldiers in thirty or forty canoes, attacked and destroyed the Royal Niger Company's trading depot at Akassa. The company counter attacked with the aid of the forces of the British Niger Coast Protectorate which claimed jurisdiction over Nembe.

Nembe was destroyed and Koko fled to the remote village of Etiema where he died in 1898.

The brief war with the Nembe drew attention to the Royal Niger Company's illegal monopoly in the delta, and was a factor leading to the revocation of the company's charter in 1899, when the Protectorate of Southern Nigeria was formed.

- *Central Africa:* Tyo rebelled unsuccessfully.
- The Chokwe were defeated by the Lunda.
- The *Sud-Kamerun Gesellschaft* was established.
- The territory near Kivu Lake and the Ruzizi and Mfumbiri Mountains were occupied by Germany (October).
- Richard Kandt explored Rwanda and Burundi.
- *Eastern Africa:* Sudanese mutineers were defeated by Indians at Mouli (August).
- There was a famine in Busoga and Bunyoro.
- Civil war erupted amongst the Masai.
- Muhammed 'Abdullah Hassan, a Somali nationalist leader, was prosecuted by the British government for harboring a thief. Muhammed responded by denouncing British sovereignty and declaring a jihad — a holy war — against all infidels.
- Mwanga, the former king of the Ganda kingdom, was captured. He was exiled to the Seychelles Islands.
- Mkwawa, the leader of the most protracted east African resistance to German occupation, died.

Mkwawa was the son of Munyigumba. It was Munyigumba who united the numerous Hehe clans into a well organized and aggressive military force in what is today southern Tanzania.

Munyigumba died in 1879. Upon his death, Mkwawa briefly fled north while a subordinate chief usurped power. Mkwawa soon returned, however, and drove the usurper out. Mkwawa then proceeded to consolidate his position by military means.

Mkwawa continued his father's aggressive policies, first fighting the Ngoni to a negotiated truce in 1881, and then raiding for cattle and ivory in all directions. During the 1880s, Mkwawa began to expand Hehe control eastward just as the Germans were advancing inland.

In 1891, Mkwawa annihilated a German column and emerged as the main obstacle to German occupation of southern Tanzania. Mkwawa relentlessly harassed trading caravans, German patrols, and Africans who accommodated the Germans. The Germans mounted ever larger forces against Mkwawa, and finally stormed his main fort in 1894.

After the loss of his main fort, Mkwawa resisted for four more years. But, in 1898, with his capture imminent, Mkwawa, the great Hehe leader, committed suicide rather than submit to capture. With Mkwawa's death, Hehe resistance to German aggression came to an end.

- *Southern Africa:* The British commenced military operations against the Ngoni in North Rhodesia (January).

The main body of Ngoni (of Zambia) were relatively independent until 1898 when they were defeated by the British. But even then, a Ngoni chief was appointed administrative head of the region.

In 1890, Mpezeni, the king of the Ngoni, granted a generous concession to a lone German trader, Karl Wiese. However, aside from this concession, Mpezeni was generally able to ignore the increasing European imperialistic pressure at the same time that the same forces were reducing his neighbors to colonial dependents.

Mpezeni's complacency was shattered in 1897. European manipulation outside his knowledge transferred Wiese's concession to a chartered British company, which attacked him without warning in 1898.

Mpezeni offered little resistance and was quickly conquered.

- Kruger was re-elected as President of the Transvaal with a large majority (February 9).

• The Lawlev treaty was negotiated between the Barotse and the BSA Company.

• A Legislative Council with elected and official members was formed in South Rhodesia.

• Khama, the ruler of the Ngwato, drove his son Sekgoma II into a long exile beginning in 1898. This exile created a legacy of political bitterness which outlasted their eventual reconciliation.

• The Ngoni in the Fort Jameson area were subjugated.

• An Anglo-Portuguese expedition against the Yao chief Mataka was initiated.

• Chinsinga aided the Portuguese in conquering the Ngoni.

Chinsinga became King of the Makanga kingdom of Mozambique in 1893. At this point in time, the Portuguese government ceded administration of the region to a chartered company, which lacked the resources to control it. Chinsinga allied with the company in 1895 and assisted it in conquering the Ngoni chiefdom north of Makanga in 1898.

• A railway from Beira to Umtali was completed.

• Jacobus Johannes Fouche was born.

• Bishop Dupont became a chief of the Bemba.

• In 1898, Bhunu, the ruler of Swaziland, was implicated in the murder of a Swazi official. Bhunu was forced to flee the country to avoid arrest by the Afrikaners. Bhunu eventually paid a fine and was reinstated as king.

• William Schreiner became prime minister of the Cape Colony.

Schreiner tried to ease the growing friction between the Imperial Government and the Transvaal, helping to arrange an abortive conference between Alfred Milner and Paul Kruger on the eve of the South African War.
In 1900, he resigned his ministry and returned to his law practice when his cabinet split over the handling of Afrikaner rebels in the Cape Colony.

• Thaba Bosiu was seized by Lerotholi.

Masupha, the ruler of Thaba Bosiu, clashed with his brother's successor, Lerotholi, the King of the Sotho *(see 1905)*. Lerotholi stormed Thaba Bosiu, arrested Masupha and deposed him. Lerotholi subsequently dismantled the fortifications of Thaba Bosiu. With this dismantlement, the legend of Thaba Bosiu came to an ignominious end.

• Albert John Luthuli (c.1898-1967), a Nobel prize winning South African nationalist, is believed to have been born in this year.

Albert Luthuli was born in Zimbabwe in the late 1890s of South African parents. As a child, he returned to Natal with his mother and was educated in mission schools.
Luthuli taught at a mission college for fifteen years, until persuaded by kinsmen to assume a minor Zulu chiefship which he had inherited (1935). Frustrated with his political impotency as a government-payroll chief, he joined the ANC in 1946, and soon became president of its Natal branch.
During the mass Defiance Campaign of 1952 in which the ANC joined with the Indian National Congress, Luthuli became the leading advocate of passive resistance as a political tactic. Because of his political activities he was deposed from his chieftainship by the government. He was then elected president-general of the nation-wide ANC, replacing J. S. Moroka (1952).
Upon his election, Luthuli was promptly restricted to his own town by the government. However, power within the ANC had already been assumed by leaders of the Congress' Youth League, such as Nelson Mandela.
Luthuli's role as ANC leader was largely a moral one. Luthuli's ability to administer the ANC was greatly hampered by his repeated government bannings. His first two-year ban was renewed in 1954, and near its expiration, in 1956, Luthuli became one of many Africans arrested for treason. Released in 1957, Luthuli was permanently banned in 1959.
In recognition of his moderating influence on South African protest movements in the face of severe government repression and violence, Albert Luthuli was awarded the Nobel Peace Prize in 1961.
In 1967, Albert Luthuli was killed by a train while crossing tracks near his home.

• Kagubi, a Shona spirit medium and cult leader, died.

Within the elaborate system of Shona spirit mediums, Kagubi appears to have been exceptional. Whereas most important mediums of the Mhondoro cult claimed to be possessed by the spirits of prominent Shona ancestors, Kagubi was a self-made figure. He was a man with no antecedents and no successors. Kagubi was the brother of Pasipamire, the Chaminuka medium killed by the Ndebele in 1883. Kagubi rose to prominence in central Mashonaland (Zimbabwe) on the strength of his personal charisma and prophetic talents after Pasipamire's death.

In 1896, when anti–British feeling was running high throughout the recently imposed colony of Rhodesia, Kagubi initiated and led the Shona revolt around the town of Salisbury. Kagubi worked closely with the more established Nehanda medium, while other mhondoro mediums directed the Shona rising elsewhere.

Early in 1897, Kagubi was joined by Mkwati — an official of the Mwari cult — who had left Matabeleland as the Ndebele rebellion was ending there. Kagubi and Mkwati collaborated to sustain Shona fighting.

Eventually, Kagubi and the Nehanda medium were captured and hanged by the British. Hours before Kagubi's execution he was baptized a Roman Catholic taking the name Dismas — "the good thief."

• Nongqause (1841–c.1898), a prophetic spirit medium during the great Xhosa cattle-killing sacrifice of 1856, is believed to have died in this year.

Young female diviners were not uncommon among the Xhosa. Nongqause's sudden rise to prominence as a teenager was thus not in itself unusual. Early in 1856, Nongqause told her uncle Mhlakaza — an established Xhosa prophet — of a millenarian vision she had had. Important Xhosa ancestors had appeared to her with instructions about how the Xhosa could escape their many earthly difficulties.

Nongqause's story greatly impressed the Gcaleka Xhosa ruler Sarili and Nongqause's reputation grew rapidly. Working with her uncle, Nongqause acted as a spirit medium passing on the ancestors' messages.

According to Nongqause, the ancestors promised the Xhosa a millennium free of Europeans in return for sacrificing all their material wealth and ritually purifying themselves. Chief Sarili vigorously supported this plan. During ten months in 1856 and 1857, the Gcaleka Xhosa and some of their neighbors killed about 150,000 cattle and destroyed most of their crops and granaries. The result was an economic disaster in which tens of thousands of people starved or fled to the Cape Colony for work.

Nongqause herself fled to avoid retribution after the millennium failed to arrive and was soon captured by the British. The British were satisfied that she had acted merely as a dupe of Mhlakaza — who himself had died during the affair — but they imprisoned her and another

young prophetess, Nonkosi, ostensibly to protect them. Nongqause was later allowed to return to the eastern Cape Colony, where she lived out her life in obscurity. She was variously reported to have died in 1898.

RELATED HISTORICAL EVENTS

• *The Americas:* The Spanish-American War began (April 22) and ended with Spain ceding Cuba, Puerto Rico, Guam and the Philippines to the United States.

On February 15, the United States battleship *Maine* exploded in Havana killing 260 sailors. The sinking followed the publication of a letter from the Spanish Ambassador to the United States calling President McKinley spineless.

On March 21, a United States naval court determined that the *Maine* explosion was caused by external sources and, on March 28, the court's report was made public.

On April 22, the War began.

On May 1, at the Battle of Manila Bay, all ten ships of the Spanish fleet were destroyed after a long morning's naval engagement.

On May 12, the United States North Atlantic Squadron bombarded San Juan on Puerto Rico. The Battle of San Juan Hill occurred on July 1 and 2 and resulted in a United States victory.

At the Battle of Santiago Bay on July 3, 180 Spaniards and one American were killed.

Spain surrendered on August 12, 1898.

• *Europe:* An Anglo-French convention on the boundaries of Nigeria and the Gold Coast was convened (June 14).

• A secret Anglo-German agreement was reached on Portuguese African territories. Under the agreement, Britain leased Delagoa Bay while Germany obtained parts of Angola and Mozambique.

• Portugal appointed a committee to study the problems of Portuguese Africa.

• The Southern Rhodesia Order in Council established a constitution for BSA Company government.

• *Notable Deaths:* Henry Barkly (1815-1898), a British Governor of the Cape Colony and the former high commissioner for South Africa, died.

Henry Barkley was the first governor of the Cape Colony who did not have a military background. Prior to his arrival in South Africa, he held a succession of colonial governorships in British Guiana (Guyana), Australia and Mauritius.

After succeeding P. E. Wodehouse as governor of the Cape Colony in 1870, Barkly quickly annexed the diamond fields in Griqualand to prevent them from falling into the hands of the Afrikaners.

Barkly oversaw the establishment of responsible parliamentary government in the Cape Colony in 1872. The head of this inaugural government was John Molteno who became prime minister. However, Barkly soon broke with the government when it refused to assume responsibility for the diamond fields.

Barkly was asked by the secretary of state for the colonies, Lord Carnarvon, to work towards federating South Africa. But Barkly was not fully up for this task. The task would only fully be tackled after Barkly was succeeded by Henry Frere.

- George Grey (1812-1898), the former British governor of the Cape Colony and high commissioner for South Africa, died.

In 1854, George Grey succeeded George Cathcart as governor of the Cape. During his tenure, Grey brought to South Africa ideas on native policy which he had developed while governor of New Zealand during the Maori wars.

Grey advocated a single African policy for all the Euro-African governments in South Africa and worked to integrate Africans into the colonial economy.

In the eastern Cape, where the Xhosa had been annexed, Grey placed chiefs on salaries in a move to weaken their ties with their own people. After the disastrous Xhosa cattle-killing of 1857, Grey organized a food relief program and created public works projects.

In his capacity as high commissioner (1854-1861), Grey visited Natal in 1858 and encouraged the importation of indentured Indian laborers to develop the sugar industry. This policy led to a major influx of Indian immigrants into South Africa in the late 19th century.

Also in 1858, Grey mediated in the war between the Orange Free State republic and the kingdom of Lesotho. Grey obtained Afrikaner sanction for a Cape Colony-Free State federation, but this proposal was rejected by London and Grey was recalled from office in 1859.

By the time Grey reached London, the government reversed itself. Grey was reinstated. Grey returned to South Africa and spent his last year of office extending the Cape frontier towards Natal Colony.

Grey granted territory in "Nomansland" to

Adam Kok III, and began negotiations with Faku, Sarili and other Transkei chiefs which led to their eventual incorporation into the Cape Colony.

At Grey's own request, he was transferred to New Zealand to serve as governor from 1861 to 1868. After retiring from the colonial service, Grey settled in New Zealand and entered local politics. He was elected to the New Zealand parliament and served in that body from 1870 to 1890. From 1877 to 1879, Grey also served as New Zealand's prime minister.

In 1894, Grey returned to England. He died in England four years later.

1899

THE UNITED STATES

- Between 1899 and 1937, approximately 150,000 persons of African descent immigrated to the United States.
- G. H. White of North Carolina was re-elected to serve in the 56th Congress.
- The National Afro-American Council, which was founded in 1898, called for a day of fasting to protest lynchings and racial massacres.
- *The Labor Movement:* John Mitchell, the president of the United Mine Workers, testified before the Federal Industrial Commission that African Americans were encouraged to join the United Mine Workers, and objected to African Americans only when African Americans were used as strikebreakers.
- Trainmen called for the exclusion of African Americans from their profession.
- *Notable Births:* Thomas "Georgia Tom" Dorsey, a blues performer and composer who is known as the "Father of Gospel Music" was born in Georgia (July 1). Dorsey would compose such blues classics as "Tight Like That" and the blessed "Precious Lord, Take My Hand."

The "Father of Gospel Music" was Thomas Andrew Dorsey. Thomas Dorsey was born in Villa Rica, Georgia. He was the son of Thomas Madison and Etta (Plant) Dorsey. Thomas Madison Dorsey was a revivalist preacher, and the family moved to Atlanta in 1910.

Young Tom Dorsey moved to Chicago in 1918 and worked at steel mills and music gigs to earn money to attend the Chicago Musical College (also called the Chicago School of Composition and Arranging) for three years. With this musical foundation, Tom Dorsey became a successful blues musician and composer. Known as "Georgia Tom," Dorsey traveled with the Whispering Syncopators before becoming the piano player and band leader for the famous blues artist Ma Rainey.

As a blues musician, Dorsey wrote more than 200 blues songs, including "Stormy Sea Blues," "Last Minute Blues," and the music for "It's Tight Like That."

Eventually, Dorsey began to return to the music of his church heritage. He combined the traditional African American church music of the 1920s with blues chords, jazzy syncopation, improvisation, and emotional interpretation. The result was a new form of church music and Dorsey coined the term, "gospel music." This music was similar to some of the songs composed by Charles A. Tindley between 1900 and 1906, but was less dependent upon spirituals. Dorsey's first gospel song, "Someday, Somewhere," was written in 1921, however, for a long time, Dorsey could not interest anyone in his new music. Finally, in 1929, Dorsey began to get orders for "If You See My Savior."

In 1931, Dorsey founded the first ever "gospel choir" at the Ebenezer Baptist Church in Chicago, and with colleague Sallie Martin and others founded in 1932 the National Convention of Gospel Choirs and Choruses, related to the National Baptist Convention, U.S.A., Inc., which still holds annual gatherings. Martin traveled the country with Dorsey singing his songs to his accompaniment and organizing gospel choirs. Martin and Dorsey were a popular duo until 1940 when Dorsey began traveling with the soon to be legendary Mahalia Jackson.

In 1932, Dorsey's wife, Nettie, and their newborn son died. Bereft with grief, Dorsey was shattered. As part of his own healing process, Dorsey came to write what would prove to be his signature song, "Precious Lord, Take My Hand."

Second only to "Amazing Grace" as the most popular song in gospel music, "Precious Lord, Take My Hand" has been translated into over 50 languages. It has been recorded by more gospel singers than any other song.

Since 1932, "Precious Lord, Take My Hand" has been sung in countless churches throughout the United States on innumerable occasions. It is so popular that African American congregations can sing it without a score.

When sung as Dorsey intended for it to be sung, "Precious Lord, Take My Hand" is one of those powerful songs which has the capacity to transport the audience from the mournful now to touch upon the sacred forever. Just as it helped to mend the broken heart of Thomas Dorsey, this song has become the spiritual salve that is used to aid and comfort so many in their time of need. "Precious Lord, Take My Hand" is a blessed song.

In 1932, Dorsey moved from the Ebenezer Baptist Church to the Pilgrim Baptist Church, where he became the music director. On February 17, 1941, Dorsey married Kathryn Mosely. Thomas and Kathryn would come to have two children.

Over the course of his gospel career, Dorsey wrote well over 400 gospel songs. John Charles Thomas' rendition of Dorsey's "Peace in the Valley" in the 1940s became the first gospel song to make the "Hit Parade." Other famous Dorsey songs included "There'll Be Peace," "I Will Put My Trust in the Lord," and "The Lord Has Laid His Hands on Me."

So many of his songs became standards and million-plus sellers that Mahalia Jackson called him "the Irving Berlin of the religious field." He did much to shape the piano style of gospel music and to promote the careers of singers like Mahalia Jackson.

In 1943, Dorsey wrote an autobiography, *My Ups and Downs*. Dorsey was sometimes confused with the famous European American bandleader Tommy Dorsey. Once they even received each other's royalty checks.

Thomas Dorsey became a legend in his own time. He was in constant demand. In 1959, Dorsey composed the music for a seventeen part television series on the Civil War entitled "Ordeal by Fire."

Dorsey ran the Thomas A. Dorsey Gospel Songs Music Publishing Company, the first publishing house for the promotion of African American gospel music. His music was endorsed by the National Baptist Convention, U.S.A., Inc., although initially many ministers resisted Dorsey's mix of nightclub rhythms within the church environment.

In 1964, Dorsey was ordained a minister and functioned as assistant minister at the Pilgrim Baptist Church. In 1979, Thomas Dorsey became the first African American to be elected to the Nashville Song Writers Association International Hall of Fame, and, in 1981, he was named to the Georgia Music Hall of Fame.

In the 1980s, Thomas Dorsey achieved a new audience of admirers as the subject of a critically acclaimed documentary *Say Amen Somebody*.

In the history of Afro-America, few would list Thomas Dorsey as being a "great man" and yet this one man, through his songs, has arguably touched the lives of more African Americans than any political leader of the century. The beauty of Thomas Dorsey is that his legacy can be heard on almost any given Sunday in any given community where African Americans reside. Thomas Dorsey's legacy is a living legacy which continues to uplift and inspire and to heal. Thomas Dorsey *was* a great man and in a sublime way his legacy has become divine.

• Aaron Douglas, a noted artist, was born (May 26).

Aaron Douglas was born in Topeka, Kansas, and was educated at the University of Nebraska. Douglas left a teacher's position at Kansas City High School to study under Winolo Reiss in New York City.

Douglas did many illustrations for books dealing with African American subject matter, and became interested in the styles of African art and successfully managed to synthesize African designs with modern abstractions.

For many critics, Douglas ranks with the Mexican, Miguel Covarrubias, as the outstanding exponent of African American types and motifs. His work includes several illustrations for books by Harlemites of the 1920s along with murals on African American themes in Harlem's Club Ebony, Chicago's Hotel Sherman, Fisk University Library and at the 135th Street Harlem Branch Library.

During the early 1930s, Douglas studied easel painting under De Waroquier and Despiau in Paris on a Barnes Foundation grant. In 1933, Douglas had a still life and portrait exhibit at Cas Delbos Gallery in Paris.

• Edward Kennedy ("Duke") Ellington, famed musician and composer, was born (April 29).

Duke Ellington was born in Washington, D.C. At the age of 7, he began to study piano. He attended Armstrong High School in Washington, where he studied music. Ellington also studied with Henry Grant.

While in high school, Duke Ellington formed a band, the Washingtonians. In 1923, Fats Waller persuaded Ellington to come to New York. Ellington's Washingtonians worked in Harlem and at the Kentucky Club downtown. After awhile, the Washingtonians began to record as Duke Ellington's Kentucky Club Orchestra. From 1927 through 1932, the Ellington band played at the famous Cotton Club, from which they made frequent radio broadcasts.

Duke Ellington's first hit record was *Mood Indigo* which was recorded in 1930 under the original title of *Dreamy Blues.*

In 1933, Duke Ellington's band made its first European tour. It was at this time that the band was enlarged to include 6 brass instrument players and 4 reed instrument players. From that time on, Duke Ellington's band was a musical force. Ellington himself became so well known during the late 1920s and early 1930s in New York that he was one of the few African American jazz musicians to be steadily employed during the Great Depression.

In 1943, Duke Ellington and his orchestra played Carnegie Hall. The performance showcased Ellington's composition entitled *Black, Brown and Beige,* a 50 minute serious work telling the story of African American people in America. This performance helped to shift jazz from dance halls to concert music pavilions.

Duke Ellington gained a world wide reputation and is generally considered to be one of the most important musical minds and talents of the twentieth century. Ellington composed over 1,500 songs. Some of Ellington's more memorable compositions are *Solitude* (1933), *Sophisticated Lady* (1933), *In a Sentimental Mood* (1935), *Daybreak Express, Blue Ramble,* and *Blue Harlem.*

• "Sleepy" John Estes, a blues singer, was born (January 25).
• Anna Arnold Hedgeman, an activist, was born in Marshalltown, Iowa (July 5).
• Musician Noble Sissle was born in Indianapolis, Indiana (July 10).
• Clifton R. Wharton, a diplomat and Ambassador to Norway, was born.

Clifton R. Wharton was born in Baltimore. Educated in the law at Boston University, Wharton joined the Foreign Service in 1925. In the Foreign Service, Wharton served in a variety of posts in Africa and Europe, and was the first African American to head an American embassy in Europe, as Minister to Romania in 1958 and Ambassador to Norway from 1961 to 1964.

• *Notable Deaths:* In 1899, 85 African Americans were lynched.
• *Miscellaneous State Laws:* North Carolina enacted legislation to segregate railroads.
• *Miscellaneous Cases:* In *Cumming v. Richmond County Board of Education* (December 18, 1899) 175 U.S. 528, 20 S.Ct. 197, the United States Supreme Court held that an

injunction that would compel a board of education to withhold all assistance from a high school maintained for European American children was not the proper remedy for error of the board in failing to provide a high school for African American children and in turning the building and funds formerly used therefore to the use of primary schools for African American children. The Court also held that the state court's denial of an injunction against the maintenance, by a board of education, of a high school for European American children, while failing to maintain one for African American children also, for the reason that the funds were not sufficient to maintain it in addition to needed primary schools for African American children, does not constitute a denial to African Americans of the equal protection of the law or equal privileges of citizens of the United States.

• *Miscellaneous Publications:* Booker T. Washington published *The Future of the American Negro.*

• Houghton-Mifflin published two collections of Charles Chestnutt's short stories *The Conjure Woman* and *The Wife of His Youth, and Other Stories of the Color Line.* These stories along with Dunbar's *The Uncalled* were the first works of prose fiction written by African Americans to reach a mass European American audience.

• *Imperium in Imperio* by Sutton Griggs was published in Cincinnati. The author was a Baptist preacher and lecturer on the race question. *Imperium in Imperio* was the first black nationalist, anti-white, and even anti-COTW published expression in American fiction. The story involved a young militant African American who formed a revolutionary secret society which was anti-white and anti-COTW. The ultimate aim of the society was to seize Texas and create a separate African American republic. Grigg's subsequent novels were toned down in their militancy and sought African American accommodations with the old plantation owners for protection from poor European Americans.

• *The Performing Arts: Sons of Ham,* by Bert Williams and George Walker, was produced at the Grand Opera House in New York City. This production initiated a ten year collaboration which lasted until Walker's death. Williams and Walker were the first successful American musical team. This duo set the trend in musical writing which was continued by such luminaries as Rodgers and Hart,

Rodgers and Hammerstein, and Lerner and Lowe. In 1906, Williams and Walker starred in *Abyssinia* by Alex Roger, Jesse Shippe and Will Marion Cook. In 1907, the duo produced *Bandana Land.*

• *Music:* Eubie Blake composed *Charleston Rag.*

• Scott Joplin composed *Maple Leaf Rag.*

• *Scholastic Achievements:* The Virginia Manual Labor School at Hanover, Virginia, was established.

• Between the years 1895 and 1899, three African Americans received doctorates.

• *Technological Innovations:* L. C. Bailey received a patent for a folding bed.

• George F. Grant, an African American dentist in Boston, received a patent for a wooden golf tee.

• *Black Enterprise:* At the Sixth Atlanta Conference for the Study of Negro Problems, it was announced that between 1870 and 1899, African Americans had paid more than $15 million in tuition and fees to private institutions, more than $45 million in indirect taxes, and a total of $25 million in direct school taxes.

• *Sports:* From 1899 to 1908, Jack Johnson, the great heavyweight champion, fought 100 bouts and lost only 3.

• W. W. Walker of the Chautauqua Tennis Club arranged an interstate tennis tournament for African American players. Staged in Philadelphia, the event attracted competitors from several nearby states. Walker became the first of a long line of great African American tennis coaches.

THE AMERICAS

• *Brazil:* Joaquim Machado de Assis published *Paginas recolhidas* and the universal classic *Dom Casmurro.*

Dom Casmurro is considered to be artistically superior to anything else written by Machado. In *Dom Casmurro,* Machado employs such novelistic elements as narrative structure, composition of characters, and psychological analysis in a manner which can only be described as genius.

In *Dom Casmurro,* the hero of the story, Bento Santiago, sought to join the two ends life and restore youth in old age. To this end, Bento had a replica of his childhood home constructed. Because the plan did not work, Bento decided to write about his past.

In writing about his past, the reader learns about what may be prompting Bento's unusual obsession. We learn that as a youth, Bento fell in love with Capitu. The two want to be together, but Bento has already promised his mother that he would become a priest. Through various machinations, Capitu convinces Bento's mother, that her son should not be a priest. Bento's mother grants his wish to leave the seminary. Bento does leave the seminary. Bento becomes a lawyer and, with his law degree, he and Capitu are united in a seemingly blissful marriage.

Capitu and Bento have a child and all seems well. Escobar, Bento's best friend, marries Capitu's best friend, and the two couples live in perfect friendship. However, as Escobar dies, Bento becomes convinced that his friend and Capitu have had an affair. This knowledge shatters Bento's world.

In *Dom Casmurro,* Bento tells his own story. The story is told smoothly and at first serenely, but as it progresses, the story becomes a tragic tale of evil, hatred, betrayal, and jealousy. This story, along with Machado's outstanding artistic abilities, have made *Dom Casmurro* into "*the* great Brazilian novel.*"

• *Canada:* Sydney, Nova Scotia received an influx of African American immigrants when three carloads of Alabamians were brought to work in the iron furnace there.

• *Cuba:* In 1899, persons of African descent represented 32% of Cuba's population.

• *Dominican Republic:* Ulises Heureaux (1845-1899), the iron-fisted dictator of the Dominican Republic, died.

Known as Lilis, Heureaux was born at Puerto Plata to a Haitian man and a woman from the Lesser Antilles.

Although raised in poverty, Heureaux acquired a good knowledge of economics, public finance, French and English. He distinguished himself in the War of Restoration(1863-1865) during which he became the close friend of the leader of the insurrection against Spain, General Gregorio Luperon.

After the restoration of Dominican independence, Heureaux became one of the outstanding leaders of the Partido Azul (the Blue Party). The Partido Azul fought against the Partido Rojo (the Red Party) which was led by the Dominican caudillo (chief or commander) Buenaventura Baez.

During Baez's infamous Regime of the Six Years (1868-1874), Heureaux successfully opposed the caudillo's forces in the south of the country. In 1876, Baez defended militarily the presidency of Ulises Espaillat.

On orders of Luperon, Heureaux terminated the presidency of Cesareo Guillermo in 1879. Heureaux then became the minister of the interior and the police during the presidency of Archbishop Fernando Arturo de Merino (1880-1882). Heureaux succeeded the Archbishop as president in 1882.

Heureaux's first term as president of the Dominican Republic lasted from 1882 to 1884. Heureaux became president again in 1887 and ruled the Dominican Republic as an iron-fisted dictator until his assassination on July 26, 1899 at Moca. The establishment of Heureaux's dictatorship led to his complete break with Luperon, who was driven into exile to Puerto Rico.

After decades of chaotic political strife, civil war, and fiscal irresponsibility, Heureaux's dictatorship provided the necessary climate for a great influx of foreign (especially the United States) capital into the Dominican Republic. Heureaux's reign also oversaw the rapid development of the sugar industry.

While progress was made under Heureaux, the die of dictatorship was cast by Heureaux and his rule would be the model for dictatorial aspirants to come. One such aspirant was one Rafael Leonidas Trujillo and Trujillo's dictatorial reign would point to Heureaux's as the model of the strong rule needed to run the "unruly" Dominican Republic.

AFRICA

• *North Africa, Egypt and Sudan:* An Anglo-Egyptian Condominium was established over the Sudan. This Condominium would last until 1956.

• An Anglo-Egyptian Convention concerning the Sudan was held (January 19).

After the Mahdist state fell to the British-Egyptian government, Zande country became the focus of aggressive imperial rivalry between the British from the northeast and Belgians from the southwest.

Yambio, the Zande ruler, struggled to remain independent while neighboring chiefs and relatives aligned themselves with the Europeans.

• An Anglo-French Convention concerning the Libyan hinterland ended the Fashoda crisis (March 21). Italy protested the large concessions made to France in the Sahara.

• The Khalifa was killed on the White Nile (November).

The Khalifa —'Abdallahi ibn Muhammed— was born in central Sudan in 1846. He was the son of a Baqqara religious leader.

During the late 1870s, 'Abdallahi joined the Islamic reformer Muhammed 'Ahmad at the latter's retreat on the Nile River.

In 1881, Muhammed 'Ahmad proclaimed himself to be the Mahdi — the Muslim redeemer. Muhammed 'Ahmad set about to construct a theocratic state modelled on that of the Prophet Muhammed. 'Abdallahi was named one of Muhammed 'Ahmad's four caliphs and was given command of a major part of the growing Mahdist army.

Over the next four years, 'Abdallahi led a wave of Mahdist victories over Anglo-Egyptian forces, culminating in the taking of Khartoum in 1885.

After the unexpected death of Muhammed 'Ahmad in mid-1885, 'Abdallahi assumed the leadership of the incipient theocratic state and moved to consolidate his position against various internal factions, while declaring himself the Khalifa al-Mahdi — the Mahdi's successor.

Over the next thirteen years, 'Abdallahi remained at Omdurman. From this center, 'Abdallahi organized a highly bureaucratic and centralized administration. 'Abdallahi maintained strict Islamic law but reinstituted many of the abuses which the Mahdi had sought to eliminate.

'Abdallahi's army continued a border war with Ethiopia and killed the Ethiopian Emperor Yohannes IV in 1889. During the 1890s, 'Abdallahi's kingdom became overextended. Agricultural disasters weakened its economy, while the modern armies of Italian, French and British imperialists threatened it from all sides.

In 1896, General Kitchener began the Anglo-Egyptian reconquest of the Sudan. 'Abdallahi's armies suffered repeated setbacks until 1898, when Omdurman fell to Kitchener and the Mahdist administration collapsed. 'Abdallahi fled south. He was killed on the White Nile in 1899.

- *Western Africa:* Sir Fredric Hodgson provoked another Ashanti-British conflict by demanding that the Ashanti surrender their sacred symbol of power — the Golden Stool — the throne of the Ashanti king. In response to this demand, the Ashanti hid the Golden Stool and besieged Hodgson's fort. It would be two months before Hodgson and his wife would be able to escape.
- Britain purchased possessions of the Royal Niger Company (August 9).
- Britain and Germany agreed on the frontiers of Togo and the Gold Coast.
- France brought Ullemmeden Tuareg and other Moorish peoples on the Niger bend under French control.
- The Gold Coast-Togo boundary was defined.
- *Central Africa:* Mahdists temporarily occupied Rejaf (June 3 and 4).
- There was a dispute between Congolese and German troops near Lake Kivu. On November 23, the Bethe-Hecq agreement was reached.
- A new labor law in Angola reintroduced forced labor.
- *Eastern Africa:* The Administrator of French Somaliland was promoted to Governor (January 9). Marchand was at Djibouti.
- The Kabaka Mwanga and Mwami Kabarega of Bunyoro were deported to Kisimayu and then to Seychelles Islands (April).

After a long guerrilla campaign against the British, Kabarega, the king of Bunyoro, was finally captured in 1899, deposed and exiled to the Seychelles.

During his exile, Kabarega became literate and converted to Christianity. Kabarega was allowed to return to Uganda as a private citizen in 1923. However, he died soon after his return.

- The "Mad Mullah" proclaimed himself the Mahdi (September) and initiated raids on British and Italian Somaliland.
- The building of Nairobi (Kenya) began.
- Lord Delamere travelled for the first time through the Kenya Highlands.
- Ankole was brought under British control.
- Boran Galla was subjected to Ethiopia.
- There was general unrest in German East Africa. 2,000 Africans were said to have been killed resisting the hut tax.
- Sir Harry Johnston was named Commissioner in Uganda.

In 1899, Henry Hamilton (Harry) Johnston went to Uganda as Great Britain's special commissioner to develop an administration for Uganda. Johnston's most notable achievement in Uganda was the signing of the Uganda Agreement in 1900 with Apolo Kagwa and other major Ganda chiefs. This uniquely detailed treaty spelled out the rights of territorial chiefs and left an indelible mark on the political history of Uganda.

- *Southern Africa:* Johannesburg Uitlanders petitioned Queen Victoria on their grievances against the Boers (March 24). Between March

31 through June 5, Milner and Kruger failed to agree on the Transvaal franchise.

• The Transvaal enfranchised immigrants after seven years residence (July 11).

• The Transvaal rejected a British proposal of joint inquiry into franchise bills.

• There was an uprising at Moroni in Grand Comoro.

• The Governor of Comoro was installed at Dzaoudzi (September 9).

• Kruger dispatched an ultimatum to Great Britain (October 9). On October 11, the Orange Free State followed Kruger's lead and, on October 12, the Boer War began. The Boer War would last until May of 1902.

In late 1899, Paul Kruger, the president of the Transvaal Republic, anticipated a build up in British troop strength. He issued Britain with an ultimatum which precipitated the South African (Boer) War. During the first year, Kruger, utilizing German armaments, led the war effort. But when Kruger's government had to retreat from Pretoria, he left South Africa to lobby for support in European capitals.

During the next few years, Kruger campaigned futilely throughout Europe. Kruger died in Switzerland in 1904, two years after the Transvaal was defeated by Britain.

• On October 15, a secret treaty of Windsor was negotiated whereby Portugal undertook to prevent transit of munitions from Delogoa Bay to Transvaal.

• The Boers were defeated at Glencoe (October 17).

• The Boers were victorious at Nicholson's Nek (October 30).

• The British initiated operations against Kazembe (October).

• The Boers captured Ladysmith (November).

• The Boers repulsed the British at Magersfontein (December 11) and, on December 15, at Colenso.

• Canadian and Australian volunteers landed in South Africa (December).

• The railroad reached Salisbury, Rhodesia.

• The Education Ordinance in South Rhodesia provided grants for mission schools.

• Silver King and Sable Antelope mines were discovered near Kafue River.

• An anti-malarial campaign in South Rhodesia was undertaken by Dr. A. M. Fleming.

• The Matabeleland Native Labour Bureau was established.

• The Rhodesia Regiment was founded.

• The last engagement in Nyasaland was undertaken against Arab slave traders.

• The Tanganyika Concessions Limited was formed.

• Theophilus Ebenhaezer (1899-1968) was born.

• Sobhuza II (1899-1982), a future Swazi king, was born.

Sobhuza was born about the same time that his father Bhunu died. As a result, Sobhuza was almost immediately proclaimed king.

During Sobhuza's youth, his grandmother Gwamile served as regent. She worked to reverse the damage that had been done during the reign of her husband Mbanzeni, who had signed away most of the country to concession-hunters. After the Boer War, the British reluctantly assumed the administration of Swaziland in 1902.

Sobhuza was formally installed as king in 1921. The next year, Sobhuza initiated an expensive but unsuccessful legal campaign in London to throw out the European concessionaires. Afterwards, Sobhuza advocated peaceful cooperation with European residents in Swaziland, while continuing to assert Swazi economic rights.

Fundamental changes took place in Swazi society during Sobhuza's lifetime and Sobhuza remained more than a symbolic leader. When Swaziland regained its independence in 1968, Sobhuza became its head of state and continued to strengthen the political power of the monarchy.

In 1973, Sobhuza assumed full executive and legislative powers and undertook to create a new constitution.

• Bhunu (c.1873-1899), the ruler of Swaziland, died.

Due to his youth at the time of his ascension to the throne, Bhunu's reign began with the assistance of regents. By the time of his ascension, Bhunu's father, Mbandzeni, had sold almost all of Swaziland's economic resources to European concession hunters.

After Bhunu (also known as Bunu, Ubane or Ngwane IV) became king, the neighboring Transvaal Republic bought up most of the Swaziland concessions to establish a legal basis for annexing Swaziland in its drive to expand to a sea port. Bhunu and his regents worked futilely to regain control of their rights, but then quietly acquiesced while the Transvaal imposed its administration on Swaziland with British consent in 1895.

In 1898, Bhunu was implicated in the murder of a Swazi official. Bhunu was forced to flee the country to avoid arrest by the Afrikaners. Bhunu eventually paid a fine and was reinstated as king.

Bhunu died on the eve of the South African (Boer) War which would cost the Transvaal its control of Swaziland. Bhunu left his infant son, Sobhuza II, as his successor.

• **Masupha** (c.1820-1899), the Sotho sub-chief and military commander, died.

Although Masupha was only a junior son of Moshoeshoe *(see 1870)*, the great Sotho chief, Masupha deemed himself a contender to the throne after Moshoeshoe's death in 1870.

During his father's reign, Masupha's military accomplishments helped him to build a powerful faction within the kingdom. In 1853, Masupha commanded the Sotho army which finally destroyed Moshoeshoe's arch-rival Sekonyela.

Masupha was defeated during the 1865 war with the neighboring Orange Free State Republic, but re-established his reputation two years later in an action which saved the Sotho from conquest by the Free State.

In 1871, the year after Masupha's brother Letsie succeeded their father as king, the British crown handed administration of Lesotho over to the Cape Colony. The Colonial government divided Lesotho into four districts, and Masupha became chief of one of them.

During the remainder of his life, Masupha controlled his father's capital Thaba Bosiu — a fortified mountain stronghold. Masupha defied Letsie's attempts to restrict his activities. His resistance to outside control set an example which seriously undermined Letsie's administration of the entire kingdom.

During the "Gun War," Masupha was the focus of resistance to the Cape Colony's attempts to disarm the Sotho. The Sotho emerged victorious, but their divided response to this war made their factional disputes even more bitter. Seemingly above the internal strife while perched upon Thaba Bosiu, Masupha ignored the political rivalries which ravaged the kingdom below.

In 1886, Masupha accepted a British magistrate in his district. A year before he died in 1899, Masupha clashed with his brother's successor, Lerotholi *(see 1905)*. Lerotholi stormed Thaba Bosiu, arrested Masupha and deposed him.

Lerotholi subsequently dismantled the fortifications of Thaba Bosiu. With this dismantlement, the legend of Thaba Bosiu came to an ignominious end.

RELATED HISTORICAL EVENTS

• *The Americas:* Helen Campbell Bannerman published *Story of Little Black Sambo. Story of Little Black Sambo* became a "classic" in both the United States and Canada.

• *Europe:* Pursuant to the Treaty of Paris, Spain relinquished Cuba.

• An Anglo-French agreement was reached on the Sudan (March 21).

• Britain bought out Royal Niger Company (August 9).

• *Africa:* Mary Kingsley published *West African Studies. See 1900.*

• *Notable Deaths:* John Mackenzie (1835-1899), a noted British missionary and imperial agent, died.

In 1858, John Mackenzie was sent by the London Missionary Society to help found a mission among the Kololo of Sekeletu in western Zambia. Colleagues who proceeded to Zambia ahead of Mackenzie were, with their families, almost completely wiped out by disease, and the Kololo mission was abandoned.

Mackenzie remained in what is today Botswana. There he opened a mission among the Ngwato of Sekgoma in 1862. With the support of Sekgoma's son, Kgama III, Mackenzie helped to build the Ngwato mission into the London Society's most successful African enterprise.

In 1876, Mackenzie transferred to Kuruman. Kuruman was an older station founded by Robert Moffat. Over the next few years, Mackenzie acted as an unpaid agent of the British government.

Mackenzie went to England in 1882 to lobby for British expansion into Botswana, returning there two years later to serve as a deputy commissioner for Tswana territories already annexed by Britain. Mackenzie was, however, soon replaced by Cecil Rhodes.

Mackenzie again went to England to campaign for total British control of Southern Africa — a cause he argued in *Austral Africa* which was published in 1887. Many of Mackenzie's proposals were eventually adopted, but since Mackenzie was unable to obtain a government post, he returned to mission work in South Africa in 1891.

1900–1915

THE UNITED STATES

• On January 20, George H. White of North Carolina, the last African American who was elected to Congress during the Reconstruction era, introduced the first bill to make lynching of an American a federal crime. The bill died in committee, and 105 African Americans were lynched in 1900.

• Booker T. Washington organized the National Negro Business League. The purpose of the National Negro Business League was to encourage business ventures by African Americans. Washington was elected president of the league by 400 delegates, representing 34 states.

• W. E. B. Du Bois attended the meeting of the African and New World Intellectuals in London. The conference's "Address to the Nations of the World" was written by Du Bois and contained Du Bois' first recorded use of the dictum "The problem of the 20th century is the problem of the color line." Du Bois also attended the first Pan-African Congress in London and was elected vice-president. The Pan-African Congress was intended to be a permanent organization protesting imperialism and working for self-government of colonized people. Du Bois, along with Monroe Trotter and other nationalistic African Americans, also supported the Democratic Party, primarily because of its anti-imperialistic stance and what they perceived to be a sympathetic attitude towards the Philippines.

• By 1900, the number of registered African American voters in Louisiana had dropped to a mere 5,320 compared to the 130,344 African American voters registered in 1896.

• William Harvey Carney belatedly received his Congressional Medal of Honor (May 23).

Sergeant William Harvey Carney, of Company C, 54th Massachusetts Colored Infantry, was awarded the Congressional Medal of Honor for his bravery during the Battle of Fort Wagner, South Carolina. When the standard bearer was killed, Carney picked up the regimental colors and led the attack to the fort. Carney was badly wounded on two occasions during the fighting.

On February 17, 1863, Carney enlisted in the army and became a member of the 54th Massachusetts Colored Infantry. He rose to the rank of sergeant and commanded Company C.

Carney earned his medal of honor only five months after he joined the army when, at the battle for Fort Wagner, the color bearer was wounded. Carney, despite his own wounds, sprang forward and seized the flag before it slipped from the bearer's grasp, an act of gallant, albeit futile, bravery.

After Fort Wagner, Carney was discharged from the army because of the wounds he had received.

For "various reasons," Carney's medal of honor was not issued until May 23, 1900.

Upon Carney's death in 1908, the flag at the Massachusetts state capitol was lowered to half mast in tribute to this brave man.

• The national secret society, International Order of Twelve of the Knights and Daughters of Tabor, founded in 1871 claimed 200,000 members in 1900.

• Booker T. Washington dispatched a team of Tuskegee graduates to Togoland in West Africa at the request of the German government. The Tuskegee graduates were commissioned to teach the Africans how to grow cotton. The project extended over a six-year period.

• *The Census:* In 1900, of the total population of the United States, there were 8,833,994 African Americans representing 11.6% of the population. 89.7% of the African Americans lived in the South and represented one-third of the total Southern population.

• Between 1900 and 1930, the native African American population increased 33.9%; the native European American population, 68.4%; foreign-born European Americans, 30.6%; and foreign-born African American population, an astounding 232%.

• In 1900, the life expectancy of African Americans averaged approximately 34 years, as opposed to the life expectancy for European Americans of 48 years.

• In the years following 1900, the South declined as an area of African American immigrant residence. In 1900, three Southern divisions, South Atlantic, East South Central, and West South Central, contained 37.2% of the foreign born African American population. By 1910, this percentage dropped by 22.5%, despite the mass immigration during the decade, and by 1930 only 14.7% of foreign born African Americans lived in the South.

• The net intercensal migration for African American males ages 15 to 34 for the decade 1890–1900, in selected states was: Alabama -12.5%; Georgia -7.6%; Mississippi -2.6%; Illinois +53.9%; Michigan +10.5%; New York +55.2%. Thus, for every 100 African American males between the ages of 15 and 34 in Alabama in 1890, by 1900 twelve of those African American males had left the state. On the other hand, for every 100 African American males between the ages of 15 and 34 in New York in 1890, by 1900, 55 more African American males had joined them.

As African American migration to the North continued, European American hostility grew. Crowds of European American toughs frequently attacked African Americans in Northern cities. On several occasions, European American citizens dragged African Americans off the street

cars of Philadelphia with cries of "lynch him, kill him."

• The percentage of African Americans living in urban metropolitan areas was in the total United States 26.6%; in the North 61.1%; in the West 66.7%; and in the South 22.1%.

• Cities having an African American population of more than 30,000 were

Washington, D.C	86,702
Baltimore	79,258
New Orleans	77,714
Philadelphia	62,613
New York	60,666
Memphis	49,910
Louisville	39,139
Atlanta	35,727
St. Louis	35,516
Richmond, Virginia	32,230
Charleston	31,522
Chicago	30,150
Nashville	30,044

• In the following cities, African Americans outnumbered European Americans:

Charleston, South Carolina
Savannah, Georgia
Jacksonville, Florida
Montgomery, Alabama
Shreveport, Louisiana
Baton Rouge, Louisiana
Vicksburg, Mississippi

• 54.5% of African Americans lived in the central city areas and represented 6.5% of the total central city residents. In the North, 2.5% of such residents were African Americans; in the West, 1.3% and in the South 29.6%.

• The percentages of African Americans and European Americans engaged in gainful occupations was 45.2% for African Americans and 37.3% for European Americans. The higher rate of employment for African Americans reflected the fact that more African American women were in the workforce than European American women.

• *Organizations:* The Washington Society of Colored Dentists was founded in Washington, D. C. (November 14). The Washington Society of Colored Dentists was the first organization for African Americans in dentistry.

• *Crime and Punishment:* In New Orleans, European American mobs assaulted African Americans, burned and robbed their homes and stores for three days.

• *The Labor Movement:* By 1900, 32,069 African Americans could claim membership in a union.

• Between 1890 and 1900, there were over

50 strikes of European American workers protesting the use of African American laborers. The European American workers demanded the discharge of African American employees and an end to the hiring of African Americans.

• The American Federation of Labor (the AFL), at its annual convention adopted a policy of creating African American locals where the existing situation — the climate of segregation — warranted it.

• The Tobacco Workers International Union gave up an attempt to forbid racial discrimination, and began to organize separate African American locals.

• There were 91,019 dues paying members in the United Mine Workers. Of this number, approximately 20,000 were African American.

• *Notable Births:* Louis "Satchmo" Armstrong, a famous jazz trumpeter, was born (July 4).

Louis Armstrong was born in New Orleans. He was a regular "second liner" of the New Orleans marching bands. A fan of the cornetist Bunk Johnson, Armstrong played tambourine, bugle and finally the cornet in the Waif's Band.

Armstrong first played cornet professionally in a trio in a saloon at age 15. In 1918, Armstrong joined Kid Ory's band. After leaving the Kid Ory band, Armstrong joined Fate Marable's band. Until 1921, he appeared in Fate Marable's band on excursion boats on the Mississippi River. It was during this time that he developed his distinctive style.

In the mid–1920s, Armstrong moved to Chicago and began to play the trumpet. Subsequently moving to New York, he appeared briefly with Fletcher Henderson. His own recording groups in the 1920s were the Hot Five and Hot Seven. It was with these groups that he produced his finest instrumental work.

In 1929, with Luis Russell's orchestra, Armstrong made his first important big-band records. In 1932, he made his first overseas tour and played at the London Palladium. Afterwards, Armstrong toured Europe. He stayed on the continent until 1935 when he took over Luis Russell's band. He led Russell's band as his own until 1946.

It was during his tenure as the leader of Russell's old band that Armstrong began to use novelty songs as well as jazz. It was also at this time that Louis Armstrong began to sing.

In 1944, Louis Armstrong took part in the first jazz concert in the Metropolitan Opera House in New York City. Also in this year he organized a sextet for the film *New Orleans*. He took his sextet to Europe in 1949 and 1952 and to Japan in 1954.

Louis Armstrong was one of America's and Europe's most popular musicians and entertainers. A direct descendant of the cornetists Buddy Bolden and King Oliver, and the predecessor of the great jazz trumpeters Eldridge, Gillespie and Davis, Armstrong was the first of the great modern jazz soloists.

• Selma Burke, a sculptor and educator, was born in Mooresville, North Carolina (December 31).

• Augusta Savage (1900–1962), a sculptress, was born.

Augusta Savage studied at Cooper Institute. She was greatly influenced by African sculpture and techniques. In 1928, she was denied entrance to the Fontainbleau School for Talented American Artists because of her race. A Rosenwald Fund grant, however, enabled her to study in France for two years.

During the 1930s, Augusta Savage organized an art studio workshop in Harlem. This workshop later became affiliated with the WPA. Through the workshop, and by her work, Savage came to exert considerable influence upon young African American artists. She is most noted for her sculptures *African Savage* and *The Tom-Tom*.

• Howard Thurman, a noted theologian, was born in Daytona Beach, Florida (November 18). Thurman founded the Church for the Fellowship of All Peoples in San Francisco and would serve as dean of Marsh Chapel at Boston University.

• Ethel Waters, a trailblazing singer and actress, was born (October 31).

Ethel Waters was born in Chester, Pennsylvania. Her first claim to fame was as the first woman to sing W. C. Handy's *St. Louis Blues*. During her career, she appeared in numerous Broadway revues, musicals and dramas, including *Blackbirds, As Thousands Cheer, At Home Abroad, Cabin in the Sky,* and *Member of the Wedding.*

Ethel Waters also appeared in the movies *Cabin in the Sky, Manhattan* and *Pinky*. Waters created the character of "Beulah" in both the radio and television series.

• Hale A. Woodruff, a noted artist, was born (August 26).

Hale A. Woodruff was born in Cairo, Illinois. He studied at the Herron Institute in Indianapolis and was sent by local citizens to Paris to continue his studies. On his return from Paris, Woodruff became an instructor at Atlanta University. Woodruff was primarily an academic landscapist specializing in Georgia scenes. He did WPA murals for Howard Junior High School and the Atlanta School of Social Work. Included in the latter were two panels of African American neighborhoods entitled *Shantytown* and *Mud Hill Row*. The *Atlanta Constitution* hailed Woodruff by saying "The young Negro artist is one of the modern masters. This exhibition is really one of the finest that will be shown anywhere."

- *Notable Deaths:* 105 (115) African Americans were lynched in 1900.
- James Augustine Healy (1830–1900), the first African American Roman Catholic bishop in the United States, died in Portland, Maine. (August 5).

James Augustine Healy was the first African American Roman Catholic priest and the first African American Roman Catholic Bishop in the United States.

James Augustine Healy was born on a plantation near Macon, Georgia. His father (Michael Morris Healy) was an Irish immigrant and his mother and his mother (Mary Eliza Smith) was a COTW slave.

In 1837, Healy's Irish planter father sent Healy to a Quaker school on Long Island, New York. In 1849, Healy graduated from Holy Cross College.

In 1852, Healy entered the Sulpician Seminary in Paris. On June 10, 1854, he was ordained a priest in Notre Dame Cathedral in Paris. Healy's first assignment as a priest was in a European American parish in Boston.

Healy later became secretary to the Bishop of Boston. When his superior died, Healy became pastor of the New Saint James Church.

Healy's prominence in the New England Catholic hierarchy continued to rise. In 1874, he was appointed bishop of Maine and was consecrated in the Cathedral at Portland, Maine, on June 2, 1875.

Although Healy served a predominately European American parish, the parishioners held him in high regard and the Bishop was only rarely subjected to racial abuse.

Healy was one of three brothers to attain distinction in African American history. His brother, Patrick Francis Healy, served as President of Georgetown University from 1873 to 1882. Another brother, Michael Healy, became a ship captain who sailed the waters of Alaska and is believed to have been the model for Jack London's *Sea Wolf. See also* James Michener's *Alaska*.

- Jefferson F. Long (1836–1900), a former Congressman from Georgia, died.

Jefferson F. Long was born a slave near Knoxville, Georgia. He moved to Macon, Georgia, where, after working for a merchant tailor, he opened a tailoring shop of his own.

From 1865 through 1869, Long was influential in the Georgia Republican Party. In 1869, he was elected to Congress. While in Congress, Long advocated the enforcement of the 15th Amendment and universal suffrage.

Long only served one term, but remained active in the Georgia Republican Party throughout his life.

- *Miscellaneous Cases: :* In *Maxwell v. Dow* (February 26, 1900) 176 U.S. 581, 20 S.Ct. 448 and 494, the United States Supreme Court overturned the 1871 decision in *United States v. Hall* by ruling that the adoption of the Fourteenth Amendment to the Federal Constitution did not have the effect of making all the provisions contained in the first ten amendments (the Bill of Rights) operative in state courts, on the ground that the fundamental rights protected by those amendments were, by virtue of the Fourteenth Amendment, to be regarded as privileges and immunities of citizens of the United States. Thus, the privileges and immunities of a citizen of the United States did not include the right of trial by jury in a state court for a state offense.
- On April 16, 1900, in the case of *Carter v. Texas* (1900) 177 U.S. 442, 20 S.Ct. 687, the United States Supreme Court held that an African American man indicted for the murder of a European American man in Texas was denied his constitutional rights because the grand jury illegally excluded African American jurors.
- *Miscellaneous State Laws:* North Carolina adopted a "grandfather clause." This amendment to its State Constitution granted descendants of people who were registered voters before January 1, 1867, exemption from other voter registration qualifications.
- A South Carolina law extended segregation to second-class railroad coaches. First class cars were already segregated.
- Virginia adopted segregation on steamships and railroads.

• *Publications:* James Walker Hood published *The Plan of the Apocalypse.*

• Paul Laurence Dunbar published a novel, *The Love of Landry*; a one-act musical sketch, *Uncle Eph's Christmas*; and a collection of his magazine articles, *The Strength of Gideon.*

• Charles W. Chestnutt published his first novel, *The House Behind the Cedars.* In this novel, Chestnutt introduced the COTW as a tragic figure, neither black nor white. The conflicted story of the child of two worlds — the "mulatto" — was later to pre-occupy many writers and filmmakers to the point of becoming a stereotypical character.

• African Americans published three daily newspapers in Norfolk, Virginia; Kansas City, Missouri; and Washington, D. C. The African Americans also published 150 weekly newspapers.

• By 1900, *The Reformer*, a weekly paper of the Virginia Organization of True Reformers (a secret African American benevolent society) which was established in 1892, reportedly had a circulation of 8,000.

• *The Black Church:* In 1900, approximately 100,000 African Americans were Catholics. There were a reported 50 African American priests.

• At the Ecumenical Missionary Conference in New York, the Reverend S. Morris, an African American Baptist, called for the use of African American missionaries because European American missionaries hampered the work of "the gospel" because they often carried their prejudices with them.

• *Scholastic Achievements:* The Sixth Atlanta Conference for the Study of Negro Problems noted that African Americans had "in a generation, (1870 to 1899), paid directly $40,000,000 in hard-earned cash for educating their children." The Conference also noted that the results of such an investment were "gratifying."

• By 1900, there were some 21,267 African American teachers and professors. In 1890, there had only been 15,100. The 21,267 teachers co-existed with 1.5 million African American school children.

• In 1900, 44.5% of all African Americans were illiterate — were unable to read. On a regional basis, the breakdown was as follows: North Atlantic, 13.8%; South Atlantic, 47.1%; North Central 21.7%; South Central, 48.8%; Western 13.1%.

• By 1900, more than 2,000 African Americans had college degrees. Over the next ten years, four doctorates would be awarded to African Americans.

• Four states, Virginia, Arkansas, Georgia, and Delaware, had state colleges which were established exclusively for African Americans.

• *The Arts:* Henry Ossawa Tanner received the Lippincott Prize from the Pennsylvania Academy of Fine Arts for his painting *Nicodemus Visiting Jesus.*

• Henry Ossawa Tanner's *Daniel in the Lion's Den* received the Silver Medal at the Paris Exposition.

• *The Performing Arts:* An establishment called The Marshall became important in the artistic life of New York. The Marshall was a hotel run by an African American and, at the turn of the century, it had become a center for the upscale fashionable life which was new to many African Americans. For nearly ten years, beginning in 1900, the Marshall was headquarters for actors, musicians, composers, writers and the better-paid vaudevillians.

• The African American song and dance team Bert Williams and George Walker opened in *Sons of Ham*, a musical comedy, which ran for two years in New York.

• *Music:* James Weldon Johnson wrote the lyrics and his brother, J. Rosamund Johnson composed the music for the song, *Lift Every Voice and Sing. Lift Every Voice and Sing* became the unofficial national anthem for African Americans. *See 1871.*

• Robert (Bob) Cole wrote the highly successful *A Shoo Fly Regiment,* a musical about African Americans in the United States forces in the Spanish-American War.

• *Black Enterprise:* By 1900, the Census reported that of African American households in Virginia some 34,234 owned their own homes while 75,895 rented their homes. These numbers represented an increase in home ownership and a decrease in home rentals amongst African Americans over the preceding decade. In 1890, only 28,621 African American households owned their own homes while 82,516 rented. Overall, approximately 24% of all African Americans owned their own homes.

• There were 1,734 African American physicians in 1900 compared to the 909 in 1890.

• There were 212 African American dentists in 1900 an increase of 92 over the 120 reported in 1890.

- In 1900, there were 21,267 African American teachers and professors; 15,528 preachers; 1,734 doctors; 212 dentists; 310 journalists; 728 lawyers; over 2,000 actors and showmen; 236 artists, sculptors and art teachers; 3,915 musicians and music teachers; 247 photographers; 52 architects, designers, draftsmen and inventors; and one — ONE — African American Congressman (G. W. White of North Carolina).
- The total value of farm property owned by African Americans was placed at $499,943,734. The average acreage of farms operated by African Americans in the United States was 51.2 acres.
- There were four African American banks in the United States.
- By 1900, some 64 African American drugstores had been established, each with a capital of at least $1,000.
- Charles P. Graves, president of Gold Leaf Consolidated Company of Montana and Illinois, a mining company, reported his property at a value of $1,000,000. Charles P. Graves was one of the first known African American millionaires.
- Booker T. Washington convened a group of African American businessmen in Boston. Together they formed the National Negro Business League. 400 delegates from 34 states elected Washington to serve as the first president.
- *Sports:* Marshall W. "Major" Taylor, became the sprint champion of the United States in bicycle racing for the second consecutive year.

THE AMERICAS

Canada

Between 1900 and 1920, Canada experienced a new wave of black immigration. Black urbanization, begun during the Civil War, had been accelerating rapidly. A search for greater job opportunities, the desire to escape from an increasingly oppressive South, and pressures exerted by industry in World War I promoted mass movement of African Americans toward the north in general and the northern cities in particular. The African American population of Cleveland, Ohio, multiplied fifty-six times while that of Chicago, Illinois, increased sixty-three fold. Although comparatively small, the African American populations of Detroit, Buffalo and Boston also grew.

As a corollary to this growth, a number of Canadian border towns also experienced an increase in the number of African Americans living within their boundaries. Such communities as Windsor, Hamilton and Saint John saw a significant increase in the number of individuals who would come to call themselves Afro-Canadians.

- In 1900, land in the Dakota Territories cost fifty dollars an acre. Comparable land in Saskatchewan, Canada sold for two dollars an acre. The lure of cheap land and a less oppressive social environment began to lure African Americans to Canada.
- *Haiti:* Dumarsais Estime (1900–1953), a future president of Haiti, was born.

Dumarsais Estime was born in a small village. He was orphaned at a young age and reared by an uncle, a magistrate and member of the national Senate. After primary and secondary education in Port-au-Prince, Estime became a mathematics teacher at his alma mater, Lycee Petion. At Lycee Petion, Estime would become the teacher of a certain Francois Duvalier, the future dictator of Haiti.

At a relatively early age, Estime became active in politics. He lost his teaching job at Lycee Petion because he opposed President Louis Borno during the United States occupation. When Borno was replaced by President Stenio Vincent in 1930, Estime became a member of the Chamber of Deputies and, for a time, served as the Chamber's president.

During his tenure as minister of education, Estime organized a system of higher education to be based on merit and improved significantly the salaries of the country's teachers. Estime also served in other positions in President Vincent's cabinet.

Vincent was replaced by the COTW President Elie Lescot. Lescot, was deposed in January 1946 by a military coup. With the backing of the only black member of the three man Executive Military Committee, Major Paul Eugene Magliore, and with support of the black intellectual community, Estime was elected president by the National Assembly.

Estime embarked on a program of reform which he labeled "socialist" but was more nationalist and populist in character. Estime restored the ban on foreign ownership of land and broke the monopoly of Standard Fruit in production of bananas, nationalizing their holdings and dividing them into seven sections that were parceled out to his supporters. Retaliation from the former owners resulted in almost total destruction of the industry.

Estime restored independence to the judiciary and the legislature, allowed freedom of the press, and encouraged formation of political parties and trade unions which were legalized and which freely criticized the government. Estime also undertook educational reform, expanding the school system. He increased the salaries of state employees, partly as a means of providing upward mobility through the civil service for blacks.

President Estime was blessed with a booming economy when he came to office. The state of the economy was largely responsible for the success of Estime's social reform programs. Haiti continued to receive United States economic assistance, while Estime made efforts to end American financial control established during occupation.

Some of Estime's policies alienated both left and right. His efforts to create and encourage a black elite came to be resented and, ultimately, became a burden on the country's fiscal resources.

Despite successful efforts to encourage tourism, much of the inordinate sums spent on development of tourist facilities was unaccounted for and squandered. Estime imposed, for the first time, an income tax that particularly hit the elite. Moreover, he at least passively encouraged the practice of voodoo and attempted to curb and Haitianize the Catholic Church.

In 1950, Estime decided to have himself reelected. He declared martial law and attempted to intimidate his opponents by mob violence. In May 1950, Estime was finally removed from office by the same junta that had paved the way for his assumption of power.

Estime left Haiti and died in New York three years later.

Estime was given a state funeral by President Paul Magloire. When Francois "Papa Doc" Duvalier came to power, Estime was named a national hero. Both Estime's widow and son served in the Duvalier regime.

AFRICA

- *North Africa, Egypt and Sudan:* Al-Liwa, an Egyptian Nationalist newspaper was founded.
- Ibrahim Abboud was born.
- The French occupied Touat, Gourar and Colomb-Bechar.
- Communication with the Lake Chad area became effective.

- A secret Franco-Italian agreement was reached on respective interests in Morocco and Tripoli (December 14).
- The Sultan of Morocco showed weakening resistance to French expansion.
- The Egyptian population of 1900 was estimated to be about 10 million.
- *Western Africa:* The French occupation of Zinder territory began.
- The British government assumed control of all Royal Niger Company territories (January 1).
- The Protectorate of Northern Nigeria replaced the Royal Niger Company. Sir Frederick Lugard was named High Commissioner. Indirect rule was instituted. This type of governance was deemed to be the "most significant development of British colonial policy" and was soon extended in numerous ordinances throughout the British Empire.

In 1900, Frederick Lugard was appointed high commissioner for Northern Nigeria, at the time a relatively small territory. From 1901 to 1903, Lugard was engaged in the systematic conquest of the Sokoto Caliphate, created a century before by Uthman dan Fodio. Lugard also annexed a good deal of territory outside Sokoto.

With limited resources at his command, Lugard was forced to rule the country through the agency of its African rulers. In doing so, Lugard sought to interfere with the internal affairs of the African kingdoms as little as possible. This policy of non-interference in internal affairs gave rise to Lugard's philosophy of indirect rule. Lugard's philosophy essentially became the basis for British administration of its African colonies.

By making a virtue out of necessity, Lugard's indirect rule policy advocated support for "traditional" African rulers and institutions whenever such support was not repugnant to British moral standards. British political officers were to use funds derived from taxation to foster the limited growth of social services and to encourage modernization of government.

Lugard's "Political Memoranda" became the Bible for British administrators. However, a number of officials misapplied the concept, viewing it as a strictly laissez-faire policy. Additionally, in most areas where it was applied indigenous African authorities had formerly lacked the degree of authority of the emirs of Northern Nigeria. Thus, indirect rule sometimes created an entirely new political system in the attempt to preserve a fictional one.

• An Ashanti uprising was suppressed by the British (November).

When, in 1900, the British demanded that the Asante surrender the Golden Stool, the symbol of Asante unity, the people unsuccessfully rebelled. Britain then dismantled the former empire and began to rule it directly.

• The Northern Nigerian Regiment was founded.
• The construction of the Carter and Denton Bridges was completed in Lagos (Nigeria).
• The Lagos to Ibadan railway was opened.
• The MacGregor Canal was cut.
• The French defeated Rabeh in the Lake Chad region.
• The Canhabaque staged an uprising against the Portuguese.
• After 1900, the Tuareg were the undisputed rulers of the southern Sahara.
• Rabeh Zubayr (c.1835–1900), the conqueror of Bornu, died.

Rabeh Zubayr was a slave of al-Zubayr Rahma Mansur before becoming a military leader in Zubayr's private slave-raiding army, operating towards the Nilotic Sudan. By 1880, Zubayr's slaving activities had been curtailed by Charles Gordon, and Rabeh took over half of Zubayr's army. His anti–European sentiments were similar to those of Muhammed 'Ahmad (the Mahdi), who was building an Islamic reform movement in the Nilotic Sudan.

Rabeh declared himself a supporter of the Mahdi. However, the two had little communication, as Rabeh had no intention of subordinating himself to another leader.

Rabeh decided to move west to carve out his own empire, and in 1892, attacked the Baghirmi state. Baghirmi allied with neighboring Wadai, but was nevertheless defeated.

Rabeh had also asked for help from Bornu which Bornu unwisely refused. The next year, Rabeh allied with Hayatu ibn Sa'id, another supporter of the Mahdi, to attack Bornu. Rabeh's forces although greatly outnumbered, were victorious through their tactical superiority, and Hashimi, the Bornu ruler, abdicated in 1893.

Hashimi was succeeded (and assassinated) by Kiyari. However, Kiyari was no more successful against Rabeh than Hashimi had been. He was captured and executed by Rabeh later in 1893.

By 1896, Rabeh had the whole state of Bornu under his control and Rabeh was well on his way to establishing a new Bornu dynasty.

Rabeh built a fortified capital at Dikwa and maintained an army of 20,000 — an army that wore uniforms and carried guns. Shortly after building his fortifications, Rabeh's ally, Hayatu, attacked. Rabeh killed Hayatu in battle.

While bettering his African counterparts, Rabeh could not check the European advance into the African interior. Baghirmi asked for French protection, and although Rabeh defeated the French a number of times in 1899, his victories were costly in men, arms and supplies.

In 1900, Rabeh was defeated by the French and killed.

• Samori Toure (c.1830–1900), the creator of the largest Mandinka Dyula (Jula) state in West Africa, died.

Samori Toure (Samory) was the creator of the largest Mandinka Dyula (Jula) state in West Africa. Samory was the last and most successful of the Dyula revolutionaries in the nineteenth century until he succumbed to the French imperial drive. Samory's two successive empires covered large parts of the Upper Niger and the interior of the Ivory Coast.

Samory was born around 1830 in Konyan (in present day Guinea). He spent his early manhood as a Dyula merchant. The Dyula were a class of professional traders who travelled and settled throughout West Africa, particularly between Senegal and the Ivory Coast. The Dyula were usually Muslims unlike most of the people amongst whom they lived.

In the 1800s, the Dyula among the Mandinka of Guinea began to seize political control. The first Dyula revolutionary, Mori-Ule Sise, launched a military campaign against his Mandinka neighbors in 1835.

Around 1853, Samory's mother was captured by Mori-Ule's soldiers. Samory went to live with the Sise to try and obtain her release. There Samory learned the skills of warfare which he was later to apply so effectively. After leaving the Sise, Samory began to amass his own following. Samory expanded his holdings by entering into various inter-chiefdom disputes, and then ruthlessly seizing power.

By the 1860s, Samory's authority was acknowledged in the Milo River region. In the 1870s, Samory continued to expand his new empire, establishing his capital at Bisandugu (Guinea), and making alliances with Dyula communities which controlled the arms traffic from the coast. By 1880, Samory was the unchallenged leader of the Dyula revolution.

Up until this time, the unifying principle

which Samory had employed was loyalty to his person. With the expansion of his empire, Samory felt that personal loyalty would not suffice and, in 1884, he attempted to turn the empire into an Islamic theocracy.

During this time, Samory modernized his army's tactics and weaponry. In 1884, Samory conquered the Sierra Leone hinterland in order to ensure the supply of arms from Freetown, the most important terminus of his caravans. In exchange for arms, Samory offered gold and ivory. The slaves that Samory captured were his most important source of capital, although these had to be exchanged for products acceptable in Freetown.

Unfortunately for Samory, his imperialistic designs coincided with those of the French, who were eager to carve out an empire of their own. First French military contact with Samory came in 1882, and the two armies battled sporadically until 1886 when they signed a peace treaty.

Samory then sent his favorite son to France on a goodwill mission. Both parties desired a respite — Samory in order to prepare to fight Tieba at Sikasso (present day Mali), and the French to fight Mamadu Lamine in the Senegambia.

Samory's attempt to take Sikasso proved to be a major disaster. The defeat decimated his army and triggered off a massive revolt in his empire in 1888. As a consequence, Samory decided to abandon Islam as a unifying principle and return to one of personal loyalty.

Before Samory could face the French, he needed to put down the rebellion and to re-establish his trade connections with Sierra Leone.

Both Samory and the French prepared for the impending conflict. The clash began in 1891 when French forces under Archinard penetrated deep into Samori's territory. In 1894, realizing he could not defeat the French, Samory decided upon a daring alternative. Samory moved his empire eastward to the Ivory Coast interior, pursuing a scorched earth policy in the lands he vacated. There he began the conquest of new lands, and briefly attempted to ally with Prempe I, the ruler of Asante in the Gold Coast.

The French military drive was relentless and, in 1898, when the British refused to sell him arms, Samory retreated into Liberia. The French captured him that year and exiled him to Gabon.

It was in Gabon that Samory died of pneumonia in 1900.

Although in the lands that he conquered Samory is remembered as a ruthless tyrant, many people consider him a hero of African resistance to European imperialism.

- *Central Africa:* A Franco-Portuguese convention on the boundary of the French Congo was held (January 23).
- A Franco-Spanish agreement was reached on the boundary of Rio Muni (June 27).
- Chad was proclaimed a French military protectorate (September 5).
- A mixed Belgian-German survey was performed for the Lake Kivu region.
- *Eastern Africa:* Between 1900 and 1904, four British expeditions were launched against the "Mad Mullah."

For twenty years, Muhammed 'Abdullah Hassan, the "Mad Mullah" led a powerful puritanical Islamic reform movement and defied the combined assaults of Ethiopian, British and Italian imperialists. Long regarded by Europeans as an irrational fanatic, today Muhammed 'Abdullah Hassan is deemed to be the first great Somali nationalist.

Muhammed 'Abdullah Hassan was born in northern Somalia during an era of popular Islamic reform movements. A precocious student, Muhammed 'Abdullah Hassan began to teach theology at fifteen and soon earned wide respect as a scholar.

During the 1880s and 1890s, Muhammed 'Abdullah Hassan travelled widely, possibly visiting Sudan, where the Mahdist movement of Muhammed 'Ahmad was in bloom.

In 1894, Muhammed 'Abdullah Hassan visited Mecca and joined the Salihiya sect of the puritanical Ahmadiya brotherhood. He then returned to Berbera, in the north of present Somalia, to introduce the reform movement.

A nominal British protectorate had been established over northern Somalia during Muhammed's absence and he became incensed by the freedom with which Christian missionaries were working in his country.

In 1896, Muhammed moved inland to escape Christian influence and to found his own pure Islamic community. Two years later, Muhammed was prosecuted by the British government for harboring a thief. Muhammed responded by denouncing British sovereignty and declaring a jihad — a holy war — against all infidels.

Supported by a steadily growing band of religious and political dissidents — a group known as the dervishes — Muhammed directed his first violent opposition against Ethiopians. The Christian empire of Menelik II was then conquering Somali territory in the east of present day Ethiopia. In 1900, Muhammed attacked an Ethiopian fort and initiated four years of uninterrupted victories. Muhammed's successes attracted to his banner even Somali who did not share his religious beliefs.

Muhammed evaded Ethiopian and British campaigns and moved to the east coast, where the Italians had established a protectorate in 1903. The combined efforts of the Italians, British and Ethiopians failed to subdue Muhammed's followers, so the Italian government offered him a compromise.

Early in 1905, Muhammed signed a treaty with the Italians which made him the ruler of a newly defined Italian protectorate on the central Somali coast.

- A Franco-Italian agreement was reached concerning the boundaries of French Somaliland (June 24). The agreement also guaranteed Italian access to the Aussa caravan route.
- On June 26, the Toro agreement was finalized.
- Pursuant to the Uganda agreement, Buganda was made a province of Uganda; Ganda was compelled to pay the hut tax for British administration; and Lukiko constituted a legislature and court of appeal.

In 1899, Henry Hamilton (Harry) Johnston went to Uganda as Great Britain's special commissioner to develop an administration for Uganda. Johnston's most notable achievement in Uganda was the signing of the Uganda Agreement in 1900 with Apolo Kagwa and other major Ganda chiefs. This uniquely detailed treaty spelled out the rights of territorial chiefs and left an indelible mark on the political history of Uganda.

When Henry Johnston negotiated the "Uganda Agreement" in 1900, Kagwa was the supreme Ganda chief and the leading signatory of the agreement. The Uganda Agreement enunciated the rights of the Ganda chiefs under the colonial administration, allotted to Kagwa an immense tract of land and brought him to the height of his power. Kagwa continued to add to his landholdings and was an enthusiastic advocate of modernization. Kagwa's prestige among the British was unrivalled.

- Around 1900, Kakunguru developed influence in Bukari. Kakunguru was recognized as Kabaka by Sir Harry H. Johnston.
- *Southern Africa:* Lord Roberts became the Commander-in-Chief with Lord Kitchener as Chief of Staff (January 10).

On the outbreak of the South African War, Roberts took command of the British forces in the Cape Colony. The first year of the war the Afrikaners fought according to orthodox theories of warfare. Roberts occupied the Orange Free State and the Transvaal and drove the Afrikaners into bush country. Declaring the war won, Roberts returned home in 1900 to wide acclaim.

- Piet Cronje surrendered at Paardeberg (February 18).
- Redvers Buller relieved Ladysmith (February 28).
- On March 13, Roberts captured Bloemfontein. However, his subsequent attempts to negotiate peace with the Boers failed.

By 1900, Louis Botha, the future South African prime minister, was commander of the entire Transvaal Republican army. He distinguished himself in a number of campaigns. When the inevitability of the Afrikaner defeat became a foregone conclusion, Botha was the first Afrikaner leader to advocate accommodation with the British.

- The relief of Mafeking occurred (May 17).

The relief of Mafeking created an international hero. Robert Stephenson Smyth Baden-Powell, the British commander, held Mafeking and withstood the Afrikaner siege for seven months. Baden-Powell's heroic stand made him a celebrity.

Eight years later, Baden-Powell would use his celebrity to start a movement which continues to this day. Robert Stephenson Smyth Baden-Powell founded a movement known as the Boy Scouts.

- Britain annexed the Orange Free State (May 24).

After Hercules Robinson retired as governor of the Cape and high commissioner for South Africa in 1897, Alfred Milner was selected for the delicate job of replacing him at a time when Anglo-Afrikaner relations were at a low ebb.

Milner started his work with a great deal of energy, learning to speak Dutch and Afrikaans, and making a good impression on Paul Kruger, the president of the Transvaal. However, Milner's British imperialistic bias hardened and he soon came to advocate British supremacy throughout South Africa.

With the support of the Secretary of State for the Colonies, Joseph Chamberlain, Milner pressured the Transvaal Republic to reform its government and to enfranchise its non–Afrikaner residents — the uitlanders. Milner threatened

British intervention and war as the alternative. A last minute conference with Afrikaner leaders failed in May of 1899 and Kruger initiated the South African (Boer) War several months later.

While the war was still being waged, Milner assumed the administration of the Orange Free State (renamed the Orange River Colony) and the Transvaal after resigning from his position as governor of the Cape Colony. At the conclusion of the war, Milner drafted the terms of the Peace of Vereeniging and signed for the British — together with Kitchener — in 1902.

- Pretoria was captured (June 5).
- The armies of Roberts and Buller united at Vlakfontein (July 4).
- Boers were steadily gathered into concentration camps. Eventually their numbers came to total 200,000 men.
- Kruger fled to Marseilles.
- Botha was defeated at Bergendal (August 27).
- Johannesburg was occupied (August 31).
- R. T. Corydon was appointed first Administrator of Barotseland and Northwest Rhodesia (September 15).
- A treaty was negotiated between the Barotse and BSA Company (October 17).
- Britain annexed the Transvaal (October 25).
- The Indemnity Act was passed by the Cape Parliament.
- November saw a number of Boer guerrilla actions.

Kitchener succeeded Roberts as commander-in-chief of British forces as the Afrikaners turned to guerrilla warfare.

- In December, mobile commandos were activated.
- Martial law was proclaimed throughout South Africa.
- African taxation was introduced in Northeast Rhodesia.
- The Basutoland "Ethiopian" Church was founded by Willie Mokalapa.
- The Labor board of South Rhodesia was established.
- The Labour tax was introduced in Nyasaland.
- Mpezeni Jere (c.1832–1900) the former ruler of the Chipata Ngoni kingdom of eastern Zambia, died.

During the great Ngoni migration out of South Africa, Mpezeni Jere was born in what is today Zimbabwe. Mpezeni was born to the chief wife of the Ngoni king Zwangendaba. As such, Mpezeni was first in line for the succession to the Ngoni kingship. However, when his father died at a later settlement in southern Tanzania around 1845, Mpenzeni's youth and inexperience aroused major opposition to his ascension.

Mpenzeni was compelled to rule with the aid of regents for a number of years. However, he remained an unpopular ruler. Pressed by recurrent food shortages in the early 1850s, Mpezeni decided to migrate west. Dissident factions refused to accompany Mpezeni, but he made no attempt to bring them into line. Instead Mpezeni led his loyal supporters south. As for the dissidents, they eventually went on to establish four additional Ngoni kingdoms in Tanzania and Malawi.

Mpezeni entered eastern Zambia and began a protracted campaign to conquer the Bemba people while building a succession of settlements. Sometime during the 1860s, Mpezeni's younger brother Mpelembe defected from him, thus weakening Mpezeni's forces.

Around 1870, Mpezeni abandoned his campaigns against the Bemba and moved into the present Chipata district farther south. From this area, Mpezeni conquered the local Chewa chief Mkanda and Mpezeni was able to build his kingdom into the greatest power in southeast Zambia.

By the late 1880s, Mpezeni's relations with his neighbors were largely stabilized and he was beginning to receive visits from European traders and concession hunters.

In 1890, Mpezeni granted a generous concession to a lone German trader, Karl Wiese. However, aside from this concession, Mpezeni was generally able to ignore the increasing European imperialistic pressure at the same time that the same forces were reducing his neighbors to colonial dependents.

Mpezeni's complacency was shattered in 1897. European manipulation outside his knowledge transferred Wiese's concession to a chartered British company, which attacked him without warning in 1898.

Mpezeni offered little resistance and was quickly conquered. Mpezeni died two years later, but his kingdom retained its structure under the rule of his son and grandson, both of whom were named Mpezeni.

RELATED HISTORICAL EVENTS

- The world population reached an estimated 1.7 billion people. There were 16 cities in the world with a population over one million.

- *The Americas:* The territorial government of Puerto Rico was established after the United States seized the island in the Spanish-American War.
- Helen Bannerman published *Little Black Sambo.*
- *Europe:* Russia suggested that France and Germany put pressure on Britain to end the Boer War (February 28). Germany rejected the proposal (March 3).
- The *Compagnie de Katanga* became the *Comite Speciale de Katanga* (June 19).
- Kruger fled to Europe (October 6), but he was denied an audience with the Kaiser.
- A Franco-Italian agreement was reached on Tunisia (December 16).
- Gottlieb Daimler (1834–1900), the inventor of the motorized vehicle, died.

Africa

- *Notable Deaths:* Mary Kingsley (1862–1900), an English explorer and writer, died.

In 1900, Mary Kingsley died and a great champion of the African people was laid to rest.

After Mary Kingsley's parents left her a modest estate, she made two trips to western and central Africa. The first, in 1893, took her to various ports as far south as Angola. From Angola, Kingsley travelled overland through the Belgian and French Congos, returning to the coast in Nigeria.

At the end of 1894, Kingsley began her second voyage which took her to Calabar (Nigeria), French Congo, Gabon and Cameroon. She travelled lightly, earning her way by engaging in petty trade.

From her travels, Kingsley became sympathetic to the position of the European traders in West Africa. Previously British opinion on Africa had been influenced either by missionaries, who believed in African cultural inferiority, or by Social Darwinism, which expressed theories of racial inferiority. Mary Kingsley denounced both views, stating that the African mentality was different from but not inferior to the European, and that attempts to meddle with African institutions were dangerous.

Because of her views, Kingsley despised western-educated Africans and opposed the spread of formal British colonialism in Africa. Instead she advocated a return to the polity of the 1880s where traders governed regions under their influence, concerned only with economics and preservation of law and order.

Mary Kingsley presented her ideas in numerous lectures and articles, and in two popular books, *Travels in West Africa* (published in 1897) and *West African Studies* (published in 1899).

Kingsley became friendly with the important trade lords of the day, and personally represented their position at the Colonial Office, frequently to Joseph Chamberlain himself.

Mary Kingsley had planned a third trip to West Africa, but instead volunteered as a nurse in the South African (Boer) War. While serving as a nurse, she caught a fever and died in 1900.

Mary Kingsley's legacy was a rehabilitated image of the African in the minds of colonial administrators after 1900 when policy became more cautious and more concerned with African social institutions.

- A. A. da Rocha de Serpa Pinto (1846–1900), a Portuguese explorer of Central Africa, died.

In 1875, the Geographical Society of Lisbon was founded to promote Portugal's image as an activist colonial power. Pinto, an army major who had served in Mozambique, was assigned to its first scientific expedition in west central Africa.

Alone, Pinto crossed the continent to the east coast, visiting the Lozi king Lewanika along the way. Pinto exaggerated this feat in *How I Crossed Africa* which was published in 1881. Despite this exaggeration, Pinto became a Portuguese national hero nonetheless.

During the following decade, Pinto undertook various assignments, including governorship of Mozambique in 1889. Pinto attempted to bolster Portugal's east African claims vis-à-vis other European powers, but was mostly unsuccessful.

1901

THE UNITED STATES

- W. E. B. Du Bois sounded a voice of opposition to Booker T. Washington's accommodationist policy. Du Bois stated that there were many African American intellectuals who refuted Booker T. Washington's position and who did not accept Washington as the popular leader of Afro-America. These intellectuals refused to accept that the African

American had to give up on attaining social equality with European Americans for the sake of economic expediency.

• President Theodore Roosevelt invited Booker T. Washington to the White House for an interview and dinner. This invitation outraged Southerners but pleased many African Americans.

• Florida and Tennessee Democrats adopted "white primaries."

• George H. White, an African American Congressman from North Carolina, ended his second term in the United States Congress. No other African American would serve in the Congress until 1928.

• Racial violence broke out in northern cities as African Americans migrated north in search of better jobs.

• *Notable Births:* Richmond Barthe, a noted artist, was born (January 28).

Richmond Barthe was born in New Orleans. He was of mixed Creole heritage. Barthe was discovered by Lyle Saxon and a Catholic priest, both of whom provided the funds for his formal art study at the Chicago Art Institute.

In 1928, Barthe essentially abandoned his painting for sculpting. During the early years of his sculpting career, Barthe concentrated primarily on bust portraiture.

In 1929, Barthe received a Rosenwald Grant to pursue his studies in New York City. Between 1933 and 1936, the Whitney Museum purchased three of Barthe's works, *Blackberry Woman, Comedian,* and *African Dancer.*

By 1936, Barthe had had six one man shows in New York City. His work ranged from portrait busts such as *Mask, Black Boy, Filipino Head, The Blackberry Woman,* and *West Indian Girl,* to African portraits. Barthe's art won him the admiration of his colleagues. He was elected to the National Academy of Arts and Letters, the first African American sculptor so honored.

• Sterling Brown, a writer and educator, was born.

Sterling Brown was born in Washington, D.C. He attended Williams College and Harvard University. Brown taught at such institutes of higher learning as Virginia Seminary, Fisk, Howard, Lincoln, Vassar, Minnesota and the New School. During the Depression, Brown served as editor for African American affairs on the Federal Writers Project, and was a staff member of the Carnegie, Myrdal study of the African American.

Brown's works include *Southern Road,* a book of narrative and lyrical poems published in 1932, much of which is in dialect and two 1928 studies of the African American entitled *The Negro in American Fiction* and *Negro Poetry and Drama.* In 1941, Brown edited *Negro Caravan,* an anthology of African American writers.

• Beauford Delaney, a painter, was born in Knoxville, Tennessee (December 31).

• Jester Hairston, a music arranger and choir conductor, was born in Pennsylvania. Hairston arranged the choral soundtracks for dozens of films and was popularly known for his appearances on the television shows *Amos 'n' Andy* and *Amen.*

• Adelaide Hall, a singer, was born in Brooklyn, New York (October 20).

• William H. Johnson, a painter, was born in Florence, South Carolina (March 18). Johnson would become the first modern African American artist to be given a retrospective by the National Museum of American Art.

• "Blind" Willie McTell was born in Georgia (May 5).

• Roy Wilkins, the long time executive director of the NAACP, was born (August 30).

Roy Wilkins was born in St. Louis, Missouri. His mother died when Wilkins was quite young. As a result of his mother's untimely death, Wilkins was raised by an aunt in St. Paul, Minnesota.

Wilkins attended the University of Minnesota where he majored in sociology. While a college student, Wilkins edited a weekly publication for African Americans entitled, *The St. Paul Appeal.* Around this same time, Wilkins became the secretary of the local NAACP chapter.

Upon his graduation from the University of Minnesota in 1923, Wilkins accepted a job as managing editor of the African American weekly, *The Call,* in Kansas City, Missouri. Soon after arriving in Kansas City, Wilkins once again became the secretary of the local NAACP chapter.

While still in Kansas City, during the 1930s, Wilkins initiated a vigorous editorial campaign against a segregationist Senator. This campaign brought Wilkins to the attention of the national NAACP.

In 1931, Wilkins joined the National Secretariat of the NAACP as assistant executive secretary. In 1932, by disguising himself as an itinerant laborer, Wilkins investigated the treatment of African Americans on Mississippi flood-control projects for the NAACP. His reporting led to a Senate investigation and an upgrading of working conditions.

From 1934 to 1949, Wilkins succeeded W. E. B. Du Bois as editor of the *Crisis*, the official magazine of the NAACP. During World War II, Wilkins served as a consultant to the War Department on the training and placement of African Americans, and he was a consultant to the American delegation to the United Nations Conference in San Francisco in 1945.

In 1949, Roy Wilkins became acting executive secretary of the NAACP when Walter White took a leave of absence. At the same time, Wilkins was made chairman of the National Emergency Civil Rights Mobilization. This organization dispatched some 4,000 people to Washington in January of 1950 in a civil rights demonstration.

When Walter White returned to the NAACP in June of 1950, Wilkins became administrator of internal affairs. Wilkins held this position until 1955 when Walter White died. Upon White's death, Wilkins was chosen to serve as the executive secretary of the NAACP. In 1965, Roy Wilkins became the executive director for the organization.

Roy Wilkins was one of the major sponsors of the August 28, 1963, March on Washington.

Beginning in 1964, a rift began to develop in the civil rights movement between moderate civil rights leaders, personified by Roy Wilkins and Martin Luther King, and more militant African Americans. This rift continued to widen. By the July 1966 NAACP annual convention, Wilkins had come to characterize the concept of "black power" as "a reverse Hitler, a reverse Ku Klux Klan." At its July, 1968 convention, a group of young radicals walked out in protest against the moderation of the NAACP.

• *Notable Deaths:* There were 130 African Americans lynched in 1901.
• Edward Mitchell Bannister (1828–1901), an African American artist, died.

Edward Mitchell Bannister was born in New Brunswick, Canada. His parents were Edward Bannister of Barbados and Hannah Alexander Bannister, a native of St. Andrews, in New Brunswick, Canada.

Bannister studied in Boston, but later moved to Providence, Rhode Island. While in Providence, Bannister helped to start the Providence Art Club (the predecessor to the Rhode Island School of Design) and became the first African American to achieve recognition as a landscape artist. Specializing in marine landscapes, Bannister was awarded a medal at the Philadelphia Centennial Exposition in 1876 for a landscape painting entitled, *Under the Oaks. Narragansett Bay* and *After the Storm* are two of Bannister's other most noted paintings.

• Hiram Rhoades Revels (1822–1901), the first African American to be elected to the United States Senate, died in Holy Springs, Mississippi (January 16).

Possibly of Croatan Indigenous American and African American descent, Hiram Rhoades Revels was born of free parents in North Carolina. He attended Quaker seminaries in Indiana and Ohio, and Knox College in Illinois.

Revels was ordained a minister of the African Methodist Episcopal Church in 1845 and for the next fifteen years, he taught and preached in the Northwestern states. During the Civil War, Revels helped to organize African American regiments. He was made a chaplain for African American troops stationed in Mississippi.

In 1866, Revels settled in Natchez, Mississippi. In Natchez, he was elected an alderman (1868) and later became a Senator in the State Legislature (1869). In 1870, Revels became the United States Senator for the State of Mississippi when he was elected by the Legislature to fill an unexpired term.

After 1871, Revels devoted his time to religious and educational activities. Revels was president of Alcorn College, and in 1876 he became the editor of the *Southwestern Christian Advocate*.

• *Miscellaneous State Laws:* Alabama adopted a "grandfather clause" for voting purposes.
• North Carolina and Virginia instituted Jim Crow laws for streetcars.
• *Publications:* Booker T. Washington published his classic autobiography, *Up From Slavery*.

Up from Slavery is a classic American success story. Its great popularity in the first decade of the twentieth century won many new financial supporters for Tuskegee Institute and for Washington personally.

• Charles Chestnutt published *The Marrow of Tradition,* a novel. *The Marrow of Tradition* was based upon actual events which occurred in Wilmington, North Carolina, during the 1898 elections, when African American voters were driven from the polls. The moral dilemma presented in the novel was central to the African American community at the time.

The moral question was: Should the African American (as represented by the protagonist Dr. Miller) retaliate against his European American oppressors with violence, or should he suppress his desire for revenge and try to win the European Americans over with Christian love and understanding. In the novel, Dr. Miller chose Christian love.

• Paul Laurence Dunbar published *The Fanatics,* a novel.

• William M. Trotter and George Forbes founded the *Boston Guardian* (also known as *The Guardian*), a militant newspaper which advocated absolute equality for African Americans. *The Guardian* was a sounding board for those espousing ideas which ran counter to those advocated by Booker T. Washington.

• Archibald Henry Grimke published *Right on the Scaffold, or The Martyrs of 1822.*

• Alberry Whitman published *The Octoroon.*

• *The Arts:* Henry Ossawa Tanner's *Daniel in the Lion's Den* was awarded the silver medal at the Pan-American Exposition in Buffalo, New York.

• *The Performing Arts:* The Coleridge-Taylor Society was founded in Washington, D. C., to study and perform the music of England's most honored black composer, Samuel Coleridge-Taylor. Coleridge-Taylor had gained a world-wide reputation with his composition *Hiawatha's Wedding Feast.*

• Bert (Egbert Austin) Williams made a recording for the Victor Talking Machine Company.

Between 1901 and 1903, Bert Williams recorded fifteen titles, primarily show tunes or comedy routines that he had done on stage. In 1910, Williams was the first African American to receive feature billing in the Ziegfeld Follies. He remained with the Ziegfeld Follies until 1919.

• *Sports:* Jimmy Winkfield won the Kentucky Derby riding His Eminence.

• Joe Walcott (1873–1935), a welterweight, became world champion. Joe Walcott would hold this title until 1904.

Joe Walcott defeated Rube Ferns and won the title at Fort Erie, Ontario, on December 18. Born in Barbados, West Indies, Walcott was sometimes known as the "Barbados Demon."

• Charles Grant, a second baseman, became the first African American baseball player in the American League. At the time,

the American League was not yet a major league. Grant played under the name Charles Tokahama, claiming he was a full-bloodied Cherokee. A former member of the black Columbia Giants, Grant played for the Baltimore Orioles until the deception was exposed.

THE AMERICAS

• *Canada:* In Canada, the African American population stood at 17,437. However, Jamaicans and Haitians were not counted in the census classification as "Negro." Of the 17,437, some 13,600 were not yet twenty-one.

• In 1901, the *Saint Paul Broadax,* an African American newspaper, began running articles in which the premier of Manitoba extended cordial invitations to all readers. This invitation sparked African American interest in immigrating to Canada.

• Edward Mitchell Bannister (1828–1901), an African American artist born in Canada, died. *See 1901: The United States: Notable Births.*

• In 1901, on the occasion of the death of Queen Victoria, Anderson Abbott composed a poem entitled "Neath the Crown and Maple Leaf (Afro-Canadian Elegy)." This poem expressed Abbott's profound sense of pride in being both black and Canadian.

• *Cuba:* The Cuban Constitution was drafted. The Cuban Constitution incorporated the Platt Amendment which gave the United States the right to intervene.

• Fulgencio Batista was born.

Fulgencio Batista (1901–1973) was born in Oriente Province of COTW parents. He received little formal education.

As a young boy, Batista had jobs as a cane cutter, railroad brakeman, carpenter's apprentice, and tailor's apprentice. In 1921, he joined the army as a private. By 1928, Batista was promoted to sergeant stenographer, a position that allowed him to become widely known among the enlisted men.

In September 1933, Batista engineered an uprising of non-commissioned officers. The revolt succeeded in deposing the United States backed President Carlos Manuel de Cespedes. The revolt also led to the establishment of the revolutionary government of Ramon Grau San Martin.

Batista overthrew San Martin in January 1934 with the approval of the United States government. Batista then installed as president the traditional politician Carlos Mendieta Montefur.

Montefur's principal task was to secure United States recognition and to bring a measure of stability to the island.

These goals were achieved and national presidential elections were held in early 1936.

The next president, Miguel Mariano Gomez, son of the republic's second president, served less than a year. When he vetoed a bill favored by Batista for a system of rural schools to be operated by the military, Batista had him impeached.

The Batista puppet was Federico Laredo Bru. During Bru's tenure, Batista implemented much of the highly publicized Three Year Plan. Legislation provided workers with pensions, workmen's compensation, and minimum wages.

Unionization of workers was encouraged through formation of the Confederation de Trabadores de Cuba. Significant gains were realized in health, sanitation, and public education, and security of tenure was given to tenant farmers.

In 1938, Batista called for a constituent assembly to write a new constitution. A truce between the warring political factions allowed Batista's most formidable political enemy, Ramon Grau, to return to Cuba.

In 1940, Batista ran for president against Grau. Batista won.

For the next few years, Batista presided over a stable and peaceful Cuba. During World War II, Cuba experienced prosperity as the chief sugar supplier to the United States and its allies.

From 1943 to 1944, Batista had two prominent Communist Party members, Juan Marinello and Carlos Rafael Rodriguez in his cabinet. In 1944, Batista's hand picked successor, Carlos Saladrigas lost the election to Ramon Grau.

For the next six years, Batista lived in self-imposed exile in Florida. However, while living in Florida, Batista was elected to the Cuban Senate in absentia.

Batista returned to power in Cuba on March 10, 1952, when he led a military coup against the regime of Carlos Prio Socarras. Batista immediately suspended the constitution, closed down Congress, and outlawed all political parties.

In November 1954, Batista held elections in an effort to legitimize his rule. Batista's only real opponent was former President Ramon Grau. Grau withdrew when he realized the outcome was rigged.

When a small pleasure boat landed in Oriente Province in December 1956 with 82 revolutionaries led by Fidel Castro, few of Batista's supporters paid much attention. However, for the next two years Castro would wage a classic guerrilla campaign against Batista. Castro eventually forced Batista to become more autocratic in his treatment of dissenters.

On the last day of 1958, Fulgencio Batista went into exile for life.

• *Haiti:* Demesvar Delorme (1831–1901), a journalist, novelist, and essayist, died.

Demesvar Delorme was born in Cap-Haitien on February 10, 1831. Delorme loved to read and received a good education in Haiti. Delorme engaged in politics, and in 1865 fought on the side on Salnave. When Salnave became president, he appointed Delorme Minister of External Relations and, later on, Minister of Public Education and Cults.

In 1868, Delorme was exiled. He went to live in Paris where he remained for ten years and published several of his works.

Delorme wrote theoretical essays that were closely related to journalism.

ASIA

• Percy Chen, a noted Afro-Chinese businessman, was born.

Percy Chen was born in Trinidad in 1901. He was the eldest son of Ch'en Yu-jen *(see 1878)*. Percy studied law in England and was made a member of the Middle Temple. Percy was called to the English bar at the age of 21. He later practiced law for several years in Trinidad.

Percy Chen went to China in the fall of 1926. He was appointed a member of the staff of the Foreign Office of the Nationalist Government and followed the Nationalist armies to Hankow during their Northern Punitive Expedition.

In 1927, Percy was commissioned by the Nationalist Government to conduct Borodin and other Russian advisors to their own country. Percy subsequently served as an advisor to the General Motors Corporation in their negotiations with the Soviet Commissariat of Heavy Industry.

AUSTRALIA

• Peter Jackson, the "Black Prince," the former Australian and British boxing champion, died. *See 1886.*

AFRICA

• *North Africa, Egypt and Sudan:* Morocco granted France control of the frontier police (July 20).

• Delcasse stated the policy of French predominance in Morocco (July 27).

• An Anglo-Italian agreement was reached regarding the Sudan frontier (December 7).

• The *tertib*, a tax on income from land and livestock, was introduced into Morocco.

• *Western Africa:* The British initiated campaigns to put down slave raiding in Kantagora and Nupe.

• The Slavery Proclamation abolished the status of slavery in Nigeria (April 1).

• Kolumbo was taken by France (April). The Baoule chiefs were compelled to submit (July).

• A Jufunco uprising against the Portuguese occurred.

• The Kingdom of Ashanti was annexed to the Gold Coast Colony (September 25). A protectorate was proclaimed.

• Yola was taken by the British (September).

In 1900, the British under Frederick Lugard took over the administration of Northern Nigeria from the Royal Niger Company, but Zubeiru, the ruler of the Fula emirate of Adamawa, refused to submit to British authority. Lugard considered him the worst slave trader in Africa, and determined to bring Adamawa under British control.

In 1901, British forces stormed and captured Yola, Zubeiru's capital, but Zubeiru escaped. He was replaced there by his brother.

Zubeiru and his followers kept on the move. He briefly attempted to ally with the French and Germans in neighboring Chad and Cameroon, but ended up fighting the Germans who massacred most of his remaining troops.

• There was an incident at Argungu between the French and the British. Captain C. V. Keyes was shot.

• The Administrator of the Gambia was made Governor.

• Samuel Johnson (1846–1901), a noted Yoruba historian, died.

Samuel Johnson's father was a Yoruba slave who had been seized at sea by the British anti-slave patrol and freed at Sierra Leone. Samuel was born in Freetown.

Samuel was educated in Freetown (Sierra Leone) and in Ibadan (Nigeria). Samuel's father was reported to be an evangelist in Ibadan in 1859.

Johnson became a school teacher and catechist until he was ordained a priest. In 1886, he was posted to Oyo, which formerly had been the predominant state in Yorubaland.

It was in Oyo that Samuel Johnson wrote *History of the Yorubas. History of the Yorubas* is a chronicle of Yorubaland from its mythical beginnings to the 19th century civil wars. Johnson finished *History of the Yorubas* in 1897.

Johnson first submitted *History of the Yorubas* to his sponsor, the CMS. CMS refused to publish Johnson's treatise. CMS claimed that the book was too long. Unwilling to take "no" for an answer, Johnson sent it to another publisher. Unfortunately, it was lost.

After his death, Johnson's brother rewrote the *History* from notes and earlier drafts. The revised version of the *History* was published in 1921.

Today, Johnson's *History of the Yorubas* remains the most definitive source of pre–19th century Yoruba history.

• *Central Africa:* Buea became the capital of Cameroon.

• *Eastern Africa:* The Uganda railway reached Lake Victoria from Mombasa.

• An Anglo-German agreement was finalized concerning the boundaries of Nyasaland and German East Africa.

• The Ankole agreement was finalized (August). Small local kingdoms were included in Ankole.

• The Italians made the Sultanate of Mijurtein, Somali, a protectorate.

• The Uganda railway influenced the settlement policies in Kenya.

• A labor bureau was established in Zanzibar.

• Sleeping sickness (trypanosomiasis) was first diagnosed in Uganda by Drs. J. H. and A. Cook.

• The last Sudanese mutineers in Uganda were rounded up.

• A British administrative officer was appointed to oversee Kakunguru at Budaka. Kakunguru was moved to Mbale.

• Cecil Rhodes' Transcontinental Telegraph Company line reached Ujiji from Abercorn.

• *Southern Africa:* Kitchener used a scorched earth policy to counter the Boer guerrillas (January). In February, Botha's raid on Natal and De Wet and Hertzog's invasion of the Cape Colony met with failure. On February 26, Kitchener and Botha met at Middleburg but failed to agree.

• A graded Civil Service was established in northeast Rhodesia.

• Solomon Plaatje launched the first independent Tswana language newspaper, *Koranta ea Bechuana*. Plaatje used the paper as a platform to oppose European encroachments on African rights.

RELATED HISTORICAL EVENTS

• *The United States:* President McKinley was assassinated (September 6). Theodore Roosevelt became the new President of the United States.
• *Europe:* Queen Victoria died (January 22). She was succeeded by Edward VII.
• *Africa:* Oreste Baratieri (1841–1901), an Italian general, died.

After serving as governor from 1892 to 1896 of Italian held Eritrea, Baratieri was named commander-in-chief over an invasion of Ethiopia.

Baratieri was overwhelmingly defeated by the Ethiopian Emperor Menelik II at the Battle of Adowa on March 1, 1896. This defeat was the worst setback ever experienced by a European power in sub-Saharan Africa.

Lucky to escape with his life, Baratieri retired in disgrace.

• Marthinus Wessel Pretorius (1819–1901), the president of both the Transvaal Republic and the Orange Free State Republic through the formative years of Afrikaner independence, died.

During the early years of his life, Pretorius participated in many of the exploits of his father, Andries Pretorius, finally settling near him in the Transvaal. When his father died in 1853, Marthinius was named commandant-general of the Afrikaners in the Transvaal.

Pretorius then worked to unify the various small "republics" of the Transvaal into the new Transvaal Republic. After a constitution was promulgated in 1857, Pretorius was elected first president of the new republic.

Pretorius was a leading advocate of unification of the Transvaal with the Orange Free State Republic, and was elected the latter's president in 1860. He resigned his Transvaal post to administer the Free State for three years. After this "sabbatical," Pretorius returned to the Transvaal where he was once again elected president.

During this period, Pretorius obtained diplomatic recognition of the Transvaal from the United States and a number of European powers and he worked to obtain a sea port for his country.

In 1871, Pretorius resigned after mis-handling the Transvaal's case in a dispute over possession of the recently discovered diamond fields. He emerged from retirement in 1877 to lead Afrikaner resistance to British annexation of the Transvaal by Theophilus Shepstone.

With Stephanus (Paul) Kruger and P. J. Joubert, Pretorius formed a triumvirate government which led the Transvaal back to independence. He then permanently retired from public life.

• Hendrik Frensch Verwoerd (1901–1966), a future South African prime minister, was born.

Hendrik Verwoerd was born in the Netherlands and came to South Africa with his family as a child. After being educated in the Cape, Southern Rhodesia (Zimbabwe), Holland and Germany, Verwoerd was appointed professor of applied psychology at Stellenbosch University in 1927.

Later Verwoerd became chairman of the University's department of sociology. Verwoerd's political career began in 1937 when he became founder and editor of *Die Transvaler*, a Nationalist party newspaper in the Transvaal. In the pages of *Die Transvaler*, Verwoerd revealed himself as anti–Semitic, anti–British and pro–Fascist.

In 1943, Verwoerd sued another paper which accused him of being pro–Nazi, but lost the case. Throughout this period, he was active in reactionary Afrikaner groups.

When D. F. Malan came to power in 1948, Verwoerd was defeated in a parliamentary election. He instead entered the senate as a government nominated member. Verwoerd was later appointed Minister of Bantu Affairs and served in that capacity from 1950 to 1958.

As Minister of Bantu Affairs, Verwoerd elaborated a segregation policy known as apartheid —"apartness." Under apartheid, Verwoerd sought to strip non–European South Africans of most of their legal rights.

Verwoerd became prime minister in 1958 when Malan's successor Johannes Strydom died. One of Verwoerd's first acts was to remove the last vestiges of non–European representation from the parliament.

Verwoerd continued Malan's drive to establish a republic, narrowly carrying a national referendum on this issue in 1960.

About this same time, government police responded to a protest demonstration by shooting down a hundred Africans at Sharpeville.

Verwoerd responded quickly by outlawing the two main African political bodies, the African National Congress and the Pan African Congress.

Shortly after banning the two African political bodies, an English-speaking farmer tried to assassinate Verwoerd. Verwoerd's survival reinforced his image as a divinely inspired leader and made his position stronger among the European South African electorate.

In 1961, Verwoerd withdrew South Africa from the British Commonwealth when it became clear that its continued membership would lead to other nations' withdrawal. A republic was then declared.

In 1962, Verwoerd initiated perhaps the most significant racial policy in the country's history — the Bantustan program. The Bantustan program was designed to include the enforced repatriation of urban Africans to "tribal" reserves, which theoretically would eventually be granted full independence.

In 1966, Verwoerd was stabbed to death on the floor of parliament by a mentally disturbed messenger.

---

1 9 0 2

THE UNITED STATES

• John D. Rockefeller pledged $1,000,000 to an agency that was being created to promote education without discrimination as to race, sex or creed. Rockefeller's gift led to the formation of the General Education Board in 1903.

• Alabama and Mississippi Democrats adopted "white primaries."

• Robert Terrell (1857–1925) was the first African American to serve as a judge in a federal capacity when he was appointed justice of the peace in Washington, D. C. A 1884 *magna cum laude* graduate of Harvard, Terrell took his law degree at Howard University Law School in Washington, D. C., in 1889.

• *The Labor Movement:* In 1902, the International Longshoremen's Association had 20,000, of whom 6,000 were African Americans.

• Wages for farm workers in South Carolina were $10.79 per month while in New York the wages were $26.13 per month.

• *Notable Births:* Marion Anderson, a concert and opera singer (contralto) who was called the "Voice of the Century," was born (February 17).

Marion Anderson was born in Philadelphia. She studied with Giuseppe Boghetti, and was given a European scholarship by the National Association of Negro Musicians.

During her career, Marion Anderson sang with many orchestras, including the Philadelphia Symphony and the New York Philharmonic.

Marian Anderson made her Town Hall debut in 1935. She sang first with the Metropolitan Opera in 1955, made a world-wide concert tour for the State Department in 1957, and in 1958 served on the United States United Nations delegation.

• Gwendolyn Bennett, a Harlem Renaissance poet, was born (July 8).

• Arna Bontemps, a poet, novelist, and librarian, was born in Alexandria, Louisiana (October 13).

• Bluesman Eddie "Son" House, Jr., was born (March 21).

• Langston Hughes (1902–1967), a poet considered by many to be the "poet laureate of Harlem," was born (February 1).

Langston Hughes' was born in Joplin, Missouri. He was educated at Columbia and Lincoln universities. He was a recipient of Guggenheim and Rosenwald Fellowships, and poet-in-residence at the University of Chicago from 1949 to 1950.

Langston Hughes early poems appeared exclusively in the *Crisis* and expressed pride in his African American heritage. Between 1931 and 1940, Hughes' poems angrily protested against the injustices perpetrated against African Americans by European Americans.

From 1940 until his death in 1967, Hughes wrote of the African American in a manner which de-emphasized the African American's relation to the European American world.

The works of Langston Hughes include *Weary Blues and Fire* (1926); *Fine Clothes to the Jew* (1927); *Not Without Laughter* (the Harmon Literary Award winner in 1930); *Ways of White Folks* (1934); *The Big Sea* (1940); *Shakespeare in Harlem* (1942); *Fields of Wonder* (1947); *Simple Speaks His Mind* (1950); *Montage on a Dream Deferred* (1951); *Laughing to Keep from Crying* (1952); *First Book of Negroes* (1952); *Simple Takes a Wife* (1953); *Famous American Negroes* (1954); *Sweet Flypaper of Life* (1955); *I Wonder as I Wander* (1956); *Tambourines to Glory* (1958); *Selected Poems* (1959); *African Treasury* (1960); *Ask Your Mama* (1961); *Fight for Freedom* (1962); *Five Plays* (1963); and *Simple's Uncle Sam* (1965).

• William H. Johnson, an artist, was born.

William H. Johnson was born in Florence, South Carolina. Johnson studied under Charles Hawthorne and George Luks at the New York National Academy of Design. Johnson won both Cannon and Hall Garten prizes given by the Academy.

In 1926, Johnson was sent to France by the New York National Academy of Design. While in France, Johnson fell under the influence of Cezanne, Rouault and Soutine.

In 1930, upon returning from Europe, William H. Johnson won the Harmon Medal for a series of French and Danish landscape scenes, and still-lifes.

Johnson returned to Florence, South Carolina and did a series of regional landscapes and portraits of African American residents. Johnson's Southern pictures are noted for their atmospheric effects and the keen eye for satire and realism.

• James Melvin "Jimmie" Lunceford (1902–1947), a jazz musician, was born.

"Jimmie" Lunceford was born in Seaside, Oregon. He studied music with Paul Whiteman's father, Wilberforce J. Whiteman, Jr., and graduated from Fisk University. Lunceford also studied at the City College of New York.

In the mid–1920s, Lunceford played reeds with the bands of Elmer Snowden and Wilber Sweatman. Lunceford began leading his own band in Memphis in 1927.

In Buffalo, from 1930 to 1933, Lunceford became nationally known. His band was among the most successful African American bands of the 1930s. Lunceford's swing arrangements were by Sy Oliver, his trumpet player, and Edwin Wilcox, his pianist.

• James Lesesne Wells, an artist, was born (November 2).

James Lesesne Wells was born in Atlanta, Georgia. The son of a minister, Wells was educated at Lincoln University, Columbia University and the National Academy of Design. Wells also taught an adult education program at the Harlem Art Workshop which was sponsored by the Harlem Public Library.

Greatly influenced by African design motifs, Wells distinguished himself in media such as wood blocks, etching and lithography, emphasizing design over human representation.

Wells had one-man shows at the Weyhe Galleries, the Delphic Studios and the Brooklyn Museum. His lithographs include a series on African design motifs, views of industrial towns, illustrations of the Bible and sketches of CCC (Civilian Conservation Corps) camp activities. Wells also had a successful career as an oil painter. His *Flight into Egypt* won the Harmon Gold Medal in 1931. Several of Wells' oils were purchased by the Phillips Memorial Gallery in Washington, D. C.

• William "Peetie" Wheatstraw, a blues musician, was born (December 21).

• *Notable Deaths:* 85 African Americans were lynched in 1902.

• James Madison Bell (1826–1902), a noted African American poet, died.

James Madison Bell (1826–1902) was an African American poet. In 1842, Bell moved to Cincinnati and, in 1854, he moved to Chatham, Canada. Bell was a personal friend of the abolitionist John Brown. In 1859, Bell assisted Brown in raising funds and recruiting followers for his tragic raid.

In 1860, Bell moved to California and, in California, his career as a poet began to be noticed. Bell's most successful poems were *The Day and the War* and *The Progress of Liberty*. In 1865, Bell left California for his native Ohio. Upon his return, he was elected a delegate to the Ohio State Convention for Lucas County. Bell later became a delegate-at-large from Ohio to the National Republican Convention.

• William Still (1821–1902), author of *Underground Railroad*, and a leading underground railroad spokesperson, died.

William Still (1821–1902) was the son of Levin Steel, a former Maryland slave who had purchased his freedom and changed his name from "Steel" to "Still" to protect his wife, Sidney, who had escaped from slavery. William Still moved to Philadelphia in 1844, and in 1847 he became a clerk in the office of the Pennsylvania Society for the Abolition of Slavery.

Between 1851 and 1861, Still served as chairperson and corresponding secretary of the Philadelphia branch of the Underground Railroad. His account of the activities of the Underground Railroad was published in 1872 under the highly appropriate title of *Underground Railroad*.

In 1864, Still was appointed post sutler (camp supply provisioner) at Camp William Penn, a military post for African American soldiers which was located near Philadelphia. Later in his life, Still was involved in the campaign against the regulation of Philadelphia streetcar lines compelling all persons of color to ride in the front of platforms.

Still's literary works included *A Brief Narrative of the Struggle for the Rights of the Colored People of Philadelphia in the City Railway Cars* (1867), and *An Address on Voting and Laboring* (1874). In 1880, Still helped to establish the first African American YMCA.

- Alberry Whitman (1851–1902), a noted African American poet, died.

Alberry Whitman was born a slave. After emancipation, Whitman went to Wilberforce University. At Wilberforce, he came under the influence of Bishop Daniel Payne. Whitman was widely read and cultivated. His memory was particularly notable.

In 1873, Whitman published his first volume of poetry. It was entitled *Leelah Misled* and was an apolitical volume of verse.

In 1877, Whitman published *Not a Man and Yet a Man* a 20 volume epic. In *Not a Man and Yet a Man*, Whitman relates the story of a COTW slave who rescues his owner's daughter during an Indian (Indigenous American) uprising. The COTW slave falls in love with the young woman and the long narrative follows the lovers travails as the slave suffers tribulations which eventually lead him to Canada and his freedom.

In 1884, Whitman published another long narrative poem, *The Rape of Florida*. *The Rape of Florida* was done in Spenserian stanzas and is focused on the European oppression of the Seminoles. The significance of the poem was that Whitman saw the Seminoles in a position analogous to that of his own people.

In Whitman's subsequent long poems, *The Octoroon* (1901) and *The Southland's Charm and Freedom's Magnitude* (1902), Whitman showed a preference for COTW. Whitman claimed that pure blacks — pure Africans — do not exist. Whitman championed the acceptance of COTWs into European American society.

It is said that Whitman's poetry was the best done by an African American before the advent of Paul Laurence Dunbar.

- *Miscellaneous State Laws:* Louisiana instituted a Jim Crow (segregationist) street car law.
- Virginia adopted a "grandfather clause" amendment for its State Constitution.
- *Publications:* In 1902, Susie King Taylor's Civil War memoirs were published. *Reminiscences of My Life in Camp* is the only comprehensive written record of the life and activities of African American army nurses during the Civil War.

- Alberry Whitman published a poem entitled, *The Southland's Charm and Freedom's Magnitude.*
- Booker T. Washington published *Character Building.*
- Paul Laurence Dunbar published *The Sport of Gods,* a novel. *The Sport of Gods* reiterated the theme that the rural African American became demoralized in the urban North.
- Mifflin Wister Gibbs published *Shadow and Light.*
- *The Performing Arts:* Gertrude "Ma" Rainey began singing the blues. *See 1886.*

Ma Rainey of the Rabbit Foot Minstrels was the first to sing the blues in a professional show. She learned a blues song from a local woman in Missouri, and audience response was such that she began to specialize in the blues.

- In 1902, *In Dahomey,* a musical with lyrics and script by Paul Laurence Dunbar and music by Will Marion Cook, became the most artistically and financially successful of all African American musicals of the time. *In Dahomey* opened to enthusiastic notices on September 2, 1902, at the Globe Theater in Boston. *In Dahomey* starred Bert Williams and George Walker. The musical ran for three years. Like all African American musicals of the time, *In Dahomey* included dancing, full orchestration and lavish, spectacular scenery. In 1907, a command performance of *In Dahomey* was given for Edward VII in London.
- *Movies:* The French film *Off to Bloomingdale Asylum,* a slapstick comedy used African Americans for the first time in a movie. The director, George Melies, described the film as follows: "An omnibus drawn by an extraordinary mechanical horse carries four Negroes. The horse kicks and upsets the Negroes, who falling, are changed into white clowns. They begin slapping each other's faces and by blows become black again. Kicking each other, they become white once more. Suddenly they are merged into one gigantic Negro. When he refuses to pay his carfare, the conductor sets fire to the bus, and the Negro bursts into a thousand pieces."
- *Music:* In 1902, the collaboration Robert Cole and J. Rosamund Johnson produced *The Red Moon,* a song which met with some commercial and critical success.
- The Victor Talking Machine Company recorded the first African American music when it recorded the Dinwiddie Quartet.

• *Sports:* Jimmy Winkfield won the Kentucky Derby for the second year in a row. Winkfield rode Alan-a-Dale to victory. With this victory, African American jockeys had won 15 out of the first 28 Kentucky Derby races.
• Joe Gans (1874–1910) became the world lightweight champion. Joe Gans would hold this title until 1908.

Joe Gans (a.k.a. Joseph Gaines) was the first American born African American to win a world boxing title. On May 12, Gans defeated Frank Erne in one round at Fort Erie, Ontario. Born in Knoxville, Tennessee, Gans was elected to the Hall of Fame in 1954. Gans retired from boxing in 1910 and died of tuberculosis the following year.

THE AMERICAS

• *Barbados:* Sir Conrad Reeves (1821–1902), the chief justice of Barbados, died.
• *Canada:* In 1902, C. W. Brown, organized a Vancouver chapter of the Colored National Emigration Association. The Colored National Emigration Association was essentially a back-to-Africa organization. However, one of the other interests of the group was the development of a black presence in the Canadian West.
• *Cuba:* The Republic of Cuba was proclaimed and United States intervention came to an end.
• *Haiti:* President Tiresias Antoine Simon Sam resigned and was succeeded by Nord Alexis as President of Haiti.
• Massillon Coicou, an Afro-Haitian poet, published *Impression et Passion*, a thoughtful, meditative collection of poetry. *See 1865.*
• An exodus which lasted from this year through 1919 brought over 90,000 immigrants from Haiti and Jamaica to Cuba.

AFRICA

• *North Africa, Egypt and Sudan:* Britain and Ethiopia agreed on the Sudan frontier (August 15).
• The Aswan Dam was opened (December).
• Algerian law provided for the special "Organization of the Southern Territories of the Sahara."
• Bu Hamara (al-Rogui), a pretender to the Moroccan throne, started a revolt at Taza.
• *Western Africa:* Bauchi was captured by

the British (February). Bornu was compelled to submit.
• A French expedition was dispatched to Sout-el-Ma, Mauritania.
• Lieutenant Moncorge and Sergeant Richard were killed by Coniaguis at Boussara, Guinea (April 18).
• There were additional French operations against Baoule. In June, a post was established at Sakassou.
• Senegal was separated from the new Protectorate area of Senegambie-Niger.
• An Oyo uprising occurred against the Portuguese.
• The British conducted military campaigns in Yola, Bornu and Zaria.
• The Zungeru made their headquarters in northern Nigeria.
• A CMS mission was opened in Zaria.
• The Coppolani mission amongst the tribes of Mauritania was established.
• In 1902, Ahmadu Bamba, the leader of the Muridiyya Islamic brotherhood, was permitted to return to Senegal. Soon after his return, followers flocked to the revival of his movement. Amidst a new rumor of a Muridiyya uprising, the French once again exiled Ahmadu. This time he was sent to Mauritania.
• Sylvanus Olympio (1902–1963), the leader of the Togolese independence movement, was born.

Sylvanus Olympio was born in Lome while Togo was administered by Germany. After World War I, Togo was partitioned between France and Britain under a League of Nations mandate. Although Olympio lived in the French-ruled — the eastern — part of Togoland, Olympio studied at the London School of Economics. In 1926, Olympio was hired by the United Africa Company, for which he later became Togoland district manager.

Olympio first became politically active as a spokesman for the re-unification of his Ewe people. The Ewe had been divided by the division of Togoland. At the same time, Olympio advocated autonomy for French Togoland within the French community. When territorial elections were held in 1946, Olympio received the backing of Togo's first political party, and became president of the assembly.

In 1947, Olympio gained international recognition and respect when he spoke before the United Nations on the issue of Ewe unity. His campaign ultimately failed, not so much because of European opposition, but because the Ghanaian leader, Kwame Nkrumah, favored integrating British Togoland into Ghana. A plebiscite in British Togoland in 1956 supported Nkrumah, and the two territories were joined the next year.

In 1954, the French, under pressure because of Togo's special mandatory status, granted the territory an executive council. The French administration consistently opposed Olympio and his party, fearing that granting autonomy would set a precedent for French sub–Saharan Africa.

Instead of supporting Olympio, the French backed Nicholas Grunitzky (see 1913), a steadfast supporter of French policies in Togo.

In 1955, elections for the territorial assembly were boycotted by Olympio's party in response to French repression, and Grunitzky's party won. The following year, the Togolese took advantage of their special United Nations status and the Ewe unification issue to force France to make Togo a republic within the French community. Grunitzky became the first prime minister.

Grunitzky's French-supported regime was highly unpopular, and Olympio was able to pressure the United Nations to retain ultimate control over the Colony until the United Nations supervised elections took place.

In the 1958 elections, Olympio's party won. As leader of the government, Olympio agitated for complete independence. In 1960, independence was achieved and Olympio became president.

Although Olympio was for the most part a popular leader, opposition formed in the north and within the radical elements of his own party. In 1961, Olympio introduced a single party state.

In a nine-month period ending in January 1962, there were three assassination attempts on Olympio's life. Olympio's downfall came as a result of his refusal to accept into the army any Togolese who were French military veterans.

One night in January 1963, a group of ex-soldiers pursued Olympio through Lome. Olympio was killed at the gate of the United States embassy where he was about to seek asylum. The soldiers afterwards claimed that he was firing upon them.

Olympio was succeeded by his long time rival Grunitzky.

- *Central Africa:* Seven Protestant missions in the Congo met to discuss common problems (June 18–21).
- Samisasa was captured by the Portuguese (August 19).
- Germans arrived in Foumbau.

- The Portuguese campaigned on the Bie plateau.
- From 1902 to 1903, anarchy and terrorism reigned in Burundi.
- Leon M'ba (1902–1967), the future leader of Gabon, was born (February 9).

Leon M'ba was born in Libreville in Gabon. M'ba was educated in Catholic schools. He worked as an accountant, journalist, and administrator, and became a dominant figure in Libreville politics.

M'ba was active in the Gabon branch of the inter-territorial party known as the RDA, led by Felix Houphouet-Boigny (see 1905) of the Ivory Coast.

In 1951, M'ba stood as Gabon's RDA candidate for deputy to the French legislative assembly. It was a period of administrative repression against the then-radical RDA, and M'ba was defeated along with most other RDA candidates. The next year, however, M'ba was elected to Gabon's territorial assembly, and in 1956 became mayor of Libreville.

In 1957, when new laws permitted a large measure of self-government for France's African colonies, M'ba's party won the territorial elections and he formed a government.

When Gabon achieved independence in 1960, M'ba continued as head of state. M'ba was a strong supporter of Houphouet, the RDA leader. When Houphouet moved to break up a proposed federation of Francophonic West African territories, M'ba did the same for a planned Central African federation. The reasoning of the two men was the same — both were leaders of comparatively wealthy countries and, as such, would have contributed more financially to any federation than they would have received in return.

After independence, M'ba was criticized for being a conservative tool of the French. In 1960, M'ba imprisoned several members of his own party, including the president of the national assembly.

Outside the party, opposition coalesced around Jean Aubame. In 1964, M'ba tried to force Aubame to resign his seat in the assembly. Army officers intervened and installed Aubame as head of state. But M'ba's close ties with the French paid off; two days later the French military was called in, and M'ba was reinstated.

By 1966, and in failing health, M'ba was spending most of his time in Paris for treatment. When he died in 1967, M'ba's hand-picked successor Albert Bongo took over.

• *Eastern Africa:* The first political meeting of European settlers of Kenya formed the Colonists' Association (January).

• A Franco-Ethiopian agreement was reached on the finance of Djibouti-Addis Adaba railway and provoked protests from Britain and Italy (February 6).

• In 1902, Taitu, the wife of Menelik, the Emperor of Ethiopia, personally led a successful military campaign against rebels in Tigre.

• The Eastern Province of Uganda was transferred to the East African Protectorate (April 1).

• The Kenya Crown Land Ordinance inaugurated European settlement of Highlands (September 27).

• The Village Headmen Ordinance in Kenya became effective.

• Joseph Chamberlain, the Colonial Secretary, visited Kenya. Chamberlain recommended an area between the Mau escarpment and Nairobi for Jewish settlement.

• The Sultan of Zanzibar recognized Italian suzerainty over Banadir.

• After a visit to London in 1902, Apolo Kagwa, the de facto leader of Buganda, was knighted.

• Hastings Kamuzu Banda, the first president of Malawi, was born.

Hastings Banda left Nyasaland (Malawi) in 1915. He worked in a hospital for a few years in southern Rhodesia (Zimbabwe) and became interested in medicine.

Banda also served as a clerk in the mines near Johannesburg while saving money for an education in the United States.

In America, Banda completed high school, college, and medical school. To be able to practice medicine in Nyasaland, Banda then went to England for further certification.

Stranded in England during the duration of the Second World War, Banda set up practice in London and met with many other future African statesmen, including Kwame Nkrumah and Jomo Kenyatta.

When the issue of the federation of the Rhodesias and Nyasaland arose in the early 1950s, Hastings Banda lobbied relentlessly against Nyasaland's inclusion in a land which was certain to be dominated by Euro-African settlers from other territories.

During this same period, Hastings Banda gained recognition in Nyasaland as a nationalist leader in exile. Disenchanted with the British Labour government's approval of the Central

African (Rhodesia) Federation, Banda moved, in 1953, to the Gold Coast (Ghana) to practice medicine.

Once in Ghana, Banda began to be besieged by requests from Henry Chipembere and other Nyasaland leaders to return to Nyasaland. In 1958, Banda succumbed to these entreaties and returned to Nyasaland. Upon his return, he was immediately elected president-general of the Nyasaland African Congress (NAC).

In 1959, rumors of an impending insurrection prompted the colonial government to declare an emergency. Banda and other Nyasaland leaders were imprisoned for over a year and the NAC was banned.

On his release from jail in 1960, Hastings Banda assumed the presidency of the new Malawi Congress Party, formed by Orton Chirwa during Banda's imprisonment. Over the next three years, Banda led the country to independence and helped to force the dismemberment of the Central African Federation.

Hastings Banda was elected prime minister of Nyasaland in 1963. In 1964, Nyasaland became and independent nation known as Malawi.

Immediately after independence, Banda clashed with his cabinet whose members objected to his autocratic decisions. Banda dismissed several members while others resigned in protest. A revolt instigated by Henry Chipembere occurred which Banda quickly suppressed. Thereafter, Banda worked steadily to concentrate power within his own office.

Malawi became a republic in 1966 and Hastings Banda became its first president. In 1971, he became president for life.

Through several elections in the 1970s, Hastings Banda reduced the national assembly to a rubber-stamp body and effectively quashed political dissent.

Banda's opening of diplomatic relations with Euro-African ruled, apartheid bound South Africa in 1967 gave Banda access to economic support from Pretoria, but served further to isolate his regime from the rest of black ruled Africa.

• *Southern Africa:* Municipal councils were established in Madagascar (March 2).

• The Peace of Vereeniging ended the Boer War (May 31). Under the Peace, the Boers accepted British sovereignty. The British promised representative government and three million pounds for restocking farms.

In 1902, Louis Botha, the future prime minister of South Africa and the commander of the

Transvaal Republican army, signed the Peace of Vereeniging which ended the Boer War. Alfred Milner, the British high commissioner for South Africa, drafted the terms of the Peace of Vereeniging and, together with Kitchener, signed it for the British.

After the peace treaty had been signed, Milner radically reformed the administration of the conquered republics. He instituted English as the language to be used in the schools in an effort to unify all of South Africa. Milner repatriated Afrikaners to their farms but offended them by encouraging new British settlement as well.

- Cecil Rhodes died.
- The Labour Party was organized in South Africa.
- The African People's Organization was founded in Capetown by Dr. Abdallah Abdurahman.
- The Broken Hill Company was formed.
- The Portuguese campaigned in the Barue region.
- Chinsinga, the ruler of the Makanga kingdom of Mozambique, was executed.

Chinsinga became King of Makanga in 1893. At this point in time, the Portuguese government ceded administration of the region to a chartered company, which lacked the resources to control it. Chinsinga allied with the company in 1895 and assisted it in conquering the Ngoni chiefdom north of Makanga in 1898.

In 1901, Chinsinga was named the company's administrator in Makanga. The next year, Chinsinga was accused of embezzling company funds. The company, with Ngoni help, invaded Makanga. Chisinga's followers failed to support him. He was captured and executed in 1902.

The execution of Chisinga brought to an end the period of family-dominated states in the Zambezi valley.

RELATED HISTORICAL EVENTS

- *Europe:* A Franco-Italian agreement was reached on North Africa (November 1).
- Spain refrained from reaching an agreement with France concerning Morocco out of fear of antagonizing Great Britain (November 8).
- The first meeting of the Committee of Imperial Defence was convened in London (December 18).
- J. A. Hobson published *Imperialism.*
- Portugal prohibited the sale of rum to Africans.

- Uganda Order-in-Council was formed.
- Abuna Mateos, the Ethiopian Bishop, visited Russia.
- *Africa:* Sigismund Wilhelm Koelle (1823–1902), a German missionary and pioneer linguist, died.

Sigismund Koelle became an agent of the Anglican Church Missionary Society, and in 1843 was sent to Freetown, Sierra Leone. While teaching at Fourah Bay Institution, Koelle published studies of the Kanuri and Vai languages. His most important contribution was *Polyglotta Africana* which was published in 1854.

In *Polyglotta Africana,* Koelle recorded many African languages and dialects. Taking advantage of Freetown's uniqueness as a haven for slaves liberated at sea by the British anti-slavery squadron, Koelle collected a comparative vocabulary of African words from over 200 informants. Koelle included biographical sketches of his informants in his introductory remarks to *Polyglotta Africana.*

Because of his remarkable accuracy, Koelle's *Polyglotta Africana* remains, even to this day, as a valuable historical and linguistic resource.

- Cecil Rhodes (1853–1902), an British South African financier and statesman, died.

Cecil Rhodes (1853–1902) first came to South Africa for health reasons in 1870. After a brief stint on his brother's cotton farm in Natal, Rhodes went to Kimberley, where diamonds had just been discovered. Starting by selling ice cream, Rhodes gradually took advantage of chaos amongst the miners to gain control of a major part of the diamond industry.

In 1880, Rhodes joined with Alfred Beit to form the DeBeers Mining Company. Eight years later, Rhodes amalgamated — merged — with his chief rival, Barnett Barnato, to found the monopoly De Beers Consolidated Mines.

Rhodes then moved into the Transvaal gold fields, founding the powerful Gold Fields of Southern Africa Company in 1887. Rhodes retained leadership of both the diamond and gold mining companies and attracted considerable additional wealth from Britain to further political enterprises.

Imbued with the ideals of what he believed to be the superior British civilization, Rhodes alternated his residence between South Africa and Oxford, England. It was from Oxford that Rhodes had obtained a degree in 1881.

Rhodes regarded education as the key to Britain's civilizing role in the world and he bequeathed a large endowment to the Rhodes scholarship fund on his death.

In 1880, Rhodes was elected to the Cape Parliament. He remained a member of the parliament until his death in 1902. While serving in government, Rhodes served on various governmental commissions. He played a major role in extending British rule over the Tswana in the northwest Cape and in Botswana.

Rhodes became obsessed with the goal of extending British rule north of the Limpopo River. In 1888, his partner Charles Rudd obtained a monopoly mining concession from the Ndebele King Lobengula. Rhodes used this concession as a lever to obtain a crown charter for his new British South African Company in 1889.

Rhodes regarded this charter as giving him a free hand north of the Limpopo and sent agents north of the Zambezi to obtain further treaties. They succeeded in gaining concessions from the Lozi king Lewanika and the Lunda chief Mwata Kazembe in 1890. These concessions laid the basis for company administration in Zambia (Northern Rhodesia) until a protectorate was declared.

Around this same time, Rhodes interpreted Rudd's concession as conferring the right on his company to occupy eastern Zimbabwe (Mashonaland). After an administration was established in Mashonaland, Rhodes' agent Leander Jameson provoked a war with the Ndebele.

Rhodes' forces easily conquered the Ndebele in 1894. This victory gave Rhodes effective control of all of Zimbabwe. In tribute to this conqueror, Zimbabwe became "Rhodesia."

In Cape politics, Rhodes' Progressive Party sought to create a British-dominated South African federation with the cooperation of Cape Afrikaners. When the Progressives won the 1890 elections, Rhodes became prime minister.

Rhodes used his office and his financial influence to extend railway ties to Johannesburg. He annexed Pondoland to the Cape and supported the Glen Grey Act. This act was designed to westernize subject African communities by granting freehold land tenure to individuals and by establishing representative government among the Xhosa.

Impatient with the conservative Transvaal administration of Paul Kruger, Rhodes secretly planned an uprising of foreign residents — the uitlanders — in the Transvaal at the same time that he authorized Leander Jameson *(see 1895)* to invade the Republic from Rhodesia.

In the fiasco that followed the Jameson raid, Rhodes' complicity was revealed. Rhodes was compelled to resign his premiership as well as the leadership of the British South Africa Company.

One consequence of the Jameson raid was that Jameson's expedition drained Rhodesia of its police force and allowed the Shona and Ndebele to revolt. Rhodes salvaged his reputation by personally negotiating a settlement with Ndebele rebel leaders while Company and Imperial forces wore down the Shona.

Rhodes' intervention in the Transvaal cost him the support of Jan Hofmeyr and other Cape Afrikaner leaders and, thereby, contributed greatly to the outbreak of the South African (Boer) War in 1899.

On Rhodes' death in 1902, leadership of the Progressive Party was assumed by Leander Jameson, the leader of the ill-fated raid of 1895.

---

1 9 0 3

THE UNITED STATES

• From 1903 to 1909, John D. Rockefeller gave some $53,000,000 to the General Education Board in four large gifts, and empowered its trustees to dispose of the principle whenever they saw fit. The Board seemed especially interested in providing means for the preparation of teachers for African American schools located in the South.

• *Political Achievements:* In 1903, Christopher Harrison Payne was appointed United States Consul to St. Thomas in the Danish West Indies. Payne would remain in this position until 1917, when the islands were purchased by the United States and became known as the Virgin Islands.

• President Theodore Roosevelt appointed William D. Crum to be collector of the port of Charleston, South Carolina.

• *The Civil Rights Movement:* Fannie Garrison Villard opposed the reaction to African Americans in the North and objected to what she saw as a regression in abolitionist sentiment.

• *The Labor Movement:* William English Walling, Lillian Wald, Jane Addams and others founded the National Women's Trade Union League.

• *Notable Births:* Ella Baker, a civil rights activist, was born in Norfolk, Virginia. Baker would become the executive director of the Southern Christian Leadership Conference and would help to set up the Student Nonviolent Coordinating Committee.

• Countee Cullen (1903–1946), a distinguished African American poet of the 1920s, was born in Baltimore, Maryland (May 30).

Countee Cullen was born in New York City. He was the son of a minister. Cullen was educated in New York City, earning a bachelor of arts degree from New York University in 1925. Cullen was also elected to Phi Beta Kappa.

Cullen received his master of arts degree from Harvard University in 1926.

Cullen's poetry began to appear in the NAACP publication, the *Crisis*, when he was only 15. In 1923, his verse was published in European American magazines and in 1928 he received a Guggenheim Fellowship.

When Cullen began to write, he was influenced by Tennyson, Millay, Housman, Robinson and Keats. He was essentially a lyrical and emotional poet.

Color was Cullen's first and arguably best collection of poetry. It was published in 1925. From a technical standpoint, Countee Cullen had no peer among his contemporary African American poets. Much of his poetry dealt with Harlem African American life, but Cullen never tried to exploit African American themes. Some of Cullen's poems, such as *The Shroud of Color* and *Heritage* reflect the author's search for his identity and his African heritage. These themes would come to dominate much of the literature during the period known as the Harlem Renaissance and Cullen would come to be one of the luminaries of the era.

• Earl "Fatha" Hines, the "Father of Modern Jazz Piano," was born in Pennsylvania (December 28). Fatha Hines developed and popularized the trumpet style of piano playing.
• Bluesman Whittaker Hudson, better known as "Tampa Red" was born (December 15).
• Trumpeter "Bubber" Miley was born (January 19).
• Jimmy Rushing, a singer, was born (August 26).
• Fredi Washington (1903–1994), a pioneering African American actress, was born in Savannah, Georgia (December 23).

Fredricka "Fredi" Washington made her first cabaret appearance in New York at 16 as a member of the Happy Honeysuckles hired by Josephine Baker — Washington's foster mother. Washington was also a chorus girl in the musical "Shuffle Along" in 1921.

While performing at the Club Alabam in Manhattan, Washington was noticed by the producer Lee Schubert, who recommended her for the co-starring role opposite Paul Robeson in the play *Black Boy* (she played the role under her stage name Edith Warren).

At the end of the play's run, with no serious productions for African American actors in view, Washington turned to dancing and toured Europe with her dance partner, Al Moiret.

When she returned to the United States, she appeared in such stage productions as *Run, Little Chillun; Great Day; Singing the Blues; Mamba's Daughters; Lysistrata;* and *A Long Way From Home* (an all African American production of Gorky's *Lower Depths*).

Her film work included roles in *The Emperor Jones; Black and Tan Fantasy; Drums in the Night;* and *One Mile From Heaven*.

Washington's best known performance was as the young COTW who passed for white in the 1934 film *Imitation of Life*. Washington's performance was so convincing that she was accused of denying her heritage in her private life.

"She did pass for white when she was traveling in the South with Duke Ellington and his band," noted Jean-Claude Baker, a restaurateur, author and friend of Washington.

"They could not go into ice cream parlors, so she would go in and buy the ice cream, then go outside and give it to Ellington and the band. Whites screamed at her, 'Nigger lover!'"

Washington's marriage to Lawrence Brown, a trombonist in the Duke Ellington Orchestra, ended in divorce. Her second husband, Anthony Bell, died in the early 1980s.

Fredi Washington's legacy is that she was one of the first African American actresses to gain recognition for her work on stage and in film. She died on June 28, 1994 in Stamford, Connecticut.

• *Notable Deaths:* 99 African Americans were lynched in 1903.
• Solomon G. Brown (1829–1903), an assistant at the Smithsonian Institution, died.

Solomon G. Brown had little formal education but a great deal of work experience. As a young man, Brown worked for Samuel F. B. Morse, the inventor of the telegraph. In 1852, Brown accompanied Joseph Henry, a Morse associate, when Henry became the first secretary of the Smithsonian Institution.

Brown became an indispensable worker who prepared most of the illustrations for scientific lectures until 1887.

• Francis Louis Cardoza (1837–1903), a noted educator, died in Washington, D. C. (July 22).

Francis Louis Cardoza was born in Charleston, South Carolina, of a Jewish father and a COTW mother. Cardoza was educated abroad and, after the Civil War, became very active in Reconstruction politics. Cardozo would come to hold several government positions including Secretary of State for South Carolina.

As an academic, Cardoza later became the principal of the Colored Preparatory High School and its successor, the "M" Street High School, in Washington, D. C.

• *Miscellaneous State Laws:* Arkansas, South Carolina and Tennessee instituted Jim Crow (segregationist) laws.

• Kentucky and Texas Democrats adopted the "white primary."

• *Miscellaneous Cases:* An Arkansas Federal Court decision in *United States v. Morris* declared unconstitutional a law which discriminated against African Americans in housing.

• *Publications:* W. E. B. Du Bois published his classic, *The Souls of Black Folk. The Souls of Black Folk* was noted for its attacks against Booker T. Washington's ideas of work and money, Washington's lack of emphasis on dignity and manhood, and Washington's failure to oppose discrimination.

• Paul Laurence Dunbar published a collection of prose entitled *Lyrics of Love and Laughter.* Dunbar also published *In Old Plantation Days,* a book of verse.

• The poet, Joseph S. Cotter, Sr., of Louisville, Kentucky, published the drama, *Caleb, the Degenerate.* This drama was concerned with the racial theories of accommodation espoused by Booker T. Washington.

• *The Performing Arts:* Wilbur Sweatman (1882–1961) and his band recorded Scott Joplin's *Maple Leaf Rag* in a music store in Minneapolis, Minnesota. Sweatman was noted for playing three clarinets simultaneously.

• *Music:* Harry T. Burleigh composed *Jean,* a popular hit.

• *Scholastic Achievements:* Archibald Henry Grimke became president of the American Negro Academy. He would serve in this capacity until 1916.

• *The Arts:* In 1903, Meta Vaux Warrick Fuller's *The Wretched,* a sculpture exhibited at the Paris Salon, made Fuller famous in Parisian art circles. *The Wretched* depicted seven types of anguish. One of the admirers of her art was none other than the great Auguste Rodin.

• *Black Enterprise:* An African American real estate developer started developing Harlem as a prime source of housing for African Americans.

• Maggie Lena Walker became the first African American woman bank president when she founded Saint Luke Penny Savings Bank in Richmond, Virginia.

THE AMERICAS

• *Cuba:* A treaty between the United States and Cuba was signed. Under the treaty, the United States acquired the naval base at Guantanamo.

• *Panama:* The United States acquired the Panama Canal Zone. This acquisition affected the lives of thousands of persons of African descent living in the area. Many more persons of African descent from the Caribbean Islands were brought into the Canal Zone to construct and operate the canal.

AFRICA

• *North Africa, Egypt and Sudan: Al-Sudan,* the first Arabic newspaper in the Sudan, began publication.

• The Sultan of Morocco borrowed 800,000 pounds from British, French, and Spanish syndicates.

• *Western Africa:* Kano offered ineffective resistance to British occupation (January).

• An Anglo-French agreement was reached concerning the boundary of Gold Coast and Ivory Coast (February 1).

• The British initiated military campaigns against Sokoto and Kano. Kano submitted (February 3).

• Great Britain completed its conquest of north Nigeria (March 15).

• J. Biker, the Governor of Portuguese Guinea, exposed contract labor scandal in Angola.

• Attahiru Ahmadu, the ruler of the Sokoto Caliphate, was killed by British forces.

Attahiru Ahmadu succeeded Abdurrahman who died shortly before the British forces under the command of Frederick Lugard began their conquest of Northern Nigeria. Due to internal dissension within Sokoto, the Sokoto army was unable to mount an effective defense against the British forces. Attahiru was forced to flee.

As he fled, Attahiru reminded the people of Sokoto that the founder of the caliphate, 'Uthman dan Fodio, had prophesied that one day the faithful would be called to take the hijra — to take flight — to the east. Attahiru soon attracted a large following of people willing to abandon their homes to join him on the hijra.

British forces pursued Attahiru. Six times the British forces engaged Attahiru's followers. Six times they were beaten back. However, on the seventh time, the British forces defeated Attahiru some 1000 kilometers from Sokoto. It was there that Attahiru was killed.

However, Attahiru's hijra did not end with his death. As many as 25,000 of his followers continued on the journey. They traveled to the Blue Nile in Sudan where they came to rest and where their descendants continue to live today.

- Zubeiru, the former ruler of the Fula emirate of Adamawa of Nigeria, died.

When Zubeiru succeeded his brother, Sanda, he was considered unstable, and probably suffered from epilepsy. He began a program of Islamic fundamentalist reform. These reforms along with the perception of him held by his people, made Zubeiru unpopular and weakened his ability to withstand the challenge of Hayatu ibn Sa'id.

Hayatu was a great-grandson of the Fula Islamic revolutionary 'Uthman dan Fodio who had created the empire of which Adamawa was a part. Hayatu came to Adamawa and attracted a large following. Zubeiru felt compelled to fight him, but was disastrously defeated in 1892. Hayatu was unable to follow up his victory however and later was killed in Bornu.

Afterwards Zubeiru's chief concern was limiting the encroachment of George Goldie's Royal Niger Company, which had assumed that its 1886 treaty with Sokoto, the seat of the empire, permitted trade with Adamawa. Zubeiru refused to acknowledge the treaty, however, and signed separate agreements in 1893 and 1897.

In 1900, the British under Frederick Lugard took over the administration of Northern Nigeria from the Royal Niger Company, but Zubeiru refused to submit to British authority. Lugard considered him the worst slave trader in Africa, and determined to bring Adamawa under British control.

In 1901, British forces stormed and captured Yola, Zubeiru's capital, but Zubeiru escaped. He was replaced there by his brother.

Zubeiru and his followers kept on the move. He briefly attempted to ally with the French and Germans in neighboring Chad and Cameroon, but ended up fighting the Germans who massacred most of his remaining troops.

Early in 1903, Zubeiru had the German resident at Marua assassinated. Zubeiru began raiding again, as the British kept him on the run.

Zubeiru was killed in 1903 by Lala warriors who were hunting down slave raiders.

- *Central Africa:* From 1903 to 1910, a railway system was constructed in the Congo Free State.
- From 1903 to 1911, the Cameroon railway was built.
- In 1903, construction of the Benguela-Katanga railway was begun.
- A German expedition against Kissabo, the King of Burundi, was initiated.
- The Congo Free State expedition to Bahral-Ghazal was launched!
- *Eastern Africa:* Lord Delamere settled permanently in Kenya (June). Lord Delamere formed Kenya Planters and Farmers Association.
- Sir C. Eliot initiated a discriminatory policy against Indian land ownership in the East Africa Protectorate.
- Berlin II Mission started work in German East Africa.
- The first cotton seed was imported into Uganda.
- Mwanga II (c.1866–1903), the last independent ruler of the Ganda kingdom, died.

When Mwanga succeeded his father Mutesa I as king — Kabaka — of Buganda in 1884, Mwanga inherited an administrative structure undergoing a fundamental transformation. Before the time of Mutesa *(see 1884),* the kings had ruled through a powerful class of hereditary territorial chiefs.

The arrival of Christian missionaries in the late 1870s gave rise to a new class of younger religiously oriented officials. Educated Catholics, Protestants, and Muslims formed distinct administrative cadres within the kingdom. Though hostile to each others' creeds, they shared the common goal of reforming Ganda society. Mwanga's often capricious dealings with these groups incurred their hostility. A four way power struggle of shifting alliances developed between him and each of the religious factions.

Mwanga's father had patronized the newly educated officials and had allowed them to undermine the traditional deference which subjects accorded the kings, giving these men unprecedented influence in the kingdom. At first Mwanga allowed this new elite to carry on as under his father, but soon he became apprehensive of the increasing influence of Christianity. His alarm mounted in 1885 when he learned of the German annexation of present day Tanzania.

Encouraged by his prime minister — his katikiro—, Mwanga rashly sanctioned the killing of the Anglican Bishop Hannington — then on his way to Buganda. The next year, Mwanga sponsored a bloody purge of Christians in order to appease the older chiefs.

Nevertheless, Mwanga afterwards elevated many Christians to positions of power within modernized military bodies. He allowed these new armies to pillage Ganda peasants unchecked. The three main religious factions coalesced into strong and distinct fighting units.

In 1888, Mwanga attempted to abolish all three religious factions in a single stroke. His plan miscarried disastrously. All three groups united to drive Mwanga out of the country.

A new king was installed in Mwanga's place. Within a month, the dominant Muslim faction staged another coup, installing yet another king. The Christians fled from the country.

A four year civil war ensued. Mwanga was assisted by the Christians in his attempt to reclaim his throne. Mwanga rewarded the strongest Christian leader, Apolo Kagwa *(see 1869),* by making him his prime minister, even though his own position remained tenuous.

In 1890, European imperial forces entered the conflict. Encouraged by their missionaries, the Catholic and Protestant Ganda aligned themselves with German and British imperial interests respectively. Mwanga signed a treaty of friendship with the German agent Karl Peters, but an accord between Britain and Germany in Europe nullified this agreement, placing Uganda within the British sphere of influence.

Frederick Lugard soon arrived to establish a British protectorate. After a complicated series of wars and treaties, Apolo Kagwa's Protestant faction emerged as the dominant force in 1892.

A formal protectorate was declared over Buganda in 1894, but Mwanga chafed at his loss of power to Kagwa and other new chiefs. In 1897, Mwanga mounted a rebellion to drive the British out altogether. Mwanga drew widespread support from traditionalists, but not in sufficient numbers to carry his cause.

Mwanga withdrew into northwest Tanzania and later returned to carry on the struggle for two additional years. In the meantime, Mwanga was formally deposed and replaced by his one-year-old son Daudi Chwa II. The regency and real power in Buganda were then assumed by Kagwa Apolo and his faction.

Mwanga was finally captured in 1898. He was exiled to the Seychelles Islands where he died in 1903.

- *Southern Africa:* Joseph Chamberlain visited South Africa. The policy henceforward was aimed at reconciliation with the Boers (February).
- The Customs Conference at Bloemfontein anticipated the later federation of South Africa (March).
- The Commission in Transvaal favored using immigrant Chinese labor in Rand mines.
- The Afrikaner Bond became the South African Party.
- Swaziland came under the government of the Transvaal.
- Tobacco was introduced into south Rhodesia.
- State education for Europeans in south Rhodesia began.
- The Rhodesia Native Labour Bureau was established.
- The Lagden Native Affairs' Commission was created.
- In Namibia, the German Governor Leutwin moved troops south against the Bondelswarts Nama, and the Herero saw an opportunity to reclaim their land.

In 1903, Hendrik Witbooi, the leader of the Oorlam Khoikhoi, personally participated in the German campaign against the Bondelswarts Nama. At that moment, however, the Herero revolted against the Germans and Leutwin was replaced by General von Trotha as military commander in South West Africa.

Witbooi had regarded his treaty with the Germans as a personal bond with Leutwin. He felt that the latter's diminished status freed him from any obligations of loyalty to the Germans. Witbooi also resented the progressive alienation of Oorlam land to European settlers.

RELATED HISTORICAL EVENTS

- *Europe:* Sir Roger Casement's report on Belgian atrocities in the Congo was published (May).
- *Africa:* George Theal completed the nine volumes of *Records of South East Africa* (1898–1903).

• Paul Belloni Du Chaillu (1831– 1903), an American explorer of west-central Africa, died.

Of French heritage, Paul Belloni Du Chaillu spent his boyhood years on the Gabon River where his father was the agent for a French trading company. At the age of twenty-one, du Chaillu emigrated to Philadelphia and became a United States citizen.

In 1855, du Chaillu returned to Gabon as an explorer under the auspices of the Philadelphia Academy of Science. Du Chaillu spent several years collecting plant and animal specimens. When he returned to America, du Chaillu reported the discovery of gorillas, but he was unable to convince the scientific community that such animals existed outside the realm of his own imagination. Du Chaillu's credibility was further undermined by the famous explorer Heinrich Barth who ridiculed du Chaillu's geographical observations.

Du Chaillu returned to Gabon in 1863. Upon his return from this trip, du Chaillu brought back indisputable evidence of the existence of gorillas. Thus, when du Chaillu next reported the even more wonderful discovery of the Pygmy people living in the forest interior, his report went unquestioned.

• Alan Stewart Paton (1903–1988), an internationally recognized South African author, was born.

Alan Paton was born and educated in Natal Province, where he served as principal of a reformatory for African boys from 1935 and 1948. During this period, Paton wrote fiction to call attention to governmental oppression of Africans.

Paton's first novel was immensely successful. It was entitled *Cry, The Beloved Country* and was published in 1948. *Cry, The Beloved Country* is a passionate statement of the alienation of Africans in their own land.

Paton's second novel, *Too Late the Phalarope,* was published in 1953. *Too Late the Phalarope* dealt with interracial romance.

Paton's writing is considered patronizing by black African nationalists. However, within the Euro-African South African political spectrum, Paton represents a radical point of view.

In 1953, Paton helped to establish the nonracial Liberal Party. The Liberal Party stood for universal suffrage.

In 1955, Paton succeeded Margaret Ballinger *(see 1894)* as the president of the Liberal Party.

Because of his writings and political activities, Paton's passport was temporarily lifted by the South African government in 1960.

In 1968, the Liberal Party dissolved in the face of new legislation which would have outlawed it.

1 9 0 4

THE UNITED STATES

At the urging of Booker T. Washington, the industrialist Andrew Carnegie financed a meeting of African American leaders. At the meeting, the Committee of 12 for the Advancement of the Interests of the Negro Race was formed. Washington pledged his support for "absolute civil, political and public equality." This pledge enabled Washington's vocal critic, Du Bois, to join in the deliberations. However, Du Bois soon found himself at odds with the perceived dictatorial manner in which Washington conducted the functioning of the Committee. Du Bois was compelled to withdraw.

The Committee of 12 had mixed success. It failed to convince the Pullman Company to reject Jim Crow — to reject segregation — but it did finance the successful lobbying effort which led to the defeat of African American disenfranchisement in Maryland. The Committee of 12 also published a number of pamphlets on African American self-help and economic achievement.

• African Americans in Augusta, Atlanta, Columbia, New Orleans, Mobile and Houston continued their protest against segregation in public transportation by boycotting street cars. In 1904, the African Americans of Houston took it one step further by organizing their own, short-lived, transportation network.

• By 1904, African Americans had been disfranchised in nearly every Southern state. According to the Populist leader, Tom Watson, African Americans could still vote in Georgia only because the powers that be in Georgia "do not dare to disenfranchise [them], because the men who control the Democratic machine in Georgia know that a majority of the whites are against them. They need the [African Americans] to beat us with."

• Charles Young (1864–1922) became a military attache and was assigned to said post in Haiti.

Charles Young was the third African American to graduate from West Point. He graduated in 1889 and was commissioned a second lieutenant in the United States Cavalry.

During the Spanish-American War, Young served as a major in charge of the Ninth Ohio Regiment, an all-black volunteer unit. Young also served in Haiti, the Philippines, and Mexico.

By 1916, Young had attained the rank of lieutenant colonel.

Charles Young was the first military person to be awarded the NAACP's Spingarn Medal. He received this award in 1916.

In 1917, at the advent of American participation in World War I, Young was forced to retire because he was suffering from extremely high blood pressure and Bright's disease. Young refused to accept this retirement. He mounted his horse at Wilberforce, Ohio, and rode the five hundred miles to Washington, D. C. to disprove that he was "physically unfit for duty." The army reinstated Young in 1918 and he was assigned to train African American troops at Fort Grant, Illinois.

In 1919, Colonel Young was dispatched as a military attaché to Liberia on a second tour of duty in that country. Young died in Lagos, Nigeria, during an inspection tour.

• *Crime and Punishment:* An African American shot and killed a European American officer in Springfield, Ohio. An angry mob of European Americans gathered and broke into the jail where the African American was being held. The mob murdered the African American, hung him to a telegraph pole and riddled his body with bullets. The European Americans then began to rampage through the African American section of town, beating and burning African Americans and African American property. For many years afterwards, African Americans shunned Springfield, Ohio.

In Statesboro, Georgia, two African Americans were accused of murdering a European American farmer, the farmer's wife and their three children. After two weeks of "safekeeping" in Savannah, Georgia, the African Americans were brought back to Statesboro, for trial. The African Americans were convicted and sentenced to be hanged. Meanwhile, the European American citizens of the town had worked themselves into a frenzy of racial animosity. Two African American women were whipped for allegedly crowding two European American

girls off the sidewalk. When the sentence was passed on the two African Americans accused of murder, a European American mob forced its way into the jail, overpowering a company of Savannah militia whose rifles were not loaded. The African Americans were then dragged out of the courtroom and burned alive. And then all hell broke loose.

One African American was whipped for riding his bicycle on the sidewalk. Another was whipped "on general principles." The African American mother of a three-day-old baby was beaten and kicked, while her alarmed husband was summarily beaten to death. The homes of African Americans were torched and the terrified African American citizens of Statesboro were forced to flee the town to save their lives.

Georgia law enforcement officials never made any attempt to punish either the mob or the mob leaders.

• *Organizations:* Sigma Pi Phi, the first African American Greek letter organization, was established at a meeting in the Philadelphia home of Dr. Henry McKee Minton (1870–1946) (May 4). Sigma Pi Phi was formed to meet the social needs of African American professional and business leaders, and to address social issues. Minton became the first grand sire archon.

• *Notable Births:* William "Count" Basie, a noted band leader, was born (August 21).

William "Count" Basie was born in Red Bank, New Jersey. As a youth, Basie was influenced by such Harlem pianists as James P. Johnson and Fats Waller.

Count Basie spent his formative musical years in Kansas City. It was there that he joined Bennie Moten's band. Upon Moten's death, Count Basie formed his own band.

Count Basie's style laid the foundation for later developments such as bop and cool jazz. From Kansas City, Basie took his band to Chicago and then to New York in 1936. In 1937, Basie's band made its first recordings for the Decca record label.

• Dr. Ralph J. Bunche, the 1950 Nobel Prize Winner, was born (August 7).

Ralph Bunche was born in a Detroit slum. Both of his parents died when he was eleven. Ralph was raised by his grandmother, an ex-slave.

As a youth, Bunche excelled in sports. He was good enough to receive an athletic scholarship to attend the University of California in Los

Angeles (UCLA). It was from UCLA that Bunche received his bachelor of arts degree in 1927.

Bunche received his masters in 1928 and his doctorate in 1934 from Harvard University. Bunche spent the years leading up to the outbreak of World War II doing post-graduate work at Northwestern University, the London School of Economics, and the University of Capetown. Bunche also taught at Howard University.

Bunche also engaged in extensive research on colonial administration and race relations. While doing his research, he traveled extensively. In 1941, Bunche entered government service, first with the Joint Chiefs of Staff and, from 1942 to 1944, with the OSS.

In July, 1945 Bunche became the first African American to serve as a division head in the Department of State. However, his career in the State Department was cut short when Bunche was named director of the Trusteeship Division of the United Nations. Bunche held this position until 1948, when he was made the principal director.

From 1948 through 1949, Ralph Bunche served as the United Nations moderator on Palestine. For his efforts in bringing peace to the region, Bunche was awarded the Nobel Peace Prize in 1950.

In 1955, Bunche was appointed Under Secretary of the United Nations, and, in 1958, he was promoted again to Under Secretary of Special Political Affairs.

During his long career with the United Nations, Ralph Bunche carried out a number of special missions. In addition to his role as moderator on Palestine, in 1960, Bunche served as a special United Nations representative to the Congo and, in 1963, he was with the United Nations Mission to Yemen.

In 1963, Ralph Bunche was awarded the Presidential Medal of Freedom.

- Dr. Charles R. Drew (1904– 1950), known as the "Father of Blood Plasma," was born (June 3).

Charles Richard Drew was born in Washington, D.C. He was a graduate of Dunbar High School and graduated in 1926 from Amherst College with highest honors.

Drew attended McGill University Medical School in Montreal, Canada. At McGill, Drew earned distinction by winning the first prize in physiological anatomy. Drew also received two fellowships in medicine and honors in athletics.

Charles Drew received his M.D. and Master of Surgery degrees in 1933. In 1935, he became

an instructor of pathology at Howard University. In 1938, Drew received a Rockefeller Fellowship and used it for postgraduate work at Columbia Medical School where he received a Doctor of Medical Science Degree in 1940.

In 1941, Charles Drew's report on the Blood Plasma Project in Britain guided the subsequent development on the project in both the United States and Great Britain. That same year, the American Red Cross set up blood banks coordinated under Drew's chairmanship.

After World War II, Drew left his position at the Blood Bank project to become chairman of surgery at Howard Medical School. Up until his death in an automobile accident, Drew wrote articles on hematology for medical journals. Drew was internationally recognized as one of the world's leading hematologists and is considered to be the founder of the "Blood Bank."

- Coleman Hawkins, a jazz musician, was born (November 21).

Coleman Hawkins was born in St. Joseph, Missouri. He began playing piano at the age of five. In 1923, he made his first records with Fletcher Henderson, with whom he played for a decade. Hawkins was the first jazz musician to attain fame as a tenor saxophonist.

In 1939, Coleman Hawkins recorded *Body and Soul*—a recording which made Hawkins famous.

- Clarence "Pine Top" Smith, a bluesman, was born (January 11).
- Willie Mae Ford Smith, a noted gospel singer, was born in Rolling Fork, Mississippi (June 23).
- Thomas "Fats" Waller (1904–1943), a jazz musician, was born (May 21).

Thomas "Fats" Waller was born in New York City. Waller's father was a minister of the Abyssinian Baptist Church in Harlem.

Fats Waller received a sound classical music training as a boy, and by the age of 15 accompanied such blues singers as Bessie Smith.

Fats Waller was the first jazz musician to use the organ successfully as a jazz instrument. In the 1920s, Waller played at theaters, night clubs and Harlem rent parties. In 1932, Waller toured Europe and won wide recognition. Waller also composed popular song hits, among the most successful of which are *Ain't Misbehavin'* and *Honeysuckle Rose.*

- *Notable Deaths:* There were 83 recorded lynchings in 1904.
- Michael Healy (1839–1904), a noted African American ship captain, died. His life

served as the inspiration for Jack London's *Sea Wolf* and was highlighted in James Michener's *Alaska*.

In 1865, Michael Healy enlisted in the United States Revenue Service, the precursor to the United States Coast Guard. In 1886, Healy was assigned to command the famous cutter *Bear* and became the chief federal law enforcement officer in the northern waters off the coast of Alaska.

• *Miscellaneous State Laws:* Kentucky passed a law which established segregation in the schools in the state, public and private. Berea, an integrated college, challenged the law. However, in *Berea College v. The Commonwealth of Kentucky*, the Court of Appeals upheld the law.

• Mississippi and Maryland instituted Jim Crow streetcar laws.

• South Carolina segregated its ferries.

• *Publications:* Booker T. Washington published *Working With the Hands*. In this year, Washington also wrote an article entitled "Cruelty in the Congo Country" for *Outlook* magazine. In this article, Washington expressed his hope that once the Congo (Zaire) was "reformed," African Americans could assume a constructive role in its development.

• In 1904, William Braithwaite published *Lyrics of Life and Love,* his first collection of poetry. This collection of poetry is notable because it stood in stark contrast to the dialect poetry that was so prevalent among African American poets of the day (*see 1872: Notable Births:* Paul Laurence Dunbar).

• *The Heart of Happy Hollow*, a collection of prose, was published by Paul Laurence Dunbar.

• James Madison Bell's collected poetical works were published.

• W. E. B. Du Bois published his "Credo" in the New York journal, *The Independent* (October 6).

• *The Arts:* Henry Ossawa Tanner's *Daniel in the Lion's Den* was awarded the silver medal at the Louisiana Purchase Exposition in St. Louis, Missouri.

• *Scholastic Achievements:* In 1904, Mary McLeod Bethune established the Daytona Normal and Industrial Institute for Negro Girls. This institution would later merge with Cookman Institute to become Bethune-Cookman College.

• Charlotte Hawkins Brown founded the Palmer Memorial Institute in North Carolina. Brown would later become the prominent leader of the National Association of Colored Women.

• John Robert Edward Lee (1870–1944), director of the Academic Department of Tuskegee Institute, became the first president of the National Association of Teachers in Colored Schools.

• *Technological Innovations:* Granville T. Woods and his brother Lyates patented the first of two improvements on railroad brakes (March 29). The second patent was issued on July 18, 1905. Both innovations were purchased by the Westinghouse Electric Company.

• *Black Enterprise:* Boley, Oklahoma, was founded.

Boley, the largest all-black town in Indian Territory, was founded in the former Creek Nation in 1904 by two European American businessmen, William Boley, a roadmaster for the Fort Smith & Western Railroad, and Lake Moore, an attorney and former federal commissioner to the region's Indigenous American tribes. Boley and Moore chose Tom Haynes, an African American, to handle promotion of the town.

Unlike Langston City, Boley was on a rail line and in a timbered, well-watered prairie that easily supported the type of agriculture familiar to most prospective black settlers. The frontier character of the town was evident from its founding. Newcomers, who usually arrived by train, were forced to live in tents until they could clear trees and brush to construct homes and stores.

During Boley's first year, Creek Indians rode several times through Boley's streets on shooting sprees that killed several people. T. T. Ringo, a peace officer appointed by townsite officials, stopped the violence. However, Boley's reputation for lawlessness continued into 1905 when a second peace officer, William Shavers, was killed while leading a posse after a gang of European American horse thieves who terrorized the town.

By 1907, Boley had a thousand residents, as well as more than two thousand farmers in the surrounding countryside, and was beginning to take on a permanent air. Boley's businesses included a hotel, sawmill, and cotton gin. Churches, a school, fraternal lodges, women's clubs, and a literary society attest to the cultural development of the town. A community newspaper, the *Boley Progress,* was founded in 1905 to report on local matters and promote town growth.

After a visit in 1905, Booker T. Washington described Boley as a "rude, bustling, Western town, {which nevertheless} represented a dawning race consciousness ... which shall demonstrate the right of the negro ... to have a worthy place in the civilization that the American people are creating." *See 1905.*

Despite its promising beginnings, Boley's spectacular growth was over by 1910. When the Twin Territories became the state of Oklahoma in 1907, the Democrats (composed primarily of European Americans from the South) emerged as the dominant political party. The Democrats quickly disfranchised black voters and segregated public schools and accommodations. Their actions eliminated the town's major appeal as a political center, and as a place where African Americans could escape the Jim Crow restrictions they faced in southern states.

Although African Americans continued to vote in local elections, political control at the local level could not compensate for marginal influence at the courthouse or the state capital, where crucial decisions affecting Boley's schools and roads were routinely made by unsympathetic officials. Moreover, after the initial years of prosperity, declining agricultural prices and crop failures gradually reduced the number of African American farmers who were then the foundation of the town's economy. Although Boley remained noted for being the location of a famous African American rodeo, it ceased to be an important center of African American life.

• *Sports:* George C. Poag (1880–1962), of Milwaukee, Wisconsin, became the first African American to win an Olympic medal. Poag, a hurdler, placed third in both the 200 and 400 meter hurdle races at the 1904 Olympics held in St. Louis, Missouri. Joseph Stadler, an African American from Cleveland, Ohio, also competed in the 1904 Olympics, but he did not medal.

• John B. Taylor, a student at the University of Pennsylvania, won the intercollegiate championship in the 440 yard dash.

• Between 1904 and 1906, Joe Walcott held the world welterweight boxing title. It was Walcott's second tenure as champion.

• Charles W. Follis formally signed on with the Shelby Athletic Association and became the first African American professional football player.

Charles W. Follis was born in Cloverdale, Virginia and moved to Wooster, Ohio, where he played at Wooster High. One of Follis' high school teammates was Branch Rickey — the man who became president of the Brooklyn Dodgers baseball team and broke the color barrier by signing Jackie Robinson to play professional baseball.

THE AMERICAS

• *Brazil:* In 1904, Joaquim Machado de Assis published *Esau e Jaco (Esau and Jacob).*

In *Esau e Jaco*, Machado added a new dimension to his treatment of symbolic and mythical elements. The novel contains more political allegories than do any of his other works. In telling the story of the struggle of two identical twins (Pedro and Paulo) for the love of a girl (Flora), Machado intertwines observations concerning the political atmosphere in Brazil around the time that the Brazilian Republic was proclaimed.

• *Canada:* William P. Hubbard became the city comptroller for Toronto.

William P. Hubbard (1842–1935) was born in Toronto, the light skinned son of Afro-Canadian parents. Hubbard worked as a livery boy in an uncle's stable and drove for George Brown.

A Torontonian, named Colonel Robert Wells, who had become interested in helping persons of African descent, became interested in William. He agreed to send William to school. At school, William learned to be a baker as well as enough mathematics to take up real estate as an alternative career.

After a long period of self-education in finance and the law, both arising from his work with property, Hubbard decided to run for alderman in a ward with little appreciable Afro-Canadian constituency. Narrowly defeated in 1892, William Hubbard won in 1894. He would serve as an alderman until 1903.

From 1904 to 1907, Hubbard served as Toronto's city comptroller. During the mayor's absence, Hubbard frequently served as the city's chief officer.

Hubbard was elected to another term as Toronto alderman in 1913. In 1914, the city honored Hubbard by having his portrait hung in the Toronto city chambers.

• Robert Walker founded the journal *Neith* in Saint John, New Brunswick.

• William Hall (1827–1904), the first person of African descent to win the Victoria Cross, died.

William Hall was born in Hants County, Nova Scotia. As a teenager, he went to sea and he later joined the British Navy. Hall was decorated during the Crimean War for his exploits at the battles of Inkerman and Sebastopol.

In 1857, when the Indian Mutiny broke out, Hall was among those who followed Sir Colin Campbell, the former governor of Nova Scotia, in relief of the British garrison under Sir John Inglis, a Nova Scotia native, at Lucknow.

Hall volunteered to join a virtually suicidal gun crew in breaching the walls of Shah Nejeef, a temple converted to a fort by the Sepoys. Continuing to load after all other members of the crew had fallen, Hall opened a gap in the wall of the fort and thereby enabled the British forces to enter.

After Hall retired from the navy in 1876, he returned to Nova Scotia. As a winner of the Victoria Cross, he became a legendary figure in Canada. In 1901, Hall was given a carriage in the procession that honored the Duke of York on his visit to Halifax.

Despite his fame, Hall was buried in an unmarked grave when he died in 1904. However, in 1947, the Hantsport branch of the Canadian Legion erected a monument to Hall and the Afro-Canadian branch of the Legion in Halifax was named for him.

• *Haiti:* Haiti celebrated one hundred years of independence (January 1).

• In 1904, *Dessalines Liberte*, the best of Massillon Coicou's dramatic works, was published. The theme of *Dessalines Liberte* was Haitian independence. *Dessalines Liberte* premiered in Paris and has since become a classic of Haitian theater. *See 1865.*

AFRICA

• *North Africa, Egypt and Sudan:* A special regime was created for Tangier (April).

• Muhammed al-Raisuli kidnapped Ion Perdicaris, the Greek resident in Tangier. The British and United States fleets were sent to Tangier.

• The United States paid a ransom of 70,000 dollars for release of Perdicaris.

• al-Raisuli was made governor of Tangier.

• Yambio, the Zande ruler, was defeated by the Belgians.

When the Mahdist state of Sudan fell to the British-Egyptian government in 1899, Zande country became the focus of aggressive imperial rivalry between the British from the northeast and Belgians from the southwest.

Yambio, the ruler of the Zande, struggled to remain independent while neighboring chiefs and relatives aligned themselves with the Europeans. In 1903 and 1904, Yambio spurned British attempts to negotiate an accommodation while Leopold's forces massed against him along his southwestern border.

Late in 1904, Yambio led a costly and futile attack on the Belgian positions. Terribly outmanned, Yambio was forced to fall back to await his fate.

• *West Africa:* A Portuguese expedition against Xura (or Churo) was initiated.

• An Anglo-French convention was convened concerning the boundaries of the Gambia, Senegal, French Guinea, Sierra Leone and Zinder (April 8).

• An Anglo-French agreement was reached on the boundaries of the Gold Coast (April 25).

• The French territory of Haut-Senegal-Niger were constituted under Governor Ponty (October 18).

• A Franco-Portuguese agreement on Guinea boundaries was negotiated (November 5).

• France recognized the West African Colonies as French West Africa with the colonial capital of Dakar (December).

• The village chief at Satiru declared himself the Mahdi. He was arrested and replaced by his son.

• A serious famine occurred in northern Nigeria.

• A French punitive expedition against the Conaguis was initiated.

• A French post was established at Agades.

• Arthur Barclay became president of Liberia.

By the time of his election as Liberia's president in 1904, Arthur Barclay had gained a reputation for honesty and competency.

When Arthur Barclay assumed office, Liberia was nearly bankrupt and the major European powers threatened to make it a protectorate. Barclay immediately moved to strengthen his hold on the country by improving relations with African political authorities in the interior, establishing a minimal administration based on indirect rule of the hinterland. Barclay also increased the power of his office by lengthening the president's term of office from two to four years.

• Leo Frobenius *(see 1873)*, the German anthropologist, made his first trip to Africa.

The anthropological field work of Leo Frobenius included twelve trips to Africa from 1904 to 1935. From these trips, Frobenius brought back to Germany many valuable pieces of Ife art.

- Benjamin Nnamdi Azikiwe, the first president of Nigeria, was born.

Benjamin Nnamdi Azikiwe was born in Northern Nigeria where his father was an army clerk. At the age of eight, his parents sent Benjamin to Iboland for education in mission schools. Benjamin later attended schools in Lagos and Calabar.

At the age of 21, Azikiwe went to the United States to attend college. Azikiwe supported himself by working as a manual laborer.

By 1930, Azikiwe had received, in addition to his undergraduate degree, a certificate in journalism from Columbia University, a master's degree in political science from Lincoln University, and a second masters in anthropology from the University of Pennsylvania.

In 1934, Azikiwe returned to Africa to edit a newspaper in Ghana. Three years later, he went to Lagos to establish the influential *West African Pilot*. It was during this time that Azikiwe became an important figure in the Nigerian Youth Movement which had come to dominate Lagos politics.

Azikiwe resigned from the Nigerian Youth Movement in 1941 for personal reasons, possibly related to his Ibo origins.

In 1944, Azikiwe joined with Herbert Macaulay, the founder of Nigeria's first political party, to bring together over forty political, labor and educational groups under the umbrella of the National Council of Nigeria and the Cameroons (NCNC).

The following year, the NCNC began a campaign of opposition to the new constitution implemented by the governor, Arthur Richards, which fell far short of nationalist expectations. During this time, Azikiwe gave support to a massive strike which brought the government to its knees. Fearing government reprisals and attempts on his life, Azikiwe went into seclusion.

Azikiwe emerged from his seclusion in 1946 as a national hero. He joined Macaulay on a tour of Nigeria to demonstrate national support for the NCNC and to raise funds for a delegation to London. Macaulay died on the tour and Azikiwe was chosen to succeed him as president of the NCNC.

In 1947, Azikiwe headed the NCNC delegation to London, although the constitution was not replaced until after the governor retired in 1948. When elections were held in 1951, Azikiwe won a seat in the Western house, but the Yoruba controlled Action Group led by Obafemi Awolowo won control of the house and prevented Azikiwe's election to the federal assembly.

Azikiwe switched to the Eastern region to run in the next elections. An NCNC victory made him chief minister (later premier) of the region.

In 1956, a government commission criticized Azikiwe for placing government funds in a bank which he partially owned. As a result, Azikiwe dissolved the house and called for new elections in which he and the NCNC received a strong vote of confidence.

In 1959, federal elections were held and Azikiwe hoped to put together a coalition with the powerful northern Nigerian leaders which would have made him federal prime minister. The office, however, went to Abubakar Tafawa Balewa. Azikiwe was forced to settle for the largely ceremonial position of governor-general.

When Nigeria became a republic in 1963, Azikiwe became president. However, the primary power continued to reside with the prime minister. Around this time, Azikiwe began to find it increasingly difficult to work with northern leaders. However, the difficulties were made irrelevant by the 1966 coup which placed Nigeria under military rule.

After a large number of Ibo were massacred in 1966 and Biafra seceded in 1967, Azikiwe joined the rebel government. Azikiwe worked to gain international recognition for the new state. When it later became obvious that the revolt had failed, Azikiwe became an advocate for reunification.

Azikiwe went abroad. He remained abroad until becoming chancellor of Lagos University in 1972.

Azikiwe re-entered politics as a presidential candidate when civilian rule was restored in 1979. However, Alhaji Shehu Shagari was elected president in 1979 and again in 1983, defeating Azikiwe both times.

- Joseph Ayo Babalola (1904–1960), a leader in the Aladura religious movement of Nigeria, was born.

Joseph Babalola was born into a Christian family in a small town in the Ilorin district of Nigeria. After attending school in Lagos, Babalola became a steamroller driver for the highways department.

One day in 1928, Babalola's steamroller stopped and Babalola had a vision telling him to preach the Gospel. Babalola returned home where he was thought to be mad and was imprisoned briefly. He eventually made his way back to Lagos, where he became associated with the Faith Tabernacle, an independent Yoruba church which had broken from the Anglican Church.

During the 1930s, Babalola led a revival which swept parts of Yorubaland. This revival became known as the Aladura movement. Although the movement involved no political protest, British officials feared its potential and put pressure on Nigerian chiefs to deny land grants to Babalola's followers.

Babalola was jailed in 1932. He was charged with participating in a witch-eradication ordeal (an exorcism). Babalola was released six months later.

Babalola and his movement remained prominent in Nigeria until Babalola's death in 1960.

• Richard Beale Blaize (1845–1904), a prominent Nigerian businessman, died.

Richard Blaize was born in Freetown, Sierra Leone, to Yoruba liberated slave parents. Blaize was raised a Christian. He received a mission education and was apprenticed to a printer.

In 1862, at the age of seventeen, Blaize went to Lagos, Nigeria. It was in Lagos, in 1863, that Blaize went to work for the government printing office. It was with the government printing office that Blaize later became the head printer.

In 1875, Blaize left the printing business to become a merchant. Blaize became a very successful merchant. By the 1890s, Blaize was the wealthiest African in Lagos. His net worth exceed 150,000 pounds.

Having achieved success, Blaize became active in the church and, to a lesser degree, in politics. Blaize financed a number of newspapers, — newspapers which frequently operated at a loss.

Blaize's death in 1904 coincided with the end of an era. In the nineteenth century, there were avenues open to freed slaves and commoners to achieve prominence in the business world. However, by the turn of the century, European merchants essentially eliminated large-scale African commerce because the African businesses simply could not compete with the Europeans' lower overhead costs.

• Wobogo, the ruler of the Mossi state of Ouagadougou of Burkina Faso, died.

Wobogo first competed with his brother Sanum for the crown at their father's death in 1850. Wobogo lost out, partially because of his youth. Forty years later, when Sanum died leaving no sons, Wobogo vied with his remaining brothers for the kingship.

Because Wobogo had led a civil war against Sanum years before and had been subsequently exiled from Ouagadougou, the council of electors was not well disposed towards him. However, they agreed to name him mogho naba (king) after his soldiers surrounded their meeting place. At his elevation, Wobogo dropped his given name, Boukary Koutou, and chose the name Wobogo, meaning elephant.

Wobogo became ruler at a time of intense French-British rivalry for the west African interior. Both nations dispatched emissaries to make a treaty with Wobogo. Wobogo signed a treaty of friendship with the British in 1894. However, he made clear his distrust of all Europeans.

Wobogo's suspicions were confirmed when French forces invaded Ouagadougou from the north in 1896. Wobogo's capital was quickly taken. When Wobogo attempted to resist, the French commander, Voulet, burned the town in retaliation.

Wobogo continued to fight, but was forced to flee when some of his vassal kings surrendered. Voulet formally deposed Wobogo early in 1897, and place his brother, Sighiri on the throne.

Wobogo appealed to the British in the Gold Coast (Ghana) for aid in respect to the 1894 treaty. The British instead came to terms with the French, demarcating spheres of influence. Wobogo carried on his campaign without help.

Repelled again, Wobogo retreated to the Gold Coast and went into exile at Zangoiri.

At his death in 1904, Wobogo was buried in the Gold Coast, but his funeral was held at Ouagadougou (in Burkina Faso).

• *Central Africa:* From 1904 to 1911, the French initiated campaigns to pacify the Fang, Bakota and Mitshogo.

• The Royal Commission of Inquiry was sent to the Congo.

• By 1904, five White Fathers' missions were already established in Rwanda.

• *Eastern Africa:* Telegraph lines were opened from Dar es Salaam to Tabora and Mwanza, and from Tanga to Korogwe.

• The Dar es Salaam to Morogoro railway was constructed.

• There was an agricultural exhibition in Dar es Salaam.

• The first power gin was built in Kampala.

• *Southern Africa:* Chinese coolie labor was recruited for the Transvaal (February).

In 1904, Alfred Milner, the British high commissioner for South Africa, introduced Chinese laborers into the gold mines of the Transvaal.

• Dr. Leander Starr Jameson became Prime Minister of the Cape Colony (February 22).

• The uprising of the Herero and Khoikhoi in German Southwest Africa began.

Shortly after his arrival in South West Africa in 1894, Theodore Leutwin defeated the powerful Khoikhoi chief Hendrik Witbooi. Afterwards, Leutwin forced Witbooi to accept a German protectorate. Thereafter, Leutwin's policy was to maintain close personal ties with African rulers, to use them against their fellow chiefs, and to make available as much land as possible for European settlement.

Leutwin's policy crumbled in early 1904. While Leutwin was occupied with a revolt of the Bondelswarts Nama, Samuel Maherero launched an unexpected Herero drive against European settlers. Leutwin had to negotiate a rapid and lenient truce with the Bondelswarts. His failure to disarm other southern peoples aroused the protests of European settlers and cost Leutwin the support of the German government at home.

After he moved against the Herero, Leutwin was surprised by a second revolt led by Hendrik Witbooi. He was replaced as military commander by the General von Trotha in April of 1904.

Von Trotha dealt the Herero a crushing blow in August and Samuel Mahehero and his Herero followers were compelled to flee east through the desert to safety.

Thousands of Herero died from hardship before Samuel Mahehero reached British Bechuanaland with only 1500 survivors. In British Bechuanaland, Samuel eventually settled under the Ngwato chief Kgama III.

It is estimated that von Trotha's extermination policy and the harsh migration killed seventy percent of the Herero. The surviving Herero still in Namibia were reunited under Hosea Kutako.

*   *   *

When the Herero revolted against Governor Leutwin in German South West Africa, Von Trotha was sent there to command all military forces. Von Trotha arrived in South West Africa (Namibia) in April of 1904. Upon his arrival, Von Trotha proceeded ruthlessly against the Herero. By August of 1904, the Herero rebellion was broken.

During the clean-up operation, Von Trotha issued an edict for which he became infamous. The edict read: "Within the German frontiers every Herero with or without a rifle, with or without cattle, shall be shot. I will not accept any woman or child; I will send them back to their people, or have them shot."

The infamous Von Trotha proclamation produced an immediate outcry in Germany and was repudiated by the Kaiser. Von Trotha ameliorated his orders somewhat, but the damage had already been done. An estimated seventy percent of the Herero died fighting or fleeing.

Von Trotha was dismissed the following year. He was blamed for having destroyed not only the Herero rebellion but also the basis for the economy of German South West Africa.

As for the Khoikhoi, Hendrik Witbooi, the Khoikhoi leader, came to fear that the policy of extermination which von Trotha was conducting against the Herero would next be applied to his own people. Acting upon a divine command, in October of 1904, Hendrik Witbooi led his people in revolt against the Germans.

Hendrik Witbooi was killed fighting a year later. His followers surrendered the next month, but the general rebellion continued until 1907.

• Rhodes University College was founded in Grahamstown.

• The first Zionist church was founded in Johannesburg by Daniel Bryant.

• Rhodesia Agricultural Union was formed.

• African taxation was introduced into northwest Rhodesia.

RELATED HISTORICAL EVENTS

• *Europe:* The *Entente Cordiale* between Britain and France settled the differences between the two countries concerning Morocco, Egypt and Newfoundland (April 8). Under the agreement, Britain recognized the Suez Canal Convention and surrendered its claim to Madagascar.

• A Franco-Spanish agreement was finalized which delimited respective zones of influence in Morocco (October 6).

• The first Algerians arrived in France to work in Marseilles sugar refineries.

• *Africa:* Francois Coillard (1834–1904), a pioneering French missionary in western Zambia, died.

After long service for the Paris Evangelical Mission in Lesotho, Francois Coillard led a party into present day Zimbabwe (Southern Rhodesia) to open a mission among the Shona.

In Southern Rhodesia, Coillard was arrested by the Ndebele king Lobengula. Lobengula expelled Coillard from the country.

On the advice of the Ngwato chief, Kgama III, Coillard then attempted to visit the Lozi kingdom in western Zambia. Arriving in the midst of civil strife, Coillard was turned back there as well. However, the Lozi king Lewanika invited him to return. Coillard did so in 1885, and the mission flourished.

Later on, Coillard played an important role in Lewanika's negotiations with British imperial factions. Lewanika himself never accepted baptism, but he encouraged the secular work of the mission.

Coillard's pioneering work helped greatly to give the Lozi a significant educational advantage over the other peoples of Zambia.

• Stephanus Johannes Paulus Kruger (1825–1904), the former president of the Transvaal Republic, died.

When Stephanus Kruger was a child his family joined the Afrikaner exodus from the Cape Colony to the northern interior. Kruger participated in battles against the Ndebele (1836) and the Zulu (1838) and then settled in the Transvaal with Andries Potgeiter's contingent.

Kruger held various minor offices in the developing Afrikaner administration, attaining some prominence by the 1850s. Kruger's reputation grew rapidly after he distinguished himself in attacks on Sechele and other African chiefs.

From 1855 to 1857, Kruger helped to form the first central government of the Transvaal and in the early 1860s was elected commandant-general of the Afrikaners and helped to quell a small civil war.

In 1865, Kruger led a Transvaal faction in assisting the Orange Free State against the Sotho king, Moshoeshoe. His reputation sagged after an unsuccessful campaign against Africans in the northern Transvaal and, in 1873, he resigned as commandant-general and returned to his farm.

During the British annexation of the Transvaal, Kruger regained his popularity by leading the resistance movement. He joined a triumvirate government in opposition to the British and was credited with negotiating the settlement which restored Afrikaner independence in 1881.

In 1883, Kruger was elected to the first of four terms as president of the Transvaal Republic. Kruger's first concerns were to remove the remaining British restrictions on Transvaal sovereignty and to secure access to a sea port. His efforts to subordinate Tswana chiefs to his west

led directly to British annexation of Bechuanaland in 1885.

The discovery of gold in the Rand in 1886 solved the country's financial problems, but it also attracted an influx of foreigners (uitlanders) who threatened to outnumber the Afrikaners in the Transvaal. Kruger's reluctance to grant these newcomers access to political rights angered the British government and invited external meddling.

In 1895, Kruger easily stopped the "raid" of Leander Jameson who was acting on the behalf of Cecil Rhodes. This success enabled Kruger to emerge with much more unified support from his own people. Thereafter, Kruger used income from the mines to equip his growing army with modern weapons, supplied by the new rail link he had established through Mozambique.

In late 1899, Kruger anticipated a build up in British troop strength. He issued Britain with an ultimatum which precipitated the South African War. During the first year, Kruger led the war effort. But when Kruger's government had to retreat from Pretoria, he left South Africa to lobby for support in European capitals.

During the next few years, Kruger campaigned futilely throughout Europe. Kruger died in Switzerland in 1904, two years after the Transvaal was defeated by Britain.

• Henry Morton Stanley (c.1841–1904), a British-American journalist, author, explorer, and pioneer colonial administrator, died.

Henry Stanley was born John Rowland in Wales. He was orphaned at an early age.

In 1859, Rowland (Stanley) took a ship to the United States and was adopted by Henry Stanley, whose name he took.

Stanley served on both sides during the American Civil War and then began a career as a journalist with the *New York Herald*. After covering Robert Napier's expedition against the Ethiopian Emperor Theodore, Stanley was assigned to locate David Livingstone in central Africa.

Lavishly backed by his newspaper, Stanley outfitted a large expedition in Zanzibar. He bullied his way to Lake Tanganyika, helping the Tabora Arabs to fight the Nyamwezi chief Mirambo along the way. His famous meeting with Livingstone at Ujiji assured his international reputation.

Stanley covered Garnet Wolseley's expedition against the Ashanti in 1873. After that he returned to East Africa to follow up the explorations of Livingstone, Speke, and Samuel Baker.

Stanley's 1874–1877 exploration of Africa was

one of the single most productive explorations ever undertaken in Africa. During this exploration, Stanley resolved many questions about the great African lakes system and traced the Congo (Zaire) River to it mouth. Along the way, Stanley visited the Ganda king Mutesa I.

During his visit with Mutesa, Stanley assisted Mutesa in a local war, and persuaded Mutesa to invite Christian missionaries to Uganda in 1875. In an incident which tarnished his reputation, Stanley was responsible for the massacre of a party of Africans.

From Uganda, Stanley entered present day Zaire and joined the Swahili trader Tippu Tip down the Congo River. Stanley's trans-continental journey revealed to Europe the commercial possibilities of Zaire.

After a rest, Stanley returned to Africa to establish an administration for Leopold's "Congo Free State." Due to Stanley's efforts, the Congo Free State won international recognition at the Berlin Conference in 1884.

Stanley's last major trip to Africa was a powerful expedition through Zaire to extricate Egypt's German governor Emin Pasha from southern Sudan. At the time, the Egyptian-Sudanese forces were cut off by the Mahdists.

Returning through East Africa, Stanley secured treaties which he turned over to William Mackinnon. These treaties served as the basis for the British protectorate in East Africa.

Returning to England, Stanley was re-naturalized as a British subject in 1892. In 1895, he was elected to parliament.

Stanley recorded his career in more than a dozen volumes, many of which were international best-sellers.

---

1 9 0 5

THE UNITED STATES

• A group of African American intellectuals organized the so-called Niagara Movement at a meeting near Niagara Falls (July 11–13).

W. E. B. Du Bois called a conference of African American leaders in Niagara Falls, Canada. The conveners issued a Declaration of Principles in which they said: "We believe that Negroes should protest emphatically and continually against the curtailment of their political rights. We believe in manhood suffrage; we believe that no man is so good, intelligent or wealthy as to be entrusted wholly with the welfare of his neighbor."

The Niagara Movement leaders went on to demand equal economic opportunity, equal education, a fair administration of justice, and an end to segregation.

For three years, the leaders of the Niagara Movement met and renewed their protests against injustice. By 1908, the Niagara Movement had won the respect and support of large numbers of African Americans, including the Equal Suffrage League and the National Association of Colored Women's Clubs.

• The Committee for Improving Industrial Conditions of Negroes in New York City and the National League of Protection of Colored Women were organized in New York. These organizations aimed at equality in economic and social spheres for African Americans.

The League for the Protection of Colored Women was founded by Mrs. William Baldwin, Jr. and Frances Kellor. It had branches in New York, Philadelphia, Baltimore, and Norfolk, Virginia. The League was biracial, with an African American field secretary. The organization grew out of an investigation of the practices of New York employment agencies toward African American women newly arrived from the South and looking for work. The organization counseled the new arrivals and helped them find housing and jobs.

• By 1905, Booker T. Washington's control of the Afro-American Council had weakened. In this year, the Council withdrew its support for the concept of a restrictive franchise for African Americans.

• Booker T. Washington served as vice-president of the Congo Reform Association. Robert E. Park was recording secretary, and G. Stanley Hall was president. Park was a sociologist and Hall was an educator.

• Through the influence of Booker T. Washington, Charles W. Anderson (1866–1938), an African American politician, was appointed collector of internal revenue for the Wall Street district of New York City.

Ohio born, Charles Anderson received his first appointment in New York City as United States gauger in the Second District where he inspected bulk goods subject to duty. Anderson received other presidential appointments until his retirement in 1934.

• *The Labor Movement:* The Industrial Workers of the World (IWW) constitution provided that "no working man or woman shall be excluded from membership in unions because of creed or color."

• Booker T. Washington visited the all black town of Boley, Oklahoma.

Boley, Oklahoma, was founded in 1904 on land owned by Abigail Barnett, an Afro-Choctaw. Boley, located in the Indian Territories, was founded to be a bastion of independent African American economic and political power. It was also a great source of racial pride.

When Booker T. Washington visited Boley in 1905, it encompassed an area of some eighty acres and was populated by some 4,000 citizens. The residents of Boley could boast to having the tallest building between Oklahoma City and Okmulgee and, most importantly of all, they relished the fact that African Americans ran the government and that half of its high school graduates went on to college.

The citizens of Boley took great pride in their community. One of the residents even wrote a song about his beloved town.

Boley Recalled in Song

Say, have you heard the story,
  Of a little colored town,
Way over in the Nation
  On such a lovely sloping ground?
With as pretty little houses
  As you ever chanced to meet,
With not a thing but colored folks
  A-standing in the streets?
Oh, 'tis a pretty country
  And the Negroes own it, too
With not a single white man here
  To tell us what to do—in Boley
                Uncle Jess, town poet

The pride that was endemic in Boley made an impression upon Booker T. Washington. A little more than two years later, Washington chronicled his observations in an article which appeared in the *Outlook* magazine on January 4, 1908. The observations made by Washington were as follows:

Boley, a Negro Town in the West
Booker T. Washington

Boley, Indian Territory, is the youngest, the most enterprising and in many ways the most interesting of the negro towns in the United States. A rude, bustling, western town, it is a characteristic product of the negro immigration from the South and Middle West into the new lands of what is now the state of Oklahoma.

The large proportions of the northward and westward movement of the negro population recall the Kansas exodus of thirty years ago, when within a few months more than forty thousand helpless and destitute negroes from the country districts of Arkansas and Mississippi poured into eastern Kansas in search of "better homes, larger opportunities, and kindlier treatment."

It is a striking evidence of the progress made in thirty years that the present northward and westward movement of the negro people has brought into these new lands, not a helpless and ignorant horde of black people, but land-seekers and home-builders, men who have come prepared to build up the country. In the thirty years since the Kansas exodus the southern negroes have learned to build schools, to establish banks and conduct newspapers. They have recovered something of the knack for trade that their foreparents in Africa were famous for. They have learned through their churches and their secret orders the art of corporate and united action. This experience has enabled them to set up and maintain in a raw western community, numbering 2,500, an orderly and self-respecting government.

In the fall of 1905 I spent a week in the Territories of Oklahoma and Indian Territory. During the course of my visit I had an opportunity for the first time to see the three races —the negro, the Indian, and the white man— living side by side, each in sufficient numbers to make their influence felt in the communities of which they were a part, and in the Territory as a whole. It was not my first acquaintance with the Indian. During the last years of my stay at Hampton Institute I had charge of the Indian students there, and had come to have a high respect both for their character and intelligence, so that I was particularly interested to see them in their own country, where they still preserve to some extent their native institutions. I was all the more impressed, on that account, with the fact that in the cities that I visited I rarely caught sight of a genuine native Indian. When I inquired, as I frequently did, for the "natives," it almost invariably happened that I was introduced, not to an Indian, but to a negro. During my visit to the city of Muskogee I stopped at the home of one of the prominent "natives," of the Creek Nation, the Hon. C. W. Sango, Superintendent of the Tullahassee Mission. But he is a negro. The negroes who are descendants of slaves that the Indians brought with them from Alabama and

Mississippi, when the migrated to this Territory, about the middle of the last century. I was introduced later to one or two other "natives" who were not negroes, but neither were they, as far as my observations went, Indians. They were, on the contrary, white men. "But where," I asked at length, "are the Indians?"

"Oh! the Indians," was the reply, "they have gone," with a wave of the hand in the direction of the horizon, "they have gone back!"

I repeated this question in a number of different places, and invariably received the same reply. "Oh, they have gone back!" I remembered the expression because it seemed to me that it condensed into a phrase a great deal of local history.

One cannot escape the impression, in traveling through Indian Territory, that the Indians, who own practically all the lands, and until recently had the local government largely in their own hands, are to a very large extent regarded by the white settlers, who are rapidly filling up the country, as almost a negligible quantity. To such an extent is this true that the Constitution of Oklahoma, as I understand it, takes no account of the Indians in drawing its distinctions among the races. For the Constitution there exist only the negro and the white man. The reason seems to be that the Indians have either receded — "gone back," as the saying in that region is — on the advance of the white race, or they have intermarried with and become absorbed with it. Indeed, so rapidly has this intermarriage of the two races gone on, and so great has been the demand for Indian wives, that in some of the Nations, I was informed, the price of marriage licenses has gone as high as $1,000.

The negroes, immigrants to Indian Territory, have not, however, "gone back." One sees them everywhere, working side by side with white men. They have their banks, business enterprises, schools, and churches. There are still, I am told, among the "natives" some negroes who cannot speak the English language, and who have been so thoroughly bred in the customs of the Indians that they have remained among the hills with the tribes by whom they were adopted. But, as a rule, the negro natives do not shun the white man and his civilization, but, on the contrary, rather seek it, and enter, with the negro immigrants, into competition with the white man for its benefits.

This fact was illustrated by another familiar local expression. In reply to my inquiries in regard to the little towns through which we passed, I often had occasion to notice the expression, "Yes, so and so?" Well, that is a 'white town.'" Or again, "So and so, that's colored."

I learned upon inquiry that there were a considerable number of communities throughout the Territory where an effort had been made to exclude negro settlers. To this the negroes had replied by starting other communities in which no white man was allowed to live. For instance, the thriving little city of Wilitka, I was informed, was a white man's town until it got the oil mills. Then they needed laborers, and brought in the negroes. There are a number of other little communities — Clairview, Wildcat, Grayson, and Taft — which were sometimes referred to as "colored towns," but I learned that in their cases the expression meant merely that these towns had started as negro communities or that there were large numbers of negroes there, and that negro immigrants were wanted. But among these various communities there was one of which I heard more than the others. This was the town of Boley, where, it is said, no white man has ever let the sun go down upon him.

In 1905, when I visited Indian Territory, Boley was little more than a name. It was started in 1903. At present time, it is a thriving town of 2,500 inhabitants, with two banks, two cotton gins, a newspaper, a hotel, and a "college," the Creek-Seminole College and Agricultural Institute.

There is a story told in regard to the way in which the town of Boley was started, which, even if it is not wholly true as to the details, is at least characteristic, and illustrates the temper of the people in that region.

One spring day, four years ago, a number of gentlemen were discussing, at Wilitka, the race question. The point at issue was the capability of the negro for self-government. One of the gentlemen, who happened to be connected with the Fort Smith Railway, maintained that if the negroes were given a fair chance they would prove themselves as capable of self-government as any other people of the same degree of culture and education. He asserted that they had never had a fair chance. The other gentlemen naturally asserted the contrary. The result of the argument was Boley. Just at that time a number of other town sites were being laid out along the railway which connects Guthrie, Oklahoma, with Fort Smith, Arkansas. It was, it is said, to put the capability of the negro for self-government to the test that in August, 1903, seventy-two miles east of Guthrie, the site of the new negro town was established. It was called Boley, after the man who built that section of the railway. A negro town-site agent, T. M. Haynes, who is at present connected with the Farmers' and Merchants' Bank, was made Town-site Agent, and the purpose to establish a town which should be exclusively controlled by negroes was widely advertised all over the Southwest.

Boley, although built on the railway, is still on the edge of civilization. You can still hear on summer nights, I am told, the wild notes of the Indian drums and the shrill cries of the Indian dancers among the hills beyond the settlement. The outlaws that formerly infested the country have not wholly disappeared. Dick Shafer, the first town marshal of Boley, was killed in a duel with a horse thief, whom he in turn shot and killed, after falling mortally wounded, from his horse. The horse thief was a white man.

There is no liquor sold in Boley, or any part of the Territory, but the "natives" go down to Prague, across the Oklahoma border, ten miles away, and then come back and occasionally "shoot up" the town. That was a favorite pastime, a few years ago, among the "natives" around Boley. The first case that came up before the mayor for trial was that of a young "native" charged with "shooting up" a meeting in a church. But, on the whole, order in the community has been maintained. It is said that during the past two years not a single arrest has been made among the citizens. The reason is that the majority of these negro settlers have come there with the definite intention of getting a home and building up a community where they can, as they say, be "free." What this expression means is pretty well shown by the case of C. W. Perry, who came from Marshall, Texas. Perry had learned the trade of a machinist and had worked in the railway machine shops until the white machinists struck and made it so uncomfortable that the negro machinists went out. Then he went on the railway as brakeman, where he worked for fifteen years. He owned his own home and was well respected, so much so that when it became known that he intended to leave, several of the county commissioners called on him. "Why are you going away?" they asked; "you have your home here among us. We know you and you know us. We are behind you and will protect you."

"Well," he replied, "I have always had an ambition to do something for myself. I don't want always to be led. I want to do a little leading."

Other immigrants, like Mr. T. R. Ringe, the mayor, who was born a slave in Kentucky, and Mr. E. L. Lugrande, one of the principal stockholders in the new bank, came out in the new country, like so many of the white settlers, merely to get land. Mr. Lugrande came from Denton County, Texas, where he had 418 acres of land. He had purchased this land some years ago for four and five dollars the acre. He sold it for fifty dollars an acre, and, coming to Boley, he purchased a tract of land just outside of town and began selling town lots. Now a large part of his acreage is in the center of the town.

Mr. D. J. Turner, who owns a drugstore and has an interest in the Farmers' and Merchants' Bank, came to Indian Territory as a boy, and has grown up among the Indians, to whom he is in a certain way related, since he married an Indian girl and in that way got a section of land. Mr. Turner remembers the days when everyone in this section of the Territory lived a half-savage life, cultivating a little corn and killing a wild hog or a beef when they wanted meat. And he has seen the rapid change, not only in the country, but in the people, since the tide of immigration turned this way. The negro immigration from the South, he says, has been a particularly helpful influence upon the "native" negroes, who are beginning now to cultivate their lands in a way which they never thought of doing a few years ago.

A large proportion of the settlers of Boley are farmers from Texas, Arkansas, and Mississippi. But the desire for western lands has drawn into the community not only farmers, but doctors, lawyers, and craftsmen of all kinds. The fame of the town has also brought, no doubt, a certain proportion of the drifting population. But behind all other attractions of the new colony is the belief that here negroes would find greater opportunities and more freedom of action than they have been able to find in the older communities North and South.

Boley, like the other negro towns that have sprung up in other parts of the country, represents a dawning race consciousness, a wholesome desire to do something to make the race respected; something which shall demonstrate the right of the negro, not merely as an individual, but as a race, to have a worthy and permanent place in the civilization that the American people are creating.

In short, Boley is another chapter in the long struggle of the negro for moral, industrial, and political freedom.

• *Notable Births:* Ivie Anderson, a singer, was born in Los Angeles, California (July 10).
• Frank Marshal Davis, a poet, was born.

Frank Marshal Davis was born in Arkansas City, Kansas. Davis was graduated from Kansas State College with a degree in journalism.

In 1931, Davis founded the Atlanta *Daily World* in Georgia and remained its editor until 1934 when he became the feature editor of the *Associated Negro Press* in Chicago.

In 1937, Davis was a Rosenwald Fellow in Poetry and a lecturer in jazz history at the Lincoln School in Chicago.

Three of Davis' collections of published poetry are *Black Man's Verse* (1935), *I Am the American Negro* (1937), and *47th Street* (1948). Davis mastered many poetic forms and was one of the first to write poetic ballads with jazz rhythm. His "Four Glimpses of Night" is a prime example of this novel ballad form.

Some of Davis' poetry was imitative but most of it was personal, honest, and unique.

• Bertha "Chippie" Hill, a blues singer, was born in Charleston, South Carolina (March 15).
• Earl "Fatha" Hines, a jazz pianist who developed the trumpet style of piano playing, was born.

Earl "Fatha" Hines was born in Duquesne, Pennsylvania. He studied piano while at Schenley High School in Pittsburgh and, later, came to work at several local clubs.

In 1927, Hines played with Louis Armstrong. Throughout the 1920s and 1930s, Hines led his own band. In the 1940s, his orchestra included many of the bop musicians such as Dizzy Gillespie and Charlie Parker.

• Lois Mailou Jones, a painter, was born in Boston, Massachusetts (November 3).
• Robert N. C. Nix, an African American member of Congress, was born.

Robert N. C. Nix was born in Orangeburg, South Carolina. He moved with his family to New York where he received his early education.

After graduating from the University of Pennsylvania Law School, Nix worked as an advocate for Federal and state departments. In 1958, Nix was elected to Congress to fill the unexpired term of a Congressman from Philadelphia.

• James A. Porter, a painter and art historian, was born in Baltimore, Maryland (December 22).
• Librarian and historian Dorothy Burnett Porter Wesley was born in Virginia (May 25). Wesley would serve as founding curator of the Moorland-Spingarn Research Center at Howard University.
• *Notable Deaths:* There were 62 recorded lynchings of African Americans in 1905.
• James E. O'Hara (1844–1905), a Reconstruction era Congressperson from North Carolina, died.

James E. O'Hara was born of free parents in New York City. O'Hara studied law at Howard University. He was admitted to the Bar in 1873.

During Reconstruction, O'Hara served a term in the North Carolina State Legislature. In 1875, he was a delegate to the North Carolina Constitutional Convention.

O'Hara was elected to Congress in 1882. He served two terms in Congress. During his second term, O'Hara worked on civil rights legislation and for equal access to public accommodations.

After failing to gain a third term, O'Hara practiced law in New Bern, North Carolina.

• Josiah T. Walls (1842–1905), a Reconstruction Era Congressperson from Florida, died.

Josiah T. Walls was born of free parents in Winchester, Virginia. By 1860, Walls had moved to Florida and had become a successful farmer.

Walls was drafted into the Confederate Army, was captured, and, by 1865, had become a sergeant-major in the Union Army.

A member of the Florida State Legislature, he was elected to Congress from 1871 to 1877, and advocated support for the Cuban Revolution.

Walls was almost ruined as a planter by severe weather conditions, and accepted the superintendence of a farm at Tallahassee State College, the predecessor of Florida Agricultural and Mechanical University ("Florida A&M").

• George Washington (1817–1905), pioneer, humanitarian and founder of Centralia, Washington, died.

George Washington was born in Virginia. His European American mother gave him up for adoption to a European American family which moved to the American frontier.

In 1850, Washington moved to the Oregon Territory and, eventually, homesteaded in present day Washington.

In 1872, Washington established Centralia when the Northern Pacific Railroad crossed his land. Today in Centralia, Washington, a city park bears his name.

- *Miscellaneous State Laws:* Florida instituted a Jim Crow streetcar law.
- Georgia became the first state to segregate its public parks.
- *Publications:* Robert S. Abbott (1870–1940) began publication of the *Chicago Defender*, the most influential and militant African American newspaper.

In 1905, Robert Sengstacke Abbott, a Chicago lawyer, decided to resume his life in print by starting up his own newspaper. The paper was entitled *Chicago Defender* and its first issue appeared on May 5, 1905. The newspaper was the first large-city African American newspaper and its timing was propitious.

It was at this time that Chicago began to receive an influx of African Americans fleeing the repressive climate of the South. The *Chicago Defender* came into existence just as the flood of African American immigrants from the South came to reside within Chicago. The newspaper served a great need and it prospered accordingly.

Abbott's *Chicago Defender* was not just a newspaper. It was an instrument for change. Abbott used the paper to crusade for the civil rights of African Americans not only in Chicago but throughout the United States.

- Booker T. Washington published *Tuskegee and Its People.*
- *The Voice of the Negro,* a respected African American magazine, began to criticize Booker T. Washington's accommodationist philosophy.
- George Edmund Hayes, an African American graduate student at Columbia University, made an extensive study of social and economic conditions among African Americans in New York City, and published it in book form as *The Negro at Work in New York City.*
- Charles Chestnutt published his last novel, *The Colonel's Dream.*
- Paul Laurence Dunbar published *Lyrics of Sunshine and Shadow.*
- *The Performing Arts:* Ernest Hogan, an African American vaudevillian and song writer, starred in *Rufus Rastus,* a musical for which he wrote the lyrics and collaborated on the music.

- The first modern jazz band was heard on a New York stage. Organized at The Marshall by Ernest Hogan (1865–1909), the band was known as the Memphis Students, a singing, playing, dancing orchestra which made use of banjos, mandolins, guitars, saxophones, drums, plus a violin, several brass instruments and a double bass. Among the twenty performers were Ernest Hogan, vaudeville comedian; Abbie Mitchell, soprano; and Ida Forsyne, dancer. The band became a sensation. One of its more daring innovations was the introduction of a dancing conductor, Will Dixon, and the first drummer (Buddy Gilmore) to perform stunts while drumming. Will Marion Cook later led the group on a European tour which lasted several months.
- The Pekin Theater, a theater owned by African Americans, was opened in Chicago. Founded by Robert Mott, the theater was important not only for stage productions, but also for its concert series. The theater ceased operations in 1916.
- *Motion Pictures:* The earliest known American film with an African American cast was the one-reeler, *The Wooing and Wedding of a Coon.* The film was a rather derogatory depiction of African Americans.
- The film *Fights of a Nation* was produced. *Fights of a Nation* was notable for its depiction of the Mexican American character as a treacherous greaser, a Jew as a briber, a Spaniard as a foppish Latin lover, an Irishman as a quarrelsome drunk, and the African American character as a razor-wielding man with natural rhythm. With regards to the African American stereotype, little would change for the next one hundred years.
- *Scholastic Achievements:* Anna T. Jeanes, the daughter of a wealthy Philadelphia Quaker, gave $200,000 to the General Education Fund to help improve rural African American schools in the South.
- *Scientific Achievements:* George McJunkin (1851–1922), a cowboy, bronco buster, Indian arrowhead collector, and explorer, was the first person to recognize bones of an extinct bison near Folsom, New Mexico. The bones alone were less significant than the spear points found with them. The presence of the spear points proved that people lived in North America over 10,000 years ago.

Black Enterprise

In 1905, Madame C. J. Walker developed a formula for a preparation which improved "the appearance of the hair" of African Americans. Convinced in the effectiveness of her product, Walker spent the next two years travelling around the country promoting it. Soon her mail order business began to grow. By 1910, she had become successful enough to establish laboratories for the manufacture of various cosmetics and hair products for African Americans. *See 1867.*

• Twenty-eight African American banks were organized in the years from 1899 through 1905.

• Ernest W. Lyon, an African American and the then United States Minister to Liberia, helped to create the New York Liberian Steamship Line. Lyon participated in this endeavor in an effort to establish closer commercial relations between the United States and Liberia.

• Alonzo F. Herndon founded the Atlanta Life Insurance Company. The Atlanta Life Insurance Company became the largest African American owned business in the nation.

• Philip A. Payton, Jr., persuaded landlords who had overbuilt apartments in the Harlem area of New York City to rent the apartments to African Americans.

By 1908, Payton controlled more than $500,000 worth of property in New York City.

• *Sports:* The Smart Set, an African American athletic club, was established in Brooklyn, New York.

• Bob Marshall was selected for the All-American football team. Marshall was a star player for the University of Minnesota.

THE AMERICAS

• *Brazil:* Jose Do Patrocinio (1853–1905), an Afro-Brazilian abolitionist, journalist, orator, poet and novelist, died.

Patrocinio was the son of a Catholic priest and planter in Rio de Janeiro Province and an Afro-Brazilian fruit vendor. Patrocinio was raised in the vicarage of Campos and on a nearby estate. It was while living on the estate that Patrocinio acquired his intimate knowledge of slavery.

After serving an apprenticeship at Misericordia Hospital in Rio de Janeiro, Patrocinio completed a course in pharmacy at the Faculty of Medicine. However, due to a lack of funds, Patrocinio was unable to pursue this profession.

Instead of pharmacy, Patrocinio joined the staff of the capital's daily, *Gazeta de Noticias.* Through this newspaper, Patrocinio soon gained prominence as an opponent of slavery.

In 1877, Do Patrocino published *Motta Coquiero. Motta Coquiero* was a story concerning the murder of a plantation owner in retaliation for a murder he did not commit. Its importance lies in the careful examination of racial tensions and conflicts on a plantation in Brazil among Euro-Brazilians, Afro-Brazilians, and COTWs.

In 1881, aided by his wealthy father-in-law, Patrocinio acquired *Gazeta de Tarde.* Under Patrocinio's leadership, *Gazeta de Tarde* would become the principal antislavery journal in Brazil until it was replaced by his equally effective *A Cidade do Rio* in 1887.

Patrocinio advanced the antislavery cause as a powerful orator, as author of fiery articles and editorials, as organizer of antislavery groups, as an abolitionist emissary to Europe, and as an effective promoter of regional movements. Some of the more notable movements which Patrocinio promoted include Ceara in 1882, Campos in 1885 and the port of Santos in 1886.

With the end of slavery in 1888, Patrocinio organized the Guarda Negra (Black Guard). The Black Guard was an association of Afro-Brazilian militants dedicated to protecting Princess Isabel. At the time, Princess Isabel's succession to the throne was threatened by a growing republican movement.

After the military revolt of 1889 and the beginning of the federal republic, Patrocinio suffered persecution from President Floriano Peixoto's government, including exile in 1892 to the state of Amazonas. Additionally, the operation of Patrocinio's newspaper, *A Cidade do Rio,* was suspended.

At the time of his death in 1905, Patrocinio was still active as a journalist.

• *Dominican Republic:* The United States seized the Dominican customs.

The 1899 assassination of Ulises Heureaux, the legendary dictator of the Dominican Republic, resulted in renewed political and financial destabilization in the country. The destabilization of the Dominican Republic was instrumental in persuading the government of the United States to take over the receivership of Dominican customs in 1905. This take over was done under what came to be known as the "Roosevelt Corollary" of the Monroe Doctrine.

AFRICA

• *North Africa, Egypt and Sudan:* Kaiser Wilhelm II visited Tangiers (March 31). The visit set off a crisis in Morocco. On May 17, Britian proposed discussions on Morocco. On

July 8, France agreed to discussions on Morocco. On September 28, France and Germany agreed to a conference on Morocco.

• The Sultan of Morocco obtained another loan from France.

• Muhammed Abduh (1849–1905), a mufti of Egypt and religious reformer, died.

• Yambio (c.1820s–1905), one of the most powerful of the late nineteenth century Zande rulers of the Sudan, died.

Yambio's father was the chief of the Gbudwe branch of the Zande in southwestern Sudan. Yambio succeeded to the chieftainship on his father's death in 1869, but by then the state had already been informally partitioned among his brothers. Arab slavers penetrating Zande country attempted to play Yambio's family factions off against each other. Yambio himself consistently refused to collaborate with outsiders and strove to consolidate the Zande unaided.

In 1870, Yambio drove an Arab slave caravan out of his territory. Shortly afterwards, Yambio rebuffed an attempted conquest by the powerful merchant prince, al-Zubayr Rahma Mansur.

The Egyptian administration being established, at that time, in Sudan eased the problem of the slavers, but it too had designs on Zande territory. In 1881, Yambio defeated an Egyptian force only to be attacked by a stronger army the next year.

Yambio was captured and held prisoner until 1884, when the Mahdists troops of Muhammed 'Ahmad freed him. The Mahdists, who were then sweeping through Sudan, wished to use Yambio as an ally in their drive towards the Congo basin. Yambio refused to cooperate and returned home to reassert his authority over the Zande.

Meanwhile, the Mahdists withdrew to consolidate their hold on central Sudan and Yambio was left to live in relative peace and prosperity for over a decade.

Yambio's peace was shattered by Mahdist raids in 1897, but he repelled their assaults. Two years later, the Mahdist state fell to the British-Egyptian government, and Zande country became the focus of aggressive imperial rivalry between the British from the northeast and Belgians from the southwest.

Once again, Yambio struggled to remain independent while neighboring chiefs and relatives aligned themselves with the Europeans. In 1903 and 1904, Yambio spurned British attempts to negotiate an accommodation while Leopold's forces massed against him along his southwestern border.

Late in 1904, Yambio led a costly and futile attack on the Belgian positions. Terribly outmanned, Yambio was forced to fall back to await his fate.

Early in 1905, Yambio's demoralized troops crumbled before a combined British-Sudanese onslaught in which Yambio was killed.

On his death, Yambio's kingdom, which fell into British hands, was partitioned among his sons.

• *Western Africa:* There was an uprising in French Guinea. French operations were initiated against Baoule, Agbas and Ebries. On June 7, the Algerian-AOF boundary was defined. French Mauritania was reorganized.

• Felix Houphouet-Boigny, the first president of the Ivory Coast, was born.

Felix Houphouet-Boigny was born the son of a Baoule chief. He received his secondary education at Bingerville before pursuing his medical training in Senegal.

Houphouet-Boigny returned to the Ivory Coast in 1925 and practiced medicine for almost twenty years, becoming a chief and a prosperous planter as well.

In 1944, Houphouet-Boigny founded an agricultural union to vent the protests of Baoule coffee farmers who were suffering under French economic restrictions. The next year, Houphouet-Boigny converted the union into the political *Parti Democratique de la Cote d'Ivoire* (PDCI).

Houphouet-Boigny, who was then considered a radical, affiliated the PDCI with the French Communist Party. In 1945, he was elected to the French constituent assemblies which designed the Fourth French Republic.

The African delegates to the assemblies, dissatisfied with the limited freedom granted to France's colonies in the new republic, met at Bamako to form an inter-territorial political party. They formed the *Rassemblement Democratique Africain* — the RDA. Houphouet-Boigny was elected president of the RDA. However, two prominent Senegalese politicians, Lamine Gueye and Leopold Senghor boycotted the conference because the French Socialist Party from which they drew support believed the RDA would be Communist dominated.

After the conference, the African politicians formed two blocs — Houphouet-Boigny's group favored autonomy for individual colonies within the French community, while the Senghor-Gueye group preferred a federation of French affiliated African states.

Houphouet-Boigny was elected to the French Chamber of Deputies, where he successfully fought two particularly hated aspects of the French colonial systems — forced labor and the *indigenat*. These two tools gave French administrators unchecked power over Africans in certain areas.

Beginning in 1949, the RDA, with Communist support organized demonstrations and boycotts throughout French West Africa. Violence erupted in the Ivory Coast, culminating in an incident at Dimbokro where thirteen Africans were killed and fifty wounded. French repression was severe, forcing Houphouet-Boigny to re-examine his policy.

Houphouet-Boigny renounced RDA links with the Communists. However, this move did not come in time to prevent the defeat of most RDA candidates in the 1951 elections to the French assembly.

Houphouet-Boigny rebuilt the RDA. This time he concentrated on cooperation with the French political and business leaders. In the 1956 election, the RDA won nine seats in the French Chamber.

Houphouet-Boigny joined the French government as a cabinet minister. In that capacity, he served until 1959.

As a minister, Houphouet-Boigny was instrumental in designing the framework for granting autonomy to France's African territories. His support of the principle of complete autonomy rather than federation stemmed from the Ivory Coast's being the richest colony. If a federation was created, the Ivory Coast would have had to contribute more to a federation than it would have received.

Although Senghor and Gueye continued to build new alliances aimed at federation, Houphouet-Boigny defeated them all.

In 1958, the hopes of the Senegalese politicians were almost realized with the formation of the Mali Federation, but Houphouet-Boigny pressured Dahomey (Benin) and Upper Volta (Burkina Faso) to withdraw at the last moment. The withdrawal of these two countries left only Senegal and Mali as partners in the Mali Federation. By 1960, the Mali Federation was no more as Mali and Senegal separated.

In 1958, the Ivory Coast achieved autonomy within the French community and Felix Houphouet-Boigny became the first president.

In 1959, the Ivory Coast became a fully independent country.

Houphouet-Boigny was later criticized for his close ties to France, his open appeals for Western capital, and his comparatively slow placement of Africans in key government positions. Houphouet-Boigny's philosophy was that economic stability is the key to political success and that French assistance is essential for sound management and organization. The measure of Houphouet-Boigny's success was the Ivory Coast's rise to comparative prosperity by the 1980s, despite a lack of exceptional natural resources.

- Siaka Probyn Stevens (1905–1988), a future president of Sierra Leone, was born.

Siaka Stevens was born in northern Sierra Leone and educated in Freetown. After serving in the national police from 1923 to 1930, Stevens worked for an iron mining company.

In 1943, Stevens founded the Mineworkers Union and took up unionism as a career. He was appointed to the protectorate assembly to represent workers. Two years later, Stevens went to Oxford to study industrial relations.

In 1951, Stevens helped the Margai brothers to found the Sierra Leone People's Party (SLPP) and became a party delegate to the protectorate assembly. Two years later, Stevens joined the executive council.

The 1957 elections that created the country's first African-controlled government made Milton Margai prime minister. Subsequently, Margai's brother Albert and Stevens withdrew from the party.

In 1960, Stevens was a member of a delegation to London sent to work out arrangements for independence. Protesting the conference's report because it did not call for new pre-independence elections, Stevens returned home and formed a new party. This party would come to be known as the All People's Congress (APC). In the furor over the election issue, Margai was temporarily jailed, but became opposition leader upon independence in 1961.

When Milton Margai died in 1964, his brother Albert became prime minister. Beset with charges of favoritism and corruption and a slumping national economy, Albert Margai proved to be less than a popular ruler.

Northerners and other dissidents rallied around Stevens, giving his APC a narrow electoral victory in 1967. However, as Stevens was about to form a new government, Brigadier David Lansana seized power. Two more coups followed before Stevens was able to become prime minister in 1968.

Three years later, Stevens made Sierra Leone a republic and became its first president.

Stevens' long survival in office was remarkable, given Sierra Leone's political volatility — a volatility which reflects ethnic factionalism and endemic economic problems. Stevens survived several coup and assassination attempts, as well as protests, demonstrations and riots.

In 1978, Sierra Leone's cherished multi-party system was abandoned with the approval of a new constitution providing for APC one-party rule. At the end of 1985, after a period of relative calm, Stevens announced his retirement. The APC selected Major General Joseph Momoh to succeed Stevens.

- *Central Africa:* There was an insurrection in the Welle district in the Belgian Congo (February). The report of the Commission of Inquiry into Belgian atrocities in the Congo exculpated Leopold II.
- Chief Machoncho attempted to kill the German administrator von Grawert. However, the attempt failed and, instead, Machoncho was shot by von Grawert.
- Mwami Kissabo was formally recognized by Germany as the ruler of Burundi (October).
- A Franco-German treaty was reached on the Cameroon frontiers.
- Simon-Pierre Mpadi, an independent church leader in Zaire, is believed to have been born in this year.

Simon-Pierre Mpadi was educated at an American Baptist Mission station in the western Belgian Congo (Zaire) and served as a Baptist catechist from 1925 to 1934.

In 1934, Mpadi joined a new Salvation Army mission and became one of its evangelists. He attended Salvation Army Bible school, but soon broke away to establish his own church in 1939.

Mpadi's Church of the Blacks revived many of the millenarian teachings of Simon Kimbangu, whose movement was then at a low ebb among the Kongo people.

For the next few years, Mpadi was harassed by the colonial authorities because his movement was thought to be dangerously revolutionary. Mpadi repeatedly escaped imprisonment and finally fled to the French Congo.

In the French Congo, Mpadi spent most of the 1940s and the 1950s in prison, until Zaire became independent in 1960. Nevertheless, Mpadi's church remained intact and by 1970 Mpadi still had about 15,000 followers.

- *Eastern Africa:* The Acting Provincial Commissioner in Ankole was speared to death (May 19). The Ankole agreement was suspended.

- The Planters and Farmers Association (Kenya) became the Colonists' Association. Delamere lost control of the Association.
- The Nandi Field Force was raised to control the Nandi tribe. An expedition was launched against Sotik and Kisu.
- The responsibility for Uganda was transferred from the Foreign Office to the Colonial Office.
- Local organizations formed the Pastoralists Association in Kenya.
- Beginning in 1905, the Maji-Maji rebellion erupted in German East Africa (Tanzania). The southern area of German East Africa was chiefly affected. *See also Kinjikitile Ngwale, below.*

During 1905, a major anti–German revolt erupted. The revolt came to be known as Maji Maji. Maji Maji swept southern Tanzania and drew in the Ngoni. Apparently motivated by a desire to preserve his authority among the Ngoni, Songea led several attacks on German positions.

The mainland territory of present day Tanzania was — along with Rwanda and Burundi — brought under German colonial rule after 1884.

Great Britain and Belgium conquered German East Africa during World War I and partitioned the territory between themselves. Belgium took Rwanda and Burundi (Ruanda-Urundi) while Great Britain took Tanganyika. These lands were taken as League of Nations trust territories.

In 1961, Tanganyika became independent. Julius Nyerere was the first prime minister.

In 1964, Tanganyika merged with Zanzibar to become the United Republic of Tanzania.

- Bishop Cassian Spiess was murdered (September).
- Early in 1905, Muhammed 'Abdullah Hassan, the "Mad Mullah," signed a treaty with the Italians which made him the ruler of a newly defined Italian protectorate on the central Somali coast. An uneasy truce ensued, but Muhammed continued to attract new adherents.
- Kinjikitile Ngwale, a religious cult leader and chief instigator of the *Maji Maji* rebellion in German East Africa, died.

Very little is known about Kinjikitile's early life. When he came to Ngarambe, in the hinterland of the central Tanzanian coast, in 1902, he was already middle-aged.

Kinjikitile's arrival was associated with strange

miracles. He soon gained renown as a prophetic cult leader. Drawing upon the established religious beliefs of the coastal peoples, Kinjikitile preached an apocalyptic message promising the ouster of the Germans if certain ritual steps were observed. Believed to be possessed by spirits, Kinjikitile came to be known by the name of a high god — Bokero.

By mid–1904 his message was spreading inland, and he was receiving pilgrims, to whom he gave sacred water (*maji*) from a special pool. Soon his special messengers were administering the sacred water over a large region. Kinjikitile insisted that the actual uprising should await his personal order, but his impatient followers spontaneously started fighting in July, 1905.

Within a month Kinjikitile was captured and hanged. Indeed, Kinjikitile was the first African executed in the uprising. After his death, the rebellion (later known as *Maji Maji* after the sacred water) spread through about a third of present day Tanzania and lasted into 1907.

- Tippu Tip (1837–1905), the most powerful of the late 19th century Arab and Swahili traders in the east African interior (Zaire), died. *See 1865.*
- *Southern Africa:* Botha formed the *Het Volk* organization to agitate for responsible government in the Transvaal.

After the Boer War, Louis Botha and his close associate, Jan Smuts, were outspoken in favor of peaceful reconciliation with the British. In 1905, Botha and Smuts founded the Het Volk party to forward their policy of conciliation and to pressure for responsible government in the Transvaal.

- The Transvaal was granted a constitution (April 25). However, this constitution was regarded by Botha as being inadequate.

In 1905, Alfred Milner, the British high commissioner for South Africa, returned to England after having initiated the restoration of representative government in the Transvaal.

- A railroad bridge over Victoria Falls was completed.
- Tshekedi Khama (1905–1959), the acting chief of the Ngwato from 1925 to 1952, was born.

Although a son of the great Ngwato chief, Khama, Tshekedi ranked behind his nephew Seretse Khama in the succession order after his own brother's death in 1925. However, Seretse was then only four years old, so Tshekedi assumed the regency — an office he held for the next twenty-seven years.

Tshekedi's position as ruler of the Ngwato was a strong one within the protectorate. The imposition of colonial rule had generally enhanced the authority of chiefs, and the Ngwato were one of the dominant societies in the thinly populated country.

Tshekedi quickly established his independence from local colonial authority. He did not hesitate to go over the heads of the local administrators in disputes. Several times, Tshekedi won major decisions in the Privy Council in London.

In the early 1930s, Tshekedi successfully resisted attempts by the British South Africa Company to reaffirm an old mining concession. In doing so, Tshekedi was also able to secure new territory for the Ngwato.

In the mid–1930s, when the South African prime minister, Hertzog pressed for South Africa's incorporation of the High Commission Territories (Bechuanaland, Basutoland and Swaziland), Tshekedi's vigorous campaigning helped to prevent such a move.

In 1944, when Tshekedi's nephew Seretse finished college in South Africa, Tshekedi asked Seretse to assume the chieftaincy formally. Seretse declined, however, in order to study in England.

In England, Seretse met and married a European woman. This marriage was without the approval of Tshekedi.

Tshekedi opposed the marriage and rejected the notion of Seretse's return to Bechuanaland with his European wife. On this issue, Tshekedi was initially supported by most Ngwato councillors. However, when Seretse did return, sentiment shifted to his favor.

Suspected of attempting to assume the chieftainship in his own right, Tshekedi went into self-imposed exile to another part of the country and renounced all claims to the chiefdom.

As a result of the furor, Seretse was restricted to England and the Ngwato were without a chief. In 1956, a compromise was reached whereby both Tshekedi and his nephew renounced their royal claims and entered private life.

- Lerotholi (1840–1905), the king of Lesotho, died.

Lerotholi became a military hero during the reign of his father, Letsie, when he commanded Sotho forces against the Cape Colony in the "Gun War" of 1880. Aware of the mistakes that the Zulu had made during their war with the British in 1879, Lerotholi adopted guerrilla tactics which effectively rendered the Cape forces impotent.

After the Gun War, Lerotholi supported the transfer of his country's administration back to the British Crown.

Lerotholi succeeded his father as king in 1891. His rule was plagued by dissident sub-chiefs who ignored the central administration. Lerotholi gradually asserted his dominance until 1898 when he overcame the last hold-out, Masupha. With the victory over Masupha, Lerotholi re-established monarchical authority.

Before his death in 1905, Lerotholi laid the basis for Lesotho's future parliament by helping to create the Basutoland National Council.

• Sigcawu (c.1860–1905), the last independent paramount chief of the Mpondo, died.

Sigcawu seized the Mpondo chieftainship on the death of his father Mqikela in 1887. Sigcawu's legal claim to the throne was marginal, but he obtained formal recognition after a year.

Sigcawu attempted to continue Mqikela's policy of maintaining friendly relations with the British administration in the Cape, but he refused to recognize a representative from the British high commissioner as a resident in his country. Sigcawu also angered the British by negotiating profitable concessions with German imperial interests.

Sigcawu's uncle Mdlangaso openly rebelled against him in 1890. This rebellion began a civil war which led to disturbances on the Mpondo borders with the British territories that surrounded the Mpondo lands.

In 1894, the Cape Colony ministry of Cecil Rhodes used the Mpondo civil war as a pretext to intimidate Sigcawu into accepting annexation.

Shortly after annexation, Sigcawu was visited by Rhodes. Sigcawu unsuccessfully attempted to obtain recognition as the sole chief of the Mpondo from Rhodes. At the time, the Mpondo had been divided into two states since the death of Sigcawu's grandfather Faku in 1867.

Instead of recognizing Sigcawu as the sole ruler of the Mpondo, Rhodes further divided the Mpondo country into small magisterial districts undermining Sigcawu's remaining authority.

Sigcawu refused to cooperate with the British administration and was, subsequently, arrested in 1895. However, he was later exonerated by a London court.

• Hendrik Witbooi (c.1840–1905), a leader of the Witbooi family of Namibia, died.

The Witbooi family was a powerful ruling family in the Oorlam branch of the Khoikhoi through the 1800s and early twentieth century. The Witboois, along with other Oorlam groups, migrated from the Cape Colony into Namibia, where they introduced Dutch language and culture.

Hendrik Witbooi is considered to be the greatest of the Witbooi chiefs. He was baptized by German missionaries in 1868 and afterwards carried a reputation among Europeans as hardworking and conscientious. Witbooi's religious devotion gave him a sense of mission.

In 1880, Witbooi narrowly escaped death during a surprise attack by the Herero chief Maherero. Witbooi emerged convinced that he was divinely ordained to conquer the Herero and to move his own people north.

During the 1880s, Hendrik Witbooi became estranged from his father, Moses Witbooi *(see 1888)* primarily over the issue of cattle raiding which Hendrik opposed. Hendrik attempted to lead a faction of Christians away from the main Oorlam community, but was stopped by the Herero and forced to remain with his father.

In 1888, Moses Witbooi was deposed and executed by Hendrik's brother-in-law, Paul Visser. Soon afterwards Hendrik defeated and killed Visser and made himself undisputed leader of the Witbooi Oorlam. Other Khoikhoi communities rallied to his banner to seek protection against their mutual enemy, the Herero.

Witbooi could not, however, gain the cooperation of the former Witbooi ally, Jan Jonker Afrikaner *(see 1889)*. But Afrikaner was killed in 1889 and Witbooi was left the strongest ruler in the southern section of Namibia.

During this period, some of the weaker African chiefs accepted German "protection." However, Witbooi resisted. But, in 1894, Witbooi was defeated by the new German administrator, Theodor Leutwin. Witbooi then signed a treaty of protection with the Germans.

Over the next decade, Witbooi worked closely with Leutwin and loaned the Germans material support in their wars with neighboring Africans. In 1903, Hendrik even personally participated in the German campaign against the Bondelswarts Nama.

Later in 1903, however, the Herero revolted against the Germans and Leutwin was replaced by General von Trotha as military commander in South West Africa.

Witbooi had regarded his treaty with the Germans as a personal bond to Leutwin. He felt that the latter's diminished status freed him from any obligations of loyalty to the Germans. Witbooi also resented the progressive alienation of Oorlam land to European settlers.

By 1904, Witbooi came to fear that the policy of extermination which von Trotha was conducting against the Herero would next be applied to his own people. Acting upon another divine command, in October of 1904, Hendrik Witbooi led his people in revolt against the Germans.

Hendrik Witbooi was killed fighting a year later. His followers surrendered the next month, but the general rebellion continued until 1907.

RELATED HISTORICAL EVENTS

• *Europe:* A Franco-German agreement was reached concerning Morocco (September 28).

• *Africa:* George Theal completed the thirty-six volumes of *Records of the Cape Colony* (1897–1905).

• Pierre de Brazza (1852–1905), a French explorer of Italian descent, died.

Born in Italy, Pierre Paul Francois Camille de Brazza became a French citizen in 1874. Beginning in 1875, de Brazza explored the region of the Ogooue River.

In 1880, de Brazza raced Henry Stanley to the upper Congo River where he signed treaties with local chiefs, most notably with the Bateke ruler, Makoko. The execution of this treaty gave France claims to the north bank of the Congo and led to the founding of the French Congo.

In 1883, de Brazza returned to the French Congo to mount more expeditions. These expeditions would greatly extend and bolster French claims in the region.

From 1886 to 1888, de Brazza was the commissioner-general of the French Congo. De Brazza's expeditions, which were quite popular in France, were greatly responsible for accelerating the European "scramble" for Africa.

• Lord Chelmsford (Frederic A. Thesiger)(1827–1905), the British commander of the forces which vanquished the Zulu King Cetewayo, died.

When the Zulu King Cetewayo *(see 1872 and 1884)* refused to comply with Frere's ultimatum to disarm, Chelmsford was named major-general over the British invasion force. One of Lord Chelmsford's regiments was quickly annihilated by the Zulu at Isandhlwana *(see 1879)* and Lord Chelmsford was immediately discredited.

Prime Minister Disraeli appointed Wolseley to supersede Lord Chelmsford. However, before Wolseley could assume his command, Chelmsford scored a victory against Cetewayo and the Zulu.

Chelmsford occupied Cetewayo's capital, Ulundi, shortly before Wolseley arrived. The war with the Zulu had been brought to an end.

Chelmsford, having restored his reputation, resigned. The capture of Cetewayo was left to Wolseley.

• Edgar Cuthbert Whitehead (1905–1971), a prime minister of Southern Rhodesia, was born.

Edgar Cuthbert Whitehead was born in Germany of British parents. He came to Zimbabwek (Southern Rhodesia) in 1928 and entered the civil service.

Whitehead was elected to the legislative assembly in 1939, but left afterwards to serve with the British army in west Africa during World War II. Afterwards, Whitehead served as Southern Rhodesia's (Zimbabwe's) high commissioner in London before returning home.

Once back in Zimbabwe, Whitehead reclaimed his old assembly seat and took a ministerial post in Godfrey Huggins' government in 1946. He retired from government because of ill-health in 1953, the same year Southern Rhodesia entered the Central African Federation.

Later, Whitehead accepted a post in Washington, D. C. As the Federation's representative.

Early in 1958, a ruling party congress removed from the Southern Rhodesian premiership Garfield Todd, who was considered too liberal. Whitehead was chosen as a compromise candidate and was recalled from America to become prime minister. In order to assume the office, Whitehead replaced another party member in an assembly seat. In an ensuing by-election, Whitehead was unexpectedly voted out of office.

Whitehead called for a general election. During the pre-election period, Whitehead restructured his entire government.

The character of Whitehead's administration was ambivalent. Although he outlawed African nationalist parties and thereby touched off an era of violent protest, he also did more to remove color bar restrictions than any previous administration.

In 1961, Whitehead sponsored a new constitution which granted Africans their first direct legislative representation. Afterwards his administration grew increasingly reactionary.

Whitehead's administration did not, however, keep pace with the conservative swing of the Euro-Zimbabwean electorate as a whole. He was voted out of office in favor of the Rhodesian Front party in 1962.

1 9 0 6

THE UNITED STATES

Two tragic incidents from 1906 left their mark on African American history. The first was an incident in Brownsville, Texas, and the second was a race riot in Atlanta, Georgia.

In August, in Brownsville, Texas, an African American soldier of the 1st Battalion of the 25th Infantry, United States Colored Troops, had an altercation with a European American Brownsville merchant. In protest, a dozen or more African American soldiers entered the town, shooting in the streets. In the melee, a European American was killed and two others, including the police chief, were wounded.

Three companies of the United States Colored Troops finally became involved in the riot. Only the firm intervention of the commander at Fort Brown prevented the melee from growing into a more deadly riot. In November, on the basis of an inspector's report which claimed that African American troops had murdered and maimed the European Americans, and the concurrent refusal of the African Americans to testify, President Roosevelt dishonorably discharged the three companies and disqualified them from future military or civil service.

John Milholland of the Constitution League and Senators Tillman, of South Carolina, and Foraker, of Ohio, spoke on behalf of the African American soldiers.

In December, Senator Foraker insisted that a full and fair trial should have preceded such drastic punishment.

*   *   *

The biggest of the Southern race riots between 1900 and 1910 occurred in Atlanta, Georgia, during the week of September 24. Days before the riot there was talk of disenfranchising African Americans. The press urged a revival of the Klan, and offered rewards for a "lynching bee."

On Saturday, September 22, a newspaper reported four assaults on European American women by African Americans. The next day, Sunday, was quiet, but on Monday, September 24, rioting erupted in Brownsville, an Atlanta suburb.

African Americans heard that rioting had begun in Atlanta and that African Americans were being slaughtered. Many African Americans sought protection (asylum) at such institutions as Clark University and Gammon Theological Seminary. Others collected firearms for their defense.

Law officers began arresting African Americans for their possession of firearms. In the course of making the arrests, one officer shot into a crowd of African Americans. The gunfire was returned. One officer was killed while another was wounded.

The news of the killing of the officer enraged European Americans who descended upon the African American community with destructive, homicidal retribution in mind. Four prominent African Americans were killed and many others were injured. J. W. E. Bowen, the president of Gammon Theological Seminary was beaten over the head with a rifle butt by a police officer. Jesse Max Barber, the editor of the *Voice of the Negro*, was forced by a European American mob to leave town. The houses of many African Americans were looted and burned.

For several days, the city was paralyzed. Factories closed. All transportation stopped. Numerous African Americans packed up their belongings and left town. Madness truly reigned.

When the madness began to subside, many European Americans recoiled in horror at what had been done. Many of the shocked European Americans confessed shame and condemned the rioters. A group of responsible African American and European American citizens came together and organized the Atlanta Civic League to work for improvement of social conditions and to prevent other riots. No action, however, was ever brought against the rioters.

As a result of the Atlanta Riot, the Afro-American Council became more militant and less amenable to Booker T. Washington's direction. At the October convention, the Council members vehemently condemned ballot restrictions, Jim Crow laws and the prevalence of mob violence.

• A race riot erupted in Springfield, Ohio.

• In Greensburg, Indiana, a European American mob rioted, destroying property and beating African Americans, in response to the conviction of a mentally disabled African American for assaulting his European American employer. Many of the town's African Americans were forced to flee from the town.

• Allen Allensworth (1842–1914) was promoted to the rank of lieutenant colonel in the United States Army.

Allen Allensworth was born a slave. He taught under the auspices of the Freedmen's Bureau, operated a number of businesses, and served as a chaplain during the Spanish-American War. At the time of his retirement, Allensworth was the senior chaplain in the army.

In 1908, Allensworth founded an all-black town named Allensworth in Tulare County, California.

• *The Civil Rights Movement:* The second Niagara conference met at Harpers Ferry, West Virginia to commemorate John Brown's raid on the federal arsenal and to issue a strong statement concerning the acquisition of civil rights for African Americans (August 16–19). This second Niagara conference published a manifesto written by W. E. B. Du Bois. The manifesto protested European American oppression of African Americans. As Du Bois wrote: "*Stripped of verbose subterfuge, and in its naked nastiness, the new American creed says: fear to let black men even try to rise lest they become equals of the white. And this in the land that professes to follow Jesus Christ. The blasphemy of such a course is only matched by its cowardice.*"

• In Macon, Georgia, several hundred African Americans met at the state convention under the leadership of William Jefferson White and formed an Equal Rights Association. The Equal Rights Association rejected Booker T. Washington's accommodationist philosophy.

• *The Labor Movement:* William H. Baldwin, president of the Long Island Railroad, encouraged a group of African Americans and European Americans to investigate the employment problems of the African American. As the Committee for Improving the Industrial Conditions of Negroes, the group tried to find jobs without racial prejudice from employers or unions.

• R. T. Sims, an African American, became a national organizer for the International Workers of the World (IWW). Sims would serve the IWW until 1919 when he left to organize a separate African American union organization.

• *Notable Births:* Josephine Baker, a famous entertainer, was born (June 3).

Josephine Baker was born in St. Louis, Missouri. At the age of 15, she ran away from home and became Bessie Smith's maid. While traveling with the great blues singer, Baker quickly established herself as a singer in her own right. After several minor parts in Broadway shows,

in 1925, Baker left the United States for Paris, France. In Paris, she starred with the "Revue Negre" and became a sensation.

Baker later went on to headline for the Folies Bergere. During World War II, she sang to raise funds for war relief, and was a nurse with the Free French Forces.

• Aviator Willa Brown was born in Glasgow, Kentucky (January 22).

• Johnny Hodges, a jazz alto saxophonist, was born (July 25).

• Jay Saunders Redding, a writer, was born.

Jay Saunders Redding was born in Wilmington, Delaware, into a closely knit, religious, middle-class family. Both of Redding's parents were graduates of Howard University and his parents insisted that all their children attend college.

Redding was on the staff of the *Brown Literary Quarterly* at Brown University. His first story, "Delaware Coon," was published in Eugene Jola's avant garde *Transition* magazine in 1928.

For the next ten years, Redding taught and attended graduate school at Brown and Columbia universities. In 1939, *To Make a Poet Black,* Redding's first book, was published. In 1950, Redding published *They Came in Chains,* a general study of the African American in the United States. Also in 1950, Redding published *A Stranger Alone,* a biographical novel. *On Being a Negro in America,* a personal study of the effects of American racism on an African American appeared in 1952.

While working for the United States State Department in India, Redding wrote *An American in India,* a detailed analysis of India's people and government. In 1958, *The Lonesome Road,* Redding's second novel, was published.

For many years Redding served on the faculty of Hampton Institute as a professor of English.

• Victoria Spivey, a blues singer, was born in Houston, Texas (October 15).

• Roosevelt Sykes, a blues singer, was born (January 30).

• *Notable Deaths:* There were 65 recorded lynchings in 1906.

• The Atlanta race riot resulted in the death of twelve people (September 22).

• Paul Laurence Dunbar, a noted African American poet, died in Dayton, Ohio (February 9). *See 1872.*

• *Miscellaneous Laws:* A Montgomery, Alabama, municipal ordinance went beyond the state Jim Crow law to require that separate streetcars be provided for African Americans and European Americans.

• Louisiana Democrats adopted the "white primary."

• *Publications:* Booker T. Washington published *Putting the Most into Life.*

• William Braithwaite published *Elizabethan Verse.*

• J. Mord Allen, a African American boilermaker and poet, had his collection of humorous dialect verse, *Rhymes, Tales and Rhymed,* published.

• *The Arts:* Henry Ossawa Tanner's *Two Disciples at the Tomb* was awarded the Harris Prize by the Art Institute of Chicago for being the most distinguished work of the 1906 art season.

• Henry Ossawa Tanner's *The Disciples at Emmaus* was purchased by the French government for 4,000 francs and paired with *The Resurrection of Lazarus* at the Musee du Luxembourg.

• The Pennsylvania Academy of Fine Arts in Philadelphia exhibited *Portraits from Mirrors,* a sculpture by Meta Vaux Warrick.

• *The Performing Arts:* In 1906, Bert Williams and George Walker starred in *Abyssinia,* a musical by Alex Roger, Jesse Shippe and Will Marion Cook.

• *The Shoofly Regiment,* a musical by Bob Cole and J. Rosamond Johnson, ran on Broadway.

• The Pekin Stock Company, the first African American repertory company, was organized in Chicago.

• *Scholastic Achievements:* John Wesley Edward Bowen, Sr., (1855–1933) became the first African American president of Gammon Theological Seminary in Atlanta, Georgia.

• R. L. Diggs earned a doctorate in sociology from Illinois Wesleyan University (Bloomington, Illinois).

• *The Black Church:* William J. Seymour (1870–1922) led the Azusa Street Revival in Los Angeles, California. This revival is considered to be the beginning of modern Pentecostalism.

From April 14, 1906, the preaching of William J. Seymour at the Azusa Street Mission in Los Angeles gave birth to a major strand in the diffusion of the Pentecostal movement among both African Americans and European Americans. Seymour's ministry emphasized the centrality of speaking in tongues as evidence of baptism in the Holy Spirit. This new development attracted both African Americans and European Americans.

C. H. Mason's experiences at the Azusa Street Mission in 1907 led him to make the practice central in the Church of God in Christ.

In 1908, G. B. Cashwell introduced the practice he had learned from Seymour to the predominantly European American Church of God, USA. Pentecostalists soon split along racial lines. However, C. H. Mason's church was incorporated and some European American leaders of segregated congregations continued to be ordained by Mason for a number of years in order to be legally recognized as ministers.

• *Organizations:* Alpha Phi Alpha, the first African American Greek letter society was organized as a fraternity (December 4).

Alpha Phi Alpha was founded at Cornell University, Ithaca, New York. The first president was George B. Kelley. The first convention, at Howard University, Washington, D. C., was held in 1908.

• By 1906, there were a number of small African American YMCAs in the District of Columbia, Philadelphia, New York City, and Baltimore.

• The first African American athletic association, the Interscholastic Athletic Association, was organized with the purpose of fostering sports in the Baltimore/Washington, D.C., area. Comprised of colleges and high schools, the first event — a track and field event — was held on May 30 at Howard University in the District of Columbia.

• *Black Enterprise:* To protest and fight against Jim Crow streetcar rules, African Americans in Austin, Nashville and Savannah, organized their own transportation companies. However, these companies were all short-lived.

• *Sports:* Bob Marshall, the University of Minnesota football star, was again selected for the All-American team.

THE AMERICAS

• *Brazil:* Joaquim Machado de Assis published *Reliquias da casa velha (Relics of an Old House).*

In 1904, Joaquim lost his beloved wife, Carolina. This loss overwhelmed Joaquim. In an attempt to relieve his pain, he wrote a very touching poem, "A Carolina." "A Carolina" would appear as an introduction to a collection of short stories, *Reliquias da casa velha (Relics of an Old House).*

• *Cuba:* The Guerrita de Agosto, a Liberal Party uprising, prompted the United States to intervene into Cuban affairs.

• *Dominican Republic:* Ramon Caceres became president of the Dominican Republic.

Under the beneficent presidency of Ramon Caceres from 1906 to 1911, the Dominican Republic experienced a brief spell of reform and modernization. Caceres' assassination in 1911 hurled the country into a new cycle of violence and financial indebtedness that persuaded President Woodrow Wilson to send in the United States Marines in 1916.

• *Haiti:* Oswald Durand (1840–1906), a noted poet, died (April 22).

Oswald Durand was born in Cap-Haitien on September 17, 1840. First a teacher, Durand later became involved in politics. He was elected a Delegate under the presidency of Salomon in 1885, a position to which he was re-elected six times.

Durand was an active advisor and a writer for several periodicals and newspapers, some of which he himself founded. He reached national fame and became one of the greatest writers.

It is written that Durand is to Haiti what Shakespeare is to England and Dante to Italy. This statement is a testament to Durand's ability to skillfully depict through his poetry all aspects of Haitian life. Love, pain, patriotism, motherland, and sadness were all key themes in Durand's writings.

Among his most celebrated works was *Choucoune,* a poem set to music which praises the beauty of Haitian women and which was acclaimed nationally and internationally. Durand also wrote a historic poem set to music, *Chant National,* which became as popular as the Haitian National Anthem.

Some of Durand's most important works are *Ces Allemands* (1872); *Chouconne* (1883); and *Rires et Pleurs* (1897).

AFRICA

• *North Africa, Egypt and Sudan:* Saad Zaghlul became the Egyptian Minister of Education.

• A dispute arose between Britain and the Porte concerning the Egyptian boundary in the Gulf of Aqaba (the Taba incident).

• The Dinshaway incident occurred. The Dinshaway incident was an affray between a British shooting party and Egyptian villagers.

• The Sultan of Morocco obtained another loan from France.

• *Western Africa:* A battle occurred between the Hausa and Jukon traders at Abinsi. Tiv joined Jukon. Together they overwhelmed the Hausa and destroyed the Royal Niger Company store.

• There was an uprising at Satiru. Many British were killed. On March 10, a punitive expedition was launched.

• On April 9, an Anglo-French convention was convened concerning the boundary of north Nigeria.

• The Colony of Lagos was amalgamated with the Protectorate of south Nigeria to form the Colony and Protectorate of Southern Nigeria (May 1).

• The French reoccupied Agades (July 7).

• Betes in Haut-Sassandra revolted. There was agitation in French Niger.

• An expedition was initiated against the Tiv in northern Nigeria.

• The Lyons missionaries (SMA) started work in Liberia.

• In 1906, Arthur Barclay, the president of Liberia, was forced to accept a British loan of 100,000 pounds secured against Liberia's custom receipts, which were, at that time, collected under British supervision.

• Birago Diop, a popularizer of African traditional literature, was born.

Birago Diop, was born in Dakar. He was educated there and in St. Louis before entering the University of Toulouse where he studied veterinary medicine until 1933.

In France, Diop met and worked with fellow poet and future Senegalese president Leopold Senghor. Senghor would later publish several of Diop's poems in his *Anthologie* (1948).

From the 1930s to the 1950s, Diop worked as a veterinarian throughout French West Africa. In 1947, Diop published a rendition of Wolof folk-tales, *Les contes d'Amadou Koumba.* The highly successful book was followed by similar volumes in 1958 and 1963. Nineteen of the stories contained in *Les contes d'Amadou Koumba* were printed in an English translation in 1966.

In 1960, Diop was appointed ambassador to Tunisia. In that year, *Presence Africaine* published a volume of his poetry, *Leurres et lueurs.*

In 1964, Diop returned to private life, opening a veterinarian clinic in Dakar.

Diop's autobiography, *La plume rabboutee,*

was published in 1978. *La plume rabboutee* illuminates the African intellectual movement in Paris in the 1930s.

- Leopold Sedar Senghor, the first president of Senegal, was born.

The rise of Leopold Sedar Senghor to power is remarkable in light of his rather humble beginnings. Although the Wolof are the predominant ethnic group in Senegal and most Senegalese are Muslims, Senghor was a Serer and a Catholic. Additionally, he was the first major political figure not to have come from one of the four communes (coastal cities) of Senegal where Africans had French citizenship and special privileges.

After being educated in Catholic schools in Senegal, Senghor went to Paris to study, and eventually entered the Sorbonne. There he obtained his "aggregation" degree — the first black African to do so.

In 1935, Senghor was appointed a teacher at Tours, transferring to Paris four years later. During that period, Senghor was one of the first African intellectuals to express discontent with French cultural assimilation.

When World War II broke out, Senghor joined the French army. He was taken prisoner by the Germans. After his release in 1942, Senghor worked with the French resistance movement.

After the war, Senghor entered politics as the protégé of the Senegalese politician Lamine Gueye. In 1945, Senghor was elected a deputy to the French legislature with the backing of the French Socialist Party (SFIO).

During this period Senghor, emerged as a major poet and cultural figure. In 1947, Senghor and Alioune Diop founded *Presence Africaine*, a Paris magazine which expressed the cultural rebellion of France's African subjects.

Leopold Senghor became a leading exponent of the philosophy of negritude, a term coined by his Martiniquais friend Aime Cesaire. It referred to the uniqueness of the African personality — neither better nor worse than that of the European, but different. Negritude became the best known cultural movement in French sub–Saharan Africa, but never caught on in the British colonies. The political and economic expression of negritude was defined by Senghor as African socialism, a concept to which he also devoted considerable intellectual energy.

In 1946, Senghor participated in the French Constituent Assemblies which shaped the Fourth Republic. Like his counterparts in other African territories, Senghor became increasingly concerned with the issue of African self-government.

Also in 1946, a group of political leaders from France's West and Central African territories met at Bamako to form the *Rassemblement Democratique Africain* — the "RDA." The RDA became an inter-territorial political party. Senghor and Gueye were persuaded by their French socialist affiliates to boycott the conference for fear that it would be Communist-dominated. The decision proved to be a mistake, for the RDA came to be controlled by Ivory Coast politician Felix Houphouet-Boigny. Houphouet-Boigny's ideas for the future of Africa were quite different from those of Leopold Senghor.

Senghor broke with Gueye in 1948 to form his own party. This break came after Senghor concluded that Gueye neglected the common people of the countryside.

An adroit campaigner among the rural populace, Senghor quickly built up a large following. Three years later his party defeated Gueye and his supporters at the polls. The new party affiliated with others in France's African territories, but outside Senegal it was not strong enough to counter Houphouet-Boigny's RDA.

Senghor's group believed that the Francophonic territories should unite in some sort of federation. Houphouet Boigny called for complete autonomy for each territory under the French umbrella.

In the 1956 elections to the French legislature, the RDA defeated Senghor's affiliates everywhere but in Senegal.

In 1957, after Senegal was permitted to hold its first legislative election, Senghor formed the new government. The next year, Senghor reunited with Gueye to form a new party, the *Union Progressive Senegalaise* (UPS). The UPS was formed to lead Senegal to total independence.

Senegal became a republic within the French community in 1959. Senghor worked actively to join Senegal to the other new republics of French West Africa in a federation. But Houphouet kept the Ivory Coast out, and pressured the leaders of Dahomey (Benin) and Upper Volta to withdraw also.

Only Senegal and the French Sudan were left to form the Mali Federation. The federation fell apart over personality and policy differences in 1960 and Senghor, his unity plan shattered, became president of Senegal.

In 1962, a dispute over economic policy brought Senghor into conflict with his long-time ally

Mamadou Dia, the prime minister. Dia's attempted coup failed and he was jailed until 1974.

Senghor overcame electoral unrest in 1963 and student riots in 1968 by maintaining a broad based coalition of supporters.

In 1970, Senghor re-established the office of prime minister. The office had been abolished after the Dia affair. Senghor selected Abdou Diouf for the position, and groomed Diouf as his successor. Meanwhile, Senghor legalized some opposition parties.

In 1981, Diouf succeeded Senghor. Senghor retired as one of Africa's most respected elder statesmen.

In 1983, Senghor was elected to the French Academy.

• Behanzin (1841–1906), the King of Dahomey (Benin) during its conquest by the French, died.

By the time Behanzin came to power in 1889, the fate of Dahomey was essentially in the hands of Europeans.

Behanzin succeeded his father, Glele, who ruled a powerful, centralized monarchy, but who could not resist the increasing French encroachment. Glele died in 1889, possibly of suicide. It is theorized that Glele did not want to negotiate with the French who had taken over the Dahomean port of Cotonou.

Behanzin adopted as his insignia the head of a shark. This symbol was adopted to indicate that he did not intend to let the Europeans penetrate his kingdom. Behanzin displayed his power by raiding the Egba for slaves in 1890. Some of these slaves were sacrificed at the funeral ceremonies for Behanzin's father, Glele.

In 1890, Behanzin's forces attacked Cotonou in an unsuccessful attempt to regain it from the French. Later in the year, Behanzin signed a treaty enabling the French to remain in Cotonou in return for 20,000 francs annually. However, the French, concerned that another European power would claim Dahomey, created a pretext for invading Dahomey by crusading against Behanzin's continued slave raiding and exporting, and against Behanzin's attacks on territory already claimed by France.

Behanzin attacked the French at Cotonou in 1892. The French were aided by Toffa, the ruler of Porto Novo—a former Dahomean dependency.

After five battles, the French occupied Abomey, the inland capital. Behanzin surrendered in 1893. He was later deported to Martinique and then to Algeria.

Behanzin's brother, Agoliagbo, ascended to the throne in 1894 to rule over a greatly reduced kingdom, as the French granted independence to its various sections. Agoliagbo was himself exiled to the French Congo in 1900.

• Suluku Konte, the Limba ruler of the Biriwa chiefdom of Sierra Leone, died (1906).

A member of the ruling Konte clan, Suluku's success as a warrior enabled him to claim the chieftaincy around 1870. At that time, the Biriwa chiefdom already controlled an important stretch of the trade route between Freetown and the northern interior.

Suluku expanded Biriwa through warfare, but also through diplomacy, for he apparently did less fighting after he became chief. Suluku maintained an elaborate alliance system with surrounding Limba, Yalunka, and Kuranko chiefdoms, marrying into a number of them.

Suluku also took care to maintain good relations with the British at Freetown. Suluku viewed the British as a powerful — but not overwhelming — neighbor.

When Samori's forces (the Sofa) invaded the Sierra Leone interior in 1884, Suluku was not powerful enough to stop them. A Sofa contingent occupied a town in Biriwa and Suluku was at first forced to pay nominal allegiance to Islam. However, Samori's forces were never able to dominate Biriwa because Suluku called on the British for intervention whenever the Sofa threatened.

By playing off the British against Samori, Suluku was able to maintain himself in power during the nine-year Sofa occupation even though many neighboring chiefs fell or became Sofa puppets. Ultimately, in 1894, the French drove out the Sofa.

In 1896, Great Britain proclaimed a protectorate over the Sierra Leone interior. Although Suluku was now limited in his external dealings, he maintained much of his power and influence. The British recognized this by making no attempt to divide up his chiefdom as they did others in the protectorate.

During the 1898 Hut Tax War, Suluku abstained from fighting, and offered to mediate between the British and Bai Bureh, the Temne rebel leader. Suluku later rebuked the British for their inability to keep the peace.

After Suluku's death in 1906, the Biriwa chiefdom was broken up into smaller chiefdoms.

• Yoko (c.1849–1906), the ruler of the Kpa Mende confederacy of Sierra Leone, died.

After divorcing her first husband and being widowed by her second, Yoko married a powerful chief in western Mendeland. As his head wife, she took an active interest in political affairs of the chiefdom, and established a reputation for charm and diplomacy. When her husband died in 1878, Yoko assumed his office, as he had requested.

Yoko made alliances with her neighbors and built a large confederacy. Perhaps the most important of these alliances was with the British who were playing a continually larger role in the politics of the Sierra Leone hinterland. Yoko aided the British in their diplomatic and peace-keeping missions, and received their support in return, including a contingent of Frontier Police stationed in her capital.

In 1886, Yoko told the Sierra Leone governor that her chief rival was leading raids which were disrupting trade with Freetown. After a British military campaign, the rival was deported.

In 1896, the British declared a protectorate over the Sierra Leone hinterland. When the Hut Tax War broke out two years later, Yoko remained loyal to the government.

After the Hut Tax War, the British permitted Yoko to increase the territory under her jurisdiction as a reward. The system of indirect rule permitted her to centralize control over the chiefs of the Kpa confederacy.

Yoko further expanded her domain by engaging in small wars which the British were powerless to stop. Her death in 1906, according to some accounts, was by her own hand because she dreaded old age.

In 1919, the Kpa confederacy was partitioned into fourteen autonomous chiefdoms.

- *Central Africa:* Kissabo's power as King of Burundi was consolidated (April).
- An agreement was reached between the Congo Free State and the Vatican which provided that each Catholic mission would include a school.
- The Mill Hill Fathers began their work in the Congo.
- *Eastern Africa:* Baron F. von Rechenburg became the Governor of German East Africa. Von Rechenburg was the first governor to speak Swahili. During his tenure, von Rechenburg developed a "plantation" colony.
- By 1906, an external agreement between France, Britain, and Italy gave international recognition to the independence of Ethiopia (July 4). See 1865.
- The Toro agreement was revised. The Toro confederacy became the Kingdom of Toro.
- Winston Churchill visited the East African Protectorate.
- Large areas in Uganda near Lake Victoria were evacuated because of the sleeping-sickness epidemic.
- The Zanzibar administration was reorganized.
- Songea Mbano (c.1836–1906), a prominent figure in the Maji Maji revolt against the Germans in 1905, died.

Songea Mbano was born in Zambia shortly after the Ngoni king Zwangendaba — who had captured his Shona parents in present day Zimbabwe — crossed the Zambezi River during his great northward migration.

Songea grew up fully assimilated into Ngoni society. During the 1850s, Songea joined the breakaway faction which settled in the present day Songea district of Tanzania.

In Tanzania, two Ngoni kingdoms developed in near proximity. Songea rose to the position of sub-chief in the branch known as Njelu by the late 1860s.

Although only a commoner chief, Songea eventually commanded the major part of the Njelu army and was effectively an autonomous ruler. When the Germans arrived in Ngoni country in 1897, they neglected the titular Ngoni ruler and negotiated instead with Songea. Songea reluctantly assented to the German occupation and cooperated with the Europeans over the next seven years.

During 1905, a major anti–German revolt erupted. The revolt came to be known as Maji Maji. Maji Maji swept southern Tanzania and drew in the Ngoni. Apparently motivated by a desire to preserve his authority among the Ngoni, Songea led several attacks on German positions.

Early in 1906, Songea surrendered to the Germans. The Germans considered Songea to be an instigator of the rebellion and summarily hanged him.

- *Southern Africa:* There was a Zulu uprising in Natal against the poll tax (February).

In 1906, many Zulu rebelled under the leadership of a minor chief, Bambatha. Dinuzulu, the paramount chief of the Zulu, had no part in the largely spontaneous affair. Nevertheless, he was once again charged with treason by the Natal government.

After a long trial, Dinuzulu was exonerated of

all charges except that of having tacitly supported the rebels. For this Dinuzulu was fined, deposed and again banished — this time to the Transvaal.

- Self-government was granted to the Transvaal and Orange River Colonies (December 6).
- The Watch Tower (Jehovah's Witnesses) movement began in Nyasaland.
- The Portuguese campaigned along the Mozambique coast.
- Thomas Mofolo published *Moeti oa Bochabela*.

The first *Moeti oa Bochabela*, appeared in a newspaper in 1906 and was later published in a translation as *Traveller of the East* in 1934.

Moeti dealt with a man searching for an alternative to traditional religion. The book revealed a strong Christian moralizing tone which characterized Mofolo's subsequent work.

- Benedict Wallet Vilakazi (1906–1947), the "Father of Zulu Poetry," was born.

Benedict Vilakazi was named Bambatha at birth after the renowned Zulu rebel leader of the day. However, Vilakazi changed his name to Benedict when he was baptized a Roman Catholic in 1918.

Through the 1920s, Vilakazi held various secondary level teaching posts. In 1934, he became the first black African to earn a bachelor of arts of degree through the University of South Africa correspondence program.

In 1935, Vilakazi was appointed the first African teacher at the University of Witwatersrand in Johannesburg. At the University of Witwatersrand, Vilakazi would teach Zulu language and literature for the rest of his life. Vilakazi also earned three advanced degrees at the University of Witwatersrand, taking his Doctorate of Literature the year before he died of meningitis.

Vilakazi co-authored, with C. M. Doke, the *Zulu-English Dictionary* in 1948. The *Zulu-English Dictionary* became the standard authority on the Zulu language.

From the early 1930s, Vilakazi also wrote and published prolifically in Zulu. Vilakazi avoided politics during his life, and his novels treat mainly historical themes.

In his poetry, Vilakazi adapted traditional blank verse forms to a modern and popular style. Two volumes of Vilakazi's poetry have been translated into English as *Zulu Horizons*. *Zulu Horizons* was published in 1962.

- Bambatha (c. 1865–1906), the leader of the Zulu rebellion against the poll tax, died.

Bambatha began as the chief of a small branch of the Zulu in northern Natal after the Zulu kingdom had ceased to exist as an independent state. In 1904, Bambatha clashed with the Natal administration over fiscal matters. Because of his incendiary activities, Bambatha was deposed in early 1906.

Bambatha fled north into Zululand proper and organized opposition to an unpopular poll tax. In Zululand, Bambatha conducted a guerrilla campaign for two months, leaving several thousand Zulu and a few dozen Europeans dead.

The Zulu paramount chief, Dinuzulu, was initially blamed for instigating the poll tax rebellion, but, after a long trial, Dinuzulu was exonerated of all charges except that of having tacitly supported the rebels. For this Dinuzulu was fined, deposed and again banished — this time to the Transvaal.

Bambatha, on the other hand, was not exonerated. Indeed, the poll tax rebellion of 1906 came to be named after Bambatha and he was found, by the government, to be responsible for it.

- Gungunyane (c.1850–1906), the last Gaza king, died.

When Gungunyane's father, Mzila, passed away in 1884, the question of succession to the throne of Gaza was unresolved. Gungunyane seized power in a coup. However, some potential rivals escaped his purge and their presence in enemy territories hampered his diplomatic efforts throughout his reign.

As king of Gaza, Gungunyane faced two key problems. First, there was the problem pertaining to the preservation of the tenuous unity of his multi-ethnic kingdom, and second, there was the problem posed by the greatly intensified Portuguese efforts to assert sovereignty over southern Mozambique.

Gungunyane sensed that his best opportunity to maintain Gaza autonomy lay with the British, whom he persistently pleaded with to establish a protectorate over Gaza. However, the Portuguese kept the British out of the region by claiming they already ruled the area. Portuguese pressure on the Gaza began in the north where Manuel de Sousa was expanding his own semi-independent empire. Meanwhile, the Chope and other Gaza subjects to the south were reasserting their own independence.

In order to avoid de Sousa and to re-establish Gaza control in the south, Gungunyane, in 1889, moved his people from the Manica highlands to near the mouth of the Limpopo River. This migration of about sixty thousand people had a tremendous impact on the entire region. The consequential economic dislocation left Gaza extremely weak.

Gungunyane did manage to suppress the Chope rebellion. However, these efforts did not manage to halt the general trend towards disintegration within Gaza.

In 1890, Gungunyane was visited by agents of Cecil Rhodes British South Africa Company. These agents sought a concession similar to the one that had been obtained from the Ndebele king Lobengula two years before. Gungunyane was anxious to comply. But in doing so, he failed to understand that he was dealing with private interests and not the British government.

In 1891, the British and Portuguese governments signed a treaty separating their zones of influence in southeastern Africa and giving the Portuguese a free hand in Gaza.

Beginning in 1891, the Portuguese mounted a major thrust to break the independent rulers of southern Mozambique. Gungunyane attempted to negotiate an accommodation with the Portuguese, but the Portuguese were not interested in accommodation — they were interested in conquest.

In 1895, Gungunyane's army was overwhelmed by the machine guns and other modern weapons of the Portuguese. Gungunyane was captured and exiled to the Azore Islands.

Gungunyane died while in exile in 1906.

RELATED HISTORICAL EVENTS

• *Europe:* The Algeciras Conference on Morocco was convened (January 16–April 8). On April 8, the Algeciras Act was signed.

• An Anglo-Belgian agreement was reached concerning the boundaries of the Congo and the Sudan (May).

• An Anglo-German agreement was finalized concerning the boundaries of Uganda and German East Africa (June 18).

• An Anglo-Italian agreement was negotiated concerning Ethiopia (December 13).

• The *Union Miniere du Haut Katanga* was established.

• The School of Tropical Medicine was opened in Brussels.

• H. W. Nevinson's *A Modern Slavery* was published. *A Modern Slavery* was an expose on contract labor in Angola.

• *Africa:* Alfred Beit (1853–1906), a German financier, died.

After working for a Hamburg diamond firm, Alfred Beit went to the diamond fields at Kimberley in 1875. In Kimberley, Beit established his own business.

Eventually, Beit amalgamated his diamond business with those of Cecil Rhodes and Barnett Barnato to form the De Beers Consolidated Mines in 1888.

Beit then invested in the developing gold mines of the Transvaal and became one of the founding directors of Rhodes' British South Africa Company. Because of his close association with Cecil Rhodes, Alfred Beit was forced to resign from the company after L. S. Jameson's raid on the Transvaal Republic in 1895.

During the remainder of his life, Beit was well known as a philanthropist.

1 9 0 7

THE UNITED STATES

• Under pressure from Legislators, on January 15, President Theodore Roosevelt revoked the civil disability of the Brownsville, Texas, soldiers. *See 1906.* After months of study, the majority of the Senate Committee upheld the President's contention as to the guilt of the accused soldiers. A highly critical minority report was authored by Ohio Senator Foraker who denounced the findings of the majority.

• William Lloyd Garrison II, the son of the great abolitionist, wrote that there had never been an affirmative majority for the abolition of slavery in the North except for the brief period when the Emancipation Proclamation was signed. Garrison also noted that Northerners had simply been more subtle in their opposition to African Americans.

• In New York, Harlem Hospital opened. Harlem Hospital became a pioneer institution in providing health care for the African American community.

• Addie Hunton (1875–1943) became the first secretary for African American student affairs for the National Board of the Young Women's Christian Association (YWCA).

• *Civil Rights Movement:* The leaders of the Niagara Movement met in Boston. They were supported by the New England Suffrage League and the Equal Rights League of Georgia.

• *Notable Births:* Lu Andrew Albert, a blues pianist who was better known as "Sunnyland Slim," was born in Vance, Mississippi (September 5).

• Charles Alston, a painter, was born in Charlotte, North Carolina (November 28). Alston would depict the African-American contribution to medicine in the entrance lobby of Harlem Hospital in New York.

• Gladys Bentley, a singer and pianist, was born (August 12).

• Cabell "Cab" Calloway, a musician and performer, was born (December 25).

Cab Calloway was born in Rochester, New York, and was raised in Baltimore, Maryland. In 1928, Calloway went to Chicago where he led the Alabamians. In 1929, he took his band to New York.

Calloway's recording of *Minnie the Moocher* in 1931 established Calloway as a novelty singer and a celebrity. He was soon seen in such motion pictures as *Singing Kid, Stormy Weather,* and *Sensations of 1945.*

In 1952, Calloway gave a bravura performance as Sportin' Life in *Porgy and Bess.*

• Benny Carter, a musician, bandleader, and arranger, was born in New York (August 8).

• Shirley Graham Du Bois, a writer and activist, was born in Indianapolis, Indiana (November 11).

• Augustus F. Hawkins, a future Congressman, was born.

Augustus F. Hawkins was born in Shreveport, Louisiana, and raised in California. A graduate of the University of Southern California, Hawkins was elected to the State Assembly in 1934. Before his election to the House of Representatives in 1962, Hawkins worked for civil rights, health, welfare, housing and labor legislation.

• Canada Lee, an actor, was born in New York (May 3).

• Robert Weaver, the first African American to serve in a Presidential cabinet position, was born.

Robert Weaver was born in Washington, D.C. He abandoned a career as an electrician because of union discrimination. He received a doctorate in economics from Harvard University and became an aide to the Secretary of the Interior in 1933.

In 1934, Weaver became an adviser to the PWA Housing Division and, in 1938, he became a Special Assistant to the Administrator of the United States Housing Authority.

During World War II, Weaver directed the Negro Employment and Training Branch of the Labor Division of the War Production Board and of the Negro Manpower Commission.

From 1944 to 1955, Weaver worked as a visiting lecturer, was professor of economics at the New School for Social Research in New York City, and directed the fellowship programs of the John Hay Whitney Foundation and the Julius Rosenwald Fund.

In 1955, Weaver became Rent Commissioner of New York. Weaver headed the Federal Housing and Home Finance Agency in 1961, and, in 1966, was named to the Cabinet as the first director of the Department of Housing and Urban Development.

Weaver authored a number of books, including *Negro Labor: a National Problem* (1946); *The Negro Ghetto* (1948); *The Urban Complex* (1964); and *Dilemmas in Urban Development* (1965).

• Dorothy West, a novelist, was born in Boston, Massachusetts (June 2).

• *Notable Deaths:* 60 African Americans were lynched in 1907.

• *Miscellaneous State Laws:* Oklahoma adopted Jim Crow streetcar and railroad laws. Oklahoma also adopted a "white primary" law. As a result, only European Americans were allowed to vote in the Democratic primaries.

• *Miscellaneous Cases:* In *Chiles v. C & O Railroad,* the United States Supreme Court held that a railroad might enforce rules requiring interstate African American passengers to occupy separate facilities, regardless of the statutes of any particular states the railroad passed through.

• *Publications:* Booker T. Washington published *The Negro in Business* and *Life of Frederick Douglass.*

• Wendell P. Dabney founded the *Union,* a newspaper to foster greater unity among African Americans in Cincinnati.

• Nat Love (a.k.a. Deadwood Dick) published his autobiography. The book was entitled *The Life and Adventures of Nat Love: Better Known in the Cattle Country as "Deadwood Dick."*

• *The Arts:* In 1907, Meta Vaux Warrick Fuller received a commission to do a series of commemorative figures illustrating the history of the African American for the Jamestown Tercentennial Exposition.

• *The Performing Arts:* In 1907, the duo of

Bert Williams and George Walker produced *Bandana Land,* a musical.

• Ernest Hogan, an African American vaudevillian and song writer, starred in *Oyster Man.*

• *Scholastic Achievements:* Alaine Leroy Locke (1885–1954) of Harvard became the first African American to be named a Rhodes Scholar.

• Anna T. Jeanes gave an additional million dollars to the General Education Board for rural African American schools in the South.

• *Service Organizations:* By 1907, the National Business League, an African American business oriented organization, had some 320 branches.

• *Sports:* John B. Taylor, of the University of Pennsylvania, won the 440-yard dash at the intercollegiate championships for the second time.

THE AMERICAS

• *Cuba:* In 1907, Cuba's Afro-Cuban population was put at 274,272. This number represented 13.4% of the total population.

• *Haiti:* Francois "Papa Doc" Duvalier (1907–1971), a future dictator of Haiti, was born.

"Papa Doc" was the name by which the Haitian dictator Francois Duvalier was known.

Francois Duvalier (1907–1971) was born in Haiti's capital, Port-au-Prince, the son of a schoolteacher.

He was educated in local schools, including the Lycee Petion, where Dumarsais Estime was one of his teachers, and the School of Medicine of the national university, where he graduated in 1934.

Duvalier worked in government service for the next ten years. He was associated with the American Sanitary Mission directing programs of preventive medicine. In 1944, Duvalier went to the University of Michigan on a fellowship to study public health, failed his course, and later attended a short course in tropical public health in Puerto Rico.

Duvalier was involved in the Sanitary Mission's malaria eradication and anti-yaws campaign.

During the 1930s, Duvalier joined a group of black intellectuals, the Griots. The Griots had begun to study and sanctify Haiti's African heritage. The group's work marked the beginning of a new campaign against the COTW elite and an emerging ideology of black power, Haitian

style. It was on this ideology that Duvalier later based his political leadership. His pro-black sentiments led to his advocacy of voodoo.

In 1946, Duvalier joined the Worker-Peasant Movement (MOP), a political party formed by a young mathematics teacher, Daniel Fignole, of which Duvalier became secretary general. Through the party, Duvalier built a political constituency in Port-au-Prince.

COTW President Elie Lescot was deposed by a military coup in 1946. Upon assumption of power by President Dumarsais Estime, Lescot's black successor, Duvalier was appointed director general of public health and later secretary of labor and public health.

When the black commander of the Presidential Guard, Paul Eugene Magliore, succeeded Estime in December 1950 after a coup, Magliore was opposed by Duvalier. Duvalier went into hiding until August 1956.

On September 7, 1956, Duvalier became a candidate to succeed Magliore. Magliore was forced to leave the country in November 1956. During the next few months, there were five provisional governments.

Duvalier waged his campaign as a representative of the Griots, proclaimed himself heir to Dumarsais Estime, and had the firm support of the military leaders.

The campaign became a two-man race between Duvalier and a wealthy COTW businessman, Louis DeJoie. With the army in full command, when the results were announced Duvalier won, and his supporters received 23 of the 37 seats in the Chamber of Deputies and all those in the Senate.

Duvalier began to organize a system of coercion, control, and patronage. He began a reign of terror which by some estimates, resulted in killing between 30,000 and 60,000 opponents during his fourteen year rule. He removed all powerful officers from the military, and in 1959 he created a militia, the tonton macoutes, over which Duvalier had absolute personal control. The tonton macoutes conducted a campaign of terror and repression against the population.

In 1963, Duvalier also created the National Security Volunteers. The National Security Volunteers were recruited from among the black underclass and were absolutely loyal to Duvalier.

The encouragement of voodoo served as a means of both recruiting rural support and spreading fear. Similarly, the tonton macoutes and the National Security Volunteers both recruited support and instilled fear. Many leaders of these two organizations were local leaders in rural constituencies.

Duvalier moved to undermine the influence of the church by expelling foreign clergy and by securing the appointment of personally acceptable Haitians to the hierarchy of the Roman Catholic and Anglican churches. Like the military, the organized church soon became an accomplice of his regime.

Duvalier institutionalized corruption which transferred enormous wealth to him, his family, and his associates. Power became increasingly personalized. Parliament was dissolved in 1961, two years before its term was up, and a unicameral legislature was decreed in the elections for which only candidates personally chosen by the president participated.

Duvalier's name was placed at the head of every ballot. All of Duvalier's candidates were declared elected, and he announced himself to be elected to another six year term of office, by virtue of the presence of his name on the ballot.

In 1963, Duvalier had himself declared President for Life, and in the plebiscite to confirm his status, it was reported that there were 2.8 million votes in favor and 3,234 against. Persons voting "no" were promptly arrested for defacing the ballot.

Although, in the beginning, Duvalier secured a considerable amount of American economic and military assistance, after 1961, this aid was finally ended by the Kennedy administration. Although Duvalier, at first managed to attract considerable private foreign investment, this too ended, and there was rapid deterioration of the economy, with growth of absolute poverty and degenerating conditions.

Duvalier was able to retain power until his death in April of 1971. Upon foreseeing his imminent death, Duvalier announced on January 22 that Jean-Claude Duvalier, his nineteen-year-old son, was his chosen successor, and in a plebiscite this was "confirmed" by a vote of 2,391,916 to 0.

• Paul Eugene Magliore, the thirty-third president of Haiti was born.

Paul Magliore was born to a black elite family in Cap Haitien. He attended primary schools there, and graduated from Lycee Philippe Guerrier.

Magliore taught at his alma mater for a year and then enrolled in Haiti's military academy, graduating in 1931. Later, Magliore took a law degree from the national university.

After graduation from military school, Magliore served as an aide-de-camp to President Stenio Vincent, as an adjutant to several regional military commanders, as governor of the national prison, and commandant of the Palace Guard. When, in January 1946, opposition to the oppressive and corrupt regime of President Elie Lescot mounted, Magliore joined with two COTW military leaders to depose the president. Magliore was instrumental in securing the election of President Dumarsais Estime, the representative of black intellectuals and other black elites. Magliore was named minister of interior. After serving as minister of interior, Magliore returned to his position as commander of the Palace Guards.

In 1950, when Estime sought to remain in office in defiance of the existing constitution, Magliore joined a military coup. The Executive Military Committee, of which Magliore was part, then dismissed Parliament and, in a revised constitution, for the first time provided for the president to be elected by universal male suffrage. Magliore was overwhelmingly elected president in December 1950, with the backing of the military, the Roman Catholic Church, and the United States.

Magliore failed to pursue policies of reform implemented in the early years of his predecessor. He concentrated on economic development, negotiating an agreement with the United States for assistance in soil conservation, cattle farming, drainage, and irrigation; and formulated a five-year plan which would be financed by foreign aid, concentrating on improvement of transportation and port facilities. His regime saw the opening of bauxite mines by Reynolds Metals as well as development of a tourist industry and attraction of foreign investment.

In 1954, however, the coffee crop began to fail, and, in October, a vicious hurricane destroyed crops and prosperity. At the same time, government projects were proving more costly than anticipated, and there was growing evidence of corruption among members of Magliore's family and some charges of politically motivated killings. A dispute arose over the date when the president's term legally ended, with Magliore insisting on May 1957 and members of the growing opposition claiming May 1956.

Magliore was soon faced with intense opposition. A student insurrection spread to strikes by unions. In November 1956, Magliore banned all public meetings and political broadcasts and publications. He finally declared a state of siege and dissolved the legislature. At that time, Magliore decided to leave Haiti for Jamaica, but he ultimately settled in New York.

• Justin Lherisson, a noted novelist, died. *See 1872.*

AFRICA

• *North Africa, Egypt and Sudan:* Al-Raisuli was outlawed by the Sultan of Morocco.

• The French physician Mauchamp was murdered at Marrakesh (March 22). Ujda were taken by the French as a reprisal (March 29).

• A French fleet bombarded Casablanca after anti-foreign demonstrations (August 4). Subsequently, Casablanca and Rabat were occupied.

• The first Nationalist Congress in Egypt under Mustafa Kamil was convened (December 7).

• The Mountains of Beni Suassen were taken by the French in further reprisal for the murder of Mauchamp (December).

• *Al-Hizb al-Watani*, the Patriotic Party, was founded by zealous Egyptian nationalists.

• *Hizb al-Umma* (Party of the Nation) was founded in Cairo as a moderate nationalist party.

• *Al-Jarida*, a moderate Egyptian nationalist newspaper, was founded.

• The Bank of Rome opened a branch in Tripoli.

• Sir Eldon Gorst became the British Agent and Consul-General in Egypt.

• *Western Africa:* A French mission was established in the southern Sahara (March).

• In June, there was an uprising against the French in Haut-Sassandra.

• A Franco-Liberian agreement on the frontiers of Liberia, Ivory Coast and Guinea was reached (September 18).

• Felix Dubois arrived at Timbuktu, having crossed the Sahara without any other European (December 8).

• There was an uprising in the Cuor region of Portuguese Guinea.

• The Northern Territories Constabulary was established in the Gold Coast.

• William Ponty became the Governor-General of AOF.

• Improvements on the Lagos Harbor for ocean vessels began.

• In 1907, the French responded to pressure from the followers of Ahmadu Bamba, the founder of the Muridiyya Islamic brotherhood, and allowed Ahmadu to return to Senegal. Ahmadu settled in the town of Diourabel where he remained under house arrest until his death in 1927.

• Muhammed Aguibu Tall (c.1843–1907), the Tukolor ruler of Dinguiray and Macina who collaborated with the French to destroy the Tukolor empire, died.

Muhammed Aguibu Tall was the son of al-Hajj 'Umar, the founder of the Tukolor empire. When 'Umar died in 1864, Muhammed Aguibu's brother, Ahmadu ibn 'Umar Tall, inherited the empire.

Ahmadu made Muhammed ruler of Segu but soon came to distrust him as being overly ambitious. Muhammed later became emir of Dinguiray which he ruled seemingly independently of Ahmadu.

When the French military leader Archinard set out to conquer the Tukolor empire, Archinard used the rivalry between the two brothers as a wedge. After the fall of Segu in 1890, Archinard contacted Muhammed and claimed that it was only Ahmadu and not the Tukolor nation whom the French were fighting. Muhammed responded amicably and formally submitted to the French the following year.

Muhammed's acquiescence to French rule, divided the Tukolor and facilitated the fall of Macina, Ahmadu's last base, in 1893. Archinard rewarded Muhammed by making him the new ruler of Macina. This was a wise move on Archinard's part since, by making Muhammed the ruler of Macina, he averted further resistance from the population. The population of Macina appeared to be far more willing to accept the substitution of one son of 'Umar for another.

Muhammed proved to be an unpopular ruler under the French colonial system. He was demoted in 1903.

• *Central Africa:* The Portuguese campaigned against the Dembo.

• An education conference was held at Douala.

• The population of Rwanda was estimated at one and a half million.

• The Bielefeld Mission was established in Rwanda.

Eastern Africa

Capuchin missionaries calculated that 6,000 to 8,000 slaves were exported annually from Kaffa (Ethiopia).

• The Uganda-Congo Boundary Commission was established. The Kivu mission successfully avoided contact with Belgian forces.

- The first Kenya Legislative Council met (August). The Council appointed a Land Board.
- The frontier of British East Africa was defined by Britain and Ethiopia (December 6).
- The Ethiopian Emperor, Menelik, became paralyzed. Lijj Iyasu was nominated as successor with Ras Tasamma as regent.
- The Education Department was established in Zanzibar. The Education Department officially prescribed Roman script for writing Swahili instead of Arabic script.
- The Commissioner for Uganda was made Governor.
- There was unrest in Bunyoro. Fifty chiefs were deported.
- Mbaruk bin Rashid bin Salim al-Mazrui (c.1820–1910), a leader of the 1895 Mazrui rebellion against the British in Kenya, was pardoned by the British government.
- *Southern Africa:* The Legislative Council was instituted in Mozambique (May 23).
- A revised constitution for the Orange River Colony was drafted (July 1).
- The Selborne memorandum proposed a federation of South Africa (July).
- An uprising in German Southwest Africa was suppressed.
- Swaziland was transferred to the jurisdiction of the High Commissioner for South Africa.
- Mahatma Gandhi began utilizing the concept of passive resistance amongst the Transvaal Indians.

In 1907, Mohandas Gandhi *(see 1869)* responded to a new pass law in the Transvaal by organizing his first passive resistance *(satyagraha)* campaign. Passive resistance became Gandhi's main strategy in all his later civil rights and nationalistic campaigns.

- The South African Labour Party was formed.
- A strike of miners occurred in the Rand.
- The Dutch Reformed Church took over missions of the Berlin Missionary Society in Rhodesia.
- Livingstone was made the capital of northwest Rhodesia.
- Responsible government was restored to the Transvaal Colony and Louis Botha was elected its first prime minister.

RELATED HISTORICAL EVENTS

- *Africa:* Michael Blundell, a leading European politician in Kenya, was born.

At eighteen, Michael Blundell migrated from England to Kenya to farm. After World War II (in 1948), Blundell was elected to the Kenya Legislative Council. Blundell soon became the leader of the European members of the Council.

From 1954, as a cabinet officer, Blundell advocated a hard line against the Mau Mau Movement.

As Kenyan independence approached, Blundell worked to establish an inter-racial political party.

In 1961, Blundell was elected to parliament on his own ticket and joined the Kenya African Democratic Union (KADU) government as minister of agriculture.

When Jomo Kenyatta's party formed a new government in 1962, Blundell retired to his farm.

- Roy Welensky, the last prime minister of the Federation of Rhodesia and Nyasaland, was born (1907).

Roy Welensky was born in Zimbabwe to a Lithuanian father and an Afrikaner mother. Welensky left school when he was fourteen and soon went to work for the Rhodesian railways.

An amateur boxer, Welensky won the Southern Rhodesian heavyweight title in 1925. In 1933, Welensky moved to Broken Hill (Kabwe) in Northern Rhodesia (Zambia). In Broken Hill, Welensky rose to leadership of the railway workers' union.

From 1938 to 1953, Welensky held a seat in the Northern Rhodesian legislative council and became leader of the unofficial opposition. Welensky cooperated closely with the prime minister of Southern Rhodesia, Godfrey Huggins, to promote a Rhodesian federation, which was achieved in 1953. Welensky was then elected to a federal legislative seat and became deputy federal prime minister under Huggins.

On Huggins's retirement in 1956, Welensky became federal prime minister, holding the post until the dissolution of the Federation in 1963. Like Huggins, Welensky spoke constantly about European-African "partnership" while, nevertheless, working to preserve European domination.

As African and British pressure to expand the African franchise mounted, he threatened to declare the Federation's independence from

Britain. However, the Federation collapsed after Northern Rhodesia and Nyasaland (Malawi) were granted majority rule and exercised their prerogative to secede. In 1964, Welensky contested a Southern Rhodesian parliamentary seat, but was badly defeated and forced into retirement.

1 9 0 8

THE UNITED STATES

On August 14 and 15, a riot in Springfield, Illinois, became terribly violent. The Illinois governor was compelled to call in some 4,200 state militia men to control the area. The riot started when the wife of a streetcar conductor claimed that she had been raped by an African American by the name of George Richardson. Richardson had been working in the area.

Before a special grand jury the woman admitted that she had been beaten by a European American man and that Richardson had had nothing to do with her injuries or with the incident. However, she refused to identify the man who had assaulted her and her recanting of her original story was simply too late. The flames of hate had been fanned and the fire could not be contained.

The feelings of hate and anger amongst the European Americans were high against Richardson. To protect Richardson, the authorities took Richardson and another African American accused of murder to another town. In fury, a mob wrecked the automobile of the owner of a restaurant whose car had been used to move the African American suspects and then proceeded to wreck havoc throughout the town. City officials made several attempts to quiet and disperse the mob, but to no avail. Finally, the governor was called and the militia troops were dispatched.

During the turmoil, more than 2,000 African American residents fled the town. Many of them went to the militia camps in search of protection. As for the mob, it proceeded to destroy the homes and businesses that comprised the African American community.

The mob burned a barber shop, lynched the barber and dragged his body through the streets.

The next night, on August 15, an 84-year-old African American who had been married to a European American woman for more than 30 years, was lynched.

Order was restored to Springfield only after the militia patrolled the streets. The toll had been great. Two African Americans were lynched, six were killed, seventy African Americans and European Americans were injured; 100 arrests were made with 50 indictments. But the alleged leaders of the riot escaped punishment, and subsequently the European American community engaged in a political and economic boycott to drive out the remaining African American residents.

In the aftermath of the Springfield riots, Oswald Garrison Villard spoke out editorially in his newspaper, *The New York Evening Post*, against the riots.

William English Walling, a European American reformer and writer, in an article, "Race War in the North" which appeared in the liberal periodical, *The Independent*, condemned the Springfield riot and those who contributed to it, inflaming race hatred and not opposing it.

Walling urged African Americans first to seek protection from proper authorities when attacked and then to defend themselves and resist to the extent that rioters would think twice before coming again. The article called for a group of citizens to stop the spread of racism that dominated the Springfield riots and threatened the entire North. Walling asserted that if racism was not stopped, the very foundations of political democracy would be threatened.

Led by Walling's close friend, Charles Edward Russell, the Liberal Club in New York City responded enthusiastically to Walling's proposals to establish a bi-racial organization for this purpose. Oswald Garrison Villard wanted to name the organization "The Committee for the Advancement of the Human Race."

- Because of the role played by the Republican President, Theodore Roosevelt, in the Brownsville, Texas incident, and encouraged by the growing Democratic party machines of the North, a large number of African Americans gave their support to the Democratic Party in 1908. Booker T. Washington, as further indication of his losing touch with most African Americans, continued to give Roosevelt his support.
- Ida B. Wells Barnett, an anti-lynching and civil rights crusader, became the first president of the Negro Fellowship League.
- Vertner W. Tandy, Sr., (1885–1949) became a registered architect in the State of New York.

Vertner W. Tandy designed the Villa Lewaro, the mansion of the hair care magnate Madame

C. J. Walker. Tandy was also known as having founded Alpha Phi Alpha fraternity at Cornell University.

- *Organizations:* Alpha Kappa Alpha, a Greek letter sorority, was founded at Howard University. The principal organizer was Ethel Hedgeman Lyle, who became the first vice president. The first president of the sorority was Lucy Slowe.
- *The Civil Rights Movement:* The Niagara Movement had its last meeting in Oberlin, Ohio.
- *Notable Births:* Thurgood Marshall, the first African American to serve on the United States Supreme Court, was born (July 8).

Thurgood Marshall was born in Baltimore, Maryland. Marshall received his bachelor of arts degree from Lincoln University and, in 1933, he received his law degree from Howard University, graduating first in his class.

From 1936 through 1961, Marshall served the NAACP as special counsel and as director of its Legal Defense and Education Fund. Marshall argued the famous cases that led to the 1954 Supreme Court school desegregation rulings.

In 1961, President Kennedy appointed Marshall to a United States Circuit Court judgeship. In 1965, Marshall was made United States Solicitor General, and, in 1967, he was appointed to the United States Supreme Court by President Lyndon Johnson.

- Frederick O'Neal, an actor, was born.

Frederick O'Neal was born in Brookville, Mississippi. He was first active in local productions of the Urban League.

After working in St. Louis where he founded (and acted with) an African American acting group called the Ira Aldridge Players, O'Neal, in 1937, went to New York.

In New York O'Neal organized and directed the New York American Negro Theater. O'Neal also starred in the play *Anna Lucasta* and other Broadway productions.

In 1945, Frederick O'Neal won the Drama Critics Award for best supporting actor.

- Trumpeter Oran "Hot Lips" Page was born (January 28).
- Ann Petry, a novelist, critic and short-story writer, was born in Old Saybrook, Connecticut (October 12).
- Adam Clayton Powell, Jr., a controversial Congressman, was born.

Adam Clayton Powell, Jr., was born in New Haven, Connecticut. Powell was the son of the famous African American minister, Adam Clayton Powell, Sr.

Powell received a bachelor of arts degree from Colgate in 1930, a master of arts degree from Columbia in 1932, and an honorary doctor of divinity degree from Shaw University in 1935.

Powell was a major civil rights activist in Depression Harlem. In 1930, Powell organized a campaign for jobs for African Americans and was successful in integrating the staff of Harlem Hospital. Powell persuaded many Harlem businesses to hire African Americans, and campaigned against the city bus lines that refused to hire African Americans. Powell also directed a relief center that dispensed food, fuel and clothing to needy African Americans.

In 1933, as chairman of the Coordinating Committee on Employment, Powell led a demonstration campaign that succeeded in forcing the New York World's Fair to hire African Americans.

In 1937, Powell succeeded his father as pastor of the Abyssinian Baptist Church.

In 1941, Adam Clayton Powell, Jr., was elected to the New York City Council and, in 1945, he was elected to the House of Representatives.

In the House of Representatives, Adam Clayton Powell quickly became noted as a civil rights leader. He personally desegregated many Congressional facilities, Washington restaurants, and theaters. Powell was the first to propose legislation to the effect that Federal funds should not be given to any project in which there was discrimination.

Powell was the first legislator to introduce legislation to desegregate the armed forces, and he established the right of African American journalists to sit in the House and Senate press galleries.

Made chairman of the House Committee on Education and Labor in 1960, the Powell Committee helped pass 48 pieces of social welfare legislation for Lyndon Johnson's Great Society Program. Powell's efforts earned him a letter of gratitude from President Johnson.

In 1967, Powell's House colleagues raised charges of corruption and financial mismanagement against him. In January, he was stripped of his chairmanship and barred from the House, pending an investigation.

On March 1, 1967, Powell was denied a seat in the House by a vote of 307 to 116, despite the committee's recommendation that he only be censured, fined and placed at the bottom of the seniority list.

On April 11, a special election was held to fill

Powell's seat. Powell, who had not campaigned; who was on the Island of Bimini; and who could not even venture to New York City because of a court judgment against him in a defamation case, received 74% of the vote cast.

• Josh White, a folksinger and composer, was born.

Josh White was born in Greenville, South Carolina. He began his career as the Singing Christian, a gospel singer. After a brief career as Pinewood Tom, he decided to use his real name.

Josh White gave concerts all over the world, made numerous records, appeared on Broadway, and starred in the CBS-TV series *Back Where I Came From*.

• Richard Wright (1908–1960), a famous writer, was born (September 4).

Richard Wright was born in Natchez, Mississippi, on a plantation. When his father deserted the family, his mother took care of the family until Wright was in his early 20s.

While in his 20s, Wright moved to Chicago, did manual jobs and joined the Communist Party. In 1937, the "Ethics of Living Jim Crow" was published in a WPA anthology, *American Stuff*. "Ethics of Living Jim Crow" was an autobiographical sketch in which the author described how the African American learned to play his role in the Southern Jim Crow system.

Uncle Tom's Children, published in 1938, as a collection of four novellas, was Wright's first book. All the stories dealt with race friction in the South, and the book was hailed by Alain Locke as the "strongest note yet struck by one of our writers in the staccato protest realism of the rising school of proletarian fiction." The four novellas are a tetraptych of protest against Southern lynch law and the plight of the African American. Despite the warm reception for this work, Wright was dissatisfied especially with the critics emphasis on Wright's compassion.

Native Son, Wright's most probing work into the plight of the lower-class urban African American was published in 1940. Like Dreiser in *An American Tragedy*, Wright focused on a murderer and expanded to an indictment of the capitalist system which created him. Bigger Thomas had much less freedom of choice than Dreiser's protagonist, and was almost totally conditioned by his environment.

Native Son was Wright's greatest achievement, and perhaps the best novel written by an African American up to that time. The influence of *Native Son* upon subsequent African American

novelists was immeasurable. In the context of American fiction, Wright belongs with the school of Chicago naturalists which began at the turn of the century with Dreiser and Frank Norris.

Richard Wright also wrote *The Outsider* (1953); *Black Power* (1954); *The Colored Curtain* (1956); *The Long Dream* (1958); and *Lawd Today* (1963).

• *Notable Deaths:* There were 97 recorded lynchings of African Americans in 1908.

• William Harvey Carney (1840–1908), a Congressional Medal of Honor winner, died.

William Harvey Carney was born in Norfolk, Virginia. He was able to receive some education and later settled in New Bedford, Massachusetts, where he was employed as a seaman.

On February 17, 1863, Carney enlisted in the army and became a member of the 54th Massachusetts Colored Infantry. He rose to the rank of sergeant and commanded Company C.

Carney earned his medal of honor only five months after he joined the army when, at the battle for Fort Wagner, the color bearer was wounded. Carney, despite being wounded, sprang forward and seized the flag before it slipped from the bearer's grasp, an act of gallant, albeit futile, bravery.

After Fort Wagner, Carney was discharged from the army because of the wounds he had received.

For "various reasons," Carney's medal of honor was not issued until May 23, 1900.

Upon Carney's death in 1908, the flag at the Massachusetts state capitol was lowered to half mast in tribute to this brave man.

• John Henry Smyth (1844–1908), a former Minister to Liberia, died.

John Henry Smyth was born in Richmond, Virginia, of a slave father, Sully Smyth. John attended a Quaker school until 1857. At the age of 14, he was admitted to the Pennsylvania Academy of Fine Arts. In 1862, Smyth attended the Institute for Colored Youth.

Smyth taught in Philadelphia public schools until 1865, when he went to England with the intention of studying under Ira Aldridge, the famous African American Shakespearean actor. However, Aldridge died not long after Smyth arrived in England and Smyth had to change his plans.

In 1869, Smyth returned to the United States and entered Howard University Law School. He graduated in 1872. Upon his graduation, he became a cashier of the Wilmington, North

Carolina branch of the Freedmen's Savings and Trust Company of Washington.

In 1874, Smyth began to practice law. The following year, he became a delegate to the Virginia State Constitutional Convention.

On May 23, 1878, Smyth was appointed minister resident and consul general of Liberia. He held this position until 1885.

After his return to the United States, Smyth became editor of the *Reformer*, in Richmond, Virginia. In 1899, Smyth was instrumental in establishing the Virginia Manual Labor School at Hanover.

• John Baxter "Doc" Taylor, a record setting quarter miler and the first African American to win an Olympic gold medal, died of typhoid pneumonia.

• *Miscellaneous Laws:* Georgia added a "grandfather clause" amendment to its State Constitution. Like the Alabama clause of 1901, however, the amendment enfranchised descendants of (Civil War) veterans.

• *Miscellaneous Cases:* The United States Supreme Court upheld the Kentucky Court of Appeals decision in *Berea v. the Commonwealth* (November 9, 1908) 211 U.S. 45, 29 S.Ct. 33, which held that segregation in all schools was constitutional. The opinion reflected the Court's attitude that segregation was a matter best left to the states.

In Kentucky, Berea College was founded in 1856. Berea College followed a policy of integration until 1908 when the United States Supreme Court upheld a Kentucky law of 1904 which required segregation of the races.

• *Publications*: In 1908, William Braithwaite's *House of Falling Leaves* was published. In this body of work, Braithwaite elaborated on his theme of mystical aestheticism. William Braithwaite also published *Georgian Verse* (1908).

• *The Performing Arts:* Freddie Keppard, a person of African and French ancestry, and his band, the Original Creoles, began playing jazz in New Orleans. Keppard took his Original Creole Band to Chicago and New York in 1913, to Los Angeles in 1914, and to Coney Island in 1915. In 1917, Keppard had a recording offer from the Victor Phonograph Company, but he turned it down because he was afraid other bands would steal his "stuff." The honor of being the first jazz band to record thus went to the European American band named Original Dixieland Jazz Band.

Scholastic Achievements

In 1908, Alain Leroy Locke became the first African American Rhodes Scholar. The impact of his selection was particularly significant because of the efforts of many European American scholars of the day to prove that African Americans were intellectually inferior and that because of this "inferiority" African Americans needed to be segregated from European Americans. Locke's selection served to dispel some of these racist notions.

• The Anna T. Jeanes fund inaugurated the Jeanes Teacher Program, to improve the quality of instruction in African American rural schools.

Virginia Estelle Randolph (1870–1958) was the first African American Jeanes teacher. Anna T. Jeanes, a Philadelphia Quaker, provided one million dollars to initiate a fund for teachers who worked with other teachers to encourage improvements in small African American rural schools. Randolph was one of the most effective educators of her day. The Jeanes teacher program was fashioned after her teaching practices in Henrico County, Virginia. Through the Jeanes movement that covered the period between 1908 and 1969, Randolph was instrumental in improving the lives of thousands of teachers, children and community residents.

• *The Black Church:* In November 1908, Adam Clayton Powell, Sr., became pastor of the Abyssinian Baptist Church in New York City. One of his first political acts in New York was to lead a campaign to force the city to rid the area (40th Street on the West Side) in which the church was then located of the prostitutes who proliferated in the locale. *See 1865.*

The Black Church

Convening in Washington, D. C., twenty-five bishops of three of the main African American churches—the Colored Methodist Episcopal, the African Methodist Episcopal Zion, and the African Methodist Episcopal churches—issued an appeal to European Americans to stop the mob violence against African Americans. The bishops also called for an end to Jim Crow laws, the peonage and convict labor systems, and all other violations of the civil rights of African Americans.

The bishops said: "We do not ask at your hands any special favors... we ask .. nothing to which we are not entitled under the law and Constitution. We ask only for that which belongs to us as a right, for justice, for equality, for freedom of action and opportunity before the law and in the industrial life of the land, North and South alike."

• *Organizations:* At Howard University, the first African American sorority, Alpha Kappa Alpha, was organized by Ethel Hedgeman and eight other students on January 15.

• Martha M. Franklin founded the National Association of Colored Graduate Nurses to improve the status and working conditions of African American nurses.

• The first convention of Alpha Phi Alpha, an African American Greek letter fraternity, was held at Howard University.

• *Black Enterprise:* Developer Allen Allensworth filed a plan for what would become the all African American town of Allensworth in Tulare County, California. Allensworth's plan was an attempt to have African Americans develop industry and a lifestyle on a par with the local European Americans.

In 1908, European American and African American land speculators combined to create the most notable westernmost all-black town, Allensworth, California. The town was initiated by the California Colony and Home Promoting Association (CCHPA), an African American, Los Angeles based land development company. CCHPA hoped to encourage black settlement in California's rapidly growing San Joaquin Valley, and it envisioned a town as the commercial center of a thriving agricultural colony.

CCHPA had no resources to purchase land, it joined with three European American firms, the Pacific Farming Company (owners of the site of the prospective town), the Central Land Company, and the Los Angeles Purchasing Company to create an eighty-acre townsite in Tulare County along the Santa Fe Railroad, about halfway between Fresno and Bakersfield. Allensworth was named for Lieutenant Colonel Allen Allensworth, chaplain of the all-black Twenty-fourth Infantry Regiment, and the highest-ranking African American in the United States Army. After his retirement, Allensworth settled in Los Angeles and he became president of the CCHPA in 1907.

Initial sales were slow, and by 1910, the town had only eighty residents. Most of the adult residents worked on ten-acre farms nearby, which they purchased for $110 per acre on an installment plan. The slow growth of Allensworth prompted Colonel Allensworth to intensify his promotional efforts.

In January 1912, Allensworth sent a letter to the *New York Age,* the nation's largest African American newspaper, promoting the townsite and linking it to Booker T. Washington's call for African American economic self-help. Allensworth suggested that his town's objectives were similar to those of Mound Bayou.

By May of 1912, Allensworth began to concentrate his recruiting efforts on his former soldiers, issuing a promotional newspaper, *The Sentiment Maker,* which specifically targeted African American military personnel.

The town of Allensworth had 100 residents in 1914. Despite their small numbers, the residents of Allensworth owned dozens of city lots and 3,000 acres of nearby farmland. Oscar O. Overt, a migrant for Topeka, Kansas, was the community's most prosperous resident native, with a 640-acre farm and four acres of town lots. In 1914, Oscar Overt became California's first elected black justice of the peace.

Allensworth also had a twenty-acre park named after Booker T. Washington, and a library named for Colonel Allensworth's wife, Josephine, and which received as its first holdings the family's book collection.

After Colonel Allenworth's death on September 14, 1914, Overt and William A. Payne, the town's first schoolteacher, attempted to establish the Allensworth Agricultural and Manual Training School, modeled after Tuskegee, to train California's African American youth in practical skills. However, the proponents failed to obtain the needed state funding primarily because urban African American political leaders feared the school would encourage segregation. The school promotion scheme was the last concerted effort to lure settlers to Allensworth. Except for a brief period in the 1920s, the town's population never exceeded 100 residents.

* * *

Today none of the surviving all-black towns are the thriving, prosperous communities envisioned by their promoters. Many, like Nicodemus *(see 1877)* and Allensworth have long been emptied of residents. In the 1990s, Boley *(see 1904),* Mound Bayou *(see 1881),* and Langston City *(see 1890)* continue to exist, but they are not dynamic centers of economic or cultural activity.

Like thousands of small towns throughout the United States, black towns were subject to the vagaries of transportation access, unpredictable agricultural productivity, detrimental county or state political decisions, and shifting settlement patterns. Moveover, towns such as Nicodemus and Allensworth, which had few African American farmers, in their hinterlands to sustain their prosperity, were especially vulnerable to decline.

No town, however, could long compete with the attraction of the big city. The urban areas lured millions of Americans — including African Americans — from farms and small towns during the twentieth century. Most of these communities began declining around 1915, the first year of the Great Migration of hundreds of thousands of African Americans from the South to the northern cities.

In addition to the nationwide social factors, the initial reason for the creation of the all-black towns may have hastened their demise. After 1915, Blacks could gain some of the political rights and job opportunities they sought by moving to northern cities rather than to the small southern or southwestern towns. The racial insularity of these all-black communities, which seemed attractive to one generation, ultimately proved to be too restricting for the next.

Nevertheless, for one brief moment, a handful of all-black communities throughout the nation symbolized the aspirations of African Americans for political freedom and economic opportunity. The existence of the all-black towns was a testament to the African American quest for dignity and liberty.

• Jesse Binga (1865–1950) founded the Binga State Bank in Chicago, Illinois.

• *Sports:* On December 26, 1908, Jack Johnson won the heavyweight boxing championship from Tommy Burns in a bout fought in Sydney, Australia. Burns explained his loss by saying "race prejudice … [and] hatred made me tense." Johnson held the title for almost seven years, eventually losing his championship to Jesse Willard in 1915.

• John B. Taylor of the University of Pennsylvania was the intercollegiate champion in the 440 yard dash for the third time. He led the American Olympic team at the London Olympics and won a gold medal for his work on the 1600 meter (4x400 meter) relay. Tragically, Taylor, who was the first African American to ever win an Olympic gold medal, died later in the year from typhoid pneumonia. He was 26 at the time of his death.

• The first intercity basketball competition between African American clubs was held between the Smart Set Club of Brooklyn, New York, and the Crescent Athletic Club of Washington, D. C. The Brooklyn club won both games.

THE AMERICAS

• *Brazil:* Joaquim Machado de Assis (1839–1908), an Afro-Brazilian writer regarded by many as Brazil's greatest novelist, died (September 29).

Joaquim Machado de Assis was born on June 21, 1839, in a slum of Rio de Janeiro. Joaquim was the son of an Afro-Brazilian painter and a Portuguese woman from the Azores. Joaquim's mother died when Joaquim was ten. The care and early education of the young Joaquim was then assumed by a kindly Afro-Brazilian woman. Joaquim's father married this woman a few years later.

Joaquim did not receive much formal education. He worked as a typesetter, proofreader, editor, and staff writer.

In 1869, Joaquim married Carolina, the sister of his friend, the Portuguese poet Faustino Xavier de Novais. This marriage followed a turbulent courtship which was opposed by Carolina's parents on racial grounds. However, Carolina, who was five years older than Joaquim, was steadfast in her love for him and Carolina's parents did eventually relent.

In 1874, Machado became employed in government service. Machado would remain a civil servant for the rest of his life.

While still very young, Joaquim began writing poetry, plays, opera librettos, short stories, newspaper articles, and translations. He was active in artistic and intellectual circles.

Some of Machado's biographers attribute Machado's success to the fact that he spent over thirty years as a government bureaucrat. It is theorized that the bureaucratic routine permitted Machado to devote himself completely to letters. Others attribute his success to the personal struggles he encountered during his difficult life. Machado's anxieties concerning his race and social origins, the epilepsy which plagued him, and his propensity for stuttering were all powerful influences on the man and his writing. Indeed, for Machado, writing itself seemed to be a relief from the insecurities and the woes that were so much a part of his life.

Machado's first volume of poems, *Crisalides (Chrysalis)* was published in 1864. This work was followed by *Falenas (Moth)* and *Contos fluminenses (Tales of Rio de Janeiro)* in 1870; Machado's first novel *Ressurreicao (Resurrection)* in

1871; *Historias da meia-noite (Midnight Tales)* in 1873; *A mao e a luva (The Hand and the Glove)* in 1874; *Americanas (American Poems)* in 1875; *Helena* in 1876; and *Yaya Garcia* in 1878.

Despite this prolific beginning, Machado had not quite found his literary voice. This would not come until after Machado suffered a major physical setback. Machado suffered a breakdown.

In 1878, Machado was sick and exhausted. He requested and was granted a leave of absence. Machado spent his leave in the resort city of Nova Friburgo, near Rio. This retreat would mark a turning point in his literary career.

During this period of recuperation, Joaquim was tenderly nursed back to health by his beloved Carolina. She took care of him by at times acting as mother, wife, nurse and confidant. Carolina gave Joaquim new life and, after Nova Friburgo, his writing would never be the same.

Upon his return to Rio de Janeiro, Machado began one of the masterpieces that characterize the second phase of his writing career. Machado began *Memorias postumas de Bras Cubas*. It is believed that Machado essentially dictated this novel to his devoted Carolina and that the dictation format is readily evident in the structure of the novel.

Memorias postumas de Bras Cubas was completed in 1881. In this novel, Machado gives the reader a fictional autobiography which is written by the dead hero. Starting with the hero's death and subsequent funeral, *Memorias posthumas de Bras Cubas* represents a complete break with the literary conventions of the time. This novel revolutionized Brazilian literature by allowing for an exploration of themes which had heretofore not been utilized. With psychological acuity, Machado was able to observe people in trivial, cynical, and egocentric conditions. His novel, in essence, became a time capsule of Brazilian society at the end of the second Brazilian empire with an accompanying psychological insight into the people of the era.

When reviewing Machado's rise to literary genius as evidenced by *Memorias postumas de Bras Cubas*, most critics interpret Machado's change in fortunes to being a consequence of his long desire for perfection and as the result of Machado's internal struggle between romantic ideals and his creative intuition. From this perspective, Machado's newly found brilliance was merely a reflection of his progression and maturation as a writer.

Other critics, however, are not so certain. For these critics, Machado's sojourn at Nova Friburgo was a cocooning experience which permitted a metamorphosis to occur, — and it was this metamorphosis which transformed the literary caterpillar which Machado had been into the artistic butterfly which he became.

Whichever analysis is correct, there is no questioning the fact that Machado's writing dramatically improved after his retreat. His first published works after this retreat was a collection of short stories. These stories were published in 1880 and include several stories which are considered to be masterpieces. Such stories as "Missa do galo" (Midnight Mass); "Noite de almirante" (An Admiral's Evening); "A causa secreta" (The Secret Cause); "Uns bracos" (A Pair of Arms); "O alienist" (The Alienist); "O enfermeiro" (The Male Nurse); "A cartomante" (The Fortune Teller), and "O espelho" (The Mirror) set a new standard for short stories in Brazilian literature.

After *Memorias postumas de Bras Cubas,* Machado wrote another Brazilian classic, *Quincas Borba. Quincas Borba* was published in 1891. In *Quincas Borba,* the hero of the story Rubiao, a teacher from Minas Gerais, inherits a huge amount of money from Quincas Borba. As he leaves for Rio, Rubiao meets a pair of con artists, Christiano Palha and his beautiful wife, Sofia. Rubiao falls in love with Sofia and, in an effort to be near Sofia, Rubiao allows Christiano and Sofia to become his closest friends.

Christiano and Sofia proceed to take Rubiao for everything that he has. In the process, a coterie of marginal and shifty people become peripherally involved. In the end, Rubiao winds up poor and insane. It is a story in which there is universal indifference in the face of human suffering and abandonment of man by the supernatural powers that be.

While both *Memorias postumas de Bras Cubas* and *Quincas Borba* were exceptional literary works, they were merely the groundwork for the ultimate work that was to come —*Dom Casmurro.*

Published in 1899, *Dom Casmurro* is considered to be artistically superior to anything else written by Machado. In *Dom Casmurro,* Machado employs such novelistic elements as narrative structure, composition of characters, and psychological analysis in a manner which can only be described as genius.

In *Dom Casmurro,* the hero of the story, Bento Santiago, sought to join the two ends of life and restore youth in old age. To this end, Bento had a replica of his childhood home constructed.

Because the plan did not work, Bento decided to write about his past.

In writing about his past, the reader learns about what may be prompting Bento's unusual obsession. We learn that as a youth, Bento fell in love with Capitu. The two want to be together, but Bento has already promised his mother that he would become a priest. Through various machinations, Capitu convinces Bento's mother, that her son should not be a priest. Bento's mother grants his wish to leave the seminary. Bento does leave the seminary. Bento becomes a lawyer and, with his law degree, he and Capitu are united in a seemingly blissful marriage.

Capitu and Bento have a child and all seems well. Escobar, Bento's best friend, marries Capitu's best friend, and the two couples live in perfect friendship. However, as Escobar dies, Bento becomes convinced that his friend and Capitu have had an affair. This knowledge shatters Bento's world.

In *Dom Casmurro,* Bento tells his own story. The story is told smoothly and at first serenely, but as it progresses, the story becomes a tragic tale of evil, hatred, betrayal, and jealousy. This story, along with Machado's outstanding artistic abilities, have made *Dom Casmurro* into "*the great Brazilian novel.*"

In 1904, Machado published *Esau e Jaco (Esau and Jacob).* In *Esau e Jaco,* Machado added a new dimension to his treatment of symbolic and mythical elements. The novel contains more political allegories than do any of his other works. In telling the story of the struggle of two identical twins (Pedro and Paulo) for the love of a girl (Flora), Machado intertwines observations concerning the political atmosphere in Brazil around the time that the Brazilian Republic was proclaimed.

1904 was an important year in the life of Joaquim Machado de Assis. In 1904, he lost his beloved wife, Carolina. This loss overwhelmed Joaquim. In an attempt to relieve his pain, he wrote a very touching poem, "A Carolina." "A Carolina" would appear as an introduction to a collection of short stories, *Reliquias da casa velha (Relics of an Old House)* which was published in 1906.

Joaquim never recovered from Carolina's death. His last novel, *Memorial de Aires,* is essentially a love story and a reminiscence of his life with Carolina. *Memorial de Aires* was published in 1908.

Joaquim Machado de Assis, frail and ill, soon rejoined his beloved Carolina. He died in 1908 not long after *Memorial de Aires* was completed.

It is important to understand the significance of Joaquim Machado de Assis in Brazilian literature and in the literature of the world. Machado de Assis was a powerful writer who connected on both an intellectual and emotional level. Most of his writing is of a psychological nature. However, the best of his work combines the social, philosophical, and historical dimensions with the psychological to make a whole.

Machado's genius at evoking the past was undoubtedly one of the secrets to his success. His stylistic traits include a simple, exact, and clear syntax and short, discontinuous sentences without rhetorical effects. Machado employs metaphor and simile in his writing. But his greatness primarily rests on the conciseness of his style. Machado's underlining philosophy is a pessimistic one that envisions man as solitary, depraved and lost. In keeping with this tragic view of life, Machado's themes embrace death, insanity, cruelty, ingratitude, disillusion, and hate.

Machado found relief from his nihilistic view of life in beauty. For Machado, heaven was — is — the aesthetic ideal.

From an ethno-centric perspective, Machado's works were not particularly enlightening. His novels centered on the activities of the upper-class Carioca society of Brazil — a society which was almost totally European. Although Machado was sympathetic to the plight of Afro-Brazilians, he did little to help them and rarely involved them in his works. This disassociation was perhaps due to Machado's acceptance into the Carioca society of which he wrote.

As for the few times when race was raised in his works, only *Yaya Garcia* and *Memorias Posthumas de Braz Cubas* were particularly notable.

In 1878, Machado published *Yaya Garcia.* In this novel, a faithful slave, Raymundo, is the only fully drawn Afro-Brazilian character that appears in any of Machado's works.

In 1881, Machado published *Memorias Posthumas de Braz Cubas.* In this work, one of the ancillary themes is the pernicious effects of slavery on both the slave and the slave owner.

In addition to his major novels, Joaquim Machado de Assis also published collections of short stories entitled *Papeis avulsos (1882), Historias sem data (1884), Varias historias (1896), Paginas recolhidas (1899),* and *Outras reliquias (1910).*

• *Haiti:* Massillon Coicou, the famed Afro-Haitian poet and the former Haitian Minister to Paris, was executed by firing squad in Haiti. *See 1867.*

- *Mexico:* Bill Pickett, the great African American bulldogger, was injured in a Mexican bullring.

Bill Pickett's most grueling bulldogging experience was undoubtedly in the Mexico City bullring on December 23, 1908. After Joe Miller, for publicity purposes, had callously bet that Pickett could "stay with" a Mexican fighting bull for fifteen minutes, during five minutes of which Pickett was to be actually wrestling with the bull. The Mexican audience, enraged at this arrogant insult to their national sport, showered Pickett and his horse with missiles ranging from fruit and cushions to bottles, brickbats, and knives. As a result, Pickett's horse was badly gored.

As for Pickett, he was severely gashed and had three ribs broken. Although he won the bet by staying on the bull's back for seven and a half minutes, he never succeeded in throwing the animal. Given the animosity of the crowd, Pickett and his horse were lucky to escape with their lives.

AFRICA

- *North Africa, Egypt and Sudan:* The National University was founded in Cairo.
- Maulai Hafid usurped his brother and was proclaimed the Sultan of Morocco at Fez (June 7).
- Abdul Aziz was defeated by the Sultan at Marrakesh (August).
- The Casablanca incident occurred (September 25). German deserters from the French Foreign Legion were taken by force from German consular officials.
- *Western Africa:* Adrar was pacified by Colonel Gouraud (December). There was an uprising in the Bissau region.
- In 1908, Arthur Barclay, the president of Liberia, agreed to permit a British officer, Major Caddell, to organize a frontier police force. Cadell used this police force to stage a coup, but Barclay managed to oust Cadell and suppress the insurgents.
- A railway was built from Bara to Kano. This railway was joined to the Lagos railway. The general manager of the Nigerian railways complained that African-owned motor transport was undermining railway profits on the Iddo to Ibadan line.
- Gabriel d'Arboussier, a West African nationalist leader, was born.

Gabriel d'Arboussier (1908–1976) was born in Jenne (Mali), the son of a French colonial administrator and his African wife. D'Arboussier was educated in France. He attended law school and, later on, he attended a school for colonial civil servants. D'Arboussier eventually returned to Equatorial Africa as an administrator.

Gabriel d'Arboussier was a Communist. As a Communist, he had strong sympathies for the nationalist movements of French West Africa.

In 1945, d'Arboussier was elected to the French Chamber of Deputies as a representative from Equatorial Africa. The next year, d'Arboussier was a key figure in organizing the *Rassemblement Democratique Africain* (the "RDA"), an inter-territorial party led by Felix Houphouet-Boigny of the Ivory Coast.

In 1947, the Ivory Coast elected d'Arboussier Councillor of the French Union. Two years later, d'Arboussier became the RDA general secretary.

At first, the RDA had strong Communist ties. In 1949, the RDA agitated fiercely against colonial administration. The resulting repression led Houphouet to cut the party's ties with the Communists, a move which d'Arboussier strongly opposed. In the resulting dispute (in 1952), d'Arboussier was expelled from the party.

Five years later, in 1957, d'Arboussier and Houphouet reconciled. D'Arboussier was elected by Niger to the Grand Council of French West Africa.

In 1959, d'Arboussier again severed his ties with the RDA over the issue of federation of French African territories which the RDA opposed.

When the union between Senegal and Mali broke up, d'Arboussier became minister of justice in Senegal. D'Arboussier became ambassador to France in 1963 and held several high diplomatic posts until 1972.

- Bai Bureh, the leader of the Temne Hut Tax War in Sierra Leone, died.

Bai Bureh was born near Port Loko in northern Sierra Leone to a professional soldier of either Temne or Lokko extraction. Bai Bureh's father sent him to a military training camp at Pendembu Gwahun. At this camp, Bai Bureh received the nickname "Kabalai" in recognition of his prowess as a warrior.

From the 1860s through most of the 1880s, Kabalai gained the reputation as a fierce and ruthless war leader of a powerful chief named Bokhari. In 1887, the elders of the Temne chiefdom, unable to find a suitable successor to Bokhari, offered it to Kabalai. From that time onward, Kabalai became known as Bai Bureh — "Bai Bureh" being the designated title of the ruler of Kasseh.

As the ruler of Kasseh, Bai Bureh became a powerful war chief. He became one of the select few who were able to sell their services to neighboring rulers.

Bai Bureh's Kasseh had had a treaty of friendship with the British in Freetown. However, Bai Bureh soon came into conflict with the British because of his continued involvement in local wars. These local wars tended to create instability and disrupted the trade within the colony.

Nevertheless, in 1891, the British allied with Bai Bureh and used 1500 of Bai Bureh's troops to defeat one of Bai Bureh's chief rivals. This alliance allowed Bai Bureh to study British fighting techniques. What he learned he soon began to employ.

The alliance with the British soon deteriorated and the relations between Bai Bureh and the British became downright hostile when, in 1893, Governor Cardew ordered Bai Bureh to pay a large fine for engaging in war and then refusing to come to Freetown to discuss it.

For the next few years, Bai Bureh had little contact with the British. However, in 1896, the British declared a protectorate over the Sierra Leone hinterland — over Bai Bureh's Kasseh.

The declaration of a protectorate was followed, in 1898, by the imposition of a hut tax on most of the protectorate. The imposition of the hut tax precipitated the famous Hut Tax War.

The Hut Tax War was essentially a protest by the indigenous people of Sierra Leone against not only the hut tax but also against their loss of freedom. Bai Bureh led the Temne campaign against the British. The Temne campaign spread from Kasseh in the north to Mende in the south and lasted for ten months.

Bai Bureh was successful at first because of his innovative use of guerrilla tactics. However, the tactics could not overcome the superior firepower and resources of the British. Bai Bureh was eventually captured.

After his capture, Bai Bureh was exiled to the Gold Coast (Ghana). He was not permitted to return to Sierra Leone until 1905. He died three years later.

- Toffa, the ruler of the Aja kingdom of Porto Novo, died.

When Toffa first ascended the throne Porto Novo was obliged to depend on Dahomey for protection from their mutual Yoruba enemies to the north. Once the Yoruba threat subsided Toffa saw in the French a means of gaining independence from Dahomey. France had previously proclaimed a protectorate over Porto Novo, but soon abandoned it (around 1868).

In 1883, Toffa asked the French to proclaim a new protectorate, and they obliged. Porto Novo thrived as a port under French protection. Toffa, meanwhile, sent insulting messages to Behanzin, the ruler of Dahomey (Benin). These taunts were ostensibly an attempt to goad Behanzin into an attack on Porto Novo, which Toffa knew the French would answer.

When the French finally did invade Dahomey in 1892, Toffa supplied porters for the French. He was rewarded for his services by being allowed greater freedom than most of his neighbors who had come under French rule. Porto Novo's limited autonomy ended with Toffa's death in 1908.

- *Central Africa:* From 1908 to 1912, many small wars by chiefs erupted in Burundi.
- The *Afrique Equatoriale Francaise* (AEF) was established by decree (June 26).
- Leopold II handed over the Congo to the Belgian government (August 20).
- The transfer was confirmed by the Belgian Act of Parliament (October 18).
- Local councils were established in Cameroon.
- *Eastern Africa:* Lord Delamere led a settler demonstration outside Government House, Nairobi, protesting Labour Policy (March).
- The Central Committee of Associations was formed in Kenya.
- A convention was held between Italy and Ethiopia on the boundaries of Italian Somalia.

In 1908, minor border skirmishes erupted into a major confrontation. Muhammed 'Abdullah Hassan, the "Mad Mullah," again raised the banner of revolt. Muhammed's international enemies were not prepared to oppose him. The British retreated to their coastal settlements in the north while Muhammed reoccupied their nominal inland possessions. The Italians, thankful for Muhammed's abandonment of the Nogal region, left Muhammed to the British.

In eastern British Somaliland, Muhammed built fortified towns, making Taleh his last headquarters.

- Italy gained the basin of the Juba River.
- The Elgin pledge was made. Pursuant to the Elgin pledge, as a matter of administrative

convenience, Indians would not be given land in the Kenya Highlands.

• There was a famine in Busoga.
• *Southern Africa:* J. X. Merriman became the Prime Minister of the Cape Colony (February 3).
• The Comoro Islands were attached to Madagascar (April 9).
• In May, the Railway and Customs conference met in Pretoria. J. C. Smuts moved for a union of South Africa and South Rhodesia.
• The National Convention in Durban and then Cape Town drafted a constitution for a Union of South Africa.

In 1908, a national convention was held to form the Union of South Africa. At the convention, John Merriman, the future South African prime minister, was the leading proponent of the unitary form of government which was adopted.

Merriman also supported the weighting of parliamentary constituencies in favor of rural areas — a policy which later greatly influenced South African politics. After the convention, Merriman pushed the resulting national unification bill through the Cape parliament.

• The first tobacco factory was constructed in Nyasaland at Limbe.
• Between 1908 and 1912, the Portuguese campaigned against the Yao in the Niassa district.

RELATED HISTORICAL EVENTS

• *Europe:* The Belgian Parliament voted to annex the Congo Free State (September 9).
• *Africa:* Slavery was abolished in Sao Tome Principe and Angola.
• Reginald Stephen Garfield Todd, a prime minister of Southern Rhodesia, was born.

Reginald Todd was born in New Zealand. He came to Southern Rhodesia (Zimbabwe) in 1934 to work as a missionary.

Todd entered politics to help advance African education and was elected to the legislative assembly in 1946. He was elevated to the premiership by a party congress in 1953, when Godfrey Huggins resigned the office in order to head the new Federation of the Rhodesias and Nyasaland.

Todd's policies towards the majority African population were not significantly different from those of his predecessors. However, he alienated the Euro-Rhodesian electorate by projecting a public image as an ultra-liberal. Todd achieved some gains in African education, land tenure, and voting rights, but he did not hesitate to use force to repress African dissent.

Widespread Euro-Rhodesian disenchantment caused Todd's government to collapse at a party congress early in 1958. Todd then served briefly in the cabinet of his successor, Edgar Whitehead.

In 1959, Todd helped to establish the multiracial Central African Party. He thereafter took a more radical stance with respect to Africans' rights, publicly acknowledging the shortcomings of his own administration and calling for sweeping legislative changes.

After Whitehead's government began to purge African political organizations in 1960, Todd called upon the British government to suspend the Rhodesian constitution in order to bring about basic democratic reform. These pronouncements shattered what was left of Todd's support among Euro-Rhodesians. His continued outspokenness led to his being restricted to his farm in 1965 and to his temporary imprisonment in 1972, followed by further restriction. The restriction order was lifted in May 1976.

---

1 9 0 9

THE UNITED STATES

• The National Association for the Advancement of Colored People ("NAACP") was founded on Lincoln's centennial birthday after the savage Springfield, Illinois race riots of the preceding year. *See 1908.* The founders of the organization were a group of African American and European American leaders, including W.E.B. DuBois and Oswald Garrison Villard. The group issued a call for a militant civil rights organization whose purpose would be to combat growing violence against African Americans (February 12).

In response to the Springfield, Illinois, race riots which occurred in 1908, William Walling, a wealthy Southerner and Socialist settlement worker (also the author of the article *Race War in the North*) along with Mary White Ovington, a Socialist humanitarian who had worked among the African Americans of New York City, and Dr. Henry Moskowitz, a social worker, met and decided to launch a campaign to assist the African Americans in the United States. Oswald Garrison Villard joined the group and on February 12 wrote their call for a conference: "We call upon all believers in democracy to join in a national conference for the discussion of present evils, the voicing of protests and the renewal of the struggle for civil and political liberty."

This group of activists was expanded and made biracial when Lillian Wald and Florence Kelly (founders of the National Women's Trade Union League), Bishop Alexander Walter of the AMEZ Episcopal Methodist Church, and William Henry Brooks of St. Marks Methodist Episcopal Church were invited to join.

Between May 31 and June 1, the National Negro Conference met in New York City. Most members of the Niagara Movement attended. However, Monroe Trotter, who was suspicious of the motivations of European Americans, declined.

In addition to the original group, some other participants in the conference were Jane Addams, William Dean Howells, Livingston Farrand, John Dewey, John Milholland, W. E. B. DuBois, and Oswald Garrison Villard. All in all, some 300 participants attended this inaugural meeting and the participants included some of the nation's most distinguished progressives and intellectuals, both African American and European American.

The participants at the National Negro Conference decided to incorporate as the National Committee for the Advancement of the Negro Race. However, before final incorporation, the name was changed to the National Association for the Advancement of Colored People — the NAACP.

The members of the new NAACP demanded equal civil, political, and educational rights, an end to segregation, the right to work, the right to protection from violence and intimidation, and criticized the nonenforcement of the 14th and 15th Amendments. A permanent committee of 40 was established to administer the affairs of the organization.

• Senator Foraker of Ohio succeeded in forcing through a bill which established a court of inquiry to pass on the cases of the discharged Brownsville, Texas, soldiers. The bill provided that all the discharged soldiers who were qualified for re-enlistment were to be deemed eligible. Any such soldier was to receive the "pay, allowances and other rights and benefits that he would have been entitled to receive according to his rank from said date of discharge, as if he had been honorably discharged ... and had re-enlisted immediately."

• Moorfield Storey stated that the African American's condition would be improved only if the South were broken up and the 15th Amendment enforced. Storey felt that the rights of the African American would have to be protected by public opinion in other parts of the country.

• Commander Robert E. Peary reached the North Pole accompanied by his "Negro assistant," Matthew H. Henson. It was the first successful polar expedition (April 6).

On their famous 1908–1909 expedition, Henson was the one who was the first to set foot on the North Pole and it was Henson who planted the United States flag at the site which is deemed to be "the top of the world." *See 1866.*

• Charles W. Eliot, the president of Harvard University, denounced any mixture of the racial stocks, and supported the South's demand for complete separation of the races.

• Thomas Wentworth Higgins, a former abolitionist, stated that it was a mistake to give suffrage to African Americans as a class. Higgins believed that no European American community would ever permit the electoral supremacy of African Americans.

• *Notable Births:* George W. Crockett, Jr., the first African American lawyer to serve in the United States Department of Labor (in 1943), was born in Florida.

• Katherine Dunham, a noted dancer, was born near Chicago, Illinois (June 22).

• Jazz vibraphonist, Lionel Hampton, was born in Louisville, Kentucky (April 12).

• The novelist Chester Himes, the creator of the characters "Gravedigger Jones" and "Coffin Ed Johnson," was born in Jefferson City, Missouri.

• Norman Lewis, a painter, was born in New York (July 23).

• Howard Swanson, a noted composer, was born in Atlanta, Georgia.

• Lester Young (1909–1959), a great tenor saxophonist, was born (August 27).

Lester Young was perhaps the single most important transitional figure in the development of bop, the significant jazz form of the 1940s and 1950s. Young played several instruments, especially tenor saxophone, with his family on the carnival circuit in the Midwest. Young appeared with Fletcher Henderson's band, with Andy Kirk in Kansas City, and from 1936 through 1940 with Count Basie.

• *Notable Deaths:* There were 82 recorded lynchings in 1909.

• Thomas Greene Bethune ("Blind Tom") (1849–1909), who gained national fame as a child piano prodigy, died.

Thomas Greene Bethune was born blind and a slave near Columbus, Georgia. His musical talents soon came to the fore and caught the attention of his owner, Colonel Bethune, who had purchased Tom in 1850.

In 1858, Blind Tom made his debut in Savannah, Georgia, and began a musical career that would span four decades.

Blind Tom was noted for his artistry and his ability to recall more than seven hundred piano pieces from memory. Over his career, it is said that he composed over one hundred musical pieces.

• George Walker, the great vaudeville performer, died. Between 1895 and 1909, Bert Williams and George Walker starred in and produced vaudeville shows throughout the United States and England. They were famous for their characterizations with Walker posing as the dandy and Williams in black-face, using a "Negro dialect."

• *Miscellaneous Laws:* Mobile, Alabama, instituted curfew laws applying only to African Americans.

• *Miscellaneous Cases:* Only once in its history has the Supreme Court invoked its contempt power. The incident occurred in 1909, when the Supreme Court cited the sheriff of Chattanooga, Tennessee, for having allowed a lynch mob to hang an African American who had been granted a stay of execution pending an appeal. However, while the sheriff was cited for contempt, there is no record of any punishment being imposed upon him.

• In the case of *Thomas v. Texas* (February 23, 1909) 212 U.S. 278, 29 S.Ct. 393, the United States Supreme Court upheld the murder conviction of Marcellus Thomas, of Harris County, Texas, but stated that "it may be that the jury commissioners did not give the Negro race full *pro rata* with the white race in the selection of the ... jurors of this case."

• *Publications:* Booker T. Washington published *The Story of the Negro.*

• William Braithwaite published *Restoration Verse.*

• On December 4 in New York, James Anderson began the *Amsterdam News.* The four page newspaper sold for a penny a copy. At the peak of its popularity, the paper claimed a circulation of more than a hundred thousand copies. The *Amsterdam News* became a major newspaper for the African American community.

• Charles Victor Roman (1864–1934) became the first editor of the *Journal of the National Medical Association.*

Charles Victor Roman was a physician, teacher, historian, and an author. Roman favored support of African American institutions and believed African and African American history should be written by Africans and African Americans.

Roman was born in Williamsport, Pennsylvania. He studied at Fisk University and Meharry Medical College, both in Nashville, Tennessee. He later directed health service at Fisk and taught at Meharry.

• *The Performing Arts:* Wade Hammond, Alfred Jack Thomas, William Polk, and Egbert Thompson were promoted to the rank of chief musician and became the first African American bandmasters in the United States Army. Previously the bands attached to African American regiments were exclusively led by European Americans.

Motion Pictures

Sigmund Lubin began production on two separate series of short comedy films featuring African Americans named Sambo and Rastus. The films had all African American casts and bore such titles as *Rastus in Zululand* and *Rastus Got His Turkey.* This series depicted African Americans as obedient, childlike characters, who were always in and out of ridiculous situations. These films would prove to be a great financial success for Lubin.

• *Music:* In 1909, W. C. (William Christopher) Handy moved to Memphis and wrote the campaign songs for Mayor Edward "Boss" Crump in 1909. These songs came to be known as *The Mayor Crump Blues* and they became the initial basis for Handy's national success when Handy transformed them into *The Memphis Blues.*

• *Scholastic Achievements:* Nannie Burroughs founded the National Training School for Women at Washington, D.C.

Nann Helen Burroughs, educator and later an active member of the National Association of Colored Women and the NAACP, became the first president of the National Training School for Women and Girls.

• Gilbert H. Jones received a doctorate in

German from the University of Jena (Germany).

• *Organizations:* The Knights of Peter Claver was founded in Mobile, Alabama. This organization was the first national African American Catholic fraternal order. The Knights of Peter Claver embraced some one hundred thousand Catholic families in the United States.

• *Sports:* Lincoln University (Pennsylvania), Hampton Institute, and Wilberforce University fielded the first African American college basketball teams.

THE AMERICAS

• *Canada:* Fleeing the increasingly oppressive environment of Oklahoma, the first bloc of Oklahoma African Americans arrived in Saskatchewan in October. This group sought out isolation from the Euro-Canadian communities, proximity to railroad lines, and distance from the United States border.

The African American settlers first took up land in the Eldon district, just north of Maidstone. Saskatoon was one hundred and fifty railroad miles to the southeast. The leaders of the all black Eldon community were Julius Caesar Lane and Mattie Hayes.

Mattie Hayes was a slim and determined woman of sixty when she arrived in Canada. She and her husband Joseph brought their ten sons and three daughters and their grandchildren from Tulsa and Muskogee along with ten other families. Until her death in 1953, "Mammy" Hayes was the mother of Maidstone — the matriarch of the community.

The government required all settlers to pay ten dollars for one hundred and sixty acres of land; to live on that land for six months in each year for three years; to clear a minimum of thirty acres on the land that was purchased; to dig a well; to build a house valued at $300; and to erect fencing worth $200.

• Two hundred African Americans immigrated to Manitoba settling as far east as the Thunder Bay area.

• *Haiti:* Jean Brierre, a poet, was born.

Jean Brierre was born in Jeremie, Haiti. After finishing school in Haiti, Brierre went to the Sorbonne (in Paris) and Columbia for his university education.

During the 1940s, Brierre held two prominent positions in Haiti. He was the secretary-general of the Union of Haitian Writers and Artists and he was the Director of Cultural Affairs in the Department of Foreign Affairs.

Brierre's books of verse include: *Le Petit Soldat* (1933); *L'Adieu a la Marseillaise* (1939), a free verse drama in tableau form on the life of Toussaint l'Ouverture; and *Nous Garderons le Dieu* (1945), poems written in memory of a fellow Haitian poet, Jacques Romain.

In 1947, *Black Soul,* Brierre's long epic poem, was published.

Brierre also edited *Province,* an anthology of Haitian verse in three volumes.

ASIA

• In the Ottoman Empire, harems were officially outlawed.

In 1909, harems were outlawed in the Ottoman Empire. The outlawing of harems brought to an end a little known chapter in African history. In the Seraglio — the grand harem of the Ottoman Sultans — the guardians of the women were always African eunuchs, and for five hundred years these black sentinels were privy to the most intimate details of one of the most powerful kingdoms on earth.

The first traces of eunuchry appear in Mesopotamia where the Tigris and Euphrates become and empty into the Persian Gulf. During the ninth century B.C.E., Semiramis, the Queen of Assyria, castrated male slaves. So also did other queens. It is even believed that the infamous Queen of Sheba castrated her male slaves.

The tradition of eunuchs traveled east, through Persia to China. Warring tribes, such as the Persians, often castrated their prisoners and offered them, along with the most beautiful virgins from amongst the conquered, to their kings.

In 538 B.C.E., Cyrus, the King of Persia, captured Babylon. Upon this victory, Cyrus proclaimed that since eunuchs were incapable of procreating and having their own families, they might be the most loyal servants.

With the advent of Christianity, the notion of chastity and the perception of women as obstacles to achieving it encouraged castration. Tertullian, the second century theologian, declared the Kingdom of Heaven open to eunuchs, encouraging many potential followers of Christ to castrate themselves.

During the Renaissance, the Catholic Church began castrating boys to preserve their soprano voices for the papal choir of the Sistine Chapel. This practice continued until 1878.

In the eighteenth century, some of the most famous opera singers were *castrati.* Such individuals as Grimaldi, Farinelli, and Nicolini all achieved fame for the quality of their unnatural but angelic voices.

In Mecca and Medina, several hundred eunuchs were employed by the holy mosques of Islam. At these mosques, the attendants had to come into contact with women who visited the mosques. Such contact was not permissible between men and women in Islamic society, especially in a holy place. Accordingly, the attendants had to be eunuchs — they had to be something less than men.

In Asia Minor (in Turkey), during the fifth century B.C.E., the priests of the Temple of Artemis in Ephesus and the Temple of Sybelle were eunuchs. Later on, the sacred function changed into a form of luxury in Greece and in Rome. As was noted by Gibbons: "Restrained by the severe edicts of Domitian and Nerva, cherished by the pride of Diocletian, reduced to a humble station by the prudence of Constantine, they (eunuchs) multiplied in the palaces of his degenerate sons, and insensibly acquired the knowledge, and at length the direction, of the secret councils of Constantius."

The custom of utilizing eunuchs lingered among the Byzantines and passed on to the Ottoman Turks. During the fourteenth century, when the Ottomans first began secluding their women, the Byzantines supplied them with eunuchs. However, soon thereafter, the Ottoman Turks established their own trade in eunuchs.

In China, castration was a well-established practice during the 1300s and 1400s. However, while the eunuchs in China were all Chinese, in the Ottoman Empire, the eunuchs were anything but Turks. After all, castration was forbidden in Islam.

At first, the Turks acquired white eunuchs from such conquered Christian areas as Circassia, Georgia, and Armenia. However, these eunuchs often proved too fragile. Their mortality rate was extremely high. Not so with the black eunuchs who apparently manifested more strength and better endurance.

According to the tenets of Islam, slaves captured in war became the property of their captor and, like all property, could be transferred. Muslim slave traders pursued certain African chiefs who willingly sold their people. Such transactions established a lucrative trade.

The majority of the slaves came from the lands of Egypt, Abyssinia (Ethiopia) and Sudan. The upper reaches of the Nile, Kordofan, Darfur, Dongola, and Lake Chad were particularly noted as being sources for slaves. The slaves were typically shipped upriver to Alexandria or Cairo, packed spoon fashion in boats. Another method of transportation was from Abyssinia to the Red Sea ports and eventually to the greatest slave emporiums in the Middle East — Mecca, Medina, Beirut, Smyrna, and Constantinople (Istanbul).

Among the slaves, some young African boys would be selected for castration. The castration would occur during the transportation of the slaves. The act of castration itself would typically be performed by Egyptian Christians or Jews since Islam prohibited the practice.

Castration was a risky operation with a high mortality rate. The mortality rate was exacerbated by the hot, arid climate which made recovery difficult. Desert sand was considered to be the most effective balm to heal the wounds so the newly castrated were buried up to their necks in desert sand until their wounds healed. The boys who survived the pain, hemorrhage, and subsequent burial became special — they became luxury items, bringing enormous profit to the slave traders. And since they had such great value, black eunuchs generally attracted only the wealthiest of purchasers. This fact contributed to their eventual positions of power and prestige.

There were three general categories of eunuchs:

Castrati — those with both the penis and testicles removed

Spadones — those with only the testicles removed

Thlibiae — those whose testicles had been crushed permanently damaging the seminal glands

In the Seraglio — the grand harem of the Ottoman Sultans — the white eunuchs served in the Selamlik — the place where the Sultan met other men. However, it was the black eunuchs who were entrusted with the harem, the most private part of the kingdom.

Because they were often privy to the most intimate secrets of the harem and also had access to the outer world, the eunuchs became some of the most powerful men in the Ottoman Empire. The chief black eunuch — the kislar agasi — exercised great political power in the court, serving as the most important link between the sultan and his mother. Officially his position was the third highest ranking officer in the empire, after the sultan and the grand vizier (prime minister).

The chief black eunuch was the commander

of the corps of baltaci, a pasha, and carried other important titles. He could approach the sultan at any time and functioned as the private messenger between the sultan and the grand vizier. The chief black eunuch had access to the valide sultana (the sultan's mother) and served as the liaison between the sultan and his mother. Any woman within the harem wanting to approach the sultan had to be screened by the chief black eunuch. He was an extremely wealthy man, greatly feared, and, consequently, the most bribed official in the whole Ottoman Empire.

If any emergency occurred, the kizlar agasi was the only person allowed to enter the harem. His duties were to protect the women, provide the necessary girl slaves for the harem, oversee the promotion of the women and the eunuchs, act as a witness for the sultan's marriage and birth ceremonies, arrange all the royal ceremonial events, such as circumcision parties, weddings and feasts, and carry out the sentence for harem women accused of crimes. It was the chief black eunuch who took the girls to the executioner — who had them put in sacks to be drowned.

In the second half of the sixteenth century, the power of the eunuchs grew. In the seventeenth and eighteenth centuries, the eunuchs, like the valide sultanas, took advantage of the numerous child sultans and mentally incompetent ones to gain political power. During the Reign of Women (1558–1687), the chief black eunuch was the valide sultana's most intimate and valued accomplice.

From the early nineteenth century until the fall of the empire, the power of the chief black eunuch declined. By the early twentieth century, his job was simply to supervise the dress of the women, making sure that it was appropriate; to accompany the women on their outings; to make certain that everything was conducted according to the rules of the Seraglio; to prohibit merchants, workers, and fortune-tellers from entering the harem; to grant or deny permission to women visitors; and to be on call in case something critical happened after midnight.

With the prohibition against harems in 1909, the demise of the eunuchs soon followed. They, along with their charges, were soon relegated to a minor footnote in history.

AFRICA

• *North Africa, Egypt and Sudan:* Press censorship was imposed in Egypt to control the nationalists (March 25).

• Bu Hamara attacked Melilla. The Spaniards replied with a force of 90,000. Bu Hamara was captured and exhibited in an iron cage, and then, literally, thrown to the lions.
• The limits of Melilla were enlarged.
• German instructors were sent to the Moroccan army.
• *Western Africa:* General Christopher Soglo was born.
• The French occupied Wadai, Chad.
• A coup led by British officer, Major Cadell, failed in Liberia.

In 1906, a British bank had loaned 100,000 pounds to the almost bankrupt Liberian government. The loan was secured against Liberia's custom receipts. A British major (Major Cadell) was dispatched to Liberia to organize a frontier force. In 1908–1909, the frontier force mutinied against the Liberian government. The mutiny failed.

• The Teachers Training College and Technical School was set up in Accra.
• Galandou Diouf *(see 1875)* entered politics in 1909 when he was elected to the general council of the four communes of Senegal (Dakar, St. Louis, Rufisque, and Goree). Diouf was a frequent critic of French policy, especially of administrative attempts to disfranchise African voters.
• Obafemi Awolowo (1909–1987), a noted representative of Yoruba interests in Nigerian national politics, was born.

Obafemi Awolowo was born into a Christian family. He was educated in mission schools and then became a teacher in Abeokuta. Determined to study law, Awolowo engaged in a number of private business concerns to raise money while studying by correspondence.

In 1944, Awolowo went to London to fulfill his dream of becoming a lawyer. While in London, he helped to found a Yoruba cultural society to promote Yoruba pan-tribalism.

It took two years for Awolowo to become a lawyer. After becoming a lawyer, Awolowo returned to Nigeria. Awolowo started his Yoruba cultural society in Nigeria as well. The society grew and Awolowo's reputation grew with it.

The Yoruba pan-tribalism movement was partially a reaction against the popularity of Nnamdi Azikiwe, an Ibo, who was the dominant figure in Nigerian nationalist politics. Azikiwe had disdained tribalism in his party, the National Council of Nigeria and the Cameroons (NCNC).

In 1951, elections were to be held under a new

Nigerian constitution for the assemblies of Nigeria's three regions. The year before Awolowo founded the Action Group (AG), a party committed to countering Azikiwe. The AG won the election in the Western region, and Awolowo formed a government.

As chief minister of the Western region, Awolowo instituted a number of reforms aimed at democratizing local government and increasing social services.

In 1954, under a new constitution, Awolowo became prime minister of the Western region. While serving in this capacity, Awolowo continued to build the AG into a national party with hopes of gaining control of the national government in the 1959 elections. The 1959 elections were to give Nigeria its first national prime minister. However, Awolowo was not successful. The party representing northern Nigeria dominated and formed a coalition with Azikiwe's NCNC. Awolowo became the opposition leader.

In 1962, Awolowo and eighteen other AG members were tried for attempting to overthrow the government. Sentenced to ten years in prison, Awolowo was released by General Gowon in 1966 and allowed to resume his leadership among the Yoruba.

When Biafra seceded in 1967, Awolowo expressed sympathy and suggested that the Western region might do the same. However, when Biafran troops invaded the Western region, Awolowo changed his allegiance to that of the national government.

Later on, Awolowo was made a federal commissioner for finance. Awolowo ultimately returned to private legal practice in 1971.

When military rule was ended in 1979, Awolowo formed the United Party of Nigeria and placed second to Alhaji Shehu Shagari in the presidential elections. In the 1983 elections, Awolowo again lost to Shagari. Shagari later was deposed by the military.

- Alhaji Ahmadu Bello (1909–1966), the most powerful leader at the time of Nigerian independence, was born.

Alhaji Ahmadu Bello was born near Sokoto. He was a direct descendant of 'Uthman dan Fodio, the legendary leader of the Islamic revolution in the Hausa states of northern Nigeria.

Bello graduated with honors from Katsina College in 1931 and became a teacher in Sokoto. At that time, the most powerful and prestigious office in northern Nigeria was the position of Sultan of Sokoto, the ruler of the Fula empire. Under the British system of indirect rule, the Sultan virtually controlled the internal affairs of northern Nigeria. When the reigning Sultan died in 1938, Bello aspired to the position, but lost to Abubakar, a rival who appointed Bello to the position of Sardauna—"leader of war"—and put Bello in charge of a section of Sokoto.

In 1943, Bello was convicted by the Sultan's court for misappropriation of the cattle tax revenues. Bello responded in a most non-traditional manner by appealing the decision to the British magistrate, who reversed the conviction.

In 1948, Bello went to England on a scholarship to study local government. Afterwards, Bello was reconciled with the Sultan.

In 1949, the Sultan chose Bello to serve as Sokoto's representative in the advisory northern assembly. The Sultan, with little Western education and no inclination for constitutional politics, was content to leave the task of party organization to Bello, who accepted it willingly.

In 1951, Bello was instrumental in forming the Northern People's Congress (NPC) as a vehicle for northern domination of federal politics. The NPC, with traditional sanction, quickly overwhelmed an older and more radical party.

Bello was elected to both the regional and national assemblies, but preferred to concentrate his energies on the north. Because of the large population in the north, the NPC became dominant in national politics.

Shortly after the 1951–1952 elections, Bello and the NPC forced the defeat of a resolution calling for independence by 1956.

In 1954, Bello became prime minister of the northern region.

Because Bello preferred to remain in the north, the position of federal chief minister fell to Abubakar Tafawa Balewa, the NPC vice-president. *See 1912.*

In 1959, after federal elections, the NPC formed a coalition with the party representing the western region, and Balewa became Nigeria's first prime minister. Remaining in the north, Bello devoted considerable energy in maintaining his status with the Sokoto Caliphate. In essence, Bello wanted to become Sultan and he did not conceal his ambition.

Bello bolstered his standing among Islamic authorities by visiting Mecca annually, sponsoring theological conventions, and building lavish mosques. He often publicly compared himself with his famous nineteenth century ancestors. His concern with traditional status and belief in natural rulers may have blinded Bello to the social forces which were tearing the fabric of Nigerian society.

In 1966, Bello and his associate, Balewa, were assassinated in a military coup which brought to an end the dominance of the north in Nigerian politics.

- Pierre Sarr N'Jie, the first chief minister of the Gambia, was born (1909).

Born in Bathurst, Pierre N'Jie was educated in mission schools and eventually became a Catholic. In 1944, after government and military service, N'Jie went to law school in London, returning home four years later to begin a successful practice.

Once back in the Gambia, N'Jie stood for election to the colony legislature in 1951, but he lost. After his defeat, N'Jie organized the United Party (UP) which enabled him to win in 1954. N'Jie served as a cabinet minister until 1956.

N'Jie's party campaigned for self-government and extension of the vote to the protectorate. After universal suffrage was initiated, the UP lost in the 1960 elections to the protectorate-based party of Dauda Jawara.

Nevertheless, because of the factionalism among Jawara's constituents, the colonial government appointed N'Jie chief minister in 1961.

In the 1962 elections, Jawara's party won again, and it was Jawara who led the Gambia to independence in 1965.

N'Jie remained in the forefront of the opposition at first, but was later removed from the legislature due to lack of attendance.

- Francis Nwia Kofie (Kwame) Nkrumah (1909–1972), the first leader of independent Ghana, was born (September 18).

Kwame Nkrumah was the son of a goldsmith. He was born in the western Gold Coast (now Ghana) and educated in Catholic mission schools.

Beginning in 1926, Nkrumah attended the Government Training College in Accra, and became a teacher.

In 1935, Nkrumah went to the United States. He studied economics, sociology, and theology at Lincoln University, and took graduate degrees in education and philosophy from the University of Pennsylvania.

After receiving his degrees from the University of Pennsylvania, Nkrumah returned to Lincoln University where he taught political science. During his academic career, Nkrumah was influenced by Karl Marx, Gandhi and particularly Marcus Garvey. Nkrumah was attracted to Garvey's advocacy of economic and political

independence as the keystone to his back-to-Africa movement.

In 1945, Nkrumah went to London to study law. There he became active in the West African Students Union, and worked with pan–Africanist George Padmore. That same year, Nkrumah and W. E. B. DuBois co-chaired the Fifth Pan-African Conference in Manchester. Meanwhile, a group of intellectuals in the Gold Coast had formed a political party, the United Gold Coast Convention (UGCC). In 1947, the members of UGCC persuaded Nkrumah to return to Ghana to lead the party. In 1948, a wave of violence swept the Gold Coast beginning with a series of angry demonstrations by ex-servicemen at Christianborg Castle. Strikes and demonstrations continued for ten days afterwards, resulting in twenty-nine deaths.

Although the UGCC had little to do with the organization of the demonstrations, its leaders attempted to capitalize on them. The government arrested Nkrumah and five others, briefly deporting them to the north. An official commission which reported on the disturbances claimed that Nkrumah was "imbued with a Communist ideology."

The disturbances prodded the government to consider constitutional reform. An official committee recommended limited responsible government, but the proposals were rejected by Nkrumah as too conservative. Upon his return, Nkrumah set about building up youth organizations, while designing a campaign of "Positive Action" which featured civil disobedience, agitation, and massive propaganda.

UGCC leaders opposed Nkrumah's campaign and his control of the youth group. In 1949, the UGCC forced Nkrumah to resign.

Nkrumah immediately transformed the youth organization into a new political party, the Convention People's Party (CPP). The CPP was mass-based and entirely loyal to Nkrumah.

In January 1950, Nkrumah initiated his Positive Action campaign. The government and the economy came to a standstill. Within a few days, demonstrators in the streets were demanding immediate self-government. Further violence ensued and the country was placed under a state of emergency. Nkrumah was arrested and sentenced to three years' imprisonment.

Nkrumah's imprisonment only served to increase his national popularity. When elections were held under a new constitution in 1951, the CPP scored a landslide victory. Nkrumah emerged from prison to become leader of government business. The next year, Nkrumah was made prime minister and permitted to form a cabinet.

Nkrumah immediately broached the question of further constitutional reform. In 1953, Nkrumah called for independence. His motion won unanimous support in the national assembly.

In 1954, the Gold Coast achieved internal self-government. Again the CPP won heavily at the polls. However, for the first time, new political parties arose to challenge Nkrumah.

The most important of the emerging political parties was the National Liberation Movement (NLM). Based in Asante, the NLM originally grew out of opposition to Nkrumah's policy of maintaining low cocoa prices. The NLM soon came to advocate a federal form of government in order to preserve Asante autonomy.

New demonstrations and violence caused the British to insist on fresh elections before independence. The CPP again emerged victorious in 1956. The following year, the Gold Coast became the first black African colony to achieve independence. Upon becoming an independent nation, the Gold Coast became Ghana.

Nkrumah quickly established himself as an authoritarian ruler. In 1957, he forced the regional opposition parties to unite, and, in 1958, he instituted the Preventive Detention Act. Under the Preventive Detention Act, imprisonment without trial was legalized.

Among those jailed under the Preventive Detention Act was Joseph Danquah *(see 1895),* a UGCC founder who had helped persuade Nkrumah to return in 1947.

Despite his authoritarian measures, Nkrumah's popularity remained high for a rather long time. In 1960, a referendum permitted the conversion of Ghana into a republic, with immense powers accruing to Nkrumah as president. Meanwhile Nkrumah poured large sums of money into lavish projects as well as Third World and pan–Africanist causes.

In the early 1960s, Ghana faced a severe economic crisis. This predicament combined with his authoritarian measures fostered popular discontent, leading to a general strike in 1961. In the following year, the first attempt was made on Nkrumah's life.

Nkrumah countered the assassination attempt by building up a large internal security force, and by making personal loyalty the primary criterion for political advancement. In 1964, Nkrumah decreed himself president for life and banned opposition parties.

Two years later, Nkrumah was deposed in a military coup while visiting Beijing.

In exile, Nkrumah took up residence in Guinea where President Sekou Toure made Nkrumah titular co-president. In Guinea, Nkrumah devoted himself to writing ideological works. During his life, Nkrumah actually produced five works on pan–Africanist and Marxist political analysis in addition to his autobiography.

Kwame Nkrumah died of cancer in Bucharest in 1972. He was buried in his home village in Ghana.

- *Central Africa:* Prince Albert of Belgium visited the Congo (April).
- A new Franco-German treaty on the Cameroon frontier was negotiated.
- The Agricultural Department was organized in the Belgian Congo.
- Jules Renkin, the Minister for the Belgian Congo, toured the country for four months.
- A government school was established in Usumbura.
- Yaounde became the capital of Cameroon after an earthquake in Buea.
- An Anglo-Belgian clash occurred near Kivu Lake (June 12).
- *Eastern Africa:* The Native Courts Proclamation was issued in Buganda (January). The Protectorate Native Courts Ordinance was enacted for the remainder of Uganda.
- The Boran Galla were driven from Wajir.
- Complete abolition of slavery was achieved in Zanzibar.
- A. M. Jeevanjee was the first Indian appointed to Kenya Legislative Council.
- A Nyabingi spirit possession cult began to pose problems for Uganda authorities. The leader Muhumsa was the widow of the former ruler of Rwanda.
- Sixty-seven Catholic mission stations were reported in German East Africa with 30,000 converts. Seventy-three Protestant stations with 11,000 converts were also reported.
- The Somalis first reached the Tana River.
- Mumia became the "paramount chief" of the new North Kavirondo district.

In 1907, the British began to use Mumia's kinsmen as headmen over his non–Wanga neighbors and then (in 1909) declared Mumia "paramount chief" of the new North Kavirondo district. In this capacity, Mumia was the most powerful African ruler in western Kenya, and Wanga influence reached its greatest extent ever.

However, the non–Luyia peoples began resisting Wanga rule thereby causing the British gradually to replace Mumia's paramount chieftaincy with alternative forms of administration.

- *Southern Africa:* Rhodesian railways linked up with the Congo railway.
- In 1909, John Jabavu and Walter Rubusana (along with the Euro-African William Schreiner) participated in a delegation to London to protest against the draft constitution of the new Union of South Africa and its failure to safeguard the African franchise.
- Elliott Kamwana introduced the Watchtower Movement to Malawi.

On his return to Nyasaland in 1909, Kamwana introduced the Jehovah Witnesses' Watch Tower Movement and preached that the millennium would come in 1914 when all Europeans were to leave Africa. Within a few months, Kamwana baptized more than 10,000 people into the movement. British authorities grew alarmed and sent him back to South Africa.

RELATED HISTORICAL EVENTS

- *The United States:* Miss Caroline Phelps-Stokes of New York, who endowed a fund for the education of Afro-Americans, died.
- *Europe:* Germany recognized France's special interests in Morocco in return for economic concessions (February 9).
- An Anglo-German agreement was reached concerning the boundaries of Uganda and German East Africa near Lake Kivu (May 19).
- Leopold II of Belgium died (December 17). He was succeeded by Albert.

Leopold II (1835–1909) was the eldest son of Leopold I, the first king of the Belgians and Leopold I's second wife, Marie-Louise of Orleans. In 1846, Leopold became duke of Brabant and, in 1853, he married Maria Henrietta, a daughter of the Austrian archduke, Joseph, palatine of Hungary.

Leopold II became the king of the Belgians on his father's death in December of 1865. Although the domestic affairs of his reign were dominated by a growing conflict between the Liberal and Catholic parties over suffrage and education issues, Leopold II concentrated on developing the nation's defenses.

Aware that Belgian neutrality, maintained during the Franco-German War of 1870, was placed in danger by the increasing strength of France and Germany, in 1887, Leopold persuaded the Belgian Parliament to finance the fortification of Liege and Namur. A military conscription bill, for which Leopold long argued, was passed shortly before his death.

* * *

In Pan-African history there are few individuals who more merit condemnation than Leopold II. It was Leopold who fostered the creation of a hell on earth in the Belgian Congo, which we know today as Zaire.

Leopold II founded the Association Internationale du Congo in 1876. This organization was formed ostensibly to explore the Congo and to bring Christianity to the region. The renowned explorer Henry Morton Stanley was employed as Leopold's main agent in the Congo and for the first decade of his interest the Congo remained a basically ignored African backwater.

During 1884 and 1885, Leopold's forces defeated an Anglo-Portuguese attempt to conquer the Congo Basin. Subsequently, at the Berlin Conference of 1884–1885, Leopold II gained recognition from the European powers (and the United States) as the sovereign of the Etat Independant du Congo—the Congo Free State. The Congo Free State that Leopold became the sovereign of encompassed an area 80 times the size of Belgium.

Leopold's interests in the Congo were primarily financial. The entire state was his private commercial domain. For years, there was a struggle to make the land profitable, but that all changed around 1891 when the production of rubber became a lucrative enterprise.

For the next thirteen years, the Congo Free State became a living hell. Cannibalism, starvation, and human mutilations (especially the buckets of severed hands) became common occurrences all for the sake of increasing rubber production. Similar to the situation which occurred on Hispaniola during the early 1500s, the cruel atrocities committed against the people of the Congo soon led to a great depopulation of the area. Leopold's exploitation of the area was simply a crime against humanity.

In 1904, exposure of the mistreatment of natives in the rubber industry marked the onset of the decline of Leopold's personal rule in the region. Great Britain, with the aid of the United States, pressured Belgium to annex the Congo state to redress the "rubber atrocities" committed while the Congo was Leopold's domain.

The Congo Free State became part of Belgium in November of 1908.

In search of wealth, Leopold reaped human misery. The images of children running into the bush as their mothers and sisters were shot down by soldiers and then eaten by cannibals was a horrific image that lingered in the minds of those who investigated Leopold's Congo. Hundreds of families were butchered. Thousands were burned in their homes. Village after village was burned and looted. The men from the village were taken off as slaves, the women and children hacked to death.

And then there were the severed hands. To prove that they had not wasted ammunition, Leopold's soldiers would chop off the hands of those they sought to punish caring not whether the victims lived or died. They would collect this gruesome evidence of their thoroughness and frugality in baskets which were then transported to the leaders that be.

For years these atrocities went unreported but eventually the world did come to see the evidence for themselves. Photographs of the survivors of the severed hands collections were graphic proof of the brutality of Leopold's Congo.

When Leopold died in 1909, his body laid in state for two days in the royal palace in Brussels and he was then given a state funeral. In tribute to Leopold, listen to the voices of his Congo.

"From our country each village had to take 20 loads of rubber. These loads were big; they were nearly as big as {a basket over three feet tall}. We had to take these loads in 4 times a month."

"How much pay do you get for this?"

"We got not pay. We got nothing ... Our village got cloth and a little salt, but not the people who did the work ... It used to take 10 days to get the 20 baskets of rubber — we were always in the forest to find the rubber vines, to go without food, and our women had to give up cultivating the fields and gardens. Then we starved. Wild beasts — the leopards — killed some of us while we were working away in the forest and others got lost or died from exposure or starvation and we begged the white men to leave us alone, saying we could get no more rubber, but the white men and their soldiers said: 'Go. You are only beasts yourselves. You are only Nyama {meat}.' We tried, always going further into the forest, and when we failed and our rubber was short, the soldiers came to our towns and killed us. Many were shot, some had their ears cut off; others were tied up with ropes around their necks and bodies and taken away. The white men at the posts sometimes did not know of the bad things the soldiers did to us, but it was the

white men who sent the soldiers to punish us for not bringing in enough rubber."

"We said to the white man: 'We are not enough people now to do what you want of us. Our country has not many people in it and the people are dying fast. We are killed by the work you make us do, by the stoppage of our plantations and the breaking up of our homes.

'We used to hunt elephants long ago and there were plenty in our forests, and we got much meat; but Bula Matari (the Congo Free State) killed the elephant hunters because they could not get rubber, and so we starved. We are sent out to get rubber, and when we come back with little rubber we are shot'."

"Who shot you?"

"The white men sent their soldiers out to kill us."

"How do you know it was the white men sent the soldiers? It might only be the savage soldiers themselves?"

"No, no, sometimes we brought rubber into the white men's stations ... when it was not enough the white men would put some of us in lines, one behind the other, and would shoot through all our bodies. Sometimes he would shoot us like that with his own hand; sometimes his soldiers would do it."

"Are the white men never going home; is this to last forever?"

• W. Cadbury published *Labour in Portuguese West Africa.* As a result, a boycott of Sao Tome cocoa was instituted.

• The Lado enclave was ceded by Belgium from Congo to the Sudan.

• *Africa:* Jan Hendrik Hofmeyr (1845–1909), an Afrikaner political leader, died.

Jan Hofmeyr rose to influence in Cape electoral politics by organizing Afrikaner farmers into a union for political action in 1878. Several years later, Hofmeyr merged this group with the Cape branch of S. J. Du Toit's Afrikaner Bond, the name by which his own party was afterwards known.

Hofmeyr took a middle course between Afrikaner nationalist and British imperialist factions. He favored maintaining ties with Great Britain, but opposed further British expansion in South Africa. Hofmeyr also supported the independence of the Afrikaner republics, but favored closer economic union among the various Euro-African states.

Hofmeyr held a seat in the Cape parliament from 1879 to 1895. He preferred to use the voting strength of his Afrikaner Bond to ally with stronger parties. Hofmeyr opposed a color bar in voting and actively sought support among African voters and politicians, notably John Jabavu.

During the administration of Cecil Rhodes (1890–1895), Hofmeyr closely supported Rhodes until the Jameson Raid. Afterwards Hofmeyr maintained his influence in parliament by working externally through the Afrikaner Bond.

In 1898, Hofmeyr used his influence to help William Schreiner come to power. Dejected by the outbreak of the South African War in 1899, Hofmeyr retired to Europe.

Later on, Hofmeyr returned to South Africa to help rebuild his party.

1 9 1 0

THE UNITED STATES

In May, despite factional disputes, a refusal of support from Booker T. Washington, lack of funds, and resignations, the formal organization of the NAACP was completed, primarily through the efforts of Oswald Garrison Villard. Moorfield Storey of Boston was elected president; William English Walling, chairman of the executive committee; Francis Blascoer, national secretary; Oswald Garrison Villard, assistant treasurer, and W. E. B. Du Bois, the only African American on the board of officers, was made director of publicity and research, and editor of *Crisis,* the organization's magazine.

A national committee of 100 and an executive committee of 30 national committee members were planned. The presence of W. E. B. Du Bois on the staff branded the organization as radical from the beginning. Many feared that it would be an irresponsible organization that would draw its main inspiration from the Niagara Movement. The organization was denounced by many European American philanthropists, and even some African Americans thought it unwise.

In November, Joel Spingarn was elected to the executive committee. His brother Arthur, a lawyer, joined the New York branch when it was organized in January of 1911.

The first local branch of the NAACP was established at Chicago. By 1912, nine branches had been established. The number of branches doubled in the years 1913 and 1914. Oswald Garrison Villard helped cover the expenses of the fledgling organization with rental fees from the New York Evening Post building. Voluntary contributions and membership fees were the principal sources of income.

The NAACP's first program advocated the widening of industrial opportunities for African Americans, sought greater police protection for African Americans in the South, and crusaded against lynching and lawlessness. The organization planned to hire lawyers to contest prejudicial laws.

Between 1910 and 1914, the NAACP was instrumental in publicizing the atrocities known as lynchings.

• The Reverend John Haynes Holmes and Rabbi Stephen Wise drew attention to lynchings in the South by constant sermons and public speeches.

The NAACP sent W. E. B. Du Bois to the International Congress of Races in London, partly to represent the NAACP, and partly to counteract Booker T. Washington, who was touring England giving lectures. It had been reported in the United States that Washington was telling English audiences that African Americans were making strides toward full citizenship.

In his speeches before the Congress in London, Du Bois made it clear that African Americans were suffering under grave legal and civil disabilities, and that only by a fierce struggle would they overcome them. Du Bois circulated a statement in London criticizing and contradicting Washington. He accused Washington of misrepresenting the truth of his dependency on certain powerful interests for philanthropy.

• Booker T. Washington's secretary, Emmett S. Scott, went to Liberia as Washington's choice for the African American member of the three man commission appointed by the President of the United States to make recommendations concerning the financial plight of Liberia and threats to its sovereignty. Washington felt that Liberia was a testing ground for the African American's ability to handle his own affairs. He believed that the country's history proved his point that political power without a firm economic basis and a body of skilled artisans was detrimental to group welfare. He urged the American government to aid Liberia, and at one time felt so strongly about the matter that he considered accepting a post as Liberian charge d'affaires in the United States.

• Julius Rosenwald, in his initial contribution to the YMCA movement among African Americans, gave $25,000 toward the erection of the Wabash Avenue building in Chicago. In succeeding years, Rosenwald's gifts amounted to $325,000 and helped to build some 13 buildings.

• In this year, over one-third of Boston's African Americans voted for the Boston Democratic gubernatorial candidate.

• In 1910, the state government of Oklahoma organized Okfuskee County where the African American population ran over forty percent. The purpose of organizing this county was to confine all the state's African Americans to one township.

• *The Civil Rights Movement:* In Boston, William Monroe Trotter led a protest against the racist play *The Clansman.*

• *The Census:* The 1910 United States Census reported that there were 9,827,763 African Americans in the United States. This number represented 10.7% of the population. Of the African Americans, twenty percent were classified as being of "mixed blood."

• The life expectancy of the average African American male in 1910 was 34 years, for African American females it was 38 years.

• 8 out every 9 African Americans in the United States lived in the region known as the South.

• One out every 4 African Americans lived in cities. 60.4% of these city dwellers resided in the central city areas. Washington, D. C., had the largest number of African Americans, with 94,000 residents. New York City's 92,000 African Americans represented 1.9% of the city's population. African Americans accounted for 52.8% of the Charleston, South Carolina, population.

• Of the African American population, 50.4% worked in farm occupations while 49.6% were engaged in non-agricultural activities.

• African Americans owned 218,972 farms, up from 120,738 in 1890. The average size of African American farms was less than ten acres.

• There were 350,000 African American factory workers.

• Only 2.5% of employed Southern African Americans and 3% of employed Northern African Americans were in the professions, including many ministers and teachers without high school or college educations.

• *Political Achievements:* Between 1910 and 1920, eleven African Americans served in the diplomatic and consular corps, including a Minister to Haiti and the Ambassador to Liberia.

• *Organizations:* The Farmers Improvement Society of Texas was founded. Inspired in part by the trend toward self-help and racial solidarity, and in part by the European American agrarian organizations then at their peak, the society first improved the homes of village and rural African Americans in the Oakland, Texas, area, and then branched out into improving farming methods, paying illness and death benefits, and providing cooperative buying and selling. The movement spread all through Texas and into Oklahoma and Arkansas. It had 21,000 members, a cooperative business making $50,000 per year, and subsidiary institutions such as an agricultural college and a bank.

• The Committee on Urban Conditions was organized in New York City (April).

In 1910, an African American graduate student in social work at Columbia University, George Edmund Haynes, and a European American woman, Mrs. William H. Baldwin, Jr., founded the Committee on Urban Conditions. The purpose of the Committee on Urban Conditions was to address the problems of African Americans in cities. It was the Committee on Urban Conditions which evolved into the National Urban League. *See 1911.*

• *Notable Births:* Leon "Chu" Berry, a saxophonist, was born in Wheeling, West Virginia (September 13).

• Chester Arthur Burnett, a blues singer who gained fame as the legendary "Howlin' Wolf," was born in Mississippi (June 10). Howlin' Wolf would become an inspiration for the British rock bands of the 1960s.

• Drummer Sidney "Big Sid" Catlett was born in Evansville, Indiana (January 17).

• Allan Rohan Crite, an artist, was born in Boston, Massachusetts.

• William "Champion Jack" Dupree, a musician, was born (July 4).

• Wilmer Angier Jennings, a painter and printmaker, was born in Atlanta.

• Ralph Metcalfe, an Olympic champion and an Illinois Congressman, was born in Atlanta.

• Pauli Murray, a writer, lawyer and theologian who became the first African American woman priest ordained in the Episcopal Church, was born.

• Bayard Rustin, a noted civil rights leader, was born in West Chester, Pennsylvania.

Bayard Rustin joined the Young Communist League (YCL) in 1936. Sent by the YCL to New York as an organizer, Rustin attended CCNY. In 1941, he left YCL to join the Fellowship of Reconciliation.

In 1942, Rustin went to California to help protect the property of Japanese-Americans who had been interned. In 1943, he was imprisoned for two and a half years for refusing to serve in the Army.

Upon his release from prison, Rustin became chairman of the Free India Committee, and was jailed several times for sitting in at the British Embassy. In 1948, in recognition of his efforts, the Congress Party of India invited Rustin to India, where he stayed for six months.

In 1947, Bayard Rustin helped organize the first Freedom Ride in North Carolina. Arrested and put on a chain gang, his subsequent expose of chain-gang life led to its abolition in North Carolina.

Rustin also directed A. Philip Randolph's Committee Against Discrimination in the Armed Forces which saw President Truman desegregate the Army in 1948.

Rustin served as Race Relations Secretary for the Fellowship of Reconciliation and helped to organize the Congress for Racial Equality. During the Montgomery Boycott in 1955–56, Martin Luther King asked Rustin to help with organization.

Bayard Rustin drew up the initial plans for the Southern Christian Leadership Conference and served as Martin Luther King's special assistant for seven years. While being very much engaged in the civil rights movement, Rustin also continued his pacifist activities. He served as executive secretary of the War Resister's League (1953–64), organizing the first London Ban-the-Bomb March in 1959, and in 1960 protesting French atomic explosions.

Rustin was the chief organizer of the August 1963 March on Washington. On February 3, 1964, Rustin directed the first New York City school boycott. Afterwards, Rustin served as executive director of the A. Philip Randolph Institute.

- Art Tatum, a jazz musician, was born (October 13).

Art Tatum was born in Toledo, Ohio. As a child, he studied violin and piano. Tatum began playing professionally on radio station WSPD in Toledo. In 1932, he came to New York as a pianist for Adelaide Hall.

Tatum's piano technique and harmonic vari-ations distinguish his playing. In 1943, Tatum formed, with Tiny Grimes on guitar and Slam Stewart on bass, what was to become one of the great jazz trios.

- Aaron "T-Bone" Walker, a blues guitarist, was born (May 28).
- Mary Lou Williams, a pianist, was born in Atlanta, Georgia (May 8).
- *Notable Deaths:* There were 76 African Americans lynched in 1910.
- William A. Harper (1873–1910), a protégé of Henry Ossawa Tanner and a gifted landscape artist, died. *See 1873.*
- Patrick Francis Healy (1834–1910), the first African American to earn a doctorate and the first African American to become a Jesuit priest, died. Healy also served as the president of Georgetown University.
- Granville T. Woods (1856–1910), an African American inventor, died.

Granville T. Woods developed an egg incubator, a system of telegraphing from moving trains, and improvements in electric railways and the phonograph. General Electric and Bell telephone purchased many of his inventions. However, Woods also marketed some of his own inventions through his own company.

- *Miscellaneous Laws:* Residential segregation ordinances appeared in a number of Southern and border state cities. In Baltimore, the NAACP had the first of these residential restrictions declared unconstitutional. However, the city enacted two others, the last of which was considered in the Louisville, Kentucky, segregation case of *Buchanan v. Warley*, in 1917.
- In addition to Baltimore (Maryland) and Louisville (Kentucky), the other cities which enacted segregation ordinances were Norfolk, Richmond, Roanoke, Greensboro, St. Louis, Oklahoma City, and Dallas.
- Oklahoma added a "grandfather clause" to its State Constitution.
- *Miscellaneous Cases:* In his efforts to help Pink Franklin, an African American sharecropper who had been convicted of murder, Oswald Garrison Villard became convinced of the need for a legal redress committee for the NAACP. One of the NAACP's first legal cases involved the arrest of an Asbury Park, New Jersey, African American for murder. The African American had been held without there being any evidence of his involvement in the crime. In one of the initial successes of the organization, an NAACP lawyer secured

his release. A similar case occurred later in Lakewood, New Jersey, and the NAACP lawyer again secured the accused's release.

• *Publications:* In 1910, W. E. B. Du Bois joined the newly formed National Association for the Advancement of Colored People (NAACP) and became the editor of its official publication, the *Crisis*, a position he held until 1934. In November of 1910, the first edition of the *Crisis* appeared. 1,000 copies were printed. By 1918, circulation had increased to 100,000.

• W. E. B. Du Bois, in an article in the *Crisis*, held that a person should have the right to choose his spouse regardless of race, but for the present, widespread intermarriage would be a social calamity.

• James Morris Webb's *The Black Man, the Father of Civilization* was published.

• *Scholastic Achievements:* By 1910, there were 100 colleges for African Americans, most of which admitted women.

• By 1910, in most of the Southern states, at least twice as much was spent per pupil on European Americans as on African Americans.

• As a result of Abraham Flexner's critical study of medical education in the United States, 3 African American medical schools were discontinued. Flexner's criticism was that these schools did not have the staffs or the resources to provide proper medical education.

• *The Arts:* George Herriman (1880–1944) published the prototype for the *Krazy Kat* cartoon (July 26). The *Krazy Kat* cartoons were popular during the 1920s, especially with intellectuals.

George Herriman, a fair skinned man, was born in New Orleans in a family classified as "Negro." The family moved to Los Angeles to escape racial labeling. Some of Herriman's friends called him "The Greek," but Herriman never openly divulged his racial background.

The Performing Arts

With the decline of African American minstrelsy and the accompanying revival of "black peril" hysteria, African Americans became limited in the forums where they could perform. Harlem soon became the Mecca for African American performers. During the decade of 1910 to 1920, Ed Hunter's Crescent Theater on 135th Street and the Lafayette were the leading African American theaters in Harlem. These theaters featured all–African American musicals, African American versions of Broadway hits and revivals of standard classics from the European theater.

• Bert Williams, the most popular vaudevillian of the era, signed a contract to perform with the Ziegfeld Follies.

• *Black Church:* There were 35,000 African American churches with 3.5 million members.

• *Black Enterprise:* The Capital Savings Bank of Washington, D. C., the first bank owned by the Grand Fountain of the United Order of True Reformers, failed. The failure of the bank led to the dissolution of the Grand Fountain Society in 1911.

• By 1910, Madame C. J. Walker, an African American entrepreneur, had become successful enough to establish laboratories for the manufacture of various cosmetics and hair products for African Americans.

There is an ongoing dispute as to who was the first African American millionairess. Some contend that Madame C. J. Walker (1867–1919) was. Some say it was Annie Turnbo Malone (1869–1957). Both women produced hair care products for black women and were developing their businesses at the same time. It is even asserted that, for a time, Walker worked as a salesperson for Malone products. In any event, by 1910, both women had become very wealthy.

• *Sports:* Jack Johnson beat Jim Jeffries in Reno, Nevada, with a 15th round knockout to retain the world heavyweight title and spoil Jeffries' comeback attempt (July 4).

The film of the Jack Johnson-Jim Jeffries heavyweight championship bout created an interstate edict against fight films, and may have convinced film producers to keep African Americans out of the movies.

• "Mother" Seames, a legendary figure in the development of African American tennis, constructed her own tennis courts in Chicago for the purpose of teaching African Americans the game of tennis.

• The Louisville Cubs, an all–African American team, was considered to be the best Southern baseball team.

• After the Detroit Tigers split a six game series with the Havana Stars, an Afro-Cuban baseball team, a ban was instituted to prevent black teams from playing against European American teams.

THE AMERICAS

- *Brazil:* Joaquim Machado de Assis' *Outras reliquias* was published posthumously.
- *Canada:* Beginning in 1910, some three hundred Oklahoma African Americans moved into the Pine Creek area of Amber Valley.

Amber Valley was the only Afro-Canadian settlement to survive both World War I and the Great Depression. The settlers who arrived in 1910 were led by Jefferson D. Edwards. While a few were able to find abandoned claims on which improvements already had been made, most needed two years or more to harvest their first crop. During the winters, the settlers returned to Edmonton to work in a meat-packing plant.

The Amber Valley settlers opened a school which served as their Methodist church as well. By 1920, the average holding at Amber Valley consisted of thirty-eight acres, three horses, two cattle and houses and fences valued at $400.

A number of the Amber Valley settlers drifted to Edmonton in the 1920s in search of Anglican or Standard Holiness religious services. These relocated Afro-Canadians gave rise to the local "blues" tradition of Edmonton. Many of the relocated Amber Valley Afro-Canadians came to marry Euro-Canadians or Canadian Sikhs.

In 1931, the opening of a post office heralded the permanency of the community of Amber Valley.

- Delos R. Davis of Amherstburg, a product of Theodosia Lyon's missionary school, became the first Afro-Canadian to be appointed King's Council in Canada.

AFRICA

- *North Africa, Egypt and Sudan:* Butros Ghali, the premier of Egypt, was assassinated by a Muslim fanatic (February 20).
- A proposal to extend concession to Suez Canal Company by forty years was rejected by the Egyptian General Assembly.
- Saad Zaghlul became the Egyptian Minister of Justice.
- Another French loan was made to Morocco.
- *Western Africa:* A French post at Agboville was occupied temporarily in revolt of Abbeys (January).
- The Kano railway was completed (March).
- French forces began their campaign to suppress Baoule, Ivory Coast.

- Beit-el-mal (Native Treasury) was established in Zaria.
- Hanns Visscher became the first Director of Education in north Nigeria.
- In 1910, Casely Hayford achieved some success when he got the government of the Gold Coast to withdraw a forestry bill which would have removed African jurisdiction over certain categories of lands.
- Around 1910, Galandou Diouf founded the Young Senegalese, an elitist pressure group which lobbied for equal pay for equal work, more political participation, and African access to scholarships for study in France.
- The Grebo rebelled against the Liberian government. The rebellion was suppressed.
- Mamadou Dia, the future prime minister of Senegal, was born.

After receiving his education at the famous William Ponty School in Senegal and later in Paris, Mamadou Dia became a teacher and a journalist.

In 1948, Dia helped Leopold Senghor organize the political party which would come to dominated Senegalese politics. As a result, Dia was rewarded with election to a number of important posts, including the French Chamber of Deputies.

Like Senghor, Dia believed in a federation of the Francophonic African states. However, the pan–Africanists Dia and Senghor were defeated by the group led by Felix Houphouet-Boigny which advocated complete autonomy within the Francophonic African community.

In 1957, Dia became vice-president of Senegal. Soon thereafter he became president of Senegal.

In 1959, when Senegal briefly united with Mali, Dia served as vice-president of the federation. When the Mali Federation dissolved in 1960, Dia became prime minister of Senegal with Senghor as president.

Dia was more radical than Senghor in his economic policy and, in 1962, Dia attempted to overthrow Senghor. The coup failed. Dia was captured, tried and sentenced to life imprisonment.

In 1974, Dia was pardoned by Senghor.

A respected economist, Dia published a number of books. He remained active in politics. However, in the 1983 elections, that returned Abdou Diouf to office Dia received less than two percent of the vote.

- Albert Michael Margai (1910–1980), a future prime minister of Sierra Leone, was born.

Albert Michael Margai was the son of a Mende trader. He was educated in mission schools and worked as a nurse and a pharmacist before going to London in 1944 to study law. He returned in 1947 to practice law in Freetown.

After serving in the protectorate assembly and on the legislative council, Margai joined his brother, Milton Margai, to form the Sierra Leone People's Party (SLPP) of which Milton became the leader.

The SLPP led Sierra Leone to independence through gradual transfer of power. Dissatisfied with his brother's highly conservative policies, Albert challenged Milton for the SLPP leadership in 1957. Albert received the support of the party leadership but backed down and permitted Milton to become prime minister in 1958.

A few months later, Albert left the SLPP to form his own party. When Sierra Leone became independent in 1961, the two brothers were reconciled and Albert became finance minister.

Milton Margai died in 1964. After Milton's death, Albert became prime minister. Albert was more radical on foreign policy matters, but his domestic policy, which favored Sierra Leone's southern (predominantly Mende) population alienated many citizens. The economy was suffering, and charges of official corruption were rampant.

There were also fears that Albert was moving to impose a one-party state upon the country. Northern citizens rallied around labor leader Siaka Stevens whose newly created party won a narrow victory in the 1967 elections.

When the governor-general invited Stevens to form a government, Brigadier David Lansana, who supported Margai, seized power. Within two days, Lansana was, in turn, overthrown by another group of officers, and Albert Margai was arrested.

In lieu of imprisonment, Albert Margai was allowed to go into exile.

In 1968, another military coup returned power to the civilians, and Margai flew home to try take power. Finding that Siaka Stevens had already been sworn in as prime minister, Margai fled to London and later died in the United States.

- *Central Africa:* Gabon, the Middle Congo, and Oubangi-Chari-Chad were federated as French Equatorial Africa (AEF) (January 15).

In 1886, the French explorer Pierre de Brazza *(see 1905)* was appointed commissioner-general of French Congo with authority over Gabon as well. Oubangi-Chari (the Central African Republic) and Chad (as the single territory Oubangi-Chari-Chad) were added to the federation in 1906. The four territories (French Congo, Gabon, Oubangi-Chari and Chad) became known as French Equatorial Africa in 1910 and the commissioner-general became governor-general.

- Extensive reforms were made in the Belgian Congo (March).

- An Anglo-Belgian agreement assigned the west shore of Lake Albert to Belgian Congo (May 14).

- Grants-in-aid was given to mission schools in Cameroon. An agricultural school was opened.

- Portuguese operations against Kasanje and Mahungo were initiated. The Lunda province was occupied.

- In 1910, Rudolf Bell, the chief of the Cameroon town of Douala, came into conflict with the German administration when the Germans moved to seize some land for colonial residential quarters. The Germans appropriation of this land was in violation of the 1884 treaty between the Germans and the Cameroon people.

- Barthelemy Boganda (1910–1959), a founding father of the Central African Republic, was born.

Barthelemy Boganda left the priesthood to marry and to enter politics. In 1946, Boganda was elected to the French Chamber of Deputies. A highly charismatic figure, Boganda and the party he organized came to dominate politics in the Central African Republic (which was then known as Oubangi-Chari).

Although considered a radical politician, Boganda viewed cooperation with France as the means to economic development. In the 1958 elections, Boganda persuaded an overwhelming majority of Central African Republic citizens to vote for autonomy within the French community. Afterwards, Boganda became prime minister.

Like Leopold Sedar Senghor in West Africa, Boganda was a strong advocate of federation. However, he was unable to secure the support of his political counterparts in the French Congo and Gabon. Accordingly, Boganda's attempts at federation failed.

Barthelemy Boganda was killed in a plane crash in 1959. He was succeeded by his cousin David Dacko.

The Central African Republic became fully independent in 1960.

• Joseph Kasavubu (1910 [1917?]– 1969), the nationalist leader in the Belgian Congo, is believed to have been born in this year.

Joseph Kasavubu was born into Kongo society in the western Belgian Congo (Zaire). During his youth, Kasavubu trained for the Roman Catholic priesthood. However, he withdrew from the seminary and became a secular teacher in 1940.

In 1942, Kasavubu entered the colonial civil service. Through the 1940s and early 1950s, Kasavubu was active in Kongo cultural societies which advocated the re-creation of the old Kongo kingdom and reunification of the Kongo people, who had been partitioned by three colonial powers.

In 1955, Kasavubu was elected president of the quasi-political Kongo association, *Abako*.

Under the leadership of Kasavubu, the mid–1950s saw the emergence of nationalist politics throughout the Belgian Congo. *Abako* soon developed into a vigorous political party dedicated to Kongo re-unification and autonomy. The Belgians began to institute democratic reforms and *Abako* became the dominant party around Leopoldville. Kasavubu himself was elected mayor of a section of the city.

Early in 1959, Kasavubu was arrested after riots in Leopoldville. Kasavubu was taken to Belgium for secret talks with the government, and then returned to his position in Leopoldville.

As nationalist activity gathered momentum in the Belgian Congo, Kasavubu and his *Abako* party came to advocate a federal structure which would grant the Kongo people a measure of autonomy.

In January of 1960, Kasavubu participated in independence talks in Brussels. In Brussels, Patrice Lumumba — a proponent of a strong unitary state — emerged as the dominant African spokesman.

Elections for the Congo were held in May of 1960. Kasavubu's party polled strongly only among the Kongo people. The premiership was offered to Lumumba and Kasavubu was made president.

Immediately after independence was achieved in July of 1960, the Congolese army mutinied and the Katanga province seceded under Moise Tshombe.

During the turmoil of the first two months of independence, the uneasy coalition between Kasavubu and Lumumba deteriorated over the issue of federalism. The two men attempted to dismiss each other from office. The military, under Joseph Mobutu, intervened. Mobutu dismissed both Kasavubu and Lumumba. Lumumba was subsequently assassinated while Kasavubu was reinstated by the end of 1960.

Between 1961 and 1965, Kasavubu remained as president and provided the only political continuity in the government while the country was torn by secessionist movements, rebellions and European intervention. Kasavubu's ability to survive politically was generally attributed to his allowing his prime ministers to play the leading role in crises.

Kasavubu's political career ended in late 1965 when General Mobutu staged a second coup and made himself president.

• *Eastern Africa:* Toro became a flourishing center for the Congo ivory trade.
• The Convention of Associations was set up by Kenya settlers.
• Mbaruk bin Rashid bin Salim al-Mazrui (c.1820–1910), a leader of the 1895 rebellion against the British in Kenya, died.

Mbaruk bin Rashid bin Salim al-Mazrui was the son of Rashid bin Salim, the last Mazrui governor of Mombasa. Mbaruk's father was overthrown by Sayyid Said, the Busaidi ruler of Zanzibar, in 1837.

Under the leadership of his father's cousin, Mbaruk and part of his family fled south to Gazi. Another branch of the family fled north. When he succeeded to leadership of the Gazi Mazrui in the mid–1860s, Mbaruk received a subsidy from the Zanzibari regime. However, Mbaruk never reconciled himself to Busaidi rule. He resisted the Zanzibari sultans at every opportunity.

During Sultan Barghash's reign (1870–1888), Mbaruk clashed repeatedly with Busaidi forces. He distrusted Barghash's offers of accommodation and spent most of these years as an outlaw, counting upon several thousand African slaves and freemen for military support.

In 1888, the chartered Imperial British East Africa Company (IBEAC) established an administration over the Kenya coast. Under its aegis, Mbaruk returned peacefully to settle at Gazi. Over the next seven years, Mbaruk cooperated with the IBEAC and occasionally lent it material support against his neighbors. This arrangement ended in 1895 when the company prepared to turn over its administration to the British crown.

Around this same time, the northern Mazrui community entered into a succession dispute. The IBEAC intervened, causing the northern Mazrui to revolt. Some of the Mazrui sought refuge with Mbaruk. Through his refusal to betray his kinsmen, Mbaruk was reluctantly drawn into the rebellion.

Mbaruk conducted a successful guerrilla campaign until early 1896, when he fled across the border into German administered territory (present day Tanzania). In the German territory, Mbaruk surrendered to Governor von Wissmann and was granted asylum.

Mbaruk's retirement to Dar es Salaam on a German pension brought Mazrui political influence in colonial East Africa to an end.

In 1907, the British government officially pardoned Mbaruk. However, Mbaruk declined the invitation to return to Kenya. He died in Dar es Salaam in 1910.

- *Southern Africa:* Botha and Hertzog founded the South African Party (April 27).
- Jameson founded the Unionist Party (May 24), and, on May 31, the Union of South Africa was proclaimed. Lord Gladstone was made the first Governor-General.
- The Union of South Africa became a Dominion (July 1).

The present day nation of South Africa was created by the Act of Union in 1910. In 1910, the British bestowed virtual independence upon its former colonies of Natal and the Cape of Good Hope and the former Afrikaner republics of the Transvaal and the Orange Free State. The Transvaal and the Orange Free State had been conquered during the South African (Boer) War.

Today the Transvaal and the Orange Free State exist as provinces in the Union of South Africa. As for the country itself, the Union of South Africa became a republic in 1961.

- Mdlangaso, the former ruler of Mpondo, was pardoned in 1910 and he was allowed to return to Mpondo land.
- The South African Party won the first elections (September 15). Botha was named prime minister.

Louis Botha played a leading role in the national convention which created the Union of South Africa. Because of his pivotal role in the nation's creation, Botha was soon rewarded by becoming the nation's first prime minister.

- Walter Rubusana became the only black African ever elected to a seat on the Cape Provincial Council. He was able to do this by allying with Euro-African politicians to win election in Thembu country.
- There was an Israelite church incident at Bulhoek.
- Moheli Island was attached to Madagascar.
- Charles Domingo, a Seventh Day Adventist missionary, began organizing in Malawi.

From 1910 to 1916, Domingo organized a chain of Seventh Day Adventist missions in northern Malawi. Around this time, Domingo also took an increasingly vocal stance against the European administration of the country. Domingo was never connected with the violent uprising of John Chilembwe *(see 1915)* in southern Malawi, but the government which at the time was greatly alarmed by dissident Africans, deported Domingo in 1916.

- Thomas Molofo published the Sotho novel *Pitseng*.
- Pixley Seme founded the first African newspaper with a national circulation, *Abantu-Batho. Abantu-Batho* was printed in four languages. Over the ensuing years, Seme edited the newspaper, practiced law, and participated in ANC activities.
- Bathoen I(Bathweng I) (1845–1910), the chief of the Ngwaketse (of Botswana), died.

Bathoen succeeded his father Gaseitsiwe in 1889, after having been the effective ruler of the Ngwaketse for almost a decade. Upon his ascension, Bathoen inherited his father's unsettled boundary disputes. His retaliatory cattle raid against Afrikaner farmers in 1884 had triggered a British expedition under Charles Warren which led to the establishment of the British Bechuanaland Protectorate in 1885.

During his reign as chief, Bathoen carelessly granted many concessions to European entrepreneurs. However, he began to recognize the danger he was creating when the British government proposed to hand over administration of the Protectorate to the privately controlled British South Africa Company.

In 1895, Bathoen joined Kgama III and Sebele in a visit to London. In London, the trio successfully blocked the proposal to turn the Bechuanaland Protectorate over to the privately controlled British South Africa Company.

Bathoen became literate soon after the London Missionary Society founded a station at Kanye in 1871. However, while learning to read from the missionaries, Bathoen resisted their attempts at conversion.

Nevertheless, Bathoen did support the missionaries and encouraged European education among the Ngwaketse. During his last years, a religious schism with political overtones developed between his supporters and opponents of the mission. Bathoen failed to heal the split before he died.

Bathoen was succeeded by his son, Seepapitso (1884–1916), an activist modernizer. In 1916, Seepapitso was assassinated by his brother, Moyapitso, in a personal dispute.

Ngwaketse administration languished under five regents until Bathoen II took office in 1928.

RELATED HISTORICAL EVENTS

• *The United States:* Mark Twain (Samuel Clemens)(1835–1910), the great American novelist, died. *See 1884.*
• *The Americas:* Joaquim Barreto Nabuco de Araujo (1849–1910), a distinguished Brazilian abolitionist, died.

Joaquim Nabuco is credited with being the principal advocate for the elimination of slavery in Brazil. He was born in Pernambuco, where his father had served as senator under Dom Pedro II.

Nabuco studied at the Dom Pedro College and received a law degree from the University of Recife. Entering journalism, he took up the cause of abolition, publishing many articles denouncing slavery.

After serving two years in Washington with the Brazilian Foreign Service, Nabuco entered politics, winning a seat in the Chamber of Deputies in 1878. There he launched a violent attack on slavery and became one of its most vocal critics.

Nabuco's advocacy brought him into constant conflict with the emperor. The emperor wished to proceed quietly and cautiously on the slavery question. However, Nabuco's persistent and eloquent oratory would not let the matter rest.

Nabuco also founded and was president of the Brazilian Anti-Slavery Society. In this capacity, Nabuco set up a network of abolitionist clubs all over Brazil.

Nabuco served as correspondent for the Brazilian newspaper *Journal of Commerce* in London from 1882 to 1884. Re-elected to Parliament in 1884, Nabuco played a leading role in getting the abolition bill through the Parliament in spite of clashes with his own Conservative Party.

When the republic was established in 1889, Nabuco was hostile at first and retired temporarily from active politics. However, he was soon brought back into politics when his talents as an astute negotiator were needed to settle a dispute over the Brazil-British Guiana border. It was Nabuco who argued Brazil's case before the Italian King Vittorio Emanuel III.

Nabuco was next appointed to serve in London but was quickly moved to Washington in 1902 as the first ambassador of republican Brazil. Nabuco died while in Washington, D. C.

• *Europe:* A British and German Conference on the Lake Kivu-Mfumbiro region was held (February).

------ **1911** ------

THE UNITED STATES

In October of 1911, the National Urban League was founded. The National Urban League merged the Committee on Urban Conditions Among Negroes, founded in 1910 by George Haynes and Mrs. William Baldwin, Jr.; the National League for the Protection of Colored Women, organized by Mrs. Baldwin and Frances A. Kellor in 1905; and the Committee on Industrial Conditions of Negroes in New York, founded in 1906 by John Scottron, Fred Moore, Eugene Roberts, William Bulkley, Abraham Lefkowitz and William Schieffelin.

George Edmund Haynes and Eugene Kinckle Jones served as the first executive officers of the Urban League. The organization received financial support from Julius Rosenwald, Mrs. William H. Baldwin, Booker T. Washington, Kelly Miller, Roger N. Baldwin, Robert R. Moton, and L. Hollingsworth Wood.

The Urban League tried to open new opportunities for African Americans in industry and to assist newly arrived African Americans in their problems of adjustment in urban centers.

Branches were opened in many large cities to meet migrants, direct them to jobs and lodgings, and to offer information on how to live in the city. The league developed a program for training young men and women for social work, established fellowships to support students at the School of Philanthropy in New York, and established part fellowships to make possible in-service training at the league's national office in preparation for field work. In the 1920s and 1930s, the league sponsored publicity to convince businessmen to hire African Americans.

• Booker T. Washington was severely beaten in New York City for allegedly approaching a European American woman. This incident caused both radical and conservative African American leaders to rush to the defense of Washington, and for a while, because of this incident, tension was reduced between these two factions.

• W. E. B. Du Bois joined the Socialist Party.

• William Henry Lewis (1868–1949) was appointed to the position of Assistant United States Attorney General by President William Howard Taft (November 26).

• Samuel J. Battle became New York City's first African American police officer (June 28).

• *Organizations:* Jane Edna Hunter organized the Working Girls' Home Association (Phillis Wheatley Association) in Cleveland to assist African American women in finding employment.

• The Negro Society for Historical Research was founded by John Edward Bruce and Arthur Schomburg.

• The first African American fraternity to be chartered as a national organization, Kappa Alpha Psi, was founded at Indiana University.

• *The Labor Movement:* To protest the hiring of African American firemen, European American firemen went on strike at the Cincinnati, New Orleans, and Texas Pacific Railroads.

• *Notable Births:* Librarian and children's storyteller Augusta Baker was born (April 1).

• David Roy Eldridge, a jazz trumpeter, was born.

David Roy Eldridge was born in Pittsburgh, Pennsylvania. As a child, he learned to play drums and the trumpet. Eldridge appeared with Horace Henderson in 1926. Later he played with Speed Webb, Jack Whyte, Elmer Snowden, and other bands.

In 1933, Eldridge organized his own band while continuing to occasionally play with the bands of Teddy Hill and Fletcher Henderson.

In the 1940s, Eldridge played with Gene Krupa, Artie Shaw and the Benny Goodman Sextet. Eldridge is ranked as one of the most influential and important jazz instrumentalists.

• Mahalia Jackson, the legendary gospel singer known as the "Queen of the Gospel Song," was born (October 26).

Mahalia Jackson was born in New Orleans. Her father was a minister, and she became acquainted with gospel songs at an early age.

Upon moving to Chicago at the age of 16, Mahalia's religious convictions became stronger and her reputation grew.

Jackson began recording in 1934. She started with the independent "race record" market and was instantly a smash. It was during this time that Jackson became associated with the legendary Thomas A. Dorsey *(see 1899),* the "Father of Gospel."

Jackson achieved national prominence in 1945 with *Move On Up a Little Higher. Move On Up a Little Higher* enabled Jackson to become the first gospel star to carry the message to a wider audience beyond the black religious community. When one of Jackson's records was recognized as a masterpiece by the French recording industry, Jackson was courted by and signed by the major record label Columbia. With Columbia, Jackson would record over a dozen internationally acclaimed albums.

Jackson's fame spread across the entire spectrum of African American music. She could fit into any jazz or gospel festival.

Jackson appeared in films like Nat King Cole's *St. Louis Blues,* the glitzy Lana Turner melodrama *Imitation of Life,* and the highly successful performance documentary *Jazz On A Summer's Day.*

By the 1960s, Jackson so defined her field that to use the words "Mahalia Jackson" and "gospel music" in the same sentence was considered to be redundant.

To her credit, Mahalia Jackson used her music as part of her efforts on behalf of the civil rights movement. A key supporter of Dr. Martin Luther King, Jr., Mahalia sang her mentor Thomas A. Dorsey's song "Precious Lord, Take My Hand" at King's funeral in 1968. This same song would be sung at Jackson's own funeral after her death on January 27, 1972. At Mahalia's funeral, the song was sung by Aretha Franklin, one of the inheritors of Mahalia's divine vocal legacy.

• Robert Johnson, one of the finest performers of country blues, was born (May 8).

• Jo Jones, drummer, was born (October 7).

• Butterfly McQueen, an actress noted for her role in the movie *Gone With the Wind,* was born in Tampa, Florida (January 8).

• James B. Parsons, the first African American appointed to a lifetime federal judgeship, was born in Kansas City, Missouri.

• Historian Frank Snowden was born in Virginia. Snowden's work would become a leading source on Africans in ancient history.

• *Notable Deaths:* There were 67 African Americans lynched in 1911.

• In May 1911, European Americans hanged two African Americans from a railway bridge across the North Canadian River, just below the all-black town of Boley, Oklahoma.

• James Bland (1854–1911), the popular African American songwriter of such songs as *Carry Me Back to Ole Virginny*, died (May 5).

James Bland was born of free parents in Flushing, New York. His father, Allen M. Bland, was a college graduate and an examiner in the United States Patent Office.

Bland was educated at Howard University. After his college career, Bland became a famous minstrel entertainer. In 1881, Bland left the United States for Europe where he enjoyed fame for 20 years.

During his career, Bland wrote over 700 popular songs, among them *Carry Me Back to Ole Virginny*; *Oh, Dem Golden Slippers*; and *In the Evening by the Moonlight*. However, out of the hundreds of songs he wrote, only 38 were ever copyrighted.

One of the great ironies, in 1940, Bland's *Carry Me Back to Ole Virginny* became the state song for the flag state of the Old South. *Carry Me Back to Ole Virginny* became the state song for Virginia.

• Frances Ellen Watkins Harper (1825–1911), an African American poet and orator, died.

Frances Ellen Watkins Harper was an African American activist in the abolitionist movement. In her day, Harper's lectures and poems were very popular. Her literary models were Longfellow, Whittier and Mrs. Hemans. In addition to anti-slavery poems such as *The Slave Mother* and *Bury Me in a Free Land*, poems noted for their simplicity and directness, Harper also wrote propaganda for the feminist movement. Her biblical narratives, such as *Truth* and *Moses*, were not well received. One of her more successful works was *Sketches of a Southern Life* (1873), a series of verse portraits of African Americans in the South.

• James Theodore Holly (1829–1911), an African American educator and a Bishop of the Episcopal Church, died.

James Theodore Holly was born in Washington, D.C., of free African American parents. In 1844, Holly moved to New York and attended school there.

In 1851, Holly and his bride Charlotte moved to Canada. In this same year, Holly organized the Amherstburg Convention. Between 1851 and 1853, Holly served as associate editor of the *Voice of the Fugitive*, an anti-slavery publication which was published in Windsor, Canada.

In 1854, Holly was appointed to the post of public school principal in Buffalo, New York. He was instrumental in arranging the National Emigration Convention of Colored Men at Cleveland, Ohio, and, in 1854, he led a group of African Americans who wanted to go to Haiti.

Upon returning from Haiti, Holly made a report to the Immigration Convention. In 1857, Holly published *A Vindication of the Capacity of the Negro Race for Self-Government and Civilized Progress*, a lecture based on the history of Haiti.

In 1861, Holly returned to Haiti with another shipload of emigrants. Embarking from Philadelphia, the emigrant contingent numbered 2,000. By the time their ship arrived in Port-au-Prince, only a third of the original 2,000 survived.

In 1861, Holly was consecrated Bishop of Haiti by the Episcopal Church.

• *Miscellaneous Cases:* In the case of *Bailey v. Alabama* (January 3, 1911) 219 U.S. 219, 31 S.Ct. 145, the United States Supreme Court held that peonage was unconstitutional. Under the peonage practiced in Alabama, a laborer was essentially compelled to labor (farm) to repay the seed money and food that was advanced to him. If a laborer failed to farm or to repay the money, it was deemed to be prima facie evidence of his intent to defraud the employer/lender — it was deemed to be a crime. The court held that so far as the refusal without just cause to perform the labor called for in a written contract of employment under which the employee has obtained money which was not refunded, or property which was not paid for, is made prima facie evidence of an intent to defraud and therefore punishable as a criminal offense, such legislation offends against the prohibition of the Thirteenth Amendment against involuntary servitude especially since, under the local practice, the accused may not, for the purposes of rebutting the statutory presumption, testify as to his uncommunicated motives, purposes, or intentions.

• *Publications:* In 1911, a story about the lynching of an African American appeared in the papers on average once every six days.

• Booker T. Washington published *My Larger Education.*

• W. E. B. Du Bois published *The Quest of the Silver Fleece* in Chicago. In this novel, Du Bois correlated the cotton industry with structural racism. This was the first African American work to examine the economic causes of the caste system. *The Quest of the Silver Fleece* was inspired by the muckraking classics of Upton Sinclair and Frank Norris' studies of the Midwestern wheat and railroad monopolies.

• Claude McKay published his first book of poetry, *Songs of Jamaica.* McKay also published *Constab Ballads.*

• *Scholastic Achievements:* The Negro Society for Historical Research was founded by John Edward Bruce and Arthur Schomburg.

• The John F. Slater Fund, administered largely by J. L. M. Curry, began its support of county training schools, and within a decade more than 100 such institutions had been assisted.

• The Phelps-Stokes Fund was established.

The Phelps-Stokes Fund was established by the will of Caroline Phelps-Stokes for the "education of Negroes, both in Africa and the United States, and of North American Indians and of needy and deserving white students." The most notable work of the Phelps-Stokes Fund was done in Africa and African American education.

The Phelps-Stokes Fund established the Booker T. Washington Institute in Liberia in 1929. The Phelps-Stokes Fund brought several Africans to the United States each year to study. In 1942, the Phelps-Stokes Fund sponsored a conference to discuss the implications of the Atlantic Charter to Africa. Out of this conference, a report was issued. The report was entitled *The Atlantic Charter and Africa from an American Standpoint.*

In 1958, the Phelps-Stokes Fund sponsored the research and publication of a bibliography of the African people in Africa and America by Monroe Work.

One of the funds other major projects was the sponsoring of an encyclopedia of the African American under the directorship of W. E. B. Du Bois in the late 1930s.

• Richard Robert Wright, Jr., received a doctorate in sociology from the University of Pennsylvania.

• *The Performing Arts:* Sigmund Lubin produced *For Massa's Sake,* which told of a slave who sold himself to free his kind master of debt. This depiction of the Uncle Tom stereotype was quite popular in early films.

• *Music:* Scott Joplin completed his folk opera *Treemonisha.* Joplin would stage *Treemonisha* without an orchestra or scenery in 1915.

Sports

A racist supremacy controversy swirled over the scheduling of the Jack Johnson and Bombardier Wells heavyweight championship fight in London. Many European and European American racists sought to use the fight as a way to prove which race was superior once and for all. A protest, led by the Reverend F. B. Meyer, the honorary secretary of the National Free Church Council, appealed to cooler heads and succeeded in having the fight cancelled because of the tensions which it had generated.

• Pitcher Andrew "Rube" Foster, later known as the "Father of Black Baseball," formed the Chicago American Giants.

• John Henry Lloyd switched to the New York Lincoln Giants, where batted .475 and joined another African American baseball great, "Smokey Joe" Williams.

THE AMERICAS

• *Canada:* Beginning in 1911, the creation and growth of Afro-Canadian settlements essentially came to a halt because of the concerted effort of the Canadian government to prevent African Americans from immigrating into the Canadian West.

However, in March of 1911, a party of two hundred African Americans arrived at the border station at Emerson, Manitoba, opposite Pembina in North Dakota. These immigrants requested admission to press on to Amber Valley in northern Alberta where other relatives had preceded them. Canadian officials subjected the African American immigrants to the most rigorous examination possible and found, contrary to expectations, that they could not stop a single member of the group. But surprisingly, not one had less than $300 which was $100 more than the law required. Additionally, all were in excellent health, and all had documentary proof of good moral standing.

• *Haiti:* Antenor Firmin (1850–1911), a theoretician, commentator, novelist, died.

Antenor Firmin was born in a modest family in Cap-Haitien on October 18, 1850. Firmin founded in Cap-Haitien a political and literary publication, *Le Messager du Nord*. Firmin engaged in teaching, politics, and served in several diplomatic functions.

Firmin is mainly acclaimed in Haitian literature for his book on the equality of the human race through which he refuted the theory on the inferiority of persons of African descent. Writing in response to Gobineau's *Essay on the Inequality of Human Races,* Firmin retorted by writing *De l'Egalite des Races Humaines* (On the Equality of Human Races) in 1885 in which Firmin strongly defended the black race.

Firmin is still widely acclaimed in Haiti for his political philosophy and accomplishments. Firmin wrote essays, philosophical theories and commentaries.

Firmin's noted works include: *De l'Egalite des Races Humaines* (1885); *Haiti et la France* (1891); *Une Defense* (1892); *Diplomate et Diplomatie* (1898); *M. Roosevelt, President des Etats-Unis et la Republique d'Haiti* (1905); and *Lettres de Saint-Thomas* (1910)

- Louis-Joseph Janvier (1855–1911), a journalist and novelist, died in Paris (March 24).

Louis-Joseph Janvier was born on May 7, 1855 in Port-au-Prince. Janvier started medical school in Haiti, then completed his education in France. In 1881, Janvier was awarded a Doctorate in Medicine. He earned degrees in administration, economics, finance and diplomacy as well as a degree in law.

While in Paris, Janvier became interested in journalism and wrote several articles. However, Janvier made his reputation by publishing novels about Haitian life.

Janvier returned to Haiti after a 28 year absence but by that time he was more accustomed to France than to his native land. Janvier returned to Paris, where he died.

Janvier's principal works were *Le Vieux Piquet* (1888) and *Une Chercheuse* (1889).

Jamaica

In 1911, Marcus Garvey founded the Universal Negro Improvement Association. The avowed purpose of the organization were: (1) to promote unity among all African peoples regardless of nationality; (2) to improve the living conditions for African people throughout the world; (3) to found independent African states and communities in Africa; and (4) to found businesses and commercial enterprises which were to be owned and operated by African people.

While located solely in Jamaica, the Universal Negro Improvement Association would prove to be an unsuccessful venture. However, once Garvey moved his operations to the United States, prospects began to change.

- Claude McKay, a Jamaican writer who would become an integral part of the Harlem Renaissance, published *Songs of Jamaica.*

EUROPE

- Claudio J. D. Brindis de Sala (1852–1911), on Afro-German who became the German Court Violinist, died.

AFRICA

- *North Africa, Egypt and Sudan:* Fez (Morocco) was captured by France (April).
- In June, Spain occupied Larache and Alcazarquivir (al-Ksar al-Kabir), and, on July 1, the German gunboat *Panther* arrived at Agadir. The presence of these European powers created international tension.
- Italy annexed Tripolitania and Cyrenaica (November 5).
- Italy captured Tripoli (November 26).
- Sheikh Ali Yusuf died. The Party of Constitutional Reform in Egypt collapsed.
- Lord Kitchener became the British Agent and Consul-General in Egypt.
- *Western Africa:* France detached the Territoire Militaire du Niger from the province of Haut-Senegal-Niger.
- *Central Africa:* The "Police" and "Government chiefs" were instituted in Rwanda.
- *Neukirchner Missiongesellschaft* was established in Angola.
- After 1911, civil circumscriptions were introduced in Angola.
- Mutara III Rudahigwa (1913–1959), the Tutsi king of Rwanda, was born.

Mutara III Rudahigwa became king — became Mwami — of Rwanda in 1931 after his father Yuhi IV Musinga was deposed by the Belgian administration because of his inability to work with subordinate chiefs. His father had ushered in European colonial rule around the turn of the century, but had become disenchanted and uncooperative. Mutara came to power after Belgian rule was more firmly established.

Mutara worked to enhance the prerogatives of his office within the colonial framework. He was the dominant symbol of the Tutsi supremacy within the overwhelmingly Hutu country.

After World War II, the Belgians began to institute democratic reforms with the aim of raising the status of the Hutu. By the mid–1950s, Hutu demands for political and social equality were reaching a crisis level within the country. Mutara worked to forestall democratization but he died mysteriously at the capital of Burundi in mid–1959.

The Belgians claimed that Mutara had suffered a heart attack, but many Tutsi believed he had been assassinated. Mutara's death touched off a political revolution.

At his funeral, Mutara's brother Kigeri V Ndahindurwa was proclaimed king by the Tutsi monarchist faction. However, politicization of the Hutu majority was proceeding rapidly and culminated in a violent uprising at the end of the year. The new king was driven out of the country and many thousands of Tutsi were massacred.

- *Eastern Africa:* Sayyid Khalifa ibn Harub became the Sultan of Zanzibar following the abdication of Sayyid Ali because of increasing British domination.
- Zanzibar was controlled by a British Resident who was answerable to the Governor of the East African Protectorate.
- The British Indian silver rupees were made the standard coinage of Zanzibar.
- The Native Tribunal Rules recognized traditional councils of elders in Kenya.
- The first meeting of the Convention of Associations of Kenya settlers was convened.
- Ras Tasamma died. Lijj Iyasu ruled Ethiopia with a Council.
- Permanent patrol of Kings African Rifles against Ethiopian gun-runners were instituted in Acholi.
- Rinderpest in Karamoja destroyed 70% to 90% of the cattle.
- Shaaban Robert (1911–1962), a Tanzanian poet, was born.

Shaaban Robert's father converted to Christianity during the German occupation of Tanganyika (now Tanzania). However, Shaaban Robert remained a Muslim and lived in a substratum largely divorced from colonial rule.

As a school teacher, Shaaban Robert published poetry and prose. His work was in Swahili language.

Shaaban Robert's poems drew upon traditional Swahili verse forms. He treated a broad spectrum of modern themes.

Shaaban Robert's greatest poetic work was the posthumously published *Utenzi wa Vita vya Uhuru* ("epic of the war of freedom") about World War II. His prose included literary and philosophical essays, a biography of the Zanzibari singer Siti Bint Saad, and his own autobiography, *Maisha Yangu,* published in 1949.

- *Southern Africa:* The West Pondoland District Council was formed.
- Isiah Shembe, the founder of the Nazirite Baptist Church, announced some revelations. He established a holy village near Durban and developed into one of the most prominent Zulu figures of his time. Upon his death in 1935, Shembe was revered as a black messiah.

RELATED HISTORICAL EVENTS

- *The United States:* Franz Boas, a professor of anthropology at Columbia University, published *The Mind of Primitive Man. The Mind of Primitive Man* was Boas' most influential work and authoritatively disproved the arguments for the superiority of any race over another.
- Irving Berlin wrote *Alexander's Ragtime Band. Alexander's Ragtime Band* took advantage of the national popularity of African American ragtime music of the early twentieth century.
- *Europe:* Italy declared war on Turkey in order to seize Tripoli (September 29).
- A Franco-German convention was held (November 4). France was to have a free reign in Morocco in return for territory in the Congo for Cameroon.
- Caseley Hayford published *Ethiopia Unbound.*
- Maurice Delafosse published the three volume *Haut Senegal-Niger. Haut Senegal-Niger* was Delafosse's best known work. *Haut Senegal-Niger* is sometimes listed under the name of Delafosse's supervisor, Francois Clozel. *Haut Senegal-Niger* is considered to be one of the best scholarly sources for parts of the Western Sudan.
- *Africa:* Olive Schreiner published *Women and Labour.*

In her later life, Schreiner was an outspoken advocate of greater rights for women. Her 1911 book *Women and Labour* argued against the "sex parasitism" of men.

- Stephanus Jacobus Du Toit, a pioneer of Afrikaner nationalism, died.

Stephanus Jacobus Du Toit was raised and educated in the western Cape Colony where he became an ordained minister in the Dutch Reformed Church in 1875.

Du Toit wrote prolifically on Calvinism but

he is best known as an advocate of Afrikans language nationalism.

In 1876, Du Toit founded the first Afrikans language newspaper, *Die Afrikaanse Patriot*. The next year, Du Toit published an Afrikans history of South Africa which was the forerunner of modern Afrikans nationalist historiography.

During the British occupation of the Transvaal Republic from 1877 to 1881, Du Toit encouraged republican resistance. Afterwards, Du Toit served as the Transvaal's superintendent of education.

Later on, Du Toit advocated Afrikaner-British cooperation and opposed many of the policies of Paul Kruger, the Transvaal president during the 1890s.

Du Toit also played a critical role in the founding of the Afrikaner Bond, a moderate Cape Colony political party.

1912

THE UNITED STATES

There were three Presidential candidates in 1912: Woodrow Wilson, a Democrat born in the South, made only vague concessions to African American concerns. William Howard Taft had thoroughly alienated African Americans. As for Theodore Roosevelt, Roosevelt, while appealing to African Americans in the North, had refused to seat African American delegates from the South at the Progressive Party Convention. Roosevelt had also allowed Southern European Americans to exclude the NAACP's platform amendment calling for the repeal of unfair discriminatory laws and the complete enfranchisement of African Americans.

W. E. B. Du Bois withdrew from the Progressive Party to support Woodrow Wilson. Du Bois' rationalization for supporting Wilson was that while Wilson was a Virginian, and was long president of a college which did not admit African American students, Wilson was a cultivated scholar and, therefore, Du Bois felt that Wilson would treat the interests of African Americans with farsighted fairness. Du Bois wrote: "Wilson will not be our friend, but he will not belong to the gang of which Tillman, Vardaman, Hoke Smith and Blease are the brilliant expositors. He will not advance the cause of an oligarchy in the South. He will not seek further means of Jim Crow insult, he will not dismiss black men wholesale from office, and he will remember that the [African American] .... has a right to be heard and considered, and if he becomes Presi-

dent, by the grace of the black man's vote, his Democratic successors may be more willing to pay the black man's price of decent travel, free labor, votes and education."

Wilson also gained the support of the NAACP, the National Independent League, and the Colored National Democratic League.

In his first formal statements on African Americans, Wilson said that he wished to see "justice done to the colored people in every matter; and not mere grudging justice, but justice with liberality and cordial good feeling." Wilson further stated: "I want to assure them [assure African Americans] that should I become President of the U. S., they may count on me for absolute fair dealing, for everything by which I could assist in advancing the interests of their race in the U. S."

Upon winning the Presidential election, Wilson's first Congress sent to the Administration the greatest flood of bills proposing discriminatory legislation against African Americans that had ever been introduced into a United States Congress. The legislation advocated segregation of public carriers in Washington, D. C.; the exclusion of African Americans from Army and Navy commissions; separate accommodations for African American and European American federal employees; and the prohibition against any immigration of persons of African descent.

The election of Woodrow Wilson and the increasing discrimination associated with the Democrat Wilson administration also had the effect of accelerating the decline in the influence of Booker T. Washington. The defeat of the Republican Party in the presidential election of 1912 spelled the end of Washington's power as a dispenser of political patronage. With his patronage power gone and his policy of accommodation so discredited, Washington's days as "the" national African American leader were numbered.

• The International Conference on the Negro met at Tuskegee.

• Julius Rosenwald was appointed to the Board of Trustees of Tuskegee Institute.

• *The Civil Rights Movement:* In 1912, the NAACP had eleven branches with a total of 1,100 members. At the first meeting of the formally incorporated NAACP in January, Oswald Garrison Villard was chosen chairman of the board of directors.

• In New York, the NAACP desegregated New York theaters and in New Jersey Palisades Amusement Park.

• *The Labor Movement:* In 1912, only the following unions in the American Federation of Labor (AFL) had a significant number of African American members: United Mine Workers (40,000 African American members); Teamsters (6,000); Cigar Makers (5,000); Hotel and Restaurant Employees (2,500); Carpenters (2,500); Painters (250).

• The Southern District of the Forest and Lumber Workers Union of the IWW convened in Louisiana. About half of the 35,000 members were African Americans, but there were no African Americans at the convention.

• Bill Haywood, who was attending asked why, and was told that integrated assemblies were contrary to Louisiana law. "If it's against the law, the law should be broken," Haywood responded, and the convention was integrated.

• *Notable Births:* Dorothy Height, a leader of the National Council of Negro Women, was born in Richmond, Virginia (March 24).

• Blues guitarist Sam "Lightnin'" Hopkins was born in Texas (March 15).

• Nina Mae McKinney, an actress, was born in Lancaster, South Carolina (August 27).

• Willard Motley (1912–1965), an author, was born.

Willard Motley was born into a middle class family in Chicago, Illinois. After high school, Motley spent the 1930s as a transcontinental drifter and odd-jobs man. At the age of 29, he began writing what was to become his first and most successful novel, *Knock on Any Door,* published in 1947 after six years of writing and revising.

Motley wrote in the tradition of the Chicago naturalists, which included Norris, Dreiser, Anderson, Farrell, Algren, and Wright. A perfectionist, Motley produced only three more novels: *We Fished All Night* (1951); *Let No Man Write My Epitaph* (1962); and *Let Noon Be Fair* (1966). Significantly, none of Motley's novels dealt with race or African American life as a main theme.

• Gordon Parks, Sr., a *Life* magazine photographer and film director, was born in Kansas.

• *Notable Deaths:* 63 African Americans were lynched in 1912.

• Memphis real estate tycoon, Robert R. Church, Sr., died (August 2).

• John Wesley Gaines (1840–1912), a clergyman, author, and a leader in the establishment of the African Methodist Episcopal Church in the South, died.

John Wesley Gaines was born a slave on the plantation of Gabriel Toombs. He was licensed to preach in 1865. Afterwards, Gaines helped to organize churches for the African Methodist Episcopal (AME) Church. Gaines was the founder, treasurer, and president of the board of trustees of Morris Brown College in Atlanta, Georgia, which opened in 1885. In 1888, he became a bishop of the AME Church.

Gaines published two notable works. *African Methodism in the South* was published in 1890 and, in 1897, *The Negro and the White Man* was published.

• Susie King Taylor (1848–1912), an African American woman who became a nurse in the United States Army and served with the First Regiment of the South Carolina Volunteers, died.

Susie King Taylor was born a slave on a plantation near Savannah, Georgia. In 1902, Taylor's Civil War memoirs were published. *Reminiscences of My Life in Camp* is the only comprehensive written record of life and activities of African American army nurses during the Civil War.

• *Miscellaneous Laws:* A housing segregation law was passed in Louisville, Kentucky. The law provided that city blocks with a majority of African Americans were designated as black blocks, and those with a majority of European Americans were designated as white blocks. African Americans were not permitted to move into white blocks, and vice versa. Baltimore, Richmond (Virginia), and Atlanta soon followed Louisville's lead. African American ghettos were thereby sanctioned by law and became well established in many parts of the country.

• *Publications:* Booker T. Washington published *The Man Farthest Down; a Record of Observation and Study in Europe.*

• James Weldon Johnson published *The Autobiography of an Ex–Colored Man.*

The Autobiography of an Ex–Colored Man was the first novel by an African American to become a permanent part of American literature. It was remarkably free of the melodrama which had marked most of the previous novels by African

Americans. Despite the title, the book was definitely not an autobiography.

The narrative of *The Autobiography of an Ex–Colored Man* consists of a series of episodes in which the hero runs the gamut of African American experiences in the United States. Although the race question appears, it never becomes a major theme. *The Autobiography of an Ex–Colored Man* is probably the first African American novel to deal with African Americans in their own environment and not in relation to European Americans. Johnson's novel pointed the way to the "new Negro movement of the Harlem Renaissance."

- Claude McKay published *Constab Ballads.*
- The first edition of *The Negro Yearbook* was published.
- Carlotta Bass bought and began publishing the newspaper *California Eagle.*

Carlotta Bass (1880–1969) ran the *California Eagle* for forty years. In 1952, she was the Progressive Party vice-presidential candidate.

- *Scholastic Achievements:* Carter G. Woodson received a Ph.D. from Harvard, becoming the second African American to earn a doctorate in history.
- *Music:* W. C. Handy published the first blues composition, *Memphis Blues* (September 27).
- *Technological Innovations:* Garrett A. Morgan received a patent for a safety hood and smoke protector.

Morgan demonstrated the utility of his innovation in 1916 by rescuing workers trapped in a smoke-filled tunnel of the Cleveland, Ohio, waterworks.

In 1923, Morgan fixed his name in history by inventing the three-way automatic traffic signal.

- *The Black Church:* J. W. E. Bowen asked for African American bishops in the Methodist Church "because the true elevation of a race to a higher level would have to come from within."
- *Sports:* Jack Johnson beat Fireman Jim Flynn in Las Vegas to retain the world heavyweight title. The fight was stopped by police in the ninth round (July 4).
- Howard Porter Drew, an African American sprinter for UCLA, won the AAU championship in the 100 yard dash (September 12). Theodore Cable of Harvard University was the inter-collegiate champion in the hammer throw.

THE AMERICAS

- *Cuba:* There was a short lived racial uprising led by the Agrupacion Independiente de Color.

In 1912, there developed a racial movement opposed to the prohibition of organizations based on race, known as the Independents of Color. The movement's leaders, Pedro Ivonet and Evaristo Esternoz, perished in the struggle. United States troops landed, but the Cuban government opposed this intervention. That same year the lease turning over Guantanamo Bay to the United States for an indefinite period was signed.

- *Haiti:* The Haitian Federation of Soccer was formed (January 30).
- The Haytian American Sugar Company (HASCO) was created as a corporate entity at Wilmington in the State of Delaware with a capital of five million dollars (August 5). Its objective was the production and sale of sugar and other related goods in Haiti and in the United States. The founders were Charles Steinheim, John A. Christie and Franck Corpay. HASCO became one of the major Haitian industries with a high level of employment.
- An explosion at 3 am destroyed the National Palace and killed President Cincinnatus Leconte and three hundred soldiers (August 8). General Tancrede Auguste succeeded Leconte as President of Haiti.

EUROPE

- Samuel Coleridge-Taylor (1875–1912), the gifted Afro-English composer, died (September 1). *See 1875.*

AFRICA

- *North Africa, Egypt and Sudan:* The Sultan of Morocco signed a treaty making Morocco a French Protectorate (March 30). Marshal Lyautey became the first Resident-General. On August 12, the Sultan abdicated.
- On November 27, a Franco-Spanish convention was held to discuss the respective zones in Morocco. The Spanish zone was to be governed by a Khalifa of the Sultan.
- From 1912 to 1925, the French gradually penetrated and occupied Morocco.
- *Western Africa:* The West Africa Currency Board was constituted.
- There was an uprising in Abeokuta.
- William Harris began his ministry.

While in a Liberian jail, William Harris received a "call" from the angel Gabriel to become a prophet. Emerging from prison in 1912, Harris donned a white robe and a turban and began carrying a staff in the shape of a cross. His white beard completed the Biblical image.

Harris began to walk the Liberian coast preaching Christianity and condemning idol worship.

• Alhaji Abubakar Tafawa Balewa (1912–1966), the first prime minister of Nigeria, was born.

Alhaji Balewa was born the son of a slave in northern Nigeria. Balewa obtained a teacher's certificate at Katsina and then attended the school of education of the University of London in 1945.

Upon his return to northern Nigeria, Balewa advanced to a senior position in the education department, one of the first northerners to achieve so high a position in the civil service. Shortly thereafter, Balewa was appointed to the council of the emir of Bauchi, and then to the first Northern Region House of Assembly. This Assembly elected him to the Nigerian legislative council.

In 1949, Balewa militantly represented northern interests in talks on constitutional reform. At the same time, he worked for moderate reform within his own northern region.

In 1950, Balewa incurred the wrath of many of northern Nigeria's traditional rulers by instigating an investigation (and initiating the reform) of the institution of "Sole Native Authority," whereby there were no checks on the power of the emirs within their own communities.

In 1951, Alhaji Balewa joined Ajhaji Ahmadu Bello, the Sardauna of Sokoto— the traditional ruler of northern Nigeria— in forming the Northern Peoples Congress (NPC) as a vehicle for establishing northern dominance in national politics. After the implementation of a new constitution in 1952, Balewa became a federal minister.

As a federal minister, Balewa enhanced his reputation as a highly intelligent hard worker. His star began to rise.

In 1957, Balewa became chief minister. After an NPC victory in the federal elections of 1959, Balewa emerged as prime minister. Nigeria became an independent nation in the next year.

In 1962, Obafemi Awolowo, the leader of the Western region, was charged with plotting to overthrow Balewa's government. Awolowo was imprisoned. However, political unrest and violence persisted and continued to plague Balewa's administration.

In 1966, a military coup was staged in Nigeria. Alhaji Balewa was killed in the coup.

• Edward Blyden (1832–1912), considered by many to be the most important Western-oriented African intellectual of his time, died.

Edward Wilmot Blyden was born in the West Indies. He went to the United States in 1850 for theological training. Repelled by the racial discrimination so prevalent in 1850s America, Blyden emigrated to Liberia after a relatively brief stay in the United States.

Once in Liberia, Blyden became active in Liberian politics serving as secretary of state from 1864 to 1866. In 1871, Blyden was driven from Liberia because of his close association with Liberian president Edward J. Roye.

During the 1870s, Liberia became bitterly factionalized along color (skin tone) lines. Roye happened to be the first dark skinned president of Liberia. Roye's and Blyden's COTW (fair skinned) opponents charged Blyden with committing adultery with Roye's wife. Blyden was dragged through the streets of Monrovia by a mob and nearly lynched. Roye himself was deposed and drowned fleeing his enemies a few months later.

Blyden fled to Sierra Leone. In Sierra Leone, Blyden established a newspaper. Within a few months, he was appointed government agent to the interior. In this capacity, Blyden made two important trips into the northern interior. First he went to Falaba, the capital of the Yalunka state of Solima. Next he went to Timbo, the capital of Futa Jalon.

Blyden returned to Liberia in 1874. Once again, he immersed himself in politics and education. Blyden served as ambassador to England from 1877 to 1878 and again in 1892. Blyden also served as president of Liberia College from 1880 to 1884.

In 1885, Blyden ran for the presidency of Liberia. After losing the election, he returned to Sierra Leone.

Blyden's legacy is an intellectual one rather than a political one. His ideas on race relations foreshadowed the philosophy of Aime Cesaire and Leopold Senghor. Blyden believed that blacks and whites had equal, but different, potentials, and that blacks could only attain their full potential in Africa.

Given his philosophy, Blyden became an advocate for a back-to-Africa movement. In this regard, he was a trailblazer for Marcus Garvey.

Blyden believed that the only way blacks could control their destinies was through Pan-African nationalism. He advocated the creation of a vast West African nation, or at least larger political groupings than those of colonial West Africa. Blyden hoped to accomplish this by linking Liberia with Sierra Leone, by encouraging European imperialism (which Blyden perceived as a tool for unifying the multitude of African peoples), by developing black racial pride, and by promoting Islam.

Although Blyden was a Christian minister, he felt that Christianity was unsuitable for Africa because of the discrimination practiced in the Christian churches.

Blyden's philosophical and political writings were voluminous. His best known work was a volume of essays, *Christianity, Islam and the Negro Race* which was published in 1887. Blyden was also a scholar in Arabic and classical languages.

Blyden's belief that a British take-over of Liberia would promote African unity apparently involved him in an attempted coup in 1909. In 1906, a British bank had loaned 100,000 pounds to the almost bankrupt Liberian government. The loan was secured against Liberia's custom receipts. A British major was dispatched to Liberia to organize a frontier force. Three years later, in 1909, the frontier force mutinied against the Liberian government.

After the mutiny was suppressed, Blyden was implicated as an accomplice. Because of his age and because he had ostensibly acted out of a higher motive, the sanctions imposed on Blyden for his involvement in the attempted coup proved to be minimal. However, Blyden was demonized in Liberia and essentially exiled to Sierra Leone.

Blyden died penniless in Sierra Leone.

• *Central Africa:* The German Residency was moved from Usumbura to Kitega (August 15).
• The African Inland Mission (AIM) started work in the Belgian Congo.
• Alexis Kagame, a noted Rwandan historian and philosopher, was born (1912).

Alexis Kagame is considered to be the leading Rwandan historian and collector of oral tradition. He is a member of the ruling Tutsi minority of the former kingdom. Much of his writing reflects his strong Tutsi bias. Among his many works are *La Poesie Dynastique du Ruanda* which was published in 1951 and *Le Code des Institu-*

tions Politiques du Ruanda Precolonial which was published in 1952.

Kagame is perhaps most widely known for his exposition of African philosophy in *La Philosophie Bantu-rwandaise de l'Etre* which was published in 1956. With *La Philosophie Bantu-rwandaise de l'Etre* earned Kagame a doctorate at the Gregorian University of Rome. In *La Philosophie Bantu-rwandaise de l'Etre*, analyzed Rwandan life philosophy in Western terms and set forth the notion of 'life force' in the Bantu concepts of *Munta, Hantu, Kintu* and *Kuntu.*

• Mwambutsa IV, the future king of Burundi, was born (1912).

While still an infant, Mwambutsa was named king — Mwami — of Burundi when his father Mutage IV unexpectedly died in 1915. Shortly afterwards, the German administration of the country was replaced by a Belgian one.

Through the ensuing years, Mwambutsa's power was largely circumscribed by the colonial authorities, and by powerful internal factions which pre-dated colonial rule. Mwambutsa's education was limited and he developed an unsavory reputation as a playboy.

By the late 1950s, as Burundi moved towards independence, Mwambutsa's own influence was slight, but members of his family dominated the nationalist movement. When Burundi became self-governing in 1961, one of Mwambutsa's sons, Louis Rwagasore, was made prime minister. However, Rwagasore was soon assassinated and a chain of violent coups was set off.

In 1962, Burundi gained its independence as a constitutional monarchy. Mwambutsa gradually moved to concentrate real power in his own hands. Military officers of the country's majority Hutu population attempted a coup in October, 1965. It failed, but Mwambutsa fled the country, eventually settling in Switzerland.

Mwambutsa's nineteen-year-old son Charles Ndizeye usurped the kingship the following July, and was installed as Ntare V. Mwambutsa's protests from abroad fell on deaf ears.

Ntare V was deposed later in 1966 by Michael Micombero, the man who Ntare had made prime minister. After the king was deposed, the country was proclaimed a republic.

• *Eastern Africa:* The Tanga railway reached Moshi.
• The *Uganda Herald* began publication.
• The Uganda Witchcraft Ordinance was enacted.
• The southern half of Lado enclave was ceded from the Sudan to Uganda as West Nile

Province. The Bari-Lotuka area was ceded to the Sudan.

• *Southern Africa:* The South African Cabinet was reconstituted (February 1). J. C. Smuts became the Finance Minister (June).

• The Comoro Islands were formally annexed to Madagascar (July 25).

• Botha resigned on December 2 but, on December 20, he formed a new cabinet without Hertzog. In Botha's new cabinet, J. C. Smuts was the Defence and Finance Minister.

• The South African Defence Act provided for a force of 27,500.

• The African National Congress was organized in South Africa.

In 1912, the organization which is today known as the "ANC" was born.

The South African Native National Congress became the organization which is today known as the African National Congress (the "ANC").

The South African Native National Congress was organized in 1912 on the initiative of Pixley Seme. Seme wanted a national union of black South Africans as an alternative to the Euro-African dominated Union of South Africa, which was formed in 1910.

Over one hundred delegates to the Congress met in 1912. At Seme's suggestion, the delegates patterned the new organization after the United States Congress. John Dube was one of the delegates who responded to Pixley Seme's call to form an African union. He was elected the first president of the new organization.

The ANC was first known as the South African Native National Congress. It changed its name to the African National Congress — the "ANC" — in 1923.

During its first decades, the ANC operated mainly as a protest organization. In the 1950s, it developed into a major mass movement. The ANC served as a model for political movements in many colonial territories north of the Zambezi River. However, with South Africa, it had little impact on the government's discriminatory and repressive legislation.

In 1959, Robert Sobukwe broke away to form the more militant Pan African Congress, but both the Pan African Congress and the African National Congress were banned by the South African government in 1959.

For over thirty years, the leaders of the African National Congress operated underground. Many of its leaders, including Nelson Mandela, were imprisoned or forced into exile.

In February 1990, South African President F.

W. de Klerk released African National Congress leader Nelson Mandela after Mandela had been imprisoned for almost 28 years. De Klerk also lifted the ban on the ANC and other anti-apartheid groups and de Klerk pledged to begin negotiations toward a new national constitution.

In July of 1991, the African National Congress held its first open conference inside South Africa and elected a strong multiracial leadership, blending leaders from exile and those from grass roots groups inside the country.

In December of 1991, the South African government and various political groups, including the ANC, met in Johannesburg at a Convention for a Democratic South Africa and began efforts aimed at framing a non-racial constitution for South Africa.

The efforts were successful and on May 10, 1994, Nelson Mandela, the leader of the ANC, became the first black African president of South Africa.

• The Northern Rhodesia Police was formed.

"Northern Rhodesia" is today known as Zambia. Northern Rhodesia was first administered by the British South Africa Company in two sections: North-Eastern and North-Western Rhodesia. These regions were united under a single Northern Rhodesian administration in 1911. The territory became a crown colony in 1924. From 1953 to 1963, Northern Rhodesia formed a part of the Federation of the Rhodesia and Nyasaland.

In 1964, Northern Rhodesia became an independent nation as Zambia, with Kenneth Kaunda as its first prime minister.

• The *History of the Basuto* by D. Frederic Ellenberger was published.

History of the Basuto is considered to be the classic authority on early Sotho history. Unfortunately, Ellenberger generally failed to identify his sources and *History of the Basuto* is additionally marred by an unsatisfactory blend of original and unoriginal information. Nevertheless, so many Sotho read Ellenberger's work that it became difficult for historians to collect oral traditions which had not been recorded (or influenced) by Ellenberger's history.

• Walter Max Ulyate Sisulu, a leader of the African National Congress, was born.

Walter Sisulu was born in the Transkei. Sisulu had a brief mission education before going to Johannesburg to work in various jobs. In 1940, Sisulu joined the African National Congress and devoted his full energies to politics.

Impatient with the moderate leadership of the ANC, Sisulu joined with Oliver Tambo, Nelson Mandela, and others to form the Youth League within the Congress in 1944. The Youth League helped to vote A. B. Xuma out of the presidency of the ANC in 1949 in favor of J. S. Moroka.

Dissatisfied with Moroka, the Youth League then helped to make Albert Luthuli president in 1952. With the ascension of Luthuli, the control of the ANC rested mostly in the hands of the leaders of the Youth League.

In 1952, Sisulu organized the national Defiance Campaign and was afterwards "banned" by the government. Four years later, Sisulu was among the many African nationalists arrested for treason. After a prolonged trial which attracted world-wide attention, all the defendants were acquitted in 1961.

In 1962, Sisulu was re-imprisoned for a technical violation of his house arrest. Sisulu escaped to Botswana, but was re-captured and sentenced to life imprisonment at Robben Island for sabotage.

RELATED HISTORICAL EVENTS

• *Europe:* The French Senate ratified the Moroccan agreement (February 10).

• A decree defining French citizenship in West Africa was issued (August 12).

• Turkey ceded Tripoli to Italy pursuant to the terms of the Treaty of Ouchy (October 28).

• A Franco-Spanish convention was reached concerning the boundaries of their respective Moroccan protectorates.

— 1 9 1 3 —

THE UNITED STATES

• In 1913, a cotton depression was felt throughout the South.

• Most of the segregation legislation introduced in Congress during the previous year failed to pass, but Wilson, by executive order, segregated most of the African American federal employees so far as eating and restroom facilities were concerned.

• Oswald Garrison Villard asked President Wilson to appoint a National Race Commission to study the status of African Americans. Wilson refused. In addition, Wilson appointed European American men to posts traditionally given to African Americans (i.e.,

Ambassadors to Haiti and to Santo Domingo).

• The executive board of the NAACP advised all branches and groups seeking affiliation with the national organization to include European American members in order to meet the requirements of the national association.

• Booker T. Washington continued to use his influence in an attempt to discredit the NAACP and to halt fund raising. The "radical" element responded with personal attacks against Washington. The splintered civil rights movement would not begin to be reconciled until after Washington's death in 1915.

• By 1913, approximately 100 old-age homes and orphanages had been established through African American charity.

• Daniel Hale Williams became a charter member of the American College of Surgeons.

• *Organizations:* Young women of the Alpha Kappa Alpha sorority split away and formed the Delta Sigma Theta sorority. Julia Quander, president of Alpha Kappa Alpha, incorporated and established national chapters for both colleges and alumnae. Thus, Alpha Kappa Alpha and Delta Sigma Theta both became national associations of collegiate women of African descent whose influence would spread across forty states and into Africa and Haiti. In time, Delta Sigma Theta would have 800 chapters and a membership of 175,000.

• The forerunner of the National Dental Association, the Tri-State Dental Association, was organized in Virginia. The fledgling effort would become the top professional organization for African American dentists.

• The National Negro Retail Merchant's Association was organized.

• *The Labor Movement:* The National Alliance of Postal Workers, an African American group of mail clerks, was organized.

• *Notable Births:* Lionel Hampton, a jazz musician, was born.

Lionel Hampton was born in Louisville, Kentucky. He was raised in Chicago, Illinois, where he played drums in the *Chicago Defender* Boys' Band. In 1928, Hampton moved to California and played in the Paul Howard Orchestra. It was there that he began to play the vibraharp.

In 1930, Lionel Hampton made his first recorded solo on vibraharp. The record was *Memories of You* and it was recorded with Louis Armstrong.

Lionel Hampton organized his own band in Los Angeles and later played on records with Benny Goodman, Gene Krupa and Teddy Wilson. Hampton formally joined the Goodman band in 1936 and stayed until 1940, when he again organized his own orchestra.

In 1942, Hampton's record of *Flyin' Home* was a great hit, and established him in the big-band field.

Hampton was perhaps the first jazz musician to feature the vibraharp or the vibraphone.

- Robert Hayden, a poet, was born (August 4).

Robert Hayden was born in Detroit, Michigan. He was educated at Wayne State and the University of Michigan. In 1940, Hayden joined the faculty of Fisk University and, in 1946, he published *Heartshape in the Dust,* his first collection of poems.

In 1947, Hayden received a Rosenwald Fellowship and, in the following year, he published *The Lion and the Archer,* his second volume of poems.

A Ballad of Remembrance, another volume of poetry, was published in 1962.

Hayden is one of the most widely translated African American poets.

- Clara Stanton Jones, the first African American to serve as president of the American Library Association, was born in St. Louis, Missouri.
- Archie Moore, the great boxing champion, was born in Mississippi.
- Jesse Owens, the legendary track and field star who won four gold medals at the 1936 Berlin Olympics, was born in Alabama.
- Rosa Parks, the woman who helped launched the civil rights movement of the 1950s and 1960s, was born in Alabama (February 4). Parks' refusal to give her seat to a European American man in Montgomery, Alabama in 1955 led to the bus boycott, the emergence of Martin Luther King, Jr., and the birth of the modern Civil Rights Movement.
- Blues pianist Joe Willie "Pinetop" Perkins was born (July 7).
- *Notable Deaths:* There were 52 recorded lynchings of African Americans in 1913.
- Educator and missionary Fanny Jackson Coppin, one of the first African-American women to graduate from college (1865), died in Philadelphia (January 21).
- Harriet Tubman (c.1821–1913), the legendary "conductor" on the Underground Railroad, died in Auburn, New York (March 10).

Harriet Tubman was a legendary conductor on the Underground Railroad. For the first twenty-eight years of her life she was a slave. In 1844, while she was working as a field hand, she was forced by her mother to marry John Tubman, a free African American. In 1849, fearing the prospect of being sold to the Deep South, Tubman escaped.

Tubman became associated with the Underground Railroad. The Underground Railroad ferreted slaves from slavery in the Southern states to freedom in the northern United States or in Canada. Sometimes Harriet was compelled to encourage her timid charges forward by using a loaded revolver as an added incentive for continuing on the Railroad.

Harriet Tubman worked, for a time, with John Brown and other abolitionists. During the Civil War, she assisted the Union cause by serving as a cook, guide, spy and nurse.

After the Civil War, Tubman became active in establishing schools for the newly freed slaves of North Carolina.

In 1869, Sarah Hopkins Bradford published *Scenes in the Life of Harriet Tubman.* This book was later revised in 1886 and retitled *Harriet, the Moses of her People.*

- Charles E. Nash (1844–1913), a Reconstruction era Congressperson from Louisiana, died.

Charles E. Nash was born in Opelousas, Louisiana. Nash was a bricklayer by trade. During the Civil War, Nash joined the Chasseurs d'Afrique Regiment of the Union Army, and rose to the rank of sergeant major.

After the war, Nash was appointed the United States Custom Inspector for Louisiana. In 1874, he was elected to the House of Representatives.

After serving one term in Congress, Nash returned to Louisiana and became a town postmaster.

- *Miscellaneous Laws:* Virginia Democrats adopted the "white primary."

Publications

In an editorial entitled "A Philosophy for 1913," W. E. B. Du Bois presented a New Year's resolution in the form of a creed which re-dedicated the NAACP's *Crisis* magazine to its commitment to confront bigotry and discrimination. The eloquence of DuBois is undeniable:

I am by birth and law a free black American citizen.

As such I have both rights and duties.

If I neglect my duties my rights are always in

danger. If I do not maintain my rights I cannot perform my duties.

I will listen, therefore, neither to the fool who would make me neglect the things I ought to do, nor to the rascal who advises me to forget the opportunities which I and my children ought to have, and must have, and will have.

Boldly and without flinching, I will face the hard fact that in this, my fatherland, I must expect insult and discrimination from persons who call themselves philanthropists and Christians and gentlemen. I do not wish to meet this despicable attitude by blows; sometimes I cannot even protest by words; but may God forget me and mine if in time or eternity I ever weakly admit to myself or the world that wrong is not wrong, that insult is not insult, or the color discrimination is anything but an inhuman and damnable shame.

Believing this with my utmost soul, I shall fight race prejudice continually. If possible, I shall fight it openly and decidedly by word and deed. When that is not possible I will give of my money to help others to do the deed and say the word which I cannot. This contribution to the greatest of causes shall be my most sacred obligation.

Whenever I meet personal discrimination on account of my race and color I shall protest. If the discrimination is old and deep seated, and sanctioned by law, I shall deem it my duty to make my grievance known, to bring it before the organs of public opinion and to the attention of men of influence, and to urge relief in courts and legislatures.

I will not, because of inertia or timidity or even sensitiveness, allow new discriminations to become usual and habitual. To this end I will make it my duty without ostentation, but with firmness, to assert my right to vote, to frequent places of public entertainment and to appear as a man among men. I will religiously do this from time to time, even when personally I prefer the refuge of friends and family.

While thus fighting for Right and Justice, I will keep my soul clean and serene. I will not permit cruel and persistent persecution to deprive me of the luxury of friends, the enjoyment of laughter, the beauty of sunsets, or the inspiration of a well-written word. Without bitterness (but also without lies), without useless recrimination (but also without cowardly acquiescence), without unnecessary heartache (but with not self-deception), I will walk my way, with uplifted head and level eyes, respecting myself too much to endure without protest studied disrespect from others, and steadily refusing to assent to the silly exaltation of a mere tint of skin or curl of hair.

In fine, I will be a man and know myself to be one, even among those who secretly and openly deny my manhood, and I shall persistently and unwaveringly seek by every possible method to compel all men to treat me as I treat them.

- Archibald Henry Grimke published *The Ballotless Victim of One-Party Governments.*
- Benjamin Brawley published *A Short History of the American Negro.*
- James Weldon Johnson published his poem, *Fifty Years. Fifty Years* commemorated the fiftieth anniversary of the Emancipation Proclamation.
- Paul Laurence Dunbar's *Complete Poems* were published. *See 1872.*
- Oscar Micheaux published *The Conquest.*

Certain novels by African American authors of the 1910s ignored the existence of the color line, maintaining that there was no barrier that hard work and diligence could not overcome. Oscar Micheaux's *The Conquest* and *Forged Note* (1915); Henry Downing's *The American Cavalryman* (1917); and Mary Etta Spencer's *The Resentment* (1920) were prominent examples of this genre. These writers accepted the American success story. In their novels, the protagonists were frequently African Americans playing European American roles. The heroes were modeled on European American heroes — the Western pioneer, the empire builder in *The American Cavalryman* and the hog king in *The Resentment.*

This color-blind trend, right after James Weldon Johnson's *Autobiography of an Ex-Colored Man,* resolved the ambiguity which had plagued the African American novel. Subsequent writers would either accept the irrefutable fact of their racial heritage or they would ignore it.

- William Stanley Braithwaite began editing the *Anthology of Magazine Verse.* The *Anthology of Magazine Verse* included works by African American and European American poets.
- Henry Edwin Baker (1859–1928), an African American who was then an assistant examiner in the United States Patent Office, published the first separate list of African American inventors, the *Negro Inventor.* Baker used his position in the patent office to discover and publicize the inventions of African Americans. This was quite a feat at the time because a patent holder's race is not recorded on patent applications. Despite this obstacle, Baker was able to uncover some 400 African American innovators.

Scholastic Achievements

The Julius Rosenwald Fund was founded by Julius Rosenwald, president of Sears Roebuck. The fund lasted until 1948. While its funding lasted, the fund expended over five million dollars ($5,000,000) on African American colleges, provided a wide assortment of scholarships and fellowships for African Americans; and supported many special projects.

The Julius Rosenwald Fund was not set up specifically for African American education and, accordingly, it expended some $22.5 million on non–African American related school grants. However, included in the African American projects which it did fund were a program set up in the 1920s to give financial assistance to African American medical students and a contribution which enabled the United Negro College Fund to be created in 1944.

The sculptors Richmond Barthe and Augusta Savage, the painter Charles White, historian John Hope Franklin, choreographer Katherine Dunham and composer William Grant Still were some of the notable recipients of Rosenwald Fellowships.

- *The Arts:* William Scott exhibited his art work at the Paris Salon (1912–1913).

The Black Church

Noble Drew Ali, the adopted name of Timothy Drew (1886–1929), formed the Moorish Science Temple in Newark, New Jersey. The formation of the Moorish Science Temple is believed to be the precursor to the reappearance of Islam among African Americans.

Noble Drew Ali taught that people of African descent were not Ethiopians, but the descendants of the Moabites of the Bible whose homeland was said to be Morocco. W. D. Fard, the founder of the Nation of Islam in the early 1930s, was originally a member of the Moorish Science Temple.

- *Black Enterprise:* The Atlanta State Savings Bank was chartered in Georgia.
- *Sports:* Howard B. Drew was again the AAU champion in the 100 yard dash.
Theodore Cable repeated as the intercollegiate champion in the hammer throw.

THE AMERICAS

- *Barbados:* Hugh Worrell Springer, a future governor-general of Barbados, was born.

Hugh Springer was the third black, native born governor-general of Barbados. A graduate of Harrison College in Barbados in 1931, Springer received a bachelor of arts and a masters degrees from Oxford University.

In 1938, Springer became a barrister following studies at Inner Temple. In 1939, he returned to Barbados to practice law and teach the classics. Springer soon became active in politics and the trade union movement.

Springer was elected to the Barbadian House of Assembly in 1944. He also served as secretary general of the newly formed Barbados Labour Party (BLP) and, with Sir Grantly Herbert Adams, was instrumental in organizing the Barbados Workers Union (BWU), becoming its secretary general in 1944. In addition, Springer became a member of the Barbadian Governmental Executive Committee, along with Adams.

Springer resigned all of these positions in 1947 to become registrar of the new University of the West Indies (UWI), near Kingston, Jamaica, where he remained until 1963.

Springer was awarded a Guggenheim Fellowship and became a fellow in the Harvard Center for International Affairs from 1961 to 1962. From 1962 to 1963, Springer was a visiting fellow at Oxford and from 1963 to 1966, he served as director of the Institute of Education for the University of the West Indies.

Between 1966 and 1980 Springer held posts as assistant secretary general of the British Commonwealth, director of the Commonwealth's educational liaison unit, and secretary general of Commonwealth Universities.

In February 1984, Springer again returned to Barbados to serve as governor general.

- *Canada:* Anderson Ruffin Abbott (1837–1913), the first Canadian-born person of African descent to receive a license to practice medicine in Canada, died in Toronto.

Anderson Abbott was born in Toronto. His father was the wealthy Afro-Canadian real estate broker Wilson Abbott *(see 1876)* and his mother was Ellen Toyer Abbott.

Anderson Abbott studied at the Toronto Academy which, at that time, was operated in conjunction with Knox's College. Anderson Abbott ultimately graduated from Oberlin College in Ohio before taking a degree in medicine at the University of Toronto in 1861.

In 1863, Anderson Abbott was appointed a surgeon in the Northern (Union) army. After the war, he opened a practice in Chatham. In Chatham, Abbott served as president of the Wilberforce Educational Institute from 1873 until 1880. He was a vocal opponent of the public segregated schools and became coroner for Kent County in 1874.

Anderson Abbott was an associate editor of the British Methodist Episcopal Church's local publication, *The Messenger,* as well as a writer for the *Planet.* After living in Dundas, where he was assistant editor of the local *Banner,* and briefly in Oakville, Abbott moved to Toronto in 1890.

In 1894, Abbott became surgeon-in-charge at the Provident Hospital and Training School in Chicago, the first such institution for African Americans in the United States.

In 1901, on the occasion of the death of Queen Victoria, Abbott composed a poem — "Neath the Crown and Maple Leaf (Afro-Canadian Elegy)," for *The Colored American Magazine.* In this poem, Abbott expressed his pride in his dual — his Afro-Canadian — heritage.

In 1906, Anderson Abbott condemned the creation of a new segregated all-black school in Saint John. This integrationist activism would later lead Abbott to support the Niagara movement of W. E. B. DuBois in opposition to Booker T. Washington's manual training school. Abbott also embarked upon writing a general history of Afro-Canadians which sought to encourage racial pride.

Anderson Abbott died in Toronto in 1913.

• *Martinique:* Aime Cesaire, a noted author, was born in Martinique.

Aime Cesaire was educated at the Lycee de Fort-de-France in Martinique, and at the Lycee Louis le Grand, Ecole Normale Superieure and Faculte des Lettres Superieure in Paris.

While in Paris, Cesaire and his fellow student Leopold Senghor founded the literary movement which became known as "Negritude."

Cesaire continued his education at the Sorbonne and remained in France as Martinique's representative to the French parliament.

Cesaire returned to be a faculty member of the Lycee de Fort-de-France from 1940 to 1945.

Cesaire was a Communist member of the two French constitutional assemblies of 1945 and 1946. Subsequently, Cesaire was Communist deputy from Martinique between 1946 and 1956. Breaking with the Communists over the Soviet invasion of Hungary in November 1956, Cesaire continued to be a deputy but as an independent.

Subsequent to 1974, Cesaire was aligned with the Socialist Party in the French National Assembly.

After 1956, Cesaire was president of the Parti Progressive Martiniquais, a party he founded which advocated "autonomy" for Martinique. He was mayor of Fort-de-France from 1945 to 1983, and, although re-elected in 1983, his election was invalidated by the Tribunal Administratif. Thereafter, Cesaire was president of the Regional Council of Martinique.

Cesaire was the leading intellectual of the French Antilles. A well-known poet, he was also author of several historical studies and a leading figure in the Francophone "Negritude" movement.

In 1939, Cesaire published a prose work which rejected French culture for Martinique. The work was entitled *Cahier d'un Retour au Pays Natal.*

In 1946, Cesaire published *Les Armes Miraculeuses,* his first collection of poems. *Les Armes Miraculeuses* dealt with the tropical beauty of Martinique.

Cesaire's subsequent collections of verse, *Soleil Cou Coupe* and *Ferrements* were published in 1948 and 1959 respectively.

Cesaire's first play, *La Tragedie du Roi Christophe*, was completed in 1963. *La Tragedie du Roi Christophe* was about Henri Christophe, the 19th century dictator of Haiti.

EUROPE

• William Scott exhibited his art work at the Paris Salon (1912–1913).

ASIA

• In Beijing, China, Ch'en Yu-jen (Eugene Chen) *(see 1878)* became the editor of the English language journal, *The Peking Gazette.*

AFRICA

• *North Africa, Egypt and Sudan:* Maulai al-Mahdi, the Khalifa of the Spanish Protectorate of Morocco, arrived in Tetuan (April).

• Al-Raisuni led the opposition to the Spanish Protectorate.

• A Legislative Assembly, which superseded previous bodies, was created in Egypt with wider powers.

• al-Zubayr Rahma Mansur (1830–1913), an Arab slave trader who built his own principality in southeastern Sudan, died.

Al-Zubayr was raised and educated in northern Sudan. He first entered southern Sudan to trade and to raid for slaves in 1856. By the mid–1860s, al-Zubayr was the virtual master of the

Bahr al-Ghazal province. Al-Zubayr controlled Bahr al-Ghazal through military conquests and an elaborate system of alliances with local chiefs.

In the early 1870s, al-Zubayr's efforts to expand his activities to the south were frustrated by the fierce resistance of the Zande chief Yambio and the increased efforts of the Egyptian-Sudanese administration to curb slaving. Afterwards, al-Zubayr maintained an uneasy alliance with the Egyptians in a drive to conquer Darfur to the north.

In 1875, while visiting Cairo to complain to the Khedive Ismail about Sudanese officials al-Zubayr was forcibly detained. Al-Zubayr nevertheless received the title "Pasha" and served the Egyptian government in various capacities.

In 1899, al-Zubayr returned to Sudan to become a progressive farmer and a government adviser under the new Anglo-Egyptian administration.

- *Western Africa:* Dissension and local civil war occurred concerning the building of a Friday Mosque at Porto Novo.
- There was an additional uprising at Abeokuta.
- Indirect rule was established in the Gambia.
- In 1913, Galandou Diouf *(see 1875)* enlisted the support of the Young Senegalese to engineer the 1914 election of Blaise Diagne *(see 1872)* as the first black African to be sent to the French Chamber of Deputies. Subsequently, Diouf became the mayor of Rufisque.
- William Harris expanded his ministry into the Ivory Coast and Ghana.

In 1913, William Harris, the Christian evangelist, entered (walked into) the Ivory Coast. In the Ivory Coast, his following grew rapidly due, in no small measure, to Harris' growing reputation as a faith healer.

Harris did not stop in the Ivory Coast. He continued his walk. He walked all the way to the Gold Coast (Ghana) before returning to the Ivory Coast.

Back in the Ivory Coast, Harris attracted over 100,000 followers.

- The foundations for the National Congress of British West Africa were laid.

An increasingly vocal advocate of African control of governmental structure, Casely Hayford and colleagues from other British West African colonies planned, in 1913, a National Congress of British West Africa. The National Congress of British West Africa was organized to press for African political representation and equality in employment.

World War I delayed the formation of the National Congress of British West Africa. It would not begin functional operations until 1920.

- Sourou Apithy, an independence leader and future president of Benin, was born.

Sourou Migan Apithy was born in Porto Novo. He was educated in mission schools before going to France where he received a degree in political science and economics and worked as an accountant.

In 1945, Apithy was Dahomey's representative to the French constituent assembly to decide the shape of the Fourth Republic. The next year, he was elected to France's Chamber of Deputies where he served until 1958.

In 1946, Apithy co-founded the inter-territorial party, the RDA. However, because of the RDA's communist affiliations, Apithy separated from the group in 1948.

The 1957 elections were held to decide the make-up of Dahomey's first territorial assembly. Apithy's party won, but his margin was so narrow that he formed a coalition, becoming president of the executive council (prime minister) in 1958.

At the end of 1958, Apithy contemplated attending a conference to set up the Mali Federation. The conference was the idea of the Senegalese politician Leopold Sedar Senghor. However, pressure from the Ivory Coast leader Felix Houphouet-Boigny on the other coalition members forced Apithy to pull out of the conference at the last moment. The coalition subsequently broke up.

After the elections of 1959, Hubert Maga, an ally of Houphouet-Boigny, formed a new government. Popular unrest in 1960 caused a government shake-up and Sourou Apithy became vice-president.

Maga was overthrown in 1963. When civilian rule was restored, Apithy became president and head of state with Justin Ahomadegbe Tometin as vice-president.

In 1965, Apithy himself was forced into exile. A period of political chaos followed. Attempts were made to impose order by instituting a rotating presidency to be shared by Apithy, Maga and Ahomadegbe. However, before Apithy could take his turn as president, another coup occurred and returned Benin to military rule. The three presidents were arrested and detained until 1981.

• Nicolas Grunitzky (1913–1969), the first prime minister of Togo, was born.

Nicolas Grunitzky was born in central Togoland to an important African family with Polish blood. He studied in France, where he became an engineer.

In 1937, Grunitzky returned to Togoland. During World War II, Grunitzky supported Charles de Gaulle against the Vichy government in France.

In 1946, Grunitzky formed a pro–French political party to counter that of his anti-colonialist brother-in-law, Sylvanus Olympio. Grunitzky's party was heavily defeated in the elections for the territorial assembly.

Over the next few years, the French administration became adamantly opposed to Olympio. French opposition of Olympio helped Grunitzky to win election to the French Chamber of Deputies in 1951.

In the 1955 elections to the territorial assembly, Olympio's party boycotted the contest to protest French oppression, and Grunitzky's party won, giving him control of the assembly.

A former German colony, French Togoland was administered as a United Nations trust territory. Because of its special status, Togolese nationalists were able to force the French into making Togo a republic with limited autonomy. The French hoped to forestall total independence which they feared would set a precedent for Francophonic Africa.

In 1956, Grunitzky was made prime minister, but, lacking local support, was highly unpopular. Sylvanus Olympio pressured the United Nations to maintain Togoland's trust territory status until new elections were held.

In 1958, Grunitzky was swept out of office. He was returned to power after Olympio's assassination in a 1963 military coup, but again he found himself highly unpopular.

In 1967, Etienne Eyandema, the man who overthrew Olympio, ousted Grunitzky on the fourth anniversary of Olympio's death. Thereafter, Grunitzky went into exile in the Ivory Coast.

Grunitzky died in the Ivory Coast in 1969 following an automobile accident.

• *Central Africa:* An Anglo-German agreement was reached concerning the frontier of Nigeria and Cameroon.
• Bakongo rose up against the Portuguese. Military activities centered around Vila Luso.
• A hospital was founded at Lambarene by Albert Schweitzer.

• The Methodist Mission of South Congo (MMSC) began work in the Belgian Congo.
• The Portuguese went to war with the Congo. The war would last until 1918.
• *Eastern Africa:* Zanzibar was incorporated into the British East African Protectorate with control transferred from the Foreign to Colonial Office (July 1).
• Ras Mikael became the effective ruler of Ethiopia.
• Cotton became Uganda's principal industry, providing over 50% of exports, fifty-seven markets were officially gazetted.
• The Buganda agreement was negotiated.
• 5,536 Europeans were reported in German East Africa of whom 4,107 Germans.
• After many years of debility, Menelik, the Emperor of Ethiopia, died (December 12).

Menelik II (Menilek) (1844–1913) was the King of Shoa from 1865 to 1889 and the Emperor of Ethiopia from 1889 to 1913.

Menelik was born Sahle Mariam in 1844. He was the heir to the throne of the Shoa (Shewa) kingdom of central Ethiopia. Up until 1855, Shoa was virtually an independent kingdom. However, in 1855, Theodore II, proclaimed himself to be the Emperor of Ethiopia and proceeded to re-assert imperial control over central Ethiopia. Theodore occupied Shoa and made Menelik a prisoner. Menelik spent the next decade under Theodore's paternal tutelage.

In 1865, Menelik escaped from Theodore and returned to Shoa. In Shoa, Menelik was proclaimed *negus*— king — of Shoa.

The collapse of Theodore's regime in 1868 was followed by a civil war which allowed Menelik to build Shoa into one of the strongest powers in Ethiopia.

In 1872, Yohannes IV, a new emperor from the northeast, seized power. However, Menelik maintained an uneasy autonomy in the south. Menelik expanded his control over the Galla-speaking regions and dealt with Europeans as an independent ruler, inviting foreign technical assistance and importing large numbers of modern firearms.

In 1878, Menelik was persuaded to acknowledge Yohannes as the Emperor of Ethiopia. But this acknowledgment was not an overwhelming vote of approval. Indeed, Menelik's own strong position was too solid for Menelik to completely subordinate himself to Yohannes.

Around this same time, European imperialists began to encroach upon Ethiopia from all sides. The Italians saw Menelik as an ally against

Yohannes, while the French saw him as a potential ally against the British who were, at the time, advancing into southern Sudan. During the 1880s, continued arms imports gave Menelik the best-equipped African army in northeast Africa.

By 1887, Menelik occupied the predominantly Muslim province of Harar. In Harar, Menelik appointed his cousin, Makonnen, as the governor of the province. Makonnen was the father of the future emperor, Haile Selassie.

The Italians occupied the Eritrean coast in 1885 and began to push inland. When Yohannes went to war with them two years later, Menelik stayed neutral. In 1889, Yohannes died while fighting the Mahdists in the west. The death of Yohannes created a power vacuum which Menelik quickly sought to fill.

Menelik had himself proclaimed the *negus nagast* — the emperor. Menelik then signed a friendship pact with the Italians known as the Treaty of Ucciali (Wichale).

The Treaty of Ucciali was a controversial document because it existed in two radically different versions. One version was in Amharic while the other was in Italian. According to the Amharic version, Italy merely offered its services as Ethiopia's diplomatic intermediary with the outside world. However, pursuant to the Italian version, Menelik recognized an Italian protectorate over Ethiopia. The irreconcilable difference between the two documents led to an Italian invasion of Ethiopia in 1895.

After some initial setbacks, Menelik, who was now supported for the first time by most Ethiopians, launched a counter-offensive in 1896. This counter-offensive resulted in a major Ethiopian victory at Adowa. As a result of this crushing Ethiopian victory, the Italians were compelled to execute a new treaty — a treaty which acknowledged Ethiopia's complete independence.

Despite his overwhelming victory over the Italians, Menelik did not pursue the eviction of the Italians from Eritrea. Instead, he turned his attention to Kenya and Somalia.

However, Menelik's defeat of the Italians did serve to enhance Ethiopia's international reputation and prompted an influx of new foreign diplomats. By 1906, an external agreement between France, Britain, and Italy gave international recognition to the independence of Ethiopia.

In addition to preserving his country's independence, Menelik laid the basis for Ethiopia's modern administration and development. In 1886, Menelik established the present capital of Ethiopia — Addis Adaba — and began to build modern bridges and roads. Menelik continued Theodore's work of replacing hereditary territorial rulers with trained, appointed governors.

During the 1890s, Menelik reformed the tax system, created a national currency, established a postal system, and initiated a railway line. After 1900, Menelik built telegraph and telephone lines and founded a national bank (1905). Menelik also promoted secular education, hospitals, and a government press.

Throughout his career, Menelik maintained tight personal control over all government activities. However, in 1906 , Menelik's health declined, so he appointed a cabinet to administer for him. Within two years, Menelik was virtually paralyzed. As Menelik lost control of his health, court factions began to vie for control of the succession. Having no surviving sons to succeed him, Menelik designated a grandson, Iyasu V, to succeed him (1908), while his wife Taitu worked to nominate her own candidate.

After many years of debility, Menelik died in 1913.

From an historical perspective, Menelik II is generally acknowledged as one of the greatest rulers of Ethiopia. Menelik is credited with not only preserving Ethiopia from European conquest but also with expanding Ethiopia to its modern extent. Menelik also is credited with laying the foundation for the modern administration and development of Ethiopia.

- *Southern Africa:* Troops fired on striking miners at Kleinfontein (July).
- The Cape Federation of Trades was founded.
- The Natives Land Act was enacted.

Considered a lucid orator, Solomon Plaatje, a leader of the organization that would become the ANC, became part of a delegation to London to oppose the new South African land bill.

- Gandhi was arrested after a demonstration. *See 1869.*

Mahatma Gandhi's South African civil rights campaign reached a climax in 1913 when he was imprisoned. While in prison, he met with South Africa's deputy prime minister, Jan Smuts and succeeded in obtaining some legal concessions for the Indians of South Africa. Shortly afterwards, Gandhi departed for India where he would begin his series of nationalistic campaigns which would led to India becoming an independent nation in 1947.

- The Salvation Trust Limited was formed.
- There was a famine in Mozambique.

• The Nguru migrated into Shire Highlands.

• Dinuzulu (c.1869–1913), the king of the Zulu during the dismemberment of the Zulu nation, died.

Dinuzulu became king when he was fifteen years old in 1884. By the time Dinuzulu became king, Zululand had recently been partitioned into sections of varying degrees of independence, and Dinuzulu's father, Cetewayo, had just been crushed by Zibhebhu, the leader of a rival faction of the Zulu royal family.

Dinuzulu was quickly installed as king by loyalists in his father's Usuthu faction. Dinuzulu then obtained military assistance from Afrikaners in the Transvaal Republic to drive Zibhebhu's party out of the country.

Unfortunately for Dinuzulu, the Afrikaners, as allies, proved to be far worse enemies than Zibhebhu. The Afrikaners proceeded to carve the "New Republic" out of northwestern Zululand as compensation for their services. The British government intervened, but the negotiated settlement between the British and the Afrikaners, ignored Zulu concerns.

By 1888, the New Republic territory was absorbed into the far larger Transvaal Republic, and the British had annexed Zululand. The British divided Zululand into magisterial districts with Dinuzulu's reluctant assent. However, Dinuzulu largely ignored the new magistrates because their authority undermined that of his own officials.

Dinuzulu repulsed a punitive force led by the family enemy, Zibhebhu. For this action and other non-compliance, Dinuzulu was tried by the British government. Dinuzulu was convicted of treason and banished to St. Helena Island with many of his councillors.

In 1895, Dinuzulu received a free pardon. However, the efforts of the Natal colonial government to annex Zululand delayed his return home until 1898.

Upon his return, Dinuzulu found Zululand (which by then had become a part of Natal), little more than a subdivision within the Natal government. As for his position, Dinuzulu had been relegated to the status equivalent to that of a local headman or a government "induna."

"Induna" is a widespread southern African term usually referring to a councillor or military commander. The organization of the Zulu, Ndebele, Ngoni and other Ngoni-derived states' armies into regiments gave rise to the misleading European assertion that *induna* translates as "general." However, even in the most militaristic states the title *induna* was freely applied to all levels of civil and military officials.

Dinuzulu suffered greatly from his reduced status. The European government suspected him of using his hereditary title to foment trouble. At the same time, many Zulu regarded him as a government dupe. Dinuzulu soon became known (perhaps unjustly so) as a shiftless drunk.

In 1906, many Zulu rebelled under the leadership of a minor chief, Bambatha. Dinuzulu had no part in the largely spontaneous affair. Nevertheless, he was once again charged with treason by the Natal government.

After a long trial, Dinuzulu was exonerated of all charges except that of having tacitly supported the rebels. For this Dinuzulu was fined, deposed and again banished — this time to the Transvaal.

Dinuzulu died a broken man in the Transvaal in 1913.

RELATED HISTORICAL EVENTS

• *Europe:* An Anglo-German agreement was reached concerning the Portuguese colonies (November 20).

• There was an Arab Congress meeting in Paris.

• *Africa:* John Gordon Sprigg (1830–1913), the man who for four times served as prime minister of the Cape Colony, died.

John Sprigg began his career as a parliamentary reporter in England. He migrated to South Africa in 1858.

Sprigg was elected to the Cape parliament for the first time in 1869.

Sprigg initially supported the Cape's first prime minister, John Molteno, but broke with him in 1875 over the issue of South African federation. Sprigg supported South African federation.

In 1878, Governor Frere dismissed Molteno's ministry and named Sprigg to form a new government.

Sprigg's ministry was soon confirmed in a general election. Afterwards, Sprigg led the move to incorporate the diamondfields (Griqualand West) into the Colony.

Sprigg's government fell when Sprigg refused to support Cecil Rhodes' group in its bid to extend a railway through the diamond fields and when his government's attempt to disarm the Sotho led to the financially disastrous "Gun War."

During Sprigg's next ministry, the Cape

parliament, in 1887, passed a franchise qualification bill which effectively denied the vote to
all but a few Africans. In 1889, Sprigg worked to
extend a railway link to the Orange Free State,
with which the Colony formed a customs union.

In 1890, Sprigg's government fell over the
issue of railway connections with Natal and the
Transvaal. Sprigg served as treasurer in Rhodes'
ministry in 1893 and returned to power in 1896
after Leander Jameson's raid on the Transvaal
discredited Rhodes' government.

Two years later, Sprigg resigned from office
after Governor Milner dissolved the parliament
in the heat of factional crisis. The peak of
Sprigg's career came during his last ministry
when he successfully resisted Milner's attempt
to suspend the Cape's constitution as a prelude
to unifying South Africa.

  • Garnet Wolseley (1833–1913), a British
  military officer who served in the Asante War
  of 1873 and the Zulu War of 1879, died.

After considerable military service in European and Asian wars, Garnet Wolseley was given
command of an expedition against the Asante
kingdom. Wolseley occupied the Asante capital
at Kumasi and brought the king Kofi Karikari
to terms. Afterwards, Wolseley served briefly as
administrator and commander in Natal.

Wolseley became the first British administrator in Cyprus in 1878. However, he was recalled
to South Africa by Disraeli after the initial
British disaster in the Zulu War at Isandhlwana
in January of 1879.

Disraeli named Wolseley "High Commissioner for South-East Africa" and gave him
broad civil and military powers over Natal, the
Transvaal and neighboring African territories.

Wolseley arrived in Zululand shortly after
Lord Chelmsford had occupied the Zulu capital,
Ulundi, in July 1879. He was left only with the
task of capturing the Zulu king Cetewayo,
whom he deposed and sent to Cape Town as a
prisoner.

In lieu of annexing Zululand for the British,
Wolseley partitioned it into thirteen territories,
and named an independent chief for each territory. This partition would have an important
bearing on Zulu politics for the next thirty years.

From Zululand, Wolseley went to the Transvaal. In the Transvaal, Wolseley conquered the
Pedi chief Sekhukhune, one of the last Transvaal
holdouts against European rule.

Despite his success at subduing the African
chiefs, Wolseley could not appease the Transvaal Afrikaners who had been brought under

British rule in 1877. Afrikaner grievances led to
an anti–British revolt in 1881—a year after
Wolseley left the Transvaal.

In 1882, Wolseley suppressed the revolt of
Arabi Bey in Egypt. He returned to the Nile two
years later to try to relieve General Gordon,
whom the Mahdists had besieged at Khartoum.
However, he arrived there a few days after Khartoum fell.

Wolseley wrote books on history and held
other commands until 1895, when he became
commander-in-chief of the entire British army.
By then his judgment and mental abilities were
faltering. He was ousted soon after the outbreak
of the South African War, in which the British
experienced early setbacks.

---------- 1914 ----------

THE UNITED STATES

  • Marcus Garvey formed the United Negro
  Improvement Association (UNIA) which
  aimed to unite people of African descent
  under the motto "One God! One Aim! One
  Destiny!" UNIA's divisions and subsidiaries
  later included the African Legion and the
  Black Cross Nurses.

It was while in Jamaica, in 1911, that Garvey
founded the Universal Negro Improvement and
Conservation Association and African Communities League — the Universal Negro Improvement Association (also known as "UNIA"). The
purpose of the UNIA was to promote black
unity through racial pride and to build a strong
black nation in Africa.

While confined to Jamaica, the Universal
Negro Improvement Association would prove
to be an unsuccessful venture. However, once
Garvey moved his operations to the United
States, prospects began to change.

  • In 1914, a dispute developed between
  Oswald Garrison Villard and W. E. B. Du Bois
  over Du Bois' handling of the *Crisis.* In January, Villard resigned as chairman of the executive board and became chairman of the
  finance committee and treasurer. Joel Spingarn succeeded Villard as chairman.

  • By 1914, Monroe Trotter had left the
  NAACP and attacked both Washington and
  Du Bois.

  • Two of Booker T. Washington's most
  loyal supporters, S. John Williams of Chicago
  and John Q. Adams of St. Paul, Minnesota,

became officers in their local NAACP branches.

• A delegation headed by Monroe Trotter obtained an audience with the President to protest segregation. The conference ended when Wilson ordered Trotter out of his office for what Wilson deemed to be insulting language.

• The Spingarn Medal awards were instituted by Joel E. Spingarn, Chairperson of the Board of Directors of the NAACP, to call to the attention of the American people the existence of distinguished merit and achievement among African Americans.

• Led by Alfred Sam, hundreds of African Americans from Oklahoma set sail for Africa.

• Oscar Over, a resident of Allensworth, California, became a justice of the peace.

• *Organizations:* The NAACP reached a membership of over 6,000 with 50 branches. Subscriptions to *Crisis* magazine, the official publication of the NAACP, reached 31,540.

• African American students founded Phi Beta Sigma fraternity and incorporated Omega Psi Phi fraternity at Howard University.

• *Notable Births*: William Ellisworth Artis, a sculptor, was born in North Carolina.

• Romare Bearden, an artist, was born.

Romare Bearden was born in Charlotte, North Carolina. He studied under George Grosz at the Art Students League in New York City. Bearden used various styles including social realism and abstraction. In the 1960s, Bearden became known for his photo montages. *Street Corner, He is Arisen* and *The Burial* are among his most famous works.

• Jazzman Herman "Sonny" Blount, who became known as "Sun Ra," was born in Birmingham, Alabama (May 22).

• Kenneth B. Clark, a psychologist, was born.

Kenneth B. Clark was born in the Panama Canal Zone. He received his doctorate from Columbia University and became one of the foremost psychologists in the United States.

Clark prepared much of the research used in the famous school desegregation cases argued before the United States Supreme Court.

Clark's books include: *Desegregation, An Appraisal of the Evidence; Prejudice and Your Child;* and *Dark Ghetto.* In 1961, Clark received the Spingarn Award.

• Ernest Crichlow, a painter and illustrator, was born in Brooklyn.

• Owen Dodson, an author, was born.

Owen Dodson was born in Brooklyn, New York. Dodson was educated at Bates College and Yale University. Two of his plays were produced at Yale, *Divine Comedy* and *Garden of Time* (1939).

Dodson taught drama at Spelman College in Atlanta and was on the faculty of Howard University. Dodson's group, the Howard Players, often toured such locales as Norway, Denmark, Sweden and Germany.

Dodson's plays have also been performed off–Broadway. In 1946, *Powerful Long Ladder,* a book of poems, was published, and in 1951, his first novel, *Boy at the Window,* was issued.

In 1962, *The Summer Fire,* a short story, won a Paris Review Prize. In 1964, *A Bent House,* Dodson's second novel, and *Cages,* Dodson's second book of poems, were finished while Dodson was on a Guggenheim Fellowship.

• William Clarence "Billy" Eckstine, a singer, was born in Pittsburgh, Pennsylvania (July 8).

• Ralph Ellison, an author, was born.

In 1914, the author of *Invisible Man*, was born. Ralph Ellison was born in Oklahoma City, Oklahoma, a few years after the territory became a state.

As a young man, Ellison came to idolize the jazz musicians of the day. He was impressed by their improvisational art which expressed their individualism within the collective of a jazz band.

Ellison attended Tuskegee Institute from 1933 through 1936. He matriculated with the intention of studying classical music with the notion of pursuing music as a career. But he did not achieve that goal.

A need to earn a living and the chance to study sculpture soon took Ellison to New York City. In 1937, Ellison met renowned African American writer, Richard Wright. It was Wright who asked Ellison to write a review and later some fiction for the *New Challenge* magazine. It was also probably Wright who introduced Ellison to the politics of the left. Ellison began writing in earnest in 1939 and worked on WPA projects. Ellison also edited *The Negro Quarterly* in 1942.

Beginning in 1952, Ellison held teaching and writer-in-residence positions at Bard, Rutgers, University of Chicago and Yale.

Ellison's *Invisible Man*, which was published

in 1952, was Ellison's major success. *Invisible Man* is considered by many to be the most ambitious novel that was ever written by an African American. Although the background of the novel was an African American one, Ellison was primarily concerned with the spiritual condition of modern urbanized man.

In *Invisible Man* the nameless protagonist at first has a rather unrealistic trust in the motives of others. The protagonist was dismissed from a Southern black college for disillusioning one of the founders by showing him the world in which African Americans really live.

In New York City, the "Invisible Man" distinguishes himself by rousing a crowd at an eviction and is picked by Communist leaders for a political role. Ultimately, the protagonist realizes that the Communists are merely using him as a symbol of the African American; as a person, he is invisible to them just as he is to other European Americans. During a surrealistic Harlem riot, the "Invisible Man" realizes that he must contend with people of both races.

By beginning his novel with a prologue inscribed in the language of his protagonist, Ellison provides his readers a fiction derived from the classic description of double consciousness by W. E. B. DuBois. "It is a peculiar sensation," DuBois wrote in *The Souls of Black Folk*, "this sense of always looking at one's self through the eyes of others. ... One ever feels his twoness, — an American, a Negro, two thoughts, two unreconciled strivings; two warring ideals in one dark body. ..."

The "Invisible Man" comes to experience DuBois' observation on a very profound level. He experiences the painful contradictions of African American life as he seeks the fulfillment promised by the American Creed. However, he discovers that the universality of the American Creed is only a pretense founded on the willed blindness of European Americans to the visibility of African Americans. To a certain extent, the American Creed works only because it applies to all except for the invisible others — the African Americans.

Invisible Man won the 1953 National Book Award. In the *New World Journal* poll of 100 United States writers, *Invisible Man* was selected as the most important American novel since World War II.

In 1964, Ellison's *Shadow and Act,* a miscellaneous collection of short articles and essays was published. This collection would be followed some twenty-two years later with *Going to the Territory.*

Ralph Waldo Ellison died on April 16, 1994.

• Jean Blackwell Hutson was born in Florida (September 4). Hutson would serve as curator of the Schomburg Center for Research in Black Culture in New York City.

• Joe Louis (Barrow), future heavyweight champion of the world, was born in Lexington, Alabama (May 13). Louis would win some 68 bouts, 54 by knockout.

• John "Sonny Boy" Williamson, a blues harmonica player, was born (March 30).

• *Notable Deaths:* 55 African Americans were lynched in 1914.

• James Lewis (1832–1914), the Civil War hero of the Battle of Port Hudson, died.

When the Union troops occupied New Orleans in 1862, James Lewis (1832–1914) abandoned the Confederate ship on which he was serving as a steward, raised two companies of African American soldiers, and led the First Regiment of the Louisiana National Guard during the battle of Port Hudson.

After the Civil War, Lewis became active in Louisiana politics and received a number of federal appointments.

• *Publications:* Fenton Johnson published a book of poetry entitled *A Little Dreaming.*

• Timothy Thomas Fortune established the *Washington Sun.*

• *Scholastic Achievements:* In Baton Rouge, Louisiana, a group of 47 students and 9 faculty members opened a new campus of Southern University.

• *The Performing Arts:* The Lafayette Stock Company was formed in Harlem for the promotion of African American theater.

• *Movies:* Oscar Michaeux founded Oscar Michaeux Pictures with studios in New York City. Michaeux produced *The Wages of Sin* and *The Broken Violin*, both of which featured all African American casts. Michaeux was the first African American film producer and his film company was the first all African American company. Michaeux's films were designed for an African American audience and were shown primarily in the inner city and Southern black communities.

• *Darktown Jubilee,* the first movie to star an African American — the talented vaudevillian, Bert Williams — was met with hisses, catcalls, boycotts, and caused a race riot in Brooklyn, New York. Williams would never again appear in a film. *Darktown Jubilee* was one of the first movies to use an African

American actor rather than European American actors in blackface.

• The fourth movie version of *Uncle Tom's Cabin* was directed by William Daley for World Pictures. *Uncle Tom's Cabin* featured Sam Lucas in the title role. Lucas was the first African American actor to play Uncle Tom. Several of the other minor characters were also played by African Americans. This movie set the trend to use African Americans rather than European Americans wearing burnt cork to play African Americans or Africans in motion pictures.

• *Coon Town Suffragettes*, a Sigmund Lubin film, satirized the feminist movement by portraying a shantytown setting with African American washer women trying to keep their fun-loving husbands out of saloons.

• *Music:* W. C. Handy's most famous song *The St. Louis Blues* was composed in 1914 with the original title of *The Saint Louis Woman*.

• *The Black Church:* Around 1914, Father Divine (a.k.a. George Baker) proclaimed himself God as he established his movement. Divine was tried on a charge of insanity in a Valdosta, Georgia, court on February 27, 1914, on the grounds that his claim to be God was clearly aberrant. Father Divine was convicted but not incarcerated.

Black Enterprise

According to the National Negro Business League, there were 40,000 African American businesses in the United States. At the League's convention, Boley, an all-black town in Oklahoma, pointed to its self-government and its African American elected officials. Boley also had a $150,000 high school, cement sidewalks and attractive residences. Boley had a Masonic Temple, an electric light plant and waterworks, and some 82 business concerns. Among the business concerns were a bank, three cotton gins and a telephone system. Boley, Oklahoma, was touted as an example of what African American self-help and racial cooperation could accomplish.

• *Sports:* Jack Johnson won a 20-round referee's decision over Frank Moran at the Velodrome d'Hiver in Paris to retain his heavyweight title (June 27).

• Howard B. Drew broke the world's record in the 100 yard dash and the 220 yard dash.

THE AMERICAS

• *Canada:* By 1914, Oklahoma African

Americans shifted their focus from Canada to the northern cities of the United States as areas where they might best pursue their dreams.

• *Jamaica:* Marcus Garvey moved the United Negro Improvement Association (UNIA) to New York. The UNIA aimed to unite people of African descent under the motto "One God! One Aim! One Destiny!" UNIA's divisions and subsidiaries later included the African Legion and the Black Cross Nurses.

It was while in Jamaica, in 1911, that Garvey founded the Universal Negro Improvement and Conservation Association and African Communities League — the Universal Negro Improvement Association (also known as "UNIA"). The purpose of the UNIA was to promote black unity through racial pride and to build a strong black nation in Africa.

While confined to Jamaica, the Universal Negro Improvement Association would prove to be an unsuccessful venture. However, once Garvey moved his operations to the United States, prospects began to change.

AFRICA

• *North Africa, Egypt and Sudan:* Sir Henry McMahon became the British High Commissioner in Egypt.

• The Egyptian Legislative Assembly prorogued — adjourned — never to meet again (October 18).

• Martial law was proclaimed in Egypt (November 2), and, on December 17, a British Protectorate was instituted for Egypt.

• Abbas II was deposed (December 18). Hussein Kemal was installed as Khedive.

• The *Code de l'Indigenat* of Algeria was modified.

• Motor vehicles were first used in the Sahara.

• *Western Africa:* Northern and Southern Nigeria were amalgamated (January 1). The Executive and Legislative Councils for Nigeria were established.

• There was an uprising north of Porto Novo (January).

• There was an uprising in Niger (July). The civil unrest would last until 1916.

• Britain and France occupied Togo (August 8) causing the Germans to capitulate (August 26).

• The Convention of Lome provided for the division of Togoland into British and French sectors (September 2).

• Egbaland was incorporated into the Protectorate of Nigeria (September 16).

• Blaise Diagne became the first black Senegalese to be elected to the Chamber of Deputies.

In 1914, Francois Carpot was defeated by Blaise Diagne. Francois Carpot was born in St. Louis, Senegal, in 1862. He was a member of the upwardly mobile *metis* merchants who were successfully challenging the Bordeaux traders for control of Senegalese politics. However, both the *metis* merchants and the Bordeaux traders were entirely French oriented. As a result, Carpot was never considered a representative of African — of black Senegalese — interests.

In 1914, Ahmadu Bamba, the founder of the Muridiyya Islamic brotherhood, supported Blaise Diagne, a radical politician. With Ahmadu's support Diagne was elected to the French Chamber of Deputies.

With his victory over Francois Carpot, Blaise Diagne became the first "black" African to sit in the French Chamber of Deputies, and it was Blaise Diagne who set a new course in Senegalese politics.

Diagne used his new position to institute a number of reforms in Senegal. One of Diagne's reforms was to buttress the right of French citizenship shared by inhabitants of the four communes of Senegal (Dakar, Saint Louis, Goree, and Rufisque).

• All Nigerian forces were combined into the Nigerian Regiment of the West African Frontier Force.

• The French occupied Tibesti.

• A railway from Port Harcourt to Udi was completed.

• The Gold Coast Regiment served in the conquest of Togo and Cameroon.

• Sir F. D. Lugard became the Governor General of Nigeria.

• Kofi Busia (1914–1978), a Ghanaian nationalist leader and a former Ghanaian prime minister, was born.

Kofi Busia was born to an Ashanti royal family. He attended Oxford and returned to Ghana (then called the Gold Coast) to become one of the first African assistant district commissioners in 1942.

In 1946, Busia returned to Oxford to earn a doctorate in sociology. Three years later, Busia became a lecturer at the University College of the Gold Coast, where he wrote an important study of Ashanti rulers.

In 1951, Busia was elected to the legislative council from Ashanti. From that point onwards, Busia was in the forefront of the organization of a number of parties dedicated to opposing Kwame Nkrumah.

As Ghana moved towards self-government, Busia was elected to the national legislature in 1954. In that year, Kwame Nkrumah's party won most of the seats, and Nkrumah was made chief minister. Busia then went to London to argue for the postponement of Ghana's independence.

When independence came in 1957, Nkrumah instituted repressive measures against his opponents. This repression caused Busia to go into a self-imposed exile in 1959.

Nkrumah was deposed in 1966 by the military. The military ruled Ghana until 1969 when Busia was elected prime minister.

Once elected prime minister, Busia began exhibiting many of the same dictatorial qualities for which he had so virulently condemned Nkrumah. Ghana also faced an economic crisis. The crisis and Busia's repression led to a military coup in 1972.

After the coup, Busia went to England. He remained there until his death in 1978.

• Ovonramwen, the ruler of the Edo kingdom of Benin at the time of the British conquest of 1897, died.

When Ovonramwen's father, Adolo, died in 1888, Ovonramwen secured his position as the new oba — king — by killing off leaders of rival factions, destroying whole villages in some cases.

Ovonramwen also strengthened himself by expanding the nobility in order to reward friends, and to placate some of his enemies. Nevertheless, the power of the many Benin palace chiefs remained sufficiently great that Ovonramwen could not entirely subdue opposing factions.

The kingdom which Ovonramwen inherited had recently been reduced in size because of Nupe and British encroachment. The British, who were quickly bringing the Niger delta states under their control, presented the major threat. When Ovonramwen asserted his authority by placing restrictions on trade to the coast, the British attempted to enforce a protectorate over Benin.

A British mission to Benin city in 1892 secured the desired treaty, although it is unlikely that Ovonramwen was aware of its provisions for the surrender of Benin's sovereignty. Ovonramwen ignored the treaty's restrictions as well as British demands that he honor it.

The British came to see Benin as a challenge —

the last important state in southern Nigeria to elude British control. Ovonramwen's extensive use of human sacrifice in Benin rituals gave them an added excuse for intervention.

In January 1897, J. R. Phillips, acting consul-general of the Niger Coast Protectorate, set out for Benin to warn Ovonramwen that he was assembling a military expedition to depose him if necessary. Phillip's party was massacred on the orders of a group of palace chiefs who opposed the oba.

In response, the British quickly assembled 1500 troops and launched an assault. The British overcame heavy resistance before reaching Benin City, which Ovonramwen abandoned.

Resistance continued until August when Ovonramwen surrendered. Although the British consul-general, Ralph Moor, at first offered to let Ovonramwen remain as chief of Benin City, the offer was withdrawn largely due to a misunderstanding between the two men. Subsequently, Ovonramwen was deported to Calabar.

After Ovonramwen's death in 1914, his son, Eweka II, was restored to office by the British.

• *Central Africa:* German troops from East Africa penetrated the Congo in spite of the Belgian declaration of neutrality (August).
• Chief Rudolf Manga Bell was hanged in Douala (August 8).

Rudolf (Rudolph) Douala Manga Bell (1873–1914) was the son of the chief of the town of Douala. He was educated at the gymnasium in Ulm, Germany. He returned to Cameroon in 1896 and succeeded his father in 1908.

In 1910, Bell came into conflict with the German administration when the Germans moved to seize some land for colonial residential quarters. The Germans appropriation of this land was in violation of the 1884 treaty between the Germans and the Cameroon people.

In 1913, Bell was divested of his title. The following year, at the beginning of the First World War, the Germans accused Bell of fomenting a rebellion in the interior and of trying to enter into contact with the neighboring French, in collaboration with Martin-Paul Samba.

Bell was hanged at Douala on the same day that Samba faced a firing squad at Ebolowa.

• The Cameroon campaigned against the Germans. On August 29, Nigerian troops occupied Tebe. Nsanakang was occupied (August 30). Douala surrendered (September 27). The French captured Victoria, Cameroon (October 2).

• The Germans defeated a Belgian attempt to take Kisenyi in Rwanda (October 4).
• The Germans defeated a Belgian attack on Rwanda (December 2).
• The first general tax was collected in Rwanda.
• The Methodist Mission of the Central Congo (MMCC) began its work.
• A campaign against sleeping-sickness was inaugurated in Cameroon.
• Martin-Paul Samba (c.1870–1914), a Cameroon resistance leader, died.

After receiving an American missionary education, Martin-Paul Samba, in 1899, entered into the service of Curt von Morgen, a German ethnographer working in German Kamerun (Cameroon). Morgan took Samba back to Germany, where he was educated and enrolled in the German imperial army as an officer.

Samba returned to Cameroon in 1895 and took part in German "pacification" of the country, but became disillusioned with colonial rule. Tradition says that Samba had been promised the governorship of the colony, but that it was later refused him.

Samba left the army and collaborated with Rudolph Doula-Manga Bell to organize a revolt. Drawing on his military experience, Samba trained soldiers from among the Boulou people.

When France declared war on Germany in 1914, Samba sent a message to the governor of the French Congo informing him of his intention to attack the Germans. The message was intercepted by the Germans who captured and executed Samba. Bell was executed on the same day. Both are remembered today as national heroes in the Cameroonian anti-colonial struggle.

• *Eastern Africa:* The Central Railway reached Kigoma on Lake Tanganyika from Dar es Salaam (March).
• The East African Indian National Congress was organized (March).
• The Kabaka Daudi Chwa came of age (August).

In 1914, Daudi Chwa II formally became king of the Ganda, ending the regency of Apolo Kagwa *(see 1869)*. The new king began to demand curbs on Kagwa's power. Lesser Ganda chiefs — resentful of the terms of a 1900 agreement — also opposed Kagwa's dominance. As the new British administration became more settled, it too became disenchanted with him.

• The British bombarded the Dar es Salaam

wireless station (August 8). The town subsequently surrendered.

• The H. M. S. *Pegasus* was disabled by the German cruiser *Konigsberg* in the Zanzibar harbor (September 20).

• The Anglo-Indian expedition of 8,000 was ambushed by General Lettow-Vorbeck in attack on Tanga (November).

After service in Cameroon and South West Africa, Paul Emil Lettow-Vorbeck was given command of colonial forces in German East Africa (present day Tanzania) on the eve of World War I in 1914.

A British naval blockade quickly isolated the Germans there. Governor Schnee advocated declaring German East Africa neutral. However, Lettow-Vorbeck, who was determined to tie up allied troops as long as possible, took the initiative by raiding Kenya.

• Abamalaki, a separatist movement in Uganda, began.

• Ras Mikael was crowned Negus of Wallo and Tigrai.

• Iyasu became the Emperor of Ethiopia.

Menelik, the great Ethiopian Emperor, spent his last years on the verge of death while political factions grappled to name his successor. Tafari Makonnen (Haile Selassie) was a strong candidate, but he pledged his support to Iyasu, Menelik's grandson and Menelik's personal choice as his successor.

Supported by the Galla army of his Muslim father, *Ras* Mikael, Iyasu ascended to the throne in 1914. Iyasu's reign upon the throne was a turbulent one. Iyasu became increasingly sympathetic to Islam. He was said to have commissioned a fake genealogy to prove he was descended from the Prophet Muhammed rather than Solomon — the traditionally purported ancestor of the Christian Ethiopian kings.

Iyasu's apparent interest in transforming Ethiopia into an Islamic state alarmed the largely Christian nobility. When Iyasu moved to replace Tafari Makonnen (Haile Selassie), who was then the governor of the predominantly Muslim Harar province, with a Muslim, a coup was mounted against him.

Under the leadership of Tafari *(see 1892)*, in 1916, a Shoa faction deposed Iyasu and replaced him with Empress Zauditu.

• After working as a school teacher and government official, Musajjakawa Malaki helped to found a separatist revival movement in Uganda which emphasized rejection

of European medical techniques. The movement developed into a formal church, "The Society of the One Almighty God," or the Malakite Church.

• *Southern Africa:* The South African Federation of Trades declared a general strike (January). Martial law was proclaimed.

• The Indian Relief Act was enacted (June). The Act was the result of an agreement between Smuts and Gandhi concerning Indian problems.

• The Northern Rhodesian Police occupied a German post at Schuckmannsberg, Caprivi strip (August).

• South African troops destroyed German coastal wireless stations at Luderitz and Swakopmund, German Southwest Africa (August 10).

• A patrol from German Southwest Africa violated Union territory (August 21).

• The Germans attacked Karonga (September 8).

• There was an abortive pro–German rebellion in the Transvaal (September). Martial law was proclaimed. On October 27, Beyer's commando was destroyed by Botha. On November 12, De Wet was routed, and, on December 20, the rebellion was declared at an end.

As South Africa's first prime minister, Louis Botha's main problem was countering his conciliatory, pro–British image among the Afrikaner political factions. In 1914, before Botha could support Britain in World War I, he had to suppress an armed Afrikaner uprising.

On the outbreak of World War I, Christiaan De Wet, a hero of the Boer War, and other notable Afrikaners joined in a widespread Afrikaner rebellion against the administration of Louis Botha. At the time, Botha was preparing for an invasion of German West Africa as an act demonstrating South Africa's wartime alliance with Great Britain. Botha quickly suppressed the rebellion and rounded up its leaders.

De Wet was tried and convicted of high treason. After serving a short prison term, he retired to his farm. As for Botha, he went on to lead the South African forces against German South West Africa. Botha conquered German South West Africa and attached it to South Africa.

• The Grand Comoro became a French colony.

• 7,500 South Africans independently went to Europe to fight Germany.

• In 1914, John Dube, the president of the

South African Native National Congress (the precursor of the "ANC") led an unsuccessful deputation to London to protest against new discriminatory legislation.

• Hertzog broke from Louis Botha's and founded the National Party. *See 1866.*

RELATED HISTORICAL EVENTS

• *Europe:* The conflict that became known as World War I broke out in central Europe (June–August).

On the outbreak of World War I, Horatio Kitchener, the British general who commanded the reconquest of the Sudan and who brought the South African War to a successful end, became British Secretary of State for War.

In 1916, Kitchener was drowned when a ship carrying him to negotiations in Russia was sunk off the Orkney Islands.

• Extensive autonomy was granted to Portuguese Colonies.

• The *Journal of Egyptian Archaeology* was first issued.

• *Africa:* Jacobus Hercules De la Rey (1847–1914), an Afrikaner general in the South African War, died.

Like most Transvaal Afrikaners, Jacobus De la Rey was a farmer. De la Rey served in the Volksraad — the legislature — and participated in various military campaigns, including the Anglo-Transvaal War (1880–1881) and the suppression of the Jameson Raid of 1895.

During the South African War (the Boer War), De la Rey earned an international reputation when he commanded a series of brilliant victories over British forces.

After the Boer War, De la Rey participated in the national union convention and, in 1910, was elected to the first Union Senate.

Jacobus De la Rey was an early supporter of J. B. M. Hertzog's nationalist party and was suspected of complicity in the 1914 rebellion against the government of Louis Botha.

Although De la Rey was shot by police when his car encountered a cordon set to catch rebels, De la Rey was never confirmed to be a rebel.

• Frederick Sleigh Roberts (1832–1914), the British commander-in-chief during the first phase of the South African (Boer) War, died.

Frederick Roberts early military career centered mainly on India. In 1868, he served in Robert Napier's expedition in Ethiopia. By 1885,

Roberts was commander-in-chief of the British army in India. Roberts then held a similar post in Ireland from 1895 to 1899.

On the outbreak of the South African War in 1899, Roberts took command of the British forces in the Cape Colony. The first year of the war the Afrikaners fought according to orthodox theories of warfare. Roberts occupied the Orange Free State and the Transvaal and drove the Afrikaners into bush country. Declaring the war won, Roberts returned home in 1900 to wide acclaim.

Subsequently, Roberts was made commander-in-chief of the entire British army. In South Africa, however, the war entered a new phase as the Afrikaners turned to guerrilla fighting. Command of the British forces was then assumed by Kitchener, Roberts' former assistant.

1915

THE UNITED STATES

• In 1915, farm labor wages fell to 75 cents per day, or less. Boll weevils devastated the cotton crop. There were major floods during the summer. As a result of the decline in the farm economy coupled with the growth in the Northern war industries, African Americans increased their migration North.

About 2,000,000 African Americans migrated from the Southern states to Northern industrial centers during the "great migration" which began in this year.

• The NAACP unsuccessfully tried to prevent the showing of D. W. Griffith's *Birth of a Nation.* The film was based on the violently anti–African American book by Thomas Dixon entitled *The Klansman. Birth of a Nation* told a distorted story of African American emancipation, enfranchisement and debauchery of innocent women. The NAACP also tried to counteract its influence by making their own film, *Lincoln's Dream,* but the project never materialized. However, three years later, the NAACP convinced several states to ban Griffith's film arguing that it fostered race hatred at a time of national crisis.

Fearing increased violence against African Americans, the NAACP tried unsuccessfully to prevent the showing of D. W. Griffith's *Birth of a Nation* because the movie portrayed African Americans in derogatory racial stereotypes and perpetuated the myth of "Negro rule" during

Reconstruction. The civil rights activist William Monroe Trotter was arrested and jailed for picketing the film.

 • Professor Ernest Everett Just received the first Spingarn Medal for his research in the field of biology (February 12).
 • The NAACP employed two legislative agents to keep track of all anti–African American bills introduced in Congress. In the first three months of the year, 6 Jim Crow bills for Washington, D. C. were introduced and an anti-interracial marriage bill for the capital was passed by the House. The NAACP, by canvassing and distributing literature, contributed to the House defeat of an immigration bill forbidding even literate persons of African descent from entering the country.
 • African Americans protested President Wilson's order for the occupation of Haiti by the United States Marines.
 • North Carolina Democrats adopted a "white primary."

By 1915, almost all of the Southern states provided for "white primaries."

 • A faction of the Louisiana State Republican Convention refused admission of African Americans to the convention in the Grunewald Hotel in New Orleans.
 • Oscar DePriest was elected alderman in the densely populated African American section of Chicago, the South Side.
 • Private Stephen Little, Colored Light 12 Infantry, was killed in action near Nogales, Arizona. The military camp was subsequently named in his honor (November 26).
 • Dr. Robert Russa Moton was elected principal, Tuskegee Normal and Industrial Institute, succeeding the recently deceased Booker T. Washington (December 20).
 • *Organizations:* The Association for the Study of Negro Life and History was founded by Dr. Carter G. Woodson in Chicago (September 9). The first meeting was held in the office of the Wabash Avenue YMCA, Chicago.
 • *The Ku Klux Klan:* The modern Ku Klux Klan began in earnest when a local chapter in Fulton County, Georgia, was chartered.

The Ku Klux Klan that was born during the Reconstruction era essentially died from lack of interest once the federal troops had been withdrawn, Jim Crow laws instituted, and African Americans disfranchised.

However, beginning in 1915, the interest in the Klan experienced a resurgence, not just in the South, but also in the North and Midwest, as European Americans organized to protect their interests against the flood of African American immigrants to the North and the flood of immigrants from southern and eastern Europe throughout the country.

Additionally, after the end of World War I, many African Americans returned to the South from Europe with notions of equality on their minds, the European Americans utilized the Klan to keep these "enlightened" African Americans beleaguered and oppressed.

By 1924, the membership in the Klan had reached 4.5 million people. Its membership was composed of self-described "white male persons, native-born Gentile citizens."

Primarily Democrats, the Klan often controlled local and state politics. However, in Indiana, the Klan actually controlled the state by using its positions in the Republican Party.

The ultimate decline of the Klan was attributable to the scandals which plagued the organization during the 1920s. By 1925, scandals had discredited top officials in the Klan. Newspaper exposes detailing the widespread corruption within the Klan eventually caused membership to dwindle and the power of the Klan to subside.

 • *The Labor Movement:* The Railwaymen's International Benevolent and Industrial Association was established.
 • *Notable Births:* Elizabeth Catlett, a sculptor and printmaker, was born in Washington, D. C. (April 15).
 • Claude Clark, Sr., an artist, was born in Georgia.
 • Trumpeter Harry "Sweets" Edison was born in Columbus, Ohio (October 10).
 • Eleanora Fagan, a singer who became a legend under the stage name Billie Holiday ("Lady Day"), was born in Baltimore (April 7). More than any other singer, Billie Holiday came to epitomize the essence of the blues and her singing was the quintessential expression of the blues.
 • Gospel preacher C. L. Franklin was born in Mississippi (January 22).
 • John Hope Franklin, an historian, was born.

John Hope Franklin was born in Rentiesville, Oklahoma. He was educated at Fisk and Harvard University where he received a doctorate in 1941. Franklin taught at North Carolina State, Howard and Brooklyn College, and the University of Chicago. Franklin's books include: *Free Negro in North Carolina* (1943), a study of the social status of the African American in North Carolina in pre–Civil War times; *From Slavery to Freedom* (1947); *Militant South* (1956); *Reconstruction After the Civil War* (1961); and *The Emancipation Proclamation* (1963).

Franklin is considered one of the leading Reconstruction revisionist historians who followed Du Bois' example in *Black Reconstruction* of re-evaluating the social position and political performance of the post–Civil War Southern African American.

- Ernest Kaiser, a bibliographer, was born in Virginia (December 5).
- McKinley Morganfield, the blues singer who is better known as "Muddy Waters," was born in Mississippi (April 4).
- Hughie Lee-Smith, a painter, was born in Eustis, Florida (September 20).
- William "Billy" Strayhorn, a songwriter, arranger, composer, and pianist, was born in Dayton, Ohio (November 29). For 28 years, Strayhorn would work with Duke Ellington's band. Among his more famous compositions are *Satin Doll* and *Take the 'A' Train*.
- Gospel singer "Sister" Rosetta Tharpe was born in Cotton Plant, Arkansas (March 20).
- Margaret Walker, a poet and novelist, was born in Birmingham, Alabama (July 7). Among her works are *For My People* and *Jubilee*.
- *Notable Deaths:* From 1900 to 1915, some 1,100 African Americans were lynched.
- In 1915, 69 African Americans were reported to have been lynched.
- Mifflin Wistar Gibbs (1823–1915), an African American who established *Mirror of the Times*, an abolitionist newspaper in San Francisco, California, died.

In addition to establishing *Mirror of the Times,* the first African American newspaper in California, Mifflin Gibbs was also the first African American to serve as municipal court judge in Little Rock, Arkansas (1873).

The life and career of Mifflin Gibbs was a unique and varied one. Gibbs founded the *Mirror of the Times* in California in 1855. However, in 1866, Gibbs was elected to the city council of Victoria, British Columbia. In 1869, Gibbs completed his law studies at Oberlin College in Ohio. And, in 1873, Gibbs became a municipal judge in Little Rock, Arkansas.

The wanderings of the peripatetic Gibbs did not end in Arkansas. He later held a number of federal positions culminating in his being named the United States Consul in Madagascar.

In 1902, Gibbs published a biography entitled *Shadow and Light.*

- Robert Smalls (1839–1915), Civil War hero and Reconstruction Era Congressman, died.

Robert Smalls was the son of Robert and Lydia Smalls, slaves of the McKee family. Smalls was allowed to acquire a limited education. Smalls moved with the McKee family to Charleston, where he became a waiter.

In 1861, Confederate authorities pressed Smalls into the service of the Confederate Navy. He became a member of the crew of the *Planter*. In 1862, in the absence of Confederate officers, Smalls navigated the *Planter* into the line of the blockading Federal squadron outside Charleston harbor. The Federal forces, upon receiving the *Planter*, made Smalls a pilot in the United States Navy, commissioned him a captain, and then promoted him to commander.

At a meeting of African Americans and Northerners in 1864 at Port Royal, Smalls was elected to the National Union Convention. Smalls became a delegate in 1868 to the State Constitutional Convention, and served in the State House of Representatives. Between 1870 and 1874, Smalls served as a State Senator.

In 1875, Smalls was elected to Congress and served until 1887. While in Congress, Smalls spoke against the election tactics of South Carolina Democrats and supported a bill to provide equal accommodations for the races on interstate conveyances.

From 1865 to 1877, Smalls served in the South Carolina State Militia, rising to the rank of Major General. While in office, in 1877, he was convicted of accepting a bribe. However, he was pardoned by Governor W. D. Simpson.

In 1895, as one of the African American members of the South Carolina Constitutional Convention, Smalls made an attempt to prevent the disenfranchisement of African Americans within the state. He was not successful.

For the last 20 years of his life, Smalls lived in Beaufort where he was the collector of duties at the local port.

- Henry McNeal Turner (1834–1915), a Bishop of the African Methodist Episcopal Church of Georgia, died in Canada (May 8).

Henry McNeal Turner worked in the cotton fields after his father's death and was apprenticed to a blacksmith. Turner learned to read at 15, and he was later employed by a law firm where he learned to write.

In 1853, after joining the Methodist Episcopal Church, he received a license to preach. Turner became a successful revivalist among African Americans and was ordained a deacon in 1860 and an elder in 1862.

Installed as pastor of the Israel Church in Washington, D.C., Turner was made an army chaplain by President Lincoln in 1863. In this capacity, Turner was attached to the First Regiment of Colored Troops.

Upon the conclusion of the Civil War, President Andrew Johnson appointed Turner chaplain in the regular army. Turner subsequently resigned in order to build up the African Methodist Episcopal Church in Georgia.

Turner was one of the founders of the Republican Party of Georgia. He was elected a delegate to the Georgia Constitutional Convention of 1867.

In 1869, Turner was appointed Postmaster at Macon, Georgia, by President Grant. He eventually relinquished this post because of the opposition voiced by European Americans in the area.

Serving as a customs inspector and government detective, Turner then, in 1876, became manager of the African Methodist Episcopal Book Concern in Philadelphia.

From 1880 through 1892 Turner served as Bishop of the AME Church in Georgia. After 1892, Turner served as chancellor of Morris Brown College in Atlanta, Georgia.

Turner traveled widely. He visited South and West Africa where he introduced African Methodism. In his later years, Turner became an advocate for the return of African Americans to Africa.

Turner founded several periodicals during his career. In 1889, he founded *The Southern Christian Recorder* and, in 1892, he founded the *Voice of the Missions.*

Turner also authored *The Genius and Method of Methodist Policy* which was published in 1885.

• James Milton Turner (1840–1915), a noted educator and the former Minister to Liberia, died.

James Milton Turner was born a slave in St. Louis County, Virginia, on the plantation of Charles A. Loring. Turner's father, John Turner (also known as John Colburn) was removed from Virginia by Benjamin Tillman after the 1831 slave insurrection which was led by Nat Turner. John Turner fell under the tutelage of a Benjamin Tillman who taught John veterinary medicine.

With these new skills, John Turner was able to purchase his freedom and, in 1843, he purchased the freedom of his wife and their young son, James Milton Turner.

At age 14, James' parents sent him to Oberlin College in Ohio. During the Civil War, he served as a Union officer's servant. After the War, Turner settled in Missouri and directed his attention to public education for African American children.

In 1866, James Turner was appointed to the Kansas City School Board. He was authorized to conduct a school for African Americans during the winter — the first such school reported to be operating in the state of Missouri. Turner was subsequently reappointed to his school board position in 1868.

Later on, Turner became interested in the Negro Institute which was located in Jefferson City, Missouri. He gave and collected money for the Institute and served as trustee for the renamed Institute — Lincoln University.

During Reconstruction, Turner became involved in Republican politics. On March 1, 1871, Turner was appointed to be the minister resident and consul general to the Republic of Liberia. Turner would hold this post until 1878.

In 1886, Turner presented to President Cleveland a claim of the African American members of the Cherokee Nation. He secured $75,000 of the federal funds allotted to the Cherokee Nation for the Afro-Cherokee people.

In 1915, Turner was killed in an explosion in Ardmore, Oklahoma. His body was transported back to St. Louis, Missouri, where a funeral was conducted by the African American Masons was the largest ever held for an African American in the city.

• Booker T. Washington (1856–1915), President of Tuskegee Institute and a noted educator and African American leader, died in Tuskegee, Alabama (November 14).

On November 14, 1915, Booker Taliaferro Washington (c.1856–1915), the founder of Tuskegee Institute and the most prominent African American leader of the late nineteenth and early twentieth centuries, died.

Booker T. Washington was born a slave on the plantation of James Burroughs near Hale's Ford, Virginia. Washington spent his childhood as a houseboy and servant. His mother, Jane, was a cook on the Burroughs plantation. Washington's father was a European American — a man Washington never knew.

With emancipation in 1865, Washington moved with his family to West Virginia. In West Virginia, Washington worked briefly in the salt furnaces and coal mines near Malden. Quickly, however, Washington obtained work as a houseboy in the mansion of the wealthiest European American man in Malden, General Lewis Ruffner. There, under the tutelage of the general's wife, Viola Ruffner, a former New England schoolteacher, Washington learned to read. He also attended a local school for African Americans in Malden.

From 1872 to 1875, Washington attended Hampton Institute in Hampton, Virginia. Washington arrived at Hampton after having walked almost 500 miles to get there. At Hampton, Washington came under the influence of the school's founder, General Samuel Chapman Armstrong. Armstrong inculcated in Washington the work ethic that would stay with Washington throughout his adult life. This work ethic would also become a hallmark of Washington's educational philosophy.

Booker T. Washington, who worked his way through Hampton by serving as a school janitor, was an outstanding student during his stay at the school. In recognition of his abilities, Washington was placed in charge of the Indigenous American students who also attended Hampton.

After graduation, Washington returned to Malden, where he taught school for several years and became active as a public speaker on local matters, including the issue of the removal of the capital of West Virginia to Charleston.

In 1881, Washington, with a start up fund of $2,000, founded a school of his own in Tuskegee, Alabama. Beginning with a few ramshackle buildings and a small sum from the state of Alabama, Washington built Tuskegee Institute into the best known African American school in the nation. In the first two decades of Tuskegee Institute, over 40 buildings were erected on the campus — most of these were erected by the students themselves.

While not neglecting academic training entirely, Tuskegee's curriculum stressed industrial education, training in specific skills and crafts that would prepare students for jobs.

Washington built his school and his influence by tapping the generosity of northern philanthropists. He pursued and received donations from wealthy New Englanders and from some the leading industrialists and businessmen of his time. Men such as Andrew Carnegie, William H. Baldwin, Jr., Julius Rosenwald, and Robert C. Ogden were all major contributors to Tuskegee and to Washington's career.

In 1882, Washington married his childhood sweetheart from Malden, Fanny Norton Smith, a fellow graduate of Hampton Institute.

Two years later, Fanny died as a result of injuries suffered in a fall from a wagon. Subsequently, Washington married Olivia A. Davidson, a graduate of Hampton and the Framingham State Normal School in Massachusetts. As Olivia Washington, Davidson would hold the title of lady principal of Tuskegee.

Olivia Washington was a tireless worker for the school and an effective fund-raiser in her own right. However, she was always rather frail and she died in 1889.

Booker T. Washington's third wife was Margaret James Murray, a graduate of Fisk University. As Margaret Washington, Murray would also serve as the lady principal of Tuskegee.

Margaret Washington was a leader of the National Association of Colored Women's Clubs and Southern Federation of Colored Women's Clubs.

Booker T. Washington's reputation as the principal of Tuskegee Institute grew through the late 1880s and the 1890s. Washington's school was considered the exemplar of industrial education. At the time, industrial education was viewed as the best method of training the African Americans who were either born in slavery or were the sons and daughters of freed slaves.

Washington's control of the purse strings of many of the northern donors to his school increased his influence with other African American schools in the South. Washington's fame and recognition as a national African American leader was derived from the impact of a single speech Washington delivered before the Cotton States and International Exposition in Atlanta *(see 1895)*. This important speech, often called the Atlanta Compromise, is the essence of Washington's philosophy regarding racial advancement and sets forth his political accommodation with the predominant racial ideology of the day — an ideology which relegated African Americans to a "second class" citizenship. For the next twenty years, until the end of his life, Washington seldom deviated publicly from the positions taken in the Atlanta Compromise.

In the Atlanta Compromise, Washington urged African Americans to "cast down your bucket where you are." By this he meant that African Americans should commit themselves to the South and that they should accommodate to the segregation and discrimination imposed upon them by custom and by state and local laws. Washington asserted that the races could exist separately from the standpoint of social relationships but should work together for mutual economic advancement. Washington advocated a gradualist advancement of the race, through hard work, economic improvement, and self-help. This message resonated with European Americans both north and south and found almost universal acceptance among African Americans. Even W. E. B. DuBois *(see 1868)* later one of Washington's harshest critics, wrote to Washington after the Atlanta Compromise speech and called it "a word fitly spoken."

While Washington's public stance on racial matters seldom varied from the Atlanta Compromise, privately, he was a more complicated individual. His voluminous private papers, document an elaborate secret life that contradicted many of his public pronouncements. For instance, few knew that Washington secretly financed test cases to challenge Jim Crow laws.

Washington held great power over the African American press, both north and south. He secretly owned stock in several newspapers.

While Washington himself never held any political office, he became the most powerful African American politician of his time as an adviser to presidents Theodore Roosevelt and William Howard Taft and as a dispenser of Republican Party patronage amongst African Americans.

With his network of informants and access to both northern philanthropy and political patronage, Washington could make or break careers. He was the central figure in African American public life during the twenty years in which he lived after the Atlanta Compromise. No other African American (not even Martin Luther King) has exerted similar dominance over African American affairs.

In 1900, Washington founded the National Negro Business League. The purpose of the National Negro Business League was to foster African-American business and create a loyal corps of supporters throughout the country.

Indirectly, Washington influenced the National Afro American Council, the leading African American civil rights group of the day.

The publication of Washington's autobiography, *Up from Slavery*, in 1901 spread Washington's fame even more in the United States and abroad. *Up from Slavery* is a classic American success story. Its great popularity in the first

decade of the twentieth century won many new financial supporters for Tuskegee Institute and for Washington personally.

In addition to *Up From Slavery*, Washington's other published works include *The Future of the American Negro* (1899), *Character Building* (1902), *Working With the Hands* (1904), *Tuskegee and Its People* (1905), *Putting the Most into Life* (1906), *Life of Frederick Douglass* (1907), *The Negro in Business* (1907), *The Story of the Negro* (1909), *My Larger Education* (1911), and *The Man Farthest Down; a Record of Observation and Study in Europe* (1912).

Washington remained the dominant African American leader in the country until the time of his death from exhaustion and overwork in 1915. But other voices rose to challenge Washington's conservative, accommodationist leadership. William Monroe Trotter, the editor of the *Boston Guardian,* was a persistent gadfly. Beginning in 1903, with the publication of W. E. B. DuBois' *The Souls of Black Folk,* and continuing for the rest of his life, Washington was criticized for his failure to be more publicly aggressive in fighting the deterioration of race relations in the United States, for his avoidance of direct public support for civil rights legislation, and for his single-minded emphasis on industrial education as opposed to academic training for a "talented tenth" of the race.

Washington, however, was adept at outmaneuvering his critics. At times, he even resorted to the use of spies to infiltrate organizations critical of his leadership, such as the DuBois led Niagara Movement. Washington's friends called him "the Wizard" for his mastery of political intrigue and his exercise of power.

Washington's leadership ultimately gave way to new forces in the twentieth century which placed less emphasis on individual leadership and more on organizational power. The founding of the National Association for the Advancement of Colored People (NAACP) in 1909 and of the National Urban League in 1911 challenged Washington in the areas of civil rights and for his failure to address problems related to the growth of an urban black population.

The defeat of the Republican Party in the presidential election of 1912 also spelled the end of Washington's power as a dispenser of political patronage. Nevertheless, Washington remained active as a speaker and public figure until his death in 1915 at Tuskegee.

Washington's place in history is the subject of much controversy. While Washington was the first African American to appear on a United

States postage stamp (in 1940) and commemorative coin (in 1946), until recently, Washington's conservative philosophy of accommodation to segregation and racism in American society caused his historical reputation to suffer. For three generations, African Americans, who took their inspiration from those who were more outspoken critics of segregation and the second-class status endured by African Americans, rejected Washington's leadership role. Indeed, amongst the African American intelligentsia, Washington, because of his racial philosophy, has largely been relegated to the recesses of the African American consciousness — his leadership being considered to be anathema to the notion of black pride.

However, the lessons of Booker T. Washington's life are far more subtle and far more profound than a general dismissal would indicate. Washington's career as an accommodationist political leader raises issues which haunt people of African descent throughout the world. In all too many instances, and in all too many places, people of African descent are led by leaders who are often more concerned with accommodating the powers that be than with advancing the progress of African people. Additionally, even with the theoretically more strident civil rights organizations of the late twentieth century, there is always a concern that the advocacy of the organization must be tempered in order to maintain the financial support of non–African American benefactors.

In reviewing the history of African people throughout the world since Washington's death, one is often struck by the underlying uncertainty associated with black leaders. In a world dominated by European and European American power and influence, — indeed, in a world where European and European American power and influence has repeatedly been used to "create" new black leaders — there have been very few black leaders who could honestly assert that they were not, in a very major way, accommodationists.

The legacy of Booker T. Washington is that his path to success — his path to leadership — has become a well worn road which has seen the footprints of many.

- *Miscellaneous Laws:* The trend of Southern legislation was exemplified by a South Carolina labor code which prohibited textile factory owners from allowing laborers of both races to work in the same room, to use the same entrances, stairs, pay windows, lavatories, drinking cups, or water buckets.
- For the first time in any state, Oklahoma law required separate phone booths.
- *Notable Cases: Guinn v. United States,* declared "grandfather clauses" in the Maryland and Oklahoma constitutions null and void (June 21).

In *Guinn v. United States* (June 21, 1915) 238 U.S. 347, 35 S.Ct. 926, the United States Supreme Court pronounced in violation of the Fifteenth Amendment and thus unconstitutional the suffrage provisions of the Oklahoma and Maryland Constitutions. The NAACP had challenged Oklahoma's "grandfather clause." Morfield Storey argued the case for the NAACP.

More specifically, the Court held that the exemption from the literacy test prescribed by the Oklahoma Constitution which exempted any person who, on January 1, 1866, or at any time prior thereto, were entitled to vote under any form of government, or who at that time resided in some foreign nation, and their lineal descendants, was a denial or abridgment of the right to vote on account of race, color, or previous condition of servitude, contrary to the provisions of the Fifteenth Amendment. The Court noted that the invalidated Oklahoma provision created a standard which, as a necessary result, re-created and perpetuated the very conditions which the Fifteenth Amendment was intended to destroy.

The case of *Guinn v. United States* is also notable because it was the first major legal victory for the NAACP.

- *Publications:* W. E. B. Du Bois' book, *The Negro,* was published. *The Negro* dealt with African American history from ancient Egypt to the present. Du Bois, writing from the Marxist point of view that both white workers and blacks were exploited by white capital, predicted the unification of the exploited classes against white capital.
- Oscar Micheaux published *Forged Note.* See 1913.
- Archibald Henry Grimke published *The Ultimate Criminal.*
- In 1915, Carter G. Woodson was a moving force behind the creation of the Association for the Study of Negro Life and History. He became its director and editor of its primary publication, *The Journal of Negro History.*
- *Scholastic Achievements:* Between 1915 and 1919, eight African Americans received

doctorates. Four received their doctorates from African American institutions and four were from integrated universities.

• In 1915, Meharry Medical College was incorporated in Nashville, Tennessee. Founded in 1876, Meharry joined Howard University Medical School, Shaw Medical School, and the Medical Department of the University of West Tennessee as medical schools for African Americans.

• Xavier University in New Orleans, an African American Catholic college, was founded by Katherine Drexel and the Sisters of the Blessed Sacrament as a high school (September 27). The school became a college in 1925.

• *The Arts:* Henry Ossawa Tanner's *Christ at the Home of Lazarus* was awarded the gold medal at the Panama-Pacific Exposition which was held in San Francisco.

The Performing Arts

The Karamu Theater in Cleveland, Ohio, was founded by Russell and Rowena Jellifes as part of a private philanthropic social welfare center. The Jellifes were upper-class European Americans. Karamu is a Swahili word meaning "center of enjoyment" or "center of community." The theater was a recreation center for inner city dwellers, both European American and African American. The Jellifes encouraged drama and theater, especially among the African Americans. The great African American actor, Charles Gilpin, founded a stock company, Gilpin Players, which produced and wrote plays especially for the Karamu house.

During the 1930s, the Karamu Theater premiered almost all of Langston Hughes' plays. The Jellifes retired in 1963, leaving the Karamu a generous endowment to continue its productions. Although not exclusively an African American theater, the Karamu, which also houses a superb collection of African art, remained one of the best and most dynamic African American theaters in the United States.

• Anita Bush (1883–1974), a dancer and actress, organized the Anita Bush Players, a professional African American stock dramatic company. The Anita Bush Players opened at the Lincoln Theater, in New York City, on November 15, with *The Girl at the Fort*. They had a short but successful run, and by December 27, had transferred to the larger Lafayette Theater, where they became the Lafayette Players.

• *The Radio:* Hattie McDaniel (1895–1952) made her radio debut.

Hattie McDaniel was the first African American to win an Oscar. She was named best supporting actress for her portrayal of Mammy in *Gone With the Wind*. McDaniel was born in Wichita, Kansas, and moved to Hollywood in 1931. She made her movie debut in *The Golden West* in 1932, and appeared in more than three hundred films during the next two decades. Her career was built on the "Mammy" image, a role she played with dignity.

• *Music:* Scott Joplin, an African American, composed a ragtime opera, *Treemonisha*.

• Jelly Roll Morton published *Jelly Roll Blues*. *Jelly Roll Blues* was the first published jazz arrangement.

• *The Black Church:* The National Baptist Convention of the United States of America was incorporated. E. P. Jones was the first president.

• The Church of the Redemption, the first verifiable spiritual congregation, was founded in Chicago.

• *Sports:* Jack Johnson lost the heavyweight boxing championship in a bout with Jesse Willard. He had held the title for almost seven years.

Jess Willard, a European American prizefighter, defeated the African American champion, Jack Johnson. It was rumored that Johnson threw the fight to relieve the racial tensions which had built up by his reign as champion and to escape punishment for a charge that he had violated the Mann Act.

• Joseph E. Trigg manned the number seven oar for Syracuse University varsity rowing team.

THE AMERICAS

• *Canada:* On November 29, the Militia Council resoundingly repeated an order that had first gone out on October 19, that "colored men are to be permitted to enlist in any battalion."

• In Saint John, all restaurants and theaters closed their doors to Afro-Canadians.

• *Haiti:* United States troops invaded Haiti (July 28).

Between 1911 and 1915, there were six presidents of Haiti. The last of them, Vilbrun Guillaume Sam, ordered the execution of many of his jailed opponents. In retribution, Sam was dragged out of the French embassy and torn to pieces by an enraged mob. On the day that Sam was publicly dismembered (July 28, 1915), the United States Marines landed in Haiti for what would prove to be a nineteen year stay.

Three thousand United States Marines led by Admiral Caperton of the cruiser *George Washington* arrived in Port-au-Prince. Through this action, backed by United States President Woodrow Wilson, Haiti came under the military occupation of the United States of America.

Explanations of the reasons for the United States invasion of Haiti have varied. The pretext was the rioting preceding the murder of President Sam which the United States considered to be a threat to United States citizens and property in Haiti. There may also have been a desire to prevent the French from invading Haiti in retaliation for the violation of the French embassy.

Additionally, there was some concern on the part of the United States about Germany which, with World War I underway, was in search of ports in the Americas from which it could strike British and French vessels. The ports of Haiti seemed to be prizes which the Germans would not likely pass up. This seemed especially probable because Germany had, at various times, asserted its right to protect the sizable German merchant community in Port-au-Prince.

As for the French and British, the American investors had bought out the French interest in Banque Nationale while the British were still interested in Haiti and often acted as protectors of the increasingly important Syrian-Lebanese merchant group that dominated much of Haiti's commercial life.

Interests in the United States had long been frustrated at the difficulties in penetrating the Haitian economy. The combination of these fears and frustrations, when added to the strategic hegemony that the United States was establishing in the Caribbean, gave enough impetus to justify the invasion and the occupation, which lasted nineteen years.

Those who defend the United States occupation refer to the political and financial stability that it brought. There were also material gains. Health conditions improved; roads, hospitals and schools were constructed; and more foreign investment flowed into Haiti. However, under the occupation, the interests of the United States came first. Accordingly, the old Haitian policy against foreign ownership of Haitian land was reversed — a reversal which led to a great resentment from the Haitian people.

Provoking even more resentment was the United States policy of favoring the COTW elite as evidenced by the installation in the presidency of a series of COTWs. Rural anger at the imposition of the corvee, a system of obligatory labor drafts, caused a cacos revolt in 1918 led by habitants such as Charlemagne Peralte, who was killed after a violent campaign by the United States Marines. Nationalistic fervor increased after the revolt, and President Franklin D. Roosevelt finally withdrew United States troops in 1934.

• Senator Sudre Dartiguenave was elected President by the Haitian Constituent Assembly (August 12).

• Edmond Laforest, a noted poet, died. *See 1876.*

AFRICA

• *North Africa, Egypt and Sudan:* The Ottoman Turks were driven back from the Suez Canal (February 4).

• The Sanusi revolted in southern Tunisia (March 24).

• By October, the revolt had spread to Hoggar.

• The Spanish recognized al-Raisuni as the governor of many Moroccan tribes.

• *Western Africa:* There were uprisings in Beledougou near Bamako, and in Goumbou and Nara regions against recruitment (March).

• The administration of Portuguese Guinea was re-organized and decentralized (August 15).

• Rebellion and guerrilla warfare began in Dahomey (August 22). The war would last until February of 1916.

• There was a revolt in Dedougou (November).

• The Sanusi rebels reached Agades (December 13), and, on December 28, Bilma.

• There was a religious revival in Opobo led to the formation of Christ's Army and the Delta Church.

• William Harris was expelled from the Ivory Coast.

In 1913, the Christian evangelist, William Harris, entered the Ivory Coast. In the Ivory Coast, his following grew rapidly due, in no small measure, to Harris' growing reputation as a faith healer.

Harris continued his walk. He walked all the

way to the Gold Coast (Ghana) before returning to the Ivory Coast.

In the Ivory Coast, Harris attracted over 100,000 followers. The French, who at first were supportive of his mission and his sermons on the work ethic, now became alarmed. After a few disruptive incidents in 1914, the French realized the movement's potential threat.

In 1915, Harris was expelled to Liberia and his Ivory Coast churches were destroyed. In Liberia, Harris continued to preach but he no longer attracted a large following.

In the Ivory Coast, Protestant and Catholic missionaries competed to recruit the new Christians that had been left behind by Harris. However, many of Harris' converts refused to join the established churches and chose to maintain separatist churches of their own.

Today, there continue to be thriving separatist churches in the Ivory Coast and Ghana which recognize William Wade Harris as their founder.

- The Gambia constitution was revived.
- Modibo Keita (1915–1977), the future president of Mali, was born.

Modibo Keita was a member of the Keita clan which ruled the ancient empire of Mali. He was born in Bamako and was educated at the William Ponty School in Senegal.

Graduating in 1920, Keita worked in the educational system before entering politics. In 1945, Keita and Mamadou Konate, who at the time represented French Sudan (Mali) in the French Chamber of Deputies, formed a political party which affiliated with the French Socialist Party (SFIO).

In 1946, Keita helped organize the Francophonic inter-territorial party known as the RDA, organized to press for more rights for the African colonies, and became a supporter of RDA leader Felix Houphouet-Boigny *(see 1905)* of the Ivory Coast.

During this time, Keita built his reputation as a left-wing opponent of colonialism. In 1947, while in Paris, Keita was arrested and imprisoned for a month for political activities.

In 1948, Keita was elected to the Sudan territorial assembly. Because of the RDA's radical stance, the French administration repressed it and its leaders, including Keita. In 1950, the French effectively exiled Keita by assigning him to a post in the remote interior.

Houphouet gave in to French pressure by renouncing radicalism and breaking RDA ties to the French Communist Party. French repression eased up and Keita was allowed to return.

In 1956, Keita was elected to the French Chamber of Deputies. He also came to hold a number of positions in French cabinets.

Around this time, Houphouet-Boigny became increasingly conservative. Because of this conservatism, Keita eventually broke with Houphouet-Boigny although he did remain in the RDA. The principal dividing issue was federation amongst the French West African territories. Houphouet-Boigny opposed federation.

In 1956, Keita became the leader of the RDA. The next year, the RDA won the elections for the territorial assembly.

In 1958, French Sudan (Mali) became a self-governing republic, however, Keita remained in the French government.

Keita's energies within Africa were directed at establishing a federation in opposition to Houphouet-Boigny and the RDA. In March 1959, Keita's party was again successful at the polls and Keita became the president of the new Mali Federation.

The federation scheme was a disaster. Houphouet-Boigny refused to let the Ivory Coast join and pressured Dahomey (Benin) and Upper Volta to withdraw. Only Senegal, and Mali were left, and the unit which they formed in 1959 broke up the next year.

Keita's anti-colonialism brought communist foreign aid, but scared off Western capital (which had little to attract it anyway) and throughout his presidency Mali remained a proud but poor country.

In 1963, Keita won the Lenin Peace Prize. Although he remained popular with the masses, Keita was the victim of a military coup in 1968. Keita was imprisoned in Mali until his death in 1977.

- James Hutton Brew (1844–1915) died.

The Brew family comprised a Gold Coast (Ghana) elite which was long prominent in trade, politics and the professions. The Brew family were the Fante descendants of Richard Brew (c.1725–1776) an Irish merchant who lived on the Gold Coast. Because of their dual heritage, the Brew family had the early advantage of Western education. This advantage enabled them to play important roles in Gold Coast (Ghana) activities for over two hundred years.

James Hutton Brew was the son of Samuel Collins Brew *(see 1881)*. James Brew became one of the earliest West African nationalists and a pioneering journalist.

Brew was an active participant in the Fante confederacy movement which lasted from 1867 to 1872. The purpose of the Fante confederacy movement was to reconstitute Fante government along national lines. The Fante confederacy movement was largely responsible for drawing up the confederacy's constitution. However, the confederacy movement was soon undermined by the annexation of the Gold Coast to the British Empire.

After the Gold Coast became a British colony, James Brew became a journalist. He pursued this profession as means of exerting political pressure. In the course of being a journalist, Brew established a number of newspapers in the 1870s and 1880s. After 1888, Brew lived in England where he continued to lobby for African rights against European encroachments. However, Brew's English sojourn was not entirely nationalistic. He also represented European business interests in the Gold Coast.

• *Central Africa:* Mwambutsa became the Mwami — the King — of Burundi.

While still only an infant of three years of age, Mwambutsa was named king — Mwami — of Burundi when his father Mutage IV unexpectedly died in 1915.

"Mwami" is the title used by the kings of Rwanda and Burundi and of Msiri, the Yeke king of southern Zaire.

• The British liaised with the Belgians to co-ordinate the war against the Germans in East Africa (February).

• Germans defeated Belgian attacks on Kisenyi (May).

• Chad was placed under a French civil governor (May 14).

• Garna, Cameroon, surrendered to Nigerians and the French (June 11). The Ngaundere were captured (June 29). Douala was captured (September 30). The fortress of Banyo was taken (November 5).

• Unrest in Belgian Congo resulted in twenty-one armed operations.

• The Congo Evangelistic Mission (CEM) started work in Katanga.

• The southern part of the Huila plateau was brought under Portuguese control.

• *Eastern Africa:* A railway was constructed from Voi to Taveta, Kenya, to facilitate the British attack of German East Africa.

• Begember and Gojjam were put under the control of Ras Mikael.

• South Africans, based on Karonga, advanced on Neu Langenburg (Tukuyu).

• Two four and a half ton British ships, *Mimi* and *Toutou*, captured German gun-boat on Lake Tanganyika.

• *Southern Africa:* South Africa troops occupied Swakopmund in German South West Africa (January 13).

In 1915, Jan Smuts assisted Louis Botha in occupying German South West Africa. As a reward, the British then gave Smuts command over their forces in east Africa.

• There was an uprising in Nyasaland led by John Chilembwe (January 23).

• Windhoek was occupied by Botha (May 12).

• Christian de Wet surrendered at Bloemfontein (June 21).

• Germans in Southwest Africa surrendered to Botha (July 9).

• Anti-German riots in South Africa followed the sinking of the *Lusitania* (October).

• Hertzog's Nationalist Party gained a majority in the South Africa Parliament (October 20).

• Daniel Malan began to edit *Die Burger*, the National Party's first newspaper.

• Balthazar Johannes Vorster was born (December 13).

• The War on War Group broke away from Labour Party in Johannesburg. The International Workers of Africa (IWA) was formed. The IWA newspaper was called the *International*.

• Port traffic in Beira reached 200,000 tons.

• In Zimbabwe, Matthew Zwimba founded his own church. Zwimba's Original Church of the White Bird Mission (Shiri Chena Church) incorporated both Christian and traditional Shona symbolism and was the first of a large number of independent churches among the Shona.

• John Chilembwe (c.1870–1915), the leader of the rebellion in Nyasaland, was killed.

John Chilembwe is a legendary figure in the history of Nyasaland, a land which is today known as the country of Malawi. Chilembwe's controversial career became the inspiration for a considerable literature.

Little is known about Chilembwe's birth and early years. What is known is that by the early 1890s, Chilembwe was a student at the Church of Scotland Mission at Blantyre in southern Nyasaland.

In 1892, Chilembwe attached himself to

Joseph Booth's new Baptist mission. Through the 1890s, Chilembwe became very close to Booth, acting as his steward, interpreter, and leading pupil. Chilembwe was soon baptized by Booth, and absorbed many of the latter's views on the equality of races.

In 1897, Chilembwe accompanied Booth to Britain and the United States. In the United States, the two separated. Chilembwe remained in Virginia to attend an African American Baptist seminary.

The details of Chilembwe's American sojourn are not known. However, it seems likely that Chilembwe became imbued with the concepts of the growing nationalistic African American thought.

Chilembwe returned to Nyasaland in 1900 as an ordained minister of the National Baptist Convention and established the Providence Industrial Mission. Over the next fourteen years, Chilembwe's following grew steadily. He preached orthodox Baptist doctrines and stressed the value of Western morals and work ethic.

Around 1911, Chilembwe began experiencing a number of health, personal and financial difficulties. Suffering from asthma and beset by personal problems, Chilembwe's outlook on life began to change. Chilembwe came to resent the poor treatment of African laborers at the hands of European settlers. He saw this problem being exacerbated by the influx of Africans from Mozambique into southern Malawi in 1913. The breaking point occurred in 1914 when the British army began to conscript Africans for service in World War I.

Chilembwe began to protest vocally against the European oppression of Africans. These protests led Chilembwe to organize an armed rebellion against the local European settlers of Nyasaland.

In January of 1915, Chilembwe initiated his rebellion. His plans were carefully executed, but his ultimate objectives were never clearly defined. In late January, several hundred of his followers attacked European farmers and killed a number of them.

The Europeans retaliated. The retaliation was harsh and unmerciful. Chilembwe fled, but was found and killed.

In the aftermath of his death, Chilembwe's missionary movement was largely exterminated.

RELATED HISTORICAL EVENTS

- By 1915, much of the world was at war.

EPILOGUE

There are those who believe that yesterday was better. They will claim that yesterday was more moral, that yesterday had more values.

Perhaps for some people in some places at some time, this assessment is true. But for the majority of the world, yesterday is best left in the past.

In the reading of history, one of the most intriguing aspects is mankind's evolving consciousness of certain fundamental truths. The great quest of mankind is to discover the truth and, after discovering it, to learn how to accept it.

By 1915, mankind had come to accept the truth that slavery is evil. To be certain, slavery was not dead. Indeed, it continues to exist even to this day. But, for the majority of mankind, the concept of slavery as a legalized, state sanctioned institution, was deemed to be a monstrous evil that could no longer be tolerated in the modern world.

Having accepted the truth that slavery was evil, there arose another truth that mankind needed to discover and accept. The next truth was that the subjugation of a people anywhere, endangers the freedom of people everywhere. Mankind's discovery of this truth would begin in earnest in 1915 as much of the world became involved with a nightmare known as the Great War.

Persons of African descent from around the world would participate in, and be affected by, the "Great War." Their participation in this endeavor, along with the opportunities that the War created, would lead to renewed efforts by African people all over the globe to obtain equality and liberty.

BIBLIOGRAPHY

As the writer of this book, I am indebted to the scholars who took the time and made the effort to preserve the history of individuals of African descent. I am particularly indebted to five sources of information without which this book could not have been written. Those sources are *The Chronological History of the Negro in America* by Peter M. Bergman and Mort N. Bergman; *Chronology of African History* by G. S. P. Freeman-Grenville; *Dictionary of African Historical Biography* by Mark R. Lipschutz and R. Kent Rasmussen; *Black Firsts: 2,000 Years of Extraordinary Achievement* by Jessie Carney Smith; and *Biographical Dictionary of Latin American and Caribbean Political Leaders* edited by Robert J. Alexander. To the authors of these sources, as well as the sources that follow, I am compelled to express my deepest gratitude.

Afro-American Encyclopedia. North Miami, Florida: Educational, 1974.

Alexander, Robert J., ed. *Biographical Dictionary of Latin American and Caribbean Political Leaders.* New York: Greenwood, 1988.

Ashe, Arthur R., Jr. *A Hard Road to Glory: A History of the African American Athlete 1619–1918.* New York: Warner, 1988.

Bartlett, John. *Bartlett's Familiar Quotations.* Boston: Little, Brown, 1992.

Bergman, Peter M. and Mort N. Bergman. *The Chronological History of the Negro in America.* New York: New American Library, 1969.

Boorman, Howard L., ed. *Biographical Dictionary of Republican China.* New York: Columbia University Press, 1967.

Burns, E. Bradford, ed. *A Documentary History of Brazil.* New York: Alfred A. Knopf, 1966.

Burns, Monique. "Two of World's Greatest Lovers — Elizabeth Barrett and Robert Browning — Were Descendants of Blacks." *Ebony,* May 1995.

Carruth, Gorton. *What Happened When.* New York: Harper & Row, 1989.

Chronicle of America. New York: Chronicle, 1988.

Counter, S. Allen. "The Henson Family." *National Geographic,* September 1988.

Cowan, Tom and Jack Maguire. *Timelines of African American History: 500 Years of Black Achievement*. New York: Perigee, 1994.

Crim, Keith, ed. *Dictionary of World Religions*. San Francisco: Harper & Row, 1989.

Croutier, Alev Lytle. *Harem: The World Behind the Veil*. New York: Abbeville, 1989.

da Costa, Emilia Viotti. *The Brazilian Empire: Myths and Histories*. Chicago: University of Chicago Press.

Davidson, Basil. *Africa in History*. New York: Collier, 1991.

Diggs, Ellen Irene. *Black Chronology*. Boston: G.K. Hall, 1983.

Dirksen, Everett McKinley and Herbert V. Prochnow. *Quotation Finder*. New York: Harper & Row, 1971.

Edwards, Paul, ed. *The Encyclopedia of Philosophy*. New York: Macmillan and Free Press, 1967.

Encyclopaedia Britannica. *The Annals of America*. Chicago: Encyclopaedia Britannica, 1968.

Encyclopaedia Britannica. *Great Books of the Western World: Darwin*. Chicago: Encyclopaedia Britannica, 1971.

Everett, Susanne. *History of Slavery*. Secaucus, New Jersey: Chartwell, 1991.

Franklin, John Hope. *From Slavery to Freedom: A History of Negro Americans*. New York: Vintage, 1969.

Freeman-Grenville, G.S.P. *Chronology of African History*. London: Oxford University Press, 1973.

_____. *The Chronology of World History*. Totowa, New Jersey: Rowman and Littlefield, 1978.

Fuentes, Carlos. *The Buried Mirror*. New York: Houghton Mifflin, 1992.

Gonen, Amiram, ed. *The Encyclopedia of the Peoples of the World*. New York: Holt, 1993.

Hamilton, Kenneth Marvin. *Black Towns and Profit: Promotion and Development in the Trans-Appalachian West, 1877–1915*. Chicago: University of Illinois Press, 1991.

Harris, Joseph E. *The African Presence in Asia*. Evanston, Illinois: Northwestern University Press, 1971.

Harter, Eugene C. *The Lost Colony of the Confederacy*. Jackson: University Press of Mississippi, 1985.

Henry Ossawa Tanner. An art catalogue prepared by the Philadelphia Museum of Art, 1991.

Hoover, Mildred Brooke, Hero Eugene Rensch, Ethel Grace Rensch, and William N. Abeloe. *Historic Spots in California*. Revised by Douglas E. Kyle. Stanford, California: Stanford University Press, 1990.

Illustrated History of South Africa. Pleasantville, New York: Reader's Digest, 1988.

Irwin, Graham W. *Africans Abroad*. New York: Columbia University Press, 1977.

Jenkins, Everett, Jr. *Pan-African Chronology*. Jefferson, North Carolina: McFarland, 1996.

Katz, William Loren. *Black Indians: A Hidden Heritage*. New York: Atheneum, 1986.

_____. *The Black West*. New York: Simon & Schuster, 1996.

Kennedy, James H. "Whistling Dixie in Brazil." *Americas*, January-February 1987.

Klein, Herbert S. *African Slavery in Latin America*. New York: Oxford University Press, 1986.

Kunitz, Stanley J. and Vineta Colby, eds. *European Authors: 1000–1900*, New York: Wilson, 1967.

_____. and Howard Haycraft, eds. *British Authors of the Nineteenth Century*. New York: Wilson, 1936.

Lewis, David Levering, ed. *W. E. B. Du Bois: A Reader*. New York: Holt, 1995.

Lincoln, Abraham. *Speeches and Writings 1859–1865*. Library of America, 1989.

Lipschutz, Mark R. and R. Kent Rasmussen. *Dictionary of African Historical Biography*. Berkeley: University of California Press, 1986.

Logan, Rayford W. and Michael R. Winston, eds. *Dictionary of American Negro Biography*. New York: Norton, 1982.

Machado de Assis, Joaquim. *Epitaph of a Small Winner*. New York: Noonday, 1990.

Magill, Frank N., ed. *Masterpieces of African-American Literature*. New York: HarperCollins, 1992.

Markus, Julia. *Dared and Done: The Marriage of Elizabeth Barrett and Robert Browning*. New York: Alfred A. Knopf, 1995.

Mason, Antony, Anne Mahon, and Andrew Currie. *World Facts & Places*. London: Tiger, 1993.

Mazrui, Ali. *The Africans: A Triple Heritage*. Boston: Little, Brown, 1986.

Murphy, Larry G., J. Gordon Melton, and Gary L. Ward, eds. *Encyclopedia of African American Religions*. New York: Garland, 1993.

Murray, Jocelyn, ed. *Cultural Atlas of Africa*. New York: Facts on File, 1981.

Nairn, Bede and Geoffrey Serle, eds. *Australian Dictionary of Biography*. Carlton, Victoria, Australia: Melbourne University Press, 1983.

Pakenham, Thomas. *The Scramble for Africa.* New York: Random House, 1991.

Parker, Geoffrey, ed. *The World: An Illustrated History.* New York: Harper & Row, 1986.

Perkins, George, Barbara Perkins, and Phillip Leininger, eds. *Benet's Reader's Encyclopedia of American Literature.* New York: HarperCollins, 1991.

The Pilgrim Press. *The New Century Hymnal.* Cleveland: Pilgrim, 1995.

Ploski, Harry A. and James Williams. *The Negro Almanac: A Reference Work on the African American.* Detroit: Gale, 1989.

Rogers, J.A. *World's Great Men of Color.* New York: Macmillan, 1972.

Sadie, Stanley, ed. *The New Grove Dictionary of Music and Musicians.* London: Macmillan, 1980.

Salzman, Jack, David Lionel Smith, and Cornel West, eds. *Encyclopedia of African American Culture and History.* New York: Simon & Schuster and Columbia University Press, 1996.

Schutt-Aine, Patricia. *Haiti: A Basic Reference Book.* Miami: Librairie Au Service de la Culture, 1994.

Sloan, Irving. *The American Negro: A Chronology and Fact Book.* Dobbs Ferry, New York: Oceana, 1968.

Smith, Jessie Carney. *Black Firsts: 2,000 Years of Extraordinary Achievement.* Detroit: Gale, 1994.

Smithsonian Institution. *Handbook of North American Indians.* Volume 5. William Sturtevant, general editor; David Damas, volume editor. Washington, D. C.: Smithsonian Institution, 1984.

Stafford, Edward Peary. "The Peary Family." *National Geographic,* September 1988.

Suchlicki, Jaime. *Historical Dictionary of Cuba.* Metuchen, New Jersey: Scarecrow, 1988.

Tenenbaum, Barbara A., ed. *Encyclopedia of Latin American History and Culture.* New York: Scribner's, 1996.

Thurston, Herbert and Donald Attwater. *Butler's Lives of the Saints.* New York: Kenedy, 1956.

Thybony, Scott. "Against All Odds, Black Seminole Won Their Freedom." *Smithsonian,* August 1991.

Trager, James. *The People's Chronology.* New York: Holt, 1992.

United States Code Annotated. Saint Paul, Minnesota: West, 1987.

Utley, Robert M. and Wilcomb E. Washburn. *Indian Wars.* New York: American Heritage, 1977.

Wade, Harold, Jr. *Black Men of Amherst.* Amherst, Massachusetts: Amherst College Press, 1976.

Waldman, Carl. *Atlas of the North American Indian.* New York: Facts on File, 1985.

Winks, Robin W. *The Blacks in Canada.* Montreal: McGill-Queen's University Press, 1971.

Wintz, Cary D., ed. *African American Political Thought: 1890–1930: Washington, DuBois, Garvey, Randolph.* Armonk, New York: Sharpe.

The Works of Elizabeth Barrett Browning. Hertfordshire, England: Wordsworth, 1994.

The Works of Robert Browning. Hertfordshire, England: Wordsworth, 1994.

INDEX

In an effort to make this index as easy to use as possible, after each entry there are two references. The first reference is to the year in which the entry appears. The second reference, in parentheses, is to the specific page on which the entry appears.

Names that are European in origin are inverted and thus alphabetized by the last name of the individual. Names that are African, Arabic, or Asian are not inverted. Thus, "Muhammed Bello" appears in this index under the letter "M."

Barnett, Ida Wells (Ida
B. Wells) 1892 (260–
261), 1895 (288),
1908 (398); bio 1892
(260–261)
Barotse *see* Lozi
Barotseland 1878
(145), 1884 (188,
189), 1885 (198),
1890 (245), 1892
(265), 1900 (341)
Barreto, Tobias, bio
1889 (229)
Barrett, Edward 1889
(230)
Barrett, Elizabeth *see*
Browning, Elizabeth
Barrett
Barrios, General 1865
(14)
Barrow, Joe Louis *see*
Louis, Joe
Barrundia, Jose Fran-
cisco 1865 (13)
Barth, Heinrich 1865
(20), 1872 (92), 1903
(361); bio 1865 (20)
Barthe, Richmond
1901 (343), 1913
(442); bio 1901 (343)
Barue 1874 (107), 1892
(267), 1902 (355)
Basanga 1891 (254)
Basel Mission 1887
(212)
Basie, William (Wil-
liam "Count" Basie)
1904 (362), 1909
(409); bio 1904 (362)
Basorun 1888 (220)
Bass, Carlotta 1912
(435)
Basuto 1865 (18)
Basutoland 1865 (18),
1868 (52), 1870 (71,
72, 73), 1871 (85),
1875 (121), 1879 (150,
151), 1880 (157), 1883
(180), 1884 (188),
1885 (199), 1887
(216), 1891 (257),
1900 (341), 1905
(381, 382)
Basutoland "Ethiopian"
Church 1900 (341)
Basutoland National
Council 1905 (382)
Basutoland Protec-
torate 1868 (52),
1879 (151), 1885
(199), 1887 (216)

Basutoland Records
1879 (151), 1883
(180)
Bateke 1880 (155),
1905 (383)
Batelas 1897 (310)
Batembuzi *see* Tem-
buzi
Bates College 1914
(449)
Batetela 1895 (292)
Bathoen I (Bathweng I)
1885 (198), 1889
(235), 1895 (294),
bio 1910 (426–427)
Bathoen II 1910 (427)
Bathweng I *see*
Bathoen I
Bathurst 1909 (412)
Batista, Fulgencio, bio
1901 (345–346)
Baton Rouge
(Louisiana) 1900
(332), 1914 (450)
Battle, Samuel J. 1911
(428)
Battle Creek (Michi-
gan) 1883 (175)
*Battleground of the Rai-
son River* 1872 (89)
Batugenge 1892 (264)
Bauchi 1902 (352),
1912 (436)
Baumann, O. 1892
(264)
Baumfree, Isabella *see*
Truth, Sojourner
Bayamo (Cuba) 1868
(48)
Bayol 1889 (232)
BEAC *see* British East
Africa Company
Beach College (Beach
Institute; Claflin
College; Claflin
Institute) (Orange-
burg, South Car-
olina) 1867 (38),
1870 (64)
Beagle, H.M.S. 1882
(170, 171)
Bear 1886 (200), 1904
(364)
Beard, Andrew J. 1892
(261), 1897 (309)
Bearden, Romare, bio
1914 (449)
Beaufort (South Car-
olina) 1915 (457)
Beaufort County
(South Carolina)

1866 (27), 1874
(106), 1880 (153)
Bechet, Sidney 1879
(147), bio 1897
(306–307)
Bechuanaland 1866
(31), 1873 (102), 1883
(178), 1885 (198),
1889 (235, 236, 238),
1890 (245), 1892
(266), 1895 (294),
1897 (312), 1904
(369, 370), 1905
(381), 1910 (426); *see
also* Botswana
Bechuanaland Explo-
ration Company
1888 (222)
Bechuanaland Protec-
torate 1874 (108),
1885 (198), 1895
(294), 1897 (312),
1910 (426)
Beckwith, Joseph 1875
(116)
Beckwourth, James
(Jim) P., bio 1867
(36–37)
Beckwourth (Califor-
nia) 1867 (36)
Beckwourth Pass 1867
(36, 37)
Bedford Springs (Penn-
sylvania) 1882 (165)
Beecher, Catherine
1896 (306)
Beecher, Henry Ward
1887 (215), 1896
(306); bio 1887 (215)
Beecher, Lyman 1887
(215), 1896 (306)
Beecroft, John 1866
(29)
beet 1894 (278)
Begemder 1915 (465)
Behanzin 1883 (178),
1889 (232), 1890
(243), 1892 (263),
1894 (279), bio 1906
(389), 1908 (407)
*Behind the Scenes by
Elizabeth Keckley,
Formerly a Slave, but
More Recently a
Modiste and Friend
to Mrs. Abraham
Lincoln; or Thirty
Years a Slave and
Forty Years in the
White House* 1868
(47)

Beijing (China) 1878
(140, 141, 142), 1909
(416), 1913 (443)
Beira 1898 (320), 1915
(465)
Beirut 1909 (412)
Beit, Alfred 1880 (156),
1887 (214), 1888
(222), 1897 (312),
1902 (355), bio 1906
(392)
Beit-el-mal 1910 (423)
Bel Air (Haiti) 1882
(166)
Beledougou 1915 (463)
Belgian Congo 1883
(178), 1885 (200),
1887 (215), 1890
(246), 1905 (380),
1909 (416, 417), 1910
(424, 425), 1912
(437), 1913 (445),
1915 (465); *see also*
Congo; Zaire
Belgium 1865 (12),
1874 (105), 1875
(119), 1876 (124),
1878 (144), 1883
(178), 1885 (200),
1888 (221), 1889
(233), 1890 (246,
247), 1891 (255,
256), 1892 (264),
1894 (279, 280, 282),
1895 (292), 1899
(326), 1900 (339,
342), 1903 (360),
1904 (366), 1905
(378, 380), 1906
(392), 1907 (396),
1908 (407), 1909
(416, 417, 418), 1910
(424), 1911 (431,
432), 1912 (437),
1913 (445), 1914
(453), 1915 (465);
Parliament 1890
(247), 1908 (408),
1909 (417)
Bell 1866 (30)
Bell, Alexander Gra-
ham 1881 (159),
1882 (166)
Bell, Anthony 1903
(357)
Bell, Dennis 1898
(312)
Bell, James Madison
1902 (350), 1904
(364); bio 1902 (350)
Bell, Rudolf Manga